D0151017

ENCYCLOPEDIA OF ANCIENT LITERATURE

James Wyatt Cook

Facts On File
An imprint of Infobase Publishing

For our newest granddaughter,
Shaina Anne Cook

Encyclopedia of Ancient Literature

Copyright © 2008 by James Wyatt Cook

Facts On File, Inc.
An imprint of Infobase Publishing
132 West 31st Street
New York NY 10001

Library of Congress Cataloging-in-Publication Data

Cook, James Wyatt.
   Encyclopedia of ancient literature / James Wyatt Cook.
      p.   cm.
   Includes bibliographical references and index.
   ISBN 978-0-8160-6475-5 (hc : alk. paper)   1. Literature,
Ancient—Encyclopedias.   I. Title.
   PN621.C66 2008
   809'.1—dc22   2007016016

Facts On File books are available at special discounts when purchased in bulk quantities for businesses, associations, institutions, or sales promotions. Please call our Special Sales Department in New York at (212) 967-8800 or (800) 322-8755.

You can find Facts On File on the World Wide Web at http://www.factsonfile.com

Text design by Rachel L. Berlin
Cover design by Salvatore Luongo

Printed in the United States of America

VB BVC 10 9 8 7 6 5 4 3 2 1

This book is printed on acid-free paper and contains 30% post-consumer recycled content.

CONTENTS

ACKNOWLEDGMENTS

Large projects need lots of help. As is always the case, my principal helper on this book has been my spouse of a short 54 years, Barbara Marie Collier Cook. My first line editor and sometime coauthor, she reads my screed with patience and even with enthusiasm. This tome is a more readable and better book because of her attention and suggestions. My editor at Facts On File, Jeff Soloway, has steadied me throughout the process of bringing a book this size to fruition. So has my agent, Jodie Rhodes, who in the course of representing me professionally has also become my friend. I cannot praise enough the principal copy editor of this tome, Elin Woodger. Her attention to detail and pursuit of excellence has many times corrected matters of fact and excised authorial solipsisms. Once she has even corrected a long-cherished but mistaken conflation of Greek mythic figures.

Albion College has generously supported this effort with a congenial workspace and a dedicated printer. The wonderful staff members of the Stockwell-Mudd libraries have regularly produced virtually instant answers to my many questions and have cheerfully fulfilled unusual requests. I cannot express my gratitude enough to John Kondelik, Peggy Vogt, Mike Van Houten, Alice Wiley Moore, Marion Meilaender, Carolyn Gaswick, Michelle Gerry, Cheryl Blackwell, Becky Markovich, Jennie Thomas, Claudia Diaz, Pat Engleter, Mary Koch, Bev Brankovich, Yvette Eddy, and Marilyn Kniburys for their enthusiastic cooperation and encouragement.

The Reverend Dr. Leon White gave careful consideration to the entries on the Bible and provided crucial feedback that significantly improved them; any lingering deficiencies are mine. Professor Emeritus Robert G. Henricks of Dartmouth kindly pointed me in the direction of the best available sources for filling in at least some of the gaps in my knowledge of ancient Chinese literature. He also led me to understand that, owing to archeologists' recent discoveries of early and hitherto lost versions of Chinese texts, this is the golden age of the study of ancient Chinese literature. As always, too, I am indebted to my blood brother, P. Lal, poet, translator, and publisher in Kolkata, India, for illuminating ancient Indian letters for me, especially with his magnificent verse translations of the *Mahabharata* and the *Bhagavad Gita*.

I wish also to remember both the late Emily Stern, who taught me Latin and with whom I read Cicero and Virgil, and the unflappably patient Mary E. McKinney, with whom I labored at Greek.

I am also deeply indebted to the hundreds of editors, translators, and writers whose books and whose contributions to specialized reference volumes gave shape to my understanding of the underlying interrelatedness of the literature of the ancient Eurasian world. Though I have cited many such editors and authors by name in entries where I have specifically included their ideas, for the others whose influence is of a more general nature, I gratefully acknowledge having consulted their work in the following reference volumes:

Eschenburg, Johann J. *Manual of Classical Literature*. Philadelphia: E. C. & J. Biddle, 1850.

Hornblower, Simon and Anthony Spawforth, eds. *The Oxford Classical Dictionary*. 3rd ed. New York: Oxford University Press, 1999.

Mair, Victor H. editor. *The Columbia History of Chinese Literature*. New York: Columbia University Press, 2001.

New Catholic Encyclopedia. New York: McGraw-Hill Book Company, 1967.

INTRODUCTION

It has often struck me that, when Ecclesiastes offers the opinion in the Hebrew Bible that there is no end to books and that much study is wearisome for the flesh, the author must have been trying to compile an encyclopedia of ancient literature. As far back into the mists of history as one can peer, there are at least allusions to prior books or to earlier poets. As soon as people perceived that they *could* invent systems of symbols to represent words, syllables, phonemes, or variations in pitch, they started to *do* it. Almost everywhere in the old world and in some places in the new, people invented such systems as long as 5,000 years ago—the Chinese perhaps as long as 7,000 years ago. Though at first they probably employed writing systems to keep records for purposes of taxation, inventory, and the like, they soon began to employ such systems to record their national or tribal stories—their myths, their genealogies, and their histories. Many of the stories that entered the record early and that still remain in it have to do with famous men and women—often rulers or military leaders, but sometimes artists and poets—who achieved divine or quasi-divine status. Not much later, artists began, like Sappho, to sing songs of themselves.

Most of the earliest surviving works are in verse, and much was originally set to music. That fact alone suggests a prewriting tradition of reciting aloud and singing the stories that have survived. So does the widespread appearance of similar stories explaining cosmology. One notes, for example, that the Roman sky god, Uranus, had a precisely functional and linguistically cognate counterpart in the ancient South Indian sky god, Varuna. Their stories spring from a lost but clearly common oral source. Examples of such sources are to be found in the *Nart Sagas*. These contain stories that have survived the ages in oral form and only recently been recorded in writing.

There are, of course, major differences between then and now. Modern readers think of *literature* as occupying the same territory as *belles lettres*—novels, poems, short stories, and artsy memoirs. For the ancients, the literary arena was much broader. Geography, physics, court cases, mathematics, the praise of athletes, history, cookbooks, philosophy, and war songs as well as drama and intensely emotional lyrics all were lumped under the rubric of literature. So were explanations of how the universe got started and books on farming and beekeeping. For a modern writer, trying to bring a sense of such matters to a general audience composed principally of high school and college students and teachers, the problem becomes one of selection.

This work deals mainly with primary texts. Although teaching young people to write research papers requires that they have recourse to journals and scholarly commentary, the result of such papers is "commentary on commentary"—a useful phrase coined by Richard Brown of the Newberry Library. This book, instead, is meant to acquaint learners with what they may expect to find in broadly literary, ancient texts and to give the same learners an introductory overview about the people who wrote the works and the traditions in which those writers developed. For readers wishing to pursue an interest into the secondary literature concerning it, I have tried to include references in the bibliographies at the end of each entry to the most recent scholarly translations into English. When no English translation is available, I have selected a Spanish, Italian, or French translation on the theory that, in polyglot contemporary America, many readers may have one of those European languages as a first or second tongue. Such scholarly editions of the primary texts almost always survey the most useful secondary literature, and the Internet is also a fruitful source of supplemental bibliography. Beyond that, however, for those readers whose interests *do* lead them into the thicket of critical discussion concerning the languages and literatures of the ancient world, at the end of this encyclopedia, I have provided a bibliography in two sections. The first section lists important secondary works addressing the literatures covered in this encyclopedia. The second section lists and lightly annotates indispensable bibliographic resources for conducting both apprentice and advanced scholarship in most of the languages and literatures discussed in these pages.

In the entries themselves, I have tried to give a fair sample of as many ancient literary traditions as I could get a handle on in the time available to write this book. As a starting point, I have included a generous sample of Greek and Roman letters from their beginnings well into the Christian era. I have tried both to cover and to go significantly beyond the classical canon suggested by scholars such as Harold Bloom. Nonetheless, significant

coverage is devoted to all the writers and works commonly encountered in high school and college classes, such as *The Iliad, The Odyssey, The Aeneid*, the works of the great Greek dramatists, and more. Note that some famous works have been translated under more than one title. To make this book as accessible as possible to students, I have always tried to choose the title most familiar to modern readers—which in some cases is an English-language title and in some is the original-language title or transliteration.

With respect to the ancient texts of Hindu India, I have tried to hit the high spots. Indian letters contain an inexhaustible trove of treasure. The full and unexpurgated text of the *Mahabharata*—India's national epic—is only now becoming *fully* available in English for the first time. Bringing that work to fruition will require 16 volumes, each almost 4 inches thick. Beyond Hindu writings, I have also included entries about Buddhist and Jain scriptures.

Scholarship in ancient Chinese studies has blossomed in the last two decades. Archaeological digs at Ma Wang Dui and elsewhere have unearthed the earliest known versions of classic Chinese Confucian and Taoist texts. As a result, wonderful translations of many ancient Chinese texts are now available for the first time, and more appear each year. As I said in the preface, this is the golden era of ancient Chinese studies, and of course a good deal of literary cross-pollination occurred between China and India—especially with respect to Buddhist texts.

Japanese literature starts late. The Japanese borrowed Chinese characters and adapted them to represent the Japanese tongue. The earliest surviving work of Japanese literature is the *Kojiki* (*Record of Ancient Matters*), which appeared in 712 C.E.

Elsewhere, particularly in South America and Mesoamerica about the time of Socrates and Plato in Greece, writing was also flourishing. Though much of what was written has yet to be deciphered fully, it seems that the records of kings and gods and matters of astronomy and cosmology occupied the thoughts of Zapotec and Mayan writers just as such matters interested the ancient Sumerians and Babylonians. The ancestors of Incan culture also devised a method for keeping track of all sorts of numerical matters—including tax records—with a system of knotted strings. Whether they also adapted this system to represent language is unclear, but an entry on quipu is included, just in case.

Although documents representing Western Hemisphere traditions exist, the ones we know well date to shortly before the period of European contact. Technically, one could define *ancient* as describing the moment that a language ceases living exclusively in the mouths of its speakers and achieves symbolic representation. Such an operational definition, however, is an impracticable basis for a one-volume reference work, so I have largely ignored the literature of languages whose written representation begins much later than the fall of the Western Roman Empire. The literature of sub-Saharan Africa represents a similar case. These literatures are covered in two companion volumes published by Facts On File, *Encyclopedia of Medieval Literature* and *Encyclopedia of Renaissance Literature*.

Egypt, of course, developed its hieroglyphic system of writing very early. I have chosen to represent the literature of Egypt with a description of *The Egyptian* Book of the Dead. A discussion of the Hebrew Bible, of representative Apochrypha, and of the Dead Sea Scrolls represents my principal forays into ancient writing in Hebrew.

In addition to brief biographies of writers and sometimes-lengthy overviews of representative works, I have tried to provide useful definitions of literary terms. Readers may trace cross-references of interest by pursuing the words in SMALL CAPITAL LETTERS to other alphabetically listed entries where those terms occur and, by following the guide thus provided, may achieve a more comprehensive view of subjects of particular interest. I have also tried to present topical entries, such as the one defining *patristic exegesis* and others dealing with Greek stage conventions and like matters, to assist those readers who are trying to grasp the points of view of ancient writers.

Many of the works that deal with the origins of the universe and human beings and books that explore ethical matters occupy the status of Scripture in their cultures. Some of the books are so revered that their adherents consider them to have been without authors and to have existed from eternity. Others assert the divine inspiration of human authors.

Despite my occasional moments of panic when it seemed unlikely that I could actually read enough about the aspects of these subjects that were unfamiliar to me, I hope that readers will perceive how much I have enjoyed bringing them these articles and synopses. I have had the opportunity both to return to texts more than half forgotten and to peruse new ones that I might never have read otherwise. Mostly, it has been great fun.

—J. W. C.
Albion, Michigan
February 10, 2007

Writers Covered, by Language of Composition

AKKADIAN

Anonymous authors of the Akkadian version of
The Gilgamesh Epic

BABYLONIAN

Hammurabi

CHINESE

Ban Biao
Ban Gu
Ban Zhao
Confucius (Kongfuzi, K'ung Fu-Tzu, Kongfuzi,
    Master Kong [K'ung])
Ji Kang (Hsi K'ang)
Jia Yi (Chia Yi)
Lie Yokou (Lieh Yü-k'o)
Lü Buwei (Lü Pu-wei)
Mei Sheng
Mencius (Mengzi, Meng-tzu)
Mozi (Mo Tzu)
Qu Yuan (Ch'ü Yüan)
Sima Qian (Ssu-ma Ch'ien)
Sima Xiangru (Ssu-ma Hsiang-Ju)
Song Yu (Sung Yü)
Tao Qian (T'ao Ch'ien, Tao)

Wang Chong (Wang Ch'ung)
Yang Xiong (Yang Hsiung)
Yüan Ming
Xunzi (Hsün Tzu)
Zhuangzi (Chuang Tzu, Chuangtse, Kuang Tzu)

EGYPTIAN

Anonymous authors of Book of the Dead

GREEK

Achilles Tatius
Ælius Aristides
Æschines
Aeschylus
Aesop
Agathias of Myrina
Alcaeus (Alkaios)
Alkman (Alcman)
Andocides (Andokides)
Antiphon of Rhamnus
Anyte
Apollonius of Rhodes (Apollonius Rhodius)
Aratus of Soli (Aratos of Soli)
Archestratus
Archilochus
Archimedes

Aristides of Miletus
Aristophanes
Aristotle
Arrian (Flavius Arianus)
Athanasius
Athenaeus
Barnabas
Basil, St.
Bion of Smyrna
Callimachus
Callinus of Ephesus
Chrysostom, St. John
Clemens Romanus
Ctesias of Cnidos
Demosthenes
Dinarchus
Dio Cocceianus Chrysostomus
Diodorus Siculus
Diogenes Laertius
Dionysius of Halicarnassus
Diphilus
Donatus, Ælius
Empedocles
Epicharmus of Cos
Epicurus
Epigenes the Sicyonian
Eratosthenes
Erinna
Euclid
Euhemerus
Euripides
Eusebius of Caesarea
Flavius Josephus (Josephus, Joseph ben Matthias)
Galen (Claudius Galenus)
Gorgias of Leontium
Gregory of Nazianzen, St.
Hanno
Hecatæus of Miletus
Hedyla
Heliodorus of Emesa
Hephæstion of Alexandria
Hermes
Heraclitus of Ephesus
Herodotus
Hesiod
Homer

Iambichlus of Syria
Ignatius
Isæus
Isocrates
Jerome, St. (Eusebius Hieronymus Stridonensis)
Julian (Flavius Claudius Julianus, Julian the
    Apostate)
Julius Pollux (Polydeuces of Naucratis, Egypt)
Korinna
Leonidas of Tarentum
Libanius of Antioch
Longus
Lucian of Samosata
Lycophron
Lysias
Meleager of Gadara (Meleagros)
Melinno
Menander
Mimnermus of Colophon
Moiro
Moschus of Syracuse
Musæus 1
Musæus 2
Nicander of Colophon
Nossis
Oppian of Corycus
Origen
Orpheus
Palæphatus
Papias
Parthenius of Nicaea
Pausanias
Philemon
Philetas of Cos (Philitas of Cos)
Philostratus, L. Flavius (Philostratus the
    Athenian)
Photius
Phrynicos of Athens
Pindar
Plato
Plotinus
Polyænus
Polycarp
Porphyry
Praxilla
Proclus of Byzantium

Procopius
Ptolemy (Claudius Ptolemaeus)
Pythagoras of Samos
Quadratus
Sappho
Simonides of Ceos
Socrates
Solon
Sophocles
Strabo
Telesilla
Thaletus of Crete
Themistius Euphrades
Theocritus
Theognis
Theophrastus of Eresus
Thespis of Ikaria
Thucydides
Tyrtaeus
Xenophon of Athens
Xenophon of Ephesus
Zosimus

HEBREW–ARAMAIC–SYRIAC

Josephus, Flavius (Josephus, Joseph ben
     Matthias)
Mani

JAPANESE

Lady Kasa
Kakinomoto no Hitomaro
Princess Nukata
Ōtomo no Yakamochi
Yamanoue no Okura
Yosami

LATIN

Augustus Caesar
Ausonius, Decimus Magnus
Avianus, Flavius
Boethius, Anicius Manlius Severinus
     (St. Severinus)
Caesar, Julius

Calpurnius, Titus Siculus
Cicero, Marcus Tullius
Claudian (Claudius Claudianus)
Curtius, Quintus Rufus
Damasus, Pope
Eutropius, Flavius
Frontinus, Sextus Julius (Iulius Frontinus,
     Sextus)
Gallus, Gaius Cornelius
Horace (Quintus Horatius Flaccus)
Isidore of Seville
Juvenal (Decimus Junius Juvenalis)
Livius Andronicus
Livy (Titus Livius)
Lucan (Marcus Annaeus Lucanus)
Lucilius, Gaius
Lucretius
Macrobius (Macrobius Ambrosius Aurelius
     Theodosius)
Marcus Aurelius Antoninus
Martial (Marcus Valerius Martialis)
Nemesianus (Marcus Aurelius Olympius
     Nemesianus)
Ovid (Publius Ovidius Naso)
Pacuvius, Marcus
Persius (Aulus Persius Flaccus)
Petronius Arbiter
Phædrus the Fabulist (Phaeder, Gaius Iulius)
Pictor, Q. Fabius
Plautus, M. Accius
Pliny the Elder (Caius Plinius Secundus)
Pliny the Younger (Gaius Plinius Caecilius
     Secundus)
Polybius
Proba
Propertius, Sextus Aurelius
Prudentius, Aurelius
Quintilian (Marcus Fabius Quintilianus)
Quintus Smyrnaeus (Quintus Calaber)
Rutilius, Claudius Numantianus
Sedulius, Caelius
Seneca, Lucius Annaeus
Silius Italicus (Tiberius Catius Silius Asconius)
Statius (Publius Papinius Statius)
Suetonius
Sulpicia

Tacitus
Terence (Publius Terentius Afer)
Tibullus, Albius
Turnus
Valerius Flaccus
Valerius Maximus
Varro, Marcus Terentius
Virgil

OLD PERSIAN (AVESTAN)

Zoroaster

SANSKRIT

Buddha
Pāṇiṇi
Vyāsa (Krishna Dvaipāyana;
    Vedavyā)

SUMERIAN

Anonymous authors of the Sumerian version of
    the *Gilgamesh Epic*

AUTHORS' TIME LINE

Dates	Author	Dates	Author
Before 2350 B.C.E.	Anon. Egyptian Book of the Dead (Reu Nu Pert Em Hru [Chapters of Coming Forth by Day])	fl. sixth century B.C.E.	Aesop Epigenes the Sicyonian Musæus 1 Thespis of Ikaria
ca. 2300 B.C.E.	Anon. *The Gilgamesh Epic* (Sumerian language)	ca. mid-sixth century B.C.E.	Theognis
ca. 2250 B.C.E.	Hammurabi, King of Babylon	fl. ca. 594 B.C.E.	Solon
fl. ca. 1500 B.C.E.	Vyāsa (Krishna Dvaipāyana, Vedavyā)	fl. ca. 590 B.C.E.	Mimnermus of Colophon
ca. 1300 B.C.E.	*The Gilgamesh Epic* (Akkadian Language)	ca. 563–ca 483 B.C.E.	Buddha
		ca. 556–468 B.C.E.	Simonides of Ceos
		551–479 B.C.E.	Confucius
fl. ca. 1250 B.C.E.	Orpheus	fl. ca. 550–500 B.C.E.	Pythagoras of Samos
fl. eighth century B.C.E.	Homer Hesiod	fl. ca. 536 B.C.E.	Anacreon
		525–455 B.C.E.	Aeschylus
fl. seventh century B.C.E.	Alkman Thaletas of Crete	ca. 518–ca. 438 B.C.E.	Pindar
		512–476 B.C.E.	Phrynicos of Athens
fl. ca. 684 B.C.E	Callinus of Ephesus	fl. 500 B.C.E.	Hanno Hecatæus of Miletus Heraclitus of Ephesus
fl. ca. 680 B.C.E.	Archilochos		
b. ca. 650 B.C.E.	Sappho (Psappho)	fl. ca. late sixth or early fifth century B.C.E	Epicharmus of Cos (Epicharmus of Sicily)
fl. ca. 647 B.C.E.	Tyrtaeus		
ca. 630–ca. 580 B.C.E.	Alcaeus (Alkaios)	ca. fifth century B.C.E.	Myrtis Korinna
ca. 630–ca. 553 B.C.E.	Zoroaster (Zarathustra Spitama)		

Dates	Author	Dates	Author
	Praxilla	ca. 340–ca. 278 B.C.E.	Qu Yuan (Ch'ü Yüan)
	Telesilla	ca. 330–270 B.C.E.	Philetas of Cos (Philitas of Cos)
496–406 B.C.E.	Sophocles		
fl. ca. 485–ca. 380 B.C.E.	Gorgias of Leontium (Leontini, Sicily)	b. ca. 315 B.C.E.	Aratus of Soli (Aratos of Soli)
484 or 480–406 B.C.E.	Euripides	fl. ca. 312 B.C.E.	Xunzi (Hsün Tzu)
ca. 480–ca. 425 B.C.E.	Herodotus (Herodotos)	ca. 310–ca. 270 B.C.E.	Theocritus
ca. 480–ca. 411 B.C.E.	Antiphon of Rhamnus	ca. 310–ca. 235 B.C.E.	Callimachus
ca. 480–390 B.C.E.	Mozi (Modi, Moti, Mo Tzu)	b. ca. 305 B.C.E.	Apollonius of Rhodes (Apollonius Rhodius, Apollonios Rhodios)
469–399 B.C.E.	Socrates		
ca. 468–ca. 396 B.C.E.	Andocides (Andokides)	fl. 300 B.C.E.	Euclid
ca. 460–ca. 401 B.C.E.	Thucydides	fl. ca. 300 B.C.E.	Lieh Yü-k'o
458–379 B.C.E.	Lysias	fl. early third century B.C.E	Lycophron
ca. 448–ca. 380 B.C.E.	Aristophanes		
fl. ca. 440 B.C.E.	Empedocles	fl. third century B.C.E.	Anyte of Tegea
ca. 436–338 B.C.E.	Isocrates		Hedyla
ca. 429–ca. 357 B.C.E.	Xenophon of Athens		Moiro
ca. 428–ca. 348 B.C.E.	Plato		Moschus of Syracuse
fl. ca 400 B.C.E.	Ctesias of Cnidos		Nossis
fl. fourth century B.C.E.	Archestratus	fl. ca. 294–ca. 281 B.C.E.	Leonidas of Tarentum
	Erinna		
	Euhemerus	fl. ca. 290–223 B.C.E.	Song Yu (Sung Yü)
	Isæus	ca. 287–212 B.C.E.	Archimedes
fl. ca. fourth century B.C.E.	Pāṇini	ca. 285–194 B.C.E.	Eratosthenes
385–322 B.C.E.	Aristotle	254–184 B.C.E.	Titus Maccius Plautus
ca. 385–322 B.C.E.	Æschines	239–169 B.C.E.	Quintus Ennius
ca. 384–322 B.C.E	Demosthenes	fl. ca. 230 B.C.E.	Livius Andronicus
ca. 371–ca. 289 B.C.E	Mencius (Mengzi, Meng K'o or Meng-tzu)	fl. 225–200 B.C.E.	Pictor, Quintus Fabius
		201–169 B.C.E.	Jia Yi
ca. 371–ca. 287 B.C.E	Theophrastus of Eresus	ca. 200–ca. 118 B.C.E.	Polybius
fl. ca. 368–ca. 265 B.C.E.	Philemon	fl. second or third century B.C.E	Xenophon of Ephesus
ca. 360–ca. 290 B.C.E.	Dinarchus	fl. second century B.C.E.	Melinno
ca. 355–ca. 290 B.C.E.	Diphilus		
fl. ca. 350 B.C.E.	Zhuangzi (Chuang Tzu, Chuangtse, Kuan Tzu)	ca. 195–ca. 159 B.C.E.	Terence (Publius Terentius Afer)
ca. 350 B.C.E.	Anon. author *Discourses of the States* (Guo yu; Kuo yü)	ca. 180–102 B.C.E.	Lucilius
		177–119 B.C.E.	Sima Xiangru (Ssŭ-ma Hsiang-ju)
ca. 342–292 B.C.E.	Menander	d. 149 B.C.E.	Mei Sheng
341–271 B.C.E.	Epicurus	fl. ca. 146 B.C.E.	Nicander of Colophon

Dates	Author	Dates	Author
ca. 145–86 B.C.E.	Sima Qian (Ssŭ-ma Ch'ien)	23–79 C.E.	Pliny the Elder (Caius Plinius Secundus)
116–27 B.C.E.	Marcus Terentius Varro	26–102 C.E.	Silius Italicus (Tiberius Catius Silius Asconius)
106–43 B.C.E.	Marcus Tullius Cicero		
ca. 100–44 B.C.E.	Gaius Julius Caesar (Gaius Iulius Caesar)	ca. 27–66 C.E.	Petronius Arbiter (Gaius Petronius [?], Titus Petronius [?]
fl. ca. 100 B.C.E.	Bion of Smyrna Meleager of Gadara (Meleagros)	27–97 C.E.	Wang Chong (Weng Ch'ung)
fl. first century B.C.E.	Dionysius of Halicarnassus Sulpicia Turnus Valerius Maximus	34–62 C.E.	Persius (Aulus Persius Flaccus)
		37–ca. 101 C.E.	Flavius Josephus (Josephus; Joseph ben Matthias)
ca. 99–55 B.C.E.	Lucretius (Titus Lucretius Carus)	39–65 C.E.	Lucan (Marcus Annaeus Lucanus)
86–35 B.C.E.	Sallust (Caius Sallustius Crispus)	ca. 40–ca. 96 C.E.	Quintilian (Marcus Fabius Quintilianus)
84–54 B.C.E.	Caius Valerius Catullus	ca. 40–103/4 C.E.	Martial (Marcus Valerius Martialis)
70–19 B.C.E.	Virgil (Vergil, Publius Vergilius Maro)	ca. 46–ca. 120 C.E.	Plutarch
69–26 B.C.E.	Gaius Cornelius Gallus	ca. 55–ca. 117 C.E.	Tacitus, Publius (?) Cornelius
65 B.C.E.–8 C.E.	Horace (Quintus Horatius Flaccus)	ca. 60–130 C.E.	Papias Quadratus
63 B.C.E.–14 C.E.	Augustus Caesar		
59 B.C.E.–17 C.E.	Livy (Titus Livius)	ca. 61–ca. 112 C.E.	Pliny, the Younger (Gaius Plinius Caecilius Secundus)
ca. 56–ca. 19 B.C.E.	Tibullus, Albius		
ca. 53–15 B.C.E.	Sextus Aurelius Propertius	ca. 70–ca. 160 C.E.	Caius Suetonius Tranquillus
53 B.C.E.–18 C.E.	Yang Xiong (Yang Hsiüng)	ca. 86–160 C.E.	Arrian (Flavius Arianus)
43 B.C.E.–17/18 C.E.	Ovid (Publius Ovidius Naso)	d. ca. 90 C.E.	Gaius Valerius Flaccus
fl. ca. 40 B.C.E.	Diodorus Siculus (Diodorus of Agyrium)	d. 96 C.E.	Statius (Publius Papinius Statius)
ca. 15 B.C.E.– ca. 50 C.E.	Phaedrus the fabulist (Gaius Iulius Phaeder)	ca. 90–168 C.E.	Ptolemy (Claudius Ptolemaeus)
ca. 4 B.C.E.–65 C.E.	Seneca, Lucius Annaeus	fl. ca. first–second century C.E.	Juvenal (Decimus Junius Juvenalis?)
fl. first century C.E.	Titus Siculus Calpurnius Parthenius of Nicaea Quintus Rufus Curtius	first & second centuries C.E.	Barnabas Clemens Romanus (Clement)

Dates	Author	Dates	Author
	Diognetus	fl. late third	Nemesianus
	Ignatius	century C.E.	(Marcus Aurelius
	Hermas		Olympius Nemesianus)
	Papias	fl. fourth	Decimus Magnus
	Polycarp	century C.E.	Ausonius
	Quadratus		Libanius of Antioch
fl. second	Achilles Tatius	fl. ca. fourth	Flavius Avianus (Avienus)
century C.E.	Julius Pollux	century C.E.	Damasus
	(Polydeuces of		Ælius Donatus
	Naucratis, Egypt)		Flavius Eutropius
	Pausanias		Palæphatus
	Polyænus		Themistius Euphrades
d. 103/4 C.E.	Sextus Julius Frontinus	329–389 C.E.	St. Gregory of
ca. 120–ca. 180 C.E.	Lucian of Samosata		Nazianzen
121–180 C.E.	Marcus Aurelius	ca. 329–370 C.E.	St. Basil
	Antoninus (Marcus	ca. 331–363 C.E.	Julian (Flavius Claudius,
	Annius Verus)		Julianus, Julian
b. ca. 125 C.E.	Apuleius		the Apostate)
ca.130–ca. 201 C.E	Galen (Claudius	ca. 339–397 C.E.	St. Ambrose
	Galenus)		Ælius Herodianus
ca. 130–220 C.E.	Pacuvius, Marcus	ca. 347–420 C.E.	St. Jerome
fl. ca. 150 C.E.	Hephæstion of	b. 348 C.E.	Aurelius Prudentius
	Alexandria		(Clemens)
	Oppian of Corycus	fl. ca. 350 C.E.	Proba, Faltonia Betitia
	(Oppian of Apamea,	ca. 354–407 C.E.	St. John Chrysostom
	Syria?)	354–430 C.E.	St.Augustine, bishop
ca. 150–230 C.E.	Dio Cocceianus		of Hippo
	Chrysostomus	365–427 C.E.	Tao Qian (T'ao Ch'ien)
ca. 117–189 C.E.	Ælius Aristides	ca. 370–ca. 404 C.E.	Claudian (Claudius
ca. 184–255 C.E.	Origen		Claudianus)
fl. ca. third	Quintus Smyrnaeus	fl. late fourth	Ammianus Marcellinus
century C.E.	(Quintus Calaber)	century C.E.	
fl. ca. 200–250 C.E.?	Diogenes Laertius	d. ca. 400 C.E.	Heliodorus of Emesa
ca. 205–270 C.E.	Plotinus	fl. ca. fourth–fifth	Longus
fl. ca. 210 C.E.	L. Flavius Philostratus	century C.E.	
	(Philostratus the	fl. fifth century C.E.	Claudius Numantianus
	Athenian)		Rutilius
d. ca. 330 C.E.	Iambichlus of Syria		Sedulius, Caelius
216–ca. 276 C.E.	Mani	fl. early fifth	Macrobius (Macrobius
223–262 C.E.	Ji Kang (Hsi K'ang)	century C.E.	Ambrosius Aurelius
ca. 233–ca. 305 C.E	Porphyry		Theodosius)
ca. 264–340 C.E.	Eusebius of Caesarea	412–485 C.E.	Proclus of Byzantium
ca. 295–373 C.E.	St. Athanasius	fl. ca. 450–550 C.E.	Musæus 2

Dates	Author
480–526 C.E.	Ancius Manlius Severinus Boethius (St. Severinus)
fl. ca. 500 C.E.	Zosimus
fl. sixth century C.E.	Agathias of Myrina Procopius
d. ca. 550 C.E.	Cosmas Indicopleustes
ca. 560–636 C.E.	St. Isidore of Seville

Dates	Author
ca. 660–ca. 733 C.E.	Yamanoue no Okura
ca. 718–785 C.E.	Ōtomo no Yakamochi
fl. seventh century C.E.	Kakinomoto no Hitomaro
fl. seventh century C.E.	Princess Nukata Yosami
ca. 810–ca. 893 C.E.	St. Photius
fl. eighth century C.E.	Lady Kasa

A

Academic sect of philosophy (Platonic Philosophy)

The label *Academics* applied to the followers of PLATO and his successors. In the fourth century B.C.E., Plato had lived near Athens and founded a school at a public gymnasium named in honor of an Athenian hero, Academus. The school survived at that location until the first century B.C.E. Thereafter it moved elsewhere. An outpost survived at Byzantium until well into the Christian era.

Plato and his immediate successors had subscribed to the view that the ultimate constituents of reality were ideas. Physical objects were the reflections of an eternal and ideal form. Human perceptions of objects were reflections of reflections of those ideal forms. Plato and his immediate successors, therefore, are considered idealists.

Later Academics became identified with skepticism. The most rigorous Academic skeptics argued that knowledge itself was finally impossible and that the philosopher must therefore be prepared to suspend judgment indefinitely. Later still, the Academics softened that view, deciding that whatever proved convincing, though perhaps impossible to prove, was in and of itself a sufficient ground for drawing a philosophical conclusion and for taking action. In essence, this is the view espoused by one of the most notable Roman adherents of the later Academic school, CICERO.

See also ARISTOTLE.

Bibliography

Sharples, R. W. *Stoics, Epicureans, and Skeptics: An Introduction to Hellenistic Philosophy*. London and New York: Routledge, 1996.

Acharnians, The Aristophanes (425 B.C.E.)

First produced at the Athenian festival of LENAEA, ARISTOPHANES' comedy, *The Acharnians,* appeared under the playwright's pseudonym, Callistratus. Though the play's appearance may not have been its author's first attempt at winning the comedy competition's top prize, *The Acharnians* is the first of his comedies to have achieved that goal. We know that Aristophanes had earlier written two comedies, but neither has survived.

A political play, *The Acharnians* directly expresses Aristophanes' passionately held conviction that the Peloponnesian War should have ended before it started. The action is set at the Athenian hill called Pnyx where the assembly of the people—the *ecclesia*—held its meetings. As many as 20,000 Athenians could gather there to consider the city's business in direct, participatory democracy. Across from the great amphitheater, as it was represented for this performance, stood three houses. One purportedly belonged to the principal character, Dicaeopolis, one to the tragedian EURIPIDES, and one to the Athenian general Lamachus.

Dicaeopolis represents Aristophanes' notion of the good Athenian citizen who, unlike many of his fellows, has come early to the assembly to do his duty. Others who should be there are still in the marketplace, trying to escape being marked by a vermilion-colored rope. This device was used to identify those who tried to shirk their civic responsibilities.

In his opening soliloquy, Dicaeopolis declares his intention to assure that the members of the assembly speak of nothing but a peaceful end to the Peloponnesian War. This noble intention, however, is thwarted by the Herald of the assembly, who refuses to acknowledge speakers favoring peace and calls instead for a report from a diplomatic party, recently returned from the court of the Athenians' former enemies, the Persians. The ambassadors report that the Persians have offered the Athenians gold to support their conflict with Sparta and the other cities of the Peloponnesians, but a Persian in their company makes it clear that the ambassadors are lying.

Seeing that peace for Athens is a foolish hope, Dicaeopolis gives money to another member of the peace party, Amphitheus, to secure a private peace between Sparta and the members of his family. While Amphitheus is gone, a group of Thracian mercenaries are introduced as potential allies against the Spartans. They seem capable only of thievery, and they confirm this by stealing a sack of garlic from Dicaeopolis.

Amphitheus returns and reports that he was set upon by a group of old men, charcoal burners, from Acharnae. Veterans of the battle of Marathon whose grapevines have been cut by the Spartans and their allies, they had tried to prevent Amphitheus from bringing the treaty. He has nevertheless succeeded and brings three bottles of wine that stand for three potential treaties with the Peloponnesians. Tasting them, Dicaeopolis rejects the first two, but the third treaty is a 30-year truce both on land and sea. This one he accepts and ratifies by drinking the bottle's contents in a single gulp. He decides to celebrate the festival of the rural Dionysia. Still afraid of the pursuing Acharnian charcoal burners, though, Amphitheus flees.

The CHORUS enters in the guise of the Acharnians, searching for Amphitheus. They make clear that they want revenge for their ruined vineyards and that they wish to continue the war. Dicaeopolis reenters with his daughter and servants and begins the ceremony of the rural Dionysia. Throughout the play and especially in this section, a good deal of sexual humor and punning contrasts with the play's serious political subject.

The Acharnians begin pelting Dicaeopolis with stones because he has concluded a separate peace. He tries to get them to listen to his reasons. They refuse and are about to stone him when he tells them that he has one of their fellow citizens hostage. He goes in and brings from his house a basket of Acharnian charcoal, which the Acharnians, whose stupidity is the butt of a good deal of joking, recognize as their fellow citizen.

Fearing that Dicaeopolis will carry out his threat to disembowel the basket of charcoal, the Acharnians agree to throw down their stones and listen to him, particularly in view of his promise to speak with his head on an executioner's block so that they can behead him if he fails to convince them. Before assuming that position, however, Dicaeopolis goes to the house of his neighbor, Euripides, who is composing a tragedy. He begs Euripides for the rattiest, most miserable old costume in his collection, a beggar's staff, a little basket with a lighted lamp inside, a little pot with a sponge for a stopper, and some herbs for a basket. Having secured these items, he also asks for a little chervil, but the annoyed Euripides locks the door on him.

Then Dicaeopolis puts his head on the block and begins his speech. He traces the history of the quarrel that has all Greece in arms and argues that because the conflict grew from such petty issues, history proves the parties to the quarrel to have no common sense. Half of the Acharnians are convinced by his argument, but the others consider it insolent, and the Acharnians begin quarreling among themselves. Dicaeopolis's allies seem to be winning, so his opponents call the general, Lamachus, forth from his house to assist them. Dicaeopolis and Lamachus trade insults, and Dicaeopolis accuses the general of enriching himself at the expense of the Athenian state by pressing for a continual state of war. The general illustrates the point by arguing for perpetual war, and exits.

The people now approve Dicaeopolis's actions. The chorus directly addresses the audience in support of the benefit that the satire of a comic poet brings them when he exposes the ploys and plotting of a crooked politician like Cleon—a demagogue whom Aristophanes often denounced in his plays.

Having made his private treaty and having convinced the populace of the benefits of peace, Dicaeopolis marks out a little square that he announces to be his marketplace. All are welcome to trade there. The first to arrive is a Megarian. The city of Megara at this epoch was a mutinous Athenian dependency. The Athenians had ruthlessly suppressed a revolt there, and the Megarians suffered terrible privation. Aristophanes illustrates this by having the first trader to arrive at Dicaeopolis's little market offer his two starving daughters for sale by disguising them as little pigs. Not deceived, Dicaeopolis saves the children, buying them for a quart of salt and a bunch of garlic.

As the play proceeds, Aristophanes seizes opportunities to lampoon other aspects of Athenian life of which he disapproves, particularly informers. When a Boetian trader arrives to do business at his little market, Dicaeopolis trades an Athenian informer for his wares. Seeing that Dicaeopolis has acquired useful and edible goods, his neighbor, the general Lamachus, sends a slave to buy an eel.

Other Athenians, seeing the benefits of the private peace that Dicaeopolis has concluded, try to trade with him for some of it, but he refuses all offers. As the action of the play nears its end, Lamachus is called off to duty and Dicaeopolis to a Dionysian feast. In a mock argument, both prepare for their respective duties, Lamachus by arming and Dicaeopolis by preparing food and drink. As the play concludes, both return—Lamachus wounded in an accident on his way to battle, Dicaeopolis roaring drunk and accompanied by two attentive courtesans. The representative of war endures torment, and the representative of peace enjoys the pleasures of the flesh. The chorus celebrates his triumph, and the play ends.

Bibliography

Aristophanes. *The Complete Plays*. Translated by Paul Roche. New York: New American Library, 2005.

Achilles Tatius   See GREEK PROSE ROMANCE.

Acontius and Kidippe   Callimachus (third century B.C.E.)

Included in the *Aetia* (Origins) of CALLIMACHUS, *Acontius and Kidippe* is a story of young love and trickery.

Having fallen in love at first sight with the lovely young Kidippe, a maiden whom many young men have sought to wed, Acontius learns from the god of love, Eros, a trick by which he might win her. As Kidippe walks with her nurse in the annual procession to the temple of Apollo on the island of Delos, Acontius writes on an apple the words: "I swear by Artemis to marry Acontius." He throws the apple in the path of the nurse, who picks it up and hands it to Kidippe. Kidippe reads the words aloud, and, realizing that she has pronounced a binding oath, throws the apple away.

One after another, the mothers of eager suitors try to arrange a marriage with Kidippe for their sons. When, however, the days appointed for the weddings arrive, Kidippe becomes deathly ill, and the weddings are called off. After three such incidents, Kidippe's father consults the oracle of Apollo at Delphi. There he learns that the gods consider the apple oath binding.

Yielding to the divine will, the parents arrange the marriage, and the young people are wed. Callimachus closes his story by tying it to the theme of the volume in which it appears. Addressing his friend, Cean, Callimachus explains that Cean's clan, the Acontiadae, sprang from the union whose story the poet has just told. As the story ends, the poet also alludes to a series of related incidents that also take their origins from the story he has just told.

Bibliography

Callimachus. *Aetia*. Translated by C. A. Trypannis. Loeb Classical Library. Vol. 421. Cambridge, Mass.: Harvard University Press, 1975.

Achilles Tatius   See Greek Prose Romance.

Adelphi (The Brothers) Terence (ca. 160 B.C.E.)

Following a prologue in which Terence defends himself against an apparent charge of having stolen his plot from Plautus and in which Terence cites as his source a different part of Diphilus's play *Synapothnescontes* than the one that Plautus used, the play proper begins.

Micio begins the play with a substantial soliloquy. In it we learn that his adoptive son—really his nephew—Aeschinus has not returned home all night. We also discover that Micio's brother Demea has given his son Aeschinus to Micio to rear. Demea has kept his other son, Ctesipho, at home. Micio and Demea, however, disagree about child-rearing techniques. Micio favors an indulgent and permissive regimen for Aeschinus, whereas Demea favors a stricter upbringing for Ctesipho. Demea has often criticized Micio for his laissez-faire attitude.

Demea now enters, however, and in scene 2 reveals that during the night Aeschinus has broken into a private home, beaten members of the family, and carried off a slave girl—a musician. Demea blames Micio, who staunchly defends both his parenting and a young man's right to such high-spirited behavior. In scene 3, though, we learn that Micio truly is distressed by Aeschinus's actions and pretended otherwise for his brother's benefit. We also learn that Aeschinus has informed his adoptive father of his intention to marry.

Act 2 opens with the entry of Aeschinus; his servant Parmeno; the music-girl he has kidnapped; and Sannio, a procurer who has paid 20 *minae* of silver for the girl and has been holding her as a thrall. After having Sannio struck for his presumption in buying a free woman, Aeschinus offers to restore Sannio's money and end the matter. Sannio thinks over the offer, but he is reluctant to accept it lest Aeschinus use the law to defraud Sannio of his money. Micio's slave, Syrus, enters and reveals that he knows enough about Sannio's shady business to ruin him unless he accepts Aeschinus's offer—indeed unless he accepts half the offer. Ctesipho, who is in love with the music-girl, enters praising his brother for his kindness. Aeschinus brushes off the praise, sends his brother in to his beloved, and goes to the market with Sannio to get his money.

In act 3, the plot takes an unexpected twist with the appearance of two women, Sostrata and Canthera. They are in urgent need of a midwife to help deliver a child whom Aeschinus has fathered with Sostrata's daughter, Pamphilia. However, a servant, Geta, enters and, reporting that Aeschinus has kidnapped a music-girl, and Sostrata concludes that he has abandoned the mother of his child. Sostrata goes to seek assistance from an aged kinsman, Hegio.

Scenes 3 and 4 reveal Demea in search of Ctesipho. The father has heard that his son was involved in the music-girl incident. Demea encounters Syrus. Syrus tries to throw Demea off the scent by telling him that his son is in the fields attending to his father's business. Convinced, Demea is just about to forget the whole affair when, in scene 6, he encounters Hegio, who is a member of his tribe and also Pamphilia's kinsman. Hegio tells the whole history of the relationship between Aeschinus and Pamphilia, and what a cad the young man is to desert her for the music-girl. (At this point, from offstage, we hear Pamphilia's cries of labor pain and her prayers to Juno—the patron goddess of childbirth.) Demea promises to intervene on Pamphilia's behalf with Micio, and Hegio reports the good news to Sostrata.

Act 4 finds Demea trying to obtain news of Ctesipho's whereabouts from Syrus. Though Ctesipho is in fact hiding nearby, Syrus sends the lad's father on a wild goose chase in search of him. In scene 4, Hegio and Micio have straightened out the entire matter between them, and they go to tell Sostrata that Aeschinus is true to his promises to Pamphilia.

Aeschinus, however, is unaware of this happy outcome and has learned how his feelings have been misrepresented to Sostrata and Pamphilia. In scene 5, he rushes to Sostrata's house and pounds on the door so that he can straighten out the confusion. His father Micio, however, is there ahead of him. Deciding that his adoptive son will benefit from worrying a bit longer, Micio misleads the young man. Pamphilia must, he says, marry a near relative who has come to take her away to Miletus. Without confessing that he argues for himself, Aeschinus asks Micio to consider the feelings of the young man who has fathered Pamphilia's child. He weeps. His tears touch his father's heart, and the older man confesses that he knows everything, promising that Aeschinus and Pamphilia will wed.

In the two scenes that follow, Demea and Micio encounter one another, and Micio explains the outcome. Demea asks if Micio is pleased with Aeschinus's match with a penniless girl. Micio admits that he is not, but that one must accept what life brings and try by art to cure it. Demea has the impression that Aeschinus, the music-girl, and Pamphilia are all to live under the same roof in a ménage à trois. He is as yet unaware that Ctesipho loves the music-girl.

Act 5 opens with Demea's soliloquy in which he regrets having spent his life worrying about money and wearing himself out about trifles while his cheerful brother has spent an easy life. Worst of all, Demea finds that both the boys he fathered now avoid him and seek out Micio as their confidant. Acting on this reflection, he immediately begins treating both sons and slaves with generosity and kindness. Encountering Aeschinus, who is chaffing at the delays involved in wedding preparations, Demea tells him to have the wall between the neighboring houses thrown down and the bride brought over. For the first time in his life, his son calls him "charming." Demea likes the effect.

He next talks his initially resistant 65-year-old brother Micio into marrying Sostrata. That accomplished, Demea enlists Aeschinus as an ally and talks Micio into freeing his slave, Syrus, and his wife as well. When an astonished Micio wonders at Demea's sudden change, Demea confesses that his behavior is intended as an object lesson. The reason that the two younger men love Micio most arises from his foolish indulgence. Although Demea consents to a union between Ctesipho and the music-girl, he makes that his last concession to youthful folly. Demea offers to advise the young men in curbing their extravagant behavior in future so that they can live genuinely happy rather than merely self-indulgent lives. Taking Demea's point, the young men accept his guidance, and the play ends.

Bibliography

Terence. *Works: English and Latin.* Translated by John Barsby. Cambridge, Mass.: Harvard University Press, 2001.

———. *Terence, the Comedies*. Translated by Palmer Bovie et al. Baltimore: Johns Hopkins University Press, 1992.

Ælius Aristides (ca. 117–189 C.E.) *Greek prose writer*

A SOPHIST philosopher and celebrated orator, Ælius Aristides was born at Hadrianapolis in the Roman province of Bithnia on the Bosphorus Sea to the family of Eudamon, a priest of Zeus. He moved to Smyrna (also called Myrrha, now Izmir in Turkey), where he established his reputation as a scholar, and became a public hero following Smyrna's destruction by an earthquake in 178. Ælius wrote to the emperor Marcus Aurelius describing the devastation, and the emperor was so moved that he had the city rebuilt. A grateful citizenry erected a statue in Ælius's honor.

Fifty-four of Ælius's public speeches survive in full, together with a few fragmentary remains. They suggest that he was as accomplished an orator as some of his golden-age predecessors. He also wrote a two-scroll treatise on oratorical style that distinguished between the high style appropriate to political speeches and the ordinary style employed for other purposes.

Another example of his writing also survives. Ælius was afflicted by a serious and recurring illness, perhaps psychological in nature. In his *Sacred Tales*, he describes the way in which the Greek god of medicine, Æsclepius, visited the sufferer in his dreams and prescribed cures for his ailments. Although Ælius rejected most proffered public honors, when the citizens offered to appoint him to the office of priest of Æsclepius, he accepted.

Some of Ælius's letters also survive. His writings are available in good English translations.

Bibliography

Aelius Aristides. *The Complete Works*. Translated by Charles A. Behr. Leiden: Brill, 1981–86.

"Aelius_Aristides." Available online. URL: http://www.nndb.com/people/761/000096473/. Accessed January 13, 2006.

Behr, Charles A. *Aelius Aristides and the Sacred Tales*. Amsterdam: A. M. Hallkert, 1968.

Horst, Pieter William van der. *Aelius Aristides and the New Testament*. Leiden: Brill, 1980.

Aeneid Virgil (30–19 B.C.E)

For most of the last decade of his life, VIRGIL, who had withdrawn from the city of Rome into the congenial countryside of Campania near Naples, worked on his great Latin EPIC, *Aeneid*. Inspired by the form and content of his incomparable Greek predecessor, HOMER, Virgil self-consciously sought to create a national epic for the emergent Roman Empire under the rule of its first emperor, AUGUSTUS CAESAR.

As one strategy among many to achieve that end, Virgil sought to link the dynasty of ancient Troy in the person of its surviving prince, Aeneas, with the newly created Roman imperium—and with the victorious heir of a man who, though perhaps emperor in fact, was never emperor in name, JULIUS CAESAR. Thus, in the English translation of Allen Mandelbaum—one unparalleled in its poetic reflection of Virgil's original—Virgil begins with his statement of epic purpose: "I sing of arms and of a man: his fate / had made him fugitive. . . ."

Then, after alluding to his hero's difficult voyage and his facing not only maritime dangers but also the unremitting wrath of Juno, the queen of the gods, Virgil tells how the Trojan prince came at last to the Lavinian shores of Italy, bringing his gods with him. "From this," says Virgil, "have come the Latin race, the lords / of Alba, and the ramparts of high Rome."

In the *Aeneid*, Virgil assumes on the part of his readers a close familiarity with the names, roles, and relationships of a large cast of characters familiar to his audience but not to a modern one. To assist a modern reader less familiar with such matters, therefore, before summarizing the epic's action, I provide a grid with the names and roles of the characters that appear in this précis of Virgil's poem.

WHO'S WHO IN VIRGIL'S *AENEID*

	Role	Allied with
Gods and Immortals		
Allecto	A Fury from the underworld who foments trouble for the Trojans at Juno's behest	Latins
Apollo	Sun god and god of physicians and artists	
Calliope	Muse of epic poetry	
Cerberus	Three-headed watchdog of Hades	
Charon	Immortal boatman of the river Styx who conducts the shades of the dead into Hades	Everyone
Clio	Muse of history	
Cupid	God of love	
Cymodoce	Sea goddess who reports to Aeneas the situation at the Trojans' camp when it is attacked by Turnus	Trojans
Diana	Goddess of the hunt and sister of Apollo	Latins
Erato	Muse of lyric poetry	
Furies (Harpies)	Hellish immortals who plague humankind	
Iris	Goddess of rainbow and divine messenger	
Juno	Queen of gods; wife and sister of Jupiter	Latins
Jupiter	King of the gods	Trojans
Juturna	Italian goddess of fountains; sister to Turnus who protects him in battle	Latins
Minerva	Goddess of wisdom	

(continues)

WHO'S WHO IN VIRGIL'S *AENEID* (continued)

	Role	Allied with
Minos	Judge of the dead in the underworld	
Neptune	God of sea and earthquake	Greeks
Polyphemus	A Cyclops on Sicily	
Proserpina	Goddess of the underworld who must spend six months there and six on Earth	
Tiberinus	The god of the Tiber River	Trojans
Venus	Goddess of love; mother of Aeneas	Trojans
Vulcan	Blacksmith of the gods	Trojans

Trojans: Their Allies, Descendants, and Enemies in Africa and Italy

Aeneas	A Trojan prince who will found the Roman state; son of Venus	
Acestes	Son of a Trojan mother and a Sicilian river-god; hosts Aeneas in Sicily	
Achates	Survivor of fall of Troy, companion of Aeneas	
Amata	Queen of the Latins; opposed to a Trojan marriage for her daughter Lavinia; pawn of Juno in opposing Aeneas	
Anchises	Aeneas's father; dies enroute to Italy	
Andromache	Former wife of Trojan hero Hector; now companion of Pergamus in Mysia	
Anna	Dido's sister	
Arruns	Trojan who sneakily slays Camilla from ambush	Trojans

	Role	Allied with
Ascanius (also called Iulus)	Aeneas's son and heir	Trojans
Avernan Sibyl	Prophetess of Apollo who guides Aeneas through the underworld	
Beroë	Aged Trojan woman whose shape Iris takes to encourage the women to fire Aeneas's ships.	Juno
Caieta	Aeneas's nurse; buried near Rome	
Camilla	Warrior maiden, leader of the Volscians; a favorite of the goddess Diana, she is slain from ambush by the Trojan Arruns	Latins
Deiphobus	Trojan who married Helen of Troy after the death of her husband Paris	
Dido	Queen and builder of Carthage; lover of Aeneas but deserted by him	
Drances	Adviser to King Latinus who urges that the king withdraw his support from Turnus and support Aeneas	Trojans
Evander	King of the Greco-Italian city of Pallanteum	Trojans
Helenus	Trojan survivor; prophet who predicts Aeneas will succeed in quest for Rome	
Iarbas	Moorish king; suitor of Dido; granted land for building Carthage	
Ilioneus	Trojan survivor; emissary from Aeneas to Dido	
Laocoön	Trojan prophet killed by sea serpents upon advising against bringing the Trojan horse within city walls	
Latinus	King of the Latins; father of Lavinia	
Lavinia	Princess of the Latins destined to marry Aeneas	

(continues)

WHO'S WHO IN VIRGIL'S *AENEID* (continued)

	Role	Allied with
Lausus	Latin warrior killed in battle; son of Mezentius	Latins
Mezentius	Latin warrior killed in battle; father of Lausus	Latins
Misenus	Trojan drowned in surf on landing at Avernus	
Nautes	Senior Trojan who encourages Aeneas to settle the less adventuresome Trojans in Sicily	
Palinurus	Trojan steersman who falls asleep, falls overboard, and is murdered by brigands on reaching shore	
Pallas	Son of King Evander of Pallanteum; killed by Turnus while supporting Aeneas in battle	Trojans
Pandarus	Giant Trojan warrior, killed by Turnus	
Priam	King of Troy killed during Greek sack of city	
Polydorus	Murdered Trojan prince, son of Queen Hecuba, whose ghost appears to Aeneas	
Romulus	Descendant of Aeneas and founder of Rome	
Rutulians	Latin opponents of Aeneas led by Turnus	
Sychaeus	Former husband of Dido, with whom she is reunited in the underworld	
Teucer	Cretan founder of Troy; gives Trojans their alternative name, "Teucrians"	
Tolumnius	Latin soothsayer who misinterprets signs and leads the Latins to break a truce	Latins
Turnus	Principal Italian enemy of Aeneas and suitor for the hand of the Latin princess, Lavinia	Latins

	Role
Greeks in the *Aeneid*	
Achaemenides	Greek castaway who warns Aeneas about hostile Cyclops on Sicily and whom the Trojans rescue
Chalcas	Greek prophet who accompanied the fleet to Troy
Helen	Wife of King Menelaus of Sparta; eloped with Paris to Troy.
Menelaus	King of Sparta; first husband of Helen
Pyrrhus	Greek warrior; slayer of Trojan king Priam
Sinon	Greek spy who opens the Trojan horse once it is within the city's walls.

Book 1

In keeping with epic convention, Virgil calls on the Muse to explain the root of Juno's enmity, and in response, the Muse begins speaking through the poet and explaining the wrath of the goddess. Juno favors Carthage, a city on the North African coast that has been her candidate for domination of the Mediterranean world. Prophecy has foretold, however, that Rome will eventually surpass Carthage. Knowing this prediction, Juno does all within her very considerable power to delay that outcome, including harassing a small band of Trojan War survivors as their fleet attempts to cross the Mediterranean Sea. (See MUSES.)

Juno is also annoyed (for background on Trojan War, see entries on *ILIAD* and *ODYSSEY*.) that Athena (Minerva) can seemingly achieve more carnage at sea than can the queen of the gods. Juno therefore appeals to Aeolus, the god of the winds, for a hurricane, promising him a wife from among her sea nymphs in recompense. Aeolus complies, and the Trojans instantly find themselves in shallow water off Sicily in the teeth of a tempest. Aeneas watches as ship after ship goes down. However, Neptune, the Roman god of the sea, reproves and calms the raging winds. Aeneas is then able to collect the remaining seven vessels of his squadron and bring them to harbor off Libya on the North African coast.

Ashore there, Aeneas successfully hunts seven deer—one for each of his remaining ship's crews. As they feast, the scene shifts to Heaven, where Venus, the goddess of love, is asking her father, Jupiter, why he has allowed such evil to befall her son and favorite, Aeneas. Jupiter comforts her and predicts the future for Aeneas and his descendants. Aeneas will become the king of Latium. His descendant, Romulus, will found Rome, and Rome will have "empire without end" and be ruled by a Trojan emperor. Even Juno will then hold the Romans dear.

The scene then shifts back to North Africa, where Aeneas and his companion Achates are trying to find out where they have made landfall. Disguised as a Thracian huntress, Venus encounters them and speaks to them. Though Aeneas does not recognize his mother, her voice gives her away as a goddess. She explains that they are in the domain of Dido, the widow of Sychaeus, and the object of the unlawful passion of Sychaeus's murderer, her brother Pygmalion. Fleeing her brother's embraces, Dido and her followers have built the city of Carthage. Eventually Aeneas recognizes the goddess as his mother and reproves her for her disguises.

Entering the city shrouded by a mist, Aeneas and Achates make their way to Dido's temple honoring Juno. There they find the history of the Trojan War movingly depicted in sculptures. As the refugees stare in wonder at their own history, the arrival of the beautiful Dido interrupts them. She sits in state dispensing legal decisions. Then, through the throng at the foot of her throne, the Trojans are amazed to see arrive many of the comrades whom they had thought lost at sea. Restraining their desire to greet their comrades, Aeneas and Achates remain concealed in their supernatural mists to observe what welcome their countrymen may find with Dido.

The eldest of the Trojans, Ilioneus, reports to Dido the objectives of their voyage and the disasters that they have suffered en route. He asks to be allowed to repair the fleet and continue the expedition. Dido willingly grants his request and wishes aloud that Aeneas, too, were present. The concealing fog dissipates and reveals Aeneas, godlike in his masculine beauty. He greets Dido. Startled, she returns his greeting, invites him to join her at her palace, and sends provisions for the other Trojans to the beaches. Aeneas instructs Achates to send gifts for Dido to the palace with Aeneas's son Ascanius.

Venus, however—always trying to give Aeneas an advantage in case matters turn sour—substitutes Cupid in the form of Ascanius. As a result of the arrival of the winged god, Dido falls hopelessly in love with Aeneas. As her heart becomes ensnared, a great banquet progresses, and following much drinking and entertainment, Dido asks Aeneas to recount the history of his wanderings from the beginning. Thus, having begun in the epic fashion in the middle of the story, Virgil jumps back to its start as the second book begins.

Book 2

Aeneas tells how the desperate Greek invaders of Troy, advised by Minerva, hit upon the stratagem of a large wooden horse, supposedly an offering for their safe return home, but in fact a ruse to get some of their best men inside the gates of Troy. The Trojans, thinking the Greek fleet has sailed, open their gates and sightsee on the battlefield. The prophet Laocoön advises destroying the horse, but the gods have determined otherwise. As the crowd admires the horse, a young Greek captive named Sinon is dragged in. Although in fact Sinon is part of the conspiracy to get the horse inside Troy, he persuades the Trojans instead that he was supposed to be sacrificed to ensure the Greeks a fair passage home. He avoided that fate, he explains, by escaping his bonds and hiding in a muddy pond until the Greeks had sailed. The Trojans believe and pity him.

Sinon convinces them that all along the Greeks' only hope had lain in the favor of Pallas Athena (Minerva), but that when they had violated her shrine, the Palladium, at Troy, the goddess had switched sides and the Greek cause was doomed. On the advice of the Greek prophet Chalcas, says Sinon, the Greeks had constructed the horse as atonement for stealing the statue of the goddess. He convinces the Trojans that the horse had been constructed so it could not be brought within Troy's gates. Should the Trojans harm the horse, the prophecy predicts their destruction. Should the horse somehow "climb the walls," however, the Trojans would eventually rule the Greeks.

As if to confirm Sinon's false words, two great sea serpents slither ashore and encircle and kill the prophet Laocoön and his two children. The Trojans take this horror as divine confirmation of what Sinon has told them, and they immediately set about breaching their own walls so that the horse can be brought into the city. Late at night, Sinon opens a trapdoor in the horse to free the Greek warriors hiding within its hollow interior. They in turn open Troy's gates to the Grecian troops that have come up from their hiding places and from the returned ships.

Now Aeneas movingly describes the sack of Troy and the Trojans' fruitless attempts at resistance. He pictures the capture of the Trojan women and the death of King Priam at the hands of the Greek warrior, Pyrrhus. He explains how, at last, he encounters Venus, his mother, who tells him to see about preserving the surviving members of his own family: his father Anchises, his wife Creüsa, and his son Ascanius (also often called by his alternative name, Iulus). Aeneas finds them and persuades his father to accompany him. Carrying the old man on his back, holding his son by the hand, and with his wife and other companions following, he sets out through the burning city. Everyone but Creüsa makes it. When he misses her, the frantic Aeneas runs back, searching everywhere until he encounters her ghost, who tells him that his fate has destined him for a new bride on the banks of the Italian river Tiber. Aeneas tries three times to embrace his wife's shade, but his circling arms encounter no substance. So, now at the head of band of refugees, Aeneas makes for the relative safety of the nearby mountains as the second book ends.

Book 3

The third book finds the Trojan exiles building a fleet to carry them on a voyage across the Mediterranean Sea in search of a new home. Aeneas attempts a landing in Thrace, but when he offers sacrifices and tries to uproot a small tree, its roots bleed. A second attempt produces the same result. (In the Middle Ages, Dante will borrow this device when describing the hellish fate of suicides.) A third attempt produces the voice of the dead Trojan prince Polydorus, who warns Aeneas that he must sail on as it was the Thracian king who murdered him. (See *Hecuba*.)

Another landing on the Mediterranean island of Delos again produces disappointment as the island's tutelary deity, Apollo, advises them to sail on to Crete, the island from which the archetypal Trojan ancestor, Teucer, had sailed when he founded the city of Troy. When the Trojan wanderers obey, however, they are plague-stricken immedi-

ately on landing. Prepared to sail back to Delos in search of further prophecy, Aeneas is spared that necessity as the Phrygian household gods that he has carried with him from Troy appear in a dream with a message from Apollo: Italy will be the Trojans' new home. They will not win it easily, however. Storms and an inadvertent war with the Harpies (also called the Furies) await them on their journey. This last episode earns them the enmity of the Furies, who promise that the Trojans will not reach Italy before famine has made them gnaw their tables.

Coasting Greece, the exiles winter on the Island of Leucadia, near the temple of Apollo, standing close by the promontory from which, much later, an unlikely legend reports that a lovelorn SAPPHO leapt to her death. With spring, the Trojan wanderers take to their ship once more. Making landfall in Mysia near the city of Buthrotum on the river Xanthus, Aeneas and his crew encounter Andromache (see *ANDROMACHE*,) the widow of the Trojan hero Hector. Now the companion of Pergamus, founder of the city Pergamum, Andromache is making offerings to her dead husband. Mutually startled at the encounter, the Trojans and Andromache are exchanging news when another Trojan survivor, prince Helenus, comes down from the city to welcome his countrymen.

In the following discussion, Aeneas and his voyagers learn that Italy is still a long and difficult voyage away. Its route, part real and part mythic, follows a portion of the one that Odysseus sailed in Homer's *The ODYSSEY*. More encouraging is the information Helenus shares with Aeneas about his ultimate destination. Aeneas will know he has arrived at his fated destination when he finds a "huge white sow" suckling 30 white piglets beside a secret stream and under the branches of an ilex. Helenus also discounts the Harpies' warning about gnawing at the tables.

Continuing his prophecy, Helenus instructs Aeneas to shun the eastern coasts of Italy, which are already occupied by Greeks, and suggests coasting Sicily on the south and not attempting the Straits of Messina. Then, when the Trojan wanderers arrive at Cumae, a point near modern

Naples, they must consult the sibyl who inhabits a cave at Avernus. She will tell Aeneas what he needs to know next.

After further leave-taking and receiving gifts from his former countrymen and from Andromache, Aeneas and his band resume their journey. At long last they sight in the distance the hills of Italy and eventually Mt. Etna on Sicily. They camp nearby and encounter a member of Odysseus's crew who was forgotten and left behind when they escaped the Cyclops's cave. This castaway, Achaemenides, tells again the story of the Cyclops. The Trojans accept Achaemenides as a passenger and, in the nick of time, escape from the land of the Cyclops Polyphemus and his kin, for the one-eyed giants had become aware of the Trojans' presence. Aeneas reports the balance of the voyage up until the point that the hurricane drove the Trojans ashore in Africa, and Book 3 ends.

Book 4

Book 4 opens with renewed focus on Dido's obsessive passion for Aeneas—a feeling that she shares with her sister and confidant, Anna. "I know too well the signs of the old flame," she remarks prophetically, but she also repeats her resolve not to remarry. Anna, however, counsels Dido otherwise and feeds her hope for a union with Aeneas. As she studies the signs of the future in her sacrifice, Virgil inserts ominous references to fire and flame as Dido's behavior increasingly reveals her as one in the grip of an irresistible and burning passion.

Juno, seeing an opportunity to avoid fate, proposes a truce with Venus. Let Aeneas and Dido rule in Carthage; the Roman Empire may never happen. Venus, however, sees through the ruse and suggests that Juno put her proposition before Jupiter. Juno, who is goddess of marriage, then announces her intention to isolate Aeneas and Dido during the next day's planned hunt, and to see them united in marriage. Venus cunningly assents.

When a sudden thunderstorm interrupts the next day's hunt, Dido and Aeneas, separated from their party, end up in the same cave. What occurs there, which with Roman golden-age taste Virgil does not report, Dido calls marriage. Rumor, however, is swift to fly to every corner. It reaches the Moorish king, Iarbas, who had granted Dido the right to settle and is as enamored with her as she is with Aeneas. Iarbas prays to Jupiter for redress, and Jupiter sends Mercury to remind Aeneas, who has dallied the winter away with Dido, that he must be on his way to Italy. Mercury's appearance terrifies Aeneas and has the desired effect.

Yet Aeneas is torn between what he knows to be his destiny and duty and his passion for Dido. He gives secret orders for the fleet to be readied, but Dido intuits his intention and rages at him. Aeneas defends himself, pleading that it is not his own free will that requires him to sail to Italy. She rejects his pleas and dismisses him, promising to haunt him forever. She takes to her chamber, from which she can watch the frenzied preparations on the beach as Trojans ready themselves for their voyage. Sending Anna as her messenger, Dido pleads that Aeneas will at least come to see her once more, but he remains adamant in his purpose.

At last driven mad by her obsession—a madness that Virgil depicts with great deftness, verisimilitude, and tact—Dido prepares to end her life. She disguises her intention, however, pretending that she is about to employ magic to win Aeneas back. She has her sister build a funeral pyre in the inner courtyard of the palace. On it are heaped Aeneas's abandoned weapons and clothing, the bed the lovers had shared, and Aeneas's effigy. Once she has performed the witchcraft associated with her design, a sorrowful Dido once more considers her options and rejects them all but suicide.

At just that moment, Mercury once again visits Aeneas to stiffen his resolve for sailing. Terrified at the god's appearance, Aeneas gives the order, and the Trojans sail for Italy. Seeing him sail, Dido invokes terrible curses on him. Then, sending a servant to bring her sister Anna, Dido mounts the funeral pyre, seizes Aeneas's sword, and falls upon it. Her astonished servants spread the word, and Anna rushes to the spot, where she finds Dido still breathing but in agony. Juno takes pity on her and sends the goddess of the rainbow, Iris, to release Dido's spirit from her body.

Book 5

From the departing ships, as Book 5 begins, Aeneas sees the conflagration of Dido's funeral pyre without knowing what it means. Once again assailed by storms, the fleet is forced ashore on Sicily in the friendly realm of Acestes, son of a river god and a Trojan mother. Acestes welcomes the wanderers, and Aeneas declares a day of feasting and competitions in honor of the anniversary of the death of his father Anchises, who had passed away the previous time the fleet had harbored there.

Virgil honors the aesthetic principle of *varietas*—variety in composition—in Book V by departing from the main line of the story to detail a sailing competition among four of Aeneas's galleys. Virgil here shows himself to be an accomplished sporting commentator in the tradition of PINDAR. To the delightful account of the race with its triumphs and disasters, he adds poetic lists of prizes, which he describes. He closes this section with a description of a galley, disabled in the race, as it limps late into shore. Footraces follow, with cheating and fouling, and then comes brutal boxing followed by archery. Finally the Trojans demonstrate their skill as cavalry troops.

Juno, however, has not abandoned her enmity toward the Trojans. She sends Iris disguised as an aged Trojan woman, Beroë, who appeals to the weariness of the Trojan women, encouraging them to burn the ships so that they will not be able to venture further on the sea. The women fire the ships, but in answer to Aeneas's prayer, Jupiter sends a deluge that extinguishes the fires, saving all but four vessels. Then, however, a senior member of the expedition, Nautes, advises Aeneas to allow those who are worn out with seafaring to become colonists in Sicily and to proceed to Italy only with those whose hearts are eager for more war and for fame. During the night, the shade of

Aeneas's father, Anchises, comes as Jupiter's messenger and seconds this counsel.

Those Trojans who wish to do so remain in Sicily, and the rest repair the ships and once more set sail. Venus invokes Neptune's protection for the seafarers, and the sea god promises that they will reach the harbor of Averna safely with the loss of only one more Trojan. This prophecy is fulfilled when the helmsman, Palinurus, falls asleep at the steering oar, falls overboard, and apparently drowns while the fleet sweeps on its way and Book 5 ends.

Book 6

In Book 6, the Trojans arrive at the cave of the Avernan sibyl—a fear-inspiring prophetess of Apollo. Under her terrifying urging, they make their sacrifices and address their prayers to the sun god. Aeneas promises Apollo that he will build temples and shrines to the god and his sister Diana when the Trojans have established their kingdom.

The sibyl begins to prophecy war, a foreign wedding, and an unlikely path to safety via a Greek city. When the prophetic ecstasy has departed from the sibyl's breast, Aeneas asks permission to descend through her cave into the underworld so that he can once more consult the shade of his father, Anchises. The sibyl warns Aeneas that few who make that descent return. Nonetheless, she instructs him to pluck the golden bough of Proserpina, which will protect him and enable him to return to the upper world. Before he undertakes the horrid descent, however, she instructs him to bury a dead friend. Surprised, the Trojans discover on the beach the body of their comrade Misenus, pounded to death by breakers. As they prepare his funeral pyre, Aeneas locates and plucks the golden bough.

After the funeral rites have been observed, Aeneas prepares to descend through a wide-mouthed cavern whose vapors pour forth, killing birds that attempt to fly over it. As the sibyl guides Aeneas through the airless cave on the path to Hades, Virgil speaks in his own voice, calling upon the gods of the underworld, the "voiceless shades," and upon Phlegeton and Chaos to help him reveal what lies below. Again, the model of Homer guides Virgil on his obligatory epic journey into the underworld.

Virgil's Hades is an even more frightening place than Homer's. At the entrance to the underworld, Aeneas encounters the personifications of Grief, Cares, Diseases, Old Age, Fear, Hunger, Poverty, Death, Trials, Sleep, Evil Pleasures, War, the Furies, and Strife. He also encounters many of the monsters of ancient mythology—Gorgons, Harpies, Chimaera, Centaurs, and Geryon—and sees the shades of the recently dead, all pleading to be allowed into Hades. But those for whom the rites have not been performed must wait 100 years for entry.

In Hades, Aeneas encounters the shade of his helmsman, Palinurus, who reports that he did not in fact drown. He had twisted off the ship's rudder and managed to make landfall when barbarians discovered and killed him. Palinurus pleads that Aeneas will find his body and bury it or use his influence with the gods so that his restless spirit can find peace.

Next, Charon, the helmsman of the river Styx, challenges Aeneas and the sibyl, but on seeing the golden bough, he ferries them across. The three-headed guard dog of Hades, Cerberus, also threatens them, but the sibyl tosses him a drugged honey cake, and he falls asleep. As they descend, they pass the souls of infants, the place where Minos passes judgment on the newly arrived shades. Then the pair arrives at the Fields of Mourning, where, among the shades of tragic women, Aeneas recognizes and speaks to that of Dido. He once more assures her that he left against his will, but, unmoved, she moves off to find the shade of her husband, Sychaeus.

Aeneas passes comrades and enemies from the Trojan War, including Deiphobus, the Trojan who married Helen of Troy after the death of Paris. (In Virgil's version, Helen betrays Deiphobus to her first husband, the Greek king of Sparta, Menelaus, who kills the Trojan.) Urged on by the sibyl, Aeneas comes next to the place where those guilty of crimes against the gods are punished. Following descriptions of some of the sufferers there, the pair passes on to the Groves of Blessedness. Amid those fortunate enough to spend eternity there, Aeneas finds his father Anchises in a pleasant green valley. As he earlier had done with his wife's ghost, Aeneas fruitlessly attempts to embrace his father's shade.

Among the matters Anchises explains to Aeneas is the fact that reincarnation is possible for those who have had all their guilt absolved over a very long time. Then Anchises prophecies what the future holds for Aeneas and his descendants. Aeneas will marry Lavinia. They will produce a race of kings who will build and rule cities—Romulus among them—and eventually Rome will extend her boundaries over all the world under Caesar and his successor, Augustus, who will reinstitute a golden age on Earth. Anchises also previews for Aeneas the activities of the Romans during what was, for Virgil, its more recent history. Then Virgil has Anchises utter the words that surely summarize the author's own view of Rome's role in the history of the world: "Roman, these will be your arts: / to teach the ways of peace to those you conquer, / to spare defeated peoples, tame the proud." (*Aeneid* 6:1135–37).

Anchises tells Aeneas of the wars he has still to face and advises him on how to respond to each circumstance. He then conducts Aeneas and the sibyl to the gate of ivory through which false dreams enter the world above, and through it the mortals pass back into the world of the living. Aeneas immediately boards his ship and sails north to Caieta—a spot on the coast south near Rome named for Aeneas's nurse, whom he buried there as Book 7 begins.

Book 7

Having conducted Caieta's funeral, Aeneas sails north to the mouth of the Tiber River. As the Trojans arrive there, Virgil once again invokes a muse, this time Erato the muse of lyric poetry. In Latium, where the Trojan adventurers have now arrived, Latinus rules. His only offspring is a daughter, Lavinia, whom he had hoped to give in marriage to a promising successor. When candidates came forward, however, and when Latinus consulted the oracles, the portents proved uniformly unfavorable. A voice informed him instead that a stranger was coming as a son-in-law who would raise the names of his descendants above the stars.

Having come ashore, the Trojans use wheat cakes as platters for a slender meal, and after eating the fruits from them, they eat the cakes. Aeneas's son Ascanius—now more usually called Iulus—quips that they have eaten their tables after all.

The next day, an embassy of 100 Trojans go to pay their respects to King Latinus and request that they be permitted a peaceful settlement in their chosen new home. Latinus welcomes them, and they recount their story and present their gifts. Latinus begins thinking about a husband for his daughter. He sends the emissaries back with rich gifts after telling them of his desire for a son-in-law.

As the Trojans settle in and begin building houses, Juno observes them and grows angry at her own apparent weakness. She realizes that she cannot keep Aeneas and Lavinia apart since Jupiter and fate have decreed their union, but the goddess can delay the wedding and still exact a high price in human blood. Juno enlists the service of the Furies, and one of them, Allecto, stirs up trouble for Aeneas and Latinus. Latinus's wife, Amata, had favored one of Lavinia's former suitors, Turnus, whom Virgil pictures as the king of Artea and the Rutulian people. Amata does her best to dissuade Latinus from matching Lavinia with Aeneas. When that fails, she pretends to be possessed by Bacchic madness and conceals Lavinia in the mountains to forestall the wedding. Her frenzy provokes a kind of mass hysteria among the matrons of Latium, and they join their queen in her wild passion.

Having provoked this furor, Allecto assumes the form of an aged priestess and seeks to incite Turnus. He ignores her until she appears to him in her own demonic form; then, driven mad by her provocation, he calls his people to arms and sets out to drive the Trojans from Italy and to support his claim to Lavinia by force of arms.

Still inciting the locals, Allecto embroils the Trojans and the local shepherds in a bloody battle over a pet stag that Ascanius had wounded. She then reports to Juno, and Juno dismisses her, saying that she can handle what else needs doing herself. With her incitement, the war spreads through the region, and Virgil recites a lengthy litany of the names and accomplishments of those who join Turnus's cause against the Trojans. Others, however, flock to the standard of the Trojans.

Book 8

In Book 8, the god of the Tiber River, Tiberinus himself, appears to Aeneas and advises him to form an alliance with King Evander of Pallanteum—the Greek city of the earlier prophecy. Following the instructions of Tiberinus, Aeneas sets out with two galleys, going upstream against the Tiber's current, and as they row, they come upon the promised sign, the white sow with her piglets. Arriving by river at Pallanteum, the Trojans interrupt a festival, receive a warm welcome, and find allies for their cause. In a lengthy digression, Virgil has King Evander tell the story of the fire-breathing, cattle-thieving monster, Caucus, whose destruction by Hercules (see *HERACLES*) was the occasion for the founding of the current festival. As it winds down, Evander takes Aeneas on a walking tour of the city as he recounts something of its history, and finally everyone retires for the night.

The reader, however, finds Aeneas's mother, Venus, wakeful and busy on his behalf. From her husband, Vulcan, she requests god-forged weapons and armor with which to arm her son and his followers. After a restful night in his wife's arms, Vulcan enters his workshop in the bowels of the Sicilian volcano, Mount Etna, and gives orders for a massive shield for Aeneas. It is the first of a suite of armaments that Venus gives her son to prepare him for his coming battle. In addition to the shield, she presents him with a helmet, a sword, a brass breastplate and back armor, greaves to protect his lower legs, and a spear. The shield, however, is Vulcan's major achievement. On it he has pictured the future of Italy and the coming victories of the Romans down to the time of Augustus. Aeneas, of course, does not discern their meaning as he slings the coming history of his descendants upon his shoulder.

Book 9

In the meantime, as Book 9 opens, Juno is pressing Turnus not to hesitate but to attack the Trojan camp. Turnus takes her advice, and from the battlements of their fortress, the Trojan garrison sees the dust cloud raised by the Rutulian troops. The Trojans mount a defense, and the gods rally to their aid, turning their beached ships into sea goddesses before the Rutulians' eyes. Turnus claims this as a good omen for them.

The Trojans, for their part, send messengers to summon Aeneas. These messengers, after first slaughtering several of the enemy in their sleep and commandeering their arms, go off in search of their commander. A squadron of Turnus's cavalry spots them, and one of them misses his way. His companion, however, gets away but then, missing his friend, turns back in time to see him captured. He attempts a rescue, and both are killed. When the Rutulians march against the Trojan camp the next morning, the heads of the two emissaries adorn their pikestaffs. As Virgil describes the battle, he calls again upon Calliope, the muse of epic poetry, and all her sisters to inspire him to sing nobly of carnage and mayhem. Ascanius makes his first kill, and Apollo himself congratulates the lad but warns him to make no further war.

Then Virgil follows Turnus's successes as he cuts his way through the melee. Mars, the god of war, joins the fray, giving heart to Turnus and his allies. The gates to the fortress open briefly to admit Trojans caught outside. Turnus enters with them. He and the giant Trojan Pandarus duel, and Turnus is victorious. He then hacks his way through many Trojan enemies. At last the captains of the garrison rally their Trojan troops, and,

little by little, Turnus is beaten back toward the river Tiber. Finally, almost overwhelmed, Turnus leaps into the Tiber, which bears him back to his comrades.

Book 10

As Book 10 opens, the scene shifts to Jupiter's palace on Mount Olympus, where a council of the gods is taking place. The father of the gods wants to know why this war is occurring against his will. Venus pleads the case for the Trojans and asks that at least her grandson, Ascanius, be spared. Juno, for her part, thinks that the Trojans are unjustly enjoying the protection of Venus and Jupiter and complains that she is within her rights to support the enemies of the Trojans. Jupiter, annoyed that the Trojans and the Latins cannot settle their differences peaceably, withdraws his special protection and says that the warring parties can fight out their differences and "the Fates will find their way."

In the meantime, Aeneas has traveled to Tuscany and also made an alliance with the Tuscans. Together, Trojan and Tuscan ships sail toward the Trojan encampment. Virgil names their leaders and describes their 30 ships. Aeneas's fleet encounters the sea goddesses into whom his beached ships were transformed, and one of the goddesses, Cymodoce, speaks to him and gives him a full report, warning him to prepare to fight Turnus's forces at dawn and defeat the Rutulians.

Both Trojans and Rutulians see Aeneas's fleet arrive, and Turnus leads his forces against them, hoping to slaughter Aeneas's forces as they disembark. Virgil follows the bloody progress of Aeneas through Turnus's troops. Next the poet turns his attention to the victories of Aeneas's Pallantean allies under the command of their general, Pallas. Eventually Pallas and Turnus face off with spears, and Turnus kills his enemy. The report of Pallas's death reaches Aeneas, who, leaving a trail of devastation and carnage, goes seeking Turnus across the battlefield.

Jupiter and Juno now discuss Turnus's fate, and Juno pleads for her champion's life. Jupiter grants her plea, but with conditions. Not satisfied with the outcome, the goddess once again takes matters into her own hands, fashioning a phantom in the shape of Aeneas. The phantom encounters Turnus and flees before him, and Turnus follows on. The phantom boards a ship, and Turnus follows. Once he is aboard, Juno cuts the anchor cable, and the wind blows the ship with its unwilling passenger out to sea. Turnus prays that Jupiter will return him to the battle, but Juno prevails, and the ship bears the frustrated warrior to safety.

Ashore, the battle rages on, and Virgil once again follows the fortunes of the principal remaining heroes, and he ends the book with Aeneas's twin victories over the giant Latin, Lausus, and Lausus's father, Mezentius—the last significant threats to the Trojans.

Book 11

As Book 11 opens, Aeneas announces his intention to attack the citadel of Turnus, but first he must bury his dead and send the body of the heroic Pallas back to his father, King Evander. Along with the body, Aeneas sends an escort of 1,000 men and such of Pallas's arms as Turnus had not taken after killing Pallas. When Latin emissaries come to Aeneas seeking permission to collect their dead from the battlefield, Aeneas gives that permission and offers to make peace—except with Turnus himself. The emissaries view the offer favorably, and they promise to carry it home.

Virgil shifts his scene to the arrival of Pallas's funeral cortege at home and touchingly evokes the grief of his father, Evander. Next he describes the funeral pyres on which all the combatants burn their dead. In the meantime, the emissaries advise making peace, and King Latinus, who had been drawn into enmity with the Trojans against his will, now offers them a generous realm where they can build their towns and enjoy friendly relations with their neighbors. One of his advisers, Drances, an enemy of Turnus, reminds the king of his earlier intention to betroth his daughter Lavinia to Aeneus. Drances calls on Turnus to renounce his intention to marry the girl. Turnus furiously

refuses, announcing his willingness to face Aeneas in single combat.

Then news comes that the Trojans and their allies are marching on the city. The Latins again prepare to do battle, and Turnus will lead the defenders. Among his allies are the Volscians, who are led by a warrior maiden named Camilla. She volunteers to set a cavalry trap for the Trojan forces, but the goddess of the hunt, Diana, finds this distressing. Camilla is a votary of the goddess and dear to her. The goddess knows that Camilla will fall in this fight, and she commands that anyone who wounds Camilla must suffer Diana's vengeance.

Virgil follows Camilla's progress through the fight, describing the many who are felled by her weapons. At last, however, she falls victim to a sneak attack from the Trojan Arruns and dies. True to her word, the goddess Diana avenges her favorite by killing Arruns with an arrow. Now, as Book 11 closes, Turnus and Aeneas catch sight of each other just at sundown, and the confrontation Virgil has been seeking must wait another day.

Book 12

Book 12, opens with Turnus's raging. He is anxious to confront Aeneas and settle the matter of his marriage to Lavinia once and for all. King Latinus attempts, not for the first time, to dissuade Turnus. The king patiently explains that fate has already determined the outcome of the entire matter, that it is fruitless to offer further resistance to the Trojans, and Latinus blames himself for letting Turnus and the queen dissuade him from a course of action upon which he had already embarked. Turnus, however, will not turn aside from his own fatal course and insists on a duel. Even Queen Amata tries to stop him, but to no avail. Turnus sends his challenge to Aeneas: Let the issue be decided by single combat.

Now, however, Juno intervenes once more. She counsels a minor deity, the Italian goddess of fountains, Juturna—who is also Turnus's sister—to save her brother. This Juturna does by making a sign appear in the skies. A Latin soothsayer,

Tolumnius, interprets the sign to mean that the Latins will defeat the Trojans, and he summons the Latins to battle, upsetting the preparations for the single combat. Virgil takes an authorial gamble in once more deferring the climax of the action. As the battle begins to rage, Aeneas tries to calm his Trojans by saying that the right of battle is now his and his alone. At that moment, however, an arrow pierces the Trojan commander. Aeneas quits the field to tend his wound, and the battle once more rises to fever pitch amid scenes of mayhem and carnage. Turnus deals out death across the plain.

Distressed by her son's wound, Venus heals Aeneas magically. Totally restored to full strength, Aeneas arms for battle and, seeking out Turnus, sends one Latin hero after another to the world of shadows. Juturna tries to protect her brother by becoming his charioteer and keeping him away from Aeneas, and many a Trojan and Latin fall as the heroic enemies, hindered by their divine protectors, try to find one another in the field.

Frustrated by the Latins' failure to observe any of their treaties, Aeneas orders the destruction of Latinus's city. Meanwhile, Turnus hears the panicked cries from the city. He tells his sister, still in the guise of his charioteer, that he has long since recognized her, and he insists that she stop interfering. Now news comes of Queen Amata's suicide. Turnus flees from his sister's protection and goes to fulfill his promise of single combat. Aeneas, too, finds his way to the field, and with all eyes upon them, in line 945 of the final book of the *Aeneid*, the adversaries first fling their spears at one another, and then, amid an epic simile that compares them to two charging bulls, join in hand-to-hand combat. Turnus's sword breaks, and Aeneas pursues him around the field five times. Then Juturna supplies Turnus with another sword, and Aeneas recovers the spear that he had thrown at first. They turn to face each other in a final contest.

Watching from Olympus, Jupiter asks Juno what other tricks she has in store to prolong the contest. Juno confesses that she has interfered and promises to stop if Jupiter will prom-

ise that the Latins can keep their own name and not be called Trojans or Teucrians. Jupiter assents, and Juno gives up her long-fought rearguard action. Jupiter sends a Fury to call off the protection that Juturna has been offering her brother. Grieved, Juturna plunges into a river. The final confrontation takes place, Aeneas vanquishes his foe, and just as he is about to let Turnus live, he sees that Turnus is wearing a belt that he had taken as a battle trophy from Aeneas's ally, Pallas. Infuriated, Aeneas plunges his sword into Turnus's chest, and as much of the *Aeneid* as Virgil was able to finish before his death ends in line 1271.

When Virgil saw that the end of his own life was approaching, he gave orders for the destruction of his never-finished epic. Happily for the subsequent history of Western letters, his instructions, perhaps on the Emperor Augustus's instruction, were ignored, and his poetic masterpiece, the national epic of ancient Rome, lives to attest to his talent.

New translations of Virgil's Aeneid and critical commentary on it continue to appear as the bibliography below suggests.

Bibliography

Conte Gian Biaggio. *The Poetry of Pathos*: *Studies in Virgillian Epic*. Edited by S. J. Harrison. Oxford and New York: Oxford University Press, 2000.

Kallendorf, Craig. *The Other Virgil: Pessimistic Readings of the* Aeneid *in Early Modern Culture*. Oxford and New York: Oxford University Press, 2007.

Ross, David O. *Virgil's* Aeneid: *A Reader's Guide*. Malden, Mass. Blackwell, 2007.

Virgil. *Aeneid*. Translated by Stanley Lombardo. Indianapolis: Hackett Publishing Co., 2005.

———. *The Aeneid of Virgil*. Translated by Allen Mandelbaum. Berkeley: University of California Press, 1971.

———. *The Aeneid*. Translated by Edward McCrorie. Ann Arbor: University of Michigan Press, 1995.

———. *The Aeneid*. Translated by Frederick Ahl. New York: Oxford University Press, 2007.

Ziolkowski, Jan M., and Michael C. J. Putnam, eds. *The Virgilian Tradition: The First Fifteen Hun-*

dred Year. New Haven, Conn.: Yale University Press, 2007.

Æschines (ca. 385–322 B.C.E.) *Greek prose writer*

One of three sons born to a schoolmaster and a priestess, Æschines early became, successively, a soldier, an actor in tragedies, and a clerk. He had distinguished himself for valor in military campaigns, and though his family's circumstances were humble, they had come from good stock. His brothers had made names for themselves in diplomatic service, and later Æschines' fortunes also improved when he too became a diplomat and subsequently an orator and politician.

The central question for Athenian diplomacy during Æschines' time was whether to appease or oppose Philip of Macedon's expansionist ambitions. Æschines belonged to the party advocating appeasement, and this conviction put him on a collision course with a much greater statesman and orator, DEMOSTHENES, who supported opposing Macedonian expansionist ambitions. The ensuing disagreement between the two orator-statesmen ripened into a full-blown personal hatred.

Demosthenes accused Æschines of being Philip's paid agent. Although this seems not to have been the case, in the end Æschines became discredited and embittered, left Athens, and ended his life in exile.

Three of Æschines' speeches have come down to us: "Against Timarchus" (345 B.C.E.), "On the Embassy" (343 B.C.E.), and "Against Ctesiphon" (330 B.C.E.). The first of these speeches was given in connection with a suit that Æschines had brought against Demosthenes' ally Timarchus on the grounds of leading an immoral life. The object of the suit was to deflect another that Demosthenes had brought against Æschines, accusing him of working for Philip. Æschines won his suit against Timarchus, thus denying Demosthenes a powerful ally in his campaign against Æschines.

"On the Embassy" is Æschines' defense against Demosthenes' further accusation that Æschines was guilty of treason when both he and Æschines had been members of an embassy to Philip. Although Demosthenes failed to prove that contention and Æschines won the case, the proceedings nonetheless left Æschines an object of popular mistrust among the Athenians.

Æschines' last surviving speech, "Against Ctesiphon," had its genesis in the profound hatred that the less-able Æschines felt for the more gifted Demosthenes. Ctesiphon had proposed that the Athenians honor Demosthenes with a golden crown in recognition of his long and meritorious service to the city. Æschines brought a lawsuit alleging the illegality of Ctesiphon's motion. As the case was not heard for six years, it had the practical effect of blocking Demosthenes' honor. When the case did finally reach the docket, however, the court dismissed its technical correctness and found for Demosthenes on grounds of popular sympathy.

Disappointed and exasperated, Æschines left Athens and died in exile. In the judgment of history, despite genuine abilities and an accurate view of long-range Greek affairs, Æschines allowed his vanity and his admiration for Philip and his son Alexander to cloud his judgment and render him ineffectual.

Bibliography

Æschines. *Æschines.* Translated by Chris Carey. Austin: University of Texas Press, 2000.

———. *The Speeches of Æschines.* Translated by Charles Darwin Adams. New York: G. P. Putnam's Sons, 1919.

Harris, Edward Monroe. *Æschines and Athenian Politics.* New York: Oxford University Press, 1995.

Aeschylus (525–455 B.C.E.) *Greek dramatist*

Born to a distinguished Athenian family in an era before Athens achieved preeminence in the Grecian world, Aeschylus, who flourished during the rise of Athens, performed notable military service at the battles of Salamis (480 B.C.E.) and Marathon (490 B.C.E.). What little we know of his life is contained in a short biographical preface to a manuscript of one of his plays. Beyond the information included there, a small body of unconfirmed tradition also surrounds his personal history. He is thought, perhaps on the basis of the focus on religion and philosophy that one finds in his works, to have been a member of the Pythagorean brotherhood—a group interested in science, philosophy, and religion. He may have been initiated into the secrets of the Eleusinian mysteries in connection with the worship of the god Dionysus, and may also have been charged with impiety for having revealed something about the nature of those secrets to noninitiates.

In considering Aeschylus's dramatic career, we are on surer ground. Dramatic performance in Athens was part of the civic worship of Dionysus and took place during the two festivals of the god celebrated in that city each year. For a dramatist, having one's plays performed was the result of an entry's surviving a competition. Each entry included three tragedies and a satyr play. The plays selected further competed against one another in performance at the festivals. Aeschylus began entering the contests in 499 B.C.E. His first victory in the contest came in 484 B.C.E., and his last in 458 B.C.E. with the three plays comprising his ORESTEIA: AGAMEMNON, The CHOEPHORI, and The EUMENIDES. His entries won first place 13 times.

In all, Aeschylus is known to have written some 90 plays. Of these, only seven survive: the three named above and The SUPPLIANTS (also called The Suppliant Women, ca. 492 B.C.E.), The PERSIANS (472 B.C.E.), The SEVEN AGAINST THEBES (467 B.C.E.), and PROMETHEUS BOUND (ca. 478 B.C.E.). These surviving examples reveal the playwright's overwhelming interest in religious matters, which provide the focus of all his surviving work as he examines theological issues through the lens that human behavior provides. Eugene O'Neill, Jr., considers that Aeschylus's Oresteia presents "one of the greatest and most purified conceptions of godhead . . . [of] Western European civilization."

As a dramatist, Aeschylus enjoys a reputation as an innovator: He emphasizes the dramatic scenes and downplays the importance of the CHORUS IN GREEK THEATER. ARISTOTLE credits Aeschylus with introducing a second actor to the stage, and Aeschylus also emulated SOPHOCLES' introduction of a third, thereby heightening the verisimilitude of the action and lessening the declamatory and choral aspects of Greek theater. All Greek dramatic performance was also poetic, and Aeschylus's mastery of the inherent musical qualities of his language and of apt imagery contributed significantly to his outstanding mastery of his craft and to his continuing reputation among lovers of theater. Together with the plays of Sophocles and EURIPIDES, the dramas of Aeschylus provide the only surviving examples of ancient Greek tragedy.

See also CONVENTIONS OF GREEK DRAMA; SATYR PLAYS; TRAGEDY IN GREECE AND ROME.

Bibliography

Aeschylus. *The Complete Plays.* Translated by Carl R. Mueller. Hanover, N.H.: Smith and Kraus, 2002.

Oates, Whitney J., and Eugene O'Neill, Jr. *The Complete Greek Drama: All the Extant Tragedies of Aeschylus, Sophocles and Euripides, and the Comedies of Aristophanes and Menander. . . .* New York: Random House, 1938.

Aesop and the fable genre (fl. sixth century B.C.E.) *Greek prose writer*

Whether or not Aesop was a real person is a matter of debate. A large number of fables have clustered around his name nonetheless. Among the ancients, some said he was a Phrygian slave, eventually set free because of his talent. Others thought him to have been a retainer and friend of Croesus, the king of Lydia. The best probability is that once either a fact or a tradition associating him with the composition of animal fables emerged, subsequent fables—likely collected from many sources—became associated with his name. We know that some of the fables were recounted earlier by other writers. HESIOD tells the fable of "The Hawk and the Nightengale." AESCHYLUS recounts "The Eagle Wounded by an Arrow Fletched with Its Own Feathers" and mentions that it was already an old story. A portion of "The Fox Avenging his Wrongs on the Eagle" also appears in a fragment from the Greek poet ARCHILOCUS.

The Roman poet PHÆDRUS, writing in the first century C.E., retold some of the stories in a popular Latin edition of five books. So, at about the same time, did Babrius, telling 123 fables in Greek verse, using the scazon meter (see QUANTITATIVE VERSE). Since then, the stories associated with Aesop have been retold many times, and they remain available in many attractive translations. The corpus of stories has continued to grow over the centuries.

William Caxton produced the first version of Aesop's stories in English in the late 15th century, and the Frenchman Jean de La Fontaine's 17th-century versions remain justly famous. An interesting recent translation of some of the tales has been taken from the New York Public Library's manuscript catalogued as "NYPL Spenser 50." This is a manuscript version of Aesop that once belonged to the Medici family of Florence.

"The true fable," said George Fyler Townsend, the 19th-century translator (from the Greek) of almost 300 fables associated with Aesop's name, "aims at . . . the representation of human motive, and the improvement of human conduct." It seeks to accomplish these goals without giving unwelcome advice and by making the reader or hearer recognize virtue or vice in the behavior of animals with which particular characteristics have become identified. Donkeys, for example, are patient, foxes tricky and clever, rabbits timid, wolves cruel, and bulls strong. Although brief, fables are carefully constructed to make their moral point clearly, palatably, and sympathetically. A fable aims to teach morality by showing the consequences of particular patterns of behavior, to teach the hearer to admire virtue and despise vice, and to recognize the symptoms of each in the reader's or hearer's own behavior.

Among the stories attributed to Aesop and retold by many are fables familiar to most school children: "The Tortoise and the Hare," "The Lion and the Mouse," "The Wolf in Sheep's Clothing," "The Goose that Laid the Golden Eggs," "The Fox and the Grapes," "The Ant and the Grasshopper," "The Dog and the Wolf," "The Donkey in a Lion's Skin," "The Boy and the Wolf," and "The Country Mouse and the City Mouse." Three of these tales are described below.

"The Country Mouse and the City Mouse"

On a visit to his country friend, a city mouse finds life in the country too tame and not luxurious enough. On a return visit to his friend in town, the country mouse finds himself faced with all sorts of tasty dishes to choose from. Just as he starts to snack, however, someone opens the cupboard door, forcing the mice to flee. After the same thing happens again, the country mouse, still hungry, decides to return to his simple but safe life in the country.

"The Goose [sometimes Hen] that Laid the Golden Eggs"

A couple owns a fowl that lays a golden egg each day. Hoping to get rich quick, they kill the bird to get at the source. No gold, however, is found inside. They have destroyed the source of their good fortune.

"The Tortoise and the Hare"

A male hare makes fun of a female tortoise's short legs and slow progress. The tortoise assures the hare that she can win a race between the two. Certain of victory, the hare take a nap while the tortoise keeps moving. The hare oversleeps and finds that the tortoise has won the race by sticking to the goal.

See also FABLES (APOLOGUES) OF GREECE AND ROME.

Bibliography

Aesop. *The Medici Æsop: NYPL Spencer 50 . . .* Translated by Bernard McTeague. New York: New York Public Library, 2005.

Aesop's Fables. Translated by George Fyler Townsend. New York: George Munro's Sons, 1890.

Aetius   See ACONTIUS AND KIDIPPE; CALLIMACHUS.

Agamemnon   Aeschylus (458 B.C.E.)

Agamemnon is the first play in a trilogy, the ORESTEIA, which won the first prize for TRAGEDY at the Athenian City Festival of the god Dionysus in the year of the play's composition. Together with *The* CHOEPHORI and *The* EUMENIDES—the other plays of the trilogy—this work is regarded as AESCHYLUS's masterpiece. In this series of tragedies, Aeschylus traces the unfolding of a curse on the house of Atreus.

The curse originated when, after winning his bride, Hippodamia, in a crooked chariot race, Atreus's father, Pelops, withheld the reward he had promised his accomplice, Myrtilus, and threw Myrtilus into the sea instead. This resulted in divine curse on the house of Pelops that manifested itself in the enmity that arose between Pelops's two sons, Atreus and Thyestes.

As a result of their mutual hatred, Thyestes seduced Atreus's wife, Aethra. In revenge, Atreus killed Thyestes' children and served their cooked flesh to their father at dinner. Horrified, Thyestes cursed Atreus and his descendants. The operation of this curse across the subsequent generations provided grist for many a Greek playwright's mill.

After seducing his sister-in-law, Thyestes involved himself in an incestuous entanglement with his daughter, Pelopia. From this union sprang Aegisthus, whom we meet as the lover of Clytemnestra in *Agamemnon.* Later Aegisthus and Thyestes conspired to slay Atreus.

Atreus left three children: Agamemnon, king of Mycenae; Menelaus, king of Sparta; and Anaxibia, the wife of Strophius, king of Phocis. Menelaus married Helen, and Agamemnon married her sister Clytemnestra. When Helen ran off with Paris, a prince of Troy, Menelaus gathered a force representing all the realms of Greece to get her back. Agamemnon was the supreme commander of the force.

The Greek fleet gathered at Aulis, where they found themselves trapped by on-shore winds. A soothsayer explained that unless Agamemnon sacrificed his own child, Iphigenia, to appease the gods, the invasion force would permanently languish.

Torn between civic duty and familial affection, Agamemnon eventually yielded to public pressure and sacrificed his daughter. The curse on the house of Atreus, which had reactivated with Helen's infidelity, was being fulfilled again. The sacrifice proved efficacious, however, and the Greek fleet sailed.

Outraged at her daughter's death at Agamemnon's hands, Clytemnestra quickly allowed herself to be seduced by Aegisthus, and she and her paramour held sway in Mycenae during the 10 years of the Trojan campaign. It is in the 10th year that the play, *Agamemnon*, opens with a watchman's soliloquy.

Wearily watching the night away, the watchman suddenly sees a signal fire flare in the distance—a fire that means the Greek forces have overcome Troy and that the fleet will soon be arriving home. The watchman rushes to inform the queen.

The CHORUS rehearses the events leading up to the Trojan War and then reflects upon the weakness of old age. That done, sections of the chorus undertake the dance-like movements of strophe and antistrophe as its members describe the auguries that accompanied the Greek fleet's departure for Troy. They recount the circumstances surrounding Agamemnon's sacrifice of Iphigenia and the flight (or kidnapping) of Helen. The members of the chorus also regret that their advanced age and weakness had disqualified them from participating as soldiers in the campaign.

The chorus, representing the weight of public opinion, knows the resentment that Clytemnestra nourishes against her husband for sacrificing their child. They also know about the queen's relationship with Aegisthus. They then break up into smaller choral units to present a variety of viewpoints. They consider Agamemnon's role in the affair. They look at the situation from Iphigenia's perspective. They pass judgment as commentators, and they review once more the events leading up to the fleet's departure for Troy.

Clytemnestra appears, and the leader of the chorus addresses her. She reports Troy's overthrow. When the chorus asks when this happened, she amazes them by saying that Troy had fallen that very night. To satisfy their incredulity, she details the complex system of mountaintop signal fires that carried home news of the Greek victory so speedily.

For the chorus's benefit (and that of the audience) Clytemnestra imagines the circumstances within Troy's walls, both from the point of view of the defeated Trojans and from that of the victorious Greeks. Presciently, however, she hopes that the Greek soldiers will "reverence well" Troy's gods. In the event, of course, they did not. Instead, they provoked the Trojan deities (who were also those of the Greeks). In retaliation, the gods sent a ferocious storm that sank many Greek ships and scattered the fleet all over the Mediterranean.

In the next scene, the fleet arrives at Mycenae. A herald comes to announce the army's imminent disembarkation and officially announce the victory. Clytemnestra masks her real feelings before the herald, proclaiming herself to be a faithful spouse and overjoyed at her husband's safe return. The chorus, of course, knows that she is lying.

The herald next reports on the ferocious storm that scattered the Greek fleet and destroyed many ships. He notes the disappearance of Menelaus and his ship on the return voyage. His fate is as yet unknown. The chorus once more considers the role of Helen as the agent of an adverse fate in implementing the curse afflicting the house of Atreus.

Agamemnon enters, followed by his war prize and concubine, the captive Trojan priestess of Athena and princess, Cassandra. He gives an arrival speech in which he singles out Odysseus as his most loyal supporter in the field. Then he promises due recompense both to his men and to the gods and heads for home. Clytemnestra meets him on the way and fabricates the history of a lonely, long-suffering, faithful soldier's wife, pining away in sometimes near-suicidal depression and solitude for a decade while her husband was at war. She explains that, fearing the possibility of civil insurrection, she has sent their son Orestes to his uncle Strophius, the king of Phocis. Still pretending, Clytemnestra declares her love and invites Agamemnon to step down from his chariot and walk upon a purple tapestry that the queen's women have prepared for the occasion. At first Agamemnon refuses, explaining that the gesture savors too much of an Eastern potentate rather than a Greek soldier. Clytemnestra, however, implores his indulgence, and to humor his wife, Agamemnon steps down from the chariot and, followed by his spouse, walks on the carpet into the palace.

The chorus sings a song of foreboding. Then Clytemnestra reappears and invites Cassandra into the palace. Possessed of the gift of second sight, however, Cassandra foresees danger and, distracted in a prophetic fit, hints darkly at Clytemnestra's plot. As the chorus continues to comment, Cassandra chants to Apollo and then describes her vision of Clytemnestra and Aegisthus's upcoming murder of Agamemnon, who will be stabbed in his welcoming bath in the next phase of the curse on the house of Atreus.

Still interacting with the chorus, Cassandra beholds the specters of the slaughtered children of Thyestes serving as spectators to the events. She next grieves at her own approaching death at the hands of Clytemnestra. She nonetheless stoically enters the palace, and the voice of Agamemnon is heard from within describing his murderers' attack upon him.

The chorus hesitates in confusion. As they continue to temporize, the palace doors swing open, and a blood-smeared Clytemnestra emerges. The corpses of Agamemnon and Cassandra lie side by side within. Clytemnestra describes the details of her deed. The chorus expresses shock at her callousness, but Clytemnestra defends her act as justifiable vengeance for the death of her daughter at Agamemnon's hands. Clytemnestra and the chorus engage in a prolonged debate about whether or not her crime was justified. She identifies herself as the helpless instrument of fate, fulfilling the curse on the house of Atreus—helpless, and thus innocent. She predicts that the shades of Agamemnon and of his daughter Iphigenia will embrace by the hellish waters of the underworld's river Acheron. Clytemnestra prays that with her deed, the curse on the house of Atreus will end. Her prayer, however, is doomed to fail.

Aegisthus appears and recounts again the curse on the house of Atreus and its origins. The chorus disapproves of Aegisthus's role in the proceedings. He warns its members to accept him as the city's ruler or they will suffer punishment. The chorus and the new king exchange insults and come to the brink of civil war before Clytemnestra intervenes. They calm down, but the mutual snarling continues as the chorus expresses the hope that Orestes will soon appear and set matters right.

Aeschylus's play explores the inexorable operation of fate and the roles human beings play, willy-nilly, in achieving fate's outcomes. Compared with some of his earlier work, this first play in Aeschylus's last trilogy reveals the apex of his command of the resources afforded him by his stage, the dramatic tradition within which he operated, and the poetic resources of the language in which he wrote.

Bibliography

Aeschylus. *Agamemnon*. Translated by Howard Rubenstein. El Cajon, Calif.: Granite Hills Press, 1998.

———. *Oresteia. English and Greek*. Translated by George Thompson. New York: Everyman's Library, 2004.

Agathias of Myrina (fl. sixth century C.E.)
Greek historian and poet

A Christian jurist or lawyer who wrote in Greek at Constantinople late in the HELLENISTIC AGE, Agathias also was an author and editor. Perhaps his best-remembered work is a continuation of a history written by PROCOPIUS. In Agathias's continuation, he usefully describes otherwise unknown Sassanid Persian customs and institutions during the reign of the Roman Emperor Justinian, which was the overarching subject of his work.

As a poet, Agathias achieved a considerable contemporary reputation as the author of EPIGRAMS. He edited a collection of epigrams by others, and he also penned a collection of historical biographies that enjoyed a considerable reputation.

Bibliography

Agathias. *The Histories*. Translated by Joseph D. Frendo. New York: de Gruyter, 1975.

Cameron, Averil. *Agathias*. Oxford: Clarendon Press, 1970.

———. *Agathias on the Sassanians*. Washington, D.C.: Dumbarton Oaks Papers, nos. 23–24, 1975.

Ajax Sophocles (ca. 440 B.C.E.)

Likely the earliest of SOPHOCLES' extant dramas, the TRAGEDY of *Ajax* rests on a story drawn from uncertain early EPIC sources. In *The ILIAD* of HOMER, Ajax figures as a warrior second in prowess only to Achilles. The sources from which Sophocles draws the raw material for his play, however, address events that occurred between the times covered in *The Iliad* and those covered in Homer's *The ODYSSEY*.

Following the death of Achilles, Ajax competed for the hero's weapons and armor. The competition ended in a draw between Ajax and Odysseus, and the Greek generals chose to award Odysseus the prize. Feeling slighted, dishonored, and furious, Ajax blames Agamemnon and Menelaus for his loss, and he intends to murder them during the night. The goddess Athena, however, is displeased with Ajax; she finds him overly prideful, and she objects to the violence of his intended vengeance. She therefore addles his wits so that in his madness he mistakes the animals on which the Greek forces rely for food as the soldiers themselves. Ajax attacks the beasts, killing some and taking others to his tent where, thinking they are his enemies, he tortures them.

As Sophocles' drama opens, Odysseus is cautiously combing the area near Ajax's encampment when he hears the voice of the goddess Athena—invisible to Odysseus but not to the audience—who asks him what he is doing. He replies that he is tracking Ajax, whom Odysseus suspects of having slaughtered all the herds and flocks captured from the Trojans. In the ensuing exchange between the two, we learn that Ajax had intended to murder the generals and their guards, but that the goddess had deceived his senses so that he thought the animals were the men.

Athena leads Odysseus to Ajax's tent and calls for him. In a humorous exchange in which Odysseus appears afraid of Ajax, Odysseus tries to persuade Athena not to disturb the madman. The goddess cautions Odysseus against cowardice and promises that she will make him invisible to Ajax's eyes.

Still wildly distracted, Ajax emerges with a bloody whip in his hand. He thinks that he has killed both Agamemnon and Menelaus and that he holds Odysseus prisoner. Ajax plans to flog him unmercifully before he kills him. Athena objects, but Ajax insists and withdraws to carry out his plan.

Odysseus reflects on human weakness, and Athena warns him to consider Ajax's example of the consequences of uttering "proud words against the gods." Athena disappears, Odysseus exits, and the CHORUS, clad as Ajax's soldiers and subjects, sing of his misery. Then Ajax's wife, Tecmessa, whom Ajax had won in battle, enters and, from her own point of view, tells the story of Ajax's mad behavior the previous night. The chorus responds sympathetically. As she finishes her tale, Ajax is heard lamenting offstage. He has returned to his right mind and feels ashamed and almost suicidally depressed because of his folly and loss of honor on the one hand, and, on the other, because his enemies have escaped him. He begins to court death. Tecmessa tries to dissuade him by making him think about what her fate will be if he is no longer alive to protect her. Her family is dead, and Ajax and their child are all she has.

Ajax asks to see his son, Eurysaces, and tells Tecmessa that his half brother, Teucer—the Greeks' greatest archer—will protect the youth. Ajax seems determined to take his own life. He makes Tecmessa take the child and leave, and then he closes the doors. The chorus grieves at what they think is coming.

Armed with a sword, Ajax reenters, and so does Tecmessa. He announces his intention to seek absolution from Athena, bury his sword in the earth, and become a pilgrim of sorts for a while. The chorus is much relieved at this speech and is happy that Ajax seems to have put aside his blood feud with the sons of Atreus, Agamemon and Menelaus. (For the curse on the house of Atreus, see *AGAMEMNON*). Ajax exits on his journey.

A messenger enters to announce Teucer's return. We learn that Teucer had instructed the messenger to see that Ajax did not leave his quarters before Teucer's arrival. The prophet Calchas had predicted that if Ajax left his tents, Teucer would not again see him among the living. In the same speech, the messenger reports that Ajax had offended the gods by suggesting that he could win battles without their aid, relying solely on his own strength. Athena plans Ajax's death, though if he can make it through this one day, he stands a chance of survival.

Tecmessa learns of all this and sends everyone off in several directions to seek Ajax and bring him back. The scene shifts, and the audience finds him first. He is alone in prayer and contemplating suicide. After bidding daylight and earthly joys a final farewell, he falls on his sword and perishes.

Portraying a search party, the chorus takes the stage, looking here and there, but Tecmessa finds her husband's body and covers it with her cloak. The chorus mourns, while she considers what may become of her. Teucer enters, grieves for Ajax, and suddenly remembers the child Eurysaces, who has been left alone in the tents. He sends for him lest an enemy carry him off.

Teucer uncovers his brother's body and grieves over it. The leader of the chorus finally interrupts the grieving, advising Teucer to consider the funeral. At this moment, the king of Sparta, Menelaus, son of Atreus, enters with his retinue. He orders Teucer not to bury Ajax, but to leave him where he lies. Depriving a corpse of a proper burial is a crime against the gods. However much one hates one's enemy, when that enemy dies, enmity dies with him. The spirit of an unburied person is doomed to wander between two worlds and cannot enter the underworld. Menelaus pridefully rehearses the crimes of the living Ajax and declares his intention to punish the dead man for them. He forbids Teucer to bury his brother on pain of death. This theme is a frequent one in Greek drama; we see its operation again, for example, in Sophocles' ANTIGONE.

Teucer, however, is unruffled by Menelaus's order. He points out that Menelaus has no authority over him, nor over Ajax. Teucer will bury the body properly, and if Menelaus imagines he can do something about it, he can try.

The chorus grows nervous as the tempers of the Greek captains rise, accompanied by threat and counterthreat, boast and counter-boast. With a final exchange of insults, Menelaus and his retinue exit. The chorus predicts a battle will soon follow.

Tecmessa and Eurysaces enter and begin performing funeral rites. Teucer commands that the troops stand guard until he has dug his brother's grave. The chorus frets about the events to come.

Teucer and Agamemnon enter almost simultaneously, and Agamemnon berates Teucer with bitter sarcasm that makes the chorus shudder and wish both warriors would show better judgment. Teucer reproves Agamemnon and reminds him of Ajax's accomplishments in the Trojan War. Teucer cautions Agamemnon against presuming to attack him.

Odysseus now enters and calms the ruffled waters with wise counsel. He explains the sacrilegious folly of dishonoring a brave dead man whom one hated while alive. After further discussion of this issue, everyone accepts Odysseus's counsel—though Agamemnon does so grudgingly—and the funeral proceeds with full honors.

Bibliography

Sophocles. *Ajax*. Translated by Shomit Dutta. Cambridge and New York: Cambridge University Press, 2001.

Akkadian (Babylonian–Assyrian)

An ancient Semitic language with several dialects, Akkadian died out in early antiquity, well before the Common Era. It was, however, a literary as well as a spoken tongue, and its surviving documents are preserved in CUNEIFORM writing. Among these documents one finds an Akkadian version of the earliest surviving EPIC—*The GILGAMESH EPIC*. Taken from an even earlier Sumerian version of the legend of the historical Gilgamesh, King of Uruk, the epic contains a version of the flood legend later appearing in the HEBREW BIBLE as the story of Noah.

Bibliography

Diakonoff, I. M., ed. *Early Antiquity*. Chicago and London: The University of Chicago Press, 1991.

Alcaeus (Alkaios) (ca. 630–ca.580 B.C.E.)
Greek poet

Like his contemporary, the poet SAPPHO, Alcaeus was born in the city-state of Mytilene on the island of Lesbos in the Aegean Sea. Also like Sappho, Alcaeus composed verses written in the local Aeolic dialect and intended to be sung and self-accompanied on a lyre. While Sappho's name is more widely recognized than that of Alcaeus, more of the latter's poetry has survived. The fragmentary remains of Alcaeus's verse suggest that he did not principally celebrate the passion of love, as did his more famous female contemporary. Instead, in addition to the hymns that he addressed to Apollo, Hermes, Hephaestus, and the demi-gods Castor and Polydeuces, we find fragments of political verse written to oppose the despotic ruler Myrsilus. This political stand resulted in a period of exile for the poet. After Myrsilus was overthrown, however, Alcaeus's friend Pittakos came to power. Criticizing his erstwhile comrade's exercise of authority resulted in two more periods of exile for the poet, though in the end Pittakos and Alcaeus apparently reconciled.

In addition to his political diatribes, some of the fragments of Alcaeus's verse celebrate the joys of wine and drinking. Wine, he suggests, is an antidote to grief. A soldier's delight in weaponry also appears in descriptions contained in a fragment of verse called "The Armory." In it Alcaeus describes "shining helmets" with "horse-hair plumes." He details polished bronze armor designed to protect the chest and back and also that worn on the lower leg. The armor is "strong to stop arrows and spears." He catalogues broad swords and shields in the same fragment of verse (Z 34).

A celebrated description of a shipwreck in a storm survives in a pair of fragments preserving parts of the same poem: "The Ship: I and II." Alcaeus invented a three-line stanza—the alcaic stanza. (See QUANTITATIVE VERSE.)

Alcaeus also produced mythological narratives drawn from the familiar material surrounding the Trojan War. An especially long (49-line) middle section of such a narrative survives in which the poet recounts the violation of the Trojan princess and priestess Cassandra by the Greek warrior Ajax.

The fact that Sappho and Alcaeus were contemporaries gave rise to later suggestions that, as well as being fellow poets, they were lovers, or at least friends. Others have suggested that they were professional rivals.

Bibliography

Martin, Hubert, Jr. *Alcaeus.* New York: Twayne Publishers, Inc., 1972.

Rayor, Diane J., trans. *Sappho's Lyre: Archaic Lyric and Women Poets of Ancient Greece.* Berkeley: University of California Press, 1991.

Reynolds, Margaret. *The Sappho Companion.* New York: Palgrave, 2000.

Romilly, Jacqueline de. *A Short History of Greek Literature.* Translated by Lillian Doherty. Chicago: The University of Chicago Press, 1985.

Alcestis Euripides (438 B.C.E.)

A tragicomedy, *Alcestis* was first presented as the fourth in the series of plays EURIPIDES entered in the GREAT DIONYSIA at Athens in 438. Ordinarily, an entry comprised three tragedies and a satyr play, but here Euripides varies the formula with a potentially tragic story that nonetheless has a happy ending.

An old tale lies behind the action of *Alcestis.* The ruler of the gods, Zeus, became annoyed with his son, Apollo the sun god, for Apollo's revenge slaying of the Cyclops who had forged Zeus's thunderbolts. As a punishment, Apollo was sentenced to serve as a slave to a mortal. He performed this service in the house of Admetus, the admirable king of Thessaly, who treated Apollo with great kindness. As a reward, Apollo interceded with the Fates to renegotiate the appointed date for Admetus's premature death. Driving a hard bargain, the Fates agreed to an extension, providing someone could be found to die early in the king's place. Most of Admetus's friends and kinfolk, including his father and his mother, refused. His wife Alcestis, however, agreed, and the play opens on the day appointed for her death.

Apollo begins by recounting the action summarized above, and as he ends his speech, Death enters with a drawn sword. The two confer, with Apollo unsuccessfully trying to persuade Death to delay taking Alcestis. They exit, and the CHORUS and a servant from the palace take the stage. The servant reports Alcestis's calm and courageous behavior as she prays for her children and her husband and wishes them farewell. The servant predicts that Admetus would be better off dead than alive, having lost such a spouse. Admetus, the servant reports, is weeping while, stricken with her final illness, Alcestis hovers on the brink of death.

As the chorus prays for her reprieve, Alcestis enters, supported by Admetus. She is chanting and reporting her premonitory visions of her death. She then makes a last request. She asks Admetus not to remarry because a stepmother might be unkind to her children. Admetus promised to wear mourning for the rest of his life, to give up partying, and to sleep with a carved image of Alcestis. She places her children's hands in her husband's, bids them all farewell, and dies. Admetus gives orders respecting her funeral, and the chorus grieves.

Heracles, in this play a comic character, now enters. He is en route to fulfilling the eighth of the labors that Eurystheus had imposed on him—taming the carnivorous horses of Diomedes. Although in mourning, Admetus welcomes Heracles as a guest, not admitting that his wife has died. The chorus reproves the king for entertaining a visitor while in mourning.

Alcestis's body is carried in procession, and her ancient father-in-law, Pheres, arrives. He compliments Admetus on marrying a woman who would die for him. The egocentric Admetus tells Pheres he is unwelcome and that the old man should have made the sacrifice rather than Alcestis. Pheres explains to Admetus his own responsibility for himself, and the argument between them escalates as the chorus tries to calm the two down. The exchange ends with Admetus cursing his father.

Meanwhile, back at the palace, Heracles is abusing Admetus's hospitality by getting roaring drunk. From a disapproving servant he learns that Alcestis has died. Realizing the strain he has placed on his host's hospitality, Heracles instantly sobers up and resolves to ambush Death, descend into the underworld, and bring Alcestis back to the land of the living.

Admetus returns home, and he and the chorus grieve. Heracles enters, leading a veiled woman.

He blames Admetus for not confessing the death of his wife. Then he explains that he must continue on his quest but that he wishes to leave the woman for Admetus to take care of. Admetus recognizes a shape like that of Alcestis and asks Heracles to leave the woman with someone else. After much hemming and hawing during which Admetus fails to recognize his restored Alcestis, Heracles unveils her, and the miracle is revealed. Heracles has overcome death. Admetus may not, however, hear his wife speak until the third dawn has risen and she has been purified from her consecration to the gods of the underworld. Proclaiming his happiness, Admetus leads Alcestis into the palace, and the chorus chants of the capacity of the gods to bring about the unexpected.

See also COMEDY IN GREECE AND ROME; CONVENTIONS OF GREEK DRAMA; TRAGEDY IN GREECE AND ROME; SATYR PLAYS.

Bibliography

Euripides. *Alcestis* [Greek and English]. Translated by D. J. Conacher. Wiltshire, U.K.: Aris & Phillips, 1988.

———. *Alcestis. Three Tragedies of Euripides.* Translated by Paul Roche. New York: Mentor, 1973.

Alexandrine Age   See HELLENISTIC AGE.

Alkman (Alcman) (fl. seventh century B.C.E.) *Greek Poet*

According to the literary historian Herbert Weir Smyth, the Spartan poet Alkman was the "chief cultivator" and perhaps the creator of "early choral poetry." Born at the Lydian city of Sardia in Asia Minor, Alkman migrated to Sparta—possibly as a prisoner of war who had been enslaved. His poetic mastery led to his rising to become the official teacher of the state choruses of Sparta.

Six books (each book was a scroll) collecting Alkman's poems circulated through the Greek world long after his death. Organized by type, these included songs that display special respect for and gallantry toward women. Called *parthe-*

neia, these songs were sung by choirs of boys or virgins. Next came a book of hymns in honor of the gods the Spartans especially reverenced: Zeus, Hera, Artemis, and Aphrodite. Two other books contained *hyporchemes* (songs associated with ritual dance and addressed to gods) and *paians* (songs in praise of the gods—especially Apollo). A fifth book contained songs called *erotika* (erotic songs), a subgenre of choral song that Alkman invented. Finally, the works that survived among the ancients included a book that brought together his *hymeneia* (songs associated with wedding processions).

Alkman was regarded as an unprecedented master of the complexities of Greek metrics. Later Greek grammarians at Alexandria in Egypt viewed him as the premier exemplar of Greek melic poetry. His choral songs were still performed at Athens as late as the time of Pericles, and Herbert Weir Smyth presents evidence of his works still being read in the second century of the Common Era. (See PERICLES AND FABIUS.)

Said to have lived to a ripe old age, Alkman was buried in Sparta near the tombs of those whose lives he had celebrated in funeral poems. Only fragmentary remains of his works are now extant.

Bibliography

Davenport, Guy, trans. *Archilochus, Sappho, Alkman: Three Lyric Poets of the Late Greek Bronze Age.* Berkeley: University of California Press, 1980.

Smyth, Herbert Weir. *Greek Melic Poets.* New York: Biblo and Tannen, 1963.

Almagest   See PTOLEMY.

alphabet

Originally developed to represent the consonant sounds of ancient Hebrew and related tongues like Phoenician, Moabite, and Aramaic, the alphabet, which first appeared around 1000 B.C.E., achieved a distinct advantage over other systems of writing such as CUNEIFORM and HIEROGLYPHS. Using a finite number of symbols to represent, first, the consonants and initial vowels of a language and later the interior and final vowels as well, the alphabet proved much more efficient than systems of writing that represented ideas, as did many hieroglyphs and cuneiform markings; that used symbols that represented syllables; or that combined all three systems. Instead of needing thousands of ideograms, as Chinese did and does, for instance, to represent words and phrases, the alphabet can infinitely recombine its relatively few symbols to represent all the possible sound combinations of a language.

From its place of origin in the vicinity of ancient Israel, the alphabet seems to have been carried by Phoenician traders and others throughout the Mediterranean world, eventually becoming the accepted system for representing languages as disparate as Greek, Latin, Hungarian, Russian, Arabic, and Korean. Over time, the forms of letters modified, and additions were introduced to represent sounds that occurred in some languages but had been absent from the tongues earlier represented. Thus, though the alphabet was invented once and once only, those who later adopted it made modifications. St. Cyril, for example, changed the form of some letters and introduced some new ones when he brought his Cyrillic alphabet to the speakers of Slavic languages, including Russian. Sometimes, too, the form of letters modified, or the sounds they represented shifted, as was the case in the development of the runic alphabet to represent the Scandinavian languages of the Germanic heroic age.

Writing seems to have been twice introduced into the ancient Greek language. It appeared first as Linear B—a syllabary with 87 characters—during the ascendancy of Minoan civilization. When that civilization fell victim to a devastating natural disaster—likely an earthquake with an accompanying series of tsunamis—the syllabary then used by the speakers of Greek disappeared. A true alphabet appeared in the Greek literary world on the island of Lesbos at about the time that the poet SAPPHO flourished. The Greeks wrote their script to be read back and forth "as the ox ploughs" and represented vowels as well as consonants with alphabetic symbols. From the Greeks, alphabetic writing spread throughout the rest of Western Europe.

The efficiencies of alphabetic script have not been lost on scholars and politicians looking for ways to represent their languages. In the 15th century C.E., scholars commissioned by King Sejong of Korea adapted from Arabic an alphabet to represent the Korean language, and since the 19th century, Japan has had two systems for representing the language, the ancient one ideographic and the modern one alphabetic.

Bibliography

Daniels, Peter T., and William Bright. *The World's Writing Systems*. New York: Oxford University Press, 1996.

Ambrose, St. (ca. 339–397 C.E.) *Roman poet-hymnodist*

A Roman aristocrat born at Treves, Ambrose grew up in a Christian family. He studied the liberal arts, law, and the Greek language. By about his 30th year, he had been appointed as governor of Liguria and Aemilia, making his headquarters at Milan.

A dispute between the eastern and western branches of Christianity was rapidly heading toward schism in the church, and, when the eastern party's Arian bishop of Milan, Auxentius, died, the two factions began to quarrel violently over his successor. As governor, Ambrose evenhandedly put down the violence and, as the only person trusted by both factions, soon found himself involuntarily drafted to become the bishop of Milan.

Though he professed Christianity, Ambrose had never been baptized. As soon as that important formality was attended to, Ambrose assumed the cathedral throne. Seeing God's will in the chain of events leading to his sudden elevation from layman to bishop, Ambrose took his responsibilities very seriously, becoming a champion of the rights, privileges, and spiritual precedence of the church in disagreements with temporal authority.

Not a particularly original Christian thinker, Ambrose followed such predecessors as Philo, ORIGEN, and St. BASIL in interpreting scripture. More original are his discussions of morality, Christian duty, and asceticism, especially the Christian devotion to virginity. He is particularly remembered as a hymnodist and is credited with founding the European tradition of spiritual song. He was, beyond that, a splendid preacher with a gift for finding uplifting allegory in scriptural text. It was his pastoral eloquence rather than his original thinking that provided the insights into scripture that converted St. AUGUSTINE of Hippo to Christianity.

Writing of his mentor in the faith, St. Augustine once observed that St. Ambrose was a silent reader. Augustine viewed this habit as something of a novelty, since reading aloud was the more usual practice at that time.

Bibliography

"Ambrose, St." New *Catholic Encyclopedia*. Vol. 1. Edited by William J. McDonald et al. New York: McGraw-Hill, 1967.

Brown, Peter. *Augustine of Hippo: A Biography*. Berkeley and Los Angeles: University of California Press, 2000.

Ammianus Marcellinus (fl. late fourth century C.E.) *Greek historian*

Born to a Greek family in Syria at Antioch, Ammianus Marcellinus pursued an adventurous military career as a young and middle-aged man both in Europe and in Asia Minor. That career early included a stint as a member of the emperor Costantius II's personal bodyguard. When the soldiering phase of his life ended and after a period of travel, he settled in Rome to work on what was to become the last major work in Latin about the history of the Roman Empire.

Beginning with the reign of the emperor Nerva (ruled 96–98 C.E.), in 31 books (papyrus scrolls) Ammianus followed the fortunes of the empire through the reign of the emperor Valens (ruled 364–78). Collected under the title *Rerum Gestarum*, ([A History] of deeds done), some 18 books of Ammianus's chronicle survive. These effectively continue earlier Roman histories written by TACITUS and by SUETONIUS.

Though some consider *Rerum Gestarum* stylistically inferior owing to the fact that Latin was Ammianus's second language, and though its facts are sometimes contradicted by better data, his digressions are often amusing, and he is an instructive commentator on historical events. This observation especially applies the closer the historian's narrative comes to his own time. His colorful descriptions of military action are action-packed and gripping, and he does not spare the rough edge of his tongue when he considers the behavior of Roman citizens, regardless of their rank, to be inappropriate.

Moreover, he is evenhanded in treating religious matters. While Ammianus was likely a pagan, posterity remains uncertain about the historian's private religious beliefs. We know that while on the one hand he admired the pagan emperor JULIANUS (Julian the Apostate), on the other, Ammianus deplored that ruler's harsh repression of the Christians. Additionally, the historian strongly favored religious toleration.

The portion of Ammianus's work that survives examines closely the emperors under whose reigns he served actively. This period includes the overlapping reigns of Constantius II and his cousin Julianus, mentioned above. They served uneasily together as a major and a lesser Augustus (that is, as co-emperors) and seemed headed toward civil war when Constantius died, leaving Julianus as uncontested emperor.

In his final major discussion, Ammianus treats in detail the invasion of the Roman Empire from beyond the Danube River by two separate contingents of Goths in 376 C.E. Ammianus describes their eventual victory over the Romans at the Battle of Hadrianople in 378—the battle in which Valens fell. Desultory notes thereafter perhaps suggest Ammianus's intention to continue the history. Some of the matters described are datable as late as 390, but apparently the historian's energies could no longer sustain the labor necessary to a continuation of his task.

Ammianus's work was admired by and a major source for the celebrated 18th-century British historian, Edward Gibbon.

Bibliography

Ammianus Marcellinus. *Ammianus Marcellinus with an English Translation.* Translated by John C. Rolfe. 3 vols. Cambridge, Mass.: Harvard University Press, 1956.

Walter Hamilton, ed. and trans. *Ammianus Marcellinus: The Later Roman Empire (A.D. 354–78).* Harmondsworth, U.K.: Penguin Books, 1986.

Amphitryon Titus Maccius Plautus (ca. second–third century B.C.E.)

Though by PLAUTUS's day the story of Amphitryon, the Theban general and foster father of Hercules (see HERACLES,) had already been long familiar to the theatergoers of Greece and likely those of Rome as well, Plautus's version does not appear to draw upon a single theatrical source. Instead, in his *Amphitryon*, Plautus creates a new theatrical genre—a tragicomedy. Tragedy often featured gods, and comedy featured slaves. Both figure importantly in *Amphitryon*.

That this double-natured theatrical type had its genesis on a Roman stage is utterly appropriate, for as the play's recent translator, Constance Carrier, reminds us, "the idea of twins" fascinated Roman culture. In *Amphitryon*, doubling is the order of the day. Beyond the conceptual framework of the tragicomic action, the principal male characters appear as doubles. The king of the gods, Jupiter, takes the shape of the general Amphitryon, so that the randy god may have his way with Amphitryon's already pregnant wife, Alcmena.

The god Mercury, who speaks a lengthy prologue explaining the concept of tragicomedy to the audience, doubles as Amphitryon's slave, Sosia, by taking on the latter's appearance and household functions.

Following Mercury's prologue, act 1 begins with the real Sosia's return from the Thebans' victorious battle against the Teleboans. Sosia has been sent by his master to tell Amphitryon's wife, Alcmena, of the victory and that she should expect her husband's immediate return. Sosia notices, however, that the night sky's constellations have not moved for hours and that night is continuing much longer than usual. The audience soon discovers that Jupiter has commanded the stars to stand still while he indulges his passion for Alcmena. To assure their privacy, Jupiter has stationed his son, Mercury, at the door of the house in the shape of Sosia.

Invisible for the moment, Mercury listens as the real Sosia rehearses his message for Alcmena. Sosia plans to spice up his report and its consequences with some believable lies. Mercury listens to Sosia's rehearsal and then, in the slave's own shape, confronts him. Mercury has all the advantages of omniscience and thus can pass all the tests that Sosia can imagine to prove that he is not confronting himself. Finally the real Sosia becomes so rattled that he begins to doubt his own identity, and he runs away in fright. Mercury gloats at the prospect of Sosia's report to Amphitryon and the confusion that report will produce.

Mercury then explains to the audience that Alcmena is expecting two children. Amphitryon has fathered one of them, a 10-month baby. The other, a seven-month baby, is Jupiter's offspring. Jupiter has arranged matters so that Alcmena will bear both children at one lying-in and forestall any gossip about their mother's behavior.

Jupiter as Amphitryon and Alcmena take the stage. Alcmena pleads with her supposed husband not to rush away. Jupiter, however, explains that his place is with his troops and that he must leave. He releases the stars from their suspended state, and the long night and the first act end together.

As the second act opens, Sosia fruitlessly attempts to explain his twin at home to Amphitryon. He thinks that Sosia is either drunk or mad. As the real master and slave approach Amphitryon's house, Alcmena enters. She feels sad about her husband's sudden departure. When she sees him approaching, she wonders if he claimed to be leaving to test her fidelity. She goes to meet him, and when he greets her as if he has been long away, she thinks he mocks her.

Amphitryon swears that he has not seen her for months. As Alcmena details the way they spent their time together the day before, Amphitryon becomes convinced of her infidelity. She is able to give him details of his recent battle, however, and when he challenges her, she produces the golden bowl that Amphitryon had received as a trophy of victory. He unseals the box that he thinks contains the bowl, and it has vanished. Finding the box empty, Sosia is convinced that Amphitryon was indeed at home with his wife the previous day, and that he had left the bowl in her safekeeping.

Amphitryon now feels certain that his wife has betrayed him, and the virtuous Alcmena spiritedly defends her chastity. Amphitryon sends for her kinsman, Naucratis, who spent the previous day with him, to convince her of his absence. The play seems destined for a tragic outcome.

Jupiter in the guise of Amphitryon takes the stage as act 3 opens. He speaks a brief prologue and declares his intention to rescue Alcmena from her husband's accusations. He also tells the audience that he means to arrange an easy delivery when Alcmena bears her half-brother twins.

Alcmena, in the meantime, has decided to leave her jealous husband, packed up her belongings, and left the house with her maids. In the guise of Amphitryon, Jupiter tries to soothe her. She resists his blandishments. Jupiter-as-Amphitryon claims that he meant everything as a little joke. Alcmena says his joke has wounded her heart. When her celestial lover calls on himself to curse Amphitryon, however, she relents, urging him to pray instead to bless Amphitryon, and the two make up their quarrel.

The real Sosia enters, and Jupiter-Amphitryon calls on the slave to support the joke excuse. Momentarily confused, Sosia deems it in his best interest to second whatever his apparent master says. Jupiter sends Sosia to invite Amphitryon's colleague, Blepharo, to dinner, and Jupiter and Alcmena enter the house together.

Mercury as Sosia takes up his station to guard their privacy. The real Amphitryon approaches. Mercury-Sosia, feigning drunkenness, climbs on the roof and pretends not to recognize Amphitryon. The two quarrel.

At this point a 272-line hiatus occurs in the surviving manuscript. In the missing section, it seems that Alcmena and Jupiter come from the house; two apparent Amphitryons are therefore on stage. Then Blepharo arrives and cannot decide which of the two is the real one. At some point Alcmena, on the point of delivery, goes inside to give birth. The two Amphitryons quarrel over who is Alcmena's husband and who is her seducer. As the text resumes, Mercury dumps a bucket of water on the real Amphitryon's head. Blepharo, confused and exasperated, tells the two Amphitryons to share the wife, and he exits.

Just as a thoroughly confused and despairing Amphitryon is about to take violent action and murder all concerned, a thunderclap causes him to faint on his doorstep, and his chambermaid Bromia rushes out. She bears the news that it thundered in the house at the same instant that an apparently supernatural voice told Alcmena to have no fear.

Bromia now reports further strange occurrences. In the midst of the thunder, voices, and resultant confusion, Alcmena painlessly bore her offspring. One was a normal baby, but the other—as the audience knows, the demigod Heracles—was so big that they couldn't swaddle him. Moreover, two great snakes came crawling from the pool in the atrium of the house in the direction of the children's cradle. Heracles leaped from the cradle, grabbed a snake in each hand and squeezed the monsters to death.

Immediately thereafter, Bromia reports, Jupiter admitted to having shared Alcmena's bed and claimed Heracles as his own. Finding that his own son is the half-brother of a demigod, Amphitryon considers himself honored rather than ill-used. Another clap of thunder signals the appearance of Jupiter on the roof. Jupiter address-

es Amphitryon, clears Alcmena of blame, claims Heracles as his own, and promises that the half-god will bring Amphitryon's house undying fame. Amphitryon assents gladly to the operation of the divine will. He calls on the audience for applause, and the play ends.

Bibliography

Plautus. *Amphitryon.* Translated by Constance Carrier. In *Plautus: The Comedies.* Edited by David R. Slavitt and Palmer Bovie. Vol. 1. Baltimore: The Johns Hopkins University Press, 1995.

Anabasis   See XENOPHON OF ATHENS.

Anacreon (fl. ca. 536 B.C.E) *Greek poet*

Anacreon was an early Greek lyric poet whose very slender literary remnants (if any are genuine) and long-standing reputation reveal that his specialties included love poetry and tender sentiments on the one hand and derisive satire on the other. In his own time, Anacreon shared the palm with PINDAR as the two best lyric poets of the age and one of the best nine poets to have flourished in early Greek literature.

Like SAPPHO, among others, Anacreon probably wrote a class of erotic poems called *Parthenia*, or songs in praise of virgins. In addition to love, Anacreon's pleasure in the company of others and praise of wine form the subjects of the softer poetry included in the corpus of verse called *Anacreontic*. A seemingly irresolvable problem of attribution, however, surrounds the poems associated with Anacreon's name as none of them can be attributed to his hand with certainty. His most expert editor, J. M. Edmonds, using a system of analysis too complex to detail here, has concluded that the poems numbered 18a, 18b, 21, 22, 26, 37, and 46 are the oldest in a collection of Anacreontic verse, the composition of whose individual pieces spans at least six centuries. Writers who lived long after Anacreon have been identified as the authors of some of the later poems.

While simply being the oldest does not assure that the above poems came from Anacreon's hand or even that they are better art than the younger examples, their age does make them more likely candidates as surviving instances of the poet's own song. "Poem 18a" is a Dionysian poem in which a speaker, crowned with grape leaves, celebrates the beneficent effects of wine on a passionate lover. "Poem 18b," instead, celebrates the beauty of a grove in a rural landscape. "Poem 21," a famous Greek drinking song, returns to the theme of imbibing. The earth drinks from the stream, the tree from the earth; the sea drinks the river; the sun drinks the sea, and the moon the sun. Why, the poet asks his comrades, should they object if he too would be drinking?

"Poem 22" is a pretty compliment to a woman the poet admires. He begins with two examples of metamorphosis. The Titaness Niobe was changed to stone; in Greek versions, the betrayed wife of Tereus, Procne, turned as she does here into a swallow (in Latin versions, she became a nightingale). The poet, too, wishes he could undergo a transformation. He would like to become a mirror so his love would gaze on him, her vest so she could wear him, a wave to bathe her cheek, a jar of her hairdressing, her necklace, her bustier to cover her bosom, or even her sandal so she could set her foot on him.

"Poem 26" compares the devastation wrought at the fall of Troy and the sack of Thebes to the poet's destruction by arrows of the god of love, Eros, fired at the poet from his beloved's eyes. The last in this series, "Poem 27," asserts that, just as a horse's brand or a Phrygian's hat make their owners recognizable, so the poet can identify a lover by an infallible, brand-like sign.

Despite the uncertainties surrounding the authorship of Anacreontic poems, they have exercised considerable influence in the subsequent history of Euro-American letters.

Bibliography

J. M. Edmonds, ed. and trans. *Elegy and Iambus . . . with the Anacreontea.* Vol. 2. Cambridge, Mass.: Harvard University Press, 1954.

Analects Confucius (ca. 380 B.C.E.)

First compiled by Confucius's students as a collection of the master's sayings, Confucius's *Analects* probably did not begin to acquire their modern form until a century or more after the sage's death in 479 B.C.E. The *Analects* is the only document bearing Confucius's name that he actually had a hand in composing, though he did edit older classics. The notes that comprise the *Analects* were drawn from his teaching. Essentially a collection of Confucian fragments, in its current form the *Analects* contains 20 chapters, which in turn contain 497 sections. If a principle of organization underlies the current form of the work, however, it was only apparent to whoever organized it.

The scholar Burton Watson has suggested that the most useful approach to the *Analects* is to regard them as scripture rather than as history or as philosophy. Then, instead of looking for a unified and systematic approach to governing a society or one's self, one can regard the *Analects*' maxims as a set of precepts that might be invoked to guide one's decisions in day-to-day living. For the long period during which Confucianism was the state religion of China, the *Analects* did in fact occupy the place of scripture in Chinese society. Thinkers in East Asia who have memorized the entire work and who have spent years contemplating its meaning suggest that the more one thinks about the *Analects*, the deeper the meaning becomes.

Central to a nascent understanding of the *Analects* is a grasp of what Confucius meant by two terms: *the way* and *virtue*. *The way*, suggests Confucius's translator, D. C. Lau, means something like the sum total of truth about human beings and their place in the universe. Understanding *the way* can be either an individual or a state accomplishment. When a state has a corporate understanding of *the way*, that understanding implies a humane and compassionate system of governance. When an individual understands *the way*, following it presupposes striving to lead an exemplary life, preferring what is right to profit, and choosing death over dishonor.

For either an individual or a state to arrive at such understandings, however, requires a rigorous program of conscious effort directed to that end. One knows when one arrives at *virtue* because one loves one's fellow human beings and treats them as one would treat oneself. At the same time, self-interest is the most insidious of vices. One must carefully guard against it. One must also temper one's benevolence with learning, otherwise one risks becoming foolishly benevolent and serving the lesser rather than the greater good.

One must be intelligent, and one must be wise. Some are born wise; others acquire wisdom through experience, study, and effort. Above all else, one must be honest with oneself if one wishes to acquire wisdom.

Beyond that, one who is virtuous is also courageous, and one must be reliable in both word and deed—but not to the degree such that hewing to the truth will bring others into harm's way. One might, for example, lie to save a child from being kidnapped and turned into a mercenary soldier. The injunction to tell the truth is thus tempered by the service of a higher good.

Another of the virtues promulgated by the *Analects* is reverence. Reverence can be displayed either toward one's superiors in the social order or toward the gods. In both instances, one does well to display the attribute and wisely keep one's distance from those—human or divine—to whom reverence is due.

On the subject of the divine, Confucius twice in the *Analects* mentions a concept called *t'ien ming*. Lau gives the meaning of the phrase as "the decree of Heaven." Although Confucius considered that decree very difficult to understand, it does seem that he credited an overarching, rational standard to which all virtues were subordinate and by which one must strive to measure one's thoughts and actions. Lau uses the word *destiny* to describe that standard, but he also suggests that it is within human capacity to understand *why* destiny operates as it must, and he opines that human beings need not bother to fathom *ming* if that word occurs without the modifying *t'ien*. That would be like trying to describe the physics of a parallel universe to which our instruments of observation and measurement have no access. To approach Confucius's analogy more closely, explaining *ming* would be like drawing a map of Heaven.

For Confucius, to achieve an individual understanding of *the way* is not enough. Once a person has mastered *the way*—and of course in Confucius's society it was always a male person—that person must put his understanding to work for the good of the common people by participating in government. It is the participation of the initiates in government that provides the moral example by which the common people can measure their own progress toward *the way*. Thus, a paternalistic government was the Confucian ideal.

Portions of the *Analects* address the rightness of older precepts and establish tests by which a student can accept or reject them. Confucius examines the utility of moral generalizations by considering the adequacy of the specific rules by which the generalizations are put into effect. The example can serve here of endangering a child by telling the truth when a lie would protect her. The universality of applying the generalization "always tell the truth" is overcome by the situational consequence of putting the rule into effect.

Bibliography

Confucius. *The Analects* (Lun yü). Translated by D. C. Lau. Harmondsworth, U.K.: Penguin Books, Ltd., 1979.

———. *The Analects of Confucius* (Lun Yu). Translated by Chichung Huang. New York: Oxford University Press, 1997.

———. *The Analects of Confucius: A Philosophical Translation*. Translated by Roger T. Ames and Harry Rosemont. New York: Ballantine Books, 1999.

———. *The Essential Analects*. Translated by Edward Slingerland. Indianapolis: Hackett Publishing Co., ca. 2006.

Sim, May. *Remastering Morals with Aristotle and Confucius*. New York: Cambridge University Press, 2007.

ancient Chinese dynasties and periods

The factual and, for the earliest periods, the perhaps partly mythical history of the dynasties of ancient China begins about 2100 years before the Common Era. Historians have further subdivided some of the dynasties into periods of time or have grouped them both geographically and by traditional names that have become associated with them. The following table provides an overview of the major features of that system through the beginning of the eighth century C.E. for all but the Tang dynasty, which resumed power after a hiatus and continued until the early 10th century. The rough cutoff for literary figures and works discussed in these pages is the end of the first Tang ascendancy.

Some of the complexities of the political situation during certain periods of Chinese history are reflected in the occasionally contemporaneous existence of multiple dynasties.

Dynasties and Periods	Time Frame
Xia (Hsia; perhaps partly mythic)	ca. 2100–ca. 1600 B.C.E.
Shang or Yin (mostly factual)	ca. 1600–ca. 1028 B.C.E.
Zhou (Chou)	ca. 1027–256 B.C.E.
Western Zhou	ca. 1100–771 B.C.E.
Eastern Zhou	ca. 770–256 B.C.E.
Spring and Autumn period	722–468 B.C.E.
Warring States period	403–221 B.C.E.
Qin (Ch'in)	221–207 B.C.E.
Han	206 B.C.E.–220 C.E.
Western, or Former, Han	206 B.C.E.–8 C.E.
Xin (Hsin)	9–23 C.E.
Liu Xuan (Liu Hüsan)	23–25 C.E.
Eastern, or Later, Han	25–220 C.E.

Dynasties and Periods	Time Frame
Three Kingdoms	220–265 C.E.
Wei (in North China)	220–265 C.E.
Shu (in Sichuan [Szechwan])	221–263 C.E.
Wu (in the Lower Yangtze Valley)	222–280 C.E.
Jin (Chin)	265–420 C.E.
Western Jin	265–316 C.E.
Eastern Jin	317–420 C.E.
Southern and Northern Dynasties	420–589 C.E.
Sixteen Kingdoms (North China)	304–439 C.E.
Northern Dynasties	386–581 C.E.
Northern Wei (Tabgatch)	386–534 C.E.
Eastern Wei	534–550 C.E.
Northern Qi (Ch'i)	550–577 C.E.
Northern Zhou	557–581 C.E.
Southern Dynasties + Wu + Eastern Jin = The Six Dynasties	420–589 C.E.
Song (Sung; a.k.a. Liu or Former Song)	420–479 C.E.
Qi (Ch'i)	479–502 C.E.
Liang	502–577 C.E.
(Chen) Ch'en	557–589 C.E.
Sui	581–618 C.E.
Tang (T'ang)	618–684 and 705–907 C.E.
Zhou (Empress Wu)	684–705 C.E.

Bibliography

Mair, Victor H. *The Columbia Anthology of Traditional Chinese Literature*. New York: Columbia University Press, 1994.

Andocides (Andokides) (ca. 468–ca. 396 B.C.E.) *Greek Prose writer*

The son of a prominent Athenian family, Andocides became a statesman and an orator. The four surviving examples of his orations are distinguished by their straightforward style and lack of ornament and also by their clarity. He is positioned at a moment of transition between early orators who, like him, were not professionals and later ones who were. His speeches are also particularly valuable because of the light they shed on the history of his epoch. One of his orations criticizes the unscrupulous Athenian statesman Alcibiades. The playwrights AESCHYLUS, ARISTOPHANES, and EURIPIDES shared Andocides' low opinion of Alcibiades.

Another surviving oration of Andocides is one that he delivered in 390 in support of concluding a peace with Sparta. Sparta and Athens had been fighting the Corinthian War for four years at the time of this speech.

The other two surviving examples of Andocides' oratory are speeches that he made in his own defense. During the Peloponnesian War, just before Athenian troops were due to depart on a mission to Sicily, numerous phallic shrines bearing statues of the god Hermes (and thus called hermae) were desecrated. This sacrilege deeply offended the Athenians, and in the subsequent investigation, members of Andocides' family as well as the orator himself were implicated. Andocides at first confessed but later retracted his confession and fled from imprisonment in Athens. One of the two other surviving examples of his rhetoric is a speech he made in an unsuccessful bid to be allowed to return from this self-imposed exile. The other is also an example of self-defense. When Andocides finally did return to Athens, he was barred from attending the ceremonies connected with the Eleusinian mysteries. When he nonetheless attended, he was charged with impiety, and in the last of his orations, he defended himself against these charges.

A portion of Andocides' defense rested on revisiting and reinterpreting the events connected with the hermae affair. Another rested on his denying the factual basis of assertions made in the accusation against him, and a third rested on his argument that it was in the best interests of the Athenian state to find him innocent. His interesting speeches are now all available in good English translations.

Bibliography

Andokides. *On the Mysteries*. Edited and translated by Douglas M. Macdowell. Oxford: Clarendon Press, 1962.

Gagarin, Michael, and Douglas M. MacDowell, ed. and trans. *Antiphon and Andocides*. Austin: University of Texas Press, 1998.

Andria (The Woman of Andros, The Girl from Andros) Terence (166 B.C.E.)

To bring his first play, *Andria*, to the Roman stage, TERENCE combined elements of two plays by the Greek comic playwright MENANDER. Like other representatives of the Roman comedy, *Andria* was composed in verse, set to music and, in this case, scored for two accompanying flutes. The music's composer, as we learn from a surviving production notice, was a slave named Flaccus, and the principal actors were Lucius Ambivius Turpio and Lucius Atilius Praenestinus. The Megalensian Games, held at Rome in April in honor of the great goddess, Cybele, provided the occasion for the performance.

The play introduces a device that was to become a signature in Terence's drama—the double plot. In this maiden effort, however, critics generally concur that the doubling lacks the organic unity that Terence would soon achieve in handling it.

After a prologue that announces Terence's sources and the names of Roman playwrights who have preceded him in mining two Greek plays to achieve one Roman production, the play opens with a dialogue between the elderly Athenian Simo and his former slave, now a freedman, Sosia.

Simo has always been very proud of his son, Pamphilus, who has behaved well all his life. Even after Chrysis—a woman from Andros—moved next door and eventually became a courtesan, Pamphilus, who sometimes accompanied her lovers to the house, always behaved respectably as far as his father could ascertain. In due course, therefore, Simo performed his fatherly duty and decided to betroth Pamphilus to Philumena, the daughter of a respectable family headed by Chremes. He neglected, however, to mention the matter either to his son or to the bride's family until the day of the wedding.

Before that day arrived, however, Chrysis died, and at her funeral pyre a woman, who proved to be her sister Glycerium, almost jumped into the flames. Pamphilus prevented her, and the two collapsed into each other's arms, revealing that they were lovers and that Pamphilus had already engaged himself to wed her.

It turns out that a slave, Davus, is privy to Pamphilus's affair with Glycerium. Simo sniffs this out and warns Davus not to interfere in his efforts to match Pamphilus with Philumena. Davus, however, knows that Glycerium is already about to bear Pamphilus's child, so he opts to continue his support for Pamphilus.

In the meantime, Glycerium's maid, Mysis, goes in search of a midwife while praying that Glycerium will have an easy delivery. As she leaves the house, Mysis overhears Pamphilus raging about his father having just told him that he must marry Philumena this very day. When Mysis challenges Pamphilus on the subject, however, he firmly announces his resolve to honor his commitment to Glycerium, and Mysis continues on her errand in search of a midwife.

The parallel plot begins its development in the second act. There we find that another young gentleman, Charinus, a good friend of Pamphilus, is in love with Philumena. We find Charinus's slave Byrria reporting to his master Philumena's proposed match with Pamphilus. The two young men meet, and Charinus begs Pamphilus not to wed Philumena. Pamphilus assures his friend that he has no desire to do so and enlists him as an ally to spoil his father's plans.

Davus arrives and reports that no wedding preparations are going forward at Chremes' house, so both young men take heart. Davus advises Pamphilus to agree to marry when his father next asks him. He can rest assured that Chremes will never agree to the match.

Simo encounters his son in act 2, scene 5, and announces his intention that his son marry. Pamphilus agrees to obey his father. The slave Byrria, however, has stationed himself where he can overhear the conversation, and he thinks that Pamphilus will wed Philumena.

As act 3 opens, Glycerium goes into labor, and, overhearing her cries and prayers, Simo is convinced that he is the victim of a plot hatched by Davus to prevent his marrying Pamphilus off to Philumena. In the following scene, the midwife Lesbia announces that "Pamphilus has . . . a bouncing boy." Simo accosts Davus with his theory that the birth is a fake, and Davus encourages the old man in his delusion, at the same time instructing him to prepare his house for a wedding feast and to spend some money on the preparations.

In act 3, scene 3, Simo and Chremes finally meet, and Chremes demands an explanation for all the rumors he has been hearing. Simo argues in favor of the marriage. Hesitant at first, Chremes grudgingly agrees. The pair encounters Davus, who learns that all his arrangements have backfired. Scene 4 of the third act ends with Davus's despairing soliloquy on the failure of his plotting. The final scene of the act features Pamphilus and Davus. The former blames Davus for his mismanagement of the affair, and Davus promises to find a solution.

As act 4 opens, Charinus is blaming Pamphilus for ruining his hopes for a union with Philumena. The slave Davus continues to search his mind for an unraveling of the imbroglio that he has apparently caused. In the next scene, he has the servant Mysis lay Pamphilus and Glycerium's child on the doorstep of Simo's house. Chremes, however, arrives and discovers Mysis in the act. Davus feigns ignorance of the entire affair. Under Chremes' cross-questioning, Mysis admits that Pamphilus is the child's father. More confusion follows until Davus finally explains to a puzzled Mysis that his odd behavior and conversation was the only way to instruct Chremes in what the plotters wanted him to know.

In scene 5 of Act 4, an heir of the deceased Chrysis, Crito, is introduced as just having arrived from Andros. Crito knows that Glycerium is not really the sister of Chrysis but that she is instead an Athenian citizen. This is significant because it means that, under Athenian law, the father of her child must marry her.

In act 5, the cross-examination of Crito reveals that Glycerium is in fact the long-lost daughter of Chremes himself, taken to Andros by his brother Phania in an attempt to avoid the wars. Pamphilus is able to convince Chremes that Glycerium is truly his daughter by telling him that her birth name was Pasibula. Certain of his fatherhood, Chremes confers upon Pamphilus the dowry of 10 talents that he had reserved for his elder daughter.

In a secondary subplot, Simo has had his slave, Davus, clapped in irons because of his interference in the matter of Pamphilus's wedding. Pamphilus goes to rescue his staunch supporter.

Free at last to marry Philumena, Charinus wins Chremes' approval and, with the younger daughter's hand, a dowry of six Athenian talents.

See also SELF-TORMENTOR, THE.

Bibliography

Terence. *Works*. English and Latin. Edited and translated by John Barsley. Cambridge, Mass.: Harvard University Press, 2001.

Andromache Euripides (ca. 425 B.C.E.)

In *Andromache*, EURIPIDES follows the postwar lives of several persons involved in the Trojan War. The title character, Andromache, is the widow of the Trojan hero Hector, whom Achilles had killed in single combat. She has been bestowed as a prize of honor upon Achilles' son, Neoptolemus, whose mistress she becomes. With her, Neoptolemus fathers a son, who, though nameless in the play, is called Molossus elsewhere.

Neoptolemus, however, also has an official family. His wife, Hermione, is a Spartan princess, the daughter of Menelaus and Helen. Hermione plots against Andromache and her son, planning with her father to murder them while Neoptolemus is away on a religious pilgrimage to the temple of Apollo at Delphi. It is at this point that Euripides begins his play.

Andromache recounts her history, the death of her husband, the murder of her son Astyanax, her own subsequent enslavement, the birth of Neoptolemus's child, and Hermione's unrelenting abuse. Learning of Hermione's plot to conspire with her father Menelaus to murder Andromache and her child, Andromache hides her son while she finds sanctuary at the altar of the goddess Thetis. A maidservant enters to repeat the warning about the threat to Andromache's life and to tell her that Menelaus has discovered the son.

A CHORUS of women rehearses Andromache's woe, and Hermione enters and berates Andromache, accusing her of gross immorality and evil intentions—including that of supplanting Hermione as Neoptolemus's consort. After an exchange of bitter words, Hermione exits. The chorus reviews the action and the history behind it, and Menelaus enters with Andromache's son. He threatens to kill the boy if Andromache doesn't leave her sanctuary: One of them must die.

Andromache remonstrates with Menelaus, suggesting that he consider the consequences if Neoptolemus returns and finds his son dead. Menelaus, however, is unmoved, and, after bewailing her fortune, Andromache leaves the altar and embraces her son. Menelaus captures and binds her, then tells her that it will be up to Hermione if the boy lives or dies. Menelaus takes perverse pride in having tricked Andromache and sets out for the palace with his two prisoners. The chorus passes judgment on the behavior of Hermione and Menelaus, calling it "Godless, lawless, and graceless."

Now Menelaus reenters with his sword drawn. He is conducting both mother and son to their place of execution. In a touching scene, the child pleads with Menelaus as his "dear friend" to spare his life. Menelaus is merciless. The execution, however, is interrupted by the arrival of the father of Achilles and grandfather of Neoptolemus, the aged Peleus. He and Menelaus engage in a boasting contest about who has more authority in the present circumstances. They cast aspersions upon each other's behavior and relations and threaten each other. The chorus eventually has enough of this fruitless argument and advises them to stop it lest they kill each other. Peleus, however, outblusters Menelaus and succeeds in rescuing the captives.

A nurse now enters with the news that Hermione, distressed at her father's departure and fearful of Neoptolemus's possible reaction to her attempt on the lives of his son and mistress, is threatening to hang herself. Her servants try to dissuade her, and as they do, Orestes, the son of Agamemnon and Clytemnestra, arrives as a traveler. His arrival provides a point of connection between the now-finished first story and the second part of the play's double plot.

Orestes says that he has decided to see how his kinswoman, Hermione, is getting along. The distraught Hermione embraces his knees in the traditional Greek gesture of supplication, and Orestes recognizes her. She tells him her story and regretfully suggests that the advice of bad women led her to persecute Andromache. Orestes reveals that Hermione had been promised to him as a wife in the first place. Since her situation is so threatening, he promises to take her home to her father. As they go to make preparations, Orestes reveals that he has already arranged for the death of Neoptolemus at the temple of Delphi. He makes this plan more credible by reminding the audience that he has already slain his mother, Clytemnestra, in revenge for her murder of Agamemnon. The pair departs on their journey.

Peleus reenters and learns the whole story from the chorus. A messenger then enters and recounts the story of Neoptolemus's death at the hands of an armed squadron of men at Delphi. The messenger and his companions have returned the body of Neoptolemus to his grandfather for burial.

Distraught by all his afflictions, the old man laments his situation and throws his royal scepter to the ground. At this point, his wife, who is also the goddess Thetis, appears above the stage as a *dea ex machina* (goddess from a machine). Her speech knits up many of the play's loose ends. She tells Peleus to take Neoptolemus's body back to Delphi and bury it there as a reproach to the Delphians. Andromache, the goddess says, must migrate to the land of the Molossians to marry their ruler, Helenus. There, her son by Neoptolemus will found a long and happy line of rulers. As for Peleus himself, Thetis intends to make him a god and her eternal consort. She gives him detailed instructions about what he must do in this connection. Finally, she pronounces that all she has ordained is the will of Zeus.

The chorus ends the play by making Euripides' favorite point: The gods often do things that people have not expected.

Bibliography

Kovacs, David, ed. and trans. *Euripides: Vol. 2: Children of Heracles; Hippolytus; Andromache; Hecuba.* Cambridge, Mass.: Harvard University Press, 1995.

annalists and annals of Rome

Almost from Rome's beginnings as a polity, its citizens kept written records of noteworthy events. At first these tended to take the form of straightforward accounts of the facts. According to CICERO in his work *De Oratore*, from the very founding of the city, the chief of the College of Pontifices, or *pontifex maximus*, listed the notable events of each year on lead tablets that he then posted in his house so that citizens could consult them. A list of the serving magistrates was also compiled annually, and less important public events were noted on linen and kept in the temple of Juno Moneta.

The kings of early Rome promulgated laws—some of them established on the model of Grecian laws imported by an embassy sent to Greece to learn about Greek governance. A lawyer named Papirus made a collection of these laws during the reign of King Tarquin the Proud (ruled 534–510 B.C.E.). Family journals and funeral orations also were collected, but as these were often edited to elevate the reputations of family members, their historical accuracy was suspect.

Hardly any examples of such early records survive. When the Gauls sacked Rome in 385 B.C.E., most of the annals were lost in the general conflagration. A new group of annalists soon emerged, however. Sometimes, these recorders, including a pair named Cneius Naevius (d. 201 or 204 B.C.E.) and QUINTUS ENNIUS, preserved their annals in verse. In addition to such verse annalists, prose annalists also appeared. Among these was QUINTUS FABIUS PICTOR and Marcus Portius Cato, the elder. Cato's largely lost work *Origenes*, or *De Origenes*, which examined the early history of Rome, discussed the city's early kings, reported the beginnings of the states of Italy, and detailed the first and second Punic wars against Carthage and the Roman victory over the Lusitanians (today's Portuguese) in 152 B.C.E. Such fragments as do survive from these and other annalists are readily available.

More significant remnants have survived from historians and annalists of the first century before and the first after the Common Era. MARCUS TERENTIUS VARRO was the most productive scholar of the epoch. Other such Romans, as Quintus Pomponius Atticus, began trying their hands at the production of universal histories. Still others began to set out the contributions that their own lives made to the events of their times. Principal examples of such autobiographical histories are the commentaries of JULIUS CAESAR and the memoirs of AUGUSTUS CAESAR.

Historians in the modern sense of that term also emerged at about this time. SALLUST and LIVY stand with Julius Caesar in the first rank of such figures. Following the death of Augustus in 14 C.E., major writers such as TACITUS, both PLINY THE ELDER, PLINY THE YOUNGER, and SUETONIUS emerged among a growing cadre of respectable historians. The emperor Claudius became a notable memoirist.

From about 160 C.E., however, after the halcyon days of the empire under the Antonine emperors—a period of western European history thought by some to have been the happiest ever enjoyed by that fractious subcontinent—the writing of history became politicized to such a degree that anything potentially unflattering to the emperor in power or to his adherents exposed historians to mortal danger. Nonetheless a hardy few, including the fourth-century historian AMMIANUS MARCELLINUS undertook the writing of respectable history, ignoring the attendant perils. Ammianus is generally considered to have been the last of the great Roman historians. In the third and fourth centuries, however, a group of six writers serially authored the official history of the empire. Their collection detailed the lives of the emperors from Hadrian to Carus. In order of their appointment to the post, they were: Aelius Spartianus, Vulcatius Gallicanus, Julius Capitolinus, Trebellius Pollio, Aelius Lampridius, and Flavius Vopiscus. As a group, they were known as *Scriptores Historiae Augustae* (writers of the imperial history). Their work survives.

The writing of history with a different focus received considerable impetus from the ascendancy of Christianity as the official religion of the late Roman Empire. EUSEBIUS wrote a *Universal History* in Greek that St. JEROME translated into Latin. Another Christian historian, Flavius Lucius Dexter, dedicated to St. Jerome a history setting forth a chronology of notable events beginning from the birth of Christ and ending with the author's own times. An even more ambitious universal history was that composed by Prosper Aquitanus. His work, *Chronicon*, tracked events from the creation of the world to the capture and sack of Rome by the Vandals' most notable king, Gaiseric (sometimes Genseric), in 455 C.E.

Bibliography

Ammianus Marcellinus. *Ammianus Marcellinus with an English Translation*. Translated by John C. Rolfe. 3 vols. Cambridge, Mass.: Harvard University Press, 1956.

Cato, Marcus Portius. *Origenes*. (Fragments in Latin and French.) Edited and translated by Martine Chassignet. Paris: Belles Lettres, 1986.

Cicero, Marcus Tullius. *Cicero on Oratory and Orators*. Translated and edited by J. S. Watson. Carbondale: Southern Illinois Press, 1986.

Ennius, Quintus. *Annali: Libri 1–8*. Naples: Liguori, 2000.

Eusebius. *The Church History*. Translated by Paul A. Maier. Grand Rapids, Mich.: Kregel Publications, 1999.

———. *The Essential Eusebius*. Edited and translated by Colm Luibheid. New York: New American Library, 1966.

Hamilton, Walter, ed. and trans. *Ammianus Marcellinus: The Later Roman Empire (A.D. 354–78)*. Harmondsworth, U.K.: Penguin Books, 1986.

Livy. *The History of Rome, Books 1–5*. Translated by Valerie M. Warrior. Indianapolis: Haskett Publications, 2006.

Mariotti, Scevola, trans. *Il Bellum Poenicum e l'arte di Nevio*. (The Punic War and the Art of Naevius.) 3rd ed. Edited by Piergiorgio Parroni. Bologna: Pàtron, 2001.

Varro, Marcus Terrentius. *Opere*. (Works.) Edited by Antonio Traglia. Torino: UTET, 1974.

Annals of Spring and Autumn (*Chunqiu, Ch'un Ch'iu*) Confucius (ca. 500 B.C.E)

One of the five canonical texts of early classic Confucianism, the *Annals of Spring and Autumn* contain a partial chronicle of principal happenings in CONFUCIUS's native but otherwise relatively minor Chinese state of Lu. In brief and unembellished entries, Confucius made note of matters of interest that occurred in Lu between 722 and 484 B.C.E. At the head of each entry, he recorded the year, month, day, and season of the noted event's occurrence. Confucius included summer under spring and winter under autumn, thus giving rise to the common title of the work.

Listed in the *Annals*' pages are natural phenomena such as meteor showers; political events such as raids by warriors from other states, victories and defeats in feudal warfare, or treaties resolving disagreements with other states; and such unfortunate occurrences as deaths from natural causes and from murders.

Modern readers may find it odd that such a bald recitation of events would assume great importance in the Confucian canon, but Confucius thought that the work would make his reputation. His view of the *Annals*' importance was shared by his successor philosopher, MENCIUS, who opined that the work struck "rebellious ministers and bad sons" with terror. For the Chinese, important commentary had a way of grafting itself onto the essential material of a text, and this occurred in the case of Confucius's annals just as it did with the BOOK OF ODES that he compiled.

A disciple of Confucius named Zuo (Tso) took the sketchy vignettes of the *Annals* and filled them out by adding more details about the incidents and discussing their significance. Confucius's base composition, then, served as a road map to such consequential events in the history of the state of Lu as would prove edifying to those willing to take the trouble to look where Confucius had pointed. Known as the ZUO ZHUAN (*Tso Chuan*), or Zuo's commentary on the *Annals*, this work's clarifying prose has long been considered the most important of three such explanatory addenda. The two others, both composed in the fifth century B.C.E., do not enjoy the general acclaim that Zuo's work does. The authors of those lesser commentaries were Ku-liang and Kung-Yang.

Bibliography

Giles, Herbert A. *A History of Chinese Literature*. New York: Grove Press Inc., 1958.

Legge, James, trans. *The Confucian Classics,* vols. 5 and 6. 7 vols. Oxford: Clarendon Press, 1893–95.

anthologies of Greek verse

From as early as the second century B.C.E., persons with literary interests began compiling anthologies of epigrams and short poems by earlier authors. We know the names of some of the earliest anthologists, such as Polemo Periegetes and MELEAGER OF GADARA in Syria (fl. ca. 100 B.C.E.). We also know the name and something of the contents of Meleager's anthology. It was entitled *Stephanos* (The Garland, or The Crown), and it included examples of the work of 46 poets. Later anthologists continued to follow Meleager's example. Among those we find Philippus of Thessalonica (fl. ca. 80 C.E.) and Diogenianus of Heraclea (fl. ca. 120 C.E.). None of their anthologies, however, survives.

Other anthologies did survive, though, in the late ancient and early medieval periods, and subsequent anthologists, such as Strato of Sardis (fl. second or third century C.E.), used their contents as the basis for new collections of their own. Others, such as DIOGENES LAERTIUS (fl. ca. 220 C.E.), found new principles upon which to base their collections. Diogenes collected poems that celebrated famous men. AGATHIAS OF MYRINA, himself an epigrammatist of note, formed a collection called *Kuklos* ("cycle" or "collection") and organized it into seven sections according to subject.

Like the works of their predecessors, the collections of these men have disappeared into the mists of literary history. No anthology, in fact, survives that was compiled before the 10th century. From that epoch, however, and from the 14th century, two representative collections survive: respectively, the collection of the otherwise unknown Constantine Cephalas and a seven-book collection by a monk dwelling at Constantinople, Maximus Planudes. In addition to that miscellany, Planudes also collected the FABLES of AESOP.

Bibliography

Eschenburg, Johannes J. *Manual of Classical Literature.* Edited and translated by N. W. Fiske. Philadelphia: E. C. & J. Biddle, 1850.

Antigone Sophocles (ca. 422 B.C.E.)

The story of Antigone, the daughter of Oedipus by his wife and mother, Jocasta, tells the final episode in a series of events also treated by AESCHYLUS in *The SEVEN AGAINST THEBES*. As the legend has it, the sons of Oedipus by Jocasta, Eteocles and Polynices, were reared by their uncle Creon and succeeded to his power while he was still living. Although they were supposed to rule by turns, the brothers fell out and ended up hating each other. When Eteocles became king, he exiled Polynices. Enraged, Polynices gathered a military force in Argos and besieged his native city. Aeschylus tells the story of that battle and how the war between the brothers fulfilled a curse upon them that they would die by each other's hands. As that play ends, the elders of Thebes have decreed that Polynices' body cannot be buried because he had invaded his native city. His sister, Antigone, disobeys their edict.

As SOPHOCLES handles the same material, after the battle in which the brothers die at each others' hands, Creon reassumes the city's throne. He issues an edict granting a hero's funeral to Eteocles, but decrees that Polynices' body must remain unburied. Without the benefit of a proper funeral, the Greeks thought, a dead person's spirit could not find rest in the underworld but would be condemned to wander as a forlorn ghost for all eternity. Unswerving in her view of her sisterly duty, therefore, Antigone opposes her will against that of her uncle and king, confident in the god-ordained justice of her cause. This situation is further complicated by Antigone's love for her cousin, Creon's son Haemon, and Haemon's for her.

The play opens as Antigone and her sister Ismene discuss their brother's announced funeral arrangements, and Antigone announces her determination to disobey Creon. Ismene vainly tries to dissuade Antigone and convince her of the folly of defying the state.

The sisters exit, and the CHORUS fills in the audience on the background of the situation as they remind their hearers of the material that appeared in *Seven against Thebes*. Creon then enters, fills in the material from *OEDIPUS TYRANNUS* that the audience needs to follow the current play, and reasserts his decision vis-à-vis the burials.

A guard rushes onstage and, after excusing himself as well as he can, reports that someone has disobeyed Creon's prohibition and performed the burial ritual by sprinkling dust on Polynices' corpse. The guards have no clue as to who the perpetrator might be.

The credulous chorus suggests that a god may have done it. Creon scornfully rejects that theory and dismisses the guard with threats. The chorus gossips about the goings-on, and a guard reenters, dragging along Antigone, whom he has caught attempting to bury the body after the guards had cleaned off the dust of her first effort. After a discussion of the apparent conflict between human and divine law in this case, Creon condemns Antigone to death. Ismene comes forward, and though she has not disobeyed Creon's edict, she asks to die as well rather than be bereft of her sister.

As Creon and Ismene discuss Creon's sentence, Ismene asks him if he will slay his own son's betrothed. Creon is inflexible, and Antigone cries out to Haemon that his father wrongs him in depriving the young man of his bride.

Haemon enters and respectfully attempts to dissuade his father from executing Antigone, not on the grounds of the young man's love for her, but rather on the grounds of the dark rumors that have been circulating among the citizens. The citizens are displeased with Creon's judgment, says Haemon, and wisdom should heed that displeasure. Creon asserts the authority of high office and disregards his son's good advice. He repeats his determination to execute Antigone. Haemon responds that Antigone's death will destroy another, and Creon, interpreting his son's words as a threat, calls for Antigone to be executed

before Haemon's eyes. Haemon promises that his father will see him no more and exits.

Creon announces his intention to deal with Antigone by imprisoning her in a cave with only as much food "as piety prescribes." As Antigone is led away, the chorus weeps for her and tries to comfort her by reminding her that, as mistress of her own fate, her death will be glorious—even godlike. Antigone perceives these well-intentioned but ill-conceived remarks as mockery. She reviews her own behavior and that of Creon and concludes that she has done the proper thing. Creon orders her led away, and the chorus draws analogies to similar fates suffered by predecessors from the annals of Greek mythology.

The blind prophet, Teiresias, now enters, led by a boy. He tells Creon that the city of Thebes has been polluted by carrion from the unburied corpse of Polynices. He warns Creon that he stands on the edge of a fatal decision, and advises him to allow the burial. Creon pridefully refuses and insults Teiresias. The seer foretells the death of one of Creon's children as the exchange of a corpse for a corpse.

Teiresias exits, and the citizen chorus advises Creon to release Antigone and bury Polynices. Finally he agrees to accept their advice, orders Polynices' burial, and rushes to release Antigone. The chorus prays to the gods, but a messenger arrives bearing sad tidings. Creon's wife Eurydice appears, and the messenger makes his report.

The body of Polynices was buried, but as the soldiers finished that task, they heard a loud voice wailing at the blocked entrance to Antigone's cavern prison. When the guards entered the prison, they found that Antigone had hanged herself and that Haemon was embracing her suspended body. Creon entered and called out to Haemon. Furious with his father, Haemon drew his sword and rushed at Creon, who fled to avoid its stroke. Desperate, Haemon fell on his sword and committed suicide. As he died, he once again embraced the corpse of Antigone.

Haemon's mother, Eurydice, reenters the palace. The chorus imagines that she wishes to grieve in private, but they hear no keening and send the messenger to investigate.

Creon reenters, bemoaning his own folly. The messenger returns with the news that Eurydice has also committed suicide, and the palace doors swing open to reveal her corpse. Creon continues grieving and is led away. The chorus ends the play with advice: "Wisdom is the supreme part of happiness." The gods must be strictly reverenced, the boasts of prideful men are punished harshly, and in old age those who have been chastened like Creon may finally learn wisdom.

The fates of Antigone, Haemon, Eurydice, and Creon must have instilled in the Athenian audience the tragic emotions of pity and fear that ARISTOTLE described in his POETICS. Whether or not this play also takes the next step in the emotional progression that Aristotle attributes to successful tragedy—that is, catharsis, an emotional cleansing that drains the audience of pity and fear—the reader will have to decide.

See also TRAGEDY IN GREECE AND ROME.

Bibliography

Bloom, Harold, ed. *Sophocles' Oedipus Plays: Oedipus the King, Oedipus at Colonus, and Antigone.* New York: Chelsea House, 1996.

Nardo, Don. *Readings on Antigone.* San Diego, Calif.: Greenhaven Press, 1999.

Sophocles. *The Complete Plays.* Translated by Paul Roche. New York: Signet Classics, 2001.

Antiphon of Rhamnus (ca. 480 B.C.E.–ca. 411 B.C.E.) *Greek prose writer*

An orator and rhetorician, Antiphon is thought to have composed an early essay on rhetoric. He was also reputed to have worked very profitably among the earliest political and legal ghostwriters. Some 15 of his speeches, delivered either by their author or by others, still survive. Of these, three were actually delivered during the trials of court cases. The others seem instead to be imaginary speeches, perhaps teaching examples. Both THUCYDIDES and CICERO discuss aspects of Antiphon's career.

Antiphon commanded Athenian troops during the Peloponnesian Wars and was an influential member of the Council of 400 during the time of near-oligarchic rule instituted temporarily at Athens during those conflicts. He died by execution for treason against Athens.

Bibliography

Cicero, Marcus Tullius. *Cicero's Brutus: Or a History of Famous Orators.* Translated by E. Jones. New York: AMS Press, 1976.

Gagarin, Michael, and Douglas M. MacDowell, trans. *Antiphon and Andocides.* Austin: University of Texas Press, 1998.

Strassler, Robert B., ed. *The Landmark Thucydides: A Comprehensive Guide to the Peloponnesian War.* Translated by Richard Crawley. New York: Simon and Schuster Touchstone, 1998.

Antiquities of the Jews   See JOSEPHUS, FLAVIUS.

Antisthenes   See LIVES OF EMINENT PHILOSOPHERS.

Antonius Diogenes   See FICTION AS EPISTLE, ROMANCE, AND EROTIC PROSE.

Apocrypha, the

As Professor W. D. McHardy explains in his introduction to the second volume of the New English Bible, the meaning of the word *apocrypha*—the Greek word for *hidden*—has shifted over time as it applies to biblical writings allied with but now excluded from the canonical writings included in the HEBREW BIBLE and NEW TESTAMENT. I follow McHardy's explanation here.

Early in the Christian era, the works considered apocryphal were thought too important to be shared with the public at large and were thus reserved for those who believed most strongly in the Christian faith. In this sense they were *hidden* from public view. Later, however, the meaning of the word *apocrypha* shifted. It came to be applied to those books that, though they were candidates for inclusion in Scripture and indeed had sometimes been included, ultimately were rejected because they might promote heresy or because their origins were dubious. St. JEROME's fifth-century translation of the Bible, known as the Vulgate, became the standard for the ancient world and, in the version authorized by Pope Clement VII, remains the authorized Roman Catholic text. Jerome used the term *apocrypha* to apply to books that early Christians venerated but had not been included in the Hebrew Scriptures—even if they had been written in the Hebrew language.

Though the form and the content of the Apocrypha have shifted from time to time, as set out in the New English Bible, they include 15 titles: the First and Second Books of ESDRAS (two titles); Tobit; JUDITH; the rest of the chapters of the Book of Esther; the Wisdom of Solomon; Ecclesiasticus, or the Wisdom of Jesus son of Sirach; Baruch; A Letter of Jeremiah; the Song of the Three; Daniel and Susanna; Daniel, Bel, and the Snake; the Prayer of Manasseh; and the First and Second Books of the Maccabees (two titles).

In McHardy's view, knowledge of the Apocrypha is crucial for an understanding of the background of the New Testament. I have selected the first and second books of Esdras and Judith for closer attention elsewhere in this book. The first provides an example of the uneasy marriage of history and prophecy, and the second offers a wonderful story of how a heroine rescues her people from certain destruction—a story that has inspired much great art through the centuries.

The Book of Tobit describes the doings of Tobit and his son Tobias and how they unwittingly played host to the Archangel Raphael. The apocryphal chapters of the Book of Esther are taken from a Greek text that undergoes many changes in the Hebrew version. As told in the Apocrypha, the Hebrew woman Esther marries the Persian ruler Artaxerxes (ruled 464–425 B.C.E.). When the king's regent, Haman, launches a genocidal initiative against the Jews, Esther successfully intercedes to save her people.

In the Wisdom of Solomon appears "The Promise of Immortality" for the godly. This is followed by discussions of divine wisdom, the evils of idolatry, and an analysis of the pattern of divine justice. The following book, Ecclesiasticus or the Wisdom of Jesus Son of Sirach, differs from its prose predecessors. Following a brief prose preface, the rest of the 51-chapter work appears in psalm-like verse. It opens with a continuation of the preceding discussion of wisdom and then turns to consider the role of divine providence in human affairs. The voice of the poet is magisterial, and the verse is presented in the form of an address of a father to a son. This mode continues as the poet considers prudence and self-discipline. Then a personified, allegorical Wisdom speaks in praise of herself. (This device was imitated in the Renaissance by Desiderius Erasmus in his seriocomic work *The Praise of Folly*.) Next appears "Counsels upon Social Behaviour." This section of the poem opens with a lamentation: "Any wound but a wound in the heart! / Any spite but a woman's!" There follows a misogynistic attack on women who are insufficiently subservient to their husbands. Then comes a series of examples of bad and good behavior, followed by a discussion of "True Piety and the Mercy of God" and an examination of "Man in Society." A series of portraits of "Heroes of Israel's Past" and a prayerful epilogue end Ecclesiasticus.

A series of short books follows the lengthy Ecclesiasticus. The first is Baruch, which is set in Babylon in the fifth year after the Chaldeans had captured and razed Jerusalem and taken its people captive. The prophet Baruch explains to the people that their captivity is just punishment for their transgressions but that they have reason to hope. A Messiah, "the Everlasting," is coming, and Israel will benefit from his arrival.

A Letter of Jeremiah next discusses the folly of idolatry. Following that comes the Song of the Three—a prose and verse addition to the Book of Daniel, which, by quoting the beatitudes of praise that the Hebrews sang amid the flames, embellishes the miracle of the Hebrews' survival in the fiery furnace of their Chaldean captors.

Another episode follows that is famous in the annals of art history as a subject for paintings: Daniel and Susanna. This book recounts the shameful episode of a group of elders who spy upon the naked Susanna at her bath. They try to force her to yield to their lust by threatening to accuse her of being with a man. She refuses. The elders carry out their threat before the assembly. The judges believe the accusation and condemn Susanna to death. As she is being led to the place of execution, God inspires Daniel to intervene. He interviews the elders separately. They give conflicting testimony that exposes their lie, and, rather than Susanna, her accusers are put to death.

In Daniel, Bel, and the Snake, the Hebrew prophet Daniel exposes the fraud of the priests of the idol Bel. Cyrus, king of Persia, was convinced that the idol was a living god because all offerings of food and drink were consumed when left with the idol in a sealed room. Daniel sprinkled the floor of the room with ashes before the door was sealed. On the next day, he showed the king the footprints of the priests and their families, who, of course had been the real diners. Daniel next destroys a huge serpent that the king revered as a deity. The Babylonian people, however, force the king to hand Daniel over and try to feed him to the lions, but God sends angels to protect him, and he triumphs once again.

The next book, entitled the Prayer of Manasseh, contains the verse petition of a repentant sinner seeking absolution. The final two books of the Apocrypha, the First Book and Second Book of the Maccabees, trace the history of the hereditary high priests of the Jews from the time of Philip of Macedon and Alexander the Great (fourth century B.C.E.) and tell of the resistance offered by Jewish insurgents to their gentile overlord. Such resisters included Mattathias, who refused to participate in heathen sacrifice or permit others to do so. The First Book of Maccabees chronicles the military campaigns of Judas Maccabeus and his brother Jonathan, who, as the high priest of the temple at Jerusalem and an ally of Alexander, successfully led the Jewish forces against Apollonius, Alexander's enemy. The Second Book of the Maccabees continues to recount such military exploits under the direction of later high priests such as Jonathan's successor, Simon. It also recounts the further successes of Judas Maccabeus against his enemies, particularly his triumph over Nicanor, the commander of a gentile army's detachment of elephants.

The books of the Maccabees end with a direct address by their author to his readers. He hopes they will take pleasure in the variety of literary styles that he has offered them.

See also GNOSTIC APOCRYPHA AND PSEUDE-PIGRAPHA.

Bibliography

The Apochrypha. The New English Bible. Vol. 2. Edited and translated by the appointees of the Joint Committee on the New Translation of the Bible. Oxford and Cambridge: Oxford and Cambridge University Presses, 1969.

Apollonius of Rhodes (Apollonius Rhodius, Apollonios Rhodios) (b. ca. 305 B.C.E.) Greek poet

The ancient sources concerning the life of Apollonius of Rhodes give conflicting information about many aspects of his biography. Apollonius's most scholarly modern editor and translator, Peter Green, however, has constructed from that ancient confusion what he considers to be a likely sequence of events, and here I follow Green's discussion—though not his preferred Greek spellings.

The first indigenous poet of Alexandria, Apollonius was born there between 305 and 290 B.C.E.—probably nearer the earlier date. He was a student of the poet CALLIMACHUS while Callimachus was still an unknown schoolteacher in the Alexandrian suburb of Eleusis and perhaps became his assistant after Callimachus joined the staff of the library at Alexandria. Perhaps between his 18th and 20th years, Apollonius gave a public reading of his juvenilia that was ill-received. Having nonetheless decided to become a poet and having chosen the subject of the voyage of Jason and the Argonauts, Apollonius moved to the island of Rhodes, perhaps to become more expert in his knowledge of seafaring and lend greater credibility to his epic. There he composed poems about Rhodes and also about the islands of Kaunos and Nidos. After a sojourn on Rhodes that lasted between 13 and 20 years, he returned to Alexandria as tutor to the prince who would become Ptolemy III. He also occupied the post of chief librarian at the great library of Alexandria.

Continuing his literary career, Apollonius penned verses commemorating the founding of the cities of Alexandria and Naukratis and a poem about origins entitled *Kanabos*. As a librarian, he was also responsible for promoting scholarship. He fulfilled that duty by writing about HOMER, HESIOD, and ARCHILOCUS.

A long-running literary debate concerns whether or not Callimachus and Apollonius participated in a vitriolic literary quarrel over the superiority of LYRIC POETRY versus EPIC poetry. Green's careful consideration of the evidence leads him to conclude that there is no reason to suppose that the two might *not* have disagreed about their preferred literary modes with some acerbity. Though Callimachus did pen one brief epic, *HECALE*, he clearly prefers short, epigrammatic poems, densely packed with subtle allusion. Likewise, Apollonius clearly preferred the longer, more expansive mode of the epic. A commonplace bit of wisdom concerning academic disputes holds that their bitterness is inversely proportional to their consequentiality, and Green suggests that in the pampered, hothouse environment of the Alexandrian library, opportunities for such scholarly disagreement would have been rife. The fact that Apollonius wrote a scathing critique of the work of his predecessor librarian, Zenodotus (fl. 285 B.C.E.) suggests that his temperament may have been quarrelsome.

Ancient sources tell us that, on his death, Apollonius was buried next to Callimachus.

Green posits that this burial was in a private cemetery for library staff.

Bibliography

Green, Peter, ed. and trans. *The Argonautika of Apollonios Rhodios*. Berkeley: University of California Press, 1997.

Apollonius of Tyana   See *LIFE OF APOLLONIUS OF TYANA, THE*.

apologues   See FABLES OF GREECE AND ROME.

Apology of Socrates (Defense of Socrates) Plato (399 B.C.E.)

In one of the world's great miscarriages of justice, SOCRATES, in his 70th year, was accused of corrupting the youth of Athens and of impiety. The accusation arose in part from confusion in the minds of many people, a confusion that identified Socrates with the Sophist philosophers, whose position Socrates abhorred. In part the charge arose from Socrates' low opinion of poets. That opinion had offended Meletus, the poet who was Socrates' chief accuser.

In any case, the high-minded and religious Socrates was brought to trial on trumped-up charges before a panel of 501 judges of the Athenian heliastic court—a court whose judges were annually appointed from among the Anthenian male citizenry. A 30-vote majority convicted him. Though no penalty was specified for conviction on the charges that Socrates faced, a guilty verdict led to a second proceeding in which both the accusers and the accused could propose a penalty. The judges then decided between the two penalties proposed; no compromise was admissible. The accusers proposed death. Socrates at first proposed being maintained at the public expense by being allowed to take his meals at the *prytaneum* (the town hall where guests of state were entertained). This penalty was essentially a reward for the services that Socrates had provided for Athens. That proposal, however just it might have been, was a rhetorical ploy. Socrates then ran through a list of potential alternatives: exile, imprisonment, paying a fine. As he had no money of his own, he suggested he could afford a fine of one *mina* of silver. His friends, however, suggested that he propose a fine of 30 silver *minae*—a sum they would guarantee.

The court imposed the death penalty—probably thinking that Socrates would choose to escape into voluntary exile rather than be executed. The judges also probably never expected the sentence to be carried out. When it was, PLATO wrote up the proceedings that had led to his teacher's execution. In the opinion of Howard North Fowler, a distinguished classical scholar and translator of the *Apology*, both its form and its content, as well as what we know from other sources about Socrates' characteristic method of discourse, suggest that Plato followed closely Socrates' actual speeches in his own defense and with respect to his sentencing.

In his own defense, Socrates first refutes the truth of his accusers' assertions. He then apologizes if he fails to follow the expected forms for speaking to the court since it is the first time he has been there. He points out that he has long been the victim of false accusations. He objects that he has no opportunity to cross-examine his accusers. He nonetheless intends to answer the long-standing accusations of persons not before the court. Scoffing at Aristophanes' unflattering theatrical portrayal of his stage Socrates, the real one calls on the many members of the panel of judges who have spoken directly with him or who have heard him speak to dismiss the accusations of impiety on the basis of what they have actually heard him say. Moreover, he points out that he does not undertake to educate people for money.

Though Socrates himself always claimed to know nothing, he does admit to being wiser than some and calls on Apollo's Pythian oracle at Delphi as a witness, for that oracle had said no living man was wiser than Socrates. He admits, however, that he has made enemies by showing people who thought themselves to be wise that they were not. And he does consider himself wiser than others who think they know something. So he went in search of wisdom. He looked among the politicians and public men, among the poets, and the artisans, but he found precious little wisdom. His method of investigation, however, made his informants aware both of their own lack of wisdom and of Socrates' certainty of that deficiency. As a result, his inquiries brought him many enemies. Also as a result of those same inquiries, however, he concluded that only the god is wise, and that human wisdom is of little or no account. Thus, Socrates concludes, the god Apollo has called him wise because Socrates recognizes that he is not so. Nonetheless, in the god's service, Socrates continues to search for wisdom, and in consequence he survives in a continual state of poverty. Also, the young men to whom he teaches his methods have also begun participating in his inquiry, and their search for wisdom has led to the charge that Socrates is corrupting the youth. Those making such accusations, however, have also prejudiced the minds of the jurors against Socrates on similar grounds.

Now Socrates turns on his accusers, and in lieu of the prohibited cross-examination, he conducts a mock dialogue with them, speaking both his own and their parts. He excoriates Meletus for a lack of seriousness and for his carelessness in even bringing such a laughable accusation before an important tribunal. If, Socrates says, he corrupts youth (which he does not) he does so involuntarily. As he has no criminal intent, he is guilty of no crime.

Socrates next addresses the accusation of impiety and, step-by-step, demonstrates that he is a believer in the gods. Among other proofs, he cites his distinguished military service in defense of the state at the battles of Potidea, Amphipolis, and Delium, pointing out that he served his military commanders by remaining at his station just as he served the gods who had called him to the practice of philosophy. It is therefore his divinely appointed task to continually call the attention of the citizens of Athens to their mistakes and follies. He is the gadfly of the gods. He will remain faithful to that assignment even if it costs him his life. He admonishes his judges to look to the perfection of their souls.

Socrates reminds his judges of the one occasion in which he himself had served in the senate. His was the only voice raised against the senate's admittedly illegal condemnation of 10 generals who, owing to bad weather, had failed to gather up the bodies of drowned sailors after the battle of Arginusae (406 B.C.E.) during the Peloponnesian War. On that occasion, the senate threatened Socrates with impeachment and death, but he preferred death to voting for the senate's illegal action. He then proposes that the senate question the relatives of the youths he supposedly has corrupted to see if any of them agree with such an assessment of his conduct. He refuses to bring his children (two of whom were still minors) to court and plead for his life as their sole support. Such behavior, he says, would be disgraceful for such a person as himself with a reputation for both wisdom and courage. In closing, Socrates reasserts his belief in the gods and leaves it to God and the jurors to decide his fate.

After the jury has brought in a verdict of guilty, Socrates suggests that some votes have been bought by his accusers to avoid having to pay a hefty fine if too few votes had been cast against him. His suggestions concerning a penalty as they are outlined above follow the guilty verdict.

When the court condemns him, Socrates says that, while he has been condemned to death, his accusers have been convicted by truth of "villainy and wrong." He also prophesies that a far more grievous punishment will come upon those who have condemned him than the death that he will suffer. He says he has already restrained men who will force those who have condemned him to account for their actions. Though those who voted against him may have done so to avoid just such an outcome, their efforts to do so will prove unavailing.

Further, Socrates mentions a divine monitor—a sort of spirit that has always supervised his speech and behavior. That spirit has not censored anything he has spoken at the proceedings. Socrates concludes from this that his death as a result of this trial is a good thing. He next considers death itself. The dead either will have no consciousness of anything—in which case death will be "a wonderful gain"—or it will be a migration of the soul to another place where opportunities will abound to meet the famous persons who have earlier died, who have become immortal, and are happier than living people in this world.

No evil, Socrates concludes, can afflict a good person in this world or the next. He dies in the conviction that God will not neglect him. He asks his judges for a single favor. He requests that the jurors will correct Socrates' children in the same fashion that Socrates has tried to show the jurors their own failings. If the jurors grant that request, he says, both Socrates and his sons will have received just treatment at the jurors' hands.

Socrates says that the jurors go to live and he to die. Only God knows which has the better lot.

Bibliography

Fowler, Harold North. *Plato with an English Translation.* Vol. 1. Cambridge, Mass.: Harvard University Press, 1953.

Apostolic Fathers of the Christian Church, The: Barnabas, Clemens Romanus (Clement), Diognetus, Ignatius, Hermas, Papias, Polycarp, Quadratus (first and second centuries C.E.)

In its current form, the *Apostolic Fathers of the Christian Church* brings together a collection of 10 very early Christian writings, sometimes called *The Sayings of the Father*, that, after much debate, were finally excluded from the official canon of the NEW TESTAMENT. For many early Christians, however, both these and other texts that antedated the establishment of the New Testament's contents enjoyed the status of Scripture.

As the state of scholarship respecting the status of early texts has changed and sometimes improved, the editors of the collection have found reasons to add or delete selections. The most recent and authoritative English-language version of the texts include the following selections:

1 The FIRST LETTER OF CLEMENT TO THE CORINTHIANS

2 The SECOND LETTER OF CLEMENT TO THE CORINTHIANS

3 The LETTERS OF IGNATIUS to the Ephesians, to the Magnesians, to the Trallians, to the Romans, to the Philadelphians, to the Smyrneans, and to the Smyrneans' bishop, Polycarp

4 The LETTER OF POLYCARP TO THE PHILIPPEANS

5 Martyrdom of Saint Polycarp Bishop of Smyrna (MARTYRDOM OF POLYCARP)

6 The DIDACHE, or the Teaching of the Twelve Apostles

7 The EPISTLE OF BARNABAS

8 FRAGMENTS OF PAPIAS AND QUADRATUS

9 The EPISTLE TO DIOGNETUS

10 The SHEPHERD (of Hermas).

The documents' latest English translator, Bart D. Ehrman, cautions readers that many uncertainties surround these compositions. Nowhere, for example, does the First Letter of Clement name the author, though the tradition that Clement penned it is very ancient.

From the perspective of ancient Christians and from that of the European editors who first published the documents as a collection in the 17th century, the writings that were formerly and are currently included in the collection were supposed to have been composed by authors who personally knew and were perhaps themselves the companions or disciples of the apostles of Jesus Christ. Thus, thought the editors, the documents had been composed shortly after the books of the New Testament. The historical accuracy of all these assumptions is very much

open to question, and in some cases, such as those of Barnabas and 2 Clement, the credited authors demonstrably did not write the works.

Nonetheless, the documents originated early in Christian history, and at the very least they shed light on some of the matters that then concerned ordinary believers and potential converts. The works also presage what finally became Christian orthodoxy some centuries later when Christianity had become the state religion of Rome and after such church councils as that of Nicaea had done their winnowing respecting what was and was not to be regarded as Scriptural.

Bibliography

Ehrman, Bart D., ed. and trans. *The Apostolic Fathers.* 2 vols. Cambridge, Mass.: Harvard University Press, 2003.

Appendices to Book of Changes (ca. 210 B.C.E.)

Formerly attributed to CONFUCIUS but apparently composed by later Chinese scholars, these appendices seem designed to bring the central document of DAOISM, BOOK OF CHANGES (Yijing, *I Ching*), under the umbrella of Confucian doctrine. To do this, the *Appendices* try to bring Confucian order to Taoist cosmology. Most think that the *Appendices* fail to achieve this objective and that they confuse rather than clarify the issue.

Bibliography

Watson, Burton. *Early Chinese Literature.* New York: Columbia University Press, 1962.

Apuleius (Lucius Apuleius) (b. ca. 125 C.E.)
Afro-Roman Prose writer

Born in Roman Africa, likely in the city of Madauros, to a well-to-do Greek-speaking family, Apuleius studied both at Carthage and in Athens, mastering colloquial rather than literary Latin as a second language. After completing his education, Apuleius traveled widely through the Mediterranean world and established his residence at

Carthage. There he undertook a career as a scholar, philosopher, and writer, composing his works both in Latin and in Greek. The genres in which he worked included songs for performance, works for the stage, satires and riddles, orations, and philosophical dialogues.

Of this considerable body of literature, Apuleius's works in Greek and his poems in both languages have all perished. Only a representative body of Latin prose remains. These remnants include a work describing the sidereal universe and the meteorological phenomena that occur in it—*De Mundo* (Concerning the world or the cosmos). His *Florida* contains examples of his oratory. Two other surviving works concern themselves with philosophy and religion, and one offers an amusing apology for the author in marrying a wealthy widow.

The philosophical work, *De Platone et eius dogmate* (About Plato and his doctrine), contains a biographical sketch of PLATO and outlines Platonic ethics and metaphysics as they were taught in Apuleius's day. The religious work, *De Deo Socratis* (Concerning the God of Socrates) explains the nature and function of *daemones*, the spiritual beings that act as go-betweens for human beings in their interactions with the divine. SOCRATES supposed that he enjoyed the regular services of one such being.

The *Apology*, a work that many scholars consider autobiographical, defends Apuleius against a charge brought against him by the relatives of his wife, Prudentilla. Her former heirs, disappointed in their expectations of an inheritance, accused Apuleius of having used black magic to win her hand.

Contemporary readers, however, principally remember Apuleius for having penned what many deem to be the only complete example of the Roman novel still surviving. This work, entitled *Metamorphoses* by Apuleius but renamed *The GOLDEN ASS* (or *The Golden Ass of Lucius Apuleius*) by its subsequent editors, is a first-person narrative that reports what happens to a Greek named Lucius when, while traveling, he arrives at a place full of witches. When he asks for a demonstration of witchcraft, the obliging witch accidentally turns him into a golden-colored donkey. After his transformation, the rest of the story details his adventures during his travels and reports many of the stories that he hears along the way. Eventually the Egyptian goddess, Isis, restores his human shape, and Lucius becomes her devotee.

Other works have sometimes been ascribed to Apuleius, but most of these are now definitively held to be spurious. Discussion continues about the authenticity of a philosophical work, *On Interpretation* (*Peri hermeneias*).

Bibliography

Apuleius. *The Apologia and Florida of Apuleius of Madaura*. Translated by H. E. Buttis. Westport, Conn.: Greenwood Press, 1970.

———. *Apuleius: Rhetorical Works*. Translated and annotated by Stephen Harrison, John Hilton, and Vincent Hunink. Oxford: Oxford University Press, 2001.

———. *Florida: Apuleius of Madauros*. Edited by Vincent Heinink. Amsterdam: J. C. Gieben, 2001.

———. *The God of Socrates*. Edited by Daniel Driscoll. Gilette, N. J.: Heptangle Books, 1993.

———. *The Golden Ass, or The Metamorphoses*. Translated by W. Adlington. New York: Barnes and Noble Books, 2004.

———. *Metamorphoses*. Edited and translated by J. Arthur Hanson. Cambridge, Mass.: Harvard University Press, 1989.

Londley, David, and Carmen Johansen. *The Logic of Apuleius* [*Peri hermeneias*]. Leiden and New York: E. J. Brill, 1987.

Aqueducts of Rome See FRONTINUS, SEXTUS JULIUS.

Aratus of Soli (Aratos of Soli) (b. ca. 315 B.C.E.) *Greek poet*

The subject of three useful ancient biographies, Aratus was born in Cilicia to Athenodorus and Letophilia. An older contemporary of the poet

CALLIMACHUS, Aratus studied with the grammarian Menecrates of Ephesus, with the philosophers Timon and Menedemus, and later with the Stoic Zeno. Likely through this last connection, Aratus was invited to the court of Macedonia. There the king of Macedonia, Antigonus (ruled 276–239 B.C.E.), commissioned Aratus to write a poem on the subject of astronomy. Aratus not only did so, he also managed to preserve for posterity much of the ancient Greeks' knowledge of that science, even though the poet was not himself an astronomer.

As his sources, Aratus employed two prose treatises written by a student of PLATO, the astronomer and mathematician Eudoxus of Cnidus (ca. 390–337 B.C.E.), relying marginally on his *Enoptron* (Things Visible) and principally on his *Phaenomena* (The Starry Sphere.). Aratus entitled the resulting poem *Phaenomena kai Diosemaiai* (The Starry Sphere and the Signs of the Weather). Of this poem in turn, CICERO translated over 730 lines as a youth into Latin verse, but, as the literary historian G. R. Mair tells us, only 670 lines of that poem remain. Other Latin translations, however, were later undertaken, and a full version by Festus Avienus survives. Commentaries by mathematicians on Aratus's work are also extant.

The poem itself opens with an introductory section followed by a description of the axis of the stellar sphere. Following this, the poet devotes almost 300 lines to a discussion of the constellations observable in the northern sky. The next section of the poem addresses the constellations south of the ecliptic and ends with the discussion of "fixed stars"—those beyond which the Greeks thought there were no more spheres. The poet, for reasons of piety, declines to discuss the planets that bore the name of the deities of the Greek pantheon: Cronus (Saturn), Zeus (Jupiter), Ares (Mars), Aphrodite (Venus), and Hermes (Mercury).

The poet next turns his attention to the circles of the celestial sphere and a technical discussion of the ecliptic and the signs of the Zodiac. There follows an increasingly technical discussion of the risings and settings of stars and their relation to the setting of the sun.

In the section entitled "The Signs of the Weather," another very technical discussion of the Metonic Cycle and the Metonic calendar appears together with a catalogue of the influence of various stars on terrestrial and on nautical activities. The Metonic cycle, named for the Athenian astronomer Meton (fl. fifth century B.C.E.), is based on a period of about 19 years, or almost 235 lunar cycles between the times the new moon appears on the same day as it did at the cycle's beginning.

Excellent English translations of the poem are available.

Bibliography

Aratus, Solensis. *Phaenomena*. Edited and translated by Douglas Kidd. New York: Cambridge University Press, 1997.

———. *Sky Signs: Aratus Phaenomena*. Translated by Stanley Lombardo. Berkeley, Calif.: North Atlantic Books, 1983.

G. R. Mair, trans. *Aratus*. In *Callimachus and Lycrophon; Aratus*. Cambridge, Mass.: Harvard University Press, 1921.

Arbitration, The Menander (ca. early third century B.C.E.)

Hope still remains that further fragments of *The Arbitration* may come to light among papyri dating to the HELLENISTIC AGE and the period of Roman rule over Egypt. What is currently known to survive of *The Arbitration* represents about half of one of the Greek playwright MENANDER's most skillfully crafted plays. Typical of the playwright's palette, *The Arbitration* features young lovers caught in the toils of a seemingly intractable problem; conflicts and misunderstandings between generations; and stock though nonetheless individualized characters that include cooks, prostitutes, drunken and crafty slaves, confidence artists, flatterers, and braggart soldiers.

Though only a fragment of the first act survives, on the basis of what follows, on what we know from other examples, and on the Roman playwright PLAUTUS's later adaptations of Menander's plots, the first act was probably preceded by a prologue that both established the problem the play will address and introduced the principal as well as some of the comic secondary characters.

The problem is that about 10 months before the action of play, a drunken man at an all-night Athenian festival sexually assaulted the play's heroine, Pamphila. Five months after her arranged marriage—during most of which time her husband had been away—she bore a baby conceived from that rape. She and her nurse have been trying to conceal that fact from her returned husband. They abandoned the baby with some objects, leaving it where it would surely be found.

Among the other principal characters, there is Pamphila's husband, Charisius. Formerly a sedate and somewhat priggishly philosophical young man, the newly married Charisius has suddenly taken up with a harp-girl (a perfect entertainer & courtesan) named Habrotonon. At an extravagant rate, he rents her as a companion from a dealer in such commodities. Charisius has installed Habroton in a rented house that he also occupies, leaving his spouse Pamphila and her nurse alone next door in his own house. The rented house belongs to Chaerestratus, who also lives there.

Also uncharacteristically, Charisius has begun spending lavishly to hire cooks. One of these, a lewd and foulmouthed cook, serves as interlocutor in the first act, commenting on the action and cross-questioning the servant Onesimus about Charisius's strangely unusual behavior. Meanwhile, Charisius's new father-in-law, the shrewd and matter-of-fact businessman Smicrines, finds his son-in-law's unaccustomed profligacy deeply troubling. After complaining about Charisius's spendthrift ways, a curious Smicrines goes to visit his daughter to see if he can find out what is happening. The cook advises Charisius of Smicrines' arrival.

Most of act 2 survives. As it begins, Smicrines is just about to enter his daughter's dwelling when he is interrupted by the arrival of the charcoal burner Syriscus; Syriscus's wife, who is carrying a baby; and the truculent goatherd Davus. The men ask Smicrines to adjudicate a case they have been arguing. After expressing his wonder that slaves argue cases, Smicrines consents.

Davus tells Smicrines that, about a month before, he had found a baby exposed in the scrubland nearby together with a necklace and some other ornaments. At Syriscus's urgent request, Davus turned the baby over to him and his wife, who had recently lost a child of her own. Now, however, Syriscus has laid claim to the objects found with the child. Davus argues that although he has given up the child, he is under no compulsion to give up the objects. Syriscus counters that the objects may be the key to the child's identity and that if Davus sells them, any hope that the child may one day discover his parentage will be totally lost. Smicrines decides the case in favor of Syriscus.

Now in possession of the objects, Syriscus shows them to the servant Onesimus, who recognizes them as belonging to Charisius; they had been lost while the young man was drinking.

As act 3 begins, we discover that Onesimus has revealed the secret about the baby to Charisius and that now the servant is afraid to show his master the objects found with the exposed child. The harp-girl, Habrotonon, expresses her dismay at being kept at a distance by Charisius. She had thought he wanted to become her lover.

With each passing moment, the audience becomes surer that Charisius is the father of his wife's child since each new circumstance makes clearer that it was he who had violated her at the festival of Tauropolia. Nonetheless, Menander strings out that certainty with new revelations about Charisius's fatherhood. Habrotonon remembers the girl ravished at the festival because she was the friend of a friend. She agrees to take the ring and the child in to Charisius and claim that he gave the ring to her while she was still a maiden. The conspirators think there will at least be a generous reward, and perhaps, if Charisius believes them, Habrotonon will receive her freedom as the mother of his child.

The rest of act 3 is missing. We know, however, that an increasingly angry Smicrines returns, having collected detailed evidence of his son-in-law's spendthrift ways. We also know that, confronted with his own signet ring, Charisius acknowledges paternity of the baby, and in the resultant hubbub the party that the cook was preparing for breaks up. Not having been paid, the cook tells all he has seen to Smicrines, but he embroiders his tale, alleging that Charisius intends to buy Habrotonon's freedom and violate his marriage contract with Pamphila. A thoroughly outraged Smicrines resolves to see justice done, and the act ends.

Much of act 4 has also been lost, but we know its beginning to have principally involved an extended argument between father and daughter as Smicrines argued her unsuitability for a *ménage à trois*. Smicrines also pointed out that Charisius could not afford to sustain such an extended household. Pamphila, however, is unconvinced by all her father's arguments and refuses to abandon her husband.

As the fragmentary text resumes, Menander gives us an encounter between Habrotonon and Pamphila. Habrotonon recognizes Pamphila from the festival, assures her that she has Pamphila's baby, and explains that its father is none other than Charisius. Charisius overhears everything and is torn by guilt and self-hatred, and Onesimus overhears his master's self-reproach. After further business in which Habrotonon convinces Charisius that he and his wife are indeed the parents of this child, act 4 concludes.

Act 5 is also fragmentary. We can guess that manumission from slavery awaits Habrotonon and probably Onesimus. The Smicrines subplot, however, continues its development as a now irrational Smicrines reenters, prepared to kidnap his daughter and too angry to listen to anyone. Onesimus, however, explains to him that, being far too occupied otherwise to give attention to each person in the world, the gods have put in each person character that can either guard or ruin a person. Onesimus advises Smicrines to propitiate that genuine deity by doing nothing foolish. Gradually the arguments of the other characters begin to overcome Smicrines' misunderstanding of the complex situation as the last surviving fragment of the play peters out.

Bibliography

Menander. *Menander*. Edited by David R. Slavitt and Palmer Bowie. Philadelphia: University of Pennsylvania Press, 1998.

———. *Menander* [English and Greek]. 3 vols. Translated and edited by W. G. Arnott. Cambridge, Mass.: Harvard University Press, 1979–2000.

———. *The Plays and Fragments: Menander*. Translated by Maurice Balme. Oxford and New York: Oxford University Press, 2001.

Archestratus (Archestratos of Gela)   See HEDUPATHEIA.

Archilochus (Archilochos) (fl. ca. 680 B.C.E.) *Greek poet*

Born in Paros, perhaps to a slave woman, the poet Archilochus later moved to Thasos. For a time he followed the calling of a mercenary soldier. A story is told of him that when his beloved Neobule and he wished to marry, her father Lycambes refused permission. Furious with Lycambes for refusing his permission and with Neobule for obeying her parent, Archilochus so effectively lampooned both of them in satiric verse that father and daughter committed suicide by hanging themselves. Among the fragments of his work remaining to us, we find a portion of the verse that produced this unfortunate result.

The other fragments of Archilochus's work include elegies, hymns, and iambic verses. As his recent biographer, Frederic Will, suggests, the fragments reveal a poet finely attuned to his senses. His terse word pictures evoke both visual and tactile responses. In English it is difficult to illustrate the way Archilochus matched the musicality of his verse to its images and to its function as, say, a marriage hymn or a lampoon. It is also difficult in Greek, for modern scholars are not certain of the precise pronunciation of his dialect. Nonetheless, Archilochus was thought by his successors to be a master craftsman. Twentieth-century critics also suggest that he remains particularly appealing because his surviving verse suggests an almost modern sensibility.

Archilochus's love poems catch the depth and the impact of his feeling and the way those effects surprise the poet. But he was not merely a pretty poet, he was also a soldier, and some of his surviving poems deal with war, conveying the excitement and joy of battle as well as its horrors. Frederic Will cites a brief example from Fragment 59 of the poet's work: "Seven men fallen dead, whom we hammered with feet, / a thousand killers we."

In his personal philosophy, Archilochus seems to anticipate the stoics. He faces the human condition steadily and sometimes scoffs at human foibles, satirizing the vice of miserliness, for example. Splendid English versions of the poetic remains of Archilochus are available in the translations of Richmond Lattimore and Guy Davenport.

Bibliography

Davenport, Guy, trans. *Archilocus, Sappho, Alkman: Three Lyric Poets of the Late Greek Bronze Age*. Berkeley: University of California Press, 1980.

Lattimore, Richmond. *Greek Lyrics*. Chicago: University of Chicago Press, 1960.

Will, Frederic. *Archilochos*. New York: Twayne Publishers, 1969.

Archimedes (ca. 287–212 B.C.E.) *Greek prose writer*

The ancient Greeks ascribed a broader purview to the field of literature than we moderns are accustomed to do, and writers on astronomy, physics, and mathematics were numbered among those whose works the ancients considered literary. A giant among the early practitioners of those sciences was Archimedes.

He was born at Syracuse on Sicily, and his genius served his native city and posterity in practical as well as theoretical ways. On the theoretical side, Archimedes discovered the mathematical relationship between the volumes of the cylinder and the sphere and the way to measure the circle; he wrote about the spiral, about cones and spheres, and on statics and hydrostatics as well. He also calculated the value of pi (π), working it out to many places.

To assist in the study of astronomy, Archimedes invented and fabricated a pair of astronomical globes. One was apparently stationary; the other appears to have been mechanized and to have illustrated the movements of the heavens as Archimedes understood them. This globe was taken as booty by the Roman general Marcellus after the sack of Syracuse in 212 B.C.E.

In an ancient shipwreck discovered off the Mediterranean Island of Antikythera in 1971, a mechanism for a similar moving globe was found. Studied by Derek De Solla Price, the "Antikythera mechanism," as it is known, proved to be "an arrangement of differential gears inscribed and configured to produce solar and lunar positions in synchronization with the calendar year." Price connected the device with an astronomer, Geminus of Rhodes, and placed its date of manufacture at 87 B.C.E. It may well be that Archimedes' mechanism was similar.

On the practical side, Archimedes contributed many useful inventions and ideas to the world. Among these was a device for raising water from a lower source to irrigate higher fields—an invention still used in places such as rural India and Egypt, where electric power sources are in short supply. A famous story about Archimedes relates that, while taking his bath, he cried out "Eureka!" (I have found it!) when he realized that by measuring the displacement of water he could accurately gauge the specific gravity of items immersed in it. This made possible testing whether or not the crown of the tyrant of Syracuse, Hieron, was made of pure gold or was an alloy containing base metal.

Archimedes interested himself in military science as well. He is credited with inventing siege engines and other apparatus that launched multiple weapons and that helped the Syracusans hold the Romans at bay for more than three years. One story that may be apocryphal suggests that he invented a lens to focus the sun's rays intensely at a distance and used it to set fire to a Roman fleet. While in theory this may be possible, no one before LUCIAN OF SAMOSATA seems to have told the story.

Fond of mathematical jokes and puzzles, Archimedes wrote (for Hieron's son, Gelo) a treatise proving that it was perfectly possible to work out the number of grains of sand in the world. Using material from HOMER'S *THE ODYSSEY*, he also showed that the number of Apollo's cattle must have amounted to many millions.

Archimedes' extant works survive in later editions and reconstructions produced over time by various hands.

Archimedes met his death during the Roman sack of Syracuse despite the Roman general Marcellus's orders to take him alive. Interrupted at his work by a Roman soldier, Archimedes expressed his annoyance at being disturbed; not realizing who he was, the soldier cut him down.

Long after Archimedes' death, while the Roman writer and statesman CICERO was serving as an official in Sicily, he rediscovered Archimedes' neglected tomb in 75 B.C.E. It was marked with a column bearing the image of a sphere enclosed in a cylinder.

Bibliography

Archimedes. *The Works of Archimedes: Translated into English, Together with Eutocius' Commentaries, with Commentary, and Critial Edition of the Diagrams.* Translated and edited by Reviel Netz. Cambridge and New York: Cambridge University Press, 2004.

———. *The Works of Archimedes.* Edited by T. L. Heath. Mineola, N.Y.: Dover Publications, 2002.

Rice, Rob S. "The Antikythera Mechanism: Physical and Intellectual Salvage from the First Century B.C.E." Available online. URL:http://ccat.sas.upenn.edu/rrice/usna_pap.html. Accessed February. 15, 2006.

Rose, Herbert Jennings. *A Handbook of Greek Literature from Homer to the Age of Lucian.* New York: E. P. Dutton and Company, 1934.

Argonautika, The (The Argonautica)

Apollonius of Rhodes (ca. 265 B.C.E.)

Returning in both matter and manner to the sort of EPIC that HOMER and the HOMERIDAE had penned centuries earlier, Apollonios Rhodios (APOLLONIUS OF RHODES) ignored intervening examples of rationalization, allegorizing, secularizing, and a contemporary poetic taste for arcane allusiveness. For his subject he takes the voyage of Jason and the Argonauts to the land of Kolchis in search of the mysterious and numinous Golden Fleece. This archetypal Greek voyage of exploration in the *Argo*—the first vessel the Greeks ever sailed aboard—had taken place a generation before the Trojan War and had provided a seemingly inexhaustible supply of grist for the epic mill. Apollonios adopts the same attitude toward his subject that characterized his predecessors: myth is history. (The origins of his people were inextricably entangled with early events as the myths recorded them.) Apollonios also reverts to the attitude of the earlier poets toward the immortals. He takes the gods and other immortals at face value; as the scholar and translator Peter Green has suggested, he does not, feel obliged to secularize the sacred.

Book 1

Inspired by his namesake, Phoebus Apollo, Apollonios begins his poem by recalling the circumstance that led Jason to undertake the voyage. Fording the Anauros River, Jason lost a sandal in the mud and arrived half-shod at the court of Pelias, the son of the sea god Poseidon. Recognizing in Jason the one-sandaled man whose arrival presaged Pelias's doom, Pelias invented a quest for Jason on the spur of the moment—a sea voyage to recover the golden fleece of the magic, winged ram that had carried away Phrixos and Helle, the children of Athamas, King of Thebes.

Apollonios leaves it to his readers to know the accounts of the way the ship was built by Argo according to the instructions of Athena, goddess of wisdom, and calls on all the MUSES for further inspiration. He continues his version with a lengthy recital of the names and genealogies of Jason's numerous companions on the voyage to Kolchis. That done, the story leaps ahead to the moment of embarkation and the grief of Jason's inconsolable mother, Alkimédé, as her son leaves home to join his contingent of heroes.

At the ship, Jason instructs the crew to appoint a leader. The men suggest the hero Heracles (Hercules). He, however, defers to Jason. All approve the choice, and the men launch the ship and prepare the sacrifices needed for a propitious voyage. The next morning, accompanied by the music of the proto-musician and poet, Orpheus, the voyage proper begins.

After a few days' sailing, rowing, and beaching as necessary, the ship comes at nightfall to the island of Lemnos. There the women had slaughtered all the men but one when their husbands, en masse, had preferred sleeping with captive women to sleeping with their wives. The one surviving man—an elder—had been smuggled out to sea by his daughter, and all the women lived in constant fear that he would bring a military expedition against them.

When the *Argo* arrives, however, and its crew's intentions prove peaceful, an elderly woman counsels the others to offer the government of the island to the ship's crew and settle down with them in familial amity. Jason receives the invitation of the women's leader, Hypsipyle, to come and hear this proposal. Dressed in his finest clothes, which are lovingly described by Apollonios, Jason arrives. He listens to the offer Hypsipyle outlines and accepts a part of it. Given his quest, settling down is out of the question, but repopulating the island with fresh inhabitants is not. The seafarers therefore linger on Lemnos until Heracles reproves them for neglect of duty.

Under Heracles' urging, the *Argo*'s crew leave the women. Jason asks Hypsipyle, should she bear a male child to him, that when his son grows up, she will send him to comfort Jason's parents. Setting forth once more, the crew continue eastward, sometimes receiving a fair welcome and sometimes a hostile reception, as when the aborigines of an island near Phrygia attempt unsuccessfully to seal off the ship's passage from harbor with stones. Once, driven back by adverse winds, the Argonauts have to fight the formerly friendly Doliones who, in the dark, have mistaken their friends for pirates.

During their next passage, the *Argo* is becalmed for 12 days until, urged by a goddess, the men propitiate the earth goddess Rhea with a sacrifice. Then, as they approach Mysia, Heracles breaks an oar. When they arrive, he goes to replace it, and his beloved page Hylas drowns because of a wood nymph's passionate kiss while trying to fill a water pitcher at a spring. Disconsolate, Heracles leaves the ship's company to mourn, and the author is spared trying to make the epic's challenges interesting when one member of the crew is an invincible demigod.

After setting sail, Heracles is missed, and a fight breaks out among the crew over whether or not to go after him. However, a sea god, Glaucus, appears and explains that Heracles has another fate to fulfill. Reconciled, the crew sails and rows on.

Book 2

As the sun rises and Book 2 begins, the Argonauts land at the kingdom of the Bebrykians. Their king, Amykos, is in the habit of challenging all seafarers to a boxing match. Polydeukes, son of Tyndareus, king of Sparta, accepts the challenge. After an exchange of blows, Polydeukes' superior skill results in a blow that kills Amykos. His seconds rush in to club Polydeukes, but the Argonauts draw their swords, killing some and driving the others off. The Bebrykians discover that while they were watching boxing, their enemy Lykos has led his spearmen against their unguarded orchards and villages.

The Argonauts sail on and at their next landfall visit Phineas, a blind prophet. Phineas is hounded by Harpies, who have been eating all of his food. When the Argonauts befriend him, though, the messenger of the gods, Iris, swears that the Harpies will not trouble the old man further, and the starving prophet feasts with the seafarers. In recompense, he prophesies as much as they are permitted to know about the balance of their voyage, and the reader gains a guide to the rest of the poem. An interesting facet of this part of the poem involves the fact that, since the early tellings of the Argonauts' story, the map that had contained unknown, mythic, and fabled blank spots during Homer's day had been filled in with actual places—partly as a result of Alexander the Great's conquests. Apollonios therefore adjusts the details of the story to account for more accurate contemporary geographical knowledge.

After further feasting and sacrifices, and following subordinate stories concerning local residents and myths of origin of the favorable Etesian winds. The Argonauts again embark, heeding Phineas's advice to carry with them a dove whose flight will lead them between clashing rocks through the narrow and dangerous passage that marks the entrance to the Black Sea. This tactic proves successful, and the dove shows the voyagers how to pass between rocks that open and close. As they reach the halfway point through the clashing rocks, however, a whirlpool stops their forward progress. There the voyage would have ended had not the goddess of wisdom, Athena, pushed the ship forward and free of the rocks—though the tip of the ship's poop is sheared off by the rocks' final clashing together. Athena's action has fixed the rocks in their open position so that the strait will be navigable thereafter. At least this is how Apollonios reconciles ancient myth and geographical fact.

The crew congratulate Jason on having brought them through and rejoice that the worst seems over. Jason, however, feels the responsibility of command weighing heavily on him and confesses his concern that he will not be up to the task of bringing his crew safely home. He takes heart, however, and the crew rows on through the night. At dawn the next morning, they enter the harbor at Thynias, and there they catch sight of the enormous sun god Apollo, striding home from Lykia. Awestruck, the mariners build altars and offer

sacrifices to "Dawntime Apollo," worshipping the god with singing and dancing. On the third morning, they resume their journey.

Their next landfall is among the Myriandyni, the people who had raided the villages and orchards of the slain Bebrykian boxing king, Amykos. The mariners are viewed as heroes and allies and welcomed accordingly. The Myriandyni king, Lykos, sends his son, Daskylos, with the seafarers to assure their welcome among his allies further to the east. Though the Argonauts gain a companion, however, they lose two others. Idmon is killed by the charge of a wild boar, and the helmsman, Tiphys, succumbs to a sudden illness. Others take their places, however, and the sailors overcome their grief and sail on. Apollonios catalogues the places they pass and mentions the associated historical and mythic events. They pause to pay their respects and make a sacrifice, for instance, at the tomb of Sthenelos, the sacker of Thebes. They pass the delta of the Halys River in Assyria and the land of the Amazons, whose activities Apollonios briefly describes.

The voyagers come at length to the island of Ares—a place populated by fierce birds that launch their wing feathers like arrows at passersby. The prophet Phineas had told them that, despite the danger the birds pose, the Argonauts must put in here if their journey is to succeed. Accordingly, the men lock their shields together over their heads and, so protected, row for land. Apollonios rhetorically asks why Phineas wanted them to stop on Ares' Island and proceeds to answer the question. By chance, the two sons of that same Phrixos whom the winged, golden ram had borne away to Kolchis have been sailing westward with the intention of claiming their inheritance at Thebes. In order to bring them and the Argonauts together, the gods have arranged for Phrixos's ship to be wrecked near Ares' island. There the Argonauts encounter the four survivors of the wreck—Phrixos's two sons, Argos and Melas, and two others.

All wonder at the divinely appointed meeting, and the Argonauts explain their mission, asking Argos and Melas to serve as their guides to Kolchis. Argos and Melas are struck with horror at the prospect of taking the Golden Fleece. But seeing the fearlessness and determination of the Argonauts, Argos and Melas agree to help them. They set sail and at the end of Book 2 arrive at the furthest verge of the Black Sea and the land of Kolchis.

Book 3

At the beginning of Book 3, Apollonios invokes the muse of the lyre, Erato, to inspire him, for he is about to speak of love, and he is favored by Aphrodite. He finds the muse's name "erotic," despite the false etymology. While the Argonauts remain in hiding among the reeds, the goddesses Hera and Athena conspire in a plan to assist them. They decide that Aphrodite (here known by her alternate name of Kypris) can help by making the princess Medeia fall in love with Jason. In a delightfully humorous scene, the goddesses prevail on Kypris to have her son, Eros, shoot one of his love-engendering arrows into the bosom of Medeia. Kypris bribes her son to do it with the promise of a splendid ball to play with. Eros goes off to accomplish his task.

In the meantime, the Argonauts hold a council to determine how they may best go about their task. They decide to send an embassy, including Jason, the sons of Phrixos, and their Kolchian companions to see if they can gain the fleece by peaceful means. Concealed from the eyes of the citizens by a fog sent by Hera, they march to the palace of the king, Aiëtés. There the sons of Phrixos encounter their mother, Medeia's sister Chalkíope, and others, including the king and his daughter Medeia, soon join them.

Eros also sneaks into the assembly and, crouching at Jason's feet, shoots an arrow directly into Medeia's heart. She is instantly consumed with passion for the hero. Argos, the son of Phrixos, introduces his companions and explains their mission, putting it in the best possible light. Aiëtés, however, flies into a rage and accuses the Argonauts of having come to seize his throne. Jason assures him that is not his intention. Aiëtés

suggests that if Jason can prove himself by yoking Aiëtés' brazen-footed, fire-breathing bull oxen and by spending the day, as Aiëtés does—ploughing with them, sowing dragon's teeth in the furrows, and then fighting and overcoming the fully armed warriors who spring forth from the teeth—then and only then will Aiëtés give Jason the Golden Fleece.

As Jason and his companions return to the ship, Argos, son of Phrixos, advises Jason to seek magic help from Argos's young aunt, Medeia. In the meantime, Aiëtés holds a council of his own at which he promises death and destruction for the Argonauts, blithely ignoring Apollo's prediction that his own destruction would come from the scheming of his offspring.

Apollonios next turns to describing the troubled dreams of the sleeping Medeia. In them she foresees that she will cast her lot with the strangers and go home with Jason as his wife. When she awakens, she makes several attempts to go see her sister to offer the strangers aid, but her courage fails her each time. Finally a servant observes her irresolute behavior and informs her sister, Chalkíope, who comes to Medeia and enlists her on the side of the Argonauts. Apollonios does a particularly craftsman-like job in conveying Medeia's internal conflict as she sides against her own kin with total strangers—even considering suicide as a means to end her anguish.

In the morning, however, Medeia prepares a potion to protect Jason from the bulls he must yoke and an elaborate plan for delivering it and deceiving her maids and companions. Finally she and Jason meet and speak in private. Jason asks for the promised drugs, and she gives them along with detailed instructions for taming the bulls and making the dragon's-teeth warriors kill each other. She also predicts that he will carry the Golden Fleece home with him. As they talk, Jason also falls in love.

That night, Jason performs the rituals as instructed, and the goddess of night, Hékaté, hears and grants his prayers. Back at the ship, his comrades test his bewitched arms and find them indestructible. Jason faces the bulls, finding himself to be unfazed by their fiery breath and attempts to gore him. He masters them, yokes them, and begins to plough the field and sow dragon's teeth. Four sown acres later, he unyokes the oxen, drinks a well-deserved helmet full of water from the nearby river, and looks around to see the ploughed land sprouting companies of fully armed men. Following Medeia's instructions, he hurls a boulder among them, and instantly they begin to fight each other. Jason joins the fray and sends myriads to their deaths. Thus defeated, a dejected King Aiëtés slinks back to his palace, brooding about how he might defeat the Argonauts.

Book 4

Apollonios begins Book 4—the final book of his epic—by invoking the daughter of Zeus as his muse. This presents a bit of a problem since all the Muses as well as all the goddesses mentioned above thus far are the daughters of Zeus. Perhaps he means to invoke the aid of whichever of them can best resolve his difficulties as he undertakes to unravel Medeia's motives in accompanying Jason back to Greece.

Aiëtés feels sure that Medeia is mixed up in Jason's victory. Medeia feels very frightened, but the goddess Hera "stirs her to flee." She escapes to the shore, where she attracts the attention of the Argonauts, and they send a boat for her. After boarding, she counsels immediate flight and throws herself on Jason's mercy. He promises to marry her, and she undertakes to get the Argonauts the Golden Fleece by putting its guardian serpent to sleep.

The crew row as near as they can to the shrine where the fleece is kept; then Jason and Medeia go after it together. The serpent hears them coming and hisses so loudly that people all over the region are frightened. Medeia's magic, however, hypnotizes the beast. Jason takes possession of the fleece, and the two retrace their steps to the ship, where Jason installs Medeia on the fleece as on a seat of honor. He arms the Argonauts and encourages them to weigh anchor and flee.

In the meantime the Kolchians have answered Aiëtés' call to arms, and in a massed force they speed along the riverbank in search of their enemies. When they become aware that the *Argo* has sailed, they make haste to launch their own ships in pursuit. Many hopelessly pursue the *Argo* by the same route the Argonauts had chosen. Others, however, led by Medeia's brother Apsyrtos, cut off the fugitives and force them to parley. In this desperate strait, Medeia and Jason conspire to trick and kill Apsyrtos rather than risk having Medeia returned to her father. Apollonios interjects an address to the god of love, blaming him for all the grief to follow.

Medeia and her brother meet, ostensibly in private. However, just as she pretends to agree with her brother to deceive the Argonauts, Jason steps from his hiding place and cuts down Apsyrtos while Medeia looks away. A torch signals the Argonauts, who bring their ship alongside the Kolchian ambassadors' ship and slaughter its occupants. They then flee under cover of darkness. Their pursuit by the Kolchian fleet is hindered by Hera, who sends storms.

The Argonauts' treachery, however, cannot go unpunished. Zeus decrees that they must be cleansed by the witch Kirke (Circe) before they can get home. Apollonios uses several different sources to construct a roundabout route for the seafarers to follow home: They sail up the Danube River (here, the Ister) to Istria, and thence south to the mouth of the Po (the Erídanós)—a river they follow into the territory occupied by the Celts. In reality, there is no confluence of the Po and the Rhone (the Rhódanos)—the river that the Argonauts follow back to the Mediterranean before coasting western Italy and then crossing to sail along the Egyptian coast. There is no reason to imagine, however, that Apollonios had a detailed knowledge of the geography of the Alps, or no logical reason to prevent his thinking that a confluence of rivers that *seemed* to come together might not have existed.

When the Argonauts do finally reach Kirke's home, Medeia and Jason present themselves as wretched suppliants. But Kirke is utterly unsympathetic and, though she complies with Zeus's behest to purify them, soon sends them packing. Under the protection of various immortals, they now must follow the route that Odysseus would later navigate on his roundabout return voyage from Troy (see *The ODYSSEY*). Eventually they end up, as Odysseus also did, among the Phaiakians. The Kolchians have also arrived there, and to avert further bloodshed, the Phaiakian king, Alkinoos, undertakes to decide the fate of Medeia. Since she is still a virgin, it looks as if he will return her to her father. To avoid that outcome, Medeia and Jason get Queen Arete's advice and determine that the time has come for their wedding. With gods and nymphs in attendance, they plight their troth in a cave and consummate their union on a great marriage bed spread over with the Golden Fleece. Alkinoos finds in the newlyweds' favor and refuses to return Medeia to her father. Afraid to report that outcome to their king, the Kolchians successfully plead to be allowed to remain in Alkinoos's island kingdom of Phaiakia.

The Argonauts once more resume their voyage, but they are not yet fated to return directly home. Rather, they are driven by storms to the Libyan coast, where a flood tide beaches them so far inland that they cannot get back to the sea. Just as they despair of ever seeing their homeland again, three local goddesses advise them that they must bodily pick their ship up and carry it inland until they encounter a bay. They follow these instructions, and for 12 days they march with the ship on their shoulders. Finally, exhausted and parched, they pray to the local goddesses to show them a source of drinking water. The three again appear and advise them that another traveler—Heracles, as it turns out—has preceded them and found water. The goddesses direct the Argonauts to the spring.

Their journey across the Libyan sands costs the Argonauts a pair of comrades: One dies by snakebite and another at the hand of a hostile shepherd. Eventually the Argonauts and the women who have accompanied them from Phaiakia as the handmaids of Medeia encounter the sea god Triton, who accepts a gift and offers them detailed instructions for finding a water route to the sea and sailing home. However, they still must overcome a dangerous obstacle: Medeia must bewitch the bronze giant Talus on the island of Crete. After she does so, things go smoothly for the Argonauts, and Apollonios leaves them engaged in friendly contests on the Island of Aigina. From there they reach home without further incident.

Bibliography

Apollonios Rhodios. *The Argonautika*. Translated and edited by Peter Green. Berkeley: University of California Press, 1997.

Aristides of Miletus   See *MILESIAN TALES*.

Aristophanes (ca. 448–ca. 380 B.C.E.) *Greek dramatist*

The most celebrated playwright of the Greek Old Comedy, Aristophanes was born in Athens but moved with his mother and his father Philippos to the island of Aegina during his childhood. By 427 B.C.E., however, he was back in Athens pursuing the vocation of playwright under an assumed name. Although his first comedy, *Daitaleis* (The Banqueters) has not survived, we know that it won the second prize in the comic competitions that year and that it satirized citified education and its products.

In the Old Comedy, playwrights felt licensed—even compelled—to include topical material and to attack contemporary politicians and their policies. This Aristophanes did in his second play, which is also lost, entitled "The Babylonians." He apparently took issue with the repressive policies of the Athenian leader Cleon (d. 422 B.C.E.), particularly as they applied to Cleon's threat to slaughter or enslave the inhabitants of the city of Mytilene on the island of Lesbos when it revolted against its Athenian overlords. Cleon was briefly a popular figure among the Athenians for his resolution in pursuing the Peloponnesian War.

Cleon was not amused at Aristophanes' satiric portrayal, and in 426 B.C.E., it seems he brought charges of high treason against the playwright, whom he also falsely accused of having been born a foreigner. Aristophanes, however, was apparently untroubled by the demagogue's enmity as, in 425 B.C.E., still using an assumed identity, he brought to the stage the first of his surviving comedies, *The Acharnians*. This work, which argued for a peaceful resolution of the issues that had produced the long war, won first prize in that year's comis contest, suggesting that at least some influential Athenians had come over to Aristophanes' view of matters.

Perhaps encouraged by this success, Aristophanes dropped his pen name and under his own produced a violent invective against Cleon, against the faults of democratic government, and against the war—another first prize winner, *The* KNIGHTS (424 B.C.E.). Aristophanes' most recent editor and translator, Jeffrey Henderson, says that the playwright regularly "promoted the views" of the "conservative right"—landowners and old, wealthy families.

The following year saw the production of *The* CLOUDS, and in the year 422 B.C.E. came *The* WASPS. Next, in 421 B.C.E., the comedy *Peace* came to the stage, but no peace came to Athens. Here a six-year hiatus occurs in the record, though Aristophanes almost certainly continued writing and producing throughout the period. Our knowledge resumes, however, in 414 B.C.E. with his production of *The* BIRDS—a second-prize winner—and of the now-lost *Amphiarus*. *The Birds* is especially important in the playwright's development as it introduces his thereafter-continuing emphasis on the theme of a political utopia.

As the Peloponnesian War dragged on, and as political invective and satire produced little impact upon the decisions of a series of Athenian politicians with respect to the war, Aristophanes perhaps lost faith in the capacity of that sort of drama to sway political events. His next play, LYSISTRATA (411 B.C.E.), represents a flight into utopian fantasy. At the same time, the play is an early document in the literature of women's liberation.

About the same time appeared *The Thesmophoriazusae* (WOMEN AT THE THESMOPHORIA)—a play departing from politics altogether and ridiculing the tragic playwright EURIPIDES and his portrayal of wicked wives. About six years later (405 B.C.E.) came a play much beloved by 20th-century audiences, perhaps because it is set in Hades: *The* FROGS, in which Euripides' ghost figures prominently. After another gap in the record, this time of 13 years, there appeared another fantasy about the Athenian women seizing power from the men: *Women at the Thesmophoria* (also called *The Assembly Women* or *The Parliament of Women*). In 388 B.C.E. appeared the last of the plays of Aristophanes still in existence: *Plutus* (*Wealth*).

We know that Aristophanes wrote further comedies. Papyrus fragments of lost plays—almost 1,000 lines of them—survive, leading to a list in Henderson's edition of some 39 or 40 titles, including the plays we have and those whose names, at least, we know. We also know that the aging playwright continued to develop and change. We have direct evidence and critical accounts suggesting that toward the end of his career, Aristophanes introduced to the Athenian stage the sorts of plays that in the aggregate would become known as the New Comedy. In *Plutus*, for example, Aristophanes innovatively dispenses with the chorus, and in the lost play *Cocalus*, which was produced by his son Araros, he is said to have introduced many devices in addition to those of rape and recognition (earlier used in Euripides' ION) that became standard in the New Comedy.

In his SYMPOSIUM, PLATO depicts Aristophanes as among his work's banqueters. Plato characterizes the playwright as genial, urbane, and intelligent.

See also COMEDY IN GREECE AND ROME.

Bibliography

Henderson, Jeffrey, ed. and trans. *Aristophanes*. 4 vols. Cambridge, Mass.: Harvard University Press, 1998–2002.

Oates, Whitney J., and Eugene O'Neill, Jr., eds. *The Complete Greek Drama*. Vol. 2. New York: Random House, 1938.

Aristotle (385–322 B.C.E.) *Greek prose writer*

A teacher, philosopher, and polymath, Aristotle was among the deepest thinking and most influential of all philosophers through the ages.

A Macedonian by birth, Aristotle was the son of a physician who ministered to King Amyntas II of Macedonia—a connection that would later benefit the philosopher. When he was 22 years old, Aristotle moved to Athens to study with PLATO, whose pupil he remained until he was 42. On Plato's death, Aristotle moved to the Troadian community of Assos for three years, then on to Mytilene on the island of Lesbos, where he remained until 344 B.C.E. In that year King Philip of Macedonia, the son of Aristotle's father's former employer, invited Aristotle to become the tutor to his son Alexander. Accepting, Aristotle occupied that office until 335 B.C.E., when Alexander, enroute to becoming surnamed "the Great," set out on his conquest of Asia.

Returning to Athens, Aristotle founded a school of philosophy in a garden sacred to Apollo—the Lyceum. Owing to his practice of strolling about in deep discussion with his students, his school and its adherents became known as the PERIPATETIC SCHOOL OF PHILOSOPHY. At the Lyceum, Aristotle collected a substantial library of scrolls, founded a museum of natural history, and shared his thinking with his students.

That thinking covered the entire field of human knowledge as it was then constituted. Over time, he came to disagree fundamentally with his former teacher, Plato. Whereas Plato had conceived of the nature of reality as understood by people to be the perception of a reflection of a reality that was constituted by immutable ideas, Aristotle came to think of the physical world as material, and he preferred methods that were more empirical than Plato's. Understanding the nature of reality required experiment, not merely reflection

and debate. Thus, Aristotle was responsible for moving philosophy in the direction of natural science.

Some of what survives of Aristotle's work was probably reconstituted in ancient times on the basis of the notes that his students took during his lectures and his discussions with them. To this class of his work belong his treatises on ethics (see NICHOMACHEAN ETHICS, THE) and on politics—works probably collected and edited, in the first instance, by his son Nicomachus and, in the second, by his student Eudemas.

The work of Aristotle that most directly addresses the literary arena includes his POETICS and his *Rhetoric*. The *Rhetoric* reflects the deep and abiding interest of the Greek world, especially at Athens, in the arts of public speaking and persuasion—skills crucial to exercising influence in a democracy. I treat the *Poetics* in greater detail elsewhere in this volume.

Beyond his forays into the literary realm, however, Aristotle's surviving discussions address a daunting array of topics. In his *Organon* (six treatises on the science of reasoning), he establishes a series of categories or predicates purporting to exhaust the analytical statements that can be offered about a subject. Moving on to a theory of interpretation, he offers his views on the relation of language to thought, accompanying those views with a discussion of grammar and an analysis of philosophical discourse. In the section of the *Organon* entitled "Prior Analytics," he makes what is probably his most important contribution to philosophy, his invention of the syllogism as a method for the examination of philosophical questions. In the section entitled "Posterior Analytics," Aristotle propounds a theory of knowledge, addressing its definition, its acquisition, the way one can be certain of its truth, and the way knowledge can be expanded and systematically arranged. The *Organon* also contains Aristotle's discussions entitled "On Sophistical Refutations," "On Coming to Be and Passing Away," and "On the Cosmos."

From the point of view of the modern discipline of physics, Aristotle's title *Physics*, as his translators Philip H. Wicksteed and Francis M. Cornford suggest, is misleading. In *Physics*, Aristotle's principal interest is the realm of nature and natural philosophy. Everything that moves or undergoes change concerns him here. In his discussion, he raises such questions as "What is motion?" "What is time?" or "What does one mean by 'becoming'?" He considers the differences between mind and matter and the nature of the four Greek elements: earth, air, fire, and water. He also examines the issues of whether or not change is purposeful, and, if it is purposeful, does that imply the necessity for a theology to explain the physical world and its processes? He thought it did.

In his work *On the Heavens*, Aristotle begins his description of a theory of the universe that remained generally credited, at least for literary purposes, until the 17th century C.E. (He completes the description in his *Metaphysics*.) He describes a finite, spherical universe with the earth at its center and bounded by the fixed stars. Beyond the universe, only the incorporeal—probably divine—can exist. Moving inward from the fixed stars, we find a series of nine crystalline spheres that turn like a system of gears, impelled by a force called (in Latin) the *primum mobile*—an unmoved or first mover. Imbedded in each sphere are stars, or a planet, or the sun, or the moon.

Little escaped becoming an object of Aristotle's close consideration. The weather and phenomena that he considered related to it received his attention in his *Meteorologica*, in which he examined topics studied in modern meteorology, such as snow, rain, storms, rainbows, and the aurora borealis. Beyond this, his work addressed some of the concerns of modern astronomy: shooting stars, comets, and the Milky Way. Elements of geology also piqued his interest, and in *Meteorologica* he wrote about earthquakes, coastal erosion, and the origin and saltiness of the sea.

Aristotle considered questions connected with the existence, nature, and survivability of the individual human spirit in his essay "On the Soul." He also lectured on "Sense and Sensible Objects," "Memory and Recollection," "Sleep and Waking," and "Dreams," and he concerned himself with the topic of "Prophecy in Sleep," in addition to considering "The Length and Shortness of Life," "Youth and Old Age," "Life and Death," and "Respiration." He devoted further attention to the last-named subject in his essay "On Breath."

Animals attracted Aristotle's enduring attention, and his studies of and reflections on them, their history, their parts, their movements, their progression, and their generation occupy five bilingual books in a 23-volume modern edition of his work.

Partly because of Aristotle's productivity, some works have become traditionally associated with his name even though they were actually written by anonymous members of the peripatetic school of philosophy that he had founded. Such writings include most of the 38 books (scrolls) included in the collection entitled *Problems*. Among many other matters, these address such topics as "chills and shivering," "sexual intercourse," "harmony," and the physical effects of eating fruit.

In the 14 books of his *Metaphysics*, Aristotle undertakes to apply his extraordinary logical and analytical abilities to developing a theology that underpins physical reality. As one of Aristotle's modern editors, Hugh Tredennick, observes, in this attempt, Aristotle ironically ends up with a position that closely approximates the thought of his teacher, Plato—a position that Aristotle had long since rejected. In essence, he refutes a central principle of his entire philosophic position. As a materialist, Aristotle was committed to the precept that no form can exist without matter. But in the final analysis, his conception of the supreme and underlying metaphysical reality turns out to exist in immaterial form.

A series of ethical works appears among those traditionally assigned to Aristotle. Two of these, *The Nicomachean Ethics* and *The Eudemian Ethics*, are generally accepted as genuinely Aristotelian. His son Nicomachus edited the first from Aristotle's notes. The second was probably written from lecture notes taken by Aristotle's student Eudemus of Rhodes, a celebrated philosopher in his own right. Modern scholarship attributes other ethical writings associated with Aristotle's name, such as the *Great Ethics*, the *Tract on Virtues and Vices*, and several other minor works, to anonymous members of the Peripatetic school.

While Aristotle's *Nichomachean Ethics* explores the nature of human character, his *Politics* examines the science of human welfare and happiness and the role of the state in securing those benefits. The state is different from the family, but it nonetheless springs from aggregations of families. Various constitutional arrangements characterize different states—principally monarchy, oligarchy, and democracy—but in all of them, citizenship implies a willingness to participate in the state's decision-making and judicial procedures. Lastly, Aristotle turns his attention to describing ideal politics, imagining the best sort of constitution and prescribing the characteristics of education for citizenship.

Like many another ancient volume, a work of Aristotle's that had been lost for millennia surfaced at OXYRHYNCHUS in 1890. This work, "The Polity of the Athenians," once belonged to Aristotle's otherwise lost private collection of 158 constitutions of ancient city-states. Among his other lost records is a list of dramatic performances acted at Athens.

Bibliography

Aristotle. *The Basic Works of Aristotle*. Edited by Richard McKeon. New York: Modern Library, 2001.

Wicksteed, Philip, F. M. Cornfield, et al, eds. *Aristotle* [Works, Greek and English]. 23 vols. Cambridge, Mass.: Harvard University Press, 1926–95.

Arrian (Flavius Arianus) (ca. 86–160 C.E.)
Greek prose writer

A provincial Greek from Bithynian Nicomedia, Arrian studied philosophy with the Stoic Epictetus (see STOICISM) and later became an officer in the Roman army. He attracted the favorable atten-

tion of the Roman emperor Hadrian, was promoted to the senatorial aristocracy of the empire, and eventually rose to become consul and legate in the province of Cappadoccia.

As a literary figure, Arrian is credited with having published the lectures of Epictetus, which he had apparently memorized as Epictetus delivered them, and summaries of the same lectures organized into a little guide to Stoic philosophy. Beyond that, on the model of XENOPHON OF ATHEN's *Anabasis*, he published a memoir of Alexander the Great. Still in the manner of Xenophon, Arrian prepared a treatise on the subject of hunting that purported to take account of new methods and technology and to bring Xenophon's similar discussion up to date.

Also interested in geography, Arrian prepared a guide (*Periplous*) to the region around the Euxine Sea as well as a commentary on India, *Indika*, of which a portion survives.

Bibliography

Arrian. *Arrian with an English Translation*. 2 vols. Edited and translated by P. A. Brant. Cambridge, Mass.: Harvard University Press, 1976–83.

———. *The Lamp of Epictetus: Being Arrian's Lectures of Epictetus to Young Men*. London: Methuen and Company, 1938.

———. *Periplous Ponti Euxini*. Edited and Translated by Aidan Liddle. London: Bristol Classical, 2003.

Ronan, James, editor. *Alexander the Great: Selections from Arrian, Diodorus, Plutarch, and Quintus Curtius*. Translated by Pamela Mensch. Indianapolis: Hackett Publishing Company, 2005.

Art of Love, The (Ars Amatoria) Ovid (ca. 1 C.E.)

In *The Art of Love*, OVID undertakes to instruct both the male and female libertine population of Augustan Rome in the intricacies of finding and winning beloveds and lovers. The poet admonishes respectable persons against perusing his pages; nonetheless, the emperor, AUGUSTUS

CAESAR, apparently did so with disapprobation. The emperor's displeasure with this work, however, was not the cause of Ovid's imperial exile to Tomi on the Black Sea.

First Ovid instructs would-be lovers about what venues to frequent in their quest for beloveds. Theaters are especially likely places and are fatal to chastity. He establishes the long Roman tradition of seeking beloveds at entertainments by recounting the rape of the Sabine women in the time of Romulus. Horse races in the Circus Maximus provide many likely occasions for the sort of gallantry that leads to amatory dalliance.

For a time, Ovid explores the forbidden passions of women for near kin and for such bestiality as the unnatural passion of the Cretan queen Pasiphae for a bull. Then he returns to more ordinary circumstances.

Ovid advises a would-be lover to become acquainted with the handmaiden of the object of his affections and to suborn the servant's loyalty without making the maid the object of the lover's quest at the same time. Begin, he advises, with the mistress. Then, if one is also interested in the maid, pursue her later. He compares the lover's quest with hunting and fishing.

The poet warns would-be lovers against gold diggers. Rather than sending presents, Ovid recommends, lovers should send letters written on wax tablets. He also advises men to avoid being too well-groomed, but rather to seem clean and casually handsome. He also gives advice for seduction at convivial parties—principally to seem drunk while staying sober, to praise the beloved, and to promise her anything since Jupiter, himself a notable philanderer, "smiles at the perjuries of lovers." Ovid finds religious belief "expedient" for would-be lovers. He sprinkles his advice with many examples drawn from the annals of mythology.

Controversially, Ovid advises the use of force as a tool of seduction—again supporting his arguments with appeals to such stories as that of Achilles' forcing himself upon Deidamia and thus obtaining her lasting affection.

Beginning the second book of his *Artis Amatoriae* with accounts of his own success, Ovid shifts to recounting the story of Daedalus and Icarus and their escape from Crete on the wings of Daedalus's invention. The poet also details the way that, heedless of his father's advice, Icarus flew too near the sun, melted the wax that glued on his wings, and plunged to his death. The moral of the story for lovers emerges: Minos, king of Crete, despite his power over land and sea, could not keep a winged man like Daedalus from escaping through the air. The poet, however, means to keep the winged god, Cupid, under his control.

Avoiding anger, says Ovid, is a principal means of maintaining a love relationship since mistresses get enough of quarreling at home. Love is nonetheless a kind of warfare, says the poet, and a lover must employ similar tactics and strategies. Continuing his advice, Ovid discusses such subjects as how to achieve reconciliation when a lover has provoked his mistress's anger and jealousy.

Above all, Ovid counsels secrecy. A lover should neither tattle nor brag. After praising the joys of mutual fulfillment, Ovid announces that his task is finished, and that lovers ought to award him palm leaves and myrtle crowns for his services to them. The poet then promises women similar favors.

As he begins the third book of his work, Ovid once more emphasizes that he addresses only "wanton lovers," and that respectable women, like Ulysses' wife Penelope, are not members of his intended audience. But those women who do belong to the class of the demimonde must bear in mind the doctrines of the philosophy of seizing the day (carpe diem). Too soon, old age will rob them of their charms.

Ovid offers advice on the care and preservation of beauty. He suggests that certain hairdos go best with certain shapes of face, and he advises those who are graying to use hair dye. Keeping one's teeth their whitest is also essential.

Short women show themselves to best advantage when they lie or recline. Thin women should wear full, heavy-textured garments. Pale women should wear colorful clothes that show their complexions to advantage. Narrow bosoms should be padded. Ovid offers advice on walking and on draping garments so that a little skin shows alluringly. He advises women to learn to sing and to play suitable games. As he had done for the men, he suggests venues appropriate for seeking lovers.

Ovid is fair-minded as he advises women about amatory matters. He instructs them to avoid the very men for whom the first two books of *The Art of Love* proffers advice. If, however, a woman has taken a lover, Ovid counsels her to address him as "she." Women should also avoid appearing melancholy; lovers do not fancy melancholy mistresses.

Changing subjects, Ovid declares that, just as a lawyer's business is the law, a poet's business is love. Therefore, women should be kind to poets. They should also encourage their lovers' ardor by assuring them that rivals for their affections exist.

The poet also instructs women in the art of deceiving any watchers their husbands may set over them. Letters written in invisible ink made from milk exemplify such a tactic. Others include messages composed in the bath and concealed in one's bosom. Watchers, moreover, can be drugged, Ovid suggests.

Ovid interrupts his advice to women to recount the monitory episode of Procris, who became jealous of the breeze when she heard her husband call upon it by its name, Aura. Thinking the cooling wind her rival, the jealous Procris followed her husband Cephalus on the hunt and surprised him in the bush. Thinking her an animal, Cephalus accidentally slew her. Avoid jealousy, Ovid implies.

Returning to his task, Ovid advises women to delay granting their lovers their favors. When delay is past, however, he offers advice concerning the positions that women of different sizes and shapes might most effectively choose for lovemaking. He concludes by advising his female pupils to acknowledge him by his name—"Naso"—as their master.

Bibliography

Ovid. *The Art of Love and Other Poems.* Translated by J. H. Mozeley. Cambridge, Mass.: Harvard University Press, 1947.

———. *The Art of Love: Publius Ovidius Naso.* Translated by James Michie. New York: Modern Library, 2002.

Art of Poetry, The (Epistles 2.3) Horace (ca. 19–18 B.C.E.)

Written as the Golden Age of Latin poetry was ending and addressed as a verse letter to his friends, the Pisones, HORACE's *The Art of Poetry* contains his advice to a rising generation of poets. That advice, as well as some of Horace's own poetic practice, does not seem to have been entirely original with the author. Although Horace is universally recognized to have been Rome's premier poet, both his satiric method and his critical advice were modeled on the example of the earlier Roman poet, LUCILIUS.

The centerpiece of book 2 of his EPISTLES, *The Art of Poetry* is Horace's longest poem. He begins by drawing a comparison between poetry, painting, and sculpture. All require unity of subject matter, simplicity of treatment, and the harmonious subordination of the parts to the whole. Horace grants that artists have license to embroider nature, but they must nonetheless give unity and credibility to their creations. He lists a series of pitfalls that endanger his own poetic practice: Brevity can lead to obscurity; grandiloquence can become bombast; caution can produce too modest a result. Writers should also write about what they know and address topics that are within their capacity to handle. Language changes, so young poets should not always emulate the style and vocabulary of older ones but should adopt new terminology as their own. It is also important to select a poetic form or meter that suits the subject.

As regards dramatic poetry, tragedy requires a higher style than comedy—though even comedy can rise to anger, and tragedy can descend to the expression of grief in prose. "Either follow tradition," Horace advises, "or invent what is self-consistent."

Modern diction is important. Old-fashioned language will provoke laughter where none is intended. Stay focused on the story so that the beginning, middle, and end all work together. Moreover, if poets are penning drama, they must be careful to assign attributes to their characters that are suitable to the characters' ages and situations in life. He advises dramatists to develop their plots through action rather than having characters report offstage developments. Taste, however, assigns limits to what the dramatist should portray. Medea's murder of her own children (see MEDEA), metamorphoses from human to animal or serpentine form, or Atreus's preparing human flesh as a banquet (see AGAMEMNON) are matters best merely described. The language, too, should suit the subject, and verse forms must be appropriately selected.

Horace suggests that his contemporary Roman playwrights model their work on that of the Greeks rather than such a Roman author as PLAUTUS. Careful discrimination, however, between "coarseness and wit" and close attention to suiting the meter to the matter are more important than imitating models. Tasteful innovation is desirable. Wisdom is the fountainhead of art.

Contrasting the Greeks and the Romans, Horace suggests that while the Greeks sought glory, the Romans are too concerned with the acquisition of wealth. He reminds the Pisones that the object of poetry is both "to please and to instruct." If anything in a poem falls short of excellence, the entire effort fails. That being the case, Horace advises his friends to seek expert criticism and to revise *before* allowing publication of their verse. One cannot call back what has once been published.

Horace traces the distinguished history of poetry from the civilizing effects of the verse of the archetypal bard, ORPHEUS, through TYRTAEUS and HOMER, to PINDAR, SIMONIDES OF CEOS, and Bacchilides, to its connection with religious festivals. He says that poets have no call to be ashamed of their craft.

Horace states that an honest critic who carefully corrects a poet's work is a much better friend to the artist than someone who prefers not to offend by finding trifling errors or infelicities. At the same time, he compares bad poets who insist on reading in public to blood-sucking leeches.

Bibliography

Fairclough, H. Rushton, ed. and trans. *Horace: Satires, Epistles, Ars Poetica.* New York: G. P. Putnam's and Sons, 1932.

Horace. *The Complete Works: Translated in the Meters of the Originals.* Translated by Charles E. Passage. New York: F. Ungar Publishing Company, 1983.

Reckford, Kenneth J. *Horace.* New York: Twayne Publishers, 1969.

Atellane fables or farces (*Ludi Osci*)

A mode of drama indigenous to the Oscan city of Atella in the vicinity of Naples, the Atellane plays may at first have been extemporaneous performances. They continued to be played in the Oscan language until they migrated to the city of Rome. There they commanded a wide audience long after LIVIUS ANDRONICUS introduced regular drama to Rome and Roman playwrights began to emulate the classical drama of Greece.

Standard Latin soon replaced Oscan in these little plays, and a custom arose that permitted respectable young Romans, even those of the patrician class, to participate as players. Like the later Italian commedia dell'arte, (the comedy of the guild) Atellane farces seem to have had a stock set of characters that appeared in traditional costumes. One such stock character was Mappus. He was presented as having a large head, a long nose, and a humped back. Another was called Pappus. The classicist J. J. Eschenburg speculates that Pappus may have been borrowed from a Greek stock character, the old man called Silenus.

The popularity of Atellane farces and the financial opportunities that writing them represented encouraged playwrights who were successful in other genres—like the poet Memmius (d. 46 B.C.E.) and the fabulist Sylla—to try their hands at composing the farces. Those who seem to have enjoyed the most success with the genre and who raised Atellane farces to literary status are Quintus Novius and L. Pomponius Bono, who cooperated in writing them in the first century B.C.E. Only fragmentary remains of their works remain—about 70 and about 200 lines, respectively.

See also COMEDY IN GREECE AND ROME.

Bibliography

Charney, Maurice, ed. *Comedy: A Geographic and Historical Guide.* Westport, Conn.: Praeger, 2005.

Athanasius, St. (ca. 295–373 C.E.) *Roman-Egyptian writer*

Probably brought up in an Egyptian Christian family and educated in both classics and Scripture with a priestly career in mind, Athanasius was ordained as a deacon around 318 by the patriarch of Alexandria, St. Alexander. This patriarch was the orthodox clergyman who opposed the Arian heresy contesting the dogma that Christ the Son and God the Father were of the same divine substance. Alexander in fact excommunicated Arius himself.

In 325, Athanasius accompanied Alexander to the Council of Nicaea, where the orthodox view held by Alexander prevailed. Alexander named Athanasius his successor, and despite some opposition, the Egyptian bishops confirmed the choice. However, caught in a backlash led by Arian bishops, Athanasius found himself exiled by the emperor Constantine to northern Gaul. On assuming the imperial throne, Constantine II recalled Athanasius and restored him to his episcopal dignities, but his enemies again prevailed and deposed him. Athanasius complained, but, despite exoneration from the charges his ene-

mies brought against him at the Council of Tyre, the Arians would not allow his restoration at Alexandria. As a result, he remained in the West for a considerable period.

In Gaul and Italy, Athanasius encouraged the institution of the church and spread of monasticism. The death of his principal adversary in Alexandria, the usurping bishop Gregory of Cappadocia, and the support of the Roman emperor of the West, Constantius II, enabled Athanasius to resume his episcopal see in 346, and for a decade he was able to work productively, relatively free from dissension. He used the time he had for writing to compose discussions of the issues in the theological dispute about which he felt so strongly; *On the Decrees of the Nicene Synod* and *On the Opinion of Dionysius of Alexandria* were produced during this period.

When the emperor Constantius died in 361, however, Athanasius's enemies began once more to plot against him. Their agitations over the next few years culminated in Athanasius's forcible removal from his church by a squad of soldiers. Eluding their vigilance, he escaped to the desert, where, aided by loyal supporters, he managed to continue his ministry while a fugitive. From a literary perspective, this was also a productive time for Athanasius. He penned a series of *Discourses against the Arians* and a history of their movement. He also wrote his famous LIFE OF SAINT ANTHONY and a pair of epistles, *Letter to Serapion* and *Letter to Epictetus.*

As a staunch traditionalist who believed in the orthodoxies of the Western Church, Athanasius found ludicrous the proliferation of creeds under the general rubric of Christianity. In his work *De Synodis* (About synods), he derided this still-continuing tendency of churches to splinter. After more vicissitudes in his status that varied as the rulers did or did not favor his point of view, and after further exiles, Athanasius resumed his episcopal throne for the final time in 364 and successfully passed it along to his designated successor, his brother Peter.

Given this history of hardships and his unwavering devotion to the orthodoxy established by the Council of Nicaea, it comes as no surprise that the bulk of Athanasius's writings address related issues. In *Discourses against the Arians*, he argues the issues involved in the orthodoxy dispute. Central among these was the question noted above concerning the identity of Christ's substance with that of God the Father. Athanasius also wrote a discourse entitled *Two Books against the Pagans*. Another work discusses the question of the divinity of Christ and the Holy Spirit: *On the Incarnation and against the Arians*.

Other works concerning Christian dogma appear in a series of letters that Athanasius wrote. Interested readers will find some of these in the bibliography below. As an author, however, Athanasius is best remembered for founding a new genre. In his *Life of Saint Anthony*, he established the model of Christian biography as an ascetic journey through life in the steps of Christ and helped to spread the monastic ideal. To that new genre—one that became the model for a flood of subsequent works—Athanasius himself added two similar works that he called letters, writing one to "the Monk Amun" and another to "Dracontius." Other less-biographical works are also called letters and are of a more usual epistolary nature. One such letter is of special importance because it contains an early list of the canonical works of the entire Christian Bible. Beyond that, Athanasius penned such scriptural exegesis as his interpretation of the Psalms in his *Letter to Marcellinus*.

A sizable body of work purporting to be by Athanasius has yet to be authenticated. Among the authentic works, some of those that argue quite abstruse theological principles may seem circular in their logic to persons who do not already share Athanasius's convictions. His work lent special impetus to monasticism and to many Christians' deciding to live lives of chastity and asceticism.

Bibliography

Athanasius. *The Life of Antony and The Letter to Marcellinus*. Translated by Robert C. Gregg. New York: Paulist Press, 1980.

———. *The Life of Saint Anthony*. Translated by Robert C. Gregg. Edited by Emilie Griffen. San Francisco, Calif.: Harper, 2006.

———. *On the Incarnation [of the Word of God]; De incarnatione verbi dei*. Introduced by C. S. Lewis. Crestwood, N.Y.: St. Vladimir's Seminary Press, 1998.

———. *Select Treatises of St. Athanasius in Controversy with the Arians*. Translated by John Henry Cardinal Newman. New York: AMS Press, 1978.

Atharva-Veda (original form ca. 1000 B.C.E.; current form ca. 200 B.C.E.)

The Atharva-Veda is a collection of very ancient hymns of India whose singing seems often to have been the special responsibility of a subcategory of Hindu soothsayers—usually those employed as court magicians. Materials contained in the Athara-Veda often also appear elsewhere in Hindu religious texts. Priests of the Atharvan sect made extravagant claims for the place that the Athara-Veda occupies in the Hindu canon; they sometimes call it the Bhrama-Veda, or the Hymn of God. Though the composition of the work is traditionally assigned to VYĀSA, the legendary author of the *MAHABHARATA*, the Atharva-Veda is clearly the product of a long process of literary accretion, and while a historical Vyāsa may be responsible for some of it, other—likely many other—voices produced its songs over centuries.

The first group of hymns in the document includes medicinal charms against fever, jaundice, coughing, constipation, and numerous other indispositions the flesh is heir to. Some of the charms are supposed to be chanted or sung along with administration of medicinal herbs to restore health. There are also songs to be sung to protect cattle from bovine diseases and charms to be recited against snakebite and poisonous insects. In addition, there are charms meant to enhance personal appearance and allure. Among these we find a pair intended to promote hair growth, and another charm to promote virility. Charms against psychological afflictions like mania and all those attributed to demonic possession are also included.

Incantations designed to achieve longevity and health appear in the Atharva-Veda's second section, and another round of curses against demons occupies the third. The fourth section contains charms for acquiring a wife or a husband and charms to promote conception, assure male progeny, make women sterile, prevent miscarriage, and promote an easy childbirth. Several charms address finding one's beloved and assuring passionate lovemaking.

The fifth section of the Atharva-Veda contains a series of charms specifically pertaining to royalty. The sixth addresses obtaining harmony and avoiding conflict. After that, the fairly long seventh section contains charms aimed at assuring prosperity and avoiding thieves, loss by fire, and loss by accident. A specific charm is designed to protect shepherds and their flocks from thieves and wild beasts.

In the eighth section we find incantations designed to assure forgiveness for sins and to cleanse those who have been ritually defiled. Then there are charms to ward off birds of evil omen and to avert bad or inauspicious dreams. The ninth section provides a series of prayers and curses designed to benefit Brahmans—the priestly class of Hinduism.

While each of the foregoing sections is of great sociological, historical, and religious interest, one might argue that the 10th section of the Atharva-Veda is really the most gripping of all. Here the hymns deal with the creation of the universe and with the efforts of the Brahmans to establish direct contact with the divine through revelation, contemplation, and prayer.

The hymns are accompanied by books of ritual and by commentary.

Bibliography

Bloomfield, Maurice, trans. *Hymns of the* Atharva-Veda *Together with Extracts from the Ritual Books and the Commentaries.* Oxford: Clarendon Press, 1897.

Joshi, K. L., ed. *Atharva-Vedasamhita: Sanscrit Text, English Translation. . . .* Translated by W. D. Whitney and Bhāsya of Sāyanācāya. Delhi: Parimal Publications, 2000.

Athenaeus of Naucratis   See Deipnoso-phists, The.

"Attis" (Poem 63) Catullus (ca. third century B.C.E.)

Considered by the literary historian Quincy Howe, Jr., to be one of the most "technically brilliant poems" in the Latin language, "Attis" displays the serious, most moving side of Catullus's art, recounting a touching story of sexuality, madness, and regret.

Based on the myth of Attis, the 99-line poem (the 63rd of the poet's surviving works) is connected with the worship of the Asiatic fertility goddess Cybele, also known as Agdistis, who was the earth mother or great mother. According to her myth, Cybele/Agdistis had been born physically bisexual. Intervening, the gods removed her male appendage, leaving her female. From the severed male organ grew a lovely almond tree.

Nana, the daughter of a Phrygian river god, the Sangarios, admired the blooming tree and pressed a blossom in her bosom. It vanished, and Nana found herself pregnant. The manner of his conception led to Nana's infant child, Attis, being abandoned to die. Cybele/Agdistis, however, loved the boy and inspired a male goat to supervise the baby's survival.

When he grew to manhood, Attis fell in love with a wood nymph and provoked the jealousy of the goddess who had mysteriously protected him. Cybele drove him mad so that he became one of her priestesses by castrating himself. It is just before this that Catullus takes up the matter, focusing on the behavior, emotions, and thought processes of the principal characters.

As the poem opens, a reader finds Attis in his madness sailing on a ship to the sacred grove of Cybele. There in his frenzy he castrates himself and becomes a priestess of Cybele's cult. From that moment forward, the pronouns alluding to Attis become feminine.

Adopting the role of the priestess of Agdistis Cybele, Attis calls the worshippers together and, chanting, leads the wild ceremony of worship. She continues her frenzied behavior until she and the other worshippers sink into exhausted slumber.

Attis awakens in her right mind and regrets the rashness of her act. She misses her parents and the homeland from which she sailed and finds her current situation "wretched." She recalls her former manly athletic accomplishments and sweet leisure. Now she finds herself the hopeless, unwilling, emasculated slave of her parent goddess.

Cybele, however, overhears her lament. Angered, the goddess unleashes the lions that draw her chariot—lions of her retribution. One of them charges the brooding Attis, whose madness returns as she flees into the forest where, Catullus says, Attis remained a slave until the day she died.

Ending the poem with his own prayer to Cybele, Catullus, who was sometimes the victim of his own passions, prays that the goddess will "drive others to such frenzy," leave his heart free, and stay far away from his home.

Bibliography

Catullus. *The Complete Poems for Modern Readers.* Translated by Reney Myers and Robert J. Ormsby. London: Ruskin House, 1972.

Rose, Herbert Jennings. *A Handbook of Greek Mythology: Including Its Extension to Rome.* New York: E. P. Dutton and Company, 1929.

Augustine, St., bishop of Hippo (354–430 C.E.) *Roman-African prose writer, Christian theologian*

Augustine, who was destined to become ancient Christendom's most distinguished and influential literary figure, was born in Thagaste, a highland town in the North African Roman province of Numidia (our contemporary Souk Ahras, Algeria). Augustine's pagan father, Patricius, worked hard and sacrificed much to give his son the classical education required to rise above his father's station. Despite the constant sacrifices that Patri-

cius made, his death in 372 required Augustine to interrupt his university education for a period before a wealthy local dignitary, Romanianus, came to his assistance.

Augustine's autobiography, CONFESSIONS, reveals that his mother Monica principally influenced his development. Also a saint of the Roman Catholic Church, Monica was a traditional Christian of a very conservative, African stripe. She believed, for example, that her dreams concerning Augustine's future were prophetic. Augustine did not always appreciate Monica's manner of mothering. When he was 28 years old, for instance, he sneaked off to Rome without telling her rather than face her disappointment at his desertion. In addition to being the dominant figure in her household, Monica was both long-suffering and patient. She put up with her husband's infidelities, paganism, and folly until at last he became a good husband and a Christian who appreciated her.

Augustine completed his university education at Carthage, where he became a devotee of the most radical of the heretical offshoots of the Christian religion, the Manichaeans (see MANICHAEAN WRITINGS). He would profess that allegiance for some years, until about the time he moved to Rome.

Augustine taught for a time in Thagaste, then returned to Carthage, where he taught rhetoric until 383 C.E. While living in Carthage earlier, in the year his father died, Augustine had formed a relationship with a woman. There were degrees of wedlock in ancient Rome, and the second-degree marriage that Augustine contracted with his spouse was effectively a form of concubinage—a relationship that, though it had legal status, could easily be dissolved. The woman, whose name Augustine never mentioned in *Confessions*, bore him a much beloved son, Adeodatus (a name that means "God's gift"). Augustine lived with the woman until the year 385. Then, as the Roman law allowed, he sent her away to free himself to contract an advantageous first-degree marriage with the daughter of a wealthy family. That marriage never took place, however.

After moving to Rome in 383, Augustine made friends with Quintus Aurelius Symmachus, another immigrant to the city, and in 385 Monica joined her son there. Symmachus, then prefect of Rome, appointed his friend Augustine to become the professor of rhetoric at the university in Milan—a role that also involved operating as an imperial press agent, for Augustine was expected to spread official propaganda. Symmachus needed a non-Catholic for the position. He had tried and failed to convince the emperor to acknowledge the old religion as well as the Christian religion, and the usual ill feelings that arise from arguments about religion were dividing the citizens of Milan.

As a professor, Augustine had expected secular success. He had not anticipated that his position would bring him into contact both with the philosophy of Neoplatonism and also with the second most influential person in his life, the Roman Catholic bishop of Milan, St. AMBROSE.

Under the influence of PLATO's followers, Augustine rejected the Manichaeans. Then, convinced by the cogency of Ambrose's sermons, he converted to mainstream Christianity in late August 386. Shortly thereafter, Augustine left Milan for a while, returning the following March, and in April 387 he was baptized. He had already begun an ambitious program of writing that would occupy him for much of the rest of his life.

Many of Augustine's writings, of course, concerned religion, and he wrote against Neoplatonism. The life of the blessed, divine providence and the soul's immortality were among the subjects that occupied his mind and his pen in 386–7. In the latter year, he also began writing about music. That same year, his mother died in Ostia and was initially interred there. Canonized as Saint Monica, her relics now rest both in Rome in the church of San Augostino, and in an Augustinian monastery near Arras, France.

In 388, Augustine turned his attention to subjects that included the soul's greatness and the problem of reconciling freedom of the human will with the doctrine of divine omniscience—especially divine foreknowledge with differences in Christian and Manichaean views of life and death. That year, too, he returned to Africa, going first to Carthage and then to Thagaste.

In 389, Augustine wrote about teaching and about the true religion. The following year, 390, brought twin disasters: the deaths of Augustine's close friend, Nebridius, whom he had known from childhood, and of his much-beloved son, Adeodatus.

In 391, Augustine moved to the North African seaport city of Hippo Regius, where he meant to establish a monastery. While that work was beginning, he still found time to write. The advantages of religious belief occupied him for a while. Then in 391–92 he turned his attention again to his continuing examination of the problem of free will and to taking up the cudgels against the Manichaeans once again. The year 392 saw Augustine's debate against the Manichaean apologist, Fortunatus, and he completed his commentaries on the first 32 Psalms. Commenting on the others would take him until the year 420.

A sermon that Augustine gave at the Council of Hippo in 393 addressed the subjects of faith and the Christian creed. The next year saw his commentary on and explanation of Christ's Sermon on the Mount as well as a series of lectures at Carthage explaining Paul's letters to the Romans and the Galatians as well as examining the subject of lying.

If Augustine was still entertaining the notion of a retired monastic life, his appointment as bishop of Hippo in 395 ended that ambition. It did not, however, seem to interfere with his ambitious program of composition. Several religious treatises that included the first part of his famous *On Christian Doctrine* (completed in 426) were written in 396, and 397 saw the beginning of Augustine's remarkable autobiography and perhaps his most celebrated work—his *Confessions*.

Further works in 398–99 opposed the Manichaeans, while another commented on the Book of Job. Augustine also wrote an educational treatise on how one could give basic Christian instruction to uneducated persons. He began another great work, *On the Trinity*, in 399, though it was not finished until 20 years later.

The subjects of the good of marriage and the blessedness of virginity held his attention in 401, as did the issue of the Donatist heresy and the literality of the stories in the Book of Genesis. The Donatists were a deeply fundamentalist group of African Christians who rejected the authority of Rome. Augustine authored the edict against them issued by the Council of Carthage in 405.

In 406, Augustine wrote about identifying demons, and in 407–8 he began a study of St. John the Evangelist. Later in the same period, he listed arguments useful in countering those of pagans and wrote about the utility of fasting in the Christian life. The subjects of baptism, further diatribes against heretics, and continuing an ongoing stream of letters occupied much of 410–12. In the latter year, he addressed the subjects of the grace of the NEW TESTAMENT and the issue of the spirit and the letter in Scripture.

The armies of the Goths, however, had given the world more to think about than the finer points of theological debate. In 408 and 409, the Gothic leader Alaric had twice besieged Rome, cutting off the city and—as the great biographer of St. Augustine, Peter Brown, puts it—starved "its citizens into cannibalism." On August, 24 410, Alaric's hordes broke through the city's defenses. They spent the next three days plundering, raping, and burning. For a time, however, life in Hippo did not seem much affected.

Augustine's greatest work, CONCERNING THE CITY OF GOD AGAINST THE PAGANS, began appearing in serial form in 413. Books 1–3 were published, and Augustine began drafting books 4 and 5.

The year 414 at last saw the appearance of On the Trinity and also a series of Homilies on the Gospel According to St. John. The following year produced a further series of tracts, including one about the perfection of human justice. Books 6–10 of The City of God came out as well.

In 417, The City of God, books 11–13, and anti-Pelagian and anti-Donatist works appeared among other less-important works by Augustine. He clearly took very seriously not only his leadership role in the church but also his role as the pastor of his flock. Among the works that he wrote addressing congregants' concerns were considerations of marriage, sexual desire, and adulterous marriage. Augustine wrote about the soul and its origins and penned a spate of biblical commentary. He reconsidered the subject of lying and criticized the critics of Scripture in such tracts as his Against the Adversaries of the Laws and the Prophets. At the center of his interests during these years, however was The City of God, book 17, which appeared in 420 after books 14–16, which he had also finished in the interim.

Among such other antiheretical tracts as Against Julian and further blasts against the Donatist heretics, the year 421 saw the production of one of St. Augustine's most charming and readable works, his Enchiridion to Laurentius. In this work, in simple and straightforward style, Augustine tells the addressee how to lead a Christian life and avoid the pitfalls of secular controversy and worldly attractions. He also wrote a tract about what a good Christian does to care for the mortal remains of the dead.

The final books of The City of God appeared over the next five years: book 18 in 425, and books 19–22 in 427. These were followed by further arguments against various groups of heretics and against the Jews, which continued to appear as late as 430. Important among the later documents were Augustine's Retractions (427), in which he acknowledged mistakes and commented on matters about which he had changed his mind.

The events that attended on the dissolution of the Western Roman Empire now reached the province of Numidia. The Vandals—like the Goths, another set of Germanic tribesmen—began ravaging the seacoast of Numidia, and in August 430 they besieged Hippo. Augustine fell victim to their attack and was buried on August 28.

Both Augustine and his unofficial literary executor, Possidius, made heroic efforts to catalogue Augustine's works in chronological order with explanatory commentary. Augustine, however, felt that his work as a Christian controversialist took precedence over a private project to catalogue and comment on his own letters and sermons. As a result, he died before that work was finished. Possidius wrote a life of Augustine that contained a definitive list of the saint's formal works of theology.

Between the fifth and the 20th centuries, certainly most and perhaps all of Augustine's original manuscripts perished. Copyists preserved his writings until the advent of the printing press, and thereafter the task passed to editors, translators, and publishers. In his letters, however, much became foreign, strange, and perhaps incomprehensible to the medieval copyists. As a result, as Peter Brown tells us, the copyists abbreviated or altogether neglected certain letters and sermons until many of them disappeared. Almost miraculously, however, some of Augustine's later writings—works thought to have been lost—surfaced quite recently. In 1975, the Viennese scholar Johannes Divjak discovered 27 previously unknown letters of Augustine in a mid-15th century manuscript preserved at Marseilles. In 1990, the Parisian researcher François Dolbeau made a similar find at the Municipal Library in Mainz: 26 sermons that were either unknown or known only through extracts. Some of these date from the beginning of Augustine's bishopric in 397. Others can be traced to the winter of 403–4—a moment when the African Church chose to assert its authority against the Donatist heresy and against persistent paganism.

Bibliography

Augustine, St., Bishop of Hippo. *Augustine's Commentary on Galatians.* Translated by Eric Plumer. New York: Oxford University Press, 2003.

——. *The Augustine Catechism; Enchiridion on Faith, Hope, and Love.* Hyde Park, N.Y.: New City Press, 1999.

——. *The City of God.* Translated by Maureen Dodds. New York: Modern Library, 1993.

——. *Concerning the City of God against the Pagans.* Translated by Henry Bettenson. London and New York: Penguin Books, 2003.

——. *Confessions.* Translated by F. J. Sheed. 2nd ed. Indianapolis: Hackett Publishing Company, 2006.

——. *The Immortality of the Soul; The Magnitude of the Soul; On Music; The Advantages of Believing;* *On Faith in Things Unseen.* Washington, D.C.: Catholic University of America Press, 2002.

——. *Instructing Beginners in the Faith.* Translated by Raymond Canning. Edited by Boniface Ramsay. Hyde Park, N.Y.: New City Press, 2006.

——. *On Christian Teaching.* New York: Oxford University Press, 1997.

——. *Political Writings.* Edited by E. M. Atkins and R. J. Dodaro. New York: Cambridge University Press, 2001.

——. *The Retractions.* Translated by Mary Inez Bogan. Washington, D.C.: Catholic University of America Press, 1999.

——. *Sermons to the People: Advent, Christmas, New Year's, Epiphany.* Translated by William Griffen. New York: Image Books/ Doubleday, 2002.

Brown, Peter. *Augustine of Hippo: A Biography.* Berkeley and Los Angeles: University of California Press, 2000.

O'Donnell, James J. *Augustine: A New Biography.* New York: Ecco of HarperCollins Publishers, 2005.

Augustus Caesar (Octavian, Gaius Julius Caesar Octavianus) (63 B.C.E.–14 C.E.)
Roman emperor, prose writer

The son of a so-called new man (*novus homo*)—that is, of a first-generation senator whose family had just risen from the commonality—Augustus Caesar, born Octavian, enjoyed the advantage that his mother, Atia, was JULIUS CAESAR's niece.

Octavian was a 17-year-old pursuing his studies at Apollonia in Illyricum when his granduncle Julius Caesar was assassinated at the Roman Senate on March 15, 44 B.C.E. Learning that in his will Caesar had named him as his adoptive son and heir, Octavian hurried to Italy to protect his interests. Julius Caesar's subordinate and friend, Mark Antony, (Marcus Antonius), proved reluctant to acknowledge Octavian's rights, but the young man moved decisively to command the loyalty of Caesar's troops. With their help, he outmaneuvered Mark Antony, successfully resisting Antony's attack on the walled city of Mutina (modern Modena) and subsequently seizing the Roman consulship (the headship of state) by force. Once in office, Octavian put the provisions of Caesar's will into effect.

In view of that success, Mark Antony and another aspirant to power, Marcus Aemilius Lepidus, joined forces with the young Octavian, and the three shared the rule of the Roman world. Octavian took over the Roman possessions in Africa and also governed Sicily and Sardinia in the Mediterranean. Antony ruled in Gaul, and Lepidus governed in Spain. Elsewhere in the Roman world, the three defeated their opponents Brutus and Cassius in the East; Sextus Pompey, son of the great Pompey, whom Julius Caesar had driven into Egypt; and also any who dared oppose them on the Italian peninsula itself. In 40 B.C.E., Octavian assumed the title Imperator.

Gradually, Octavian consolidated his power. He forced Lepidus into retirement and misstated the facts concerning Antony's actions in Egypt. This led the credulous Roman Senate to declare war on Antony and his mistress, Queen Cleopatra of Egypt. Rome's navy destroyed Antony and Cleopatra's flotilla at the battle of Actium in 31 B.C.E., and Alexandria was captured the following year. After mopping-up operations were completed, Octavian returned to the city of Rome in 29. For the first time in many years, the Roman world was at peace.

Almost another 10 years were to pass before Octavian felt the time to be right for officially acknowledging that he was the first of a new series of hereditary emperors of Rome. He spent that decade putting in place the institutions that made rule of the Mediterranean world a practical possibility, in the process turning Rome from a sprawling brick town into an imperial city of gleaming marble. He extended the rule of Rome over vast tracts of land by military action, and astute massaging of the diplomatic relationships that Rome maintained with friendly nations made possible the somewhat fictive claim that Rome ruled the known world. Octavian received the title Augustus (esteemed or revered) in 27 B.C.E.

Historians variously date the moment at which Augustus's imperium became hereditary rule to 31 or to 14 B.C.E.—the defeat of Marc Antony in the first instance and the official accession to power of Octavian's adoptive son Tiberius in the second. Tiberius exercised actual power well before Augustus Caesar's death.

From a literary perspective, Augustus is best remembered as a patron of letters. Both VIRGIL and HORACE, for example, benefited from his patronage and his largesse, and literature flourished under his reign. The period of his rule is remembered as the golden age of Roman letters. He also affected the output of OVID, exiling the poet to Tomi on the Black Sea, where Ovid both finished his METAMORPHOSES and composed his TRISTIA.

Also an author himself, Augustus wrote a now-lost autobiography. There survives, however, the record of his public accomplishments that he himself penned to serve as his epitaph. That record was originally engraved on pillars of bronze that stood before his tomb in Rome. The inscriptions were often copied and translated. We still have them both in Latin and in Greek as *Res gestae divi Augusti* (Deeds accomplished by the divine Augustus). Imperial and kingly deification was a standard practice among many ancient Asian, Middle Eastern, Egyptian, and, later, Roman, societies.

Bibliography

Cooley, M. G. L., ed. *The Age of Augustus.* Literary texts translated by B. W. J. G. Wilson. London: London Association of Classical Teachers, 1997.

Everitt, Anthony. *Augustus: The Life of Rome's First Emperor.* New York: Random House, 2006.

Raaflaub, Kurt A., and Mark Tobler, ed. *Between Republic and Empire: Interpretations of Augustus and His Principate.* Berkeley: University of California Press, 1993.

Ausonius, Decimus Magnus (fl. fourth century C.E.) *Roman Poet*

Born to the family of a physician resident in Bordeaux in the Roman province of Transalpine Gaul, Decimus Magnus Ausonius received a typically Roman education in rhetoric and then became a professor of that subject himself. After teaching for almost 30 years, he became tutor to the Roman emperor of the West, Gratian. When Gratian succeeded to the throne, he appointed Ausonius to be the prefect of his Praetorian Guard.

Quite apart from his twin careers as teacher and public official, Ausonius was also a prolific poet of the academic variety. The standard English edition of his principally didactic works runs to almost 800 pages. A glib and easy versifier, he made any subject grist for his poetic mill. His particular forte was writing verse catalogues of events, people, and places. These treated such subjects as his relatives, the consuls of Rome, renowned cities of the world, professors who taught in Bordeaux, and many others. Though his poetic inspiration was pedestrian, his formal expertise was masterly, and he seemingly delighted in overcoming challenges by accomplishing difficult technical feats in verse metrics.

At least two of Ausonius's poems have engaged the interest of subsequent generations of readers. The first of these, his *Mosella,* traces his path on a journey to and along the Moselle River. His descriptions of the things he encounters are genuinely charming. He describes the journey to reach the river, and on arriving, he addresses the river. He then describes the fish that live in it; reflections in the water; scenery, vineyards, and dwellings along the riverbanks; the river's tributaries; and, finally, the river's confluence with the Rhine, where he bids the charming watercourse farewell.

The second poem by Ausonius that has attracted scholarly interest, *Ephemeris,* is one in which he follows his own schedule of activities through a typical day. Historians, however, find more of interest in it than do literary critics.

Ausonius also wrote verse letters and EPIGRAMS. He was a careful and reliable teacher and public servant, grateful for the honors and offices that his pupil, Gratian, heaped upon him late in his life. He did produce creditable prose—as in a paean of thanks to his imperial patron for making Ausonius a consul of Rome. As a poet, however, he mainly proved to be a skillful hobbyist.

Bibliography
Ausonius, Decimus Magnus. *The Works of Ausonius.* Edited by R. P. H. Green. New York: Oxford University Press, 1991.

Avesta (Zoroastrian scriptures)   See
Gāthās

Avianus, Postumius Rufus Fes (fl. ca. fourth century C.E.) *Roman poet*

A translator, poetic geographer, and fabulist, Avianus is best known for rendering into late Latin the astronomical work *Phaenomena kai Diosemaiai* (The Starry Sphere and the Signs of the Weather) by the Greek poet ARATUS OF SOLI. Avianus's version is sometimes entitled *Carmen de Astris* (Song of the stars). Beyond this, he translated into 1,392 Latin hexameters Dionysius of Charax's *Description of the Inhabited World*—a work itself deriving from ERATOSTHENES' geographical writings. He also composed a very long navigational poem designed to lead its reader along the northern coast of the Mediterranean from Cádiz in Spain to the Black Sea. Only 700 lines of this poem survive.

Two other poetic efforts can be confidently ascribed to Avianus. One contains 42 rather amateurish FABLES written in elegiac stanzas (see ELEGY AND ELEGAIC POETRY). The other derives from an eight-verse inscription that he addressed to an Etruscan deity, Nortia. This inscription was discovered in Rome.

Bibliography
Avianus. *The Fables of Avianus.* Translated by David R. Slavitt. Baltimore: Johns Hopkins University Press, 1993.

Eschenburg, J. J. *Manual of Classical Literature.* Translated by N. W. Fiske. Philadelphia: E. C. & J. Biddle, 1850.

B

Bacchae, The Euripides (ca. 407–406 B.C.E.)
Composed shortly before the playwright's death
while EURIPIDES was away from Athens and the
guest of King Archelaus of Macedonia, *The Bacchae* probably was not quite finished by the time
Euripides died. The play focuses on the pre-
Christian mystery religion that celebrated the god
Dionysus.

Dionysus was the offspring of the king of the
gods, Zeus, and a human mother, Zeus's paramour, the Theban princess Semele. Tricked by
Zeus's jealous spouse, the goddess Hera, Semele
asked Zeus to prove his love for her by showing
himself to her in his proper form. Bound by his
own oath to do so, Zeus revealed himself as a flash
of lightning that incinerated Semele. Before this
happened, however, he rescued from her womb
the demigod he and Semele had conceived together, and he enclosed the infant in his own flesh.
Later the child was mysteriously reborn from Zeus
himself and became the god Dionysus.

A cult grew up around this twice-born deity.
Its adherents drank wine, sacrificed the god, and
were purified by the bull's shed blood. Believers
who participated in this ritual were thought to be
cleansed of their sins and, like the god himself, to
undergo a mysterious rebirth. Celebrants practiced their rites in secret, and noninitiates who

dared to observe the Dionysian mysteries ran the
risk of having the frenzied worshippers tear them
to pieces. Such had been the fate of the archetypal
musician-poet ORPHEUS.

A long-standing tradition holds that Euripides
himself either became an adherent of the cult or
had somehow been able to observe its rituals. In
any case, the Dionysian cult and the excesses of
some of its devotees, called Bacchae, provide the
material for this, the last of the playwright's tragedies. It was performed in Athens in 405 B.C.E.

As the play opens, the god Dionysus has
assumed human form and is visiting his mother's
home in Thebes, "The Tomb of the Lightning's
Bride." He has come to Greece to do what he has
already done in Asia, to teach his dances and his
rituals to new worshippers so that men may see
god manifest in the flesh. Dionysus is angry with
the Thebans for scorning his new religion. To
punish Thebes, he has made converts of many of
their women, including the queen mother, Agave.
Her son, Pentheus, the city's ruler, is a chief persecutor of the new faith, and Dionysus intends to
teach him a cruel lesson.

Having acquainted the audience with this
background, Dionysus departs, and 15 women
dressed as his worshippers cautiously take the
stage. When they are sure no one is about, they

begin to perform the Dionysian rites. They sing a series of genuinely lovely lyrics that invite the god to join them. Instead, clad like the singers in the fawn skins that identify Dionysus's worshippers, the blind and ancient prophet Teiresias enters. He demands that someone summon the even more ancient and now-retired king of Thebes, Cadmus, Pentheus's grandfather. Cadmus appears, also clad as a worshipper. The two old men inform the audience that they are the only male Theban worshippers of the god, and they set off together toward the mountains where the rites will be celebrated. They see King Pentheus and his bodyguard approaching, and conceal themselves to eavesdrop.

Pentheus vents his annoyance that this new cult has swept through the women of the town, and he promises to shackle and imprison all he finds participating. He has also heard of the arrival of a stranger claiming to be the god himself. He intends to capture the stranger and execute him for blasphemy. His annoyance redoubles when he discovers his own grandfather, Cadmus, lurking nearby with Teiresias, dressed in fawn skins and crowned with ivy. Pentheus chides Teiresias. The audience hears the chorus accuse Pentheus of sacrilege.

Teiresias tries to convert Pentheus to his point of view, and the chorus and Cadmus second his appeal. Cadmus points out the political advantage of the association of the god with the Theban royal house, and he attempts to crown Pentheus with an ivy wreath. Pentheus refuses, and he exits after sending half his guard to dishonor Teiresias's shrine to the god and the other half to seek out and arrest the stranger calling himself Dionysus. In another round of lovely hymns, the maidens of the CHORUS celebrate the god.

The soldiers reenter with Dionysus among them, and Pentheus returns. The soldiers marvel that Dionysus has come willingly and laughing, and the god's captors announce that the maidens whom the king had already imprisoned have been set free by miraculous means.

Pentheus cross-examines Dionysus. The god poses as a Lydian to whom the Dionysian mysteries have all been divinely revealed. He refuses Pentheus's demand that he recount those mysteries. Only the faithful, he insists, can know such matters. Out of patience, Pentheus orders Dionysus's hair to be cut, takes away his wand of religious office, and has him cruelly bound and imprisoned. Dionysus warns Pentheus that in imprisoning him, he is imprisoning a god, but Pentheus stands firm.

Now the chorus sings songs of worship, rehearsing Euripides' version of the Dionysian rites. As they finish their song, they throw themselves to the earth, and Dionysus, alone and unbound, enters from the castle. He greets his worshippers and bids them rise. He tells them that Pentheus never bound or imprisoned him. Rather, the god has confused Pentheus with an illusion, and the king bound and imprisoned a bull. The god has worked other miracles as well, but Pentheus has not been impressed, and he enters demanding to know how his prisoner escaped.

After more verbal sparring between the god and the king, a messenger arrives from the region of Cithaeron, but he fears to deliver his message until the king assures him of his safety, whatever news he brings. Pentheus agrees, and the messenger reports that he has seen the Bacchae, led by the king's mother and her sisters, who engage in the mysteries, perform miracles, and overcome villagers who attempt to interrupt them in their celebrations. The messenger advises the king to relent and accept the new god. Pentheus resolves to take up arms against the worshippers, and Dionysus warns him not to. Pentheus cannot, however, be dissuaded. At last the god gives up on him and readies Pentheus himself as a sacrifice.

Pentheus suddenly becomes irresolute and experiences difficulty in making decisions as the god leads him on. After more choral hymns, Pentheus, now disguised as a female Bacchante, begins to see Dionysus's shape shift into that of a sacrificial bull. His manner of speaking shifts as well. Dionysus sends the king to his approaching, terrible fate.

The chorus of Bacchae begins singing a hymn presaging the death of uninitiated spies on their mysteries.

A messenger from the mountain where Pentheus has gone now confirms that during the song, the Bacchae have killed the king. The messenger reports the details: The god himself pointed out the interloper to the women. His aunts, Autonoe and Ino, and his own mother, Agave, not recognizing their nephew and son and totally overcome by religious delusion, tore Pentheus apart. This the messenger describes in gory and graphic detail. Agave, the audience learns, is returning with Pentheus's still-unrecognized head impaled upon her wand.

Agave enters, proud of her conquest and thinking that she displays the head of a young lion. She calls for her son Pentheus so that he can mount the lion's head on the palace wall. She shows it to her father Cadmus. Slowly the old man leads her from her religious frenzy and has her look upon the head. At last she recognizes her son and repents her deed.

Just at this point in the play, a page is missing from the manuscript upon which all later editions of *The Bacchae* are based. Editors speculate that the missing page contained a speech by Agave and a deus ex machina appearance of Dionysus in which he probably passed judgment on the city of Thebes for not accepting his divinity. As the text resumes, the god does say that if everyone had acknowledged his divinity in time, all would have been well. Cadmus, Agave, and her sisters all go into voluntary exile. The chorus reminds the audience of the gods' unpredictability.

The unfeeling cruelty of gods in their dealings with men is a theme that emerges more than once in Euripides' later plays. One sees another instance of it, for example, at the end of HELEN, where Zeus rewards his daughter, Helen of Troy, for her cruelty in starting the Trojan War and causing the deaths of so many troublesome mortals, thereby reducing their numbers. It may be that the old playwright had concluded that human beings were merely the playthings of the gods.

Bibliography

Euripides. *Bacchae; Iphegenia at Aulis; Rhesus*. Edited and translated by David Kovacs. Cambridge, Mass.: Harvard University Press, 2002.

Oates, Whitney J., and Eugene O'Neill, Jr., editors. *The Bacchae: The Complete Greek Drama*. Vol. 2. New York: Random House, 1938.

Bacchides (Two Sisters Named Bacchis)
Titus Maccius Plautus (ca. late second century B.C.E.)

Based on MENANDER's play *The Double Deceiver*, of which only traces exist, PLAUTUS's *Bacchides* concerns a pair of twin sisters who have the same name, one living in Athens (Bacchis A) and one dwelling on the island of Samos (Bacchis B). Both are courtesans, and both are consumed with a passion for money. Two young and foolish men, both Athenians, love the women ardently. Pistoclerus loves Bacchis A, and Mnesilochus loves Bacchis B.

As the play opens, Bacchis B arrives from Samos at her sister's house in Athens. We learn that Bacchis B has been employed by a soldier named Cleomachus to serve him exclusively for a year. We also discover that Mnesilochus, who has been away at Ephesus but will soon return, lives next door to Bacchis A. Mnesilochus has written to his friend Pistoclerus asking his help in prying Bacchis B loose from her arrangement with Cleomachus.

The sisters also think that Bacchis B would stand to gain more from involvement with Mnesilochus than with the soldier, so in the first scene they also try to recruit Pistoclerus in scheming against Cleomachus. The scene involves much amorous punning as Bacchis A bends Pistoclerus to her will while keeping his ardor within bounds. He ends up paying for a welcoming banquet for Bacchis B.

The second scene features a debate between Pistoclerus and the slave Lydus, who has also been Pistoclerus's teacher. Striking a series of tragic poses, Lydus reproves his former pupil for his interest in a courtesan and for wasting his father's money. Pistoclerus, of course, ignores the older man's advice.

As act 2 opens, Chrysalus, the slave of Mnesilochus's father, arrives from Ephesus with Mnesilochus. Encountering Pistoclerus, Chrysalus learns that Bacchis B still prefers Mnesilochus to her soldier, and that both sisters are living right next door to Mnesilochus and his father Nicobolus. Pistoclerus explains that Chrysalus must find the money to buy Bacchis B's contract from the soldier Cleomachus. Chrysalus immediately begins to scheme to pry the money out of the father for the son's benefit. He will convince Nicobolus that money actually in Mnesilochus's possession has been banked for safe-keeping.

Much of the attraction of this and other scenes depends upon witty wordplay and on the double takes that Plautus allows his characters as the playwright has them step out of character to comment, for instance, on the acting of the others or on the playwright's talent. Plautus's use of doubling extends beyond reduplicating the roles of his characters to using actors both as participants and as observers.

As the third scene opens, Nicobolus steps out his front door. Chrysalus greets him with the intention of fleecing him of the above-mentioned money Mnesilochus needs. The slave invents a complex cock-and-bull story to convince the old man that the money his son had really collected had been deposited with a rich man in Ephesus to protect the cash from pirates. Chrysalus goes to tell Mnesilochus that he can use the cash. The slave does worry, however, about what will happen when Nicobolus learns of the trick.

Act 3 opens with the lines that the Florentine poet Dante Alighieri borrowed as the motto posted above the gates of Hell in his *Inferno*: "Abandon all hope all who enter here." The moralistic teacher-slave Lydus speaks the lines, comparing the door of Bacchis A's brothel to the gates of Hades and saying that all who enter there have already abandoned all hope. Lydus, addressing the audience, threatens for the second time to tell Pistoclerus's father what his son is up to.

In the second scene, the returning Mnesilochus mouths a series of dull aphorisms in praise of friendship and then encounters Lydus together with his master, Philoxenus, the father of Pistoclerus. Lydus is carrying out his threat and informing on the son. Philoxenus is much more

philosophical about his son's moral lapse than the straitlaced Lydus expected. Lydus responds with a diatribe about the sorry condition of morality and blames the father for approving the son's sensuality. Seeing Mnesilochus, Lydus makes self-deluding and unflattering comparisons between Pistoclerus and his friend. Mnesilochus, Lydus thinks, tends strictly to business.

Lydus tells Mnesilochus about the way that Pistoclerus has behaved in the brothel with Bacchis A, and Mnesilochus mistakenly concludes that his friend has been fondling Bacchis B. He resolves to return the filched money to his father (which he does) and to intercede on behalf of Chrysalus. In the next scene, however, when Mnesilochus confronts Pistoclerus, the matter is cleared up. Both Bacchides are in their house.

As act 4 opens, we meet a stock figure of Roman and Greek comedy, the parasite. He introduces himself as the parasite of the soldier Cleomachus. The parasite is searching for Bacchis B to discover whether she will repay Cleomachus or leave with him. The parasite bangs on a door; Pistoclerus answers, and the parasite states his business. Pistoclerus tells him that Bacchis B will not be returning home and threatens the parasite with a beating. Now, Pistoclerus reflects, Mnesilochus needs money again.

Scene 3 opens with a song sung by Mnesilochus. Ancient drama had many of the characteristics of opera or musical comedy, and Plautus often employs *cantica* (songs). In his aria, Mnesilochus expresses regret at his behavior and its consequences. He really is upset because he does not have the money to buy Bacchis B's contract. Pistoclerus enters and tries unsuccessfully to cheer up his friend. In scene 4, Chrysalus enters, comparing himself favorably with the slave characters who inhabit Greek (as opposed to Roman) comedies. They only manage to provide their masters with small sums, whereas Chrysalus manages large ones. He is flabbergasted to learn that Mnesilochus has returned all the money to his father and kept none for himself. Nonetheless, Chrysalus agrees to bilk his master of enough money to accomplish Mnesilochus's purposes.

Chrysalus has Mnesilochus write his father a letter in which he tells the exact truth about the way in which his son and his slave are plotting to relieve the old man of large sums of cash. Chrysalus instructs Mnesilochus to remind the master of his promise not to beat his slave. Rather, as part of his plot, Chrysalus wants Nicobolus to tie him up.

In scene 6, Chrysalus, who has been wondering how to make his master angry, finds Nicobolus already in that condition. Chrysalus hands over the letter of confession and waits while Nicobolus rushes off to bring assistance and ropes to bind Chrysalus. When he returns with servants from the house, Chrysalus insults Nicobolus and tells him that he will soon be voluntarily giving money away to save his son from danger.

When Nicobolus wants to know the sort of danger that threatens his son, Chrysalus leads him next door. They open the door a crack, and Nicobolus observes the drunken orgy that is in progress with his son as a prime participant. Chrysalus assures him that the girl is no courtesan and promises that Nicobolus will soon learn who she is.

Now in search of Mnesilochus, the boasting soldier Cleomachus appears and he brags to the audience about his martial prowess. Chrysalus tells Nicobolus that the soldier is Bacchis B's husband. The slave manages matters so that Nicobolus promises to buy out the contract for 200 pieces of gold.

In act 4, scene 9, Chrysalus enters spouting verse in EPIC style. He switches to a dirge for King Priam of Troy and then begins declaiming Greek mythology like an orator or lecturer—at once illustrating his own and Plautus's mastery of several literary styles. Chrysalus draws a series of parallels between the fall of Troy and the situation that is beginning to resolve itself under his creative hand. After reading another letter ostensibly from his son, Nicobolus coughs up a second 200 gold coins.

In the meantime, Pistoclerus's father, Philoxenus, enters, reflecting on his own misspent youth and on his reformation. Now Nicobolus enters in a rage. He has learned the truth from Cleomachus and is thoroughly disgusted with himself, his slave, and his son.

The two old men decide to demand the money from the two sisters. They create an uproar at the Bacchides' door, and when the sisters answer, they perceive an opportunity for further profit and behave seductively. Philoxenus succumbs first, admitting that he has fallen in love with Bacchis B. Bacchis A exerts her charm on Nicobolus, and after holding out against it for a time, he also succumbs. The Bacchides lead the fathers inside to share a couch with the women and with their sons.

The comedy ends with the entire company of players assuring the audience that, if the old men had not been worthless since boyhood, they would never have fallen victim to the sisters' charms.

Bibliography

Plautus. *The Two Bacchides*. Translated by Edward H. Sugden. In *The Complete Roman Drama*, vol 2. Edited by George E. Duckworth. New York: Random House, 1942.

———. *Two Sisters Named Bacchis*. Translated by James Tatum. In *Plautus: The Comedies*, vol. 2. Edited by David R. Slavitt and Palmer Bovie. Baltimore and London: Johns Hopkins University Press, 1995.

"Ballad of Sawseruquo, The" (possibly ca. 3000 B.C.E.)

A representative of an ancient body of folklore, the NART SAGAS, the first fragment of "The Ballad of Sawseruquo" tells of how the Nart hero Sawseruquo stole a firebrand from and then overcame and destroyed a seemingly invincible giant. As it now exists, the story is told in the Circassian language.

The Narts, a group of legendary protohumans, are freezing and need fire, so Sawseruquo steals a firebrand from a sleeping giant. On awakening and missing the firebrand, the giant, who is a shape-shifter, stretches himself in all directions until he overtakes Sawseruquo on his winged steed, but the giant does not know him. The giant threatens to eat the man he finds if he will not tell him what sort of man Sawseruquo is.

Sawseruquo, who has much in common with tricksters in many folk traditions, promises to teach the giant about his quarry's games and amusements. These games involve a series of attempts to destroy the giant; but the trickster insists that he is merely showing the giant ways to have fun. First Sawseruquo throws an iron meteorite at the giant's head, but the giant easily butts it away and thinks this iron sphere-butting game is fun. Then Sawseruquo shoots white-hot arrows into the giant's mouth; the giant chews them up and spits them out, not only finding the game to be jolly, but also claiming that it has cured his sore throat. Next the giant swallows red-hot plowshares and vomits them up with no harm and much amusement. At his wits' end, Sawseruquo explains a game that involves standing in the deepest spot in "seven turbulent seas" where the giant cannot touch bottom. The giant must stand there for seven days and nights, allowing the water to freeze around him. He does, and then he heaves and sets himself free.

Sawseruquo explains that the giant has not waited long enough, and that if he allows the ice to set more firmly, it will increase his strength. The giant, who seems to be a mental dwarf, agrees. This time he cannot free himself. Sawseruquo mounts his winged horse and flies off to get the giant's sword. At last, too late, the giant recognizes both his own folly and the identity of Sawseruquo.

Returning with the sword, Sawseruquo lops off the giant's head. He then takes the stolen firebrand to those of the Narts who have survived both cold and heat while he has been away.

The recent translator of many Caucasian Nart Sagas, John Colarusso, has pointed out the similarities between this story and Prometheus's theft of fire in Greek myth (see PROMETHEUS BOUND). The confrontation between Sawseruquo and the giant is also reminiscent of Gilgamesh and Enkidu's conquest of the giant Humbaba in the Hittite EPIC OF GILGAMESH.

Bibliography

Colarusso, John. *Nart Sagas from the Caucasus: Myths and Legends from the Circassians, Abazas, Abkhaz, and Ubykhs*. Princeton, N.J.: Princeton University Press, 2002.

Ban Gu, Ban Biao, and Ban Zhao   See *HISTORY OF THE FORMER HAN DYNASTY*.

Basil, St.   (ca. 329–370 C.E.)

Born to an upper-class Christian family at Pontus in Asia Minor, Basil received a Roman patrician's education at Constantinople and Athens. Employed as an imperial administrator until about 358, Basil gave up his career to join other members of his family at Amnesi in Pontus. There the family all dwelled together as Christian ascetics in a community led by Eustathius of Sebaste. A strong supporter of the Nicene Creed, Basil was ordained a priest in 365. Five years later, he became a bishop, and throughout the rest of his life he attempted to repair certain of the doctrinal divisions that seemed to plague every religious community at that time.

From a literary perspective, Basil, who followed the teachings of ORIGEN, first compiled an anthology of the latter's works—the *Philocalia of Origen*. He next drew from the NEW TESTAMENT a collection of 1,533 verses addressing the subject of morals and proper behavior—his *Moralia*. Over time, he prefaced that compilation with two essays: "On the Judgment" and "On the Faith."

To young people still very much under the sway of Hellenistic polytheism, he addressed a celebrated work *Ad adolescentes, de legendis libris Gentilium* (To young men on [the subject of] reading the books of the Gentiles). This work discussed the utility of the Pagan classics to a Christian education and remained influential well into the European Renaissance.

Basil next turned his attention to the exposition of orthodox dogma, writing against the Arian heresy in three treatises contradicting the position taken by their apologist, Eunomius of Constantinople. This was followed by a work on the Holy Spirit (*De Spiritu Sancto*). Basil's most notable work—one that became a model for many that followed—is entitled *On the Hexameron.* Concerning the six days of creation as reported in the Bible, and incorporating into that explanation the views of Greek science, Basil attempted to account for the creation and processes of the universe. Over 300 of Basil's letters also survive, as do a number of his sermons and works of dubious attribution.

The Roman Catholic Church venerates as saints not only Basil himself but also several other members of his immediate family.

Bibliography

Basil, Saint, Bishop of Caesarea. *Ascetical Works.* Translated by Monica Wagner. Washington, D.C.: Catholic University of America Press, 1980.

———. *On the Holy Spirit: St. Basil the Great.* Translated by David Anderson. Crestwood, N.Y.: St. Vladimir's Seminary Press, 1980.

———. *On the Human Condition* [Sermons]. Translated by Nonna Verna Harrison. Crestwood, N.Y.: St. Vladimir's Seminary Press, 2005.

———. *St. Basil on the Value of Greek Education.* Edited by N. C. Wilson. London: Duckworth, 1975.

Bhagavad Gita Vyāsa (ca. 1500 B.C.E.; current form ca. 150 C.E.)

The Bhagavad Gita is a 701-line portion of the fifth book of the immense Indian EPIC, the MAHABHARATA. Its attribution to VYĀSA is traditional and probably reflects the customary submergence of the individual identities of ancient Indian poets in a Vyāsan persona. There is no way to be sure, but it seems likely that the poem, at least in the form we have it, was composed around the second century C.E.

The Bhagavad Gita, in any case, is sometimes called The Song of God, though its theological ramifications need not concern us here. It is nonetheless one of the most popular of all Indian liturgical passages and nurtures the spiritual lives of millions of people in India and elsewhere, in addition to supporting their devotion to high standards of truth and fairness. From a Hindu perspective, the verses of the Bhagavad Gita are canonical and have the authority of Scripture. Others find in it a work that calls for a mystical or an ascetic interpretation. Still others examine it for its philosophical and dialectical implications. Here we focus on the narrative.

The poem is organized as a series of questions and answers. The first exchange occurs between the questioner, the blind king Dhritarashtra, and Sanjaya, one of the three narrators of the *Mahabharata.* In answer to Dhritarashtra, Sanjaya is describing the events taking place on the sacred battlefield of Kurukshetra. There two enormous armies are drawn up and awaiting the command to commence hostilities.

Sanjaya names the heroes of the opposing force and then the commanders of his own forces. Then the order is given for the troops to form ranks, and as they do, trumpets blow and kettledrums sound. As in such Western medieval battle epics as *The Song of Roland,* the trumpets, here made of conch shell, have names: Endless Victory, Honey Tone, and Jewel Blossom. The enormous noise heartens the troops, and as the battle is about to begin, the reader meets two of the poem's principal heroes: Krishna (the Hindu deity) and Arjuna. Getting Arjuna to fight is the main narrative object of the poem.

Arjuna has Krishna drive him out in Arjuna's chariot to reconnoiter so that Arjuna can know his enemy before fighting. Arjuna finds his kinsmen facing each other in the ranks of both armies. Disheartened by this discovery, Arjuna refuses to fight, saying that he will not kill his kinsmen lest he destroy his own happiness. He understands that his kinsmen's minds are clouded by greed, but, unlike them, Arjuna and Krishna recognize the immorality of the contest. Arjuna prefers to die at their hands rather than participate in his kinsmen's sinful folly. He flings away his bow and quiver and refuses to fight.

Krishna reproves Arjuna's decision as "unmanly and disgraceful." Moreover, it is at odds with heavenly will. Arjuna implores the divine Krishna for grace and illumination. Arjuna wants what is best, but he is determined not to fight.

Krishna preaches Arjuna a lengthy sermon about the temporality of the physical person and the indestructibility of the atman (soul) that vivifies the body. The true self, Krishna insists, can neither slay nor be slain. "As a person throws away [old] clothes and puts on [new]," so the "embodied Self throws away this lifetime's body and enters another that is new." If Arjuna persists in his cowardly behavior, he will lose his dignity and leave his fate unfulfilled. He must fight. His mind must achieve poise, and he must be calm, steady, and free from desire. When he brings himself under appropriate control, he will achieve tranquility and overcome sorrow. He will find eternal unity with Bhraman.

Arjuna, however, finds Krishna's sermon confusing, so Krishna attempts clarification. He explains that each person must follow either the contemplative Yoga of knowledge, or the Yoga of action and work. Arjuna's path is that of action. He must work, but work selflessly to avoid the traps set by selfish action. He must crush both hope and ego, and he must fight.

Arjuna has now become interested in the moral implications of Krishna's discourse and asks what drives people to do evil despite what they truly wish. Krishna replies that greed and anger destroy judgment, dwelling in the senses and the intellect. Krishna describes the following ascending hierarchy: flesh, senses, mind, intellect, and atman.

Krishna now reveals to Arjuna that, though both of them have lived through many incarnations, Krishna, because he is divine, can remember all his. Arjuna cannot. Krishna is at once man and the god who comes in every age to "protect the good and destroy the wicked." Krishna now explores a series of seeming contradictions, explaining how all of them are resolved if a person overcomes his senses; understands the true nature of work; avoids ignorance, disrespect, and disbelief; and finds strength in discipline.

Still not clear about the best way to follow, Arjuna asks Krishna if renunciation or activity is the better course. Krishna says that both are good, but work is better. Either path followed selflessly leads to tranquility. Greed spoils both. Those who selflessly focus on the atman recog-

nize Krishna as "the giver of ritual and religious discipline, the creator of the three worlds, and the refuge of all beings" will find peace, escaping the continual cycle of rebirth.

In the next section of the poem, Krishna focuses on the benefits of meditation. Then he turns to the benefits that accrue from worshipping Krishna and the kinds of persons who can successfully do so. These include those who sorrow, those who seek truth, those who seek bliss, and those who are wise. Few people achieve wisdom. Those who do achieve it recognize that all things come into being during the eons-long "day of Brahman," and all things cease to be during the eons-long "night of Brahman."

Now Krishna reveals to Arjuna his true nature, at once immanent and transcendent. He describes himself as "the ritual . . . the sacred gift . . . the holy food . . . the sacred fire . . . and offering . . . the father and mother of the world . . . the goal of knowledge . . . Om . . . the supporter . . . the refuge . . . the lord . . . the silent witness . . . the origin . . . the dissolution . . . the storehouse and the seed . . . death and salvation . . . what is and what is not."

All who worship, Krishna says, even though they may not know it, worship him. Therefore Arjuna should immerse himself in thoughts of Krishna.

Convinced by what Krishna has taught him, Arjuna confesses his faith. Yet he still wishes to know more and asks Krishna to explain his divine powers. Krishna agrees to explain them "in orderly form." These powers are many, involving numerous manifestations in the form of gods, scriptures, such human faculties as intelligence, and such animal faculties as consciousness. Krishna is priest and worshipper, the sun and the ocean, the Himalayas, the fig tree, the best of horses, the strongest of elephants, the thunderbolt, the crocodile, the Ganges, the first principle, and so forth. It is sufficient for Arjuna, however, simply to know that Krishna exists and that he sustains the world.

Converted now, Arjuna prays that Krishna will reveal himself in his supreme form. Krishna endows Arjuna with godlike vision so that he may see Krishna in his true form and glory. In the lengthy passage that follows, Arjuna describes what he sees, and the awesome nature of his vision destroys the inner peace he had achieved, for he has seen Krishna not only as the creative but also as the destructive principle in the universe. Arjuna calls for pity.

Krishna now commands Arjuna, telling him that, even if he refuses to fight, none of the enemy soldiers he pities will survive. Krishna tells Arjuna to destroy them and enjoy their kingdom. Arjuna falls down before Krishna and worships him, begging him now to show him his peaceful form. Again Krishna complies, and Arjuna regains his composure.

Before he fights, however, Arjuna craves further instruction. Krishna willingly provides it, explaining the nature of knowledge and the knowable. He grants the knowledge that makes achieving perfection possible. He continues, explaining divine and demonic natures as they appear in people. He also explains the utility of the scriptures and the three devotions.

When Krishna finally explains the way of salvation, Arjuna has learned all he needs to know and at last agrees to follow Krishna's instructions. He will fight.

Bibliography

Chatterjee, R. K. *The Gita and Its Culture.* New Delhi: Sterling Publications, 1987.

Vyāsa. *The Bhagavad Gita.* Translated by P. Lal. Kolkata, India: Writers' Workshop, 1968.

———. *The Bhagavad Gita: The Original Sanskrit and an English Translation.* Translated by Lars Martin Fosse. Woodstock, N.Y.: YogaVida.com, 2007.

Bible   See HEBREW BIBLE; NEW TESTAMENT.

biography, Greek and Roman

Several sorts of works with varying degrees of biographical focus appeared in ancient Greece and Rome. Particularly notable among the Greco-Roman works was PLUTARCH's *PARALLEL LIVES*, in which the Greek historian paired a biographical sketch of a notable Roman with one about a famous Greek. As the classicist C. B. R. Pelling points out, however, biographical writing appeared in many genres among both Greeks and Romans.

Such genres included EPICS like HOMER's *The ODYSSEY*, in which a largely fictive and mythological narrative centers on the partly true events in the life of an historical individual. Pelling also points to funeral orations and dirges as forms of biographical writing that celebrated the accomplishments of the deceased. Included in Pelling's list are Ion of Chios (ca. 480–421 B.C.E.) and Stesimbrotus of Athens (fl. fifth century B.C.E.). Ion reports his conversations with such famous persons as AESCHYLUS and SOPHOCLES in his *Visits*. Stesimbrotus's surviving fragments give particulars about the Athenian politicians Themistocles and Pericles. The biographer reputedly wrote about THUCYDIDES as well, but no example of that work has survived.

XENOPHON OF ATHENS's *CYROPÆDIA* and his *Memorabilia*, which dealt respectively with the education of the Persian ruler Cyrus and with the death of SOCRATES, proved important in their own right and also as examples for later writers to follow. Numerous quasi-political biographies dealing with such figures as Alexander the Great looked to Xenophon as a model, mixing the writing of biography with praise. PLATO's accounts of Socrates' life and conversations in several dialogues also contributed a string to biography's lyre. Pelling credits ARISTOTLE with contributing cultural and ethical history to the concerns of biographers. In picturing Socrates as notoriously ill-tempered and Plato as a plagiarist, the celebrated musician and musical theorist Aristoxenus of Tarentum (fl. fourth century B.C.E.) contributed the maliciously scandalous story to the biographer's arsenal.

The sort of biographies about writers that, when little is actually known about their subjects, draw unsupported inferences from the writers' works may be traceable to a writer on the lives of poets, Chamaeleon of Heraclea (fl. sixth–fifth century B.C.E.). References to one such work survive, but the work itself is lost.

Once the HELLENISTIC AGE got underway in Alexandria, Egypt, scholars at the Ptolemaic library there introduced a mode of biographical writing in which brief notes about a famous person's life, acquaintances, associates, and so forth introduced scholarly commentaries on the subject's works. A particularly interesting example of later Greek biography is THE LIFE OF APOLLONIUS OF TYANA by L. FLAVIUS PHILOSTRATUS (Philostratus the Athenian). The book tells of a pagan Greek wise man whose career in many ways parallels that of Jesus Christ—most notably describing Apollonius's resurrection from the dead. An early Platonist critic of Christianity, Celsus (fl. late second century C.E.), accused the Christians of borrowing for the emergent Christian scriptures' accounts of Apollonius's raising the dead, of his having himself been resurrected, and of his having ascended bodily into heaven. The work also displays characteristics of hagiography—biographies of the lives of saints, which would become standard Christian fare. Philostratus also composed a series of *Lives of the Sophists* that included portraits of rhetoricians and orators from the time of Protagoras in the fifth century B.C.E. until the early third century C.E.

DIOGENES LAERTIUS's discussion of the lives and writings of 82 Greek philosophers and other notable persons has been transmitted to us in 10 books (manuscript scrolls). Among these, Book 3 deals exclusively with PLATO and Book 10 with EPICURUS.

Differences in the practices and emphases of national biography arose from the divergent histories and customs of the Greeks and the Romans. In terms of genre, however, one naturally finds many overlaps. Funeral orations, for example, extolled the departed. Autobiography featuring political spin appears in works such as JULIUS CAESAR's COMMENTARY ON THE GALLIC WARS (*De bello Gallico*).

Roman emperors also often wrote a species of autobiography. Numbered among such imperial authors we find AUGUSTUS CAESAR, his successor Tiberius, Claudius, Hadrian, and MARCUS AURELIUS ANTONINUS. Writing in Greek, the last-named emperor most closely approximated the modern autobiography of self-exploration and discovery in his *To Himself* (MEDITATIONS). A succession of civil servants, the "writers of imperial history," found employment penning the lives of Roman emperors from Hadrian to Carinus.

Competing politicians or their surrogates wrote quasi-biographical sketches focusing on the failings of their opponents or on their own or their constituents' virtues. A fiery exchange of such political biography appeared after the death of Marcus Porcius Cato, the staunchest defender of the Roman Republic and its constitution. Cato had committed suicide rather than accept Caesar's pardon for opposing him. CICERO and Iunius Brutus wrote panegyrics (poems of praise) honoring the great republican. These were answered by Caesar himself and by his aide-de-camp, Hirtius, who had also written the eighth book of Caesar's *Gallic Wars*.

Among other Roman biographers we find the name of MARCUS TERENTIUS VARRO—ancient Rome's most important and productive scholar. Varro penned some 700 biographical sketches (*Imagines*) of famous Greeks and Romans, appending an appropriate EPIGRAM to each. He also compiled the lives of many famous poets.

St. JEROME—himself no mean biographer, as his *On Illustrious Men* demonstrates—named Cornelius Nepos (ca. 110–24 B.C.E.) and SUETONIUS among others as Roman biographers worthy of note. Though the surviving works of Nepos are fragmentary, we know that they originally included about 400 lives of illustrious men, many of whom were military and not all of whom were Roman. Suetonius also wrote about famous men. He sorted his subjects into categories that included historians, orators, philosophers, grammarians, and rhetoricians. Though this work does not entirely survive, St. Jerome borrowed from it some of his own examples of poets, orators, and historians.

The cruelty of punishment in the Roman world, especially as it was practiced by deranged men such as the tyrant emperor Nero, gave rise to another subcategory of biography—works focusing on the fortitude of the martyred as they died. Often, as in the case of Christian martyrs, these works expanded to include discussion of the exemplary lives the faithful led before being crucified, torn by wild beasts, burned, or sacrificed in unequal contests against professional gladiators. Not all martyrs, however, were by any means Christian. Death was a regular part of Roman spectacle, and philosophical pagan martyrs had also died during the pre-Christian era. Accounts of such heroic passings became popular, and when the arenas did not fulfill the public appetite for stories of martyrdom, the genre moved from biography to fictive romance.

Bibliography

Caesar, Julius. *The Conquest of Gaul*. Translated by F. P. Long. New York: Barnes and Noble Books, 2005.

———. *The Gallic War*. Translated by H. J. Edwards. Mineola, N.Y.: Dover Publications, 2006.

Cicero, Marcus Tullius. *Cicero on Oratory and Orators*. Translated and edited by J. S. Watson. Carbondale: Southern Illinois Press, 1986.

Diogenes Laertius. *Lives of Eminent Philosophers* [Greek and English]. Translated by R. D. Hicks. 2 vols. New York: G. P. Putnam's Sons, 1925.

Jerome, Saint. *On Illustrious Men*. Translated by Thomas P. Halton. Washington, D.C.: Catholic University of America Press, 1999.

Marcus Aurelius. *Meditations*. Translated by Maxwell Stansforth. London and New York: Penguin Books, 2005.

Nepos, Cornelius. *A Selection, Including the Lives of Cato and Atticus*. New York: Oxford University Press, 1989.

Pelling, C. B. R. "Biography, Greek" and "Biography, Roman." In *The Oxford Classical Dictionary*, 3rd ed. Edited by Simon Hornblower and Antony Spawforth. Oxford: Oxford University Press, 1996.

Philostratus the Athenian. *Apollonius of Tyana*. Edited and translated by Christopher P. Jones.

Cambridge, Mass.: Harvard University Press, 2006.

Plato. *The Last Days of Socrates*. Translated by Hugh Tredennick and Harold Tarrant. New York: Penguin Books, 2003.

Plutarch. *The Lives of the Noble Grecians and Romans*. Translated by John Dryden with revisions by Arthur Hugh Clough. New York: The Modern Library, 1932. Reprinted as *Greek and Roman Lives*. Mineola, N.Y: Dover Publications, 2005.

———. *Plutarch's Lives* [Greek and English]. 11 vols. Translated by Bernadotte Perrin. Cambridge, Mass.: Harvard University Press, 1959.

Varro, Marcus Terentius. *Opere di Marco Terenzio Varro* (Works of Marcus Terentius Varro). Edited and translated into Italian by Antonio Traglia. Torino: Unione tipografico editrice torinese, 1974.

Xenophon. *Cyropaedia* [Greek and English]. 2 vols. Edited and translated by Walter Miller. Cambridge, Mass.: Harvard University Press, 1953.

———. *The Shorter Socratic Writings*. Translated and edited by Robert C. Bartlett. Ithaca, N.Y.: Cornell University Press, 1996.

———. *Xenophon's Cyrus the Great: The Arts of Leadership and War* [Selections]. Edited by Larry Hedrick. New York: Truman Talley Books, 2006.

Bion of Smyrna (fl. ca. 100 B.C.E.) *Greek poet*

A lesser pastoral poet often named with—but never thought to equal—THEOCRITUS, Bion of Smyrna is more often considered a peer of another bucolic poet, MOSCHUS OF SYRACUSE. Bion's surviving work includes a substantial fragment of a pastoral poem in the Doric dialect of ancient Greek. In it, a shepherd responds to the request of his colleague by singing about the love of the hero Achilles for Deidameia, the daughter of Lycomedes.

One complete poem also survives. This work laments the death of the beautiful youth Adonis, who was cherished both by the goddess of love, Aphrodite, and by the queen of the underworld,

Persephone. Zeus decrees that the deified Adonis (known in Syria as Thamuz) should be annually resurrected, spending part of the year on Earth and part in Hades. Adonis is one of many pre-Christian, resurrected deities of the Mediterranean world. An anonymous Greek hand later imitated Bion's poem.

Bion died by poisoning, and his death inspired an anonymous lament for the poet. That poem became the model for the 17th-century English poet John Milton's more powerful threnody, *Lycidas*.

See also PASTORAL POETRY.

Bibliography
Bion of Phlossa near Smyrna. *Bion of Smyrna: The Fragments and the Adonis*. Edited by J. D. Reed. New York: Cambridge University Press, 1997.

Birds, The Aristophanes (414 B.C.E.)

The most celebrated of ARISTOPHANES' utopian comedies, *The Birds* won the second prize at the GREAT DIONYSIA in the year of its first performance. In this inventive drama, Euripides imagines that two Athenians, Euelpides and Pithetaerus, have become so frustrated with Athens that they have decided to initiate a movement to put the birds in charge of the universe. To that end, each man has acquired a bird as a guide to help them find Tereus, a human being who was changed into a bird, usually called a hoopoe. In this play, however, Tereus has become the character Epops—from the hoopoe's Greek ornithological name *upupa epops*. Euelpides has a jay and Pithetaerus a crow.

The play opens with the two Athenians trudging along, guided by the birds perched on their shoulders. Complaining that they are lost and cannot now find their way home, both men become aware that their birds are trying to get their attention. Hearing birds in the vicinity, Euelpides shouts, "Epops!" A huge bird named Trochilus appears from a thicket, inquiring who is calling his master. The men are so startled that their bowels evacuate. They learn that Trochilus, too, has once been a man, the slave of Tereus. When Tereus changed into a hoopoe, Trochilus became a "slave bird" so he could continue to serve Tereus. In the confusion, the birds that have guided the Athenians to their destination have flown away, and the travellers find themselves in the presence of Epops/Tereus.

Euelpides and Pithetaerus explain that they want Tereus to advise them where to settle, and they describe the sort of society they seek. They want a place where hospitality is so widespread that they seldom need to purchase food or prepare meals, a place where parents are offended when their friends *do not* take amorous liberties with their children,

Epops makes a pair of suggestions, but the Athenians reject them. They wonder what life among the birds might be like. Epops makes it sound attractive, and Pithetaerus suggests that the birds found a city in the sky and require tribute from human beings for allowing the smoke of their sacrifices to ascend through the air. Epops likes the idea and suggests calling a parliament of the birds, who, he says, he has taught to speak since becoming one of them. He speaks to Procne, who was changed from a woman into a nightingale, and she warbles a beautiful song. Epops himself then sings an invitation to the birds of the air to gather. Members of the CHORUS in costumes representing different birds come flocking in.

When the birds discover that hated human beings are present, they decide to peck them to pieces and deal with Tereus/Epops later. The Athenians are terrified, but Epops persuades the birds to listen to the men's proposal. The birds agree, and the Athenians begin their speeches. The birds, they say, existed before the gods or even before the earth, and they cite AESOP as their authority. With example after far-fetched example and authority after irrelevant authority, the two convince their feathered listeners that the primeval and natural masters of the universe were birds. By degrees, however, the birds' primacy has been so far forgotten that now they are prey for humans and disregarded except as a food source or a nuisance.

The Athenians' far-fetched yarn and their flattery earn the confidence of the birds, and the birds ask how they can regain their earlier ascendancy. (Throughout this section, Aristophanes is clearly satirizing people who uncritically accept whatever myths and authorities fit in with their belief system.) The Athenians advise that, first, the birds must build a brick wall around the entire region of space that separates the heavens from the earth and demand that the gods restore their empire. They are also to require that no man can sacrifice to a god without at the same time making an appropriate sacrifice to a bird—a sacrifice like that of a male gnat to a wren.

What will happen, the birds ask, if men refuse to recognize their deity? Sparrows, the Athenians reply, must then eat up all the human beings' seed corn. The goddess Demeter's failure to replace it should convince people of the birds' divinity. Other convincers include having birds peck the eyes out of farmyard animals and fowls. When the gods cannot restore sight, people will realize the truth.

The Athenians further propose, however, that the birds not merely punish people for failing to recognize their divinity, but rather that the birds also win human allegiance by rewarding their beliefs. The birds will identify the richest mines, predict the weather before sea voyages, and reveal the location of hidden treasures. These prospects so excite Euelpides that he announces his intention to buy a trading vessel and a spade to dig treasure.

Pithetaerus also recommends that the birds promise to add 300 years to the human life span. Euelpides is now utterly persuaded that birds will be better gods and kings than the Olympian pantheon. Pithetaerus also describes the benefits that will accrue from not having to build temples and from needing to sacrifice only a few kernels of grain. All agree to make their demands of the gods and to explain to human beings the benefits of recognizing the birds as their gods.

Pithetaerus and Euelpides have left the stage during the chorus's demanding and explaining, and the two now return to the stage, having grown wings in the interim. They decide on a name for the new city that the birds are building in the air. It is to be called Nephelococcygia (Cloud-Cuckoo City), and its patron goddess will be Athena Polias (senile Athena)—satiric barbs at Aristophanes' fellow Athenian citizens.

No sooner has the city been established, however, than members of what Aristophanes considered to be the parasitic classes begin to arrive and ply their trades. First a priest comes, then a poet. Next, a seller of oracles arrives on the scene, closely followed by a real estate developer who wishes to survey the plains of the air and parcel them out into lots. An inspector comes and then a dealer in decrees. Pithetaerus beats them off. Then a messenger comes to report that the city's wall has been built. He describes the ingenious construction methods that various breeds of birds have invented to make the wall a reality.

Lowered from a machine, Iris, the Olympian goddess of the rainbow and the gods' messenger to mankind, passes through Nephelococcygia on her way to instruct people what sacrifices they must offer the Olympians. The birds accost her, explaining that they have taken over as gods. Iris warns the birds not to arouse the wrath of the Olympians, and the machine flies her away.

A herald announces that bird mania has seized the human population, whose members are now imitating birds in everything. He tells the birds that they can expect an immigration of 10,000 people. Pithetaerus, who is the city's leader, instructs that wings be prepared for the new immigrants.

The first to arrive is a parricide who wants to kill his father and take his wealth. Pithetaerus dissuades him, gives him black wings, and sends him off to be a soldier in Thrace. Next, the poet Cinesias arrives and, over Pithetaerus's strenuous objections, insists on reciting his dull verse. He is not qualified for wings. An informer arrives who wants wings to help him gather fodder for lawsuits and denunciations. Pithetaerus whips him away.

The Titan Prometheus (see TITANS), masked to conceal his identity from a vengeful Zeus, next arrives. Prometheus, who was always a friend of mankind, has now decided to befriend the birds, and he warns Pithetaerus that both the Olympian gods and the barbarian gods, whom he lumps under the term *Triballi*, are sending emissaries to sue for peace with the birds because people have ceased sacrificing to the old deities. Prometheus advises refusal until the gods give the symbol of their office, the scepter, to the birds and until they give a woman named Basilea to Pithetaerus in marriage. Then, borrowing an umbrella to shield him from the gaze of Zeus, Prometheus departs.

Now the emissaries of the gods arrive: Poseidon, Heracles, and Triballus. After some mock disagreement, the emissaries agree to the conditions that Prometheus counseled. Equipped with the scepter of Zeus and clad in a splendid robe, Pithetaerus marries Basilea and becomes the new king of the gods—who are now the birds.

Bibliography

Aristophanes. *The Complete Plays*. Translated by Paul Roche. New York: New American Library, 2005.

Boethius, Anicius Manlius Severinus

(St. Severinus) (480–526 C.E.) *Roman prose writer, poet*

Also known in the Roman Catholic hagiology as Saint Severinus, Boethius, the vastly influential polymath and statesman of the late Roman Empire, was the scion of a Roman patrician family, the Anicia. When his father died during his boyhood, Boethius was reared in the family of another influential Roman, the prefect and senator Quintus Aurelius Memmius Symmachus. Symmachus saw to Boethius's careful education in the fields of language, literature, mathematics, and philosophy. Boethius eventually married Symmachus's daughter, Rusticiana. Possibly also

through the influence of Symmachus, Boethius early came to the attention of the Ostrogothic conqueror and king of Italy, Theoderic, who employed Boethius in a series of increasingly responsible public offices.

In the year 510, at the age of 30, Boethius served as sole consul—Rome's most prestigious but by this time mainly ceremonial office. Thereafter, however, he headed the civil service of Rome and became the chief of the officials who served Theoderic's court. In 522, Theoderic further honored Boethius by appointing his two sons to serve together as the consuls of Rome.

The continual bickering of sixth-century Christians over the abstruse question of whether or not Christ was or was not of one substance with God the Father seems to have initiated the series of events that eventually led to Boethius's downfall. Theoderic was an Arian Christian, a position deemed heretical by Western Christianity, but one that had been supported in the late fifth century by the Byzantine patriarch Acacius. The eastern and western branches of the church split on the issue in 484, and Boethius's desire to see the empire unified again seems to have given his enemies an opening to undermine Theoderic's confidence in his chief official. Perhaps Theoderic suspected him of sympathizing with the persecution of Arians. In any case, Boethius's enemies accused him of corruption in office and perhaps of treason. Boethius claimed that their evidence was falsified, but he was nonetheless found guilty and sentenced to death.

Boethius exercised his right of appeal to the Roman Senate, and while that appeal was pending and he was in prison, he wrote his most celebrated work, *The CONSOLATION OF PHILOSOPHY*. In that work, in whose pages Boethius conducts a dialogue with Lady Philosophy, he not only comforts himself as he faces his own mortality, but in a series of lyrics he also reveals himself to be a gifted poet. In due course, the Senate found, not surprisingly, for the king's view of Boethius's guilt, and Boethius was first tortured and then clubbed to death in the city of Pavia.

Mastery of the Greek language had become unusual among sixth-century Romans, but Boethius had learned the language thoroughly. Fearing that ancient Greek philosophy was an endangered species, Boethius undertook to rescue it by setting himself the ambitious goal of translating all of PLATO and all of ARISTOTLE. Though he failed to achieve that objective fully, he nonetheless did translate and comment on the scholar and philosopher PORPHYRY's *Introduction to the Categories of Aristotle*. He also completed translations of Aristotle's treatises on logic, including *Analytics*, both *Prior* and *Posterior*, *On Interpretation*, and *Topics*. He also commented on CICERO's *Topics*.

Boethius's interests extended as well to music and mathematics, and he prepared textbooks on both these subjects. The one on music was still in use as late as the 18th century, and those on mathematics and number theory served for 1,000 years as important school texts. Beyond that, he may also have written on astronomy.

It would be difficult to exaggerate Boethius's intellectual importance to the Middle Ages and to the Renaissance. His *Consolation of Philosophy* attracted such distinguished translators as King Alfred the Great, who rendered it into Anglo-Saxon, and Geoffrey Chaucer, who provided a similar service for the readers of Middle English. More importantly, in addition to his own contributions to the field of logic, Boethius's translations and commentaries on Aristotle and Porphyry were the principal vehicles that preserved any knowledge of Aristotle for the European Middle Ages. Medieval debates concerning the nature of reality were grounded in Boethius's remarks about Porphyry. A much-quoted description of uncertain origin fixes the place of Boethius in the intellectual edifice of the Western world. The quotation proposes that he was "the last of the Romans" and "the first of the scholastics."

Bibliography

Boethius. *Boethian Number Theory: A Translation of the De institutione arithmetica*. Translated by Michael Mann. Amsterdam: Rodopi, 1983.

———. *The Consolation of Philosophy*. Translated by Richard H. Green. Minneola, N.Y.: Dover, 2002.

———. *Fundamentals of Music*. Translated by Calvin M. Bower. New Haven, Conn.: Yale University Press, 1989.

———. *In Ciceronis Topica* [On the *Topics* of Cicero]. Translated by Eleanore Stump. Ithaca, N.Y.: Cornell University Press, 1988

———. *On Aristotle On Interpretation: 1st and 2nd Commentaries*. Translated by Norman Kretzman. London: Duckworth, 1998.

Herberman, Charles G., et al. "Boethius." *The Catholic Encyclopedia*. Vol. 2. New York: The Encyclopedia Press, 1913, pp. 153–160.

Book of Changes (Yijing, I ching)
(ca. 800 B.C.E)

Originally thought to have been composed by the founder of the Chou dynasty, King Wen, and at first a work separate from Confucian doctrine, over time the *Yijing—Book of Changes*—became incorporated into the Confucian canon as one of its five classic documents. The *Book of Changes* fulfills a function not performed by the other four Confucian foundational documents.

As it now exists, the heart of the work is a handbook for foretelling the future directions of the universe. The handbook contains brief, cryptic predictions organized under a series of 64 hexagrams composed of broken and unbroken lines. By casting a series of numbered objects called *divining stalks*, whose odd numbers stood for broken and even for unbroken lines in the hexagrams, diviners selected a particular hexagram, found the prediction listed under it, and then offered their interpretations about not so much the course of coming events but, rather, of general tendencies in the universe.

The balance of the *Book of Changes* is made up of commentaries called *the ten wings*. These treat questions concerning the nature of the cosmos and attempt to address such metaphysical issues as the nature of being and reality. They also sometimes explain the metaphors involved in the interpretations of the hexagrams. The *Book of Changes* is the only one of the five central texts of Confucianism that directly addresses such issues.

See also ANCIENT CHINESE DYNASTIES AND PERIODS; *APPENDICES TO BOOK OF CHANGES*.

Bibliography

Giles, Herbert A. *A History of Chinese Literature.* New York: Grove Press, 1923.

Idema, Wilt, and Lloyd Haft. *A Guide to Chinese Literature.* Ann Arbor: Center for Chinese Studies, University of Michigan, 1997.

Shaughnessy, Edward L., trans. *I Ching: The Classic of Change.* New York: Ballantine Books, 1998.

Watson, Burton. *Early Chinese Literature.* New York and London: Columbia University Press, 1962.

Book of Lord Shang (*Shangjun shu, Shang-chün schu*) (ca. 400 B.C.E.)

Principally in essay form, the *Book of Lord Shang* represents a prose, legalist subcategory of ancient Chinese literature. An imperial advisor, Wei Yang, whom the Ch'in (Qin) emperor ennobled as lord of the region of Shang in the Huang Ho basin, probably wrote the book's 24 brief essays. All of these essays address the subject of practical politics and the courses of action that rulers must implement to create a strong and healthy state. The central message requires, first, the encouragement of agriculture to provide the economic basis for a strong government. Second, it advises a program of aggressive warfare to enhance state power and further contribute to the treasury.

With respect to relationships between the ruler and the ruled, the ruler must put in place a system of carrots and sticks. He must generously reward compliance with his programs and brutally punish noncompliance. One wonders whether the 20th-century Chinese Cultural Revolution under Mao Zedong might have drawn inspiration from the *Book of Lord Shang.*

The literary historian Burton Watson quotes Lord Shang as assuring his reader that "mercy and benevolence are the mother[s] of error." Lord Shang promulgates an active program of cruelty and repression.

Bibliography

Duyvendak, J. J. L., trans. *The Book of Lord Shang: A Classic of the Chinese School of Law.* Union, N.J.: Lawbook Exchange, 2002.

Idema, Wilt, and Lloyd Haft. *A Guide to Chinese Literature.* Ann Arbor: Center for Chinese Studies, University of Michigan, 1997.

Watson, Burton. *Early Chinese Literature.* New York: Columbia University Press, 1962.

Book of Odes (*Shi jing, Shih Ching*) (ca. 700–600 B.C.E.)

One of the five foundational documents of Chinese Confucianism, in its current form the *Book of Odes* contains 305 rhymed songs. Some of the individual songs may well be older than the dates given above for the collected version. One of the songs alludes to a datable solar eclipse that occurred on August 29, 775 B.C.E. Five others reportedly date to the Shang dynasty (ca. 1600– ca. 1028 B.C.E.).

Said to have been selected by CONFUCIUS himself from a collection containing some 3,000 ballads, the poems are organized according to four principal topics. First appears a group of ballads that reflect the lives and customs of common people from around the feudal states comprising the Chinese Empire. The literary historian Herbert A. Giles tells us that local nobles would periodically forward examples of these ballads to the imperial court. There the chief musicians of the realm would examine the songs carefully and, on the basis of their analysis, report, first, what customs prevailed in the states and how the people comported themselves. Second, the royal musicians would report their opinions concerning whether or not the emperor's subordinate officials in the various states were ruling well or wickedly.

The second group of odes in the collection included those composed for performance at ordinary entertainments in the subordinate states. The third group contained special odes written for performance at conventions of the feudal nobility. The fourth group contained poems of praise and poems intended to accompany sacrifices on religious occasions.

A number of the poems are love verses on the sorts of subjects that occupied couples everywhere in the days before the intervention of technology in the natural consequences of lovemaking. Maidens expressed concern about their virtue and their parents' attitudes toward their behavior. They encouraged or reproved their lovers. Wives repined about the high hopes they once entertained for their married lives before their husbands strayed. Good marriages are celebrated.

Warfare is another subject treated in the *Book of Odes*. So are the passage of the seasons, agricultural pursuits of various sorts, and hunting. Grievances against public officials and too-frequent military conscription also appear among the topics represented. Lovely nature poems appear frequently.

A significant strain of misogyny reveals itself in the way women and girls are drawn in the poems. The different treatment of girl and boy babies in the imperial household makes clear, for example, that the boys are destined for rule and the girls for household tasks. Moreover, clever women are considered dangers to the state since, despite their intelligence, the ancient Chinese considered them to be untrainable.

The representation of those who tilled the soil was sympathetic, and the public provision for widows by leaving some grain standing or sheaves unbound or handfuls uncollected is reminiscent of passages both in the Babylonian CODE OF HAMMURABI and in the Hebrew scriptures.

The ancient Chinese view of God also becomes manifest in the odes. That view is not incompatible with many other ancient views. The Chinese thought of God—or the ruler of the pantheon of gods—as human and masculine and at least sometimes corporeal. He was considered kind and loving and thought to be a friend to the downtrodden. He disapproved of bad behavior, and he found the odor of burnt offerings pleasing.

Confucius had a very high opinion of the odes and encouraged all who aspired to public office, including his own son, to commit them to memory. He saw in their implications the foundations of statecraft and thought that initiates who both knew the odes by heart and understood the subtleties of their implications should conduct diplomacy. After Confucius, in fact, such knowledge and understanding became requisite for public officials, and for a long time the language of the odes was also the language of diplomacy as officials communicated their negotiating positions and expectations by means of quoting relevant passages.

Given the centrality of these poems to the conduct of government, it should be no surprise that commentators soon burdened the odes' primary texts with a heavy weight of allegorical and symbolic interpretation. Mastery of that commentary, too, became an expectation for those who aspired to public office.

After the ruler of the state of Ch'in (Qin) brought all of China under his absolute dominion in 221 B.C.E., the old ways of doing business seemed inappropriate, especially since criticism of state policy was one of the functions of the odes. Therefore, in 213 B.C.E., the Han emperor approved a plan to burn all the ancient books so they could not serve as a platform for political dissidents. That plan was carried out with significant effect. Fortunately for literary posterity, however, the suppression of older literature was not altogether successful, and much, including the *Book of Odes*, survives for the edification of contemporary readers and scholars.

Bibliography

Barnstone, Tony, and Chou Ping, eds. *The Anchor Book of Chinese Poetry*. New York: Anchor Books, 2005.

Birch, Cyril, ed. *Anthology of Chinese Literature*. New York: Grove Press, 1965.

Connery, Christopher Leigh. *The Empire of the Text: Writing and Authority in Early Imperial China*. New York: Rowman and Littlefield Publishers, 1998.

Giles, Herbert A. *A History of Chinese Literature*. New York: Grove Press, 1958.

Idema, Wilt, and Lloyd Haft. *A Guide to Chinese Literature*. Ann Arbor: Center for Chinese Studies, University of Michigan, 1997.

Book of Rites *(Chou Li, I Li, Li Chi)*
(ca. 100 B.C.E.)

One of the five classics of the Chinese Confucian canon, the *Book of Rites* is an idealized behavioral guide. Its first section, *Chou Li*, gives a romanticized account of Chou (Zhou) dynasty bureaucracy. (See ANCIENT CHINESE DYNASTIES AND PERIODS.) This section has often proved useful to later statesmen in search of authoritative precedent for their policies.

I Li, the book's second section, prescribes detailed rules for all facets of the public behavior of aristocrats. If one is in doubt about how to comport oneself at weddings, archery contests, funerals, banquets, sacrifices, and the like, one need only consult the *I Li*. Suppose, for example, that one is an official escort for a corpse whose eternal resting place is more than a day's journey away. Everyone knows, of course, that the cortege must proceed only during the daylight hours and never travel at night. What, however, must it do in the event of a solar eclipse? The *I Li* provides unembellished but detailed, straightforward, factual guidance: The funeral procession must stop on the left side of the road and wait until the sun reappears before proceeding.

The principal section of the *Book of Rites* is the *Li Chi*. Longer and more varied in content than the other sections, it sometimes resembles the *I Li* in providing careful guidance for such matters as household management or naming a newborn. Beyond that, however, the *Li chi* also contains formal considerations of topics like education, music, or the place of ritual in the scheme of human existence.

Two other included essays, respectively entitled "The Great Learning" and "Doctrine of the Mean," have been influential in the subsequent history of Chinese thinking. Another considers the principles by which a true Confucian should live: "Behavior of a Confucian."

The literary historian Burton Watson calls particular attention to the *Li Chi*'s regular effort to reconcile ancient, pre-Confucian funeral ritual with the work's contemporary Confucian belief concerning death. Though the old rituals incorporated the burial of funeral goods with the deceased, then-contemporary Confucian belief did not suppose that such items as musical instruments or dishes would be of any comfort to the departed, nor did they credit a surviving spirit. Rather, such rituals expressed the wishes of survivors that such objects *could* still benefit their dead loved one. Confucian belief held that human wishes should not be suppressed but, instead, directed in a positive way. The inclusion of grave goods in burials gives comfort to the living. At the same time, grave goods should not be items that living persons would find useful. So the goods might consist of items that are either worn out or unfinished.

Many passages of the *Li Chi* take the form of anecdotes attributed to or concerning CONFUCIUS and his disciples, but these appear to be parables and not to be taken literally. In its current form, legend has it that two cousins named Tai the Elder and Tai the Younger prepared the *Li Chi*. It purports to be a compilation drawn from the work of Confucius and his disciples. Tai the Elder reduced his source materials to 85 sections. Tai the Younger, rejecting material that had already appeared elsewhere, winnowed the work further to 46 sections. Later scholars then had their way with the text, so that the work as we have received it acquired its current form around 200 C.E. Its most recent English translator, James Legge, terms the work an "encyclopedia of ancient ceremonial usages."

Bibliography

Giles, Herbert A. *A History of Chinese Literature.* New York: Grove Press, 1958.

Legge, James, trans. *Li Chi: Book of Rites: An Encyclopedia of Ancient Ceremonial Usages, Religious Creeds, and Social Institutions.* Edited by Ch'u Chai and Winberg Chai. New Hyde Park, N.Y.: University Books, 1967.

Watson, Burton. *Early Chinese Literature.* New York: Columbia University Press, 1962.

Book of the Dead (Reu Nu Pert Em Hru, Chapters of Coming Forth by Day) (before 2350 B.C.E.)

Apparently already ancient as a traditional body of oral funerary material even before HIERO-GLYPHS had been invented, at least some of the texts collected in the Book of the Dead seem to have originated outside Egypt, somewhere in Asia. Physical evidence of the burial practices described in the collection of scrolled papyri and monumental inscriptions that constitutes the book does not exist among the aboriginal inhabitants of Egypt. Rather, that evidence begins to appear contemporaneously with the arrival from the east of unknown Asian conquerors who, following their conquest, eventually established the pharaonic dynasties that ruled Egypt for millennia (ca. 3100/3000 B.C.E.–ca. 550 C.E.). At least parts of the book seem to have been already widely known—perhaps in oral form—before the first of those dynasties.

The Egyptologist E. A. Wallis Budge argues that over time, the Book of the Dead came to reflect the beliefs not only of the conquerors but also of the conquered and of the various other peoples who came to compose Egyptian society in the dynastic period. Central to that system of beliefs is faith in the resurrection of the human dead in the afterlife. the Book of the Dead reflects the belief that King Osiris—at once a god and a man—had suffered death and perhaps the dismemberment (in early versions) but certainly (in later ones) the mutilation of his body, which had been embalmed. His sisters, Isis and Nephthys, had, however, given Osiris magical objects that warded off all harms in the afterworld. The sisters also recited a series of incantations that conferred everlasting life upon Osiris. His followers believed that, like Osiris, who had conquered death, they would live forever, perfectly happy in perfect bodies. Budge quotes words addressed by the god Thoth to Osiris, who "makes men and women to be born again."

Within the framework of ancient Egyptian religion, people considered the Book of the Dead to be of divine origin and to have been written down by the god Thoth, who was the scribe of the Egyptian pantheon. Like the sacred writings of all major religions, however, the text of the Book of the Dead endured many human emendations, additions, and deletions over its long history. Papyri and inscriptions representing various stages in the development of the book reveal many changes, some intentional and some apparently owing to scribal error.

As the major text of Egyptian religion, however, the Book of the Dead always retained its central purpose: the protection of the dead in the next life. There, after being judged and found worthy, and after being reborn in a perfect body, the dead would again see their parents, enjoy material comforts akin to those of this world, be free from onerous labor, and participate in many of the same pleasures they had enjoyed while living. To help achieve those ends, the book or portions of it were recited on a person's death. Reciting specific chapters conferred specific benefits on the departed. Reciting chapter 53, for example, protected the deceased from tripping and falling in the other world and assured access to heavenly food rather than to offal. Chapter 99 named all the parts of a magic boat. These names the deceased needed to know to qualify as a master mariner and enable him or her to sail in a magic boat across the heavens as the sun god Ra did each day. Reciting chapter 25 restored a dead person's memory. This made possible recalling one's own name—a central requirement for immortality. It also called to the deceased's mind the names of the gods he might encounter in the afterlife. Reciting other chapters conferred upon the deceased the power to transform oneself into the shapes of other creatures: birds, serpents, or crocodiles, for example. Though considerations of space here prohibit more than a tiny representative sampling of the whole, at least one compelling example deserves a fuller treatment.

The eternal survival of a fully self-conscious individual in the afterlife was contingent upon a last judgment. This was not something that occurred at the end of time, but rather came soon after a corpse's entombment. The deceased is represented as entering the presence of an enthroned Osiris and other deities, including Thoth and the dog-headed god, Anubis. Anubis weighs the heart of the deceased on a scale in which the heart is counterbalanced by a feather. Thoth records the result of the weigh-in. If the heart is light enough, the justified deceased is admitted to the presence of the enthroned Osiris—sometimes portrayed wrapped as a mummy since Osiris also died and was reborn—and into the company of immortals. If the heart fails the test, a tripartite monster with the head of a crocodile or other carnivore, the forepart of a hyena, and the rear quarters of a dog eats the candidate, and the failed soul simply passes from existence.

To assure access to the text in the next world, copies of the book or portions of it were sometimes buried in the coffins of dead persons, sometimes inscribed upon the walls of a tomb, sometimes written on the inside of the coffin, or sometimes placed within a hollow wooden statue of the god Osiris. As Egypt's fortunes waned—especially in the face of Roman expansion and the introduction of Christianity, and finally after the Arab conquest of Egypt in 642 C.E.—deceased persons increasingly had to make do with less and less of the text. Toward the end of the survival of the old religion the book had detailed, just snippets of the text were buried with the departed.

As it is known today, the Book of the Dead survives in three major versions or recensions. The oldest of these is the Heliopolitan Recension, whose text is to be found in hieroglyphic inscriptions at the Pyramids at Saqqara. These date from the fifth and sixth dynasties (ended ca. 2350 B.C.E.). One finds these texts occurring as cursive hieroglyphics on coffins as late as the 11th and 12th dynasties (2081–1756 B.C.E.). The fullest version of the Book of the Dead appears in the Theban Recension. This text occurs both written on papyrus and painted on coffins in hieroglyphs from the Eighteenth to the Twenty-second Dynasties (ca. 16th–10th centuries B.C.E.), and written in hieratic script on papyrus in the Twenty-first

and Twenty-second Dynasties. The final version of the text is that of the Saïte Recension, which appeared in various scripts on tombs, coffins, and papyri from the Twenty-sixth Dynasty until the demise of the ancient Egyptian religion. This version was widely employed after the Greek Ptolemy family, to which Cleopatra belonged, assumed the role of pharaohs in Egypt.

Bibliography

Budge, E. A. W., ed. and trans. *The* Book of the Dead: *An English Translation of the Chapters, Hymns, Etc. of the Theban Recension.* London: Routledge & Kegan Paul, 1899. Reprint, New York: Barnes and Noble, 1969.

Diakonoff, L. M., ed. *Early Antiquity.* Chicago: University of Chicago Press, 1989.

Edwards, I. E. S., C. J. Gadd, and N. G. L. Hammond, eds. *The Cambridge Ancient History.* 3rd ed. Cambridge: Cambridge University Press, 1970.

Parkinson, R. B. *Voices from Ancient Egypt: An Anthology of Middle Kingdom Writings.* Norman: University of Oklahoma Press, 1991.

Books from the Foundation of the City [of Rome] *(Ab urbe condita libri)*
Livy (28–ca. 9 B.C.E.)

LIVY began the composition of his 142-book history of Rome sometime shortly before 27 B.C.E. and, as the classicist John Briscoe tells us, had completed the first five books by 25 B.C.E. Surviving portions of Livy's history include books 1–10 and books 21–45, though 41 and 43–45 have suffered losses. From time to time, more fragments continue to surface. A formerly unknown fragment, for example, was discovered as late as 1986.

In addition to what remains of Livy's text, there are also ancient summaries of parts of his work. These abridgments include the "OXYRHYNCHUS Epitome," written on papyrus and summarizing books 37–40 and 48–55. Additionally, there are ancient summaries called *Periochae* that date to around the early third century C.E. Though not necessarily always accurate, comparative readings of the surviving text and the summaries suggest that we can place a good deal of confidence in them. I rely heavily on them for the précis of the extant books below.

Stylistically, Livy is the most elegant and effective of the historians of Rome. In the early sections, as he traces Rome from the legendary arrival of Aeneas, a prince of Troy, Livy relies heavily on legendary and mythic materials. The closer he comes to his own times, the fuller his accounts become. It is very clear that Livy is interested in identifying what qualities have determined both the Roman character and the Roman political system. His sympathies are drawn to the Roman Republic, though he seems to think that the imperial sovereignty of Augustus is a necessary expedient for Livy's own epoch.

The first book of Livy's history begins, then, with the arrival of Aeneas and recapitulates VIR-GIL's accounts of Aeneas's accomplishments (see AENEID). Livy follows the reign of Aeneas's son, Ascanius, and his descendants in the region of Alba. He recounts the birth of Romulus and Remus and Romulus's construction of the city of Rome, his establishment of the Roman Senate, his warfare against the Sabines, his reverence for Jupiter, his administrative arrangements for the Roman people, and his erection of a temple to the two-faced god Janus. This temple was always open when Rome was at war and closed when she was at peace. Romulus was able to close the temple and enjoy a peaceful reign. Livy traces innovations through several generations, telling about conquests, the incorporation of defeated tribes into the populace of Rome, the creation of new senators and aristocrats, and the construction of a city wall and sewers.

In Book 2, Livy recounts the rape of the virtuous Roman heroine Lucretia by Sextus Tarquin—one of the most famous of Roman stories. The Tarquin line, whose members had made themselves kings, were dethroned and the Roman republic established as a result of the public outrage at Lucretia's rape and suicide. The author recounts the way in which Lucius Iunius Brutus thwarted the several attempts of the Tarquin line to restore the monarchy by guile and by force of arms. Livy tells of the creation of the institution of the tribunes of the people and of the burial alive of the unchaste vestal virgin, Oppia. The rest of book 2 gives accounts of a series of wars.

Book 3 tracks such internal difficulties of the Roman state as riots about agrarian laws and rebellion by exiles and slaves. It also covers external wars. The book traces the new institutions established for governing Rome more effectively, including the introduction of a code of laws in 10 tables. The Decimvirs (a committee of 10 men), who were charged with this responsibility, thereafter became the administrators of justice. Livy tells how they did this fairly at first but later became corrupt. When one of them, Appius, tried to corrupt Virginia, the daughter of Virginius, the common people forced the Decimvirs to resign, jailing the two worst ones, Appius and Oppius, who subsequently committed suicide. (In the 14th century, Geoffrey Chaucer told the story of Virginia's abduction in "The Man of Law's Tale" [*The Canterbury Tales*].) After further description of warfare, Livy recounts the unfair decision of the Romans when, asked to judge a land dispute, they found for neither party but temporarily took the land themselves.

Books 4 and 5 consider the establishment of new civic offices, such as that of censor, and the operations of the temporary office of dictator under Quintius Cincinnatus. At this time, a rebellion of slaves took place, and the Roman army was first put upon a professional footing. Military innovations were also introduced, such as erecting winter quarters and having cavalrymen ride their own horses (as opposed to army mounts).

Called upon to mediate in a war between the Clusians and the Gauls, the Romans were found to be partial to the Clusians. As a result, the Gauls attacked and occupied Rome; the Romans capitulated and agreed to ransom themselves. As the gold was being weighed, the dictator Camillus arrived with an army, drove the Gauls out of Rome, and exterminated their army.

Book 6 examines one of a recurrent series of executions, which took place whenever someone was suspected of attempting to gain royal power. The victim in Book 6 is Marcus Manlius, who was executed by being thrown from the Tarpeian Rock—a regular method of legal execution in archaic Rome. The same book records the successful campaign by the Roman commoners to gain the right to elect the consuls rather than have them appointed by the senate and patricians.

Livy first makes use of extended scenic descriptions in Book 7. In addition to describing single combat, the historian recounts such memorable events as leaping on horseback into an artificial lake. He also discusses the enlargement of the Roman population and the organizational expedients developed to deal efficiently with the increase. The history of the army, the near revolt of the garrison at Capua, and its return to duty and patriotism also interest Livy in this book. So do successful military operations against several tribal peoples.

Rebellion and successful negotiation are major themes of Book 8, which documents how the rebellious Campanians obtained a consul to represent their interests at Rome. Livy revisits the theme of a vestal virgin put to death for corruption—this time for incest. For the first time, a Roman official, Quintus Publilius, occupied an office for a period of time beyond his term. Rome fought against the descendants of the Sabines, the Samnites; and the dictator, Lucius Papirius, wished to punish Quintus Fabius, the victor, for disobeying orders. Reason prevailed.

In Book 9, Livy describes continued battles with the Samnites and the Roman expansion of power by fighting against other native tribes of Italy, including the Apulians, Etruscans, Umbrians, Marsians, Pelignians, and Aequans. Alexander the Great was conducting his conquests during the time that book 9 covers, so Livy digresses to assess the comparative strength of the Romans and Alexander's army. Livy concludes that Alexander did well to carry his campaign of world conquest eastward to Asia instead of westward to Italy. The Romans could well have been his match.

Book 10 continues the discussion of the wars. Eventual victory fell to Rome, which now had mastery of most of the Italian peninsula. A census of the population found 262,322 Roman citizens in 291 B.C.E.—the 461st year of the history of the Roman people.

Highlights from the summarized accounts of the lost books (11–20) include the founding of the temple of the deity of medicine, Aesculapius, on the island of the Tiber River following a terrible plague. When the Romans imported the god's image from Epidaurus, a gigantic serpent that the Romans believed to be the god himself came along and took up residence in the temple (Book 11). The year 281 B.C.E. saw the first athletic games staged in Rome.

Books 12–14 trace the attempts by the Molossian king, Pyrrhus of Epirus, to assist the Grecian inhabitants of the southern Italian city of Tarentum in their military challenge to Roman supremacy on the Italian pennisula. Essentially a mercenary leader, Pyrrhus brought both troops and eight elephants into Italy. As the Roman soldiers had not seen elephants before, the beasts' appearance threw the Romans into disarray, and they were defeated. Nonetheless, Pyrrhus remarked that the dead Roman soldiers had all fallen facing the enemy. Eventually, however, the elephants were slain, and after years of hard effort, Pyrrhus was forced to leave Italy in 273 B.C.E. Two years later, as Book 15 reports, the Tarentines were finally defeated. Rome granted them both peace and freedom.

Books 16–18 detail the Roman conduct of the first Punic War against the North African city of Carthage. Book 20 traces the incursion of transalpine Gauls into Italy and their defeat in 236 B.C.E. For the first time, Roman troops advanced north of the River Po, and the Roman army numbered more than 300,000 men.

As earlier noted, the closer Livy gets to his own time, the longer and more circumstantial his discussion of events becomes. When we again arrive, then, at the books still extant, we find

Books 21–30 occupied almost exclusively with discussions of the second Punic War and with descriptions of the personalities and leadership capacities of such major figures as the Carthaginian general Hannibal; Fabius Maximus, the Roman dictator who thwarted Hannibal with caution and delay; and Scipio Africanus, the Roman general who won the war.

Picking up at Book 37, after a hiatus in the extant version, the summaries recount the slaughter of Romans in Spain. Then the Romans gained victory in Lusitania (modern Portugal) and founded a colony there. In Book 38, Livy tells the story of how a high-ranking female prisoner, the queen of Galatia, killed a Roman centurion who had assaulted her. On being set free, the queen carried the centurion's head home to her husband.

Book 39 mentions the abolition of the rites of the cult of Bacchus in Rome. The Romans continued mopping up in Spain.

A break in the summaries occurs at this point, and they resume with book 46, which records the Roman population as 337,022, according to a census. The book reports a throne usurped in Egypt and the various campaigns of the Roman army in Europe and in the Middle East. A notable achievement of the years 167–160 B.C.E. was the draining of the Pontine marshes and their reclamation as farmland.

Book 47 describes the lead-up to the third Punic War. While they denied their hostile intentions, the Carthaginians nonetheless hoarded timber for ship building and fielded an army.

Among the interesting historical details that Livy pauses to describe in this book are the funeral instructions left by Marcus Aemilius Lepidus, the chief of the Roman senate. He limited the money his sons could spend on the occasion, remarking that the dignity of the funerals of the great had its origin not in expenditure but in the parade of ancestral portraits that preceded the bier of the deceased. Livy also remarks on the unusual number of Roman women who were poisoning their husbands.

Despite Carthaginian claims to the contrary, the Romans became convinced of their intention to make war. The Romans sent an army to Carthage, where they made such exorbitant demands that the Carthaginians were forced to take up arms.

Military history occupies most of the next several books. The Numantine War succeeded the third Punic War, and a former shepherd turned military commander staged a successful revolt against the Romans in Lusitania. Livy's vivid narrative makes clear the increasingly international focus of Roman affairs as the once local and regional power came to dominate the affairs of the Mediterranean world.

After describing the rigorous military discipline of the great Roman general Scipio Africanus in Book 57, Livy turns his attention for a while to the political situation in Rome, describing the ambitions of the Gracchus family and the illegalities they attempted to achieve them. So incensed did members of the upper class become at the Gracchi's assault on their prerogatives that they incited a riot in which Gaius Sempronius Gracchus was murdered and thrown into the Tiber. Further wars and the subsequent careers of members of the Gracchus family occupy several further books.

Book 61 records the founding of the colony of Aquae Sextae (contemporary Aix-en-Provence, France), named for the six waters of its hot and cold springs. In the next several books, accounts of military actions in Africa and against the tribal peoples of northern Europe grow more frequent, while the population of the city of Rome approached 400,000. In Book 68, the name of Gaius Marius, one of the greatest heroes of Roman arms, is mentioned in connection with his being made consul (the Roman head of state and its military commander in chief) for the fifth time.

Book 70 emphasizes political events at Rome, diplomatic missions abroad, and also contains reports of military actions in Syria. With Book 73, readers find themselves being drawn into accounts of the run-up to the Roman civil wars that culminated with the election of Julius Caesar as dictator for life. Book 78, however, concentrates on the revolt of Mithradates VI Eupator, king of Pontus, in Asia and tells of the arrangements he made to have every Roman citizen in Asia slaughtered on the same day.

Back in the city of Rome, says Book 79, the consul Lucius Cinna was using violence and force of arms to force "ruinous legislation" through the Senate. Livy interpolates the sad story of a soldier who killed his brother, not recognizing him until he stripped the body of its armor. Then he built a pyre to cremate his brother and committed suicide, his body burning together with his sibling's.

All the peoples of Italy were granted Roman citizenship in 89 B.C.E.—a fact Livy belatedly reports in Book 80. Cinna and Marius had become consular allies, and together the two conducted unprecedented military operations within the city against their political enemies, then appointed themselves consuls. Marius died on January 15, 87 B.C.E. Livy considers the question of whether the good or ill Marius did for Rome weighs most heavily in the balance of Marius's life accomplishments. As a general, he had saved the state from foreign enemies. As a politician, he had ruined the state with his untrustworthiness, even devastating the Roman state with warfare within the city walls.

Books 81–90, still setting the stage for the Roman civil wars, follow the remarkable career of Lucius Cornelius Sulla. Sulla successfully commanded Roman armies, resisted the political opposition of Marius by threatening Rome with his troops, and waged successful war against dissident peoples of Italy. Having overcome all opposition, Sulla had himself made dictator. In that capacity, he forcibly settled his veterans on the confiscated lands of communities that had proved hostile to Rome. As dictator, he also restored control of the government to the Roman senate and reformed the criminal courts. Thinking he had saved the republic, he retired from public life in 79 B.C.E. Sulla likely shortened his life by a retirement spent in unbridled dissipation. He died in 80 B.C.E.; his reforms survived him by about a decade.

In Book 90, Livy turns his attention to the career of Gnaeus Pompeius—Pompey—the sometime father-in-law and colleague and later the enemy of Julius Caesar. With Pompey's arrival on the scene, Livy begins to describe the Roman civil wars in earnest. As his source, he used LUCAN's unfinished CIVIL WAR (*Pharsalia*); the content of that EPIC can be read in the entry for the work. (See also Julius Caesar's The CIVIL WARS.) The summaries end with book 142, in which we find described the participation of Rome's first emperor, AUGUSTUS CAESAR, in the funeral of the Roman general Nero Claudius Drusus, who died in the field in 9 B.C.E. of injuries sustained when his horse threw him.

In the books that survive intact, Livy makes much use of direct discourse, with descriptions that are apt and colorful. He is the unanimous choice among modern historians for best prose writer of Roman history.

Bibliography

Livius, Titus. *History of Rome*. Translated by D. Spillan and Cyrus Edmonds. New York: Harper and Brothers, Publishers, 1875.

———. *The History of Rome: Books 1–5*. Translated by Valerie M. Warrior. Indianapolis: Hackett Publishers, 2006.

———. *Livy*. 13 vols. Translated by B. O. Foster. Cambridge, Mass.: Harvard University Press, 1939.

Braggart Soldier, The (Miles gloriosus) Titus Maccius Plautus (ca. second–third century B.C.E.)

Though braggart soldiers had appeared earlier on the Greek and Roman stage, perhaps none so exaggerated the type to an audience's delight as did PLAUTUS's hero, Pyrgopolynices. The recent translator of the play, Erich Segal, renders the braggart's name as "terrific tower taker."

To whet his audience's appetite for more of the self-admiring character, Plautus defers the play's prologue in favor of a dialogue between Pyrgopolynices and his overtly fawning but covertly contemptuous slave, Artotrogus—another character type, the parasite who in this case is paid to be an admirer. Segal speculates that Pyrgopolynices proved especially attractive to Roman audiences since almost all the men had been soldiers, and custom required modest silence from veterans concerning their military exploits. A braggart soldier, therefore, was a universal object of scornful satire.

As the play opens, Pyrgopolynices, in contrast with Roman expectations, is admiring his shield and sword and feeling sorry for the weapons because they temporarily lack the sort of heroic action that he alone can give them. To his master's face, Artotrogus flatters the soldier's ego by describing impossible deeds, like punching out an elephant, while sniggering about them in asides to the audience. He also keeps track of the impossible numbers of foes that Pyrgopolynices either killed or would have killed had the circumstances been right. Beyond that, Artotrogus praises the conceited soldier's good looks and his appeal to women.

The two go off to enlist new recruits for the army, and the speaker of the belated prologue, Palaestrio, takes the stage. Palaestrio, who is another of Pyrgopolynices' servants, explains that the play is drawn from Greek models that featured the *alazon*—a braggart who is a fraud, a lecher, and a cheat as well. Palaestrio also explains that the play is set in Ephesus, a city to which his master has forcibly abducted a young woman, Philocomasium. She had been the concubine of Palaestrio's former master, Pleusicles, in Athens before her abduction. When the braggart took the girl, Palaestrio set out by ship to inform his former master. Pirates, however, attacked Palaestrio's vessel, and he himself was captured. By chance, which always plays a major role in such mannered comedies, those same pirate-kidnappers gave Palaestrio to Pyrgopolynices as a slave.

Knowing Philocomasium's whereabouts, Palaestrio was able to smuggle a letter to Pleusicles, who immediately came to Ephesus and now is lodging right next door at the home of an elderly friend, Periplectomenus. Palaestrio has been able to tunnel through the shared wall of the two houses to the bedroom of Philocomasium, who can crawl back and forth and, eventually, pretend to be her own twin.

As the play begins, Periplectomenus reports to Palaestrio that someone from the braggart soldier's household has spotted Philocomasium through the skylight while she was visiting the adjoining residence and kissing Pleusicles. The old man appoints Palaestrio to devise a plot to outfox the neighbors. Palaestrio cogitates histrionically and formulates a scheme. He invents a newly arrived twin sister for Philocomasium—the sister that she herself will represent to the confusion of her captor and his household.

Palaestrio's next task is to discover *which* of his master's servants saw the girl. The slave Sceledrus immediately resolves that problem by sharing with Palaestrio that it was he. Palaestrio artfully convinces Sceledrus that he did not see the girl, first by going inside and reporting Philocomasium's presence at home, and then, while Sceledrus guards the next door, by bringing the girl from her abductor's house.

Despite the fact that Sceledrus knows of no possible passage between the houses, he insists that he believes the evidence of his eyes and will not be dissuaded, until Philocomasium has a thought. She says she remembers dreaming that her twin sister had arrived from Athens and was staying next door in Ephesus and that, just as Sceledrus had done, a slave who confused the sisters accused her of infidelity. Philocomasium goes into the braggart's house, and Sceledrus, now beginning to doubt his eyes, moves over to guard that door.

The girl soon appears at the door of the other house, and, when accosted by Sceledrus, pretends not to know him or Palaestrio, explaining that her name is Dicea. Still unconvinced, Sceledrus grabs the girl and tries to drag her into the braggart's house. She swears that she will go inside if Sceledrus will release her. He does, and she skips into the house next door. Palaestrio sends Sceledrus to bring a sword so they can force her out. When Sceledrus goes to bring it, he finds Philocomasium within, relaxing on her couch. At last the story of twin sisters convinces him.

Periplectomenus now appears, however, to avenge the insult to his guest. He threatens to have Sceledrus whipped for his discourtesy and false accusations. Sceledrus explains his confusion and abjectly begs forgiveness. When Periplectomenus grants it, Sceledrus thinks he won it too easily and decides to make himself scarce for a few days to let the incident blow over lest his master sell him.

Now the would-be rescuers of Philocomasium get together to confer about their next moves. Her lover, Pleusicles, apologizes to the 54-year-old Periplectomenus for involving an older person in a juvenile love affair. Periplectomenus replies that he still has a goodly portion of youthful energy, spirit, and appetite for love. He explains that he has never married so that he can preserve the freedom to pursue his appetites without responsibilities. He has no need of children since he has plenty of relatives to inherit his estate. In that expectation, all his kinsmen are attentive and compete in entertaining him. As a result, his hopeful relatives effectively support Periplectomenus.

Periplectomenus would continue discussing this sort of matter, but Palaestrio interrupts him and returns the discussion to the issue at hand. He has a plan for rescuing Philocomasium and duping the braggart Pyrgopolynices into the bargain. They will recruit a courtesan and her maid. Periplectomenus will pretend the courtesan is his wife. The wife will feign an ardent attraction for the braggart soldier—who can never say "no" to a woman. The maid and Palaestrio will act as go-betweens, and, to give the entire matter greater plausibility, he will take Periplectomenus's ring to the braggart soldier as a token of the courtesan's affection.

Some stage business between Palaestrio and another of the soldier's slaves, Lurcio, follows. Then the courtesan, Acroteleutium, and her maid, Milphiddipa, enter. Acroteleutium holds forth on the subject of her mastery of the arts of wickedness and expresses her willingness to dupe the soldier and separate him from a healthy share of his money. She and Palaestrio, for the audience's benefit, run through the plan once more. Acroteleutium shows that she has utterly mastered the deception.

Palaestrio sets out with the ring in search of Pyrgopolynices to set the plot in motion.

Pyrgopolynices enters with Palaestrio. When the latter has his master's attention, he tells him of Acroteleutium's passion, describing her as both wife and widow—a young woman married to an old man. His lechery aroused, Pyrgopolynices agrees to get rid of Philocomasium and to entice her to leave his house by allowing her to keep all the gold, jewels, and finery that he has given her.

The maid, Milphidippa, appears and, knowing that the men are listening but pretending not to notice them, praises Pyrgopolynices' looks extravagantly. Flattered, the soldier starts to fall for the maid, but Palaestrio warns him off, saying that he gets the maid when his master gets the mistress. Palaestrio then privately instructs Milphidippa to feign, on behalf of her mistress, an overwhelming love for Pyrgopolynices.

Palaestrio encourages Pyrgopolynices to stand at stud, but only for a substantial fee. His children, says Palaestrio, live for 800 years. Pyrgopolynices corrects him; they live for a millennium. Feigning shock, Milphidippa wants to know Pyrgopolynices' age. He tells her that Jove was born of the earth on the day of creation. Pyrgopolynices was born the next day. Milphidippa exits to bring her mistress, and Palaestrio once more advises his master in the art of gently disposing of Philocomasium by allowing her to go with her sister and mother and to take along all the presents he showered on her.

Pyrgopolynices is lecherously distracted by thoughts of the twin and the mother. He also expresses interest in the ship's captain who brought the women to Ephesus.

Acroteleutium now enters, and Palaestrio instructs her in her role. She is to say that, in her ardor for Pyrgopolynices, she has divorced her current husband so they can marry. Moreover, she is to say that she owns Periplectomenus's house since it was a part of her dowry and the divorce settlement. Having coached the woman, Palaestrio turns to Philocomasium's lover, Pleusicles, telling him to disguise himself as a ship's captain. Pleusicles has already done so. He must now call for Philocomasium and say he is taking her to her mother. Palaestrio will carry luggage to the harbor, and the entire company will be off for Athens and out of Pyrgopolynices' control.

Pyrgopolynices reenters, delighted at his success in enticing Philocomasium to leave without a fuss. He says he even had to give Palaestrio to her to seal the bargain. The slave feigns shock and disappointment.

Now the maid and her mistress enter and, pretending not to see Pyrgopolynices, flatter his ego by praising him. He, of course, thinks their praise is only his just reward. He starts to go to the women, but Palaestrio convinces him not to be so easily won. When Palaestrio remarks that every woman loves the soldier at first sight, Pyrgopolynices shares the tidbit that the goddess of love, Venus, was his grandmother.

The women now dupe the soldier into believing that the house is part of the divorce settlement. Before he understands this, however, he reveals his cowardice by expressing his concern that the husband might catch him with Acroteleutium.

Now Pleusicles, dressed as the sea captain and with a patch over one eye, comes to collect Philocomasium and her baggage. Philocomasium pretends to be reluctant to leave, but obeys her mother. Palaestrio in the meantime carries a trunk full of treasure from the soldier's house.

More stage business follows as Philocomasium pretends to faint with grief at parting. Palaestrio bids farewell to the household gods and his fellow slaves as lackeys continue to carry out trunks of treasure. Palaestrio feigns inconsolable sorrow at leaving Pyrgopolynices, and after extended farewells, he races away.

Now, encouraged by a boy from the house next door, Pyrgopolynices enters in the expectation of enjoying a love tryst with Acroteleutium. Instead he encounters the men of the household, who overcome him, carry him out, and beat him. His cowardice exposed, Pyrgopolynices begs to be released, and after a few more blows and a bribe of 100 drachmas, the men of Periplectomenus's household release the braggart soldier.

Sceledrus returns from the harbor with the news that Philocomasium's ship has sailed and that she was the sweetheart of the man with the eye patch. Pyrgopolynices realizes that he has been "bamboozled" by Palaestrio, but he accepts the outcome philosophically, concluding that "there would be less lechery" should lechers learn from his example. He and his slaves leave the stage as he calls upon the audience for applause.

Direct stage descendants of the braggart soldier in later European theater include such characters as the stock character Scaramuccia in the Italian commedia dell'arte. The type also underlay such English theatrical characters as Nicholas Udall's Ralph Roister Doister and Shakespeare's Falstaff; braggart soldiers appeared in virtually every national theater of Europe.

Plautus. *The Braggart Soldier (Miles Gloriosus)*. Translated by Erich Segal. In *Plautus: The Comedies*. Vol. 1. Edited by David R. Slavitt and Palmer Bovie. Baltimore: Johns Hopkins University Press, 1995.

bucolic poetry   See PASTORAL POETRY.

Buddha and Buddhism

A major religion of Asia and beyond, Buddhism was founded by Siddhartha Gautama (ca. 563–ca 483 B.C.E.). The son of Suddhodana and Maya Gautama, Siddhartha was born at Lumbini in the Nepal valley. His titles, Buddha (the enlightened one) and Sakyamuni (sage of the Sakya clan), were bestowed on him by public proclamation.

When he reached the age of 29, Buddha left his wife and son to spend five years in meditation and in trying to achieve enlightenment. Following a strict ascetic regimen, he found what he sought, coming to understand how to overcome pain, how to become a vessel for truth, and how to achieve rebirth.

Knowledge, he believed, and the practice of four truths could overcome pain, which he identified with human existence. The identity of existence and pain was the first truth. The second was that desire causes pain. If one can overcome desire, one will no longer suffer—the third truth. To overcome desire—the fourth—one must follow the eightfold path whose elements were these:

1 One must gain right knowledge of the four truths above.

2 One must rightly resolve to restrain malice.

3 One must cultivate right speech, which will be both true and kindly.

4 One must behave rightly and respect life, property, and decency.

5 One must labor at the right occupation.

6 One must strive to rid the mind of evil qualities and habits and keep and cherish the good ones.

7 One must exercise right control of one's sensations and thoughts.

8 One must learn right contemplation in four stages.

    a   Isolation that leads to joy.

    b   Meditation that leads to inner peace.

    c   Concentration that leads to bodily happiness.

    d   Contemplation that produces indifference to both happiness and misery.

Buddha's teaching first attracted a following of men and then, at the request of his foster mother, Mahaprajapati, a group of women who, as monks and nuns, were willing to commit themselves to a monastic life. In their monasteries, they practiced abstinence from sexual intercourse, theft, causing harm to living creatures, and boasting of human accomplishments or perfection. Buddha also founded a third order for the laity. The initiates agreed to be kind, speak purely, be generous in almsgiving, eschew drugs and intoxicants, and be faithful to their spouses. They also were to be instructed in the eightfold way. Buddha did not promulgate any theories concerning the nature of deity, nor did he deny any conceptions of deity that other religions already espoused.

As Buddhism developed, it sent missionaries in all directions. Some went to western Asia and even into Macedonia in the Grecian archipelago. Others went to Ceylon, where the faith proved triumphant. As the Buddhists encountered the adherents of other faiths over the next several centuries, a good deal of mutual exchange of ideas and doctrines occurred. As a result, we see Buddhist elements in Zoroastrianism, Gnosticism, and elsewhere. At least by the first century C.E., and almost certainly earlier, Buddhism found a congenial reception in China, where it developed a regional variant by melding with traditional Chinese ancestor worship. We also see in Buddhism an accretion of elements of several religions and of the polytheistic beliefs of the Indian subcontinent.

Just before the beginning of the Common Era, warfare and political dislocations caused the adherents of Buddhism to fear that the doctrinal splintering that was already well advanced in the Buddhist faith would gain impetus. The monks of several monasteries perceived, moreover, that the centuries-long practice of entrusting Buddha's teachings to memory and oral preservation subjected Buddhist doctrine to unintentional corruption. Moreover, oral transmission ran the risk of losing all the teachings in the event of warfare. Accordingly, some 500 monks from several monasteries met to confer. They undertook to record, in the Pali language of northern India, what became the Buddhist canon: the *Theravāda* (The elder's tradition). It contained the three essential texts of Buddhism: the *Abhidhamma Pitaka* (Treatises); the *Sutta Pitaka* (The sermons of Buddha); and the the *Tripitaka* (Three Baskets). (See BUDDHIST TEXTS.)

Just as in the parallel case of the Christians, writing down these matters provoked further controversy, especially about the Buddhists' monastic rules. It seems that, unbeknownst to the authors of the canonical texts, Sanscrit versions of some of the material may have existed already, and that these varied from the canon. Even in the absence of alternate texts, monastic practice varied enough to provoke disagreement. In the late third century C.E., therefore, a group of schismatics adopted another text, the *Vaipulya Pitaka*, as the authoritative statement of Buddhist belief. The regional monarch, however, found the work heretical and burned it.

A further period of text making followed in the early fifth century C.E., when a Buddhist monk and scholar named Buddhaghosha wrote the *Visuddhimagga* (way of purification), which incorporated the teaching of the conservative Burmese school of Buddhism.

Bibliography

Banerjee, Biswanath, and Sukomal Chaudhuri, eds. *Buddha and Buddhism*. Kolkata, India: Asiatic Society, 2005.

The Buddhism Omnibus. New York: Oxford University Press, 2005.

Olson, Carl. *The Different Paths of Buddhism: A Narrative Historical Introduction*. New Brunswick, N.J.: Rutgers University Press, 2005.

Williams, Paul, ed. *Buddhism: Critical Concepts in Religious Studies*. 8 vols. New York: Routledge, 2005.

Buddhist texts

Although not an official part of the Buddhist canon, the oldest surviving Buddhist documents are *The Edicts of Asoka*. Asoka of Maurya (ruled ca. 273–232 B.C.E.) became the most celebrated Buddhist monarch of ancient India. Shortly after his conquest of the territory of Kalinga on India's east coast, Asoka began his career as a Buddhist.

Enormous carnage had attended his conquest. Literally hundreds of thousands of persons perished either in military engagements or as a result of captivity and starvation. Sickened at that outcome, Asoka issued edicts and had them engraved on stone; many are still extant. As his objective in issuing his edicts, Asoka said that he wanted his sons and grandsons to avoid the error of undertaking wars of conquest. He observed: "All animate beings should have security, self-control, peace of mind, and joyousness."

Asoka's edicts are exclusively ethical documents. Theological considerations—apart from a reverential attitude—are absent from them. Anxious to have his ethical concerns shared by as many as possible, and concerned about the cure of bodies as well as souls, Asoka dispatched medical missionaries to Ceylon, to regions elsewhere in India, and to Syria, Egypt, Cyrene, Macedonia, and Epirus.

With respect to ancient Buddhist canonical texts, the earliest and most complete collection to survive is one preserved in the Pali language: the *Tripitaka* (Three Baskets). It contains three systematic bodies of Buddhist doctrine. First it contains the *Vinaya pitaka*—the five books, or basket, of monastic discipline. The second work is the *Sutta pitaka*—the five collections, or basket, of Bhuddha's popular discourses or sermons. Four of these are single-volume works, and the fifth contains 15 subordinate works. The third body of doctrine—the *Abhidhamma pitaka*—contains seven books of psychological ethics and rarefied philosophy.

Numerous such early noncanonical works as handbooks and commentaries also survive in various languages. Perhaps the most important among these is the Pali encyclopedic *Visuddhimagga* (The way of purification) of Buddhaghosha.

Noncanonical early Buddhist literature also contained five ancient biographies of the Buddha and short stories whose object was to explain good and bad karma and the effects of each. A verse manual, the *Dhammapada*, organizes 423 verses into 26 chapters. This work is a devotional and instructional pamphlet that young persons in monasteries memorized and chanted as a way of internalizing the Buddhist monastic discipline. Its central message is: "Abstain from all evil; accumulate what is good; purify your mind." The *Dhammapada* holds that ignorance is the highest form of impurity; that suffering will cease only when the desire for things does; and that greed, ill-will, and delusion will make a happy life impossible.

As Buddhism spread throughout Asia, translation became a flourishing industry. The literary historian P. V. Bapat counts 4,566 translations—not all of them ancient—into Tibetan, and about the same number—again, not all ancient—into Chinese. Recent finds in Tibet of Sanskrit manuscripts dating to the fifth or sixth century C.E. and earlier have shed new light on the nature of the transmission of Bhuddhist texts to that region.

Like other major world religions, Buddhism has split and fragmented over time. Sometimes it has incorporated into its creed aspects of older religions practiced in the regions into which it has spread. As it has done so, texts reflecting such ideological melding have appeared. Many of these, however, such as the texts of Tantric Buddhism, are beyond the purview of this discussion.

Bibliography

Banerjee, Biswanath, and Sukomal Chaudhuri, eds. *Buddha and Buddhism.* Kolkata, India: Asiatic Society, 2005.

Bapat, Purushottam V., ed. *2500 Years of Buddhism.* Delhi, India: Publications Division, Ministry of Information and Broadcasting, 1959.

The Buddhism Omnibus. New York: Oxford University Press, 2005.

Coomeraswamy, Ananda. *Buddha and the Gospel of Buddhism.* New Hyde Park, N.Y.: University Books, 1964.

Olson, Carl. *The Different Paths of Buddhism: A Narrative Historical Introduction.* New Brunswick, N.J.: Rutgers University Press, 2005.

C

Caesar, Julius (Gaius, Iulius Caesar)
(ca. 100–44 B.C.E.) *Roman general, writer, statesman*

The scion of the most distinguished of Roman patrician families, Julius Caesar traced his lineage through Ascanius (also called Iulus, the founder of Rome's predecessor city, Alba Longa) to the Trojan prince Aeneas, legendary originator of the Roman state. Through Aeneas, Caesar could also claim descent from Aeneas's mother Venus, the goddess of love, and her paramour Anchises, a prince of Troy. This distinguished if partly fanciful ancestry became one of Caesar's principal tools of propaganda as he sought to make of himself what he eventually, if briefly, became: the master of Rome, permanently appointed dictator of the city and its dominions.

Caesar's work as a military historian, memoirist, and commentator constitute his most important and virtually only surviving contributions to the literature of his epoch. His COMMENTARY ON THE GALLIC WARS (*De bello Gallico*) comprises seven books to which an eighth was added, probably by his lieutenant, Aulus Hirtius. A similar work describes Rome's CIVIL WARS (*De bello civili*). Beyond these military works, Caesar authored other books that are now lost. These included a pair of treatises on predicting the future through signs and auguries: *Auguralia* and *De Auspiciis*. A lost work on a similar subject, *De motu siderum*, investigated foretelling the future by observing the motions of heavenly bodies. Another volume collected speeches given before judges, and still another answered a legal work of Cicero. Caesar is reported to have published his letters, now almost all lost except for a few that CICERO preserved.

A collection of Caesarean ephemera is also credited to this remarkable Roman, though some suspect that those writings were identical with his military commentaries. Caesar is also said to have composed a TRAGEDY, *Oedipus*, whose publication Rome's first emperor, AUGUSTUS CAESAR, refused to license.

Caesar's family provided a signal example of heroic leadership for him to emulate. His uncle by marriage, the general Marius, saved the Roman state from destruction at the hands of barbarian hordes within two years' time twice, first in 102 B.C.E. at Aquae Sextae (Aix-en-Province, France) and then in the following year just south of the Brenner Pass on the road to Verona.

Concerning Caesar's early education, we know that he was tutored at home by a clever and well-educated man named Marcus Antonius Gnipho, but beyond that we have principally the testimony of Caesar's own intellect and accomplishment to assure us that he became very well educated indeed. He spent his late adolescence and acquired his first political experience during the period of the Roman Civil Wars (89–82 B.C.E.) With respect to his political education, Caesar learned early to associate himself with powerful people, as he did when, rejecting the match that his family had arranged for him, he married Cornelia, the daughter of the most powerful Roman of the era, the consul (head of state) Lucius Cornelius Cinna.

The vicissitudes of the political situation, however, soon cost Cinna his power and his life when the troops he led against his rival, the soon-to-be dictator Sulla, mutinied and murdered Cinna. Sulla initiated a program of reprisals against members of the Marian party that Cinna had represented—a party with democratic proclivities. Cinna's son-in-law was then only 20, and his name was not on the list of those whom Sulla had put to death. The dictator did demand, however, that Caesar divorce his wife. This Caesar refused to do, remaining married to her until her untimely death nine years later. In reprisal, Sulla stripped Caesar of a priesthood of Jupiter to which he had been appointed and confiscated both the dowry that Cornelia had brought him and his own property. Through his connections, perhaps principally through the college of the Vestal Virgins, Caesar was able to procure Sulla's grudging pardon.

Concluding that the moment was propitious to perform his obligatory military duty to Rome, in 80 B.C.E. Caesar sailed off to Asia Minor to serve with distinction as aide-de-camp to Minucius Thermus, Sulla's legate in the area, against Sulla's old enemy, Mithradates VI Eupator, the Persian-named but Hellenistic king of Pontus. Caesar continued serving in the East until Sulla's death in 78 B.C.E. He then returned to Rome, where, attempting to begin a legal career, he unsuccessfully argued two cases before the Roman Senate. Back-to-back failures convinced him that he needed to hone his oratorical skills, so, perhaps on CICERO's

advice, he sailed for Rhodes to study with a master named Molo. On the way, pirates captured Caesar and held him for 38 days until his ransom arrived. His subsequent study with Molo apparently proved fruitful, for thereafter Caesar came to be regarded as among the foremost orators of his day.

When Caesar returned to Rome, probably in the winter of 74–73 B.C.E., he threw in his lot with the parties agitating for the overthrow of the Roman constitution that Sulla had imposed. That document simply did not provide adequate mechanisms for the successful government of a fractious city-state or a perennially dissatisfied Italian peninsula, nor did it offer a superstructure supporting the governance of a far-flung empire. External pressures were also building on the constitution. Spain was in armed rebellion against Roman rule, and a slave leader named Spartacus and his army threatened to undermine Roman authority on the Italian peninsula itself. One of a pair of joint consuls, Marcus Licinius Crassus, ended the Spanish threat and joined his forces with those of his co-consul, Gnaeus Pompeius (Pompey), to defeat Spartacus.

With their armies camped just outside the walls of Rome, Crassus and Pompey—between whom no love was lost—collaborated in 70 B.C.E. to overthrow the Sullan constitution and with it oligarchic rule in Rome. The following year, the Roman Senate named Julius Caesar quaestor for Spain—a role in which the young man would learn the day-to-day details of provincial and civic finance and management, not to mention having the opportunity to hone the skills of military leadership.

On Caesar's return to Rome, he was soon drawn into close association with Pompey, who, though ostensibly in retirement, was still in a position to pull the strings that controlled Rome. Though the Senate sat and debated, in reality it was the popularly elected tribunes of Rome who held the reins of popular power, and Pompey controlled the tribunes. Pompey was appointed and given adequate resources to clear the Mediterranean of pirates—a job he successfully performed with great dispatch. That done, he renewed hostilities against the troublesome Mithradates, extending Roman influence to the Euphrates River. Asia Minor became entirely subject to Rome, as did Syria and Judea.

Having completed his responsibilities in Spain, in 65 B.C.E. Caesar took the next step in the Roman hierarchy of public offices: He became an *aedile curule*. This office carried with it membership in the Roman Senate and responsibility for the oversight and maintenance of various civic necessities in the city—enforcing certain laws and imposing certain fines. Two years later, he rose to the position of pontifex maximus—the leading member of the college of priests responsible for the observance of religious practices in Rome. His friend Cicero at that time served as consul—the Roman head of state.

Caesar's political career now continued to follow one of the paths that typically led to civic positions of the highest authority and responsibility. The year 62 B.C.E. saw his elevation to the post of praetor—an official post second in rank only to that of consul and involving both civil and military leadership responsibilities. The following year saw his ascension to the rank of propraetor—a capacity in which he became the governor of a province, in his case of Further Spain. Before leaving Rome, he established himself in the good graces of the two most powerful men of the era: Pompey and the fabulously wealthy Crassus, who lent Caesar the equivalent of almost a million dollars to settle his debts so that he could depart Rome for Spain. There he was obliged to further hone his military skills as he marshaled both land and sea forces against barbarian uprisings.

The next year, Caesar returned to Rome to stand for election to the consulship. As a returning successful general, he was entitled to a triumph—a victory parade—but he could not stand for election to office without giving up both his military command and the celebration he had earned. He confounded his enemies who had arranged the dilemma by resigning his military offices unhesitatingly and abandoning the tri-

umph. Despite the machinations of the Roman senators who hated his resistance to government by oligarchy, Caesar became consul in 59 B.C.E. In that role, he cemented alliances with both Crassus and Pompey, and the three men became the leaders of the Roman world, supported in this period by the influence of CICERO. When the senate resisted such necessary measures as buying private lands to reward returning veterans, Caesar went over their heads directly to the Roman people, who obliged the senators to perform their consul's will. This method became Caesar's standard practice.

It was also standard practice to reward a consul with the governorship of a province following his year of service. The senate was anxious to trim Caesar's sails and had passed a bill limiting the current consuls to service in Italy. Caesar turned this limitation to advantage by becoming the governor of a province that was on the Italian peninsula, but not under the authority of the senate: Cisalpine Gaul, the area between the Po River and the Alps. Military considerations also prompted the senate to tack onto Caesar's responsibilities the Gallic provinces beyond the Alps—Transalpine Gaul.

From the moment that Caesar assumed his Gallic proconsulship, we have in his own voice a detailed account of his activities and their significance in his *Commentary on the Gallic Wars*, which covers the period from 59 to 49 B.C.E. The same period includes his invasions of Germany and Britain. The sequence of military engagements that occupied these years seems all the more impressive when one realizes that in addition to his role as general, he also had to preside as the chief judge of the provinces whose oversight he exercised. At least one historian, E. Badian, however, is at pains to point out that more than 1 million of Caesar's Gallic and Germanic enemies were slain during his proconsular campaigns. Another million were forced into bondage and displaced. Badian also compares the damage Caesar's forces did to both the social fabric and the environment of northern Europe with the damage wrought by the European invasion and conquest of the Americas 15 centuries later.

Pompey, Crassus, and Caesar exercised de facto power throughout the Roman world during this entire period, and in spring 56 B.C.E., the three met at the Cisalpine city of Lucca with many of their senatorial and magisterial supporters in attendance. The agreements reached at this conference confirmed Caesar in his proconsulship of Cisalpine and Transalpine Gaul for another five years and added to his subject domains the province of Illyria that lay to the north and east of the Adriatic Sea. The rest of Rome's foreign dominions became subject to the military rule of Pompey and Crassus. The triumvirate continued to exercise executive power in the Roman world.

While the preeminent rulers of Rome were all off in the provinces, the city of Rome descended into near anarchy. When Crassus was killed in military action in the East, elevating Pompey to dictator became a compelling option. It was a decision that Caesar subscribed to since he had the rebellion of the splendid Gallic leader Vercingetorix to contend with.

Now, however, a breach opened between Caesar and Pompey as each pursued his own interests and Pompey, in particular, sought to nullify Caesar's actions. As long as Caesar held public office, he was proof against any trumped-up charges that might be brought against him. If, however, a hiatus occurred in his public service, Caesar would be at the absolute mercy of Pompey, who could arrange to pass whatever laws he wished. This included ex post facto laws that made crimes of formerly noncriminal acts.

As the situation developed, Pompey held the reins of political power against a politically defenseless Caesar, but Caesar commanded an army of seasoned veterans likely to prove invincible against any opposing power. Caesar attempted to ameliorate this seemingly irresolvable impasse by offering to dismiss several legions of his troops and retain proconsulships in Cisalpine Gaul and Illyria until he had been elected consul in Rome again. The senate firmly rejected

that offer, and from that instant, the situation descended into the internecine hostilities in Italy and Spain that Caesar describes in his commentary *The Civil Wars*.

In that commentary, we learn of Caesar's decision to cross the Rubicon River with the legions that marched with him—a decision that made him guilty of high treason against the Roman state since it was forbidden for a general to bring his troops onto Roman soil. We learn, too, of his subsequent victories over Pompey in Spain, Africa, and at Pharsalus in Greece. Pompey fled to Egypt, and Caesar followed, arriving to the horrid spectacle of his adversary's severed head, presented to him as a mark of loyalty on the part of a group of Alexandrian assassins. The same people, however, soon besieged Caesar, who, though in grave danger, was eventually relieved by Mithradates of Pergamum and a force of Syrians and Jews. The Romans' combined forces then turned against the forces of the Egyptian boy king, Ptolemy. The Egyptians lost, and their king drowned in the Nile.

Caesar tarried in Egypt (though not for long) with that country's queen of Greek—not African—ancestry, Cleopatra Ptolemy. He then took a circuitous route to Italy, putting down rebellion along the way. In Italy, his alliance with Cicero and his presence calmed an explosive situation. That done, he led a force to Africa to put down rebellion in the Roman provinces there.

Throughout this period, Rome named Caesar dictator four times. In February 45 B.C.E., the Roman senate took an unprecedented step, conferring that title on Caesar for life. A final battle remained to be waged—the Battle of Munda in Spain. On March 17, 45 B.C.E., Caesar commanded a vastly outnumbered force against an army led by Pompey's son. Caesar won and is said to have considered the battle the most dangerous in which he participated.

Although, as permanent dictator, Caesar adopted the dress of the ancient kings of Rome, he refused to assume their titles. Some, however, have suggested that he had something even greater in mind. The descendant of a goddess, he aspired to deification—an honor not without precedent among the monarchs of Asia. He also began to yearn for another foreign campaign. Faced with the prospect of a still-young dictator for life, Caesar's enemies began to coalesce about him. Some of them were disappointed in their own expectations; others were suspicious of having an absentee god as supreme ruler; a few clung to the ancient principles of a Roman republic. As every high school student knows, on the ides of March (the 15th) 44 B.C.E., a coterie of conspirators struck Caesar down.

Some think that Caesar was forewarned. His second wife, Calpurnia, whom he had been constrained to divorce to seal his alliance with Pompey by marrying Pompey's daughter, sent him a monitory note. Either uninformed or overconfident in his power, however, he chose to ignore both warning notes and premonitions. Arguably the most remarkable individual that western Europe has ever known, Caesar fell to the knives of his assassins.

Bibliography

Bradford, Ernle. *Julius Caesar: The Pursuit of Power.* London: H. Hamilton, 1984.

Fowler, W. Warde. *Julius Caesar and the Foundation of the Roman Imperial System.* New York: G. P. Putnam's Sons, 1908.

Fuller, J. F. C. *Julius Caesar: Man, Soldier, and Tyrant.* New York: Da Capo Press, 1991.

Kamm, Antony. *Julius Caesar.* New York: Routledge, 2006.

Meir, Christian. *Caesar.* Translated by David McLintock. New York: Basic Books, HarperCollins, 1995.

Callimachus (ca. 310–ca. 235 B.C.E.) *Greek poet*

Born in the Greek colony of Cyrene in Egyptian Libya to a couple named Battus and Megatima, Callimachus studied grammar and philosophy in his native city and at some juncture migrated to Alexandria, the intellectual center of the Greek-Egyptian world under the Ptolemaic pharaohs. The Ptolemies were of Greek origin.

After an apparent period of poverty, Callimachus became a schoolteacher in Eleusis, an Alexandrian suburb, but he aspired to be recognized as a poet and critic. Thereafter he somehow came to the attention of Ptolemy II, who had established the ancient world's finest library at Alexandria. Ptolemy employed Callimachus as a functionary in the library—probably as a cataloguer of manuscripts. Callimachus's surviving work includes an example of his work in the library, *Pinakes* (tables). Lost, however, are many of his prose works—catalogues about foreign cultures, language, geography, the origins of cities, and natural wonders that Callimachus seems to have written for the benefit of the library's users.

Callimachus's poetic reputation rests most securely on his EPIGRAMS, 64 examples of which survive. He was particularly fond of shorter forms, and conducted a notable literary feud with his pupil, APOLLONIUS OF RHODES, who preferred longer ones. Callimachus pithily remarked: "The bigger the book, the greater the nuisance." In keeping with his preference, he wrote hymns and elegiac verse addressed to various deities of the Greek pantheon, and several of these survive. He also wrote about local religious traditions, as we know from the fragmentary remains of his elegiac *Aetia* (causes or origins). This piece was long but composed of linked short pieces with some traces of direct descent from Callimachus. These include the love elegy ACONTIUS AND KIDIPPE and a translation of The LOCK OF BERENÍKÊ by the Roman poet CATULLUS that makes possible a reasonably confident reconstruction of the original.

It was to the love elegies of Callimachus that the Roman poet OVID looked when seeking a model for his METAMORPHOSES. Notable, too, are the poet's "HYMNS TO ZEUS, APOLLO, ARTEMIS, AND OTHERS." Callimachus did try his hand at the EPIC, and we have fragmentary remains of his HECALE, which treats legendary material associated with Theseus, the king of Athens.

Although Callimachus's literary remains are often in a very fragmentary state, a trio of synopses and commentaries on his work also survive that convey further important information. One of them, for example, is the source of what is known about his *Artemis of Leucas*, only a snippet of which has survived.

Above all else, Callimachus participated by example in an ongoing debate between those who preferred poems in the traditional mode and those who preferred shorter, more carefully polished work. He appeared at an historical moment when the epic tradition had little that was innovative to offer, and the great Athenian tradition of TRAGEDY had likewise enjoyed its heyday. Bookish, precise, subtle, careful of nuance, and unerringly tasteful, Callimachus's lyrics—though they may not have proved widely popular—reinvigorated the poetic production of Greece by their grace, multilayered allusions, and musicality. If his poetry seemed snobbish or overly erudite to some—and it did—it nonetheless provided models for poetic innovators in the Western tradition from Catullus and Ovid to Ben Jonson, T. S. Eliot, and Ezra Pound.

Bibliography

Callimachus. *Callimachus: Hymns, Epigrams, Select Fragments.* Translated by Stanley Lombardo and Diane Rayor. Baltimore and London: Johns Hopkins University Press, 1988.
———. *The Poems of Callimachus.* Translated by Frank Nisetich. Oxford and New York: Oxford University Press, 2001.
Ferguson, John. *Callimachus.* Boston: Twayne Publishers, 1980.
Trypannis, C. A. *Callimachus: Aetia, Iambi, Lyric Poems, Hecale, Minor Epic and Elegiac Poems and Other Fragments.* The Loeb Classical Library. Vol. 421. Cambridge, Mass.: Harvard University Press, 1925.

Callinus of Ephesus (fl. ca. 684 B.C.E.)
Greek poet

Based on four slender surviving fragments, Callinus of Ephesus seems to have been the earliest known elegiac poet in the Greek language.

Two sorts of poems commonly get lumped under the rubric *elegiac.* The earlier sort, to which Callinus's fragments belong, are war songs. The latter sort laments mournful events. What the two kinds of elegies share in common in the Greek language is their poetic form. The elegiac verse is composed of two dactylic lines, the first of hexameter and the second of pentameter.

In one of the surviving fragments of Callinus's elegies, the warrior-poet encourages his fellow soldiers to fight bravely against their enemies from the city of Magnesia, located in Asia Minor on the Hermus River in Lydia. According to later authorities, the Ephesians overcame the Magnesians.

See also ELEGY AND ELEGIAC POETRY and QUANTITATIVE VERSE.

Bibliography

Edmonds, J. M., ed. and trans. *Elegy and Iambus . . . The Greek Elegiac and Iambic Poets from Callinus to Crates. . . .* Vol 1. Cambridge, Mass.: Harvard University Press, 1954.

Calpurnius, Titus Siculus (fl. first century C.E.) *Roman poet*

A minor Roman poet who was very likely a contemporary of the Emperor Nero, Calpurnius composed PASTORAL POETRY in imitation of VIRGIL and THEOCRITUS. Seven of his poems survive. Three of them, *Eclogues 1, 5,* and *7,* are concerned with events during the reign of Nero, the death of his predecessor Claudius, and Nero's accession to the throne. The last of these describes the wonderment that strikes a shepherd named Corydon, who, while visiting Rome, attends games sponsored by Nero at a newly constructed amphitheater. The attractions of life in the capital city estrange Corydon from his former rural existence.

Although *Eclogues 1* and *7* above rely heavily on the observations of a single speaker, *Eclogues 2, 3, 4, 5,* and *6* are presented in dialogue and treat the sorts of subjects that more usually appear in pastoral poetry. In the second eclogue, shepherds sing of their love for the same country maiden. The third draws a rather farfetched comparison between a stubborn woman and an ornery cow and contains a plea for forgiveness by Lycidas, who has beaten his beloved Phyllis in a paroxysm of jealousy. The fourth combines rural themes with extravagant praise of the benefits that Nero's rule has brought to country life. It also contains a request that the shepherd Meliboeus bring to the attention of Nero the verse of Corydon and his colleague Amyntas. Some have speculated that Meliboeus stands for the emperor's tutor, SENECA. The fifth pastoral gives advice about tending sheep and goats, and the sixth contains a staple of the pastoral mode, a singing contest. The ill temper of the contestants and judges and their resultant dispute, however, causes the contest to abort.

A principal benefit of Calpurnius's pastoral work derives simply from its survival. It was published in Venice during the early days of printing (1472) and helped transmit the pastoral genre to the Renaissance.

Another poem, *De laude Pisonis* (In praise of Piso), which seems to celebrate the actions of the person who led the conspiracy that brought Nero down, has also sometimes been attributed to Calpurnius.

Bibliography

Dunlop, J. E., ed. *Latin Pastorals by Virgil, Calpurnius Siculus, Nemesianus*. London: Bell, 1969.

Keene, Charles Haines, ed. *The Eclogues of Calpurnius Siculus and M. Aurelius Nemesianus*. Hildesheim: G. Olms, 1969.

Cato the Elder　See ORIGINES.

Catullus, Caius Valerius (84–54 B.C.E.)

Roman poet

Catullus was the scion of an aristocratic family from Verona, in the Roman province of Cisalpine Gaul, who, on reaching his majority, spent an extended period in the city of Rome. There he soon became involved in the city's society, pleasures, and vices. A gifted poet, he at once associated himself with a group of writers known as the *new poets*. The group's members differed from their predecessors in that, instead of looking backward to earlier Roman and Greek heroic models or to public affairs for their subjects, they looked principally to their own colorful biographies. The literary historian Quincy Howe, Jr., also finds evidence of the influence and learned allusion of the epigrammatic Alexandrian Greek poet CALLIMACHUS—a predecessor whose work Catullus certainly knew. Others find evidence of the influence of Roman epigram as practiced about a half century before Catullus. A language rich in colloquial usage also marks the poet's work, as does a mastery of many subjects—some quite scholarly.

Although Catullus's private behavior was undoubtedly libertine, he was nonetheless a romantic idealist who regarded love as the highest and most ennobling of human emotions. He also thought of fidelity to one's beloved as a high calling. Regrettably, but interestingly, the older, aristocratic, and unprincipled woman with whom he fell in love, Clodia Metelli, the wife of a distinguished provincial administrator, took a more pragmatic and sensualist view of extramarital liaisons. To the idealistic poet's extreme chagrin, Clodia—called Lesbia in Catullus's verse—entertained at least five other lovers besides Catullus. CICERO considered her a notorious slut.

Those of Catullus's poems that address this relationship (including poems 2, 3, 5, 7, 51, 72, and and 76) chronicle his growing distrust, his disappointment, and his manful efforts to continue loving his mistress and maintain his ennobling view of love in the face of incontrovertible evidence of her infidelities. His poems also evidence the disappointment and nervous exhaustion that accompanied the effort.

His own extracurricular activities, also reflected in his verse, included the employment of both female and male prostitutes (poem 32). To one of the latter, a youth named Juventus, Catullus appears to have temporarily transferred his affections from Clodia (poem 48). Unwisely, however, Catullus introduced Juventus to a friend named

Aurelius, with whom Juventus had an affair before moving on to another acquaintance, one Furius (see poems 15 and 24).

Catullus left Rome for about a year in 57 B.C.E. He traveled as a civic official to the Black Sea province of Bithnyia, doubtless hoping to improve his already enviable financial situation. Poems 10 and 28 make clear that this hope, too, was doomed to disappointment. Beyond that, word reached him in Bithnyia that his brother had died in the nearby region of the Troad. Poems 68 and 101 reveal his feelings about this tragedy and his journey to mourn at his brother's tomb.

Although service in Bithnyia did not improve Catullus's financial position, he nevertheless could afford to have a private ship built to take him back to Italy. Once there, he returned to his familial villa, whose substantial ruins—now a tourist attraction—still grace the peninsula of Sirmione on the western shore of Lake Garda not far from the city of Verona.

Catullus's surviving work reveals that, for a time at least, his political opinions favored the party opposed to JULIUS CAESAR. As an aristocrat, Catullus objected to Caesar's preferment of sycophantic commoners to responsible posts and found offensive the outrageous manner in which such persons behaved (see poems 29, 41, 43, 57, 94, 114, and 115). In the final analysis, however, Catullus seems to have changed his mind about Caesar.

Catullus died at about the age of 30. Known at least by reputation and by the occasional comments of persons who had read his poems since he flourished, his complete poems have come down to us in a unique manuscript discovered in the Capitoline library of Verona in the 14th century. He was the most influential lyric poet of his epoch.

See also "ATTIS" (POEM 63).

Bibliography

Catullus. *Catullus: The Complete Poems for Modern Readers.* Translated by Reney Meyers and Robert J. Ormsby. London: George Allen and Unwin Ltd., 1972.

cento

Cento—an English word—has two meanings. First, it can be a collection of translations by many hands of the works of an author. In the 19th century, for example, the Bohn Cento was the only complete translation available in English of the 366 poems comprising Petrarch's *Canzoniere*.

The second meaning alludes to a poem or collection of poems that an author has constructed by borrowing lines from one or more other authors and arranging them to express the arranger's thoughts and emotions. The Roman aristocrat FALTONIA BETITIA PROBA, who was one of only two women poets noted among the ancient Romans, became a renowned author of centos. (For the other known Roman female poet, see SULPICIA.) Proba borrowed lines from VIRGIL to construct poems on biblical subjects.

Employing the cento technique asserts an author's familiarity with the work of others and invites comparison—an invitation that implies an author deserves to be considered in the same league as the poet who originally wrote the lines.

Chariton of Aphrodisias   See GREEK PROSE ROMANCE.

Chinese classical literary commentary

The history of Chinese literature is long. The nature of Chinese writing is often both ambiguous and allusive. Language changes, and meaning becomes slippery. Readers frequently need clarification to help them understand what old texts mean, and ancient scholars were often able to earn their livings supplying that need. For all those reasons, writings that explained, clarified, or amplified basic texts soon became necessary adjuncts to the texts themselves, and the literary historian Haun Saussy has traced a long and rich tradition of such Chinese explanatory or exegetical writing for us.

Saussy points to the BOOK OF CHANGES as the Chinese classic that has benefited most from successive layers of explanatory writing. As each successive generation of readers found earlier versions difficult, new explanatory material clarified the older text and the former glosses.

CONFUCIUS's ANNALS OF SPRING AND AUTUMN (Chunqiu, or Ch'un Ch'iu) provided a skeletal framework upon which a body of helpful commentary could be and needed to be erected so that readers would know why Confucius had selected the original entries in the book. Among the most important and fundamental examples of that sort of amplifying commentary are those that appear both in the fifth century B.C.E.'s ZUO ZHUAN (Tso chuan; Commentary of Zuo) and, almost 700 years later, in Luxuriant Dew of the Springs and Autumns (Chunqiu Fanlu [Ch'un-ch'iu fan-lu]) by Dong Zhongshu (Tung Chung-shu; ca. 125 C.E.).

A third sort of commentary that one encounters is lexical analysis that offers familiar, contemporary synonyms for words that have fallen into disuse or that have changed their meanings over time. Examples of such works include those of the first–second century C.E. lexicographer Xu (Hsü) Shen's Erya (Ehr-ya; Approaching elegance) and his Shouwen jiezi (Shou-wen Chieh-tzu; Explication of characters simple and complex).

Eventually, of course, the sheer mass of such commentary threatened to overwhelm the primary documents the comment was supposed to clarify, so that scholars since the ancient period have spent much time and effort winnowing the commentators' output—sometimes even suggesting that their work had once and for all arrived at definitive interpretations of the meanings of ancient texts. The nature of linguistic and social change, however, suggests that such self-confidence is misplaced.

Bibliography

Saussy, Haun. "Classical Exegesis." In The Columbia History of Chinese Literature. Edited by Victor H. Mair. New York: Columbia University Press, 2001.

Chinese ethical and historical literature in verse and prose
(ca. 1766 B.C.E.–ca. 200 C.E.)

The very oldest surviving examples of Chinese writing appear on bronze containers and on "oracle bones" that were used for predicting the future. Tens of thousands of ancient examples of writing on wood and bamboo strips have also been discovered periodically. Later ancient Chinese writing on less-durable paper (invented in China ca. 100 C.E.), has for millennia been preserved in China, however, by a laborious and error-prone process of recopying and editing earlier manuscripts. We know, for instance, that CONFUCIUS edited the now-lost texts of earlier masters. Many other early versions of important documents have long been thought to be irretrievably lost.

In 1973, however, Chinese archaeologists exploring a site at Mawangdui (Ma-wang-tui) uncovered a treasure trove of 50 of the earliest Chinese manuscripts known to exist. Written on silk, the rediscovered manuscripts make possible correcting many errors that had crept into later versions of the documents over the course of centuries. Perhaps ironically, that find has made the late 20th and early 21st centuries the great age of the study of ancient Chinese literature.

Among the manuscripts discovered at Mawangdui (Ma-wang-tui) were two copies of the verse Daodejing (Tao Te Ching)—the foundational text of Daoism and what one of the manuscript's translators, the scholar Victor Mair, considers to be the document central to all Chinese religious and philosophical thought. Received opinion attributes the authorship of the Daodejing to Laozi (Lao Tzu), but Mair believes the document to have coalesced from a preliterate oral tradition.

Also among the manuscripts unearthed at Mawangdui (Ma-wang-tui) was the earliest known version of the BOOK OF CHANGES, or Yijing (I Ching). This work was apparently originally a collection of brief oracular sayings arranged under a series of interpretative hexagrams. Those initiated into its proper use employed it to ascertain the direction of change in the ongoing processes of the universe. Later the followers of Confucius added commentaries to the oracles and co-opted the work as one of the five documents central to Confucian thought.

Another work whose origins disappear in the mists of preliterate history is the BOOK OF ODES, or *Shijing* (*Shih Chi*). In its current form, it contains 305 songs, selected, according to tradition, by Confucius himself from an earlier collection of more than 3,000 lyrics, perhaps compiled around 600 B.C.E. Confucius is also credited with having edited the odes' musical settings, but these are now apparently lost irretrievably. Also among the five documents central to Confucianism, the book contains songs critical of government policy, corrupt officials, and military conscription. Though it was suppressed both in ancient times and in Maoist China, the work has nonetheless survived.

We find a third ancient book crucial to the edifice of Confucian doctrine in the *Book of History*—the *Shiji*. The earliest sections of this work date to late in the Zhou (Chou) dynasty, a dynasty begun in ca. 1100 B.C.E. As a compilation of documents with commentary, and perhaps beginning around the eighth century B.C.E., the work expanded over time. Again, tradition has it that Confucius himself edited this work by assembling and commenting on the documents that comprise it. While this may well be true, it is also the case that later hands have added or substituted their own emendations. Autocratic leaders over the course of history have often tried to suppress points of view critical of their agendas. This was the case with the *Book of History* when, after the unification of China under the first Qin emperor (221 B.C.E.), he commanded that all copies of the writings supporting Confucianism be destroyed. Though much in the *Book of History* escaped this edict, chapters 28–32 of its later sections disappeared. Later forgers attempted to remedy the defect.

The fourth document in the ancient corpus of essential Confucian thought is a historical text chronicling important events that occurred in the feudal fiefdoms of China between the years 722 and 481 B.C.E. This work suffered the same fate at the hands of the first Qin emperor as did the *Book of History*. Portions survived, however. The principle surviving section is entitled *Spring and Autumn Annals* (*Chunqiu*). Other portions of the original document are preserved in the sixth chapter of *Grand Records of the Historian*, or *Shiji*. A historian, SIMA QIAN (Ssu-ma Ch'ien), compiled these records about 100 B.C.E. Bits of this document have also been recovered from tombs and elsewhere as inscriptions on bamboo strips.

Apart from Confucius, the most respected of the ancient Chinese ethical thinkers is MENCIUS (Mengzi or Meng Tzu). Mencius differed from Confucius in that the former thought that human nature was fundamentally good while Confucius thought it bad but remediable. Like Confucius, Mencius traveled about looking unsuccessfully for a ruler willing to implement his social programs. Also like Confucius, Mencius's followers compiled a posthumous anthology of his sayings, *The Mencius* (*Mengzi*), and recorded his conversations with rulers. Not highly regarded at first, Mencius came to be ranked second only to Confucius among the ancient sages, and the record of his life and sayings came to be viewed as an ancient Chinese classic. His life overlapped that of PLATO in the West for a period of some two decades.

The names of some other ancient Chinese writers and the subjects they wrote about have survived. These include SunZi, KuanZi, WuZi, and WenZi—writers on war, political philosophy, and related subjects. Although the extant documents bearing the names of these authors have been shown to be forgeries written long after their ostensible authors had died, the forgeries prove instructive nonetheless.

In addition to the classical philosophical and behavioral canon outlined here and commentaries on it, the literary historian Christopher Leigh Connery lists the following literary genres as being recognized by the ancient Chinese: CI (TS'U) POEMS (sung poetry) and FU POEMS (verse recited without singing); astronomy, calendrical writing, and divination; military texts; and medical commentaries and cures. Many of the genres that modern European readers and writers value—novel, memoir, introspective confessional verse, and the like—either did not exist or were actively devalued as having little merit by the ancient Chinese.

Included in the received canon we do find the work of the fourth–third century B.C.E. moralist Dan Gong (Tan Kung), some of whose reflections appear in the *Book of Rites*. Surviving as well from the third century B.C.E. is the work of XUNZI, whose views were diametrically opposed to those of Mencius. Xunzi considered the fundamental nature of human beings to be irremediably evil and deserving of harsh governmental restraint.

Another work, much revered for reasons that have more to do with its title than its content, has been ascribed to the hands of Confucius and a collaborator. The work is entitled the CLASSIC OF FILIAL PIETY (*Xiao jing*).

The texts included in the Chinese classical canon had above all a moral focus that eventually did what Confucius had hoped they would: They became the organizing principles of Chinese government. After the emperors had extended their sovereignty over lesser kings and warlords, as Connery tells us, the emperors sat like quiet fountains of power whose principal duty was the appointment of capable officials. Those officials proved their capacity by demonstrating their mastery of the canonical texts in the Confucian tradition. They conducted diplomacy by quoting from the canon passages of poetry that would clarify the officials' negotiating positions and the outcomes desired *if* their negotiating partners had also mastered the same essential body of moral poetry, philosophy, history, and so forth. Confucius expressed the opinion that anyone who had not mastered the *Book of Odes* would have nothing to say.

Connery makes this major point—one that anyone interested in ancient Chinese letters must bear in mind: In the generations following Confucius's death, the ancient Chinese literary canon became a regulatory corpus of material governing every aspect of Chinese public and many facets of Chinese private life. The canon taught people right and moral thinking and behavior. Literature that merely expressed private feeling or dissident thought was perceived to be self-indulgent, of little worth, excessive, and even dangerous.

See also SHIHJI.

Bibliography

Confucius. *The Analects of Confucius (Lun Yu)*. Translated by Chichung Huang. New York: Oxford University Press, 1997.

Connery, Christopher Leigh. *The Empire of the Text: Writing and Authority in Early Imperial China*. New York: Rowman and Littlefield Publishers, 1998.

Giles, Herbert A. *A History of Chinese Literature*. New York: Grove Press, 1958.

Idema, Wilt, and Lloyd Haft. *A Guide to Chinese Literature*. Ann Arbor: Center for Chinese Studies, University of Michigan, 1997.

Watson, Burton. *Early Chinese Literature*. New York: Columbia University Press, 1962.

Choephori, The Aeschylus (458 B.C.E.)

The second TRAGEDY in AESCHYLUS's trilogy ORESTEIA, the first-prize winner in the last year Aeschylus competed in the Athenian City Festival of the god Dionysus, the GREAT DIONYSIA, *The Choephori* takes up the examination of the continuing effects of the curse on the house of Atreus where its predecessor play, AGAMEMNON, leaves off. (For a detailed account of the curse, see the entry for *Agamemnon*.)

When Agamemnon's wife Clytemnestra and her paramour, Aegisthus, murdered Agamemnon on his victorious return from the Trojan War, Agamemnon's son, Orestes, was in exile at the court of his uncle, Strophis, the king of Phocis. *The Choephori* opens with a returned Orestes praying at the tomb of his father and laying a lock of his own hair as a sacrifice on the grave. His friend Pylades accompanies him, and the two are interrupted by the arrival of Orestes' sister Electra, accompanied by the CHORUS. The chorus reflects upon the sorry state of affairs in the city of Mycenae since the murder of its king and on the portents of disaster yet to come that reflect the anger of the dead in the underworld and bode ill for the city. The members of the chorus instruct Electra in the proper form of a prayer for vengeance, for the restoration of the children of Agamemnon to the throne of Mycenae, and for the prompt return of her brother Orestes, who has momentarily hidden himself away.

Electra notices Orestes' hair and identifies it as his. She imagines that he has sent it in honor of his father, but she hopes that he has laid it there himself. She also sees and identifies his footprint, but when he himself reappears, she nevertheless doubts his identity until he offers proofs. The siblings speak of their unhappy state and of their hope for vengeance and restoration to power. The leader of the chorus cautions them against spies who will report their words, but Orestes tells how Apollo's own oracle has foretold that to avoid an adverse fate, he must slay his father's murderers. Otherwise he will die slowly, friendless, cursed, and horrified. The children thirst for vengeance, and the chorus thirsts for the deaths of the murderers of Agamemnon. Orestes vows that if he can kill his mother, he will "dare to die."

Electra laments the curse on the house of her grandfather Atreus—a curse under which her generation continues to suffer. Orestes promises that together they will end the curse. The chorus reports that Clytemnestra had dreamed of nursing a fatal serpent at her breast—a foreshadowing of her death at the hands of her own son.

Orestes plans to arrive at the palace in disguise with Pylades and to strike down Aegisthus at the first opportunity. The chorus draws comparisons with events from legend and mythology, and the scene shifts from Agamemnon's tomb to the palace gate. Orestes seeks admission. Clytemnestra greets him and offers hospitality. Orestes identifies himself as a merchant from Phocis who bears a message from its king, Strophius. In that disguise, he tells Clytemnestra that Orestes is dead

and that Strophius wants to know whether or not to send home Orestes' remains. Appearing deeply moved, Clytemnestra offers shelter to her visitors and sends a nurse to find Aegisthus. The nurse reports to the chorus that Clytemnestra is only pretending to grieve. In her heart, she is glad her son has died. Moreover, she has instructed the nurse to tell Aegisthus to bring with him a spear-armed bodyguard. Clytemnestra is less gullible than her son imagines.

The chorus, however, advises the nurse to change Clytemnestra's instructions and tell Aegisthus to come alone. She goes, and the chorus prays to Zeus for the success of Orestes' enterprise and the restoration of the commonwealth.

Aegisthus enters alone and goes to meet his guests. The chorus rejoices as Aegisthus's cries for help are heard offstage. (The Greeks disapproved of death onstage.) Clytemnestra enters and is confronted by Orestes bearing a sword dripping with Aegisthus's blood. Clytemnestra grieves, and Orestes threatens her. She pleads her motherhood and the care she gave him as an infant. Moved, Orestes seeks advice from Pylades: Can he spare his mother? Pylades says no, and Orestes leads the pleading Clytemnestra to die at Aegisthus's side. Her pleading turns to threats and curses. Orestes remains firm in his intention and thrusts her into the palace. While he is killing her offstage, the chorus celebrates the restoration of Mycenae's freedom.

The central doors of the palace swing open. Holding his sword in one hand and in the other displaying the robe that had immobilized Agamemnon and kept him from defending himself, Orestes stands over the bodies of Aegisthus and Clytemnestra. The chorus celebrates the return of freedom to the city of Mycenae.

Now that the deed is done, however, Orestes begins to have second thoughts that prey upon his sanity. He begins to suffer from hallucinations, seeing serpents, and despite the chorus's assurances that he has done the right thing, his sense of guilt drives him to and over the brink of madness. Overwhelmed by his haunting visions, he resolves to go as a suppliant pilgrim to the temple of Apollo in Delphi in an effort to be released from his maddening sense of guilt.

The chorus ends the play by reviewing the operation of the curse on the house of Atreus: Thyestes' eating the cooked flesh of his own children; Agamemnon's murder; and now a third event whose outcome is still in question—will Orestes go mad, or will he escape the toils of the curse? (See *The Eumenides.*)

Bibliography

Aeschylus. *Oresteia. English and Greek.* Translated by George Thompson. New York: Everyman's Library, 2004.

chorus in Greek theater

In connection with the theater of the Greek world and its center at Athens, the chorus was usually a group of men—rarely, apparently, women—who sang and danced. As Greek theater had its origins in religious liturgy, the chorus also sprang from associated ritual occasions and participated in both tragic and comic performances.

Greek theater had much of the flavor of opera about it, and the choral parts of the play were usually chanted, often accompanied by dance-like movements either of the entire chorus or of halves of the chorus moving and singing together as they participated in the plots, explained matters to the audience, and represented public reaction to events.

The chorus had a leader, and in the earliest surviving Greek dramas, the parts that were spoken or sung were shared by a single actor, the leader of the chorus, the whole chorus in unison, or halves of the chorus operating separately to sing and dance a strophe and an antistrophe. These might be thought of as the verses of a song alternately performed by halves of a larger group of singers. As they sang the strophe, the choristers danced to the right of stage for two verses, as they sang the antistrophe, they danced back to their customary location.

As the number of actors on the Greek stage increased from one to two to three, the importance of the chorus diminished. Whereas both early Greek COMEDY and TRAGEDY prominently featured the chorus, comedy eventually dispensed with the chorus altogether, as in the plays of MENANDER. In later tragedy, the choral songs often represented the responses of public opinion to a drama's major action or served to underline the central message of a play in a final song.

Athenian citizens vied to be selected as members of the choruses. Eminent citizens considered it a matter of honor to pay the wages of the chorus members, and the playwrights in whose productions the choruses sang and danced also trained them to perform. A fringe benefit of this system for Greek theater arose from its contribution to a knowledgeable audience who thoroughly understood the fine points and the conventions of the performance.

Both comedy and especially tragedy remained closely connected to the religious roots from which they had sprung. Thus, serving as a chorus member fulfilled a spiritual as well as a civic obligation.

See also CONVENTIONS OF GREEK DRAMA.

Bibliography

Ley, Graham. *A Short Introduction to the Ancient Greek Theater.* Chicago: University of Chicago Press, 1991.

Chrysostom, St. John (ca. 354–407 C.E.)
Greek prose writer

Under the tutelage of the polytheistic SOPHIST LIBANIUS OF ANTIOCH and early identified as a literary prodigy and a genius, John was educated at Antioch. Finding himself attracted to a life of Christian asceticism, for a while John became a hermit, but then he took holy orders, becoming a priest at Antioch in 386. Called to Constantinople as its patriarch in 398, John reluctantly accepted the assignment. His nickname, Chrysostom, means the golden-tongued or golden-mouthed one, and he felt himself to be much more effective as a preacher than as a church administrator.

Ironically, his success in extending the influence of his bishopric led John into difficulties.

Theophilus, the bishop of Alexandria in Egypt, had ambitions of his own, and they conflicted with the expansion of a Christian power base at Constantinople. That rivalry plus the active enmity of the empress Eudoxia and other envious bishops in Asia led to his banishment. Once recalled, he was banished a second time in 404. He retired to Armenia, where he spent the last three years of his life.

John's surviving works are numerous, with more than 300 discourses and orations and more than 600 homilies. In addition, a substantial selection of his letters and treatises survive. If they are sometimes too flowery for our contemporary taste, they are nonetheless distinguished by their thoughtfulness, rich imagery, and clarity of style. He was perhaps the most prolific writer of the Eastern Church Fathers.

Among the subjects John addressed we find the nature of God, repenting of wrongdoing and its connection with the care of the poor, explanations of passages of Scripture, warnings against pride, cautions against attempts to turn Christians into Jews, and justifications of the Christian religion. A generous selection of his work is available in English translation.

Bibliography

Chrysostom, St. John. *Apologist: John Chrysostom.* In *The Fathers of the Church.* Vol. 48. Translated by Margaret A. Schatkin and Paul W. Harkins. New York: The Fathers of the Church, 1980.

———. *Commentary on St. John the Apostle and Evangelist, Homilies 1–47.* In *The Fathers of the Church.* Vols. 33 and 41, 1957–1960. Translated by Sister Thomas Aquinas Goggin. Washington, D.C.: Catholic University of America Press, 2000.

———. *Discourses against Judaizing Christians.* In *The Fathers of the Church.* Vol. 68. Translated by Paul. W. Harkins. Washington, D.C.: Catholic University of America Press, 1984.

———. *Homilies on Genesis 18–45.* Translated by Robert C. Hill. Washington, D.C.: Catholic University of America Press, 1986.

———. *On Repentance and Almsgiving.* Translated by Gus George Christo. Washington, D.C.: Catholic University of America Press, 1998.

Laistner, Max Ludwig Wolfram. *Christianity in Pagan Culture in the Later Roman Empire, Together with St. John Chrysostom's Address on Vainglory and the Right Way for Parents to Bring up their Children.* Translated by Max Ludwig Wolfram. Ithaca, N.Y.: Cornell University Press, 1951.

Cicero, Marcus Tullius (106–43 B.C.E.)
Roman prose writer and poet

Cicero was the eldest son of a well-to-do landowning family of Roman citizens of the knightly class at Arpinum in Volscia. Nevertheless, he did not belong to the class of hereditary aristocrats, the *optimates*, from which members of the Roman Senate were customarily drawn. Following a first-rate education in philosophy and rhetoric at Rome and in Greece, and following a period of military service, Cicero entered first the Roman court system and then senatorial politics. He did so as a "new man"—someone principally supported by his merits rather than by his lineage. He subsequently rose to become respected and revered as a lawyer, a leader, and a politician.

In the latter role, he served successively as a quaestor (a financial official) in Sicily (75 B.C.E.), as an aedile in charge of the grain supply for the Roman metropolis (69 B.C.E.), as praetor (magistrate of justice) in the city of Rome (66 B.C.E.), and finally as consul (64–63 B.C.E.). When he served as consul, Cicero became the legal head of the Roman Republic. In that capacity, he staved off an attempt by Catiline (Lucius Sergius Catilina) to overthrow the state.

As the Roman Republic disintegrated owing to an antiquated system of administration unsuited to the task of managing a world empire, Cicero remained a staunch republican as long as he reasonably could, serving as the conscience of the Roman senate. When it became clear the republic could not continue, however, and after the wars occasioned by the assassination of the dictator JULIUS CAESAR in 44 B.C.E., for a short time Cicero became a political mentor and adviser to Caesar's grandnephew, the young Octavian (who would later become AUGUSTUS CAESAR, the first emperor of Rome [27 B.C.E.]).

Eventually, however, largely because of his outspoken criticism of Mark Antony's ambitions in a series of addresses called *Philippics*, Cicero became a political liability to the ambitious Octavian. When Octavian found it expedient to join forces with Marcus Aemilius Lepidus and Mark Antony, as part of their deal, he agreed to the judicial murder of Cicero. Agents of Mark Antony implemented the agreement, killing Cicero near one of his country estates in 43 B.C.E.

Beyond the busy political life implied in the brief summary above, Cicero also undertook a formidable program of writing and publishing. Apart from inconsequential juvenilia, he polished and published the orations he had given defending or prosecuting persons accused in legal proceedings—often perfecting his arguments after the fact. He wrote about the art of rhetoric, about political science, about philosophy, and about theology. He was also a poet of respectable talent and accomplishment, and much of what we know of his life is preserved in a series of letters to his friend Titus Pomponius Atticus. That series began in 68 B.C.E. and continued with occasional interruptions almost until Cicero's death. The famous Italian poet and humanist Petrarch recovered most of these uncatalogued letters in the Capitoline Library of Verona during the 14th century. Petrarch considered that the revelation in the letters of the personal details of Cicero's private life tarnished the statesman's public image.

Perhaps Cicero's most lasting contribution to European and Euro-American English letters appears in his carefully crafted and balanced prose style. That style emerged as the model toward which prose writers aspired—whether or not they knew its origin—in Europe and in America as late as the mid-20th century.

As time permitted in his busy schedule, Cicero wrote important works throughout his majority. His *De inventione* (Topics for speeches) appeared before 81 B.C.E. *De oratore* (Concerning the orator) followed in 55. He spent four years preparing *De re publica* (On the State, 51 B.C.E.). He devoted another nine years to writing *De legibus* (On the law, 43 B.C.E.)

A hiatus in public service combined with a series of personal crises to spur Cicero to an unparalleled period of literary production. In 46 B.C.E., he divorced his wife of more than 30 years, Terentia, and hastily married his younger second wife, Publilia. In 45 B.C.E., Tullia, the adored daughter of his first marriage, died of complications arising from childbirth. When Publilia seemed relieved at losing a rival in Tullia, Cicero immediately divorced his second wife.

As therapy, perhaps, for the stress occasioned by both public and private turmoil, Cicero embarked on a maniacally ambitious writing program. The years 45 and 44 B.C.E. saw the drafting of *Hortensius; Academica (Academic Treatises), De finibus bonorum et malorum* (On Supreme Good and Evil), *Tusculanae disputationes* (TUSCULAN DISPUTATIONS), *De natura deorum* (ON THE NATURE OF THE GODS), *De divinatione* (On Divination), *De fato* (Destiny), and *De officiis* (About duties).

The second president of the United States, John Adams, said of Cicero: "All ages of the world have not produced a greater statesman and philosopher combined."

Bibliography

Cicero, Marcus Tullius. *Cicero on Oratory and Orators*. Translated and edited by J. S. Watson. Carbondale: Southern Illinois Press, 1986.

———. *Letters to Atticus*. 4 vols. Edited and translated by D. R. Shackleton Bailey. Cambridge, Mass.: Havard University Press, 1999.

———. *On Duties*. Edited by M. T. Griffen and E. M. Atkins. Cambridge: Cambridge University Press, 1991.

———. *On Moral Ends*. Edited by Julia Arinar. Translated by Raphael Woolf. Cambridge: Cambridge University Press, 2001.

———. *Philippics*. Edited and Translated by D. R. Shackleton Bailey. Chapel Hill: University of North Carolina Press, 1986.

———. *The Nature of the Gods, and On Divination*. Translated by C. D. Yonge. Amherst, N.Y.: Prometheus Books, 1997.

———. *The Republic and The Laws*. Translated by Niall Rudd. Oxford and New York: Oxford University Press, 1998.

Everitt, Anthony. *Cicero: The Life and Times of Rome's Greatest Politician*. New York: Random House Trade Paperbacks, 2001.

ci (ts'u) poems or songs

Because the *ci* verse form originated as song lyrics, in the beginning of the genre, at first, in ancient times, the line length was determined by the tune to which the song was performed. Over time, however, the tunes of the songs disappeared, and the uneven line lengths of the original songs became the pattern on which new poems—intended to be spoken or read silently—evolved. As a result, small subgenres of *ci* poems might be grouped together under the title of a long-forgotten song, but the poems' subject matter would have nothing to do with that title. It had simply become a versifying label.

Once separated from song, *ci* lyrics soon generated conventions of their own. They often concerned love—a subject deemed unworthy of classical verse. Often, women spoke words of the lyric, even though there was every likelihood that the verse had been written by a man. The language employed in *ci* verse also approximated more closely the common parlance of the Chinese person in the street. Whereas the more formal SHI verse might contain lofty intertextual allusions to earlier verse that would be recognized by educated cognoscenti who had committed large bodies of classical verse to memory, *ci* was likely to be relatively free from such intellectual freight.

Bibliography

Victor H. Mair, ed. *The Columbia Anthology of Traditional Chinese Literature*. New York: Columbia University Press, 1994.

Civil War (Pharsalia) Lucan (ca. 65 C.E.)

Using LIVY's now-lost books on Rome's civil wars as his source, LUCAN undertook the writing of an EPIC poem on that subject. Before he could complete the project, however, the emperor Nero, jealous of Lucan's accomplishment, forbade the poet to read his poem in public or even to share it with friends. Lucan joined a conspiracy against Nero, and, despite the poet's cooperation with the authorities when the plot was discovered, he was compelled to commit suicide. Thus, we have nine complete books and part of a 10th.

A recent translator of Lucan's poem, P. F. Widdows, suggests that two tenable views exist with respect to Lucan's design for completing his epic. The more probable of these views holds that the poem would have concluded with the suicide of Cato. Lucan admired Cato as the representative of the republican ideal that perished with the appointment of JULIUS CAESAR as dictator for life and with the subsequent ascent of AUGUSTUS CAESAR to the imperial throne. Cato had committed suicide rather than accept Julius Caesar's pardon for resisting his agenda. In a less likely scenario, thinks Widdows, Lucan might have planned to extend the action through Caesar's assassination. Others have argued for a still grander design that would have traced the conflict to the Battle of Actium and Augustus Caesar's victory over Marc Antony and Cleopatra in 31 B.C.E.

As it stands, the poem is a masterpiece of pessimism that traces the decline of a great republic and the destruction of its heroes and heroines. The villain of the piece is Julius Caesar, who attracts Lucan's passionate contempt.

Book 1

Book 1 begins with a statement of epic purpose, but instead of invoking the muses, Lucan alludes to the failure of the agreement of Julius Caesar, Pompey (Gnaeus Pompeius), and Marcus Licinius Crassus to share the government of Rome and its dominions and the universal guilt borne by all parties to the conflict. In the highly oratorical style that characterizes the entire poem, Lucan blames the citizens for allowing themselves to be led into fratricidal conflict, and he calls upon them to look upon the consequent and still visible ruin of cities and farmland. At line 33, however, the poet interrupts himself to suggest, perhaps unconvincingly, that all the horror and cost of the war was worthwhile given that the conflict ultimately resulted in the rule of Emperor Nero. Under Nero, Lucan hopes and prays that peace may spread through the world. In that hope, Nero becomes the singer's muse and his inspiration. (Line numbers allude to the Widdows translation.)

Lines 67–80 suggest that the underlying first cause of the civil war was universal disorder. All things came apart. The more immediate and local causes, however, were the formation of the first triumvirate of Caesar, Pompey, and Crassus (ll. 81–97), Crassus's death in battle (53 B.C.E.); the death in the year following of Julia, who was both Caesar's daughter and Pompey's wife; and the resultant and growing discord and mistrust between the two leaders (ll. 98–192). Beyond that personal rivalry, however, Lucan blames the wealth of Rome, its concentration in the hands of a relative few, and its consequent undermining of Roman morality as the governing classes and the electorate sold their influence and votes. Meanwhile, the poor suffered all sorts of indignities.

His introduction finished, Lucan tells how Caesar, returning with his army from Transalpine Gaul, paused at the boundary of the Roman state proper, the River Rubicon. The poet reports that there Caesar encountered the allegorical figure of Roma, weeping and disheveled. She tried to dissuade Caesar from breaking the law by illegally leading armed troops into her territory. Caesar, however, insisted on the purity of his motives. In the first act of warfare, he crossed the Rubicon. At this point, Lucan pictures Caesar as a marauding lion.

Lines 252–286 describe Caesar's occupation of Rimini (Arminium) and the reaction of the town's citizens. There Caesar's allies, the Roman tribunes, and the governor of Sicily, Curio, come and encourage Caesar to proceed despite the fact that Pompey means to resist his efforts (ll. 287–324).

Lucan's preference for the oratorical mode now appears as Caesar addresses and encourages his troops and then hears an answering speech by a centurion, Laelius, who expresses the soldiers' viewpoint (ll. 325–433). Encouraged by his troops' approval, Caesar calls his legions, both native and foreign, from as far away as the Rhine River, leaving the borders of the empire unprotected.

The poet next describes the fearful rumors that led the senate and the citizens of Rome to panic and abandon the city, then turns to a digression in which he recounts the fearful portents of impending disaster. New stars and meteors appeared. Lunar and solar eclipses occurred. Wild animals entered the city. Cattle talked. A supernatural being, a Fury, appeared, and Rome's great military hero Marius raised his head from his ruined tomb.

Priest and seers are summoned, consult the omens, and pronounce dire predictions. As *Book 1* ends, a Roman woman runs in a trance through the city, darkly predicting events that will occur in the coming warfare.

Book 2

As book 2 opens, Lucan tells the god Jupiter that human foreknowledge of coming disaster is a bad thing and that people would be better off without it. The entire city of Rome goes into mourning. First the women and then the men lament the coming disaster. The men can think of nothing worse than civil war. The digression begun in book 1 continues with an old man who recalls in lengthy detail the former civil war between Marius and Sulla. The old man has been an eyewitness to the bloody horrors that Romans can now expect to see again: executions and suicides, massacres of prisoners, and the Tiber River filled with the corpses of the slain.

When the long digression ends, Lucan returns to contemporary action. A fearless Brutus visits his kinsman, the stoic defender of republican values, Cato. Brutus seeks Cato's advice concerning whom to support in the coming strife. Cato, after predicting that his own death will atone for the sins of the Romans, opts to support Pompey against Caesar, and his words excite in Brutus's heart "an excessive and ominous passion."

Lucan now expands his audience's view of the character of Cato. First the poet recounts how Cato had passed his former wife Marcia along to his friend Hortensius so that Hortensius could sire offspring. Marcia arrives directly from Hortensius's funeral to plead that Cato remarry her. He does so, though in his current state of stoic renunciation, consummating the remarriage is out of the question. Lucan chooses this occasion to underscore Cato's unwavering virtue and self-mastery. For Lucan, Cato personifies the ideals of the Roman republic.

Beginning an account of the military maneuvers of the combatants—first those of Pompey—Lucan interrupts himself with a mytho-geographic discussion of Italy's Apennine Mountains and the rivers that spring from them. That done, he recounts Caesar's successes in northern Italy against Pompey's generals. The poet next describes the fruitless resistance of Pompey's loyal Domitius, whose soldiers deserted and whom Caesar embarrassed by releasing Domitius after his defeat.

Returning the action to Pompey's camp, Lucan indulges in a further oratorical interlude as he has Pompey address his troops. Pompey emphasizes Caesar's criminality. He justly boasts of his own military prowess, including his major triumph of ridding the Roman Mediterranean of pirates in only two months—a fraction of the anticipated time. His strength now, however, is depleted. He is outmanned and in danger of being outmaneuvered. Therefore he withdraws to Brundisium (Brindisi), which is defensible and which is also a seaport from which, if necessary, he can escape.

An historical description of Brundisium and then another address by Pompey follows. He sends representatives, his son Gnaeus and the consuls of Rome, Lentulus and Marcellus, to enlist allies in Asia Minor, Scythia, and in Greece.

Then Lucan describes Caesar's attempts to block the harbor at Brundisium and cut off Pompey's escape route. Pompey, however, was no mean military tactician, and he successfully countered this action. All but two ships of his fleet broke free of the harbor. No sooner was he at sea than the city's citizens threw open their gates to welcome Caesar's forces. Book 2 ends with a dark foreshadowing of Pompey's eventual death in Egypt.

Book 3

As book 3 opens and the fleet sails eastward, Pompey watches Italy recede. Overwhelmed with weariness, he falls asleep, and a frightful vision of his deceased but still jealous spouse, Caesar's daughter Julia, visits him. She tells him that she has special permission to dog his footsteps wherever they may lead until he rejoins her in the underworld, leaving behind his current wife, Cornelia.

Having safely crossed the Adriatic, Pompey reaches Epirus—a country to the northwest of ancient Greece. Lucan now turns his attention to Caesar. First Caesar sends a fleet with infantry and cavalry to pacify Sicily, for Rome's supply of grain depended on Sicilian production. Then Caesar marches his forces toward the almost deserted city of Rome. Such senators as are still in residence assemble to hear a "private citizen's" demands. Lucan sneeringly reports their cowardice. They are willing to make Caesar a king or a god and to subscribe to any cruelty he might inflict. Lucan, who hates Caesar, notably remarks that Caesar is ashamed to impose things that Rome would have assented to.

Metellus the tribune, however, does try to stop Caesar's raiding the Temple of Saturn and confiscating its treasure. Lucan, sneering again, notes that no degree of honor could rouse the Romans to resist, but money has found a defender. Caesar refuses to have Metellus killed, and the consul Cotta finally dissuades Metellus from continuing his futile efforts. Caesar then pillages the temple of the accumulated Roman wealth of centuries.

Now Lucan lists the allies who have rallied to Pompey's cause throughout the eastern Mediterranean, Asia, and North Africa, salting his account with ethnographic and geographic details about the peoples in his catalogue. He credits the Phoenicians, in passing, for the invention of the ALPHABET. News of the Civil War has spread as far as India. Once again, however, the poet sounds the note of foreboding. All the kings assembled under Pompey's standard are fated "to share in [his] . . . disaster" and to march in his funeral train.

Turning once more to Caesar, Lucan follows his march from Rome, across the Alps, toward Spain. At the city of Massilia (Marseilles), the citizens attempt to declare their neutrality and offer their town as a place for negotiation. Angered, Caesar attacks, only to find that the Massilians have made speeches only to buy time and that their city is strongly fortified against him.

Caesar makes preparations for a siege, cutting down a sacred wood in the process. Some think that this will anger the gods, but, if it does, the gods give no sign. Weighing his options, Caesar decides to leave the siege of Massilia to his lieutenant, Trebonius, and Caesar himself continues toward Spain. Lucan describes, as Caesar had done in his own version of *The* CIVIL WARS, the stout defense of the Massilians and their destruction of the Roman siege-engines and entrenchments. Consequentially, Decimus Junius Brutus builds a fleet to launch a successful attack.

Lucan devotes the balance of book 3 to a description of the battle that focuses both on its most horrifying and lurid details and on the courage of the combatants. As the Roman fleet wins total victory, this section of the poem recalls the great battle scenes in such earlier epics as VIRGIL'S *AENEID* and HOMER'S *The* ILIAD.

Book 4

Book 4 follows Caesar's fortunes in Spain. It details the difficulties Caesar faces in besieging the city of Llerda (today's Lleida), first because of the terrain, and second because of torrential rains and flooding. Lucan decides that Fortune is only pretending to have deserted Caesar, for the rains soon cease, and Caesar's customary success in battle returns.

The poet details the story, also told by Caesar, of the way that the Roman soldiers of the two opposing armies, many of whom are friends and townsmen, fraternize in the camp of Pompey's supporters until, reminded of their duty, Pompey's troops massacre their visitors. In response, Caesar cuts off the Pompeian supporters from their supplies of both food and water. Starvation and thirst force Pompey's general, Afranius, to surrender to Caesar, who raises his blockade; the men soon recover. Lucan intervenes with an apostrophe (oratorical address) to gluttony. Its folly is illustrated by how little food and water the soldiers require to return to health. Caesar disbands Afranius's troops and sends them home, and Lucan considers them lucky. For them, the fratricidal war is finished.

On the island of Curicta (now Krk) in the Adriatic Sea, however, matters were not going equally well for Caesar's commander there, Gaius Antonius, the brother of Caesar's friend, Marcus Antonius (Mark Antony). A Pompeian fleet has cut off his grain supply by blockading his island. Lucan details Antonius's countermeasures, but an attempt to run the blockade fails. Vulteius, the commander of a trapped raft full of Caesar's soldiers, advises them to commit suicide rather than surrender, which gives Lucan another chance to indulge his oratorical impulse in Vulteius's stoic speech. Heeding his words, the soldiers resist Pompey's forces as long as they can. When they see that further resistance is futile and that they will be taken prisoner, Caesar's men kill one another and themselves, to the great admiration of the Pompeian commanders.

Now Lucan turns his attention to another theater of war, the North African coast and Libya, where Caesar's governor of Sicily, Curio, has arrived to secure the area. The reader is treated to a digression about local mythology, for it was nearby that Hercules fought against the son of the earth goddess Gaia and defeated him by holding him aloft. Curio also finds himself near the site where the great Roman general, Scipio Africanus, pitched his first camp as he led his troops to victory against Carthage. Curio takes this as a fortunate omen, and he pitches his camp on the same site. At first his campaign enjoys some success against the troops of Pompey's general in Libya, Varus. A king of neighboring Numidia, Juba, however, is Varus's ally. Juba has assembled an enormous international army in support of Pompey. Juba also proves to be the superior tactician. He ambushes Curio and routs his forces, and Curio commits suicide in shame.

Lucan ends book 4 with a consideration of Curio's life and career. He finds much that was worthy of praise in the unfortunate general. He had been a man of great ability and sometimes had championed justice and right. His rectitude, however, had been overcome by greed, and Curio sold himself and Rome to Caesar's party for great wealth. Thus Lucan finally judges Curio a traitor to the cause of Rome—one greater than the cause of Caesar.

Book 5

Book 5 shifts the scene to Epirus in northwestern Greece, where Lucan imagines that the consuls of Rome call together the Roman senate in exile. One of the consuls, Lentulus, anticipates the speech that the late Renaissance British poet, John Milton, has Satan make in *Paradise Lost* when Satan assures the fallen angels that "the mind is its own place" and that it can "make of Hell a Heaven." Where the senate convenes, Lentulus assures his hearers, there Rome will be. All Caesar has in Italy are buildings and territory. Flattering their sense of self-importance, Lentulus calls on the senators to make Pompey their commander in chief. Like most overawed senators, they heed the head of state's advice.

At line 59, Lucan details the honors that the Senate in exile doles out to Pompey's allies. One that Lucan disapproves of is their conferring Egypt on the boy king Ptolemy, thus helping him to thwart his father's intention that he should be

coruler with Cleopatra. This decision also contributes to Pompey's murder on landing in Egypt.

At the end of the meeting, one of the senators, Appius Claudius Pulcher, seeks news of the future from the oracle of Apollo at Delphi. Again Lucan digresses to provide a bit of mythological history. He explains how, at the time of the great flood, only one peak of Parnassus poked a bit above the waters. The poet then reports the way in which Apollo had established the shrine, and Lucan speculates about the mode of operation of the prophecies that emanate from Delphi. As the reports from Delphi are trustworthy and fixed by fate, prayer is fruitless, and none is allowed. Moreover, inhaling the essence of divine truth that emanates from the gaseous depths beneath Delphi (and, as Lucan posits, ultimately from heaven) is dangerous. The consequent ecstasy that shakes the priestesses who serve as oracle shortens their lives.

Appius coerces the priestess to consult the oracle despite her desire not to do so and her attempt to deceive him. In the grip of a genuine divine ecstasy, the priestess Phemonoe knows not only all the future, but all the past as well. Finally, she focuses in on Appius's personal future and lets him know that he will not participate in Rome's crisis but will "rest alone" in a valley on the coast of Euboea.

Lucan interrupts to inquire why the god Apollo would not assent to reveal the future of Rome, and to propose answers to his own question. Maybe the gods have not yet decided Rome's fate. Appius, meanwhile, remains blissfully unaware that he has just received forewarning of his own death.

Lucan now returns to Caesar, who, as other sources tell us, has led his army back to northern Italy, where he faces a mutiny among his troops. They air their complaints as Lucan once more waxes oratorical. As the poet has Caesar prepare his response, he judges that Caesar would have approved of any atrocity that his soldiers wished to commit to keep their allegiance. Caesar offers his unarmored breast to the swords of his troops and talks them out of their mutiny; they execute the ringleaders of the abortive rebellion themselves.

Lucan now reports Caesar's trip to Rome, where, in addition to the dictatorship that has already been conferred, he also becomes consul—the head of state. Caesar pretends to be reluctant to accept but bows to public pressure.

Tracing Caesar's journey to Brindisi and his voyage from there to Greece, Lucan reports how Caesar and Pompey pitch their camps near one another not far from Dyrrhachium (now Durazzo). Anxious to press his enemy, Caesar is delayed by the failure of Marc Antony to arrive with his army. Ever moved to demoniac activity in Lucan's pages, Caesar sneaks away alone and hires a fisherman, Amyclas, to take him back to Brindisi so he can encourage Antony. A hurricane-force gale, however, nearly scuttles the ship, strips it of its sails, and forces it back again to the shores of Greece. Lucan's power as a poet appears in sharp relief in his wonderful description of the storm and its effects on men and ships. Caesar makes a speech into the teeth of the gale, and a huge wave deposits the ship safely ashore at the only possible spot for such a landing.

On Caesar's return, his officers reprove him for taking such a risk and tempting the gods. The storm, however, eventually blows itself out and Antony is able to bring reinforcements across the Adriatic.

In the meantime, Pompey has been growing concerned about the safety of his wife Cornelia in the present doubtful circumstances, and he tells her that he is going to send her to the island of Lesbos to assure her safety. Shocked, Cornelia makes a speech describing the situations that this decision will imply for her. She agrees to it, but makes Pompey promise not to come to her if he loses. Where she is, his enemies will seek him. Oppressed by foreboding, she unhappily sets sail, and book 5 ends with Lucan's dark prophecy of the gods' cruel plans for the couple.

Book 6

Book 6 begins with descriptions of Caesar's attempts to force the issue and bring Pompey to a decisive battle. When that strategy fails, Caesar marches suddenly on the Greek coastal city of Dyrrhachium. Pompey manages to relieve the city, and Caesar constructs massive earthworks surrounding both Pompey's forces and the landward approaches to the city. This feat of military engineering, says Lucan, outdoes the walls of Troy or Babylon. The poet regrets that such an enormous labor was dedicated to destructive purposes when the same effort might have produced a causeway across the Hellespont or a shipping canal across the Grecian peninsula.

Once Pompey's scouts detect Caesar's work, which he had successfully begun in secret, Pompey begins constructing a countering series of fortifications. Yet despite occasional individual encounters, no general action follows. Pompey, however, cannot bring in enough fodder for his starving horses. He is cut off from land supply, and the weather keeps his grain ships from arriving. The animals' rotting carcasses spread disease among the hungry troops. Finally, however, the wind shifts, and the grain ships relieve Pompey's men and their surviving animals.

A failed harvest now begins to starve Caesar's army. Pompey chooses this moment and the weakest point in Caesar's encircling defenses to attack. At first, success seems at hand. The outnumbered defenders are on the point of deserting their posts when a centurion, Scaeva, rallies them so that they hold on until Caesar sends reinforcements. Lucan lavishes a gory description on Scaeva's single-handed heroism as he fights until, gutted with sword thrusts and pin-cushioned with spears, he begs to be taken in his dying condition before Pompey. A soldier named Aulus tries to do so, and Scaeva, boasting of his prowess, cuts Aulus's throat. At this moment, Caesar's forces arrive. Lucan praises Scaeva's courage but denies him glory because he has displayed all that heroism in defense of the tyrant, Caesar.

Now Pompey succeeds in breaking through Caesar's lines at another spot and is on the point of defeating Caesar decisively, but, apparently not recognizing his advantage, he fails to follow through. Lucan blames Pompey's forbearance for the ultimate demise of the Roman republic and for the slaughter in the battles yet to come before the end of the Roman civil wars. As it is, Caesar retreats into Thessaly, and, ignoring the advice of his officers, Pompey pursues him.

Lucan follows with an epic digression that, in a virtuoso poetic performance, details the geography and the mythical history of the region of Thessaly. There both armies encamp, and another digression ensues. This one describes the remarkable powers of Thessaly's witches, who can "dislocate the orderly workings of nature" with their magic arts. One in particular, the witch Erictho, is the most despicable of the lot. Living among tombstones, she has compelled the ghosts to leave their graves. She can hear the conversations that take place in the underworld. The very gods fear the ghastly sacrifices she makes them. She is a cannibal who feeds on the dead in whatever state of decomposition she finds them. If she requires fresh blood for her potions and incantations, she will commit murder to get it.

When Pompey's forces encounter Erictho, Pompey's son, Sextus, asks her to foretell the war's result. Flattered by Sextus's manner and by his praise of her powers, Erichtho willingly complies. Choosing a corpse from among the piles of fallen soldiers, she drags it to the cave in which she lives—one that Lucan suggests is on the boundary between the upper world and the underworld. This portion of the poem is Lucan's equivalent of the more usual epic feature of a descent into the underworld. The Pompeians who have come to hear the prophecy tremble with fear. Erichtho reassures them of their own safety and then begins to work on the corpse. Having restored it to a zombie-like life, she invokes the powers of darkness to restore the body's spirit so it can speak. She threatens those powers—the Furies—saying that she can punish them if they refuse. The Furies acquiesce, and the corpse returns to life, passing backward through the process of death.

Erichtho demands that the corpse clearly predict the future course of the war. The corpse responds that the shades of famous persons from the Roman republic are saddened because they know the outcome of the war. The shade of Scipio Africanus anticipates the death of his kinsman, Mettelus Scipio. Likewise, Marcius Porcius Cato, the censor, foreknows the suicide of his descendant of the same name. Those among the dead who conspired against the republic, however, are pleased since they know that empire will replace the republic. Pluto himself is busy preparing implements of torture in preparation for the arrival of Julius Caesar, who will be the victor in the war. Pompey, on the other hand, will have a place in the Elysian Fields—the most pleasant of Hell's neighborhoods.

Having uttered his prophecy, the soldier waits while Erichtho performs the necessary rites. She builds a funeral pyre. He mounts it. She lights the fire and leaves him to burn. For the protection of her guests, Erichtho has lengthened the night so they can safely return to their camp.

Book 7

Book 7 opens with evil portents for the Pompeian cause. The sun god sadly drives his chariot into the heavens, and Pompey has dreamed of the time that he entered Rome in triumph. This dream, however, forecasts an opposite outcome. Pompey, who once triumphed in Rome, is destined to be denied the grief of her citizens on his death.

Pompey's soldiers grow restive. They want action, so do his allies. Cicero advises him to fight Caesar's forces. Pompey explains his strategy of delay and war by attrition, but he grudgingly yields to the pressure of his subordinates and advisers. Lucan suggests that Pompey has abandoned his post in taking this position.

At once, portents of disaster begin appearing: meteors, pillars of flame, waterspouts, and fireballs appear. Weapons dissolve. The battle standards grow impossibly heavy. A sacrificial bull knocks over the altar and escapes. A lake grows bloody. Ghosts appear. Even in Italy, signs appear that presage the tyrant Caesar's victory.

Now Lucan devotes 20 lines to a description of the organization of Pompey's massed forces as they advance to the field of Pharsalia. Seeing them coming, Caesar experiences a moment of fear, but iron resolution quickly replaces his qualms, and he (and Lucan) seize that moment for him to make an eloquent address to his troops. He disparages the prowess of his enemies. He also counsels his troops to press the attack against fellow Romans only as long they stand and fight. If they flee, they are to be allowed to escape. When he finishes, Caesar orders the destruction of a defensive earthwork and a general advance.

Seeing Caesar's forces on the march, Pompey speaks to his soldiers. He emphasizes that they have the advantage of numbers, and he appeals to them that they will not let him be enslaved in his old age. Heartened by his address, his troops take the field.

Lucan interrupts with a prediction of the consequences of the battle. He eloquently explains its future effects and then turns his attention to the ways in which the battle has undone the work of the past, encouraging the conquered peoples on the fringes of the Roman empire to continue their resistance to Roman power. He interrupts this reflection with a statement of his heartfelt credo: "There are no gods governing mankind. . . . We are swept along by chance . . . to say that Juppiter [sic] reigns is a lie."

Lucan curses the Caesarian soldier Crastinus for hurling the first spear, and the battle is underway. Lucan describes infantry and cavalry engagements. Pompey's foreign allies flee the battle. Their flight strikes fear into Pompey's Roman forces, but they stand and fight. The poet cannot bear to describe the horror of the internecine fray.

Lucan praises Caesar's generalship grudgingly, but he bemoans the criminality of his objective. Caesar has instructed his troops to leave the commoners alone and seek out the senators. They obey, and many a noble Roman falls victim to their swords.

Brutus, disguised as a common soldier, goes seeking Caesar, hoping to kill him. Lucan explains that he is not yet fated to succeed. The flower of Roman nobility falls instead. Brother

fights brother, and father kills son. Lucan regrets that his generation does not have the chance to fight for the preservation of the republic.

At last, finding the situation hopeless and horrified at the bloodshed, Pompey flees, praying that his flight will end the carnage. Lucan interrupts the progress of the poem to address Pompey, mourning his reversal of fortune and consoling him with the observation that his fall has been the choice of the gods. The poet advises the fleeing leader to "choose a country to die in" from among his former conquests.

Arriving at the town of Larisa, Pompey advises the townspeople, who encourage him to mount further resistance, that he has been beaten and that they should transfer their loyalty to Caesar. At the same time, Pompey finds the affection of the people gratifying.

Caesar's victory gives Lucan another opportunity for oratory. His victory speech finished, Caesar encourages his men to loot the enemy camp. But night brings guilty dreams to the victors, and Caesar especially suffers from pangs of conscience, alleviated only by the thought that Pompey had survived the battle. Caesar leaves the victims of the battle unburied and sits regarding the evidence that the gods have favored his cause. Lucan provides posthumous comfort for the fallen of Pharsalia. Though Caesar has denied them a funeral pyre, they have taken permanent possession of the earth of the battlefield until the day that the earth itself perishes in the universal conflagration that will also be a pyre for those dead soldiers. The same mood informs Lucan's reflections on the scavenging of birds and beasts of prey among the fallen.

Lucan closes the seventh book with a reflection on Thessaly as he considers how long it will take for evidence of this massacre to cease affecting the activities of farmers and herdsmen. He observes that the gods have ordained equal guilt for Munda, Sicily, Mutina, and Actium. (The last-named battle, which Antony and Cleopatra lost, left Augustus Caesar the unchallenged ruler of the Roman world.)

Book 8

Book 8 begins by tracing Pompey's circuitous route to the seacoast. His effort to maintain his anonymity is foredoomed, for he is famous, and along the way he meets many persons who know him. Lucan reflects on the bitterness of former fame.

Taking ship, Pompey sails to Cornelia at Lesbos, and on his arrival she faints. Pompey reproaches her with the suggestion that what she misses and weeps over is her former greatness. Cornelia, however, suggests that the jealousy of Pompey's first wife, Caesar's deceased daughter Julia, is the root cause of the civil war.

The citizens of Lesbos welcome Pompey and pledge their support. Pompey addresses a last prayer to the gods who seem to have deserted him. He prays for more welcomes like that of Lesbos and also asks that, having welcomed him, people will allow him to leave.

Pompey and Cornelia set forth upon the Mediterranean, and in an effort to alleviate his mental distress, Pompey questions the ship's captain concerning stellar navigation. The captain explains the rudiments and asks for a destination. Other than avoiding Thessaly and Italy, Pompey instructs the captain to go where the winds will take the ship.

Then Pompey, who has begun formulating a plan for his future, sends his ally, King Deiotarus, to ask another friend, the king of Parthia, to secure an Asian country for him to retire to. Pompey is convinced that Caesar will grant such a request. Pompey continues his voyage upon a sea that he himself had made safe from the depredations of pirates. As he sails, something of his old self-confidence returns. He begins to consider saving Rome and which of his allies is equal to the task of helping him. He asks his retinue for advice on choosing among Libya, Parthia (northeast modern Iran), or Egypt. Lucan puts in Pompey's own mouth the pros and cons of the assessment he has requested. Pompey opts for Parthia.

His advisers demur, however, and in a long speech raising objections to a Parthian exile, one of them, Lentulus, suggests that Pompey seek refuge with the boy king of Egypt, Ptolemy. Among his objections is the notorious lust of the king of Parthia and the danger into which Cornelia's virtue would fall there.

Lentulus's arguments carry the day, and the ship proceeds toward Ptolemy's encampment. Informed of Pompey's impending arrival, Ptolemy assembles his advisers. One, Acoreus, advises Ptolemy to welcome Pompey. The other adviser, Pothinus, however, argues for assassination. Both arguments give further opportunities for oratory. Pothinus's arguments prevail, and the Egyptians lay their plot against Pompey's life.

Pretending to welcome Pompey, the Egyptians bring a small craft to his vessel and invite him to join them. Cornelia smells a plot and asks to be included, but the unsuspecting Pompey goes alone. The craft has hardly pulled away from the larger vessel when, in the full view of Cornelia and of his son, two Roman mercenaries serving with Ptolemy cut him down. He dies manfully, and as he dies, Lucan imagines the general's final thoughts.

Cornelia blames herself for interrupting Pompey's intended voyage toward Parthia. She faints; her companions catch her, and her ship weighs anchor.

Meanwhile, the assassin Septimius saws off the still-conscious Pompey's head and pitches his body overboard. Lucan makes the details of the assassination as gory as possible, including a description of the mummification of Pompey's head.

Pompey's body washes ashore, and one of his former soldiers, Cordus, who had witnessed the assassination, hunts for the body, finds it, cremates it as well as he can, and buries the remnants. An outraged Lucan cites Pompey's glories and, cursing the land of Egypt, complains at the inglorious funeral accorded him.

Book 9

As the ninth book begins, Pompey's spirit ascends to the lunar circle, the sphere in which the souls of heroes abide. There the spirit adjusts to its new and marvelous circumstances for a while before revisiting Pharsalia's field.

Marcus Porcius Cato, a confirmed Stoic and the staunchest of Roman republicans, had suspended judgment between the causes of Caesar and Pompey. On Pompey's death, however, he concludes that Pompey's had been the better cause. Cato takes it upon himself to rally Pompey's scattered forces and continue the war against Caesar. Cato manages to assemble 1,000 shiploads of Pompey's forces. By chance, his flotilla encounters the returning squadron carrying Cornelia and Pompey's son Sextus, but he does not know they are aboard.

Lucan retrospectively recounts Cornelia's lament against Fortune for having denied her the opportunity to lament her husband and bury him with due solemnity. She assigns her son Sextus the mission of continuing his father's struggle. She tells him that if Cato takes up the cudgels, Sextus may learn by following him. Their ships continue to Africa, where Cato is by then encamped. With him they find Sextus's elder brother, Gnaeus. Sextus tells Gnaeus about the manner of Pompey's death. In his grief and anger, Gnaeus envisions the extirpation of all Egyptians, living and dead.

Burning her husband's gear and mourning in a traditional fashion, Cornelia conducts a memorial service for Pompey at which Cato eulogizes the departed general. Though Pompey may have fallen short of the high republican ideal that Cato set, he was nonetheless the best Rome had to offer and was never motivated by personal gain.

Now a band of Cilicians whom Pompey had converted from the practice of piracy threatens to resume their old trade. This occasions an exchange of oratory between them and Cato. Cato's eloquence wins the day, calming the Cilicians, and they remain with the Pompeian loyalists as Lucan develops an extended epic simile comparing their debarkation to a swarm of honeybees.

Lucan next describes a victory for Cato and, subsequently, the unfriendly shoals of an area called the Syrtes. There a storm destroys some of Cato's fleet. The balance makes it safely to Lake Triton, whose mythical history Lucan recounts. From there they pass on to Libya. Once in harbor, Cato challenges the soldiers to a grueling overland march through the desert, persuading them with his inspiring oratory that they should welcome the challenges that "snakes, thirst, and the heat of the desert" will present.

The expedition sets out. The men are tormented by thirst and by sandstorm, but Cato's model of endurance encourages them. Lucan then takes poetic license with the location of the temple of "Juppiter [sic] Hammon." He moves it into the expedition's line of march so as to give Cato the chance to refuse to consult its oracle and to bear witness to his Stoic faith. Encouraged by his adjutant Labienus to consult the oracle, Cato replies that nothing men do is done without the gods' direction. All men from their birth know as much about the gods' wills as men are meant to—nothing. God permeates everything and resides in human virtue. The only certainty men possess is the certainty of death.

On the grueling march, Cato sets the standard for endurance. When water is found, he is always the last to drink. One exception to this rule occurs when the expedition encounters a spring full of poisonous serpents. Cato assures the men that the poison will hurt them only if the snakes bite them and that the water the snakes swim in is utterly harmless. He illustrates his point by, for the first and only time, being the first to take a drink on the long, dry march.

There follows a lengthy digression on the snakes of Libya, on their varied kinds, and on their mythic genesis from the blood scattered from the Gorgon's head after Perseus cut it off. Among them are fearsome flying dragons and the flying Jaculus—the javelin snake. Another variety is the parias, which only touches the ground with its tail.

At every step on the march, Lucan assures his readers, a soldier dies from snakebite whose poison instantly and utterly dehydrates him—or, in one particularly horrifying instance, liquefies him. Grisly examples proliferate. Not surprisingly, the soldiers begin to lose heart and long for the comparative safety of the battlefield at Pharsalia.

Cato heartens the troops by his example, taking no heed of the danger, and encouraging the dying to endure their suffering in silence. Finally, the healers of the indigenous Psylli are able to offer antidotes and expertise to the army. They accompany the troops with their knowledge and their equipment. The troops arrive safely at the city of Leptis and spend the winter there.

Shifting his attention to Caesar, Lucan finds him, sometime earlier, trying to follow Pompey through the Mediterranean. Caesar plays tourist and visits the site of Troy. There he offers sacrifice, prays that the gods will crown his ventures with success, and promises to rebuild a "Roman Troy."

Caesar tracks Pompey to Egypt, where he is presented with Pompey's preserved head. Rather ungraciously, Lucan assures his reader that Caesar feigns grief over Pompey's death while secretly rejoicing. The poet puts in Caesar's mouth a "sham speech." He complains that Egyptian presumption has deprived him of the one privilege of civil war—that of sparing the defeated general. He mutters that if Ptolemy loved Cleopatra, Caesar would reply in kind and send the king his sister's severed head.

Caesar gives orders for a proper funeral and a tomb for Pompey's head and ashes. No one, says Lucan, believes that Caesar's grief is genuine.

Book 10

The incomplete 10th book of Lucan's *Civil Wars* follows Caesar's progress to a hostile Alexandria, where Caesar visits the tomb of Alexander the Great. Lucan, however, is no admirer of Alexander, whom he considered a mad adventurer insatiable in his pursuit of power.

Ptolemy comes to Alexandria and is taken into protective custody by Caesar. Cleopatra also manages to gain access to him. She now becomes the target of Lucan's oratorical invective. The poet rather ironically blames her for distracting

Caesar from the war he was fighting. Using both her beauty and her intelligence, she begs Caesar for his protection, and he confers it.

Now Lucan digresses to describe the beauty and luxury of Cleopatra's palace, the magnificence of her personal beauty and attire, and the opulence of the banquet she prepares in Caesar's honor. There follows the now obligatory sequence in which Caesar and the wise Egyptian Acoreus discuss Egyptian ethnography, geography, and religion. Acoreus discourses learnedly about theories concerning the source of the Nile River. Its actual source still lies shrouded in mystery, as Acoreus explains.

Meanwhile, the Egyptian boy king's adviser, the wily Pothinus who had arranged for Pompey's murder, now hatches plots against the lives of both Caesar and Cleopatra. By means of a love potion, as Pothinus thinks, she has become Caesar's mistress. She has also married her brother, whom she and Caesar have in protective custody. (Marriage between siblings was a common matter among the rulers of some ancient nations.) Pothinus decides to mount an attack on Cleopatra's palace, kill both her and Caesar, and rescue Ptolemy.

Rather than attack at night, the Egyptians wait for morning. Caesar sees the army gathering in the distance and organizes his personal bodyguard to defend the palace. Knowing that the Egyptians will try to liberate Ptolemy, Caesar sends an emissary to explain that if he dies, Ptolemy dies. The Egyptians slay the messenger. Their attempts to storm the palace, however, prove ineffectual. They try an attack by water where a section of the palace extends into the sea, but again they cannot prevail against Caesar's seasoned generalship—which here Lucan seems to admire. Caesar burns the Egyptian ships, though he preserves one of them and escapes on it to the island of Pharos, whose possession blockades the Egyptian ships. He then takes the treacherous Pothinus prisoner and gives him the same death he had administered to Pompey.

Cleopatra's younger sister, Arsinoe, now raises troops of her own, and her general, Ganymede, succeeds in isolating Caesar and a small force on the breakwater of Pharos. All seems lost until Caesar spots a miraculously surviving Scaeva—the hero of Dyrrachium—plugging a breach against the Egyptians. At this point, Lucan's *Civil War* breaks off.

Every discussion of Lucan's epic notes QUIN-TILIAN's judgment that, as full of energy and memorable epigram as the poem is and however great the talent it reveals, the poem may well be considered a better model for oratory than for epic poetry.

Bibliography

Lucan. *Civil War*. Translated by S. H. Braund. New York: Oxford University Press, 1992.

———. *Lucan's Civil War*. Translated by P. F. Widdows. Bloomington and Indianapolis: Indiana University Press. 1988.

———. *The Civil War: Books I–X*. Translated by J. D. Duff. New York: G. P. Putnam's Sons, 1928.

Civil Wars, The Julius Caesar (ca. 45 B.C.E.)

The governmental structures of republican Rome had long proved inadequate to cope with the responsibilities that ruling the Mediterranean world imposed. As a result, during the first century B.C.E., de facto power tended to migrate away from the senate and consuls (heads of state) of Rome toward the hands of the wealthy, the militarily capable, and the most politically astute. Three such men were the incomparably wealthy and militarily able Marcus Licinius Crassus; the superb general Gnaeus Pompeius, known as Pompey; and the astute military and political strategist and tactician, JULIUS CAESAR. These three formed an alliance known to history as the First Triumvirate. They were bound together by mutual interests, by Crassus's money—a loan from which had enabled Caesar to leave Rome to assume command of Spain—and by kinship ties. Caesar was also father-in-law to Pompey, who was married to his daughter Julia.

As matters developed, Crassus went to lead the Roman forces in the East; Caesar became the proconsul (civil and military governor) of the Gallic provinces both south and north of the Alps, and Pompey became both the governor of Spain and the head of state in Rome itself. Although the three leaders were able to work cooperatively for a considerable time, their alliance eventually frayed and then unraveled. In 53 B.C.E., Crassus died in military action in the East. He had been effective in averting disagreements between his two colleagues. Further distancing Pompey from Caesar, Pompey's wife Julia—Caesar's daughter—had died in 54 B.C.E.

By manipulating matters at Rome, Pompey sought to strip Caesar of all political office and, simultaneously, of his military command. This would have left Caesar exposed to prosecution under ex post facto legislation that could have resulted in his exile or execution. In an effort to avoid armed confrontation, Caesar wrote to the Roman senate offering to disband his legions if Pompey would do the same. Pompey controlled the senate, which passed a measure requiring Caesar to disband his army, then encamped just outside Rome's Italian territory on the banks of the little Rubicon River. Caesar's supporters, the tribunes of the people, vetoed the senate's action. The senate overrode the people by declaring a state of emergency—legislation that concentrated all power in Pompey's hands. Caesar's allies, the tribunes, escaped to join him, and Caesar broke Roman law by leading his forces across the Rubicon to begin the civil wars that eventually led to the establishment of imperial government in Rome.

It is the story of that series of conflicts that Caesar tells in *The Civil Wars*. Less carefully crafted than his COMMENTARY ON THE GALLIC WARS, *The Civil Wars* achieves an attractive sense of immediacy and, sometimes, of urgency by being reported in the present tense.

Book 1

Caesar begins his narrative by reporting the political maneuvering outlined above, He then details the military skirmishes, the levying of troops, and the occupying of towns. He reports the way in which he had dealt generously with the senators of Rome and their children, all of whom he had brought before him. He complains of the way they had cooperated with Pompey against him, and then he had released them all.

Pompey in the meantime had drafted troops and was moving south through the Italian Peninsula. Some of his troops, however, deserted him and joined Caesar's forces. Pompey's army fled to the port of Brundisium (modern Brindisi). Pursuing him, Caesar sent a letter suggesting that the two parley at Brundisium. When Caesar arrived there, he prepared to besiege the city, though he tried again to arrange a conference. Pompey responded that, in the absence of the consuls, no negotiation could take place, so Caesar decided he must attack. Pompey, however, hastily withdrew his forces during the night, losing two shiploads of soldiers that Caesar's forces captured.

Considering the entire strategic situation in the Mediterranean, Caesar decided not to pursue Pompey and instead dispatched forces to Sardinia and Sicily, where they found that the forces of Pompey had left. Caesar also sent forces to Africa and Spain. After levying further troops, he returned to the city of Rome. There he found the senate paralyzed by its fears both of him and of Pompey. Caesar withdrew to Gaul.

After detailing the divided allegiances of Gallic tribesmen, Caesar recounts his preparations for a major offensive against Pompey's forces in Spain—the province that Pompey still governed and toward which, Caesar knew, Pompey himself was marching. He reports engagements between his troops and Pompey's in the vicinity of Llerda (today's Lleida) in Spain, and how the guerrilla tactics of Pompey's troops—learned while fighting against Lusitanian (Portuguese) irregulars—initially threw Caesar's troops into a panic. His forces rallied however, and soon found themselves in a more favorable military position, though hard-pressed to find enough rations.

Caesar interrupts his narrative about the battle of Llerda to describe a naval engagement off Marseilles (then called Massilia)—one fought between the squadron of Caesar's subordinate, Decimus Brutus, and an ally of Pompey's, Domitius. In a pitched battle, the unseasoned forces of Decimus Junius Brutus finally managed to gain the upper hand against Domitius and inflict heavy losses on his forces.

In the meantime, Caesar's situation at Llerda was improving. His fortifications were nearly complete, and local tribes submitted to his authority and supplied him with badly needed grain. Caesar describes his eventually successful efforts in getting both cavalry and infantry across a dangerously swollen Ebro River and the race between his forces and his enemy's to occupy easily defended narrow passes in mountainous country. Caesar's military successes the next day led numbers of his opponents, many of whom had friends or relatives among Caesar's forces, to consider honorable surrender. When the troops began to fraternize, however, Pompey's commander Afranius put a stop to it, killed those of the enemy who had accepted invitations to visit friends in Pompey's soldiers' camp, and demanded an oath of allegiance. Caesar, on the other hand, dealt kindly with the strangers in his camp and accepted the allegiance of those who did not wish to return to Pompey's forces.

In the ensuing confrontation, Caesar totally outmaneuvered Afranius, isolating his forces so effectively from supplies that for four days Afranius could not feed his animals. Desperate, Afranius at last threw himself on Caesar's mercy. After thoroughly reproving Afranius for his obstinacy in not accepting Caesar's earlier overtures for peace and for his outrageous behavior in killing the invited guests of his soldiers, Caesar told him that his only objective was to have Afranius disband his army and go home. Arrangements were made to achieve this, and it was so ordered.

Book 2

As the second book of *The Civil Wars* opens, Caesar returns to the siege of Marseilles—a responsibility that he had entrusted to his deputy commander, Gaius Trebonius. A reader may be particularly impressed by Caesar's descriptions of the military technology possessed on both sides. Catapults were capable of throwing 12-foot-long, iron-pointed poles that could penetrate wooden defenses several inches thick. To protect infantry from missiles and arrows fired from above, a mobile, 60-foot-long shed with a roof a foot thick was constructed. It could also provide level footing over uneven ground. In addition to arrangements for an infantry siege of Marseilles, preparations were made for another naval engagement. Caesar's fleet was again under the command of his subordinate, Decimus Junius Brutus, who again enjoyed the victory.

Perceiving themselves on the brink of being overcome by Caesar's technical superiority, the citizens rushed out and begged him to spare them. Caesar had not wished to sack Marseilles, so he agreed, and his soldiers relaxed. Two days later, however, the citizens suddenly flooded out of the city's gates and attacked Caesar's unarmed soldiers. Their principal targets, however, were Caesar's offensive and defensive technology: sheds, siege towers, and the like, to which they set fire, destroying some of them. The next day, the citizens attempted to repeat this success but encountered a prepared soldiery who killed many of them and drove the others back within the city's walls.

The citizens thought it would take the Romans a long while to repair the damage they had done. Within a few days, however, despite a shortage of materials that required invention and ingenuity to overcome, new and better Roman defensive measures were in place; therefore the citizens of Marseilles once again surrendered, this time in reality. Despite their treachery, Caesar accepted their surrender on the same generous terms he had earlier offered.

In the meantime, some of the citizens of Spain who had prospered under Caesar's earlier proconsulship of the region began to expel Pompey's forces from the cities in which citizens loyal to Caesar were in control. On seeing his

forces decimated by their divided allegiances, the leader of Pompey's soldiers, Varro, simply surrendered his remaining troops to Caesar. Caesar appointed representatives to govern western Spain. Then news reached him that, back in Rome, Marcus Lepidus had nominated Caesar to become dictator. Caesar returned at once to the capital city.

At the same time that the above events were taking place, another of Caesar's subordinate commanders, Curio, the governor of Sicily, had led a relatively small but nonetheless powerful force from Sicily to Africa. Although a detachment of 10 ships had been stationed to oppose him, their commander saw the futility of engagement, beached his small armada, and fled. Curio marched inland to within sight of the camp of Pompey's subordinate, an officer named Varus. There, despite minor defections among Curio's troops to Pompey's side, Curio achieved stunning successes against Numidian cavalry and infantry. Concern nonetheless increased among Curio's soldiers that they should be fighting for Pompey instead of Caesar. Curio quelled this emergent dissatisfaction with a stirring address to the troops in which he assured them that they were indeed fighting for the right cause and on the winning side. Caesar reproduces the speech in detail and reports that it had the desired effect. The heartened soldiers routed the enemy in battle the next day until Varus's forces heard that Pompey's African ally, King Juba, was marching toward him with reinforcements.

Also learning of Juba's approach, Curio sent cavalry to harass Juba's forces during the night. Catching them unaware, Curio's cavalry was able to reduce the numbers of Juba's Numidians significantly. Learning of that attack, Juba responded by sending reinforcements that included 2,000 cavalry, his best infantry, and 60 armored elephants—the ancient precursors of tanks.

Underestimating both the size and the fortitude of Juba's reinforcements, Curio led his men on a forced march against Juba's army. In the ensuing disaster, Curio's forces were destroyed and Curio himself chose to die fighting rather than face Caesar after his defeat. The survivors surrendered to Varus, but over Varus's objections, Juba claimed many of them as spoils of war, putting some to death and enslaving others.

Book 3

Back in Rome during 49 B.C.E., Caesar exercised his dictatorial powers by bringing order to Italy, taking steps to curb inflation and calm fears of a general debt amnesty, and supervising elections. Having restored order and bolstered public confidence, he resigned the dictatorship. He then went to Brindisi, meaning to lead his forces against Pompey's in Illyrium on the northeastern shore of the Adriatic. Pompey himself at this time was with his troops in Macedonia.

In Brindisi, however, a shortage of shipping dictated that Caesar proceed with an army much reduced in numbers. He could embark only 15,000 legionaries and 500 cavalry to face a superior force that Pompey had assembled during Caesar's first Roman dictatorship.

Caesar began marching southward, sometimes encountering resistance and sometimes being welcomed. His swift progress in the direction of the city of Durazzo spurred Pompey to move northward by forced marches in an attempt to fortify Durazzo against Caesar. As the armies approached one another, Caesar sent a message offering a cessation of hostilities and an opportunity for both Pompey and him to submit their rival claims to the judgment of the Roman senate.

Though Caesar's situation on land was tenable, Pompey's naval squadron under the command of Bibulus had succeeded in blockading the coast and denying Caesar reinforcements. Attempts at a negotiated settlement failed, and the opposing armies seemed on the brink of a decisive engagement. One of Pompey's commanders, Labienus, declared that only Caesar's beheading could bring peace.

At this crucial moment, Caesar interrupts his war narrative to describe in the third chapter of book 3 the machinations of Marcus Caelius Rufus, who was a praetor—the official immediately subordinate to the consuls. Caelius proposed to cancel or reduce debts—a proposal entirely unacceptable to powerful creditors. In response, he was stripped of his praetorship. He made an unsuccessful attempt to seize power by force of arms and was killed during the fighting.

Meanwhile, in Illyrium, Pompey's admiral in the southern Adriatic, Libo, had successfully blockaded the harbor at Brindisi and boasted that he could prevent reinforcements from joining Caesar's forces on the Balkan Peninsula. Mark Antony, Caesar's commander at Brindisi, successfully routed Libo and put an end to the blockade. But still no reinforcements reached Caesar. At Caesar's urgent request, Mark Antony and others sent the necessary troops, and the weather seemed to cooperate with them. The wind not only prevented Pompey's ships from intercepting them but drove 16 of his vessels ashore and wrecked them. Antony's reinforcements arrived, forcing Pompey to withdraw to a more secure defensive position to avoid being caught between two armies.

Pompey now called on the Roman commander in Asia, Scipio, to send forces to Macedonia against Caesar and his allies. Scipio responded so rapidly that news of his coming coincided with his arrival. Caesar's forces, however, dealt successfully with the threat that Scipio posed.

Pompey's son, Gnaeus, who commanded the Egyptian fleet, now sailed in force to Illyrium and harassed Caesar's forces there until, failing to take the port city of Lissus, he was forced to withdraw his fleet to the Mediterranean.

Caesar, in the meantime, successfully implemented a strategy to surround and blockade Pompey's forces near the city of Durazzo. Though he maneuvered in ways that he hoped would tempt his opponent to fight, Pompey refused to do so. Caesar chose to make Pompey's reluctance to do battle a propaganda tool that would diminish Pompey's status in the eyes of his foreign allies. However, Pompey would neither fight nor withdraw from Durazzo, where all his war matériel and supplies were stored. As the stalemate continued, punctuated by skirmishing, both sides adopted defensive strategies and looked to improve their protective fortifications. Warfare by a process of attrition developed—a sort of warfare that Caesar considered innovative.

Caesar now interjects the story of two Gallic brothers, Raucillus and Egus, whose extortionate behavior toward their own subordinates made them so unpopular that they decided to desert Caesar and defect to Pompey. As the brothers had earlier enjoyed Caesar's confidence, they knew all his plans, and they shared them with Pompey. As a result, Pompey was able to mount successful attacks on Caesar's weakest points. This was a very dangerous engagement for Caesar's cause, and only the timely arrival of Mark Antony and his forces kept this engagement from escalating into a disaster.

Caesar then quickly assessed Pompey's new situation and devised a plan to mount a surprise attack. This plan miscarried, and Caesar almost lost everything. He was saved, however, by Pompey's delay in pressing his advantage. Nonetheless, Caesar suffered a signal defeat, and Pompey's success led his troops to honor him with the title imperator.

Caesar determined that a tactical retreat was in order and conducted it so successfully that Pompey's pursuing army could not catch up with his main column and suffered significant losses at the hands of Caesar's rearguard cavalry.

Caesar's ally Domitius inadvertently learned from some of the Gauls who had deserted to Pompey that Pompey was secretly marching against him. Spurred by that intelligence, Domitius hastened to join forces with Caesar, and in their combined strength the two marched on the fortified town of Gomphi. The citizens of Gomphi, having heard exaggerated reports of Pompey's successes, refused to admit Caesar's forces and sent to Pompey for help. Caesar quickly took the town, allowed his troops to plunder it, and resolved at one stroke the supply shortage from which his army had been suffering. Having taken the citizens prisoner, Caesar moved on to the town of Metropolis. Metropolis at first offered resistance, but when they heard from the captive

citizens of Gomphi what had resulted from their refusal to submit, the people of Metropolis opened their gates to Caesar. It was in the vicinity of this town that Caesar chose to take his stand against Pompey.

Meanwhile, Pompey and his ally Scipio had joined forces in Thessaly. So certain were Pompey's supporters of their coming military success that they began arguing about who would receive what political office as a reward for their good services to their leader. This discussion impeded laying practical plans for conducting the battle looming before them. When they did finally address that issue, their overconfidence led them to make foolish strategic and tactical decisions.

Caesar describes the disposition and order of battle of both armies as they massed for the decisive confrontation of the Illyrian campaign. He then criticizes Pompey's tactics in having his soldiers stand firm to await the charge of Caesar's troops rather than themselves charging to meet the enemy. In any case, Caesar's superior generalship and the dedicated courage and skill of his troops won the day, and Pompey's forces were driven inside their camp.

As Caesar's forces began mopping-up operations, Pompey stripped himself of all insignia of his rank and, with an escort of 30 cavalry, fled to the coast, boarded a grain ship, and set sail. The next day, Caesar accepted the surrender of Pompey's forces and ordered that none of them be mistreated nor any of their possessions plundered. Caesar reports that his losses numbered 200 men, 30 of whom were seasoned centurions. Pompey's losses numbered 15,000 killed and 24,000 who surrendered.

Caesar briefly describes Pompey's voyage from island to island in the Mediterranean and how, after abandoning a plan to flee to Parthia, Pompey sailed instead to Egypt, landing at Pelusium, a city on the Mediterranean Sea at the easternmost mouth of the Nile River. There Pompey found an army belonging to Egypt's boy king Ptolemy engaged in civil conflict with the forces of his sister, Cleopatra. He sought the protection of Ptolemy's advisers, who controlled the young king and pretended to welcome Pompey. When Pompey boarded a small ship with a bodyguard they sent him, however, a Roman officer in Ptolemy's service and the chief of the king's bodyguard, Achillas, murdered him. They also apprehended and later killed Pompey's adjutant, Lucius Lentulus.

Arriving at Alexandria in Egypt, Caesar found himself unwelcome. He nonetheless sought to mediate in the dispute between Ptolemy and Cleopatra. As it happened, Ptolemy was himself in Alexandria, and Caesar took him into protective custody. Very soon thereafter, he received word that the army previously stationed at Pelusium was marching on Alexandria. Efforts to negotiate ended in the deaths of the Roman ambassadors. Caesar occupied the Island of Pharos, which controlled the approach to Alexandria from the Mediterranean, thereby insuring his grain supply, and ends his account of the Roman Civil Wars by describing the events leading up to the Alexandrian War.

Bibliography

Caesar, Julius Gaius. *Caesar: The Civil Wars*. Translated by A. G. Peskett. Cambridge, Mass.: Harvard University Press, 1951.

———. *The Civil War: With the Anonymous Alexandrian, African, and Spanish Wars*. Translated by J. M. Carter. Oxford and New York: Oxford University Press, 1997.

———. *War Commentaries of Caesar*. Translated by Rex Warner. New York: New American Library, 1964.

Canfora, Luciano. *Julius Caesar: The People's Dictator*. Translated by Marian Hill and Kevin Windle. Berkeley: University of California Press, 2007.

Classic of Filial Piety (*Xiao Jing, Hsiao Ching*) Confucius (?) and Zengzi [Tseng Tzu] (?) (ca. 210 B.C.E.?)

Unlikely to have been authored by either CONFUCIUS or Zengzi (Tseng Tzu) *Classic of Filial Piety* is an unprepossessing little handbook of rules that govern relationships. Just as the father whose word is law is the head of the family, so the Chinese emperor is the head of the larger empire, and his word is law for the extended family of his subjects.

Either in the smaller or the larger of these spheres, the greatest sin or crime conceivable for a child or a subject to commit was that of being unfilial. In both circumstances, failing to observe one's filial obedience could be punished by death. Failing to observe the rules of filial piety in the larger state was seen as planting the seeds of anarchy. Of course, there were degrees of unfilial behavior, and according to the handbook these could be subdivided into 3,000 separate offences, for each of which one of five punishments was prescribed.

Bibliography

Editorial Department of the Complete Works of Confucian Culture. *Xiao Jing: Classic of Filial Piety*. Translated by Lu Ruixiang and Lin Zhihe. Jinan Shi: Shandong you yi shou she, 1993.

Giles, Herbert A. *A History of Chinese Literature*. New York: Grove Press, 1958.

Claudian (Claudius Claudianus) (ca. 370–ca. 404 C.E.) *Roman poet*

Almost certainly born in Egypt, perhaps at Alexandria, Claudian had Greek as his first language. At some point, however, he mastered Latin as well, and it was in his second tongue that, during the last decade of his life, he wrote the works that earned him universal recognition as the final major poet of the Western Roman Empire and of polytheistic religion.

Claudian migrated to Rome around 395 C.E. He was well connected with the noble ancient Roman family of the Anicii—the family to which BOETHIUS would later belong. Two brothers of that family, Probinus and Olybrius, became the joint civic heads—the consuls—of the Roman state in that same year. In their honor, Claudian composed a panegyric (a poem of praise). Probably also through their influence, he soon moved to Milan as an official at the court of Stilicho. As regent during the minority of the Western Roman Emperor Honorius, Stilicho—a Germanic Vandal by heritage—was the West's de facto ruler.

Claudian became the court poet who celebrated the achievements both of the young Western emperor Honorius and, especially, of the poet's hero, Stilicho. For them he wrote a series of panegyrics that illustrate one pole of Claudian's poetic range. We find examples of the other pole in Claudian's invectives against Rufinus—the official whom Emperor Theodosius had appointed as protector of Honorius's elder brother, Arcadius, named by his father as emperor of the Eastern Roman Empire. Doubtless perceiving in Rufinus a challenge to his own ambitions, Stilicho had him killed in the presence of Arcadius. Claudian's two invectives vilifying Rufinus were published in 396–7, after his murder—a form of political whitewash for Stilicho's action.

Until around 400, Stilicho maneuvered to unify the East and the West under Honorius's sole rule. As a part of that strategy, Honorius married first one and then the other of Stilicho's daughters, but neither union produced an heir. Claudian wrote five poems celebrating Honorius's first marriage to Maria.

Another target of Claudian's poisoned pen was Arcadius's chief minister in the Eastern Roman Empire, the eunuch Eutropius, against whom Claudian wrote two books. By all accounts other than Claudian's, Eutropius was a wise and effective ruler in the East, becoming consul in 399. By allying the Eastern Roman Empire with Alaric the Goth, Eutropius contrived to maintain the East's independence against Stilicho's plots. In the year of Eutropius's consulship, however, a conspiracy against him succeeded, and he was deposed and executed over the objections of St. John Chrysostom. Claudian's invective against Eutropius appeared the same year.

Poems commemorating the victories of the arms of Stilicho and his generals also occupied Claudian's pen. Only the first book of the earlier of them, *The War against Gildo,* survives. That unfinished work in epic style tells the story of the rebellious Prince Gildo of Mauretania. He had also been commander of the Roman forces in Africa. When he rebelled, Gildo successfully cut off the supply ships that carried grain bound for Rome. Employing Gildo's own brother against him, Stilicho was able to break the embargo starving the city. The classicist Maurice Platnauer speculates that Claudian himself may have suppressed the second book of this poem rather than risk offending Stilicho with praises of Gildo's brother Macezel, who saved Rome.

In a kind of pocket epic running only 647 lines, Claudian celebrates Stilicho's personal victories over the Goths. The poem's introduction is memorable, for in it Claudian boasts none too modestly about a brass statue of him that the senate and emperor had dedicated at Rome. Otherwise the poem praises Stilicho's military prowess and superior tactics in overcoming the Getae, as Claudian denominated the Goths. The poem particularly celebrates Stilicho's victory over the Gothic leader Alaric at the Battle of Pollentia (402 C.E.). The celebration proved premature. The same Alaric beleaguered the city of Rome in 408 and 409, and conquered and sacked the city in 410.

Incomplete poems on mythological subjects also survive from Claudian's pen. One of these, *The Rape of Proserpine,* was again in the epic mode. Claudian's poem follows the action from Pluto's preparations to seize the daughter of the harvest goddess, Ceres, through Proserpine's actual kidnapping and her wedding to Pluto in Hades, and well into the distraught Ceres' search for her daughter and the responses of the other gods to the situation.

Among Claudian's shorter poems, one is addressed to Christ the Savior. Whether or not Claudian was a Christian, however, is a matter that has been much debated with no clear resolution. Such fathers of the church as St. Augustine and Orosius thought not.

Claudian's models seem to be poems by such writers as Lucan and Statius. His methods reflect those of schools of rhetoric in the late Roman manner and feature formal addresses of some length. His mastery of Latin idiom attains the highest level. If his surviving works seem marred by their propagandistic flavor, they also provide glimpses of his contemporaries and of important events.

Among Claudian's shorter works we find genuinely charming poems about animals and people. A poem describing the porcupine exemplifies the former category. The latter appears in a portrait of an old citizen of Verona who has blessedly spent his entire life on his native plot of land.

We know that Claudian married another client of the imperial family. A verse letter to Stilicho's wife Serena, also the adoptive daughter of the emperor Theodosius, essentially thanks her for having arranged his marriage. In that letter, too, Claudian invokes fair winds to prosper what is presumably his wedding voyage. If such classicists as Vollmer and Maurice Platnauer are right in dating the poem to 404, however, Claudian's voice falls silent immediately thereafter. This leads Vollmer to suggest that the poet died on his honeymoon.

Bibliography

Claudian. *Claudian's Panegyric on the Fourth Consulate of Honorius.* Edited and translated by William Barr. Liverpool, U.K.: Cairns, 1981

———. *"De raptu Proserpinae." Broken Columns: Two Roman Epic Fragments.* Translated by David R. Slavitt. Philadelphia: University of Pennsylvania Press, 1997.

———. *Panegyricus de Sexto Consulatu Honorii Augusti.* (Panygyric on the Sixth Consulate of the Emperor Honorius.) Translated by Michael Dewar. New York: Oxford University Press, 1996.

———. *Rape of Proserpine.* Liverpool, U.K.: Liverpool University Press, 1959.

Platnauer, Maurice, ed. and trans. *Claudian with an English Translation.* 2 vols. New York: G. P. Putnam's Sons, 1922.

Clouds, The Aristophanes (423 B.C.E.)

In a three-entry contest at the GREAT DIONYSIA in Athens in the year of its composition, ARISTO-PHANES' *The Clouds* disappointed the expectations of its playwright by taking third place. Because of a scornful allusion in the play's surviving text to this unexpectedly disapproving reaction of the Athenian citizenry to his comedy, we know that Aristophanes modified the version we now have after the play's first performance.

The play is set in an Athenian street before the houses of two neighbors. One of the houses belongs to Strepsiades, who is almost bankrupt with gambling debt. So is his son, Phidippides. The other house belongs to the great Athenian thinker SOCRATES. His house is jocularly labeled "the Thoughtery." There the SOPHISTS think great thoughts.

The play opens with a wakeful Strepsiades lying abed worrying about his debts. His sleeping son talks in his sleep about his dreams of the horse and chariot races that are impoverishing him and his father. Waking Phidippides, Strepsiades advises his son to go next door to learn from the Sophists how to win lawsuits justly or otherwise. Fearing that such knowledge would interfere with his love of horses and racing, Phidippides refuses. His furious father throws him out. The son blithely announces that he will go to live with his more sympathetic uncle, Megacles.

Phidippides exits, and Strepsiades decides to educate himself with the Sophists. He knocks and declares his intention to become a pupil. The disciple who admits him praises Socrates for solving such a problem as "how many times the length of its legs can a flea jump?" or as "does a gnat buzz through its proboscis or anus?"

Impressed with such wonders, Strepsiades pleads to be admitted. The door to the Thoughtery opens, revealing wan and emaciated men in various attitudes of contemplation and meditation. The disciple shows Strepsiades such devices as celestial globes and maps and explains their utility. A naive realist, Strepsiades is not impressed. He finds Socrates suspended in a basket, "traversing the air and contemplating the sun."

On learning who Socrates is, Strepsiades explains his problems and his errand, swearing by the gods to pay any fee Socrates may name. Socrates reveals that the gods are not much reverenced in the Thoughtery. Instead the initiates converse with the clouds, which they regard as spirits or guardian deities.

There follows a long and rather tedious discussion between Socrates and Strepsiades, punctuated by scatological humor. Socrates sees and hears goddesses and thunder in the clouds. Strepsiades instead sees mist and hears flatulence. Nonetheless, hoping to learn to defraud his creditors, Strepsiades enrolls as Socrates' student.

Here the action is interrupted by the leader of the CHORUS, who berates the Athenians for their judging this play, a favorite of Aristophanes', unworthy of a first or second prize. Then, in the character of the clouds themselves, the chorus explains to the audience that it owes the clouds divine reverence, reminding the Athenians that the clouds had thundered their disapproval when the Athenians had elected as their general Cleon, Aristophanes' deadly enemy and a chief supporter of the Peloponnesian War—a war the playwright despised.

Following the choral interlude, Socrates and Strepsiades reenter. The lessons are not going well. Strepsiades wishes only to learn how to bilk his creditors, and Socrates is attempting to teach his unwilling pupil the complexities of QUANTITATIVE VERSE.

Finally Socrates decides that Strepsiades is too old to learn and retain new material. Strepsiades decides to try again to persuade Phidippides to study with the Sophists. This time he succeeds, and after teacher and pupil get off to a bad start, Socrates calls upon two quarreling allegorical characters, Just Discourse and Unjust Discourse, to take over the instruction of his reluctant pupil. The two Discourses exchange insults until the chorus has had enough. The chorus leader asks that each state his position without interruption. They agree, and Just Discourse speaks first. He praises the good old days, careful education, children who knew how to behave, and high standards of sexual conduct for young people.

When his turn comes, Unjust Discourse makes the case for wasting time, for immodest and unchaste behavior, and for becoming the sort of citizens that comprise the audience witnessing the play. Looking out over the audience, Just Discourse sees that Unjust Discourse is right, and concedes the argument to him. He decides to join the ranks of the debauchees.

Strepsiades turns Phidippides over to Unjust Discourse as the young man's tutor.

As the day of financial reckoning approaches for Strepsiades, he goes to the Thoughtery to reclaim his son. Socrates assures the father that the son has mastered Sophistry and that the two can now win as many cases as they choose.

When the two are alone, Phidippides confuses his father with arguments far from the point under discussion. Strepsiades is impressed and thinks that now no one can best him in a lawsuit. His creditors begin to arrive, and Strepsiades refuses to pay them, confident that he will win when they bring suit. When the creditors have gone, Strepsiades confidently enters his house. In a few moments, however, he comes rushing out, followed by Phidippides, who is beating his father. It seems that the father asked for the son to sing, the son refused, they argued about songs and poems, and their disagreement over literary matters first grew heated and then led to blows. Phidippides uses his newly learned debating skills to assert his right to beat his father.

Disillusioned, Strepsiades complains bitterly to the clouds, from which he thinks all his troubles have come. Answering for them, the chorus assures the old man that he is the source of all his own troubles. Strepsiades resumes his faith in the old gods. Phidippides, however, denies Zeus, claiming that Whirlwind is the ruler of the world.

Convinced now that all his troubles proceed from Socrates, Strepsiades sets fire to the Thoughtery and attacks it with an axe as the source of blasphemies. The chorus, with a single spoken line, troops from the stage, and the play ends.

Generally speaking, the Athenians' original unfavorable judgment of the play seems more accurate than its author's unshakeable conviction that it represented his best work.

Bibliography

Aristophanes. *The Complete Plays*. Translated by Paul Roche. New York: New American Library, 2005.

Code of Hammurabi, *King of Babylon,* (ca. 2250 B.C.E.)

Jewish and Christian readers of the HEBREW BIBLE may associate the Code of Hammurabi with the summary phrase "An eye for an eye; a tooth for a tooth." That association does not much miss the mark, for the 21st through the 23rd chapters of the Book of Exodus, in which Moses details the laws that God dictated to him, share much in common with the statutes that the Babylonian King Hammurabi promulgated.

Just as Moses credited God with having presented the leader of Israel with a legal code that included 10 commandments inscribed in stone, so Hammurabi credited the Babylonian sun god, Shamash or Shamshu, with having given the king the stone tablet on which the Code is inscribed. Unlike the tablet of Moses, that of Hammurabi has been found: A French archaeological expedition unearthed it in December 1901 and January 1902 on the acropolis of the ancient city of Susa on the Tigris River, where the three broken pieces of the tablet had apparently been brought from Babylon as plunder around the year 1100 B.C.E. The Code's translator, Robert Francis Harper, believes that corroborating evidence points to the existence of several copies of the Code at crucial locations. The original now reposes in the Louvre Museum in Paris.

In addition to a bas-relief picturing Hammurabi receiving the Code from Shamash, the tablets contain a prologue, 282 laws governing a wide variety of interactions, and an epilogue filled with curses invoked against anyone who in the future may change, efface, or subvert Hammurabi's divinely ordained legislation.

The first of Hammurabi's laws prescribes the death penalty for false accusation and the third exacts the same penalty for false witness. The second law addresses the crime of sorcery. It requires the same test that applied to witches in Europe as late as the 18th century C.E.: A person accused of sorcery must throw himself into a river. If he drowns, he is held to have been a sorcerer, and his accuser inherits his estate. If he floats or swims, he is innocent; his accuser is then put to death, and the accused inherits the accuser's estate.

Judges who alter their judgments are in danger of having to pay 12 times the original fine and losing their jobs. Stealing is divided into a number of subcategories. Stealing a slave is a capital offense, but returning a fugitive slave earns a reward of "two shekels of silver."

If a person is robbed and the robber escapes, a sworn affidavit itemizing the loss requires that the state reimburse the victim. Stealing from a burning house while pretending to help earns the perpetrator the penalty of burning with the house. Soldiers whose property is occupied by others while the soldiers are away must recover the property on their return. Officers of government are especially protected from attempts to seize their property, but they are also prohibited from transferring public property in their charge to their wives and daughters. Fines imposed on persons for breaches of trust range from five to 12 times the value of the property entrusted.

Some of the laws governing concubinage and marriage seem quite enlightened and even modern. If a man leaves a concubine who has borne him children, he is required to support the children. Either party to a marriage could initiate divorce, and the payments that accompany the separation are specified. If, for instance, a woman grows to hate her husband and an inquiry into the matter determines that she has performed her part of the marriage contract, the husband must return her dowry and the wife must go to her father's house. When widows choose to remarry, Hammurabi's Code protects the interests of the children of the first marriage. If husbands give their wives property outright, then children of those marriages can make no claims on that property against their mother.

The property rights of unmarried priestesses are also carefully stipulated. Should they predecease brothers, however, the brothers inherit. The responsibilities of adoptive fathers are also carefully specified.

Other laws reflect a rigidly hierarchical social structure. Husbands of barren wives can take concubines, or the wives can present their husbands with the wives' own maidservants. If the maidservant bears children, she gains status equal to that of the wife. If she also proves barren, however, the wife can sell her. Several laws stipulate the rights of masters over their slaves. Punishments that masters can take against slaves for denying their condition of servitude, for example, include mutilation by cutting off an ear.

The "eye-for-an-eye" and "tooth-for-a-tooth" portion of Hammurabi's Code also exists. It begins with the 196th injunction and runs through the 201st. What an eye or a tooth was worth, however, depended on the relative social ranks of those concerned. Only when persons of equal rank were involved were the penalties the same.

Hammurabi's Code also governs the practice of physicians and veterinarians, providing rewards for successful and punishments for unsuccessful surgeries. If a physician succeeds in saving a man's life or eye, he receives as his fee 10 shekels of silver if the man is upper class, five if he is a former slave, and two if the patient is currently a slave. A similar set of judgments applies to unsuccessful operations. If an upper-class person dies or is blinded by an operation, the physician's fingers are cut off. If the deceased patient has been a slave, the physician has to provide a replacement slave.

Laws governing trade, pasturage, and tenant farming also appear in the Code.

The magnificent edition of Hammurabi's Code prepared by Robert Francis Harper should be consulted by anyone with an interest in this ancient document. Not only does it contain the CUNEIFORM original of the text, it also provides a transliteration and a translation as well as other fascinating editorial material.

Bibliography

Harper, Robert Francis, ed. and trans. the Code of Hammurabi *King of Babylon about 2250* B.C. Chicago: The University of Chicago Press, 1999.

comedy in Greece and Rome

The first entire Greek comedy to survive into modern times is The ACHARNIANS by ARISTOPHANES (performed 425 B.C.E.) The play typifies the comedy of this early period in that its essential thrust is political. It names such contemporary politicians as Cleon, and, like other representatives of what critics call Greek old comedy, it pillories them. The *Acharnians* also exposes the addictive effect that politics in the form of sitting on juries produces in old men. As the literary historian Peter Wilson suggests, this sort of comedy was rooted in making fun of or in roughly satirizing representatives of the male citizens of Athens who exercised unprecedented power as members of the mass assembly of Athenian citizens (the *ecclesia*), or the council of 500 who referred matters to that assembly, or the system of citizen courts frequented by the old men of *The Acharnians* that sometimes brought together as many as 2,001 judges to hear cases.

The ongoing warfare between Athens and Sparta or other city-states during the exhausting Peloponnesian Wars also drew comedic scorn from Aristophanes in his *LYSISTRATA*. In this play, in an effort to make the men stop fighting, the women withhold their sexual favors and occupy the treasury to force an end to the seemingly perpetual conflict. Such comedies were associated with city festivals, particularly the Athenian festival of LENAEA, where two of Aristophanes' plays, *The Acharnians* and *The KNIGHTS* won back-to-back first prizes in 425 and 424 B.C.E.

The period of the Greek Old Comedy came to a sudden close with Sparta's defeat of Athens in 404 B.C.E. Athens was no longer the democratic ruler of a far-flung empire, and political theater gave way to the battle of the sexes or to class warfare. We see this shift in the late dramas of the long-lived Aristophanes with his *Ecclesiazusae* (WOMEN AT THE THESMOMORPHIA, *The Assembly Women*) and *Plutus* (*Wealth*)—plays that are now counted among examples of early Middle Comedy. Only fragmentary remains of other Greek middle comedies survive, but the observations of historical critics suggest that perhaps the plays became less bawdy in costume and language. Similar sources suggest that, in the Middle Comedy, philosophers became a favorite butt of stage sarcasm. Mythology, too, seems to have become a subject of burlesque.

Stock characters—a feature that became a staple of Greek New Comedy—also made their appearance at this juncture, though the seeds of types like the *miles gloriosus* (see *The* BRAGGART SOLDIER are also observable in such a figure as Lamachus in Aristophanes' *The Acharnians*.

For millennia, literary historians had to rely on surviving lists of ancient Greek stage props and on the imitations of Greek New Comedy by the Roman playwrights PLAUTUS and TERENCE to guide their speculations about the characteristics of New Comedy. No example of the type and only tiny fragments had survived. Then, in the 20th century, archeologists and others discovered more and more fragments. The capstone of a series of finds was achieved with the appearance of a virtually complete text of MENANDER's comic play DYSKOLOS. That text confirmed the conclusions that literary historians had already drawn. The plots of the plays often involved stock situations in which more or less clueless young people fell in love but faced difficulties posed by members of the older generation. Minor characters were drawn from a reservoir of such stock characters as cooks, slaves, parasites, and difficult old persons. A good deal of slapstick like that in the final act of *Dyskolos* was also featured in the plays. All difficulties were always resolved by a happy ending.

The rediscovery of other fragments of new comedy offer hope that other, more complete representatives will be discovered. We also find evidence of a tradition of private performance of comedies or of comic scenes at banquets and other entertainments in Greece, but no specific examples of these have as yet appeared.

In Italy, where one must remember that the Greeks had established colonies well before the foundation of Rome, a mode of comedy appeared as early as the second century B.C.E. It displayed Greek influence but was indigenous to the Oscan city of Atella in the vicinity of Naples; thus, it became known as the ATELLANE FABLES OR FARCES. These may first have begun as extemporaneous performances, and they continued to be played in the Oscan language at Atella until they migrated to the city of Rome. There they commanded a wide audience long after LIVIUS ANDRONICUS had introduced the regular drama to Rome, and Roman playwrights had begun to emulate the classical drama of Greece.

Standard Latin soon replaced Oscan in these little plays, and a custom arose that permitted respectable young Romans, even those of the patrician class, to participate as players. Like Greek New Comedy and the later Italian *commedia dell'arte*, Atellane farces seem to have had a stock set of characters that appeared in traditional costumes. One such stock character was Mappus. He was presented as having a large head, a long nose, and a humped back. Another was called Pappus. The classicist J. J. Eschenburg speculates that Pappus may have been borrowed from a Greek stock character, the old man called Silenus.

The popularity of Atellane farces and the financial opportunities from writing them encouraged playwrights who were successful in other genres—such as the poet Memmius (d. 46 B.C.E.) and the fabulist Sylla—to try their hands at composing the farces. Those who seem to have enjoyed the most success with the genre and who raised Atellane farces to literary status are Quintus Novius and L. Pomponius of Bononia, who cooperated in writing such farces in the first century B.C.E. Only fragmentary remains of their works remain—about 70 and about 200 lines respectively.

A custom arose of having young Romans of respectable families perform in short, farcical pieces at the end of the Atellane plays. These afterpieces were called *exordia*.

Livius Andronicus, mentioned above as the father of the regular Roman drama, wrote both TRAGEDY and comedy. No comedy survives in any but fragmentary condition, but the fragments suggest that he borrowed heavily though not slavishly from Greek New Comedy.

It would be hard to exaggerate the importance of Plautus in the annals of Roman comedy. His plays, of which there were many—possibly more than 50—are the earliest examples of mainstream Roman theater to survive. Plautus initiated modern musical comedy. He borrowed his plots and his character types from Greek New Comedy, but he often treated them innovatively, heightening aspects of plotting. For example, he emphasized doubling his situations so that not just one but two couples of young lovers would complicate his comic situations. Moreover, Plautus also either borrowed from Greek Old Comedy or independently reintroduced a strain of risqué humor. He also drew recognizable, satiric portraits of his contemporary Romans.

Only six plays survive to represent the work of the other most famous of Roman comic playwrights, Terence. Like Plautus, Terence modeled his plays on Greek originals. Stock situations also typified his plays: shipwrecks, mistaken identities, kidnapping by pirates, disguises, separations and reunions, and young lovers kept apart by venal elders all figured prominently. Characters were also a predictable lot: old misers, lickspittles, blusterers, foolish youngsters, and hypocrites peopled Terence's stage. A part of the playwright's charm, however, arises from his ability to make his characters fresh and engaging within the confines of their predictability.

Silent mimes and pantomime with spoken lines also became popular in Rome. These comic types became immensely popular. Such a notable Roman politician as JULIUS CAESAR subsidized their public performances generously, and the various branches of comedy continued to be performed in Rome until the city's fall in 410 C.E.

After the fall of the city of Rome, such performances continued despite a general ban on theatrical performance. They spread, moreover, through the provinces. Their bawdy humor provoked at least three sorts of responses from Christians. The first was ineffectual disapproval. The second was to create a comedy based on the legends of the church or on incidents in the Bible. The major impetus for the continued development of this kind of comedy came from Constantinople and the Eastern Roman Empire. For example, the Christian bishop, Apollinaris of Laodicea, took the model of the comedy of Menander and adapted to it several domestic stories from the Bible, creating a kind of scriptural comedy.

The third sort of Christian response occurred in the monasteries. There, a racy monastic farce developed that amused the monks by exploiting potential double meanings in liturgical language. They might, for instance, take a phrase like *cor meum eructavit* (my heart lifts up) and apply it to a resounding belch.

The first recorded instance of such farcical material actually being performed in churches proper, however, does not occur until the 10th century, when a patriarch of Constantinople, Theophylact, introduced farces, complete with singing and dancing, to houses of worship. It seems likely that similar instances had occurred earlier.

The influence of Greek and Roman comedy has survived, informing the theater of both the Middle Ages and the European Renaissance. It remains alive and well today, as one can observe in television's situational comedy and, on Broadway, in such productions as *A Funny Thing Happened on the Way to the Forum*.

Bibliography

Charney, Maurice, ed. *Comedy: A Geographic and Historical Guide*. Westport, Conn.: Praeger, 2005.

Conte, Gian Biagio. *Latin Literature: A History.* Translated by Joseph B. Solodow, Don Fowler, and Glenn W. Most. Baltimore: Johns Hopkins University Press, 1994.

Eschenburg, J. J. *Manual of Classical Literature.* Translated by N. W. Fiske. Philadelphia: E. C. and J. Biddle, 1850.

Henderson, Jeffrey, ed. and trans. *Aristophanes.* 4 vols. Cambridge, Mass.: Harvard University Press, 1998–2002.

Menander of Athens. *Dyskolos, or The Man who didn't Like People.* Translated by W. G. Arnott. London: University of London, Athelone Press, 1960.

Slavitt, David R., and Palmer Bowie, eds. *Plautus: The Comedies.* 4 vols. Translated by Constance Carrier *et al.* Complete Roman Drama in Translation. Baltimore: Johns Hopkins University Press, 1995.

Terence. *Works: English and Latin.* Translated by John Barsby. Cambridge, Mass.: Harvard University Press, 2001.

Wilson, Peter. "Powers of Horror and Laughter: The Great Age of Drama." In *Literature in the Greek and Roman Worlds: A New Perspective.* Edited by Oliver Taplin. New York: Oxford University Press, 2000.

Commentary on the Gallic Wars Julius Caesar (ca. 50 B.C.E.)

JULIUS CAESAR's own account of his campaigns against the Celtic tribes of Gaul, apart from being of inestimable value from the viewpoint of subsequent generations of historians and readers, had important political and propagandistic value for Caesar's own generation and for his political career. The text gives evidence of a level of editing and thoughtful composition more careful than Caesar lavished on his other extant work, THE CIVIL WARS.

Book 1

The first chapter of *Commentary on the Gallic Wars* describes the geography of the country denominated *Gaul,* its three parts, and the inhabitants of each. These peoples include the Belgae, whom Caesar judges to be the toughest soldiers; the Aquitani; and the Gauls themselves, who are further subdivided into tribes. Among the Gallic tribes, Caesar deems the Helvetii to be the bravest. The superior valor of the Belgae and the Helvetii stems from similar causes. They are the most distant from merchants, whose wares tend to make people effeminate, and they are nearest the Germans, whom the Belgae and Helvetii constantly fight.

Caesar next traces the circumstances that led to a confrontation between the Gauls and his legions. Considering that the 38,590 square miles of their territory was too confining a space for a people of their valor and accomplishments, the Helvetii had decided to undertake a mass migration. Of the two routes available to them, one was mountainous and militarily too dangerous, and the other lay through lands occupied by the Romans and their allies. The Helvetii sent ambassadors to Caesar, requesting permission to march through the latter territory. Suspicious of their motives and fearing that they would ravage any countryside they passed through, Caesar first delayed giving them an answer while he made defensive preparations, and then he refused his permission.

Anticipating that the Helvetii would try to force their way through, Caesar hurried to Italy to raise additional troops. By the time he returned with them to Transalpine Gaul, the Helvetii were already on the move and pillaging the territory of the Romans' allies, the Aedui, the Ambarri, and the Allobroges.

Caesar's forces pursued the Helvetii, catching up with them at night after the main body of their forces had crossed the Saone River, a tributary of the Rhone. Caesar surprised the rear guard—a clan called the Tigurini—and decimated them. He derived particular satisfaction from this action since the Tigurini had killed Caesar's father-in-law's grandfather three generations before. In a single day, Caesar bridged the Saone and came up on the main force. The

Helvetii parlayed, and the adversaries exchanged threats and counterthreats. Caesar demanded hostages to assure the Helvetii's good behavior. They refused.

The second chapter explains how Caesar's forces shadowed the Helvetii as they marched through the domain of the Aedui. It also notes the failure of the Aedui to supply the Romans with grain as they had promised and the way that Caesar uncovered a plot to block the supply. Eventually, accidentally misled into imagining that the Romans were afraid of them, the Helvetii attacked the Roman forces. Caesar details the subsequent battles, whose upshot was the utter rout of the Helvetii.

The survivors among them, whom Caesar numbers at 130,000, were ordered to retrace their steps to their original lands and were obliged to repair or rebuild anything they had damaged or destroyed on the way. As the Helvetii were absolutely destitute of supplies, Caesar arranged for grain to sustain them on their journey home. He explains that he did not wish their former lands to remain vacant since they formed a buffer against the even more warlike Germans. According to a census Caesar had taken, 110,000 Helvetii made it home.

Chapter 3 details the way in which the leaders of several tribes of Caesar's Gallic subjects came in secret to complain of their treatment at the hands of a Germanic king, Ariovistus, who was occupying their lands and ensuring their compliance with his orders by taking their children hostage. Caesar exchanged letters with Ariovistus, who refused to parley and who boasted of the unparalleled prowess of his German warriors. About then, Caesar received complaints that Ariovistus was forcibly settling another group of Germans, the Harudes, in Gallic territory. Caesar decided that the time had come to deal with Ariovistus. By forced marches, he raced the Germanic forces to the stronghold of Besançon, which the Romans occupied. As they regrouped, the Roman soldiers began to hear and believe stories about the invincibility of the German forces. The officers began inventing reasons for needing to take leave, and finally Caesar rallied

them with examples of previous Roman successes against Germanic troops. He also shamed them by announcing his willingness to face the Germans with only his reliable 10th Legion. Taking heart, the Romans resumed their march and, six days later, encamped 22 miles from the main body of the German forces.

Now Caesar reports the parlays, the proposals and counterproposals, and the eventual tactical ruses of the Germans that preceded a general engagement of the two armies. Caesar describes the battle and its vicissitudes. He reports that the defeated Germans fled 15 miles to the Rhine. Ariovistus escaped by boat, losing family members in the melee and rout. The Suebi, another Germanic tribe who were waiting on the eastern shore of the Rhine to be resettled in Gaul by Ariovistus, tried to return east to their original homelands, but their former sponsors in the vicinity turned on them and killed many of their fellow Germans.

Book 2

Having fought two major wars in one season, Caesar quartered his troops for the winter and crossed the Alps to Cisalpine Gaul to perform his duties as judge and magistrate. There, as Book 2 opens, Caesar began to hear disturbing reports that the Belgae were in arms and restless. Accordingly, Caesar raised two new legions and in early summer sent them north across the Alps. As soon as he could, Caesar set out for the Belgian frontier, where he arrived unannounced about two weeks later. There he discovered that a Belgian army of more than 300,000 men were already marching against him and were not far off. A series of defensive maneuvers soon put Caesar in command of the situation, and the vast army that faced him withdrew. Though its rear guard behaved as a disciplined unit, the vast bulk of the troops straggled as an undisciplined mob making its way home as quickly as it could. The Roman cavalry, once it had overcome the rear guard's resistance, harried the mob and killed thousands. Total victory for Caesar's forces required only a few more tactical successes and a demonstration of the Romans' superiority in military technology. The hostile forces surrendered. Caesar ensured their compliance with the terms of surrender by demanding and receiving 600 hostages.

Now, among the Belgians, only the tribe of the Nervii resisted Caesar's dominion. The second chapter of Book 2 describes the Romans' campaign against them. This time Caesar's opponents succeeded in catching his forces at a disadvantage as they engaged in preparing defensive positions. So desperate, indeed, did the Romans' situation become that an accompanying detachment of Roman African Numidians decamped for home. On arriving there, they reported the defeat of the Roman forces and the loss of all their baggage.

Caesar reports that he seized a shield and personally rallied his troops, forming a square to defend against attacks from any direction. As his soldiers were losing heart and were in danger of being overwhelmed, Caesar's doughty 10th Legion arrived to reinforce them. Their presence, Caesar says, "changed everything." Heartened, even the wounded rose from the ground to continue the fight. When the battle finally ended, of a force of 60,000 Nervii, Caesar reports that barely 500 survived. Caesar treated the survivors with consideration and mercy, allowing them to keep their territory.

The third chapter deals with the false surrender of the Aduatuci tribe. After seeing Caesar's siege engines, they begged for leniency, which Caesar granted. The Adatuci surrendered large quantities of arms, but during the night they sallied forth from their town and attacked the Roman positions. Caesar had prepared for that eventuality, easily defeated the Aduatuci, and sold the entire population of their city, 53,000 persons, into slavery as punishment for their duplicity.

Shortly thereafter, Caesar received word from his subordinate commander, Publius Crassus, that the several tribes of Gallic people who occupied the Atlantic coast had also submitted to Roman authority so that all of Transalpine Gaul was at peace.

Book 3

In the high Alps themselves, however, indigenous Gauls were harassing Roman trade routes, we learn as Book 3 opens. Caesar describes the way he sent forces under Galba to pacify the region and how the Gauls again feigned a peaceful alliance and then mounted a ferocious attack. When the Roman defensive position seemed desperate, Galba's troops broke out in a surprise attack that routed their Gallic enemies, the Seduni and the Veragri.

Book 3's second chapter reports the "impulsive decision" of the Atlantic coastal Gauls under the influence of the powerful Veneti to abrogate their treaty with Rome and even to imprison Rome's envoys—ambassadors who were supposed to enjoy diplomatic immunity. Caesar details the difficulties he faced in pacifying the coastal peoples who used tides to their advantage, abandoned towns by sea, and moved their forces along the coast, and whose ships were superior to the Roman craft. Caesar's commanders, however, finally discovered a weakness in the Gauls' vessels: They were difficult to row. Destroying their rigging left them vulnerable to Roman attack. By this means, the coastal Gauls were once more pacified. Caesar then reports the successes of his subordinate commander, Sabinus, who pretended cowardice to lure another set of rebellious Gallic tribes into attacking him—a mistake that led to their decimation.

In the meantime, as Caesar tells us in chapter 3, he sent Publius Crassus to pacify Aquitania—about a third of the Gallic land area. Crassus succeeded in this commission after fighting pitched battles against not only the Gauls resident in Acquitaine but also reinforcements the Gauls had recruited from Spain. In the course of this discussion, Caesar describes an institution among Gallic fighting men called *soldurii* (a cognate of the Old French source word for English *soldier*). *Soldurii* swore an oath not only to share all the good things in life but also to die together either in battle or by suicide. Caesar observes that he has never heard of anyone who broke his vow.

The success of Crassus in subduing the Aquitanian Gauls who took the field against him encouraged others to submit voluntarily. Some tribes, distant from the action, refused to submit, thinking that the arrival of winter would protect them from Roman incursions. In this hope many were disappointed, for Caesar himself led mopping-up operations against them and had subdued most before the onset of winter obliged him to suspend operations against the few remaining holdouts.

Book 4

In 55 B.C.E., as we learn in Book 4, two Germanic tribes, the Usipetes and the Tenchtheri—under military pressure from a third, more warlike tribe, the Suebi—crossed the Rhine with the intention of occupying Gallic territory. After describing the characteristics of the Suebi and other Germanic peoples, Caesar reverts to a frequent theme: the mercurial nature of the Gallic decision-making processes. Their penchant for jumping to conclusions, Caesar thinks, leads them to act—particularly in military matters—in ways that they often regret immediately after taking action. Caesar frequently turns this perceived weakness to Roman advantage.

Next Caesar recounts his dealings with the Germans. Seeking to delay the Romans while they awaited their own cavalry, the Germans held the Romans in parlay. After agreeing to defer action, the Germans treacherously attacked a Roman cavalry unit. The next day, the German ambassadors returned, apologizing for the "mistake." Caesar, who had mistrusted them from the beginning, was not to be deceived twice. He imprisoned the ambassadors, whose ranks included the principal German leaders, and mounted a surprise attack on the main body of their forces, slaughtering many. The rest, trapped on a promontory, tried to escape by swimming the Rhine, and most drowned. The loss of almost 430,000 men ended the Germanic threat for the moment. Their captive leaders chose to join Caesar rather than risk their lives among the Gauls whom they had invaded.

Given the warlike disposition of the Germanic tribes, Caesar considered it expedient to cross the Rhine with a show of force. Moreover, some of the Germans, the Ubii, had requested Roman protection against the Suebi. Caesar declined an offer to have his troops transported over the river in German boats. Instead, he and his engineers designed and, in 10 days, built a bridge capable of withstanding the Rhine's current. Above the bridge, he also had bulwarks built to impede any logs and tree trunks that the Germans might float down in an effort to destroy the bridge, whose clever design Caesar reports in detail.

The Roman incursion, which lasted only 18 days, achieved all its objectives. The Ubii were no longer threatened. The Suebi and their allies the Sigambri, thinking the Romans intended to attack them, abandoned their towns and moved deep into the forests, where they massed in expectation of a Roman attack. Instead, Caesar destroyed their towns and crops. Then his forces returned to Gaul, destroying the bridge as they withdrew.

On the understanding that his enemies had received help from their allies in Britain, Caesar next formulated a plan to send an expeditionary force to that island. Knowing next to nothing about it, he set about finding out what he could from traders who went there. The traders reported his plans in Britain, and, while he prepared 80 transports for a channel crossing, deputations began arriving, offering hostages to secure Caesar's friendship.

When the Roman infantry actually arrived off the coast of Britain, however, a hostile defensive force was waiting for them. Caesar's cavalry had missed the tide for sailing and had not yet arrived. Caesar describes the difficulties of the infantry's landing, their courage, the defensive tactics of the Britons, and the eventual success of the Roman infantry. When the defenders had been defeated, they sent emissaries to Caesar. Although the Britons had enchained Caesar's ambassador, Caesar displayed his usual forbearance, accepted their apologies and excuses, and looked forward to the Britons' peaceful submission.

Weather, however, proved to be a more formidable foe than had the island's defenders. A storm forced most of Caesar's late-arriving cavalry to return to the Continent, and very high tides made him suspect his transports were not seaworthy. When the Britons realized that his expeditionary force was effectively cut off, they began to hatch plots against the Romans on the theory that a Roman failure would insure their island from further incursions. After a few other engagements against the Britons, all occasioned by their treachery, Caesar decided to take the risk of crossing the channel on doubtful transport before winter weather closed that option to him. The Romans made the crossing without incident, but when the first ships reached the Continent, local Gauls harried the disembarking legionaries until the Roman cavalry was ashore. Then the Gauls took flight with much loss of life.

At the end of Book 4, Caesar, as he often does, reminds his readers of his unparalleled services to the Roman state by reporting the senate's decrees of public thanksgiving on receipt of his reports.

Book 5

As Book 5 begins, Caesar details the preparations he ordered for his second invasion of Britain. Now that he knew about the channel and what to expect on the other side, in addition to repairing his small fleet, he designed a new kind of cargo transport and ordered 600 of these and 28 new warships to be built for a channel crossing from Boulogne, where the distance to Britain was only 28 miles.

He interrupts the narrative concerning Britain to recount his activities to pacify the ever-fractious Gauls and his decision to take along the most untrustworthy among them on the second invasion of Britain. He was chiefly concerned about an old enemy, Dumnorix. Dumnorix tried everything to avoid going to Britain. When Caesar remained firm, Dumnorix tried to sneak away; Caesar sent cavalry after him and had him killed.

Leaving his adjutant, Labienus, with three legions and 2,000 cavalry to fortify the Gallic dominions on the Continent, Caesar and a fleet of almost 800 warships sailed to Britain. Though Celtic fighters had massed to confront the invaders, the sight of so large a flotilla frightened them, and Caesar met no opposition to his initial landing. Skirmishing soon began, however, and Caesar describes these engagements. He also describes the geography of the eastern side of Britain and some of the customs of the people, like wife sharing.

The Britons agreed on the appointment of a warlike chieftain, Cassivellaunus, as the overall commander of their forces, and he successfully harried the Roman army with lightning chariot raids. Not all the Celtic tribes, however, universally admired Cassivellaunus, and several defected, placing themselves under Roman protection. Disheartened by these desertions and by Roman victories, Cassivellaunus himself asked for the terms of surrender and accepted them.

After the British Celts agreed to send annual tributes to Rome, Caesar and his entire expeditionary force withdrew to the Continent. There a drought had produced a poor harvest, and Caesar found it necessary to disperse his troops around the occupied territory. Many Gauls were discontented with the occupation of their territory, and with the Romans dispersed as they were, the Gauls agreed to attack all the Roman winter camps at the same time so that one could not be summoned to the others' aid.

One Gallic leader, Ambiorix, joined in the general uprising, but, as he explained, he was grateful to Caesar for past kindness and support. He therefore warned the Roman commander Sabinus that a great army of Germans had crossed the Rhine and were moving to attack within the next few days. After a prolonged council of war and much disagreement, Sabinus determined to lead the greater part of the garrison to a better fortified position. As he was doing so, it was necessary for the entire army to march through a long, deep ravine. As soon as all the Romans were within it, Ambiorix had his warriors attack the Romans at both entrances to the ravine. Finding his situation desperate, Sabinus requested a conference with Ambriorix. When he arrived at the meeting place, however, Sabinus was killed. Only a few of his soldiers escaped to tell the story of the destruction of a Roman army.

Ambriorix's success heartened other Gauls, who joined him in mounting an attack on the winter camp of those Roman troops commanded by CICERO's brother, Quintus Tullius Cicero. As Ambriorix had done with Sabinus, they attempted to lure Q. Cicero out of camp by guile, but Cicero did not rise to the bait. The Gauls attacked the Roman camp, using tactics they had learned from the Romans. The Romans, however, held out, and Caesar recounts the story of two rival centurions, Vorenus and Pullo. Forever arguing about who was the better soldier, the two sallied out alone against the enemy, saved each other's lives, and returned safely to camp.

By promising his freedom and riches to a Gallic slave, a Roman loyalist Gaul named Vertico sent his servant unnoticed through the Gallic lines with a message to Caesar wrapped around the servant's spear shaft. Caesar immediately marched to Cicero's rescue with a relatively small band of Romans. Through deception and superior tactics, he was able to draw off the Gauls attacking Cicero and defeat them decisively. Similar tactics and determination by Labienus led to the defeat of another dangerous Gallic force and the death of their leader, Indutiomarus.

Book 6

The Roman yoke, however, still lay heavy on the necks of the subjugated Gauls, and revolutionary violence was far from over. Book 6 reports the steps that Caesar took to suppress the revolutionaries or to dissuade them from taking up arms. Having dealt with the Gauls, however, Caesar learned that the German Suebi were once more in arms. The Ubii, another Germanic tribe, did not want Caesar to think they were not observing the agreements they had made with the Romans, so they became the Romans' eyes and ears, keeping Caesar apprised of the Suebi's movements.

The second chapter begins with a discussion of the customs and characteristics of the Gauls and the Germans. The priestly classes, called the Druids, and the military classes, the knights, ruled the Gauls. Polytheists, whose gods Caesar calls by Roman names, the priestly classes enjoyed all sorts of privileges, including freedom from taxation, and they taught the doctrine of transmigration of the soul. The knights brought to battle with them contingents of armed warriors, and knightly prestige and status rested on the number of followers who accompanied the knights to battle. The Gauls considered themselves to be the descendants of Dis, the god of the underworld. The magistrates suppressed any news that they considered might not be good for their people to learn.

The Germans, on the other hand, had no priestly class. Caesar tells us they worshipped objects and phenomena like the sun and the moon and fire. They derived prestige from controlling vast tracts of wasteland and from forcing their neighbors off land that they coveted for their own. Caesar describes a vast forest whose extent is unknown except that it stretches east for more than 60 days journey. He describes some of the fauna of this forest, such as elk and the now-extinct giant aurochs.

In the third chapter, Caesar turns his attention to describing his tactics in pursuing and punishing Ambiorix. Leaving Q. Cicero in charge of the Roman army's baggage and a small garrison and promising to return on a fixed day, Caesar warned Cicero not to send any troops outside the fort walls. Cicero, however, began to doubt the wisdom of Caesar's instructions. He finally sent troops out to gather grain. As it happened, a force of marauding Germans of the Sigambri tribe, seeking booty at the suggestion of some Gauls, arrived at Cicero's camp that very day. In the ensuing attack, the diminished garrison held firm. Veterans among the foraging party, caught outside by the German attack, opted to form a flying wedge and fight their way back to camp. They achieved this with no losses. New recruits instead chose first to defend the high ground. They were forced off it and also tried to cut their way through to the fort, but they were hampered by their adversaries, and only a few reached safety. Only Caesar's arrival the next day kept the garrison from total panic.

In his search for Ambiorix, Caesar once again had recourse to a scorched earth policy, devastating the land of the Gallic Eburones. Ambiorix and a bodyguard of four trusted companions, however, still managed to elude the Roman dragnet.

In the winter of 53–52 B.C.E., while Caesar was south of the Alps and his Transalpine troops all in winter quarters, the Gauls decided on an all-out effort to rid themselves of the Roman yoke. Their choice for leadership fell upon a young Gaul of the Arvernian tribe, Vercingetorix. He was to become the most celebrated warrior his people had ever known.

A savagely no-nonsense ruler, Vercingetorix used fear of his ruthlessness to instill iron discipline in the Gallic tribes under his sway. With his troops shoveling their way through blocked Alpine passes, however, Caesar was able to surprise the Gauls and throw their expectations into disarray. Vercingetorix responded to Caesar's remarkable tactics by changing his strategy and instructing his allies to make every effort to cut off the Roman grain supply. He also instructed the Gauls to burn down those of their own cities that would be impossible to defend. These expedients proved so successful that the Romans were sometimes hard put to keep from starving.

Despite such difficulties, Caesar showed his usual military acumen by successfully laying siege to the city of Bourges, most of whose inhabitants perished in the Roman victory. Moreover, the city was abundantly supplied with grain—a circumstance that solved the Roman food crisis. In addition to describing the tactical and strategic situations as the war against Vercingetorix and his supporters developed, Caesar is always careful to keep readers informed about the politi-cal situation among the Gauls, so that readers understand the currents and crosscurrents of public opinion and the truths and falsehoods that shape it.

Caesar next describes the battle for the walled city of Gergovia—a battle that ended in the Romans' tactical withdrawal and with the Gauls still in possession of the town. By forced marches, then, Caesar led his legions to a place where they could still ford the meltwater-swollen Loire River—a crossing the Gauls had thought impossible.

Book 7

In the first three chapters of Book 7, the Gauls secretly plan a rebellion under the leadership of the Carnutes. They seek Cenabum and kill its Roman population. In the fourth chapter of Book 7, Caesar turns his attention to describing the campaigns of his colleague Labienus, whose troops were conducting simultaneous, imaginative, and successful operations along the River Seine. The revolt of the Aedui against the Romans, however, heartened those Gauls whose allegiance still wavered, and the Roman position became less and less tenable.

The Aedui contested the supremacy of Vercingetorix, but when all the Gallic representatives voted on the issue, Vercingetorix emerged as supreme commander. Then began preparations for a final confrontation between the combined strength of the Gallic tribes and their Roman adversaries. The Romans were not entirely without allies; perhaps ironically, the Germanic tribes whom they had overcome honored their treaties. The Romans and their Germanic allies roundly defeated the best hope of the Gauls, their massed cavalry.

Vercingetorix now retreated to the citadel of Alesia. From there he sent representatives to all the Gallic tribes, calling on them to send reinforcements and explaining how dire his own supply situation had become. He collected all the available grain and began to dole it out in small increments, explaining that by that expedient he might make his supplies last for 30 days or a bit longer.

In the meantime, Caesar began to use superior Roman technology to construct trenches, ramparts, battlements, towers, and breastworks to impede any attack that his enemies might initiate. Caesar's military innovations included stakes embedded in the ground in such a way that enemy attackers would necessarily impale themselves on them. Various inventive booby traps were also put in place. The net result was that the Roman forces could not be surrounded.

All the Gauls, even those whom Caesar had found absolutely reliable in his campaigns against the Britons, responded to Vercingetorix's call for Gallic unanimity in his support. Though they did not respond as generously as he had asked, the sheer numbers of Gallic enemies massed against Caesar were nonetheless daunting—8,000 cavalry and 250,000 infantry. But they were slow in coming, and this resulted in the defenders of Alesia expelling from the city all who were either too old or too young to fight. The Romans, however, would not receive them.

Caesar recounts the ferocious battle that followed. Although the issue was often in doubt, the Romans eventually won the day. Vercingetorix instructed his subordinates to either put him to death or turn him over to the Romans. The Gauls chose the latter course, Caesar made arrangements for governing the subdued Gallic tribes, and Book 7 ends. We learn from other sources that Vercingetorix was forced to march as an enslaved captive in Caesar's victory parade and later put to death.

Book 8

Book 8, which tells the end of the story, comes to us not from Caesar's pen but from that of his subordinate, Aulus Hirtius. In a charming and modest prefatory letter to the eighth book, Hirtius reveals that he reluctantly wrote the book after acceding to the repeated requests of Caesar's friend, Lucius Cornelius Balbus. Hirtius also says that, fully acknowledging his own incapacity compared to Caesar's ability, as substitute author he continues the story only until the moment of Caesar's death.

Hirtius details the mopping-up operations against a Gallic tribe, the Bellovaci, who had the ingenuity to cover their withdrawal with a conflagration that disguised their movements. However, as the Bellovaci under their leader, Correus, attempted to rout the Romans in a surprise attack, the tide of battle turned against them as the Romans overwhelmed the surprise attackers.

In the second chapter, Hirtius tells of Caesar's scorched earth policy against the adherents of the still-fugitive Ambiorix. He also reports the way in which the squadrons of Caesar's subordinate commander, Gaius Fabius, intercepted the forces of another fugitive Gallic leader, Dumnacus, as he attempted to flee across the Loire river. Fabius's forces routed and destroyed most of the Gauls. Dumnacus himself, however, escaped to plot further mischief against the Romans.

Hirtius next reports the Roman successes at Uxellodunum, where a force under the command of the Roman general Caninius killed or captured all his Gallic enemies who faced him in the field. Nonetheless, the Romans could not bring the town itself to surrender until they managed to divert its water supply. After numerous townspeople had died of thirst, the city finally submitted. Caesar decided to make an example of Uxellodunum to discourage others from determined resistance. He had the hands cut off all who had borne arms and then released them so that others could learn from their example. Despite this, further examples follow of Caesar's capacity for the exercise of mercy.

Then Hirtius follows Caesar's progress though the Cisalpine provinces as he makes his way toward a Rome in which, as his second term as Cisalpine and Transalpine proconsul drew to a close, Caesar's political enemies were busily attempting to strip him of power.

Bibliography

Caesar, Julius. *The Conquest of Gaul.* Translated by F. P. Long. New York: Barnes and Noble Books, 2005.

———. *The Gallic War.* Translated by H. J. Edwards. Mineola, N.Y.: Dover Publications, 2006.

———. *War Commentaries of Caesar.* Translated by Rex Warner. New York: New American Library, 1964.

Canfora, Luciano. *Julius Caesar: The People's Dictator.* Translated by Marian Hill and Kevin Windle. Berkeley: University of California Press, 2007.

Concerning the City of God against the Pagans St. Augustine, bishop of Hippo (413–425 C.E.)

As a Christian spokesman, St. AUGUSTINE, bishop of Hippo, had written against many of the opponents of Western Christian orthodoxy, both those Christian splinter groups that he considered heretics and those older faiths that represented pagan idolatry. In Augustine's view, however, no group presented a greater danger to Christian belief than did high-minded and virtuous Roman intellectuals. These men were often Neoplatonists who were also devoted to the austerely virtuous life that they found modeled both in the writings of revered thinkers and by citizens in the early days of the Roman Republic. These men were the very kind of intellectuals who had weaned Augustine himself away from the absurdities of Manichaeanism (see MANICHAEAN WRITINGS) between the time when he arrived in Milan and the moment that St. AMBROSE made Augustine a Christian convert.

Augustine's classical education had equipped him with a comprehensive mastery both of the texts upon which the Neoplatonists based their arguments and of their preferred rhetorical approaches to conducting their arguments. Moreover, as his most notable biographer Peter Brown has demonstrated, Augustine understood that the strongly held viewpoints of these conservative, pagan thinkers were grounded in an antiquated literature. Of that literature, Augustine himself was also a perfect master. To the bishop, it seemed that his adversaries took an essentially romantic view of ancient Roman ethical practice. The practice they admired had never really existed.

Nonetheless, like the Christians, the salvation of souls was the ultimate objective of these virtuous pagans in the waning days of the Western Roman Empire.

To anticipate and counter the arguments of such erudite opponents, Augustine undertook what he described as "a giant of a book." In *Concerning the City of God against the Pagans*, he adopted a plan that rested on his mastery of classical texts. Ignoring the then-contemporary mystery cults that shared with Christianity many such features as raising the dead, Augustine takes aim at the ancient traditions on which the thought of his opponents was based. He makes point-by-point comparisons between such classics of Rome as VIRGIL's *AENEID* and Christian Scripture. Always he compares the utility of pagan answers with the helpfulness of those proposed in the Bible. Using this method, the first 10 books of the *City of God* effectively but respectfully demolish the intellectual basis of his opponents' paganism. Particularly, Augustine pays tribute to the Neoplatonist author PORPHYRY's failed attempt to find a path by which the human soul could be set free.

Whereas Augustine's opponents conceived of their Roman ancestors' virtues as divinely privileged, Augustine instead saw those same Romans as laboring like all other human beings under the burden of original sin. His opponents had idealized the undoubted virtues of the early Roman state because they were what they had to work with.

The saint is not above a bit of sarcastic criticism when he considers those virtues exaggerated, as is the case when he discusses the famous chastity of the Roman matron Lucretia. Nonetheless, Augustine grants that Roman virtues had made the Roman Empire, with all its faults, better than any of its predecessors. He argues, however, that the Romans had an ulterior motive for their obsession with virtue: They lusted after glory. They suffered, in other words, from the archetypal sin of Satan.

Though he doesn't put it just that way, Augustine does pursue the subject of excessive and diabolic pride. In their obsession with the pursuit of ancestral pagan virtues, the Neoplatonist intellectuals of Rome were continuing to draw on the same sources that motivated the old Romans' obsession with glory. Those sources, as Augustine firmly believed, were the demons, fallen from heaven, who tried continually to drag human souls with them to Hell when the last judgment came.

In marshalling his arguments, Augustine, as Peter Brown convincingly demonstrates, moves the seat of glory from the human imperium—from Rome as a concept—to the heavenly City of God.

Bibliography

Augustine, St., Bishop of Hippo. *Concerning the City of God against the Pagans.* Translated by Henry Bettenson. London and New York: Penguin Books, 2003.

Brown, Peter. *Augustine of Hippo: A Biography.* Berkeley and Los Angeles: University of California Press, 2000.

Confessions St. Augustine, bishop of Hippo (written ca. 397–401 C.E.)

Often called the world's first modern autobiography, St. AUGUSTINE's *Confessions* tracks the moral, spiritual, emotional, intellectual, and psychological development of one of the most imposing figures who ever graced Christendom. From a religious viewpoint, the work is also an extended address to God—and thus a prayer, a profession of faith, a reflection on the operation of Divine Providence, and a hymn of praise.

Book 1

Following a lengthy invocation in which his ecstatic adoration of Deity manifests itself, Augustine arrives at his birth in the sixth chapter of the first book. He knew, he says, only how to suckle, be satisfied with pleasant things, and to cry when he was hurt. Later he learned to smile and to make his wants known by crying. When adults did not fulfill his whims, he became angry and punished them by crying more.

Thinking back on matters that he cannot remember—the desires that he felt in infancy—Augustine thinks that even as a baby he must have been both manipulative and sinful. In Book 1, chapter 9, he recalls the circumstances of his early schooling and how he was whipped if he was slow to learn. He recalls being punished for preferring play to school, and says that adults are not punished for analogous preferences.

In chapter 10, Augustine remembers his childhood sins, and in the following chapter he tells his readers that soon after birth he became a catechumen in the Roman Catholic church—one marked out for Christian instruction although his baptism was deferred. Here too we find the first substantial passage about his mother, Monica, a devoutly Christian woman who headed a household unanimous in its faith except for Augustine's father, who at this stage still believed in the old Roman religion.

In chapters 12 and 13, Augustine confesses that he "detested" his schoolwork, particularly the study of the Greek language, though he liked Latin. He excoriates the grammar schools for filling children's heads with poetic fictions—fictions he had liked as a child. He did not, however, enjoy translating them from a tongue in which he was not already reasonably fluent, and Latin was his native tongue. He prays for forgiveness for the vanity of studying literary fictions, and that theme carries through the end of Book 1, chapter 17. There he wishes that he had been studying Scripture instead of the ancient poets, and he remarks that there is more than one way to "sacrifice to . . . offending angels."

Given the sorry state of his boyish soul, Augustine cannot imagine a condition that God would have found more offensive. The symptoms of that state were to be found in his love of games, in a love of food and wine that prompted him to steal from his parents, and a desire for winning that led him to cheat.

On the positive side, as Augustine reports in chapter 20, he found delight in truth, developed a good memory, learned to speak well, found friendship consoling, and avoided "suffering, dejection, and ignorance." He thanks God for these freely given gifts and prays that he may yet perfect them to the degree that he may be with God.

Book 2

As the second book begins, Augustine avers that he wants to recall his failings, not because he loves them, but because he wants to love God. He confesses that as a youth he ran wild through various "shady loves." He admits to lustful and shameful actions in his boyhood. Matrimony might have saved him, but his parents were focused on his education, not on the state of his soul's well-being and the realities of postpubescent adolescence. His 16th year—a year the family could not afford to send him to school—proved especially difficult for the young Augustine.

His mother tried to redirect his course, but he despised her advice, favoring the approval of his wicked companions. If he could not match them in vice, he pretended to that sin rather than be laughed at for chastity.

The fourth chapter of Book 2 contains the famous episode of the pear tree, in which Augustine and his companions stole a neighbor's pears—not because they were hungry, but for the sheer thrill of stealing and wasting food. They took pleasure in their crime. In chapter 5, still in the context of the pear episode, Augustine traces the origin of sin to the human desire for such lesser goods as "tactual tactile sensations," defense of honor, and friendship. In search of them, the human creature deserts the higher goods of God's eternal love and companionship.

In the following chapter, Augustine discourses on the operation of pride, lust, and covetousness as a failed effort to emulate the power that belongs to God alone—the archetypal sin of Satan. Chapter 7 gives thanks that, despite such failings, God cured him. Nonetheless, Augustine still suffers anguish at the thought of his sinful folly in having participated in the theft of the pears. He is still ashamed, though he has long been forgiven and, at the moment of composition, is serving as the bishop of Hippo. He closes the book by confessing that, in his youth, he wandered into the desert of selfishness and became estranged from God.

Book 3

Book 3 opens with Augustine's arrival in Carthage—ostensibly to continue his studies. He confesses that he immediately plunged into love affairs. He also cherished the theatrical depiction of love affairs (chapter 2), in which he imaginatively participated. Augustine confesses that he even managed to conduct an affair in church, for which, along with his other lapses, God punished him—though not as much as he felt he deserved. Moreover, he and his fellow students of oratory and rhetoric conspired to behave demonically.

The third chapter reports Augustine's first acquaintance with the doctrines of Manichaeanism and the attractions those teachings held for him. The reader also comes to understand more deeply Monica's concern for her son, and Augustine reports a dream that predicted his conversion to Christianity.

In chapter 4, we learn that it was CICERO's *Hortensius*, rather than Scripture, that converted Augustine into a true seeker after wisdom. And yet, the saint confesses, the name of Christ was absent from his search. Augustine tried to read the Scriptures but found that they failed to meet Cicero's test for truth. He found the Bible's style off-putting, and he had not yet learned to see beyond its surface. This theme occupies the following several chapters, after which Augustine turns his attention to the issue of evil habits. This issue occupies a significant portion of his thought here and elsewhere. If one can successfully form good habits, one makes considerable headway in protecting oneself from temptations.

Book 4

The 16 chapters of Book 4 detail Augustine's last years in Carthage as a student of Manichaeanism and as a young teacher of rhetoric. With respect to the latter activity, he characterizes himself as "conquered by cupidity" and as "a vendor of victorious verbosity." It is in this book, too, where the reader first learns of the woman with whom Augustine lived for some years. Though he characterizes the union as an unlawful one, that characterization is from a Christian perspective rather than that of Roman law. Certain arrangements of concubinage, of which this apparently was one, were sanctioned by a degree of legality. Roman custom acknowledged as legal the sort of arrangement that Augustine had with this unnamed woman, who bore him his only and much beloved son, Adeodatus. Augustine's biographer, Peter Brown, calls the couple's relationship a "second-class marriage." Augustine was faithful to the woman, and she remained with him until near the time of his final reconversion to the Christianity of his early boyhood in Milan. Such a degree of relationship was very easy to terminate, and had Augustine not converted, his social standing makes it improbable that he would have married the unnamed woman. Rather, as finally did happen, a suitable match would have been arranged for him.

Also in Book 4, Augustine confesses his interest in numerology and all sorts of magic arts, including astrology. When a young friend died, Augustine was deeply affected and depressed at the passing of a young person of such promise.

In the following chapter, Augustine reports his return to his birthplace, Tagaste, where he again established himself as a teacher of rhetoric. As he formed new friendships, his depression passed. He takes the opportunity to point out in the ninth chapter that one's friendship with God can last forever. The next three chapters trace the transitory nature of material things, treat God as the source of all beauty, and explain that things are lovable only because of the presence in them of their Creator.

In the 13th chapter, Augustine speaks of some books he wrote on the subject of "the beautiful and the fitting," but what, beyond their subject, may have been in them, he says, has slipped from his memory. He does recall that he addressed

those books to a person named Hierus—a man Augustine admired. As Augustine continues confessing his misapprehensions, it becomes clear that he remembers perfectly well what he wrote in the books, but he has become ashamed of their contents. He insists, however, that in his error he was striving toward God, who was not yet ready to accept him until he had been punished for his sinful life in some measure. God eventually did administer this punishment, though Augustine thinks it was too mild.

Book 5

In Book 5, Augustine says that all the time he sought God, God was right before him. Yet Augustine was still immersed in Manichaean thinking. Eventually he came in contact with a Manichaean thinker named Faustus—a man he had been very anxious to meet. Augustine remained impressed with Faustus as long as he heard him preach. When he at last had the opportunity to question Faustus privately, though, he discovered that Faustus was a slick public speaker with only superficial learning to support his public utterances, and he began to feel doubts about the Manichaeans. When he discovered that Faustus was aware of his own ignorance and willing to admit it, Augustine found Faustus once again attractive and gave him the benefit of the doubt as a man, but the doctrines upon which Augustine had pinned such hopes began to lose their appeal.

Chapter 8 of Book 5 recounts Augustine's decision to go to Rome to teach. His mother tried to dissuade him from going; failing that, Monica tried to persuade Augustine to take her along. To escape her entreaties, Augustine lied and slipped away, boarding a ship and sailing off. Although Monica blamed her son for the deception, she nonetheless prayed for his continued well-being. In chapter 9, Augustine reports that he fell dangerously ill in Rome. He considers that he was in peril of hellfire, since he had not yet been baptized. He continued consorting with the Manichaeans in Rome after his recovery, but he had become disenchanted with their doctrines, and at this stage found himself attracted to the philosophical descendants of PLATO, the ACADEMIC philosophers. Then his thinking turned once again to Catholicism. His religious thinking, however, was in a state of confusion as he conflated doctrines from the several philosophies and religions that he knew. He had reservations both about Mary's presumptive virginity and about the truth of many biblical passages.

The hope of finding a better-behaved class of students had been among Augustine's objectives in going to Rome. What he found there, however, were students who broke their word, who did not pay their fees, and who often simply disappeared. At just about that time, Symmachus, the prefect of Rome, required a master of rhetoric in Milan, and Augustine enlisted his friends to help him get the job. He succeeded and went off to Milan, where he met St. AMBROSE, the Christian bishop of Milan. Under the influence of Ambrose, Augustine resumed the Christian status of catechumen—the road upon which his parents had initially started him.

Book 6

In the meantime, as we learn in Book 6, Monica had come to join Augustine. She came to revere Ambrose and unquestioningly accepted his authority when he instructed her to abandon the African custom of revering the saints by bringing offerings of food to their shrines. In this book, too, we learn that Augustine considered St. Ambrose's habit of silent reading to be a novelty. Reading aloud was the more common practice in the ancient world.

During this period, Augustine began to understand Catholic doctrine correctly, and his doubts started evaporating. Nonetheless, a Christian vocation had not yet occurred to him. He longed, he reports, for "honors, wealth, and [an advantageously arranged] marriage." But little by little Augustine became infused with an obsession for God that eventually overcame such competing notions—but not quite yet. In the 13th chapter of Book 6, Augustine reports that, largely through his mother's efforts, a suitable girl had at last been found for him, and although he was still involved with his African concubine, a marriage was in prospect. The girl, however, was still two years shy of the Roman marriageable age of 12, so no immediate arrangements were on the horizon, and in the event, no marriage ever took place. Nonetheless, when the betrothal occurred, the African woman, says Augustine, "was torn from my side," leaving him with a "wounded heart." On her part, she vowed to God never to know another man, and she left Augustine and his son. Despite this painful separation, and despite his betrothal, Augustine soon found himself another woman. He characterizes himself as "a slave of lust."

Book 7

Book 7 traces Augustine's philosophical and religious development, beginning from about the age of 30. In this book, Augustine considers such questions as whether or not a God who is totally good can be the source of evil. Since this is a logical impossibility, Augustine next wonders why God permits evil to exist. Yet amid his questioning, he is also aware of a growing faith in the teachings of the Catholic church.

As Augustine's faith grew, so did his contempt for astrologers and numerologists. In the seventh chapter of Book 7, he admits that the principal barrier to his total conversion was the deadliest of all the sins, his pride. Yet little by little, God administered the healing ointment of faith, and Augustine's pride diminished. As it did so, his understanding of God matured, and with fuller understanding came a deeper faith. That faith did not reach its full maturity, however, until Augustine came to see that Christ was the mediator between the human and the divine. This was a step that Augustine was still not able to take. While he was ready to acknowledge Christ as the greatest person in the history of the world, and even accepted the virgin birth as literal truth,

Augustine did not yet grasp the meaning of the phrase "the Word made flesh."

Book 8

When Augustine read the writings of St. Paul, however, this too began to clarify, and, as Book 8 reports, he began to consider entering the priesthood. But as he was still enthralled by women, he sought help from Simplicianus, a mentor of St. Ambrose. Simplicianus congratulated Augustine on having read the Platonist philosophers and having avoided the error of the others. He told Augustine about Victorinus, an even wiser Christian who had converted when he read the Scriptures with the intention of rebutting them. Yet Augustine remained torn between the attractions of the flesh and those of the spirit.

It was at this moment that Augustine first learned from a Christian named Ponticianus about the existence of St. ATHANASIUS's *The LIFE OF SAINT ANTHONY* and its miraculous effect in leading two young men into the monastic life. Under the influence of that story, Augustine famously prayed: "Give me chastity and self-restraint, but not just yet." (Book 7, chap. 7) A deeply troubled Augustine concluded that he was weighed down by habit and original sin.

Seeking a sign of providential will, Augustine opened the Scripture at random and chanced upon Paul's letter to the Romans, 13.13: "Not in revelry and drunkenness, not in debauchery and wantonness, not in strife and jealousy; but put on the Lord Jesus Christ, and as for the flesh, take no thoughts for its lusts." Convinced now of his Christian vocation, Augustine went directly to his mother and told her of his decision to enter the church. That decision, says Augustine, pleased her more than further grandchildren would have done.

Book 9

Book 9 reports how Augustine gave up teaching rhetoric and how he continually excoriated himself for his former misdeeds and credulous acceptance of Manichaean doctrine. He sought counsel from Ambrose about what he should read next, and Ambrose advised him to read "Isaias the Prophet." Augustine, however, did not then understand the book and decided to try it later when he had improved his understanding of the language of Scripture. He submitted his own name as well as that of his son, Adeodatus, then 15 years old, among those who would soon be baptized.

We also learn of the discovery of the preserved bodies of two Christians, Protasius and Gervasius, who had been martyred in the time of Nero. The baptism of Augustine and Adeodatus occurred, and together with Monica they set out for Africa. At the port of Ostia near Rome, however, Monica died. Augustine digresses to tell something about his mother's life. He recounts the way in which she fell into the habit, first, of taking a sip of wine each day. Little by little, the amount increased until she was drinking two full cups. When a maid called the young Monica a "wine-biber," Monica was so stung by the truth of the characterization that she never touched another drop.

In the ninth chapter, Augustine goes on to report how by her patience and care, she was able to manage a difficult and irascible husband so that, unlike the husbands of her friends, he never beat her. Eventually, rather, she made him not only a model husband but also a Christian.

In the 10th chapter, Augustine recounts his final conversation with his mother. In the course of the conversation, the minds of the two joined in a sort of Platonic ascent from the material to the spiritual worlds until they contemplated the realm of Heaven itself. Monica finally confessed to Augustine that, since his conversion to Catholic Christianity, she felt that her mission in this world had been accomplished and she eagerly looked forward to the next. She instructed him to bury her body anywhere and to remember her at the Lord's altar, wherever Augustine might be. She died five days later at the age of 56. Augustine buried her at Ostia, where a fragment of an inscription from her tomb was discovered within the past century. Monica is a saint of the Roman

Catholic Church. Some of her bones were eventually moved to an Augustinian monastery in France; other relics repose in a sarcophagus in the Church of San Augostino in Rome.

The rest of Book 9 is an encomium to Monica, to her life, and to the meaning that her life and that of her husband, Patricius, came to have for Augustine as his understanding of his faith matured.

Book 10

Having dwelt at length upon the history of his sins and mistakes during the first 39 years of his life, Augustine turns his attention in Book 10 to exploring the sort of person he has become in the hope that interested readers may find something in the story of his internal life that will encourage them in their search for spiritual health.

First, Augustine conducts a 19-chapter inquiry into the nature of memory and its wonderful capacities. He next considers the role of memory in living "the happy life." On the question of the happy life, Augustine is not sure that everyone wishes to be happy, for the truly happy life is to be found only in God. At last, however, he makes clear that, somehow, God now dwells in and throughout Augustine's life and has always dwelled in Augustine's memory.

The 27th chapter of book 10 bursts forth as a paean of joy and gratitude that the God whom Augustine sought so long elsewhere had been within him always.

Augustine's impassioned statement of his faith occupies the next two chapters of the 10th book. Then, with chapter 30, Augustine turns his attention to God's expectations for him. These include the saint's continued rejection of "the concupiscence of the flesh," a sincere effort to heal the spiritual diseases within him, eating a modest diet just sufficient to sustain life, and the rejection of all things that might present temptations. He considers these from the point of view of each of the senses to which temptations appeal. He is convinced that his own speech is a source of temptation since, unless he is careful, he may stray from God's truth and allow intellectual pride to creep in. Augustine concludes that overcoming such temptations requires the mediation of Christ.

Book 11

In Book 11, Augustine first assures God that the writer of the *Confessions* is well aware that God foreknows everything Augustine will say. It is Augustine who benefits from his book's extended meditation, for all that he says increases his love of his creator. The balance of the book contains an extended consideration of creation and of the nature of time. Among the conclusions Augustine reaches, we find that God simply brought heaven and earth into being from nothing with a creative word—though that word is not of the nature of human speech. There was no time *before* that creative word since time, too, is God's artifact. Augustine struggles manfully to understand the nature of time, wondering if human perception of time's passage is a function of the mind's operation rather than an external datum. Finally, however, Augustine must rest content with the mysteries that time and eternity pose, and he prays that he may rise above time to be with God in eternity.

Book 12

Opening Book 12, Augustine observes that the "poverty of human understanding" often finds expression in "rich talk," since "inquiry talks more than discovery." Then he considers the biblical story of creation in the context of a tripartite discrimination that he borrows from the Septuagint Old Testament. He discriminates among earth, the observable heavens, and the extratemporal Heaven of God. He notes that he has believed God's books, but he finds their words "exceedingly mysterious."

As he considers those mysteries, Augustine's rhetorical posture shifts from that of the penitent in the confessional to that of the Christian controversialist. He imagines contradictors, puts arguments—not always seemingly apposite—in their mouths, and with seemingly sophistic and increasingly metaphorical arguments, sustained principally by his faith, calls on God to judge between his point of view and that of his hypothetical objectors. At the end of Book 12, Augustine seems well aware that his hypothetical arguments really have failed to clarify the issues he has addressed. As a transition to the next section, he prays that, from among the possible points of view he has attempted to explicate, he may be divinely inspired to select the right one.

Book 13

In Book 13, then, Augustine turns away from controversy and back to prayer. He conducts a partly mystical, partly allegorical, and partly analytical discussion of the account of creation as it appears in the book of Genesis. That discussion employs the methodology of PATRISTIC EXEGESIS in an effort to clarify the multiple layers of meaning that the initiated can tease from Scripture. This final book of Augustine's *Confessions* lays bare the saint's faith in the mysteries implicit in the Scriptures. He views the words of Genesis not as he did as an uninitiated admirer of Cicero in the lecture halls of Carthage, but as a fully mature devotee of his faith as versed as was his mentor, Saint Ambrose, in the explication of Scripture for the benefit of those who believe. As Augustine says in the 34th chapter, he has looked at the biblical text concerning the creation of the world with "a view to its figurative meaning."

With chapters 35–38, Augustine reaches the seventh day—the Sabbath—in his discussion of the seven days of the Creation. He opens this final section with a prayer for God's peace. He explains that, figuratively speaking, the seventh day is the paradigm for eternity and has no end. Neither man nor angel, Augustine concludes, can finally give or receive the actual understanding of the mysteries of Scripture. Only the Creator can open the door to divine wisdom.

Bibliography

Augustine of Hippo. *Confessions.* 2nd ed. Translated by F. J. Sheed. Indianapolis: Hackett Publishing, 2006.

———. *St. Augustine: Confessions.* Translated by Vernon J. Bourke. New York: Fathers of the Church, 1953.

Brown, Peter. *Augustine of Hippo: A Biography.* Berkeley and Los Angeles: University of California Press, 2000.

Confucius (K'ung Fu-tzu, Kongfuzi, Master Kong [K'ung])
(551–479 B.C.E.)

The son of a poor but aristocratic family dwelling in the ancient Chinese state of Lu (now part of Shandong [Shantung] province), Confucius early impressed his contemporaries with his precocious learning and wisdom. A teacher who prepared young Chinese men for government service, he came to advise the rulers of his native state.

A master of ritual, music, and statecraft, Confucius rose through a succession of increasingly responsible positions in state government and also founded a school that accepted promising children even if they could not pay tuition. Civil strife in Lu prompted Confucius to seek more peaceable circumstances in the state of Qi (Chi) (517 B.C.E.). There he sometimes taught and sometimes consulted with the local grandee. Lack of regular employment, however, constrained him to wander with his disciples in search of patronage for a period of 14 years. He traveled to the states of Wei, Chen, Cai, Chu, and Song. Confucius had hoped to find a nobleman somewhere who would be willing to implement Confucian theories of statecraft, but in that hope he was disappointed.

Finally, in 484 B.C.E, Confucius was recalled to Lu. There too, however, his hopes to find a government willing to follow his precepts were disappointed. He spent the rest of his life teaching and perhaps editing older writings, though it is not altogether clear whether or not he himself wrote down his own teachings. After his death, certainly, his students collected his precepts and reminiscences about his actions in what became known as the ANALECTS of Confucius.

Confucius's personal life during his last few years was tragic. Both his wife and his only child, a son named Li, predeceased him, in 485 and 483 B.C.E., respectively, as did two of his closest disciples, Yan Hui and Zi-lu. Li's son Zi-si, however, survived his father, and through him until at least the year 1997, the direct line of Confucius survived through 77 generations. It may still survive.

After Confucius's death in 479, all of his disciples save one observed a three-year period of mourning. One disciple, Zi-gong, maintained a solitary vigil in a shack at Confucius's graveside for three additional years.

The philosophical tradition and the former Chinese state religion associated with the name of Confucius became, like many religions, a work in progress assembled around the name of its founder. The principal teachings of the Confucian position involve the application of a situational ethic that demands good will and generosity, respect for others and their views, mutual kindness, and personal exertion in achieving those ideals. Taken together these elements constitute the tao (or dao)—the *way* that Confucius espoused.

Bibliography

Confucius. *The Analects of Confucius (Lun Yu).* Translated by Chichung Huang. New York: Oxford University Press, 1997.

———. *The Analects of Confucius: A Philosophical Translation.* Translated by Roger T. Ames and Harry Rosemont. New York: Ballantine Books, 1999.

———. *The Essential Analects.* Translated by Edward Slingerland. Indianapolis: Hackett Publishing Co., 2006.

Sim, May. *Remastering Morals with Aristotle and Confucius.* New York: Cambridge University Press, 2007.

Consolation of Philosophy, The Anicius Manlius Severinus Boethius (ca. 525 C.E.)

Written in prison in the city of Pavia, Italy, while its author, BOETHIUS, was under sentence of death and awaiting the outcome of an appeal pending before the Roman senate, *The Consolation of Philosophy* is a remarkable document from every point of view. It is not least remarkable since it was in all likelihood written without recourse to any book other than that of Boethius's own memory.

As the literary historian and translator V. E. Watts tells us, the work belonged to an ancient literary subspecies, the *consolatio*. This was a quasi-medical treatise whose authors sought to produce a sort of literary cure for the psychological or spiritual malaise from which they were suffering. At the same time, the book belongs to the kind of dialogue practiced by PLATO and to the sacred dialogue in which a human being discusses an issue with a spirit in order to gain new insight. *The Consolation of Philosophy* also displays certain characteristics of Menippean SATIRE—particularly in its alternation of verse and prose passages and those passages in which Boethius describes himself ironically.

Much critical discussion has been devoted to the question of why, in the extremity of his condemnation, Boethius—who was almost certainly a professing Christian, whose family had been Christian for 200 years before him, and who, as St. Severinus, has been canonized by the Roman Catholic Church—appeals to philosophy rather than to faith for comfort. As a modest addition to that discussion, I suggest that Boethius had been a lifelong student of philosophy, not of theology. It strikes me as altogether probable that, faced with his own rapidly approaching mortality, he found a greater probability of comfort in proceeding from what he *knew* seasoned with what he *believed* rather than vice versa. He may also have found more solace in the ancient philosophers' careful thinking on great issues than in the petty quarrels of fifth- and sixth-century theologians about such hair-splitting and finally unknowable issues as the essential nature of Christ's substance—the issue over which thousands, possibly including Boethius himself, died at the hands of their fellow Christians. Finally, the pragmatic if slender possibility of a senatorial exoneration still lingered while Boethius worked on his treatise. Any hope of a possible reprieve might very well have foundered on the too-direct expression of a Christian sentiment that could be construed as critical of King Theoderic's Arian convictions.

Book 1

Book 1 of *The Consolation of Philosophy* begins with a poem in which Boethius bewails his treatment at the hands of fickle Fortune, who early lifted him high and then, in an instant, took everything away from him. As he is ruminating on that issue, an awe-inspiring woman appears to him in his prison. Her size varies from that of a normal human being to that of a goddess whose head sometimes reaches the heavens.

Finding Boethius in the company of the MUSES who have been inspiring his poems, Lady Philosophy angrily asks why "these hysterical sluts" have been allowed near Boethius's bedside. She drives them away and recites her own poem about the unhealthy condition of Boethius's mind and spirit. She then wipes his eyes, and his grief at his situation instantly evaporates.

Nonetheless, Boethius blames Lady Philosophy for his current situation. He took seriously, he says, the responsibility of philosophers to become the governors of men, as Plato required in *The* REPUBLIC. Boethius proclaims his honesty in restraining the greed of his fellow civil servants. Their thirst for vengeance has landed him in this jail where he awaits his execution. He rehearses the history of his imprisonment, proclaiming his innocence all the while.

A fifth poem follows this discussion. The verse takes the form of a questioning prayer. Why is it that God orders the heavens and the earth in predictable cycles, it asks, but leaves governing the affairs of people to unpredictable Fortune?

Lady Philosophy tells Boethius that in his present diseased state of mind, he has lost the capacity to be calmly rational but is undergoing all sorts of conflicting emotions from one moment to the next. Philosophy promises relief through her administration of gentle remedies. She reminds him that the world is subject to the governance of divine reason and not happenstance. In the final poem of Book 1, Lady Philosophy urges Boethius to rid himself of joy, fear, hope, and grief, so that he may clear his mind.

Book 2

As book 2 opens, Lady Philosophy explains to Boethius that Fortune is responsible for having lulled Boethius into regarding her as his friend. When Fortune suddenly then turned against him, his mind became unsettled. Now, however, he must look squarely at Fortune and understand that she has fully displayed her normal behavior, which is to be constantly changing. Since that is the case, neither her disappointments nor her favors should hold any terror or happiness for Boethius. Speaking in Fortune's voice, Lady Philosophy reviews with Boethius the role that she has played in his life since birth. Everything he had really belonged to Fortune, so he has no cause to complain when she takes it all away.

Asked to reply, Boethius confesses that while Lady Philosophy speaks, he feels better. As soon as she stops, however, he falls again into a deep melancholy. Lady Philosophy reviews the extraordinary favors that Fortune has bestowed on Boethius throughout his life. Had she still remained with him, his death would eventually have ended his relationship with Fortune.

Now Lady Philosophy summarizes the blessings that Boethius still enjoys: the health and well-being of his father-in-law Symmachus, the devotion of his wife, and the good characters of his sons. Lady Philosophy tells Boethius to dry his tears, for he is still a happy and fortunate man. Besides, she reminds Boethius, misery and happiness are all relative, not absolutes. Beyond that, she continues, true happiness is to be found within, not in the external gifts of Fortune. Happiness, she explains, "is the highest good of rational nature," and it cannot be taken away. Moreover, she reminds Boethius, he believes in the immortality of the human mind.

Lady Philosophy next rehearses a litany of the many things that Boethius might count among his blessings—not only such things as wealth and possessions, but also beautiful views and enjoyments. Philosophy assures him that even had Boethius not owned such things, they would still have pleased him, and it was because they did that he wished to possess them. She praises the gifts of God and nature that cannot be taken away, and she blames lusting after wealth and mastery—things that can pass in an instant.

She next considers high office and power. She suggests that these rarely find themselves in the possession of honest and virtuous persons, but when they do, the honor associated with holding office arises from the virtue of the holder, not from the office held. Thus, when unworthy persons occupy high office, the office does not make them worthier, it merely makes evident their failings and incapacities. A poem about the failings of the mad Roman emperor Nero illustrates Lady Philosophy's point.

She next tries to put human affairs in their proper perspective by comparing the size of the spherical Earth with the heavenly sphere and then noting that the habitable part of the earth is smaller still, so that the affairs of men are hardly considerable when compared with a universal scale. Even the fame of the Roman Empire has not yet penetrated the Caucasus Mountains. She then applies a similar comparison to time, making the point that any period of time is inconsiderable when compared with eternity. An eternal mind, freed from its temporal, earthly prison will rejoice in its liberty.

Lady Philosophy ends Book 2 with the discussion of a paradox. Bad fortune is better for people than good fortune. Bad fortune instructs people in the fragility of happiness and teaches them to bear adversity, whereas good fortune misleads

people into foolish confidence and opens them to just the sort of spiritual malaise that afflicts Boethius. Lady Philosophy then sings of a universal order bound together and ruled by divine love. True human happiness would result if the hearts of human beings were subject to the same rule of love.

Book 3

As Book 3 opens, Boethius confesses that he is feeling better. Lady Philosophy's remedies have begun to take effect. He begs for more, and she promises to help him dispel the shadows of happiness that cloud his sight so that he may directly observe the pattern of true happiness. Her argument here partially recasts that of Plato in his famous allegory of the cave in book 7 of *The Republic* and in his dialogue *The Timaeus*. In part, it supplements that argument by drawing upon the religious aspects of the Neoplatonism of such thinkers as PLOTINUS and PROCLUS OF BYZANTIUM.

In essence, Lady Philosophy leads Boethius to perceive that the earthly things that make people happy are merely the shadows of truly eternal things that human beings dimly recall from a preexistent state. Philosophy reminds Boethius that in *The Timaeus*, Plato recommended prayer invoking divine aid even in small matters. Boethius agrees, and in a hymn Lady Philosophy invokes the Creator who is the divine archetype of—and whose mind contains—the universe. To the sources listed above, Lady Philosophy now adds language and rhetorical constructions reminiscent of the *Gloria* from Christian liturgy and of the Gospel according to St. John. The prayer solicits the privilege of a direct vision of godhead.

Lady Philosophy leads Boethius to agree that goodness and happiness are identical and an essential attribute of God and that goodness is the means by which God rules the universe. As Book 3 ends, however, she introduces the problem of evil and raises the question of whether or not an omnipotent God whose nature is goodness can do evil. Boethius is sure God cannot, since evil is foreign to God's nature. With that issue still hanging, Lady Philosophy sings a song that recounts the story of ORPHEUS's descent into Hell to recover his beloved wife Eurydice.

Book 4

Book 4 addresses the problem of evil head-on. Despite God's goodness, evil still exists in the world and often goes unpunished—or at least so it seems to Boethius. Lady Philosophy, however, denies the truth of his analysis. Goodness is what makes a person human. When people pursue wickedness, they dehumanize themselves and destroy their capacity for rising toward godhead, so that wicked behavior instantly involves its own punishment. Her next poem recalls the way that, in HOMER's *The Odyssey*, the witch-goddess Circe turns Odysseus's crewmen into animals—a passage often treated as an allegory of what happens when human beings allow their passions to overcome their reasons. Though such lapses may not hurt the body, says Lady Philosophy, they "cruelly wound the mind."

When the wicked are punished for their wickedness, that punishment is good and relieves their suffering. Lady Philosophy also acknowledges punishments after death—some with "penal severity" and some with "purifying mercy." But the discussion of such matters is not on her current agenda. Instead, she wants to see the wicked brought to justice in the same way that persons who are ill are brought to physicians. The object of correction being to cure rather than punish their wickedness, the wicked deserve sympathy rather than hatred.

Boethius remains unsatisfied on one point. Given that God seems sometimes to reward the wicked and ignore the good and vice versa, how does one distinguish between Divine Providence and chance occurrences?

Lady Philosophy's reply is one of the touchstones of thinking about the difference between an eternal and a temporal point of view. In God's mind, there is an eternal and immutable plan for everything. Thought of as God's extratemporal intention for the universe, this plan is called Providence. Thought of as outcomes of events for individual objects and sentient creatures in time, the plan is Fate. Fate itself, since it occurs within time, is subject to Providence.

Book 5

As Book 5 gets underway, Boethius asks about chance and has Lady Philosophy resolve an issue that forever troubles the minds of faithful believers. How can a God who is all good and all powerful allow awful things, like the death that awaits Boethius, to happen to good people, one of whom Boethius knows himself to be?

With respect to chance, Lady Philosophy denies that there is any such thing as a causeless event. At the same time, she defines *chance* as an unexpected event arising as a result of a coincidence of unrelated causes. She also defends the notion of freedom of the human will, which, if it chooses to follow the path established for it by Divine Providence, paradoxically achieves greater freedom. If, however, it pursues a lesser good—its own will for itself—it paradoxically loses freedom.

Boethius then turns to a vexing perplexity. How can one reconcile the freedom of the human will and God's universal foreknowledge? The answer, again, has to do with the difference between the perceptions of the creature, living in time, and the Creator, extant in an extratemporal and changeless now. For the creature, existence has a beginning and an end, and the events of life proceed serially. For the Creator, existence is and simultaneously was and will always be. Thus, events pass before the mind of the creature as film passes through a camera, one frame at a time, so to speak. For the Creator, instead, all events are always there, and because of the Creator's goodness, all apparent evil and injustice are always and continually reconciled into the good and justice of a perfect creation. The concept of *foreknowledge*, therefore, is a function of the creature's perception of the passage of time. The Creator's knowledge is at the same time perfect, timeless, and immediate. Evil, finally, is nothing—a shadow, an appearance.

Thus, Lady Philosophy has consoled Boethius. However horrible the end that awaits him at Pavia among his torturers and executioners, in the mind of the Creator, Boethius's apparently undeserved punishment is part of a perfect fabric that always has made, is now making, and always will make its contribution to the goodness of God's perfect plan for God's creation.

Bibliography

Boethius. *The Consolation of Philosophy.* Translated by Richard H. Green. Mineola, N.Y.: Dover, 2002.

———. *The Consolation of Philosophy.* Translated by V. E. Watts. 1969. Harmondsworth, U.K.: Penguin Books, 1981.

conventions of Greek drama

Unlike today's theater, Greek drama was performed as part of a noncommercial, public, religious celebration. In Athens, state-sponsored dramatic performances appeared twice annually at festivals in connection with the worship of the god Dionysus, the god of wine and the harvest. The first, the festival of LENAEA, occurred in midwinter and invited the god's annual resurrection to assure the regreening of the earth. The second, sometimes called the City Dionysia and sometimes the GREAT DIONYSIA, roughly corresponded to Christian Easter and celebrated the return of spring in March and April.

In preparation for these ceremonies, playwrights competed by submitting manuscripts of works they hoped to perform. A randomly chosen Athenian official considered the submissions and chose from among them three examples of TRAGEDY and a SATYR PLAY by a single dramatist for performance on each day of the festival. The dramatists whose works were so chosen for performance then competed against one another for three prizes—first, second, and third—awarded by group of judges selected by a complex process designed to prevent the possibility of fraud or threat.

The Athenian state hired three actors per set of plays to present the principal characters, and such prominent Athenian citizens as Pericles (ca. 490–429 B.C.E.) underwrote the training and expenses of the choruses, which numbered from as few as 12 to as many as 500. (See CHORUS IN GREEK THEATER.) These choruses, often accompanied by instruments, sang, danced, interacted with the actors, and recited on-stage commentaries on the action, providing the points of view of ordinary people on the action, or filling in background that an audience might need to understand the play. Sometimes the chorus might present a particular political or religious point of view. Above all, perhaps, the chorus helped establish and track the play's mood and its sometimes-subtle variations.

Occasionally too, the chorus's point of view influences both that of the principal characters and the action of the play. A choral innovation practiced by a playwright named Agathon—a younger contemporary of Euripides—met with the disapproval of ARISTOTLE. Agathon apparently used the chorus in an attempt to achieve variety by introducing material that had nothing to do with the action of the play. Aristotle found that such a practice destroyed the effect of the play. The literary historian Philip Whaley Harsh suggests another important function of the chorus. Because of the numbers of people and the training involved, preparing the chorus also prepared a passionately interested and knowledgeable audience that was sensitive to theatrical subtleties.

Despite the religious purpose of the festivals, the plays' material was by no means limited to pious subjects. Some plays, such as SOPHOCLES' *OEDIPUS TYRANNUS* or Euripides' *The TROJAN WOMEN*, drew their sources from ancient legend and history. Less frequently, recent or nearly contemporary history provided the subject, as in AESCHYLUS's *The PERSIANS*. Again unlike later commercial drama, the plays—even the winners of the first prize—did not enjoy long runs on the Athenian stage. Although many of them were later staged repeatedly in the provinces throughout the Mediterranean sphere of Grecian influence, at

Athens they were performed once and once only for the festival competition.

Though both legendary and historical material was considered to be factual, Greek dramatists exercised considerable license in their presentation of subjects so that the motivation of character and the selection or invention of supporting incident might vary widely within the general outlines of a story, and such treatments sometimes responded to or commented on contemporary political circumstances. Such was the case for both tragedy and COMEDY. ARISTOPHANES' LYSISTRATA, for instance, mocked the predilection of Athenian men for making war and neglecting their women.

Performance conventions in the Greek theater included the wearing of masks by the actors, who typically presented more than one role. The masks were large and painted to represent the general character of the person being portrayed. By around 300 B.C.E., a knowledgeable audience member might recognize as many as 28 separate masks. It is possible, as well, that the masks were designed to serve as megaphones, making the voices of the actors more audible to persons at considerable distances from the stage.

Beyond these conventions, and certain others that I discuss in connection with Aristotle's POETICS, Greek drama was invariably performed in verse, much of which was sung or chanted. Greek and Latin meters are defined by arbitrary rules of syllable length. Unlike English prosody, which is determined by accent—the degree of emphasis given to a syllable—Greek and Latin prosody is said to be *quantitative*. (See QUANTITATIVE VERSE.) The basic structure of the verse line was iambic— a short syllable followed by a long one. In drama, two iambs were said to constitute a metric foot. Three such double iambic feet made up the base measure of the Greek dramatic line, though of course considerable variation was possible, desirable, and frequent. In the hands of skillful dramatists, the character of the verse reinforced the emotional effects of the text and action. Regrettably, the effect cannot be accurately approximated in English. Suffice it to say that the general effect

of this line, though decidedly poetic, is nonetheless conversational.

Another convention of Greek theater that has been the subject of much good-natured theatrical spoofing in succeeding centuries employed a piece of stage machinery to suspend a character representing a god above the stage—the famous deus ex machina, or god from a machine. The time-honored spoof presupposes that a playwright, like Euripides in his ORESTES, has so complicated the play's situations that no human agency can unravel those situations and bring the play to a close. Divine intervention thus becomes necessary. While this circumstance did sometimes occur, more usually Greek playwrights employed a god's descent from Olympus in more sophisticated ways. A god might, for instance, predict the future or lend his or her dignity to a statement of the significance of the action. Finally, a god's appearance from above makes for a spectacular conclusion.

Bibliography

Marsh, Philip Whaley. *A Handbook of Classical Drama*. Stanford, Calif.: Stanford University Press, 1944.

Oates, Whitney J., and Eugene O'Neill, Jr. *The Complete Greek Drama: All the Extant Tragedies of Aeschylus, Sophocles and Euripides, and the Comedies of Aristophanes and Menander, in a Variety of Translations*. New York: Random House, 1938.

Cosmas Indicopleustes (Ctesias) (d. ca. 550 C.E.)

Born in Egypt in the city of Alexandria, Cosmas became a Christian monk and traveled widely throughout portions of the ancient world, principally in Ethiopia and India. Cosmas was both an observant geographer and a biblical literalist. His major work, *Christianike Topographia* (Christian Topography), a geographical treatise composed on 12 papyrus scrolls, attempts to reconcile his observations with his beliefs by presenting the earth in the form of a flat parallelogram on a single plane. Cosmas thought this the only view of the world consistent with the text of the Bible.

Only in the 20th century with the advent of space flight did the last of Cosmas's defenders—the members of the Flat Earth Society—finally yield to the overwhelming evidence against him.

See also GEOGRAPHY AND GEOGRAPHERS, GREEK AND ROMAN.

Bibliography

Cosmas Indicopleustes. *Christian Topography of Cosmas.* Translated and edited by J. W. Mc Crindle. London: The Hakluyt Society, 1897.

Crito Plato (399 B.C.E.)

In this dialogue by PLATO, SOCRATES awakens in prison a few days before his death sentence (see *APOLOGY OF SOCRATES*) is to be carried out, and is surprised to find his lifelong friend Crito sitting with him. Crito has come to persuade Socrates to allow his friends to hire bodyguards to spirit him away from prison and from Athens. A certain ship will be arriving from Delos in a day or two, and Socrates is condemned to die on the day after that ship arrives.

Socrates reports a dream of a woman in white. Quoting HOMER, the woman advises Socrates that he will "come to fertile Phthia"—that is, he will die—on the third day.

Crito begins presenting his arguments. His own reputation is suffering because people are saying that he and his associates are unwilling to spend the money that would assure Socrates' escape. Moreover, Crito argues, Socrates is not doing the right thing in betraying himself when he could save himself, and he will be abandoning his family just when his children need him to supervise their educations. Crito urges that Socrates should allow his friends to arrange his escape that very evening. No delay is possible.

Socrates, however, has already thought through his circumstances and is proof against Crito's importunities. He argues that what the many have to say is of no consequence and that what

Crito and Socrates must decide is whether or not it is right for Socrates to escape. Crito concurs. Socrates then leads Crito to see that, even if the law has condemned the philosopher in error, since he has agreed to abide by the judgment of the law, it is still a wrong to evade the law's force.

Socrates assumes the justice of the laws of Athens, and points out that, if the now condemned man find the laws of Athens onerous, he has had 70 years to pull up stakes and look for a more congenial dwelling. Since he has not, indeed since he prefers death to exile, he has supported the Athenian law and must perforce obey it. If he fails to do so, Socrates thinks, by his example he will make himself guilty of just what he has been charged with—corrupting the youth.

Having finished his arguments, Socrates invites Crito to speak if he has anything further to say in objection to what the philosopher has said. Crito can offer no argument. Socrates advises that they continue along the way that God has led them.

Bibliography

Plato. "Crito." In *Plato with an English Translation.* Translated by Harold North Fowler. Cambridge, Mass.: Harvard University Press, 1952.

Ctesias of Cnidos (fl. ca 400 B.C.E.) *Greek historian*

Born in Asia Minor, the Greek physician Ctesias practiced for an extended period at the Persian court at Susa. He also undertook to write a history of Assyria and Persia and another of India, all in the Ionian dialect of Greek. Though fragments of his single-scroll *Indica* and his 23-scroll *Persica* survive, we know his work principally from an abstract prepared in the late ninth century C.E. by the patriarch of Constantinople, Photius.

With respect to Persian and Assyrian history, Ctesias's accounts do not always accord with those of HERODOTUS and XENOPHON OF ATHENS, and critical opinion is divided on the comparative reliability of the historians. While Persica has been translated into both French and German, it has not yet appeared in English. With respect to Ctesias's discussion of India, it is richer in fable than in history.

Bibliography

Ctesias. *Ancient India as Described by Ktesias the Knidean.* Translated by J. W. McCrindle. 1882. Reprint, Delhi: Manohar, 1973.

cuneiform

In the Near East, city-states as a form of political entity emerged about 5,000 years ago. With that emergence came an accompanying need for keeping records and for using propaganda to achieve political cohesion and bring the ruled into line with the rulers' agendas. As the American scholar Denise Schmandt-Besserat has discovered, before actual writing systems developed, objects used for one purpose were sometimes employed to communicate something else. Though we are not sure what objects carried what messages, the historian I. M. Diakonoff, whose discussion I abridge here, suggests that a bundle of arrows might conceivably have been used to convey a declaration of war. Schmandt-Besserat also discovered three-dimensional objects enclosed in clay containers. Their shapes seem to anticipate several of the pictorial signs used in Mesopotamia that developed between about 3000 and 2400 B.C.E. into the cuneiform (wedge-shaped) writing system that speakers of the Sumerian language employed to mark on soft clay. That clay then hardened and was sometimes intentionally or inadvertently fired so that remarkably well-preserved representations of early Sumerian documents survived. The cuneiform signs seem on the one hand to represent syllables and half syllables and on the other to establish conceptual categories within which the linguistic information is organized. The Sumerian tongue does not seem to have any surviving descendants.

Three very early archives containing clay tablets—two from the ancient city of Uruk (con-temporary Warka) and a third from an area currently called Jemdet-Nasr—have been uncovered. These archives date to the period 2900–2750 B.C.E—the so-called protoliterate period. From these documents, we learn that both the speakers of Sumerian and the genetically related but linguistically separate speakers of another tongue, AKKADIAN, both called themselves the *black-headed people.* They worshipped several local deities who all seem to have been subordinate to a chief god, Enlil—a deity whose worship was centered in the city of Nippur. There priests, whose leader was titled *en,* seemed to be in charge of civic as well as ritual affairs in a society whose worship and activity was directed toward maintaining the fertility of the land and controlling the society's food supply, crafts, and commerce. As yet, the emergent ability to write does not seem to have been applied to self-consciously literary production.

That distinction belongs to the second stage of the next period of Sumerian history, the so-called Early Dynastic Period, ca. 2750–2400 B.C.E. Before, that self-conscious literary activity emerged, however, a kind of proto-history first appeared in the form of a Sumerian "king list," which purported to list all the rulers of the black-headed people since the beginning of the world. The list divides into two segments—those priests and warlords who ruled before the flood (probably not the same as Noah's flood, about which more later) and those who ruled after the flood. The antediluvian part of the list is certainly mythical. The postdiluvian part contains both rulers who were probably mythical and real ones verifiable from other sources. Moreover, the later king list enumerates both warrior kings and priest rulers and treat persons who ruled simultaneously over different parts of the country—Uruk, Ur, and Kish—as having ruled serially. Included in the list is a verifiable ruler of Kish named Aka.

Aka and his conqueror, Gilgamesh, the latter of whom the king list names as belonging to the first dynasty of Uruk, figure as characters in the first self-consciously literary work that we know existed and that continues to exist, *The GILGAMESH EPIC.* The version known to us today was composed in the Akkadian language about 1,000 years later, but the historical Sumerian Gilgamesh was deified shortly after his death, and his accomplishments became the subjects of many Sumerian songs as well of the Akkadian EPIC still widely translated into many languages and studied regularly. Both literature and history, then, can be said to begin in Sumer.

Bibliography

Diakonoff, I. A., ed. *Early Antiquity.* Chicago and London: University of Chicago Press, 1991.

Van de Mieroop, Marc. *Cuneiform Texts and the Writing of History.* London: Routledge, 1999.

Curtius, Quintus Rufus (fl. first century C.E.) *Roman historian*

Until recently, various scholars argued that the biographer Quintus Curtius Rufus flourished under one or the other of several Roman emperors from the time of AUGUSTUS CAESAR (d. 14 B.C.E.) to that of Theodosius (d. 395 C.E.), but some consensus has recently emerged. As the historians Barbara M. Levick and Ronald Syme explain, most now agree that Curtius is the same person as a proconsul of Africa, Curtius Rufus, who died in office and who had first come to power in Rome as praetor with the support of the emperor Tiberius (42 B.C.E.–37 C.E.). Both TACITUS and PLINY THE YOUNGER mention Curtius Rufus.

As an author, Curtius penned a romanticized biography of Alexander the Great in 10 books. The first two of these and portions of others have perished. Without inventing detail, Curtius exaggerates facts gleaned from earlier historians to invigorate the narrative. He follows the method of many of his predecessors by analyzing events rather than tracing a single thread from beginning to end. He also adopts the strategy of many ancient historians of putting likely-sounding speeches in the mouths of his characters. As in the rest of his work, these speeches seem to stem from

the work of previous writers, some of whom scholars have identified, though he rarely names his sources. Curtius's admiration of Alexander is evident throughout.

Bibliography

Curtius, Quintus Rufus. *The History of Alexander.* Translated by John Yardley. New York: Penguin, 1984.

Gergel, Tania, ed. *Alexander the Great: Selected Texts from Arrian, Curtius, and Plutarch.* New York: Penguin, 2004.

cyclic poets See HOMERIDAE.

Cyclops Euripides (ca. fifth century B.C.E.)

The only whole surviving example of a SATYR PLAY—an often bawdy, farcical drama that accompanied three tragedies to complete an entry in the annual Athenian dramatic festivals—EURIPIDES' *Cyclops* draws its plot from HOMER's *The ODYSSEY.* To depict Homer's story of Odysseus's encounter with the one-eyed giant goatherd Polyphemus, Euripides simplifies the plot somewhat. He also makes tactical changes in the landscape that will adjust Homer's story to the realities of staging the tale in Athens—notably by not having Polyphemus's cave sealed with a stone and by providing it with a second entrance.

Beyond that, as we learn from the editor and translator of *Cyclops,* David Kovacs, the playwright assimilates Polyphemus's contempt for the gods to the views espoused by SOPHISTS such as Callicles in PLATO's *Gorgias* (see GORGIAS OF LEONTIUM). In Euripides' version of the story, Polyphemus has no respect for any god.

Finally, Euripides supplies a full chorus of the half-human, half-goat satyrs, absent from Homer's version, which fit the play to the genre that it represents. Silenus, a satyr who opens the play with a prayer to the god Dionysius, leads the members of the CHORUS. In this prayer, we learn that a shipload of satyrs, while attempting to rescue the young Dionysus from Tuscan pirates, wrecked near Mt. Etna on Sicily. We also learn that Polyphemus has pressed the satyrs into slavery as house servants and shepherds.

As the younger satyrs drive the sheep home, their father Silenus sees that a Greek ship has beached and that their crew, led by Odysseus, is coming in search of food and water. Silenus tells Odysseus that Polyphemus is a cannibal, and Odysseus barters for food. Silenus has meat and cheese and asks for gold. Odysseus, however, has only wine—a superior trade good, in the opinion of the satyrs.

Seeing the Cyclops coming and no way for the Greeks to escape, Silenus tells them to hide in Polyphemus's cave. They do so, but Silenus at once betrays them to Polyphemus, who immediately begins preparations to eat them. Reappearing on stage, Odysseus objects to Polyphemus that Silenus is lying by saying the Greeks were trying to steal Polyphemus's property, and he appeals to the laws of hospitality. The traveler is under Zeus's special protection, and those who receive strangers inhospitably are subject to divine punishment.

Polyphemus makes clear that he shares the views of the Sophists when they say that laws are made by the weak to restrain the strong. As Polyphemus is one of the latter, he takes no account of the laws of men or of gods. He drives Odysseus and his men into the cave again. After an interval, Odysseus emerges to report the carnage he has witnessed within as Polyphemus killed and ate his two fattest crewmen. Odysseus, however, has with him a wine sack that refills itself magically. He gives some to Polyphemus, who, having never before experienced wine, drinks himself into a stupor. Odysseus also tries to enlist the chorus of satyrs in an escape attempt. He explains his plan to harden an olive stake in the fire and drive its hot point into the Cyclops's eye.

After a choral interlude, the drunken Polyphemus enters, having acquired a new respect for Dionysus, the god of wine, and having become that deity's devotee. With him comes an also drunken Silenus. Polyphemus asks Odysseus his name. Odysseus replies, "Noman." Polyphemus is so pleased about having learned to drink wine that he grants "Noman" the favor of being eaten last. Polyphemus eventually drinks so much that he becomes lecherous and selects an unwilling Silenus as the object of his affections. Together they reenter the cave.

Odysseus tries to enlist some satyrs to assist in the attack on Polyphemus, but the satyrs are too cowardly to participate—a congenital characteristic of satyrs. Odysseus and his men, therefore, do the deed alone. The chorus cheers them on, and Polyphemus, bloody and blinded, emerges from the cave. A game of hide-and-seek follows as the chorus of satyrs misdirects the Cyclops in his search for his Greek enemies.

Odysseus and his men make for the ships. Once there, just as in Homer, Odysseus pridefully reveals his true name. This is a mistake. Names are magic, and someone who knows a person's name can curse that person. In Homer's version, this is what Polyphemus does, calling on his father Poseidon, god of the sea and the earthquake, to punish Odysseus. Here, however, the play ends with Polyphemus going offstage to throw huge rocks at the departing ships, which carry off both Greeks and satyrs.

Bibliography

Kovacs, David, ed. and trans. *Euripides: Cyclops; Alcestis; Medea.* Cambridge, Mass.: Harvard University Press, 1994.

Cynicism

Now more of an attitude and a way of life than a formal philosophy, Cynicism as a school of thought looks particularly to Diogenes of Sinope (ca. 410–ca. 320 B.C.E.) as its founder. Diogenes preached and practiced a life of severe asceticism. His chief principle was to live a natural life. He is remembered for dwelling in a tub and for carrying around a lantern during daylight hours trying to find an honest man. *Cynos* is the Greek word for dog, and, as Diogenes was thought to live like a canine, the word *cynic* was applied to him and to those who subscribed to his principles over time.

The historian DIOGENES LAERTIUS attributes the honor of founding both Cynicism and STOICISM to Diogenes of Sinope's teacher, Antisthenes.

Not only did Cynics reject a comfortable style of life and luxuries, they also rejected observing social conventions—particularly those that involved distinctions in rank. Thus, the story is famously told of a visit to Diogenes from the Macedonian ruler and world conqueror, Alexander the Great. When Alexander asked Diogenes if there were anything the king could do for the Cynic, Diogenes replied that Alexander could move a little so that his shadow would not block Diogenes' sunlight. The classicist John L. Moles suggests that Diogenes' viewpoint rejected all conventional behavior but stressed individual freedom, happiness, self-sufficiency, and living in harmony with nature.

Cynicism remained influential throughout ancient times, though its practitioners did not always go to Diogenes' extremes. The movement waned in the two centuries before the Common Era, but it revived soon afterward and attracted a large following. Some have claimed that Jesus of Nazareth subscribed to the Cynics' program, though that view may have originated in mixing up Christian and non-Christian ascetics. Nonetheless, the principles of pre-Christian cynicism proved profoundly influential in early Christian ascetic and monastic movements and seem to have influenced St. Paul's thinking about the behavior of Christians toward each other and toward non-Christians.

The Cynical viewpoint also deeply influenced ancient literature. Diogenes himself composed a lost work, *Politeia* (Republic) that DIOGENES LAERTIUS summarized. The philosophical position of STOICISM derived the ethical part of its structure from Cynical thinking, arriving at the position that only virtue is good and that virtue is all one requires for happiness.

The attitudes of the Cynics did not only appear in philosophical tracts. We find elements of their program in PLATO's Socratic dialogues and XENOPHON OF ATHENS's *Memorabilia*. For example, Socrates' famed physical hardihood and his rejec-tion of the opportunity to avoid execution both recall the Cynic program.

Menippean SATIRE was a kind of verse satire in Greek written by the early Cynic philosopher Menippus of Gadara (fl. third century B.C.E.). Though only the titles of a few examples survive, the ancients generally thought that Menippus's work exercised influence on that of the Romans HORACE, SENECA, and VARRO. Roman COMEDY, too, benefited from the expression of Cynical attitudes in the plays of PLAUTUS and TERENCE.

We find further evidence of the Cynics' disenchantment with conventional norms in the writings of LUCIAN OF SAMOSATA and PLUTARCH, and in *The GOLDEN ASS* by APULEIUS.

Bibliography

Cutler, Ian. *Cynicism from Diogenes to Dilbert.* Jefferson, N.C.: McFarland and Company, 2005.

Deming, Will. *Paul on Celibacy and Marriage: The Hellenistic Background of 1 Corinthians 7.* Grand Rapids, Mich.: William B. Eerdmans Publishers, 2004.

Desmond, William D. *The Greek Praise of Poverty: Origins of Ancient Cynicism.* Notre Dame, Ind.: University of Notre Dame Press, 2006.

Downing, Francis Gerald. *Cynics, Paul, and the Pauline Churches: Cynics and Christian Origins.* New York: Routledge, 1998.

Navia, Luis E. *Classical Cynicism: A Critical Study.* Westport, Conn.: Greenwood Press, 1996.

———. *Diogenes of Sinope: The Man in the Tub.* Westport, Conn.: Greenwood Press, 1998.

Cyropædia Xenophon of Athens (after 394 B.C.E.)

A mixed-genre, largely imaginary story about the education and career of Cyrus the Great (ruled 559–529 B.C.E.), the son of King Cambyses I of Persia, XENOPHON OF ATHENS's *Cyropædia* (The Lessons of Cyrus—both those he learned and those taught) displays elements of history, philosophy, biography, love stories, and other literary types as well. Above all, it combines historical romance with educational fiction.

Though, for example, *Cyropædia* purports to picture Persian institutions and characters, in drawing an idealized constitutional monarchy, Xenophon has in fact chosen to transplant the government, the educational practices, and the military management and tactics of Sparta into Asia. He has also introduced certain Greek characters under thin Persian disguises. Xenophon's revered teacher, the philosopher SOCRATES, for example, appears lightly veiled as the Persian, Tigranes. Also transplanted into an Asian setting are the Greek ideals of the equality of citizens' rights before the law and respect for freedom of speech. Xenophon undertakes to picture what has never existed in fact: an "ideal monarchy" ruled by "an ideal monarch" and governed according to "Socratic principles."

Cyropædia also contains, much important factual matter, however. Contemporary scholars are grateful for Xenophon's unique and accurate descriptions of the Armenians and Chaldeans—people Xenophon had come to know well when, as a youth, he successfully led 10,000 Spartan mercenaries home after serving in a disastrous Persian military adventure.

Book 1

In his first chapter, after asserting that it is easier to rule any animals than it is to rule people, Xenophon enumerates the peoples of Asia who became Cyrus's subjects, either through voluntary assent or through conquest. After Xenophon explains why he has chosen Cyrus as a subject, he next discusses the educational arrangements and orderly life of young male aristocrats. They live communally for 10 years, learning the skills necessary to the successful conduct of warfare. Then they graduate into the ranks of the military, where they serve as required until they are 55 years of age. Thereafter, they become the elders who administer society and who settle questions of law and punishment.

In the second and third chapters, Xenophon turns his attention to the affectionate and precocious child Cyrus, who, with his mother Mandane,

is living at the court of his maternal grandfather, Astyages, the king of the Medes. Mandane warns her son that the lessons he may learn at court will smack of tyranny rather than kingship.

The apple of his grandfather's eye, Cyrus gains early experience in hunting and riding, displays a willingness to be treated as a full equal of his playfellows, and gives early evidence of his leadership qualities and bravery in a surprise cavalry skirmish with enemy Assyrian troops. Upon Cyrus's completion of his 10 years among the boys, and after he piously consults the oracles of the gods, he immediately assumes command of an army of 31,000 men. Of these, the first 200 are noblemen whom Cyrus has hand-picked for their virtue and military proficiency. Then Cyrus and his father, King Cambyses I, discuss the importance and efficacy of prayer and the tendency of the gods to favor people who are both industrious and careful.

Cyrus and Cambyses then consider issues concerned with military leadership. Foremost among them, they address providing for the health and well-being of the soldiers and assuring their adequate provisioning and armament. An important part of good military leadership, says Cambyses, requires first that the leader avoid raising false hopes, and next that he avoid saying things about which he is not perfectly certain. The discussions of the father and the son range widely over the differences in the ways one behaves toward friends and toward enemies. Friends deserve respect and orderly behavior, whereas a good commander regularly seeks opportunities to outwit and deceive the enemy. Cambyses analyzes the ways in which the lessons that Cyrus learned as a boy hunter can be applied in warfare. Above all else, the king counsels his son to continue consulting the will of the gods through the interpretation of omens.

Book 2

In the second book of *Cyropædia*, Cyrus leads his army of Persian peers and commoners to Media to assist the Medes in their struggle against an enormous alliance of enemies. That alliance includes the Lydians, the Phrygians, the Cappadocians, the Arabians, the Assyrians, and others. On learning that the combined forces of Persians and Medes will be greatly inferior in numbers, Cyrus rules out the strategy of a war of attrition to be fought at long distance with slings and arrows. Rather—although no mention is made of Spartan tactics—Cyrus opts for arming the common soldiers in the manner of the Spartan Hoplites. Each man will be equipped with body armor, a helmet, a small shield for the left arm, and a short sword or scimitar for fighting in close quarters with a largely unarmored enemy who depends, in close encounters, upon the weight of its numbers to overcome its foes.

Cyrus then organizes his army with a chain of command. Every five men will be led by a corporal, every 10 a sergeant, and every 50 a lieutenant. Captains will each be in charge of 100, colonels of 1,000, and generals of 10,000. Cyrus provides ladders of promotion for those who demonstrate their competence and valor, as well as monetary prizes to encourage the victorious. He then arranges the order of battle and provides for training, drill, and plentiful food. To further achieve cohesiveness, loyalty, and morale, Cyrus himself regularly invites representatives of every rank to dine with him in his tent. He recognizes, however, that every army contains soldiers who are vicious and lazy. He is at pains to see such persons identified and weeded out from among his soldiery.

Other topics addressed in this section involve the constituents of valor and the way that male children from a very early age seem to display an instinctual preference for playing with weapons. If a reader is acquainted with Xenophon's personal history as the youthful leader of 10,000 Greek mercenaries, such a reader will be hard-pressed not to see the vestiges of Xenophon's own generalship in Cyrus's arrangements.

The second book ends with a description of the stratagem that Cyrus employed to force the king of Armenia to send his accustomed tribute to the Medes. Covering his intention to invade the Armenians with a hunting party near their border, Cyrus manages to have a group of his soldiers secretly infiltrate nearby wooded uplands during the night. Then, from just over the horizon, he calls up cavalry in support of his ostensible hunters and traps the Armenian king between two jaws of the resultant pincer.

Book 3

Book 3 begins with a description of the Armenian king's alarm when he discovers himself surrounded and with no option but to obey Cyrus's demand that he present himself at the Persian camp for trial. Cyrus acts as judge, the king promises to tell the truth, and by his testimony about his practices in similar circumstances, he admits that he deserves a death sentence.

Before Cyrus pronounces that sentence, however, Tigranes, the crown prince of Armenia and the Socratic figure in Xenophon's fiction, intercedes on his father's behalf. He argues that Cyrus, having outwitted his father at every turn, has taught the Armenian king discretion with respect to the Persian and that his fear of Cyrus has converted him from disloyalty to loyalty and friendship. He further argues that all of this makes the Armenians stronger and more trustworthy allies than they were previously.

Convinced by Tigranes' arguments and by the king's conciliatory offer to let Cyrus take as much of his army and his treasure as he wishes, Cyrus reinstates the king into his favor, taking half the army on his campaign and leaving half to defend Armenia. Cyrus insists that the king pay double tribute to make up for being in arrears, and asks that the king loan Cyrus 100 talents to cover the current expenses of his army. That concluded, all have dinner.

In a veiled allusion to the death of Socrates at the hands of the Athenians, Cyrus asks Tigranes about a man who used to hunt with them when they were boys together. Tigranes replies that his father had that noble and good man put to death, accusing him of corrupting Tigranes. Tigranes reports that the man had excused the king for acting from ignorance, doing wrong against his will.

Tigranes becomes the general of the Armenian force allied with Cyrus's army, and Cyrus commands his army to seize the Chaldean mountains that lie along the border of Armenia and build a fort. From it the Persians and the allies can keep an eye on their friends, the Armenians, and on the Chaldean foe.

Defeating the Chaldean defenders of the mountains in a brief skirmish, Cyrus treats his prisoners hospitably, sending them home to discuss with their countrymen whether they would prefer to be the Persians' friends or foes. They accept the offer of friendship. Then Cyrus negotiates a mutual-assistance pact between the Armenians and the Chaldeans. The former get to rent pasturage for their flocks in the Chaldean highlands, and the latter are allowed to rent land for farming on the Armenian plain. He assures the peaceful observance of the pact by keeping control himself of the mountain fortress that commands the pastures and the fields. The Armenians and Chaldeans agree to a treaty of mutual defense and grant each other the right of intermarriage. Finally, Cyrus asks that the Chaldeans and the Armenians accompany his ambassador to the king of India, from whom Cyrus hopes to secure a donation in support of his defense of Asia (today's Middle East). Many Armenians voluntarily present money to Cyrus in support of his objectives, and Cyrus sends the money with his significantly larger army to the Median king, Cyaxares—Cyrus's uncle and his superior officer in this campaign. Following a break for some recreational hunting, Cyrus distributes a portion of the money to his captains for sharing among those of their men they found deserving.

Now perceiving that his troops are ready for battle, Cyrus sets the arguments for immediate action before Cyaxares, who agrees that the time is ripe for action.

Book 4

As Book 4 begins, Cyrus's army takes the field and encamps partly out of sight of the Assyrian host. Xenophon describes the way in which the rival commanders encourage their troops. In the midst of a discussion of tactics, Cyaxares sends an order to attack. Cyrus, though he considers the time unripe, nonetheless obeys, charging the enemy with paeans and shouted encouragement. After a successful first encounter with those of the enemy who appeared outside the defensive perimeter of the Assyrian breastworks, Cyrus's troops retreat out of the range of such missiles as stones and arrows. There Cyrus praises and rewards their bravery before setting sentries, dining, and retiring for the night.

The next day, Cyrus persuades his uncle to allow him to pursue the fleeing enemy with a contingent composed entirely of volunteers. The Assyrians have left the cavalry of a subject people, the Hyrcanians, as the rear guard to cover their retreat. The Hyrcanians, however, are in the field with their entire families, according to the custom of the Asians. They decide it would be prudent to switch sides and join forces with Cyrus. Cyrus accepts the offer.

Practically everyone among the Medes and the Persians volunteer to accompany Cyrus—some because they admire him, and some in hope of gain. The host marches off in pursuit of the enemy, and Xenophon details a report of a heavenly light that shines through the night on Cyrus and his army.

Cyrus gives his orders to his host, now enlarged by the Hyrcanians, and he cautions his men not to turn aside from the battle to plunder—a mistake that has resulted in many a defeat. He cautions everyone to return before nightfall. Frightened by the advance of Cyrus's host, all the enemy who can flee before it do so. Those caught in the tents of the encampment prove to be mostly quartermasters, servants, and cooks. Cyrus, who had taken the field without provisions, is glad to gain control of a supply of food good for a month or more. He orders the prisoners to prepare a meal to feed whoever returns victorious from the fray, friend or foe. He again advises his men to avoid plundering, even though much in terms of money, objects, and slaves might be theirs for the taking.

Cyrus now becomes convinced of the advantage of cavalry—an advantage that, until now, the Persians have not enjoyed. They rely on the horsemen of subject peoples, but Cyrus considers this a defect in need of remedy. He proposes that his men become virtual centaurs—half horse, half man—with the added advantage of being able to separate the halves at will. He offers his prisoners the opportunity to resume their accustomed lives and dwell at peace under the Persians' protection. They accept.

In the meantime, back at the camp of the Medes, Cyaxares, who had been drinking and carousing with his boon companions, discovers that the vast majority of his forces have volunteered to accompany Cyrus. In his anger, he recalls both them and Cyrus and his men. When this message reaches Cyrus, he has no intention of humoring his uncle's foolish and wrathful petulance. Instead, he writes Cyaxares a letter in which he patiently explains how all his actions have been in his uncle's interests. Then the tone of the letter shifts as Cyrus makes clear that he has at his disposal the means to respond forcibly to any threats his uncle might consider. He closes by assuring Cyaxares that he and his men will return as soon as they have completed the task they set out to accomplish—one that benefits Cyaxares as much as anyone.

With this pointed message, on the advice of Cyaxares' soldiers, Cyrus sends his uncle some captured women as a gift. Having done this, he gives his allies among the Medes and the Hyrcanians first choice of the spoils of battle, and the Persians content themselves with what is left. He then frees those of the prisoners whom the Assyrians had forced into slavery, and assigns them as squires to his newly mounted cavalry officers.

There now arrives an Assyrian suppliant—an old man named Gobryas. He explains that his friend, the Assyrian king, has fallen in the battle and been succeeded by his son. The new king is the murderer of the old man's son, and the old fellow's sworn enemy. Gobryas begs Cyrus to accept him into his service so that he can hope to avenge his son's death. This story is touching-

ly told, with the sentence structure reflecting the old man's sobs as they interrupt his narrative. Cyrus accepts Gobryas's offer of assistance, and the fourth book ends with an account of the division of the spoils. Among them are the women captured in the camp. The second loveliest is sent to Cyaxares. The loveliest, however—Panthea, the wife of Abradatas of Susa—is kept for Cyrus.

Book 5

As Book 5 opens, however, Cyrus refuses to accept Panthea, or for that matter even to look at her. He explains that he is afraid her beauty might keep him from his duties. Then he and his friend Araspas have a discussion about whether love is an irresistible passion or a matter of will. Araspas argues the latter position, but Cyrus considers love an irrational form of bondage. Araspas, however, thinks he can "put his hand in the fire," and not be burned. He proves to be wrong in this.

In the meantime, Cyrus offers his Median volunteers the opportunity to return to Cyaxares. All of them opt to remain in the field with Cyrus. So do the Hyrcanians, and on the following morning, all set out for the castle of Gobryas. Arriving there, they find that Gobryas is as good as his word, putting all his vast wealth and possessions at their disposal and offering his daughter as a bride for Cyrus—an offer Cyrus declines for himself but accepts for some worthy member of his retinue.

Gobryas learns that, though he owns more than Cyrus appears to, Cyrus and his Persians are the better men in their valor and simplicity of life. At a council of war, Cyrus first explores with Gobryas the possibility of gaining other allies among those whom the current Assyrian king has injured. Finding that such persons do exist, Cyrus proposes marching straight to Babylon and attacking it. There the greatest number of the enemy will be concentrated, and there a disciplined attacking force will have the greatest opportunity to strike fear into the hearts of the defenders.

In preparation, Cyrus sends Gobryas to recruit an ally, Gadatas, from among the Assyrian king's enemies. By trickery, Gadatas occupies an Assyrian border fortress and turns it over to Cyrus. Cyrus in turn presents the fortress to the Hyrcanians, whose allies, the Sacians and Cadusians, in turn swell Cyrus's ranks.

The Assyrians, however, discover Gadatas's duplicity and mobilize an army to invade his territory. Cyrus postpones his plan to march straight to Babylon and instead marshals his forces to support Gadatas. Xenophon next describes in detail Cyrus's organization of a night march as the allies move to defend Gadatas's land from the Assyrians. In passing, the reader learns of the pains that Cyrus takes to remember the names of anyone to whom he gives directions.

Thus far, everything has favored Cyrus and his allies. Now, however, treachery makes an appearance. One of Gadatas's cavalry officers, the commander of a fortress in Gadatas's territory, thinks he can win Gadatas's place and fortune by advising the Assyrian king where and how he might capture Gadatas and overcome the small force accompanying him in advance of Cyrus's larger army. The Assyrian king takes possession of Gadatas's fortress and prepares a trap to capture him. As Gadatas flees the pursuing Assyrians, he is on the point of being captured when he encounters Cyrus and the main body of his forces. Harried by pursuing Persians, several Assyrians fall, including the traitor.

Cyrus's Cadusian allies, marching in the rear, have missed the fight. Chagrined, they set forth on their own, without informing Cyrus, to pillage the countryside. They encounter a superior force of Assyrians, however, who kill many of them and capture the spoils they were carrying. The surviving Cadusians flee to Cyrus, who welcomes them, attends to the wounded, and, blaming no one, turns the entire incident into a useful object lesson.

Cyrus then proposes to the Assyrian king a treaty under which the soldiers of both sides agree to leave the farmers in peace to tend their fields and to confine their warfare to men at arms. This agreement applies only to crops and not to husbandry. Domestic animals are regarded as fair game for either side.

Now accompanied by Gadatas, Cyrus marches his army not to Babylon but, rather, to a planning session with his uncle, Cyaxares. When, the two meet with their retinues, however, the grandeur of Cyrus's cavalry puts Cyaxares to shame. Cyrus undertakes to placate his uncle by convincing him that all Cyrus has done has been in Cyaxares' interest, reviewing everything he has done since he assumed command. After detailing his activities, Cyrus draws from Cyaxares an admission that his nephew has done nothing blameworthy. Nonetheless, the uncle confesses that it is Cyrus's very successes that cause him chagrin, for Cyrus is performing the offices that he himself had rather do. Nonetheless, the two are reconciled and, to everyone's relief, exchange the customary kiss between relatives in full view of the army. Then, while Cyaxares goes to dine and rest, Cyrus begins laying his plans for his next campaign.

Book 6

The next day, Cyaxares also joins the planning and assumes the chair. All agree that continuing the war is in the allies' best interests, and preparations include plans for building new fortresses and siege engines. Cyrus redesigns chariots to turn them into killing machines. Having set the plans in motion, Cyrus seeks a spy. His choice falls upon Araspas the man with whom he had discussed whether or not love is irrational. By this time, Araspas is ardently in love with Panthea, but she repulses his advances, for she is devoted to her husband. When Araspas threatens to force her, she complains to Cyrus, who reproves Araspas. This becomes widely known throughout the camp. Cyrus sees an opportunity to use Araspas, who will pretend to flee his general's wrath and desert to the enemy.

Among those taken in by this ruse is Panthea herself. She goes to Cyrus and advises him to send for her husband, Abradatas, whose loyalty to the current Assyrian king has been undermined by the king's effort to separate Panthea from her husband. Cyrus follows her advice, and Abradatas soon arrives at the head of 1,000 cavalrymen. A new design for Abradatas's chariot suggests to Cyrus a plan for manned siege engines pulled by eight oxen yoked together.

At this juncture, ambassadors arrive from the Indian king, bringing a contribution of money to Cyrus's cause. The Indian king also promises more, should Cyrus need it. Returning spies report that, on the Assyrian side, King Croesus of Lydia has been appointed field marshal for the Assyrians and their allies. These include Thracians, Egyptians, Cyprians, Cilicians, Phrygians, Lycaonians, Paphlagonians, Cappadocians, Arabians, Phoenicians, and, under duress, Greek islanders from Ionia and Aeolia.

Faced with such a foe, Cyrus's soldiers begin showing signs of panic, and Cyrus undertakes to calm them. The men attribute their restlessness not to fear but to the work that still lies ahead. In preparation for the long overland march that his army must undertake, Cyrus advises that only water should be drunk with dinner, no wine. Then, though wine may be consumed after dinner, it must be in ever diminishing amounts until everyone has become a teetotaler for the remainder of the campaign.

Preparations made, the army marches forth along with its supply wagons, camp followers, and equipment. After several days of marching, they begin to see signs that the enemy is in the vicinity, and news comes that Croesus is in the field with his host. At this moment as well, the spy Araspas returns with information about the numbers of the enemy and the enemy's battle order, strategy, and tactics. Based on the extent of the front—24,000 feet—and the depth of the formation—30 men—the opposing army is estimated at about 360,000 men.

Facing this army, Cyrus stations his heavily armed infantry in the vanguard, his spearmen behind them, his archers third, and veteran infantrymen in the rear so that the most doughty fighters are stationed front and rear, and projectiles

may be thrown and fired over the heads of the front rank. He also deploys the camp followers and baggage trains in the rear to give the impression of greater numbers, and he stations troops mounted on horses and camels in the rear of the baggage trains. Abradatas claims the privilege of leading the charioteers, but the Persians grumble. They cast lots for the honor, and Abradatas wins. Panthea brings him armor for his body and his arms, a plumed helmet, and a tunic, and as she arrays him in them, she weeps, calling him her "best jewel." Threading this love story through his account of the war is one of the marks of Xenophon's talent as a writer of historical fiction.

Book 7

In Book 7, the opposing armies draw near one another. Croesus begins a flanking movement, designed to box in the Persians on three sides. He has not, however, taken into account Abradatas's chariots with their armed and slashing wheels. Neither is Croesus aware that a detachment of camels will be facing his cavalry. Horses are deathly afraid of camels.

Charging into the midst of the Egyptians, Abradatas and his companions create carnage until their very success forces the wheels from their chariots, and all are overwhelmed by the Egyptian infantry and slain. Eventually, Cyrus's tactics overcome even the superbly disciplined Egyptian forces, who, even after they can no longer strike a blow, remain in defensive formation behind their shields. Cyrus gives them the opportunity to join him and take up residence in Persia as subjects and landholders. When the Egyptians discover they can do so with honor and that Cyrus will meet the condition that they not have to fight against Croesus, to whom they had sworn allegiance, the Egyptians accept his proposition.

The remainder of Croesus's defeated army flee toward Sardis during the night, and the next day Cyrus leads his forces against the city. Again victorious, Cyrus accepts Croesus's surrender in person. The two parlay, and Croesus advises Cyrus to benefit by sparing the city from sack and plunder. Cyrus agrees, then asks Croesus to clarify his relationship with the god Apollo, who had pronounced oracles deemed favorable to Croesus. Croèsus admits that he has offended the god by putting his oracle to a test before reposing trust in Apollo, and that thereby he has incurred the god's enmity. After further parlay, Croesus becomes Cyrus's friend, and thereafter Cyrus takes his former enemy with him wherever he travels.

Missing Abradatas, Cyrus inquires about him. He is informed of his death and told that his funeral is even now underway. A touching interview between Cyrus and Panthea follows in which she blames herself for encouraging her husband to join Cyrus. Cyrus assures her of his continuing friendship and of proper escort to whatever destination she chooses. As soon as he is gone, however, Panthea plunges a knife into her heart and expires on her husband's corpse.

Xenophon now recounts the wisdom of one of Cyrus's generals, Adusius, in settling a civil war among the Carians without bloodshed. Impressed by Adusius's statesmanship, the Carians request that Cyrus appoint him as their satrap (regent or governor). Another commander, Hystaspes, subdues a portion of Phrygia. Then those Assyrian allies who had resisted Cyrus begin falling like dominoes. Greater Phrygia, Cappadocia, and Arabia submit to the force of his arms, and their warriors swell Cyrus's ranks as he marches toward Babylon. As usual when discussing warfare, strategy, and tactics, Xenophon deserts fiction and romance for history, and the following account is accurate.

Arriving at Babylon, the Persians and their allies surround the city to survey the walls. The Babylonians conspire to attack the resultant thin line of troops as soon as Cyrus begins to withdraw beyond missile range. A deserter, however, brings Cyrus news of this plan. Cyrus has his men maneuver to provide continual cover against such an attack as they withdraw by stages beyond the range of enemy arrows and stones.

Babylon is an enormous city—more than 60 miles in circumference. It is walled with brick cemented with bitumen, and a hundred brass gates provide access. Moreover, the very broad and deep Euphrates River flows through it. Convinced that the walls are impregnable, Cyrus sets about building watchtowers and earthworks. The Babylonians find his efforts entertaining, for they feel secure protected by their walls and their river. Out of their sight, however, Cyrus sets the majority of his men to digging an enormous trench that will enable him to divert the river's course. When the trench is ready, Cyrus waits until the Babylonians are celebrating a festival at which most of the city's inhabitants carouse and become drunk.

On that night, Cyrus has his men breach the restraining levee. The Euphrates flows into the trench, and Cyrus's army enters the city along its bed. Those who recognize them as Persians fall to their swords. In the darkness, however, many of the revelers think the Persian troops to be their fellow citizens and call out greetings, which the Persians return as they make their way straight to the royal palace. There they find the king of the Babylonians, Belshazzar, preparing to defend himself with his dagger.

Cyrus leaves killing the king to Gobryas, whose son Belshazzar had killed, and to Gadatas, whom Belshazzar had castrated. After the palace falls, the Persian cavalry rides about the city warning the inhabitants to stay indoors, for anyone found outside will be cut down. Not until the next day do many citizens Babylon realize that their supposedly impregnable city has fallen.

Ever pious, Cyrus calls on the magi—the priests of Babylon—to select the first fruits of the booty for the gods. Then he distributes houses and official quarters among those he thinks most deserving and makes arrangements for tribute and governance.

Having subdued much of Asia, Cyrus now thinks that he is entitled to become its king. Yet even in this he manages matters in such a way that the suggestion seems to come from his loyal followers. So Cyrus moves into the royal palace of Babylon and, having taken up residence there, sets about organizing his court. Realizing that he is likely to be the object of the citizens' hatred, he decides upon a personal bodyguard of eunuchs and those whose fidelity to him he can most confidently ensure with the promise of riches. For a household garrison, he selects 10,000 Persian spearmen, whose generous salaries are to be paid by the Babylonians, whom Cyrus intends to keep poor to make them more submissive and docile.

Calling his Persian peerage together, he encourages them to continue to pursue the moral imperatives whose practice has made them great. He also advises that they not share with others the military practices that have made them virtually invincible in the field.

Book 8

As the last book of Xenophon's masterpiece opens, one of Cyrus's companions, Chrysantas, rises to speak, concurring in Cyrus's view and emphasizing the role of discipline and the need for continued obedience to Cyrus. Chrysantas also underscores the duty of the peers to attend Cyrus at his court.

Xenophon now details Cyrus's administrative arrangements for governing his vast empire. His success as a military commander leads him to model his civil service on the army. After discussing the policy with which Cyrus manages his retinue, Xenophon notes that the king becomes even more pious, virtuous, temperate, considerate, and self-disciplined than he had been previously. He adopts the costume preferred by the Medes and has his associates do the same. He tries to assure his personal safety by making his powerful associates better friends to him than to each other. He entertains them, feeds them lavishly, and employs them as his eyes and ears in intelligence gathering. The model of kingship that he chooses is that of the good shepherd who, while deriving benefit from his flocks, keeps them happy and contented.

Cyrus demonstrates to Croesus, who was often accounted the richest king of antiquity, that treasures in the hands of Cyrus's friends and allies are like money in his own bank account. If he ever needs it, he can call on them and they will willingly give more than he needs. This contrasts with Croesus's practice of storing his wealth in a treasury.

Xenophon continues to describe Cyrus's arrangements as those of an ideal ruler of an ideal state—including his establishment of a board of public health and a public medical dispensary, all of whose services are available to any citizen free on demand.

Cyrus's first state public appearance in Babylon—designed to inspire awe and wonder and also to provide maximum security for the monarch—draws from the author a detailed and loving description. So do the subsequent descriptions of Cyrus's receipt of petitions; the sacrifices made to Zeus, the Sun, the Earth, and the tutelary heroes of Syria; and the games and races that follow.

Next comes the story of a former farmer, Pheraulas, whom Cyrus has made a rich man in consideration of his loyal service. Burdened by his unaccustomed wealth, Pheraulas gives it all away to a Sacian acquaintance in exchange for being maintained as a guest. Thus both dwell happily together.

Xenophon next turns his attention to illustrating Cyrus's preference for good deeds over warfare. He tells how the king honors his friends and how he establishes a matchmaking service to see that his loyal officers marry appropriately and well. He also accounts to all his friends for the possessions that he has in store and explains to them that his wealth is there for his friends when they have need of some of it.

In due course, Cyrus decides that he wishes to return to Persia. He organizes a grand caravan for that purpose, giving detailed instructions for pitching tents and arranging for security, meal preparation, and so forth.

On the way home, Cyrus turns aside to visit his uncle, Cyaxares, and to present him with a state residence of his own in the city of Babylon. Cyaxares proposes that Cyrus marry his daughter and accept the Median kingdom with her as a dowry. Pending the approval of his father and mother, Cyrus accepts his first cousin as his bride—a degree of relationship still highly valued for spouses among some societies in the Middle East.

After visiting his father Cambyses, agreeing that Cambyses should rule for life and then be succeeded by Cyrus as king of Persia, and after obtaining his parents' permission to marry his cousin, Cyrus departs, picking his new bride up along the way to Babylon. Here Xenophon yields to the temptation to insert a little authorial joke. Some historians, he says, claim that Cyrus married his mother's sister. Xenophon quips: "But that maid must certainly have been a very old maid."

Once back in Babylon, Cyrus sets his hand to organizing his far-flung empire for stability, assigning authority for civil matters to a satrap but leaving military garrisons in charge of defense and establishing a system of inspections to assure that each element of his government fulfills its duties. That done, Cyrus establishes the archetypal pony express—one so organized that the mail throughout his far-flung empire moves both day and night. Xenophon calls it "the fastest overland traveling on earth."

Further conquests, says Xenophon, extend Cyrus's empire from Syria to the Indian Ocean. Xenophon also credits him with the subjugation of Egypt, though in fact it was his son Cambyses that accomplished that feat. At its greatest extent, Cyrus's empire stretches from the Indian Ocean in the east, to the Black Sea in the north, to Cyprus and Egypt on the west, and south to Ethiopia.

Cyrus arranges his own life so that he dwells all year in a part of his empire where, at the season of his residency, the weather is springlike. Late in his long life, he comes to Persia for the seventh time. There a phantom appears to him in a dream and predicts his coming death. Accordingly, Xenophon reports, Cyrus makes the appropriate sacrifices and prays. After a couple of days, during which his appetite fails him, Cyrus calls his relatives and friends to his bedside, and with them he reviews his life and the motives for his various actions. He names his firstborn son, Cambyses, his successor. Cyrus then asserts his belief in the immortality of the soul and enjoins upon his survivors the duty to be reverent. He then gives directions for his burial. He wants no state funeral but merely instructs that his unclothed body should be committed to the earth.

Cyrus then laments the sad state of morals in his old age, for he thinks that people have become less trustworthy and more dishonest in their financial dealings. Their physical fitness has declined. Male behavior has become more effeminate; the display of wealth is shameful; and they have neglected useful weapons and military tactics that Cyrus invented, such as the scythed chariot and close combat. Now, Cyrus laments, Asian wars must be conducted with the assistance of Greek mercenaries if they are to succeed. When Cyrus has pronounced his views on these subjects, Xenophon's book ends.

The historical Cyrus died in 529 B.C.E. following a military campaign in central Asia. His son, Cambyses II, buried him at Cyrus's royal residence at Pasargadae, a location to the northeast of Persepolis in modern Iran. His tomb can still be seen there.

Bibliography

Xenophon's Cyrus the Great: The Arts of Leadership and War [Selections]. Edited by Larry Hedrick. New York: Truman Talley Books, St. Martin's Press, 2006.

Xenophon. *Cyropaedia* [Greek and English]. 2 vols. Edited and translated by Walter Miller. Cambridge, Mass.: Harvard University Press, 1953.

D

dactylic hexameter   See QUANTITATIVE VERSE.

Damasus (fl. fourth century C.E.) *Roman poet*
Elected Pope Damasus I on October 1, 306, amid violence and controversy, Damasus is remembered as an important pope under whose pontificate Latin became the principal liturgical language of the Roman church and who appointed St. JEROME to prepare the official canon of the Scriptures that was approved by the Roman Council of 382. In addition to these administrative contributions to the development of Christian literature, Damasus was himself a minor poet who wrote Latin hymns and EPIGRAMS, both rhymed and unrhymed. They have not been translated.

Bibliography

"Damasus I." In *New Catholic Encyclopedia*. New York: McGraw-Hill Book Company, 1967.
Ferrua, Antonio, ed. *Epigramata Damasiana* [Damasian epigrams]. Rome: Pontifical Institute of Christian Archaeology, 1942.

Daode Jing   See LAOZI.

Daoism (Taoism)

A Chinese philosophy based on the attempt of human beings to conduct their lives in a manner consonant with the "natural, eternal, spontaneous, nameless and indescribable" original principle of the universe. The word *dao* (*tao*) means "the way." It is the way that individuals and nations must follow if they are to live in consonance with nature—or, perhaps better, to emulate the natural processes that are native to the universe. Thus, while Daoism is sometimes thought to imply inactivity, in fact it implies *natural* activity. That activity is characterized by doing what is simple, by acting spontaneously, by tranquil living, by behaving meekly, and by only taking actions that are consonant with essential nature itself. As is the case with many Chinese printed and spoken words, many overlapping meanings are implied by a single character or utterance. Thus, Daoism presents an alternative to the busy program of beneficent social action that CONFUCIUS espoused.

The central tenets of Daoism are contained in a little book called the *Laozi* (also *Daode Jing, Tao Te ching*). The book itself is slender, its roughly 5,250 words deployed in 81 sections and running to 105 pages, including illustrations and generous-sized typeface in one of its most recent English translations. Nonetheless, it has spawned as many as 700 learned commentaries in China alone, and it is the Chinese book that has been most often translated into other languages.

Bibliography

Henricks, Robert G. *Lao-Tzu: Te-Tao Ching: A New Translation Based on the Recently Discovered Ma-wang-tui Texts.* New York: Ballantine, 1989.

Mair, Victor H., trans. *Tao Te Ching: The Classic Book of Integrity and the Way: Lao Tzu.* New York: Bantam Books, 1990.

Wing-Tsit Chan, trans. and ed. *A Source Book in Chinese Philosophy.* Princeton, N.J.: Princeton University Press, 1963.

Daphnis and Chloe　See Pastorals of Daphnis and Chloe.

Dead Sea Scrolls, The　(ca. 375 b.c.e.–ca. 70 c.e.)

The Dead Sea Scrolls are a collection of eight groups of ancient papyrus, leather, and (in one case) metal manuscripts first discovered and excavated clandestinely by some Bedouin tribesmen. Later, often in competition with the Bedouin, professional archeologists were authorized to investigate known and likely sites. The documents described by the catchphrase *Dead Sea Scrolls* began coming to light in 1947 and continued emerging from underground as late as 1977. It is conceivable that more will be found someday. Here I principally follow the discussions of the theologian Florentino García Martínez and of the historian, translator, and linguist Geza Vermes, who are among the most balanced, scientifically reliable, and authoritative of the scrolls' editors.

The following collections each contributed a share to the wide variety of materials somewhat inaccurately lumped together under the designation Dead Sea Scrolls:

1　Papyri recovered from Wâdi Daliyeh, also called the Samaria Papyri. Mainly legal documents, these manuscripts are written in the Aramaic language and bear dates between 375 and 335 b.c.e. They were discovered together with human remains and a variety of possessions that suggest the papyri belonged to a band of refugees fleeing the destruction of Samaria by the conquering troops of Alexander the Great. It seems that the refugees were trapped in the cave by pursuing Macedonian soldiers who set a fire at the cave's entrance, exhausted the cave's oxygen, and suffocated its inhabitants.

2　The Qumran Papyri: Papyri in the Aramaic, Hebrew, and Greek languages found in 11 caves near Khirbet Qumran. These manuscripts were partly recovered by the Bedouin and partly by the archeologists. They are of extraordinary interest to students of religion and the focus of discussion here.

3　The Masada Manuscripts: Discovered while excavating the fortress at Masada destroyed by the Romans in (73/74 c.e.). These manuscripts are in the Hebrew, Aramaic, Greek, and Latin languages. Some of them contain biblical texts. One of them is a copy of "Songs of the Sabbath Sacrifice," a work also found in several copies at Qumran.

4　The Manuscripts of Murabba'at: These documents include contracts and letters signed by the Hebrew revolutionary Bar Kokhba, who fought against Rome from 132 to 135 c.e. Most of the other documents also originate early in the first century c.e. and appear in Aramaic,

Greek, Hebrew, and Latin. Among this collection, a single PALIMPSEST was discovered that dates to the seventh century B.C.E.

5 The Manuscripts of Nahal Hever: Originating in two caves dubbed the Cave of the Letters and the Cave of Horror, this collection also contains a significant trove of documents relevant to Bar Kokhba, the leader of the second Jewish revolt against Rome (132–135 C.E.). The collection also contains an archive belonging to the family Babata. These two sets of documents are written in Aramaic, Greek, Hebrew, and Nabataen (an offshoot of the Aramaic tongue and an ancestor of Arabic). Beyond this, fragmentary biblical remains were discovered with bits of text from Numbers 20:7–8, and from Psalms 15 and 16. Investigators also found a partial Greek manuscript of a text called The *Twelve Prophets*. The 12 prophets were traditionally Hosea, Joel, Amos, Obadiah, Jonah, Micah, Nahum, Habbakuk, Zephaniah, Haggai, Zechariah, & Malachi.

6 The Manuscripts from Wâdi Seiyâl: This group includes documents of dubious or clandestine provenance.

7 The Manuscripts from Nahal Mishmar: Though investigators found much earlier handicraft on this site, they recovered only two or three papyrus sheets.

8 The Manuscripts from Khirbet Mird: The contents of this site differ markedly from those above. The items found on this site were a part of the collection of a Christian monastery of Castellion. Its documents, written in Greek, Christian Palestinian Aramaic, and Arabic, date to the Byzantine and Arab periods of Palestinian history—significantly later, in other words, than the documents from the other sites.

The documents described above have all been submitted to a rigorous scientific regimen of radiocarbon analysis and, later, to the even more precise dating method of accelerator mass spectrometry, which also has the advantage of being less harmful to the manuscript. The results produced by these laboratory tests have been further cross-checked by paleographers—experts in dating the handwriting that appears on the manuscripts. The three sorts of analysis converge exactly, determining the period beyond which no manuscript from Qumran or Masada could have been copied. No document postdates 68 C.E., according to Martínez, or around 70 C.E., according to Vermes.

The significance of that date arises, Martínez argues, from its exclusion of Jewish-Christian or Zealot origins for the documents in the treasure troves. Readers can expect to learn little, if anything, new about the activities of early Christians during the years between the crucifixion of Christ and the appearance of the earliest of the Christian gospels, ca. 70 C.E.

With respect to the documents from the Qumran caves, Martínez convincingly argues—and Vermes agrees—that they all come from the religious library of a Jewish sect of believers who dwelt and worshipped together, who avoided contact with other branches of Judaism, and who followed a unique calendar and a set of rules of behavior peculiar to themselves, called *halakhah*. The sect seems to have followed the precepts that had evolved from those of an early Zadokite priest of the temple, Onias III (served 187–175 B.C.E.). Onias had resisted the introduction into Judea of Greek religion and institutions under the rule of the Syrian successors of Alexander the Great.

To illustrate that premise, Martínez has undertaken to construct a composite of the several copies of documents typifying the collection. He advises his reader that the copies show the effects of hundreds of years of editing and revision.

First among the documents Martínez includes is what he calls "The Rule of the Community." This details the specifics of required behavior during worship and guidelines for leading a good life in general. It also provides specifics about the group's organization, about discipline within the sect, and about appropriate conduct when interaction with persons outside the sect proves necessary. Also included here are essays on theology, reflections on biblical history, explanations of biblical passages, moral advice, and discussions of liturgy. The literary form of the rule, says Martínez, is unprecedented in ancient Judaism but one that continued to develop among a wide spectrum of early Christians and in later monastic communities. That spectrum included the Gnostics as well as other communions eventually deemed heretical. Parts of the document are in prose and parts in verse.

Some of the rules of the community are reminiscent of those practiced by the followers of EPICURUS in ancient Athens. Community members were expected to correct one another, but their reproaches were to be delivered meekly and compassionately; no anger, muttering, or "spiteful intent" was allowed. Exclusion from "the pure food" of the community—whether an actual or a metaphorical communion—for short or long periods, depending on the seriousness of the offence, were apparently frequent. Excommunication and even death were also a part of the system. One could be punished for falling asleep in the general meeting of the society or for "giggling inanely."

Following the "Rule" comes what Martínez labels "The Damascus Document." (For the belief system it represents, others label this document a "Zadokite text.") The text presents a picture of a deity much offended by the behavior and attitudes of his creation—a God of wrath who punishes the manifold transgressions of human beings. People are encouraged in those transgressions by the Hebrew God's demonic adversary, Belial. This document also outlines the manner in which the community enforces discipline among its members and the consequences of failing to submit to that discipline.

As seems usual in such religious communities, those in the seats of leadership interpreted and explained the will of God to their followers. The document also seems to contain prescrip-

tions for diagnosing and treating conditions such as leprosy and gonorrhea.

Beyond the rules already described, there is another set of rules from the *halakhah*. These are important because they distinguish the community at Qumran from mainstream Judaism. These are rules governing even the minutiae of day-to-day living.

Still another set of manuscripts addresses the subject of eschatology—that branch of theology that concerns itself with the end of the world. In a section that Martínez labels "The War Scroll," the final battle between "the sons of light" and "the sons of darkness" becomes the subject of a detailed prophecy that results, predictably, in the victory of the former. For the righteous survivors of the final battle, "The Rule of the Congregation" emerges. Among the subjects addressed is convocation for planning the conduct of further warfare. Another is the breaking of bread and the drinking of wine.

Then a New Jerusalem is described in some detail, and other texts contain further prophecies concerning the question of final things as the world winds down. One should note that many if not most of the manuscripts above existed in several copies and showed evidence of editorial emendation over time.

Another broad category addressed by the Dead Sea Scrolls is literature that interprets and explains the meaning of Scripture: exegetical literature. Chief among these ancient texts we find the Temple Scroll. This enormous document measures some eight meters (over 26 feet) long. Perhaps predictably, the explanation of difficult passages results in the promulgation and refinement of ever more rules of conduct in all departments of life. These include such matters as purifying a house in which someone has died, rules governing the sacrifice of animals, and rules prohibiting the ingestion of blood when dining on flesh.

Notable among the Temple Scroll's instructions to YHWH's (the Hebrew name of god—the Old Testament name for the supreme and only true deity) faithful are those relating to the consequences of straying from the faith and worshipping other gods. Prophets or interpreters of dreams who propose the worship of other gods must be put to death. If the people of an entire city have revered another deity, the faithful are instructed "to put to the sword all the inhabitants of that city." Their animals must also be destroyed and the city and its contents burned.

Among other matters addressed in the scroll, we find instructions for the elevation and behavior of kings. We also learn of the offerings that are required from hunters, fishermen, and farmers, and the form of encouragement that priests must give soldiers advancing to battle. Other examples of exegetical literature appear in commentaries on such books of the Bible as Isaiah, Hosea, and Micah, and upon such apocryphal scriptures as Nahum.

Still other important classes of documents appear among the Dead Sea Scrolls. One of these is what Martínez labels "para-biblical literature." This class contains quite disparate materials. First we find "Paraphrases of the Pentateuch," which interweaves direct quotations from what has come to be regarded as received Scripture with formerly unknown material, both more and less connected with Scripture. Other subclasses of the para-biblical material, including the "Genesis Apocryphon" and the "Book of Jubilees" embroider basic stories from the Bible with extra-biblical detail. At a more distant remove from what has subsequently been defined as received Scripture, we find pseudepigrapha—writing that is falsely ascribed to biblical characters. Examples of this class of material take now-received Scripture as a starting point but tell nonbiblical stories about biblical characters. These stories may be older than, contemporary with, or more recent than received Scripture, but no one can be sure.

Of particular interest to biblical scholars anxious to trace the development of Scripture during the proto-Christian period are manuscripts like that labeled "Pseudo-Ezekiel," which preserves hints of connections with the development of very early Christianity. Other manuscripts in this category include the "Aramaic Testament of Levi," the "Books of Enoch," and the "Book of Jubilees"

named above. Beyond this, we find examples of other apocrypha, such as "Pseudo-Samuel," "Pseudo-Jeremiah," "Pseudo-Daniel," and "Tobit" in both Aramaic and Hebrew.

Further classes of literary texts represented in the Dead Sea treasure trove include poems such as a series of "Apocryphal Psalms," a number of quite lovely hymns of praise, and some less lovely hymns designed to be sung as a protection against demons. There are also several "Wisdom Poems." These include one warning against the "Wiles of a Wicked Woman" and one predicting the arrival and nature of the "Messianic Apocalypse." Beyond these poetic texts, one also finds a series of liturgical texts and a group of texts relating to astronomy, calendars, and the casting of horoscopes and physiognomy.

A final scroll contains a mystery. This one consisted of two sheets of totally oxidized copper rolled up together. To decipher the Hebrew writing—from apparently pre-200 C.E.—on the sheets, it was necessary to cut them very carefully into parallel strips. While the translation is often difficult, and while experts wonder whether the scroll's contents are true or fictitious, the scroll seems to contain detailed directions for finding an enormous quantity of hidden Zadokite treasure. A group of inscriptions on ceramic shards and on a wooden tablet completes the finds.

Among other conclusions about the scrolls' scholarly, literary, historical, biblical, and religious significance, Geza Vermes draws the following ones: The scrolls' discovery initiated a new scholarly discipline, Hebrew codicology—the study of Hebrew manuscripts. The finds have shed new light on both the text and the canon of the Bible. Though the central message of the HEBREW BIBLE is unaffected, the discoveries have fundamentally altered scholarly thinking about the history of the text. Most importantly, given the variety of texts discovered—several previously unknown—the concept of a definitive Bible seems to have still been in process of formation, and the books that eventually would be included in the biblical canon—including the Hebrew Bible—had not yet been finally identified (although all the books of the Hebrew Bible except Esther are represented among the scrolls at Qumran). These facts, of course, point conclusively toward the subsequent role that both Jewish and Christian communities played in winnowing through the material that for many adherents of both faiths would come to constitute the infallible word of God.

It appears that the community of whose library the scrolls are the remnant was either the main or a splinter group of the separatist society of Essenes—Jews devoted to a rigorously strict religious discipline. As none of those persons who deposited the materials ever returned to collect them at the place where, 2,000 years later, they were found, theories that posit a Roman massacre of the Essenes seem viable.

As regards the relationship of the Dead Sea Scrolls and the NEW TESTAMENT, Vermes notes the following. First, there are basic similarities of language (as a single instance, both use the phrase "sons of light.") Next, both the Essenes and Jewish Christians thought of themselves as "the true Israel," and both expected the arrival of the Kingdom of God at any moment. Both communities also saw their recent history as the fulfillment of Hebrew Bible prophecy. Similarities in the structure and governance of the communities lead Vermes to speculate that the early Jewish Christians modeled their institutions on those of the Essenes. The two communities also shared a belief in the healing of all debilitating conditions, including death, for the faithful at the world's end.

Finally, Vermes is struck by the diversity and originality that characterized what the Indian poet P. Lal has called scribal *transcreations* of older texts at the Essene community of Qumran. That freedom of scriptural expression leads Vermes to speculate that the utter subjugation of the Jewish state to the Romans after the general (later emperor) Titus destroyed the temple at Jerusalem (70 C.E.) led the rabbis to hunker down and enforce a nononsense orthodoxy that included mandatory allegiance to a received Scripture. This point of view seemingly passed along to the Christian Church in its various manifestations in Europe and Asia. The ecclesiastical historian Karen L. King, however,

points to the survival and proliferation of a more diverse early Christian literature such as GNOSTIC APROCHRYPHA AND PSEUDEPIGRAPHA before the official definition of a New Testament canon.

Owing to many complexities, including scholarly ineptitude and rivalries, translation and publication of all the Dead Sea Scrolls has been a scandalously drawn-out affair.

Bibliography
Davies, Phillip R., et al., editors. *The Complete World of the Dead Sea Scrolls.* New York: Thames and Hudson, 2002.

Davila, James R. *The Dead Sea Scrolls as Background to Postbiblical Judaism & Early Christianity: Papers from and International Conference at St. Andrews in 2001.* Boston: Brill, 2003.

King, Karen L. *What is Gnosticism?* Cambridge, Mass.: The Belknapp Press of Harvard University Press, 2005.

Martínez, Florentino García, ed. *The Dead Sea Scrolls Translated: The Qumran Texts in English.* Translated by Wilfred G. E. Watson. Leiden: Brill; and Grand Rapids, Mich.: Eerdmans Publishing Company, 1996.

Ullmann-Margalit, Edna. *Out of the Cave: A Philosophical Inquiry into the Dead Sea Scrolls Research.* Cambridge: Mass.: Harvard University Press, 2006.

Vermes, Geza. *Scrolls, Scriptures, and Early Christianity.* New York: T&T Clark International, 2005.

———. *The Complete Dead Sea Scrolls in English.* New York: Allen Lane, The Penguin Press, 1997.

Deipnosophists, The (Sophists at Dinner) Athenaeus of Naucratis (early third century C.E.) *Greek prose writer*

Most of what we know about Athenaeus of Naucratis must be ferreted out or inferred from the pages of his rambling, sometimes comic, partly lost cookbook in the Greek language, *The Deipnosophists* (Sophists at Dinner). It is the oldest book on the subject of cooking that survives largely intact in a Western European language. From its pages, we learn that Athenaeus was an Egyptian of Greek extraction born late in the second century C.E., in the city of Naucratis. Later he moved to Rome during a period in which intellectually fashionable Romans admired all things Greek, learned the Greek language fluently, and preferred their reading material in that language.

The pages of *The Deipnosohists* reveal their author as an omnivorous reader and an indefatigable collector of anecdotes that he weaves together into an invaluable if disorganized treasure trove of otherwise unavailable information about the ancient world. All of these data are loosely arranged about the central topic of food. The standard, bilingual edition of this ancient work runs to seven substantial volumes.

Oddly, recipes rarely appear in the work, but the practices of Greek, Persian, Roman, and especially Sicilian cooks—and many others too—appear frequently. We learn as well about their specialties, and we are treated to descriptions of elaborate, expensive feasts and the entertainments that accompanied them. We hear about the music and the instruments on which it was played. Athenaeus also describes the furnishings of the dining rooms and the menu cards that the guests were given. He discusses good and bad wines, gluttony and fastidiousness, and he considers the medical treatments available to cope with ailments arising from excess eating and drinking or from over-dieting.

In planning his work, Athenaeus had before him the models of PLATO's SYMPOSIUM and the *symposium* of XENOPHON OF ATHENS. Both of those works, however, focus the readers' attention on the drinking party that follows dinner, the *symposium*: from Greek *potos* (drink) and *sym* (together). Plato's is tightly woven, focusing on the content of the conversation and on the personalities of the guests. Xenophon reports conversations collected from several banquets in different times and places.

Athenaeus seems at first to want to adopt Plato's plan, but Athenaeus's compulsion toward inclusiveness stretches his description of both the main course and the drinking party of his first banquet at Rome, taking 10 of the 15 manuscript scrolls that contain the version of the work transmitted to us. A second banquet runs from book 11 to book 14, and Athenaeus squeezes a third banquet into book 15.

Among the attendees at Athenaeus's banqueting we find, of course, the host, Larensios. He, like several others present, is named for a real person, the Roman pontifex minor (whose function was a priestly one), Publius Livius Larensis. Also present at the gathering was one of the most famous physicians of the ancient world, GALEN of Pergamum, whose medical writings formed a standard part of the curriculum for physicians at least until the end of the 18th century. The principal speaker in the discussions is a politician and jurist, Ulpian of Tyre, who wrote voluminously on legal subjects and who died at the hands of soldiers in the imperial palace in 228 C.E.—a detail that Athenaeus spares his readers.

Against Ulpian, Athenaeus sets up a foil, the cynic (see CYNICISM) philosopher Cynulcus, who opposes Ulpian with uncouth, ironic mockery. Affecting to loathe widely learned persons, Cynulcus nonetheless reveals that he is one of them. Joining him in his attacks, but also turning on Cynulcus from time to time, we find Myrtilus of Thessaly, who outdoes Cynulcus by loathing all philosophers.

One must understand that although Athenaeus assigns the names of real persons to some of his banqueters, their performances are not based on actual occurrences. They merely provide an extended opportunity for Athenaeus to pursue his encyclopedic interests. The fact, for example, that Cynulcus and Myrtilus are paired invokes a literary commonplace also evident in the Menippean SATIRE of the New Comedy in Greece (see COMEDY IN GREECE AND ROME). This becomes self-evident when one discovers that Myrtilus is the son of a shoemaker. Cynics and shoemakers are often paired by their poverty and humble origins as in *The* FERRYBOAT of LUCIAN. Many other diners are also present.

The interaction among the characters, one must fairly say, is not the principal focus of interest in *The Deipnosohists*. The conversation principally consists of the pedantic citation and recitation of stories and incidents from a seemingly inexhaustible store of miscellaneous erudition. Sometimes, however, the stories the diners tell are genuinely amusing, as when in book 2 Athenaeus has one of his speakers tell a story attributed to Timaeus of Tauromenium. A group of young men got so drunk that they imagined themselves at sea on a sinking ship, though they were really in town in a house. They nonetheless threw out all the furniture and crockery to lighten the load. In the morning, when the town constabulary answered neighbors' complaints, the officers took pity on the still inebriated young fellows and told them to make sacrifices at the local altars as soon as they had sobered up. The lads promised to do so if they ever made port. Moreover, they looked upon the constables as their saviors and as sea deities and promised to construct altars to them.

Apart from descriptions of cooks and cookery and the recognition of the connection between civilization and fine dining, then, and aside from the occasional retellable vignette, the main value of *The Deipnosophists* arises from its contribution to our knowledge of matters that would have been forgotten without it. It makes important contributions to what we know about both Middle and New Comedy in Greece and broadens our knowledge of Greek life both during the classical ages and later, when Rome ruled the Hellenistic world.

Bibliography

Athenaeus. *The Deipnosophists.* 7 vols. New York: G. P. Putnam's Sons, 1927.

Demosthenes (ca. 384–322 B.C.E.) *Greek prose writer*

The greatest orator and one of the greatest statesmen of democratic Athens, Demosthenes was the son of a manufacturer of furniture and swords. His father died in Demosthenes' early childhood, leaving the boy a sizable fortune and appointing three guardians to oversee it. The guardians wasted much of the lad's inheritance. Early perceiving their breach of trust and determined to have justice, a very young Demosthenes began practicing oratory and rhetoric, studying under Isaeus, an expert on inheritance law.

Whether or not a story is true respecting his practicing oratory with stones in his mouth, he is known to have overcome a speech defect. By the time he was 20, he felt ready and sued his guardians. He won, and after further suits, he recovered a little of his money from Aphobus and Onetor, two of the guardians. His speeches on these occasions survive.

Owing to a fast-growing reputation for legal oratory, Demosthenes became a professional writer of orations for several private clients engaged in litigation, and he also instructed others in litigation and oratory. Apparently his personality was waspish and dour, perhaps influenced by the unfriendly litigiousness among politicians that characterized the legislators and city leaders of his time. In his professional capacity, he helped the statesmen of his era in their public disagreements with one another, and some of the speeches he wrote for such persons drip with vitriol. The orations of the foregoing sort divide themselves into those addressing private matters and those addressing semipublic matters. A theme emerges from them that became the center of Demosthenes' political stand once he began in 354 to speak for himself—as he did in that year's oration "On the Navy Boards"—on matters important to the Athenian state. Athens, as the historian J. H. Vince describes Demosthenes' stand, must remain "committed to a policy of honor and high ideals."

Athens in the mid-fourth century B.C.E. found itself in a complex and delicate military and political situation. Though the Athenians depended on a citizen soldiery, they had successfully confounded Theban ambitions on the Grecian peninsula, but subsequently Athens had lost her most important possessions. Though weakened, the Persian Empire remained a continuing threat, as did bands of marauding mercenaries.

Most dangerous of all, the expansionary ambitions of Philip of Macedon and his son Alexander the Great, though still not entirely clear, loomed on the horizon and excited Demosthenes' prescient alarm. Philip was building a virtually invincible professional army—one that his successor Alexander would forge into the most formidable pre-Roman military force of the ancient world. To a probably foredoomed effort to counter that force, sometimes with skillful diplomacy and alliance building and sometimes with military action, Demosthenes dedicated the rest of his public life, and the balance of his surviving oratory attests to his efforts to contain and restrain Macedonian ambitions.

Sixty of Demosthenes' orations survive. In addition, we possess an erotic essay that he penned, several letters, and 56 paragraphs called *Exordia*. These are the opening paragraphs of speeches. Some of these appear in the orator's surviving speeches, and some of these introduced works now lost. In this reference work, it is possible to describe only the most celebrated of Demosthenes' orations to give a sense of his subjects and method. Because of his long-standing feud with Æschines and universal admiration of the speech, I have selected for this purpose his oration On the Crown, which provides an outstanding example of his art.

Eventually Demosthenes was accused of misappropriation of public funds. The Greek historical biographer Plutarch suggests that Demosthenes took a bribe in exchange for his silence. The matter is vexed, and the statesman's intentions may well have been honorable, but the Athenians found him guilty. He was fined two and half times the allegedly misused amount and, like his enemy Æschines, went into exile. Eventually the citizens of Athens recalled him and found a way to remit the fine they had imposed.

The political scenario, however, that Demosthenes most feared for Athens had come to pass. Alexander of Macedonia (Alexander the Great) had made himself the master of all Greece. As a result, Demosthenes and all the members of his party who had opposed Macedonian ambitions were sentenced to death.

According to Plutarch, Demosthenes sought refuge in the temple of Poseidon in Calauria. There a search party sent by Alexander's general, Antipater, discovered him. Rather than be taken and subjected to whatever punishments might be in store for him, Demosthenes took poison and died before the sea god's altar.

Bibliography

Plutarch. *Greek and Roman Lives*. Translated by John Dryden with revisions by Arthur Hugh Clough. Mineola, N.Y.: Dover Publications, 2005.

Vince, J. H. et al., trans. *Demosthenes*. 6 vols. Cambridge, Mass.: Harvard University Press, 1954.

De Rerum Natura (On the Nature of Things) Lucretius (ca. first century C.E.)

A poem in six books explaining the materialistic views that Lucretius and Epicurus shared about the nature of the universe, *On the Nature of Things* excoriates religion as the principal blight responsible for clouding the human intellect. That view of the misguidance offered by religion does not prevent Lucretius from invoking mythology or from addressing Venus, the goddess of love, as the muse of his poem. Love, as he thinks, is after all the force that drives the animal and vegetable kingdoms, making the earth productive with life. From an allegorical point of view, moreover, Venus is the goddess that brings peace.

Book 1

Lucretius promises to explain how nature brings into being and at last dissolves into their atomic constituents all living creatures. He credits Epicurus with being the first to expose the disadvantages that religion entails for people and the first to put down religion by suggesting that its deceptions, because they prevent people from recognizing the truth of natural processes, are in fact impious. He cites human sacrifice as an example of such impiety. Such sacrifice destroys something brought into being by the natural processes the gods have established.

Lucretius exhorts people not to fear terrors after death. Body and soul die together, and there exists no afterlife, no judging, no rewards, and no punishments. On the contrary, his first principle holds that no *thing* is produced by divine power from nothing. All things require specific seeds for their generation, and all things die or dissolve, returning their elements to the common pool. Those elements eventually recombine to form new things, living or inanimate, sentient or insentient.

Lucretius is not an atheist. He believes (or says he believes) in the gods. He merely agrees with Epicurus that as immortal and perfect beings, gods must be perfectly happy and totally unconcerned with human affairs.

The poet continues to discuss the composition of wind, water, and solids, concluding that all things are composed of a mixture of atoms and void—an assertion that in a sense presages the experimental knowledge of modern science. Lucretius's predecessor, Epicurus, grants that some sorts of matter may be everlasting and recombinable into new objects when their old objects wither away. He also asserts that the survival of anything after the countless ages that the universe has existed proves that something must be indestructible.

The notion of the persistence of species interests Lucretius, but of course evolutionary change does not occur to him.

Space, he argues, must be infinite in all directions and must contain an infinite store of matter.

Book 2

In the second book, Lucretius argues that, of all the things that men value, only reason is genuinely profitable, for only reason can overcome human appetites and superstition. As for matter, it is always in motion, always being tossed about in infinite space, and all things accessible to human perception are formed from it, though its motion is not always apparent to people.

Lucretius argues against those who believe that the gods made the world with the benefit of people in mind, citing the many faults that, from a human perspective, exist in the universe. He cites the multiplicity of forms within the species of things as evidence of the unpredictable variability of the universe, and he argues for a similar variety in the shapes of their essential atoms. Moreover, Lucretius attributes the pleasure or displeasure that human beings take in different substances to the conformity or nonconformity of the substances' constituent atoms to human sensory apparatus.

Lucretius attributes qualities such as hardness and softness to the relative degree to which atoms are "hooked" together. The harder substances are composed of closely hooked atoms and the softer of more loosely hooked atoms. Nonetheless, he argues, there is a limited number of shapes that atoms can come in since the things that are composed of them are in fact limited in their variability. Though he does not use this example, absolute zero sets the limit for the possibility of cold, and at the other extreme, Lucretius would argue for a limit beyond which temperature cannot rise.

Within those limits, Lucretius argues for the variability of speciation and acknowledges that, like individuals, species come into being and pass away. As for extant species, the earth—which Lucretius recognizes as round—is properly venerated as their source and mother, not some extraterrestrial deity. Similarly, Lucretius denies the possibility of the kinds of shape-shifting of one thing into another or of double-natured things such as the Minotaur or other monsters that OVID traces in his *METAMORPHOSES*.

Lucretius argues at some length that atoms must be colorless, and he associates the perception of color with the sense of touch rather than sight. He also posits that atoms are without temperature, sound, moisture, odor, or sensibility. Sensation, he suggests, is a quality that arises only in living creatures composed of the insensate atoms. The physical heavens—that is, the sidereal universe—and Earth are the parents of the human species. No intervening deity is necessary to accomplish the requisite natural processes. Upon the deaths of Earth-born creatures, their atoms are eventually dispersed and become available for recombination into other forms.

Given the infinitude of space, Lucretius argues, other worlds beyond our own must exist. In making that assertion, Lucretius anticipates the multiplicity of universes suggested by modern physics and string theory.

As he ends Book 2, Lucretius emphasizes that nature does not require gods to operate creatively. Natural processes and infinite time are enough to account for all existence. Similarly, however, all things and all natural processes also wear out and decay. The human race and animals and plants are all subject to this same fate. All sentient—and, for that matter, insentient—nature is destined for the tomb.

Book 3

The third book begins with an encomium to Epicurus as Lucretius's intellectual forebear who has driven away the terrors of superstition by assuring the world of the self-satisfaction and happiness of the immortal gods and their utter disinterest in the affairs of human beings. Lucretius next examines the nature of mind and spirit, finding both to be natural functions of the body and coexistent with it. He locates the mind in the breast because of the changes in feeling that occur there in moments of terror or ecstasy, and he concludes that the spirit is associated with the mind, and that both directly influence the state of the body. He believes the mind to be composed of very small, round, weightless particles. Lucretius affirms that mind is composed of four substances: breath, heat, air, and a fourth nameless and extremely tenuous substance that disperses the effects of mind through the body. The blending of these four substances is critical to sensation. Moreover, their admixture varies from species to species and individual to individual and the relative proportions accounts for differences in temperaments. Lions have more of heat, stags of cold breath, and so forth. Human predispositions are traceable to similar causes.

If, however, these predispositions lead to faults in human beings, reason can overcome those faults. Soul and body must dwell together for either to live. Separated, both die. Lucretius points to the failure of the mental faculties as well as the physical during the aging process to illustrate the codependency of body, mind, and soul. The influence of alcohol and the results of epilepsy also reveal codependency. Thus, when the body dies by degrees, losing capacity after capacity, the soul does likewise and does not remain intact to leave the body at death.

After listing examples of the death of the soul in bodies dismembered on the field of battle, Lucretius argues against the immortality of the soul on the grounds that it retains no memories from a state prior to an individual's physical birth. Moreover, the similarity of physical and character traits from one generation of animals to the next—fierceness in lions, for example—demonstrates that mind and body are coexistent. Like the soul, the mind cannot survive outside the body. From time to time, Lucretius rejects mythical stories, like that of a crowd of immortal souls awaiting mortal bodies to transmigrate into.

Having made his case, Lucretius asserts that, given the truth of all he has said, death means nothing to human beings. They experience nothing memorable before birth, and they will experience nothing after death. That which does not exist can feel nothing. If all ends in sleep and rest, the poet asks, where is the bitterness in that?

As for the punishments myth ascribes to hell, they exist rather in life. Some are torn by passion; others have their ambitions disappointed. Others still are discontented no matter what they have or achieve. Those punished by guilty consciences suffer their pangs on earth. Ascribing such torments to some eternal place of punishment is no more than fearful projection of what for many are their just deserts. The wise go gently into the good night of death. Those who suffer from the consequences of their appetites or behavior would do well to seek the consolations of philosophy, which would teach them to lighten and bear their burdens. The net effect of book 3 is to reconcile people to the realities of the human condition.

Book 4

Lucretius begins Book 4 with a none-too-modest encomium on the power of his verse and its benefit for those of his readers who allow themselves to become enlightened by it.

Having clarified mind and soul for his readers, Lucretius now turns his attention to the phenomenon of vision. He explains that very thin, colored films are continually thrown from the surfaces of things. When they encounter the organs of human vision, people see them. When they encounter reflectors such as mirrors or the still surface of a pool, they are reproduced almost unchanged. The poet lingers over the necessary fineness of the component atoms of such images and the speed at which they travel, and he marvels at how quickly such images reach our eyes. By similar means we hear, touch, taste, and smell.

Lucretius explains that distortions in human perception of distant images arise from the corners of the images being rubbed off by their passage through the air. He accounts more accurately for the reasons that our shadows move with us. A substantial discussion addresses optical illusions and what we today understand as phenomena arising from the refraction of light. He also discusses our seeming perceptions while dreaming.

Lucretius argues that logical reasoning finally depends on the senses. (If he were writing today, he would doubtless include as sensory extensions the microscopes, telescopes, other scientific instruments, and perhaps sophisticated mathematical computations that allow us to understand better the micro and macro components of physical reality.)

Next he treats the other senses, explaining sound—by which he principally means the voice—and hearing. He explains the phenomenon of echo and attributes myths relating to nymphs as nonscientific attempts to account for echo. Then Lucretius passes on to taste, explaining it as the result of food particles being squeezed through the pores of the palate. Smooth particles, he thinks, give rise to pleasant and rough particles to unpleasant tastes, but the pleasure one derives from flavor ends at the palate. He also accounts for differences in food preferences among various species and from individual to individual and for the way that health or illness affects one's perceptions of flavor.

Treating smell, Lucretius explains that odors are made of larger particles than sights or sounds, and therefore are harder to perceive and do not travel as far. Different creatures react differently to different odors, such as vultures to carrion and bees to honey.

Next, Lucretius accounts for mental images—composed of even finer particles than the physical ones. Mental images often arise from recombining physical ones that have entered the mind. These combinations, Lucretius thinks, account for the notions of ghosts, centaurs, three-headed dogs like Cerberus, and other double-natured creatures such as Scylla (see OVID's *METAMORPHOSES*). Such combinations also account for dreams.

The poet then considers conscious thought and the ability of the mind to conjure up instantly that which it wishes to address. He concludes that all the images (representing the input of every sense) in the mind are instantly accessible, but that the mind must voluntarily attend to them to call them up in useful sequences. An inattentive mind may find itself considering irrelevant images and unintentionally draw false conclusions.

Digestion and motion now occupy Lucretius's attention. Food replaces the body's waste products and fuels the body the way coal fuels a furnace. Drink extinguishes the heat that the stomach generates in digestion. Motion results from our willfully emulating the images of motion that we have perceived. When one wishes to move, the image strikes the mind, the mind strikes the spirit, and the spirit strikes the body, which moves.

There follows a discussion of sleep and dreaming. Sleep occurs when a part of the spirit withdraws from the body and another part, necessary to continued life, sinks deeper into the body. The mind dreams of the interests of the day, says the poet. Likewise, horses dream about racing, dogs about hunting or guarding, birds about flying, and human beings about that which most concerns them. In youth, this is likely to be sex.

The same "seed" that causes young people to dream about passion is responsible for the onset of waking physical desire and for the mind being wounded with the pangs of love. There follows a discourse on lovesickness and its ill effects. Even when desire is satisfied, it soon returns. Lovesickness wastes life, strength, and wealth. It leads to consuming jealousy and a guilty conscience. Given the delusions that accompany falling in love, Lucretius counsels that one avoid it altogether. Love deludes the lover into thinking that his beloved is the most beautiful of all women. Lucretius thinks that one woman is much like another. Moreover, he thinks that women know it and are at pains to conceal the fact.

Nonetheless, women as well as men, he finally grants, are subject to passion. So are the members of the animal kingdom. He next discusses the reasons that some children take after their fathers and some their mothers and some resemble both parents. This depends on the proportion of seed received from each parent.

Barrenness results from the seed of one parent or the other being either too thick or too thin. This situation may change in the course of a marriage, or it may be resolved by changing one's spouse. The sort of food one eats can also influence fertility, as can the position assumed when copulating.

True love, Lucretius concludes, arises from the habit of loving.

Book 5

Book 5 begins with another encomium on the benefit that human beings derive from the thought of Epicurus, who freed them from the chains of theocratic superstition and modeled a way of life free from debauchery and excess. Then follows Lucretius's declaration that he follows in Epicurus's footsteps and expands his work by teaching nature's laws.

The poet continues by announcing his intention of showing that the universe, too, had a beginning and will have an end. (For Lucretius the universe, though infinite, was nonetheless geocentric.) He announces his intention to account for the existence of matter and its arrangement into earth, sky, sea, stars, the sun, and the moon. He promises to account for the variety of human languages and for the origins of the fear of the gods in human hearts.

Lucretius also means to explain planetary and stellar motions and to disprove any notion that they are in any way volitional or divinely arranged for human convenience. He argues that the universe and everything in it will be destroyed. He pronounces it impossible that the gods can exist in the universe. Rather, he says, they live in a kind of hyperspace between universe and universe and do not intervene in natural processes. As they have no interest whatever in human creatures, the gods did not create the universe for people. Doing so could bring them no possible benefit.

Rather, the world is the accidental product of the movement of atoms. Or, if it is not, some other automatic mechanism explains its existence, for the gods would derive no benefit from having created the world or the people in it. Moreover, the world is far too imperfect to have been the product of divine creation. Lucretius cites a series of such imperfections, including disease and natural disasters. Most significantly, the world is itself mortal, as one can see from the ongoing process of the destruction of parts of it.

Lucretius says that if one believes the legends about the prior destruction of the earth by flood and fire, that destruction proves its mortality and susceptibility to disaster. As for the earth's beginning, he ascribes it to an accidental assemblage of atoms and matter that eventually compressed into the universe as we have it. The details here are not crucial, since the processes of planetary formation are better understood now than then. The central issue for Lucretius is that no divine fiat brought the world into being.

Recalling that for Lucretius Earth was the center of the universe, a reader observes him struggle with various possibilities to explain the apparent celestial motions caused by Earth's rotation. Air currents, tides of ether, or even the quest for food are among the possibilities the poet offers. His estimates of the sizes of celestial bodies—all of which he thinks are about the size we perceive—are totally inaccurate, but he admits that he is not sure about these matters. Instead, he offers a variety of alternatives that occur to him to explain the observable phenomenon of the sky's visible motion.

The variable lengths of days and nights equally mystify the poet, but again he offers theories to account for them. Perhaps the sun runs slightly different routes, some longer, some shorter. Perhaps air is thicker in some places than in others and makes the sun slower or faster. He does better with the moon, for the reflection of sunlight as the source of the moon's illumination does occur to him. As he is not sure, however, he also theorizes the possibility that the moon is darkened by the shadow of a passing satellite—not a bad guess for a lunar eclipse—and he suggests that a part of the moon emits light and a part does not. His wildest surmise suggests the production of a brand new moon each day, each one emitting a different amount of light. Now Lucretius turns his attention to solar and lunar eclipses, and this time the possibilities he entertains include the right ones in both instances.

Next Lucretius attempts to account for the emergence of life on a hitherto lifeless earth. Grasses came first, he says. Then came trees, and then birds and animals, arising in different unspecified places by means of unspecified processes. He guesses wrong when he opines that animals could not have arisen out of salt pools but right when he asserts that they could not have fallen from the sky. While much uncertainty surrounds his account of the origins of animal life, of one thing Lucretius is certain. All the metamorphoses that mythology reports in its discussion of centaurs and other monsters made from the combination of two or more species such as Scylla, who is a girl-dogs-fish creature, never existed and could not exist.

Likewise, there are no rivers of gold, flowers that bloom with jewels, and other such wonders.

On the other hand, he declares, early men were hardier, lived longer, and lived naked in unheated caves. They were more likely than in Lucretius's day to be eaten by wild beasts, but less likely to die in battle against other people. Then civilization began to grow. Dwellings and clothing appeared. Social contracts were informally or formally drawn that let neighbors dwell in peace and mutual amity.

Lucretius next speculates on the origin of language, which he believes arose from a codification of the sorts of sounds that animals and birds use to express their emotional states. He locates the origin of fire in lightning or in the accidental rubbing together of dry sticks or branches—dispelling the myth of the Titan Prometheus (see *PROMETHEUS BOUND*). People learned to cook from watching things soften in the heat of the sun.

Next, highly capable men began to organize societies, and kings built cities to house and protect groups of neighbors and their animals and to store their crops. They also established systems of redistribution of goods among their subjects. Then gold was discovered, and the desire to accumulate wealth followed. This in turn led to dissension, warfare, assassination, and crime. People responded with laws and magistrates for the general well-being.

Next, says Lucretius, men created gods, fabricated idols, and attributed human characteristics to their creations. They imagined them to be both alive and immortal. Then, however, people attributed to gods their own predisposition toward wrathfulness, and thereafter religion became a bane to the human race. True piety that honors real gods, says Lucretius, arises from surveying all things "with mind at peace" and from understanding and accepting the natural processes of the universe. Nonetheless, he understands how natural disaster and bad conscience both terrorize human beings and lead them to attempt to curry favor with the gods through prayer and sacrifice.

Continuing his natural history of the development of human society in the world, Lucretius suggests that people accidentally discovered metals and their properties of being forged and shaped into useful and decorative objects. He speculates that bronze and copper were more valuable than gold, and then iron replaced bronze. Animals were domesticated, and people discovered which ones could and could not be tamed. Lucretius imagines in detail a scenario in which lions and boars throw friend and foe alike into confusion as they frighten horses and draught oxen and indiscriminately attack anyone. He talks of the development of weaving and the art of cultivating fields. Both clothing and diet improved as a result of such innovations. Lucretius imagines that singing developed from human imitation of the birds, and then that people learned to make and play various musical instruments.

The scenarios that Lucretius ascribes to human history introduce a novel concept, the idea of technological progress. The Greek and Roman religious view of things imagined that an idyllic golden age came first and that it was followed by ages of silver, bronze, and iron—each one worse than those prior. Lucretius sees things getting better and better.

Book 6

As Book 6 begins, Lucretius credits Athens with introducing and disseminating the cultivation of grain crops and with promulgating laws for governing the state. He then returns to his praise of Epicurus as the great discoverer of truth. His philosophy encouraged people to live modestly in amity with their neighbors and freed his followers from the burden of religious superstition. Errors such as attributing natural disasters to the will of the gods keep people in a state of continual fear, says Lucretius. Moreover, such superstitious claptrap degrades the true gods. Fortunately, in their omnipotence, the true gods are not susceptible to insult, and they are neither wrathful nor vengeful. Human beings should therefore approach their altars with their minds at peace.

Many of the phenomena that have caused human beings to ascribe vindictiveness and wrath to divine temperaments arise from phenomena observable in the sky. Thunder and lightening, windstorms and hurricanes occur, and since people do not understand their causes, they attribute them to divine wrath. Lucretius therefore undertakes to offer natural explanations for them.

Thunder results, he says, from clouds' clashing together or when a wind shatters a cloud like a popped balloon. Lightning has the same source if the clashing clouds contain the "seeds" of fire. The clouds' collision strikes out lightning as a flint strikes sparks from metal. When a cloud bursts, the same phenomenon results.

Lucretius also considers the source and effects of thunderbolts—phenomena that the religion of the Greeks and Romans ascribed to the wrath of Zeus and his Roman counterpart, Jupiter. Thunderbolts emanate from thick and piled-up clouds, which are especially full of the seeds of fire. The winds whirling inside the clouds collect the seeds until the thunderbolt is formed and then drive it forth. After further speculations of this sort, Lucretius firmly asserts that thunderbolts are utterly natural, not supernatural, phenomena. He bolsters his argument by asking why, if the gods cast the thunderbolts, they do not strike the guilty.

The poet continues by discussing the source and nature of waterspouts, rainfall, rainbows, snow, wind, hail, frost, and ice. He also offers natural explanations for earthquakes, which he attributes to subterranean watercourses and winds. Lucretius does not neglect volcanic eruptions, attributing them to superheated subterranean wind that eventually melts basalt and blows it together with unmelted rock into the air. When enough matter has been ejected, the sea rushes in to quench the fires within, and the cycle begins anew.

Lucretius next offers suggestions to explain the annual flooding of the Nile, and one of them—rainfall near the river's source—has since proved correct. He also considers places, such as the region of the Avernan lake near

Cumae outside Naples, where the concentration of invisible volcanic gases still proves fatal to birds. Though the superstitious consider such places entrances to the underworld and the realm of the spirits of the dead, Lucretius asserts that the phenomenon is utterly natural, pointing out that many natural elements prove poisonous to life. In support of that argument, he provides many examples.

After discussing possible reasons for daily variations in the temperatures of certain bodies of water, Lucretius turns his attention to the nature of the magnet, whose force he attributes to invisible particles—an explanation not really too far off the mark. When he tries to explain the details of magnetic attraction, however, Lucretius is forced to exercise excessive and not very convincing ingenuity. He does report that the force of magnets can sometimes attract and sometimes repel.

Addressing the causes of diseases, Lucretius considers the seeds of illness to be airborne and capable of settling on water and on crops. He gives a graphic description of a plague in Egypt that appears to have been smallpox. It rivals the famous description that Giovanni Boccaccio gave in his *Decameron* of the bubonic plague at Florence during the 14th century. According to Lucretius, so devastating was the plague he describes that ordinary arrangements for dealing with the dead were rendered useless. Temples and sanctuaries were so overwhelmed with corpses that, even in devout Egypt, both the power of the gods and their worship were disregarded. With this somber description, Lucretius ends *De Rerum Natura*.

Bibliography

Lucretius. *De Rerum Natura*. Translated by W. H. D. Rouse. Cambridge, Mass.: Harvard University Press, 1953.

————. *On the Nature of Things*. Translated by Cyril Bailey. New York: Barnes and Noble Books, 2005.

————. *On the Nature of Things*. Translated by W. E. Leonard. Mineola, N.Y.: Dover Publications, 2004.

deus ex machina   See CONVENTIONS OF GREEK DRAMA.

Dialogues of the Dead Lucian of Samosata (ca. 150 C.E.)

In his *Dialogues of the Dead*, LUCIAN OF SAMOSATA's characteristic method strips the shades of people in the underworld of all the pretenses, wealth, and differences in status and reputation that distinguished one person from another. Even differences in physical beauty and intelligence are gone when nothing survives but skull and bones and mindlessness.

In the 13th dialogue of the collection, the shade of Diogenes the Cynic (see CYNICISM) encounters that of Alexander the Great. The two had been acquainted in life. Diogenes expresses some surprise that Alexander has died like everyone else, since, as a matter of policy—as he elsewhere tells his father, Philip of Macedon—Alexander had encouraged the story that he was the son of the Egyptian god Ammon, a counterpart of Zeus.

It appears that Alexander himself had half believed the stories of divine paternity, but his death has convinced him that all such rubbish is "moonshine." He tells Diogenes, however, that his corpse is currently lying in Babylon but will soon be moved to Egypt, where he will be counted among the gods.

Diogenes accuses Alexander of still nursing vain hopes of developing into an Osiris or an Anubis—that is, into Egyptian deities who were resurrected from the dead. The philosopher reminds Alexander of the riches and veneration that were his while he lived, and Alexander weeps. Diogenes expresses surprise that Alexander's teacher, ARISTOTLE, did not better instruct the king concerning the impermanence of fortune's favors. Alexander proclaims Aristotle "the craftiest of all flatterers" and an "imposter."

Diogenes prescribes deep and repeated drinks of the waters of forgetfulness from the river Lethe to relieve Alexander's melancholy nostalgia for the trappings of his earthly life and to protect him from those in the underworld that still bear him grudges.

In the dialogue that precedes the one above, two famous generals dispute over the order of precedence that each should be accorded in Hades. One is, again, Alexander; the second is Hannibal, the Carthaginian general who threatened Rome. Also participating in the discussion are the Roman general, Scipio Africanus, who eventually defeated Hannibal, and one of the judges of Hades, Minos. Hannibal is able to participate in the debate since, he says, he has improved his time in the underworld by learning Greek. The two rivals present their cases, citing their accomplishments. As Minos is about to judge, Scipio interrupts, presents his credentials, and ranks Alexander first, himself second, and Hannibal third. The equanimity with which a judge of the dead in Hades concurs in Scipio's ranking underscores its utter meaninglessness under the circumstances.

Even the highly respected SOCRATES occasionally suffers the edge of Lucian's wit in the *Dialogues of the Dead*. In the 21st dialogue, the three-headed guard dog of Hades, Cerberus, expresses the view that the equanimity with which Socrates faced death was merely a sham act put on for effect. Once the philosopher found himself among the dead, his demeanor was entirely different as he wailed, wept, and gnashed his teeth. In the 20th dialogue, the shade of Socrates encounters that of the Cynic Menippus—a favorite character of Lucian's and one who figures prominently in many of his works. Socrates inquires what the Athenians think of him. Menippus replies that it is Socrates' good fortune to be considered remarkable and omniscient—though in truth Menippus thinks that Socrates knew absolutely nothing. Socrates responds that he kept telling the Athenians precisely that, but that they thought he intended his disclaimer of knowledge as irony.

The *Dialogues of the Dead* make abundantly clear that Lucian's skepticism allows no exceptions to death, the common fate of all humanity.

Bibliography

Lucian. *The Works of Lucian*. Vol. 1. Translated by H. W. Fowler and F. G. Fowler. Oxford: The Clarendon Press, 1905.

Dialogues of the Gods Lucian of Samosata (ca. 150 C.E.)

In choosing the dialogue as the vehicle for his SATIRE, LUCIAN OF SAMOSATA selected a particularly effective form. He took the dialogue, which PLATO had developed as a means of enlivening philosophical discourse, and interwove within it the spirit of comedic discourse from the stage of the Greek New Comedy (see COMEDY IN GREECE AND ROME). This combination resulted in a flexible satiric instrument with a broad register of effect. His dialogues can elicit an amused and sympathetic smile—as is the case with many of his *Dialogues of the Gods*. Lucian's dialogues can also engage both the intellect and a reader's sense of irony, as they do in "Zeus the Tragedian." Beyond that, some of Lucian's other dialogues can.ne in on moral issues in ways that evoke a deeply sardonic response from thoughtful readers, as is the case with the satirist's "Voyage to the Underworld."

In *Dialogues of the Gods*, Lucian elaborates on stories from mythology, setting the Olympian gods of the Greeks in circumstances that deflate their awe-inspiring qualities and expose their all-too-human foibles. In picturing them, Lucian draws on HOMER and HESIOD for their attributes and attitudes, and for their appearance, he draws on on famous statues of them that were fabricated 500–600 years before his time. For example, in the seventh dialogue of the collection, Lucian uses satire to imagine a conversation that occurs between the blacksmith of the gods, Hephaestus, and the sun god, Apollo, on the occasion of the birth of Hermes, son of Maia. Hermes would become both the messenger of the gods and the patron deity of thieves.

As Hephaestus exclaims like a bachelor uncle over the sweet baby, Apollo takes an altogether more jaundiced view of the infant. Hardly able to stand, baby Hermes has already stolen the sea god Poseidon's trident and the sword of the war god Ares. Hephaestus remains unconvinced until he notices that his own blacksmith's tongs are missing. Hermes, moreover, has thrown the god of love, Eros, in a wrestling match, and has invented a tortoiseshell lyre.

With wings on his feet, baby Hermes can transport himself anywhere in a twinkling, and his mother says he will not spend a night at home but instead goes off to herd the dead around the underworld. Convinced at last, Hephaestus sets about finding his tongs in the infant's crib. One is amused at the surprising ineptitude of the Olympians and at the enterprising energy of the baby god.

We find much more elaborate satire in "Zeus the Tragedian," or, as the translator Lionel Casson has rendered it, "Zeus the Opera Star." Here the nub of the piece arises from the conflicting viewpoints of the Stoic and the Epicurean philosophers concerning the authority or even the existence of gods in the universe. The style of the piece arises in part from Lucian's tongue-in-cheek parody of the CONVENTIONS OF GREEK DRAMA, with its sometimes overblown rhetoric and declamatory bluster combined with such inconsequential and homey activity as talking to oneself and pacing back and forth. In part, too, the style derives from Lucian's picturing the gods as famous statues representing them and from his portraying them as living on the smoke from human beings' burnt offerings.

As the dialogue begins, Zeus and Athena exchange high-flown, worried rhetoric until Zeus's wife Hera reproves them for posturing when she knows that Zeus is merely in love again. For once, however, she is wrong. Zeus is worried that human beings may stop worshipping the gods. That fateful decision hangs on the outcome of an ongoing debate between the Stoic philosopher Timocles and Damis the Epicurean. Hera admits the justification for the tragic style of speech.

Zeus calls for a general meeting of divinities. Hermes calls them together. His first attempt is regarded as too simple, given the gravity of the situation. He tries again, this time in the Homeric style, though he has to hum through some of the requisite metrical feet.

The gods—or rather their gold, silver, ivory, bronze, and stone images—gather and take their places according to the value of their materials. Apollo, who comes in his representation as the Colossus of Rhodes, presents a problem. The statue is too large for the auditorium, so Zeus advises him to just stoop and listen. The hall is crowded with Greek, Roman, Celtic, Egyptian, Scythian, Persian, and Thracian deities. Since they don't share a common language, Zeus signals with his hand for silence.

After outlining the problem, Zeus calls for responses from the assembly. The first to rise is Momus, who says that he cannot blame men, since the only concern that the gods have for them is whether or not they are offering the burnt sacrifices whose aromas sustain the gods. Zeus pronounces Momus a malcontent and cedes the floor to the sea god, Poseidon. Poseidon recommends striking Damis with a thunderbolt. Zeus says that such a solution rests in the hands of the fates and that the gods lack the power.

Apollo has a better idea. Though the Stoic Timocles is very bright, he makes poor speeches. He needs a mouthpiece, someone he can whisper to who will then present his ideas clearly and forcefully. Momus finds that idea ludicrous.

Apollo responds with one of his famously perplexing oracular statements that Momus interprets: Apollo is a quack and the assembly of gods brainless crickets, mules, and asses for believing him. Hermes now arrives to let the gods know that the debate is resuming. Zeus commands the hours to roll back the clouds and open heaven's gates so the gods can listen in.

Damis insists that chance, not the gods, is in charge of everything. Timocles calls on the crowd to stone him, and Damis asks why the gods do not act for themselves if his opinion is so offensive. He suggests that if the gods were real, they would visit a horrible death on a sinner like Timocles.

Timocles appeals to the orderly processes of the universe, and Damis admits the order but rejects the necessity for divine intervention to achieve it. Timocles appeals to the authority of HOMER. Damis admits his poetic superiority but rejects his credentials as an expert on the matter under debate. He then points out the skepticism of EURIPIDES, to whose authority Timocles next appeals. Finally Damis points to the multitude of gods, objects, animals, nature spirits, skulls, cups, and bowls that various people worship.

Beaten on that score, Timocles turns to oracles, and Timocles demonstrates their double-sided nature. Whatever happens, the oracle can be construed to have predicted it.

Among the gods, panic at the pending proof of their inconsequentiality becomes widespread, and Timocles begins grasping at straws. The satire ends with Timocles reduced to a laughing-stock and the gods themselves convinced of their insignificance.

Bibliography

Lucian. *Selected Dialogues.* Translated by Desmond Costa. New York: Oxford University Press, 2005.

———. *Selected Satires of Lucian.* Edited and translated by Lionel Casson. Chicago: Aldine Publishing Company, 1962.

———. *The Works of Lucian of Samosota.* 4 vols. Translated by H. W. Fowler and H. G. Fowler. Oxford: Clarendon Press, 1905.

Dialogues of the Sea Gods Lucian of Samosata (ca. 150 C.E.)

In his *Dialogues of the Sea Gods,* LUCIAN OF SAMOSATA often invigorates myths that were already ancient in his time with new details or with new points of view that ancient poets such as HOMER, HESIOD, and others had neglected to supply. Though the SATIRE of these dialogues is sometimes less pointed and less diverting than that in *DIALOGUES OF THE GODS,* Lucian's readers nonetheless benefited from the amplification of familiar stories.

Such amplification appears in Lucian's treatment of the familiar encounter of Homer's Odysseus with the Cyclops Polyphemus, whom Odysseus blinds (see *The ODYSSEY*). In Homer, Polyphemus prays to his father, the sea god Poseidon, that Odysseus be punished, and Poseidon becomes Odysseus's implacable enemy as a result. Lucian expands the Cyclops's prayer for revenge into a conversation between Polyphemus and Poseidon.

In Lucian's version, Polyphemus complains like a whimpering child to his father about Odysseus's (who at first said his name was Noman) getting the Cyclops drunk and blinding him. After all, Polyphemus had not done anything but kill and eat a few of Odysseus's crew.

Poseidon's responses to his son's complaints, though sympathetic, also reveal that he knows that Polyphemus is not very bright. When Polyphemus reports that Odysseus finally taunted by saying that "Not even Papa can put this right," the sea god replies that, while curing blindness is not within his power, those who sail the seas are. Odysseus "is not home yet," Poseidon concludes.

Polyphemus figures prominently in another dialogue featuring minor deities. Famous in the annals of classical and postclassical literature well into the Renaissance is the unrequited passion that one-eyed Polyphemus felt for the sea nymph Galatea. The story has been told and retold many times, but Lucian's take on the relationship seems unique. He imagines that Galatea has accepted Polyphemus as a lover and defends her choice when her sister Doris upbraids her.

Against Doris's complaints that Polyphemus is ugly, one-eyed, wild, and shaggy, Galatea replies that, though she does not love Polyphemus, he is a god's son, after all. She also notes that wildness and shagginess are not altogether unbecoming in a man, and that he sees as well with his one eye—attractively placed in the middle of his forehead—as most people do with two. Galatea suggests that Doris is just jealous.

At this point, the sisters' claws start showing in earnest. Doris says that Polyphemus, who is a goatherd, admires Galatea only because her white skin reminds him of milk and cheese. Galatea responds that she, at least, has a lover whereas her sisters do not. Moreover, Polyphemus is musically talented.

Doris then plays music critic, comparing Polyphemus's singing to the braying of an ass. She also mocks his homemade, tuneless instrument made from a stag's skull, and says that even Echo would not repeat the song. Moreover, Polyphemus has foolishly given Galatea a bear cub as a pet.

Galatea again reminds her sister of Doris's loneliness. Doris closes the contest by suggesting the worst thing she could wish her sister would be that she fall in love with her lover.

A final example to provide the flavor of *Dialogues of the Seagods* reveals Lucian's famous skepticism. In Homer's *Odyssey*, Odysseus must hold down the sea god Proteus, who is a shape-shifter, until Proteus has gone through all the transformations of which he is capable—transformations that include changing from his original form as a seal to a lion to water to fire. Only when he has exhausted his entire bag of tricks does Proteus yield to Odysseus's demand that he foretell the future and that he reveal the fate of Menelaus, the king of Sparta.

In Lucian's fourth dialogue in the collection, the speakers are Proteus and Menelaus. As the encounter begins, Menelaus feels puzzled. He can understand, he says, Proteus, as a seagod, being able to change into water. He can even accept the idea of Proteus's shifting into a tree or a lion. The god's capacity to become fire, however, exceeds the Spartan's capacity for belief.

Proteus suggests that he can become fire again, and Menelaus can try to confirm the evidence of his eyes by testing whether or not his flesh will burn in Proteus's fire. Menelaus rejects that course of action as too rash an experiment. Nonetheless, despite the earlier visual evidence, he still doubts the capacity of a single sea god to become *both* fire and water.

Bibliography

Lucian. *The Works of Lucian of Samosata.* Vol. 1. Translated by H. W. and F. G. Fowler. Oxford: Clarendon Press, 1905.

diatribes   See SATIRE IN GREECE AND ROME.

Didache: The Teaching of the Twelve Apostles Anonymous (ca. late first–early second century C.E.)

The manuscript containing the *Didache* (MS Hierosolymianus, preserved in the Library of the Holy Sepulcher in Constantinople/Istanbul) is also among the source documents for three other sections of THE APOSTOLIC FATHERS OF THE CHRISTIAN CHURCH: the FIRST LETTER OF CLEMENT TO THE CORINTHIANS, SECOND LETTER OF CLEMENT TO THE CORINTHIANS, and EPISTLE OF BARNABAS. Nonetheless, the *Didache's* association with the writings contained in *The Apostolic Fathers* remained undiscovered and unrecognized until 1873, when a Greek scholar, Philotheos Bryennios, recognized the text as a very early Christian document—one of the earliest now included among the writings of the Apostolic Fathers. As the scholar of early Christianity, Bart D. Ehrman, suggests, this means that the *Didache* antedates some of the books of the NEW TESTAMENT. Moreover, Ehrman points out, the work likely achieved near-canonical status among early Christians before disappearing from the record sometime following the fourth century.

The *Didache's* two titles attest to the importance of the book's contents for early churches. The first translates as above: "The Teaching of the Twelve Apostles." The second title is more specific: "The Teaching of the Lord through the Twelve Apostles to the Gentiles." Its contents lead Ehrman to think that the work is the earliest surviving manual for churches.

The work begins by contrasting two opposing paths that a person might follow through life. One is the path of life, the other of death. Those who would tread the first must follow God's commandments, particularly those enunciated by Jesus to love God, to love one's neighbor as oneself, and to avoid treating others as one would not wish to be treated. It also repeats without attribution Jesus' injunctions in the Sermon on the Mount.

The second chapter of the work repeats the prohibitions of the Ten Commandments together with some other specific injunctions against pederasty, magic, and abortion, and against duplicity of word and thought, spitefulness, and pride. It requires parents to teach children the reverential fear of God. One must hate hypocrisy. It also instructs the faithful to confess so that they do not come to prayer with "an evil conscience." This is the path of life.

The path of death includes pursuing every manner of sinfulness prohibited in the Ten Commandments. Beyond that, those who tread death's path include "corrupters of what God has fashioned who turn their backs on the needy," those who "oppress the afflicted," and those who "support the wealthy." It also seems to involve eating foodstuffs that have been sacrificed to false gods.

Beyond discriminating between the two paths, the *Didache* is the earliest surviving manual describing the proper procedures for baptism. Running water is preferred, but any water will do. Adult recipients of the sacrament of baptism should fast for a day or two in advance of the ceremony.

The eighth section advises fasting on Wednesday and Friday but not on Monday and Thursday, which are the days the "hypocrites" fast. This section also mandates praying the Lord's Prayer three times each day. Similarly, the ninth section prescribes the form of the Eucharist and limits communion to the baptized.

The faithful are next advised to welcome those who teach the truth but to turn away from others. It also suggests that itinerant apostles should be welcomed but should be turned away if they stay as long as three days. Itinerant apostles who are unwilling to work should be shunned. Prophets and the poor, however, deserve community support. Before celebrating the Eucharist on the Lord's Day, all quarrels among members of the community must be settled. Bishops and deacons are to be elected by the congregations.

Finally, the *Didache* describes the last days of the world: The sky will split or stretch, a trumpet will sound, and the saved will be resurrected. In essence, the document gives to early churches and Christians all they need to lead holy and responsible lives. Interestingly, at this early moment, no mention is made of a church hierarchy that parallels the Roman imperium. Neither is any mention made of a Christian nation in this world. That distinction is reserved for believers in the world to come.

Bibliography

Didache: The Teaching of the Twelve Apostles. *The Apostolic Fathers*. Vol 1. Edited and translated by Bart D. Ehrman. Cambridge, Mass.: Harvard University Press, 2003.

didactic poetry

In the ancient Greek and Roman worlds, didactic poetry—that which undertakes to teach lessons of some sort—was understood to include poems of all sorts. The classical object of poetry was both to please and to instruct. Thus, for example, one can regard HOMER as a didactic poet since from his pages one can draw lessons concerning the consequences of overweening pride, learn the history of the Trojan War, learn something of seamanship, and learn of the foibles of the gods. Homer's principal object, however, was probably to entertain his listeners.

Among both Greeks and Romans, however, there were many writers who intentionally emphasized the instructive element of their verse. HESIOD in his *WORKS AND DAYS* teaches an approach to conflict resolution, provides a picture of an ancient farming community that continues to interest historical anthropologists, and instructs his readers in the proper seasons for planting and harvesting. From Hesiod's THEOGONY a reader learns the genealogy of the Greek gods.

In Rome, VIRGIL and LUCRETIUS both undertook to instruct the readers of their verse in ethics and morality as well as in, in Virgil's case, rural economy. In four books of Dactylic Hexameter verse (see QUANTITATIVE VERSE), Virgil follows Hesiod's example. Virgil's GEORGICS teach predicting the weather, planting crops, cultivating grapes and olives, animal husbandry and the care of cattle, and beekeeping. In the six books of hexameters that constitute his DE RERUM NATURA, Lucretius instructs his readers in the philosophical position of EPICURUS and about the operations of the natural world. He teaches about a world that operates without the intervention of gods.

While one could give many examples, suffice it to say that didactic poetry in the ancient world, and for that matter in all periods, emphasizes instructing its readers while providing them as well with the pleasure of reading verse.

didactic satires (silloi, lampoons)

Only slender fragments remain to illustrate this distinctively Greek sort of ancient satiric verse, and the names of only two writers are associated with it: Xenophanes of Colophon, of whose work nothing remains, and Timon of Phlius, who was both a skeptic philosopher and a playwright. The surviving fragments of lampoons are his work.

As the commentators describe the genre, silloi satirized ignorant persons who pretended to knowledge or capacities that they did not possess. Such poems taught by modeling and poking fun at behavior to be avoided. It seems that the author of such verse would select an appropriate section from a distinguished poet and apply it laughably to the person being satirized. Timon of Phlius (fl. ca. 320–230 B.C.E.) seems to have been highly accomplished at doing this, and his work reportedly attracted favorable notice from early commentators.

Bibliography

Eschenburg, J. J. Manual of Classical Literature. Translated by N. W. Fiske. Philadelphia: E. C. & J. Biddle, 1850.

Dinarchus (ca. 360–ca. 290 B.C.E.) Greek
prose writer

Born in Corinth, Dinarchus moved as a youth to Athens. Because he was not an Athenian born, Dinarchus could neither hold political office nor practice law by arguing before the Athenian courts. Nonetheless, his strong suit was oratory, and he made a lucrative living by ghostwriting the orations that others made in arguing before the courts.

Though we know the titles of 87 orations purporting to be his, Dinarchus really authored perhaps around 60 of them, and of these only three survive. On the strength of these, historians of oratory judge his work to have been of inferior quality. Despite that, the second-century rhetorician, Hermogenes, listed Dinarchus as belonging to a select group of 10 Athenian orators.

Dinarchus's only personal appearance in the Athenian courts, the classicist George Law Cawkwell tells us, occurred when the orator, having gone blind, filed suit against his friend and host Proxenus when Dinarchus's money disappeared from Proxenus's house.

Though Dinarchus's surviving work has been translated into Latin and French, no English translation is yet available.

Bibliography

Dinarchus. Dinarque. Edited by Michel Nouhaud. Translated by Laurence Dors-Méary. Paris: Belles Lettres, 1990.
Eschenburg, J. J. Manual of Classical Literature. Translated by N. W. Fiske. Philadelphia: E. C. & J. Biddle, 1850.

Dio Cocceianus Chrysostomus
(ca. 150–230 C.E.) *Greek prose writer*

The "Chrysostomus" following Dio Cocceianus's name is a nickname meaning "the golden-tongued." This soubriquet arose from the Stoic philosopher and rhetorician's reputation for flowery and effective writing and speaking.

Born to a wealthy family at the city of Prusa in Bithynia, Dio traveled to Rome, where he enjoyed the favor of the emperor Vespasian. When Domitian became emperor, however, Dio's open criticism led to his exile from Rome and also to his banishment from the comforts of his extensive property in Bithynia. Reduced to extreme poverty, he journeyed from place to place, earning a bare living by whatever means came to hand as he wandered far and wide in the ancient world. We know he journeyed as far away from Rome as Borysthenes, to the north of the Black Sea and near modern Odessa in Russia. He also lived for a while in Thrace, southeast of the Carpathian Mountains along the lower Danube River. There he became interested in the Getae, the technologically primitive people among whom he resided, and wrote their history.

Following Domitian's death in 96 C.E., Dio's banishment ended. The emperor Nerva welcomed him back to Rome, and after Nerva's short reign, Dio became close friends with his successor, Trajan.

As a thinker, Dio was at first a sophist, rejecting the views of all philosophical schools. By the time he returned from exile, however, he had come to believe in a composite philosophy that merged Platonism, STOICISM, and CYNICISM. Above all those schools, however, he had come to value eloquence rather than argument as the vehicle through which people might achieve moral improvement. He took upon himself, therefore, the character of an exhortatory moralist, preaching the good life to all who would listen and doing his best to connect moral conduct with nationalism and the great achievements of the Greeks throughout history. His model of connecting patriotic and moralistic fervor has been popular with many preachers and politicians ever since.

About 80 of Dio's Greek essays and speeches on a variety of topics survive, though a pair of those once ascribed to him has been reassigned to his student, Favorinus. Dio's principal modern editor and English translator, J. W. Cohoon, classifies Dio's surviving works as follows: sophistic works, political works, and moral works. To those categories one might add works of a literary character—both fiction and literary criticism.

To the first category—sophistic—belong such tongue-in-cheek essays as "Eulogy of Hair" (as opposed to baldness); "Eulogy of a Parrot"; and "In Praise of a Gnat." Also in this category we place Dio's 11th discourse in which he undertakes to prove by sophistic argument that the Greeks never captured Troy. This instance clearly illustrates, as Dio intended it should, the inappropriateness of trying to resolve questions of empirical fact, such as whether the earth is flat or round, by debate, syllogism, and appeals to Scriptural authority.

In the category of political works, one finds, for instance, at least seven substantial discourses on the subject of kingship and several on the benefits of peace between warring factions. Portions of other discourses that exhort the citizens of various places to moral probity also discuss the political dimensions of moral action. "On Law" (discourse 75) and "On Freedom" (discourse 80) fall into this category.

Also exemplifying Dio's moral works, a reader finds essays such as the 69th discourse, "On Virtue." In discourses 14 and 15, Dio considers slavery and freedom. The 23rd asserts as its title "The Wise Man is Happy." Discourse 17 treats the topic of covetousness, and number 25 discusses "The Guiding Spirit." Dio's 12th discourse, also called his "Olympic Discourse" is subtitled "On Man's First Conception of God." Early Christian commentators sometimes perceived connections between Dio's moral program and that of the NEW TESTAMENT.

In at least one instance, early readers discovered a storytelling bent in Dio's work, and the ancients split his seventh discourse, the "Euboean Discourse," into two parts. Having done so, they published the first part as a pastoral romance, "The Hunters of Euboea," and it has ever since continued in its separate status as a representative of that genre.

Under the heading of literary and artistic criticism, we also find in Dio's 52nd discourse a comparison of three plays on the same subject: the PHILOCTETES of AESCHYLUS, SOPHOCLES, and EURIPIDES. As only Sophocles' play has survived, this essay is valuable for what we learn of the two lost plays as well as for its insights when comparing the playwrights' work.

Dio's reputation may have suffered because of the loss of works of his own. His *History of the Getae* has not come down to us, nor has another historical work, "On Alexander's Virtues." Lost as well are some philosophical writings, including a consideration of "Whether the Universe is Perishable," a "Defense of Homer" addressed to Plato, and several other works as well.

Bibliography

Cohoon, J. W. *Dio Chrysostom*. 5 Vols. Cambridge, Mass.: Harvard University Press, 1960.

Dio, Chrysostom. "*The Hunters of Euboea.*" In *Three Greek Romances*. Translated and edited by Moses Haddas. Indianapolis: Bobbs Merrill, 1964.

Diodorus Siculus (Diodorus of Agyrium)
(fl. ca. 40 B.C.E.) *Greek historian*

The author of an enormous (40 books) assemblage of historical information in the Greek language, Diodorus Siculus announced his intention to present in his work, entitled *Library,* a synopsis of all known history. Though he failed to achieve that object, he gave very full accounts of his native island, Sicily, and of ancient Greece up until around the mid-third century. Also included in the early books are important and useful discussions of Egypt, India, and Abdera near the Hellespont. Based on internal evidence, it seems that the composition of this extended compendium required about 30 years.

From around the time of Rome's confrontation with Carthage during the first Punic War (ended 241 B.C.E.), Diodorus found more and more reliable source material about Roman history and shifted his principal focus thereafter to Rome. He attempted, not always successfully, to synchronize events in the Roman arena with those in Greece. He carried his account down to the year 60 B.C.E.

Of the 40 books (manuscript scrolls), the contents of 15 survive intact. These include Books 1–5 and 11–20. Fragments of some of the others also exist. In terms of length, the surviving portions of Diodorus's *Library* of history exceeds any other ancient historian's work. The standard Greek-English edition runs to 11 volumes. The first book deals with Egypt and its rulers and ethnography. The second book details the history of Assyria and furnishes descriptions of India, Scythia, Arabia, and the known islands of the ocean. In Book 3, Diodorus turns his attention to Ethiopia, African Amazons, Atlantis and its inhabitants, and the origins of the gods. The fourth book concerns itself with the mythical history of Greece and includes discussions of the principal Greek deities, of Theseus of Athens, and of *Aeschylus's The SEVEN AGAINST THEBES*. Book 5 looks at peoples in the western Mediterranean and at the ethnography of the islands of Crete and Rhodes.

The fragmentary remains of the sixth through the 10th books indicate that in them Diodorus traced events from the time of the Trojan War down to 480 B.C.E. The sixth book is especially interesting as it contains most of our record of *Sacred Scriptures*, a utopian novel by EUHEMERUS. Although the novel describes a fictive voyage to an island in the Indian Ocean, Diodorus apparently thought the work a report of an actual expedition.

In the 11th through the 20th books Diodorus examines Greco-Roman events, principally from 480 through 301 B.C.E. The fragmentary remains that survive of the 21st through the 40th books indicated that the historian pursued these interests down through 60 B.C.E.

In the extant sections of the work, beyond merely cataloguing events, Diodorus assesses the characters of chief figures in his narrative. He also reveals his moral bias that history should instruct people in how to live virtuously and displays his belief in a "great-man theory" of history.

As a historiographer, however, Diodorus strikes some of his critics as not very discriminating in weighing the authority or reliability of his sources. His translator and editor, C. H. Oldfather, dissents from that view, suggesting that Diodorus chose his sources carefully but picked a confusing method of presentation. A good deal of scholarly debate continues about the identity of some of those sources. Translations of the most interesting sections of Diodorus's work continue to appear regularly as independent volumes.

Bibliography

Diodorus Siculus. *Diodorus of Sicily.* 11 vols. Translated by C. H. Oldfather, C. L. Sherman, et al. Cambridge, Mass.: Harvard University Press, 1935.

———. *Diodorus Siculus: Books 11–12.37.1; Greek History 480–431 B.C., the Alternative Version.* Translated by Peter Green. Austin: University of Texas Press, 2006.

———. *The Antiquities of Asia. A Translation with Notes of Book II of the Library of History of Diodorus Siculus.* Translated and annotated by Edwin Murphy. New Brunswick, N.J.: Transaction Publishers, 1989.

———. *The Antiquities of Egypt. A Translation with Notes of Book I of the Library of History of Diodorus Siculus.* Translated and annotated by Edwin Murphy. New Brunswick, N.J.: Transaction Publishers, 1990.

Sacks, K. *Diodorus Siculus and the First Century.* Princeton, N.J.: Princeton University Press, 1990.

Diogenes Laertius (fl. ca. 200–250 C.E.)
Greek prose writer

Little is Known of Diogenes Laertius's personal life. One account suggests that the form of his name is backwards. Another has it that he was born at the town of Laerte in the Roman province of Lycia in Asia Minor and later became a foreign resident in Athens. Though the story may be apocryphal, at some point in his Athenian residency, Diogenes appears to have lacked the means to pay the tax imposed on nonnative residents. The penalty for nonpayment required that the delinquent person be sold into slavery. The historian J. J. Eschenburg reports that this actually happened to Diogenes but that the debt was redeemed and he regained his freedom.

Diogenes interested himself in the history and development of Greek thought and in the lives of Greek thinkers. He collected and summarized biographical material and examples illustrating the thought of 82 Greek philosophers and statesmen from the time of the early Greek philosopher Thales of Miletus (b. ca. 624 B.C.E.) through that of Diogenes' probable contemporary, the philosopher EPICURUS (d. 270 B.C.E.).

Considering its intrinsic merit, Diogenes' work has proved disproportionately important, for the writings of all the preceding authorities on whom he depended for his material have vanished from the record and only his LIVES OF EMINENT PHILOSOPHERS survives to bear witness to their greatness. Some scholars, however, doubt the work's attribution to Diogenes.

Bibliography

Diogenes Laertius. *Lives of Eminent Philosophers.* Translated by R. D. Hicks. New York: G. P. Putnam's Sons. 1925.

———. *Lives of the Philosophers.* Translated by A. Robert Caponiari. Chicago: Regnery, 1969.

Diogenes of Sinope   See CYNICISM; LIVES OF EMINENT PHILOSOPHERS.

Dionysius of Halicarnassus (fl. first century B.C.E.) *Greek historian*

In 30 B.C.E., the literary critic and historian Dionysius of Halicarnassus migrated from his Grecian homeland to join a small but influential colony of Greek intellectuals living in Rome under its first emperor, AUGUSTUS CAESAR. The influence that Dionysius and his Grecian comrades enjoyed stemmed from the high regard of their Roman conquerors for the language, literature, and intellectual accomplishments of the Greeks. Well-bred young Roman boys devoted time to the mastery of the Greek language—often before undertaking the formal study of their own.

Dionysius clearly earned a portion of his living by teaching, but the broad range of the issues and interests addressed in his surviving works suggests that he also enjoyed generous, though anonymous, patronage to support his work in the Greek language. His translator, Stephen Usher, suggests that the emperor himself would have had political reasons for anonymously encouraging Dionysius's work. The emperor, perhaps, did not want his propagandistic purposes with respect to the conquered Greeks to become evident.

However that may be, the breadth of subjects treated by Dionysius is impressive. Perhaps the most influential of these is his essay On Literary Composition. In addition to advising aspiring writers to study the best authors of the past and to discussing how to achieve a unified, pleasing, and sonorous effect, Dionysius generously illustrates his argument with examples from the past. To this practice we owe the preservation of the one complete surviving ode of Sappho, her Hymn to Aphrodite.

Posterity also remembers Dionysius for his *Antiquities of Rome*. This work of history, written in Greek, may have been penned to help reconcile conquered Greece to Roman mastery. Dionysius additionally wrote penetrating assessments of the style and practice of several of his predecessors, including the orators Demosthenes, Lysias, Isocrates, Isæus; and the historian Thucydides. Fragmentary remains exist of his *Memoirs of the Attic Authors*. Finally, several of his letters, in which he comments on various authors, have come down to us.

Bibliography

Dionysius of Halicarnassus. *On Literary Composition*. Edited by W. Rhys Roberts. New York: Garland, 1987.

——. *The Three Literary Letters*. New York: Garland, 1987.

Usher, Stephen, ed. and trans. *Dionysius of Halicarnassus: Critical Essays*. 2 vols. Loeb Classical Library. Nos. 465, 466. Cambridge, Mass.: Harvard University Press, 1974.

Diphilus (ca. 355–ca. 290 B.C.E.) *Greek dramatist*

Though the playwright Diphilus is represented only by fragmentary remains, we know him to have been a prolific writer during the period when the Greek New Comedy flourished (see Comedy in Greece and Rome). He is said to have written about 100 comedies; of these, we know the titles of about 60. Diphilus's plays have suffered the fate of the entire Greek New Comedy except for some of the plays of Menander; all others have disappeared. Some of the titles survive, however, and they suggest that Diphilus sometimes drew on mythical sources for his plots, as was the case with his *Theseus*. He seems also to have been among the playwrights who took bawdy license with the biography of Sappho, improbably giving her lovers such as her contemporary, the elegist and satirist Archilochus or the natural philosopher Hipponax, who lived a century later than she did.

We can acquire a general sense of the shapes of some of Diphilus's plays by looking at those by the Roman playwrights Terence and Plautus, who modeled some of their still-extant work on plays that Diphilus had written. Such plays include Plautus's *Mostellaria* (*The Haunted House*), *Rudens* (*The Rope*), and his *Casina* (*A Funny Thing Happened on the Way to the Wedding*). Terence's *Adelphoe* (*The Brothers*) also preserves echoes of Diphilus's work.

Beyond this, a few scraps of iambic verse attributed to Diphilus are quoted in ancient references to him, though there is some controversy over whether or not these are the work of the same Diphilus.

Bibliography

Gerber, Douglas E., ed. and trans. *Greek Iambic Poetry From the Seventh to the Fifth Centuries*

B.C. Cambridge, Mass.: Harvard University Press, 1999.

Eschenburg, J. J. *Manual of Classical Literature.* Translated by N. W. Fiske. Philadelphia: E. C. & J. Biddle, 1850.

Hornblower, Simon, and Antony Spawforth, ed. *The Oxford Classical Dictionary.* Oxford: Oxford University Press, 1996.

Discourses of the States *(Guo yu, Kuo yü)* Anonymous (ca. 350 B.C.E.)

Organized according to the state to which the included material pertains, the *Discourses of the States* contain a good deal of such legendary and mythic material as the "Kung-kung flood myth," in which a god of that name causes a flood. In its original form, this tale is a version of the widespread myth of the world's total inundation. In the *Discourses of the States,* however, the familiar story—like that of Noah—becomes less mythic, more humanized, and set in a historical period.

Proverbial material, too, abounds: "To follow goodness is to ascend; to follow evil is to plummet." Anecdotes regularly lead to elaborate speeches, sometimes boring but more often lively. The speeches offer predictable advice: Rulers who heed good ministers succeed, those who do not fail. States rise and fall on this pattern. Demonstrating this point is the central and often too evident didactic purpose of the work, and in its pages history tends toward moralizing fable.

While the work addresses events in the three states of Qi (Chi), Zhou (Chou), and Lu, matters in a fourth state—Chin—receive the lion's share of the anonymous author's attention. He follows at length the difficulties of Jin's (Chin's) foolish Duke Xian (Hsien). Among other difficulties that he faces, the duke becomes besotted with an evil mistress, Lady Li, who wishes to displace the duke's heir, Shen-sheng. Eventually Lady Li succeeds in her plot by making it appear that the son had planned to poison his father. Mortified to be thought guilty of such an offense, Shen-sheng hangs himself.

Much attention focuses as well on the initially unpromising but eventually triumphant career of a younger son of Duke Xian Chonger (Ch'ung-erh), who became revered as Duke Wen of Jin.

The literary historian Burton Watson makes the point that the lively, dramatic style of this work became a regular feature of subsequent Chinese historiography—a feature that makes reading Chinese history entertaining as well as instructive.

Bibliography

Durrant, Stephen. "The Literary Features of Historical Writing." In *The Columbia History of Chinese Literature.* Edited by Victor H. Mair. New York: Columbia University Press, 2001.

Watson, Burton. *Early Chinese Literature.* New York: Columbia University Press, 1962.

Donatus, Ælius (fl. fourth century C.E.)
Roman prose writer

Literary history remembers Æius Donatus as the teacher of St. JEROME, as an influential grammarian, and as a commentator on the works of TERENCE and VIRGIL. Only fragmentary remains of these commentaries survive, though later editors included portions of Donatus's commentaries in their own work, so that some idea may be gained of the shape of portions (but not the whole) of both commentaries. A section of the commentary on Virgil, for example, survives in the manuscript of Virgil that once belonged to the Renaissance poet Petrarch.

Because Donatus's grammatical compositions were used as school texts as late as the 12th century however, they survive more or less intact. One of these was a primary school grammar text entitled *Ars minor* (The lesser treatise). It introduces students to the eight parts of speech by means of a series of questions and their answers. His other work, *Ars Maior* (The greater treatise), is addressed to more advanced scholars and offers stylistic advice about effects to be sought and flaws to be avoided in speaking.

Bibliography

Chase, Wayland Johnson. *The* Ars Minor *of Donatus, for One Thousand Years the Leading Textbook of Grammar.* Madison: University of Wisconsin Studies in the Social Sciences and History, 1926.

dynasties, Chinese See ANCIENT CHINESE DYNASTIES AND PERIODS.

Dyskolos (The Bad Tempered Man, The Man Who Didn't Like People)
Menander (ca. 316 B.C.E.)

For students of ancient Greek theater, the 20th century might be considered the age of MENANDER, for it was during that century, beginning in 1905, that significant portions of the lost plays of the early Greek comic playwright began to surface. Then in 1957, an almost complete, 10-page manuscript of Menander's *Dyskolos* was found in Geneva. The manuscript of the verse play, which as late as 1969 belonged to the classicist Martin Bodner, was edited, and a Greek version was printed in 1959. In 1960, W. G. Arnott prepared an English translation of that edition for stage production. Though Arnott was obliged to supply some missing lines here and there, what he produced may be as close to Menander's original as we shall ever come.

As *Dyskolos* opens, the god Pan speaks the prologue outside the front door of his shrine. The audience learns of the people-hater named Knemon, who married a widow with a baby boy. The wife, Myrrhine, subsequently bore Knemon a daughter, but Knemon and his wife never got along. So when her son, Gorgias, came of age and moved to his natural father's estate, the wife deserted Knemon, leaving him with the daughter. The unnamed daughter is a delightful young woman, and the care she lavishes on Pan's shrine has earned her the god's favor as well as that of the nymphs who share his dwelling with him. Pan tells the audience that he has expressed that favor by putting a wealthy young fellow under a spell

and that, even as Pan speaks, the young fellow and his parasite (a stock comic character named Chaireas) are approaching.

As the first scene opens, we learn that the wealthy young man, Sostratos, has just told Chaireas that he has fallen in love at his first sight of the daughter. Sostratos admits that he sent another servant, Pyrrhias, to negotiate with the girl's father about a wedding.

At that moment, Pyrrhias appears, running for his life away from Knemon, who is not yet on stage. Knemon has driven Pyrrhias off before he can even state his business. Uttering antisocial sentiments, Knemon arrives on stage and expresses his displeasure when he finds Sostratus loitering about his property.

Now the daughter enters with a pitcher, searching for somewhere she can draw water to heat for her father's bath. Overwhelmed by her beauty, Sostratus offers his help, and she accepts it. As he gets the water, her half brother's servant, Daos, who suspects Sostratus of dishonorable intentions, observes him. The act ends with the arrival onstage of a drunken chorus of Pan's votaries, who entertain the audience with their revels.

As act 2 begins, Daos warns the half brother, Gorgias, that Sostratus is lurking about and is up to no good. Just at that moment, Sostratus returns with the intention of speaking to Knemon himself when Gorgias interrupts Sostratus with a mystifying lecture about being neither prideful because of his wealth nor disdainful of poor folks. When Sostratus asks Gorgias to explain his purpose, Gorgias says that he suspects Sostratus of evil intentions with respect to his half sister and, therefore, of making Gorgias his enemy. In reply, Sostratus declares that his intentions are honorable. He has fallen in love with the girl, is willing to marry her without dowry, and promises to cherish her for life. He is perturbed at Gorgias's misconstruction of his intentions.

His opinion of Sostratus totally changed, Gorgias explains the difficulties posed by Knemon's misanthropy. Although the old man is wealthy, he has no servants except one old woman, Simike.

He only speaks voluntarily to her and to his daughter, and he is resolved to marry her only to someone with a disposition like his own. This, Gorgias thinks, means the girl will marry no one. Nonetheless, if Sostratus is resolved to persist in his attempt, he must first shed his fine clothes and pose as a common laborer. This is his only hope of not being driven off as soon as Knemon sees him.

Once clothed as a laborer in a leather jerkin, Sostratus warms to his task. Moreover, he imagines that, having been reared by such a father as Knemon, the girl will be free of the sort of prejudices that an aunt or a nurse might have nourished in her. The young men exit.

After a brief interval, another stock character of Greek New Comedy appears. A cook named Sikon takes the stage, dragging along a sheep he clearly intends to butcher as a sacrifice at Pan's altar. Another stock figure, Getas, the slave of Sostratus's father Kallippides, also enters bearing a load of pots, pans, rugs, cushions, and mattresses in preparation for a sacrifice at Pan's temple. The women of the household will be in attendance at the ceremony.

Getas reports to Sikon that he thinks he has seen the god Pan put chains on Sostratus's legs, dress him in a leather jerkin, give him a spade, and make him start digging. Sikon thinks the upcoming sacrifice will make all this turn out well and promises Getas a good meal at the sacrifice. Getas mutters that, although Sikon is a wonderful cook, Getas does not trust him. A performance by a choir ends the act.

Act 3 begins with Knemon's appearance from his door, speaking over his shoulder to someone inside the house. As he speaks, a great crowd of participants in the sacrifice engulfs him. This group includes Sostratus's sister and his mother; her friends, relations, and slaves; and a flute-girl named Parthenia, who is playing a double flute. Knemon curses the crowd as Getas and Sikon appear, complaining about the group's late arrival and sniping at one another.

Annoyed at all the hubbub, Knemon grouses that the only part of the sacrifice that the gods will get are the incense, the sacrificial cakes, the end of the sheep's backbone, and the guts. The worshippers will eat and drink everything else. He goes back inside his house.

Discovering that the arriving servants have forgotten a boiling pot, Getas tries to borrow one from Knemon, who snarlingly tells him that he does not have one. Getas insults Knemon and leaves, as Knemon threatens him and slams the door. Sikon thinks he can do better and tries a second time to borrow a pot. Knemon whips Sikon for bothering him, and Getas pokes fun at the cook for his empty bravado. Sikon decides to roast the mutton rather than boil it.

Sostratos enters. He is sore and weary from his unaccustomed physical exertion, and he complains that neither Knemon nor the girl has appeared. He will have to try again tomorrow. He also wonders about the mysterious way he seems drawn to the vicinity. Sostratos then encounters Getas, who explains the preparations for the sacrifice and tells Sostratus that his mother is there and that his father is expected. Sostratos decides that it would be good policy to invite Gorgias and Daos to share the sacrificial meal.

Knemon's elderly servant Simike now appears. She has accidentally dropped both a pitcher and a pitchfork down the well, and she knows that Knemon will soon want the pitchfork. Getas suggests that she jump in too. Knemon appears and tells Simike that he is going to lower her into the well using the same rotten rope that cost her the pitcher in the first place. This is an idle threat. Knemon prepares to descend into the well himself. He articulates his feelings of loneliness, but when Getas offers a bucket and rope, Knemon curses Getas for speaking to him.

Sostratus and Gorgias end the act as Gorgias says he must not come to the feast because he must attend to his mother, and Sostratus understands. Another choral interlude follows the action.

Act 4 opens with a shrieking Simike calling for help. Knemon has fallen down the well trying to retrieve his lost objects. Sikon suggests that she drop a heavy stone down on top of him.

Simike cries out for Gorgias, who comes, calling on Sostratus for assistance. Knemon's predicament convinces Sikon that the gods really exist.

Knemon's daughter is heard off stage, first lamenting her father's predicament and then joyously exclaiming at his rescue. Sikon calls on the women at the sacrifice to pray that Knemon has a broken leg and will have a permanent limp.

In a lengthy soliloquy, Sostratus describes the way that Gorgias rescued his stepfather Knemon from the well while Sostratus stayed ineffectually above, trying to comfort the nameless daughter.

Gorgias and the daughter wheel a splinted and bandaged Knemon onto the stage on a couch. Knemon's ordeal has somewhat sweetened his disposition, though when Sostratos tries to assist, Knemon addresses him as a "nincompoop." Gorgias lectures Knemon, pointing out that living alone has almost done him in. He needs help.

Knemon confesses that he is difficult and asks Gorgias to bring Knemon's estranged wife, Myrrhine, who never speaks. With everyone assembled, Knemon makes a lengthy speech. He explains that he thought he could be the one person in the world who was independent, but his near-fatal accident has demonstrated that he needs someone standing by. He observes that he adopted his mode of life out of disgust for "the petty calculations" that people made to "assure a petty profit." Out of gratitude for Gorgias's selfless risk in rescuing him, he names Gorgias heir to half his estate. The other half he reserves as his daughter's dowry, charging Gorgias with the responsibility of arranging a suitable match for her.

Then, remarking that people should not say more than necessary, he gives his daughter advice: If people were all kind to one another, there would be no need for law courts and war would cease. Everyone would have enough to get by and be content.

Gorgias agrees to Knemon's requests and, over Knemon's objections, introduces Sostratus as someone who helped rescue him. Mollified, Knemon notes that Sostratus is sunburnt and asks if he's a farmer. Sostratus, who has had one day's experience on the farm, is able to answer truthfully that he is. Satisfied that Sostratus is not an idle, wealthy nobleman (which, of course, he is), Knemon puts his seal of approval on the marriage that Gorgias suggests. Gorgias pushes Knemon's couch back inside.

When Sostratus assures Gorgias that his father will confirm his choice of bride, Gorgias performs the ceremony of betrothal between the two young people. No sooner is he finished than Sostratus's father, Kallippides, appears. Gorgias knows the wealthy old fellow and is amazed. Sostratus praises Kallippides as an honest farmer. He thinks, however, that it will be a good idea if his father eats lunch before the young people break the news of the betrothal. The stage empties, and another choral interlude ends the act.

In act 5, Kallippides has willingly given his consent to Sostratus's wedding. When, however, Sostratus proposes a second union between Gorgias and Kallippides' daughter, the father balks. He does not want both of his children marrying paupers. But after Sostratus lectures his father on generosity, somewhat improbably, Kallippides drops his objections. Gorgias then surprises Sostratus by refusing on the grounds that he should not take so much when he and his father have "so little." Both Sostratus and Kallippides argue with Gorgias, who soon agrees to the union.

Now pleased, Kallippides announces a dowry of 15,000 pounds for his daughter, but when Gorgias wishes to confer 5,000 on Sostratus with his sister, Kallippides and Sostratus refuse it, preferring that Gorgias keep his estate together.

Sostratus proposes a grand party for the evening. Knemon will be invited, though his acceptance is dubious. Simike, on the other hand, goes willingly. As everyone else prepares for the party, the cook Sikon and the slave Getas conspire to annoy Knemon by begging to borrow things. Then they pester him about going to the party, keeping him awake and forcing him to dance with them. Finally Knemon yields in self-defense. Several servants carry him into the shrine, and Sikon speaks the epilogue, calling on the audience to applaud.

Dyskolos is the only virtually complete example of Greek New Comedy to survive. It confirms scholary conclusions already reached on the basis of surviving lists of stage props and on surviving imitations of Greek comedies by such Roman comic writers as PLAUTUS and TERENCE. The plots of the plays often involved more-or-less clueless young people in love but faced with difficulties often posed by members of the older generation. They and the minor characters were drawn from a reservoir of such stock characters as cooks, slaves, parasites, and difficult old persons. A good deal of slapstick, like that in the final act of *Dyskolos*, was also featured in the plays. All difficulties were always resolved by a happy ending. The frequent rediscovery of fragments of new comedy offer hope that other, more complete examples will be discovered.

See also COMEDY IN GREECE AND ROME.

Bibliography

Handley, E. W., ed. *The Dyskolos of Menander.* Cambridge, Mass.: Harvard University Press, 1965.

Menander of Athens. *Dyskolos, or The Man who Didn't Like People.* Translated by W. G. Arnott. London: University of London, Athelone Press, 1960.

E

Eclogues Virgil (37 B.C.E)

A collection of 10 dactylic hexameter (see QUAN-TITATIVE VERSE) poems in the PASTORAL mode, most of VIRGIL's *Eclogues* celebrate the attractions of a stylized, poetic, and largely mythical rural life. The first and the ninth of them, by contrast, are autobiographical in their content. Following JULIUS CAESAR's assassination, the Roman conspirators against him, Brutus and Cassius, were defeated at Philippi. To pay the victorious troops, lands were allotted to veterans. Virgil's ancestral estates near Mantua were among the lands seized as a part of that distribution.

In the first eclogue, we meet of the goatherd Tityrus—probably Virgil himself–who conducts a dialogue with another dispossessed goatherd, Meliboeus. As "Eclogue I" opens, Meliboeus mentions that the two shepherds are outcast from their country and its "sweet fields," but that Tityrus nonetheless woos "the woodland Muse" and teaches the woods to echo the name of the shepherdess, Amaryllis. She is also silently present.

Tityrus answers that a god has won him his peace. This passage probably pays a compliment to Octavian (AUGUSTUS CAESAR), who either restored the confiscated lands or who granted Virgil others. Meliboeus, however, apparently has not experienced the same good fortune, and he bemoans the fate that denies him the sight of his native place.

"Eclogue II" features the shepherd Corydon singing his grief at the failure of a beloved boy, Alexis, to return his passion. The eclogue looks for its inspiration to THEOCRITUS's third and 11th IDYLLS, which deal with similar laments. Following many promises of delights if Alexis would only return Corydon's feelings, another shepherd, unnamed, reproves Corydon for his folly in suffering as he does and in neglecting his work while he suffers. Corydon will find another Alexis, so he should stop moping about and get busy at his necessary chores.

"Eclogue III" is modeled on the fourth and fifth *Idylls* of Theocritus. It features a singing contest between two shepherds—in this case, Menalcas and Damoetas. The eclogue begins with the two chiding one another for various misdemeanors—destroying newly planted vines and stealing a goat, for instance. Damoetas, however, explains that he won the goat fairly in a singing contest. Menalcas doubts this assertion and makes fun of Damoetas's singing ability. This exchange leads to a wager in which Damoetas stakes a cow and Menalcas a pair of engraved cups made from beech wood. They invite a passing neighbor, Palaemon, to judge their song. He accepts the invitation, and, turn and turn about, the shepherds sing their lines celebrating country activities, pleasures, ill fortune, and their passions. Having heard their songs, Palaemon declares the contest a tie and suggests that they both leave off singing.

The opening of the "Eclogue IV" addresses the Sicilian Muses—that is, the Greek pastoral poets of Sicily, including Theocritus—and declares the eclogue's intention to address a loftier subject. A new age has begun. The goddess of justice, Lucina, has returned to earth, and a golden age has begun under the aegis of Apollo the sun god. Though the heightened rhetoric of these passages were likely addressed to Augustus Caesar, whom Virgil admired unabashedly, some Christians have perceived unintended foreshadowing of the coming of Christ and the Virgin Mary in these lines.

"Eclogue V" contains another singing contest, this time between the shepherds Menalcas and Mopsus. Mopsus begins, singing of the death of Daphnis, a character in Theocritus's first *Idyll*. In Theocritus's version, the archetypal Sicilian shepherd, Daphnis, refused to love. The goddess of love, Aphrodite, therefore punished him by making him the victim of unrequited love. When Daphnis dies of his hopeless ardor, Aphrodite tries unsuccessfully to revive him. Virgil has Mopsas sing of Daphnis's death, funeral, tomb, and epitaph.

Menalcas admires Mopsas's song and thinks his own singing may not measure up. Menalcas sings instead of Daphnis's transfiguration and deification when he arrives in heaven. Menalcas also celebrates the annual sacrifices of milk, olive oil, and wine that shepherds make to Daphnis's memory. He further suggests that shepherds can now use Daphnis's name as they do those of other gods to swear by when they make vows. The shepherds end the eclogue by exchanging gifts in honor of one another's songs.

The sixth eclogue, which Virgil addresses to his friend, the critic Quintilius Varus, admonishes Varus that Virgil is not yet ready to sing "of kings and battles,"—that is, to write an epic.

Nonetheless, Virgil assures his friend that Apollo will find no poem more welcome than one dedicated to Varus. Then, calling on the Muses, Virgil writes of two lads, Chromis and Mnasyllos, who catch the drunken satyr Silenus asleep in a cave, bind him with his own Bacchic garlands, and demand a song as the price of his release. The water nymph Aegle joins them and paints the satyr's face with crimson mulberries. Amused, Silenus promises the boys their song and the nymph "another kind of reward." Silenus begins his song, singing of the beginning of the universe; the making of the earth; the origins of the forms of mountains and landscape features; the appearance of the sun, clouds, and showers; and the arrival of living things—the woodlands and the animals.

Next, Silenus briefly summarizes mythical history, alluding to but not telling stories like those of the rule of Saturn, of Prometheus's theft of fire from the gods, of Pasiphae and the bull. Continuing with a catalogue of myths, Silenus alludes to Virgil's friend Gallus, who established the elegiac poem in the Latin tongue (see ELEGY AND ELEGAIC POETRY), and to the Greek poet, HESIOD, whose *THEOGONY* and *WORKS AND DAYS* provided the models whose contents Virgil's report of Silenus's song briefly summarized. (Virgil assumed that his audience would know these works by heart and that the briefest of allusions to them would be enough to evoke the full texts of the stories in his readers' minds). Silenus continues singing the old mythical songs until the end of the day, when the shepherds had to take their flocks to the fold.

The shepherd Meliboeus opens the seventh eclogue, telling how Daphnis and he happened upon a singing match between Corydon and Thyrsis. After a 20-line introduction, Corydon and Thyrsis alternately recite or chant four-line verses. Corydon calls on the nymphs of Libethra to inspire his song. Thyrsis calls on the shepherds of Arcadia to crown him and rise above Codrus, a poet whom Corydon had named as his model. Corydon next addresses a song and a series of gifts, including a marble statue, to the Grecian nymph Delia. Thyrsis outdoes him by making an offering of milk and cakes, to the Roman god of masculinity, Priapus, and the promise of a golden statue if the flock flourishes.

Corydon calls on the nymph Galatea to come to him when her bulls are in their stalls. Thyrsis hopes that his steers will go home and that Galatea will find him bitter, rough, and worthless. Corydon prays for a pleasant summer and protection from the heat. Thyrsis prays for a good fire within to ward off the winter's chill.

Corydon crafts a pretty compliment to the handsome boy, Alexis, saying that in his absence the rivers would dry up. Thyrsis says that the parched fields and brown grass would all recover and be green again as, when his Phyllis arrives, Jupiter will rain down showers.

Linking his stanza to Thyrsis's, Corydon pays his compliment to Phyllis, who loves hazels; therefore, Apollo's own favorite plants, myrtle and laurel, will not compete with hazels. Thrysis abandons the direct reflection of the preceding verse in his final effort, suggesting that a visit by the handsome young Lycidas would make the loveliness of the trees in the woods, hills, and plains pale in comparison with his beauty.

As judge, Meliboeus decides that Corydon is the clear winner of the singing contest.

Virgil dedicates "Eclogue VIII" to his friend Cneius Asinus Pollio, the governor of Cisalpine Gaul, who had just defeated the troops of the Parthini in the Roman province of Illyricum (39 B.C.E.). Once again Virgil presents the reader with a singing contest—this time between Damon and Alphesiboeus. Throughout these eclogues, which are among the most finely crafted of all Roman lyrics, Virgil takes the greatest care to maintain his readers' interest with variety of style and content.

Early in the morning, the shepherd Damon begins his song with an address to the morning star. In that address, we learn that his beloved Nysa has spurned him and that, resolved to die, he calls on the gods to hear him. As each of the stanzas of Damon's song ends, he repeats a refrain: "Begin with me, my flute, a song of Mae-

nalus!" (Mt. Maenalus in Arcadia was a venue sacred to the Muses.) Nysa, the reader learns, has been married to Mopsus. Damon thinks the wedding a mismatch and compares it to the mating of griffons and mares or to hounds drinking with the deer they hunt.

Damon rehearses the history of his love, how from his 11th year he loved Nysa. Now he has discovered love's essential inhumanity. He compares love's ruthlessness to that of Medea when she murdered her children (see MEDEA). The world has been turned upside down: Oak trees bear golden apples; owls vie with swans. Damon wishes that the world would all become ocean. He will plunge from a mountain peak into the waves. He ends his song, varying the refrain to close the poem, then calls on Alphesiboeus to begin.

Begin he does, calling for water and wool to wreathe the shrines and try his magic at warming up the mood. Only songs that can do so are lacking. Alphesiboeus mimics the device of using a refrain, and his stanza length—stanza for stanza—matches that of Damon. Songs, he insists, have magical powers; they can draw the moon from the heavens, change men into swine, or burst a snake in the meadow. As he sings, Alphesiboeus, following "Idyll II" of Theocritus, tells how a girl weaves a magic spell to call her lover, Daphnis, home to her. The refrain invokes the spell to call the lover home from town until that of the final stanza notes the success of her effort by announcing that Daphnis is on his way.

In "Eclogue IX", Virgil assumes the persona of Menalcas, and the subject shifts from the mythic and the amatory to the seizure of his own lands discussed above. The shepherds are lamenting their expulsion from their ancestral lands, and Lycidas expresses surprise. He had heard that Menalcas (Virgil) had saved some of the farms with his appeals. In the ensuing disputes, the shepherd Moeris suggests, both he and Menalcas were lucky to escape with their lives.

Moeris sings an old song recalling the ancient pastoral tradition, but Lycidas changes the tune. There is no point, he implies, in looking to the heavens for the old constellations. The comet that appeared on the death of Julius Caesar and that was thought to be his soul on its way to its deification symbolizes a new order of things. Yet there is hope that new generations will inherit their ancestral lands.

Moeris feels less hopeful but also philosophic in the face of adversity. Time robs us of everything, he says, memory included. He has now forgotten the old songs—though Menalcas can still repeat them. The shepherds and farmers who work the land take solace in the thought that a new master will still need them.

In "Eclogue X", Virgil does a friend a favor. He composes a love poem that his friend and fellow poet, G. Cornelius Gallus, can send to win back the heart of a woman, Lycoris, who had been his mistress but had deserted him. In the poem, Virgil as the shepherd Menalcas has Gallus complain that military duty has kept him away from his love. He will, he promises, return to the poet's imaginary Arcadian life—one he wishes to share with Lycoris. Yet the singer recognizes that it is the god, Love, not human lovers, who conquers all. He hopes that Lycoris will yield to Love and once more love Gallus.

Bibliography

Virgil. *Eclogues and Georgics.* Translated by James Rhodes. Mineola, N.Y.: Dover Publications, 2005.

———. *Eclogues, Georgics, Aeneid I–VI.* Translated by H. Rushton Fairclough. Cambridge, Mass.: Harvard University Press, 1967.

Electra Sophocles (ca. 410 B.C.E.?)

In *Electra*, SOPHOCLES develops a play from the same material treated by AESCHYLUS in *The CHOEPHORI* and by EURIPIDES in his *Electra*. The death of Orestes' father, Agamemnon, at the hands of his mother, Clytemnestra, and her paramour, Aegisthus, must be avenged. In Sophocles' version, Orestes, who lives because his sister Electra saved him by sending him to his aunt and uncle, and his companion, Pylades, arrive in the city of Mycenae accompanied by a tutor called Paedagogus, who urges the youths to lay their plans for vengeance quickly. Orestes reveals that his plans are already laid and that Apollo has revealed to him the necessary course of action. Paedagogus is to gain entry to the house with an urn ostensibly containing Orestes' ashes and gather intelligence. In the meantime, Pylades and Orestes will visit Agamemnon's tomb and sacrifice locks of their hair as a funeral tribute.

Electra is heard lamenting and chanting within. She is recalling her father Agamemnon's murder. Members of the CHORUS come to comfort her in her constant grieving. They remind her that Orestes lives to seek vengeance—a vengeance on which Electra's imagination is unswervingly fixed. From the chorus we learn that Aegisthus is away and that, though Orestes has often promised to come, he never has.

Electra's sister, Chrysothemis, enters and tries to dissuade her from angry and vengeful thoughts. Electra tells her that her inaction and her lack of wrath betray their father. Chrysothemis informs her sister that Clytemnestra and Aegisthus have determined to imprison Electra in exile if she does not cease her vengeful chanting. The sisters exchange points of view about the respective paths they have chosen to follow in the wake of their father's murder.

Then Chrysothemis tells Electra about Clytemnestra's dream. Clytemnestra dreamed that Agamemnon took his royal scepter and planted it near the hearth. From it sprang a fruitful tree that overshadowed all Mycenae. The dream has made Clytemnestra fearful. Electra tells Chrysothemis to pray for Orestes' arrival; the chorus encourages her to do so, and she agrees. The chorus then remarks upon the vengeful Furies who lie in wait for Clytemnestra and upon the multigenerational history of curses on the progeny of Pelops and Atreus.

Clytemnestra now enters and attempts to justify her murder of Agamemnon to Electra, saying that her doing so was just vengeance for his sacrificing Electra's sister Iphigenia to gain a fair wind for the Greek fleet assembled at Aulis to sail against Troy. Electra rejects that argument and accuses her mother of being motivated by her lust for Aegisthus. Following a further exchange of insult and impatience between mother and daughter, Clytemnestra prays to Apollo that he will uphold her in prosperity and do the same for those of her children who bear her no ill will.

Paedagogus arrives and inquires if the palace is that of Aegisthus. On learning that he is in the presence of the queen, he reports that Orestes is dead. He follows this news with a convincingly circumstantial account of an accident in a chariot race in which Orestes ostensibly died. Clytemnestra is, on the one hand, moved at the report of the death of her son, and, on the other, relieved that his desire for vengeance no longer threatens her. Electra is downcast at the disappointment of all her hopes. As she laments, her sister Chrysothemis brings news that Orestes lives and is present. She reports that while visiting her father's tomb, she found evidence of fresh funeral sacrifice and a lock of their brother's hair. Electra, however, recounts Paedogogus's story, and Chrysothemis is convinced of her error. She joins Electra in plotting revenge against their father's murderers. Again the chorus advises restraint, and while Electra remains firm in her resolve, Chrysothemis vacillates, then decides not to participate after all.

Orestes and Pylades now enter, in disguise and carrying a funeral urn. Orestes tells Electra that what remains of Orestes is in it. She requests the urn and grieves over it. Orestes surprises Electra by being stirred to pity. Eventually he confesses that the ashes in the urn are not Orestes' own but a "fiction" bearing his name. He reveals himself as her brother. He then counsels her to restrain her joy and to pretend to be grieving his death. Paedogogus enters and cautions them not to give the plot away with their rejoicing. Electra remains outside while the men go in and kill Clytemnestra. Orestes emerges with bloody hands, and Aegisthus is observed approaching in the distance. Orestes reenters the palace.

Aegisthus arrives and asks for the Phocian strangers who have reported Orestes' death. Electra, each of her utterances bristling with double meaning, says they await him within. The palace doors open, revealing a shrouded corpse near which Orestes and Pylades stand. Aegisthus assumes it to be that of Orestes, but when he removes the face cloth from the body, he realizes into whose power he has fallen. Orestes and Pylades force Aegisthus into the house to kill him on the spot where Agamemnon had died. The chorus ends the play with a reference to the end of the curse that for generations had plagued the house of Atreus. (See *AGAMEMNON*.)

Sophocles' version of the story contains virtually no weighing in the balance of justice Agamemnon's sacrifice of Iphigenia against his murder by Aegisthus and Clytemnestra. Nor does a viewer find evidence that Orestes feels any guilt or regret at the prospect of becoming the instrument of justice in slaying his mother. There is none of the disagreement between the vengeful Furies and the Olympian goddess of wisdom, Athena, that one finds in Aeschylus's version of the story, and finally, there is no need for balloting by an Athenian jury that comes within a single vote of consigning Orestes to the hands of vengeance. Sophocles ends the curse on the house of Atreus definitively with the deeds of Orestes.

Bibliography

Sophocles. *The Complete Plays*. Translated by Paul Roche. New York: Signet Classics, 2001.

elegy and elegiac poetry

Applying the terms *elegy* and *elegiac* principally to poems of mourning and lament represents a late development in the history of the elegiac genre. Among the earliest Greek practitioners of the genre, *elegiac* applied to the meter of the verse in which the poem was composed rather than to its subject matter. The elegiac verse was composed of two dactylic lines, the first of hexameter and the second of pentameter. The elegy seems to have been a development from the EPIC genre. On the one hand, it came to be used for poetry sung or recited during the drinking party, or symposium, that followed the main course of a banquet. Typical poems treated such subjects as the pleasures of wine, of love, and of abundant living. On the other hand, the elegiac stanza reflected its epic roots by serving as the meter for war songs and songs recited together by troops as they marched into battle.

The earliest Greek elegists are customarily dated to the seventh century B.C.E. Included among them we find such poets as CALLINUS OF EPHESUS and TYRTAEUS. The poems of both Callinus and Tyrtaeus—an Athenian schoolteacher who became a Spartan general—were war songs that inspired troops to acts of courage. About a century later, THEOGNIS used the meter to offer advice to young aristocrats and introduces the note of lamentation by bewailing the injustice of the lower classes having replaced the aristocrats in important offices and depriving them of their hereditary privileges and wealth. Among Roman elegists ALBIUS TIBULLUS was the form's foremost practitioner.

Otherwise, the elegiac verse was also used in more extended poems to report historical action. We see at least a fragmentary example of this sort in the remains of SIMONIDES OF CEOS's elegy on the Battle of Plataea.

See also PASTORAL POETRY; QUANTITATIVE VERSE.

Bibliography

Edmonds, J. M., ed. and trans. *Elegy and Iambus . . . The Greek Elegiac and Iambic Poets from Callinus to Crates . . . .* 2 vols. Cambridge, Mass.: Harvard University Press, 1954.

Taplin, Oliver. *Literature in the Greek and Roman Worlds: A New Perspective.* Oxford: Oxford University Press, 2000.

Empedocles (fl. ca. 440 B.C.E.) *Greek poet*

Empedocles was a distinguished Greek-Sicilian philosopher, naturalist, and poet who is remembered best for the probably apocryphal story that, in an effort to discover if he had become a god, he committed suicide by jumping into the Sicilian volcano, Mt. Etna. While Empedocles had in fact boasted of his divinity, that boast may well have been a form of literary hyperbole or simple egoism. On the other hand, his hubris may have stemmed from a genuine conviction that he was actually an immortal who, in punishment for some Olympian transgression, had been condemned to sojourn for a time on earth before being welcomed back among his peers. As for his demise, it seems more likely that he died from altogether less romantic causes while traveling in the Peloponnesian peninsula of Greece.

Approximately 500 lines representing two of his poems—*Physics* and *Purifications*—have come down to us in such fragmentary condition that one cannot always be sure which lines go with which poem. Empedocles belonged to the school of philosophy that had been propounded by PYTHAGORAS OF SAMOS—one that believed in the reincarnation of souls—and he asserted his recollection of previous lives as a young man, a maiden, a bush, a bird, and a fish.

In *LIVES OF EMINENT PHILOSOPHERS*, the third-century B.C.E. historian of philosophy DIOGENES LAERTIUS credits ARISTOTLE with naming Empedocles as the inventor of rhetoric and attributing to him an unfinished poem on Xerxes' invasion of Greece, a hymn to Apollo, tragedies, and political discourses. Diogenes also reports assertions contemporary with Empedocles that he could perform magic and was also a physician.

Bibliography

Diogenes Laertius. *Lives of Eminent Philosophers.* Vol. 2. Translated by H. D. Hicks. New York: G. P. Putnam's Sons, 1925.

Empedocles. *The Poem of Empedocles.* Translated by Brad Inwood. Toronto: University of Toronto Press, 2001.

———. *The Extant Fragments.* Cambridge, Mass.: Haskett Publishing Co., 1995.

Encountering Sorrow (Li sao) Qu Yuan (ca. 300 B.C.E.)

A lengthy dramatic narrative poem, *Encountering Sorrow* is the principal surviving example of the work of Qu Yuan (Ch'ü Yüan) and the most famous poem in the history of Chinese literature. Qu is the earliest Chinese poet whose name we know. Many commentators think that *Encountering Sorrow* traces the poet's response to having lost the confidence of his ruler and employer as a result of slander.

After introducing the poet and tracing his genealogy, the poem reports Qu's efforts to follow the "right way"—that is, the way of the Confucian gentleman. Qu employs the imagery and symbolism of gathering flowers associated with several virtues to underscore his own righteousness. The poet frets about the influence that his slanderers, Chieh and Chou, enjoy with the king. Qu worries not so much about his own situation as about the dangers to the king that will follow from heeding the advice of depraved counselors. In his depression, his thoughts turn to exile and to suicide. It would be best, he thinks, to die in the cause of virtue.

A long section follows in which Qu Yuan compares his situation with those of historical persons who provide examples and counterexamples of following the sort of path he has marked out for himself. Then he traces his route into exile and the physical and spiritual preparations that he made for the journey. He imagines himself traveling through the sky in a dragon-drawn chariot. Although he is turned away from Heaven's gate, he experiences moments of joy. Then he looks down and sees his old home in the distance. The fleeting moment of happiness passes, and despite the earlier efforts of a person named Ni Xi to cheer up the poet, depression claims him.

A four-line *luan*—a concluding section that in some ways resembles the last lines of a Renaissance Italian ode—ends the song. Instead, of addressing the poem in his last lines, however, Qu Yuan reaches a firm conclusion. His life is finished. He is alone and unknown. He longs for his own home. As no ruler will employ him to help administer a just regime, his purpose in life is doomed to remain unfulfilled. He resolves to seek out a certain P'eng Hsien, who had earlier ended his life by drowning.

Although one of the poem's translators, Burton Watson, much admires the work, he is put off by Qu's self-righteousness and melodramatic sense of injured merit. Other sorts of works also appear in Qu's verses. One finds ritual songs; a series of verse riddles on the subjects of Chinese history, cosmology, and myth; and a poetic dialogue between Qu and a fisherman in which the latter encourages Qu to remain among the living and continue to do his job. Several of the poems deal with the ritual activities of a priest or a shaman.

The literary historian Victor Mair explains that the verse riddles make up a particularly perplexing set of poems from Qu Yuan's pen, the *T'ien wen*. That title can be rendered into English as "Heavenly Questions" or "Divine Conundrums." The work poses a series of unanswered questions about cosmology, myth, the rise of civilization, and the founding of societies by demigods.

For students of ancient literature, tangled critical issues arise from this text. Some light has been shed, however, by applying the methods of comparative mythology to the work. The riddle poems of *Heavenly Questions* find parallels in such other mythical traditions as those of the ancient Indo-European and even of North African peoples. Such verses may have been connected with induction into cults and with sacrifices. Typical of the questions the work asks are queries like these: Who measured heaven? How many miles does the sun travel? How did the husbandless goddess of fertility conceive nine sons? Is the distance greater from north to south, or from east to west? Mair translates a generous sample of the poem in his work listed in the bibliography below.

Bibliography

Barnstone, Tony, and Chou Ping, eds. "The Verses of Chou." In *The Anchor Book of Chinese Poetry*. New York: Anchor Books, 2005.

Mair, Victor H., ed. *The Columbia Anthology of Traditional Chinese Literature*. New York: Columbia University Press, 1994.

Ssu-ma Ch'ien (Sima Qian). *Records of the Grand Historian.* Vol.1. New York: Columbia University Press, 1961.

Watson, Burton. *Early Chinese Literature.* New York: Columbia University Press, 1962.

Ennius, Quintus (239–169 B.C.E.) *Roman playwright*

A trilingual poet and playwright, Quintus Ennius was the most important figure in the archaic period of Latin literature—the period, that is, when the Latin language was still in its formative stages. Though his literary remains are fragmentary and though we have those fragments largely at second hand, his celebrity and accomplishment made his work the object of imitation and of scholarly study well into the Common Era. As a single example, in his AENEID, VIRGIL borrowed freely from Ennius's *Annals.*

Ennius was born on the Sallentine Peninsula of southeastern Italy—then called Calabria—at Rudiae (modern Rugge). His parents spoke the Italic language called Oscan. Beyond his native tongue, Ennius also mastered Greek and archaic Latin during his childhood. This trilingualism caused him to describe himself as having "three hearts."

We learn from the editor and translator E. H. Warmington that Ennius joined the Roman army after finishing his education. As a soldier, he achieved the rank of centurion (one who commanded 100 men) and came to the attention of Marcus Porcius Cato, the elder. Then a quaestor (a judicial official) of the Republic, Cato rose to become the chief of the Roman State, its consul. According to tradition, Ennius tutored Cato in Greek literature and perhaps in the Greek language as well.

In any case, for a considerable period, Ennius continued to enjoy the patronage of Cato, who took the younger man with him to Rome. There Ennius supported himself, according to St. JEROME, by maintaining the precinct sacred to the goddess Tutilina—also called the "guardian goddess." He also gave lessons in the Greek language,

began publishing his own verse, and became a playwright. In that capacity, he seems to have written a few examples of comedy and some 20 tragedies, all based on Greek models that he freely translated. The fragmentary remains of several of the tragedies also suggest that Ennius particularly revered EURIPIDES.

The known tragedies of Ennius listed by the classicist H. D. Jocelyn included: *Achilles, Ajax, Alcmaeon, Alexander* (here the alternate name of the Trojan prince, Paris), *Andromache, Andromeda, Athamas, Cresphontes, Erectheus, Eumenides, Hectoris Lustra, Hecuba, Iphigenia, Medea, Melanippe, Nemea, Phoenix, Telamon, Telephus, and Thyestes.* (I have normalized Jocelyn and Ennius's Old Latin spellings.) He may have written a comic *Telestis* in addition to his two authoritatively attributed comedies, *Cupuncula* and *Pancratiastes.* Beyond those works, Jocelyn reports that Ennius also tried his hand at historico-tragedy in a play about the notable rape of the Sabine women (*Sabinae*) and another concerning the Roman siege and conquest of the Greek city of Ambracia, whose name is also the title of Ennius's play.

Poetry in archaic Latin had been composed in accentual verse, relying on the sort of stressed and unstressed syllables that English typically uses (see SATURNIAN VERSE). Ennius was responsible for initiating the importation into Latin from Greek of a metrical system based on the length of syllables. Syllable length was determined either by the actual duration of a syllable's sound or by an arbitrary system for determining vowel length. (See QUANTITATIVE VERSE.)

Among his contemporaries and several generations of his successors, Ennius's reputation rested chiefly on a quantitative dactylic hexameter EPIC, his *Annals.* In this masterwork, Ennius traced the history of Roman military successes from Rome's beginnings down to the Roman campaign against the Istri (178/77 B.C.E.). We are not certain that the 18-book poem was finished when Ennius died. Being of a bibulous disposition, Ennius is said to have remarked that he never worked on that poem unless he had been drinking heavily—a habit that killed him in the end when he died of gout.

During his career, Ennius became friends with and wrote about some of the most celebrated Romans of his day. These included Scipio Africanus, the conqueror of the Carthaginian general Hannibal, and Marcus Fulvius Nobilior, the conqueror of Ambracia and the hero of Ennius's play of the same name. Partly as a reward for celebrating his father, Nobilior's son Quintus helped Ennius to become a Roman citizen in 184 B.C.E. and to obtain a grant of land.

E. H. Warmington speculates that in some of Ennius's other works, the poet showed too great an admiration for the freethinking of EPICURUS and his followers. As a result, the poet may have lost the support of his earliest patron, Cato. Warmington suggests Cato came to think that Ennius's admiration for the Epicurean position, which held that the gods were uninterested in human affairs, and the poet's presentation of such ideas in his *Epicharmus* and *Euhemerus (Holy History)*, constituted a danger to the religious values of the Roman Republic. *Epicharmus* was a dream vision in which the poet imagined that he had died and awakened in heaven, where mysteries were revealed to him. *Euhemerus* proposed the view that the pantheon of deities worshipped throughout the Mediterranean world had once all been remarkable human beings to whom their successors had ascribed supernatural powers.

In addition to the works outlined above, Ennius wrote at least four scroll-length works of SATIRE; a number of EPIGRAMS; and a work on gastronomy, *Hedyphagetica*, a volume that APULEIUS read which borrowed much of its content from the *HEDUPATHEIA* of ARCHESTRATUS of Gela (fl. fourth century B.C.E.).

Bibliography

Ennius, Quintus. *The Annals of Ennius Quintus.* Edited with commentary by Otto Skutsch. Oxford: Clarendon Press; New York: Oxford University Press, 1985.

Warmington, E. H., ed. and trans. *Remains of Old Latin: Ennius and Caecilius.* Vol. 1. Cambridge, Mass.: Harvard University Press, 1935.

Entrepreneur, The   See MERCHANT, THE.

epic

The epic style of poetry has deep roots in the past of many cultures. Apparently epics arose in the ancient world from oral recitations of stories—many older than writing itself. These stories recount the deeds of heroes and gods, and they report facts and myths of central importance to the cultures that produced them. The epics of HOMER, *The ILIAD* and *The ODYSSEY*, established the characteristics of the model for the ancient Mediterranean world, and VIRGIL imitated and polished their form for his Roman national epic, *AENEID*.

In ancient Greece, epics remained popular well into the HELLENISTIC AGE. In the third century B.C.E., for instance, APOLLONIUS OF RHODIES, in his *ARGONAUTIKA*, returned to the characteristic genre of Homer, putting aside such developments as a tendency to allegorize the contents of epics that post-Homeric practitioners of the genre had developed.

As polished by Virgil in his *Aeneid*, the form of the epic became largely fixed. The action begins in the middle of things, and later in the poem, flashbacks transport the reader to what had happened earlier. The poet invokes the MUSE, asking her to sing through him. Poets also state their epic purposes early in the song. Other features characterize the form. A reader usually finds a descent into the underworld; gods or other supernatural beings play significant roles. The action regularly includes military and amorous encounters, but beyond that it is of great importance in the development of a national or supranational mythos. These attributes continued to characterize the work of epic poets throughout the ancient Mediterranean world and, in western Europe, right through the

Middle Ages and well into the early modern period.

The Middle Eastern prototype is *The GIL-GAMESH EPIC* of ancient Sumer—the oldest written epic known (before 3000 B.C.E.) and the source of some of the plot for the story of Noah in the HEBREW BIBLE. In ancient India, the *RAMAYANA* and the *MAHABHARATA* arose as national epics of high religious significance. The *Mahabharata* enjoys the distinction of being the world's longest known epic poem. In India, a series of shorter works, the *Puranas*, also appeared.

Bibliography

Homer. *The Iliad*. Translated by Robert Fitzgerald. New York: Farrar, Straus, and Giroux, 2004.

———. *The Odyssey*. Translated by Edward McCrorie. Baltimore: Johns Hopkins University Press, ca. 2004.

Lal, P. *The Mahabharata of Vyasa condensed from Sanskrit and Transcreated into English*. New Delhi: Vikas, ca. 1980.

Narayan, R. K. *The Mahabharata: A Shortened Modern Prose Version of the Indian Epic*. Chicago: University of Chicago Press, 2000.

Virgil. *Aeneid*. Translated by Stanley Lombardo. Indianapolis: Haskett Publishing, 2005.

Epicharmus of Cos (Epicharmus of Sicily) (fl. ca. late sixth or early fifth century B.C.E.) *Greek dramatist*

A very early writer of COMEDY, Epicharmus is credited by some with being the founder of the genre. Several Mediterranean islands, including Cos in the eastern Aegean group called the Sporades, claim to be the birthplace of Epicharmus. The most authoritative view presumes Sicilian origin—a possibility that gains credence from the fact that the exceedingly fragmentary remains of his work are in the Sicilian dialect of Doric Greek. J. J. Eschenberg calls Epicharmus "a professor of . . . Pythagorean philosophy" at the court of the tyrant Hiero in Sicily about 470 B.C.E., a date that conflicts with other estimates.

It seems that Epicharmus's comedies were known at Athens and that his work gave impetus to the development of Athenian comedy. The number of known fragments of Epicharmus's work has recently grown owing to their discovery among the OXYRYNCHUS papyri. As a result of these finds, it has become possible to say something about the subjects and nature of his lost comedy. The classicist Kenneth James Dover suggests that "mythological burlesque" was a feature of the playwright's comedy, and that Heracles and Odysseus figured among his comic heroes. On other issues, such as the number of actors he employed in each play and whether or not there may have been a chorus, discussion still continues. Dover considers the CHORUS a likelihood.

Bibliography

Dover, Kenneth James. "Epicharmus." In *The Oxford Classical Dictionary*. Edited by Simon Hornblower and Antony Spawforth. Oxford: Oxford University Press, 1996.

Eschenberg, J. J. *Manual of Classical Literature*. Translated by N. W. Fiske. Philadelphia: E. C. & J. Biddle, 1850.

Kirkhof, Rainer. *Dorische Posse, Epicharm und Attische Komodie* [Doric Farce, Epicharmus and Attic Comedy]. Munich: K. G. Saur, 2001.

Epicurus (341–271 B.C.E.) *Greek prose writer*

Epicurus was the son of an Athenian couple, Neocles and his wife Chaerestrate, who had moved to the island of Samos. On Samos, Epicurus studied philosophy and other subjects from age 14 through 18 with a Platonist tutor named Pamphilius. He then traveled to Athens to perform a mandatory two-year period of military service.

While Epicurus fulfilled that duty, his parents suffered political oppression on Samos. To escape it, they migrated to Colophon, a city in Asia Minor. There, in 321, Epicurus joined them, and for the next decade he continued his studies both independently and under the tutelage of Nausiphanes.

That teacher believed in the precepts of the atomists—a school of philosophers who held that the universe is composed of tiny, indivisible, indestructible particles. Epicurus may have benefited from other instruction as well, perhaps, that of Praxiphanes, who followed the teachings of ARISTOTLE (384–22 B.C.E.)

In 331 B.C.E., Epicurus moved to Mytilene on the island of Lesbos, where he began to propound his own philosophical system. His ideas, however, did not receive a favorable hearing, and after only a year he moved to the city of Lampsacus, located not far from the Hellespont in Asia Minor. In Lampsacus, his views enjoyed a much more encouraging response, and with his earnings and a retinue of followers, he was able to migrate to Athens in 306. There Epicurus purchased a sizable house with a walled garden and founded a private school of philosophy called "the garden" that was also a community of like-minded individuals of both sexes. His was the first philosophical academy in Greece to welcome women as well as men.

Contrary to the accusations of his detractors—of whom there have been many—and contrary to the popular association of Epicurus's name with the aphorism "Eat, drink, and be merry, for tomorrow you may die," the goal of Epicurus's communal society was, as his biographer George A. Panichas assures us, "the moral perfection of the individual." The regimen of Epicurus's group savored more of monastic asceticism than of the sybaritic license attributed to its founder and its members by Epicurus's detractors and by posterity. Meals were sparse, alcoholic beverages were in short supply, and water was the principal liquid refreshment. Though the community was hierarchically organized, apparently anyone was free to correct anyone else if one member perceived a fault in another. Such correction was offered firmly but, as Panichas says, with "gentleness, persuasion, sympathy, [and] compassion." Epicurus's regimen proposed as a principal object the avoidance of pain and suffering. This included physical, mental, emotional, and ethical pain. Living a good life that strove in all its departments to achieve a concerned balance toward oneself and toward others was the goal of Epicurean wisdom. The society he founded endured as a fellowship for some 700 years and gained numerous adherents throughout ancient Greece and Rome.

Epicurus's writings apparently encompassed some 300 "books." From the early Greek perspective, a book was a manuscript scroll, usually papyrus, of a more or less standardized length. Only a few of his compositions, however, have survived to come down to us directly; these writings are preserved in the 10th book of DIOGENES LAERTIUS's biography of Epicurus. They include his 40 *Principal Doctrines* as well as a letter on the subject of natural philosophy addressed to a contemporary named Herodotus, another on meteorology addressed to a certain Pythocles, and a third on theoretical ethics addressed to a correspondent named Menoeceus.

In the first of these letters, Epicurus sums up his conclusions about the physical nature of the material universe and points out the benefits that arise for human beings from understanding physical science. Among these he includes a reduction in both superstition and skepticism about the existence of an essentially indescribable deity. In his "Letter to Pythocles," Epicurus offers explanations for observable celestial events, like the orbits of planets, eclipses, falling stars, and the formation of clouds. He again endorses an empirical rather than a magical or superstitious approach to understanding the natural world.

In "Letter to Menoeceus," Epicurus discusses theology and ethics. He makes clear that he believes in an "immortal and blessed God" but suggests that believers should believe about that God only such things as support both immortality and blessedness. Epicurus also suggests that believers should avoid attributing to God their own partisan preferences. Here, too, he famously remarks, "Death is nothing to us," and he summarizes his views about the virtuous life.

Good English translations of these documents and of Epicurus's other writings and surviving fragments are accessible through the website listed in the bibliography below.

Beyond the few surviving texts, our knowledge of the writings and thinking of Epicurus comes principally from the celebrated materialistic poem DE RERUM NATURA (*On the Nature of Things*) written by his subsequent admirer, the Roman Titus LUCRETIUS Carus (ca. 95–55 B.C.E.). Other remnants appear elsewhere among later Roman and medieval writers. From these sources we learn at least the titles of some of Epicurus's estimated 300 books (varying from 1 to 37 scrolls in length) and with them something of the range of his thought. A sampling of those titles includes: *On Atoms and Void, On Benefits and Gratitude, On Choice and Avoidance, On Diseases and Death, On the End, On Fate, On the Gods, On Gratitude, On Human Life, On Images, On Just Dealing, On Justice and Other Virtues, On Kingship, On Music, On Piety, On Touch,* and *On Vision.*

Although Epicurus does not appear to have acknowledged his indebtedness to earlier thinkers, he nonetheless occupies an important place in a line of Greek atomistic and materialist philosophers. That line stretches from Thales (ca. 625–546 B.C.E.) through Anaximander (ca. 611–546 B.C.E.), Anaximenes of Miletus (fl. sixth century B.C.E.), Heraclitus (ca. 544–484 B.C.E.), the versifying philosopher Parmenides (ca. 540–470 B.C.E.), EMPEDOCLES (fl. ca. 440), and Anaxagoras (500–428 B.C.E.). The line culminates in the work of Leucippus (fl. ca. 430 B.C.E.) and his friend Democritus (fl. ca. 400–357 B.C.E.). All these thinkers, like Epicurus, shared the essential premise that the world and all in it arose from natural and material origins. Though some were deists, they denied mythical theories of divine origins, and they developed their ethical viewpoints from the mutual benefit of good behavior for members of the community rather than from divine commandments. Perhaps inevitably, the adherents of successive pre- and post-Christian religions, along with astrologers, magicians, and spiritualists, vilified the views of these Greek materialist philosophers.

For 21st-century readers, Epicurus raises numerous relevant issues. For example, he defends the concept of the soul's mortality—body and soul die together. For him death holds no threat, since it means only the end of sensation. He perceives happiness as the highest good, and not far behind happiness comes friendship. The known precepts of Epicurus have sparked interest, admiration, and heartfelt criticism ever since their author enunciated them. His views address issues still controversial after almost 2,500 years.

Never very strong, Epicurus died after two painful weeks of suffering excretory difficulties. He met his own death with equanimity, firm in the conviction that he had nothing to fear.

Bibliography

Cook, Vincent. "Epicurus & Epicurean Philosophy." Available online. URL: http://www.epicurus.net/index.html. Downloaded May 19, 2005.

Epicurus. *Epicurus, the Extant Remains.* Translated and annotated by Cyril Bailey. Westport, Conn.: Hyperion Press, 1979.

———. *The Essential Epicurus: Letters, Principal Doctrines, Vatican Sayings, and Fragments.* Translated and edited by Eugene O'Connor. Buffalo, N.Y.: Prometheus Books, 1993.

———. *The Epicurus Reader: Selected Writings and Testimonia.* Translated and edited by Brad Inwood and L. P. Gerson; introduced by D. S. Hutchinson. Indianapolis, Ind.: Hackett, 1994.

———. *Letter on Happiness.* Translated by Robin Waterfield. San Francisco, Calif.: Chronicle Books, 1994.

Koen, Avraam. *Atoms, Pleasure, Virtue: The Philosophy of Epicurus.* New York: Peter Lang, 1995.

Panichas, George A. *Epicurus.* New York: Twayne Publishers, Inc., 1967.

Sharples, R. W. *Stoics, Epicureans, and Skeptics: An Introduction to Hellenistic Philosophy.* London and New York: Routledge, 1996.

Warren, James. *Facing Death: Epicurus and His Critics.* Oxford and New York: Clarendon Press, 2004.

Epigenes the Sicyonian (fl. ca. sixth century B.C.E.)

We have no knowledge of any Greek TRAGEDY before Epigenes. Mentioned by the historian

HERODOTUS and by the Byzantine lexicographers Suidas and Photius as the inventor of the tragedy, he was thought to have flourished on the island of Sicyon. According to a rhetorician of Constantinople, Themistius (fl. fourth century C.E.), Epigenes developed a sort of operatic proto-tragedy on the island of Sicyon. That dramatic presentation celebrated in choral song the sufferings of a legendary king of Argos, Adrastus, whom the people of Sicyon honored as a deity.

Bibliography

Eschenberg, J. J., and N. W. Fiske. *Manual of Classical Literature*. Philadelphia: E. C. & J. Biddle, 1850.

epigram, Greek and Latin

Originally meaning a brief inscription on buildings, tombstones, or votive offerings, the verse epigram became a favorite mode of expression for numerous ancient authors. Some of the early authors named as writers of epigrams include AESOP, ANACREON, SIMONIDES OF CEOS, and the playwrights AESCHYLUS and EURIPIDES.

In the HELLENISTIC AGE, the epigram's brevity gave opportunities for skillful poets, such as the Greek CALLIMACHUS, to indulge their preference for short, pithy, emotionally intense, highly allusive, striking verses as opposed to the more extended and, perhaps, less effective EPIC. That ancient genre, in Callimachus's opinion, had largely run its course. (See *EPIGRAMS*.)

Among others who wrote Greek epigrams in the HELLENISTIC AGE, we find LEONIDAS OF TARENTUM. Around 100 of Leonidas's widely admired epigrams are extant. As the epigram gained in popularity, the numbers of those who opted to compose in the genre mushroomed correspondingly. A particularly talented practitioner around the mid-first century B.C.E., MELEAGER OF GADARA, gathered together a collection. He included a selection of his own epigrams together with those of 45 others. Entitled *Stephanos* (The Garland), it became a model for later similar collections throughout the ancient and early modern worlds. The subject matter of many of the poems was amorous, sometimes steamily so.

In the Latin language, the history of early epigrammatic inscription on tombstones and elsewhere parallels that of the Greek. In its earliest recorded stages, Latin versification was based, like modern English, on accent rather than, on the arbitrary definition of the length of syllables, as in ancient Greek. That accentual system plus a preference for alliteration characterized Latin SATURNIAN VERSE, as the ancient system is known.

Around the beginning of the second century B.C.E., the Roman poet and playwright QUINTUS ENNIUS introduced a version of the Greek system into Latin prosody. He also composed a series of dignified epigrams that exhorted people to observe high-minded civic values. Under the influence of a growing Roman popular taste for all things Greek, epigrams in the Greek manner steadily gained in popularity among both writers and readers. CATULLUS composed memorable examples on subjects that included love. MARTIAL's work in the idiom (see *EPIGRAMS*) made it broadly popular. Moreover, among the Roman upper classes there was a vogue for the composition of the epigram that contributed to its becoming the principal genre of the time. Over time, too, the subject matter deemed appropriate for epigrams broadened so that everything from the noblest to the most obscene topics became grist for their mill.

The epigram retained its popularity well into the Christian era and even into the 21st century. Numerous Christian epigrams appear in both the Latin and the Greek languages on the native peninsulas and throughout the two cultures' diaspora—particularly at Byzantium (Constantinople), where the genre endured and where anthologies of work in both languages were compiled.

Bibliography

Callimachus. *Callimachus: Hymns, Epigrams, Select Fragments*. Translated by Stanley Lombardo and Diane Rayor. Baltimore, Md., and London: Johns Hopkins University Press, 1988.

Eschenburg, J. J. *Manual of Classical Literature.* Philadelphia: E. C. & J. Biddle, 1850.

Taplin, Oliver. *Literature in the Greek and Roman Worlds: A New Perspective.* Oxford: Oxford University Press, 2000.

Epigrams Callimachus (third century B.C.E.)

In his own epoch, CALLIMACHUS was most famous, though not universally admired, for his EPIGRAMS. Of these brief, pithy, often humorous, and always polished poems, 64 examples survive. These treat a broad array of subjects in an equally broad spectrum of emotional registers always perfectly suited to both the subject and the way the poet handles it, as we see in examples of brief epitaphs. The first of these, epigram 1, evokes the poet's sadness as he recalls his friend and brother poet, Herakleitos of Halikarnassos, whose poems are deathless "nightingales" that are beyond the grasp of the king of the underworld. The fourth of Callimachus's epigrams briefly reports the pious act of Leontikos, who found an anonymous body washed up on the beach and, in an act of piety, buried it. The tears Leontikos shed, however, were for his own mortality.

Among the epitaphs in Callimachus's collection of funereal epigrams we find number 16—an epitaph for the common grave of the poet's father and son. It evokes sympathy for the poet's ironic double loss through its understatement. The following epitaph, epigram 17, is Callimachus's own. In it, he reports: ". . . his line / was verse, his diversion wine." It is a nonsentimental, minimalist, and amusing autobiographical verse epitaph.

Some of the epigrams contain quite elaborate jokes. In epigram 24, for instance, a passerby calls on the dead Charidas to answer questions about the underworld. The questioner learns the bad news: The underworld is dark, there is no way out, and its king, Pluto, is a myth. The good news, however, is the low cost of living.

A series of epigrams seem designed to accompany votive offerings presented on the altars of the gods. Among these, some seem designed to accompany real gifts, and others, like the portrait and intimate apparel of a streetwalker named Simone offered to Aphrodite, seem fictive.

Epigrams 45–57 deal self-mockingly yet touchingly with Callimachus's various infatuations with beautiful young men and his remedies against the god of love, Eros. Epigram 58 brings that theme together with an assertion of the poet's refined tastes in the literary and personal realms. A reader finds that he "hates the poems" that comprise the ancient Greek cycle of epics. Similarly, the poet dislikes heavily trodden highways, drinking from public fountains, and promiscuous lovers. He therefore rejects a handsome man named Lysanias.

The 59th through the 63rd epigrams continue to chronicle Callimachus's literary tastes and his preferences for the new, brief, and pithy polished over the extensive, familiar, and careless. In the 62nd epigram, the poet praises Aratos of Soloi, who writes "terse, subtle tokens of long effort at night."

The 64th of the surviving epigrams is an admonitory poem based on the experience of a certain Pittakos of Mytilene. It advises against overreaching in seeking a wealthy mate and also, presumably, against trying anything unsuited to one's situation and capacities.

Bibliography

Callimachus. *Callimachus: Hymns, Epigrams, Select Fragments.* Translated by Stanley Lombardo and Diane Rayor. Baltimore, Md., and London: Johns Hopkins University Press, 1988.

Epigrams Martial (ca. 86–ca. 98 C.E.)

MARTIAL's 14 books of *Epigrams* were instant successes from the moment the first book appeared. A part of their popularity, of course, stemmed from the fact that the EPIGRAM was already by far the most popular literary genre among Romans. The poet CATULLUS had brought the verse genre into vogue in Rome, and a series of other poets, whose works are almost totally lost, followed him in the practice of the genre. Some of their names survive principally because Martial points to them as sources of his inspiration: Lentulus Gaetulicus, Domitius Marsus, and Albinovanus Pedo. Moreover, the composition of epigrams was a popular pastime among the social elite of Rome.

Martial, however, gave the genre a form that would characterize the epigram for centuries. First of all, his subjects were regularly drawn from the real life of the city. An epigram might describe one of the great public spectacles—the "circuses" that the powerful afforded to keep the common people entertained. It might be a personally designed verse that he had written on commission—in effect, a greeting card by Martial. An epigram might contain a recognizable caricature of a person, but it would more likely contain a stylized character type. Martial moved the stock theatrical characters of the Roman comedies into his verses and added types to the cluster: to misers and parasites, to the vainglorious and the con artists, Martial added self-important poets, plagiarists who *borrowed* Martial's work without crediting it, and fading beauties who found lovers only with increasing difficulty. In this epigrammatic presentation of character flaws made funny through exaggeration, Martial gave the Renaissance a model for a favorite prose form: the *character*.

A technique that Martial perfected involves his concluding an epigram with a witticism that gave a brilliant final point to the whole performance. Such a tag appears in *Epigrams* 8:13, addressed to his friend Priscus, who had apparently asked why Martial did not wish to marry a wealthy wife. Martial's reply: "I don't want to be my wife's wife." Then, with amusing double entendre, Martial continues: "The matron should be under her husband," followed by the tag: "That's the only way a man and a woman can be equal."

The literary historian Gian Biaggio Conte summarizes received opinion concerning Martial's typical epigrammatic pattern: He describes the subject of his poem, human or otherwise, establishing an expectation—often unconscious—in his reader. Then, in the end of the poem, he surprises his reader with a humorous paradox. Beyond this, Martial used the real language of real people. Some of that language is humorously obscene, and his subject matter never shies away from the earthier practices of the Roman population.

While all those aspects of Martial's verse made him a popular poet, it was his mastery of deploying the evocative power of language to touch not only his readers' sense of humor but also their heartstrings that sets him among the great poets of the Western tradition. He can evoke sadness, he can be polished, or he can be solemn and funny at the same time.

Sometimes he was also political. While that tendency contributed to his popularity for a time, it also necessitated his rewriting the 10th book when the Emperor Domitian's successors repudiated Domitian's memory after his death. Martial scrambled to excise from the 10th book certain passages that praised Domitian immoderately. The book was reissued, but the damage had been done. Martial found it expedient and healthy to retire from the Rome he loved to his native Spain. There he languished unhappy for a while until he died.

Bibliography

Conte, Gian Biaggio. *Latin Literature: A History.* Translated by Joseph B. Solodow, Don Fowler, and Glenn W. Most. Baltimore, Md.: Johns Hopkins University Press, 1994.

Martial. *Epigrams.* 3 vols. Edited and translated by D. R. Shackleton Bailey. Cambridge, Mass.: Harvard University Press, 1993.

———. *Select Epigrams.* Edited by Lindsay and Patricia Watson. Cambridge and New York: Cambridge University Press, 2003.

Sullivan, J. P., and A. J. Boyle, eds. *Martial in English.* Selections. New York: Penguin Books, 1996.

Epistle of Barnabas, The Anonymous
(ca. 70–135 C.E.)

Though some scholars have argued for a narrower time frame within which the Epistle of Barnabas can be dated, internal evidence suggests that the document must have been written between the destruction in 70 C.E. of the temple built by Herod in Jerusalem and the construction on its site of a new one in 135. The attribution both of the letter and its embedded tract to Barnabas, the associate of the apostle Paul, seems to have occurred retrospectively. EUSEBIUS, the third-century bishop of Caesarea, considered the attribution wrong, and the document's militant anti-Jewish content seems inconsistent, according to the church historian Bart D. Ehrman, with what we know of Barnabas's views. Other evidence points to the possibility that the epistle was composed in Alexandria, Egypt, though some commentators have offered Asia Minor and Syro-Palestine as alternatives. In Egypt, the letter of Barnabas was included as Scripture in a NEW TESTAMENT manuscript (Codex Sinaiticus).

Whatever the occasion for the epistle's composition, from the point of view of subsequent Judeo-Christian relations, it is just as well that the work was finally excluded from the text of the New Testament, for the work argues that, inspired by an evil angel, the Jewish religion has always erred by misunderstanding its own scriptures and that it continues to do so. In the fourth chapter, for example, the epistle argues against persons who claim that the covenant between God and God's people belongs both to Jews and to Christians. In support of such views, the author argues that though God inscribed the Ten Commandments on a stone tablet with his own finger, when the Jewish people erred by worshipping idols, the tablet was smashed and, with it, so was the Jews' covenant with the Lord. This event, says the epistle, prepared the way for the new covenant between God's "beloved, Jesus" and the Christian people.

Having presented a series of arguments along these lines, the epistle's author reminds his readers of the two paths of light and darkness—the first maintained by "the light-bearing angels of God," and the other by "the angels of Satan." From that point, the epistle essentially repeats the views about the way of life and the way of death proposed in the *DIDACHE: THE TEACHING OF THE TWELVE APOSTLES*. Then, after admonishing his readers that judgment day is near at hand, the Epistle of Barnabas's author salutes his readers lovingly and ends his letter.

See also *APOSTOLIC FATHERS OF THE CHRISTIAN CHURCH, THE*.

Bibliography

Epistle of Barnabas. In *The Apostolic Fathers*. Vol. 2. Edited and translated by Bart D. Ehrman. Cambridge, Mass.: Harvard University Press, 2003.

Epistles Horace (ca. 20–15 B.C.E.)

Rather than real letters, HORACE's epistles are dactylic hexameter poems (see QUANTITATIVE VERSE) written as if they were verse epistles and addressed to various friends and acquaintances and persons of note. For Horace, the epistolary poem was not only a departure from his previous practice in his *ODES* and in his often-satiric *Epodes*, it was also likely a new genre altogether. To be sure there had been earlier verse letters, but to make a systematic collection of them seems unprecedented.

Two sets of Horatian *Epistles* appeared. In the first set, the poet adopted the philosophical perspective of an aging person who has advice and encouragement to offer on the conduct of life. He also wishes to recall portions of his personal history. Taken as a group, the letters of the first collection offer their addressees an overview of the benefits of a life conducted at a distance from Rome's urban confusion and in a pleasant and withdrawn place, both geographically and psychologically. They are the work of a Horace more serene than the poet of his *SATIRES*.

In Epistle I.1, Horace asserts his independence from all formal philosophical schools and his capacity either for engagement in or for withdrawal from civic affairs. At the same time, he seems uneasy with a life that wavers between restraint and damaging self-indulgence. As in Epistle I.8, he also yearns for Rome when he is at Tivoli and vice versa. He gives an impression of wanting to be both teacher and exemplar, but at the same time, he seems aware that his own imperfections may disqualify him for the task.

In the letters of the second book, Horace directs his attention to artistic and especially literary matters. He first concerns himself with Roman theater and the tendency of the theatergoers of the Augustan age to give preference to the early dramatists of the old Roman theater. Horace even presumes to lecture the emperor, AUGUSTUS CAESAR, about his preference for staged spectacle over the private reading of poetry.

Horace composed his longest epistolary poem as the centerpiece of the second book, his famous literary-critical epistle, THE ART OF POETRY, which is included in this volume as a separate entry.

Bibliography

Fairclough, H. Rushton, ed. and trans. *Horace: Satires, Epistles, Ars Poetica.* New York: G. P. Putnam's and Sons, 1932.

Horace. *The Complete Works: Translated in the Meters of the Originals.* Translated by Charles E. Passage. New York: F. Ungar Publishing Company, 1983.

Reckford, Kenneth J. *Horace.* New York: Twayne Publishers, 1969.

epistles   See FICTION AS EPISTLE, ROMANCE, AND EROTIC PROSE.

"Epistle to Diognetus, The" (ca. 150–190 C.E.)

Not incorporated into the body of material comprising the writings of the APOSTOLIC FATHERS OF THE CHRISTIAN CHURCH until the 18th century, the 12-chapter epistle to the pagan Diognetus includes 10 chapters of a letter answering the inquiries of its otherwise unknown addressee. Diognetus wanted to know more about the Christians and their God. He queried their reasons for rejecting the religious observances of both the Jews and the Greeks. He wondered why, if the beliefs of the Christians were true, they had appeared so comparatively late in history. The polished answer to many of his questions is one of the distinguished literary documents of late second-century Christianity.

Chapters 11 and 12, however, were clearly written by a different though also uncertain author. As historian of Christianity Bart D. Ehrman tells us, they appear to derive from a homily rather than from a letter. As compared with the epistle's earlier sections, chapters 11 and 12 take a more generous view of the Jewish religion as a precursor of Christianity, especially as regards the validity of Jewish law and the prophets.

After greeting Diognetus and encouraging him to prepare his mind to receive information that will make him a new person, the author points out that the gods Diognetus currently worships have been fabricated by artisans and are deaf, blind, dumb, and decaying. Those made of stone and ceramics, moreover, get neglected while those made from precious metals are safeguarded.

The letter's author next points out where he thinks the Jews go astray in such matters as "their anxiety over food," superstitions concerning the Sabbath, and the practice of circumcision.

In the fifth chapter, the author enumerates the excellences of the Christians, who may dwell anywhere, speak any language, work at any trade or profession, and marry and have children like everyone else, and though they observe the laws of their homelands, they are everywhere persecuted and repay the evils they suffer with good. Wherever they live, however, they are the citizens of heaven.

Christians, says the author in the sixth chapter, are to the world as the soul is to the body, and he explains that analogy in some detail, concluding that this is the role that God has assigned them and they cannot rightfully abandon it. The author then addresses the means by which God chose to convey Christian truth to the world and explains Christ's role and identity as "the craftsman and maker of all things."

Chapter 8 begins by asking this question: Before Christ came, "what person . . . had any idea what God was like?" The chapter and the one following continue by expostulating on the ways in which God revealed his nature to human beings through Christ, and how Christ's sacrifice brought people the promise of immortality. The 10th chapter instructs Diognetus in what he must do if he desires to acquire Christian faith and escape the fires of eternal condemnation.

The 11th chapter differs markedly in style and vocabulary and changes the subject, discoursing, first, on the role of the author as "a teacher of the nations." Next, the writer considers the embodiment of the logos—God's word—in Christ as he worked among his disciples and as he offers grace to those who will accept it. In the 12th chapter, the writer concludes by counseling the acceptance of the "true, comprehensible word" and its accompanying salvation.

Bibliography

"Epistle to Diognetus." In *The Apostolic Fathers.* Vol. 2. Edited and translated by Bart D. Ehrman. Cambridge, Mass.: Harvard University Press, 2003.

Epistulae ex Ponto   See TRISTIA AND EPISTULAE EX PONTO.

epode

Originated by the Greek lyric poets ARCHILOCHUS and ALCAEUS, the epode is a lyric verse form in which a long line is followed by a shorter one. Sometimes the word *epode* is also applied to the third stanza in a group of three. The sequence of stanzas in such a composition goes: strophe, antistrophe, epode. The versification of the epode varies from that of the two preceding stanzas.

The Roman poet HORACE was famous for his *Odes* and *Epodes*—especially for the way he gave the form fresh vigor as he celebrated the renewed centrality of the state in the imperial order established by AUGUSTUS CAESAR.

Eratosthenes (ca. 285–194 B.C.E.) *Greek poet/prose writer*

Born on the island of Cyrene, Eratosthenes studied with CALLIMACHUS, spent several years in Athens as a student, and then, at the invitation of the Greek pharaoh, Ptolemy III, moved to Alexandria as royal tutor. He followed APOLLONIUS OF RHODES as the director of the great library at Alexandria.

A gifted polymath, Eratosthenes wrote a great deal. His originals, however, probably went up in smoke in one of the successive disasters that afflicted the library's collections, including their ultimate destruction by fire. Even direct quotations from his manuscripts have mostly been lost. We know his work, then, at third and fourth hand.

Eratosthenes is known for his *Chronology*—a work that tried to ascertain the important dates of literary and political history and prehistory. He wrote learnedly about mathematics, particularly prime numbers. ARCHIMEDES regarded Eratosthenes as his mathematical peer. He also wrote two philosophical works, one about PLATO and another about the philosopher Ariston. Beyond those subjects, he turned his attention to geography. In this field, he was the first to arrive mathematically at an accurate estimate of the circumference of the earth, which he knew to be round.

On the strictly literary front, Eratosthenes made contributions to at least two fields. As a literary critic, says the first-century Roman biographer SUETONIUS, Eratosthenes was the first to designate himself a *philologos*—a lover of words, or philologer. In that capacity, he wrote a substantial discussion of ancient comedy and issues associated with it. He also both wrote and wrote about poetry. He took issue with the ancient formula that the object of poetry was "to please and to instruct," arguing that only pleasure was the object of poetry. He authored lost EPICS: *Hermes* told of the juvenile adventures of the god and of his wanderings among the planets. Another treated the murder of the poet HESIOD and the punishment of his killers. Beyond that, Eratosthenes wrote an ELEGY dealing with the story of Icarus, the mythological inventor of human-powered flight.

Only small fragments remain to hint at Eratosthenes' admirable talent.

See also GEOGRAPHY AND GEOGRAPHERS, GREEK AND ROMAN.

Bibliography

Fraser, P. M. *Eratosthenes of Cyrene*. London: Oxford University Press, 1971.

Lasky, Kathryn. *The Librarian who Measured the Earth*. Boston: Joy Street Books, 1994.

erotic prose   See FICTION AS EPISTLE, ROMANCE, AND EROTIC PROSE.

Esdras, The First and Second Books of (in the Apocrypha) (ca. 200–300 C.E.)

The first book of Esdras begins by tracing the history of the Jewish people's Babylonian exile and, at the order of the Persian king Cyrus the Great, their eventual return to Israel. First Esdras describes the honored status the Jews enjoyed under the rule of the Persian Empire, beginning with King Cyrus (ruled ca. 548–529 B.C.E.), who, in keeping with his policy of religious conciliation with his subject peoples, authorized rebuilding the Temple of Solomon that the Babylonians had razed.

An interesting aspect of First Esdras appears in its frequent recourse to and quotation from documents contained in various royal repositories in Persian territory. These include letters to and from the Persian rulers Darius, Cyrus, and Artaxerxes. If the documents—quoted in detail with cross-references to their archival repositories— are authentic, they affirm the historicity of the activities described. If the documents are fabricated, their citation nonetheless lends an air of authenticity to the events as narrated.

The First Book of Esdras concludes, first, with the emergence of the prophet Ezra as the chief conserver and interpreter of God's law for the repatriated Jewish people and, second, with a considerable xenophobic diatribe about the necessity for those Jewish men who had taken foreign wives to send the women away.

The Second Book of Esdras opens with a 19-generation, patrilineal genealogy of the prophet Ezra, tracing his line to Aaron of the tribe of Levi. This is followed by Ezra, speaking in his own voice and describing the way that the Lord called him to preach while Ezra was a prisoner in Media during the reign of Artaxerxes (d. 242 C.E.). Ezra preaches that the Lord is displeased with the Jews and is transferring his favor to another people—the Gentiles—who have accepted a new prophet, the Son of God.

Ezra next prophesies concerning the mystery of human destiny. His recital contains a report of a conversation with the angel Uriel and revelations by the archangel Jeremiel. Jeremiel grants Ezra visions and describes some of the awful events that will presage the end: Persia will have become a trackless desert, the sun will shine at night, "trees will drip blood," "nations will be in confusion," and the very courses of the stars will change. Waking from the dream in which he envisioned all this, the prophet is very naturally upset, but more and worse is to come. In a series of dream visions, the balance of the book describes the trials to be visited on humanity during the last days. Among these is an allegorical vision whose meaning an angel interprets for Ezra. Finally, the angel utters a series of prophecies of doom but promises the salvation of the chosen people. Though they are never named, Ezra unmistakably thinks the Christians to be the chosen ones.

See also APOCRYPHA, THE.

Bibliography

The First Book of Esdras and The Second Books of Esdras. In *The Apocrypha. The New English Bible*. Vol. 2. Edited and translated by the appointees of the Joint Committee on the New Translation of the Bible. Oxford and Cambridge: Oxford and Cambridge University Presses, 1969.

Ethical Essays   See MORALIA.

Euclid (fl. 300 B.C.E.) *Greek prose writer*

Though no information concerning the details of Euclid's life survives, he is credited with having written one of the most popular books of all time. It seems fairly certain that Euclid incorporated the work of his predecessors into his *Elements* (of mathematics) and that his successors emended his work. For two millennia, nonetheless, students of both plane and solid geometry and of the theory of numbers have studied from volumes bearing his name.

Beyond this best-known of his writings, two other works by Euclid also survive, *Optics* and *Phaenomena*. The title of the first work indicates its content, except that the science of optics among Euclid's contemporaries dealt primarily with theories of vision rather than also with the properties of light. The second work applies spherical geometry to the study of astronomy. Other works dealing with music whose authorship remains in dispute have also sometimes been attributed to Euclid.

Although older commentators confidently assert that Euclid lived at Alexandria at the time of the Greek pharaoh, Ptolemy I, this assertion lacks reliable authority even though it may be so.

Bibliography

Artmann, Benno. *Euclid and the Creation of Mathematics.* New York: Springer, 1999.

Euclid. *Dedomena: Euclid's Data, or, The Importance of Being Given.* Translated by Christian Marinus Taisbak. Copehhagen: Museum Tusculanem Press, 2003.

———. *The Euclidean Division of the Canon: Greek and Latin Sources.* Translated and edited by André Barbera. Lincoln: University of Nebraska Press, 1991.

——— et al. *The Mathematical Writings of Euclid, Archimedes, Apollonius of Perga, and Nichomachus of Gerasa.* Franklin Center, Pa.: Franklin Library, 1985.

———. *Euclid's* Phaenomena: *A Translation and Study of a Hellenistic Treatise in Spherical Astronomy.* Translated by J. L. Berggren and R. S. Thomas. Providence, R.I.: American Mathematics Society, 2006.

———. *The Thirteen Books of Euclid's Elements.* 3 vols. Translated by Thomas L. Heath. Cambridge: Cambridge University Press, 1926.

Euhemerus (fl. fourth century B.C.E.) *Greek prose writer*

Perhaps a native of Messene, Euhemerus ranks among the early Greek mythographers and utopian novelists. Though the texts and most commentary on them have been lost, extant fragments suggest the shape of a fascinating novel. It bore the ambitious title *Hiera Anagraphe* (Sacred Scriptures), though that title would lead a modern reader astray concerning its contents.

Preserved principally in the summary by DIODORUS SICULUS in the sixth book of his *Library*, Euhemerus's story imagines taking a voyage to a fantasy island in the Indian Ocean—the island of Panchaea. On the island, he finds a golden column containing inscriptions recording the deeds of Uranus, the Greek deity personifying the heavens, of Cronus, who personifies time, and of Zeus, the king of the Greek pantheon of gods. Through the record on the column, Euhemerus discovers that each of the three gods had once lived as men and ruled as kings. Their divinity had been bestowed on them by their admiring subjects who had elevated their leaders to the status of gods—as the credulous often did and do.

Another successor who may have been led astray by the supposed reality of Euhemerus's imagined voyage was the third century C.E. Christian apologist Lactantius, who, in his *Divine Institutes,* used Euhemerus among others to try to persuade sophisticated pagans of the falsity of their gods.

Euhemerus gave his name to the *ism* that attributes the origins of the gods to admirable people—euhemerism. The subgenres of voyages to nonexistent places and descriptions of utopian and distopian societies have continued to thrive from Euhemerus's time to our own.

Bibliography

Diodorus Siculus. *Diodorus of Sicily.* 11 vols. Translated by C. H. Oldfather, C. L. Sherman, *et al.* Cambridge, Mass.: Harvard University Press, 1935.

Winiarczyk, Marek. *Euhemerus von Messene: Leben, Werk, und Nachwirkung.* [Euhemerous of Messene: Life, Work, and Influence.] Munich: Saur, 2002.

Eumenides, The Aeschylus (458 B.C.E.)

The final TRAGEDY in AESCHYLUS's ORESTEIA, the only surviving complete trilogy from the theater of ancient Greece, *The Eumenides* takes its name from a euphemism applied to the Greek mythical beings, the Furies, when addressing them in prayer. One did not want to offend these avenging deities, born from the blood of the mutilated pre-Olympian god Uranus, by addressing them with a name they might find unflattering. Thus, one prayed instead to "the kindly ones," which is what *eumenides* means.

The first two plays in *Oresteia*, which won first prize at the GREAT DIONYSDA—the Athenian City Festival of the god Dionysus—in the year of their composition are AGAMEMNON AND THE CHOEPHORI. The entire sequence of plays centers on the effects of a curse on Atreus and his descendants over a series of generations (detailed in *AGAMEMNON*). In *Agamemnon*, the curse manifested itself when, during, the Trojan War, the Greek general Agamemnon had to sacrifice his daughter Iphigenia to secure a favorable wind for the fleet to sail east, leading to his wife Clytemnestra's subsequent hatred and infidelity and her murder him upon his return from the war.

In *The Coephori*, Agamemnon and Clytemnestra's son, Orestes, is forced by oracular prophecy to avenge his father's death by killing his mother and her paramour, Aegisthus. The fact of his having become a matricide, however, begins to drive him mad, and as *The Coephori* ends, Orestes undertakes a pilgrimage to the temple of Apollo at Delphi to seek counsel from the prophet Loxias and, he hopes, to gain absolution and an end to the curse, which has been afflicting generation after generation of the descendants of Atreus.

The Eumenides opens with the Pythian priestess of Apollo praying at the temple to the Olympian gods and to those who preceded them. She goes to the central altar and immediately returns shaking with fear, for on the altar the Furies are sleeping in the fearsome shapes of Harpies, and a man, Orestes, is also there. She characterizes him as "one abhorred by heaven."

The priestess exits, and the central opening doors of the inner stage reveal Orestes embracing the altar and the Furies sleeping nearby. The sun god Apollo and the gods' messenger, Hermes, appear. Apollo comforts Orestes, promises him his protection, instructs him to make a pilgrimage to Athens and embrace the altar of Athena there, and sends Hermes with him as a guard. They exit, and the ghost of Clytemnestra enters to try to awaken the sleeping Furies by pleading the cause of a mother murdered by her son's hand. The drowsy Furies—represented by the CHORUS—slowly awaken and lament that Orestes has escaped them. They blame Apollo, and in the ensuing discussion, the immortals discuss the merits of the case: Who is worse, a wife who kills a husband or a son who kills a mother to settle the score? The outcome is a draw. The Furies refuse to relinquish their quest and set out on Orestes' trail.

The scene shifts to Athens, where Orestes is clinging to Athena's altar and praying. The Furies enter, having tracked him down by following the smell of blood like hounds. Athena, the goddess of wisdom, enters, having come from her altars at Troy to hear the arguments of the adversaries. The Furies plead their case and ask Athena to serve as judge. She asks if they will be content with her judgment, and they assent. The goddess then turns to Orestes, commanding him to identify himself, give his genealogy, and make his defense. He complies, but Athena avoids making judgment, characterizing the dispute as too weighty even for her wisdom. She exits to empanel a jury of 12 Athenian citizens, and the arguments begin afresh. Aeschylus momentarily digresses into the science of etiology or origins. The jury, we soon learn, is the original of the *Areopagus*—the revered court of wise judges who convened on Ares Hill in Athens.

Apollo testifies in support of Orestes. It was Apollo's will that Orestes carried out, and that should absolve him of bloodguilt. Questioned by the leader of the chorus, Orestes admits that he slew Clytemnestra, that he cut her throat, and that he was impelled to do so by the oracles of Apollo. Apollo, in his turn, asserts that he was performing the will of Zeus. The question is difficult and the arguments of both sides weighty.

Eventually, however, the jurors cast their ballots, and as they do so, Apollo and the leader of the chorus of Furies continue the argument. Athena casts the final vote in favor of Orestes. When the votes are counted, perhaps predictably, they tie: six for and six against Orestes. This means that Orestes has won. He is absolved of his guilt, and the curse on the house of Atreus has ended.

The Furies are very displeased. They feel that the younger gods, the Olympians, have disdained them, and they threaten vengeance on the city of Athens. Athena, however, in her wisdom, offers the older deities a new role in the Olympian order of things. They will no longer be the Furies, wreaking vengeance on malefactors; rather, they will become "the kindly ones"—the Eumenides— in keeping with what people had formerly called them to keep their fury at bay. Happy with that solution, the former Furies agree, and the play ends in a triumphant parade and a paean of praise for the city of Athens.

Bibliography

Aeschylus. *Oresteia. English and Greek.* Translated by George Thompson. New York: Everyman's Library, 2004.

Euripides (484 or 480–406 B.C.E.) *Greek dramatist*

According to the Library of Congress's online catalogue, between the turn of the 21st century and the moment of this writing, some 49 separate translations into modern languages have been done of plays by Euripides. He exemplifies a writer whose work was perhaps undervalued in his own time, but whose reputation and popularity have been on the rise ever since.

We know little about Euripides' life, however, that is demonstrably factual. Apparently born at Salamis, his exact birth date is a matter of conjecture. His first tragedies (perhaps including the lost *Daughters of Pelias)* were performed at Athens at the GREAT DIONYSIA in 455 B.C.E. Between that competition and the time of his death, he probably wrote 88 plays, of which 19 or 20 are extant. The authorship of one of them, *Rhesus,* remains in dispute, and that play has not been included in the Loeb Classical Library's bilingual edition of his complete works.

Though four groups of his plays—three examples of TRAGEDY and a SATYR PLAY—were regularly selected to compete with those of two other tragedians at the annual Athenian festival (perhaps 22 times), Euripides' entries won first place only four times. In 408 B.C.E., he moved to the court of King Archelaus of Macedonia, where he remained until his death. One of his English-language translators, Richmond Lattimore, suggests that the foregoing is all that can confidently be said about Euripides' life. Lattimore regards other assertions about Euripides as "fanciful gossip." One such repeatedly made assertion, however, says that Euripides initially abandoned painting for playwriting. Another holds that he died as a result of being torn to pieces by Archelaus's hunting dogs.

Nevertheless, Lattimore suggests that the frequency, vehemence, and discrimination with which the comic poets of Athens, including ARISTOPHANES, ridiculed and parodied Euripides means that the playwright's work made a more lasting impression on them than the work of his more successful competitors.

Euripides' surviving works include: *ALCESTIS, ANDROMACHE, THE BACCHAE, Children of Heracles, CYCLOPS, Electra, HECUBA, HELEN, HERACLES, HIPPOLYTUS, ION, IPHIGENIA IN AULIS, Iphigenia among the taurians, MEDEA, ORESTES, The Phoenecian Women, The Suppliant Women,* and *The TROJAN WOMEN.* Additionally, in 1905 a fragment of papyrus, with a portion of Euripides' play *Hypsipyle* was discovered at the world's most important literary trash heap at the Egyptian site of the ancient city of OXYRHYNCHUS.

As the titles of his works suggest, Euripides mined the rich vein of Greek legend, as did many another writer before and after him. The Greeks accepted this body of legendary material as historical, and to a considerable degree it probably was. Euripides, however, treated that material differently from other playwrights. He highlighted the stressful effects of their internal conflicts on his characters. He tended to raise uncomfortable questions about the received views on religion and morality and conduct a concomitant social criticism. He was especially successful at portraying women as both heroines and villains. He often modified his legendary material—as others also did—to accommodate the requirements of his stagecraft. The quality of his verse was also widely admired among his contemporaries and his successors.

SOPHOCLES is said famously to have remarked that he himself portrayed men as they ought to be whereas Euripides showed them as they are. Literary history echoes that judgment concerning Euripides' realism. At the same time, his plays display compositional faults. Because he overloads his plots and sometimes his characters, his connections do not always work. He sometimes gets carried away with the beauty of his verse and fails to integrate it into the play at hand.

As a mole on the cheek of a great beauty sets off her loveliness, however, so Euripides' flaws principally serve to highlight the dramatic genius of a poet-playwright who originated the problem play, was a master of character portrayal, and, in the context of tragedy, pointed the way toward romantic comedy.

Bibliography

Euripides. *The Complete Plays.* Translated by Carl R. Mueller. Hanover, N.H.: Smith and Kraus, 2005.

Grene, David, and Richmond Lattimore, eds. *Euripides: The Complete Greek Tragedies.* Vol. 1. Chicago: University of Chicago Press, 1955.

Kovacs, David, ed. and trans. *Euripides.* 5 vols. Loeb Classical Library. Cambridge, Mass.: Harvard University Press, 1994–2002.

Eusebius of Caesarea (ca. 264–340 C.E.)
Greek prose writer

Although he became the bishop of Caesarea in Palestine, Eusebius did not believe in the physical resurrection of Christ. Rather, he subscribed to the belief of the Arians—eventually condemned as heretical—that Christ was the best of all created things, the Logos or God's word incarnate, but not the same substance as the Creator. He further argued that Christianity was not a new idea. The central idea of Christianity—righteous living—had been implicit in the HEBREW BIBLE all along, and the Logos had inspired and appeared to prophets before. What was new about Christians was their organization into a church, their pious behavior, and their expanding influence. After the council of Nicaea produced what must have seemed to Eusebius a confrontationally radical creed, his pronouncements on the central disagreement between the official and the Arian views of doctrine became more ambiguous and restrained. It does not seem that he ever fully subscribed to the Nicene Creed.

As a writer and Christian apologist and historian, nonetheless, Eusebius was virtually without peer in early eastern Christianity. Though no complete list of Eusebius's writings survives, the church historian J. Stevenson categorizes his known Greek writings under three headings: (1) writings about Holy Scripture, including efforts to establish and improve the text of Scripture (textual criticism), writings that explain Scripture (exegesis), and efforts to describe the physical details of the places discussed in Scripture (biblical topography); (2) writings that undertake to prove and defend the truth of the Christian religion (apologetics); and (3) works about church history and works in praise of the emperor Constantine and his own place and that of the Roman Empire in promoting the spread of Christianity.

In the first category, we find, first, Eusebius's *Gospel Questions and Solutions* (before 312 C.E.). In this work, he compares differences in the text of editions of the Bible. Of 10 books that he wrote providing a full indoctrination into the Christian faith, four survive with the title *Eclogae propheticae* (Prophetic eclogues). He also wrote a surviving but uneven guide to the geography of the Bible, *Onomasticon*. Several more of his works on the same subject have not survived.

Eusebius made his principal contributions to the second category, the field of Christian apologetics. Before 303, he wrote 25 books defending Christianity against the attacks of the Neoplatonist Porphyry. He likewise defended the Christian faith against the comparisons that an official named Hierocles had drawn between Christ and Apollonius of Tyana (see PHILOSTRAIUS, L. FLAVIUS and LIFE OF APOLLONIUS OF TYANA). The titles of these works are, respectively, *Against Porphyry* and *Against Hierocles*. In a similar vein, he argued on behalf of his predecessor, ORIGEN, defending him from the attacks of another Christian apologist, Methodius.

Still in his role of Christian apologist, Eusebius authored his *Praeparatio* (Preparation), a 15-book attack on the mythic beliefs of the pagans and on their faith in oracles and astrology. In the same book, Eusebius explains Jewish scripture, drawing examples from non-Jews and non-Christians in support of their accuracy. Beyond that, he authored *Demonstratio* (Demonstration), a work in 20 books (of which 10 survive) that explains Christ's fulfillment of Hebrew prophecy and discusses the incarnation of Godhead in Christ's person.

In the third category of Eusebius's literary output, we find his *Chronicle* of the history of the world down to the year 303. Having dealt in that book with the history of several nations, he next applied a similar method to a 10-book history of the church in which he traced the succession of Roman emperors and the succession of bishops at Alexandria, Antioch, Jerusalem, and Rome through the year 324. The last two sections of the book—those dealing with the persecution and martyrdom of Christians after 303—strike Stevenson, whose argument I follow here, as additions by another hand.

According to the ecclesiastical historian Kirsopp Lake, Eusebius may well have served as the chief theological adviser to the emperor Constantine, though assertions that he took an active role in government as a member of Constantine's council are probably not true. In any case, Eusebius saw the operation of Providence in the rule of Constantine and in the spread of Christianity as a result of the emperor's adoption of the creed as the Roman state religion. It was therefore in a spirit of admiration that, probably between 337 and 339, Eusebius undertook his *Life of Constantine*, a work full of praise and applause for the emperor.

Bibliography

Eusebius of Caesarea. *The Church History*. Translated by Paul A. Maier. Grand Rapids, Mich.: Kregel Publications, 1999.

———. *The Essential Eusebius*. Edited and translated by Colm Luibheid. New York: New American Library, 1966.

———. *Life of Constantine*. Translated by Averil Cameron and Stuart G. Hill. Oxford: Clarendon Press, 1999.

———. *Onomasticon: The Place Names of Scripture*. Translated by R. Stephen Notley and Zev Safari. Boston: Brill, 2005.

Philostratus the Athenian. *Apollonius of Tyana*. Edited and translated by Christopher P. Jones. Cambridge, Mass.: Harvard University Press, 2006.

Eutropius, Flavius (fl. fourth century C.E.)

At the request of the Roman emperor Valens (ruled 364–78), Eutropius, a historian, prepared an outline history of Rome from the time of its mythical founder Romulus through that of the emperor Jovian (d. 364). The work is principally remembered for its matter-of-fact, bare-bones, and often-incomplete recitation of events.

Bibliography

Watson, J. S. *Justin, Cornelius Nepos, and Eutropius*. Translated by John Selby Watson. London: G. Bell, 1876.

F

fables of Greece and Rome (apologues of Greece and Rome)

Brief didactic stories or poems, often about animals, fables or apologues that convey a moral or predict the consequences of human behavior seem to have been a feature of the storytellers' art since telling stories began. The long line of practitioners of the fable genre stretches back to the ancients, particularly to the Greek fabulist AESOP (ca. 700 B.C.E.) as well as ARCHILOCHUS, Stesichorus, and HESIOD; to ancient India before those archaic Greeks; and finally into the mists of preliterate, oral storytelling.

The Greek teacher and principal figure in PLATO's dialogues, SOCRATES, is known to have translated some of Aesop's fables into verse. Thereafter, Demetrius Phalereus collected a body of fables together, and since his time, newly written or newly discovered fables from various sources tended to gravitate toward Aesop's name whether or not he had actually written them. Such additions are known as *Aesopian* or *Aesopic fables*. Other collections were also circulated or read aloud in Greece in elegiac verse (see ELEGY AND ELEGIAC POETRY).

In Rome before 50 C.E., a freedman named Phaedrus (sometimes Gaius Iulius Phaeder) issued fives book of fables in iambic verse. Largely drawn from Aesop, this collection also included fables from other later Alexandrian Greek sources and some drawn from the author's personal experience. Whereas the fable had earlier been used principally for such illustrative purposes as pointing up a moral or making a satirical point, Phaedrus's contribution raised the fable into a literary category in its own right.

Around 100 C.E., a Roman scholar named Valerius Babrius collected 123 Aesopic fables—many from Phaedrus's versions—and retold them in Greek choliambic or Scazon meter (see QUANTITATIVE VERSE). Babrius and Phaedrus are the principal sources for the central Aesopic fables that have come down to us from ancient times, though later scholars and storytellers throughout the Middle Ages added to the fable genre, often assigning their additions to Aesop's authorship.

Bibliography

Aesop. *The Complete Fables: Aesop.* Translated by Olivia and Robert Temple. New York: Penguin, 1998.

———. *The Medici Aesop: NYPL 50 from the Spenser Collection of the New York Public Library.* Greek and English. Translated by Bernard McTigue. New York: New York Public Library, 2005.

Babrius and Phaedrus. *Babrius and Phaedrus Newly Translated into English, Together with an Historical Introduction and a Comprehensive Survey of Greek and Latin Fables in the Aesopic Tradition.* Cambridge, Mass.: Harvard University Press, 1984.

Phaedrus. *The Fables of Phaedrus.* Translated by Paul F. Widdows. Austin: University of Texas Press, 1992.

Fasti Ovid (ca. 7–8 C.E.)

An incomplete calendrical poem (a poem that uses the calendar for its framework), OVID'S *Fasti* traces Roman festivals and other annual events that took place in the capital city. Interested in the city's culture and the development of its yearly celebrations—many deriving from the otherwise largely defunct indigenous religion of pre-Roman Italy—the poet attempts to account for the origins of each event and the history of the mode of observance peculiar to each celebration or festival. He also offers an explanation of specific terminology associated with each event.

From the models available to him for such an enterprise, Ovid chose CALLIMACHUS's now-lost poem concerned with the origins of things, *Aetia*. In addition to the popularity of antiquarian topics, Ovid may also have sought to defuse the imperial disapproval that at last drove him into exile. The emperor AUGUSTUS CAESAR's blood uncle and adoptive father, JULIUS CAESAR, had been responsible for reforming and regularizing the Roman calendar. Augustus himself was both the head of the Roman Empire and the chief priest of the state religion. A poem, therefore, that dealt with the origins and development of native religious festivals during each of the calendar's 12 months and one whose first draft was dedicated to Augustus may well have been aimed at improving Ovid's standing with his ruler. Unfortunately, the emperor sent the poet into exile before the poem was ready for publication, and even after rededicating *Fasti* to Augustus and Tiberius's successor, Germanicus (better known as Caligu-

la), Ovid proved to be too near the end of his life for the poem to help end his exile.

Fasti, by universal consent, is not among Ovid's most successful works. Only six of the original 12 books survive, and while it would be tedious for readers to follow summaries of each of the six, what follows will convey an idea of what goes on.

Though March had been the first month of the original archaic Roman year, January came first in the current calendar. Obligingly, the two-faced god Janus, god of doorways, for whom the month is named, appears to the poet. The god carries a key that signifies his responsibility as the deity who begins all things, so that one of his faces looks forward to what will be and the other backward to what was. There follows a series of questions and answers. Ovid wants to know, for instance, why the first day of the New Year was not a holiday for the Romans. Janus replies that not working on the year's first day would set a bad example. After a further series of questions and answers, Ovid asks Janus why the door to the temple sacred to him is always left open during wartime. Janus's answer suggests that the temple doors remain open to welcome home the troops fighting abroad. During peacetime, they are closed to protect the citizens within the city's walls, keeping them safely within.

Six other days of the month of January get special attention from Ovid. Among these was the January 11, on which Rome celebrated the feast of the *Agonalia*. As an aid to understanding the purpose of this holiday, Ovid considers the various etymologies that might underlie the name. Did a priest ask if he should strike the sacrificial animal by saying "Agone"? Did it, rather, allude to the sacrifice of lambs? Is it associated with the anticipatory suffering of the victim? Or did it allude to the Greek term for the games that used to be played as a part of the festival in bygone days? Ovid settles on the explanation that the name of the holiday is associated with an antiquated word for sacrificial animals, *agonia*. With that theme in mind, Ovid moves into a consideration of the history of sacrifice itself.

Passing on to January 13—a day that Augustus had selected to provide entertainments for the people of Rome—Ovid rehearses a story also told in VIRGIL's AENEID, the story of the alliance formed between the Trojans under Aeneas and the Greek Arcadian exile, King Evander. Ovid tells of Evander's arrival in Italy and has him prophesy the greatness of the Emperor Tiberius and his mother Livia.

We also find associated with the festival of January 13 a tale of Hercules and Cacus. People liked stories about the popular Greek superhero, so Ovid gave them one that he set near Evander's city on the Tiber River. In it Hercules overcomes Cacus, a huge son of Vulcan.

Ovid associates February with *februa*, a word connected with purification rituals. March is the month of Mars, father of Romulus, the legendary founder of the city. Ovid fancifully develops a false etymology for April, associating it with the word *aperit* (it opens). So April is a time for beginnings. Venus is its tutelary deity, so it is also the month for love.

Waxing inventive once more, Ovid associates May with *majestas* (majesty)—a personification of which the Romans considered as a god. June, of course, is the month of the queen of the gods, Juno. Into each of the six months whose texts are still extant, Ovid weaves real and mythical history, old Roman legend, and his own invention.

Fasti underlies a part of the conception of such later works as Edmund Spenser's 16th-century poem *The Shepherd's Calendar.*

Bibliography
Ovid. *Fasti*. Translated and edited by A. J. Boyle and R. D. Woodward. New York: Penguin Books, 2000.

Fayan *(Fa yen)* Yang Xiong (ca. 1 C.E.)

YANG XIONG's *Fayan* (Exemplary Words, or Discourses on Method) is a dialogue between Yang and an unnamed questioner. Yang organized his work into 13 sections and paid homage to the ANALECTS of CONFUCIUS by using that work as his model. Yang's deference to the *Analects*, however, extended beyond merely emulating the work's rambling order and its conversational tone. He also adopted Confucius's style and reproduced the great sage's diction. As a result, Yang's work seemed stilted and archaic even in its own time.

Considering differences between the FU POEMS that appear in the foundational Confucian document, the BOOK OF ODES, and those that he himself had written, Yang concluded that the beauty of the poems in the *Book of Odes* led readers to appreciate and emulate the rules for the conduct of life that the verses espoused by criticizing vice. The *fu* verse of his own epoch, on the other hand, was beautiful, but the object of that beauty was to lead people away from a consensus view of goodness and toward indulgence in private, sometimes depraved, codes of ethics. He considered contemporary *fu* "ineffective as a form of persuasion."

Nonetheless, as Christopher Leigh Connery tells us, Yang made at least two more attempts to bring *fu* up to its former standards. Before giving up the form altogether, he wrote a poem, "*Chieh ch'ao*" (Dissolving ridicule). Though similar to *fu*, the work founded a new genre: the "essay of rejection." A final try joined together that novel mode with a verbally spare, morally serious, philosophically instructive poem in classical tetrameter, "Chu p'in *fu*" (Rhapsody on expelling Poverty).

Bibliography
Ming, Lai. *A History of Chinese Literature*. New York: The John Day Company, 1964.

Owen, Stephen. *Readings in Chinese Literary Thought*. Cambridge, Mass.: Harvard University Press, 1992.

Connery, Christopher Leigh. "Sao, Fu, Parallel Prose, and Related Genres." In *The Columbia History of Chinese Literature*. Edited by Victor H. Mair. New York: Columbia University Press, 2001.

female Greek lyricists: (Anyte of Tegea, Erinna, Hedyla, Korinna, Melinno, Moiro, Myrtis, Nossis, Praxilla, Telesilla) (fl. ca. 640–323 B.C.E.)

The fifth century successors of SAPPHO, female lyricists including Korinna, Myrtis, Praxilla, and

Telesilla, continued the practice of such archaic Greek poets as Sappho herself and ANACREON. Only fragmentary remains represent these female lyricists. For explanations of the verse forms alluded to in this entry, see QUANTITATIVE VERSE.

Korinna tells us that the MUSE of the dance, Terpsichore, inspired her to sing to the "white-robed women of Tanagra," that the city "delighted in [her] voice," and that she sang "the excellence" of both male and female heroes. She is known to have composed long narratives in the Boetian dialect of Greek. Her poems sometimes focused on heroes and heroines from her own locale and sometimes retold the ancient myths, or "father-songs" as she called them, often placing them in a new context. A tradition suggests that she instructed PINDAR in composition.

Of the work of Korinna's elder contemporary, Myrtis, no example and only a single paraphrase survives. Myrtis was said to have instructed both Korinna and Pindar.

Represented by few surviving samples, Praxilla was born at Sicyon. She wrote hymns, drinking songs, and choral lyrics. Among her surviving lines are a few that seem to place the earthly things that death will cost her in order of preference: sunlight; "shining stars"; the moon; "ripe cucumbers, apples, and pears."

Telesilla came from the Greek region of Argos. Only nine fragments survive to attest to her work in choral lyrics—songs that she composed for performance by choirs of girls. A poetic meter that she perhaps originated bears her name—the telesilleion. The fragments suggest that perhaps the praise of the deities Artemis and Apollo figured prominently in her verse.

Erinna's place of birth is uncertain and is variously given as Lesbos, Rhodes, Teos, and Telos. Erinna (fl. mid-fourth century B.C.E.) is known to have written a poem in a dialectical blending of Doric and Aolic forms of Greek. Entitled *The Distaff*, the work contained 300 EPIC hexameter lines and represented its author at age 19, spinning and weaving at her mother's behest. Some fragments of Erinna's poem survive. The poets and critics of the HELLENISTIC AGE warmly regarded her work.

They considered her to be on a par with Sappho, whose work Erinna consciously emulated, and with HOMER.

The work of the early third century B.C.E. lyricist Anyte of Tegea is represented by a few (18) surviving funerary EPIGRAMS, some of which remember animals. She is reputed to have been among the originators of pastoral representation of undomesticated landscape.

Dating from approximately the same period, the Greek colonial poet from southern Italy, Nossis, thought herself to be an heiress of Sappho. Among other verse, she wrote love poetry, and what survives of her work is to be found in about a dozen anthologized epigrams, some of which seem written to accompany offerings for the altars of the gods. A number of the epigrams comment on the representational qualities of portraits. In one of these, she addresses a stranger sailing to the island of Mitylene, Sappho's home. Nossis names herself as a friend both to Sappho and to the Muses.

Moiro of Byzantium also lived in the third century B.C.E. Her sparse literary remains confirm that she at least, wrote epigrams and also composed verse in hexameters. One hexameter poem explains how the eagle became the god Zeus's symbol and how doves became the harbingers both of summer and of winter.

Dwelling at Athens, Hedyla was Moiro's approximate contemporary. The one surviving example of her work concerns the wooing of the sea nymph Scylla, who elsewhere, though not in Hedyla's fragment, metamorphoses into a monster. Scylla's wooer is a merman named Glaucus. The poem's meter and form is that of the elegiac couplet.

Mellino, a second-century poet, though writing in Doric Greek, celebrated the power of Rome in five Sapphic stanzas. Melino presents the earthly goddess Roma as an Amazon-like figure who subordinates the people of the world to Rome's martial power.

Bibliography

Gow, A. S. F., and D. L. Page. *The Greek Anthology: Hellenistic Epigrams*. Vols. 1 & 2. Cambridge: Cambridge University Press, 1965.

Rayor, Diane J., trans. *Sappho's Lyre: Archaic Lyric and Women Poets of Ancient Greece.* Berkeley: University of California Press, 1991.

female poets of ancient Japan (*Lady Kasa* [fl. 8th c., c.e.], *Princess Nukata* [fl. 7th c. c.e.], *Yosami* [fl. 7th c., c.e.])

Literacy came late to Japan. Not until the eighth century c.e. were poems written down in a collection, though some of the individual works in that collection antedate it. Nonetheless, poetry was alive and well and being sung and remembered long before it achieved written form. At the court of the Japanese emperor and also at gubernatorial courts in the provinces, there seems to have been a class of women—court poets—whose function it was to compose poems to be performed at state occasions.

Posterity owes the survival of 29 of Lady Kasa's poems in the pages of Japan's first and best poetry anthology, the MAN'YŌSHŪ, to a popular genre of ancient Japanese verse called poems of mutual inquiry. These were poems exchanged between lovers, and Lady Kasa was one among many of the paramours of the poet ŌTOMO NO YAKAMO-CHI. Whereas the lady was in love with the poet, the poet was in love with love. At some point in their relationship, Lady Kasa realized this and wrote a wonderful little poem telling him just what it felt like to realize that, though she loved him, he did not love her. She expected that their love would feed both their spirits. Instead, she found him to be a starveling with no emotional nourishment to offer her.

On the other hand, the love between the poet Princess Nukata and her former husband, the crown prince who became Emperor Temmu, survived her second marriage to another husband. A pair of poems of mutual inquiry which appear in the *Man'yōshū*, represents their exchanges. On a royal hunt, the prince waves a sleeve at her. She fears that her chaperone will notice and reproves his audacity, but the prince's response acknowledges his continuing adoration.

Yosami was the wife of the poet KAKINOMOTO NO HITOMARO, who died while far away from her. Her poem tells how she awaits him in vain and learns that he has been buried "in the Ravine of the Stone River." She invokes the clouds, asking them to hover above his resting place so that she can see them and remember her husband. This poem is also preserved in the *Man'yōshū*.

Bibliography

Keene, Donald. *Seeds in the Heart: Japanese Literature from Earliest Times to the Late Sixteenth Century.* New York: Henry Holt and Company, 1993.

1000 Poems from the Man'yōshū: *The Complete Nippon Gakujutsu Shinkokai Translation.* Translated by the Japanese Classics Translation Committee. Mineola, N.Y.: Dover Publications, 2005.

Ferryboat, The (The Tyrant) Lucian (ca. 150 c.e.)

A COMEDY in the manner of ARISTOPHANES, LUCIAN's little drama has a longer title in Greek—one that means "The arrival of the ferryboat." Its principal subject concerns role reversal in the underworld, where the rich and powerful and the poor and powerless each get their just desserts.

As the play opens, Charon, the ferryman of the dead, is complaining to Clotho, one of the fates who determine the course and end of each human life. Hermes, the messenger of the gods who conducts the shades of the newly dead to the shores of the River Styx for transport to the underworld, is very late with the current passengers, and Charon suspects the god of negligence. Clotho defends Hermes, whom she then spies herding the ghosts of the dead toward the river. The god is perspiring and agitated. Hermes explains that one of the convoy ran away and it has been necessary to chase him down and bring him in chains. The entire consignment of the dead, 1,004 of them, is now ready for embarkation.

Clotho and Charon board them by cohort: 300 exposed infants; 398 "unwept dead"—those over 60 years old; 84 killed in battle; eight lovelorn suicides;

several who died attempting coups d'état; one murdered by his wife and her lover; 16 victims of pirates; women and those drowned at sea; victims of fever; and Kyniskus, a cynic philosopher who is the only shade who seems pleased to be there. The shade who had to be dragged along in chains proves to be a nonhistorical tyrant named Megapenthes, who continues to plead for a reprieve from his fate, even offering Clotho a bribe.

Megapenthes, whose name suggests the high esteem in which he holds himself, imagines that he will prove to be above being judged in hell. Clotho reminds him that death is no respecter of persons.

A cobbler named Mikyllus now pushes forward and complains of being made to wait to board last. He is a foil for Megapenthes. Being without possessions of any kind, Mikyllus has nothing to regret leaving behind. In fact, he has been laughing at the grief of Megapenthes and other rich people in the assembly of ghosts who grieve at leaving their belongings.

Clotho tells Mikyllus to board, but Charon countermands her, saying the boat is already full. Mikyllus jumps into the Styx, proposing to swim, but Clotho prevents him, and the ferryman perforce drags the cobbler aboard. As there is no seat for him, they put him astride Megapenthes' neck.

The philosopher Kyniskus confesses that he doesn't have the fare—a penny (an obole) usually buried with the dead. Charon lets him earn his passage by rowing. While the other dead regret the people and possessions left behind, Mikyllus seems to be enjoying himself. Hermes suggests that he groan and lament about something for the sake of conformity. Obliging, Mikyllus regrets that he will never again go hungry or half-naked and cold. On arrival, he also has no way to pay his fare. Charon accepts his loss philosophically and returns to ferry across all the day's dead animals.

The off-loaded passengers now trudge off toward the place of judgment. Kyniskus and Mikyllus link arms and are confronted by the Fury Tisiphone, who brings them before the judge of the dead, Rhadamanthys. Kyniskus asks to be examined first so that he may credibly bear witness against someone else. No one brings accusations against him, and when the judge examines his skin for marks of former sins, none can be found, though there are some traces of former marks. Kyniskus explains that the study of philosophy by degrees cleansed his soul of the marks of his former sins. Rhadamanthys adjudges him worthy of the Elysian Fields in the islands of the blessed—the best situation one can hope for in the underworld. He can go there as soon as he has testified. Mikyllus receives the same judgment.

Now, however, Megapenthes comes before the bar of judgment. Kyniskus accuses him of overthrowing the state and seizing power, of 10,000 murders (confirmed by the appearance of a multitude of ghosts shrieking against Megapenthes), of innumerable rapes and sodomies, of treachery, and of overweening pride. Megapenthes admits the murders but denies the other accusations.

Kyniskus has Hermes call Megapenthes' couch and lamp to testify against him. These objects confirm Kyniskus's accusations. Rhadamanthys considers a fit punishment, but Kyniskus has a suggestion. Whereas most of the dead drink of the waters of forgetfulness from the River Lethe, Megapenthes instead will be condemned to remember his misdeeds and to recall the power and delight he once enjoyed, all the while being chained alongside Tantalus from whose lips the water of a spring forever recedes, and beyond whose reach a bunch of grapes forever dangles.

Bibliography

Lucian. *The Works of Lucian of Samosata*. Vol. 1. Translated by H. W. Fowler and F. G. Fowler. Oxford: Clarendon Press, 1905.

fiction as epistle, romance, and erotic prose

At some very early stage in the development of imaginative literature, using correspondence to tell stories became widespread. Thus, the boundaries, if there ever were any, between reportage and fiction blurred. This proved to be especially true in the period from the mid-second century B.C.E. until the early fourth century C.E. During that span of time, writers used the epistolary method in a variety of imaginative ways. One such was a series of letters home from an imaginary voyage "beyond Thule"—that is, from a point beyond the northernmost boundary of the known world. This was authored by the Greek Antonius Diogenes (fl. second century C.E.). No longer extant, it seems to have contained reports of a series of wildly imaginative happenings on a voyage to places where no one had gone before. Quotations from the work survive in the pages of St. PHOTIUS.

Antonius Diogenes' work apparently inspired both imitators and satirists. One finds an example of the latter in LUCIAN's work, *True Histories* (second century C.E.). That work cleverly parodies both the literary heirs of Diogenes and the miracles reported in the Christian Scriptures.

Related to these developments, the writers of romance fiction were quick to perceive the suitability of exchanges of letters between lovers as a way to spin a good story. The result was the epistolary novel. Practitioners of this form in the ancient world included the perhaps fictive Aristaenetus of Nicaea, who was credited with a series of erotic letters.

The Greek PARTHENIUS in the first century B.C.E. prepared a prose collection of melancholy erotic stories. He did this work at Rome, to which he had been taken as a military prisoner.

Iambichlus of Syria (d. ca. 330 C.E.) may be considered the founding author of a form still very much with us—the prose, erotic, adventure romance. His novel was entitled *The Loves of Rhodane and Sinonis* in 39 books. A few fragments and a summary survive.

Fully surviving examples of the ancient genre were penned by Heliodorus of Emesa (d. ca. 400 C.E.) and Longus (fl. ca. fourth–fifth century C.E.). Their works include, respectively, the *Ethiopian Story of Theagenes and Chariclea* in 10 books and PASTORALS OF DAPHNIS AND CHLOE. As Heliodorus was a Christian bishop, the erotic elements

of his story are much repressed as his hero and heroine resist the attractions of the flesh and wait for their formal union.

Another ancient writer of romance was XENOPHON OF EPHESUS (dates unknown), who prepared a five-book romance entitled *The Story of Anthia and Abrocomas*. Chariton of Aphrodisia, about whom nothing else is known, prepared the extant *Love Story of Chaeras and Callirrhoe*. Finally, Eumathius of Egypt penned the tale of *Hysmine and Hysminias*.

See also GREEK PROSE ROMANCE.

Bibliography

Hadas, Moses, trans. *Three Greek Romances*. Indianapolis: Bobbs Merrill, 1964.

Heliodorus of Emessa. *An Ethiopian Romance*. Translated by Moses Hadas. Philadelphia: University of Pennsylvania Press, 1999.

Lucian. "True Histories 1 & 2." In *Selected Dialogues*. Translated by Desmond Costa. New York: Oxford University Press, 2005.

Parthenius of Nicaea. *The Selected Fragments and the Erathika Pathemata* [Melancholy Erotic Stories]. Edited by J. L. Lightfoot. Oxford: Oxford University Press, 1999.

First Letter of Clement to the Corinthians, The (ca. first–second C.E.)

Included as the first selection in the current form of the *APOSTOLIC FATHERS OF THE CHRISTIAN CHURCH*, and unlikely to have been written by Clement, this long and diffuse letter in the Greek language was written by someone in authority (though not yet papal authority) in the church at Rome to the church in Corinth, Greece. A group of usurpers have overthrown the established authorities of the Corinthian church, and the Roman author of the letter reproves the rebels for their disorderly behavior, urging them to restore the church to its former order and the former officials to their posts.

The letter's author gives examples of the orderly behavior of HEBREW BIBLE's priests and prophets, of the natural order of the universe, and even of the orderly and periodic rebirth of the mythical phoenix (perhaps here a symbol of the resurrected Christ) to encourage the dissident Christians of Corinth to conform to divine expectations for orderly, Christian behavior based on "brotherly love," rather than on personal advantage and ambition.

In his discussion of the letter, its most recent and authoritative English translator, Bart D. Ehrman, suggests that the missive's digressiveness conforms to a rhetorical form commonly employed by orators in Greece and Rome to counsel "peace and harmony" in disorderly city-states. Ehrman suggests that the letter, whoever wrote it—and Clement himself does remain an undemonstrated possibility—is notable on several counts. It demonstrates, first, close familiarity with Jewish Scripture but does not yet have a canonical NEW TESTAMENT to rely on. It nonetheless quotes Jesus' words on the basis of oral tradition and specifically cites chapter 47 of Paul's first letter to the Corinthians.

Next, the letter provides an early instance of an attempt to assert the authority of the church at Rome over a congregation elsewhere when as yet no hierarchical organization had been established.

Finally, the epistle anticipates what would later become the orthodox view of the apostolic succession: Jesus appointed the apostles, who named their successors. The usurpers of Corinth had deposed those persons, called presbyters, and had thus erred by intervening in the orderly succession of authority traceable to Christ himself.

Bibliography

"First Letter of Clement to the Corinthians." In *The Apostolic Fathers*. Vol. 1. Translated by Bart D. Ehrman. Cambridge, Mass.: Harvard University Press, 2003.

Fragments of Papias and Quadratus
(ca. 60–130 C.E.)

Included among the writings of *The* APOSTOLIC FATHERS OF THE CHRISTIAN CHURCH we find the fragmentary remains of the writings of Papias and Quadratus, two early second-century Christians. Later Christian writers, including EUSEBIUS OF CAESAREA, thought that Papias had been important. The adjective chosen by the scholar of early Christian history, Bart D. Ehrman, to describe both Papias and Quadratus is *proto-orthodox*—that is, both these early Christians took positions that later came to characterize the orthodox views of a better-organized Christian church.

Sometime between 110 and 140, Papias, the bishop of Hieropolis in Asia Minor, authored a five-volume work entitled *Expositions of the Sayings of the Lord*. Only fragments of it, however, have survived—principally as quotations in the works of such other writers as Eusebius and Ireneus. Some ancients held the view that Papias had been personally acquainted with Jesus' disciple, John the son of Zebedee, but Papias himself denied this. Rather, he collected the sayings of the apostles from others who had heard them, preferring the testimony of eyewitnesses of apostolic preaching to the written word. Almost all commentators agree that Papias was a companion of Polycarp (see LETTER OF POLYCARP TO THE PHILIPPEANS).

Papias played a role in the foundation of millenarian thinking—the notion that after the second coming, Christ would literally reign on earth for 1,000 years and establish an earthly paradise. Eusebius seems to have thought this a silly idea and found Papias exceedingly unintelligent. Nonetheless, Eusebius quotes him.

Among the fragments surviving is a tale that Judas Iscariot survived hanging and thereafter suffered horribly from disgusting physical ailments. Papias further recorded that the apostle John and his brother James were killed by the Jews, and he detailed later miracles, including a resurrection from the dead and the use of Jesus' name as an antidote against a deadly poison.

The single fragment from Quadratus is also preserved by Eusebius in his *Ecclesiastical History*, 4.3. According to Eusebius, the fragment came from a defense of the Christian religion that Quadratus sent to the Roman emperor Aelius Hadrian. The fragment attests the truth of such miracles as raising from the dead, and Quadratus insisted that some of those thus raised still survived at the time of the writing.

Bibliography

Fragments of Papias and Quadratus. In *The Apostolic Fathers*. Edited and Translated by Bart D. Ehrman. Cambridge, Mass.: Harvard University Press, 2003.

Frogs, The Aristophanes (405 B.C.E.)

Though modern critics generally regard *The Frogs* as one of ARISTOPHANES' weaker plays, it nevertheless won the first prize for COMEDY at the festival of LENAEA in the year of its production. Moreover, in response to unprecedented public demand, the play enjoyed a second performance the following week.

The play posits that the god Dionysus missed the tragedies produced in the god's honor by the recently deceased playwright, EURIPIDES at the Athenian festival of the GREAT DIONYSIA. Dionysus therefore decided to descend into Hades and bring Euripides back to the land of the living. The play begins after Dionysus has reached this decision. Since the god does not know the way to Hades, he and his slave Xanthias seek the advice of the Greek hero and immortal, Heracles (Hercules). Heracles had earlier journeyed to the underworld (see Euripides' HERACLES).

Costuming makes a major contribution to the play's fun and to its silliness. As Dionysus and Xanthias appear on stage, Dionysus has donned the lion skin of Heracles over the god's own saffron-colored silk robe. Dionysus also carries a huge club and is wearing a pair of high boots of the sort tragic actors wore to increase their stature on stage. His appearance is utterly bizarre. His slave, Xanthias, enters mounted on a donkey. Xanthias is burdened with an enormous load of baggage for the journey, and a significant portion of the early stage business concerns his efforts to gain relief from this cargo.

Thus costumed, the pair arrive at the door of the house of Heracles, who collapses with laughter at the sight of Dionysus. The god explains his longing for Euripides and inquires the way to Hell. Before giving directions, Heracles suggests a number of living poets as substitutes, but Dionysus is firm. Next Heracles offers several quick roads to Hades. These include hanging, death by drinking hemlock as SOCRATES did, and leaping from a high tower. Finally, however, Dionysus asks Heracles to point the way that the hero had earlier followed.

Heracles explains that the way is long and that Dionysus will need two obols (coins) to pay a ferryman. Now knowing the route, the god and his slave set out. Xanthias complains again about the weight of his burden and suggests hiring a porter. A funeral passes, and Dionysus asks the deceased to help bear the burden. The corpse sits up and bargains over the fee. Dionysus finds the requested two drachmas—much higher than the ferry fare—too expensive, so Xanthias must again shoulder the entire load.

The pair soon arrives at the shore of the Stygian lake and hails the ferryman of the dead, Charon. Charon accepts Dionysus as a passenger but refuses to take a slave, so Xanthias has to carry the luggage the long way round the lake. Charon also makes a reluctant Dionysus row.

As they cross the lake, they first hear from offstage and then encounter the chorus of frogs from which the play takes its name. The frogs accompany the crossing by singing a ditty whose refrain, "Co-äx, co-äx, co-äx; / Brekekekek co-äx," has been adopted as a cheer for the athletic teams of a famous Ivy League university.

Dionysus joins the frogs in their song, and a contest ensues to see whether the god or the amphibians can sing louder. Dionysus wins, the boat arrives at the far shore, and Xanthias trudges in from offstage.

Having arrived in Hell, the two travelers look about in search of father beaters and perjurers. Looking in the direction of the audience, they think they see many. They next see a phantom, Empusa, who devours travelers at the behest of

Hecate, goddess of the night. Dionysus is very frightened, but the apparition disappears.

The pair next encounter a group of Dionysian revelers celebrating the Eleusinian Mysteries, and the travelers join their dance. When the dance ends, the two enquire the way to the dwelling of Dis, god of the underworld, and they discover themselves to be at its gate. Their knock is answered by Aeacus, formerly king of Aegina but now the judge of the dead.

Dionysus introduces himself as Heracles, and Aeacus flies into a rage. Heracles, in his earlier trip, had choked Cerberus, the three-headed guard dog of Hell. Aeacus, who was the dog's caretaker, bore the blame and suffered the punishment. Aeacus therefore threatens Dionysus with horrible tortures and departs to arrange them. Dionysus, who by this time has emerged as a thoroughly cowardly deity, quickly doffs his lion skin, giving it and his club to Xanthias, so that master and slave exchange roles.

Just then a maid who serves the queen of the underworld, Persephone, enters. She invites Xanthias/Heracles to join her mistress at a feast in his honor. He is reluctant until she mentions dancing girls, at which point he accepts the invitation. Dionysus, however, insists that master and slave exchange costumes once again.

As soon as the god resumes the aspect of Heracles, however, a landlady enters. Heracles still owes her money for food and lodging during his journey years earlier. Dionysus wants to switch costumes again. As soon as he does, Aeacus predictably reappears with two muscular slaves. Undoubtedly recognizing that the costume exchanges are growing tedious, Aristophanes introduces a twist.

Athenian law only accepted as true the testimony of slaves if it had been elicited under torture. Thus a master's willingness to allow his slave to be tortured was often construed as a mark of the master's innocence. Xanthias/Heracles quickwittedly offers Dionysus as a victim and lists a number of horrible torments that he is willing to have his ostensible slave endure. Aeacus accepts his offer, promising to pay damages if the treatment disables Dionysus.

Dionysus objects, warns everyone that he is immortal, and reveals his true identity. Xanthias encourages Aeacus to proceed with the torture since, if Dionysus truly is immortal, he will not feel pain. Dionysus counters that Heracles is also immortal. Aeacus decides to beat each one in turn. Both feel the blows but pretend not to. They disguise their cries by quoting verses that begin with: "Oh, Lord!" and "It hurts!" and "Oh!" Finally, unable to decide about them, Aeacus takes them before Dis, leaving the decision to the lord of the underworld. The CHORUS closes this section of the play with a song that blends satire of contemporary political affairs in Athens with appeals to Athenian patriotism.

As the action resumes, Aeacus and Xanthias discover they have much in common and embrace as friends. A clamor offstage, however, interrupts their affectionate exchanges. The noise proves to be an argument between the shades of AESCHYLUS and Euripides. They are disputing the question of which one had been a greater tragedian. The greatest one is allowed to occupy a throne in Hell until one even greater arrives.

Xanthias asks why SOPHOCLES does not enjoy the privilege. Aeacus explains that Sophocles is satisfied to defer to Aeschylus, but that, should Euripides carry the day, Sophocles will dispute his victory. Thus, in a play that is a contest within a contest and that contains a series of contests between Dionysus and the frogs, Dionysus and Xanthias, and a potential contest between Euripides and Sophocles, a final contest now plays out. It begins as a rancorous argument between the two playwrights, but under Dionysus's direction, it becomes a contest in which the two compare their skills by discussing their works, exchanging insulting judgments, and by quoting from their own verse. With admirable critical judgment, Aristophanes finds lines from the work of each poet that, at least out of context, seem inept or pompous.

The contest begins with Aeschylus's praying to Demeter while Euripides, whom Aristophanes more than once accuses of atheism, prays to the ether, to his vocal chords, to reason, and to his nostrils that "scent and sneer." While the cognoscenti of Athens may have found delight in the extended exchange between the two poets, a less involved reader from a later age may find it rather wearing.

As the contest continues, Dionysus is unable to decide which of the two poets deserves the prize. Finally, the god decides to weigh the verse in a balance, as one might weigh cheese. This procedure produces an invariable result. Aeschylus's verse is always weightier and thus more meritorious. Yet still the god cannot make up his mind.

Pluto tells Dionysus that he must decide or return to the land of the living empty-handed. Dionysus, forced to judge, says that he will choose the poet his soul desires. Euripides reminds the god that he had come to rescue him, but Dionysus chooses Aeschylus. Pluto invites the travelers for a farewell dinner, the chorus sings them on their way, and the play ends with a typical dig at Aristophanes' enemy, the Athenian demagogue Cleophon.

Modern critics of the play have often been hard-pressed not to see the literary judgment of Aristophanes himself in Dionysus's preference for the work of Aeschylus.

Bibliography

Aristophanes. *The Complete Plays*. Translated by Paul Roche. New York: New American Library, 2005.

———. *The Frogs. The Complete Greek Drama*. Vol. 2. Edited by Whitney J. Oates and Eugene O'Neill, Jr. New York: Random House, 1938.

Frontinus, Sextus Julius (Sextus Iulius Frontinus) (d. 103/104 C.E.) *Roman historian*

A Roman military governor, politician, and public official, Sextus Julius Frontinus first served as consul in the city of Rome around 72 or 73 C.E. He filled that office twice more in the years 98 and 100. Immediately following his first consulship, he became the governor of Britain, where he suppressed local resistance to Roman rule. In 86, Frontinus served as proconsul of Asia. In 97, under the emperor Nerva, he became the civil servant in charge of the construction and maintenance of the system of aqueducts that supplied the city of Rome with water.

A partly surviving monument to Roman ingenuity and engineering, the aqueducts brought water from as far away as 60 miles via a system of conduits that sometimes ran along structures 100 feet high. Frontinus wrote a surviving discussion of the history, workings, problems, maintenance, administration, and political initiatives of the Roman water supply. The work, *De Aquis urbis Romae* (Concerning the water system of the city of Rome), richly documents the workings of Rome's civil administration.

Frontinus also wrote *Strategemata*, a still-preserved work about military training, command, tactics, and strategy. Another work on the same subject is now lost, as are treatises on land surveying, though portions of the latter may be incorporated into other works. In his own time, Frontinus was properly considered to be a person of remarkable distinction. His literary style was straightforward and unadorned with rhetorical flourish.

Bibliography

Frontinus, Sextus Julius. *The Stratagems; and The Aqueducts of Rome*. Translated by Clemens Herschel. Edited by Mary B. McElwain. Cambridge, Mass.: Harvard University Press, 1993.

fu poems

The ancient Chinese genre of *fu* verse was the earliest that provided opportunities for poets to display at once their lyricism, their talents at painting word pictures, and their narrative capacities. Variously translated as *descriptive poems, prose poems, rhyme prose*, or *rhapsody, fu* poems made up approximately a fourth of the material included in the BOOK OF ODES (*Shīing*). That work identifies the mode of the *fu* poem as "descriptive." Moreover, it identifies the poet SONG YU, (Sung Yu) (290–223 B.C.E) as one of the two originators of the form.

Several of Song's *fu*—or at least portions of them—have often been anthologized in English: *The Summons of the Soul* (*Zhao Hun* [Chao Hun]) the authorship of this poem is sometimes assigned to Song Yu's uncle); *The Nine Changes* or *Nine Arguments* (*Jiu Bian* [*Chiu pien*]); and a rhapsody entitled *The Wind*.

Virtually any describable subject is grist for the *fu* poet's mill. Song Yu's uncle, QU YUAN, the author of China's most celebrated poem, *Li sao* (ENCOUNTERING SORROW), also anticipated such aspects of the *fu* mode as the tone of lament that characterized early examples.

Other famous *fu* appeared in the second and third centuries B.C.E. The first one that has a firm date assigned to it is a poem on the evil omens that accompany the appearance of an owl. It was written by JIA YI (Chia Yi) in 174 B.C.E. The same poet lamented the loss of Qu Yuan in his *fu* entitiled "*Grieving for Qu Yuan.*"

Fu expanded its expressive capacities in the hands of Mei Sheng (?–140 B.C.). Mei abandoned the mournful cast that his predecessors had lent the genre, making his *fu* at once more lighthearted and more lyrical.

A court poet of the Han dynasty, SIMA XIAN-GRU (Ssu-ma Hsiang-ju) rose to new heights of lyricism and introduced a new theme in a pair of *fu* celebrating imperial hunts. The subject matter of the genre expanded further as the poet Ban Gu (Pan Ku); (32–92 C.E.) used the *fu* poem to describe the capital cities of the Han dynasty. That experiment spawned a practice that continues to this day—writing *fu* that describe and celebrate places.

Fu continued to be written and anthologized throughout the period treated in these pages—a period ending roughly at the eighth century C.E. Authors since have never stopped penning examples of the genre throughout the subsequent history of Chinese letters.

Bibliography

Lévy, André. *Chinese Literature, Ancient and Classical.* Translated by William H. Nienhauser, Jr. Bloomington and Indianapolis: Indiana University Press, 2000.

Sung Yu. "The Wind." Translated by Burton Watson. In *The Columbia Anthology of Traditional Chinese Literature.* New York: Columbia University Press, 1994.

——— or Qu Yuan. *The Nine Songs* [selections]. Translated by David Hawkes. In *Anthology of Chinese Literature.* New York: Grove Press, 1965.

G

Galen (Claudius Galenus) (ca. 130–ca. 201 C.E.) *Roman prose writer*

Born in Pergamum in the Roman province of Mysia in Asia Minor, Galen began the study of medicine in his home city and continued his studies in Smyrna, in Corinth, and at Alexandria. In 157 he accepted a post in his native Pergamum as chief physician to the gladiators who fought in the amphitheater there. Subsequently he emigrated to Rome, where he became both the physician and the close companion of the emperor MARCUS AURELIUS. He continued in the post of imperial physician during the reigns of both the emperors Commodus and Severus.

From a literary perspective, Galen was an indefatigable writer on philosophical and medical subjects. (Curricular concerns and variant methodologies had not yet divided the scientific from the literary disciplines.) He dissected animals with great care and recorded what he learned by doing so. He wrote substantially if theoretically on the subject of human physiology, and, in addition to his own medical treatises (83 survive, some preserved in Arabic versions), he authored 15 commentaries on the work of his predecessor, the great Greek physician Hippocrates.

The works of Galen remained an integral part of the European medical curriculum as late as the 18th and early 19th centuries. A partial idea of the range of Galen's medical and philosophical writings can be gleaned from the bibliography below. It contains only recent English translations from the corpus of his work, together with representative scholarly commentary.

Bibliography

Galen. *On Examinations by which the Best Physicians are Recognized.* Translated from the Arabic by Albert I. Iskandar. Berlin: Akademie Verlaag, 1988.

———. *On My Own Opinions.* Edited and translated by Vivian Nutton. Berlin: Akademie Verlag, 1999.

———. *On the Properties of Foodstuffs (De alimentorum facultatibus).* Translated by Owen Powell. Cambridge: Cambridge University Press, 2003.

———. *On Semen.* Edited and translated by Philip De Lacy. Berlin: Akademie Verlaag, 1992.

Hankinson, R. J., ed. and trans. *Galen On Antecedent Causes.* Cambridge and New York: Cambridge University Press, 1998.

———. *On the Therapeutic Method.* Oxford: Clarendon Press; New York: Oxford University Press, 1991.

Johnstone, Ian. *Galen on Diseases and Symptoms.* Cambridge and New York: Cambridge University Press, 2006.

Rocca, Julius. *Galen on the Brain: Anatomical Knowledge and Physiological Speculation in the Second Century A.D.* Leiden and Boston: Brill, 2003.

Gallic Wars   See COMMENTARY ON THE GALLIC WARS.

Gallus, Gaius Cornelius (69–26 B.C.E.)
Roman poet

Except for nine lines recovered in 1978 in a papyrus fragment (papyrus Qasr Ibrîm), none of Gallus's works has survived. Posterity nonetheless remembers him as the poet who popularized the ELEGY AND ELEGIAC POETRY in Latin, as he composed four books of verses in elegiac meter. These works told of his love for an actress, Volumnia Cytheris, whom Gallus called by the pseudonym Lycoris in his verses. In these poems, he is thought to have begun the practice of celebrating the subservience of a lover dominated by the will of his mistress.

Gallus was a friend of VIRGIL, who in his *ECLOGUES* praised Gallus's poetic accomplishment. We also learn from Virgil that Volumnia Cytheris tired of Gallus and deserted him.

Born in humble circumstances in Foro Iulii (contemporary Frejus, a market town founded by JULIUS CAESAR), Gallus rose to become the prefect of Egypt under Rome's first emperor, AUGUSTUS CAESAR. As Egypt's prefect, Gallus strengthened and extended Rome's mastery of its province. He became too impressed with his own accomplishments, however, and began erecting statues to himself and having his deeds commemorated in inscriptions on stone as the ancient pharaohs had done. Offended by such hubris, Augustus recalled Gallus from Egypt, and he was forbidden to enter the emperor's presence. Gallus was subsequently accused and convicted by the senate for crimes against the Roman state. He died by his own hand.

Bibliography
Manzoni, Gian Enrico. *Foroiuliensis Poeta: Vita e Poesia di Cornelio Gallo*. [The Poet from Forum Iulii: The Life and Poetry of Cornelius Gallus.] Milan: Vita e Pensiero, 1995.

Ross, David O. *Backgrounds to Augustan Poetry: Gallus, Elegy and Rome*. New York: Cambridge University Press, 1975.

Stickler, Timo. *Gallus Amore Peribat? Cornelius Gallus und die Augusteischen Herrschaft in Äegypten* [Did Gallus Die for Love? Cornelius Gallus and the Augustan Rule in Egypt]. Raden, Westfalia: Leidorf, 2002.

Gāthās   Zoroaster (ca. 600 B.C.E.)

The entire surviving corpus of literary work of the founder of a major religion, the Persian prophet ZOROASTER, is found in a group of 17 poems containing 900 lines in total. The *Gāthās*, as they are called, are the most sacred part of the Avesta, or Zoroastrian scripture. The poems have traditionally been arranged according to their meter. Most of the poems invoke the Zoroastrian god of light, Ahura Mazda, calling for the divinity's help. The help required includes the acquisition and protection of cattle and land with its attendant prosperity. Assertions of praise also accompany the expectation of the achievement of bliss.

The poet-prophet prays to understand the mind, intentions, and requirements of the deity. He asserts that all his actions are undertaken with the will of the deity in mind. In other verses, he praises the deity for the goodness of creation. Zoroaster expects that good will eventually conquer evil and that human beings have an important role to play in achieving that outcome. They must choose between serving the forces of light and serving the forces of darkness, and that choice has eternal and universal consequences. The final outcome remains in doubt, and the believer must strive to serve the forces of light. In the event that light and goodness finally triumph, the believer can look forward to rebirth and immortality.

Not numbered among those religions in which one is required to love one's enemies, Zoroaster's verse asks when the deity will strike down the malicious and give victory to the devout and the righteous. The verses suggest that sacrifice has been replaced with worship and praise of the divinity.

The Zoroastrian universe revealed in the verses is a place of a positive, divinely burning fire. Yet the Zoroastrians also envision a hell—a place of darkness inherited by the unrighteous.

The prayers of the prophet are not limited to requests for the souls of human beings. The souls of "the mother cow" and of the ox are proper objects of the deity's concern and protection.

In a series of 20 questions with multiple parts, Zoroaster raises the issues that have always concerned people: Who ordered the stars in their courses? Who keeps the earth in its place? Who established the winds and the waters? On what grounds do armies gain victories? Have false gods ever been good masters?

In the same section, Zoroaster also raises some questions that may imply a period of exile in his own lifetime. He complains of being cast out and prays for friends and succor. He prays that his enemies' hostility may recoil upon them. He excoriates false gods, blaming them for defrauding mankind of happiness and immortality.

The prophet also includes some private prayers, invoking the deity in the hope that his daughter and her husband will achieve happiness in their marriage.

Bibliography

The Hymns of Zoroaster. Translated into French by Jacques Duchesne-Guillemin and from French to English by M. Henning. Boston: Beacon Press, 1963.

Geography (*Geographika*) Strabo (ca. 7 C.E.)

Destined to become one of the premier geographers of the ancient world, Strabo (ca. 64 B.C.E.– ca. 24 C.E.) was born to a prominent family of Roman citizens in the town of Amasia in Pontus. He studied at Rome and traveled in Egypt, Italy, Greece, and Asia, noting as he traveled some the material that he would organize into his valuable Greek-language *Geographika*, or *Geography*.

Preserved in 17 books, with a short section missing from the seventh volume, Strabo's work first occupies two of them with anticipatory matter. In his first book, Strabo argues that geography is a science worthy of inclusion under the general heading of philosophy in that word's etymological sense of "the love of wisdom." This, he maintains, is true despite the faults of earlier writers on the subject who took no pains to give accurate and scientific accounts of their subject rather than mythic ones. He goes on to review such geographical information as is contained in HOMER and others who preceded him. Strabo includes astronomy under geography and credits Homer with founding both sciences in his discussions of Odysseus's voyages around the Mediterranean (see *The Odyssey*). Strabo also includes natural history as a subfield under geography, and so proposes to give accounts of the flora and fauna that he encountered on his travels. He merged this material with similar accounts from his predecessors' work.

In reviewing the accomplishments of such earlier geographers as ERATOSTHENES, Strabo is careful to point out their errors. A Stoic philosopher himself (see STOICISM), Strabo is especially hard on those who intermingle "romancing" with observation. He devotes most of the first two books to debunking his predecessors— though he also praises them when he thinks they merit praise. Then, in the fifth and last chapter of the second book, he at last turns his attention to his own conclusions. He points out that, although a traveler across a sea or over plains may think that what surrounds him is flat, in fact the earth is spherical. He also makes clear, however, that for him the universe is geocentric.

Nevertheless, since Strabo's principal objective in this section of his work is to describe the imaginary transfer of portions of the surface of a sphere to a plane surface, his scientific weaknesses do little damage. Those failings apart, however, he is a fine geopolitical observer.

Central to Strabo's thinking is the political fact that the city of Rome holds sway over much of the known world. Thus, a major geopolitical theme runs through the whole of his work. He is an imperial apologist who lived under the reigns of AUGUSTUS CAESAR and Tiberius. Moreover, the audience that Strabo envisioned for his work was one composed principally of civil servants with administrative responsibilities for the areas he discussed.

He admits the limitations under which he labors. Though he says he has traveled further to the east than any of his predecessor geographers, he confesses that some had been further west. He has not traveled in Italy very far north of Rome, and he has seen neither northern Europe nor Britain. He neglects, moreover, most reliable, firsthand Roman accounts of the places he discusses, though he did look at JULIUS CAESAR's work and at a few others. His firsthand acquaintance with Greece is likewise very limited.

Strabo concludes his second book by briefly noting nations, seas, and countries and by making remarks on their climates. In the third book, beginning in the west with Iberia, Strabo undertakes his account of Europe—an account that will occupy him through the 10th volume. He relies chiefly on sources external to himself. In the fourth book, he turns his attention to Gaul. The Roman administrative divisions of its Gallic empire organize his discussion. He also looks at Britain, Thule, and the Alps. Julius Caesar and POLYBIUS are his principal guides.

Italy and its outlying islands are the subjects of Strabo's fifth and sixth books. He ends this section with a description of the magnitude of the Roman Empire. One of Strabo's modern translators, W. Falconer, observes that the section on Italy is marred by his failure to consult the best authorities available to him.

In his seventh book, Strabo turns his attention to the tribes whose homelands border the Danube. A portion of this book is lost, though efforts have been made to restore its content by consulting later summaries. In this discussion, ethnography emerges as a principal concern as Strabo discusses some of the customs of the peoples dwelling in the region.

Books 8, 9, and 10 concern themselves with Greece and the surrounding islands, including Crete and other islands in the Aegean Sea. These books are characterized by a principle of organization somewhat different from that of the former seven. In part, this is owing to the reverence that Strabo felt for Homer. When Homer has described the physical features of a location, Strabo puts the poet's description above both his own eyewitness account and the accounts that others had provided to the geographer.

With the 11th book, Strabo turns his attention to the countries lying east of the Don River. He follows Eratosthenes in dividing Asia, first into the regions lying north and south of the Taurus River's east-west flow and then subdividing northern Asia into four sections. The geographer treats the northern three of those sections in the 11th book. He discusses such matters as the lay of the land, the occupations of the people, and the distances in *stadia* between one location and another (one *stadion* equaled 600 feet, though the length of a foot was somewhat variable). Strabo gives the distance from Ephesus to Smyna, for example, as 320 stadia.

Books 12–14 concern themselves only with Anatolia—still in the part of Asia lying north of the Taurus. Strabo's authorities for these books are principally such historians as Patrocles and Aristobulus, who traced the Asiatic campaigns of Alexander the Great.

With the 15th and 16th books, Strabo moves south of the Taurus River and into regions of Asia that he never personally visited. He covers both India and Persia in book 15, falling victim occasionally to the very propensity for "romancing" that he had blamed in others, as when he identifies an Indian people, the Sydracae, as the descendants of Bacchus because grapevines proliferate in their country. He also recalls the perhaps otherwise unnoted military campaigns of Hercules (see HERACLES) in the region. Strabo's accounts of Indian agriculture, local customs, and elephant training are both informative and entertaining.

Similarities in climate lead Strabo into a digression concerning Egypt and Ethiopia in which he concludes that the sun in these warm regions does not approach the earth more closely than elsewhere. Rather, he suggests it shines more perpendicularly. He also suggests that the dusky complexions of the inhabitants of these regions are not the result of sunlight, for sunlight cannot reach children in the womb.

After concluding the 16th book with accounts of Arabia, the Indian Ocean, and the Red Sea, Strabo turns his full attention in the 17th book to Egypt, Ethiopia, and the north coast of Africa. These were regions in which Strabo had traveled extensively, so in addition to the discussions of previous authors, he presents much eyewitness material here. Strabo concludes his great work with another brief consideration of the extent of the Roman Empire.

Bibliography

Birley, Anthony Richard, ed. *Anatolica: Studies in Strabo*. Oxford: Clarendon Press, 1995.

Bunbury, E. H. *A History of Ancient Geography among the Greeks and the Romans*. Vol. 2. New York: Dover Press, 1959.

Dueck, Daniela. *Strabo of Amasia: A Greek Man of Letters in Augustan Rome*. New York: Routledge, 2000.

Nicolet, Claude. *Space, Geography, and Politics in the Early Roman Empire*. Ann Arbor: University of Michigan Press, 1991.

Strabo. *The Geography of Strabo*. 3 vols. Translated by H. C. Hamilton and W. Falconer. New York: G. Bell and Sons, 1903–06.

geography and geographers, Greek and Roman

Greek and Roman knowledge of geography, at first undoubtedly local and very limited, expanded with seafaring and with increasingly far-flung military and trading expeditions. One can draw a useful estimate of the ancient, well-informed, Mediterranean dwellers' assessment of the extent and character of the world they lived in by considering a map of the world drawn by the Egyptian geographer and astronomer PTOLEMY in the second century C.E.

On Ptolemy's world map, the westernmost landmarks are the Fortunate Isles (the Canary Islands). In the northwest, Thule is mentioned— perhaps identical with the Shetland Islands, though some have argued for Iceland. Much of the Scandinavian peninsula is absent from Ptolemy's map, as are place names to the north of Scythia (now Russia and former Soviet dependencies), a region Ptolemy thought to be inhabited by a people called the Hyperboreans, whom VIRGIL mentions in his *GEORGICS*. Amber traders from what is today's Lithuania had traveled south at least as far as the edges of Greek and Roman spheres of influence by Ptolemy's time, but perhaps the scholar was unaware of those merchants or of their origins.

As one might expect, the European and African areas around the shores of the Mediterranean, including Asia Minor, Europe as far north and west as military expeditions had penetrated, and Asia as far east as Persia (Iran), are fairly accurately depicted on Ptolemy's map. East from that point, however, matters become a good deal more speculative. Ptolemy at least has a notion of the locations of places as far distant to the North and East as Kashgar (now the Chinese city of Shufu) and beyond that to the northwestern corner of China near the terminus of the Great Wall. The most easterly point on Ptolemy's map is also the southernmost point in Cambodia. Ptolemy had no idea whatever of the existence of the Pacific Ocean.

Moving back west at a southerly latitude about 10 degrees below the equator, Ptolemy's notions remain essentially fanciful until he reaches the southern tributaries of the Nile River. About then, his map becomes reasonably accurate. Then, moving west, it once more grows blank until it reaches the Atlantic Ocean, where it represents the Atlantic coastline toward the north quite accurately. Ptolemy's map attempted to include land encircled by water beyond the known land masses. He succeeded in representing about a third of the earth's land area with variable accuracy.

Despite its flaws, Ptolemy's map tried with some success to depict actual geographic features. The ancients also invented other sorts of maps, though it is not always possible to ascribe them to the hands that drew them. One sort was a "T in O" map. Imagine a circle with the horizontal bar of a T touching the circle's circumference on two sides and the vertical bar touching the horizontal bar at the top and the circle's circumference at the bottom. The circle's circumference represented the river of ocean that was thought to flow all the way around the earth's continents. The T represented the waters that separated the three continents known to Europeans, Asians, and North Africans from one another. As time progressed, T in O maps became more valuable for their biblical or allegorical value than for their geographical usefulness. The Christians saw the T as identical with Christ's cross. Some maps put Jerusalem directly at the top center of the map where the bars of the T touched. The top of the map—above Jerusalem—was east, the direction where Heaven was thought to lie.

Most pre-Christian Greek, Roman, and Egyptian astronomers and geographers knew the earth was a sphere. Not until Christian geographers tried to reconcile actual geography with biblical descriptions of geography did some, such as COSMAS INDICOPLEUSTES, seriously come to imagine that the earth had to be flat.

A third and very ancient sort of map was a zonal map. This separated the known and the unknown world into frigid, temperate, and torrid zones. Animal life, the ancients thought, could exist only in the temperate zone.

Pre-Ptolemaic Greek geographers inhabited a quasi-literary twilight zone. They constructed coastal itineraries, some real and some fanciful, describing harbors and water sources, landmarks, and encounters with people and animals. Called *peripluses,* these navigation guides were written by such authors as Hanno (fl. ca. 500 B.C.E.). Hanno claimed to have translated a document originally written in the Punic tongue of Carthage. This work described the places encoun-

tered by voyagers southbound from the Mediterranean along the Atlantic coast of Africa. Some of its points of interest were real, but others seem to be fanciful.

Hecatæus of Miletus, also writing about 500 B.C.E., introduced a degree of scientific rigor into the *periplus.* Starting at the Straits of Gibralter and sailing around the Mediterranean into and around the Black Sea and then back again along the southern shore of the Mediterranean, Hecatæus's work sometimes wanders from its course to investigate the inhabitants of Mediterranean islands and inland peoples as well. Some of the work probably rests on the author's personal experience and some on information from other sources. The fragmentary nature of what survives obscures the matter.

A third very ancient *periplus*, that of Scylax of Caryanda (fl. sixth century B.C.E.), is said to have been commissioned by Darius I of Persia. Only descriptions of the work survive, but apparently Darius directed Scylax to sail down the Indus River to its mouth and report what he learned. The later writers noted above referred to the work, as did others, including ARISTOTLE.

XENOPHON OF ATHENS's *Anabasis* contributes to geographic information as it recounts the story of the way Xenophon led 10,000 Greek mercenaries home from Persia via overland routes. Pytheas of Massilia (ca. 380–ca. 310 B.C.E.), who authored both a *periplus* and a description of the ocean, composed other early geographical works, now lost.

The earliest Greek, however, to move geography from the realm of observational narrative and reportage to the level of science, was the Alexandrian scholar, librarian, and mathematician, ERATOSTHENES. Eratosthenes not only knew that the earth was a sphere, he also made a very accurate calculation of its circumference. He divided his work into three parts: physical geography, mathematical geography, and political geography.

Roman geography generally was more advanced than that of its Greek forebears. The most notable geographical work of the ancient

Western world, in fact, appeared from the pen of Strabo, who, though born in Amaseia in Pontus, migrated to Rome. A 17-book work entitled *Geographika* (GEOGRAPHY) survives almost entirely intact (chapter 7 is partly lost). It is a treasure trove of information about the known world as it was in the first century C.E.

About the same time, the first century Persian Dionysius of Charax was commissioned by Rome's first emperor, AUGUSTUS CAESAR, to prepare a description of the East as a text for the education of his stepson, Tiberius. Dionysius composed the most consciously literary (in the modern sense) of all the ancient geographies, his *Description of the Habitable World*, in DACTYLIC HEXAMETER verse (see QUANTITATIVE VERSE).

Both geography and ethnography are represented in TACITUS's *Germania*, a description of Germany that was much admired by the 18th-century historian Edward Gibbon.

Bibliography

Blomqvist, Jerken. *The Date and Origin of the Greek Version of Hanno's Periplus: With an Edition and Translation.* Lund: Liber Läromedel/Gleerup, 1979.

Bunbury, E. H. *A History of Ancient Geography among the Greeks and the Romans.* New York: Dover Publications, 1959.

Hecataeus of Miletus. *The World According to Hecataeus.* London: John Murray, 1874.

Peretti, Aurelio. *Periplo di Scilace: Studio sul Primo Portolano del Mediterraneo.* Pisa, Italy: Giardini, 1979.

———. *Ptolemy's Geography: An Annotated Translation of the Theoretical Chapters.* Princeton, N.J.: Princeton University Press, 2000.

———. *Ptolemy's Map of Ceylon.* Colombo: Survey Dept., Sri Lanka, 1978.

Ptolemy, Claudius. "Facsimile World Map." In *World 2000, A Millennium Keepsake Map.* Washington, D.C.: National Geographic Society, 1998.

———. *Geography, Book 6: Middle East, Central and North Asia, China.* Translated by Helmut Humbach and Susanne Ziegler. Wiesbaden: Reichert, 1998.

———. *The Geography.* Translated by Edward Luther Stevenson. Mineola, N. Y.: Dover, 1991.

Thompson, J. Oliver. *History of Ancient Geography.* New York: Biblo and Tannen, 1965.

Georgics Virgil (30 B.C.E.)

VIRGIL grew up in the Italian countryside between Cremona and Mantua in the Roman province of Cisalpine Gaul. There he acquired a love of the land, of rural occupations, and of rustic living that remained with him throughout his life. Given that bent and given that such earlier important Greek and Roman authors as HESIOD, ARATUS, and LUCRETIUS had provided useful poetic models for discussions of farming, animal husbandry, meteorology, astronomy, and other aspects of the natural world in both real and mythologized states, it was perhaps inevitable that Rome's most accomplished poet should address his talent and his individual vision to the production of a similar work.

The *Georgics* comprise four books of dactylic hexameter verse (see QUANTITATIVE VERSE) dedicated to Virgil's friend, Gaius Maecenas, who was a great patron of poets and the close friend, adviser, and deputy of Octavian, who became the first Roman emperor, AUGUSTUS CAESAR. At the outset of the first book, Virgil announces what the subjects of each book will be. First he will discuss the right time for plowing the soil so that the crops will be "happy." Second, he will discuss tending vines, olives, and trees. Third, he will address the issue of animal husbandry—the care and breeding of cattle. Finally, he announces, he will consider the subject of beekeeping.

Having established his subjects, Virgil next piously invokes the sun, moon, and stars and the tutelary deities under whose care the weather favors farming and the earth produces abundantly. Finally, before beginning his discussion of tilling the soil, Virgil addresses Augustus, who is infallibly destined for deification and stellification, asking that the emperor make Virgil's course smooth so that he may teach not only farming to the country folk but also proper religious respect for both their emperor and their gods. In the Georgics, a reader finds both Virgil's personal piety and, beginning here and leavening the poem throughout, his belief that the gods incline favorably toward those who respect and propitiate them.

Virgil teaches that new fields should be plowed in the early spring in each of two years, but not before the careful farmer has studied the land to see what sorts of plants—trees or grasses or fruiting plants—spring naturally from the land. Thereafter, the fields should lie fallow in alternate seasons after reaping. He tells what crops enrich the land and which ones exhaust it. He speaks of enriching the soil with manure and with ashes and of occasionally firing the fields. He advises turning the soil and breaking up clods, and he counsels farmers to pray for moist summers and sunny winters. He speaks of sowing and of irrigating, and he notes the benefit that derives from the fact that Jupiter made husbandry a difficult occupation.

During the Golden Age, when Saturn ruled, men did not till the fields and the earth gave freely of its bounty. When Jupiter took over, however, the Age of Iron began, and "toil conquered the world." But the goddess Ceres taught people to plow, hoe, weed, and drive away the birds. Virgil advises farmers concerning the equipment they will need to do the job and makes useful suggestions like that of training an elm tree to grow into the shape necessary for the stock of a plow.

Virgil sets forth the proper times of year for performing each task for each crop. He next explains the signs of the weather and how a farmer can interpret them. He advises that certain tasks, such as sharpening stakes and pitchforks or making ropes and baskets, be undertaken during rainy periods.

Virgil emulates HESIOD's *WORKS AND DAYS* in explaining what days are lucky or unlucky for particular tasks. He enumerates the meteorological misfortunes that can afflict the farmer, such as windstorms, floods, and lightning strikes. Farm-

ers must be ever vigilant for signs that help them predict foul weather, so Virgil provides a list that includes bird calls, the direction of the wind, sea signs, different sorts of clouds, the apparent moods of cattle, and the color of the moon. The appearance of the sun at morning and evening, too, will predict the coming weather.

The poet also takes up supernatural signs and their apparent connection with earthly events. Particularly, he lists all the unusual signs that appeared in connection with the murder of JULIUS CAESAR: volcanic eruption and earthquake; mysterious voices and specters; interruptions in the flow of rivers; floods; lightning from a cloudless sky; and, especially, "fearful comets," which the ancients regularly viewed as portents of disaster.

Virgil ends the first book with a prayer addressed to the gods and heroes of Rome. He lists the manifold wars and woes that afflict his nation and prays that the gods will not hinder the young prince, Augustus Caesar, in his efforts to set matters right and end the "unholy strife" raging through the world.

As Book 2 opens, Virgil invokes Bacchus as god of the vine and addresses the forest saplings and the olive trees since these will concern the poet here. He speaks of the various ways that farmers can encourage trees to grow. He discusses lopping off and planting suckers and grafting fruiting branches onto non-fruiting trees. This last Virgil illustrates by saying that apple boughs have been successfully grafted to plane trees, walnuts to arbutus, and pears to ash trees. Then he gives instructions for doing the grafting.

Virgil next discusses the varieties of grapes and other fruits that one finds in varying locations around the known world. He mentions that not all soils are suitable for all fruits. Having looked around the world at the wonderful variety of fruits and trees that different regions produce, he concludes that nowhere can one find such various riches as in Italy, where the climate makes possible two harvests a year and the land is rich in minerals and in vigorous people.

Virgil now turns his attention to the variety of soils that one encounters in Italy and the advantages of each for different sorts of farming. He tells prospective farmers how to judge each sort and what will be most profitable to plant in it. Once a soil is selected for growing grapevines, Virgil explains how to design the arbors, trench the soil, and plant the vines. He celebrates spring as the time for planting, and he advises fertilizing, protecting the new plantings with porous stone or rough shells, and periodic hoeing. Above all, the leaves of the new vines must be protected against the depredation of browsing animals. Virgil suggests that goats are sacrificed to Bacchus and that goats' connection to the origins of tragedy stem from the tendency of the animals to destroy grapevines. (See TRAGEDY IN GREECE AND ROME.) In addition to hoeing, pruning is a necessity. Growing grapes requires constant vigilance. Virgil suggests that a carefully tended small farm is more profitable than an ill-tended large one.

Olives, on the other hand, require virtually no attention once established. This is also the case with numerous trees that yield wood for various enterprises, including shipbuilding and the manufacture of spear shafts.

Following a paean of praise for the lives of the hard-working husbandmen, Virgil now addresses the MUSES of his inspiration, calling on them to grant him the happiness not merely of describing the farmer's life, but to live it as well. Not for him is the life of kings who war, amass wealth, are swayed by flattery, and often find themselves exiled from their homelands. That said, Virgil returns to a final description of the joys of the husbandman's life—the last survival, as he thinks, of the pleasures, if not the ease, of life as it was lived during the Golden Age.

Virgil begins Book 3 by invoking, first, the rustic Italian female deity, Pales, whom herdsmen and urbanites alike had already anciently celebrated. In the same invocation, Virgil addresses the sun god, Apollo, as the shepherd of Amphrysus, invoking the legend that Zeus had once required Apollo to serve for a time on the banks of the river Amphrysus as the slave and shepherd of King Admetus of Pherae in Thessaly.

Then the poet announces his intention to erect a temple (that is, compose a poem) in which his emperor will reign as its deity. He predicts something of the shape of the poem—enough to indicate that it will be an EPIC—and then he returns to the poem at hand.

If one aspires to breed horses or bullocks, that person should attend most carefully to the characteristics of the breeding females. The best cows will be fierce-looking with ugly heads, thick necks, large dewlaps, long flanks, crooked horns, and shaggy ears. They will be between four and 10 years old. Among such breeders, Virgil advises, set loose the males.

With respect to male horses, Virgil gives a series of behavioral and bodily characteristics that a breeder should look for. Above all, the breeder should take care that the animal be spirited and not too old.

Virgil allows himself to digress here to discuss the history of chariot racing and horse racing. Then he returns to giving advice about the care of potential dams and of pregnant females. As the latter near the time of their delivery, they should not be allowed to pull heavy loads, leap, run fast, or swim in or ford swift streams.

Next Virgil details the care of calves, which should be divided early into those to be kept for breeding, those that will become working animals, and those that are to be kept sacred for sacrifice. He discourses on the steps to be taken in accustoming bullocks to the yoke for plowing.

Offering advice for training horses occupies Virgil next. He spends particular care in discussing the distractions that mares present for stallions and cows for bulls. All nature, the poet announces, is subject to the torments of love. After a lengthy digression on this subject, the poet reminds himself to return to his theme, and he turns his attention to sheep and goat herding.

Give the animals soft herbage until the pastures can sustain them. Then let them graze near water and find them shade in the midday heat. Be sure that they drink enough water. In this section, Virgil achieves variety by discoursing on the herding practices of the shepherds of Libya in Africa and Scythia (part of present-day Russia) on the cold and snowy Eurasian steppes.

If one is raising sheep for wool, Virgil warns against sires and dams with even a spot of black on them anywhere, even the tongue. Here he does not miss an opportunity to mythologize by recalling that Pan wooed and won the Moon (Selene) with a downy fleece.

Next he advises shepherds on the proper feeding and care of animals whose principal function is giving milk. He also offers counsel on breeding and caring for dogs and on the advantages to be reaped from that activity.

Snakes are a plague for the herdsman, and Virgil offers advice on avoiding them and on killing them. Following his discussion of dealing with serpents, Virgil deals with the diagnosis and treatment of various animal diseases. In one of the poem's most lurid passages, he pictures the symptoms and outcomes of plagues that can decimate herds and flocks and bankrupt their owners. He cautions against attempting to use either the flesh or the hides of plague-stricken animals lest the disease jump to human beings.

The final and most charming book of the *Georgics* considers beekeeping—"the wondrous pageant of a tiny world," as H. Rushton Fairclough's translation has it.

Bees need a shady spot near good water, one protected from winds, predatory birds, and lizards. Likewise, the flowers where they gather nectar must be fenced off from browsing goats. The poet tells what flowers one may set out to attract a swarm of honeybees. He describes a warring swarm, though he misinterprets some of his own observations. To keep a swarm in a hive, the beekeeper must tear the wings from the "monarch." Then the swarm will stay near home. He advises planting *laurustinus* to attract bees.

Virgil digresses to tell a story about the archetypal beekeeper in Tarentum in southern Italy. He then enumerates the qualities of bees. They have children in common and own communal property—both house and food. They have a fixed division of labor: gathering honey, hive and comb building, care of the young, and so forth. Some are sentries and soldiers who, when necessary, also drive the drones from the community. Membership in the various subcommunities is in part determined by age, with the young bearing the burden of hunting food and the old the home tasks. Bees do not engage, he says, in conjugal embraces. (Virgil does not seem aware that the queen bee—whom he calls the "king"—lays all the eggs of the hive or that she mates with the drones.)

Virgil explains the use of smoke in gathering honey and how the bees will redouble their efforts to make more to sustain themselves through the winter. Like people, however, bees can suffer disease. Virgil explains how to identify a hive with sickly bees and what to do to restore them to health. If an entire swarm of bees falls ill, then there is a remedy that involves the putrid blood of a slain bullock, which can, as the poet thinks, engender bees.

Apparently running short of material directly relevant to his announced subject, Virgil chooses to fill out most of the rest of Book 4 with the bullock-blood story, much of it mythical, and to trace it back to its Egyptian and perhaps Indian origins. The tale involves transformations, trips to the underworld, and the story of Orpheus and Eurydice. Amid all this, Virgil follows the tale of a shepherd, Aristaeus, son of a nymph, Cyrene. Aristaeus's bees were stricken and dying, and Aristaeus undertook the journey outlined above in an effort to get at the root of the problem. After many adventures, including trying to make the sea god Proteus reveal the secret, the young man's mother, Cyrene, who has known the source of the problem all along, reveals that Aristaeus's own heart's sorrow is the cause of his bees' illness. If he will lay his sorrow aside and make appropriate sacrifices, his bees will recover. He does, and they do, breeding as promised in the blood of a sacrificed bullock.

In the last lines of the last book, Virgil announces his own name, saying that in youth's boldness, he sang of Tityrus, thereby connecting the last eclogue to the first and bringing his composition full circle.

Bibliography

Virgil. *Eclogues and Georgics.* Translated by James Rhodes. Mineola, N.Y.: Dover Publications, 2005.

———. *Eclogues, Georgics, Aeneid I–VI.* Translated by H. Rushton Fairclough. Cambridge, Mass.: Harvard University Press, 1967.

Gilgamesh Epic, The (Sumerian language: ca. 2300 B.C.E.; Akkadian language: ca. 1300 B.C.E.)

Among the remarkably diverse CUNEIFORM literary remnants of ancient Sumer, both king lists and fragments of stories attest to the historic existence of Gilgamesh, a king of the Sumerian city of Uruk. The state of development of those fragmentary tales suggests that, even as early 2300 B.C.E., verse accounts of the historic activities of Gilgamesh and mythical stories about his superhuman accomplishments were beginning to coalesce into a kind of proto-EPIC. Of this Sumerian version, 175 lines survive. A millennium later, the process of development begun in Sumer had resulted in a full-blown epic written in the AKKADIAN tongue. Episodes also appear in Hittite poems.

The credit for preservation of *The Gilgamesh Epic* belongs in large part to Assurbanipal, the last great ruler of the Assyrian Empire. A formidable military leader who subdued Egypt, he also was intensely interested in antiquities—particularly literary ones. He therefore dispatched scholars to search the long-neglected and sometimes buried libraries of Babylon, Nippur, and Uruk. Assurbanipal commissioned his scholars to translate what they discovered into the language he spoke, Akkadian. Among the works thus preserved, of course, was *Gilgamesh*. Except for the emendations of modern scholars, who rediscovered the texts at Nineveh in the 19th century and who continue to work at correcting and enlarging them with newly discovered fragments older than the Akkadian version, Assurbanipal's version gives us the poem essentially in the form we know it.

The first sentence of the epic addresses Gilgamesh, identifies him as the "lord of Kullab," and recalls his praiseworthiness. Then, shifting to the past tense, the opening recalls his virtually omniscient mastery of geography, secret mysteries, and the state of things before the flood. We learn that he traveled far, learned much, and engraved his history on a stone. We also learn that he was two-thirds god and "one-third man." A paragraph of praise is devoted to his building walls and the temple of Eanna, dedicated to the Sumerian god of the firmament, Anu, and to Ishtar, the goddess of love.

As the epic proper opens, we find that the people of Uruk are worn out with Gilgamesh's warlike energy, dispirited because his military levies deprive them of their sons, and angry that his sexual appetites require all the women to sacrifice their virginity to him before they marry. Responding to the people's prayers, the goddess of creation shapes a wild man named Enkidu who will be able to tame Gilgamesh.

Enkidu lives with the beasts of the fields and the forests until one day a trapper sees him. Frightened, the trapper reports the wild man to his father, complaining that Enkidu ruins his traps and helps the beasts escape. The father suggests that the trapper ask Gilgamesh for a temple courtesan to seduce Enkidu. If she succeeds, he says, the beasts will reject him. The plan succeeds, and Enkidu finds himself much diminished in strength and unwelcome among the beasts. At the courtesan's urging, he accompanies her to Uruk, where he intends both to challenge Gilgamesh and become his companion. The courtesan predicts that Gilgamesh will learn from his dreams that Enkidu is coming.

Gilgamesh first dreams that a meteor falls. He tries to lift it but cannot at first. All the people and he himself find themselves drawn to the meteor with feelings of love. With help, Gilgamesh finally manages to bring the meteor to his mother Ninsun. (Later we will discover that Gilgamesh is her son by his tutelary god, Lugulbanda.) Gilgamesh dreams a second dream of an axe for which he feels a powerful attraction. Ninsun interprets both dreams. She tells Gilgamesh that the meteor is his brother—a comrade who will rescue him in necessity.

For a while, Enkidu lives with the shepherds, where he learns to eat bread and drink wine. Eventually hearing of the way Gilgamesh offends his people by demanding to be first with their women, however, Enkidu goes off to Uruk to challenge the king. Enkidu confronts the king as he is coming to a bride's home to claim his right. The two supermen fight, and Gilgamesh prevails. Enkidu acknowledges the king's superior strength. The two heroes embrace and become best friends.

The chief god of the Sumerian pantheon, Enlil, decreed Gilgamesh's mortality and his authority over his people, and Enkidu, interpreting a dream for his friend, explains to Gilgamesh both the extent and the limits of his power.

Gilgamesh decides to go the forest, raise monuments to himself and to the gods, and destroy the evil giant who lurks there—a giant named Humbaba, who may stand for the military enemies of Uruk. Enkidu tries to dissuade his friend, but Gilgamesh fearlessly insists. He invokes the sun god Shamash, praying for his aid and approval in his undertaking, and then begins his preparations for the dangerous enterprise. Ninsun, Gilgamesh's mother, also prays that the sun god will protect both Gilgamesh and her adoptive son Enkidu as well. To Enkidu she entrusts Gilgamesh's safety.

After much advice from Uruk's counselors, the two set out. They cover immense distances in a very short time and eventually come to the forest of Humbaba. Enkidu counsels immediate attack before Humbaba can don all seven layers of his armor, but Humbaba sees them coming and withdraws into the forest. In due course, nonetheless, Gilgamesh fells a towering cedar tree. This provokes Humbaba, who is the guardian of the forest, and Enkidu grows fearful. He describes the horrors of Humbaba to Gilgamesh, confesses that he himself is frightened to death, and suggests they go home. Gilgamesh restores Enkidu's

courage, however, and the two confront Humbaba, cutting down seven cedars at his dwelling.

It seems that some episodes of this portion of the tale are lost, for in the next scene we find Humbaba pleading that Gilgamesh will spare his life. Enkidu counsels his friend against this. Nonetheless, both strike Humbaba, who dies, and they offer the giant's head to the god Enlil as a sacrifice. Enlil, however, is furious. The god reproves the two killers and distributes Humbaba's former glory among wild creatures. The episode with Humbaba in the forest may belong elsewhere in the epic. Its exact place in the story is unclear, and segments seem missing.

In the next section of the epic, the goddess of love, Ishtar, offers herself to Gilgamesh as his wife. Gilgamesh replies doubtfully. He cannot offer her appropriate presents and recalls that she has made the same offer to others. Each time, he reminds her, she tired of her lovers and punished them in unpleasant ways. Why, he asks, would she not treat him in the same fashion?

Angered, she prays that her father Anu will create the Bull of Heaven to destroy Gilgamesh. Anu replies that, if he does so, there will be seven years of famine and drought. Ishtar replies that she has enough grain and fodder stored to preserve the people and the cattle through the famine, and her father complies with her request. Once created, the Bull of Heaven falls to earth. There its very snorts slay hundreds. Enkidu confronts the Bull, grabbing it by the horns. Holding the Bull, he tells Gilgamesh to kill it with a sword thrust between the nape of its neck and its horns. Gilgamesh does, and the two sacrifice the Bull's heart to Shamash, the sun god. Ishtar is furious, but Enkidu cuts off the Bull's thigh and throws it at her.

That night, Enkidu dreams that the gods sit in council. Despite the fact that the sun god instructed the two comrades to cut the cedar and kill Humbaba, the gods decide that Enkidu must die as a punishment. He falls sick and curses the gate of the forest and the courtesan who first led him to Uruk. The sun god, Shamash, reproves him, and he calls back his curse on the woman.

In his final illness, Enkidu has a vision of the afterworld. Its inhabitants are like birds, covered with feathers. They sit in darkness. The kings who are there had been treated as if they were gods while they lived. They and the priests, who also ruled in ancient Sumerian society, are now the servants in the underworld and perform the menial labor. After lying sick for 12 days, Enkidu addresses his last words to Gilgamesh. Gilgamesh gives a eulogy before the assembled counselors of Uruk. Then, touching his friend's heart and finding it stilled, Gilgamesh shrouds Enkidu's body and gives vent to his grief. The king orders a statue of Enkidu made from precious materials and presents it as a votive offering to the gods.

Driven now by his fear of death, Gilgamesh undertakes a pilgrimage in search of Utnapishtim, a human being reputed to have "entered the assembly of the gods." Reaching the entrance to the underworld, Gilgamesh confronts half-human, half-dragon creatures called the Scorpions, who recognize the king's partly human, partly divine nature. They interrogate Gilgamesh, who explains his reasons for coming. The Scorpions admit him to the underworld—a descent into which has ever afterward characterized all epics and raises the probability that the pre-Homeric Greeks knew a version of *Gilgamesh* at least in oral form.

For 11 leagues, Gilgamesh presses on in utter darkness. Finally, light appears, and after the 12th league, he arrives at the garden of the gods. There he encounters the sun god, Shamash himself. Shamash assures the traveler that he will never find the eternal life he seeks. Gilgamesh begs to be allowed to see light of the sun, though in other ways he may not differ from other dead men.

An atypically sudden transition, suggesting the loss of intervening text, takes the reader to a description of the woman of the vine, Siduri, who sits with her golden bowl and vats at the edge of the garden of the gods. Fearing the appearance of Gilgamesh whose face is drawn with despair and who, like the Greek hero Hercules (see HERACLES), is dressed in animal skins, the woman bars her door against him. Threatening to break it

down, Gilgamesh identifies himself, explains that he is in mourning, and prays that the woman will give him eternal life. She rationally explains to him his duties as a human being: stay clean, well fed, and happy; please your wife; and delight in your children. At his request, she tells him where to find Urshanabi, the ferryman of Utnapishtim. Utnapishtim is the literary prototype of the biblical Noah, and Urshanabi is perhaps a literary ancestor of the ferryman of the dead, Charon, in Greco-Roman myth as well. Siduri tells Gilgamesh that he will find Urshanabi building an ocean-going ship.

Seeing Gilgamesh coming, Urshanabi greets him and asks about his wild and forlorn appearance. Gilgamesh requests that the ferryman carry him over the river of death. Urshanabi tells him that when Gilgamesh destroyed "the things of stone" (perhaps ballast?), he also destroyed the safety of the ship. Nonetheless, Urshanabi gives Gilgamesh instructions for preparing the lumber with which to make 120 poles. When these are finished, they carry them aboard ship and sail to the edge of the waters of death. Now Gilgamesh must take a pole, and without touching the water push himself as far as he can. When he has used the 120th pole, he strips, holds his arms out, and drapes his clothing so the ship will sail. In this fashion, he comes at last to the dwelling of Utnapishtim, the only mortal to whom the gods have granted eternal life.

There follows the usual ritual challenge in which Utnapishtim finds it difficult to believe that as disheveled and dispirited a person as he has before him could possibly be Gilgamesh. Gilgamesh repeats his explanation of his mission and asks Utnapishtim how he qualified for the gods' unique favor.

In reply, Utnapishtim tells Gilgamesh the story of the flood. Disturbed by the constant uproar of humankind, the gods decided to destroy people. The god Ea, however, pitied Utnapishtim and instructed him to tear down his reed house and build a boat with the materials. A squarish sort of boat, its length and beam were to be equivalent— 120 cubits on a side—and the deck roofed over.

Ea charged Utnapishtim to take aboard the seed of all living creatures.

Utnapishtim expressed concern about how he will explain his behavior to his fellow citizens, and Ea gave him a cover story in which the boat builder was the one whom the gods decided to punish, and his fellow citizens were those who will be spared. Then, assisted by many helpers whom he wined and dined, Utnapishtim finished in seven days, loaded up his seven-decked ship with nine compartments per deck, and battened down the hatches. Then heaven unleashed its fury, and the storm came. For six days and nights it howled. Then on the seventh day, the weather calmed, and Utnapishtim looked out on a water world. In the distance, he spotted the mountain of Nisir, where the boat grounded and held fast for another seven days. Then he released a dove that found no perch and returned. A swallow came back as well. But when the next day he released a raven, it found food and a perch. Utnapishtim ordered a general disembarkation and ordered a sacrifice. From the aroma of the cooking meat of the sacrifice, however, the instigator of the flood, the god Enlil, was excluded. He nonetheless arrived and, finding himself shunned, complained that he had ordered the destruction of all people. Ea gently reproved Enlil and explained that a dream had revealed the coming flood to Utnapishtim. In an act of contrition, Enlil granted Utnapishtim and his wife the privilege of eternal life.

Gilgamesh's next adventure anticipates that of Odysseus in HOMER's The ODYSSEY when the poet has the hero try to stay awake for nine days and nights rather than let anyone else handle the ship. Utnapishtim suggests that if Gilgamesh can avoid sleeping for six days and nights, the gods may assemble and entertain his request. Almost immediately, Gilgamesh falls asleep and remains so for seven days. Anticipating this outcome, Utnapishtim has his wife bake a loaf of bread each day so that when he wakes Gilgamesh on the seventh day, he will be able to convince the hero by the bread's condition that he really slept that long.

That accomplished, Utnapishtim reproves Urshanabi and banishes him for bringing Gilgamesh. The immortal orders Urshanabi to bathe Gilgamesh, give him new garments that will always remain fresh, and take him home. As a consolation prize, Utnapishtim tells Gilgamesh of a flower that, when eaten, will restore youthful vigor to old men. Thorny and growing underwater, the flower is difficult and dangerous to pick. Gilgamesh nonetheless tries, and though his hands are painfully pricked, he obtains the flower. Then Urshanabi bathes him, and the flower's fragrance attracts a serpent that steals and eats it and immediately sheds its skin.

Gilgamesh's quest has proved unsuccessful. Urshanabi takes the king home. Once there, he engraves the story of his adventures on a stone.

In the epic's final chapter, Gilgamesh dies, and the people grieve for him in an eight-line threnody. Each line ends with either "he will not rise again," or "he will not come again." His funeral complete, and his praises once more sung, his epic ends.

Gilgamesh has been said to be the world's first tragic hero. Almost but not quite a god, despite heroic efforts, and against insurmountable odds, he aspired to godhead, but in the final analysis he was human. In the end he suffered humanity's common destiny. Only his story has achieved a measure of immortality.

Bibliography

George, A. R. The Babylonian Gilgamish Epic. Critical Edition and Cuneiform Text. 2 vols. Oxford and New York: Oxford University Press, 2003.

Hines, Derek, trans. Gilgamesh. New York: Anchor Books, 2004.

Sandars, N. K., ed. and trans. The Epic of Gilgamesh. Baltimore, Md.: Penguin Books, 1964.

The Epic of Gilgamesh: A New Translation, Analogues, and Criticism. Translated by B. R. Foster.

The Sumerian Gilgamesh Poems. Translated by Douglas Fraye. The Hittite Gilgamesh. Translated by Gary Beckman. New York: Norton, 2001.

gnomic poetry and prose

From very early in Greek literary history—at least from the fifth century B.C.E., pithy maxims (gnomes) came to be expressed in verse and in prose. These sayings, frequently only one line, were memorable and quotable, and they tried to formulate important truths in ways that would make them easy to call to mind. Thus, their authors seem to have thought of them as broadly instructive, and readers and hearers valued the gnomic verse or prose lines both for their aptness and for their educative value.

From AESOP we draw such examples as: "Familiarity breeds contempt" (from "The Fox and the Lion"); "The gods help them that help themselves" (from "Hercules and the Wagoner"). From THEOGNIS: "No man takes with him to Hades all his exceeding wealth" (*Elegies* l.725). From ARISTOPHANES: "You cannot teach a Crab to walk straight" (*Peace* l.1083.) From THUCYDIDES: "We secure our friends not by accepting favors but by doing them" (*The PELOPONNESIAN WAR* 2.40).

Roman writers also made their contributions to the genre. LIVY gives us "better late than never" (from *History* 4.23), and SENECA loaned Shakespeare the often-quoted "What fools these mortals be" (from *Epistles* 1.1.3).

Gnostic apocrypha and pseudepigrapha (Nag Hammadi manuscripts)

The discovery of the first-century DEAD SEA SCROLLS electrified students of first-century Judeo-Christian developments. Likewise, for students of religious developments during the next two centuries, the discovery in 1945 of fourth-century Christian manuscripts at Nag Hammadi in Egypt shed new light on the variety of Christian belief and the wealth of religious literature that had been excluded from received Scripture after the fourth-century institutionalization of an official form of Christianity as the state religion of the Roman Empire.

Without becoming embroiled in the technicalities of the argument, suffice it to say that the Nag Hammadi GOSPEL OF THOMAS seems to contain previously unknown historical utterances of Jesus Christ. Further evidence of primitive stages of traditions surrounding Jesus emerges from *The*

Dialogue of the Savior, Apochryphal James, and a manuscript preserved in Berlin, *The Gospel of Mary.* The ecclesiastical historian Karen L. King studies these texts and related ones with a view to establishing a more accurate interpretation of the relationship between early Christianity, early Gnosticism, and other communities subsequently deemed heretical by the Roman church and its authorities. King lists and revisits 44 such works in an effort to place them and the communities of belief that produced them in a more historically accurate context—one that sees the works as the product of alternate communities of faith rather than the work of heretics who were excluded from Christianity altogether and perhaps also from Judaism.

The contents of the Nag Hammadi manuscripts deserve an important place in the literary history of the ancient world. They continue to occasion much discussion and controversy among the learned and the faithful alike.

Bibliography

King, Karen L. *What is Gnosticism?* Cambridge, Mass.: The Belknap Press of Harvard University Press, 2005.

Meyer, Marvin, et al., eds. *The Nag Hammadi Library in English.* Translated by Douglas M. Parrott et al. San Francisco, Calif.: Harper & Row, Publishers, 1988.

gods of ancient Greece   See THEOGONY.

Golden Ass, The (Metamorphoses)
Apuleius (second century C.E.)

Often called the only Roman novel to survive in its entirety, APULEIUS's colloquial Latin, framework tale of a Greek named Lucius who accidentally gets turned into a golden-coated donkey when he becomes too interested in magic has continued to delight readers for almost 2,000 years. In the form that Apuleius gave his book to the world, the text apparently looks back to earlier Greek progenitors for inspiration and some of its material. The careful and comic way in which Apuleius has woven together borrowed material with his own sense of the amusing and the bizarre, however, gives the world a prototype of what would become the picaresque novel during the European Renaissance.

Book 1

Borrowing a device from EPIC poetry, *The Golden Ass* begins in the middle of things with the conjunction *but*. The effect suggests that the speaker is continuing a conversation about the literary device of tying tales together by embedding them in a framework, as did Aristides of Miletus, who wrote a number of now-lost racy stories. The putative author of Apuleius's story, the Greek traveler Lucius, speaks in the first person and provides the reader with something of his history. Then, cautioning the reader to pay attention so that delight in the story can follow, Lucius begins the tale proper.

On a business trip to Thessaly, Lucius encounters two other travelers who are passing the time with storytelling. He asks to join them and does so just in time to hear one of the companions pooh-poohing the notion of the efficacy of magical incantations. Lucius reproves the speaker with a not-altogether-relevant account of a sword swallower whom he has just seen perform. Then he promises to credit the stories of his new companions and invites them to dine at the next inn at his expense.

One of Lucius's traveling companions, Aristomenes, passes the time by recounting an earlier experience. In the course of buying and selling cheese, Aristomenes had encountered his missing friend Socrates—not the famous philosopher of the same name. Filthy, almost naked, and penniless, Socrates explained that he had been enchanted by and become the love slave of a powerful witch named Meroe. Meroe had turned a competing innkeeper into a frog and, by witchcraft, extended a rival's pregnancy for eight years and performed other wicked wonders. She had also deprived Socrates of everything he had.

Aristomenes got Socrates cleaned up, and the two checked into an inn for the night. Around midnight, the doors to their room burst open, and Meroe and a confederate witch, Panthea, appeared. They plunged a sword into Socrates' neck, collected the blood in a sponge, and pulled his heart out through the wound. Then they healed the wound with a sponge, which, with magical incantations, they instructed to return to the sea via a river. The two witches then urinated all over Aristomenes and departed.

Fearing that he would be crucified for having murdered Socrates, Aristomenes tried to leave the inn. The innkeeper, however, would not unlock the gate. The next morning, to his amazement, an apparently unscathed Socrates rose and reported that he had dreamed exactly what Aristomenes had witnessed. The two then set out on their journey together. When, however, they encountered a river and stopped to eat, Socrates grew pale. He stooped to drink from the river, the wound in his throat opened, the sponge fell into the river, and Socrates fell dead.

Bidding his traveling companions farewell after hearing the story, Lucius spends the night in the town of Hypata at the home of a notorious miser named Milo. After reporting his doings at Hypata, Lucius goes to bed hungry, fed on nothing but Milo's incessant chatter.

Book 2

As Lucius awakens, Book 2 begins. He recalls that he is in Thessaly, the epicenter of magic arts, and he is obsessed with a desire to learn more about them. He reports that he thought everything he encountered to have been changed by witchcraft from something else; he expected statues and pictures to speak and animals to utter prophecies. Suddenly, he encounters a couple whom he fails to recognize but who call him by name. They prove to be his aunt Byrrhena and her husband, and he accompanies them to their sumptuous residence. Byrrhena warns Lucius against the love charms of Milo's wife, Pamphile, whose name suggests that she falls for every man she meets. The aunt cautions her nephew that Pamphile changes those who reject her into some sort of animal.

This warning only inflames Lucius's desire to learn more of witchcraft. He decides to woo Milo's maid, Photis, and to evade any amorous connection with Pamphile. The wooing opens with an exchange of clever sexual double entendre in which the metaphor of cooking applies to amorous activity. Photis and Lucius agree to become lovers; the aunt Byrrhena sends food and wine for a small banquet, which Lucius reserves for Photis and himself.

As the household gathers for the usual evening conversation in lieu of dinner, Lucius reveals that before he left Corinth, a Chaldean prophet had predicted that on this journey, Lucius would gain reputation and become a long and unbelievable story recorded in several books (scrolls of papyrus). Milo asks the name of the Chaldean, whom he recognizes. Milo tells a story about him, and Lucius, bored and annoyed, excuses himself, retiring to his banquet and amorous encounter with Photis. That encounter Lucius describes in detail, explaining that it is the first of many.

Lucius next reports the events of a banquet at his aunt's home and a macabre story of witchcraft practiced on the bodies of the dead and told by one of the banquet's guests. The guest, who wears bandages, says that he had volunteered as a watchman to assure that witches did not mutilate a corpse awaiting burial. Although a strangely behaving weasel appeared in the room briefly, in the morning the corpse remained unmarked. The watchman was so well paid that he unthinkingly offered his services whenever they might be required. The relatives of the bereaved widow beat the watchman soundly for uttering such a bad omen.

As the corpse was carried to its funeral, an old man accused the widow of having murdered the husband and produced an Egyptian seer capable of restoring life to the corpse so that it could testify in the matter. This was done, and the corpse confirmed the accusation against his widow. It continued, reporting that while its watchman

slept, the witches had indeed tried to mutilate the corpse. Because, however, the watchman had the same name, the incantations worked on him rather than on the corpse. The witches had sliced off the watchman's nose and ears and replaced them with wax ones. The watchman confirmed the truth of this story, and ever since, he has worn bandages to conceal the shame of his mutilation.

Returning to Milo's house, Lucius discovers three stout fellows beating at the door. Lucius draws a concealed sword and fights them, eventually killing all three. Photis admits him to the house, and the second book ends.

Book 3

The opening of Book 3 finds Lucius arrested and conducted through the streets by the magistrates to the place of tribunal. All along his route, he passes crowds of people who roar with laughter. The chief of the watch, who was an eyewitness to the deaths, accuses Lucius of murder before the magistrates. The onlookers keep laughing.

Lucius explains that he was trying to protect the household of his host, but the widows of the slaughtered men demand justice. The authorities doubt that one person could have killed three such hardy youths, and they prepare to torture Lucius to extract the names of his confederates. The widows demand that the corpses be uncovered to inflame the crowd's desire for justice. The laughter grows.

When Lucius pulls the covering cloth off the corpses, he discovers three blown-up wineskins covered with gashes. The magistrates explain that Lucius has been used in a ceremony honoring the god of Laughter—an annual holiday. They make it up to him by granting him special honors, naming him the patron of the holiday, and making a bronze image of him. Lucius thanks them for the honor but modestly rejects having his statue erected.

Milo actually feeds Lucius something after this day's events. When Photis appears in Milo's chamber, she confesses that she was the cause of Milo's embarrassment and invites him to beat her. He refuses, but he wants to know the reasons for her behavior. In reply, Photis reveals the secrets of the house and confirms Lucius's aunt's assessment of the witchcraft of his hostess, Pamphilia.

Photis explains that she was trying to collect some hair of Pamphilia's current love at the barbershop, but that the barber prevented her from doing so. Rather than admit her failure, she had collected some blond hair from some wineskins and given it to Pamphilia. When Pamphilia tried to use the hair to summon her lover, she instead brought the wineskins to life, and it was their human apparitions that Lucius had slain. He became, she tells him, a "bag slayer."

Lucius begs Photis to help him observe Pamphilia at her incantations. Photis does so, and Lucius watches Pamphilia change herself into an owl. Lucius now wants a jar of Pamphilia's magic ointment that will let him change into a bird. This Pamphilia secures for him, assuring him that she knows the formula for changing him back into himself. Lucius daubs himself generously with the ointment and forthwith transmutes into an ass. Pamphilia blames herself for bringing the wrong ointment, but she assures Lucius that, as soon as he eats some roses, he will become himself once more.

Assured that Photis will bring the flowers in the morning, Lucius goes off to stable himself with his horse and Milo's donkey. Both animals attack him, and he retires to a far corner, contemplating the revenge he will take when he resumes his proper form. He notices roses on the altar of a household deity, but just as he stretches his neck to eat them, his own slave beats him off, and then a band of robbers attacks the house. They find so much booty that they require the three animals to carry it off, and Lucius now finds himself hustled off to the mountains carrying a heavy load. Chancing upon a garden with roses, Lucius is about to eat when it occurs to him that, should he resume his proper shape, the outlaws would kill him. He decides to bear his misfortune awhile longer as Book 3 ends.

Book 4

After several attempts at escape in early Book 4, and after seeing his companion donkey killed when he feigned death, Lucius decides to become a model jackass. Soon he finds himself at the headquarters of the band of brigands.

As the evening meal wears on, another troop of robbers arrives. These tell the tale of how they lost their leader, Lamachus, who committed suicide after his own men cut off his right arm in an effort to rescue him. Among their other exploits, the second group of robbers reports how they acquired a bear's skin and disguised one of their number as an animal. Putting him in a cage, they delivered him to a nearby aristocrat, Demochares. The thieves claimed the bear was a gift from a friend. Demochares put the man in bear's clothing under guard in his house. In the middle of the night, that man, Thrasaleon, left his cage, killed his guards and the gatekeeper, and let the rest of the robbers into the house. After they had stolen a load of treasure and were returning for a second, a servant in the house discovered that the bear was loose, roused his many comrades, set the dogs on Thrasaleon, and destroyed him.

On their next venture, the robbers capture a maiden whom they hold for ransom. Finally dissuaded from bewailing her fate by an old woman assigned to her, the girl tells the tale of how she was kidnapped from her wedding and had a vision of the death of her pursuing groom at the hands of the brigands. The old woman advises the girl not to credit dreams, and then tells a tale of her own, perhaps the most famous in *The Golden Ass*—the story of Cupid and Psyche.

Once upon a time there was a girl named Psyche, so beautiful that the adherents of the goddess Venus began to transfer their worship to the lovely human being. This enraged the real goddess, who convinced her son Cupid to make Psyche fall in love with the meanest, most miserable man on earth.

Psyche, in the meantime, pined for a husband and prayed to marry. An oracle, however, instructed her father the king to expose the girl on a mountain crag to be carried off by a snaky monster in a funeral-wedding. Everyone except Psyche grieved at her fate, but the girl herself, though shaken, faced it bravely. She was bound on the crag and abandoned, but as Book 4 ends, Zephyr, the west wind, wafts her gently to the valley below and lays her tenderly upon a flowery bank.

Book 5

Awakening in a magnificent park crowned by a royal palace, Psyche realizes, as Book 5 opens, that she is in the private precinct of some god. As she marvels at the splendors of the place and its many treasures, a disembodied voice tells her that everything she sees belongs to her. The voice advises her to rest and bathe, and then her invisible servants will dish up a royal feast. They do this and also entertain her with music from an equally invisible source. Late at night, a husband whom she never sees comes to bed with her, and her wedding is consummated. This routine goes on for a long time.

In the meantime, her parents who know nothing of Psyche's fate, wear themselves out with grief, and her sisters leave their husbands in an effort to console their parents. They set out to try to find traces of their sister.

One night, Psyche's invisible husband tells her that her sisters are nearing the cliff. He warns her neither to answer their calls nor even to look in their direction if she hears them. Should she do so, the husband will be bitterly pained, and Psyche will cause her own destruction.

Psyche, however, feels resentful, preferring freedom of action to the benefits of her luxurious prison. Knowing this, her invisible husband, whom she can feel as well as hear, tells her to do whatever she wishes, but to remember his heartfelt warning when she belatedly regrets her decision. Psyche pleads and wheedles, and finally her husband relents, saying that she can converse with her sisters, comfort them, and give them valuable presents. However, she must not, under any circumstances, take her sisters' ruinous

counsel to try to discover what her husband looks like. Otherwise both her good fortune and her husband would be lost to her.

When the sisters arrive and Psyche hears their lamentations, she has Zephyr bring them to her. Psyche evades the sisters' inquisition, loads them with rich gifts, and has Zephyr take them home. There the sisters begin to envy Psyche's good fortune and to complain bitterly about it. They connive to keep their sister's existence and good fortune a deep secret, and conspire to find a way to punish what they are pleased to call her pride.

Psyche's husband warns her of the plot and orders her not to speak to her sisters if they come again. By this time Psyche is pregnant, and her husband warns her again, this time most urgently, not even to answer her sisters when they call, or disaster will certainly follow. Psyche, however, thinks she can handle the situation and implores her husband to permit another visit from her sisters. They congratulate her on her pregnancy, saying that the baby will be an absolute "Cupid." They inquire further about her husband, and, forgetting the details of her former story, Psyche fabricates a new one. Catching her in the lie, the sisters conclude that she must be married to a god and envy her the opportunity to bear a god's child.

On their next visit, the sisters tell Psyche that they now know the truth about her husband. He is a "monstrous snake" that will eat her as soon as she has borne the child. The artless Psyche believes them, and the sisters encourage her to bring a lamp to her hitherto pitch-dark bedroom and to cut off the snake's head by its light. Following their instructions, Psyche illuminates her husband, the god Cupid himself, beautiful in slumber. Handling his bow and arrows, she pricks herself with one of them and is at once consumed by a fiery passion. The oil lamp sputtered a drop of hot oil onto Cupid's shoulder. The god awakes, and, finding himself betrayed, instantly flies off. Psyche grabs a leg and holds on until her strength fails, then drops to the ground.

Cupid explains that in loving her, he has disobeyed the edict of his mother, Venus, wounding himself with one of his own arrows so he would love Psyche faithfully. He promises to avenge himself upon the sisters, but as for Psyche herself, he is leaving her. She attempts suicide by drowning, but the river will not receive her and sets her ashore. There the god Pan finds her. He counsels her to cease mourning, to attempt suicide no more, and instead to pray to Cupid and to worship and flatter him, for Cupid is a "pleasure-loving and soft-hearted youth."

Psyche goes to the house of one of her sisters and tells her what has happened, but she adds the lie that Cupid had announced he would now wed this sister. The sister immediately travels to the crag where Psyche had been exposed, leaps off, and dismembers herself on the rocks—no gentle Zephyr for her. Psyche repeats the process with the second sister with the same outcome.

A seabird, meanwhile, goes to Venus and complains that the entire household of the goddess is getting a bad reputation since Cupid has a girlfriend. Venus demands a name, and the bird names Psyche.

Furious, Venus confronts Cupid and utters numerous threats. She swears to punish Cupid, and she then enlists Ceres and Juno to help her find Psyche and vent her fury upon her. The other two goddesses try to dissuade Venus, but succeed only in offending her as Book 5 ends.

Book 6

The opening of Book 6 finds Psyche traveling about the world, making sacrifices at the altar of every god and goddess in her desperation to regain her husband. Ceres discovers Psyche tending her altar and warns Psyche to consider her safety. Psyche prays for sanctuary, but Ceres denies it and sends her packing.

Psyche next prays to Juno as the patron of pregnant women, but the immortal blood (called *ichor*) that flows in the veins of the gods proves thicker than Juno's pity for Psyche, and that goddess also rejects Psyche's supplications. Psyche resolves to surrender and throw herself on Venus's mercy.

In the meantime, Venus borrows the services of the messenger of the gods, Mercury, from Jupiter. The goddess gives Mercury a poster with Psyche's name and description and sends him around the world in search of someone who can reveal her whereabouts. Eight kisses from Venus herself is the reward offered for information leading to Psyche's apprehension.

Psyche, however, is already at Venus's door, where Venus's servant, Habit, recognizes her. Habit drags Psyche inside by the hair and takes her to Venus, who turns her over to Trouble and Sadness for torture. The goddess also cites Roman law to declare the offspring of Psyche's union illegitimate.

Then Venus gave Psyche a great pile of mixed seeds and orders her to sort them all by evening. A humble ant, pitying the girl her impossible task, calls squadrons of his fellows, and the ants quickly accomplish the job for her. Venus attributes the miracle to Cupid, tosses Psyche a crust of bread, and stomps off. Cupid, also in solitary confinement, is in Venus's house.

Venus next sets Psyche the task of procuring a hank of wool from a flock of nearby wild, golden sheep. This time a reed, stirred by the wind, instructs Psyche how to procure what she seeks. Not at all mollified, Venus sets Psyche another task. She must bring a phial of freezing water from the source of two rivers of Hell, the Styx and the Cocytus. When Psyche comes to the place, she discovers snakes everywhere, and the water itself speaks and warns her off.

This time the eagle of Jupiter himself comes to Psyche's aid and fills the vial for her. Still unsatisfied, Venus sends Psyche to hell for a jar of Proserpine's beauty. Psyche decides on suicide as the quickest route to the underworld, but the tower from which she is about to jump speaks and tells her of an alternate route to take and the price of admission to hell—two barley cakes soaked in mead and two coins in her mouth. The tower also tells her of the snares that she will encounter and of attempts that will be made to delay her journey and to relieve her of the coins and the cakes. She must not fall for any of them.

One cake she must feed to Cerberus. Then, when she comes into Proserpine's presence, Psyche must resist her invitation to dine as a guest but must sit on the floor and eat only bread, make her request, and feed Cerberus the other cake as she leaves. With the two coins, she must pay her passage to the boatman of the Styx—one coming and one going.

Finally, Psyche must not look into the jar she is carrying or think curiously about the treasure of divine beauty. Psyche heeds all the tower's counsel except the last two. She yields to the temptation to open the jar. There is nothing in it but deathlike sleep, which instantly overcomes her.

Cupid, however, now cured of his burn from Psyche's oil lamp, escapes and finds Psyche. He carefully wipes the sleep off her and awakens her with a little prick of his arrow, then sends her off to fulfill Venus's orders, promising to take care of everything else himself. He rushes off to Jupiter and appeals to the king of the gods. Despite the fact that Jupiter had often been wounded by Cupid's arrows in the chief god's interminable series of amours, Jupiter grants Cupid's request for assistance on two conditions: Cupid must know how to take precautions against his competitors, and he must give Jupiter an outstandingly beautiful human girl in repayment.

Jupiter calls a meeting of all the gods and announces that Cupid is to keep Psyche forever. He reconciles Venus to his decision, makes Psyche an immortal, and a wedding banquet ensues among the gods.

At the robbers' headquarters, Lucius in asinine form has overheard this tale, and just then the robbers return. They mistreat Lucius and, as he has gone lame, decide to do away with him. Lucius resolves on flight and breaks loose. The old woman tries to restrain him, but the captive maiden tears the strap from her hand and jumps on Lucius's back, and the two gallop off.

The girl promises her mount many rewards if he carries her safely home. The robbers, however, intercept the pair and resolve upon a horrible death for the two of them as the sixth book ends.

Book 7

As Book 7 opens, Lucius overhears the robbers discussing the robbery at the house of his host, Milo. Lucius learns that the authorities have decided to prosecute him for the crime, and that his slave had been tortured though he knew nothing. Lucius concludes that fortune truly favors the wicked and the undeserving. He would like to testify in his own defense, but he can only bray. Moreover, as the robbers intend to kill him, he has a more pressing problem.

As he considers it, a new recruit appears among the robbers. He introduces himself as Haemus of Thrace, son of Theron, and launches into telling the next story in the book. It concerns the history of his former robber band, the way the emperor ended it by edict, and his subsequent escape to the camp of his new comrades. He rips open the rags he is wearing, and 2,000 gold pieces pour out. He gives them to the band and offers his own services as their leader. The robbers welcome him in that role, but when they outline their plans for killing the ass and the maiden, Haemus suggests that a more profitable course would involve selling the maiden into prostitution.

Haemus proceeds to get his new comrades thoroughly drunk, smuggles food to the maiden, and kisses her on the sly. Lucius prudishly disapproves of this behavior until he discovers that Haemus is in reality Tlepolemus, the young woman's bridegroom. When the robbers are all dead drunk, he binds them, sets the girl on Lucius's back, and leads the pair home. Once the rescued girl and ass are safely there, Tlepolemus leads a posse of townspeople back to the camp, where they kill all the robbers. He and his in-laws next determine to reward Lucius. They decide to set him free so that he can roam about performing stud service, and they entrust a herdsman with the task. The herdsman and his wife, however, yoke Lucius to a grinding mill and set him to crushing grain—including the barley that his grateful would-be benefactors had meant for Lucius's feed.

When Lucius is utterly worn out from over-work, the herdsman at last sets him free. Just as he is about to begin his career as a stud, however, the resident stallions object and attack him. Then he is forced to carry wood down the mountain, directed by an uncaring boy who overloads him, beats him bloody, and ties a knot of thorns to his tail so that his suffering is constant. Then the boy sets Lucius on fire, and only a puddle of muddy water saves him.

Finally, the boy accuses Lucius of attempting to rape human beings, and the herdsman instructs the boy to destroy the ass. As the boy sharpens the sacrificial axe, a more parsimonious country fellow recommends castration instead. As the boy is about to perform this office, a she-bear attacks him, and Lucius breaks away. A stranger finds him and rides him straight into the midst of the herds-men who had ordained his emasculation. They accuse the rider of thievery and, finding the boy dismembered by the bear, also of murder. The boy's parents schedule Lucius for death on the day following, and during the night the mother tor-tures him. Lucius saves himself by befouling her, and Book 7 ends.

Book 8

The next morning, a groom arrives to announce the untimely death of Charite, the maiden Lucius had tried to rescue. The groom tells the sad tale of how a rival and brother of Charite's husband, feigning friendship, had murdered the husband on a boar hunt. On learning the news of her husband's death, Charite went mad. The murderer, Thrasyllus, however, unable to con-tain his impatience, proposed marriage to Charite before her time of grieving had passed. Charite put him off, and her husband's ghost paid her a nocturnal visit, warning her that Thrasyllus had killed him.

Pretending to accept Thrasyllus's impious pro-posal, Charite lured him to her chamber. There a trusted maid gave him a soporific in wine. Charite first blinded him and then seized his sword. With sword in hand, she ran to her husband's tomb and committed suicide. Chastened at last, the blinded Thrasyllus locked himself in the same tomb to starve himself to death.

As their employers have died, the herdsmen are suddenly without wages. They load up their goods and trek off. They need Lucius for a pack animal, and he is reprieved. As they march off, news of ferocious wolves in the neighborhood makes them huddle together and move fast, with Lucius right in the middle. Though no wolves attack, the workers on an estate mistake them for bandits and set the dogs on them. Then the neigh-boring farmers assault them with rocks. Matters get sorted out, and the group travels on.

They pause, but a man-eating snake devours one of their number, and the herdsmen hasten on again. They finally find refuge in a town where they learn about a notable crime. To avenge herself on an adulterous husband, the accountant of an estate, his wife destroyed his records, his baby, and herself. The owner of the estate punished the husband by smearing him with honey and tying him to a fig tree that har-bored a nest of ants—with painful and predict-able results. Lucius's group does not linger there.

In due course, they arrive at a city where they decide to settle. They rest the animals for three days and take them to the market to sell. A per-verted worshipper of a notorious Syrian god-dess, Atargatis, buys Lucius after considerable tomfoolery. The chief of a bevy of catamites, the purchaser expects that Lucius will carry their goddess about while her worshippers flagellate and mutilate themselves before taking up a col-lection among the bystanders. They load the offerings on Lucius, who now discovers that he is both a temple and a storehouse. On their return home, they revel in forbidden pleasures. These are inopportunely discovered when Lucius attracts a party searching for a stolen donkey with his brays. His masters manage to flee, beat-ing Lucius unmercifully when they get the chance. They stop short of killing him, however, since they need him to carry the image of their goddess.

Book 9

Book 8 ends with Lucius in danger of being slaughtered so a cook can use his thigh to replace a stolen haunch of venison. He escapes this fate as Book 9 opens, by interrupting a banquet and being locked away. Because his masters fear that he might contract rabies in the stables, they lock him in a bedroom, where for the first time in years, he sleeps like a human being. The next morning, he passes their test for asinine gentleness and once again bears the goddess forth. The group spends the next night at an inn, where Lucius overhears the next story he reports. It is an account of an unfaithful wife who deceives her husband by hiding her lover in a jar when the husband unexpectedly returns home and about the way wife and lover continue a successful deception.

After making light of the prophecies and soothsaying of his group of mountebank masters, Lucius tells how they are caught stealing a golden cup from a temple and imprisoned. Lucius is sold as a pack animal again, this time to a miller who is also a baker. He harnesses Lucius to a grindstone and sets him again to hard labor.

Lucius reports the sorry condition of both the human and the animal slaves at the mill. Then he turns to a report about the wife of his master the baker—a vicious drunkard, adulteress, sadist, and shrew. Lucius's highly sensitive ass's ears overhear much of her conversation with another woman, her confidante, and he reports a tale within a tale. It concerns a jealous husband, Barbarus, a slave, Myrmex, a wife of easy virtue, and her admirer. Barbarus sets Myrmex as a guard over his wife's virtue. The would-be lover, Philesitherus, overcomes the reluctance of both slave and mistress with gold. While the tryst is in progress, Barbarus unexpectedly returns home. Myrmex holds his master at bay with the excuse of a mislaid key while Philesitherus makes his escape through the bedroom window. In the confusion, however, the lover forgets his sandals, which Barbarus discovers the next morning. Guessing the truth, Barbarus hauls the sandals and Myrmex

off to the authorities, but the shrewd Philesitherus intercepts them and beats Myrmex, accusing him of taking the shoes from the public bath. The ruse is successful, and the conspirators deceive Barbarus on all fronts.

The next tale, concerning the miller's wife, mirrors aspects of the one just told. The miller's wife, thinking her husband safely away for the evening, entertains a young lover at a sumptuous banquet. When the miller returns unexpectedly, she hides her paramour under a wooden tub and asks her husband why he is back so soon. The miller reports that his friend the fuller and he had discovered the fuller's wife in similar circumstances. She had hidden her friend in a wicker cage used to fumigate clothes with sulfur. The young man's sneezes revealed his hiding place. The fuller would have killed the youth had the miller not assured him that the sulfur's fumes would accomplish the same object. The miller reports that he smoothed matters over, advising the wife to stay for a while with a female friend until her husband's anger had cooled. Then he had returned home immediately.

As the miller's wife reluctantly serves her husband a dinner she had prepared for her lover, Lucius's keeper leads him past the tub where the young man is hiding. Lucius steps on the lad's exposed fingers, and the lover cries out. The miller discovers him, but keeps his temper. He explains that he too is attracted to the young man, so he arranges a ménage à trois. The three will share one bed. However, the miller locks the wife away elsewhere, and on the next morning he has the boy thrashed by his servants and divorces his wife. The wife hires a witch to soften her husband's heart. When her charms fail, however, the witch tries to charm the ghost of a murdered woman to destroy the miller.

One day, a strange woman shows up and privately interviews the miller. After a long time, his subordinates, needing supplies, discover him hanging dead from a rafter in a locked room with the woman nowhere to be found. When his daughter comes to the miller's funeral, she reveals that her father had told her what happened in a dream, and this is how Lucius learns the truth of the matter.

Auctioned off again, Lucius becomes the property of a market gardener, and of course his meager circumstances lead once more to a new story. This time, when his new master is about to receive a reward from a wealthy landowner, portents of disaster appear. A chicken lays an egg from which a full-fledged chick emerges. The ground opens, and a fountain of blood gushes forth. Wine boils, and other strange signs appear. These predict the deaths of a thieving rich man, his neighbor's three sons, and the suicide of their father.

As Lucius and the gardener leave the home of the landowner, a soldier unsuccessfully attempts to commandeer Lucius, beating the gardener into the bargain. Forced to defend himself, the gardener bests the soldier, takes his sword, and rides off. The soldier confides his shame to some fellows, and they plot revenge. They accuse the gardener of thievery and discover both him and Lucius hidden in a friend's house as the ninth book ends.

Book 10

As Book 10 begins, Lucius, now laden with the soldier's weaponry, arrives at the soldier's station and there overhears a tale that, as usual, he shares with his readers. A stepmother conceives a violent passion for her stepson and displays all the symptoms of lovesickness—considered a dangerous disease among the ancients. She propositions her stepson. Though he is shocked, he decides it is best to put her off rather than flatly refuse her. He tells her to wait until his father is away, and then he seeks advice from a trusted teacher. The teacher counsels immediate flight.

In the meantime, the stepmother has managed to send the husband off. She tries to collect on the young man's promise, but he puts her off with repeated excuses. When she realizes that his acquiescence was insincere, her love turns to hatred. With a slave, she plots the boy's murder. They prepare a poisoned cup, but by chance the woman's own son by her first marriage drinks it. Far from caring, the wicked stepmother sends for her husband, accusing his son of murdering hers to punish her for refusing to yield to the young man's lust.

Convinced, the father appeals to the magistrates for a judgment against his own son. They duly summon the young man to appear. They also examine the slave who had prepared the poisoned cup. The slave testifies against the son. Almost all the jurors think the son is guilty, but one keeps them from voting and invoking the sentence of being flogged, sewn into a sack, and thrown into the sea. The dissenting juror proves to be the doctor who had sold the slave the poison. He had suspected foul play, had the slave seal the money paid for the poison with his ring, and had preserved the means for proving his allegation in court. The slave nevertheless maintains his innocence in spite of torture.

The doctor then admits that he gave the slave not poison but a coma-inducing drug, mandragora, and that the supposedly dead youth will soon come to. Such proves to be the case. The stepmother is exiled, the slave crucified, the doctor permitted to keep the money, and the father has two fine sons.

Now Lucius experiences a bit of good fortune. Two slaves, brothers who are cooks, buy him, and he contrives to feed on the gorgeous food they bring home from banquets until he is caught. At first they think an ass would not eat such fare, but, made suspicious by his increasing girth, they catch him eating human fare. This proves to be a source of amusement, not only to the slaves but also to their master and his guests. Then it occurs to someone that Lucius might also enjoy a drink of wine and mead. Indeed he does. The slaves' master pays them quadruple what they had paid for Lucius, and then has someone teach him a number of tricks, including gesturing with his head to indicate his likes and dislikes, wrestling, and dancing.

Lucius interrupts his story about himself to give details about his master and then returns to his own adventures, explaining that his master has profited from exhibiting him. Among those who admire him is a lady who, like Pasiphae, the queen of Crete who had yearned for a bull, conceived an unnatural passion for the golden ass—one that she consummates in a detailed encounter with Lucius. Learning of it from the slave, Lucius's master decides that there is money to be made from his jackass's new trick, and a condemned woman is found for the occasion.

Lucius interrupts his story with an account of the woman's condemnation. It is a story that begins with the birth of a female child. Ordered to expose the child to its death, the mother instead gives it to neighbors to rear. When the girl nears marriageable age, its real mother tells her son that the girl is his sister lest he commit incest with her. The brother, a noble youth, receives his sister into his own home and arranges a marriage for her. The brother's wife, however, thinks the sister might be a rival and begins to plan her death—a deed the sister-in-law accomplishes in a loathsome manner.

The brother's wife, who is also an adulteress, now turns her venom on her husband, who has fallen ill after his sister's death. The wife hires a physician to poison her husband and contrives to get the physician to poison himself into the bargain. The physician, before dying, confesses the entire affair to his wife. The brother of the murdered girl also dies from poison. The doctor's wife attempts to blackmail the guilty widow. Unfortunately by this time the wife has become a serial murderess. She wheedles poison from the doctor's wife and uses it to poison her and also a daughter who is the legal heir to her husband's fortune. The doctor's wife, however, lives long enough to confess the whole sordid story to the district governor. The governor sentences the woman to be torn by wild beasts.

It is this convicted murderess who is to become Lucius's unnatural bride. Lucius strives to think of a way to commit suicide instead. Although he cannot, he reminds himself that it is now the season for roses to bloom. Perhaps he can resume his natural form.

Turning his attention to a description of the preliminary entertainments that have been prepared as a prelude to the main event that would feature him and the murderess, Lucius lingers lovingly on the show's details—scantily clad dancers representing goddesses and all sorts of magnificent pageantry. Addressing his readers as "cheap ciphers" and worse, Lucius offers yet another associative transition, as he recalls that since the beginning of the world, juries have been subornable for a price. He gives a series of illustrations that includes the jury that granted the armament of the slain Achilles to Ulysses instead of to Ajax.

Calling himself back to the main story, Lucius admits that he cannot bear the thought of participating in such a shameful display. Watching his chance, he bolts and runs six miles before finding his way to a deserted stretch of beach where he spends a night of restful sleep, watched over by a resplendent moon to end Book 10.

Book 11

As the 11th and last book begins, a refreshed Lucius awakens with the premonition that his asinine troubles may be nearly over. After bathing in the sea in a ritual purification, he prays to the queens of heaven and hell, whoever they may be. In response, a divine face emerges from the sea, followed by the full form of a goddess. Lucius lovingly describes her appearance and dress and the object that she carries. She identifies herself by the various names by which her worshippers in different parts of the world address her. Her true name, however, is Isis, and the Egyptians worship her with proper rites.

Isis explains to Lucius that the day of his salvation is at hand. He is to join a procession in her honor, reverently pluck from the hand of her priest a garland of roses, and reassume his human form. He must remember and keep secret the fact that the rest of his life is pledged to the celibate service of Isis. After his death, he will continue to serve her among the privileged souls inhabiting the Elysian Fields in the underworld.

Now Lucius carefully describes the religious procession—one in which the gods of Egypt themselves participate. When the priest carrying the roses approaches, Lucius carefully edges forward. The priest, however, has been forewarned of Lucius's coming metamorphosis and offers him the garland. Lucius takes and eats it. His transformation into a naked man immediately takes place in the midst of a wondering crowd, who praise the power of the goddess.

After giving Lucius a garment, the priest lectures Lucius about the folly of his earlier human life and the price that blind Fortune had exacted for his foolishness. The priest recruits Lucius as a communicant of the religion of the goddess. As her slave, Lucius will, the priest promises, find true freedom.

The procession returns to the spot where Lucius had spent the previous night. The worshippers load a ship with offerings to the goddess, and they set the ship adrift. The goddess having been thus propitiated and blessings pronounced in Latin and in Greek, the priests declares the season for navigation officially open.

Upon learning that Lucius has lived, his townspeople welcome him home, and his former servants, returning from Hypata, manage even to identify and recover his horse that they had sold long before.

In the meantime, the requisite vows of chastity have deterred Lucius from joining Isis's order as a full-fledged priest. Now, however, he seeks to do so. His priestly mentor counsels patience as the requirements for such consecration are complex and as the act of initiation involves voluntary death and salvation.

Lucius waits patiently, and eventually the goddess makes clear to him that the day has arrived. After 10 days of fasting and fulfilling other requirements, Lucius is admitted to the priesthood of Isis. He regrets being unable to share the mysteries of his initiation with his readers. The full initiation and Lucius's ritual death and rebirth require three days. Lucius adores the goddess in prayer and in the sort of liturgical language familiar to Christians.

He then boards a ship for Rome, where Isis is worshipped under the name Campensis, owing to the location of her temple on the Campus Martius. There, after a year, Lucius dreams that, although he is an initiate of the cult of the goddess, he has not yet been admitted to the mysteries of her husband, the supreme god Osiris. Such initiation is expensive, but Lucius scrapes together the required sums by selling his ragged clothing, and he is also admitted to the cult of Osiris. Thereafter, Lucius supports himself by practicing law in the Latin language.

The Golden Ass, or *Metamorphoses,* of Apuleius ends with Lucius's being divinely prompted to undergo yet another initiation in which he becomes a member of the chief initiates of the bearers of Osiris's shrine.

As Apuleius's distinguished translator, J. Arthur Hanson, explains, critical estimates of the novel and of Apuleius's purposes in writing it rarely agree. One school considers the work a jumble of poorly organized and largely immoral stories tossed into the framework of Lucius's adventures as a donkey. This view seems to ignore both the parallels between the associative organization of parts of Ovid's *Metamorphoses* and that of Apuleius and the care that Apuleius takes to suit the subordinate tales to the development of his overarching story. Another school of thought finds in the work an extended allegory of the salvation of Lucius from the foolish errors of the flesh through the gracious intervention of the goddess Isis. A careful reader can trace parallels between Apuleius and Cervantes' *Don Quixote of La Mancha.* Various critics have taken other philosophical and literary views of the work as well. Perhaps the greatest tribute to the work is the frequency with which it is translated and read after 2,000 years.

Bibliography

Apuleius. *The Golden Ass.* Translated by P. G. Welsh. Oxford: The Clarendon Press; New York, Oxford University Press, 1997.

———. *The Golden Ass or The Metamorphoses.* Translated by E. J. Kenney. New York: Penguin Books, 1998.

———. *The Golden Ass or The Metamorphoses.* Translated by W. Adlington. New York: Barnes and Noble Books, 2004.

———. *Metamorphoses.* [*The Golden Ass.*] 2 vols. Translated and edited by J. Arthur Hanson. Cambridge, Mass.: Harvard University Press, 1989.

Gorgias of Leontium (Gorgias of Leontini, Gorgias of Sicily) (fl. ca. 485– ca. 380 B.C.E.) *Greek prose writer*

An extremely long-lived Sophist philosopher, a Sicilian ambassador to Athens, and a superb rhetorician, Gorgias of Leontium is reported to have studied with Empedocles. Serving as Leontium's ambassador to Athens in 427 B.C.E., Gorgias is credited with having introduced Sicilian oratorical conventions into Athenian rhetoric. He remained in Athens as a Sophist, teaching oratory and its application to politics. In his personal philosophy, Gorgias professed extreme skepticism and nihilism. He believed that nothing really existed or, if something did exist, it would be unknowable. If someone did manage to learn something about the nature of existence, that person would find it impossible to communicate the knowledge to anyone else.

Various figures of speech are associated with Gorgias's rhetorical innovations. Called *Gorgian figures*, these include balancing antithetical arguments one against another (on the one hand . . . and on the other . . .). He also strove to achieve euphony through the repetition of vowel sounds (assonance) and rhyming. Gorgias achieved a similar effect by using words with like endings in a series (weeping, wailing, and gnashing of teeth) a technique called *homoeoteleuton*. He also made effective use of carefully balancing similar grammatical arrangements within phrase structures (*parison*)—"servants of the undeservedly unfortunate, punishers of the undeservedly fortunate."

The classicist Donald A. F. M. Russell tells us that Agathon's speech praising the god of love in Plato' *Symposium* parodies the style of Gorgias. Also, in his dialogue entitled *Gorgias*, Plato has his character named Gorgias unsuccessfully defend the art of rhetoric and its uses against Socrates' relentless questioning.

Surviving examples of Gorgias's work, beyond a few miscellaneous fragments, include a eulogy praising Helen of Troy and a defense of Palamedes, the man who supposedly enlisted Odysseus in the Greek army against Troy by threatening to destroy Odysseus's son Telemachus. Regrettably, neither of these works is currently available in English, though recent translations from the Greek are available in Italian. The fragments appear in Spanish. In English there are recent good and accessible studies of Gorgias and his work.

Bibliography

Consigny, Scott. *Gorgias: Sophist and Artist.* Columbia: University of South Carolina Press, 2001.

Gorgias of Leontini. *Encomio di Elena; Apologia di Palamede.* Translated into Italian by Luca Càffaro. Florence, Italy: Aletheia, 1997.

———. *Fragmentos.* Translated into Spanish by Pedro C. Tapia Zúñiga. Mexico City: Universidad Nacional Autónama de Mexico, 1980.

McComiskey, Bruce. *Gorgias and the New Sophistic Rhetoric.* Carbondale: Southern Illinois University Press, 2002.

Wardy, Robert. *The Birth of Rhetoric: Gorgias, Plato, and Their Successors.* New York: Routledge, 1996.

Gorgias Plato (ca. fourth C., B.C.E.)

Usually considered a lesser Platonic dialogue, the *Gorgias* takes its title from the name of a Sophist philosopher of that name. The dialogue begins by examining the nature and the value of the art of rhetoric. It continues by expressing the hope that the eloquence of rhetoric and its persuasive power can become the handmaid of logic and morality as they are practiced in public and in private life. The Sophists generally valued rhetoric for its persuasive power and its ability to gain adherents for a cause irrespective of that cause's truth or morality.

As a final caveat to sophistic expediency, Plato ends the dialogue by describing the eternal circumstances of both righteous and unrighteous souls.

Bibliography

Plato. *Dialogues of Plato*. 2 vols. Translated by Benjamin Jowett. New York: Washington Square Press, 2001.

Gospel of Thomas, The (ca. first century C.E.)

This nonbiblical gospel was discovered largely intact among the Coptic Nag Hammadi manuscripts in Egypt in 1945 (see GNOSTIC APOCRYPHA AND PSEUDEPIGRAPHA) and earlier in extremely fragmentary condition in Greek at OXYRHYNCHUS. The Gospel of Thomas is thought to have been written in the Greek language in Syria, perhaps at Edessa, where the bones of the Christian apostle Thomas were venerated. The work was subsequently translated into Coptic. The author of the gospel was thought to have been Didymos Judas Thomas, whom the Syrian church considered to be both the twin brother of Jesus and his apostle. While some scholars consider the work a Gnostic document, others are only willing to say that some influence of Gnostic theology is apparent in it.

The importance of this document stems in part from its containing otherwise unrecorded sayings attributable with some confidence to the historical Jesus. Clear parallels appear between many of the 114 sayings reported in the Gospel of Thomas and those in the synoptic gospels of the Christian NEW TESTAMENT. According, though, to the scholar Helmut Koester of the Institute for Antiquity and Christianity, the forms of the parallel sayings suggest a greater antiquity for Jesus' remarks as they appear in Thomas than in the synoptic gospels. That antiquity may derive from the form of the remarks originating in an earlier, thus far undiscovered version of the Christian Gospels. The scholars who posit it label this version "Q." Alternatively, the earlier form of the remarks may result from their having been recorded by someone who had heard Jesus speak.

Beyond this, Thomas's importance also derives from its early date of composition at a time before Christianity became the state religion of Rome (fourth century C.E.), and before either Christian (or heretical) doctrine or an approved biblical canon had achieved definitive status.

Little commentary surrounds the largely prophetic sayings of Jesus in the Gospel of Thomas. There is conversation between Jesus and several of his disciples and between Jesus and Mary, but Jesus is here pictured as a human teacher of wisdom and not as a supernatural being—though he presents himself as someone of great authority. In and of itself, that fact is enough to occasion bitter controversy among those who subscribe to an orthodox view of Christianity and those who, instead, search in Scripture for spiritual wisdom instead of personal salvation. For those whose interest in all such early documents is principally literary and historical, the light that this document and similar ones shed on the development of first- and second-century codicology, on the history of religious texts, and on the development and mingling of religious ideas in the Greco-Roman-Persian-Egyptian Mediterranean world provides excitement and fascination enough.

Bibliography

Barnstone, Willis, and Marvin Meyer, eds. *The Gnostic Bible*. Boston and London: Shambhala, 2003.

Meyer, Marvin W., et al., eds. *The Nag Hammadi Library in English*. Translated by Douglas M. Parrott, et al. San Francisco, Calif.: Harper & Row, Publishers, 1989.

grammar and grammarians in Greece

The concept of *grammar* as it developed among the Greeks did not limit itself to the parsing of words and phrases contained in a sentence. The broader Greek notion of grammar encompassed what contemporary students of language would address in the much broader study of philology. It included the skills of correct speaking and writing, usually divided into the principles or rules of language and the interpretation of words and phrases. Grammar also addressed the composition of poetry, the study of eloquence, and the study of history and elementary philosophy.

As the discipline developed among the Greeks, grammarians devoted themselves to useful tasks and studies of different sorts. Some undertook revising classical authors in editions that accounted for changes in usage and the meanings of words in ancient texts. Others conducted commentaries on such texts or sought to resolve grammatical and philological conundrums. Still others concerned themselves with differences among the several dialects spoken in the ancient Greek world, some commenting on differences in single words or in variant grammatical forms. Poetic meter was also among the subjects of interest to ancient Greek grammarians.

An early school of Greek grammarians flourished in Alexandria, Egypt, under the leadership of Zenodotus. He was succeeded in that role, first by Aristophanes of Byzantium and next by Aristophanes' highly respected disciple, Aristarchus of Samothrace. The latter's name became a common descriptor for any renowned literary critic of the epoch, such as Crates, PHILEMON, Artemidorus, and Sosibius. Another especially severe critic of HOMER, Zoilus, lent his name to any of the more judgmental sort of literary commentators. Though we know the names of these grammarians and something of their reputations, only disconnected bits of their works survive.

After the Greek world became a part of the Roman Empire, the study of Greek grammar in the broad sense expanded exponentially. A few names of the most outstanding practitioners of the discipline must suffice as representative. Those who focused principally on lexicography included Apollonius the Sophist, Ertianus, Timaeus (immortalized in PLATO's dialogue that bears his name), and Julius Pollux (Polydeuces of Naucratis).

Julius Pollux (fl. second century C.E.) is especially remembered for a fine Greek dictionary that not only treats the meanings of words but also, in its first volume, addresses such matters as gods and kings, commerce, mechanical matters, houses, war matériel, and agriculture. The second volume discusses the age of the human race and parts of the human body, while the third examines family relationships, friends, travels, road, and rivers. The fourth book considers sciences, the fifth animals and hunting, the sixth (perhaps oddly) meals and crimes. A treatment of the trades practiced by people is the subject of the seventh book. The eighth volume considers the administration of justice, while the ninth looks at cities, buildings, money, and games, and the final book addresses such matters as furniture and household utensils. Grammar in Julius's mind was a broadly encompassing subject.

Among those who specialized in the study of dialects, Tryphon son of Ammonius, Phrynicus the Arabian, and Ælius Mœris stand out from the crowd. Apollonius Dyscolus and others wrote on specific topics of Greek syntax. Apollonius's surviving works treat pronouns, conjunctions, adverbs, and syntax in general. While it is possible to provide numerous examples, I close this entry with a notice of the grammarian Suidas, who flourished about 1000 C.E., and with a word about an anonymous source.

Although Suidas is a late figure for inclusion in this volume, his *Lexicon* is the source of considerable otherwise unknown information about the literature of the 1,700 years that preceded him. Similarly, a glossary known as the *Etymologicum Magnum* (Great Etymology) of an anonymous author preserves many otherwise lost passages from ancient authors and clarifies a large number of otherwise irresolvable mysteries from the pages of history and of mythology. The glossary also dates from about 1000.

Bibliography

Dickey, Eleanor. *Ancient Greek Scholarship: A Guide to Finding, Reading, and Understanding Scholia, Commentaries, Lexica, and Grammatical*

Treatises from their Beginnings to the Byzantine Period. New York and Oxford: Oxford University Press, 2006.

grammarians of Rome

Like their Greek literary forebears, Roman grammarians were interested both in the literature and in the history and structure of the Latin language, and thus, *grammar* was a broader study than the word implies in our contemporary English. Both Roman and Greek grammarians were persons with broad expertise in language and literature, and it was a Greek, Crates of Mallos, who is credited with sparking Roman interest in the professional study of the Latin language when Crates came to Rome in 168 B.C.E.

The earliest professional Roman grammarians included Aurelius Opilius, who wrote a nine-book commentary on early Latin authors. Antonius Gnipho, a teacher of CICERO, composed a philological discourse on the Latin language. Neither of these works has survived.

MARCUS TERENTIUS VARRO (116–27 B.C.E.), who was the most notable scholar that ancient Rome ever produced, wrote an important work in 25 books (papyrus scrolls) entitled *De Lingua Latina*, on Latin vocabulary and syntax. A significant portion of this work still exists. In the same epoch, the emperor AUGUSTUS CAESAR employed a grammarian, Valerius Flaccus, as a palace tutor. Flaccus wrote a grammar of which an abridgement is left to us. The grammarians of this early period directed their attention chiefly to the history and development of the Latin language.

After the beginning of the first century C.E., the succeeding generations of grammarians turned their attention to what we might call historical literary criticism. Quintus Asconius Pedianus (9 B.C.E.–76 C.E.) wrote commentaries on the works of Cicero, SALLUST, and VIRGIL. Handwriting was also among the topics that interested first-century grammarians, and Velius Longus wrote a surviving work on the subject. A writer on the same topic and also on HORACE's *The ART OF POETRY* was Terentius Scaurus. Marcus Cornelius Fronto, on the other hand, interested himself in synonyms and wrote a treatise on the variations in their meanings.

The somewhat later grammarian Aulus Gellius, a student of Fronto, was temporarily a resident in Athens. There he entertained his children and whiled away the long winter nights by collecting a miscellany of observations on various matter of grammatical, antiquarian, and philological interest. Entitled *Noctes Atticae* (Greek nights), more than 18 of his original 20 books survive.

Particularly prized for his citations of otherwise lost earlier authors is the third-century C.E. grammarian Nonius Marcellus. His fourth-century successor, Aelius Donatus, one of the teachers of St. JEROME, proved uniquely important for the subsequent study of Latin. When taken together, his collected grammatical essays—a compilation known as the *Ars Donati* (The art of Donatus)—form the first known systematic Latin grammar. Donatus's works provide the foundation upon which all subsequent Latin grammars have been constructed. He was also an important early commentator on the dramatic works of TERENCE.

MACROBIUS, who flourished early in the fifth century, left seven books called *Saturnalia* that contain much philological material—both his own work and much gleaned from other authors. He also wrote a detailed account exploring the likenesses and differences among Greek and Latin verbs. Though this work is lost, a later extract of it survives. His most famous work—*Commentary on the Dream of Scipio Described in Book 2 of Cicero*—is a philosophical work.

The sixth century's most important Latin grammarian was Priscianus (Priscian), who lived in Constantinople. His entire corpus of 18 books, *Grammatical Institution*, survives. Priscian's works make up the most extensive extant ancient authority on the grammar of the Latin language.

The last great figure among the ancient grammarians of the Latin language was St. ISIDORE, the Roman Catholic bishop of Seville (d. 636 C.E.). His *Etymologiae*, or *Origines*, is an encyclopedic work in 20 books. The last 10 of them are devoted mainly to etymological matters. Beyond several other treatises on grammatical topics, Isidore wrote about history and about religious subjects.

Bibliography

Asconius Pedianus, Quintus. *Commentaries on Five Speeches of Cicero.* Edited and translated by Simon Squires. Wauconda, Ill.: Bolchazy-Carducci, 1990.

Donatus, Aelius. *The Ars Minor of Donatus, for One Thousand Years the Leading Textbook of Grammar.* Edited and translated by Wayland Johnson Chase. Madison: University of Wisconsin Studies in the Social Sciences and History, 1926.

Gellius, Aulus. *The Attic Nights of Aulus Gellius.* 3 vols. New York: G. P. Putnam's Sons, 1927.

Isidore of Seville, St. *The Etymologies of Isidore of Seville.* Translated by Stephen A. Barney et al. Cambridge, and New York: Cambridge University Press, 2006.

Porter, David W., ed. *Excerptionis de Prisciano: The Source for Aelfric's Latin-Old English Grammar.* Rochester, N.Y.: D. S. Brewer, 2002.

Varro, Marcus Terrentius. *De lingua latina X; A New Critical Text and English Translation.* Translated by Daniel J. Taylor. Philadelphia: J. Benjamin, 1996.

Great Dionysia (Athenian Dionysia, Urban Dionysia)

The Athenians celebrated this most lavish and spectacular of their civic religious observances in honor of the god Dionysus in the spring, contemporaneous with the annual regreening of the earth around March. It is the festival of the pre-Christian Greek year that most closely corresponds with Christian Easter, with the Hindu Holi, or with the Iranian New Year.

During the festival, a statue of the god was carried in procession, and the high point of the observance for the crowds in attendance were three successive days of dramatic performances, each of which included three examples of TRAGEDY and a SATYR PLAY. Dramatists such as AESCHYLUS, SOPHOCLES, and EURIPIDES strove to have their plays selected for production in the competition and then, if possible, to win the competition with their four-play entries.

See also LENAEA, ATHENIAN FESTIVAL OF.

Greek prose romance

Although elements that came to characterize the novelistic Greek prose romance had appeared in the works of many early writers, those elements did not come together to produce a separate literary genre with shared characteristics until the second and third centuries C.E. The stories that belong to the romance genre sometimes contain licentious representations of love and sex. They also feature improbable accounts of shipwrecks and survival, narrow escapes from horrible dangers, the separation and unlikely reunion of lovers, unsympathetic parents, abductions, pirates, and an invariably happy ending.

Examples of the type include *Leucippe and Cleitophon* by Achilles Tatius of Alexandria, Egypt, who probably flourished in the second century C.E. A better writer who specialized in stories of repressed eroticism was the SOPHIST called Longus (fl. fourth or fifth century C.E.). Though his name is uncertain, the four-book PASTORALS OF DAPHNIS AND CHLOE recalls the love between the Sicilian shepherd, Daphnis, whom THEOCRITUS named as the inventor of PASTORAL POETRY, and Chloe, the shepherdess whom Daphnis adored. The only surviving exclusively pastoral prose romance, its story, which Longus sets on Lesbos, has inspired many artists over the centuries. Plays, operas, musical compositions, and ballets have resulted from that inspiration.

Generally speaking, not much is known about the writers who composed Greek prose romances. Those whose work has survived more or less intact include Chariton of Aphrodisias in what is now Anatolian Turkey, Eumathius (or, more properly, Eustathius) of Egypt, Bishop Heliodorus of Emesa, and XENOPHON OF EPHESUS.

Chariton (fl. late first or early second century C.E.) composed *The Story of Callirhoe,* but, except for his city and that the author is the clerk of a lawyer named Athenagoras, nothing further is known about him. The work of Heliodorus stands out among other representatives of the genre by being both better plotted than most romances and also unremittingly moral. A Syrian, Heliodorus flourished late in the fourth century C.E. and served as bishop at Tricca in Thessaly. The work for which he is best remembered is *An Ethiopian Romance*. Xenophon of Ephesus may have been the earliest among these writers, but no one knows. His romance was called *The Story of Anthia and Abrocomas*.

Even before many of the Greek stories, Romans also eagerly penned licentious examples of the romance genre. Perhaps the best known of the Roman stories is SATYRICON by PETRONIUS ARBITER.

The romance genre of the ancient world sparked renewed interest during the European Renaissance. Boccaccio's *Decameron* looks back to the literary type, as does the *Heptameron* of Marguerite of Navarre. The pastoral drama of Italy, too, takes its inspiration from the narratives of the ancient romancers. The Italian theater, in turn, influenced other European playwrights and composers, including Shakespeare and Handel, and such a 20th-century Broadway hit as *The Fantasticks* looks back through multiple theatrical lenses to this ancient genre for its source.

A useful overview of the entire Greek genre appears in Gareth L. Schmeling's modestly entitled *Chariton*.

Bibliography

Achilles Tatius. *Leucippe and Clitophon.* Translated by Tim Whitmarsh. Oxford and New York: Oxford University Press, 2001.

Chariton. *Callirhoe.* Edited and translated by G. P. Goold. Cambridge, Mass.: Harvard University Press, 1995.

Haddas, Moses, trans. *Three Greek Romances.* Indianapolis: Bobbs Merrill, 1964.

Heliodorus of Emesa. *An Ethiopian Romance.* Translated by Moses Haddas. Philadelphia: University of Pennsylvania Press, 1999.

Schmeling, Gareth L. *Chariton.* New York: Twayne Publishers, 1974.

Gregory of Nazianzen, St. (329–389 C.E.)
Greek prose writer

Born to a Christian family, Gregory was educated in Caesarea, Alexandria, and Athens. While traveling from Alexandria to Athens, Gregory narrowly escaped death in a shipwreck. This harrowing experience confirmed his already ardent faith, and he devoted his life to God and the church. Like many of his epoch, he felt drawn to a monastic vocation, but that was a calling he followed only intermittently.

The complexities of church politics and internecine Christian rivalries embroiled Gregory for much of his career. A staunch defender of Nicene orthodoxy, Gregory often found himself in the minority in the Eastern Roman Empire, and despite his best efforts to diffuse disagreements, he often found himself unwillingly at their center.

From a literary perspective, Gregory is principally remembered for the power of his orations, of which more than 40 survive. Chief among these are five *Theological Orations* that he delivered at Constantinople stating the Nicene position and contributing to the development of Trinitarian doctrine within the Roman Church.

Gregory was an unflagging correspondent, and more than 240 of his letters survive. Also extant is a collection of his theological and historical verse that is of greater biographical than poetic interest. Particularly, the Song of His Life (*Carmen de vita sua*) falls into this category. Divided into three sections it considers first the present, then the past, and then the future. The section on the past considers Gregory's forebears, his birth, his disposition, his training and education, and his behavior and accomplishments. In recounting the difficulties he faced in the church, Gregory's tone vacillates between sorrow and anger. In terms of its mode of composition and its focus, Gregory's biographical work provides an instructive contrast with the CONFESSIONS of St. AUGUSTINE.

In his final years, Gregory withdrew from the controversies that had often surrounded him and moved to his family estate at Arianzus. There he occupied his retirement with writing and with acting as the spiritual adviser of a nearby monastic community.

Bibliography

Daley, Brian, E. *Gregory of Nazianzus*. New York: Routledge, 2006.

Gregory of Nazianzus, Saint. *Autobiographical Poems*. Translated by Carolinne White. Cambridge: Cambridge University Press, 2005.

———. *Select Orations*. Translated by Martha Vinson. Washington, D.C.: Catholic University of America Press, 2003.

———. *On God and Christ: The Five Theological Orations and Two Letters to Cledonius*. Translated by Frederich Williams and Lionel Wickham. Crestwood, N.Y.: St. Vladimir's Seminary Press, 2002.

———. *On God and Man: The Theological Poetry of St. Gregory of Nazianzus*. Translated by Peter Gilbert. Crestwood, N.Y.: St. Vladimir's Seminary Press, 2001.

gushi (*ku-shih*)

Meaning simply "old [or old-style] poems," *gushi* verse had five-syllable lines. Sometimes they were not distinguishable from Chinese poems of the YUE FU BALLAD sort, but usually *gushi* were not written for singing. Sometimes a *gushi* might be embedded in a longer *yue fu*.

The most notable collection of *gushi* poems, the literary historian Robert Joe Cutter tells us, survive under the title *gushi shih-chiu shou* (19 old poems). Their author/s is/are anonymous, and they contain rather diffuse sentiments concerning the fleeting quality of life, the necessity for seizing the day, and absent lovers. They may have been extracted from longer *yuefu* (*yüeh-fu*) poems.

Bibliography

Mair, Victor H. *The Columbia History of Chinese Literature*. New York: Columbia University Press, 2001.

H

Han Feizi (*Han Fei Tzu*) Han Feizi (ca. 250 B.C.E.)

A political opponent forced the author, Han Feizi (Han Fei Tzu), to commit suicide some 15 years before the book that bears his name appeared. That work, *Han Feizi*, shares much in common with the contemporaneous INTRIGUES OF THE WARRING STATES. Both are witty, civilized, and cynical, and both provide models for subsequent students of the rhetorical arts. *Han Feizi*, in fact, devotes an essay to a consideration of the subject of the art of persuasion. Beyond that, it contains a stinging condemnation of traditional Confucian scholars and thinkers.

Moreover, the work is charming, using stories and memorable parables to clarify its arguments and delight its audience. In discussing the differences between Confucian and Mohist thinking, for example, *Han Feizi* recalls a seller of pearls who made beautiful boxes. People bought them, but they kept the boxes and returned the pearls. *Han Feizi* says that MOZI dispensed real pearls, but avoided pretentious rhetoric lest he obscure the substance of what he had to say. Presumably Han Feizi thought CONFUCIUS used high-flown rhetoric that contained little substance.

Some of *Han Feizi*'s rhetoric remains exactly apposite for those in every age and place who espouse outmoded points of view. I quote from Burton Watson's translation: "Those who preach and praise . . . high antiquity do so with much eloquence but little sincerity." *Han Feizi* goes on to say that the old ways can neither sustain the country nor be used to govern it. *Han Feizi* argues in favor of government according to a strictly enforced code of laws and against cults of personality or ancient theory and practice.

Bibliography

Puett, Michael. "Philosophy and Literature in Early China." In *The Columbia History of Chinese Literature*. Edited by Victor H. Mair. New York: Columbia University Press, 2001.

Watson, Burton. *Early Chinese Literature*. New York: Columbia University Press. New York, 1962.

———. *Han Fei Tzu: Basic Writings*. New York: Columbia University Press, 1964.

Hanji (*Han Chi, Annals of the Han*) Xun Yue (ca. 150 C.E.)

A historical digest of the events of the Han dynasty, *Han ji* drew its source material from the much more ambitious SHIHJI of SIMA QIAN and from Ban Gu's less expansive *Hanshu* (History of the Han dynasty.) *Hanji*, however, differed from its immediate models by taking the materials it borrowed and arranging them in strictly chronological order. In making this adjustment, Xun Yue (Hsün Yüeh) (148–209 C.E.) emulated early Confucian annals and eschewed the more expansive, narrative style of his sources.

Bibliography

Ch'Yun Ch'en. *Hsün Yüeh and the Mind of the Late Han China: A Translation of the* Shen-chien. Princeton, N.J.: Princeton University Press, 1980.

Mair, Victor H., ed. *The Columbia History of Chinese Literature.* New York: Columbia University Press, 2001.

Hanno   See GEOGRAPHY AND GEOGRAPHERS, GREEK AND ROMAN.

Hebrew Bible

A useful way to think of the Bible as a *literary* document involves considering the text from the point of view of the genres that characterize the writing it contains. In doing so, I follow with some additions and modifications the generic scheme proposed by William Owen Sypherd. While many books of the Bible contain representatives of several literary types, certain genres prevail in specific books.

The first books of the Hebrew Bible—Genesis, Exodus, Leviticus, Numbers, and Deuteronomy, which are grouped together as the Torah or Pentateuch—can be thought of as the earliest form of Hebrew Scripture. These books are the work of composite authorship and editing, and they were likely in process of creation from about 900 to 400 B.C.E. Received opinion identifies five anonymous authors or schools of authors who, working over half a millennium, brought the Pentateuch to its current form.

Among other genres, the Pentateuch contains foundation myths. Two separate stories of creation, for example, appear in the first chapter of Genesis. There the reader traces in the first through the ninth chapters the moment of creation, the mythical beginnings of history, explanations of the origin of death and of a fallen world, the beginnings of human language, and the sovereignty of the human race over earthly creation. The origin of the institution of marriage also appears there, as does the institution of observing the seventh day as one of rest.

In a second major thrust, the Book of Genesis recounts the lives of the founders of Israel—Abraham, Isaac, Jacob, and Esau—and the efforts of the Hebrews to establish themselves in a land to which they had migrated from somewhere in Mesopotamia. Genesis addresses a third major topic as it recounts the story of Joseph in Egypt and the way that his success there established his people for a while among the Egyptians before the Hebrews were reduced to slavery.

Exodus follows the history of the Hebrew people from the death of Joseph to Moses' construction of a tabernacle for worship. Chapters 1–11 trace the steps leading to the decision of the Pharaoh to set the Israelites at liberty. A final plague reinforces that decision, and the Israelites depart and journey to Sinai in chapters 12–19.

The story of how the Babylonian sun god, Shamash or Shamshu, gave a code of laws inscribed on stone to Hammurabi, king of Babylon (see CODE OF HAMMURABI—a story 600 years older than the Book of Deuteronomy—provides a direct analogue to and source for the Genesis account of Moses' receiving the Ten Commandments from God. Moreover, many of the legal statutes that Moses promulgates before his death in Deuteronomy come directly from Hammurabi's compendium.

History, biography, and, to a degree, genealogy (so-and-so begat so-and-so through numerous generations), prominent in the Pentateuch, continue to predominate in Joshua, Judges, 1 and 2 Samuel, 1 and 2 Kings, 1 and 2 Chronicles, Ezra, and Nehemiah. Biography and short story combine to produce Ruth and Esther, and with a generous infusion of myth, those two genres coalesce to produce Jonah's story, with his resistance to his sense of divine mission and his sojourn in the belly of a whale.

Such books as the Psalms and the Song of Songs—a love poem—inspire readers with the beauties of lyric verse as well as with their contents. Poetry of this sort, of course, is also scattered through other books, as we see in such examples as David's lament (2 Sam. 1:17 and 19–37), Deborah's song (Judges 5)—a very early war poem dating from about 1200 B.C.E.—and the duet of Moses and Miriam (Ex. 15:1–21).

From a literary perspective, the story of Job may well strike some as high drama. It contains a *psychomachia*—a struggle of the forces of good and evil for the soul of a human being. It could be considered a tragicomedy, since God allows Satan to inflict terrible sufferings on Job before Job's steadfastness defeats evil's best efforts to snare him. Depending on one's point of view, considering the deaths of Job's children, his story might also be viewed as straightforward tragedy, but that view would not be consonant with the clear intent of Job's author, which is to underscore Job's eventual triumph through steadfast allegiance to his God.

Since literary genre sometimes resides in the eye of the beholder rather than essentially in a text, one might also group Job and Proverbs together either as DIDACTIC POETRY or as FABLES.

Elements of documentable history as well as mythical history are observable in the Pentateuch. There was, for instance, a historic Joseph who rose to high administrative rank in Egypt; the site of his tomb has been identified. Nonetheless, over very long stretches of preliterate or early literate times, there is a tendency for mythical and factual history to become intertwined. While such genealogies as those in preliterate Polynesia have proved to be accurate for remarkably long periods of time—sometimes spanning several centuries—there is still a tendency for groups of originally separate stories, perhaps reporting actual happenings, to coalesce around heroic figures and take on mythical dimensions.

Such seems to be the case with Joshua and Judges, books that trace the history of Israel from

Moses' death to just before the establishment of a Hebrew monarchy. In Joshua, we read of the efforts of the Hebrews to conquer Palestine, to occupy the land on a basis equitable to the needs of each of the 12 tribes of Israel. Included in this material we find the fall of Jericho, perhaps the world's oldest city. This may well be largely actual history. We also find the sun and the moon standing still, however, and the defeat of a race of giants. History and myth both seem represented.

Judges contains a wealth of popular narrative too rich to treat in detail. Two premier stories, nonetheless, stand out from among the rest: the story of Samson and Delilah and that of Jephthah and his daughter. While in both stories the personages may well have been real, much that seems legendary has also coalesced around them. Delilah is an archetypal seductress. Samson's strength resides in his hair. He becomes weak when it is cut and regains his power as it grows back. While many a modern politician may try to emulate Sampson's feat of slaying armies with the jawbone of an ass, neither in Samson's day nor in ours has the expedient seemed destined for success. As in the story of Noah (Gen. 6:5–8:22), much of the mythical material in Samson finds analogues in *The* GILGAMESH EPIC of ancient Sumer—an epic dating from about 2300 B.C.E. in the earliest form we have it.

A similar situation presents itself in the story of Jephthah and his daughter. From the stock situations of myth, that story contains an account of a banished hero's rise to power. It also records the hero's vow to sacrifice a first-born child to appease an angry God. (Compare with EURIPIDES' *IPHIGENIA IN AULIS*.) Other elements of stories conforming to this pattern appear in the account of Jepthah: the preparation for the sacrifice, the complaint of Jephthah's daughter at her sacrificial death as a virgin, and the lamentation of the women of Israel about the death.

From a literary perspective, the Book of Ruth is among the crown jewels of biblical narrative. The story's unity adds force to its effect. The characterization of Ruth is convincing and conveys her devotion and loyalty to Naomi. Naomi's kindness and nobility of temperament and the depiction of the kindness of Boaz to both women—all these are elements that contribute to an inspirational story concerning the capacity of the human character for true dignity.

When a reader of the Hebrew Bible as literature arrives at the books of Samuel, Kings, Chronicles, Ezra, and Nehemiah, the reader has at last reached the more solid ground of mostly verifiable history. Yet the writers and the editors who recorded these histories must still be forgiven if they added a detail here and there to heighten the interest and consequence of the facts they reported.

Both Samuel and Kings were originally single books, but each was divided in the SEPTUAGINT OLD TESTAMENT version of the Bible. Samuel follows the prophet Samuel's role in the selection of the king of Israel. Its two books begin with Samuel's birth and follow the history of and legends about Saul and David through the end of David's public career. Seemingly historic episodes appear in the accounts of David and Goliath, David and Jonathan, and David's military successes. Saul's encounters with an evil spirit and the Witch of Endor may be less factual.

The books of Kings continue Hebrew history, first recounting David's naming Solomon as his successor, then detailing Solomon's reign and career. Short stories that seem grounded in fact include those concerning Solomon's wise judgments, the construction of the Temple at Jerusalem, the Queen of Sheba's state visit, and Solomon's apostasy as he reveres gods other than the Hebrew Yaweh. Kings also recounts the division of Israel into the southern kingdom of Judah, ruled by David's heirs, and the northern kingdom of Israel. The occurrences recounted in Kings bring Hebrew history down to the year 562 B.C.E.

The next four books of the Hebrew Bible, 1 and 2 Chronicles, Ezra, and Nehemiah, retrace world and Hebrew history from Adam through the prophet Nehemiah's second visit to Jerusalem, an event that occurred in 432 B.C.E. While a good deal of duplication appears, the authors and editors of these four books have also interpolated

materials from sources different from those of the earlier books. They have also shifted the geographic and political focus to Judah in the southern part of Palestine.

The Book of Esther has long perplexed and sometimes even offended biblical scholars. Such early Christians as Melito, a second-century C.E. bishop of Sardis, excluded it from the Hebrew Bible canon. St. ATHANASIUS and other fathers of the Eastern Church excluded Esther as late as the fourth century. At the end of that century, however, at the Council of Carthage in 397, Esther was finally admitted among the canonical Scriptures of the Western church. Martin Luther wished the council had not done so, for he found in Esther's pages "many heathenish improprieties." Among them, presumably, were the divorce between the Persian king Ahasuerus, who drank too much, and his wife Vashti for her disobedience to the king's orders. Luther may also have found the elevation of the Hebrew Esther into the idol-worshipping Persian royal family objectionable.

As a short story, however, with its intrigues of state; its planned destruction of the Jews in the Persian kingdom; Esther's intercession in their favor; the execution of the king's minister, Haman, who had proposed the Jew's destruction; and the joy of the Hebrew people at their reprieve, the story is gripping. It also explains the origins of the Hebrew feast of Purim.

The drama of Job follows Esther, and then come the Psalms—the loveliest extended collection of devotional poetry in the Hebrew Bible. That collection carries over into Proverbs. There, however, the emphasis shifts from devotion to instruction. Belonging to the literary genre of DIDACTIC POETRY or GNOMIC POETRY AND PROSE, Proverbs instructs people in the right conduct of their daily lives.

Ecclesiastes presents the reader with an unorthodox and speculative essay on the meaning of life. The first verse of the book ascribes the authorship to Solomon, the wise king of Israel, but that assignment is altogether unlikely. The book begins in a reflective mood. All of human life is vanity. Therefore, finding as much pleasure as possible in life is the only sensible course to follow. The central message of the third through the sixth chapters advises the reader that God has established a fixed schedule for the sequence of events in people's lives: "For everything there is a season." God has moreover, preordained what is going to happen, so that dwelling on apparent injustice in the world is an exercise in futility. The tone in the sixth chapter becomes cynical and foreboding.

A selection of wise proverbs opens chapter 7. The preacher advises readers that wisdom dictates moderation in all things. In contrast to the determinism of the sixth chapter, the eighth and ninth chapters seem to suggest that everything comes to pass as a result of chance happenings and that trying to exercise wisdom is fruitless in such a world. A series of proverbs follows in chapters 9 and 10.

Chapter 11 and the first several verses of 12 admonish the reader that one must work whatever the outcomes may be. The youthful reader should also seize the day and make the most of whatever opportunities present themselves. Chapter 12 ends with a statement approving what the preacher has said. It also contains a warning that "the use of books is endless, and much study is wearisome." Ecclesiastes' final advice is to fear God and to keep God's commandments; there will, the book warns, be an accounting.

The lovely Song of Songs—a verse duet between a bride and a bridegroom that is occasionally punctuated by a chorus of their companions—was frequently read in Jewish circles as a dialogue between Jehovah as bridegroom and Israel as bride. Christian interpreters have similarly seen the book as an allegorical dialogue between Christ as bridegroom and his church as bride. Humanist readers satisfy themselves with a more literal interpretation.

The genre of prophecy is generously represented in the Hebrew Bible. Readers find it in Amos, Daniel, Ezekiel, Habakkuk, Haggai, Hosea, Isaiah (which seems to conflate as many as three prophets of different periods), Jeremiah, Joel, Malachi, Micah, Nahum, Obadiah, and Zechariah (which may conflate two prophets). Probably

the most confusing books of the Hebrew Bible, many of the prophetic books are firmly grounded in local history, and their writers assume that readers will share a writer's familiarity with that history. Suffice it to say that Amos, Hosea, and Isaiah seem to have lived in the eighth century B.C.E. The original texts of Amos, who was a shepherd of Tekoa, are extant and date to about 750 B.C.E. He prophesies the fall of Israel and Judah and the restoration of Israel. Hosea concurs in the general dreariness of Amos's message, attributing Israel's troubles to its infidelity to Jehovah. Nonetheless, Amos sees Jehovah as a god of forgiveness, and he foresees Israel's eventual restoration.

Isaiah enjoys a reputation as the greatest of the prophets. At the same time, it is clear that all the works assembled under his name do not belong to him and that their composition spans a period of about 500 years. It is possible, however, to separate out much that is confidently attributable to Isaiah. He was an intellectual living in the city of Jerusalem under the reigns of the Hebrew kings Jotham, Ahaz, and Hezekiah. He envisioned Jehovah as characterized principally by holiness, and he wrote that the role of Israel was to fulfill God's holy purposes in the world. Isaiah's writing is by far the most polished among the prophets.

The prophets of the seventh century B.C.E. include Zephaniah, Nahum, Habakkuk, and Jeremiah. Their writings concern events beginning in 626 B.C.E. and ending with the destruction of Jerusalem. Zephaniah contains a collection of brief oracles predicting the coming destruction of Judah and Jerusalem. The prophet then encourages the Ammonites, Assyrians, Ethiopians, Moabites, and Philistines to repent of their evil ways and avoid the coming destruction. On the other hand, Zephaniah encourages the faithful in Jerusalem to rejoice.

Nahum concerns itself exclusively and vividly with the impending fall of the Babylonian city of Nineveh. Habbakuk splits into two parts. First comes a series of oracles cast in the form of a dialogue between Habbakuk and Jehovah. These oracles forecast the eventual justification of

Judah and the chastisement of its enemy. The second part asserts the teaching that the righteous will keep the faith. That part ends with a lyric of rejoicing.

The most notable and at the same time the most complex of the prophets of the seventh century B.C.E. is Jeremiah. Scholars believe that his secretary, Baruch, probably wrote the work that bears his name, which first details Jeremiah's call to become a prophet, then records his early prophetic utterances. Such material continues with the addition of his assertion that a drought is a mark of Jehovah's anger. He continues by making predictions concerning foreign nations and with the restoration of Israel. Jeremiah's personal history interrupts that discussion, which is thereafter resumed. Following a series of prophecies concerning foreign nations, a faithfully historical account describes the capture of Jerusalem and the enslavement of its population by the Babylonians.

The prophetic books of the sixth century B.C.E. include Ezekiel, portions of Isaiah discussed above, Haggai, Micah, and a part of Zechariah.

Ezekiel opens by revisiting the issue of the sin of Judah and the coming fall of Jerusalem. Several chapters follow that inveigh against foreign nations, and several more predict the restoration of the Jews after the Babylonian captivity. A final section deals with the establishment and organization of the state after that restoration. Ezekiel employs a broad spectrum of techniques in presenting this material: allegory, colorful images, impassioned speech, parable, and reports of visions.

Daniel is a bifurcated book. From a literary perspective, part of it contains a series of short narratives. Daniel visits Kings Nebuchadnezzar and Belshazzar of Babylon and Darius of Persia. Then we encounter Daniel with other Israelite wise men: Shadrach, Meschach, and Abednego. Daniel interprets dreams, and he and his companions refuse to worship a golden idol. Here too we find the story of the magic prophecy written on Belshazzar's wall, that of Daniel in the lion's den, and we hear King Darius praise Daniel's

God. The other part of Daniel contains a series of apocalyptic visions.

Haggai appeals to the people of Israel, released from the Babylonian captivity, to rebuild the temple at Jerusalem. A portion of his prophecy describes the wonderful features of the new building, and a part admonishes the people against the taint they will suffer until they undertake the work.

Micah first denounces the sins of Judah and Samaria. Then, following a series of prophecies, the book envisions a coming era of universal peace and the eventual victory and universal rule of Zion. Probably the most compelling and thought-provoking feature of Micah is its definition of what the God of Israel requires of his worshippers: "Only to act justly, to love loyalty, to walk wisely before your God."

The first part of the Book of Zechariah contains the prophet's own report of his visions. One of these imagines the Lord God Jehovah in a copse of myrtle trees, getting news from around the world. In another vision, the prophet observes four metal horns being destroyed by four blacksmiths. In still another, a surveyor traces out the footprint of a city. Zechariah also envisions the high priest of Israel as the defendant in an action brought against him by Satan as chief prosecutor before the high court of Jehovah, who acquits the high priest. Other less straightforward visions also appear: The reader finds one vision of a golden lamp stand or another of winged women flying off with a large container holding inside it the son of Judah, metamorphosed into a woman. The second part of Zechariah was composed some time later by a different hand and contains prophecies about protecting the temple and reconciling Israel with God.

Malachi condemns insincere worship and divorce, encourages payment of tithes and offerings, and predicts that the faithful will prosper. Joel, too, calls the people to repentance, envisions the final judgment in the Valley of Jehosaphat, and predicts the permanent establishment of Judah and Jerusalem.

Perhaps belonging to the fifth century B.C.E., Obadiah predicts Israel's destruction of Edom when Jehovah makes his final judgment. The book principally contains a group of oracles and thus belongs to the prophetic genre.

See also NEW TESTAMENT; RAS SHAMRA TEXTS.

Bibliography

Amit, Yairah. *Reading Biblical Narratives: Literary Criticism and the Hebrew Bible.* Minneapolis: Fortress Press, 2001.

Anderson, Bernhard W. *Understanding the Old Testament.* Englewood Cliffs, N.J.: Prentice Hall, 1975.

Bloom, Harold, ed. *The Bible.* New York: Chelsea House, 2006.

The New English Bible: The Old Testament. Oxford and Cambridge: Oxford University Press and Cambridge University Press, 1970.

Norton, David. *A History of the Bible as Literature.* New York: Cambridge University Press, 2005.

Sypherd, Wilbur Owen. *The Literature of the English Bible.* New York: Oxford University Press, 1938.

Hecale Callimachus (third century B.C.E.)

CALLIMACHUS, who preferred penning the shorter genres of poetry, may have undertaken the composition of *Hecale* to prove to his critics that he could write an EPIC poem. In its original form, *Hecale* was probably around 1,000 lines long. Its fragmentary remains comprise 326 lines.

We know that Callimachus drew his plot for the poem from a chronicle of the history of the Greek region of Attica that had also served PLUTARCH as a source for his *Life of Theseus.* As usual, however, Callimachus adapted his material to his own ends. A surviving summary of the plot as Callimachus handled it appears in an ancient *diegesis*, or digest of the story.

Fulfilling his destiny to become the king of Athens, Theseus travels to that city from Troezen. On his arrival, Medea, who had sought refuge with Theseus's father Aegeus, attempts to poison Theseus. His father, who at first did not know him, recognizes his son belatedly but in time to save him from Medea's plot. Thereafter, Theseus learns that a wild and ferocious bull is terrorizing the inhabitants of the region around Marathon. Theseus wishes to resolve the problem.

Aegeus, however, has become overzealous about his son's safety, so Theseus has to sneak away. He seeks refuge from a sudden downpour in the hut of an old woman named Hecale. She courteously entertains him, and at dawn he continues on his way to Marathon, locates the bull, and overcomes it. That done, he returns to Hecale's, only to find that she had died while he was gone. Grief-stricken, Theseus honors his hostess's memory by establishing a suburb on the surrounding land and founding there a sanctuary named Zeus Hecaleios in honor both of his patron deity and his hostess.

Apparently Callimachus de-emphasized Theseus's heroism and emphasized the interactions between Theseus and Hecale while he was her guest. This was in keeping with the conventions of Alexandrian poets, who liked to humanize the great mythical heroes of the past by setting them in ordinary circumstances and handling their folksy interactions with humor and realism. Later poets, including OVID and VIRGIL, imitated the way Callimachus handled the story.

Bibliography

Trypanis, C. A. *Callimachus: Aetia, Iambi, Lyric Poems, Hecale, Minor Epic and Elegiac Poems, and Other Fragments.* Loeb Classical Library. Vol. 421. Cambridge, Mass.: Harvard University Press, 1975.

Hecatæus of Miletus See GEOGRAPHY AND GEOGRAPHERS, GREEK AND ROMAN.

Hecuba Euripides (ca. 425 B.C.E.)

Famed for his portrayals of remarkable women in such plays as *MEDEA, ELECTRA,* and *IPHIGENIA IN AULIS,* EURIPIDES twice portrayed Hecuba, the deposed queen of a defeated Troy. She provided the playwright with his protagonist both in *The TROJAN WOMEN* and in *Hecuba.*

Hecuba has a double plot. It focuses first on the anger, grief, and frustration Hecuba feels when the victorious Greeks decide to sacrifice her daughter Polyxena at the tomb of their fallen hero Achilles. The second plot concerns the revenge that Hecuba takes for the treacherous murder of her son Polydorus. Hecuba's husband, Priam the king of Troy, had sent Polydorus, the couple's youngest son into the protection of the Thracian king, Polynester. With the lad Priam also sent an enormous treasure. When the Greeks defeated Troy, Polynester had Polydorus killed to gain control of that treasure.

As the play opens, however, Hecuba is as yet unaware of the fact of her son's death. Rather, Polydorus's ghost, hovering above the stage, opens the play with a prologue that acquaints the audience with the background to the play and with the fact that Polynester had not buried his body as Greek custom required. Instead, the murderer had the corpse thrown in the sea, where it is about to wash up on the shores of Troy.

While the Greeks consider sacrificing Polyxena, Hecuba enters, chanting prayers for the preservation of her daughter's life. As she does so, a CHORUS of Trojan women enters singing. Their song acquaints Hecuba with the Greeks' decision to sacrifice Polyxena at Achilles' tomb as a mark of the soldiers' gratitude for his heroism. Despairing, Hecuba tells Polyxena the army's decision, and the girl quakes with fright.

The Greek general Odysseus enters bearing the sentence. Hecuba reminds him that he owes her his life. During the Trojan War, when he had visited Helen in disguise, Helen told Hecuba, and she kept his presence to herself. Odysseus agrees that he owes Hecuba her own life, but not Polyxena's. He advises the old queen to make the best of a bad situation.

Polyxena, however, joins the ranks of Euripides' extraordinary women by explaining that she would rather die than live as a slave—the fate of the other surviving Trojan women. Hecuba proposes that she die in her daughter's place. When Odysseus refuses, she asks to die with her child. That option is also denied her, and she exclaims

miserably: "Not one of my 50 children left." Polyxena is led away to the slaughter. (One other child, Cassandra, still lives in fact, but she has become the personal slave and unwilling concubine of Agamemnon.)

The chorus of captive Trojan women joins the general grieving by bewailing their own fates and wondering where, in their slavery to the victorious Greeks, their destinies will lead them. As the choral keening ends, the Greek messenger Talthybius enters and asks for Hecuba. The leader of the chorus points to her. She is lying on the ground weeping, and Talthybius is shocked at her condition. He tells the queen that she must come with him to bury Polyxena's corpse. Hecuba asks him to describe the manner of her daughter's death.

Talthybius's answering speech achieves one of the great moments in the monologues of Grecian theater. He describes the way that Polyxena, led to Achilles' tomb and immobilized by the hands of her captors, demanded to be set free so she could voluntarily expose her throat and breast to the sacrificial blade. Her bravery as she suffered the fatal stroke so impressed the Greek troops that, even as Talthybius speaks, they are building a funeral pyre in Polyxena's honor.

Grieving, Hecuba reflects on her former glory and her present misery, concluding that the happiest person is the one who encounters no sorrow as he goes about his daily tasks. She then retires into a tent. Marking the passage from the first to the second part of the play, the chorus chants of the evils that have befallen Troy because of the Trojan prince Paris's illicit passion for Helen, the wife of King Menelaus of Sparta and afterward Helen of Troy.

Now a group enters bearing the body of Polydorus. Hecuba learns by sorcery that the Thracian king, Polynester, has murdered him. Although she is now only a slave of the victorious Greeks, she pleads with Agamemnon to become her ally as she seeks vengeance against Polynester, who has offended the gods by ignoring the laws of hospitality and killing her son from a motive of greed.

Sympathetic, Agamemnon explains that any assistance he provides must be secret. The Greek army perceives Polynester as an ally and would, Agamemnon fears, slaughter their own general should they learn that Agamemnon assisted Hecuba against Polynester. In the meantime, the burial of Polyxena's body is delayed so that she and her brother may be cremated and their ashes buried together.

Agamemnon summons Polynester to Troy. He comes, bringing his children with him. Claiming that she has more gold for Polydorus that she wishes to entrust to Polynester's keeping, Hecuba entices her enemy and his children into a tent full of Trojan women. Pretending to admire the children, the women separate them from their father and kill them. After Polynester has seen his offspring dead, the women turn on him with the pins of their brooches, and they blind him.

Polynester demands redress from Agamemnon and pleads his cause. Hecuba, however, convinces Agamemnon that Polynester is as false a friend to the Greeks as he was to the royal house of the Trojans. She points out that he did not bring them the gold that was their due as the victors' spoils. Convinced by Hecuba's arguments, Agamemnon condemns Polynester to death.

Hopeless, Polynester becomes inspired by the prophecies of the Thracian god Dionysus. Polynester tells Hecuba that she will die on the voyage to Greece, throwing herself into the sea from the masthead after having first been transformed into a dog with bloodshot eyes. He also predicts the death of Hecuba's only still-living child, Cassandra, along with Agamemnon at the hands of Agamemnon's wife Clytemnestra.

Agamemnon sentences the blind Polynester to a slow death by stranding him on a desert island where exposure to the elements, hunger, and thirst will extend his suffering. The play ends with the chorus of Trojan women once more anticipating their future lives as slaves.

Bibliography

Euripides. *After the Trojan War: Women of Troy; Hecuba; Helen: Three Plays by Euripides.* Translated by Kenneth McLeish. Bath, U.K.: Absolute Classics, 1995.

Hedupatheia (*Hedupathia*) Archestratus (ca. mid–fourth century B.C.E.)

Though clearly not the Western world's original writer on the subjects of cuisine and nourishment, Archestratus (fl. fourth century B.C.E.) did pen a work on that subject. A significant portion of it survives (about 330 of perhaps 1,200 dactylic hexameter lines), largely owing to the interest of CALLIMACHUS when that more famous poet was a librarian and copyist at the library of Alexandria. The works of his predecessors are almost totally lost except for a line here and there and an occasional reference.

A native of Greek Sicily, Archestratus was likely born at Gela—hence the other name by which he is known, Archestratos of Gela—but perhaps moved to Syracuse when the Carthaginians occupied his birthplace. He traveled widely through the Greek Mediterranean world during the HELLENISTIC AGE, collecting information about food and its preparation and consumption, and about dining customs. He published the results of those investigations in his lengthy poem *Hedupatheia* (Well-being). The work is also known as "Life of Pleasure," "Gastrology," "Art of Cookery," "Inquiry into the Belly," and other more and less satirical titles supplied by later readers.

It seems, however, that although Archestratus sometimes treated his subject lightheartedly, he found it genuinely interesting and thought others would also find it so. Casting his poem as an epistle to his friend Moschus, Archestratus gives instructions for pleasant dining. He recommends a company limited to four or five persons. He discusses grains and their sources and manner of preparation into various breads and cakes and suggests that Lydians and Phonicians are the best bread makers.

Archestratus lavishes a good deal of attention on seafoods and where to obtain the best examples. He recommends Ainos for mussels, Abydos for oysters, and Mitylene on Lesbos for scallops. He discusses the advantages of eels. Fish in general seem among his favorite foods. He especially recommends a sort of mixed seafood dish fried up with "fragrant green herbs and olive oil." The underbelly portions of the thresher shark sprinkled with cumin, roasted with a pinch of salt and greyish olive oil, then served with a dipping sauce earns the author's approbation. He also approves lobsters acquired in the Lipari islands or near the Hellespont.

Most of the surviving portions of the poem have to do with seafood, including among many other species red mullet and cuttlefish. When he does turn his attention to meat and fowl, Archestratus mentions such delicacies as a sausage or a "stewed sow's womb" done in cumin, vinegar, and silphium, together with whatever birds happen to be in season. Elsewhere, he approves "a grain-fed gosling."

Bibliography

Archestratos of Gela. *Greek Culture and Cuisine in the Fourth Century* BCE. Edited by S. Douglas Olson and Alexander Sens. Oxford and New York: Oxford University Press, 2000.

Heida no Are   See *Kojiki*.

Helen   Euripides (412 B.C.E.)

In this tragedy with a happy ending, EURIPIDES borrows a version of the story of Helen of Troy that HERODOTUS recounts in his HISTORIES (2.112–20), where Herodotus rescues Helen's reputation.

By way of background, in the world's archetypal beauty contest, the Trojan Prince Paris (also known as Alexandros) had chosen Aphrodite, goddess of love, as the most beautiful among the female immortals. He had selected Aphrodite over Hera, goddess of power, and over Athena, goddess of wisdom. His decision was to a degree influenced by the bribe the goddess had offered—the love of the world's most beautiful woman. (The other goddesses had respectively offered power and wisdom, but Paris was young and tired of his girlfriend, the nymph Oenone.) The difficulty with this arrangement, however, arose from the fact that Helen, the world's most beautiful woman, was, predictably, already married. She was the queen of Sparta, wife of its king, Menelaus.

In the version of the story told by HOMER, Aphrodite fulfilled her promise, and Helen fell in love with Paris, willingly accompanying him to Troy. In Herodotus's version, however, the voyage from Sparta to Troy, though still made willingly, was interrupted with a stop in Egypt. There King Proteus discovered that Paris had robbed Menelaus of his wife and his fortune, and Proteus confiscated both. For dramatic effect, Euripides further embroiders the tale by inventing a phantom Helen, furnished by Hera—a sore loser in the contest. Zeus snatches his blameless daughter, the real Helen, into the sky from Sparta, hides her in the clouds, and eventually sets her down at Proteus's palace in Egypt. The phantom, meanwhile, accompanies Paris to Troy. It is the phantom for whom the Greeks fight the war and the phantom whom Menelaus eventually recovers. For the 10 years of the war, the real Helen remains in Egypt, fending off the advances of the Egyptian successor of Proteus, his son Theoclymenus.

Euripides' play opens with a long monologue in which Helen recounts Euripides' version of events. She laments the bad reputation she suffers in the world and explains that the god Hermes has predicted that, so long as she remains chaste, she will one day be restored to Sparta. Now, however, Theoclymenus is pressing her to marry him, and Helen, to preserve her virtue, has thrown herself as a suppliant upon the tomb of her deceased protector, Proteus.

The Greek warrior Teucer, brother of Ajax, enters and thinks he sees the Helen he had been acquainted with in Troy. The real Helen learns from Teucer about the outcome of the Trojan War and about the suicide of her mother, Leda, shamed to death by Helen's behavior at Troy. Helen also learns of the deification of her brothers, Castor and Pollux, as the so-called Dioscuri; they have been stellified as the constellation Gemini. That is one version of their story. The other is that they, too, committed suicide for the same reason as their mother. Helen warns Teucer that Theoclymenus is killing all Greek males rather than run the risk of Helen's rescue. Additionally, Teucer reports the storm that separated the ships of the Greek fleet on their return from Troy and says that her husband, Menelaus, is missing and presumed dead. He exits and she grieves.

A CHORUS of Greek women, slaves to the Egyptians, enters, and they and Helen commiserate about the lengthening roll of misfortunes. Helen is principally concerned about her undeservedly scandalous reputation. She decides that since Menelaus is lost, she will die, but the chorus reminds her that reports are often untrue. They advise her to consult Theoclymenus's sister, the prophetess Theonoe. Helen agrees, and all exit.

Menelaus, clad in sailcloth, now enters. He complains that he has been at sea ever since he left Troy and that every time he nears Sparta, the winds drive him back out to open water. Now he is among the several survivors of a shipwreck on the Egyptian shore. He comes to the palace and learns that its owner kills Greeks and that Helen is within and has been there since before the war. Menelaus is surprised, as he had left the phantom Helen in a cave on the seashore.

In the meantime, Helen has learned from Theonoe that Menelaus lives and will eventually reach home. Helen sees Menelaus but does not immediately recognize him. Soon, however, they discover each other's identity, but, knowing of the Helen in the cave, Menelaus is confused and finally seems ready to reject his real wife. Just then, a servant comes to Menelaus to report that the phantom Helen has flown up into the sky. As she rose, she confessed that the real Helen is blameless. The reunited husband and wife embrace. Then follows discussion with other characters that essentially repeats the details of the story as Euripides wished the members his audience to remember it so it would displace Homer's version in their minds.

Menelaus then briefly recounts for Helen his adventures upon reaching Egypt, beginning his recitation with the formula "Why should I recount," and then recounting. After this, the reunited couple confronts the problem that occupies the balance of Euripides' play: Theoclymenus is not about to let Helen go. The couple might be able to trick the king if only his sister, Theonoe, were not effectively omniscient. Helen decides to try to enlist Theonoe as an ally. Convinced that it is their only recourse, Helen and Menelaus swear to risk it and to commit suicide together if they fail.

Theonoe enters, and the two suppliants state their case, begging that she will not assist her brother in an unjust and unholy course. Their arguments prevail, and Theonoe resolves to keep their secret and not to assist her brother in his misguided course of action. That problem out of the way, the couple now has to devise an escape plan. Menelaus's ship has been destroyed. Though Menelaus has purpose, strength, and resolve, Helen thinks better than he does. She devises the plan.

Menelaus will become a messenger reporting the death of Menelaus. Helen will tell Theoclymenus that she will marry him as soon as she has performed the funeral rites for her husband. To do that, she will need a ship and treasures to offer as propitiation to her husband's spirit. The chorus restates the central problems of the play in a song that reveals their antiwar sentiment.

Theoclymenus now enters to pay his respects at his father's tomb and to see if Helen is still seeking sanctuary there. Finding her gone, he first imagines that she has fled. He has also heard of a Greek skulking about. The king resolves to kill him if he can catch him. Just then, Helen enters clad in black, weeping and having cut off her hair. Pointing to Menelaus as the messenger, she tells Theoclymenus the story they have concocted and, when he is dubious, directs him to ask his sister. Finally, Helen agrees to marry Theoclymenus. First, though, she must follow the Grecian funeral customs for those dead at sea.

Menelaus, pretending to be the messenger, explains the customs, at the same time provisioning himself at Theoclymenus's expense for a sea voyage and a potential battle. A series of treasures, bedding, armor, live animals for sacrifice, and foodstuffs must be rowed out to the horizon and dumped overboard for the use of the deceased in the underworld. Only the next of kin can perform these rites, so Helen must go along.

As the principal characters prepare for the mock funeral, the chorus performs a beautiful song in honor of Cybele (Rhea) the goddess of the harvest and the earth's fecundity, recounting her grief at the loss of her daughter, Persephone.

Helen, Menelaus, and Theoclymenus return to the stage. Menelaus is in full armor and ready for battle. Theoclymenus gives the ostensible mourners a ship and instructs his sailors to obey Menelaus's orders. He makes one attempt to keep Helen ashore, but relents when she promises not to throw herself overboard in her grief for her first husband. The funeral party departs, and Theoclymenus begins wedding preparations.

After another lovely choral interlude, however, a messenger enters to tell Theoclymenus that Helen has left the country. As Theoclymenus's men were readying their ship for the voyage, Menelaus's surviving crew appeared, and Menelaus took them aboard as passengers. Though suspicious, the Egyptian crew felt bound by Theoclymenus's orders.

Once at sea, the messenger reports, Menelaus sacrificed a bull, praying not for the dead but for a safe passage to Sparta. His men and the Egyptian crew then fought a pitched battle on the ship's deck, and the Egyptians who were not killed leaped overboard and swam for shore. The ship sailed off with a fair wind for Greece.

Stymied in his desire for Helen, Theoclymenus declares his intention to obtain vengeance by killing his sister. As he goes to do so, he is stopped by a servant, who explains that the king's position only gives him the right to command in matters of piety, not matters of wrong. Theoclymenus is on the point of killing the servant when Helen's deified twin brothers, Castor and Pollux, appear as gods from a machine. They explain that what has happened was fated to happen and that Theoclymenus should just let it go. Realizing that further resistance to the operation of fate is pointless, Theoclymenus graciously accedes to the demands of the Dioscuri. The chorus closes the play with a lesson that Euripides frequently sought to teach: Expect the unexpected from the gods.

Bibliography

Euripides. *After the Trojan War: Women of Troy; Hecuba; Helen: Three Plays by Euripides.* Translated by Kenneth Mc Leish. Bath, U.K.: Absolute Classics, 1995.

Kovacs, David, ed. and trans. *Euripides, Vol. 5: Helen, Phoenician Women; Orestes.* Cambridge, Mass.: Harvard University Press, 2002.

Heliodorus of Emesa   See FICTION AS EPISTLE, ROMANCE, AND EROTIC PROSE; GREEK PROSE ROMANCE.

Hellenika   Xenophon of Athens (ca. 380–350 B.C.E.)

Following the lead of THUCYDIDES, XENOPHON OF ATHENS picks up the history of the Peloponnesian Wars where his predecessor historian left off—411 B.C.E.

In seven books, Xenophon chronicles the government of Athens by a council of 30 aristocrats, their overthrow as a result of Spartan intervention, and the resultant restoration of Athenian democracy in 403 B.C.E. He then recounts the history of Sparta's war against Persia and the Persians' victory in 387 B.C.E. Xenophon next flashes back to recount the war that a league of Greek states, led by Corinth, fought against Sparta in an effort to rein in Sparta's growing power on the Grecian peninsula. That segment of Xenophon's story ends with the treaty of peace that the Spartan envoy Antacidas negotiated with the Persian king Artaxerxes II—a treaty the Persians imposed on the warring Greeks, also in 387 B.C.E.

Xenophon then turns his attention to the growing influence of the city of Thebes and the developing rivalry between Thebes and Sparta. This enmity soon developed into open warfare. Thebes emerged as the victors at the Battle of Leuctra, where they mortally wounded the Spartan King Cleombrotus.

Xenophon's political preferences color his historiography. He was strongly pro-Spartan, and in his report of this battle, he neglects to mention the name of the victorious Theban general, Epanimondas. Epanimondas does, however, subsequently appear in the narrative as Xenophon traces Thebes' domination of Grecian affairs until the Thebans' defeat and Epanimondas's death at the second battle of Mantinea in 362 B.C.E.

Bibliography

Brownson, Carleton L., ed. and trans. *Xenophon: Hellenica; Anabasis.* 2 vols. Vol. 1: London: William Heinemann Ltd., 1950; Vol. 2: New York: G.P. Putnam and Sons, 1930.

Xenophon of Athens. *The Hellenica (Greek History of Xenophon: a Facing-page Critical Edition and Translation.)* Translated and edited by Donald E. Jackson and Ralph E. Doty. Lewiston, N.Y.: Edwin Mellen Press, 2006.

Hellenistic Age (Alexandrine Age)
(ca. 300 B.C.E–600 C.E.)

In 331 B.C.E., Alexander the Great founded a city near the western mouth of the Nile River in Egypt. Named for its founder, Alexandria soon rose to become one of the principal cultural and intellectual metropolises of the greater Grecian world. Before Rome outgrew it, in fact, Alexandria was for a time the largest city on the planet.

On the death of Alexander, his general in charge of Egypt, Soter the son of Lagos, became Pharaoh Ptolemy I of Egypt—a country over which he and his descendents exercised virtually absolute control for 500 years. Under his rule and that of his son and grandson, Ptolemy II, called Philadelphus, and Ptolemy III, Alexandria flourished intellectually, materially, and militarily.

Ptolemy I interested himself in matters of history as well as in the exercise of statecraft, and he himself penned a history of the campaigns of Alexander the Great. He also founded and Ptolemy II expanded what was probably the major intellectual center of the ancient world, the great library at Alexandria. There the accumulated learning of the preceding ages was deposited and catalogued by a succession of capable and devoted librarians that included Zenodotus (fl. ca. 285 B.C.E.), ERATOSTHENES (ca. 285–194 B.C.E.); and Aristarchus of Samothrace, who headed the library between ca. 180 and ca. 145 B.C.E., and who was an important editor, literary critic, and grammarian. The poet CALLIMACHUS also seems to have been employed in the library in some capacity, but probably not, as some have suggested, as chief librarian. Also sometimes mentioned as chief librarian is Callimachus's literary opponent, the epicist APOLLONIUS OF RHODES. A good deal of later Greek literature came from Egypt during the Hellenistic period.

The Greeks continued to rule Egypt until 30 B.C.E., when the last Ptolemy to rule, Cleopatra VII, took her own life after bearing Julius Caesar a child and subsequently becoming the mistress of the soon-to-be defeated Mark Antony. Both the name and the lineage of Cleopatra are exclusively Greek. Although she was the last of the pharaohs and had been born and bred in Egypt, no drop of pre-Ptolemaic Egyptian royal blood ran in her veins. Her traceable genetic heritage was thus European and Near Eastern rather than African.

Greek culture flourished elsewhere during the Hellenistic Age as well. Alexander's successes had unified Greece and Macedonia, and the previously independent city-states of Greece slowly lost their independence, becoming part of a broader national and international culture under the Grecian dynasty of the Attalids, who, as Roman allies, expanded their power from their base in Asia Minor to include lands to the east and Macedonia on the Grecian peninsula itself.

After Alexander's death, the jewel in his crown, Asia (today's Middle East), came under the dominion of another of Alexander's officers, Seleucus, who became the governor of conquered Babylonia on the death of Alexander. By means of adroit alliances and successful warfare, Seleucus I began the hellenization of much of the Asian continent. His heirs fought successfully with the Ptolemies over the control of Phoenicia and Palestine until Antiochus III brought them firmly under his control in 200 B.C.E. Ten years later, the Romans displaced him there. Throughout Asia, however, the Grecian Seleucids were successful in spreading Greek culture for decades, largely by means of founding dozens of cities.

The cultural and, particularly, literary influence of this period of hellenization of most of the ancient Mediterranean and Asian world outlasted the defeat of the Seleucids by the legions of Rome. The Roman conquest of the ancient world is one among many instances of a cultural inferior's overwhelming a cultural superior by force of arms. Greek literary culture, happily, survived the shock of Roman arms and finally became the definitive literary foundation of the Roman intellectual edifice.

Under the conditions that prevailed after Alexander's conquest had imposed the intellectual heritage of his homeland upon the known world, literary quality rarely rose to the high standard of pre-Alexandrian times. Nevertheless, literature still accomplished much. Education and literacy grew by leaps and bounds. Whereas HOMER and SAPPHO had enjoyed virtually no readership and had relied on trained memories and performance to spread their poetic fame, book (manuscript scroll) production became an increasingly lucrative enterprise during the Hellenistic period. Libraries and theaters flourished. Professional organizations grew up that included writers, all sorts of theatrical artists, and musicians. The Attalid, Ptolemaic, and Seleucid rulers pleased their citizens with many celebrations and festivals that featured opportunities for literary competition and for authors like MENANDER and THEOCRITUS to display their talents. EPIC poetry enjoyed a resurgence as exemplified by the ARGONAUTIKA of Apollonius of Rhodes. Such Philosophers as the moralist EPICURUS, and the Stoic Zeno (see STOICISM) attracted their disciples, taught them, and through them exercised a for-

mative influence of the ideas of a fledgling Christianity.

In other intellectual spheres, the sciences and the representational arts also flourished during the Hellenistic Age. The astronomer Aristarchus of Samos (b. ca. 330 B.C.E.) developed the heliocentric view of the operation of the solar system, and the anatomists Herophilus and Erasistratus (fl. ca. fourth–third century B.C.E.) respectively discovered the nervous system and distinguished between the motor and the sensory nerves. Much outstanding sculpture also survives from the period.

The ascendancy of the Roman Empire throughout much of the known world ended the political phase of the Hellenistic domination of the Mediterranean shores and Asia. Certainly, cultural influence was a two-way street, and the subject peoples under Ptolemies, Seleucids, and Attalids contributed much from their indigenous civilizations to the Hellenistic literary and intellectual climate. Nonetheless, outside the religious sphere, the intellectual ascendancy of Hellenistic Greek literary culture lasted until the fall of the Western Roman Empire.

Bibliography

Green, Peter, ed. *Hellenistic History and Culture.* Berkeley: University of California Press, 1993.

Mueller, Katja. *Settlements of the Ptolemies: City Foundations and New Settlements in the Hellenistic World.* Dudley, Mass.: Peeters, 2006.

Stephens, Susan. *Seeing Double: Intercultural Poetics in Ptolemaic Alexandria.* Berkeley: University of California Press, 2003.

Hephæstion of Alexandria (fl. ca. 150 C.E.)
Greek prose writer

Hephæstion, about whom little else is known, was the author of a manual, *About Meter*, describing the basic varieties of QUANTITATIVE VERSE. Some subsequent commentators abridged Hephæstion's work from its original 48 books down, eventually, to one. Other commentators, however, preserved various parts of the manual. As a result, we know a considerable amount about the structure and content of the original work.

Essentially, we learn that Hephæstion's analysis was relatively mechanical and simplistic and that he ignored complex meters not within his purview. His work remains valuable, nonetheless, because it contains fragments of poems that would otherwise have been totally lost.

Bibliography

Hephæstion. *Hephæstion on Metre*. Translated and edited by J. M. van Ophuijsen. New York: E. J. Brill, 1987.

Heracles Euripides (ca. 420 B.C.E.)

Assigning a date to *Heracles* involves considerable guesswork. Some argue that EURIPIDES' positive view of Athens in this play points to a date around 420 B.C.E.—before the playwright lost his faith in Athenian democracy. Others feel that the chorus of elders' discussion of old age in lines 637–700 of the play suggests the playwright is projecting his own experience of advancing age into the work, and so it is a late one.

In any case, the play's hero, Heracles (Hercules), a demigod fathered by Zeus with his paramour Alcmene and the most celebrated of all Greek heroes, is away from the city of Thebes as the play opens. He is, as a matter of fact, in the underworld capturing the three-headed guard dog of Hades, Cerberus. This is the last and most difficult of the 12 labors assigned him by Eurystheus, ruler of Argolis.

Heracles' mother's mortal husband, Amphitryon, begins the play with a prologue that seeks to unravel the genealogical, political, and mythological complexities of Heracles' situation. Having summarized the background, Amphitryon reveals that in Heracles' absence from Thebes, where his family awaits him, a stranger, Lycus, has killed Creon, the king of Thebes and father of Megara, Heracles' wife. It is Lycus's intention, moreover, to settle a blood feud by destroying all the members of Heracles' family, which includes Megara, Heracles' three sons, and Amphitryon

himself. Fearing for their lives, the family has sought sanctuary at the altar of Zeus.

Megara pleads with Amphitryon to devise some means for their safe escape. Their best hope, however, rests in Heracles' possible return from Hades. The CHORUS encourages them in their hope.

Lycus enters and demands to know how long the family will seek to prolong their lives under the protection offered by Zeus's altar. He explains that their destruction is nothing personal—merely a matter of political policy so that Heracles' children will not seek to avenge their grandfather, Creon, by killing Lycus when they grow up.

Amphitryon answers boldly. Lycus, stung by his words, orders wood to be brought and set afire to burn the family alive at Zeus's altar. Megara pleads with Amphitryon that they all face a more merciful death together. He, however, says he means to save Heracles' children if he can. Megara, who argues that there will be no return from Hades for Heracles, pleads to be allowed to return to the palace and clothe herself and her children in funeral attire so they may properly meet their deaths. Lycus agrees. Amphitryon prays to Zeus, blaming the god for not intervening.

In a long choral interlude, the chorus sings of Heracles' success in accomplishing the first 11 of the seemingly impossible 12 labors assigned him. They then call the attention of the audience to the return of his family, whose members now all are shrouded for burial. Grieving, Megara recounts the careful arrangements she and Heracles had made for the children's future—the marriages they had arranged and the principalities they would govern: Athens, Thebes, and Sparta.

Just as they have abandoned hope and are bidding farewell to their friends, they spy Heracles approaching. Arriving, he asks for an explanation. Megara recounts the whole story. Heracles prepares to take action against Lycus, but Amphitryon counsels caution owing to the tyrant's many allies.

Then the elder man asks for an account of Heracles' adventures in Hades. He learns that Heracles bested the hellhound Cerberus in a fair fight and brought him to the land of the living, and that Cerberus is kenneled in the city of Hermione. We also learn that Heracles has brought Theseus, king of Athens, back from Hades. Then, together with Heracles, the family reenters the palace.

Following another choral interlude that celebrates Heracles' triumphs and his return, Lycus and his retinue enter just as Amphitryon reappears. Lycus asks where the others are and scorns Amphitryon when he answers that they are at their household altars. With his followers, Lycus enters the house, and Amphitryon follows. Knowing that the tyrant and his followers are doomed, the chorus celebrates, and the audience hears from within the anguished cries of the slain.

The chorus celebrates Lycus's fall, but in the midst of their rejoicing, two spectral figures appear above the house. One is Iris, the rainbow and a messenger of the gods. The other, more frighteningly, is Madness, whom Iris introduces to the chorus and the audience. Iris reports that Hera, her jealousy aroused by Zeus's infidelity, has determined that Heracles, whose fate had been suspended while he was engaged on his 12 tasks, must now be made to suffer. Iris reports that Madness will infect Heracles and cause him to destroy the very children he has just been at such pains to save. The gods demand this sacrifice lest human power grow at the gods' expense.

Madness, ironically, is more compassionate than her companion and seeks to dissuade Iris. Failing, she calls on Apollo to witness that she is obeying against her will. That done, she infects Heracles, who unwittingly destroys everything he had set out to save as the chorus describes his deeds. A messenger then enters and in great detail reports what has transpired within the house. He tells how Heracles imagined himself to be slaying the sons of Eurystheus, and how, despite the pleas of his own sons, he mercilessly slew them and their mother.

The madness having run its course, Heracles falls into slumber and is bound to a stone column. Amphitryon enters and repeats the news of the events within. Finally, Heracles awakes in his right mind. A grieving Amphitryon explains what has happened. When the truth of his mad behavior dawns on Heracles, he resolves to kill himself.

Theseus now enters, and Heracles explains that throughout his life, the jealous goddess Hera has been his enemy and that she is the cause of the current horror. Theseus tries to persuade Heracles to come to Athens and accept half of all Theseus owns. Heracles, however, refuses at first and grieves piteously, finding himself unworthy to participate in the funeral rites of his family. He assigns Amphitryon that task, but promises to fulfill his filial duty by returning to bury Amphitryon. At last he accepts help from Theseus, and the play ends as Heracles is led away while the chorus of old men laments.

See also *Mad Hercules*.

Bibliography

Euripides. *Heracles. Alcestis, Heracles, Children of Heracles, Cyclops and Other Plays*. Translated by Robin Waterfield. Oxford and New York: Oxford University Press, 2003.

Heraclitus of Ephesus (544–484) *Greek prose writer*

The earliest Greek philosopher to choose prose as his medium of expression, Heraclitus proposed the view that everything is in a continual state of change. This was a clear departure from the conviction of his predecessors that changes are a function of human perception and that an immutable reality underlay the material universe. Only fragments of Heraclitus's philosophical prose survive. They are enough, nonetheless, to reveal that he was a deep and careful thinker. His expression of his thoughts, however, was condensed and cryptic. His contemporaries seem to have thought him gloomy and self-important.

Bibliography

Heraclitus. *Fragments: The Collected Wisdom of Heraclitus*. Translated by Brooks Haxton. New York: Viking, 2001.

———. *Heraclitus: Translation and Analysis.* Translated by Dennis Sweet. Lanham, Md.: University Press of America, 1995.

Hercules furens   See MAD HERCULES.

Hermas   See SHEPHERD, THE.

Hero and Leander   See MUSÆUS (2).

Herodotus (Herodotos) (ca. 480–ca. 425 B.C.E.) *Greek historian*

The earliest historian (in the modern sense of that term) whose writings have survived largely intact, Herodotus was born at Halicarnassus in the province of Doria on the southwestern coast of Asia Minor. We know his father's name, Lyxes, and that of his uncle, Panyasis, a poet who wrote an EPIC about Heracles (Hercules). The city's ruler, Lygdamis, executed Panyasis.

The same political upheavals that resulted in his uncle's execution led Herodotus to migrate elsewhere. Though trying to draw an itinerary of all his travels from the pages of his *The HISTORIES* is probably an exercise in futility, and though it remains unclear just when he undertook some of the journeys he did make, at the time of his exile or later, he certainly spent some time on the island of Samos. He also roamed Egypt, Athens, other parts of the Greek world, and perhaps some of Persia as well. He was acquainted with the Athenian statesman Pericles, and he is reported to have given a public reading of a portion of his history at Athens in 446 B.C.E.—a reading for which he was very well paid.

Though Herodotus, like many of his contemporaries, respected the religious customs of his country and also those of others, like many of his contemporaries he received with skepticism the myths that some of his predecessors treated as factual. At the same time, however, the priests of various cults, gods, and goddesses, in the places where Herodotus conducted his research, maintained many of the records that were open to his consultation. Thus, portions of his book have a decidedly religious cast.

Nonetheless, Herodotus was no religious propagandist, and he assiduously sought to discover truth and to weigh probabilities carefully. He departed from the practice of most of his predecessor epic poets and elegists—the sources of popular history—by composing in prose. The presentation of his text seems to suggest that he was writing it to appeal both to private readers and to listeners who might hear him read his work aloud.

In his unprecedented work, Herodotus focuses principally on the confrontation between the Grecian and Asiatic worlds from about the time of the last king of Lydia, Croesus (ruled ca. 560–546 B.C.E.) through the conquests of Lydia and Egypt with accounts of the rise to power of the Persian king Darius. After recounting Persia's incursions into Libya and Scythia, he turns his attention to the struggle between the Asiatic Greek world and Persia's expansionary ambitions. He traces that struggle through the famous battles of Marathon, Thermopylae, Artemesium, and Salamis to the decisive battle at Platea, which forced the Persians to withdraw.

It is likely that Herodotus composed other works. He himself mentions one of them, his "Assyrian Logoi," and ARISTOTLE seems to have known the book.

The exact dates of Herodotus's death and the composition of the *Histories* remain a matter of scholarly debate. The historian of literature Oliver Taplin speculates that the work may have been composed orally over a long period of time and later written down. Taplin also argues convincingly that Herodotus had been preceded by a group of epic poets who had chosen history as their subject and composed verse narratives on subjects similar to some of those of Herodotus. Herodotus himself alludes to one of them, HECATÆUS (Hekataios) OF MILETUS, who wrote genealogies of mythical families with the stories surrounding them. More to the point, he also seems to have written the same sort of material with which Herodotus fills out sections of his narrative—geography, ethnography, itinerary, local tales and fables, and descriptions of rare animals. Like Herodotus, moreover, the poets who preceded him in some approximation to the historical enterprise he undertook wrote in Ionic. Perhaps significantly, this was Herodotus's second dialect—a fact that serves at some level to identify Herodotus with a school of writers in the Ionic language.

In an effort to identify Herodotus's unique contribution to the enterprise of writing history, Taplin cites the assessment of the *Histories* made by Dionysius of Halicarnassus. The predecessor historians tended to focus narrowly on subjects relating to single nations or cities. They collected stories in a single frame of reference and reported what they collected without addition, subtraction, or passing judgment on the credibility of the stories they recounted.

Herodotus's unique contribution arises, first, from the synthesis he achieved within a global framework that interlinked the stories of many European and Asiatic peoples. Second, his discriminating judgment about the credibility of his material sets him apart. For the modern reader, a principal value of Herodotus's work stems from its being compelling and entertaining reading.

Bibliography

Carter, Harry, trans. *The Histories of Herodotus of Halicarnassus*. New York: The Heritage Press, 1958.

Herodotus. *The Histories*. Translated by Robin Waterford. Oxford: Oxford University Press, 1998.

Taplin, Oliver, ed. *Literature in the Greek and Roman Worlds: A New Perspective*. Oxford: Oxford University Press, 2000.

Heroides Ovid (ca. 20 B.C.E.)

A series of 21 verse letters that the Roman poet Ovid composed as if heroines of myth and legend had written them to their husbands and lovers, the *Heroides* belong to Ovid's earliest period of composition. It was the period during which the young poet found himself preoccupied with the subject of love.

First among the letters is that written by Penelope to her long-absent husband, Ulysses. She instructs him not to answer her letter but rather to return in person. She has heard the account of the Trojan War that the aged Greek general, Nestor, recounted to her son Telemachus, but in the absence of Ulysses, news of the Greek victory there brings her no comfort. She reports that her father Icarius is pressuring her to remarry, and she urges Ulysses to hurry home for the sakes of his aged father Laertes, his son Telemachus, and Penelope herself. She touchingly complains that she was only a girl when he left her, but that she will seem an aged woman upon his return.

The second letter is that of the seduced and deserted Thracian girl, Phyllis, to the son of Theseus, Demophon, who succeeded his father as ruler of Athens. Phyllis complains of Demophon's failure to honor his promise to return. Her disappointed expectations have driven her mad, and, after reproving Demophon for his faithlessness, she ends her letter by quoting the epitaph that will appear on her tomb when she dies by her own hand.

A letter from Briseis to Achilles stands third in the collection. Briseis was Achilles' captive and lover in Homer's *The Iliad*. The Greek general Agamemnon demanded her from Achilles, and rather than fight to keep her, Achilles gave her up, though in his anger he withheld his military services from the Greek cause with nearly disastrous results. Briseis wants to return to Achilles, and her letter encourages him to demand that she be restored to him.

The fourth letter is one of seduction. Written from Phaedra to her stepson Hippolytus, this letter encourages Hippolytus to overcome both his filial piety and his prudery. Even the gods give the example of loving and wedding near kin. Love, she explains, is all that matters. She begs him to yield to her impassioned entreaties.

The jilted nymph Oenone authors the fifth letter, addressed to Paris, who had left her to claim Helen of Troy as his prize for judging Venus to be the most beautiful goddess in the world's archetypal beauty contest. Oenone reproves Paris for having deserted her, quoting to him the words of promise he emblazoned on a tree with his sword when the nymph married him. Oenone prays that Helen may live to endure the same loss that the nymph experienced, and the nymph affirms that she will remain true to Paris, come what may.

Hypsipyle addresses Jason, the Argonaut (see *The* ARGONAUTIKA) in the sixth missive. On their voyage in search of the Golden Fleece, the Argonauts had tarried for a time on the island of Lemnos, from which the women had expelled all the men. The Argonauts lingered with the Lemnian women, and their leader, Hypsipyle, was Jason's beloved. Though in some versions of the story, the pair part on good terms with no regrets on either side, here Hypsipyle has learned from a traveler that Jason has married Medea, and Hypsipyle is both furious and brokenhearted. She advises Jason that she has borne him twins, and she curses his union with Medea, who will kill her children by Jason and end her life a wanderer through the world, dependent on the largesse of strangers.

The seventh letter comes from Dido, the unhappy queen of Carthage, and is addressed to Aeneas, the Trojan prince who first married and then deserted her to fulfill his fate and become the founder of Rome. The forlorn Dido tells Aeneas that her fate will be to end her own life with his forgotten sword and that her epitaph will bear only the name of her first husband, Sychaeus.

Hermione pens the eighth letter to Orestes. Here Ovid follows the version of the story in which Hermione was first betrothed to Orestes, then abducted by and forced to wed the son of Achilles, Neoptolemus (see ORESTES by EURIPIDES). Her letter begs Orestes to come and rescue her. In Euripides' play, he does so.

Ninth in the sequence is a letter from Deianira to her deceased husband Hercules. In it, she complains that he had replaced her in his affection with an Oechalian concubine, Iole. Hoping to regain his love, Deianira sent him a robe sprinkled with the blood of the centaur, Nessus, which she believed would act as a love potion. Hercules had killed Nessus when the centaur attempted to ravish Deianira. Rather than acting as a love potion, however, the centaur's blood was in fact a raging poison whose effects were so painful that Hercules chose to be burned to death rather than endure it. The accusatory tone of Deianira's letter shifts to one of self-reproach for having inadvertently caused her husband's death. She resolves to die, and her letter becomes one of farewell to her family, one of self-reproach, and her suicide note. Her performance is one of the most moving of the collection.

The 10th letter contains the deserted Ariadne's complaint against Theseus, who used her to escape the Cretan labyrinth when he killed the half-bull, half-man Minotaur, but who left her stranded on the island of Naxos when he sailed for his home in Athens. Ariadne's guilt at having betrayed her father and her love for the faithless Theseus emerge in moving counterpoint.

Canace complains of the consequences of incest in the 11th letter—one that she addresses to her brother and lover, Macareus, who is also the father of her child. Learning of the child's birth and its parentage, Canace's father Aeolus takes the child to be exposed in the wilderness, and he sends Canace a sword with instructions to use it as befits her crimes. She resolves to do so. She begs Macareus, however, to collect the scattered remnants of their infant and to enclose them with her own remains in the same sepulcher.

Returning to the story of Medea and Jason, Ovid next imagines a letter from Medea in which she rehearses the story of the Golden Fleece and her role in Jason's securing it as she participated in the murder of her brother and fled Colchis for the city of Corinth in Greece. Now Medea finds that Jason is betraying her and her two children by marrying the daughter of Creon, the tyrant of Corinth. Medea's children call their mother to come and see a procession being led by their father, who is all arrayed in gold. Medea swears vengeance in her letter to Jason, though the form it will take is as yet unclear, even to her. As every reader of Ovid knows, Medea will kill her children. The omission of that detail in her letter is more effective than a statement would have been.

Letter 13 is one written by Laodamia to her soldier husband Protesilaus, who, unknown to her, had been the first Greek ashore at Troy and the first to fall in battle. The letter is filled with tender expressions of her love, with forebodings of her husband's death, and with wishful thinking as she tries to reassure herself of Protesilaus's well-being.

The 14th letter is one written by Hypermnestra—the only one of Danaus's 50 daughters to disobey when their father ordered them to slay their husbands on the common wedding night of all 50. (See SUPPLIANTS, THE) In the letter, Hypermnestra pleads with her husband Lynceus to rescue her from the vengeance of her father, Danaus. When Hypermnestra had disobeyed her father's directive because she loved Lynceus, Danaus had accused her of filial disobedience and demanded the courts impose a death sentence. In the event she is saved.

Letter 15 is a letter from the poet SAPPHO. It is addressed to Phaon whom legend identifies as the lost lover for whom she committed suicide. It expresses her feelings of loss and longing.

The remaining six letters are pairs exchanged by lovers. The 16th is a letter from the Trojan prince Paris addressed to the wife of the Spartan king Menelaus. In it Paris tries to persuade Helen to abandon Menelaus and sail with Paris to Troy. In the 17th letter, Helen agrees to do so.

The 18th and 19th letters are exchanged between the lovers Leander and Hero. To be with Hero, Leander nightly swam the Hellespont until he drowned in a storm. In the two letters the lovers mutually declare their affection and longing for one another.

Another pair of lovers send the 20th and 21st letters—Acontius and Cydippe [See, ACONTIUS AND KIDIPPE and CALLIMACHUS]. In the first letter, Acontius declares his love for Cydippe and he anticipates the day they will marry as a result of his having tricked her into swearing to do so. In the second letter of the pair, also the final letter of the collection, Cydippe consents to abide by her involuntary bargain and marry Acontius.

Bibliography
Ovid. *Heroides and Amores.* Translated by Grant Showerman. New York: G. P. Putnam's Sons, 1925.

Hesiod (fl. eighth century B.C.E.) *Greek poet*

The son of a Greek merchant turned farmer, the poet Hesiod was born at Ascra on the lower slopes of Mount Helicon—a venue sacred to the patron goddesses of the arts, the MUSES. As he was among the earliest of known Greek didactic poets, Hesiod has often been bracketed with HOMER, though Hesiod probably wrote a decade or two later. Like Homer, Hesiod composed in the Ionic dialect of ancient Greek, though with some admixture of the Boeotian dialect that was spoken in the vicinity of the city of Thebes near the poet's home.

Hesiod's is the earliest Greek poetry that illustrates an interest in subject matter outside the EPIC tradition. His *WORKS AND DAYS* instead examines two subjects. On the one hand, it lauds the honesty of farmers who make their living by the sweat of their brow while at the same time censuring corrupt judges and their injustices. On the other hand, Hesiod's poem is a kind of farmer's almanac, suggesting which days might prove most propitious for certain kinds of farm labor. In the course of the work, Hesiod paints a fascinating picture of an eighth-century B.C.E. Greek farming community.

His second notable work, *THEOGONY*, concerns itself with the origins of the universe and of the gods. It particularly interests those who study early Greek myth with a view to tracing its development. Some think he also composed a *Catalogue of Women.* Its fragmentary remnants reveal that he (or another poet) listed goddesses who married human beings and legendary heroines of the past, detailed their exploits, and tracked their descendants, marking transitions with the repeated phrases *like her . . .* or *like her who . . .* This practice has given rise to the Greek title that translates the phrase *like her—Eoeae.* Critical opinion varies about whether this work is really Hesiod's, but it is sometimes included in collections of his work. A better though not universally accepted case has been made for Hesiod's authorship of an often-appended section entitled "The Shield of Heracles." "The Shield" begins with "Or like her who."

According to not altogether reliable reports, Hesiod is said to have been murdered by the relatives of a woman whom he either seduced or in whose seduction he somehow cooperated.

Bibliography

Hesiod et al. *Theogony, Works and Days, Shield.* Translated by Apostolos N. Athanassakis. Baltimore, Md.: Johns Hopkins University Press, 2004.

———. *Works of Hesiod and the Homeric Hymns.* Translated by Daryl Hine. Chicago: University of Chicago Press, 2005.

Nelson, Stephanie A. *God and the Land: The Metaphysics of Farming in Hesiod and Vergil* [sic], *with a Translation of Hesiod's Works and Days.* Translated by David Greene. New York: Oxford University Press, 1998.

hieroglyphs

Used for representing the ancient Egyptian language—Old, Middle, and Late Egyptian—from as early as ca. 3100 B.C.E., hieroglyphic writing employed pictorial symbols to convey several categories of linguistic information. Some of the symbols represented sounds. Called *phonograms,* such symbols stood for one, two, or three consonants. No symbols representing vowels were employed. A second category of symbol, the *logogram* represented an entire word. Logograms were accompanied by a stroke called an *orthogram,* which indicated an adjacent logogram. Another sort of symbol, a *taxogram,* was sometimes used to indicate the category to which a word belonged. A man's name, for instance, might be accompanied by a symbol that determined the category *male* for the preceding word.

Both because of their pictorial quality and because they could be written horizontally from right to left or from left to right, or vertically, hieroglyphs were aesthetically satisfying and, together with pictures, made for pleasing decoration upon any flat surface, including walls, coffins, or papyrus scrolls. They could be carved, painted, or written with a pen. For the sake of scribal speed and convenience, a cursive form of hieroglyphs developed as time went on. This form of hieroglyphic writing, called *hieratic script,* soon developed abbreviations and modified forms that replaced the aesthetically satisfying but more cumbersome ancient system, in many cases rendering the older texts virtually indecipherable to later scribes, who wrote exclusively from right to left. Hieratic script remained the standard manner of representing Middle Egyptian from ca. 2160 to ca. 1780 B.C.E.

Throughout this long stretch of time, not only was the system of representing the language changing, the language itself changed as well, and around 1370 B.C.E.—the end of the 18th dynasty—a new standard of usage as well as a changed mode of hieratic script came into widespread use. With respect both to language and to script, this process repeated itself about 500 B.C.E. Then, shortly after the beginning of the Christian era, the Egyptian language underwent a further, more fundamental change, developing into Coptic. About this time, too, a modified form of the more efficient Greek ALPHABET replaced the more cumbersome hieroglyphic system, and, except for antiquarians, everyone who was literate adopted the new style.

Bibliography

Edwards, I. E. S. et al., eds. *The Cambridge Ancient History.* Cambridge: Cambridge University Press, 1970.

Parkinson, R. B. *Voices from Ancient Egypt: An Anthology of Middle Kingdom Writings.* Norman: University of Oklahoma Press, 1991.

Schumann-Antelme, Ruth, and Stéphane Rossini. *Illustrated Hieroglyphics Handbook.* Translated by Joseph Bain. New York: Sterling, 2002.

Wilson, Hillary. *Understanding Hieroglyphs: A Complete Introductory Guide.* New York: Barnes and Noble, 2003.

Hippolytus Euripides (428 B.C.E.)

Apparently a revision of EURIPIDES' earlier unpopular play on the same subject, *Hippolytus* enjoys the reputation of being Euripides' finest play, in the view of many critics.

The play is set at Troezen, a city ruled by Theseus, king of Athens. There an aging Theseus lives with his son Hippolytus. The young man is the product of Theseus's youthful liaison with Hippolyta, queen of the Amazons, whose forces Theseus had overcome in battle. Theseus's new, much younger wife, Phaedra, also dwells at Troezen.

Hippolytus's purity of heart and his utter devotion to the virgin goddess Artemis have angered Aphrodite, goddess of love. As the play opens, we find the goddess ruminating over the way she rewards her worshippers and punishes those who resist her. Hippolytus, it seems, regards her as "the vilest of goddesses." The goddess expresses her intention to punish the young man for his disregard.

The instrument of her vengeance, she explains, will be Phaedra, his stepmother, and the goddess has long been preparing to spring her trap. Before ever coming to Troezen, Phaedra saw Hippolytus and fell violently in love with him. Phaedra even built a temple to Aphrodite to help her achieve the object of her desire. Aphrodite outlines her plan—and the skeleton of the play. She will tell Theseus about Phaedra's love for his son. Theseus will then curse Hippolytus. Theseus's patron god, Poseidon, has granted three curses to Theseus, and what he prays for will be performed. Phaedra's death, too, albeit an honored one, is a part of Aphrodite's plan. She disappears.

Hippolytus and members of his hunting party enter, singing the praises of Artemis. The leader of his party reproves the lad for his neglect of Aphrodite.

Phaedra, nearly hysterical and pale and gaunt from love sickness, is led out and lies down on a couch. Her nurse and the CHORUS exchange sentiments of concern over her illness and its unknown cause. In the course of their discussion, we learn that Theseus is away from home.

Phaedra's nurse cross-questions her and at last wrings from her the confession that she is in love with Hippolytus. She is, however, determined to die rather than disgrace Theseus and break her marriage vows. Anxious to play go-between, the nurse advises that the best way to cure lovesickness is to act on impulse and get it over with. Phaedra is appalled at the advice.

The nurse nevertheless goes to Hippolytus with the news of her mistress's passion. It is now Hippolytus's turn to be appalled, and he berates the nurse loudly enough that Phaedra can hear him from outside the house. The self-righteous Hippolytus is intent on broadcasting the nurse's treachery to all who will listen. He seizes the occasion to pronounce a diatribe against women in general. At this point, Euripides portrays Hippolytus as an excessively self-righteous woman hater.

Phaedra, in the meantime, despairing of keeping her feelings a secret from her husband, resolves to die rather than dishonor him, and she hangs herself. Theseus returns at this moment to be greeted with news of his wife's suicide but no explanation. Then he spies a suicide note in her hand. On reading it, he concludes that Hippolytus has violated his honor and invokes Poseidon's curse on him.

Hippolytus denies his guilt, swearing his innocence in both deed and thought. Unconvinced, Theseus pronounces his son's banishment, and Hippolytus leaves.

Now a messenger appears, bearing news of Hippolytus's death. As Hippolytus drove his chariot along the shore, Poseidon sent a tidal wave containing a monstrous bull. The bull's bellowing panicked the horses, and they dragged Hippolytus to his death. All this is described in bloody and graphic detail. Hippolytus may have a breath left in him, but he is certainly doomed.

The goddess Artemis now appears above the stage and tells Theseus the true story. He is conscience-stricken and disconsolate. Servants assist the dying Hippolytus to enter. Artemis explains that Aphrodite has arranged all the play's events. Father and son are reconciled, and Hippolytus's former self-righteousness evaporates. He dies, leaving a grieving Theseus full of self-recriminations for his thoughtless haste in cursing his son.

Bibliography

Euripides. *Hippolytus*. Translated by Michael Halleran. Newburyport, Mass.: Focus Publishing, 2001.

———. *Hippolytus. Three Tragedies of Euripides.* Translated by Paul Roche. New York: Mentor, 1973.

Histories, The Herodotus (ca. mid–fifth century B.C.E.)

HERODOTUS of Halicarnassus undertook researching and writing *The Histories* so that "men's actions" and the "great and wonderful accomplishments" both "of Greeks and Barbarians" would not in time be forgotten. He especially set out to examine the causes of war between the Greeks and the "Barbarians" (by whom he meant persons who did not speak the Greek language).

As Herodotus's work has come down to us, it has been subdivided by later editors into nine books, each of which those same editors have provided with a chapter title bearing the name of one of the nine MUSES. The divisions of the chapters do not always follow the organization of the book's subject matter and may have been predicated on how much text the editor or scribe could fit on a single papyrus scroll.

Book 1

In the book named for the Muse of History, Clio, Herodotus's first inquiry addresses the sources of the ongoing enmity between the Greeks and the Asians. He concludes the desire for women was at the root of the hostility. Making it clear that he has little confidence in the historicity of the mythical accounts preserved in the EPIC poems of his predecessors and the folklore of places, he nonetheless reports the kernel stories of those myths. He chooses, however, to give Persian and Phoenician versions of the stories as a corrective to the Greek spin imparted to them by his countrymen.

Herodotus tells the Persian version of the kidnapping of Io, a princess of Argos, by Phoenician sailors and her subsequent appearance in Egypt. He then tells the Phoenician version, in which Io, pregnant by the Phoenician captain, goes with him willingly to avoid the scandal on Argos. Herodotus pointedly leaves out the part of the story in which Io is beloved by the god Zeus, who changes her into a heifer to avoid Hera's wrath (see *PROMETHEUS BOUND*). He reports that Jason's taking Medea from Colchis was a kidnapping in retaliation for Io's (see *The ARGONAUTIKA*). He treats the story of Paris's (here called by his alternative name, Alexander) running off with Helen of Troy as another reprisal for Io's rape. According to folk traditions around the Mediterranean Sea, from this series of incidents arose the enmity between Greeks and Asians. Having recounted them, Herodotus turns his attention to political history as he thinks it to be true.

As he personally believes, the historic enmity between East and West had its origins in the conquest of Lydia and supplanting the rule of the descendants of Heracles (Hercules) with that of the family of King Croesus of Lydia—the first of the Asian barbarians to impose the payment of tribute on the Greeks. Unable, however, to resist a good related story, Herodotus interrupts this part of the account with the wonderful story of the singer Arion of Methymna's ride on the back of a dolphin across miles of open sea to the safety of the Grecian mainland.

Returning to pre-Croesan Lydia, Herodotus recounts the tale of Heracles' 23rd-generation descendant, Candaules, a Lydian king so besotted by the beauty of his unnamed wife that he encouraged his confidant, Gyges, to see her naked. Gyges demurred, but his king insisted, hiding him in the royal bedchamber. Having seen the wife, Gyges quickly departed. She, however, observed him leaving. Furious with her husband for so dishonoring her, she gave Gyges the choice of killing Candaules and marrying her, thus becoming king, or of being killed himself. Accepting the first alternative, Gyges became king, received the approval of the oracle of Apollo, and gave offerings of thanks to the temple at Delphi—offerings that Herodotus describes.

Next Herodotus traces the descendants of Gyges and their various wars against the Greeks until he arrives at the accession of Croesus to the throne of Lydia in about 560 B.C.E. It was the military prowess of Croesus that succeeded in bringing all the Greek colonists in Asia under his sway. The tribute they paid him made him fabulously wealthy, and meeting him became a goal of Grecian philosophers. Herodotus then launches into a story about a visit to Croesus's court by the Athenian statesman and poet SOLON.

Fishing for a compliment, Croesus asked Solon to name the person he considered to be the happiest of men. To the king's surprise, Solon did not name him. Asked for second and third choices, Solon still did not name Croesus. Finally the king asked why Solon did not include him. Solon replied that, given the vicissitudes of fortune, no living man could confidently be counted happy. Only after his death could that judgment be valid.

Though Croesus was displeased, time bore out Solon's assessment. First Croesus lost his son in a hunting accident. Then, after a lengthy description of Croesus's campaigns, a reader learns that the king came to venerate Apollo's oracle. This resulted from the Pythian oracle's having passed Croesus's test of its powers. Later on, the king himself was defeated in battle, taken prisoner, and ordered to be burnt on a funeral pyre, only to be saved by a cloudburst attributed to divine intervention. Croesus's conqueror was Cyrus the Great, king of the Persians (d. 529 B.C.E.). Herodotus reports that Croesus then remembered Solon and wished that he had rewarded him for his wisdom. No one knows Croesus's date or manner of death, though Herodotus later reports him as being among both Cyrus's military advisors and those of Cyrus's son, Cambyses. It seems likely that Croesus died in battle as a Persian ally.

Herodotus reports that Cyrus was positively impressed by Croesus's behavior and granted him any favor he chose. Croesus asked that his chains and shackles be borne to the Temple of Apollo at Delphi and the oracle questioned about the reasons for his defeat, since, because of the prediction that he would put an end to a great empire, he had anticipated success. The answer came back that he had misinterpreted the prediction and that his defeat was the gods' retribution for his ancestor Gyges' having slain Candaules.

In the rest of the first book of *The Histories*, Herodotus observes that the Lydians were the first to use coins and that they prostituted their female children until they found husbands, but that otherwise their customs are much like the Greeks'. He then shifts his attention briefly to the Assyrians, but principally to the Medes and the Persians. He tells how a good judge, Dioces, became the first king of the Medes, how he built and fortified the city of Agbatana (Ecbatana), and the manner in which he ruled his people. Dioces' son, Phraortes, subjugated the Persians to his rule and afterward several other Asian peoples until he attacked the Assyrians, who defeated his forces and killed him. His son, Cyaxares, succeeded him, but after initial successes with a highly organized army with specialized units, Cyaxares was overcome by the Scythians, who then ruled over all of Asia. They did not rule well, however, and eventually fell victim to Cyaxares' plotting. He then reestablished the power of the Medes and married his daughter Mandane to the Persian Cambyses.

Warned in a dream that the child of that union would depose him, Cambyses tried to have his son Cyrus killed in infancy. However, the servant to whom Cambyses entrusted this task, Harpagus, considered his master mad and gave the baby to a herdsman to expose in the mountains. Instead, the herdsman exchanged his wife's stillborn son for the baby and took the royal child as his own. That child would eventually become the Persian king, Cyrus.

Later, discovering that his son was alive and learning from Harpagus what had really happened, Cambyses took Harpagus's son and had the lad killed, cooked, and served to his father as a punishment. When Cyrus grew up and became king of the Persians, Harpagus conspired to help him overthrow Cambyses, and so the Medes together with the rest of Asia became subject to the Persians.

Herodotus next describes the Persian Empire together with its religion and its customs, including the Persians' willingness to adopt the customs of foreigners in matters of dress and of adding foreign deities to the pantheon of those they worship. The historian then devotes his attention to describing the Greek cities of Asia, and then to discussing the way in which Cyrus and his general and ally, Harpagus, led the Persians to bring Asia Minor as well as Ionia and several Greek islands under their sway. Herodotus also recounts the siege and capture of Babylon. Before doing so, however, he details the wonderful manner in which the city's former female rulers, Semiramis and Nitocris, had engineered flood control and improved the city's defenses. Modern scholarship has not confirmed the existence of Nitocris, and some think that the works Herodotus attributes to her were those of Nebuchadnezzar.

Nonetheless, after describing Nitocris's tomb, Herodotus returns to the conquests of Cyrus and his defeat of Nitocris's son, Labynetus. The historian then turns to cataloguing examples of the Babylonians' wealth and power, pointing out that fully a third of all the tribute paid to the Persian empire from Asia came from the country of Assyria, whose capital was Babylon. He praises the pre-Persian conquest marriage customs of the region and also their provision for the universal treatment of the sick.

The Persian's campaign against the Massagetae, who lived east of the Caspian Sea, the death of Cyrus in battle against them, and a brief account of the customs of the Massagetae ends the first book.

Book 2

Named for Euterpe, the Muse of flute playing, the second book of Herodotus's history uses the decision of Cyrus's son, Cambyses, to invade Egypt, which he conquered, as a transition to a consideration of Egypt, its people, and its customs. He reports the experiment of the Egyptian ruler Psammetichus that was designed to determine which human nation was the oldest. Thinking that the original language of mankind would spring automatically to the lips of a child that never heard language, he arranged for a shepherd to rear twin children among his flocks and for them to never hear a word spoken by another human being. When the children began to speak, their first discernible word was *bekos*. On discovering that this was the Phrygian word for bread, Psammetichus concluded that Phrygian must have been the original human language and its speakers the most ancient of peoples. Herodotus considers foolish an elaboration of the story that he attributes to the Greeks. As an experimental control, said some Greeks, Psammetichus had had the tongues cut out of all who came in contact with the children.

The historian next turns to a discussion of Egyptian religion and geography. He has clearly been an eyewitness to much that he describes. He speculates, however, about the source of the Nile without reaching a firm conclusion. He then discusses dining and toilet habits, the Egyptian custom of circumcision, the Egyptian religion, its priesthood, and its manner of sacrifice. He digresses to consider the Egyptian god Heracles, whom he concludes has to be a different figure from the heroic and also deified Greek Heracles—a conclusion he reached after traveling to the temple of Heracles at Tyre in Phoenicia and discovering it to be over 2,000 years old.

Herodotus attributes certain Greek ceremonies honoring the god Dionysus to Egyptian origin and also considers Egypt the source of the other Greek gods, erroneously thinking the differences in names a matter of language only. He then describes various ceremonies, including a festival of lights honoring the Egyptian god Osiris, who was killed and rose from the dead. Herodotus identifies Ares, the Grecian god of war, with the Egyptian deity Set—the monarch of evil who was responsible for the death of Osiris.

Next the reader learns of the Egyptians' reverence for animals and their practice of embalming cats. One discovers that the crocodile lives in peace with a bird—the *trochilus*—that pecks the leeches out of the crocodile's mouth. We also learn of flying serpents, the ibis that eats them, and other birds and animals.

Turning to Egyptian funeral customs, Herodotus gives a detailed description of the various processes of mummification practiced on the bodies of important persons, persons of the middling sort, and poor persons. Persons killed by crocodiles or through the agency of the River Nile can only have their bodies handled by priests of the Nile deity, for the deceased is regarded as more than human.

Always careful to inform the reader of the manner in which he formed his views, Herodotus turns from his personal experience and cross-questioning to matters of hearsay. What he learns and reports is a sort of history as folk legend. Among the unlikely matters reported in this section are the doings of an Egyptian queen with the same name as the suspect Babylonian, Nitocris, and a putative and otherwise unsubstantiated Egyptian invasion of Europe.

He gives the report of Helen of Troy that is the foundation for EURIPIDES' version of her story in *HELEN*. Herodotus remarks that he thinks HOMER knew this version of the story, but found the one in *The ILIAD* and *The ODYSSEY* more suitable for his artistic purposes. Herodotus himself credits the Egyptian version as more likely. If the Trojans had had Helen in their city, he thinks, they would have given her up rather than suffer a 10-year siege and their citadel's destruction.

Herodotus attributes to the Egyptians the origin of the belief in the transmigration of souls. A soul comes into being with a human's birth. On that person's death, it moves on into the body of another creature coming into being. After making the rounds of the living things on land, in the sea, and in the air over a period of 3,000 years, it comes again into a human body. (For what happens after that, see EGYPTIAN BOOK OF THE DEAD.)

Herodotus next describes the manner of building the pyramids, which he had visited. Turning to a story of special interest to his Grecian hearers and listeners, Herodotus recounts the story of Charaxus, the brother of SAPPHO, who brought home to Mytilene a courtesan from the Egyptian city of Naucratis, one Rhodopis. Sappho reproved her brother's infatuation with the courtesan, also called Doricha or Dika, in a poem now lost. Fragment 5 of the Sappho canon addresses Dika.

An interesting choice for an aside appears in the answer of the priests at Thebes to the boast of the Greek writer Hecataeus that, at a remove of 16 generations, he was descended from a god. The priests showed him—and also Herodotus— 345 statues, the likenesses of that many generations of high priests. These, they pointed out instructively, descended from a good and honorable man.

As he customarily does, Herodotus equates the Egyptian pantheon to the the Greek gods. He identifies the Egyptian god Horus with Apollo and the Greek Dionysus with the Egyptian Osiris. The latter gods have being twice born in common, and Osiris was believed to have risen from the dead. Herodotus thinks that the mysteries and worship of Dionysius have their roots in Egypt, and he is careful to omit from his account both the name of Osiris and the nature of the mysteries surrounding his worship. Other identifications include Demeter as Isis and Artemis as Bubastis.

Herodotus discusses the dynasties of Egypt and recounts his travels to view some architectural wonders, both standing and ruined. Among those standing in his day was the artificial lake called Moeris, which had two enormous pyramids topped with seated statues in its center. Among the Egyptian rulers he discusses is Psamtik I (whom Herodotus calls Psammetichus; he reigned from 663 to 609 B.C.E.). One of 12 contemporaneously ruling kings, Psamtik I consolidated his sole power with the aid of Ionian and Carian pirates who wore bronze armor, thus fulfilling a prophecy that "bronze men" would aid him in gaining the throne.

Another architectural achievement that Herodotus describes is the canal running from the Nile River to the Arabian Gulf, first dug around 1300 B.C.E. and reconstructed by Necos (Egyptian: Neco). A portion of its route paralleled that of the present Suez Canal.

Herodotus tells of the reign of Apries (Egyptian: Hophra, reigned 588–569 B.C.E.) and his overthrow by Amasis (Egyptian: Ahmose, reigned 569–529 B.C.E.). Amasis was friendly to the Greeks and married a woman from the Greek colony of Cyrene in Libya. He also conquered Cyprus—though he was not, as Herodotus says, the first Egyptian to do so.

Book 3

Book 3 of Herodotus's history (which some might say is misnamed for Thalia, the Muse of comedy) begins with a description from both Persian and Egyptian points of view of the Persian king Cambyses' invasion of Egypt about 525 B.C.E. Responding to Cambyses' offer of a royal marriage linking Egypt and Persia, the Egyptian king Amasis substituted a daughter of the predecessor he had deposed. Infuriated, said the Persian account, Cambyses invaded. The Egyptians, however, claimed (falsely, according to Herodotus) that Cambyses was the son of Cyrus by the substituted Egyptian woman. The historian next compares stories about the way Cambyses provided his soldiers with water by making a treaty with the Arabians so the army could cross the desert. Herodotus goes on to report that with his own eyes he had viewed the skeletons of the warriors slain in the final battle that gave Persia sovereignty over Egypt.

Shifting his focus, Herodotus next catalogues the distinguishing customs of the Ethiopians, whose usual age at death he reports to be 120 years. Upon dying, Ethiopians were enclosed in transparent, alabaster coffins, kept in their homes for a year, and then set up around their cities as monuments. Famine in the Persian army dissuaded the Persians from undertaking the conquest of Ethiopia.

Taking a closer look at Cambyses, Herodotus reports several of the emperor's mad acts, including arranging the murder of his brother. When Cambyses asked the supreme judges of Persia if, contrary to custom, he could marry his sister, the judges found an answer "both just and safe." There was no law, they opined, that permitted siblings to marry, but there was one allowing the king of Persia to do whatever he wanted. Accordingly, Cambyses married two of his sisters but killed one of them.

Following a rehearsal of more insane royal acts, Herodotus segues into a discussion of the continual good fortune of Polycrates, the tyrant (ruler) of the island of Samos, and of the way in which he rid himself of his political enemies by sending them on a mission in support of Cambyses together with a secret request that Cambyses not send his ambassadors back. This leads Herodotus into a consideration of the political alliances and notable crimes and activities among the inhabitants of the Greek islands and city-states and the role Polycrates of Samos played in their affairs. Herodotus justifies his lengthy digression on this subject by praising the Samians for a series of notable feats of engineering: a system of aqueducts, a harbor enclosure, and a temple complex.

Cambyses died, Herodotus explains, when an accidentally self-inflicted wound became gangrenous. A Mede, a Magian named Smerdis, who impersonated Cambyses' murdered brother of the same name, succeeded him on the throne. Then Herodotus recounts the unmasking and death of the imposter and the Persian recovery of the imperial throne. With the throne vacated and no clear successor at hand, the Persians considered whether or not to modify their form of government. A committee of seven of their foremost male citizens compared the advantages and disadvantages of a democracy, an oligarchy, and an absolute monarchy. They concluded that, when the best-qualified person sits on the throne, a monarchy is the best form of government. Otanes, the chief supporter of democracy, fearing that the others might select him as monarch, foreclosed that eventuality by refusing in advance. As a condition of his withdrawal, however, he required that he and his descendants be exempted from allegiance to whomever might become king. The others agreed to the condition.

With that decided, the six remaining members of the committee agreed that the one whose horse first neighed at sunrise would become king. Darius was one of the six, and just before sunrise his clever groom stationed a favorite mare of Darius's stallion at a spot where the stallion would whinny in greeting. A thunderclap confirmed this sign, and Darius became Persia's new king.

Herodotus next describes the way that Darius organized the government of Asia, forged loyalties through marrying multiple wives, and set up a monument to his horse and its groom. The historian then catalogues the tribute that Darius imposed on each of the 20 administrative regions (called satrapies) into which he had divided Asia, portions of Africa, and, later on, the Mediterranean islands of Asia Minor and Thessaly.

Turning his attention to a geography that, in all directions, becomes increasingly fanciful with distance, Herodotus describes Asia and the wonders he has heard of Arabia and India. He feels least confident about his store of reported information when he discusses Europe and the North—though some of his reports from that quarter do prove accurate. He points to the North as the source both of tin and of amber. The ancient Celts of Britain both mined tin and recovered it from streambeds, trading it south with the Veneti who passed it along to the Mediterranean world. The Lithuanian historian Arnolds Spekke has traced the ancient routes by which amber made its way from the Baltic to the Mediterranean areas.

Herodotus next turns his attention to the story of the Greek physician Democedes and how, by healing King Darius's foot, he gained the king's confidence. He also tells how Democedes contrives to return to his homeland by indirectly encouraging Darius to add Hellas (greater Greece including Greek possessions in Asia Minor) to his dominions. Sent as a part of an intelligence-gathering mission, Democedes escaped Persian control.

Nonetheless, encouraged by the physician's accounts of Greek wealth, Darius began a campaign of conquest against the easternmost Hellenic islands by capturing their principal prize, the island of Samos. After telling a complex tale of plot, counterplot, and the eventual Persian decimation of the population of Samos, Herodotus shifts to recounting the revolution of Babylon (521 B.C.E.) against Persian rule. Having thrown off the Persian yoke, the Babylonians boasted that Darius would retake their city "when mules bear offspring." In the 20th month of the resultant Persian siege, that very event occurred when a female mule foaled.

Herodotus ends the third book of his history by recounting the stratagems of the Persian general Zopyrus, who, by mutilating himself and conspiring with Darius to sacrifice a part of the Persian army, was able to pose as a disaffected deserter and gain command of the Babylonian forces. His sacrifice of his nose and ears and the lives of 5,000 Persian troops made possible a deception that resulted in the second Persian conquest of Babylon. As a reward, Darius made Zopyrus Babylon's governor for life.

Book 4

In Book 4—more aptly named by early editors for Melpomene, the Muse of Tragedy—Herodotus turns his attention to Darius's campaign against the Scythians. This people's homeland was in a section of what is now Russia. For 28 years, they had ruled over the highlands in the western portion of the Persian Empire. The Scythians considered themselves to be the most recently created race of human beings since they could only recount 1,000 years of history. They also thought that the land to their north was not habitable because of a continual fall of white feathers. (Herodotus felt sure this must be snow.)

The hero and demigod Heracles, reports Herodotus, fathered three boys with a half-woman, half-serpent. The youngest, Scythes, became the first king and sire of the entire Scythian people. Following this account of Scythian origins comes a lengthy account of the peoples to their east and to their north. As usual, the proportion of mythical to ethnographic detail rises with distance, but interesting admixtures of potentially factual information intrigue a reader. As an example, Herodotus details reports of a funeral custom of the Issodones—a known people. They eat the flesh of their deceased fathers, he says, and gild and preserve their heads. The latter custom was sometimes more recently observed among some eastern European Christians to preserve the relics of popularly canonized saints.

Herodotus also tells stories concerning the Hyperboreans—people dwelling beyond the north wind. This likely alludes to those ancient Baltic peoples who shipped their amber south.

The historian then attempts to describe what he thinks a map of the world should look like: two great, intersecting peninsulas. One of them contains Libya (by which at this point Herodotus seems to mean the African continent) and Asia. The second peninsula is that of Europe, which he thinks is larger. Though he has no clear idea of Europe's extent, he presents a credible account of one failed and one successful circumnavigation of Libya.

Herodotus next undertakes a catalogue of the rivers of Scythia and another of the gods of the Scythian pantheon. As is his usual practice, Herodotus normalizes the Scythian deities on the Greek model. He also discusses the Scythians' treatment of their enemies in warfare, a treatment that includes scalping. He reports the practices surrounding royal sickness and burial, and details the funeral customs practiced on the death of commoners. Among these is the custom of carrying a corpse to the homes of friends for 40 days. The friends entertain the deceased for this period

and then bury the remains. Herodotus also remarks on a Scythian steam bath that gives the bathers much pleasure. Having thus detailed what he knows of Scythia and its people, Herodotus returns to the Persian king Darius and his preparations for war against them.

Herodotus reports that Darius moved against the Scythians with a navy of 600 ships and an army of 700,000 men drawn from all the nations under Persian sway. The army marched across the Bosporus over a 20-mile-long bridge of ships. Herodotus follows the march of the army and catalogues the people it overcame in its march toward Scythia. He also tells of the provisions that Darius made for his return. Then the historian turns to the Scythians and enumerates the allies they recruited to resist the Persian onslaught.

At this point, Herodotus interjects the story of a group of Amazons whom the Greeks had captured. Having overcome and killed their captors aboard ship, the Amazons drifted ashore in Scythia. There they stole horses and began raiding the Scythian countryside. The historian details the fashion in which the Amazons eventually took young Scythian men as mates and established the separate society of the Sauromatae.

Unable to corner the nomadic Scythians for a decisive engagement, Darius eventually decided to give up his Scythian ambitions and withdrew toward the bridgehead he and his Ionian allies had established across the Ister (Danube) River. As the Persian army retreated in that direction, a Scythian vanguard attempted to persuade the Ionian rearguard contingent to destroy the bridge and withdraw in keeping with the orders that Darius had given them. Outnumbered, the Ionians pretended to agree, destroying as much of the bridge as they could quickly rebuild. Their leaders knew that they owed their offices and emoluments to Darius, and that if he were defeated at the hands of the Scythians, as the Greek rulers of Persian outposts in the Aegean, the Ionian leaders would soon be supplanted. The loyalty of the Ionians coupled with the mistakes of the Scythians enabled Darius and his host to narrowly escape destruction at Scythian hands.

In one of his associative digressions, Herodotus next recounts the tale of the Minyae, the descendants of Jason and the Argonauts by the women of the island of Lemnos (see *The* ARGONAUTIKA). Wishing to migrate to Sparta, the Minyae were first welcomed as settlers, then condemned to death for presumption, and finally fled from Sparta. The historian leaves it to the reader to draw the parallels between this story, its predecessor, and the story that follows.

In the following episode, Herodotus recounts the establishment of a Greek colony in Libya, the colony's subsequent growth, the conflict that expansion provoked with Libyan neighbors, their expulsion of the Greeks, and the appeal of their deposed queen Pheretime, to Aryandes, the Persian viceroy of Egypt, for military assistance against the Libyans. Using that appeal as a pretext, Herodotus thinks, Aryandes seized the opportunity to add Libya to the Persian Empire, planning to return Pheretime to Libya's throne as a Persian vassal. At the height of its power, that empire extended from Libya in the south and west, through Egypt, Palestine, and Mesopotamia, across the northern edge of the Arabian desert (whose dwellers were Persian allies), and east as far as the Indus River in the south and east. From there, the empire turned north through portions of what is now Afghanistan, then back east along the course of the Araxes River (the Aras River in Armenia), around the southern half of the Caspian Sea, and across the Balkans to the approximate center of the Grecian peninsula, including Macedonia.

Next Herodotus catalogues the lands and ethnography of Libya. Among those lands, he alludes to the land of the Gindanes, where, as in Homer's *Odyssey*, the inhabitants eat the fruit of the lotus. Among the other peoples he describes, we find the Ethiopian cave dwellers whose speech Herodotus compares to "the squeaking of bats." He also locates among the Libyans a tribe of dog-headed men, the *kynokepheloi*. By a complex process of myth making, they were later to become the source of legends surrounding the now-disavowed St. Christopher. Herodotus also locates

there a headless people whose eyes are in their breasts. Herodotus's remarks, however, indicate that he recognizes such folk as the product of Libyan fables.

Having devoted some 33 chapters to his discussion of Libyan ethnography, geography, and natural history, Herodotus resumes the story of the Persians' alliance with the exiled Pheretime. ("At Herodotean length" became a Greek epithet used to characterize long-windedness.) After an unsuccessful, nine-month siege of the city of Barce, the Persians tricked the citizens by breaking a truce and restored Pheretime to the throne, enslaving all those who had overthrown her. Herodotus ends Book 4 with a description of the awful death of Pheretime, an expression, as he thought, of the gods' anger at her excessive revenge against the revolutionaries of her city.

Throughout his *Histories*, Herodotus organizes his material in a highly associative and sometimes digressive fashion. This proves particularly to be the case in the fifth and sixth books of the historian's great work. Here as well, however, an attentive reader not only gains insight into the European ambitions and campaigns of the Persians and the sources of the developing enmity between Persians and Greeks, but also comes to understand Herodotus's own views on such matters as comparative systems of government and the way those systems compare and contrast with modern ones.

Book 5

Herodotus begins Book 5 (editorially named for Terpsichore, the Muse of the dance) by cataloguing the Persian general Megabyzus's campaign against the European Paeonians. Next follows an account of the misbehavior of Persian emissaries with the women of the Macedonian court and of the revenge that the Macedonian prince, Alexander the son of Amyntas, took for the insult by slaughtering the emissaries and successfully hushing up the matter.

After Herodotus details a revolt against Persian power led by Aristagoras of the island of

Miletus, he digresses to detail an ironic and unsuccessful attempt by the Spartan prince Dorieus to establish a colony, first in Libya and then in Sicily. Had Dorieus remained in Sparta, he would have soon become its king.

Returning to the main thrust of his discussion, Herodotus recounts the mission to Sparta of the tyrant of Miletus, Aristagoras, who brought with him to Sparta a bronze tablet engraved with a map of the known world. He unsuccessfully encouraged the Spartans to overcome the Persians and conquer it.

Herodotus then describes the royal road leading from Sardis in Ionian Asia Minor to the Persian capital at Susa. He explains that traveling the road involved three months' journey plus three extra days to reach Sardis from the seaport at Ephesus.

At Athens, Herodotus interjects here, Phoenician refugees led by Cadmus and arriving 60 years after the fall of Troy, first introduced the ALPHABET to the Greeks.

Herodotus then recounts the story of the way the Athenians rid themselves of despots and became a democracy. After tracing the Athenians' subsequent growth in power, Herodotus concludes that equality of the citizenry is a more effective civic arrangement than despotism because of the impetus that democracy lends to individual achievement.

Next come reports of the establishment of despots in several cities; of oracles and their interpretation; of the cold ghost of Melissa, whose burial garment was stolen, and the ghost's advice to her husband; and, eventually, of the way in which Hippias, a tyrant of Athens deposed in 510 B.C.E., encouraged the Persians to make war on the Athenians. At about the same time, after failing to interest the Spartans, Aristagoras the Milesian encouraged the Athenians to intervene against the Persians in Ionia in Asia Minor, where Athenian settlers had colonized the country. Persuaded, the Athenians sent 20 warships to the region. Those ships, Herodotus darkly declares, "were the beginning of trouble for Greeks and foreigners," for, encouraged by Athenian naval support, the Ionians began a general revolution against the Persians. Combined Athenian and Ionian forces began that uprising by attacking and destroying the Persian stronghold at Sardis. That destruction hardened the Persian king Darius's resolve to punish the Athenians.

Assisted by the Phoenicians, who were the Persians' usual naval allies, Darius's troops set off to regain control. They met forces of the Ionians and the Cyprians at sea and on land. The Ionians, encouraged by the courageous example of the men of the Island of Samos, defeated the Phoenician navy at sea. Despite the death of Artybius, the Persian commander, however the land forces did not fare so well, and after a year's freedom, the rebellious island of Cyprus fell once again under Persian control. Persian land forces also prevailed in Ionia and in nearby Aeolia. At the end of this book, Herodotus reports the death of Aristagoras of Miletus, the principal organizer of Athenian support of the Ionian revolutionaries.

Book 6

Later editors chose the name of Erato, Muse of the lyre, to adorn the section of Herodotus's history they assigned to Book 6. Using the death of Aristagoras as a transition, Herodotus turns to a discussion of Histiaeus, the tyrant of Miletus who had actually been the mastermind behind the revolt of the Ionians against their Persian overlords. Though Histiaeus had successfully deceived Darius concerning his complicity in the revolution, he failed to fool the Persian governor of Sardis, Artaphernes, who directly accused Histiaeus. Discovered in his treachery, Histiaeus fled to Miletus. There, however, the citizens repulsed him, wounding him in the thigh. He had better luck on the island of Lesbos, where the citizens of Mytilene gave him eight warships that he took with him to Byzantium. There he established a base of operations.

In the meantime, the Ionians on the islands of Asia Minor amassed a fleet of more than 200 vessels with which to face an enemy fleet of 600. The Ionians, though, were the better seamen, and the Persians feared their tactical advantage. Their commander, Dionysius of Phocaea, sought to improve that advantage by further training his Ionian seamen in the skills requisite to naval warfare, but their lack of discipline frustrated his efforts, and some of the revolutionaries began to think it best to return to Persian rule. When the sea battle was finally joined, despite heroic deeds by the Ionians, the Persians overcame them and took and sacked Militus.

The Persians spared the city of Samos because the commanders of its ships had deserted the Ionian navy. Those Samians who wished to be free of Persian domination migrated to Sicily. On all the other islands whose peoples had stood against them, the Persians implemented a policy of destroying the cities and mutilating the young men, selling both them and the women into slavery elsewhere. They removed the entire populations of the islands and settled them with loyal Persian subjects.

The Persians then sent a land and sea force under their commander, Mardonius, against the remaining cities of Ionia and from there across the Hellespont into Europe. It was this force under Mardonius that subdued the northern shore of the Aegean Sea and conquered Europe as far as Macedonia, which he also subdued. In doing so, he did something that Herodotus accounts as a wonder. Instead of co-opting or installing new tyrants in the cities he overcame, Mardonius established democratic governments. As a result of his efforts, Persian rule in southeastern Europe endured for half a century.

Heartened by Mardonius's success, Darius sent ambassadors to the cities of the Grecian mainland to propose that they buy peace by paying him tribute. Here Herodotus digresses to compare conflicting accounts of the origin of the Spartans' custom of having two kings, who were regularly at odds with one another. The historian continues this digression by discussing royal privileges, the organization of the Spartan state, some notable disagreements among her kings, and the doings of the king Cleomenes. Then the focus of the history shifts to a discussion of an armed disagreement between Athens and the island of Aegina. That done, Herodotus resumes his account of King Darius's attempt to subdue Athens and make all Greece a part of his empire.

Having taken Eretria and other cities on the large island of Euboea just off the Grecian mainland, the Persians sailed to Attica and the plain of Marathon, a place most suitable for their cavalry operations. Contrary to Persian expectations, instead of awaiting an onslaught inside their city's walls, the Athenians marched toward Marathon to meet the Persians. The Athenians sent a runner, Phidippides, to call the Spartans to arms against the Persians. Accosted by the god Pan on the way, Phidippides nonetheless covered the 150 miles in less than 24 hours and called the Spartans to arms. The Spartans replied that they could not undertake a campaign until the next full moon.

Herodotus then continues the story of one of the most notable and memorable feats of Athenian arms. While a deposed tyrant of Athens, Hippias the son of Pisistratus, was guiding the Persians to Marathon, the outnumbered Athenians, whose leaders voted 6-5 in favor of battle, arrayed themselves under the command of Miltiades for the contest at arms. Making their line strongest on the left and right, with the center only a few ranks deep, the Athenians, reinforced by men from the city of Platea, charged the Persians at a run. The Persians successfully pushed back the center, but the two flanks of the Greek army drove the Persians back and in a pincers movement closed in on those in the center. Overwhelmed, the Persians fled, and the Greeks pursued them to their ships, of which the Greeks captured seven.

Thinking that, if they could get to Athens first, they might find it unprotected, the Persians sailed there. The Athenian troops, however, rushed home and got there first. The Persians sailed for home. The adventure had cost them 6,400 men; the Athenians lost 192. Some critics have faulted the usually expansive Herodotus for cutting so short his account of one of the most important battles in the history of ancient

Greece. Arriving too late for the action, the tardy Spartans praised the Athenians for their splendid performance.

At this point, Herodotus digresses to discuss the wooing and winning of Agariste, the great-grandmother of Herodotus's good friend, the famous Athenian statesman Pericles. After tracing Pericles' subsequent genealogy, Herodotus returns to the story at hand.

A hero of Marathon, the general Miltiades, persuaded the Athenians to give him command of a fleet to begin the recapture of Athenian islands the Persians had taken. His military venture proved unsuccessful, however, and the fickle Athenians tried him for his failure. He forestalled their judgment by dying of gangrene contracted from a wound he had suffered. Herodotus ends the sixth book by telling how Miltiades had won the island of Lemnos for them.

Book 7

Book 7, bearing the name of Polymnia, the Muse of sacred music, opens with an account of the way Darius drafted troops for a much-enlarged army from all of his Asian dependencies. As Darius himself prepared to lead the next military adventure against the Greeks and also against a rebellious Egypt, his sons insisted that he name a successor before setting out. Darius selected Xerxes, the eldest son of his second marriage, since the children of the first marriage had been born before Darius became king. This provision for the succession proved fortunate, for Darius died within the year—in 486 B.C.E.—and Xerxes mounted the Persian throne.

Xerxes put down the rebellion in Egypt. Then, encouraged both by dissident Greeks and by his general, Mardonius, he turned his attention to punishing Athens. At a general council of the principal Persians, he announced his intention to bridge the Hellespont, raze the city of Athens, and subdue all of Europe. Herodotus reports that other advice and a series of prophetic dreams caused Xerxes to doubt the wisdom of his decision and waver between peace and war.

Finally, the prophetic dreams convinced him that war was the better option. After four years of preparation, in 481 B.C.E., Xerxes led a great host as far as Sardis. Herodotus describes some of Xerxes' preparations, including digging ship canals and bridging the Hellespont. He then recounts the march of the army from Sardis to the Hellespont and reports the forebodings of disaster delivered to Xerxes by his uncle Artabanus—forebodings that Xerxes ignored.

It took seven days and seven nights, reports Herodotus, for the Persian host of 170,000 to march across the bridge from Asia in Europe. Then the Persian army and the fleet began their march by land and voyage by sea toward Greece. Herodotus describes the dress and equipment of the soldiers of the various nations comprising the multitude, naming the commanders of each as well as the commanders in chief of the whole. After telling of the horses and camels that accompanied the army, he turns his attention to the navy, comprised of 1,207 triremes—armored warships propelled by three ranks of oars as well as sail. The historian continues by naming the nations that had furnished ships, the dress and equipment of the sailors, and the catalogue of their commanders. He gives special attention to the sole woman among their number, Artemisia, the tyrant of Herodotus's own city of Halicarnassus.

Herodotus next reports Xerxes' questioning a Greek exile, Demartus, about the Greeks' willingness to fight. Demartus praised the Greeks, particularly the Spartans, as fighting men and assured Xerxes that they would do battle.

Now the story follows Xerxes' line of march as, at city after city, he drafted soldiers, increasing the size of his army all along his route. At last the Persian host came in sight of the mountains of Thessaly, where Xerxes reconnoitered the outflow of the River Peneus. Then he sent heralds throughout Greece, promising to spare those who accepted his rule by sending him gifts of earth and water. Several Grecian cities did this. Xerxes sent no heralds to Athens or to Sparta, because heralds from Darius had been thrown into a pit at Athens and a well at Sparta and told to get earth and water there. Herodotus then digresses concerning the subject of the immunity of heralds from such treatment and the propensity of the gods to punish those who disregarded heralds' diplomatic status.

At this point, Herodotus expresses his opinion that Athens deserves most of the credit for saving Greece from Persian domination. As usual, the Athenians sought advice from the oracle of Apollo at Delphi to guide them in their response to the Persian threat. Also as usual, the advice of the oracle seemed ambiguous. Its central messages involved wooden forts and the island of Salamis.

The Athenian leader, Themistocles, led the contingent who thought that the wooden forts alluded to ships (which he had been provident enough to insist on building in a dispute with Aegina three years earlier) and that the island of Salamis might be an appropriate venue for a naval battle.

Herodotus tells of the efforts of emissaries from Athens and Sparta to enlist Gelo, a tyrant of Sicily, as an ally. He reports the failure of that effort and Gelo's duplicity in preparing for the victory of either the Persian or the Greek side. In similar fashion, Herodotus reports other attempts by the Greeks to enlist allies and the outcomes of those missions. Among the matters he details is the capitulation of the Thessalians to the Persians. Before that capitulation, however, it was they who told the Athenians of the narrow pass that the Persians would have to use through the mountains at Thermopylae.

Herodotus next details the numbers of Persian ships and troops that landed near Thermopylae. Herodotus's modern editors doubt the accuracy of the numbers he gives and estimate an invasion force of 300,000 men and about 750 ships. Only a few of those ships made landfall, however, before a three-day blow from the north wrecked the majority of the ships of the Persian fleet. Herodotus describes the fate of several ships that escaped the storm, and little by little, he approaches his description of the battle. He reports the way that the Spartans held against the repeated waves of Persian attacks, and how the Persians

were at a disadvantage because of the narrow pass and the greater length of the Greeks' spears. Then, however, Epialtes of Malis showed the Persians another route to the other side of the pass.

Learning that the Persians had found another way over the mountain and would soon be attacking, Leonidas, the leader of the Spartan troops, released the other allies and prepared to resist the Persians with just his own followers—men he could count on to fight to the death. All the allies left, except the 700 Thespians and Thebans, who stayed to fight beside the 300 Spartans—1,000 against the 300,000 Persians. The defenders at Thermopylae fought to the last man. Xerxes was so incensed at having so few men seriously interfere with his plan of conquest that he uncharacteristically had the fallen body of Leonidas mutilated. Herodotus, in an afterthought, recounts the way that the news of Xerxes' plans for Europe had been smuggled into Sparta, and the seventh book ends.

Book 8

Named for Urania, the Muse of astronomy, Book 8 shifts its opening focus to the war at sea that occurred simultaneously with the battles at Thermopylae. Herodotus enumerates the allies who furnished 378 ships to the Athenian fleet at Artemisium in Euboea, of which the Spartan, Eurybiades, was supreme commander. Bribes to the Athenian Themistocles and to Eurybiades overcame the commanders' initial reaction to flee when they saw the size of the fleet that the Persians were bringing against them.

A Persian tactic whose purpose was to seize the Greek fleet in a pincers movement failed when a storm wrecked the ships constituting one of the pincers' jaws. In the meantime, superior Greek tactics whittled away at the Persian ships comprising the other jaw. When the main battle was joined, the fleets were approximately equal in size.

The Persians and their allies had the worst of the battle, but the Greek losses were also numerous. Learning of the outcome at Thermopylae, the Greeks had a group of shepherds light numerous fires to deceive the Persians, and then they launched their remaining ships by night and withdrew to safer waters.

Herodotus next relates the skirmishes between the loyal Greeks of Phocis and the Greek allies of the Persians. He also recounts the Persian advance toward Athens and the army's pillaging. He then reports the apparently supernatural events that took place as the Persians were about to plunder the temple of Apollo at Delphi. Weapons stored inside unaccountably moved themselves outside, and two peaks of Mt. Olympus detached themselves amid lightning and thunder, burying many Persians in the resultant landslide and causing the remnant to withdraw.

Meanwhile, the Athenians and their allies continued mustering their fleet at Salamis. Simultaneously, in the city of Athens itself, news came that the Peloponnesians (Supporters and neighbors of Sparta on the Peloponnese peninsula) had decided not to try to defend Athens but rather to resist the Persians at the isthmus of Corinth. This caused most citizens to leave the city, save their families, and have able-bodied men join the fleet. That fleet, when assembled, was formidable.

A few Athenians remained behind and, as long as they were able, defended the Acropolis. Eventually, however, some Persians succeeded in scaling the rocks, killed the defenders, robbed the temple of Athena, and set everything afire.

Turning again to the fleet at Salamis, Herodotus reports the arguments of Themistocles of Athens that did not quite persuade the commanders of the squadrons of other cities to remain together and enjoy the advantage that fighting in the narrows gave the Greeks.

A similar council was taking place among the Persians, all of whom favored fighting the Greeks at sea except for Herodotus's countrywoman, Artemisia, who counseled against a sea fight. At this point, Herodotus whets the reader's anticipation for the outcome of the Battle of Salamis by digressing at some length to consider the preparations of the Peloponnesians to resist the Persian ground forces.

Finally, to force the Greek commanders to implement his plan, Themistocles sent a spy to the Persians with a false message: The Greeks planned to disperse. Believing the spy, the Persians moved their ships to block the Greek fleet, thus denying free passage to any who would sail away. This forced the Greeks to adopt Themistocles' plan.

The battle was long and bloody, and Herodotus lingers over the details—including one about the extraordinary bravery of his favorite Persian ally, Artemisia, in ways that suggest his greater interest in military action by sea than by land. Suffice it to say here that the Greeks won a signal victory. That triumph convinced Xerxes that retreat was in order lest his bridge over the Hellespont be destroyed and his forces stranded on the European side. He set about deceiving the Greeks about this intention, however, and sent messages by the Persian equivalent of the Pony Express—the most rapid message system of the ancient world—to the capital at Susa, informing citizens there of his misfortune. (A footnote of interest: Herodotus is the source of the motto of the United States Postal Service. "Neither snow nor rain," the historian says, nor "heat nor darkness" kept the Persian riders from getting through at full speed.)

When the news was dispatched to Susa, the general Mardonius who had advised Xerxes to undertake the European campaign feared that he might shoulder the blame. He therefore counseled Xerxes to go home and let him, Mardonius, take over in Europe, promising to subdue the Greeks. Asked for her opinion on the matter, Artemisia supported Mardonius, saying that if he failed, it would be no great matter. By destroying Athens, Xerxes had accomplished what he said he would.

Now Herodotus reports how Themistocles, playing both ends against the middle, accepted his subordinates' advice not to destroy the Persians' bridge across the Hellespont, lest the Persians, denied a road home, resume their ambitions. At the same time, Themistocles sent an embassy to Xerxes, explaining that he had persuaded the

Athenians not to destroy the bridge. Thereby the Athenian leader built a reservoir of gratitude in Xerxes that would later prove useful.

The Persians marched away to Thessaly, where Mardonius selected the men who would stay with him, and Themistocles led the navy around the Greek islands, demanding money from their inhabitants to forestall invasion and enriching himself thereby.

On its 45-day forced march back to the Hellespont, famine, plague, and dysentery beset the Persian forces returning with Xerxes. Those who arrived suffering from starvation found that a storm had broken the bridge, and they had to cross by ship. Once on the Asiatic side and provided with food, many ate immoderately and died when their systems could not stand the shock.

A detachment of Persians under the command of Artabazus returned to Europe to strengthen Mardonius's forces. Marching toward Thessaly, they besieged the cities of Olynthus and Potidea. What must have been a tidal wave wiped out the majority of the Persian besiegers, but in spring 479 B.C.E., a stalemate was reached. The Persians remained to the east of the island of Samos, and the Greeks remained west of the island of Delos. "Between them," says Herodotus, "was a space guarded by fear."

Herodotus's eighth book ends with an account of the Persian Mardonius's failed attempt to made a separate treaty with the Athenians—a treaty that would have imperiled the whole of Greece.

Book 9

Perhaps the editor who named Herodotus's ninth book for Calliope, the Muse of epic poetry, had in mind setting the historian's work on a par with the great epics of Homer. In any case, the final book in *The Histories* details the reoccupation of the Athenian region of Attica and the second destruction of Athens at Persian hands only 10 months after the first—a second destruction in part assured by the tardy response of the Spartans to Athenian pleas for assistance. Seeing that resistance was pointless without Spar-

tan help, the Athenian populace once more withdrew to Salamis, leaving an empty city to Persian wrath.

Herodotus also reports a banquet at which the citizens of the Greek city of Thebes entertained the officers of the Persian army. He describes a conversation in which one of the officers predicts disaster for the Persian army based on prophecies of which he and his fellow officers are aware, but to which Mardonius will not listen. "The most hateful of men's troubles," remarked the Persian, "is to have the wit but not the power."

Eventually the Spartans decided the time was ripe to face the Persian power once again, so with allies from the Peleponnesus and others, they marched into the region of Boetia. After feints and counterfeints, initial successes by Persian cavalry, the Persian interruption of the Spartan supply line, and the steadfastness of the Spartans in preventing a general Greek withdrawal, the battle of Plataea began in earnest. Herodotus now gives to a land battle the sort of loving attention he had earlier lavished on the sea battle at Salamis. He describes the order of battle of the armies, digresses to detail earlier battles in which various groups of combatants had participated, relates the oracles of each side and their interpretations, and rehearses the discussions held in the tents of the generals.

At Plataea, Greek tactics proved superior to Persian power. As is often the case with self-confident military powers, the Persians underestimated the skill, courage, and resolution of their enemies. Fighting from horseback, the Persian general Mardonius was killed. His loss threw the Persians into a panic. Moreover, as the Persians fought without armor, they were no match for the heavily armored Spartans, despite their superior numbers. The Persians fled, and the Greeks pursued them, hewing them down as they ran. The carnage was immense, and the Persian dead lay in heaps upon the battlefield. Of 300,000 Persians, 40,000 led by Artabazus escaped. Of the others who engaged in battle, fewer than 3,000 survived. Only 159 Greeks fell at the battle of Plataea.

Then Herodotus reports the deeds of several notable individuals, the disappearance of the body of Mardonius—apparently secretly buried—and the richness of the plunder that fell into the hands of the Greeks. He recounts as well the punishment of Thebes, whose soldiers had fought with the Persians, and the escape of the Persian general Artabazus to Asia with the remnant of the soldiers he led.

The historian turns his attention once more to the fortunes of the Greeks at sea, among the Ionian islands, and in Asia Minor, where the Greeks won another great battle on land and sea at Mycale near Ephesus on the same day of the victory at Platea (479 B.C.E.). There the Greeks destroyed both the Persian fleet and the Persian army.

Turning from warfare to a tale of love, betrayal, intrigue, and revenge, Herodotus details a love affair between Xerxes and his daughter-in-law, Artaynte, the wife of Darius, and the bloody result of the liaison as Xerxes' wife avenged the insult on a woman she knew to have been the go-between in the affair.

Herodotus concludes the final book of his history by describing the Greek mopping-up operations in Asia Minor, digressing occasionally to speak of relevant matters from the distant past. Organized principally around the central theme of the enmity between the Asians and the Europeans, Herodotus's work weaves a vast tapestry of historical events, the deliberations and deceptions of powerful persons, geography, ethnography, tales told in the expansive manner, myths that Herodotus recognizes as such, comparative reports of the same incidents from two or more points of view, portents and prophecies, and charming digressions that, in the mind of the author at least, seem always relevant to his themes and interests.

Bibliography

Herodotus. *Herodotus*. 4 vols. Translated and edited by A. D. Godley. Cambridge, Mass.: Harvard University Press, 1946.
———. *The Histories/Herodotus*. Translated by Donald Lateiner. New York: Fine Creative Media, 2004.
———. *The Histories*. Translated by Robin Waterfield. Oxford: Oxford University Press, 1998.
———. *The Histories of Herodotus of Halicarnassus*. 2 vols. Translated by Harry Carter. New York: The Heritage Press, 1958.

History of the Former Han Dynasty

(Hanshu, Han Shu) Ban Gu, Ban Biao, and Ban Zhao (ca. 50 C.E.)

To a considerable degree, *History of the Former Han Dynasty* is modeled on the SHIHJI (*Shi-chi*) (*Records of the Grand Historian*) of SIMA QIAN (Ssŭ-ma Ch'ien). Just as Sima had continued his father's history, Ban Gu's (Pan Ku's) book continues work begun by Ban Gu's father, Ban Biao (Pan Piao). From Sima, Ban Gu borrowed his general plan of organization, including annals, biographies, chronological tables, and treatises, punctuated occasionally with songs and poems. Although almost half of Ban Gu's history simply reproduces the *Records of the Grand Historian*, it nonetheless contains certain innovative features. It is, for instance, the earliest Chinese work of history to focus exclusively on an account of a single dynasty.

Beyond that focus, in the sections that he originated, Ban Gu more carefully followed his primary source material than his predecessor historian had done. As the literary historian William Nienhauser, Jr., suggests, this care appears especially in Ban Gu's biographical portraits, where he is at pains to achieve accuracy. His organization of that biographical material, however, attempts to illustrate overarching points about the moral characters of the figures he memorializes. For example, he groups together his portraits of persons who used trickery and deception to accomplish their political ends and who were later discovered and punished. He then contrasts those figures with others who achieved their ends by more admirable means and prospered. As an historian, Ban Gu strives for greater realism than did Sima Qian, but in the process he lacks some of Sima's power to use biography for illustrating general historical trends.

Probably because of the virtual identity of long sections of Ban Gu's work with parts of the *Rec-*

ords of the Grand Historian, as of this writing the entire History of the Former Han Dynasty has not been translated into English or any other Western European language. Important sections of it have been, however, and in these partial translations the interested English speaker can learn of such matters as the early political role of China in Central Asia or about the circumstances surrounding the rise to power of the usurping ruler Wang Mang (ruled 9–23 C.E.). One can see an example of Ban Gu's biographical style in a translation of a section on Yang Xiong (Yang Hsiang). One can also discover information concerning the diet and the coinage in the former Han dynasty, as well as the social distinctions between the elite and the common people

Songs, too, sometimes appear in Ban Gu's history. One charming one is a homesick song of lament by a young bride who has been married off to the king of Wu-sun—a yurt-dwelling nomad whose language she cannot speak. Another is a song of mourning sung by the parents and townspeople of a group of young men whose bad behavior had resulted in their being rounded up by the local authorities and cast into a sealed pit to die.

Ban Gu himself met with a lamentable fate. Suspected of being implicated in the treasonous activities of a general, he was imprisoned for "investigation"—presumably by torture. He did not survive his ordeal, and sections of the "Treatises" and "Chronological Tables" of his history remained unfinished. The emperor solved this problem by sending for Ban Gu's sister—Ban Zhao (Pan Chao). Atypically for a woman of the period, she was a competent scholar in her own right. The emperor ordered that Ban Zhao finish the work and instruct other Han scholars in its meaning and utility, which she did. Ban Zhao survived until about 116 C.E.

Bibliography

Ban Gu. The Han shu Biography of Yang Xiong (53 B.C.–A.D. 18). Translated by David R. Knechtges. Tempe: Center for Asian Studies, Arizona State University, 1982.

Dubs, Homer H., trans. The History of the Former Han Dyunasty by Pan Ku: A Critical Translation. Baltimore: Waverly Press, 1938- [?].

Hulsewé, A. F. P., trans. China in Central Asia: The Early Stages, 125 B.C.–A.D. 23: An Annotated Translation of Chapters 61 and 96 of The History of the Former Han Dynasty. Leiden: Brill, 1979.

Nienhauser, William, Jr. "Early Biography." In The Columbia History of Chinese Literature. Edited by Victor H. Mair. New York: Columbia University Press, 2001.

Sargent, Clyde Bailley, trans. Wang Mang: A Translation of the Official Account of His Rise to Power as Given in the History of the Former Han Dynasty. Westport, Conn.: Hyperion Press, 1977.

Swan, Nancy Lee, trans. Food and Money in Ancient China: The Earliest Economic History of China to A.D. 25: Han Shu 24 and 91, and Shiji 129. New York: Octagon Books, 1974.

Tjan Tjoe Som, trans. Po Hu T'ung. The Comprehensive Discussions in the White Tiger Hall. 2 Vols. Leiden: E. J. Brill, 1949–52.

Watson, Burton. Early Chinese Literature. New York: Columbia University Press, 1962.

———, trans. Courtier and Commoner in Ancient China: Selections from the History of the Former Han. New York: Columbia University Press, 1974.

Homer (fl. eighth or ninth century B.C.E.)
Greek epic poet

Several locations for Homer's birthplace have been proposed. These include Smyrna, Ioma, Asia Minor, and elsewhere, but no certainty attaches to any of these possibilities. Scholars have generally rejected the suggestion that Homer was blind. More likely are claims that he resided for a long time in Chios and that he died on the island of Got. Certainty on any of these matters may never emerge.

Though some have argued against his existence and others against his authorship, Homer is traditionally credited with having composed two EPIC poems on subjects connected with the

Trojan War (ca. 1200 B.C.E.) and its aftermath. *The ILIAD* derives its title from Troy's other name, Ilium or Ilion, in honor of the city's founder, Ilus. *The Iliad* is set during the last year of the 10-year war and focuses on the consequences arising from the anger of the Greek warrior hero, Achilles. The poem also interweaves a moving discourse that recounts the conditions within the besieged city, the state of mind of many of Troy's inhabitants, and accounts of episodes drawn from the war itself.

The ODYSSEY recounts the adventures of one of the Greek generals, Odysseus, king of Ithaca, as he navigates the Mediterranean Sea in an extended, thrill-packed, and dangerous voyage home. The poem also examines the passage of the hero's son Telemachus from boyhood to manhood and details the strategies and tactics of Odysseus's faithful wife, Penelope, as she holds at bay a pack of suitors who want her to acknowledge that her husband must be dead and to marry one of them.

The oldest extant poems in any Western European language, Homer's works establish the model for all subsequent epics in the Western tradition. Like Homer's, the succeeding epics begin in the middle of the action, are populated with gods and heroes, make use of flashbacks, involve a journey to the underworld, and consider matters on a grand scale—matters of national, international, or even universal importance. Their language is elevated, and the style of their versification is dignified. Homer chose dactylic hexameter as the meter that approximated the cadences of ordinary language and also imparted to his verse an underlying structure that established a reader's metrical expectation (see QUANTITATIVE VERSE). A reader or listener grew to anticipate a certain metrical pattern, and, by subtly varying his style, Homer could satisfy his reader's expectations or achieve a pleasing surprise.

Homer worked at a moment that either coincided with or slightly anticipated the Greeks' adoption of the ALPHABET to record their language. In the texts as they have been transmitted to us, scholars have discovered evidence of an ORAL-FORMULAIC TRADITION. In the formation of both Western and non-Western epic poems, it appears that older, shorter stories and legends coalesced into lengthier ones. The episodes that comprise *The GILGAMESH EPIC* seem to have come together by a similar process. Sometimes this collecting of stories was done by country poets and sometimes by professional entertainers. Many speculate that Homer was one of the entertainers who, while accompanying themselves on a stringed instrument, amused the aristocratic classes by reciting or singing lengthy retellings of the accomplishments of the hearers' forebears. The poems' length posed no impediment to their memorization as this feat was routinely accomplished by school children for more than 1,000 years.

Once the texts of such performances had been written down, they became largely fixed, and the surviving versions passed from generation to generation, usually without major revision. The evidence of a preceding oral tradition, however, can be observed in often-repeated phrases that a performer could have used to fill out the verse expectations of lines or as aids to memory. In Homer, such epithets as "rosy-fingered dawn" or "Odysseus, son of Laertes" occur with some frequency and suggest oral performance.

Over the centuries, Homer's readers, perhaps yielding to the temptation of reading the author's biography into his work, have occasionally identified the poet with the blind entertainer Demodocus, who sings at the court of Alcinous. That identification has sometimes led to the assertion that Homer was himself blind. However, during the period 1870–81, when Heinrich Schliemann undertook to find and excavate the ruins of Troy and the subsequent communities that had occupied its site, the descriptions of landmarks in his copy of *The Iliad* helped him identify the mound of the citadel. Perhaps a sighted Homer, too, had visited the famous battlefield some 400 years after the war and some 2,200 before Schliemann.

It seems that the early Greek poet HESIOD, working shortly after Homer, knew the Homeric poems and attributed them to Homer's hand. A number of emulators of Homer's manner, collectively known as the HOMERIDAE, alleged their descent from Homer and worked as entertainers. Skeptics about the existence of a single poet named Homer sometimes attribute to the Homeridae the authorship of the Homeric epics.

Bibliography

Allen, Susan Heuck. *Finding the Walls of Troy: Frank Calvert and Heinrich Schliemann at Hisarlik.* Berkeley: University of California Press, 1999.

Bloom, Harold, ed. *Homer's The Iliad* [a study guide]. Philadelphia: Chelsea House, 2005.

Homer. *The Iliad.* Translated by Robert Fitzgerald. New York: Farrar, Straus & Giroux, 2004.

———. *The Odyssey.* Translated by Edward McCrorie. Baltimore: Johns Hopkins University Press, 2004.

Schliemann, Heinrich. *Troja: Results of the Researches and Discoveries on the Site of Homer's Troy* and *in the Heroic Tumuli and Other Sites, made in the year 1882.* New York: Harper and Brothers, 1884.

Homeridae (Sons of Homer)

The word *Homeridae* refers to a group of kinsmen living on the island of Chios off the coast of Asia Minor. The natives of Chios insisted that the island was the birthplace of HOMER, and the Homeridae claimed descent from the ancient poet. As a clan, they practiced the profession of entertainers, minstrels, and poets. Often attributed to the Homeridae are later poems of uncertain authorship that were written in the manner of Homer. Those students of ancient Greek literature who doubt Homer's authorship of the EPIC poems *The ILIAD* and *The ODYSSEY* sometimes attribute them to the Homeridae.

The Homeridae have also sometimes been called the rhapsodists, and the ancients alluded to

them as the cyclic poets. The former label came about because they also composed hymns and religious introductions to their performances. The latter label resulted from the fact that the Homeridae confined the subjects of their composition to two cycles of stories: those having to do with the events associated with Greek myths of origin and those having to do with the Trojan War and its attendant events.

Bibliography

Eschenberg, Johann J., and N. W. Fiske. *Manual of Classical Literature.* Philadelphia: E. C. & J. Biddle, 1850.

Horace (Quintus Horatius Flaccus)
(65 B.C.E.–8 C.E.)

Born Quintus Horatius Flaccus on December 8, 65 B.C.E., to the family of a manumitted slave in the community of Venusia, south Italy, Horace must have been a child of unusual promise. His father collected payments at tax auctions, was probably paid on commission, and apparently accumulated a substantial estate. It was enough that he could afford to give Horace a first-rate education, sending him first to Rome, where he studied with the teacher Orbilius Pupillus. Horace reports that Orbilius did not spare the rod in supervising the boy's education.

Horace next traveled to Athens to continue his studies. The Roman Civil Wars began while Horace was there, and he joined the army of Marcus Iunius Brutus, receiving a commission as a tribune—a post that made him a commander of a cohort of cavalry. When the forces of Mark Antony and Octavian (later to become Rome's first emperor, AUGUSTUS CAESAR) defeated Brutus at Philippi in 42, Horace fled and, on his return to Italy, formally submitted to the victors' authority. He did not escape punishment for having supported the losing side and was stripped of all his Venusian property.

Perhaps through his Roman connections, Horace managed to secure a post as a clerk in the office of the quaestor—a civic magistrate. He began to supplement a slender income by publishing verses. His success as a poet brought him to the attention of VIRGIL and of the tragedian and EPIC poet Varius Rufus. They in turn brought Horace into the circle of poets generously patronized by Augustus Caesar's principal minister, confidante, and counselor, Gaius Maecenas.

Maecenas was an enlightened literary patron who understood that gifted authors need time and leisure to write. Certain of Horace's gifts after the appearance of the first book of the poet's SATIRES (35 B.C.E.), around 33 B.C.E. Maecenas conferred on the young man an idyllic property known as the Sabine Farm in the valley of the Licenza River. Relieved of financial necessity by the farm's produce, and inspired by the property's beauty to write some of his most charming verse, Horace passed a productive bachelorhood on the estate. He became a friend of Augustus Caesar and the semi-official poet laureate of his court, but he declined the emperor's suggestion that he become his confidential secretary.

Horace's second book of *Satires* appeared around 30–31 B.C.E., as did a collection of EPODES in which he brought together both newer works and some of his earlier writing. In 24 B.C.E. appeared the first three books of Horace's famous ODES, which treated the poet's reflections on contemporary Roman history. The last of the *Odes*, the 30th of book 3, reveals that Horace knew exactly how to value himself as a poet. "I have," he wrote, "completed a monument more enduring than bronze."

The next year, Horace announced that he was retiring from active participation in the Roman literary scene to study philosophy. Perhaps his military service had deprived him of an opportunity to do so at Athens. It is, however, unclear that the study of philosophy brought him the sorts of benefits that he expected. When he emerged from his self-imposed exile from the realm of poetry, he became essentially what he was before: a "spokesman . . . for education, culture, and san-

ity," to borrow the words of Horace's biographer, Kenneth J. Reckford.

Horace returned to his tasks as a writer, and the year 20 B.C.E. saw the appearance of the first book his EPISTLES. That year was also the most likely date for the appearance of the work that posterity has dubbed his *Ars Poetica* (The ART OF POETRY). In 17 B.C.E., Horace composed a series of secular songs (*Carmen Saeculare*) to be performed at the secular games of the city of Rome. In 13 B.C.E., the fourth book of his *Odes* appeared, as did *Epistles,* book 2, part 1.

Horace died on November 27, 8 B.C.E. Posterity is fortunate that Horace was among the subjects treated somewhat over a century after his death by the Roman biographer SUETONIUS. According to Suetonius, Horace was short, portly, and, after a youth during which his curling black locks moved many a young woman's heart, he went prematurely gray.

One can hardly overstate the influence of Horace's taste, good sense, and poetic mastery, not only on the expansion of the capacities of Roman verse for subtlety of expression, but also on the subsequent course of European and American letters. His work became the model for and the standard toward which such English poets as Alexander Pope and John Milton strove. They, in turn, were models for later practitioners of the art of poetry in the English language.

Bibliography

Horace. Collected Works. Translated by Lord Dunsany and Michael Oakley. New York: Dutton, 1961.

———. *The Complete Works of Horace.* Edited by Casper J. Kramer, Jr. New York: Modern Library, 1936.

———. *The Complete Works: Translated in the Meters of the Originals.* Translated by Charles E. Passage. New York: F. Ungar Publishing Company, 1983.

———. *Horace in English.* Edited by D. S. Carne-Ross and Kenneth Haynes. London: Penguin Books, 1966.

———. *The Odes of Horace: Newly Translated from the Latin and Rendered into the Original Metres.* Translated by Helen Rowe Henze. Norman: University of Oklahoma Press, 1961.

Reckford, Kenneth J. *Horace.* New York: Twayne Publishers, 1969.

"How a Man May Become Aware of His Progress in Virtue" Plutarch
(first century C.E.)

In this essay from his MORALIA, addressed to his Roman friend, Quintus Sosius Senecio, PLUTARCH attacks two principles taught by Stoic philosophy (see STOICISM). The Stoics argued, first, that only a wise person could be virtuous and that both wisdom and virtue were acquired instantly and simultaneously in a sudden transformation of a person's life. Second, they maintained that any small imperfection in either wisdom or virtue ruined the entire edifice of a person's goodness and right thinking. Dissenting from that viewpoint, Plutarch maintains that acquiring both wisdom and virtue proceeds by stages, and that people can recognize marks of their own progress.

Successful vigilance against vice in its various seductive forms is one mark of progress on the road to virtue, says Plutarch. A more serious demeanor and greater dedication to the task at hand in a course of study together with a greater compulsion to pursue it provides a sure indicator of the acquisition of wisdom. So does a calm and equable disposition—one slow to anger and patient in pursuit of virtuous goals and the acquisition of knowledge and good judgment.

The capacity, too, to hold depression at bay when progress is slow and difficult is a mark of wisdom. So is a gentle and reliable manner of dealing with others, particularly when one disagrees with them. Plutarch also counsels tracking one's words and actions to be sure that "usefulness" rather than "ostentation" characterizes them. Also, a person should have no need of the opinions or praises of others to take pride in his good deeds. The deed itself is the good and wise person's adequate reward. The more advanced one becomes in wisdom and in virtue, the less will be their conceit and the lower their opinions of themselves.

The wise and the good also do not shrink from the criticism and reproof of others when they have been foolish or vicious. Rather, they admit their mistakes and seek such help as may be necessary to rectify them. Wise persons listen to the accusations of their revilers as if their best friends were praying for their success.

Plutarch also considers the dream life of the wise and virtuous to be a mark of progress on the road to perfection when the dreams become free of vicious and foolish matter. Satisfaction with one's lot in life is another mark of wisdom and virtue. So is acting on one's judgments about what needs doing rather than simply talking about it.

Imitating persons one admires for wisdom and virtue provides another indicator that a person in on the right road. So is the ability to approach an admired person without fear and to seek that person's advice—or, in the person's absence, to ask the question: "What would Plato, Lycurgus, or whoever else one admires for wisdom and goodness have done?" If answering that question keeps one on the path to wisdom and virtue, Plutarch considers it a sure sign of progress.

Finally, a person who seeks to be both wise and good will consider all faults, great or small, as equally worthy of attention and will strive first to diminish them and at last to obliterate them altogether.

Bibliography

Plutarch. "How a Man May Become Aware of his Progress in Virtue." In *Plutarch's Moralia.* Vol. 1. Translated by Frank Cole Babbitt. Cambridge Mass.: Harvard University Press, 1960.

"How to Profit by One's Enemies"
Plutarch (ca. 96 C.E.)

Originally given as a speech, this essay (from MORALIA), addressed to PLUTARCH's Roman friend, Cornelius Pulcher (a civil administrator), takes its title from a remark of XENOPHON OF ATHENS on the same subject. An enemy, says PLUTARCH, is ever alert to find some flaw in one's life that the enemy can seize upon to do a person harm. Recognizing this, it behooves one to lead as flawless a life as possible so that the enemy may not take advantage of one's mistakes, vices, and failures.

Second, Plutarch advises people to treat their enemies kindly. At the same time, one should become acquainted with an enemy's flaws and vices and then compare oneself with the enemy to see if some of the same flaws and vices persist within oneself. If so, one should be at pains to root them out. Some have argued, for example, that during World War II, the Allies lost a good deal of moral authority when they emulated the Nazi practice of firebombing civilian populations. A similar loss of virtue might be thought to attach to the practice of torture.

Moreover, says Plutarch, when an enemy reviles a person, it can have the effect of turning that person from error if what the enemy says is true. If what the enemy says is false, Plutarch nevertheless advises a thorough self-examination of one's behavior to see what might have given rise to the calumny. The best thing to do when an enemy reviles one is to remain silent. Thus, one gains practice in patient forbearance and profits from the enemy's hostile behavior.

Responding to an enemy's hostility with kindness may sometimes negate the enmity and produce an advantage for everyone. Moreover, if one deals kindly with one's enemy, one reinforces benevolent behavior in oneself in general, reducing quarrels and thus benefiting all.

Finally, Plutarch advises his readers to study an enemy's successes as well as his failures. Thus, one may improve oneself by imitating the former and avoiding the latter.

Early Christians approved very highly of this essay, and it was among the reasons that some of them prayed that the soul of Plutarch might be excepted from the universal exclusion from Heaven thought to be the fate of non-Christian people.

Bibliography

Plutarch. "How to Profit by One's Enemies." In *Plutarch's Moralia*. Vol. 2. Translated by Frank Cole Babbitt. Cambridge, Mass.: Harvard University Press, 1962.

Huainanzi (Huai-nan Tzu) Liu An
(139 B.C.E.)

The Han dynasty of the second century B.C.E. encouraged scholars to engage in the intellectual enterprise of attempting to construct a theory of the fundamental nature of the universe—a cosmology—that would be consonant with the principles of DAOISM. The local king of Huainan, Liu An, undertook meeting this challenge by having his scholars bring together a series of treatises addressing the subject. The result of their effort, the *Huainanzi,* contains a third chapter entitled Tianwenxun "(Tien wen hsün; Treatise on the patterns of heaven). At first, as the literary historian Michael Pruett explains the chapter's content, all was formless. From archetypal formlessness, the universe shaped itself into *qi* (ch'i)—a substance composed of parts with varying compositions. The subtler constituents of *qi* drifted upward and became heaven. The heavier bits settled downward and became earth. The essences of heaven and earth emerged and became *yang* and *yin*—the archetypal masculine and feminine principles of the universe. These principles then interacted, producing fire, water, the seasons of the year, and the other characteristics that give the universe its form and content. All of this occurred spontaneously without the necessity of supernatural intervention of any sort.

Moreover, all parts of the resultant universe are linked. A stimulus in one sector will stimulate a response elsewhere—a principle eerily supported by the discoveries of modern science. As human beings are a part of this universal mix and also take part in its essential nature, a truly wise person will seek to act spontaneously and in consonance with cosmic harmony.

Elsewhere in the work, Liu An's scholars caution their readers about the mistakes and the superstition that had crept into Confucian doctrine over time. Using careful principles of textual criticism, for instance, they demonstrated that the supernatural behavior of pigs in a widely circulated Confucian story had originated with a misreading of a Chinese graph that named a day but was similar to a character used for the word *pig*. The scholars admonish the Confucian true believers that venerating ancient texts is a less reliable guide for human affairs than examining matters in the light of logic. This is particularly true for the art of ruling a nation—the topic that most centrally concerns the *Huainanzi*.

Bibliography

Ames, Roger T. *The Art of Rulership: A Study of Ancient Chinese Political Thought.* Albany: State University of New York Press, 1962.

Pruett, Michael. "Philosophy and Religion in Early China." In *The Columbia History of Chinese Literature.* Edited by Victor H. Mair. New York: Columbia University Press, 2001.

Watson, Burton. *Early Chinese Literature.* New York: Columbia University Press, 1962.

hubris

Overweening human pride, or hubris, was the characteristic that the gods in ancient European literature found most objectionable. Hubris invariably led those who displayed it into difficulty. HOMER's Odysseus, for instance, after having been given a favorable wind to send him home to Ithaca, attempted to exceed the capacities of human beings by refusing to allow any but himself to handle the ship's tiller while he stayed awake nine days and nights. He also kept to himself the knowledge that a bag he had brought on board contained all the unfavorable winds. Finally and inevitably, within sight of his goal, Odysseus dropped, exhausted. His crew, thinking that Odysseus meant to keep a treasure concealed in the bag for himself, opened it. All the imprisoned winds rushed out at once, producing a hurricane that blew the ship back to its starting point on the island of Aeolia.

Because Homer's ODYSSEY is essentially comic, that episode is only one of a series of setbacks Odysseus experiences before reaching his home in Ithaca and recovering his former kingdom and his family. Such, however, is not the case for those who display hubris with tragic outcomes.

We find such a figure in SOPHOCLES' tragedy *OEDIPUS TYRANNUS*. There Oedipus imagines that he can identify the killer of the former king of Athens and free the city from the curse of a plague that is afflicting its citizens. Although the prophet Teiresias warns Oedipus not to pursue the matter, his confidence in his own capacities eventually destroys his happiness when he discovers that he himself is the cause of the plague. He learns that he is the murderer of his father and is also the incestuous husband of his mother by whom he has fathered children. His wife and mother Iocasta commits suicide, and Oedipus blinds himself and goes into exile.

As many a tragic hero in the Greco-Roman world discovered, the gods will punish hubris.

See also TRAGEDY IN GREECE AND ROME.

hymns to Zeus, Apollo, Artemis, and others Callimachus (ca. 285 B.C.E.)

In the first of his hymns, "To Zeus," CALLIMACHUS begins by asking how one can praise the king of the gods. The poet then rehearses the god's sometimes-disputed history: Was Zeus born on Crete or in Arcadia? "Cretans are always liars," Callimachus decides and opts for Arcadia, upon whose then-waterless wasteland the Titaness Rheia (the earth) bore her son by Chronos (time). (See also TITANS.) In the instant of Zeus's birth, the parched plain brought forth water to wash the mother and her newborn. From Arcadia, Callimachus traces Zeus's journey to Crete, where he was hidden from his father, who had eaten all his previous offspring. The poet recalls Zeus's upbringing and the way the demigods called Kuretes beat upon their shields so that Chronos would not hear the baby crying.

Commenting on the beauty of the god in childhood, Callimachus passes quickly on to consider the question of Zeus's victory over Chronos and his leadership of the other Olympian gods. That leadership was owing to strength and power, Callimachus concludes, and for that reason Zeus is the exclusive patron of kings and the rulers of cities.

Having established that patronage, Callimachus points out that Zeus has not equally honored and enriched all kings, and he chooses this moment to slip into his hymn to the king of the gods a compliment to the poet's own ruler, Ptolemy II. Also called Ptolemy Philadelphos, that king had honored the poet with a responsible position in the library Ptolemy built at Alexandria. His own earthly king, Callimachus assures us, is by far preeminent in power and wealth among the rulers of the earth, and his projects are accomplished immediately. Callimachus ends his hymn with a double salute to Zeus and a prayer for both goodness and wealth since wealth alone is worthless and goodness "needs substance."

Callimachus's second hymn, "To Apollo," celebrates the patron deity of archers and poets, the deity who draws his power from the right hand of Zeus. Among the aspects of Apollo that Callimachus praises are some that later appear as characteristics of Christ. In addition to carrying out the will of Zeus, Apollo is called "pastor," a shepherd, and he is the god of light. Callimachus also celebrates Apollo's role as a founder of cities. He links that detail to his own ancestor Battus—a general with the same name as Callimachus's father. The elder Battus founded Cyrene in Libya—the city of Callimachus's birth. The poet further links his own profession as a cataloguer of books to Apollo, mentioning that the god is indexed under *Boëdrómios*, *Klários*, and *Karneîos*. Libyans like himself especially, Callimachus asserts, honor the god.

Callimachus's translator, Stanley Lombardo, suggests that the hymn's final stanza enlists Apollo as the poet's ally in support of short, pithy, and allusive poems instead of long EPIC ones. The allegorical figure Envy whispers in Apollo's ear that

Envy is "charmed by the poet who swells like the sea." Lombardo glosses this line as implying that those who are jealous of Callimachus's poetic skill suggest to Apollo that they prefer poets like HOMER, whose work is as copious as the ocean. But Apollo reproves this point of view. The god suggests that the flow of the river Euphrates, though abundant, also carries mud and refuse. The poets, who are like bees, the makers of honey and wax, are responsible for producing the honey's sweetness and light from beeswax candles, though their production be as slender as "the trickling dew" from the height of a holy spring.

Callimachus's charming "Hymn to Artemis" opens by reminding the reader that poets do well not to neglect the goddess of the hunt and recalls that beyond hunting, she enjoys dancing. Then the scene shifts, and we find a preteen goddess, sitting on the knee of her father Zeus and begging for privileges and gifts. She wants to stay a virgin forever and be known by as many names as her brother Apollo. She wants a bow and arrows—not too fancy a set. She describes the clothes she wants to wear and requests certain companions. These include 60 nine-year-old sea nymphs, daughters of Ocean, as dancing girls, and 20 wood nymphs as maids and dog tenders after the hunt.

Artemis wants all the mountains in the world and one town. She promises to fulfill her destiny to relieve the pangs of women in childbirth since she herself caused her mother no pain.

Zeus is so pleased with his little daughter that he grants her all she asks and gives her 30 cities, not just one, for herself alone, and several other cities and islands to share with other deities. He also makes her the patron deity of harbors and roads.

Artemis next goes traveling to collect her father's gifts. She gathers her retinue and goes off to Mt. Etna to watch the three Sicilian Cyclopes fashion her weapons. She next stops at Arcadia, where Pan presents her with hunting hounds. She then catches four of five golden-horned deer to pull her chariot.

Once he has her fully equipped, Callimachus sings briefly of each of the major episodes associated with the myths featuring Artemis. He ends his poem with a greeting and a prayer that she will hear his song and receive it graciously.

Other extant hymns of Callimachus include one addressed to the island of Delos—the birthplace of Apollo, another entitled "The Bath of Pallas [Athena]," and a third addressed to Demeter, the goddess of corn and patron of agriculture.

Bibliography

Callimachus. *Callimachus: Hymns, Epigrams, Select Fragments.* Translated by Stanley Lombardo and Diane Rayor. Baltimore and London: Johns Hopkins University Press, 1988.

Trypanis, C. A., ed. and trans. *Callimachus: Aetia, Iambi, Hecale, and Other Fragments.* Loeb Classical Library. Vol. 421. Cambridge, Mass.: Harvard University Press, 1975.

"Hymn to Aphrodite" (7th C. B.C.E.) Sappho

Had it not been quoted in its entirety by DIONYSUS OF HALICARNASSUS, SAPPHO's lovely, brief invocation of the goddess of love would have been totally lost to the modern world. Instead, it calls out to contemporary readers across three millennia in the voice of a female poet who sings with such unparalleled beauty that the ancients called her the 10th Muse.

Aware that few modern English readers have the qualifications to read Sappho in her original dialectical Greek, Margaret Reynolds, in her discussion of the poet, has provided for consideration not only Sappho's Aolic Greek dialect but also several English renderings of Sappho's song. Among those Reynolds offers, the translations of Mary Barnard (1958) and Suzy Q. Groden (1964) strike me as coming closest to catching the music of Sappho's verse.

The poet begins her song by invoking the goddess Aphrodite and inviting her to come in her sparrow-drawn chariot from the throne of Zeus to Sappho's aid. The goddess appears and, smiling, asks Sappho what her heart (called "mad" by one translator and "distracted" by the other) wants now.

The goddess, of course, already knows the answer to that question and promises that the woman who currently flees Sappho's love will soon become the pursuer and that, if the goal of Sappho's quest now rejects Sappho's proffered gifts, she soon will offer gifts of her own. The goddess promises that if the object of Sappho's affection does not currently return Sappho's love, she will do so soon, even if that occurs against the beloved's will.

In the poem's final stanza, the poet again asks the goddess to be her ally in pursuit of the object of her affection.

Bibliography

Reynolds, Margaret. *The Sappho Companion.* New York: Palgrave, 2001.

I

Iambichlus of Syria See FICTION AS EPISTLE, ROMANCE, AND EROTIC PROSE.

I ching See BOOK OF CHANGES.

Idylls Theocritus (mid–third century B.C.E.)
Though more than 30 poems have traditionally been included in THEOCRITUS's *Idylls*, 20th-century scholarship has reduced the number for confident attribution to the 22 cited in this entry. These poems fall into a variety of subcategories: pastorals, encomia, laments, hetero- and homo-erotic love songs, myths, and so on. Some editors and translators group them by type or theme in their editions. In the following descriptions, however, to observe the ancient poetic value of variety as an effect that poets actively sought, I shall follow the translator Robert Wells's example, using traditional order and enumeration for the 22 poems now thought to be from Theocritus's pen.

"Idyll 1: The Passion of Daphnis" is set in the countryside of Sicily. The shepherd Thyrsis and his companion, a goatherd, have been involved in a friendly contest of composition. The poem opens with Thyrsis speaking and suggesting that the goatherd, inspired by the god Pan, has already won the prize. The goatherd objects, however, saying that on the contrary, Thyrsis, inspired by the MUSES, has won for a song he just sang in an earlier match with a Libyan named Chromis, and he must take the prize for his song, "The Passion of Daphnis." If Thyrsis will sing the song again, the goatherd will give him a good milking goat and a beautiful carved wooden cup. The goatherd describes the carved wonders of the cup at length in language that reflects its extraordinary beauty. Then, reminding Thyrsis that "Hades and forgetfulness are the same," the goatherd asks the shepherd to sing.

Calling on the Muses for inspiration, Thyrsis complies with a lovely ELEGY commemorating the death of Daphnis—a shepherd whom Theocritus credits with the invention of PASTORAL POETRY. The poem imagines the dying Daphnis's farewells, disjointed but lovely goodbyes, and quasi-delirious observations to the mourners present at his death. After each stanza of two to six lines each, the singer invokes the Muses in a refrain calling on them to sing for the departed poet-herdsman.

At length, Daphnis dies and falls silent. Aphrodite, the goddess of love, attempts to revive him, but to no avail, and after the third of a series of three refrains that bid the herdsman, the Muses, and the song farewell, Thyrsis ends his song and claims his prizes. The goatherd ends the idyll by quieting the she-goats whom the elegy has aroused.

"Idyll 2: Pharmaceutria." A poem that inspired the Renaissance poet-playwright-singer Isabella Andreini to pen a similar monologue, "Pharmaceutria" recounts the efforts of a jilted young woman, Simaetha, to win back her absent lover Delphis's affections by witchcraft. As the reader learns, Delphis has not put in an appearance for 12 long days, and the speaker of the poem is busily preparing charms to win him back and punish him. She prays he will be scattered "bone by bone," that his heart will shrivel and his veins burn. She blames him for loving himself. She wants him to twist in pain, to be crushed as she crushes ashes. But each five-line verse in the poem's first part ends with a refrain addressed to a "magic wheel," asking that it force her lover home.

She then turns to recalling the history of her affair, and each refrain she calls on the "Lady Moon" to help her remember the details: how they met, how she fell in love, how she suffered, how she arranged to meet the man by sending her slave girl as an intermediary. As she recalls their conversations, the reader sees that Delphis was a lying opportunist, pretending that Simaetha barely approached him before he sought her out.

Having used her, however, Delphis's affections have now turned elsewhere, and Simaetha is prepared for either of two eventualities. Either her magic will restore him to her, or she will poison him. The poem's last four lines reveal, though, that she really expects neither of those outcomes. She knows that having vented her sense of betrayal and her anger, she must now deal with her longing and her loss.

"Idyll 3: The Lovesongs" begins with a goatherd asking a friend, Tityrus, to tend his flock while he goes off to serenade his beloved Amaryllis. He warns Tityrus to watch out for a butting goat. Then the goatherd sings a series of fruitless songs outside Amaryllis's cave. She either isn't there, or she takes no notice. He tries to comfort himself. More songs follow. First he promises to die to please her. Then he acknowledges that she does not care, but he thinks that persistence may pay off. In that regard, he thinks of a series of successful lovers but finally convinces himself he is not one of them. He decides to stop singing and lie around till the wolves eat him. That, he hopes, will satisfy cruel Amaryllis.

"Idyll 4: The Herdsmen" recounts the verse conversation of two cowherds, Battus and Corydon, whose employer, Aegon, himself an amateur boxer, has gone to Olympia to see the games. The herdsmen note that the cows miss their master, and they predict that Aegon's interest in athletics will be the ruin of him. Their wandering conversation turns first to piping and then to the beauties of Amaryllis, then back to the cows that are growing stubborn.

Battus steps on a thorn that pierces his foot, and Corydon draws it out. Then they discuss the sexual misbehavior of their master with a girl, and the poem ends.

In the risqué "Idyll 5: Goatherd and Shepherd," a goatherd, Comatas, and a shepherd, Lacon, who have been sex partners in the past, accuse each other of theft. They mutually deny their guilt and discuss having a singing contest. They also discuss their former relationship, and it becomes clear that while Comatas still has a preference for boys, Lacon has moved on to women. With not-so-veiled references to this state of affairs, they decide to have a singing contest, but in their mutual mistrust, they need an unbiased judge. They settle on Morson, a woodsman, and continue their acrimonious but now subliminal debate in alternating two-line stanzas that rhyme in the Robert Wells translation. Finally Morson stops them and announces that Comatas has won the prize—a lamb. The poem ends with Comatas's warning to his billy goat to leave the nannies alone.

In "Idyll 6: Damoetas and Daphnis," we have another singing contest between two youthful shepherds, Daphnis and Damoetas. This idyll presents an exchange between the Cyclops Polyphemus and his beloved nymph, Galatea. Daphnis begins by addressing Polyphemus and speaking as an observer who watches Galatea throw apples to tease the one-eyed giant and his sheepdog.

Damoetas replies in the voice of Polyphemus, explaining that he too can play a teasing game of love, keeping Galatea away from his cave until she promises to become his lover again. Polyphemus has admired his own looks in a pool and decided that he is not such an ugly fellow after all. When the songs have ended, the shepherds exchange a kiss, and each gives the other a prize for having sung equally well.

In "Idyll 7: The Harvest Festival," a trio of young men—Eurcritas, Amyntas, and the speaker, Simichidas—encounter another traveler, the goatherd Lycidas, while on their way to a harvest festival. They greet one another with good-natured insults, and Simichidas challenges Lycidas to a singing contest. Both men are modest about their talents, and Lycidas promises his shepherd's crook to Simichidas for his modesty.

Lycidas begins the contest, reciting a poem that he has written in the hills. It begins as a prayer for a calm sea passage to the port of Mytilene on Lesbos for Lycidas's beloved friend Ageanax. The poet imagines the joyous reunion that he and Ageanax will share and imagines the song that Ageanax will sing. He closes his song with an address to a poet of a former age, Comatas.

Simichidas next performs his song, dedicated to Lycidas as "the Muses' friend." First Simichidas confesses his passion for Myrto, but he also knows how his friend Aratus is consumed with passion for a boy named Philinus. The singer prays that Pan, the goat-footed god, may assure a happy outcome for his friend's passion. Failing that, Simichidas calls for Pan's punishment with insect bites, nettle scratches "from head to hoof," and other discomforts appropriate to a shepherd god. The singer then returns to the subject of Philenus and advises his enamored friend, Aratus, to give up on the boy and live a peaceful life.

Lycidas finds the song amusing and well-structured, presents the promised crook to Simicidas, and takes a different fork in the road. The other young men continue to the farm of Phra-

sidamus, whose attractions the poem delightfully describes. It also describes the harvest plenty, breaking the seals of four-year-old wine jars. The poem praises the wine by comparing it with vintages celebrated in myth, and the verse ends with a prayer to the goddess Demeter that the poet may be blessed by surviving another year to set his winnowing fan in the fall harvest's heap of grain.

In "Idyll 10: The Reapers," two reapers, Milon and Bucaeus, are working side by side in the grain field, bringing in the harvest. Milon notices that Bucaeus is lagging and teases him about it. Bucaeus confesses that he is suffering from loveickness for Bombyca, a girl at a nearby farm. Milon teases him, and tells him to do his job and vent his feelings in song. Bucaeus complies with a somewhat awkward 14-line effort that Milon sarcastically characterizes as "masterly."

Milon then quotes 14 better-crafted lines from the poet Lityerses as an example for Bucaeus. Milon advises his friend to keep his love-longing as a secret between Bucaeus and his mother.

In "Idyll 11: The Cyclops," Theocritus begins by telling his friend, Nicias, that the poet has learned love has no remedy. He illustrates this with a song about the love-longing that the Cyclops Polyphemus felt for his beloved sea nymph Galatea. Polyphemus traces the history of his love from the pair's first meeting. Knowing that his one-eyed visage is unlikely to please Galatea, he speaks of his skill as a shepherd and of the wealth of milk and cheeses that his careful tending of his flock of 1,000 beasts produces. He speaks of his feelings and wishes that he had been born with gills so he could seek Galatea in her watery home. He blames his mother for not proposing a match. Finally, he recalls himself to the realities of his life and the tasks at hand. He comforts himself with the thought that he will eventually find a new love. The Cyclops's voice falls silent, and the poet speaks again, saying that the giant shepherd found more relief from his love-sickness by singing than he would have found by paying a physician for treatment.

"Idyll 12: The Touchstone" or "The Beloved" opens with the poet's address to a beloved boy who has arrived after a three-day absence. The poet observes that even a single day's absence "makes a lover old." After seeking to define his feelings through a series of comparisons, the poet hopes that the god Love will "breathe equally" on him and his beloved. That would become a matter for a future song. He then prays that after 200 generations, a shade newly arrived in Hades will tell his ghost that the story of his and his beloved's mutual affection will be on everyone's lips—especially on the young men's.

In the poem's fourth and last stanza, the poet returns to the title issue of the poem. The poet introduces an address to the oarsmen of the island of Megara who honor the hero Diocles with a competition to determine which of the local boys has the sweetest kiss. That decision may baffle the judge who must decide, but, the poet implies, the kiss of the addressee of the poem would resolve the judge's dilemma as easily as a legendary touchstone in Lydia could identify "true gold."

"Idyll 13: Hylas" belongs to the category of Theocritus's work called half- or semi-epic. Hylas was the pageboy and the beloved of the hero Heracles (Hercules). The two had embarked together with the Argonauts who accompanied Jason in search of the Golden Fleece (see *The* ARGONAUTIKA). When their ship anchored at the island of Chios to replace a broken oar, Hylas went to find fresh water. The nymphs in the pool he found so admired his beauty that they dragged him into the water, where he drowned. Heracles in his grief deserted the expedition to search for the boy.

Theocritus addresses his poem to his own beloved, Nicias. He says that when the two first fell in love, they thought love existed for them alone, but this was wrong. They are neither the first nor the last to love. The poet then makes a transition to the love of Heracles for Hylas, and how in Heracles the lad had the example of the hero on whom to model the man he would become. But then the poet tells the story of Hylas's loss.

The poem's technique is masterful as it looks aside from its central incident, instead focusing first upon the dangers of the voyage. Then the poem describes the way the Argonauts made

camp. Hylas went for water; he found a pool—one lovingly described. As he dips his vessel in the water, the nymphs in their desire for him grab him and pull him in. His passing is like a shooting star.

As the sailors prepare to leave, Heracles, maddened by love, searches for Hylas. The sailors blame Heracles for deserting, but the poet explains that he came on foot at last to their destination. In using spare but imagistic and musical language to focus on the feelings of a grief-stricken Heracles, the poem implies much more about the feelings of the poet for Nicias than it could have said directly.

"Idyll 14: Aeschines and Thyonichus" is cast as a dialogue between two friends who run into each other. The first part of the poem focuses on Aeschines' breakup with his girlfriend, Cynisca. An innocent toast at a party grows into a quarrel as it becomes clear that Cynisca has two lovers at the table. Aeschines strikes her, she flees, and her other admirer, the son of Labas—nicknamed the wolf—becomes her steady lover.

Aeschines is thinking of enlisting for foreign service as a soldier. Thyonichus advises that King Ptolemy of Egypt offers good wages and opportunities at Alexandria. Aeschines, however, had better hurry. His hair is beginning to gray, and little time may be left for fresh starts.

"Idyll 15: The Festival of Adonis" opens in a suburb of Alexandria in Egypt. In a pre-Christian, Easter-like celebration, the spring festival of Adonis was celebrated each year to welcome the demigod back to earth after his annual rebirth and death in celebration of the earth's seemingly inexhaustible, self-renewing fertility.

Gorgo has called to collect her friend, Praxinoa, so that the two women can travel into central Alexandria and the royal palace there to participate in the festival. After a bit of a chat about husbands and babies, Praxinoa dresses in her best with the help of her slave, Eunoa, and the two women set off for the festival. The streets are crowded with people and horses, but the friends manage to jostle their way to the palace gate, where a mob of would-be worshippers are pushing and shoving to get in. The women are swept up in the crowd, and Praxinoa's dress gets torn, but with the help of a man who gives them a friendly push, the two friends make it into the precincts of the palace. There they find themselves overawed by the robes, tapestries, and lovely artworks. They also have a sharp exchange with a man who objects to their chatter. The high point of the festival, however, is about to begin. A talented singer appears who invokes the goddess Aphrodite, praying that she will once more conduct her beloved Adonis back from Hades to earthly life.

The song celebrates the preparations for the feast to be held in honor of the occasion and the succulent foodstuffs that have been prepared. These include desserts formed to depict incidents in Adonis's story. The song also celebrates artworks, particularly tapestries whose scenes depict the annual lovemaking between Aphrodite and the always 18-year-old Adonis. But the hymn penultimately introduces a sad note. At dawn of the following day, Adonis must float down to the sea and die for another year. Nonetheless, his annual day above ground is a triumph that no other demigod or hero has ever achieved.

When the song ends, Gorgo admires its artistry and envies the singer's gifts. But now she must rush home to prepare her husband's dinner. She bids farewell to Adonis and hopes that he will find her healthy and happy and with her friend at the following year's festival.

"Idyll 16: The Graces" is addressed to Hiero, the tyrant of Syracuse in Sicily, and is an appeal for the king's patronage for the poet. Just as the proper role of the Muses is to celebrate the gods, so that of poets is to celebrate the accomplishments of living men and to preserve the memory of those accomplishments throughout the ages, so that recollection of the men's existence will not pass into oblivion. Performing such a service for people is worthy of generous recompense, and miserly people will sooner be forgotten than will those who patronize poets. If not for the poets, sings Theocritus, the deeds of the heroes of the Trojan War would long since have vanished from human memory.

Heroes still dwell among men, however, and among them stands Hiero of Syracuse, the scourge of the African Phoenicians. The tactful poem concludes with a prayer to Zeus, god of power, and Athena, goddess of wisdom, to watch over and protect the people and leaders of Syracuse. At the very end, Theocritus says that he is one of many poets who stand ready to serve if called—to laud the name of Hiero and the Sicilians. He will not "jostle for notice." Nonetheless, his lovely poem has provided his potential patron with an extraordinary example of the poetic power of the wares Theocritus has to offer.

"Idyll 17: Encomium to Ptolemy" moves to Egypt for its theme. Ptolemy II (Philadelphus) ruled as the pharaoh of Egypt from his capital at Alexandria—a city named for its founder, Alexander the Great. Identifying Ptolemy's power on earth with that of Zeus in heaven, Theocritus begins and ends his poem with Zeus's name. Having announced his subject, Theocritus turns to Ptolemy's genealogy, beginning with his father, Ptolemy I—a general of Alexander the Great before he ruled Egypt. The Ptolemy line traces its origins back to the demigod and hero Heracles, and through him to Zeus himself. In the guise of Heracles's father, Amphitryon, Zeus sired Heracles with Alcmene. Theocritus follows the genealogy all the way down to Ptolemy I and his wife Berenice, also the product of a noble and distinguished line.

Next the poet lauds the places that are fortunate to be connected with Ptolemy II: his birthplace, Cos, in Egypt and Egypt's 33,333 cities. In addition, Theocritus lists the lands and the peoples that acknowledge Ptolemy's sway: Syria, Phoenicia, Libya, Lycia, Pamphylia, Caria, Sicily, and the Cylcades. The poet celebrates Ptolemy's sea power and his prowess as a general. He also details Ptolemy's wealth and some of its sources, his piety, the loyalty that he inspires in his subjects, and his fame. He praises Ptolemy for having elevated his parents to the status of gods, and he celebrates the double love the king feels toward his consort, who is both his sister and his wife—a relationship that also characterizes the bonds between Zeus and Hera.

The poet ends his encomium to his king by bidding him farewell. He also praises the power of his own song to rank Ptolemy's name among the gods and heroes, though he acknowledges that virtue comes only from Zeus.

In "Idyll 18: Helen's Epithalamium," though an epithalamium is a wedding hymn, the poem begins after the ceremony. Twelve young girls sing outside the bridal chamber, and their song echoes through the house. It chides the bridegroom for sleeping, perhaps because he drank too much, when he should be busy begetting an heir. The singers confess that none of them is as beautiful as Helen, or so clever at weaving, or so accomplished a musician.

They take their leave of Helen as a companion and a playmate, but they promise to dedicate a tree in her honor. As they leave, they express their good wishes, promise to come again to greet the bridal couple in the morning, and pray to Hymen, the god of marriage, to bless the couple's marriage vows—an irony in view of Helen's infidelity with the Trojan prince Paris.

"Idyll 22: The Dioscuri" is another of those categorized as half- or semi-epic. The Dioscuri were the twin sons of Leda. Named Castor and Polydeuces (Pollux in Latin), the boys were conceived when their mother coupled with Zeus in the shape of a swan. They became the patron deities of seamen, appearing to sailors as St. Elmo's fire. Later they also became identified with the constellation Gemini. The first part of Theocritus's poem celebrates the twins' role as the protector of seafarers.

The second stanza recalls, generally, the role that the brothers played as Argonauts and, particularly, a boxing match between Polydeuces and the giant son of Poseidon, Amycus. Theocritus's vivid description of the fight suggests that sports fans everywhere might be better served if television networks hired poets instead of repetitious ex-athletes as commentators.

Having given Polydeuces his due, Theocritus now turns his attention to Castor. The twins had kidnapped the fiancées of Lynceas and Idas, the sons of Aphareus. When the two attempted to recover their brides by reasonable argument, Castor told them either to reconcile themselves to the current situation or be prepared to fight. Rather than engage in a general melee, the rivals agree that the firstborn son of each family will duel. Lynceas and Castor take the field. At the first sally, their spears stick in each other's shields. They draw their swords and continue the fight. Eventually Castor emerges victorious, having slain his opponent. Idas attempts to avenge his brother, but Zeus forestalls the attempt, striking him down with a thunderbolt.

Ending the poem, Theocritus bids his subjects farewell and reminds his readers that Castor and Polldeuces cherish poets. So, the poet says, do the gods who value poems above all other gifts. Essentially "The Dioscuri" seems to be an advertisement of the poet's abilities as he seeks potential commissions.

"Idyll 24: The Childhood of Heracles" is still another idyll in the semi-epic mode. In this poem, Theocritus first recounts the incident in which the baby Heracles chokes the life out of two enormous serpents sent by Hera—the jealous spouse of his Olympian father, Zeus—to kill him and his baby brother, Iphicles. Deft distribution of the elements of the story manages to create interest in an episode well known to ancient Greek audiences.

The second section of the idyll details the way that Heracles' mother, Alcmene, calls on the blind prophet Teiresias to foretell her son's future. This, Teiresias does, after assuring the woman that she too will long be remembered among the women of Greece. Heracles is destined to be a hero, to accomplish 12 labors, to be burned on a pyre in Tracis, to live with the gods on Olympus, and to marry a daughter of Hera. The prophet tells the mother to burn the bodies of the snakes, purify the house, and sacrifice a boar to Zeus.

The end of the poem is regrettably lost, but the surviving next sections recount the heroic education of Heracles and his learning to master such battle crafts as chariot driving, warding off sword strokes, commanding men, and estimating the strength of enemies. The poem breaks off as it describes the hero's diet and his dress.

In "Idyll 26: The Bacchae," Theocritus recounts a portion of the same story that Euripides tells in his tragedy *The Bacchae*. Pentheus, the king of Thebes, resists the spread of the cult of the god Dionysus, but his mother, Agave, is a sister of the god's consort, Semele, and has embraced the religion. With her two sisters, Ino and Autonoa, Agave has gone to prepare a sacred grove for the celebration of the Dionysian mysteries. Pentheus has been secretly observing the preparations, but the women discover him. Already frenzied by their drinking in honor of the god, the women tear Penthus to pieces, with his mother administering the coup de grâce by tearing off his head.

Theocritus, apparently also a devotee of the god, approves the women's actions, calling them "an act of god."

"Idyll 28: The Distaff" addresses an ivory distaff that Theocritus has purchased as a present for Theugenis, the wife of his friend Nicias, whom the poet is about to visit in Miletus in Ionia. Though the poet considers the distaff a small gift, that it comes from a friend makes it precious.

In "Idyll 29: Drinking Song," the speaker is an aging man drinking with a former male lover. While the speaker still feels strongly about their former affection, the other man dismisses it as "slight acquaintance." The speaker advises his companion to drop the pose and cherish the memory and the emotion that survives the physical capacity for its expression. If the hearer cannot accomplish that, the speaker will not bother to cross the street to speak if the two should meet.

"Idyll 30: The Fever" gives an aging man's soliloquy on the subject of having fallen hopelessly in love again with an attractive boy. Though he advises himself against this unwelcome passion, and though he anticipates the hurtful consequences that are sure to follow from it, he is caught in the toils of a passion over which he has no control. He is, he says, "a leaf that has lived its day/His lightest breeze catches and whirls me away."

Bibliography

Theocritus. *Encomium of Ptolemy Philadelphus.* Translated by Richard Hunter. Berkeley: University of California Press, 2003.

———. *Idylls.* Translated by Anthony Verity. New York: Oxford University Press, 2002.

———. *A Selection: Theocritus.* Translated by Richard Hunter. Cambridge: Cambridge University Press, 1999.

Wells, Robert, trans. *The Idylls of Theocritus.* Manchester, U.K.: Carcanet Press, 1988.

Iliad, The Homer (ca. eighth–ninth century B.C.E.)

One of two epic poems attributed to the early poet-minstrel Homer, *The Iliad*, like its companion piece, *The Odyssey*, focuses on events that, according to tradition, had occurred during the Trojan War some 300–400 years before the composition of the Homeric poems. Whereas *The Odyssey* focuses principally on the long and difficult homecoming of its hero Odysseus and on events that involved members of his family on and near his home island of Ithaca, *The Iliad* examines events that occurred during the 10-year-long Greek siege of the city of Troy, or Ilium as it was sometimes called in honor of Ilus, the city's legendary founder. Like *The Odyssey*, *The Iliad* interweaves two principal series of events. (Throughout *The Iliad*, the Greeks are also called Danaans and Achaeans.)

The first principal series surrounds the warrior-hero Achilles and the tragic consequences that follow from his anger at being slighted by the Greek commander in chief, Agamemnon, at the siege of Troy. The second series more succinctly explores the situation of the besieged city and its inhabitants. The poet focuses on the royal family of Troy and on the mounting public and private grief it must endure throughout the Grecian siege and the city's eventual fall. In both series, the gods choose sides and play favorites, with the result that human beings become pawns in the deities' often uncaring games-playing.

Using the epic formula whose prototype appears first in Homer, the poet calls on the Muse of epic poetry, Calliope, to inspire him by making him her instrument and singing of the wrath of Achilles through him. Which god, the poet asks, provoked the quarrel between Achilles and Agamemnon? Answering this question with the parentage and name of Apollo, the poet begins the action of the epic.

In *The Iliad*, Homer makes extraordinary demands of his audience, whether listeners or readers. His cast of characters is enormous, and the poet assumes on the part of his listeners or readers a close familiarity with the names and genealogies of each person who appears in the immense verbal tapestry he weaves. To assist a modern reader less familiar with such matters, therefore, before summarizing the epic's action, I provide a table with the names and roles of the characters that appear in this précis of Homer's poem.

WHO'S WHO IN HOMER'S *ILIAD*

	Role	Allied With
Gods and Immortals		
Aphrodite	Goddess of love	Trojans
Apollo	Sun god and god of physicians and artists	Trojans
Ares	God of war	Trojans
Artemis	Goddess of the hunt and sister of Apollo	Trojans
Athena	Goddess of wisdom	Greeks
Calliope	Muse of epic poetry	n/a
Clio	Muse of History	n/a
Hephaestus	Blacksmith of the gods	Greeks
Hera	Queen of gods; wife and sister of Zeus	Greeks
Hermes	Messenger of the gods	Greeks
Iris	Goddess of rainbow; messenger	n/a
Leto	A Titaness	Trojans

(continues)

WHO'S WHO IN HOMER'S *ILIAD* (continued)

	Role	Allied With
Pasithea	Youngest of the three graces, promised as wife to Hephestus	
Poseidon	God of sea and earthquake	Greeks
Thetis	Immortal sea nymph; mother of Achilles	Greeks
Xanthus	Personified river also called Scamender	Trojans
Xanthus the horse	Immortal steed belonging to Achilles	
Zeus	king of the gods	first Trojans, then Greeks

Greeks and Their Allies

Achilles	King of Thessaly, leader of Myrmidons, and mightiest Greek warrior
Agamemnon	King of Mycenae and principal Greek general
Ajax x 2	Greek warriors of the same name
Diomedes	A principal warrior
Menelaus	King of Sparta, Greek general, husband of Helen
Nestor	King of Pylos, oldest and wisest of Greeks
Odysseus	King of Ithaca, fierce warrior and wise counselor
Patroclus	Best friend of Achilles and fierce warrior

Trojans and Their Allies

Aeneas	A Trojan prince who will found the Roman state
Andromache	Wife of Hector; Mother of Astyanax

	Role
Astyanax	Son of Hector and Andromache
Briseis	Achilles' captive and lover, demanded by Agamemnon
Chryses	A priest of Apollo
Chryseis	Daughter of Chryses, captive of Agamemnon
Deiphobus	Trojan prince, brother of Hector, son of Priam.
Dolon	Trojan who reveals information to the Greeks
Euphorbus	A Trojan who wounds Patroclus
Glaucus	A Trojan warrior
Hecuba	Wife of King Priam of Troy; Mother of Hector
Hector	Principal Trojan warrior hero
Pandarus	A foolish Trojan warrior
Paris	Son of King Priam of Troy; kidnapper and lover of Helen
Polydamus	A Trojan warrior
Priam	King of Troy, husband of Hecuba, father of Hector
Sarpedon	Son of Zeus, prince of Lycia; a Trojan ally.

Book 1

A priest of Apollo, Chryses, attempts to ransom his captive daughter, Chryseis, from the Greeks, but, ignoring the positive consensus of his troops, Agamemnon roughly refuses. Chryses prays to the god for vengeance. Hearing his prayer, an angry Apollo shoots arrows of pestilence upon the Greek army for nine days, and smoke from the consequent funeral pyres darkens the sky.

At a council held to consider the situation, Achilles advises breaking off the siege and heading for home. The prophet Calchas, having first secured Achilles' promise of protection, explains the cause of Apollo's anger. Infuriated, Agamemnon nevertheless agrees to restore Chryseis to her father if one of the other Greeks, perhaps Achilles himself, will replace her with another woman. Harsh words ensue between the two, and Agamemnon threatens to come to Achilles' tent and take his beloved Briseis.

Furious, Achilles nearly draws his sword to kill Agamemnon. He is prevented, however, by the arrival of Athena, goddess of wisdom, who tells him to rail at Agamemnon all he wants to, but not to kill him. In retaliation for Agamemnon's contempt, Achilles promises to absent himself from the battle when the Greeks need him most.

The wise and aged king of Pylos, Nestor, tries to pour oil on troubled waters. Finally, Achilles agrees to give Briseis to Agamemnon. When heralds come for her, however, Achilles repeats his vow to withhold his military services. He enlists his mother, the immortal sea nymph Thetis, in the quarrel. He asks her to intercede with Zeus so that the Greeks will fall victim to the swords of the Trojans. Meanwhile, Chryseis is restored to her father, and Apollo ends the pestilence among the Greeks.

Twelve days later, Thetis asks Zeus to confer victory on the Trojans until the Achaeans (the Greeks) treat Achilles with respect and enrich him. Despite fearing a domestic quarrel with his wife, the goddess Hera, over the issue, Zeus grants Thetis's request with an irrevocable nod. Hera indeed surmises his plot and reproves her husband, the two deities snipe at each other like crotchety human spouses, but Zeus at last silences Hera with the threat of a thrashing.

Books 2–4

To fulfill his promise to Thetis, Zeus sends a false dream to Agamemnon and encourages him to begin the final siege of Troy at once. After pretending to withdraw, Agamemnon heartens his army for the coming attack. At this point, Homer interrupts the narrative with a catalogue of the captains of the Greek host—a list that occupies the rest of the second book. (At a date much later than its composition, *The Iliad* was editorially divided into 24 books.)

The third book provides an interlude in which the armies observe a truce while Menelaus and a reluctant Paris agree to settle by single combat the issue of who gets Helen of Troy. Helen has grown tired of Paris and has once more begun hankering after her former husband, Menelaus.

By far the better fighter, Menelaus is on the verge of an easy victory when the goddess Aphrodite intervenes, spiriting her favorite Paris away from the fight and back to Helen. For Helen's roving eye, the goddess reproves her as a hussy. Everyone knows that, Paris's disappearance notwithstanding, Menelaus has won the duel, and the Greeks demand their prize.

In book 4, like rival but friendly fans at a sporting event, Zeus and Hera have been watching the duel. Zeus favors the Trojans, while Hera roots for the Greeks. Both agree, however, that Paris has lost, and Zeus agrees to the sacking of Troy provided that Hera will not object if, in the future, he wishes to have one of her favorite cities sacked. Hera names Argos, Sparta, and Mycenae as her favorites and agrees that Zeus can destroy them at his pleasure without her intervention. She then flashes down from Olympus and encourages a foolish Trojan, Pandarus, to break the truce by wounding Menelaus with an arrow.

As a physician treats the minor wound, Agamemnon urges the commanders of the Greek forces into battle. The Greek army moves forward in silence, while the Trojans encourage themselves with shouting and banging together their shields and weapons. As the battle is joined, gods preferring one side or the other encourage favored warriors. Apollo, for instance, tells the Trojan prince Hector that he should charge the Greeks and that Achilles is nursing his wrath and not fighting. Athena urges on the Greeks. Homer's descriptions of the carnage are individualized, detailed, bloody, and gripping.

Books 5–6

The gods do not merely encourage their champions; several immortals actually engage in battle. Athena, for instance, guides the spear of the Greek hero Diomedes so that it kills the truce breaker, Pandarus. Aphrodite protects her son Aeneas, who will later lead the expedition to people Rome (see AENEID). Seeing her carrying Aeneas and covering him with her cloak, Diomedes, knowing Aphrodite to be weak in battle, wounds her in her hand so that she bleeds ichor—the immortal fluid that flows in the veins of gods—and drops Aeneas. Diomedes drives Aphrodite from the field, but Apollo takes over caring for Aeneas, who rejoins the battle. Ares, the god of war, also intervenes on behalf of the Trojans. The Trojan forces beat back the Greeks and are on the verge of winning the day when Athena and Hera decide to do battle together.

Donning a helmet of invisibility, Athena, with Diomedes at her side, mounts an attack directly on the god of war Ares, who has been killing Greeks. With her help, Diomedes grievously wounds Ares, who, though he cannot die can nonetheless feel pain. The wounded god retreats to Olympus, where Zeus has the physician of the gods, Paeeon, instantly heal him, and the fifth book ends.

In the sixth book, the Trojan princes Hector and Aeneas rally their troops, and Homer breaks from recounting instances of carnage to chronicle a pause in the battle for an individual combat between the Greek hero Diomedes and the Trojan Glaucus. From formal, detailed, and respectful introductions that include relevant genealogies and summaries of the accomplishments of ancestors, the two learn each other's backgrounds. The antagonists realize that bonds of friendship between their families preclude their fighting.

During this interval, Hector goes back to the city to inform his wife, Andromache, and his mother, Queen Hecuba, of the war's progress. Hector blames Paris for all the Trojans' suffering and wishes his brother dead. He advises his mother to make sacrifices to Athena, and as she and her women comply, Hector goes to encourage Paris to join the battle. He finds him still lolling about at home where Aphrodite had left him. Helen shares with Hector her disenchantment with Paris. Having delivered his message, Hector goes home in search of Andromache. There her weeping maids report that she and Hector's son Astyonax are on the city's walls watching the battle. Hector finds them there, and in a moving scene that sets the plight of the women of Troy in bold relief, Andromache pleads with her husband to forego the war and

remain with her. He tries unsuccessfully to comfort her, but he must return to battle. On his way, he encounters Paris, now clad in full armor, and together they go to fight.

Books 7–9

The brothers fighting as a team prove so successful that Athena and Apollo decide to intervene on the Greeks' behalf. They arrange to have Hector challenge a Greek to single combat, and the fighting pauses as the Greeks seek out a champion willing to face him. When no Greek comes forward, Menelaus accepts the challenge himself. The Greeks, however, restrain him, assuring him that he is no match for the Trojan champion. The Greeks decide to choose a duelist by lot, and all put their names in a helmet. The name of the fiercest warrior present, Ajax, is drawn. The two duel fiercely with spears and then with stones, and though blood is shed on both sides, neither can overcome the other. As daylight fades, heralds from both sides intercede. The two warriors agree to suspend their fight, to exchange presents of friendship, and to resume their contest whenever the chance of battle brings them face-to-face.

The two sides withdraw to eat, rest, and confer. The Greeks decide to burn their dead and build a wall along the shore to protect their ships. The Trojans urge Paris to return Helen and the treasures he took from Sparta. Paris agrees to return the treasure with interest, but he means to keep Helen. The Trojans send heralds to offer the financial settlement and to request a truce to burn their dead. The Greeks grant the truce but refuse the money. The war will continue.

As the eighth book opens, with threats of dire consequences, Zeus warns the gods not to intervene further in the battle. Athena replies that they will henceforward only offer counsel. Zeus slyly confesses that he did not mean it anyway—a fact that he instantly demonstrates by going down to influence the battle himself. With Zeus's favor, Hector single-handedly drives the Greeks back to the staging area near their ships. Then, in response to the Greeks' prayers, Zeus changes sides, and the

Greeks begin gaining ground. The battle continues to be a seesaw affair. Athena and Hera try to intervene, but on Zeus's orders they desist, and nightfall ends the day's hostilities with the Greeks once more driven back to the staging area immediately around their ships, and the watch fires of the Trojan defenders burning all across the plains of Troy.

In book 9, faced with the Greeks' imminent defeat, Nestor of Pylos advises Agamemnon to restore Briseis to Achilles, pay him damages, and entreat him to rejoin the battle. Confessing his error, Agamemnon agrees, swearing that he has not coupled with the girl. When the offer is taken to Achilles, however, the hero refuses it. Nothing the messengers say can persuade him, and they return to Agamemnon with the news of their failure.

Books 10–12

In the 10th book, the mission to Achilles having failed, Nestor, who thinks that a Greek disaster is imminent, awakens a coterie of clever Greeks who are also able warriors. They hold a council, decide they need reliable intelligence, and send Diomedes and Odysseus to reconnoiter behind enemy lines. The Trojans are as sleepless as the Greeks, for Hector wants to know if the Greeks, having been bested in the previous day's battle, are planning to sail. A warrior, Dolon, volunteers to find out. Diomedes and Odysseus, however, detect and capture him. In an effort to save his life, Dolon provides them with everything they want to know. The Greeks kill him nonetheless and, using what they have told him, kill the king of the Thracians along with 12 of his companions and steal his horses before returning to their own camp near the Greek ships.

Book 11 begins the next day, and the battle resumes more fiercely than before, with no quarter given on either side. The Greeks have the best of it until Agamemnon himself is wounded; then, counseled by Zeus, Hector rallies the Trojan forces, and the tide of battle turns for a time against the Greeks. Back and forth the battle continues to rage, and Homer turns his poetic gaze first on one

and then on another hero, first on Trojan and then on Greek, giving an account of the battle better than that of an eyewitness—an account that speaks either to the detail of Homer's sources or, more likely, to the richness of his imagination. In the course of the battle, Achilles, watching from his encampment, sees someone wounded and taken to the tents of Nestor. Achilles sends his beloved friend, Patroclus, to find out the name of the wounded man. While Patroclus is there, Nestor convinces him that he should help persuade Achilles to aid the Greeks.

In the 12th book, Homer describes the assault that the Trojans mounted on a wall and trench the Greeks had constructed to protect their ships. The poet interrupts his account to describe the gods' unfavorable view of this fortification and their subsequent means of destroying it. The reader may here be particularly struck by the details Homer chooses to heighten the realism and pictographic quality of this description. A particularly telling instance occurs when the poet pictures the warhorses' fear of trying to jump so broad and deep a trench and the way the animals balk when urged to the attempt. As a result, almost all the Trojans dismount and assault the entrenched bulwark in five infantry companies.

Homer masterfully describes the Trojan assault on the wall. He catches the tumult and the desperation of the fight and fright of the defending Greeks at the onslaught of Hector and his Trojans. Encouraged by Zeus, the attackers finally break through and drive the defenders toward their ships in headlong flight. Once the wall is breached, however, and the Greeks routed, Zeus loses interest in the fight and turns his attention elsewhere, confident that no other god will intervene.

Books 13–14

Poseidon, the god of the sea and of earthquake, however, assumes the form of the prophet Calchas and heartens the Greek defenders, renewing their strength and their resolve. Poseidon's anger against the Trojans increases when they kill his grandson, Amphimachus, in the melee. With his encouragement, the Greeks begin to turn the tide of the battle under the very sterns of their beached vessels. After underlining the intentions of the two gods' interventions in the fight, Homer returns to his description of the carnage, evoking in his verse not only the sights, vicissitudes, and confusion of the battle, but sometimes its odors and often its noise of shouting and the ringing of the bronze and iron weapons as well.

The Trojan Polydamus perceives that despite Trojan successes, the Greeks are beginning to roll up the Trojan left flank. Polydamus therefore recommends a council to consider whether to press the attack or beat a tactical retreat. Hector agrees, saying that he will continue the fight until Polydamus has rounded up the commanders. The 13th book ends with another surge in the fighting.

As the 14th book opens, Homer has shifted the scene to the tent of the ancient king Nestor, where the old man is taking a break for wine. The increasing noise of the battle makes the old king cut short his respite, arm, and go in search of Agamemnon. Nestor finds the king and the two confer with Odysseus and Diomedes about how to save an increasingly dangerous situation. Diomedes, the youngest man present, suggests that, even though all four are wounded, they can still urge the others on, and all four go to do so. In the guise of an old man, Poseidon reminds Agamemnon about Achilles and then the god rushes into the fray with a great battle cry. The Greeks once more take heart and redouble their efforts.

The goddess Hera, in the meantime, approves Poseidon's action on the Greeks' behalf and thinks of a way she can keep Zeus occupied. She bathes and coifs and dresses, decking herself with jewels, and borrows from Aphrodite an embroidered belt into which all the love magic that Aphrodite possesses has been woven. Thus beautified and equipped with a powerful love medicine, Hera goes in search of her husband Zeus, whom she means to charm into making love with her. On her way, she recruits the god of sleep to make Zeus slumber after she has had her way with him. Sleep is reluctant, for Zeus had earlier punished him for making the chief god fall asleep when he did not want to, but Hera promises that she will marry Sleep off to the youngest of the three Graces, Pasithea. Sleep, who loves Pasithea, readily agrees, and they set off for Mount Ida, where Zeus was stopping at the moment.

As soon as Zeus catches sight of Hera, he feels inflamed by a passion for her such as he has not known since their first prenuptial encounter. She pretends to be on another errand, but Zeus wants to dispense with all other matters and make love. He says that he has not felt such a passion in any of his love affairs with mortal women—affairs that he enumerates. The two fulfill Hera's plan and Zeus's passion, while Sleep goes off to tell Poseidon that Zeus is not watching the battle for the moment. So informed, Poseidon himself marches at the head of the Greek soldiers. Ajax wounds Hector, who is carried from the fray, and the Greeks beat the Trojans back toward their own walls.

Books 15–16

As book 15 begins, Zeus awakens, sees Poseidon leading the Greeks, and accuses Hera of having tricked him. He reminds her of an earlier punishment that he had inflicted on her. Frightened, she swears that she is not responsible for Poseidon's actions. Zeus says she can prove it by rounding up Iris, goddess of the rainbow and a messenger of the gods, and Apollo, one of whose functions is to be the patron deity of physicians. Iris is to bear Zeus's message to Poseidon to get off the battlefield and go home. Apollo is to heal Hector and make him forget his sufferings so that he can drive the Greeks into confusion once more.

Zeus then outlines for Hera the events that he knows are coming. When the Trojans drive the Greeks back among the ships and reach those of Achilles, Achilles will send his best friend and companion, Patroclus, to fight. Hector will kill Patroclus and others, including Sarpedon, Zeus's son by a human mother—Laodamia. Achilles will return to the battle to kill Hector in revenge for the death of Patroclus, and Zeus will finally permit the Greeks to fulfill Athena's predictions and conquer Troy.

Those gods who favor the Trojans obey Zeus's orders rather than have a test of wills and strength. Though most acknowledge Zeus's supremacy, Poseidon does not fear Zeus's strength—only his seniority.

Now, with Apollo and a restored Hector at their head, the Trojans swarm once more toward the Greek ships. The flower of the Greek warriors stand against them, while the rest fall back again to the ships. Another Homeric description of carnage ensues, and as usual Homer details the genealogies and accomplishments of those who prevail and those who fall.

Homer often whets his listeners' and readers' appetites with previews of action to follow, and he chooses this moment to convey the news that Zeus intends to allow the Trojans to prevail until the moment that they succeed in setting fire to one of the Grecian ships. At that moment, the chief god will consider his promise to Achilles' mother Thetis fulfilled, and the Trojans will inexorably suffer their fate.

As book 16 opens, Patroclus has come weeping to the tent of Achilles. Patroclus begs Achilles to allow him to wear his friend's armor and lead Achilles' crack troops, the Myrmidons, to the Greeks' assistance. Not knowing that he is signing Patroclus's death warrant, Achilles agrees. He does, however, counsel Patroclus merely to relieve the Greek ships and not to pursue the retreating Trojans toward the city.

Homer invokes the Muses—both Caliope of epic poetry and Clio of history—to tell how fire came to the Greek ships. Ajax had been defending against firing a ship, but he was driven back, fire thrown aboard, and his ship was immediately engulfed in flame.

While the ship was being set ablaze, Achilles, who has brought 50 ships of his own, encourages his men to arm and follow Patroclus to the rescue of the fleet. Then Achilles prays to Zeus that Patroclus may save the ships and return unharmed. Zeus grants the first half of the prayer.

Seeing the armor of Achilles, the Trojans are thrown into confusion and beat a panicked retreat. Having cleared the area of Trojans, Patroclus puts out the fire at the half-burned ship. Then he turns to fight the Trojans, who, though retreating, at first yield each foot of ground stubbornly. Finally, their retreat turns into a rout. Zeus considers where best to have Hector kill Patroclus and decides that it should happen under the battlements of Troy. Patroclus, in the heat of battle, forgets or neglects Achilles' sage advice not to pursue the retreating Trojans. He very nearly overruns the battlements until Apollo himself warns Patroclus that he is not fated to become the sacker of Troy. That said, the god assumes the guise of a mortal and advises Hector to drive straight at Patroclus and kill him.

First Patroclus kills Hector's charioteer, and then 36 other Trojans, but Phoebus Apollo himself becomes Patroclus's invisible adversary. The god beats the helmet from the hero's head and dazes Patroclus so that he is at the mercy of his enemies. A spearman wounds him, and when Hector finally finds him, Patroclus is in no condition to fight. Hector gives him his deathblow. The dying Patroclus prophesies Hector's demise at the hand of Achilles.

Books 17–18

The Spartan king, Menelaus, having seen Patroclus fall, bestrides his body and kills the first man to come—Euphorbus, who had wounded Patroclus. When, however, Menelaus sees Hector coming with others, he deserts the fallen hero like "a lion . . . chased by dogs." Hector strips the body of Achilles' armor, but Ajax successfully recovers Patroclus's body before the Trojans can behead it and fling it to the dogs. In the meantime, Hector exchanges his own armor for that of Achilles. Zeus disapproves this action and vows that Hector will not return to Andromache.

The battle rages again as each side tries to gain and maintain control of Patroclus's corpse. In a touching detail of the battle, when the immortal horses of Achilles learn of Patroclus's death, they weep, refuse to move, and bow down their heads in mourning so that Zeus pities them, and in his pity he momentarily favors the Greeks. Finally, through their prayers the Greeks command enough of the god's compassion that they are able to send news of Patroclus's death to Achilles while Menelaus and the warrior Meriones bear the body from the field.

As book 18 opens, the messenger Antilochus, Nestor's son, brings the news of Patroclus's death to Achilles. Achilles mourns and, hearing his cries, his mother Thetis comes to comfort him. He vows to kill Hector, and Thetis reminds her son that his own death is fated to follow soon upon Hector's. Achilles stoically accepts his fortune. Thetis then promises to bring new armor tomorrow—armor forged by the smithy of the gods, Hephaestus. The goddess Hera, meanwhile, sends Iris to tell Achilles to help the Greeks bring Patroclus's body away from the battle. With Athena's help, Achilles' shouting frightens the Trojans enough to permit the Greeks to move the body beyond their enemies' reach.

In the meantime, Thetis goes to Hephaestus and summarizes for him—and for Homer's audience—the events at Troy. She then requests that Hephaestus craft new armor for her son. In her debt for an earlier kindness she had shown him, Hephaestus immediately sets to work, crafting new armor both effective in defending its wearer and wondrously beautiful, wrought with complex allegories of peace and war. He presents it to Thetis who instantly bears it away to Achilles.

Books 19–21

In book 19, now armed, Achilles meets with the other Greeks in general council. There, he and Agamemnon settle their quarrel, and Agamemnon restores Briseis and pays a generous settlement for the injuries and insult that his pride had inflicted upon Achilles. Achilles and Briseis mourn Patroclus, and Achilles vows to spend the day in mourning and fasting. Athena, however, sees to it that he is secretly fed on divine nectar so that his strength will not fail him in the coming fight. As he readies

his chariot and its immortal team for battle, he addresses his horse, Xanthus, urging him to bring his next passenger back alive. Granted the power of speech by Hera, Xanthus reminds Achilles that, though the team can save him this time, the hour of his death is fast approaching. Both Greeks and Trojans now prepare for the battle.

In book 20, Zeus countermands his order that the gods not participate, telling them that, although he himself will no longer intervene, they can now all do as they wish. Accordingly, the immortals choose sides. Hera, Athena, Poseidon, Hermes, and Hephaestus join the Greek cause. Ares, Apollo, Aphrodite, Artemis, and the TITAN Leto all go with the Trojans. So does the personified Trojan river that the gods call Xanthus and that men call the Scamander.

The gods, however, spend a good deal of time in planning while the men take the field. As the two armies form up to face one another, the Trojan prince Aeneas challenges Achilles to single combat. The two follow a formal pattern of insult and boasting. Achilles insults Aeneas. This gives Aeneas the opportunity to declare his lineage and credentials as a warrior worthy to oppose such a hero as Achilles. The two begin the fight, but the gods recognize that Aeneas will fall if the duel continues, and Poseidon spirits Aeneas away so that he can live to fulfill his destiny.

The armies engage, and Achilles wreaks havoc among the Trojans. Apollo warns Hector not to seek single combat against Achilles, but when Achilles slays Hector's brother, Polydorus, Hector disregards the god's warning. Athena, however, intervenes to protect Achilles from Hector's spear. With the two gods protecting their favorites, neither can do the other harm on their first encounter, so they go in search of other opponents.

As book 21 begins, Achilles' fury splits the massed forces of the Trojans into two separate bodies as he hews his way to the banks of the river Scamander (Xanthus). The river grows angry because of the burden of blood and bodies with which Achilles is loading it. The river sends a champion against Achilles, who triumphs. Then the river speaks to Achilles, asking him to do his killing on dry land. When Achilles does not comply, the river attempts to overwhelm him with a flood. Achilles flees to land, and the river pursues him with water. Achilles becomes afraid, but Poseidon and Athena assure him that it is not his fate to die in the flood. They tell him to go find Hector and kill him. Strengthened by the gods' intervention, Achilles strides against the floodwaters' current in search of his foe. Angered, the river redoubles its force, endangering Achilles again, but Hephaestus intervenes with fire and dries up the waters until Xanthus/Scamander gives up.

Ares and Athena also engage in single combat, and Athena wins easily. Some of the gods, however, are growing bored with their sport or ashamed of their disagreements with each other, and one by one, they begin to leave the battlefield.

Books 22–24

Now, in book 22, Achilles encounters Apollo and reproves the god for thwarting his intentions. He then goes searching for Hector across the plain. From the battlements of Troy, the aged Trojan king Priam sees Achilles coming and warns Hector to enter the city's gates. Hector's mother, Hecuba, seconds her husband's plea. Fearing the scorn of his comrades more than he fears Achilles, however, Hector remains outside the gates *until he sees Achilles coming. At the sight of* Achilles, Hector's courage fails him, and he runs away with his foe in hot pursuit. Apollo, however, perceives that he can no longer keep Hector from the jaws of Hades and ceases to protect him.

Athena assumes the form of Deiphobus, Hector's brother, and proposes that the two together stand and face Achilles. Hector falls for the goddess's cunning and confronts his pursuer. After the exchange of ritual insults, the two hurl their spears at each other. Neither is effective. Hector turns to ask Deiphobus for another, finds himself alone, and knows the gods have played him false. He falls in the ensuing swordplay. Before he dies, he asks that Achilles return his body for decent burial. Achilles refuses. The dogs, he says, will eat Hector's flesh and gnaw his bones. Hector

dies, and Achilles strips him of the armor Hector had taken from Patroclus.

As Achilles drags Hector's body behind his chariot back to the Greek lines, Priam and Hecuba learn of their son's death and mourn him. Andromache hears their grief, rushes to the wall, sees Hector's corpse bouncing behind the chariot, and faints. Coming to herself, she grieves for Hector, for herself, and for their son Astyanax.

Book 23 begins, and back at the Grecian ships, while the body of Hector lies scorned beside Patroclus's bier, the preparations begin for the Greek hero's funeral feast. Achilles falls asleep, and the ghost of Patroclus pays him a visit, telling him to get on with burying him so that he can get to Hades and rest. He also asks that he and Achilles be buried together in a common urn. The next morning, a long funeral procession bears Patroclus to the bier that had been erected for his burning. After sacrificing a number of Patroclus's pets and domestic animals and a dozen Trojan captives to be burned with him, they also lay these bodies upon the funeral pyre and try to ignite it. At first it refuses to burn, but a prayer carried by Iris to the winds Boreas and Zephyrus bring them to fan the flames of the pyre, and soon it burns brightly.

After the bodies have burned, the Greeks carefully gather Patroclus's bones from the center of the ashes and store them in a golden urn where those of Achilles will soon join them. The dogs, however, will not touch the nearby body of Hector, for the goddess Aphrodite preserves it from them and from decay. Then chariot races are held in honor of Patroclus. Homer describes these with relish, and his audience gains an insight into the strategy and tactics of the sport. One also learns that chariot racers can be sore losers when Menelaus complains about the foolhardy tactics employed by Antilochus. By the time the prizes are awarded, however, several of those who won pass their prizes over to others who did not, and good fellowship gets restored all around. A series of boxing and wrestling matches and foot races follow the horse racing. Then come discus throwing and archery contests. The funeral games of Patroclus anticipate the activities of later Olympiads.

In book 24, Achilles, still burning with rage at the dead Hector for the death of his beloved Patroclus, dishonors the body of Hector by dragging it three times around Patroclus's tomb. The gods are offended by this behavior. Dishonoring the dead is a major sin, as the dead belong to them and are no longer an appropriate object of human enmity. Zeus therefore summons Thetis and dispatches her to tell Achilles to give up Hector's body for decent burial. Achilles obeys, and King Priam of Troy ransoms his son's body from Achilles.

The final episodes of book 24 recount how Hermes, the messenger of the gods, escorts Priam, with the ransom on a mule wagon, within the Greek encampment. Priam kneels before Achilles and appeals to his human nature to let him take the body of his son Hector—one of 50 he has sired with Hecuba and other women of his royal household. Most of those sons now lie dead as a result of the war. Moved by pity and the memory of his own father, Achilles releases Hector's body to Priam. The hero then insists that the old king accept his hospitality overnight. Priam is reluctant, but failing to accept would insult Achilles and might provoke his wrath. Then Priam negotiates an 11-day truce with Achilles to give time for the proper performance of the rites connected with Hector's burial. After that, the fight, if necessary, can commence once more. Achilles agrees.

The focus of Homer's attention follows the old king and the body of his son back to Troy, where the grief of Hector's family and the hero's funeral occupy the end of *The Iliad*.

Bibliography
Homer. *The Iliad*. Translated by Robert Fitzgerald. New York: Farrar, Straus & Giroux, 2004.

"I more than envy him . . ."   Sappho
What remains of this poem—the 27th in Paul Roche's translation and one of the most famous of SAPPHO's works—the ancient critic Longinus preserved in a celebrated essay °LONGINUS, ON THE SUBLIME. (Longinus's authorship is sometimes questioned.) There we find four complete stanzas of Sappho's poem and the first line of a fifth verse.

In the first stanza, the speaker—presumably Sappho herself—addresses a woman who is the object of her affection. The speaker confesses that she considers the woman's male companion—a lover or husband—a god because he enjoys the privilege of sitting close to the woman whom Sappho admires. Sappho also covets his opportunity to hear the sweet sound of his partner's intimately spoken words. Her laughter makes Sappho's heart beat faster and, as Sappho shifts the focus to her internal responses, leaves the poet speechless.

Moreover, as the third stanza makes clear, the woman's presence makes Sappho feel feverish, strikes her blind, and leaves her deaf. In the fourth stanza, the poet breaks into a sweat, she shudders, and she finds herself on the point of death.

The single surviving line of the fifth stanza explains that the poet must bear all these unpleasant effects, as she has become a beggar—and the poem breaks off.

The Roman poet CATULLUS borrowed the poem's ideas and images in a four-stanza complaint, "He seems the equal of the gods," addressed to his mistress, Clodia Metelli, whom he called Lesbia. She had a husband and took other lovers, which drove Catullus nearly mad.

Bibliography
Catullus. *Catullus: The Complete Poems for Modern Readers*. Translated by Reney Myers and Robert J. Ormsby. London: George Allen and Unwin, 1972.
Sappho. *The Love Songs of Sappho*. Translated by Paul Roche. Amherst, N.Y.: Prometheus Books, 1998.

In Defense of Ctesiphon   See ON THE CROWN.

Intrigues of the Warring States (Zhan Guo Ce, Chan-kuo ts'e) (ca. 200 B.C.E.)
During the Warring States Period (403–221 B.C.E.), narrative prose writing in ancient China

developed quite rapidly. One of the early fruits of this development was *Intrigues of the Warring States,* or *The Book of the Warring States.*

The oldest copy that has survived contains 33 volumes and was edited in the first century B.C.E. by the Han dynasty scholar Liu Xiang (Hsiang). Dealing with events that occurred as early as 475 B.C.E. and proceeding in a roughly chronological order, among other matters, the *Intrigues of the Warring States* reports the eloquence with which the warring-states diplomats sought to convince their opposite numbers to withdraw from a situation in which the strongest of the states, Jin (Chin), will or will not be able to annex all the other states concerned. The principal states involved included the Zhou (Chou) imperial court and the seven rival states principally involved in the war: Zhao (Chao), Jin (Chin), Qi (Chi), Chu, Han, Wen, and Yan (Yen). A few other weaker states were absorbed by their neighbors early in the process that finally ended when Chin emerged victorious.

The task of the diplomats was to convince their colleagues that unless the weaker six states banded together to resist Chin's expansionist ambitions, they would certainly all fall separately. The author or authors of *Intrigues of the Warring States* capture the eloquence and the subtlety with which the diplomats—particularly Su Chin—negotiated an anti-Chin alliance.

An even more brilliant master of the art of persuasion, however, was Zhang (Chang) Yi, the negotiator from the state of Jin who convinced the alliance to split; the result was that Jin was able to do exactly what Zhang Yi had hoped and bring all the states under its imperial control. Before that happened however, *Warring States* traces the untiring efforts of the diplomats to create alliances that will not only hold the dominant state of Chin at bay, but also will serve the many and shifting interests of the parties to the negotiations.

Friendly persuasion, however, is not the only diplomatic art that the *Intrigues* celebrates. The fine arts of insult and posturing also play roles, as does the relative sumptuousness of the funerals of the politically important in helping diplomats decide which side to support.

Both the way that events are depicted in their narration and the use of dialogue to reflect the cleverness of the diplomats are new aspects of Chinese prose writing. The appearance of personality in the speech of the personages drawn is also a new aspect of early Chinese prose. Moreover, the speeches that the diplomats make, as Burton Watson tells us, became the models for rhetoric as it was later studied in Chinese schools. This rhetoric is summary and allusive in character and relies on all parties having studied the basic documents from which the rhetoric is drawn so that they can perceive not only what is said, but also what is hinted at and, beyond that, what is intended.

See also ANCIENT CHINESE DYNASTIES AND PERIODS.

Bibliography

Liu Hsiang, ed. *Chan-kuo tse* [*Intrigues of the Warring States*]. Translated by J. I. Crump, Jr. Oxford: Clarendon Press, 1970.

Mair, Victor H. *The Columbia Anthology of Traditional Chinese Literature.* New York: Columbia University Press, 1994.

Watson, Burton. *Early Chinese Literature.* New York: Columbia University Press, 1962.

Ion Euripides (before 406 B.C.E)

Thought to be a late work by EURIPIDES, the plot of *Ion* treats matters that no other surviving Greek drama handles. Moreover, Euripides develops that material in an uncharacteristic way. The play addresses the story of its title character, Ion, in a manner that is potentially tragic but that in fact proves to be comic. Thus the play both presages the subsequent Greek New Comedy (see COMEDY IN GREECE AND ROME) in the resolution of its plot and relies on the conventions of the older TRAGEDY in establishing the audience's expectations.

Hermes, the messenger of the gods, speaks the prologue from the temple of Apollo at Delphi. Hermes reports that Apollo raped Creusa, the daughter of a legendary king of Athens, Erechtheus. As all unions of gods and human beings were fruitful, Creusa conceived and eventually bore a son, Ion, in secret. To hide her shame, she left the child to die in a circular vase within a willow basket, but she carefully clothed him and left with him an ornament that she wore. Apollo sent Hermes to carry the baby to Apollo's temple at Delphi. There the priestess of the temple discovered the baby and thought some nymph had borne it and left it there. The priestess chose to keep the child, and she reared him in the vicinity of the temple.

In the meantime, Creusa married the Euboean demigod Xuthus. Although the couple wanted children, none came. Eventually, accompanied by trains of servants portrayed by the CHORUS, Creusa and Xuthus traveled separately to Apollo's temple to pray for the god's intercession in their plight. Hermes announces to the audience that the temple oracle will tell the couple that the child Ion is the offspring of Xuthus.

Ion enters, chanting while he cleans and decorates the temple, reverently singing all the while and celebrating his intention always to serve Apollo. Behaving like sightseers, the chorus enters as the servants of Creusa. When she arrives, she and Ion discuss her ancestry and the stories connected with her lineage. They then turn to Ion's history, and he explains that the priestess of the temple has reared him. The conversation now turns to Creusa's errand, and in the course of the discussion Creusa, tells her own story, pretending it to be another's.

Xuthus now enters. He has arrived from the cave of Trophonius, another oracle. There he learned that he and Creusa would not depart childless from Delphi. Xuthus goes to consult the Delphic oracle. Ion reflects on the injustice sometimes done by the god he serves in conceiving mortal children to satisfy his lust, and then deserting his offspring. The chorus sings, instead, of the happy outcome of the coupling of gods with humankind.

Xuthus reenters and salutes Ion as his son. Ion thinks the man has lost his wits. Ion cross-questions Xuthus and discovers that the older man did indeed have an affair in the vicinity at about the time of the lad's conception. Finally convinced, Ion greets Xuthus as his father.

In their mutual rejoicing, the pair is mindful that, though Xuthus has apparently been reunited with his son, Creusa remains childless and may well be past childbearing. They do not want to upset her by suddenly announcing Xuthus's good fortune. They agree to bring Ion to Athens as a visitor. They will then choose an opportune moment to inform Creusa. The women of the chorus, however, have been witnesses to the entire proceeding, and although Xuthus warns them to help keep the secret, the women conclude among themselves that they owe their primary allegiance to Creusa.

Now Creusa enters. Her aged tutor accompanies her. They ask the women to share news of the oracle's answer. The women hesitate, but then report the bad news. Creusa will not conceive a child. Pressed for more, however, they report that Xuthus has discovered his son. Creusa is not pleased. She calls Xuthus a "wretch of a husband."

The tutor supports her in this view, fabricating a fanciful history of Xuthus that presupposes him to have known all along about Ion and to have intentionally deceived Creusa throughout her marriage. He advises Creusa to kill Ion—an undertaking in which the tutor will happily cooperate. Creusa responds to this with a lengthy lament in which she blames Apollo for giving a child to her husband while withholding the child born to her union with the god. She then confesses all to her tutor, and in a lengthy dialogue the two determine to poison Ion at the party celebrating the reunion of the putative father and son. She gives the old tutor a box containing the poison, but warns him that her husband must not drink from the wine with which it is mixed.

Offstage, however, the plot fails. An attendant enters to report the events. The god has provided ill omens that Ion easily reads. He has all the celebrants pour out their wine cups on the ground. A flock of doves descends, and they drink from the spilled wine. The only dove to die drinks from Ion's spillage. As everyone knows that the cup was Creusa's gift, the attendant predicts that she will be executed for her attempt upon a sacred life.

Creusa rushes in, confirming that the Pythian council has sentenced her to death. The leader of the chorus advises her to seek sanctuary at the altar, where none can kill her. Ion and others enter to carry out the sentence. He and Creusa rancorously debate until he is about to tear her from the altar and take her life.

At that moment, however, the priestess of Apollo who had reared Ion intervenes. She carries with her the vase and basket in which she found the infant boy. Ion realizes that he now has the means necessary to identify his mother. Seeing the vase and basket, Creusa belatedly realizes that Ion is her son. She tells him so, but he mistrusts her. He asks her to name the other contents of the basket and vase. She describes them in detail, and Ion embraces her as his mother. She explains that Apollo is his father and that Apollo has now conferred upon Ion a human father, Xuthus.

Ion is dubious and announces his intention to consult the oracle. At that moment, Athena, the goddess of wisdom, appears and explains all, including the care that Apollo has always taken of Ion. The goddess predicts subsequent good fortune for all. Creusa is at last reconciled with Apollo, and the members of the chorus end the drama with a paean in praise of piety.

The identification of a lost child through the recognition of a token became a standard device of later Greek comedy. The device has been resurrected in literary works many times through the intervening millennia to resolve otherwise irresolvable questions of identity.

Bibliography

Euripides. *Ion.* Translated by W. S. Di Piero. New York: Oxford University Press, 1996.

Oates, Whitney J., and Eugene O' Neill, Jr., ed. *Ion.* In *The Complete Greek Drama.* Vol. 1. New York: Random House. 1938.

Iphigenia in Aulis Euripides (staged 406 B.C.E.)

Completed by EURIPIDES' son and namesake following his father's death, *Iphigenia in Aulis* elaborates on a situation that occurred at the beginning of the Trojan War. The invading Greek fleet has gathered at the port of Aulis on its way to the invasion of Troy. There, however, the fleet finds itself becalmed, and the prophet Calchas has informed the leader of the Grecian forces, King Agamemnon of Mycenae, that in order to secure an offshore sailing wind from the gods, Agamemnon must sacrifice his daughter Iphigenia to them. Pretending that he has arranged a marriage between the hero Achilles and Iphigenia, Agamemnon has summoned his wife Clytemnestra and his daughter to Aulis, where the sacrifice will occur.

As the play opens, a distraught Agamemnon is commiserating with an old servant. The general tells his old retainer that he is fortunate to be a humble person. The old man objects that leaders get the glory, but Agamemnon replies that the gods' wrath can shatter that glory in an instant. Repenting his decision to kill his child, Agamemnon has written a letter instructing Clytemnestra not to send the girl to Aulis. He gives it to the servant, instructing him to deliver the message and to turn back the chariot carrying the girl if the old man should encounter it.

The old man leaves, but he is intercepted by the king of Sparta, Menelaus, Agamemnon's brother, who has been suspiciously watchful and has taken the letter and read it. The brothers quarrel. A messenger interrupts to report that he has brought Iphigenia and Clytemnestra to the Greek camp. Agamemnon thanks the messenger but privately bewails this misfortune. Moved, Menelaus undergoes a change of heart and speaks on behalf of sparing Iphigenia. Now, however, her unlooked-for arrival has convinced Agamemnon that he is in the hands of the fates and must go through with the sacrifice. Moreover, Agamemnon feels sure that Odysseus and the army would force him to follow through should he try to avoid his fate. Agamemnon merely hopes now that he can keep word of the impending sacrifice from Clytemnestra. With her he dissembles, pretending that the wedding is to take place, describing the genealogy of the groom Achilles, and discussing the wedding arrangements.

Agamemnon proposes that Clytemnestra go home and not stay for the wedding—a suggestion she strongly rejects. Clytemnestra exits, and a CHORUS of women who have been on stage since the end of the first scene chant predictions about the progress of the Trojan War and eventual Greek victory.

Achilles, anxious for martial action, accidentally encounters Clytemnestra. He has had no news of the impending wedding. Clytemnestra speaks of it, Achilles is baffled, and both are thoroughly embarrassed. Achilles means to ask Agamemnon for an explanation. Before he can leave, however, the old servant enters and explains Agamemnon's true purpose to the mother and the purported bridegroom. He also explains that Agamemnon made an attempt to stop the sacrifice. But Achilles is angry that he has been made a pawn in the business. He swears to assist Clytemnestra by intervening with Agamemnon.

She, however, thinks that her husband is a coward afraid of the army, and that Achilles' pleas will prove fruitless. Clytemnestra goes to Iphigenia, and when the two present themselves before Agamemnon, he pretends that the wedding preparations are going forward. Clytemnestra flings the lie in his face and confronts him with her own series of truths. She never loved him, she says. He killed her first husband, Tantalus, and acquired her by force. Nonetheless, she was a true and faithful wife who kept his house and bore his children, and now he would sacrifice the life of her firstborn to recover Helen, a strumpet who fled his brother's palace with her lover. Clytemnestra darkly hints, moreover, at the welcome he will receive when he returns home from the war—his murder. To her mother's complaint, Iphigenia adds her own pleas. But Agamemnon is firm in his own resolve and has recourse to the tyrant's usual plea, public interest and patriotism. The chorus sympathizes with Iphigenia's plight.

Now Achilles enters leading a small company of armed soldiers. He reports that the army is clamoring for Iphigenia's sacrifice, and that they tried to stone him when he spoke in her defense. Nonetheless, with his few soldiers, he is prepared to confront the entire host of the Greeks in defense of Iphigenia.

She, however, has decided that dying in the Greek cause is the right thing for her to do—remarking at one point: "A thousand women are not worth one man!" She counsels that the Greeks should take her life and conquer Troy. Achilles admires her courage and regrets losing her as his bride.

Firm now in the rectitude of her sacrifice, Iphigenia comforts her mother, who at last accepts her daughter's death as inevitable. Iphigenia bids farewell to her baby brother, Orestes, and counsels her mother not to hate Agamemnon, who is acting against his own will. Clytemnestra rejects those arguments.

In triumphant certainty, Iphigenia voluntarily goes forth to meet her fate as the members of the chorus celebrate her as the "conqueror of Troy."

Bibliography

Euripides. *The Complete Plays*. Translated by Carl R. Mueller. Hanover, N.H.: Smith and Kraus, 2005.

Grene, David, and Richmond Lattimore, ed. *Euripides: The Complete Greek Tragedies*. Vol. 1. Chicago: University of Chicago Press, 1955.

Kovacs, David, ed. and trans. *Euripides*. Loeb Classical Library. 5 vols. Cambridge, Mass.: Harvard University Press, 1994–2002.

Isæus (fl. fourth century B.C.E.) *Greek prose writer*

An orator during the golden age of Greek oratory, Isæus was born in Chalchis in Euboea. He moved to Athens and studied oratory with LYSIAS and ISOCRATES. In turn Isæus became the teacher of the most distinguished of Greek orators, DEMOSTHENES.

Although 50 of Isæus's orations remained extant as late as the ninth century C.E., only 11 now survive. They are exclusively concerned with the subject of inheritance. Isæus gave these speeches before the Athenian tribunal concerned with such matters. Isæus's orations remain important sources of historical information concerning the laws governing Athenian legacies, adoption, and property transfer. They also present a dispiriting picture of the fraud and vindictiveness practiced by guardians, trustees, executors, and quarreling heirs. Isæus's lively style reportedly confirmed Demosthenes in his decision to study oratory with Isæus.

Bibliography

Isæus. *Isæus*. Translated by Michael Edwards. Austen: University of Texas Press, 2007.

Isidore of Seville, St. (ca. 560–636 C.E.)
Spanish prose writer

The last of the ancient Western Fathers of the Church, Isidore, whose father was named Severianus, may have come from Cartagena. Isidore's elder brother, Leander, had been bishop of Seville before Isidore, who succeeded his sibling to that post around 600. Isidore spent his career reorganizing the Spanish church, increasing episcopal power, and knitting close ties between clerical and temporal authority by fostering relations between the church and the Visigothic rulers of Spain.

Literature best remembers Isidore for a work of encyclopedic scope, his *Etymologies*. Written in 20 books, it provided a storehouse of ancient knowledge—particularly philological knowledge—throughout the Middle Ages and beyond. Isidore thought that tracing the origins of words would enhance their truth and help preserve and extend knowledge.

Also a historian, Isidore produced two major works of the historical genre. The first, his *Chronica maiora* (Great chronicle) traces the history of the world from its creation to 615 C.E. His other historical work, less ambitious but perhaps more valuable, is *History of the Goths, Vandals, and Suevi* (*Historia Gothorum vandalorum Sueborum*). These were Isidore's ancestors—the Germanic tribes, the Visigoths—who had centuries before arrived from the east and made Spain their own.

The work begins with an apostrophe, or address, to Spain as beautiful and fertile and the jewel of nature. Isidore deems the Goths fortu-

nate to have conquered her. His history proper begins in 49 B.C.E. and traces the tribes down to the year 624 C.E. Isidore's principal sources are known, and they are all extant. Nonetheless, his history remains our main and, after 590, sometimes our only source concerning Gothic history.

Isidore also wrote works connected with his religious vocation. These included introductions to both the Old Testament and the NEW TESTAMENT, works about the monastic rule and about church offices, a defense of Christianity against the Jews, and a work of wise maxims or *sententiae*.

See also GRAMMARIANS OF ROME.

Bibliography

Conte, Gian Biagio, et al. *Latin Literature: A History*. Translated by Joseph B. Solodow, Don Fowler, and Glenn W. Most. Baltimore, Md.: Johns Hopkins University Press, 1999.

Isidore of Seville, St. *Isidore of Seville's History of the Goths, Vandals, and Suevi*. Translated by Guido Donini and Gordon B. Ford, Jr. Leiden: E. J. Brill, 1970.

———. *The Etymologies of Isidore of Seville*. Translated by Stephen A. Barney et al. Cambridge and New York: Cambridge University Press, 2006.

Isocrates (ca. 436–338 B.C.E.) *Greek prose writer*

Born in Athens, where he studied oratory with the SOPHISTS GORGIAS OF LEONTIUM and Prodikos, Isocrates was something of an anomaly. He rarely spoke in public himself because he was very shy and had a weak voice. He became, nonetheless, a much sought-after teacher of oratory because of his mastery of eloquence and his ability to produce orations distinguished by their refinement and precision.

As a young man, Isocrates had been a friend of PLATO and a devotee of SOCRATES. A renowned patriot, Isocrates is said to have died as a result of starving himself over his grief at the Athenian loss of the battle of Chaeronea (338 B.C.E.) to Philip of Macedon. This was the battle that ended democracy in Athens.

Some 21 of Isocrates' orations survive, as do 10 of his letters. Among the surviving orations, the most famous is one that he wrote to be presented at the Olympic Games. Addressed to all the Greeks, it nonetheless praised Athens as the premier Grecian city-state. Four of the surviving speeches are written in praise of individuals or, in one case, of the entire Athenian citizenry. Others have to do with court cases and with his personal financial affairs. Isocrates also wrote an attack on the Sophists that survives.

Bibliography

Isocrates. *Isocrates II.* Translated by Terry Papillon. Austen: University of Texas Press, 2004.
———. *Isocrates.* 2 vols. Translated by David Mirhady and Yun Lee Too. Austen: University of Texas Press, 2000–2004.

Italic School of Philosophy

Founded by Pythagoras of Samos (ca. 580–ca. 500 B.C.E.) at Crotona in Italy, the Italic school enrolled as many as 600 students who lived together in a single large building and held all property in common. The members of the school, which had much in common with a monastic order, were divided into two groups: those who were initiates and those on probation. Only the initiates were allowed to know the secret knowledge of the school.

All human knowledge was grist for the school's mill and the object of their philosophical study. Pythagoras, however, particularly valued music and astronomy. He was certain that the sun and not the earth was the center of the solar system. Pythagoras is credited with the introduction of the notion of the music of spheres—music created by the friction of the crystalline spheres in which he supposed the heavenly bodies to be embedded.

The people of Crotona came to view the school with suspicion and eventually attacked and destroyed it.

Bibliography

Eschenburg, J. J. *Manual of Classical Literature.* Translated by N. W. Fiske. Philadelphia: E. C. & J. Biddle, 1850.

Itinerary of Greece *(Helladios Periegesis, Description of Greece, Guide to Greece)*
Pausanias (second century C.E.)

The only fully extant example of ancient travel literature describing Greece, the Roman PAUSANIAS's book in the Greek language offers information principally concerning statues and paintings that survived from the Greek classical period and from its predecessor, the archaic period. Pausanias was also deeply interested in the religious contexts from which the sculpture and graphic representations that he described had originated. A Grecophile, he wrote enthusiastically about ancient sites and cities in central Greece (Achaia). Additionally, he indulged a more modern interest as he also described monuments that his own emperor, Hadrian (ruled 117–138 C.E.), had constructed in various Greek locations.

Bibliography

Pausanias. *Guide to Greece.* Translated by Peter Leir. New York: Penguin, 1979.
———. *Pausanias's Description of Greece.* Translated by J. G. French. New York: Biblos and Tannen, 1965.

J

Jain texts

The Jains of India belong to one of the world's oldest religious communities. The number of believers is currently estimated to run between 3 and 4 million persons divided into two main lines of religious practice associated with two sets of teachers of divergent doctrines involving cosmography, iconography, and the history of the universe. These lines of practice are respectively called Digambaras (whose monks remain unclothed, though their nuns wear robes) and Shvetambaras (whose monks and nuns both wear white robes).

As the historian of religion Paul Dundas tells us, the Jains do not, like Christians or Muslims, regard a single prophet as their founder, and the texts that they revere do not occupy a place comparable to that of the Bible or of the Koran. On the contrary, the Jains actively discourage individual reading of their venerated texts. They think that doing so not only confers no benefit but also can be positively dangerous. Their texts need to be studied under the guidance of a qualified teacher. The principal teachers of Jain history are classed as *fordmakers*. The *fords* that they construct are the Jain communities the makers establish that create fords or crossings over the ocean of rebirth directly to the eternal state of bliss.

Jain texts begin from a preliterate oral tradition. A fordmaker directly perceived eternal, uncreated truths and preached them. His disciples each interpreted his utterances and structured those interpretations into what Dundas's translation calls "a twelve-limbed basket of the disciples." Thus, a long history of oral transmission and interpretation precedes the eventual written preservation of the truths that have been handed down over the millennia. As one can imagine, the contents of such a tradition shifts continually. Around 150 C.E., worried that the accumulated wisdom of Jainism might disappear, a Diagambara monk named Dharasena finally wrote down his recollections of Jain teachings. This work underwent further development and has been preserved as "The Scripture of Six Parts." To this was later added a "Treatise on the Passions." These works were preserved in increasingly fragile manuscripts until their eventual (and at first unauthorized) publication in the 19th and 20th centuries.

The Shvetambaras principally venerate a work that continues to be presented orally during their annual eight-day September celebration of a festival called Paryushan. This work is called the *Kalpasutra*. It is annually recited in Prakrit, a dialect that hardly anyone in the audience can understand.

The two branches of Jainism concur that texts important to both of them have utterly perished. These, called the Purvas, seem to have disappeared around 500 C.E. The Purvas also seem to have contained the most difficult portions of the Jain creed, since, unlike the surviving texts that both branches agree were originally promulgated for women, the Purvas were addressed to the more robust intellects—as the Jains imagine—of the men.

Beyond these the Shvetambaras venerate some 45 other texts as canonical. A full listing of them appears in the Dundas reference in the bibliography. The Digambaras oddly reject much of the Shvetambaras' canon, though they share a veneration for much that it contains and for the so-called Five Homages that express respect for those who occupy the "highest stage": those who are (1) omniscient, (2) liberated, (3) teachers, (4) preceptors, and (5) monks.

Jain Scripture in both branches is thought to be authorless and without beginning. It has simply always been. The central behavioral observances of both branches include nonviolence, pacificism, and a strictly observed respect for the lives of all creatures—a respect that extends, for example, to covering the mouth with a cloth lest an insect inadvertently enter and die.

Bibliography

Cort, John E. *Jains in the World: Religious Values and Ideology in India.* New York: Oxford University Press, 2001.

Dundas, Paul. *The Jains.* New York: Routledge, 1992.

Japanese literature, ancient

The word *ancient*, when applied to literature, can mean different things in different circumstances. If one limits the notion of literature to that which has been written rather than also meaning that which was sung or spoken before writing developed, then *ancient* alludes not to an arbitrarily defined time period but rather to that culturally relative moment when speech or song has been preserved in symbols.

That moment occurred in Japan toward the end of the ancient and the start of the medieval period in Europe. The oldest surviving Japanese book is the *Kojiki* (Record of ancient matters, 712 C.E.). The second oldest is the *Nihon Shoki* (Chronicles of Japan, 720 C.E.). Both books, as the historian and translator of Japanese letters, Donald Keene, tells us, allude to earlier documents in the Japanese language, but all such documents were destroyed in a conflagration that occurred in 645.

In any case, the Japanese did not develop a native system of writing to represent a language that had evidently lived exclusively in the mouths of its speakers. Then, around the sixth century C.E., Buddhism arrived in Japan, bringing with it an already well-established textual tradition (see BUDDHA AND BUDDHISM; BUDDHIST TEXTS). Rather than develop an ALPHABET—as the Koreans would do eight centuries later—or start from scratch with an idea of their own, the Japanese adapted Chinese characters to their own purposes in two ways. They first took some of the many characters (over 5,000) that stood for whole words in Chinese, ignored their Chinese meanings, and assigned phonological value to each of the characters they selected. Second, still ignoring the Chinese meanings, the Japanese assigned whole concepts to some of the Chinese characters. Thus, a single ideogram might stand for a number like 1,000 without reference to pronunciation. Though this system surely must sometimes have proved awkward, it made possible the literary preservation of important Japanese texts. Because the representation of the language was so cumbersome, however, modernizers of early Japanese books rarely agree on the details of what the texts say.

They do, however, agree on the general lineaments of the contents. Included in this volume, then, readers will find ancient Japanese literature represented by brief descriptions of the two documents named above and also by the first and most celebrated collection of Japanese poetry, the *Man'yōshū* (Collection for a Myriad Ages). That collection contains poems composed as early as the fifth century C.E. The *Man'yōshū* appeared in its first collected version around the end of the eighth century C.E.

Bibliography

Keene, Donald. *Seeds in the Heart: Japanese Literature from Earliest Times to the Late Seventeenth Century.* New York: Henry Holt and Company, 1993.

Jerome, St. (Eusebius Hieronymus Stridonensis) (ca. 347–420 C.E.) *Roman prose writer*

Born to a Christian family at Stridon in the northeastern Adriatic sector of Italy, Jerome proved to be an intellectually precocious child. At age 12, he went to Rome to study with the influential grammarian DONATUS. Following Jerome's baptism at age 19, he traveled in Gaul and, being attracted by the monastic life, he became an ascetic for a period of about two years. For reasons unknown, he then left the community he had joined in Aquileia and wandered through Asia Minor for a while. Then he briefly dwelled with a friend, Paulinus, in Antioch. Called again to the ascetic life, he isolated himself in the desert near Aleppo. There he fell ill and had a dream in which a voice reproved him for being not a real Christian but instead a follower of the thought of CICERO. On recovering, he set himself to perfect his knowledge of Greek and began the study of Hebrew.

In 379, Jerome was ordained a priest of the Church of Rome. He conferred with several of the principal Christian intellectuals of his time and then undertook an ambitious literary career in earnest. He began by translating into Latin the Greek *World Chronicle* of EUSEBIUS and a selection of the homilies of ORIGEN.

Jerome and Paulinus moved to Rome in 382. Pope Damasus I welcomed him there by appointing Jerome his secretary. Jerome continued to practice asceticism, and he also became the spiritual adviser to a group of wealthy and devout women.

By collating Origen's *Hexepla* (concerning the six days of creation and the attendant HEBREW BIBLE matter) with the then-current version of the Hebrew Bible, Jerome was able to provide Pope Damasus with corrected versions of the Gospels and the Psalms. As a Christian controversialist, he wrote in defense of the perpetual virginity of Mary the Mother of Jesus, and in a dialogue against Lucifer, he discussed the efficacy of baptism into communities of Christians deemed heretical, as well as the authority of the bishops of such communities.

To recruit for the monastic life, Jerome penned quasi-authentic biographies of Hilarion and a monk named Malchus. He also defended the Christian ideal of virginity in two books entitled *Against Jovinian.*

Perhaps Jerome's most important work of this period (393–5) was his *Lives of Illustrious Men*—a work that listed 135 authors, both Christian writers and influential heretics. The first work of criticism to consider such authors seriously as men of letters, it began with St. Peter and ended with himself.

As a Christian controversialist, Jerome conducted an ongoing and increasingly bitter argument about Origen with his former friend Rufinus. When the argument ended on Rufinus's death, Jerome expressed his satisfaction with the departure of "the scorpion." That he was an indefatigable correspondent is indicated by the survival of 117 of his letters.

All the while that he was penning the works listed above, Jerome was also engaged in his most monumental work—a new version of the Bible in Latin that would be based on sound principles of textual criticism. Moreover, with his command of both Hebrew and Greek and his unparalleled learning, he was the person in his time most qualified to accomplish the daunting task. Between 382 and 385, he revised the old Latin version of the NEW TESTAMENT by consulting the original texts of the Greek gospels. He used the Hebrew SEPTUAGINT OLD TESTAMENT as the source of his new translation of the Psalms.

Then, from 391 to 406, Jerome turned his attention to the Hebrew Bible, publishing a new translation of all the books it contained. While all this went forward, he also produced a steady stream of commentary on the texts, on his methods of translations, and explanations of problems of Scripture posed by his friends.

In his last 15 years, Jerome turned his attention to the explanation of Scripture, employing the fourfold method of interpretation favored by the church fathers and explaining biblical texts in terms of their literal meanings, their implications for a moral life, the allegorical interpretations they would support, and their anagogical import—that is, what Scripture passages taught devout Christians about future glory. In so doing, he drew upon the exegetical methods that had found favor in Antioch, Alexandria, and the rabbinical traditions.

The Roman Catholic Church considers Jerome to have been its greatest apologist in explaining sacred Scripture. His version of the Bible remained officially accepted in the Western church until well into the European Renaissance. Although recent editions of Jerome's complete extant works are available in Spanish and in French translation, none seems to have appeared in English. The bibliography below, therefore, is illustrative of work available.

See also GRAMMARIANS OF ROME.

Bibliography

Jerome, Saint. *Homilies of Saint Jerome*. Translated by Marie Ligouri Ewald. Washington, D.C.: Catholic University of America Press, 2002.
———. *On Illustrious Men*. Translated by Thomas P. Halton. Washington, D.C.: Catholic University of America Press, 1999.
———. *Patristic Scholarship*. Edited and translated by James F. Brady and John C. Olin. Toronto: Toronto University Press, 1992.
———. *The Commentaries of Saint Jerome: On Saint Paul's Epistle to the Ephesians*. Translated by Ronald E. Heine. New York: Oxford University Press, 2002.

Jewish War Flavius Josephus (ca. 75–79 C.E.)

In 67 C.E., JOSEPHUS had commanded the Jewish forces in Palestine in their battle against the Romans at Jotapata. There the Roman general, Titus Flavius Vespasian, who later became emperor, disastrously routed Josephus's army. Josephus's detractors maintain that he betrayed his army to the Romans, surrendering himself on advantageous terms while leaving his forces leaderless to suffer decimation. Others, including Josephus himself, suggest that from a very early date, he perceived that the only hope for his countrymen lay in cooperation with rather than antagonism toward the Romans. He probably perceived his action as serving the interests of a greater good—peace between Rome and Palestine. Both opinions about him may be true. Subsequent events supported his view of the matter, for when the Jews continued their resistance, the Romans sacked and leveled Jerusalem.

Josephus, in the meantime, went to Rome as a trusted and respected client of Vespasian. As a sign of that affiliation, Josephus took the Roman name Flavius. Then he undertook to fulfill the imperial request for a history, written from the Roman perspective, that would present the conquerors as destiny's favorites and reconcile the conquered Jews to their at least temporarily subordinate place in the providential scheme of things. In a word, Josephus became Rome's minister of propaganda for Palestine.

That characterization, however, does not undermine Josephus's credentials as an historian. He not only had at his disposal his personal experience as a campaigner in the war he would chronicle, he also had at hand the detailed records of the Jewish War that had been kept by Roman field commanders, as well as a large and competent staff of research assistants quartered with him in Vespasian's private palace in Rome. Before him, too, he had the model of such predecessors as JULIUS CAESAR and THUCYDIDES.

Josephus's history of the war, then, recites the events largely as they happened, but he recounts them from the perspective of conquerors wishing to pacify a subject people. First, Josephus penned a preliminary work in the Semitic tongue. This version of the history has perished. Then he amplified that version into the extant Greek work.

Josephus follows the example of Caesar in showing the might and ingenuity of Roman arms to their best advantage. He emulates the techniques of Thucydides in putting credible speeches in the mouths of commanders encouraging their troops and of other principal actors. Such speeches invariably display a high degree of mastery of oratory as taught in the ancient Greek and Roman worlds.

Bibliography

Josephus, Flavius. *The Great Roman-Jewish War (De bello Judaico): The Life of Flavius Josephus.* William Whiston and D. S. Margolioth, trans. Mineola, N.Y.: Dover Publications, 2004.

Thackeray, H. St. John. *Josephus: The Man and the Historian.* New York: KTAV Publishing House, 1967.

Ji Kang (Chi K'ang, Xi Kong, Hsi K'ang) (223–262 C.E.) *Chinese poet*

One of a circle of poets who achieved fame as the SEVEN SAGES OF THE BAMBOO GROVE, the 7' 7" tall Ji Kang was an in-law of the imperial family of the Wei dynasty (see ANCIENT CHINESE DYNASTIES AND PERIODS). He nonetheless held government service in contempt, as is clear in 18 poems addressed to Ji 's brother on the occasion of the latter's induction into the army. The same disdain for officialdom also appears in a letter he wrote to another of the seven sages, Shan (Dao Tao). Ji broke off his friendship with Shan because Shan had joined the government.

As a poet, Ji became the most celebrated member of his group. He preferred to write in an archaic style, penning lines four syllables in length. He chose this form for about half of his 60 surviving poems. Ji was an accomplished performer on the lute or zither, and one of his poetic essays carefully details the origin of the instrument, its construction, and the method of playing it. The work simultaneously bemoans how hard it is to find a friend who "understands one's music." The phrase implies the difficulty of finding someone who can properly value the unusual constellation of attributes that make up Ji 's character.

In addition to composing poems, Ji occupied his time in various ways. He is also credited with having translated certain Indian Buddhist documents into Chinese. He was an amateur blacksmith who tried to achieve immortality through a series of mystical breathing exercises, and he conducted alchemical experiments with a view to prolonging life.

Two stories are told concerning Ji 's unfortunate end. One has it that one day an important official came to call on him while Ji was working at his blacksmith's forge. Ji made the official wait while he finished his task. The offended official charged him with insubordination, and Ji was condemned to death. The other story says that Ji came to the defense of a friend, Lu An, whose brother had brought capital charges against him. When Ji helped Lu, he too was arrested, and both friends were condemned to death.

The stories agree that thousands of Ji 's disciples offered to take his place, but all to no avail. The stories also agree that before Ji met his end with equanimity, his request to play the zither one last time was granted.

Bibliography

Giles, Herbert A. *A History of Chinese Literature.* New York: Grove Press, 1958.

Ji Kang. *Hsi K'ang and His Poetical Essay on the Lute.* Translated by R. H. van Gulik. Rutland, Vt.: C. E. Tuttle Company, 1968.

———. *Philosophy and Argumentation in Third-Century China. The Essays of Hsi K'ang.* Translated by Robert G. Henricks. Princeton, N.J.: Princeton University Press, 1983.

Idema, Wilt, and Lloyd Haft. *A Guide to Chinese Literature.* Ann Arbor: Center for Chinese Studies, the University of Michigan, 1997.

Mair, Victor H., ed. *The Columbia History of Chinese Literature.* New York: Columbia University Press, 2001.

Josephus, Flavius (Josephus, Joseph ben Matthias) (37–ca. 101 C.E.) *Jewish historian*

The son of a Jewish priestly family with royalty on his mother's side, the precociously erudite Joseph ben Matthias found himself consulted for advice by rabbis when he was just 14. Wishing to learn all that he could about his Jewish faith, at age 16 Josephus undertook a program in which he proposed to spend a period of time as a member of each of the principal factions of Judaism: the Essenes, the Pharisees, and the Sadducees. From 16 to 19, he lived the life of an ascetic Essene. At age 19, he affiliated with the Pharisees, and he spent the rest of his life as an adherent of that sect. If he also mastered the doctrine of the Sadducees, he did so without joining them. His writings suggest that he fulfilled his intentions vis-à-vis the Sadducees through a program of reading rather than through direct experience.

In 64 C.E., Josephus went from Jerusalem on a diplomatic mission to Rome in an effort to convince the emperor Nero to release Jewish priests who had been sent to stand trial as dissidents. Assisted by the emperor's wife, Poppea, and by a popular Jewish actor in Rome, Josephus accomplished his mission. During this visit, he also became convinced that Rome was invincible. It was better to join the Romans than fight them.

That conviction was shaken by an unexpected Jewish victory over the Romans' Twelfth Legion in 66 C.E., and Josephus changed sides, leading Jewish forces against the Romans in 67. The outcome supported his original view, for Josephus surrendered to the forces of Vespasian in July of that year. After his defeat, Josephus predicted that Vespasian would one day become emperor—an unlikely prospect in view of the fact that all the emperors thus far, either by birth or adoption, were the heirs of JULIUS CAESAR's line. Nonetheless, the prediction gained for Josephus both Vespasian's favor and a place among the members of his staff.

The continued resistance of the Jews resulted in the outcome that Josephus had originally feared, the utter destruction of Jerusalem. Though after the war Vespasian granted Josephus an estate not far from the ruined city, Josephus instead opted to accompany Vespasian's son Titus back to Rome. There he adopted Vespasian's family name, Flavius, to indicate his status as a trusted client of the royal family. He also undertook a literary career that would last the rest of his life, becoming both a historian and a propagandist. In the latter role, he sought to present the Jewish people in the favorable light to which their distinguished history entitled them.

Josephus composed his first work, *Wars of the Jews* (ca. 75–79 C.E.), in Aramaic but issued it in the Greek language. Using Julius Caesar's COMMENTARY ON THE GALLIC WARS as his model, he slanted his account to dissuade other Roman dependencies from making the same mistake the Jews had in rebelling against Roman authority.

The work for which posterity best remembers Josephus is one that he entitled *Judaic Archeology*, now known as *Antiquities of the Jews* (published 93–94 C.E.). In addition to being the source of most of the biographical information we possess about its author, this work has as its objective ennobling the Jewish people in the estimation of learned Greeks and Romans. For his models in constructing this work, Josephus used, first, the Greek Septuagint version of the Hebrew Old Testament. This work shares much in common with the versions of the HEBREW BIBLE current in Western countries. Added to those materials, however, are others that were composed either in Greek or in Hebrew during the HELLENISTIC AGE. As his second model for his masterwork, Josephus employed the *Romaic* or *Roman Antiquities* of DIONYSIUS OF HALICARNASSUS.

For most of the first two millennia of Christianity, devout Christians pointed to Josephus's references to Jesus Christ, John the Baptist, James the brother of Jesus, and other apparent correspondences with Christian NEW TESTAMENT events as independent confirmation of biblical accounts and of the truth of Christianity. Antiquarian scholars, however, now largely agree that the passages supporting such an interpretations are all ex post facto emendations by hands other than Josephus's. His work has been doctored subsequently to create just such pro-Christian impressions.

Josephus composed the autobiographical account that usually stands at the beginning of modern editions of his *Antiquities* in about the year 100. A slightly later work in two books, *Against Apion,* first defends Josephus's account of the great antiquity of ancient Jewish culture against the disbelief of surprised Greeks. Then it proceeds to conduct a comparison between the beliefs of the monotheistic Jews and the polytheistic Greeks, awarding the prize for credibility to the Jews.

Bibliography

Josephus, Flavius. *Against Apion.* Translated by John M. B. Barclay. Boston: Mass.: Brill, 2006.
———. *Flavius Josephus: Translation and Commentary.* Edited by Steve Mason. Boston: Brill, 2005.
———. *The Great Roman-Jewish War.* Translated by William Whiston and D. S. Margoliouth. Mineola, N.Y.: Dover Publications, 2004.
———. *The New Complete Works of Josephus.* Translated by William Whiston. Grand Rapids, Mich.: Kregel Publications, 1999.

Jia Yi (Chia Yi), (201–169 B.C.E.) *Chinese poet*

Born in the city of Luoyang (Lo-yang), Jia Yi (Chia Yi) was already famed for his erudition by the time he was 18 years old. In particular, he had acquired a reputation for his ability to recite the entire BOOK OF ODES and to compose literature. Learning of the youth's precocity, the governor of Honan, Lord Wu, invited him to become one of his retinue, and he became Jia's close friend and mentor. When Wu, in turn, was summoned to the imperial court as the commandant of justice, he recommended Jia Yi as a court scholar. Emperor Wen acted on the recommendation, and Jia joined the ranks of the imperial "erudites" as their youngest member. He soon distinguished himself as their premier thinker and rapidly advanced to the post of palace counselor.

Thinking that the Han dynasty should distance itself from its predecessors by inaugurating new ritual practices, Jia Yi made a series of recommendations on that score. When Emperor Wen consulted his other advisors about the suggestions, however, they opposed Chia's advice, and when the emperor suggested that the young man be elevated to the top rank of imperial advisers, they slandered him so that the emperor's confidence was shaken. Wen therefore sent Jia Yi away from court to become tutor to the young king of Changsha (Ch'ang-sha) in the Yangtze valley.

Aware that he had fallen from favor and concerned about what he feared would be an unhealthful climate, Jia Yi traveled south. When he reached the Xiang (Hsiang) River, he remembered that the watercourse was called the River Miluo further down. He also recalled that in that very river the great poet QU YUAN (CH'Ü YÜAN) had drowned himself after his overlord had similarly demoted him. Identifying with Qu, Chia Yi composed a FU POEM entitled *A Lament for Qu Yuan.* The verse paid tribute to his predecessor poet and simultaneously complained of Jia's similar circumstances.

After three years in the uncongenial climate of Changsha, Jia Yi became convinced that he would not live long. In the midst of his depression, a bird of ill omen, an owl, appeared, and Jia Yi composed another mournful *fu* poem, "On the Owl," which reflects a good deal of early Han Daoist thinking.

About a year later, Emperor Wen recalled Jia Yi to the capital and took the opportunity to discuss with him the nature of spiritual beings. Jia's explanations so fascinated the emperor that he lingered listening late into the night and concluded that he had erred in sending the scholar away. The emperor reassigned Jia as the tutor to his youngest and favorite son, Liu Chi, who was King Huai of Liang. Wen, however, still would not entertain strategic political advice from Jia. When a riding accident took the life of King Huai of Liang, Jia Yi blamed himself for not taking proper care of his charge, fell into a deep depression, and died a year or so later at the age of 33.

Bibliography

Sima Qian [Ssu-ma Ch'ien]. *Records of the Grand Historian of China* [*Shihji*]. Translated by Burton Watson. New York: Columbia University Press, 1961.

Judith, Book of (ca. second–third century B.C.E.)

The Book of Judith, from the APOCRYPHA, recounts a story whose central episode—a famous subject for many works of art—is Judith's beheading of Holofernes.

Holofernes is the principal general of the armies of the Assyrian king Nebuchadnezzar. The general has besieged the Hebrew community of Bethulia and plans to bring the hitherto impregnable mountain town to its knees by the simple expedient of denying its people access to the spring upon which they depend for drinking and cooking water. The townspeople are on the point of surrendering and letting the Assyrian troops sack the city and reduce the population to slavery.

A beautiful and wealthy Bethulian widow, Judith, calls the town's elders together, however, and reports that the Lord has sent her a plan to raise the siege. Casting off her widow's mourning, Judith dresses and makes herself up to look her best. She then has the townsmen let her out and confronts the Assyrian guards, saying that she can show Holofernes a way to take Bethulia and other such hill towns without losing a man.

Judith tells Holofernes, who receives her courteously, that the Bethulians have sacrilegiously determined to eat unclean animals and consume God's portion of their food supply. As a religious woman, she says, she can pray that God support the cause of Holofernes against the sacrilegious Jews, and he can conquer the entire region and win over the Jews with the support she can offer.

Convinced, Holofernes gives her three successive days of safe passage from his camp so she can go to the spring, bathe, and ritually purify herself.

On the fourth night, she accepts an invitation to dine with the Assyrians. Overwhelmed by Judith's beauty and charm, Holofernes drinks more than he has ever done before and collapses in a drunken stupor. The attendants tactfully withdraw, leaving Judith alone with Holofernes. After praying, she seizes his sword and cuts off his head with two strokes. She hides the Holophernes' body behind the bed, puts his head in a bag, and, collecting her maid who is waiting outside, makes her usual nightly sortie to pray. This time, however, she goes to the gates of Bethulia, enters, and reveals the head and her courageous action.

Following Judith's instructions, the men of Bethulia attack the Assyrians, who had reported to Holofernes' tent and found him dead. The loss of their general has thrown them into such consternation that they become easy prey for the Israelite troops, who rout them and then spend a month looting their camp. Judith takes the loot to Jerusalem and gives it to the temple. Then she returns home, where she remains a widow until her death at age 105. Her courage dissuades others from attacking the Israelites for a long time.

Bibliography

"Judith." In *The Apochrypha. The New English Bible.* Vol. 2. Edited and translated by the Appointees of the Joint Committee on the New Translation of the Bible. Oxford and Cambridge: Oxford and Cambridge University Presses, 1969.

Julianus (Flavius Claudius Julianus, Julian the Apostate) (ca. 331–363 C.E.)
Roman prose writer

The emperor of Rome after the death of his uncle Constantius (361 C.E.), Julian made vigorous efforts to disestablish Christianity as the state religion of Rome—hence his soubriquet *the apostate*. His efforts in that direction were largely fruitless, perhaps in part because he reigned only briefly, dying in battle against Persia at the age of 32. Nonetheless, Julian was an intellectual and something of a philosopher. He penned a lost treatise against Christianity and also wrote a surviving, Greek-language encomium to the sun as a deity, entitled "To the Monarch the Sun." Another of his works addressed the goddess Cybele: "To the Mother of the Gods."

A number of Julian's letters also survive. In one notable one, "Against the Galileans," he advises a pagan priest on the best way to support the belief of his worshippers against the proselytizing of the Christians. Beyond this sort of religious writing, he was also the author of SATIRES. One of the most celebrated was his *Symposion*, also entitled *The Caesars*.

Julian was a generous patron of the Greek schools of philosophy, and he intended to restore the temple at Jerusalem in contradiction of biblical prediction. In the latter project, however, as J. J. Eschenburg tells us, his intentions were thwarted by a series of disasters.

Bibliography

Eschenburg, J. J. *Manual of Classical Literature.* Translated by N. W. Fiske. Philadelphia: E. C. & J. Biddle, 1850.

Julian, Emperor of Rome. *Julian's Against the Galileans.* Amherst, N.Y.: Prometheus Books, 2004.

———. *Two Orations of the Emperor Julian: One to the Sovereign Sun, and the Other to the Mother of the Gods.* Translated by Thomas Taylor. London: E. Jeffrey, 1793.

Julius Pollux   See GRAMMAR AND GRAMMARIANS IN GREECE.

Juvenal (Decimus Junius Juvenalis?)
(fl. ca. first–second century C.E.)
Roman Poet

Attempts to construct a biography for Juvenal from the literary remains of his *SATIRES* and from scarce or long-lost fragmentary evidence elsewhere have always come to nothing. As a result, we cannot even say with certainty that the tripartite Roman name usually assigned to Juvenal is correct.

We do know that the Roman poet MARTIAL addressed three EPIGRAMS to Juvenal in which he alludes to the furious pace of Juvenal's life and to his accomplishments as an orator. Juvenal's recent translator, Susanna Morton Braund, follows custom by speculating that Juvenal may have been a person of considerable wealth and social status since patronage did not seem to concern him.

Like the satirist PERSIUS before him, Juvenal's poetic voice was an angry one—at least at first. In fact, the aggressive invective of Roman satire is often cited as one of its distinguishing characteristics. The rhetorical style of Juvenal's satires and their declamatory subjects, such as recommending a specific set of actions or addresses of farewell, welcome, or comfort in adversity, also point to a rhetorical bias. As time passed, however, Juvenal's satiric art grew more subtle and began including double views of the objects of his satire. To a degree, irony replaced invective, and the stance of the author became more reflective as Juvenal tried to emulate the peace of mind characteristic of the Greek philosopher and polymath Democritus, who was known as "the laughing philosopher." A particularly attractive aspect of Juvenal's mature satiric approach arises from the double edge of his wit. The satirist is willing to satirize himself along with or as one of the objects of his disapproval.

Beyond echoes of earlier satire, Juvenal's works also reveal a broad acquaintance with the principal literary modes of the Greek and Roman world: EPIC, TRAGEDY, COMEDY, ELEGY AND ELEGAIC POETRY, and epigram. Beyond his satires' rhetorical tone, the epic manner of Juvenal's work constitutes a novelty in the satiric genre. His expansiveness contrasts sharply with the terse economy of Persius's few lines.

It is fair to suggest that the history of the satiric mode in Western letters comprises a long series of footnotes to the genre as Persius and Juvenal molded it. The vehicles for satire have expanded far beyond the Roman dactylic hexameters of Juvenal. Nonetheless, the techniques by which satire attempts to achieve moral improvement in its readers by exposing and ridiculing vice remain largely those that Juvenal developed.

The names of his literary descendants in Western letters are legion, but naming some of them will suffice to suggest Juvenal's influence. Boccaccio, Geoffrey Chaucer, Erasmus, John Donne, John Dryden, Ben Jonson, Molière, and Samuel Johnson are a few of those who learned a significant portion of their satiric art from Juvenal's example.

Bibliography

Braund, S. H. *Beyond Anger: A Study of Juvenal's Third Book of Satires.* Cambridge and New York: Cambridge University Press, 1988.

Braund, Susanna Morton, ed. and trans. *Juvenal and Persius.* Cambridge, Mass.: Harvard University Press, 2004.

Juvenal. *The Satires of Juvenal.* Translated by Rolfe Humphries. Bloomington: Indiana University Press, 1958.

———. *The Sixteen Satires.* Translated by Peter Green. London and New York: Penguin, 1998.

K

Kakinomoto no Hitomaro (fl. seventh century C.E.) *Japanese poet*
We know little about the life of ancient Japan's best-known poet, Kakinomoto no Hitomaro. We do know that he served the widowed empress Jitō (ruled 686–697, regent until 702) as her principal court poet and that all of his poems with known dates of composition appear in the second section of the earliest and greatest of all collections of Japanese poetry, the MAN'YŌSHŪ.

Hitomaro's poetry reflects his devotion to his sovereign and to the imperial family. He apparently believed ardently in the hereditary divinity of the family's members, and he frequently spoke of the empress as a goddess—one whom the tutelary deities of rivers and streams obey.

It fell to Hitomaro to compose eulogies for members of the royal family. His ELEGY on the death of Prince Takechi is the longest poem in the entire collection and lauds the young man's bravery and prowess in battle. Hitomaro's empress had lost her husband, Emperor Temmu, and as a devout and pious woman, she undertook religious pilgrimages that Hitomaro also regularly memorialized in his verse. It seems to have been the poet's task to assure that the members of the royal family and their deeds be remembered through all time.

Hitomaro's work was not entirely governed by his official responsibilities, however. One of his most deeply felt and moving elegies commemorates the death of a stranger whose body lay abandoned on a beach. The poet thinks about the man's absent wife, waiting at home for the husband who will never return and whose fate will remain forever unknown.

Bibliography

Keene, Donald. *Seeds in the Heart: Japanese Literature from Earliest Times to the Late Sixteenth Century.* New York: Henry Holt and Company, 1993.

1000 Poems from the Man'yōshū: *The Complete Nippon Gakujutsu Shinkokai Translation.* Translated by the Japanese Classics Translation Committee. Mineola, N.Y.: Dover Publications, 2005.

king lists   See CUNEIFORM.

Knights, The (Hippes, Equites)
Aristophanes   (423 B.C.E.)
The most directly political and perhaps the least theatrical of ARISTOPHANES' 11 surviving comedies, *The Knights* mounts a relentlessly rancorous

attack on the Athenian politician Cleon—a demagogue whom Aristophanes abhorred. Despite the low opinion of the play voiced by such 20th-century critics as Whitney Jennings Oates and Eugene O'Neill, Jr., the judges at the Athenian festival of LENAEA awarded the play the first prize in the festival's COMEDY contest.

An actor portraying the great Athenian leader DEMOSTHENES opens the drama. He complains about and curses Cleon, the Paphlagonian, who had pressed the Athenians to continue the Peloponnesian War and had secured the high regard of many Athenians by leading their forces to victory over 420 Spartan hoplites (soldiers) on the island of Sphacteria. Nicias, a leader of the peace party, seconds the curse by wishing the plague on Cleon, and the two commiserate, seeking a way to undermine Cleon. Neither can think of anything, so they agree to share their troubles with the spectators.

Demosthenes summarizes the situation. He and Nicias have, he says, a very brutal master named Demos. In this play, the character Demos stands for the Athenian populace at large. Demos, says Demosthenes, bought a slave—a Paphlagonian tanner. The slave, who of course represents Cleon, has pulled the wool over the eyes of Demos and is bleeding him and everyone else dry. He has managed to gather all de facto power into his own hands.

Demosthenes has Nicias steal some wine for him. With the wine, Demosthenes lubricates his wits and has Nicias steal the oracle of the Paphlagonian, who lies' indoor drunk, snoring, and flatulent. Reading the oracle's predictions, the two discover that a sausage seller is destined to overthrow Cleon and rule the city. Happily, a sausage seller enters immediately, and Demosthenes sets about convincing him of his great good fortune. He will become the ruler of Athens. The sausage seller pleads ignorance, lack of education, and dishonesty. Demosthenes explains that precisely these traits best qualify him to lead the state. He then reads the oracle and interprets it for the sausage seller. The sausage seller continues to protest, but Demosthenes has an answer for every objection. When the sausage seller asks

who will be allied with him—given that rich people fear the Paphlagonian—Demosthenes assures him that 1,000 brave knights will stand with the sausage seller against Cleon.

Cleon enters, uttering threats, and the sausage seller tries to run away. Demosthenes restrains him, however, and calls the knights to the rescue. The CHORUS rushes on stage attired as knights. They begin beating Cleon, who calls for help. The leader of the chorus explains that he deserves the beatings and enumerates some of his crimes against the people.

Seeing his candidacy supported by the knights, the sausage seller begins to out-shout Cleon. Occasionally punctuated by Demosthenes' comments, a screaming match follows between the two. The argument focuses, first, on which of the two candidates for public office is the bigger crook. Then it shifts to a series of threats about how each will harm or kill the other. The disagreement reaches a climax when the sausage seller beats Cleon with a sausage, and Cleon departs to denounce the sausage seller to the senate on grounds of his conspiring against the Athenian state. The sausage seller follows, and Demosthenes also leaves the stage.

There follows a fascinating interlude in which the chorus explains to the audience Aristophanes' reasons for not having produced a comedy under his own name until this present play. They explain that, fearing the censure and the fickle nature of the audience, Aristophanes' prior comedies were trial balloons, floated to ascertain the drift of the audience's taste and preferences. Feeling that he now has taken the measure of their taste, and confident of his victory in the competition, Aristophanes has allowed his name to be associated with his work.

This announcement is followed by two invocations to the deities Poseidon and Athena. A paean of praise follows each invocation, first in honor of the Athenians of old who would have found Cleon beneath official notice, and second in honor of Athenian horses—the steeds who carried the knights who have been Athens' hereditary protectors. The song thinly disguises a call for the overthrow of the real Cleon.

Now the chorus welcomes back to the stage the new hero of the Athenian people, the sausage seller, who reports that he has beaten the senate. In a mockery of bribing public officials, Cleon and the sausage seller have appealed to the senators' appetites for anchovies, coriander seed, and leeks. The sausage seller wins the bribery contest.

Cleon now reenters, and the competition of threats resumes where it earlier left off. Having lost before the senate, Cleon now challenges the sausage seller to a direct appeal to Demos—the allegorical figure who stands for the Athenian people.

The candidates for Demos's favor swear their love for Demos, but the sausage seller's gifts of a cushion for the old man's stone seat and some cushion-soled shoes incline Demos toward him. Eventually the sausage seller seems about to prevail, when Cleon appeals to prophecy, and Demos demands to hear the predictions for each.

The two contenders rush off and return bearing reams of prophecies. The prophecies contain gibberish, and the contestants, like ignorant preachers, interpret these dark prophecies self-interestedly.

The chorus warns Demos that he is easily flattered, fooled, and led by politicians with only their own self-interest to offer. Demos replies that he only pretends to be foolish; really he is using the politicians as his pawns. Demos's behavior, however, undermines this argument.

At last Cleon and the sausage seller compete in offering Demos things to eat. Cleon seems on the verge of winning, for he has brought a stewed hare. Before he can present it, however, the sausage seller distracts Cleon, snatches the hare, and gives it to Demos. Pressed to a decision between the rivals, however, Demos still hesitates. The sausage seller now suggests that Demos examine the baskets of the contenders. Demos will discover that the sausage seller's is empty; he has given his all. In Cleon's basket, however, Demos finds that Cleon has kept for himself the lion's share of everything he has offered Demos.

Forced to his final stratagem, Cleon says he knows the name of his successor, for the oracle has revealed it to him. He asks the sausage seller a series of questions: Where were you schooled? What did you learn? What trade did you follow? Where did you sell your sausages? The sausage seller's answers to these questions are the ones that the oracle had predicted, and a dejected Cleon knows at last that his days of demagoguery are finished. He withdraws in the face of the sausage seller's victory.

Demosthenes congratulates the victor and, as a reward for his services, asks for a minor but potentially lucrative appointment as secretary to a law court. Demos asks the name of his (that is, the city's) new steward. The sausage seller reveals that his name is Agoracritus because he has always lived in the marketplace (the *agora*) amidst lawsuits.

After yet another choral interlude, Agoracritus returns to the stage accompanied by a freshly robed, golden-crowned, rejuvenated Demos. Agoracritus explains that he has freshened up Demos on his stove. Demos shows himself now possessed of better judgment than his past toleration of Cleon displayed. Agoracritus is able to present Demos with a beautiful young girl, gorgeously dressed, who allegorically represents a 30-year truce between Athens and Sparta and its Peloponnesian allies—a truce that Aristophanes urgently hoped would eventuate.

Agoracritus pronounces an appropriate punishment for Cleon: He will be forced to become a sausage seller, exchange foul language with prostitutes, be perpetually drunk, and otherwise only be allowed to drink dirty water from the public baths. Demos approves this sentence, and the play ends.

This drama was the third in which Aristophanes pursued his enmity for Cleon. After the first of them, the playwright's now-lost *The Babylonians*, Cleon brought charges of high treason against Aristophanes. Wealthy and aristocratic, however, Aristophanes remained contemptuous of the Paphlagonian-tanner-become-demagogue whose hawkish war policies, as the playwright accurately foresaw, would be the ruin of Athens.

Bibliography

Aristophanes. *The Complete Plays*. Translated by Paul Roche. New York: New American Library, 2005.

Kojiki (*Records of Ancient Matters*)
(712 C.E.)

The oldest surviving example of ancient JAPANESE LITERATURE, the *Kojiki* came into being when the emperor Temmu (r. 672–686), perusing earlier texts soon afterward destroyed, found in them many errors. He commanded a courtier named Hieda no Are to memorize the proper versions and to write them down. The real purpose was political—to establish on record the divine status of the imperial family. The *Kojiki* is essentially a genealogy.

Many preliterate societies had specialists who were trained in memorization to serve as the repositories of the foundational poems, songs, myths, and genealogies of their cultures, and Hieda no Are seems to have been such a person. The literary historian Donald Keene, whose account I summarize here, tells us that Heida no Are memorized anything he (or, as some argue, she) read or heard on the first encounter. Hieda no Are's work came to fruition in 712, when the collection was presented at the emperor's court. The *Kojiki* transmitted the foundational myths of the Japanese tradition to the ages that followed.

Following a flowery introduction by another person, Ō no Yasumaro, who was the scribe who wrote down what Hieda no Are dictated, the first book of the three-book work begins on the High Plain of Heaven, where three gods pop into existence. The earth below is not solid and drifts about. It shows some signs of plant life.

Other gods come into being. Among them we find Izanagi and his wife, Izanami. They are charged with solidifying the fluid land below and with creating more solid earth. With a jeweled spear, Izanagi stirs the mess below until it solidifies into a place where he and Izanami can copulate. They do this, and Izanami immediately gives birth to monstrously misshapen offspring. The pair keeps trying until they get it right, and now Izanami gives birth to the principal islands of the Japanese archipelago and then to a number of lesser islands.

Izanagi and Izanami keep at their task, and she now bears the gods responsible for overseeing such natural phenomena as winds, fire, the sea, and so forth. When she bears the fire god, however, Izanami is horribly burned. In the throes of the consequent illness, she excretes and vomits, and from the solid and fluid results, more deities come into being—35 in all. Then Izanami dies. Angered, Izanagi beheads and dismembers the newborn fire god. From his blood and body parts, another 16 deities spring into being.

In a story reminiscent of those of ORPHEUS and Euridice and that of Proserpina in Greco-Roman mythology, Izanami seeks out his wife in the land of the dead. She cannot return as she has eaten there. Other parallels between the Japanese MYTHS and those of Europe and the Middle East suggest a common ancestry lost in the mists of prehistory.

Keene points out an unparalleled datum in the Japanese creation story, however. An unusual effect derives from the peculiar circumstance of the procreation and birth both of the land and of the nature gods. One of them, the sun god, is the ancestor of the Japanese emperor. This makes the emperor a blood relative of the land he rules.

The *Kojiki* contains stories of such hero-gods as Susano-o, who functions both in heaven and on earth. Susano-o is credited with having written the earliest-ever surviving Japanese poem to mark his construction of a palace for his bride.

The *Kojiki* also features fables and folk tales. One of these concerns an encounter between a clever rabbit and some slow-witted crocodiles. The rabbit tricks the crocs into forming a bridge for him. He almost makes it across the water on their backs, but the last crocodile skins him. As a trickster tricked, the rabbit suffers at the hands of several gods. Eventually another deity, Ōkuninushi, relieves the rabbit's pain. To repay the kindness, the rabbit foretells the wedding of Ōkuninushi and Princess Yagami.

Stories about Ōkuninushi—including two in which he serially dies and is resurrected—occupy the next extended portion of the narrative. In the course of his story he defeats his 80 wicked brothers. In a seeming recapitulation of the earlier story regarding the birth of the land, Ōkuninushi and his wife produce the country of Izumo. Ōkuninushi is also a bard, and he and another princess exchange some erotic songs. His wife grows jealous, and more singing exchanges result. On condition that he be revered and worshipped in Izumo, Ōkuninushi cedes control of his land to the goddess Amaterasu. She, in turn, calls upon her grandson to come down from heaven to rule, and she presents him with the imperial insignia: beads, a mirror, and a sword.

Having arrived on earth, the grandson marries a human being, but he offends her father by insisting on wedding the more beautiful younger rather than the plainer elder daughter. The father curses the new emperor and his descendants with mortality. This brings to a close both Book 1 and the mythical age of the gods.

Book 2 traces the careers of mortal but nonetheless superhuman descendants of the emperor. His grandson, Jimmu, enlarges the domain over which he rules. His conquests and encounters continue to derive from the world of myth, and he lives to be 137 years old. A genealogical section follows until we arrive at the 10th emperor, Sujin. With him, the *Kojiki*'s account apparently becomes more historical as the dates of imperial deaths begin appearing. These dates are not always certain, but it seems that Sujin died either in 258 or 318 C.E.

Book 2 also introduces the second principal character of the *Kojiki*, the angry and bloodthirsty fratricide, Yamato-takeru. He is the son of Emperor Keiko, who fathered 80 children and in old age married his own great-great-great granddaughter. Yamato-takeru slices people on the slightest provocation. This ferocity with potential rivals makes possible a considerable extension of his

father's realm. Keiko, however, does not want his violent son around the court and keeps sending him off into dangerous situations. Happily, the young man's aunt, Yamato-hime, prepares her nephew for dangerous situations with a gift of a magic sword and a bag to be opened in case of dire emergency. His charmed gifts, his unusual strength, and his luck holds out for a long time, but eventually old age catches up with him and he dies. Just as the funeral is about to start, Yamato-takeru metamorphoses into a large, white bird and flies away. Before he dies, Yamato-takeru yields to poetic impulse and composes several poems, including one celebrating the beauties of his birthplace.

In the balance of book 2, we learn of the 14th emperor, Chuai, who raided Korea—a fact seemingly confirmed by a Korean account of such an expedition in 364 C.E. The 15th emperor, Ōjin, may have sent ambassadors to China in 421 and 425. During his reign, as well, Chinese emissaries arrived bringing 10 volumes of the ANALECTS of CONFUCIUS and other Chinese works. This event marked the introduction of literacy to Japan.

Book 3 begins by recounting the reign of a Confucian emperor, Nintoku. This wise king implemented social programs, remitted taxes, and suspended military conscription for a time.

A tale of incestuous love between a prince and a princess, both named Karu, follows. It becomes the archetype for an often-recurring subcategory of Japanese tale—the love-suicide story. Prince Karu is exiled for his forbidden love. Princess Karu follows him to his place of exile. There, after he composes two love songs, they commit joint suicide.

Tales of palace intrigues and murder alternate with stories of love. One of the latter recounts how the emperor, on seeing a lovely girl, tells her not to marry till he sends for her. After 80 years of waiting, she seeks him out. (The emperor lives to be 124.) Though her fidelity moves Yūryaku to mull over marrying her, he instead gives her a pair of songs. In one of them, he regrets their not having slept together in their youth. Now, he says, *she* is too old. (Emphasis mine.)

Apart from this touching tale, Yūryaku is pictured as a monster who killed most of his own children. One who escaped that fate, Seinei (ruled 480–84 C.E.), succeeded him. With increasingly sketchy accounts of individual reigns, the *Kojiki* traces the imperial succession down to the 33rd ruler of Japan, Empress Suiko (r. 593–628).

Bibliography

Chamberlain, Basil Hall, trans. *The Kojiki: Records of Ancient Matters*. Rutland, Vt.: C. E. Tuttle Company, 1982.

Keene, Donald. *Seeds in the Heart: Japanese Literature from the Earliest Times to the Late Sixteenth Century*. New York: Henry Holt and Company, 1993.

Philippi, Donald L., trans. *Kojiki*. Tokyo: University of Tokyo Press, 1968.

L

Lady Kasa   See FEMALE POETS OF ANCIENT JAPAN.

lampoons   See DIDACTIC SATIRES.

Laozi (*Lao Tzu, Daode jing, Tao Te Ching*) (ca. 300 B.C.E.)

The oldest of the three most prominent Taoist texts, the *Laozi (Lao Tzu)* was formerly attributed to a hermit named Laozi (Lao Tze) or Lao Tan, a contemporary of CONFUCIUS. Now, however, the work as we have it is thought to be more recent, though considerable older material may be included in it. A formerly unknown silk manuscript that antedated any other version by about 500 years has recently (1973) been discovered among the trove of manuscripts (see CHINESE ETHICAL AND HISTORICAL LITERATURE IN VERSE AND PROSE). The work's alternative title, *Daode jing*, translates as: *[the] Way [and] integrity classic*.

In its current form, the *Laozi tzu* contains 81 short stanzas. These are in part old adages and in part commentary on or interpretations of the sayings. The text seems to contain the key to great though sometimes illusive wisdom. Partly this is owing to the inaccessibility of the *Dao (Tao)*—the absolute or primal principle of the universe that precedes all else—to the operation of human intelligence. Many metaphors purporting to suggest the nature of that principle are included in the *Lao Tzu*.

Accompanying these metaphors are a series of suggestions concerning what people should do and the mind-sets they should adopt to bring themselves into a harmonious relationship with the Dao. Principally, these suggestions propose a program of simplicity, natural action, and passivity—of going with the universal flow.

"The sage," in Victor H. Mair's translation of the document, "knows without journeying / understands without looking / accomplishes without acting."

Striking metaphors abound in the document. Since people are soft and flexible when they are alive and rigid when dead, the sage suggests, rigid people are adherents of death and flexible ones are "lovers of life." People who seek an "excess of praise" ultimately have none. To die but to be nonetheless remembered defines longevity. All being is grounded in nonbeing.

The wise person treats everyone well—both people who are good and those who are not. The way that one treats individuals applies as well to the way that families treat families, villages treat villages, and governments of whatever sizes treat one another. Thus, the *Lao Tzu* implies a political as well as a personal program. That program requires existing in harmony with the universe. The book recommends humility, modesty, non-assertiveness and the peaceful coexistence of nations.

In an inventory compiled by the scholar Wing-Tsit Chan, the principal concepts contained in the work include being and nonbeing, desires, the quality of being female and that of water, government, humanity and righteousness, knowledge, name, the natural, lack of strife, the concept of oneness, relativity, good and evil, certain paradoxes, reversal, simplicity, Tao, tranquility, virtue, weakness, and refraining from action.

Victor H. Mair's discussion of the state of current scholarship concerning the *Lao Tzu* (which in Mair's translation is entitled *Tao Te Ching*) is fascinating. He brings to bear linguistic scholarship that establishes cognates between the ancient Chinese language and the Indo-European languages of Europe and Asia. English, of course, belongs to the Germanic subbranch of the Western development of these languages. The languages of contemporary northern India and Russia belong to families within the Eastern branch. Mair gives several instances of cognate words and phrases, showing that the ancient Chinese language did not develop in a cultural vacuum but must have had considerable contact with languages spoken by people living to the west of China. Mair argues convincingly for a long period of oral circulation of the concepts described in the book before they came to be or even could be written down.

Beyond demonstrable relationships among words found in several languages, Mair also discusses the correspondence in concepts to be found among several of the world's religions. He particularly traces parallels between Daoism and the Yogic tradition of India and points as well to relationships between Daoism and Persian Sufism. He also finds more generic correspondences among several religions for such concepts as "vital breath," which has both verbal and ideological correspondences with the idea of *spirit* as well as with the late historian of religion Mircea Eliade's notion of "the myth of eternal return" of such spirit to its cosmic source.

Bibliography

Chen, Ellen M. *The Tao Te Ching: A New Translation with Commentary.* New York: Paragon, 1989.

Eliade, Mircea. *The Myth of the Eternal Return.* Translated by Willard R. Trask. New York: Pantheon, 1954.

Henricks, Robert G., trans. *Lao Tzu's* Tao Te Ching: *A Translation of the Startling New Documents found at Guodian.* New York: Columbia University Press, 2000.

———. *Lao-Tzu: Te-Tao Ching: A New Translation Based on the Recently Discovered Ma-wang-tui Texts.* New York: Ballantine, 1989.

Mair, Victor H., trans. *Tao Te Ching: The Classic Book of Integrity and the Way: Lao Tzu.* New York: Bantam Books, 1990.

Ma-wang-tui Han Mu Po-shu (I). [Silk Manuscripts from the Han Tombs at Ma-wang-tui (Mawangdui)]. Beijing: Wen-wu Ch'u-pan-she, 1974. [Contains photos of all the manuscripts.]

Wing-Tsit Chan, trans and ed. *A Source Book in Chinese Philosophy.* Princeton, N.J.: Princeton University Press, 1963.

Lenaea, Athenian festival of

Celebrated around January, when the days had begun to lengthen after the winter solstice, the Lenaea, or festival of the wine vats, occurred annually in honor of the god of the vine, Dionysus. Beginning with the festival of 450 B.C.E., it became customary to include a dramatic competition in the festival, which included the enactment of comedies. Two by the playwright ARISTOPHANES, THE ACHARNIANS and THE KNIGHTS, won the first prize for COMEDY at the festivals of 424 and 423 B.C.E., respectively.

See also GREAT DIONYSIA.

Leonidas of Tarentum (fl. ca. 294–ca. 281 B.C.E.) *Greek poet*

An author of EPIGRAMS in the Doric dialect of the Greek language, Leonidas enjoyed a reputation as a poet in the genre second only to that of his contemporary, CALLIMACHUS. His literary remains include about 100 fine examples of epigram. The literary historian Alan Douglas Edward Cameron explains that the epigrams of Leonidas differed from those of Callimachus. Whereas Callimachus wrote about love, Leonidas was a poet of the people. His highly wrought verse and long, ornate sentences address matters of everyday life. His poems contain epitaphs for rural folk, mariners, and fisherman, and some of his verse is dedicated to such people.

Leonidas's verse also suggests that he led a wandering life, visiting many places on the shores of the Aegean Sea and on the Grecian archipelago. Cameron proposes that Leonidas followed the philosophical doctrines of the cynic philosophers (see CYNICISM). This conclusion rests on autobiographical poems in the body of Leonidas's work that recount the poet's poverty, and on the fact that Leonidas wrote an epitaph for Diogenes of Sinope—one of the icons of the cynics' position.

Bibliography

Clack, Jerry, trans. *Asclepides of Samos and Leonidas of Tarentum: The Poems.* Wauconda, Ill.: Bolchazy-Carducci, 1999.

Leonidas of Tarentum. *The Poems of Leonidas of Tarentum.* Translated by Edward Bevan. Oxford: Clarendon Press, 1931.

Letter of Polycarp to the Philippians (ca. early second century B.C.E.)

The scholar of Christian antiquity and most recent English translator of The APOSTLIC FATHERS OF THE CHRISTIAN CHURCH, Bart D. Ehrman, suggests that we know more about Polycarp, the bishop of Smyrna, than about any other Christian of his era. In the collection of seven texts written by the Apostolic Fathers, one text is a letter that Polycarp wrote, another is a letter addressed to him, and a third is a letter written on the subject of his martyrdom.

Polycarp's Letter to the Philippians, says Ehrman, is essentially a "cover letter" written to convey a collection of the LETTERS OF IGNATIUS to the Philippians in answer to their request that Polycarp forward them. Additionally, Polycarp lets the Philippians know that he plans to honor both their request and that of the martyred Ignatius that Polycarp send on a letter from the Philippians to Antioch. Beyond that, Polycarp expresses his concern about the apparent financial chicanery of Valens, a member of the Philippian congregation. He also offers advice for dealing with the problem.

Finally, striking a chord that seems to resonate with the worries of many early Christians, Polycarp warns against those heretical teachings that doubt the reality of a future resurrection and a final judgment. Above all, Polycarp counsels right living and moral behavior, quoting both from scriptural and nonscriptural sources to lend weight to his advice.

Bibliography

Polycarp. "Letter of Polycarp to the Philippians." In The Apostolic Fathers. Vol. 1. Edited and translated by Bart D. Ehrman. Cambridge, Mass.: Harvard University Press, 2003.

Letters Pliny the Younger (ca. 62–ca. 114 C.E.)

We do not know exactly when PLINY THE YOUNGER decided to make a selection from his letters and publish them. It must, however, have been a relatively early decision, for all the surviving letters are carefully, even artfully, composed and bear witness to the superb oratorical education that Pliny received under the instruction of QUINTILIAN.

The first nine of Pliny's 10 books of letters contain missives addressed to more than 100 persons. As Pliny has organized them, the first nine books are chronological, though the order of letters within the books is not. Pliny's objective—admirably fulfilled—seems to have been to prepare an epistolary history of his life and times and of matters that he found important and interesting. The 10th book contains his official correspondence with the emperor Trajan—both Pliny's letters asking the emperor's advice and the emperor's responses.

A characterization of the author himself emerges from the younger Pliny's correspondence. He was a reliable friend and a loving husband. Like other wealthy Romans, he owned slaves. He understood, however, that they too were human beings, and he treated them with kindness and consideration. He was also impatient with others who did not. He carefully performed the duties of every office that he occupied and was a person of unimpeachable character. He was natural and unaffected and ruefully aware of his own eccentricities.

Rather than try to give a full overview of the contents of such an extensive collection of letters, what follows represents a selection of some of the more celebrated examples of Pliny's correspondence.

In book 3, letter 5, addressed to Baebius Macer, Pliny describes in absorbing detail his uncle PLINY THE ELDER's literary work and provides a list of his compositions.

Book 6, letter 16: Addressed to Cornelius TAC- ITUS, this famous letter describes the eruption of Mount Vesuvius in 79 C.E., to which the younger Pliny was an eyewitness, and the death of PLINY THE ELDER during that disaster. The elder Pliny was in command of a naval squadron stationed at Misenum in the northern sector of the Bay of Naples. His family accompanied him, including his nephew and adoptive son, Pliny the Younger. His mother was first to notice the unusual cloud over the mountains to the southeast. It seemed shaped like a tree—sometimes white and sometimes blotchy with its burden of "soil and ashes."

The elder Pliny meant to put out to sea in a warship for a closer look and invited his nephew along. He, however, had homework to do and so demurred. As a squadron of ships was readied for sea, a message came from Rectina, wife of Tas-

cus. Her house was at the foot of Vesuvius, and her only possible escape was by boat. The commander immediately sailed to the rescue, planning to pick up as many people as possible with his warships. They sailed through a fall of ashes that grew thicker and hotter the nearer they came to Vesuvius. As they approached their destination, however, they found their way blocked by debris from the explosion. He therefore changed course for Stabiae, four miles south of Pompeii, where his friend Pomponianus had a villa and an anchorage. There he greeted his friend and asked to bathe and nap so that his composure might calm his friend's anxieties.

As Admiral Pliny slept, the eruption became increasingly active, and the fallout of ash and pumice stone had almost blocked his chamber door. He awoke to violent earthquakes. He and his companions decided to reconnoiter, tying pillows on their heads to protect themselves from falling pumice stones. Arriving at the harbor under a night-black sky, he found the sea in a fury. By now the atmosphere had grown so sulphurous that it was no longer breathable. Overcome, the elder Pliny collapsed and died. Two days later, his body was found uninjured.

Letter 24 of book 6, addressed to Calpurnius Macer, reports the heroism of Arria, the wife of a neighbor at Lake Como, who discovered that her husband was suffering from a painful and incurable cancer. When she saw there was no hope, she encouraged him to commit suicide by drowning in the lake. When he did so, she roped herself to him and also drowned.

Letter 27 of book 7, addressed to Licinius Sura, reports that Pliny is predisposed to believe in ghosts because of an experience reported by QUIN- TUS RUFUS CURTIUS, who apparently encountered a woman of superhuman size. Saying that she was the spirit of Africa, she accurately predicted that he would become governor of Africa and die there. Pliny also repeats the story of a chain-rattling specter that inhabited a mansion in Athens. This visible ghost seemed to be a fettered and manacled, emaciated old man with a long beard and hair that stood up straight. Anyone who dared live in the house would infallibly grow ill from lack of sleep and die.

To test the veracity of the story, the Greek philosopher Athenodorus spent the night in the house taking notes, the ghost appeared, beckoned Athenodorus to follow it, led him into the courtyard, and then vanished. Athenodorus marked the spot. The next day, he had the city magistrates give orders to have the courtyard dug up. On doing so, they discovered a chained and manacled skeleton. They gave it a public burial, and the ghost appeared no more.

Pliny appeals to personal experience for his final example of supernatural activity. On two occasions, members of Pliny's household had dreams that someone was cutting their hair. On awakening, each found that the dream was true and that the cuttings were on the floor. Pliny interpreted these occurrences as warnings that, at the time of the murder of the emperor Domitian, the emperor had been planning to take action against Pliny for his support of the senate against Domitian. Pliny arrived at this conclusion because it was customary for accused persons to let their hair grow. He interpreted the haircuts to mean that Domitian's death had averted the danger of Pliny's indictment. This view found support in papers discovered in Domitian's death.

Perhaps the most notable exchange in the official correspondence contained in the 10th book of the *Letters* is that between Pliny, who was governor of the province of Bithnia and the emperor Trajan on the subject of persecution of Christians—letters 96 and 97. In the first letter of this pair, Pliny asks Trajan for advice concerning his handling of accused Christians. Their crime was membership in a foreign, and therefore subversive, cult. Pliny, however, is not sure whether or not simple membership is adequate grounds for the requisite death penalty. So he asks the emperor's advice—though not until he has already sentenced several Christians. Pliny wants to know if he should sentence young and old alike, if anyone disavowing Christian beliefs should be spared, and if merely being called Christian demands the sentence or if some other crime must be connected with the name before the death sentence is necessary.

Pliny explains that he has already condemned some because "their stubbornness and unshakeable obstinacy ought not to go unpunished." He has, however, sent any who are Roman citizens to stand in trial in Rome. Pliny further informs the emperor that, after he began arresting Christians, an anonymous pamphlet appeared with lists of the names of persons the pamphleteer accused of being Christians.

Pliny further informs the emperor that he has spared those who denied Christ, prayed to the Roman gods, and made offerings to a statue of the emperor. He also spared those who confessed to having formerly been Christians. From them he learned that their guilt resulted from their having met at dawn on certain days; chanted verses honoring Christ as a deity; and taken an oath of allegiance to Christ in which they promised not to steal or commit adultery, to be trustworthy in all things, and to restore any money they held in trust when so called upon. Later on the same day, they reassembled for a common meal. The former Christians reported that they had given up these practices when Pliny issued an edict banning "all political societies." Pliny tested the truth of these allegations by torturing two female slaves that the Christians called deaconesses. Based on their forced testimony, he found nothing more than "a degenerate sort of cult carried to extravagant lengths." Pliny opined that, given the opportunity to repent, a great many Christians could be reformed.

In Trajan's answer to Pliny's letter, the emperor approves of Pliny's course of action. He instructs Pliny not to seek Christians out. If, however, individuals are brought for judgment and the charges proved, they must be punished unless they recant. In that case, they are to be spared. No mass charges may be brought, nor may any anonymous pamphlets be used as grounds for laying charges.

Pliny's letters are a reliable, instructive, and entertaining storehouse of otherwise unavailable information about Roman and other matters in the second century of the Common Era.

Bibliography

Hoffer, Stanley E. *The Anxieties of Pliny the Younger.* Atlanta, Ga.: Scholars Press, 1999.

Pliny. *Letters and Panygyricus.* 2 vols. Translated by Betty Radice. Cambridge, Mass.: Harvard University Press, 1969.

——. *Letters.* 2 vols. Translated by William Melmouth and W. M. L. Hutchinson. Cambridge, Mass.: Harvard University Press, 1952.

Letters of Ignatius, The (ca. late first or early second century C.E.)

It seems that Ignatius was either the second or the third Christian bishop of Antioch in Syria. If he was second, as ORIGEN suggests, he followed St. Peter in that capacity. If, as EUSEBIUS OF CAESAREA reports, Ignatius was the third bishop, he followed Peter's successor, Euodius.

In any case, during the reign of the Roman emperor Trajan, Ignatius and other Syrian Christians were taken into the custody of a company of Roman soldiers and sent overland through Asia Minor before sailing to Rome, where the Christians were destined to face martyrdom among the wild beasts of the Coliseum. Word of Ignatius's arrest and impending execution preceded him along his route, and Christians in the cities where he stopped received permission to visit him and offer him solace. Ignatius did not want his wellwishers to try to avert his martyrdom. He looked forward to a heavenly reward.

Opportunities presented themselves for Ignatius to write to the members of the congregations of various cities. He seized those occasions to exercise pastoral care for the communities by advising them on issues close to his heart. Seven of these letters were subsequently collected— perhaps by St. Polycarp, the bishop of Smyrna—

and survived as collection for their eventual inclusion in *The* APOSTOLIC FATHERS OF THE CHRISTIAN CHURCH. The surviving letters include one to Polycarp himself, another to Polycarp's church at Smyrna, a letter to the Magnesians, a letter to the Ephesians, one to the Trallians, another to the Romans, and one to the Philadelphians.

In general, Ignatius's letters address matters of great consequence to early Christians. He is concerned with the authority of bishops and the preservation of the apostolic succession that traces that authority directly to Christ's apostles and to Jesus himself. Ignatius wants the church to speak with a single voice on matters of doctrine and theology and not to splinter on issues deemed heretical, such as the proposed nonhumanity of Jesus or, even among Christians, the then still-unsettled question of Christ's resurrection. Ignatius seems to see both the Gnostic Christians and those who, though believing Christ to be the Messiah, would nonetheless follow the old Jewish law as threats to the doctrinal Christianity of the true church. He is at first concerned about his home church in Antioch, which was undergoing some sort of upheaval at the time of his arrest. On later learning that this matter had been resolved, Ignatius encourages other churches to send representatives to participate in the celebrations marking the end of internal conflict. It was in his letter to the church at Rome that Ignatius requested there be no attempt to avert his martyrdom. Rather, he explains, he will coax the wild beasts to devour him.

In another letter included in the collection of the *Apostolic Fathers,* the LETTER OF POLYCARP TO THE PHILIPPIANS, we find a reference to Ignatius's martyrdom, but no details about the manner of his death. Later accounts of it are apparently fictitious.

Bibliography

Ignatius. "Letters of Ignatius." In *The Apostolic Fathers.* Vol. 1. Translated and edited by Bart D. Ehrman. Cambridge, Mass.: Harvard University Press, 2003.

Libanius of Antioch (fl. fourth century
C.E.) *Greek prose writer*

A SOPHIST who wrote about, taught, and practiced the art of public speaking, Libanius was the most distinguished practitioner of his calling among his contemporaries at Constantinople. His preeminence aroused the envy of his competitors, and they connived to have him banished from the city in 346 C.E. After a period during which he practiced first in Nicaea and then in Nicomedia, Libanius was called back to Constantinople, where he practiced until he retired to his native city of Antioch.

In Constantinople, Libanius benefited from the patronage of the Roman emperor JULIAN. Libanius shared with the emperor his desire to unseat Christianity as the Roman state religion and restore polytheism.

As a writer, Libanius bequeathed to posterity an autobiography that appears in his Greek *Declamations,* or *Harangues (Meletai).* More than 60 of them survive, and they are renowned for their purity of style. He also left a 13-section work of *Rhetorical Examples.* A composition that seems to have provided models for drafting practice debates is his *Arguments [responding] to the Orations of Demosthenes.*

Libanius's letters have also been collected, and they are of unusual interest. Among some 2,000 epistles, we find letters to two of the Fathers of the Christian Church: St. BASIL and St. JOHN CHRYSOSTOM. Both of these renowned figures had been Libanius's students.

Bibliography

Libanius of Antioch. *Antioch as a Centre of Hellenic Culture as Observed by Libanius.* Translated by A. F. Norman. Liverpool, U.K.: Liverpool University Press, 2000.

———. *Autobiography and Selected Letters: Libanius.* Translated by A. F. Norman. Cambridge, Mass.: Harvard University Press, 1992.

———. *Libanius' Declamations 9 and 10.* Translated by Mikael Johansson. Göteborg, Sweden: Universitas Regia Gothoburgensis, 2005.

Meeks, Wayne A., and Robert L. Wilkin. *Jews and Christians in Antiochin the First Four Centuries of the Common Era.* Missoula, Mont.: Scholars Press for the Society of Biblical Literature, ca. 1978.

Library Diodorus Siculus   See DIODORNS SICULUS.

Lie Yukou   See *LIEZI.*

Liezi (Lieh Tzu) (ca. 300 B.C.E.–300 C.E.)

A prose text of DAOISM doubtfully attributed to Lie Yukou (LIEH YÜ-K'O)—an author who may have lived a century before the version in which the document has survived was written—*Lieh Tzu* is reputed to be the easiest of all classical Taoist texts to understand.

In its eight parts, divided into 150 sections, the book explains such matters as the differences between what is real and what is illusory. It offers theories about the origins of dreams. It is something of a geography text when it discusses strange foreign countries, and it is one of numerous texts that make stereotypical jokes about foolish farmers from the region of Sung. The work also contains popular fables that convey a moral. These vary in the level of their sophistication from very straightforward to quite complex.

The translator A. C. Graham has provided an example of the simpler sort—one whose title Graham gives as "The Stupid Old Man Who Moved a Mountain." In it, an old man proposes to level two mountains that are 700 miles square and 700,000 feet tall. He means to carry away their mass in baskets and dump the earth and stones in a gulf. After working for months on the project with his son, his grandson, and a neighbor child, the old man, whose name was Mister Simple, starts for home. He encounters a neighbor named Old Wiseacre, who reproves him for his folly. Simple, however, explains that the mountain will never grow any larger, whereas his progeny will increase forever through the generations and eventually accomplish the project.

Overhearing this, the mountain spirits become concerned that Simple might really succeed in his project, and they complain to God. Impressed with Simple's sincerity and follow-through, God has supernatural beings carry away the mountains and plant them elsewhere, with the result that within his own lifetime Simple can travel across level ground for the first time.

A more sophisticated narrative from the 48th chapter concerns the master of the zither, Po-ya, and his most faithful and understanding listener, Chung Tzu-chi. Whatever is in Po-ya's mind or however he is feeling when he improvises upon his instrument, his music instantly conveys into the mind of Chung Tzu-chi. The story is a lesson in the benefits of trying to understand and appreciate the thought and accomplishment of others. It also suggests that such immediate sympathy is a quality missing from then-contemporary life and that achieving such sympathy should be a goal for everyone.

Less complex and quite touching is the third chapter's story of a traveler who returns late in life to the region of his birth. A traveling companion decides to play a joke on him and identifies as his native place a much more humble village, which has a local shrine, dwellings, and a graveyard—all places associated with the old man's ancestors. At each identification, the old man is deeply moved, and the sight of his purportedly ancestral graves touch him so that he weeps. Then his companion confesses the joke, and the old fellow feels ashamed. Worse, when he comes to the real site of his ancestors' former dwellings and their burial places, he is not nearly so deeply moved as when he was deceived. The moral: Some innocently intended jokes prove cruel.

Bibliography

Lieh Yük'o. *The Book of Lieh-Tzu: A Classic of the Tao.* Translated by A. C. Graham. New York: Columbia University Press, 1990.

Mair, Victor H. *The Columbia Anthology of Traditional Chinese Literature.* New York: Columbia University Press, 1994.

Owen, Stephen. *Readings in Chinese Literary Thought.* Cambridge, Mass.: Council on East Asian Studies, Harvard University, Harvard University Press, 1992.

Life of Apollonius of Tyana, The
L. Flavius Philostratus (ca. 210 C.E.)

At the request of the learned empress, Julia Domna, wife of the Roman emperor Septimus Severus, the scholar L. FLAVIUS PHILOSTRATUS undertook the composition of a greek biography of a second-century philosopher and sage, Apollonius of Tyana. The empress gave Philostratus certain documents purporting to be a rough memoir prepared by Damis, a disciple of Apollonius. In addition to that source, Philostratus also had access to letters written by Apollonius, some of which survive, either in their originals or in copies. Beyond that, having accepted the empress's commission, Philostratus traveled to Tyana, where a temple of the sect that the philosopher had founded still venerated his memory. Philostratus journeyed elsewhere, too, in an effort to amass as many recollections and reports concerning the sage as he could find. He read a book written by Maximus of Aegae about the work of Apollonius in that place, and he saw Apollonius's will. Finally, Philostratus read four books about Apollonius composed by one Moeragenes. Philostratus, however, rejected what Moeragenes had to say as spurious since it was not confirmed by the more reliable documents and reports that he had gathered.

Apollonius is of particular interest in an era like ours in which such documents as the DEAD SEA SCROLLS and the Nag Hammadi Manuscripts (see GNOSTIC APOCRYPHA AND PSEUDEPIGRAPHA) are reforming scholars' thinking about the shape of first- and second-century Christian communities and the writings they produced. This interest arises in part from a book written by Hierocles, a provincial governor who served the Roman emperor Diocletian. Hierocles observed that Apollonius had displayed the same degree of wisdom and performed the same range of miracles as were imputed to Jesus Christ. Understandably, early Christian zealots and missionaries took great offence at this suggestion, and Eusebius of Caesarea—the Christian bishop of that community—undertook a refutation of Hierocles. That refutation stands as the church's official position on Apollonius despite the fact that Eusebius was not himself a believer in the physical resurrection of Christ. Subscribing to that particular article of faith became requisite only after the Nicene Creed required it in 325 C.E.

A summary of the biography follows.

In a passage reminiscent of the Christian Annunciation, before the birth of her baby, Apollonius's mother receives a visit from the god Proteus in the guise of an Egyptian demon. When she asks what sort of child she will bear, the apparition answered, "Myself . . . Proteus the god of Egypt." The baby is born in a meadow where the mother has fallen asleep. Swans dance around her as she sleeps, and when they all trumpet at once, she awakes and bears her child. At that instant a bolt of lightning shoots from the sky and bounces back into heaven—a sign that local people interpret to mean that the child will transcend earthly things and come near the gods.

As a child of 14, Apollonius begins a systematic study of the Greek philosophers and their systems of thought; he finds that of Pythagoras of Samos (see Italic school of philosophy) particularly congenial. At the conclusion of his formal education, Apollonius forswears wine and becomes a vegetarian. He goes barefoot, wears only white linen, will not wear any animal's skin, grows his hair and beard long, and takes up residence in the temple at Aegae in Cilicia.

There follows a series of examples of the young Apollonius's wisdom and virtues. Among these, Philostratus tells the story of how Apollonius reforms his wild older brother by positive reinforcement and his own good example. Then Apollonius announces his intention to lead a celibate life, and Philostratus comments on the young man's mastery of his passions. Moreover, Apollonius cultivates his memory. (Though he may have lived beyond 100 years, his memory remained prodigious.) He also chooses to remain silent for a period of five years, confining his communication to gestures, nods, the movement of his hands, and so forth. During this time of silence, Apollonius begins to travel about widely. When he breaks his silence, he reproves and chastises corn merchants who are starving the people of Aspendus by withholding the harvest for export and a higher profit.

Traveling to Antioch, Apollonius attracts disciples with his unaffected manner and his wisdom, and seven choose to attend him at all times. They leave him, however, when he announces his intention to travel first to Nineveh and Babylon and then on to India. It is on this journey that his first biographer, Damis, joins Apollonius as a disciple. Damis explains that his mastery of languages will prove useful. Apollonius, however, assures him that he already understands all human tongues. He has to learn the language of the birds, however, from the Arabs as he passes through their territory.

Arriving at Babylon, Apollonius refuses to honor the king by kissing his image on arrival. Being cross-examined about this refusal, he so impresses the king's officers that that they bring Apollonius before the ruler. The king is on the point of sacrificing a horse, and as Apollonius is much opposed to blood sacrifice, he merely throws frankincense into the flames and leaves until the ceremony has ended. Asked to be the king's guest in Babylon, Apollonius accepts, provided that he might be lodged with a person of circumstances similar to his own. This done, the king offers him 10 gifts of his own choosing. Apollonius asks that a colony of formerly Greek Eretrians be permitted to remain in possession of the land they occupy, and that he be given a meal of bread and dried fruits. When the king asks why he does not accept the other gifts, Apollonius replies that it was because he has not yet made other friends.

Among his other accomplishments, Apollonius, who believes in the transmigration of souls, says he remembers his former life. He also has the gift of seeing the future. Apollonius advises the king that no cause is worth going to war over. After giving the king of Babylon much good advice, Apollonius is ready to move on to India. Before leaving, he asks the king to bestow his favor on the Magi, who are the priests of Babylon, and on the host who had housed him during his sojourn in Babylon. The king is pleased to do this and also insists on giving Apollonius camels and camel drivers for his onward journey, provisioning him with water and the necessities of desert travel and advising him on the best route to follow.

As Apollonius and Damis follow the road through the Caucasus to India, Apollonius conducts an ongoing dialogue with Damis in the manner of SOCRATES. Along the road, they pass by many places of interest, visiting some and missing others. They also encounter various people and animals, including a boy riding an elephant. Apollonius uses the incident to explain that the elephant's instinctive obedience, not the boy's power, is responsible for the great beast's willing subordination to the youngster. A lengthy and often misinformed discourse on elephants follows.

Among the tactics that Apollonius employs in instructing Damis is rewriting a line of Euripides. In its original form, the line asserts that the life of all men lies in their children. Apollonius revises the truism by substituting the word *animals* for men, thereby assigning men to their proper category.

Upon reaching the Indus River, they discover that a Persian satrap (governor) had anticipated their need for a boat and guide, and owing to his foresight, they are ferried across and arrive at last in India proper. Apollonius is delighted to discover that the Indian king, Phraotes, lives and behaves according to a code of conduct that would do credit to a philosopher. He is also surprised to discover that Phraotes, like his Babylonian hosts, speaks Greek—a useful accomplishment that avoids putting Apollonius's universal mastery of language to the test.

Having concluded that Phraotes is also a philosopher, Apollonius eagerly debates assorted topics with him, including the issue of whether teetotalers sleep better than those who drink wine moderately. (Both agree that drunkards do not sleep well.) Among the arguments that Apollonius advances in favor of drinking only water, we find one that holds that dreams dreamed under the influence of alcohol are useless for the purposes of interpreting them as guides to future events. Apollonius is adept at divination of dreams' meaning.

After assisting the king in judging difficult legal cases, Apollonius decides to leave India, where the law permits only a three-day sojourn. The king inquires about the condition of the camels that have carried them from Babylon—a matter totally outside Apollonius's notice. Damis tells the king that the camels are in such poor condition that they ought themselves to be carried. King Phraotes therefore provides new camels, a guide, and a letter of introduction to his father, Iarchus. He also tries to heap treasures on them. Apollonius accepts some linen robes and some gemstones that he intends as gifts to the gods on his return. He refuses, however, to accept any gold or treasures for himself.

Following the route of Alexander the Great, the travelers reach the furthest point of Alexander's penetration into India on the banks of the river Hyphasis. As they journey on, they comment on the flora and fauna they encounter and on the topography of the Gangetic Plain. There follows a mythic discussion of the varieties of dragons indigenous to the area and how some of them prey on elephants. Encountering Indian monks ruled by Iarchas, known as "the masters" or "the sages," Apollonius and Damis observe them levitating.

Iarchas impresses Apollonius by recounting the philosopher's personal history from childhood to illustrate the monks' knowledge of events past and present. Iarchas promises to teach Apollonius all the lore he needs to be able to do likewise. In their ensuing discussions, Apollonius and the sages consider self-knowledge and the transmigration of souls.

Turning to ethnography, Iarchas tells Apollonius that the Ethiopians had formerly been Indians but had been expelled. Then he returns to the subject of reincarnation, and, on finding that Apollonius also recalls a former existence, Iarchas asks him to tell the sage about it. We discover that, in his former life, Apollonius had been the pilot of an Egyptian vessel. Apollonius recalls a bargain that he had struck with some pirates during that time. In the event, however, he outwitted them and sailed away from the pirates and their bribes.

Iarchas reproves Apollonius for confusing abstention from injustice with justice—a failing the Indian attributes to all Greeks. From the sages, Apollonius learns that the universe is a living creature formed by God, and Iarchas promulgates the belief that natural disasters occur as punishments for the transgressions of people.

In a series of the episodes that would later lead to the Roman governor Hieron's seeing in Apollonius a prototype of Jesus Christ, Apollonius first heals an Indian boy possessed by a demon. He then restores a lame man to health, a blind man to sight, and returns movement to the paralyzed hand of a third person.

Philostratus turns his attention to reporting Apollonius's work on astrology and the proper method of sacrifice. The author also discourses on his subject's foretelling the future and the connection between knowing what the future holds and the successful practice of medicine. Apollonius and Iarchus discuss magnets and the difficulty of finding stones with magnetic properties. Iarchas attests to the actual existence of Pygmies, but other fanciful poetic peoples, such as dog-headed or shadow-footed men, he treats as poetic fancies. the firebird (phoenix) he treats as a living creature that visits Egypt every 500 years. Following discussions of this sort, Apollonius and Damis set sail for home in a ship provided by Iarchus.

As he journeys toward home, Apollonius teaches along the way, discoursing at Ephesus on the advantages of communal responsibility. Also at Ephesus, he predicts and prevents a coming plague by forestalling the demon who would have caused it. When Apollonius arrives in Ionia, Philostratus thinks, he predicts the earthquakes that the Ionians and the surrounding territories will soon suffer. These kindnesses and prophecies later cause Apollonius trouble.

Continuing his voyage toward Greece, Apollonius often stops to pay his respects at the tombs and altars of Greeks of past ages, including those of the archetypal musician, ORPHEUS, and the clever Palamedes, who had tricked Odysseus into serving in the Trojan War. Apollonius then reports to his disciples, whose number increases as he travels home, that while he had been in India he had interviewed Achilles. The ghostly Achilles reported to him that the Thessalians had neglected his tomb and the worship of his cult. Achilles permitted Apollonius to ask five questions about the Trojan War. When asked about whether or not Helen was really in Troy, Achilles replied that for a long time the Greeks thought so, but in fact Helen was, as EURIPIDES' play about her had indicated, in Egypt throughout the war.

Arriving at Athens, Apollonius lectures the Athenians on the subject of religion—particularly on their rites and ceremonies, which, through the ignorance of the priesthood, have become lax and blasphemous. Also while in Athens, he casts out another demon from a youth and rebukes the Athenians for the effeminacy of their dancing at the Dionysian rites.

Now Apollonius undertakes a religious and patriotic pilgrimage around Greece, visiting famous shrines and lecturing multitudes at the places he stops. From Greece, he sails to Crete and thence to Rome, where the emperor Nero holds sway and is imprisoning people who represent themselves as sages, philosophers, and religious leaders. Sternly warned against going to Rome with his followers, Apollonius nonetheless chooses to do so, and most of his disciples desert him in fear of the consequences of following him.

Once in Rome, by a happy chance, Apollonius makes the acquaintance of a certain Telesinus—an officer in charge of the temples of Rome. Impressed by the prophet's wisdom, Telesinus equips Apollonius with letters to the priests of the temples to reform their rites and sacrifices in accordance with his teaching and to allow Apollonius to live within the temples. His presence there soon spearheads a religious revival in Rome.

Before long, Apollonius attracts the attention of Nero's henchman, Tigellinus, who sets a constant watch on him, hoping to find cause to punish him. Instead, Tigellinus becomes afraid of Apollonius's unusual powers. Nonetheless, Nero's agents keep close tabs on Apollonius until they finally think they have cause to arrest him. But Apollonius cows them with his fearlessness and wisdom, so that Tigellinus finally decides he must be dealing with a god.

Apollonius also raises up a young woman who is being borne to her funeral, but Philostratus suggests other, more naturalistic possibilities without ruling out the possibility of her having been resurrected from the dead. Nero eventually issues a proclamation banning the teaching of philosophy at Rome, and Apollonius turns his steps toward Spain.

Philostratus himself had been to Spain and, as had Apollonius before him, had observed the advance and retreat of oceanic tides. Philostratus relies on Apollonius's explanation—one that involves the advance and retreat of spirits breathed in and out by the earth. He offers in support of that notion the assertion that the souls of the dying do not quit their bodies at high tide; he also mentions a connection with the phases of the moon. That said, Philostratus traces the course that Apollonius takes in Spain and the various altars and Greek culture that he encountered there.

In book 5, Apollonius discourses with his apostle Damis concerning the pathological egocentrism of Nero in having rescheduled the Olympic games so that he himself could compete in them and so that the celebrants could sacrifice to him rather than to Zeus. Apollonius predicts that the emperor will win in the singing contests since no one will dare compete against him. The philosopher scoffs, however, at an emperor who neglects making laws so that he can stroll about singing like a street entertainer. Soon a messen-

ger comes to Spain demanding that people sacrifice in honor of Nero's having taken three first prizes. The people performed the sacrifices as ordered, but they have no idea why they did so.

Philostratus reports that Apollonius conspired against Nero with Vindex, the governor of a Spanish province. Vindex apparently led a revolution, in which he was killed, but Nero fled nonetheless, and Apollonius accurately predicted that the reigns of those succeeding Nero or hoping to succeed him, Vitellius, Galba, and Otho, would be short. Defending Apollonius against the charge of wizardry, Philostratus suggests that his knowledge was based instead on divine revelation. Detailed knowledge of the situation and clear thinking might also be candidates for explaining his accuracy.

Apollonius travels to Sicily, and in a discussion of the relative merits of mythology as treated by poets and the *FABLES* of AESOP, Apollonius favors Aesop. The content of the stories of poets involves immorality, slanders the gods by attributing human failings to them, and encourages people to behave in similarly perverse fashions. Aesop, on the other hand, used "humble incidents to teach great truths" and used pleasing tales to make animals "interesting to mankind."

Arriving in the vicinity of Mount Etna, Apollonius next turns his attention to attempting a nonmythological explanation of the activity of volcanoes. The explanation is not very accurate, but from it Apollonius draws a useful moral. Even during and after volcanic eruption, there is plenty of unaffected earth available for holy persons to do good works.

Sailing for Greece, Apollonius has a presentiment of shipwreck and disembarks to take passage on another vessel. The one he abandoned does sink. Arriving at Athens, the philosopher is initiated into the Eleusinian mysteries of the cult of Dionysus.

Taking ship for Egypt, Apollonius rebukes a trader who is carrying images of the gods to sell in market places. He also reproves a young man who, though uneducated, has amassed wealth and spent it on a sumptuous dwelling. A glutton also feels the sharp edge of the philosopher's tongue. On his arrival in Egypt, Apollonius saves an innocent young man condemned by his own false admission of guilt because he preferred death to torture. The citizens of Alexandria, who had been expecting him, are delighted to have Apollonius in their midst.

Horse racing is all the rage in Alexandria, and the fans have, like those of some of our contemporary soccer teams, become violent to the point of murder in their devotion to their favorites. Apollonius rebukes them for their bloody-mindedness.

Vespasian (ruled 69–79 B.C.E.) desires to become the Roman emperor. On entering the city of Alexandria, he seeks out Apollonius where he is residing in a temple and prays that Apollonius will make Vespasian a king. Apollonius replies that he has already done so as he has prayed for a wise, just, noble, temperate "father of legitimate sons"—in other words, just such a person as Vespasian—to become emperor and replace Vitellius. Apollonius considers Vitellius worse than Nero, though the historical record suggests otherwise. (Vitellius ended up being dragged through the streets of Rome and killed, so the opinion of Vitellius that Philostratus attributes to Apollonius may be the result of authorial hindsight.) In any case, the issue of politics remains prominent through the rest of the fifth book. One of the speakers, Euphrates, champions the restoration of the Roman republic. Vespasian is present and a bit disconcerted at the prospect that his absolute authority might be undermined.

Apollonius, however, suggests that restoration of the republic is not an achievable goal, and he argues in favor of a beneficent monarchy. Vespasian is pleased, but Euphrates becomes Apollonius's implacable enemy. Then Apollonius lectures Vespasian on the internal checks that he must put in place to restrain any tendency to abuse his authority. Euphrates in general approves of Apollonius's remarks, but he cautions Vespasian against any philosophical position that claims a special understanding of the purposes of deity. Such philosophies falsely ascribe their own priorities to the divinity.

Philostratus fairly reveals that even Apollonius could mistake his man. When Vespasian became emperor, he repressed the freedoms that Nero had uncharacteristically granted to the Greeks. Philostratus quotes a series of three brief letters from Apollonius to the emperor in which Apollonius accuses the monarch of having fallen below the level of Nero by enslaving the Greeks.

Otherwise, while he is still in Egypt Apollonius recognizes the soul of the former Egyptian king Amasis in the body of a tame lion. Then he sets out for Ethiopia and, as he hopes, the source of the Nile River. After a series of adventures that include purifying a man who had committed an involuntary homicide, Apollonius comes to the lands of the "naked sages" of Ethiopia. An enemy, Thrasybulus of Naucratis, a henchman for Euphrates, has arrived before him and prejudiced the Ethiopian philosophers against Apollonius, so his reception is cool.

The leader of the Ethiopian sages, Thespesion, harangues Apollonius about the superiority of Egyptian wisdom to that of India and to Apollonius's own. In reply, Apollonius schools the Ethiopians in the Indo-Brahman origins of their own wisdom, and indeed of their own peoples, for they were bred from the Ethiopian exiles from India. He plays his trump card on behalf of the superiority of the Indian philosophers by pointing out that they alone among men have mastered the art of levitation to soar aloft with the sun god. Eventually Apollonius perceives that Thrasybulus and Euphrates have prejudiced the Ethiopian sages against him by claiming that Apollonius had disparaged them. One of the youngest Ethiopians, Nilus, however, recognizes Apollonius's innate goodness and wisdom and prevails on him to recount his Indian experiences in detail. Moreover, Nilus switches his allegiance to Apollonius, who, advises him to be circumspect and not to annoy the Ethiopians.

Apollonius and Thespesion meet again, and this time their conversation turns on the comparative representation of gods by the Greeks and the Ethiopians. Apollonius complains that the Ethiopians fashion their gods to resemble animals. This argument, insofar as it is, from our contemporary point of view, over an issue that is absolutely culturally determined, sheds little light on the subject. The conversation soon turns to Greek culture and institutions, and here Apollonius is able to correct some of Thespesion's impressions and conclusions. He argues, for example, that the ruler Lycurgus had pure motives for denying strangers permission to settle in Sparta.

The philosophers next turn their attention to the problem of justice in the context of Greek history. After that they agree about the immortality of the soul and about nature, essentially agreeing with PLATO in his *Timaeus*.

Having concluded those discussions, Apollonius, joined by his new disciple Nilus and with a man named Timasion as a guide, departs in search of the source of the Nile. Philostratus repeats the ancient notion that the sound of the Nile's cataract (waterfall) is literally deafening. The sojourners make their way as far as the third of the Nile's seven cataracts, and then turn aside.

In the 29th chapter of book 6, Philostratus abruptly changes the subject to the success of the Roman general and later emperor, Titus, in capturing Jerusalem in 70 C.E., and to a conversation between Titus and Apollonius. In that discourse, Apollonius offers to the young emperor one of his disciples, Demetrius, who will become a watchdog over the imperial character. Titus agrees to let Demetrius "bark" and even "bite" to keep him on the path of virtue and justice. The Greek contains a familiar play on words. Greek *cynos* (a cognate of English *canine*) means *dog*, and Demetrius was a Cynic philosopher (see CYNICISM).

Apollonius warns Titus that as long as his father, Vespasian, lives, the young man must be on his guard against his father's enemies. After Vespasian dies, Titus's near kinsmen will present the greatest danger. When Titus asks how he will die, Apollonius answers that the sea will be the agent of his death. The prophecy is fulfilled when Titus dies from eating bad fish.

Concerned that he is becoming long-winded, Philostratus leaves off detailing the journeys of Apollonius and begins instead to tell stories about his miraculous intercessions in people's lives to their benefit. He finds a fortune for one man and dissuades another from his unnatural passion for a statue of the goddess Aphrodite. He exposes charlatans and heals a young man bitten by a mad dog. He also heals the dog.

Next Philostratus considers Apollonius as an incomparable defender of liberty by setting his story in the context of philosophers who died for their beliefs. After several examples of these, Philostratus tells how Apollonius opposed the tyranny not only of Nero but also of the emperors Domitian and Nerva.

Domitian trumps up a charge against Apollonius and has him summoned to Rome. Apollonius, however, has mysterious foreknowledge of the summons and anticipates it by sailing immediately from Asia Minor for Italy. In Italy, Apollonius's friend, the philosopher Demetrius, advises him to take ship again, since Domitian certainly means to see him tried, convicted, and killed. Apollonius, however, replies that "it is the duty of the wise" to die for their principles. He compares the cruelty of tyrants and decides that the crueler sort includes those who color their murders with the trappings of legality. He remarks that a sage who knows himself will not be frightened by that which most people fear, and that he will obey his conscience wherever it leads him.

Having come to court and offered himself to the emperor's justice, he discovers that a longtime admirer and acquaintance, Aelian, is the emperor's chief officer. Aelian warns Apollonius that the emperor means to condemn him and that his indictment contains many serious accusations that range from inappropriate dress to having allowed himself to be worshipped to having predicted the future to having slandered the emperor to having performed a human sacrifice by cutting up an Arcadian boy.

As he waits among the other defendants for the emperor's court to begin, Apollonius hears their stories, cheers them up, and offers advice for their defense. He also deals adroitly with informers who are sent to try to get him to say something incriminating. When he finally comes before the emperor at a session preliminary to his trial, Apollonius learns that Domitian has indeed prejudged him. The emperor insults the philosopher by cutting off his beard and his long hair.

The emperor sends him in chains to await the formal trial. In the first clear evidence of Apollonius's superhuman nature, he miraculously removes a metal fetter from his leg and then puts it on again. Then, through the influence of Aelian, the emperor allows Apollonius to wait without bonds in a more comfortable prison.

Finally brought before the emperor, Apollonius answers the charges against him, and the emperor acquits him of them but declares his intention to hold him for a private interview. Perceiving that the emperor intends to hold him indefinitely, Apollonius quotes from HOMER's *The ILIAD*, 22.13: "For thou shalt not slay me, since I tell thee I am not mortal." Having said that, Apollonius vanishes into thin air.

Despite this apparent miracle, Philostratus quotes for the record the oration that Apollonius had composed to defend himself against Domitian's anticipated accusations. He disproves the charge of wizardry. Rather, he portrays himself as a master of the liberating arts of poetry, music, astronomy, philosophy, oratory, and voluntary poverty. He explains that he is a vegetarian and dresses without employing the skin of animals since he is against blood sacrifice. He explains the reasons that he wears (or used to wear) long hair.

The philosopher next details his religious belief: God has brought all things into being and sustains them, and God's motives are good. Human beings partake of some of the good qualities of the creator. Many human beings, however, allow their baser natures to overcome their higher impulses. To guide them away from their own follies, God sometimes sends a god to lead them in the right path. The clear implication is that Apollonius is such a being—though he does not say so.

He admits, however, that he did save the city of Ephesus from the plague. Accused again of wizardry because of his foreknowledge, Apollonius explains that his light diet makes it possible for him to see things—including future things—as if in a mirror in his mind. It was through prayer to HERACLES, says Apollonius, that the plague was averted. As for the charge that he killed a child as a sacrifice, Apollonius utterly disproves it and names witnesses who can vouch for his having been with a dying friend at the time. He next disproves a charge of seditious utterances, implicating his Egyptian enemy, Euphrates, as the man who has brought false accusations against him.

Meanwhile, Apollonius's disciple, Damis, has obeyed his master's instruction to go to Dicaerchia. It is to that destination that Apollonius is miraculously transported and encounters Damis and another disciple. At this point in the narrative, for the first time as I think, certain incidents occur that bear a truly striking similarity to the NEW TESTAMENT's account of the risen Christ's appearing to his apostles. Both disciples think that Apollonius must be a ghost. Apollonius instructs them to take hold of him and convince themselves that he is alive and has not abandoned his body. Asked about how he came so quickly to them, Apollonius attributes it to divine intervention. At this late point in Philostratus's narrative, Apollonius's disciples begin to regard him as a divinity.

The trio board a ship for Sicily, where multitudes from around the Mediterranean come to see Apollonius. Among the other wonders that Philostratus reports, we find one that suggests that, while he is in Ephesus in Asia Minor, Apollonius mysteriously witnesses the assassination of the emperor Domitian at Rome and reports it to his followers.

Having attained an advanced age—80s, 90s, or beyond 100—Apollonius dies, and wondrous circumstances surround his passing. He posthumously speaks through a disciple concerning the immortality of the soul. He also, however, reproves the disciple for being concerned about the soul's immortality while he is alive and responsible for the world he lives in, not the one his soul will inhabit.

In addition to Philostratus's biography of the philosopher, some 97 letters attributed to Apollonius also survive. His historicity, in other words, is well established. Aside from the incidental parallels mentioned above and the credulity of their respective followers, one would be hard-pressed to find much other than humanity, piety, a healthy mistrust of temporal authority, and wisdom that Apollonius of Tyana and Jesus Christ of Nazareth share in common. (For a close comparison, see Andy M. Reimer's *Miracle and Magic* in the bibliography below.) To imagine, as the anti-Christian Hieron apparently did, that the writers of certain books of the New Testament used the story of Apollonius as a model suggests Hieron's lack of literary knowledge about the myth-making of the ancient Mediterranean world. Resurrected deities abounded in those myths, and stories of miraculous happenings were very common.

There is one passage in Philostratus that criticizes the Jews for hardheadedly rejecting the polytheism practiced by most of the ancient world, but one must remember that in Judea after Alexander's conquest of the Persian Empire, an official policy of hellenizing Jewish institutions remained in place for centuries. Viewed from an exclusively literary rather than from a theological or philosophical perspective, in such circumstances it would be surprising if, around the beginning of the Common Era, elements of Greek myths associated with miraculous births, precocious childhoods, and resurrections did not infiltrate popular Jewish thinking to some degree.

Bibliography

Philostratus the Athenian. *Apollonius of Tyana.* Edited and translated by Christopher P. Jones. Cambridge, Mass.: Harvard University Press, 2006.

———. *The Life of Apollonius of Tyana.* (Contains letters of Apollonius and Eusebius's response to Hieron.) 2 vols. New York: G. P. Putnam's Sons, 1921.

Reimer, Andy M. *Miracle and Magic: A Study in the Acts of the Apostles and the Life of Apollonius of Tyana.* New York: Sheffield Academic Press, 2002.

Life of Saint Anthony, The *(The Life and Affairs of Our Holy Father Anthony)* Athanasius (ca. 360 C.E.)

The historical Saint Anthony died in 356 C.E. He was certainly not the first solitary monk, but in no small measure due to St. ATHANASIUS, Anthony became the model for the tradition of Christian anchorites—monks who chose to spend long devotional periods in isolation. Shortly after Anthony's death, Athanasius, who was the patriarch or bishop of Alexandria and who had known Anthony well, responded to requests from monks who wished to know more about the famous holy man and penned the saint's biography. It became an instant classic and the prototype for many subsequent spiritual biographies of real and of fictive Christians who, in their lives, actions, and commitments—and in their deaths and often their martyrdoms—emulated Christ's pattern for living, overcoming temptation, dying, and subsequent elevation to immortality. Beyond the ancient works that emulate it, Athanasius's book anticipates such comparatively modern descendants as John Foxe's continually updated *Book of Martyrs*, John Bunyan's *Pilgrim's Progress*, and the 15th-century. Florentine playwright Antonia Pulci's plays of *St. Francis, St. Theodora, St. Guglielma*, and *St. Anthony the Abbot*. The last-named work retells Anthony's story with Florentine local color.

Reared with a younger sister in a Christian, Egyptian family, the devout Anthony lost his parents when he was about 20 years old. Deeply moved by the concern of the early church for the care of the poor, he established his sister in a community of religious women, sold all he had, and distributed the money to the needy. He then modeled his life on that of a virtuous anchorite and other holy persons in the vicinity, working with his hands to earn his food and committing the Scriptures to a capacious memory.

As Athanasius tells the story, Anthony's reputation for goodness soon attracted the attention of the Devil, who began to tempt Anthony with guilt for abandoning his sister and with fond recollections of the more comfortable life he had led before following the Lord's assigned path for his life. Satan sent lascivious thoughts that Anthony overcame with the help of constant vigilance, Christ, the Scriptures, prayer, and fasting.

The Devil and his minions did not, however, cease their assaults on Anthony, even after he isolated himself in a tomb where he prayed and fasted. The forces of evil assaulted Anthony physically, but Anthony, now 35, resisted so heroically that his Lord appeared to him and promised to sustain him forever.

Overcoming the temptations of silver and gold that Satan placed in his way, Anthony barricaded himself inside a deserted fortress with just enough bread to sustain life for six months. He arranged to have this simple diet replenished twice yearly, and for years he subsisted on bread and water. Demons continued to try to assault him, but, as promised, Anthony was now invulnerable to their attempts. For 20 years, he continued in this fashion, his isolation broken only by occasional visits from friends. Finally, however, his friends tore the door from his dwelling, and Anthony came forth looking as fit and well as he had 20 years before. Many chose to emulate him, and the desert was filled both with monasteries and with the cells of anchorites.

Anthony illustrated the efficacy of prayer by wading untouched across a crocodile-filled stream with a group of his friends. He began preaching to others who had chosen to live the monastic life, encouraging them to contemplate the life everlasting instead of the short span of human existence. He exhorted the monks to persevere in their discipline and not to relax even for a moment. Virtuous living was all that mattered. He explained that everything God created began as good. The demons that assail human beings *chose* to become bad.

A lengthy sermon follows. It encourages Anthony's listeners to believe in the sufficiency of the Scriptures and revealed truth for every human need. Other education is superfluous since the Scriptures are all one requires to stand firm against the infinitude of temptations with which legions of demons continually try to mislead human beings. He also exposes the deceptions practiced by false prophets who wish to make money by impressing the credulous with fakery.

Anthony identifies the oracles of Hellenistic religion with demons. Even when, he says, demons come in the guise of angels, they can be driven off by prayer. Good spirits, on the other hand, can be recognized by the calm that accompanies their presence. He then details some of his own experiences in his struggles against the temptations of demons.

When Athanasius has finished describing the success of these struggles, he turns his attention to the benefit that members of Anthony's congregation derived from the saint's sermon. They loved virtue more, put away conceit, and became more careful in identifying and resisting temptation. When his sermon was finished, Anthony resumed and intensified his monastic discipline, but he nevertheless frequently shared the company of other anchorites.

Athanasius next reports Anthony's response to the persecution of the Christians of Alexandria under the pagan governor of Syria and Egypt, Gaius Galerius Valerius Maximianus, who championed resurgent paganism, martyring a few Christians but more often enslaving or mutilating them. Athanasius says that Anthony sought martyrdom, but that the Lord protected him for the benefit of others. Back in his cell, Anthony daily suffered the pangs of martyrdom as he struggled with his conscience and his sense of unworthiness. He practiced an ever more rigorous asceticism, wearing a hair shirt and never bathing so that he was tormented by vermin nesting next to and within his skin. He also moved to a more isolated dwelling place on a mountain near an oasis on a caravan route, and there he tended a small garden whose produce sustained him and relieved the hunger of the travelers that passed his way. As he grew older, passersby also brought him gifts of edibles.

Next Athanasius attributes a series of wonders to Anthony. He tamed wild beasts that harassed him at the behest of demons. He saved himself and a company of parched monks from dying of thirst by causing water to miraculously spring forth in the desert. Returning with those monks to their cloister, Anthony encountered the sister from whom he separated so many years before and found that she had become the leader of a community of nuns.

Accounts of the wonders that Anthony accomplished continue. He healed the sick; he knew the details of faraway events as they were happening; he cast out demons. All the while, he resisted the unflagging efforts of the Devil and his minions to distract him from his holy work. Anthony eventually achieved both inner and outer peace, and he punctiliously observed the mandates and orthodoxies to which Athanasius himself subscribed. Except for exhorting such heretics as the Meletian schismatics, the Arians, and the Manichaeans to reform their beliefs, he had no business with them.

During his rare appearances in populated communities, many came to see or touch Anthony, and he cast out demons and cured many of their physical and spiritual disabilities. He confounded a pair of Greek philosophers who came to test him with his wisdom, advising them to become Christian.

Speaking to two Greeks through an interpreter, Anthony conducted a scathing critique of classical Greek myth and its irrationality. He also defended faith as a more reliable test of knowledge than dialectic—that is, more reliable than arguing according to formal systems of logic and syllogism. He also pointed to the success of Christianity in gaining converts as opposed to the dying, polytheistic religions. He underscored his point by casting out demons from several sufferers brought to him for that purpose.

Sometimes when Anthony was speaking with visitors, he would suddenly fall silent and seem to be distracted. When this happened, he envisioned things either occurring elsewhere or things that would happen in the future. He predicted, for instance, the coming temporary ascendancy of the Arian heresy over orthodox Christianity.

After recounting more of Anthony's healings and predictions, Athanasius turns to the manner of his death, which the author also deems remarkable. At age 105, as he felt the approach of death, Anthony imparted his final advice to his visitors: Keep your soul from foul thoughts and avoid falling victim to any of the heresies afflicting orthodox Christianity. Concerned lest his body be mummified or otherwise treated in a manner that he considered irreverent, he commanded his followers to bury him secretly and tell no one where, since at the day of judgment he expected to resume his flesh. He gave one of his sheepskins and a worn-out cloak to Bishop Athanasius.

To the monks for whom he had written this life of Anthony, Athanasius addresses a final exhortation to share what he has written, not only among themselves and with other Christians, but also with pagans who may profit from learning of Anthony's life and be converted.

Bibliography

Athanasius. *The Life of Antony and the Letter to Marcellinus.* Translated by Robert C. Gregg. New York: Paulist Press, 1980.

———. *The Life of Saint Anthony.* Translated by Robert C. Gregg. Edited by Emilie Griffen. San Francisco, Calif.: Harper, 2006.

Pulci, Antonia. *Saint Anthony the Abbott. Florentine Drama for Convent and Festival: Seven Sacred Plays.* Translated by James Wyatt Cook. Chicago: University of Chicago Press, 1996.

Linear B

The oldest script known to represent the Mycenean dialect of the ancient Greek language, Linear B survives incised or impressed on clay tablets and other objects. The script was written on the island of Crete and on the southern portion of the Grecian Pennisula from around 1500–1200 B.C.E.

Linear B uses a somewhat mixed system to represent the sounds of language. Principally, it is a syllabary; that is, most of its symbols represent whole syllables. Additionally, some of its symbols represent entire words, Called logograms. Beyond that, Linear B uses linear strokes to represent breaks in words. One reads the script as one does English, from left to right. This differs from the system of writing the Greeks later used after they had adopted an ALPHABET to represent the individual sounds of their language. Then they began to write as the ox plows—back and forth, one line reading right to left and the next left to right. The technical word that describes this system, taken from the Greek for the pattern the ox plows, is *boustrophedon.*

Although the Linear B script was discovered early in the 20th century, it was not deciphered until 1953, when a pair of researchers, Michael Ventris and John Chadwick, figured it out. Based on examples thus far uncovered, Linear B seems to have been used for keeping records rather than for literary purposes. Agamemnon, king of Mycenae and principal Greek commander in the Trojan War, conceivably could have known it.

Because one finds syllables absent from Greek represented in the script and in Greek finds sounds that are not represented by the syllabary, it appears that the Greeks had borrowed the script from people speaking a different language—one without descendants in the modern world.

Apparently the script fell into disuse as a result of some uncertain cataclysmic event. When writing resurfaced in Greek after about 400 years, the system for representing language was the alphabet.

Bibliography

Ancientscripts.com. "Linear B." Available online. URL: http://www.ancientscripts.com/linearb.html/. Downloaded November 1, 2005.
Perlman, Paula J. "Prehistoric Documents from Crete." Available online. URL: http://ccwf.cc .utexas.edu/~perlman/myth/linb.htm.   Downloaded November 1, 2005.

Li-sao   See ENCOUNTERING SORROW.

Liu An   See HUAI-NAN TZU.

Lives of Eminent Philosophers   Diogenes Laertius (ca. 250 C.E.)

DIOGENES LAERTIUS's discussion of the lives and writings of 82 Greek philosophers and other notable persons has been transmitted to us in 10 books (manuscript scrolls). Among these, book 3 deals exclusively with PLATO and book 10 with EPICURUS.

One of Diogenes Laertius's 20th-century translators, R. D. Hicks, suggests that both Diogenes' research method—mining the secondary discussions of his predecessor compilers—and the popular taste of his contemporary readership for "personal details, anecdotes, and witty sayings" shaped the form that the *Lives* finally assumed. So did Diogenes' intention to develop a sort of history of the development of Greek philosophical thought and to some degree also political thought. If it is not the best such document to have been attempted during the several hundred years during which his predecessors wrote, it does enjoy the distinction of being the earliest of its kind to have survived intact.

Thus, whatever warts and moles the composition may display, it also constitutes a unique repository of much information that would certainly have been lost otherwise. Whatever it lacks in scholarly authority, the book makes up for in its preference for a good story and surprising details. The work, though not always sequenced chronologically, begins its prologue by peering into the mists of philosophical prehistory. Philosophy may have had its roots among non-Greek speakers: The Magi were the philosophers of Persia, the Chaldeans of the Babylonians and Assyrians; the Gymnosophists (ancient, unclothed ascetics) were the original philosophers of India, the Druids of the Gauls and the Celts. The Egyptians credit Hephaestus—who lived, according to Diogenes' sources, exactly 48,863 years before Alexander the Great—with originating philosophical thought in their realm. To substantiate the extreme antiquity of the last assertion, Diogenes informs us that 373 solar and 832 lunar eclipses occurred between Hephaestus's time and Alexander's. National pride, however, now asserts itself. Diogenes reveals that the Greeks were not only the true originators of philosophy but also the original human beings, descending, as did the most ancient of the race, directly from the gods.

Diogenes then catalogues the genealogy of more recent philosophy, beginning with early Greek poets such as HOMER and HESIOD, and then naming "sages," including Thales of Miletus, SOLON, and others. There follows an overview of the development and subdivisions of philosophy, the succession of philosophers, their schools, the places of their origin, their founders, and finally the philosophical sects.

In the opening of his first chapter proper, Diogenes turns first to Thales (ca. 625–ca. 547 B.C.E.)—both a politician and a "student of nature." From a plethora of sources, Diogenes cites a host of details about Thales and about his certain and disputed contributions to all the fields that interested him. These fields ranged from politics to astronomy and poetry. Diogenes reports Thales' birth, education, beliefs, and death, and quotes his extant letters in full. The compiler also includes sayings and lines of Thales' poems that still enjoyed currency during Diogenes' lifetime.

A letter from Thales to Solon provides the transition to a similar sort of compendium about Solon's career and contributions to Greek political and intellectual history. Diogenes devotes the rest of his chapter to those that his predecessors included among the early Greek "sages." Discussions follow of Chilon, Pittacus, Bias, Cleobulus, and Periander—all Greeks of the sixth and seventh

centuries B.C.E. Diogenes continues his first book with a discussion of Anacharsis the Scythian, who was the son of a Greek mother and the brother of a king of Scythia. Anacharsis wrote a poem that compared Greek and Scythian institutions.

Discussions of Myson, Epimenides, and Pherecydes round out Diogenes' overview of the sages, and with the second book, he turns his attention to philosophers proper. He deals first with Anaximander, about whom he knows little—some of it wrong. Then Anaximenes, Anaxagoras, and Archelaus come under review.

Next, Diogenes discusses SOCRATES, asserting that the famous teacher helped EURIPIDES master the playwright's craft. He reports that Socrates was a "formidable" public speaker—so much so that the Athenian governing council of 30 men forbade him to teach rhetoric, the subject he had introduced at Athens. Socrates was also, says Diogenes, the first philosopher to be put to death.

Diogenes reports that Socrates saved the life of XENOPHON OF ATHENS at the battle of Delium. He also says that Socrates' orderly life protected him from catching the diseases that periodically swept through Athens, decimating the population. The biographer praises Socrates' simple manner of life and reports his answers to questions that several persons put to him. Asked, for instance, if a young person should marry or not, Socrates reportedly replied: "Whichever you do you will repent it." On being told that he had been condemned to die by the Athenians, Socrates reportedly replied: "So are they, by nature."

Diogenes tells stories of the shrewish behavior of Socrates' wife Xanthippe and of the way that Socrates said he benefited from her unpleasantness and valued her not only in spite of it, but because of it. In the society of Xanthippe, Socrates said that he learned to adapt himself to the rest of the world.

Diogenes also reports the details concerning the accusations brought against Socrates, his trial, the penalties he ironically proposed when convicted of introducing gods other than those recognized, for refusing to acknowledge the official gods, and for corrupting the youth of Athens. Diogenes refers the reader to PLATO's *Phaedo* for an account of Socrates' discourse on the day of his execution. He also reports the remorse that swept through the Athenian populace for their rash action in executing one of the best among them.

Then Diogenes turns his attention to the 10 schools of moral philosophers that took their origin from Socrates. These *Socratics* principally included Plato, Xenophon, Antisthenes, ÆSCHINES, Phaedo, Euclides, and Aristippus. Biographical entries on each of them and on a group of their successors brings Diogenes' second chapter to a close.

The third book devotes itself entirely to Plato. The fourth begins with a consideration of Plato's successor as head of the Platonic Academy at Athens, Speusippus (d. 339 B.C.E.). Speusippus produced a remarkable number of memoirs and dialogues, and Diogenes catalogues a generous portion of them before turning his attention to Plato's second successor at the academy, Xenocrates; we learn that his collected works totaled 224,239 lines. Then the succession of heads of the Platonic Academy continues: Crates, Crantor, and Arcesilaus. A discussion of the SOPHIST philosopher Bion interrupts the catalogue and ends the list of the heads of the original Platonic Academy. Succeeding Arcesilaus around 242 B.C.E., Lacydes of Cyrene founded a school known as the New Academy. The fourth book closes with a consideration of the headship of the Stoic philosopher Carneades (d. 129 B.C.E.), and with a brief entry on his successor Clitomachus the Cathaginian, who was well versed in the precepts of three major schools of philosophy: the ACADEMICS, the PERIPATETICS, and the Stoics (see STOICISM).

Having treated the principal Academic philosophers, in the fifth book, Diogenes turns his attention to the Peripatetics and to their founder, ARISTOTLE, who withdrew from both the institution and the thought of the Platonic Academy during the lifetime of Aristotle's teacher Plato. Aristotle founded his own school, named, as some think, for his habit of walking up and down as he discoursed with his students in his own school. After quoting a number of Aristotle's pithier sayings, Diogenes Laertius catalogues the entire corpus of the philosopher's works—a corpus running to just under 450,000 lines. Diogenes undertakes to summarize the content of these lines in about four pages. As he had done with the followers of Plato, Diogenes now lists the disciples and successors of Aristotle.

First comes THEOPHRASTUS OF ERESUS, who succeeded Aristotle in 323 B.C.E. A famous lecturer, Theophrastus's lectures were said to draw a crowd of 2,000 auditors. His dying advice encouraged his students to continue his inquiry into right conduct. There follows a catalogue of writings and the usual line count—almost a quarter million—and his quoted last will and testament, in which he emancipated his slaves.

Strato of Lampsacus, a physicist and head of Aristotle's school, enjoys a similar though less elaborate treatment. So, except for quotation of the will, does his successor Lyco of Troas, and the next head, Demetrius, who later became the chief politician of the city of Athens. Overthrown by envious dissidents, he fled to Egypt, where, after advising the Greek pharaoh, Ptolemy Soter, Demetrius fell into disfavor with the pharaoh's successors and died, like Cleopatra, from the bite of an asp. Following the recitation of Strato's works, Diogenes adds, as he often does, a list of persons of accomplishment who have the same name as his subject. These lists are largely irrelevant to his philosophical purposes, but the science of naming—onomastics—and the possibility that like names might lead to like achievements seems to have interested Diogenes. His own namesake, Diogenes of Sinope (see CYNICISM), is the subject of the second chapter of the sixth book. The fifth, however, ends with a summary of the life and career of Heraclides, who had first been a member of Plato's Academy, had attended the lectures of the Pythagoreans, and had finally become a student of Aristotle.

With the opening of the sixth book, Diogenes Laertius, whose work is very carefully sequenced and formally organized, recurs to the time of

Socrates to consider that great teacher's contemporary, Antisthenes (ca. 445–ca. 365 B.C.E.). Antisthenes had studied with GORGIAS OF LEONTIUM, the rhetorician. After coming into contact with Socrates, however, Antisthenes so admired his teacher's physical courage and disregard of pain that Antisthenes "inaugurated the Cynic way of life." He advised enduring both physical and psychological discomfort and considered luxury a bad thing: "May the sons of your enemies," he said, "live in luxury." He believed that virtue, which he defined as the sum total of one's actions, ensured happiness; words and learning did not. The law of virtue, rather than enacted statutes, should be the wise man's guide in his public actions. He was considered among the fathers of both the Cynic and the Stoic schools of thought.

Next, turning his attention to the person for whom he had been named, Diogenes Laertius details the life and career of Diogenes of Sinope. That worthy, after a youthful brush with the law, wore out Antisthenes' resistance to accepting students, became his disciple, and devoted himself to a life of poverty and simplicity. He slept in his cloak and lived for a while in a tub. A public gadfly, Diogenes of Sinope railed against vice and indifference to vice with an unattractive self-righteousness. No respecter of persons or common courtesy, he described himself as "a Socrates gone mad." Despite his cantankerousness, Diogenes of Sinope enjoyed great respect among the Athenians and was described by the poet Cercidas as "a true born son of Zeus, a hound of heaven." The biographer Diogenes provides a substantial list of works attributed to his namesake but warns the reader that some thought he wrote nothing and others attribute just a few works to him.

Fourth-century B.C.E. Cynic successors to Diogenes of Sinope included Monimus, Onesicritus, Crates of Thebes, Crates' wife Hipparchia, Metrocles, Menippus, and Menedemus. Most of those named emulated Diogenes' simple life.

Book 7 devotes a very long first chapter to the career and thought of Zeno of Citium, the founder of the Stoic school of philosophy, about whom Diogenes Laertius reports many interesting anecdotes. It becomes clear, moreover, that the biographer admires his subject's simplicity of living and the good example that his life and teaching set for the Athenians. Once the biographical section of the chapter is finished, Diogenes next turns his attention to listing the disciples of Zeno and then to detailing the positions that the Stoics take in their physical, ethical, and logical doctrines. He discusses the subdivisions and methodology of the various branches of Stoic thought and also makes clear differences between Stoic and Peripatetic views of such matters as virtue and vice.

The Stoics, Diogenes Laertius explains, think that virtue and vice are opposite categories that preclude any middle ground, whereas the Peripatetics think that "moral improvement" occupies a position between the two. After detailing the physical doctrines of the Stoics, including their view that the world itself is animate, Diogenes ends the first chapter of book 8 and passes on in the second chapter to a consideration of those Stoics who differed in certain particulars from the views presented in the first.

Having traced the development of Ionian philosophy to his satisfaction, in book 8, Diogenes turns his attention to the development of philosophy in Italy. There the development of the discipline began with an immigrant from Phoenicia and Samos, Pythagoras (ca. 580–500 B.C.E.). Returning to Samos from an extended sojourn in Egypt, Pythagoras discovered the tyrant Polycrates in charge of the island that had become his home. Rather than submit to an uncongenial rule, Pythagoras emigrated with 300 followers to Croton in Italy and established an aristocratic constitution for Greeks in Italy. He also founded the ITALIC SCHOOL OF PHILOSOPHY. Music and astronomy were among his chief interests. Diogenes reports that the school Pythagoras founded in Italy attracted 600 auditors to his evening lectures. After recounting alternate versions of the death of Pythagoras, who may have been murdered or may have starved himself to death, Diogenes asserts that Pythagoras's school survived him for nine generations.

The balance of book 8 devotes itself to a discussion of notable Pythagoreans. Among them we find the famous EMPEDOCLES, who, according to legend, ended his life by leaping or falling into the Sicilian volcano, Mount Etna. Diogenes duly reports variants on this tale. Other successors of Pythagoras include Epicharmas of Cos; Archytas of Tarentum; the physician Alcmaeon; and Eudoxus of Cnidos, who mastered astronomy, geometry, medicine and law, and others.

In book 9, Diogenes turns his attention to those philosophers who espoused no particular school, the so-called sporadic philosophers. First among them appears HERACLITUS OF EPHESUS, who, Diogenes reports, became a misanthrope. Following him come notices of Xenophanes; Parmenides of Elea; Melissus of Samos; and then Zeno and his pupil Leucippus, both of Elea. These philosophers subscribed to the view that the human soul is material in its essence. Leucippus subscribed to and perfected the view that the universe is composed of atoms.

Diogenes attributes extraordinary longevity to Democritus of Abdera (ca. 5th–4th c B.C.E.) following Hipparchus in asserting that the philosopher, a contemporary of Plato at Athens, died in his 109th year. Democritus subscribed to Leucippus's atomic theory and believed that in their elemental whirl, atoms brought all things into being and destroyed all things in an infinitude of necessary change. Diogenes follows his predecessor compiler, Thrasylus, in enumerating the many works ascribed to Democritus.

Turning his attention to Protagoras (ca. 485–410 B.C.E.), Diogenes reports that he was the first to maintain that every question has two opposing sides. Diogenes also credits Protagoras with originating the dialectic method of discussion popularly attributed to Socrates. The biographer next turns his attention to yet another namesake, Diogenes of Apollonia. Modern editors register surprise at the inclusion of this early philosopher at this point in the narrative and also at the omission of others more relevant.

Entries on Anaxarchus, a companion of Alexander the Great, on Anaxarchus's student, Pyrrho, and on Timon, a onetime stage dancer turned philosopher, conclude book 9.

Book 10 is exclusively devoted to the life and thought of perhaps our contemporary world's most misrepresented Greek philosopher, the admirable EPICURUS. That same misrepresentation seems to have been rife during Epicurus's own lifetime, as Diogenes reports scurrilous attacks on his character, the circulation of scandalous books falsely attributed to Epicurus, and, finally, accusations of false attacks on other philosophers. Diogenes cites abundant evidence that people circulating such misrepresentations "are stark mad." In fact, Diogenes avers, Epicurus displayed "unsurpassed goodwill to all men."

With 40 of the most important articles of Epicurus's philosophical position—Diogenes brings his collection to a close. In doing so, he says, he makes the end of his notable work "coincide with the beginning of happiness." The first of them provides a good antidote for those who presume to speak on behalf of deity with respect to persons and activities deserving punishment: "A blessed and eternal being has no trouble himself and brings no trouble on any other being; hence he is exempt from movements of anger and partiality, for every such movement implies weakness."

Bibliography

Diogenes Laertius. *Lives of Eminent Philosophers* [Greek and English]. 2 vols. Translated by R. D. Hicks. New York: G. P. Putnam's Sons, 1925.

Lives of the Noble Grecians and Romans, The   See PARALLEL LIVES.

Livius Andronicus (Lucius Livius Andronicus) (fl. ca. 230 B.C.E.) *Roman dramatist*

Livius Andronicus came to Rome in 272 B.C.E., at the end of the city's war against Tarentum, a southern Italian city that had initially been colonized by

Sparta. Bilingual in Latin and Greek, Livius Andronicus earned his living by teaching those languages, by writing tragic plays about the Trojan War and Greek myths, by writing imitations of Greek New Comedy (see COMEDY IN GREECE AND ROME), and by acting in some of his own dramas.

According to the Italian literary historian Gian Biaggio Conte, around 20 fragments containing 40 verses from Livius Andronicus's plays survive—largely as a result of their having been quoted by later authors. On the basis of these survivals, we know the titles of five examples of his war tragedies: *Achilles, Aegisthus, Aiax Mastigophorus* (Ajax with the whip), *Equos Troianus* (The Trojan horse), and *Hermiona*. We also have the names of three tragedies drawn from myth: *Andromeda, Danaë,* and *Tereus.* Of Livius Andronicus's comedies, only six verses survive, and we know only one certain title: *Gladiolus* (a short sword). He also was the first translator of HOMER's *The ODYSSEY* into Latin SATURNIAN VERSE.

On the basis of what CICERO and LIVY report about him, we know that Livius Andronicus was Rome's first important playwright and literary translator. In 240 B.C.E., one of his works became the first drama ever staged in Rome. Later, in 207 B.C.E., he composed a song in honor of Juno that was performed publicly by a choir of girls as part of a citywide religious festival. For the first time in the city's history, a literary endeavor earned official recognition. The city granted Livius Andronicus public honors and acknowledged as official the playwrights' association (*collegium scribarum histrionumque*), to which he belonged. Its title was posted in the temple of Minerva on the Aventine Way. This is all that has come down to us about Livius Andronicus.

On the basis of his study of the fragmentary remains of Livius Andronicus's work, however, Gian Biaggio Conte has provided a plausible assessment of his significance. In translating Homer's *Odyssey*, Livius made a fundamental Greek text available to Roman readers. Livius's version, *Odusia*, though it is accurate and clear, is not a word-for-word plod through the Greek. It is, rather, an artistic translation that renders Homer more palatable to Roman taste than a literal translation would have. Heroes, for example, are demoted from godlike status—a notion that would have offended Romans. Moreover, in keeping with a Roman taste for pathos, Livius heightens the pathetic mood in certain Homeric passages that give him the opportunity.

Comparing the scattered fragments of the plays with the Greek originals from which Livius Andronicus drew them, Conte follows the analysis of the scholar Scevola Mariotti, who finds further evidence of emotional heightening and adaptation rather than slavish fidelity both to the language and to the mood of the original. This was a tendency also observable in the comedies of PLAUTUS and TERENCE—all drawn from Greek originals.

Although the plays of Livius Andronicus soon fell out of favor with Roman audiences, his method of dealing with his Greek originals passed along to his successors and established the essential parameters within which Roman writers subsequently adapted Greek works.

Bibliography

Beuchner, Karl. *Fragmenta poetarum Latinarum epicorum et lyricorum praeter Ennium et Lucilium.* [Fragments of epic and lyric Latin poets before Ennius and Lucilius.] 3rd ed. Stuttgart, Germany: B. G. Teubner, 1995.

Conte, Gian Biaggio. *Latin Literature: A History.* Translated by Joseph B. Solodow, Don Fowler, and Glenn W. Most. Baltimore, Md.: Johns Hopkins University Press, 1994.

Mariotti, Scevola. *Livio Andronico e la traduzione artistica; saggio critica ed Edizione delle Frammenti dell' Odyssea.* [Livius Andronicus and artistic translation: a critical study and edition of the fragments of the *Odusia*]. Urbino, Italy: Università Degli Studii di Urbino, 1986.

Livy (Titus Livius) (59 B.C.E.–17 C.E.) *Roman historian*

The son of a wealthy and possibly senatorial family of Padua, Livy received the usual Roman upper-class education. He moved to Rome at about age 30 and became a courtier of the emperor Augustus. There, though he never seems to have occupied public office, he played the role of a gadfly, openly expressing his preference for republicanism over imperial Rome. The emperor apparently appreciated Livy's honesty, for the two remained friends throughout the emperor's life.

Livy devoted himself entirely to literature— principally the writing of history. Doing so may well have been his object in moving to Rome, for it was there that he began his enormous project of tracing Rome's history from her mythical and historical beginnings down to the death and burial in 9 B.C.E. of Nero Claudius Drusus, a hero of the wars against the Germanic tribes and the stepson of AUGUSTUS CAESAR. Livy advised Augustus's grandnephew, Claudius, to become a writer of history, and Claudius did so.

Livy's history was an enormous undertaking, one that runs to 142 books, most of which survive. In addition, summaries of the work were discovered at OXYRHYNCHUS, making it possible to fill out the content of some of Livy's books that are in fragmentary condition.

Completing his great work occupied the writer for about 40 years. He survived Augustus by about three years, and at some point he moved back to Padua. There, at about 76 years old, his life work completed, he died. Inscriptions on a Paduan sarcophagus indicate the possible resting place of the old scholar.

Bibliography

Livius, Titus. *History of Rome.* Translated by D. Spillan and Cyrus Edmonds. New York: Harper and Brothers, 1875.

———. *The History of Rome: Books 1–5.* Translated by Valerie M. Warrior. Indianapolis: Hackett Publishers, 2006.

———. *Livy.* 13 volumes. Translated by B. O. Foster. Cambridge, Mass.: Harvard University Press, 1939.

Lock of Berenîkê, The Callimachus (ca. 246 B.C.E.)

The historical Berenîkê, or Berenice, was the wife of King Ptolemy III. In 246 B.C.E., Ptolemy led a military expedition to Syria to restore his sister's children to the throne of that country. At his departure, Berenîkê sacrificed a lock of her own hair on a temple altar to influence the gods to bring her husband back safely. The king did return home uninjured, but the sacrificed lock of hair mysteriously disappeared from the altar.

To solve the mystery and at the same time pay an elaborate compliment to his employers, a court astronomer named Conon asserted that he had discovered a new constellation of stars, and that the lock of hair had been taken to heaven by the gods and turned into a constellation, which was known afterward as Coma Berenices (Berenîkê's lock of hair).

CATULLUS translated CALLIMACHUS's poem on the subject into Latin. It is from this source and from an ancient *diegesis*, or summary, of the story that we know the plot of Callimachus's work, for the remains of the poem itself are extremely fragmentary.

The story continued to influence European poets at least until the 18th century C.E., when the British poet Alexander Pope made use of a similar device in his poem *The Rape of the Lock*. There, a lock of hair stolen by an ardent suitor from the coiffeur of the poem's heroine, Belinda, is taken to heaven and turned into a hitherto unobserved star. This process of stellification is one that the ancients described when the souls of such important persons as emperors left their bodies. Sometimes before and sometimes after their deaths, their living admirers deified the emperors, and, as those subjects believed, their rulers' transfigured souls were turned into new stars in the sky.

Bibliography

Callimachus. "The Lock of Berenîkê." In *Callimachus: Hymns, Epigrams, Select Fragments.* Translated by Stanley Lombardo and Diane Rayor.

Baltimore and London: Johns Hopkins University Press, 1988.

Lokāyata (*Carvaka*) (ca. 600 B.C.E.) *ancient Indic antireligious texts*

Also known as *Carvaka*, *Lokāyata*'s texts have all perished and are known only through quotations cited in arguments against them by Hindu and spiritualist Buddhist controversialists. The Hindu sage, Brihaspati, wrote the earliest of the movement's texts, the *Brihaspati Sutra*. Buddhism and Jainism may both have originally been systems of either agnostic or atheistic ethics that developed from the thinking of Brihaspati.

Sharing certain viewpoints with ancient Greek and Roman STOICISM, *Lokāyata* was atheistic and anticlerical and did not believe in human reincarnation. It was deeply critical of the priesthood, holding that the priests' true gods were their bellies, and that their spirituality was a dodge designed to help them make a living and acquire power over their flocks.

Lokāyata seems to have died out as an independent system of Indian thought around 1400 C.E.—a moment in time coincident with a resurgence of the spiritual Bhakti movement. In one of the preserved verse arguments of *Lokāyata*, its sage wonders about where the human soul would come from were it to be reincarnated.

Bibliography

Chattopadhyya, Debiprased, ed. *Carvaka–Lokayata: An Anthology of Source Materials and Some Recent Studies*. Philadelphia: Cornet Books, 2006.

°*Longinus, On the Sublime* Anonymous (ca. first or second century C.E.)

The question of the real authorship of the famous but fragmentary treatise, *On the Sublime*, is a vexed one. Until the 19th century, the author was universally held to be Cassius Longinus, a third-century author who had also written on the subject of rhetoric. For that reason, the name Longinus remains associated with the document. Objections to the traditional attribution of authorship, however, have largely rendered it untenable, and arguments for other candidates, including DIONYSIUS OF HALICARNASSUS, seem even less tenable. The dating of the essay also offers problems. Undisputed, however, is the influence that this piece of aesthetic criticism has exercised over writing for many centuries.

Apparently written at the request of the author's friend and former fellow student, Postumius Terentianus, the essay undertakes a systematic analysis of the quality that distinguishes great poetry (and great literature in general) from that of a lesser standard. That quality is sublimity. The sublime in literary works is to be found in a combination of "consummate excellence" and "distinction of language" that has the power to amaze and inspire wonder—not merely to convince and please. A reader or listener recognizes the sublime when it occurs because that person will feel as if a bolt of lightning has struck. Writers or reciters who produce such moments for their audiences are often gifted with a natural genius that has been schooled and disciplined by an acquired mastery of their art.

After a hiatus occasioned by lost text, the essay resumes with a tactic of definition by explaining what the sublime is not. It is not turgid bluster or bombast. It is not childish simplicity. It is not to be found in outbursts of authorial emotion or in its opposite, authorial frigidity—faults that display to an audience the triviality of an author's mind. So does a constant striving for novelty and exaggeration.

What is truly sublime in literature elevates and exalts and fills the reader with joy and pride, as if the reader had penned the passage. Those feelings arise from trains of thoughts, from strong emotions well expressed, from certain moving figures of speech such as apt metaphors or similes, from "noble diction" and the dignified arrangement of words.

To illustrate greatness of thought, *On the Sublime* discusses Homer and the opening of the Book of Genesis from the HEBREW BIBLE. As an example of sublimity arising from the selection and accumulation of detail, the author chooses the poem of SAPPHO that begins "To me that man equals a god . . ." The discussion of amplification (proliferating apt detail), of which the last example is a part, continues with illustrations drawn from CICERO and from DEMOSTHENES' oration ON THE CROWN. PLATO's work furnishes a further instance.

The discussion of Plato leads to the introduction of the topic of imitation as a device for achieving sublimity. The essayist advises his readers to try to think like great writers of the past.

Continuing to consider the means by which writers may achieve sublimity, the essay treats the role of imagination or visualization in the process and how that role differs with the genre in which one works. It then turns to a consideration of figures speech and, in that context, to a detailed analysis of a portion of On the Crown. Here the essayist advises the writer to try to conceal ingenuity. There follows a detailed consideration of the utility of highly technical rhetorical devices and a consideration of the use of metaphor. Next the author announces a digression in which he includes the most important and best-written part of his essay with this essential advice: Prefer flawed genius to flawless mediocrity. The former will rise more frequently and predictably to the level of sublimity.

The balance of what we have of the essay returns to a consideration of simile, hyperbole, word arrangement, and rhythm. The last two the author considers to be of crucial importance in achieving sublimity.

The essay then focuses on the devices that will undermine the sublime and result in pedestrian style and failure. Then, as the writer promises a close consideration of emotion, the essay breaks off abruptly.

See also "I MORE THAN ENVY HIM . . ."

Bibliography

Russell, Donald, and W. H. Fyfe, trans. °Longinus, On the Sublime. In Aristotle. Vol. 23. Cambridge, Mass.: Harvard University Press, 1995, pp. 143–307.

Longus *Greek prose writer*　See FICTION AS EPISTLE, ROMANCE, AND EROTIC PROSE; GREEK PROSE ROMANCE; *PASTORALS OF DAPHNIS AND CHLOE.*

Lü Buwei　See SPRING AND AUTUMN OF MR. LÜ.

Lucan (Marcus Annaeus Lucanus) (39–65 C.E.)

Lucan was born Marcus Annaeus Lucanus in Cordova, Spain, to a wealthy family. His father, Marcus Annaeus Mela, and his mother, Acilia, moved their household to Rome just seven months after Lucan's birth. There he not only enjoyed the advantages that his father's wealth made possible, but he was also apparently much loved by his uncle, LUCIUS ANNAEUS SENECA. Seneca had been the childhood tutor of the emperor Nero, and he later became both Nero's close advisor and the chief administrator of Rome, its consul. His connection with the emperor and his literary success made Seneca both the most famous Roman of his day and the wealthiest. As Seneca had lost his own son, it seems that he transferred much paternal affection to his nephew.

Lucan therefore received the best education possible, and Roman education always had as its prime objects the mastery of literature, rhetoric, and philosophy. Lucan's philosophy professor was the Stoic philosopher Cornutus (see STOICISM), and the young man was early identified as one of the leading speakers of his time. Though his juvenilia have not survived, he began writing at a remarkably tender age and published works both in prose and verse.

Lucan's family arranged a splendid marriage for him with a beautiful, rich, highly intelligent, and virtuous young woman, Polla Argenteria. After Lucan's untimely death, Polla, who lived into old age, celebrated his birthday annually. The seventh poem in the second chapter of STATIUS's *Silvae* was written for one of those celebrations.

Seneca introduced his nephew to Emperor Nero, who was only two years Lucan's senior and who admired and liked Lucan. The emperor's favor made Lucan an official of the city, a quaestor, before he reached the minimum age required to hold that office. Nero also recommended the youth for membership in one of the four colleges of Roman priests—that of the augurs, who ruled on matters of doctrine and interpreted the meanings of signs and omens. If they declared omens unfavorable, they could forbid certain assemblies. Lucan, who by this time had become an unparalleled master of the rhetorical art, acclaimed Nero's virtues and accomplishments in an address to the crowd assembled at the Neronia, a festival in the emperor's honor.

This mutual admiration society, however, did not long endure. Not satisfied with ruling the world, Nero also aspired to great artistic accomplishment. When he saw Lucan actually achieving it, the emperor grew envious. He prohibited Lucan, not only from publishing his works, but also from reading his verses to his circle of acquaintances and friends.

The emperor's pettiness so disaffected Lucan that he joined a conspiracy to overthrow Nero and kill him. Nero's spies, however, were everywhere, and they discovered the plot. Trying to save his own life, Lucan told everything. He even named his mother as a member of the conspiracy. In appreciation, Nero granted Lucan the privilege of choosing the way he would die. He made a common choice: His veins were opened while he sat in a warm bath. As he bled to death, he recited lines from his own EPIC that described a soldier who also died from bleeding. Lucan was 26. His fall brought down other members of his family with him. His father and two uncles, one of whom was Seneca, were also required to commit suicide.

Of all his works, only the poem from which the dying Lucan quoted has survived into our era. Earlier often mislabeled as *Pharsalia*, but properly titled *CIVIL WAR*, the work is an epic in 10 books. Although the poem is written in Latin DACTYLIC HEXAMETER (see QUANTITATIVE VERSE), it otherwise departs from the norms of both Greek and Roman epics in several ways. It does, however, reveal Lucan's superiority as a rhetorician. While the famous rhetorician QUINTILIAN admired the poem as an example of the art in which he himself excelled and also praised its energy, he felt dubious about the work's value as a poem. In another innovative move, Lucan deprives the gods of their customary central role in national epics. Such a critic as Lucan's translator, J. D. Duff, finds the poem full of "exaggeration and repulsive detail." Lucan considered the civil wars of Rome to have been unmitigated horrors, and his views on the central figures in the wars are often at odds with the judgments of history.

Bibliography

D'Alessandro Behr, Francesca. *Feeling History: Lucan, Stoicism, and the Poetics of Passion.* Columbus: Ohio State University Press, 2007.

Leigh, Matthew. *Lucan: Spectacle and Engagement.* New York: Clarendon Press, 1997.

Lucan. *Civil War.* Translated by S. H. Braund. New York: Oxford University Press, 1992.

———. *The Civil War: Books I–X.* Translated by J. D. Duff. New York: G. P. Putnam's Sons, 1928.

Lucian of Samosata (ca. 120–ca. 180 C.E.)
Syrian-Greek Poet

Born in the Syrian village of Samosata on the banks of the Euphrates River, Lucian came from a relatively poor family. His parents apprenticed him at an early age to an uncle who carved marble, but a broken piece of marble and a beating ended the apprenticeship at the end of the first day. So Lucian tells us.

What we know about his life, in fact, comes exclusively from what Lucian reports about himself. As Lucian reports it in his allegorical essay, "Vision," his mistress was to become Learning, not Statuary. Before he could woo her effectively, however, he first had to polish whatever Greek he had picked up from the Greek troops stationed in the vicinity and in the dealings of the Syrian merchants with their Greek masters. Having succeeded at that effort and having mastered the Greek both of his own and of former times, he worked at being a rhetorician—as a writer of speeches or a pleader of cases, perhaps. His success made it possible for him to travel in Greece and eventually in Italy and also to work in Gaul. There he proved to be a successful rhetorician and made a good living until approximately 160 C.E.

Around 160, Lucian returned to Syria for a period. A surviving poem celebrating the charms of the mistress of Lucius Verus puts Lucian in Antioch during 162–3. In 165, Lucian set out with his father for Athens, narrowly missing becoming the victim of a vendetta when he impulsively (and characteristically) bit the hand of a mountebank named Alexander. In retaliation for being bitten, Alexander tried to hire the captain of Lucian's ship to throw him overboard. Happily, the captain did not oblige.

Not long thereafter, Lucian decided to abandon his lucrative profession of rhetorician for the greater uncertainties associated with the composition of dialogue. As a skeptic and a wit with a creative imagination—and also as a person who had, as he thought, made enough money to secure his future—Lucian felt the need to put into play more of the talents with which he had been endowed. We have reason to be glad he did so, for he became perhaps the wittiest writer of the ancient world.

Although wit and satire surely proved more congenial than rhetoric, it apparently did not pay as well. After about 175 C.E., Lucian retired to Athens. Lack of funds, however, soon forced him to resume working as a rhetorician. Eventually the Roman emperor Commodus (ruled 180–92 C.E.) relieved Lucian's poverty by appointing him to a legal sinecure in Egypt.

Lucian was evenhandedly skeptical and irreverent respecting religious points of view: He equally lampooned all belief systems that credited the supernatural. Some later writers found it safer to express their own satirical doubts about Christianity under Lucian's name. One such spurious diatribe led to the assertion by the 10th-century Greek encyclopedist Suidas that God had punished Lucian for his apostasy by having a mad dog bite him so that Lucian died of hydrophobia. Lucian's

own late play about the infirmities of old age, particularly the gout from which he suffered, suggests a different final scenario, but we cannot be sure.

Lucian's surviving output is very substantial. It runs to 65 titles in four volumes in the standard edition. Some of these works address literary-critical, biographical, or, like "Vision," noted above, autobiographical topics. His essay "Prometheus" discusses the way in which he combines elements of the Old Comedy of Aristophanes with dialogue to produce satire. In an essay named for his teacher, the philosopher Demonax, Lucian sketches the character of the man. His epistolary essay "The Way to Write History" surveys the literary quirks of his contemporary historians and proposes a list of desirable qualities that ought to characterize historians and history. In his essay "True History," he parodies the incredible assertions of ancient writers. For example, on an imaginary journey, he describes vines growing from the ground that turn into women from the groin upward. The vine-women kiss the travelers, and their kiss produces a drunken state.

The works, however, for which Lucian is both best remembered and most highly valued are his SATIRES—works that puncture people's credulity, false piety, vanities, and pretenses. To represent them in this volume, I have chosen examples from DIALOGUES OF THE GODS, DIALOGUES OF THE SEA GODS, DIALOGUES OF THE DEAD, and The FERRY BOAT, (The Tyrant).

Other characteristic works belonging essentially to the same satirical category as those chosen above for fuller discussion include "Menippus," the story of a Cynic philosopher (see CYNICISM) who becomes so perplexed by the self-contradictory complexities of his discipline that he travels to the underworld to consult the prophet Tiresias—the only mortal whose wisdom the gods permitted to remain intact after death. What, Menippus wants to know, is the best life to lead on earth? Tiresias smiles knowingly and advises that the best life involves doing the task at hand as well as one can.

As one might expect, philosophers are a regular butt of Lucian's humor, and Menippus reappears on eagle's wings, flying to Olympus in "Icaromenippus," with a brief stop at the Moon. On arriving at his destination, Menippus's question about philosophers results in a divine decision to destroy all of them as useless.

In the essay "Gods in Council," Lucian mocks the human tendency to expand pantheons with the addition of newly created deities. Before the assembled gods of the Greek pantheon, Momus—pictured in HESIOD as the son of primeval night and characterized as always criticizing and finding fault—complains about the continual admission of new and foreign deities such as Dionyisius, the Egyptian Anubis, and Apis.

Against the allegations of Suidas that Lucian was anti-Christian, one can oppose the datum that only one uncomplimentary reference to early Christians appears in Lucian's works. One finds it in "Peregrine," a tongue-in-cheek narrative that reports the actual career of a Cynic philosopher of that name who had himself burnt alive in his pursuit of fame. Peregrine plays on Christian credulity to convince the faithful that he too is a god. In his characterizations of the Christians, Lucian suggests that the "misguided creatures" consider themselves "immortal for all time." Under that and similar self-delusions, they are easy prey for "adroit and unscrupulous' persons like Peregrine.

As the narrator in the piece, Lucian reports the voluntary immolation of Peregrine on a funeral pyre. As a joke, Lucian says, he reported to others that at the moment of Peregrine's death, Lucian had seen a vulture fly from the midst of the flames toward Olympus. "East or west?" his auditors immediately asked. Within a day's time, stories reached Lucian of a resurrected Peregrine, clad entirely in white, with Lucian's vulture perched on his shoulder. Lucian implies that this is an instructive example of the myth-making process in action.

Bibliography

Lucian. *The Dialogues of Lucian* [selections]. Translated by William Tooke. Edited by N. M. Penzer. London: Empire House, 1930.

———. *Selected Dialogues*. Translated by Desmond Costa. New York: Oxford University Press, 2005.

———. *Selected Satires of Lucian*. Edited and translated by Lionel Casson. Chicago: Aldine Publishing Company, 1962.

———. *The Works of Lucian of Samosota*. 4 vols. Translated by H. W. Fowler and H. G. Fowler. Oxford: Clarendon Press, 1905.

Lucilius, Gaius (ca. 180–102 B.C.E.) *Roman poet*

Lucilius was an early Roman author of SATIRES and a wealthy and aristocratic member of the literary circle that surrounded Publius Cornelius Scipio Aemilianus, known as the Scipionic circle. Lucilius is known to have produced 30 books of satires in around 1,400 verses. Only fragments survive, but their number is unusually large because of the great interest that Lucilius's unusual and archaic vocabulary excited in later lexicographers and grammarians. That interest led them to quote his works, and the surviving texts come from such quotations.

Consequently, we know that Lucilius or, more probably, his later editors organized his works by the sorts of meters in which he composed. Books 1–21 included his poems in dactylic hexameters (see QUANTITATIVE VERSE); books 22–25, less certainly, are thought likely to have contained elegiac couplets (see ELEGY AND ELEGAIC POETRY). Books 26–30 contained some poems in hexameters but principally in iambic and trochaic measures. These were the measures regularly employed by Roman COMEDY at the beginning of Lucilius's career. Therefore, such literary historians as Gian Biaggio Conte consider that books 26–30 were the earliest written. Within each set of books, the poems seem to have been organized chronologically.

Conte also makes clear that the Roman notion of satire was different from what the Greeks meant or what contemporary Americans and Europeans mean. For the Romans, *satura* evoked the idea of what we mean by *miscellany*, or poems brought together from several varying sources. Lucilius himself called his works *sermones*—informal largely autobiographical and literary discourses.

A partial reconstruction of Lucilius's work suggests that the first book contained a parody on councils of the gods that were a standard feature of EPIC. This parody developed a disparaging attack on a foe of the Scipionic circle, Lentulus Lupus.

Gastronomy and travelogue provided the focus of book 3. Book 16, by contrast, contained verses addressed to a woman in which Lucilius recalled their time together in a singularly unrepressed fashion. Elsewhere, he became a literary critic of the tongue-in-cheek, cuttingly humorous sort. He attacked tragedy, defended personal attacks in satire, and had much to say on the subject of effective style and word choice—sometimes poking fun at rhetoricians. Often, he was also an ironist and a political polemicist.

Bibliography

Conte, Gian Biaggio. *Latin Literature: A History*. Baltimore: Johns Hopkins University Press, 1994.

Evans, Lewis, and William Gifford. *The Satires of Juvenal, Persius, Sulpicia, and Lucilius*. London: G. Bell and Sons, 1901

Gruen, Erich L. *Culture and National Identity in Republican Rome*. London: Duckworth, 1993.

Lucilius, Gaius, et al. *Roman Verse Satire: Lucilius to Juvenal*. Translated by William J. Dominik and William T. Wehrle. Wauconda, Ill.: Bolchazy-Carducci Publications, 1999.

Rudd, Niall. *Themes in Roman Satire*. Norman: University of Oklahoma Press, 1986.

Lucretius (Titus Lucretius Carus)
(ca. 99–55 B.C.E.) *Roman poet*

A Roman materialist philosopher and a poet, Lucretius is chiefly remembered for his dactylic hexameter poem (see QUANTITATIVE VERSE) in six books, DE RERUM NATURA (*On the Nature of Things*). Lucretius felt convinced of the falsity of all religious belief with its accompanying notions that whatever one believes and does is God's will and that whatever contradicts one's cherished faith is evil. That kind of credulity, he thought, is the source of most human misery. The poet hoped that his monumental poem would popularize a thoroughgoing philosophical materialism in the place of such superstition.

Though most Renaissance Europeans did not agree with Lucretius about religion, they nevertheless considered his poem a reliable source of scientific knowledge. They mined it for wonders that Lucretius described as natural facts—for instance, a magnetic rock that sank ships by drawing the nails from their timbers so that their hulls disintegrated, or his assertion that people living near the source cataract of the Nile River were deafened by the roar of its falling water. Both Petrarch and Lorenzo de' Medici, for instance, used Lucretius in this way.

Virtually nothing is known about Lucretius's life. St. JEROME follows SUETONIUS in claiming that Lucretius wrote during brief periods of sanity after being driven mad by an aphrodisiac. Given the scope of Lucretius's poem and his antireligious point of view, there is reason to doubt this account.

Bibliography

Lucretius. *On the Nature of the Universe*. Translated by Ronald Melville. Edited by Don and Peta Fowler. New York: Oxford University Press, 1999.

Ludi Osci   See ATELLANE FABLES OR FARCES.

Lun Heng (*Critical Essays, Balanced Discussions*) Wang Chong (ca. 75 C.E.)

A rationalist critic of superstitious beliefs that had infiltrated Confucian teachings by the first century C.E., WANG CHUNG (Ch'ung) wrote a critique in 85 sections in which he tried to debunk popular nonscientific belief. In a typical section

(*Lun Heng, 17, Shiying*), Wang describes a wondrous *ming* plant that grew at the emperor's front door and miraculously kept track of the passage of the days of the month. In a lengthy, harsh, naturalistic critique of the assertions of the story, Wang demonstrates, first, that the *ming* plant does no such thing—not even at the behest of gods wishing to honor an emperor. Second, he discusses the natural cycle that all *ming* plants follow during the course of the year. Third, he points out the inconsistencies that the story would still contain were it true. He concludes that the emperor would still have had to consult a calendar because of the schedule on which the plant shed its pods. Only early in the month could the monarch have ascertained the date by consulting the plant.

In section 28, Wang conducts a similar analysis of a story drawn from the *Shihji* (*Records of the Grand Historian*). In this section, Wang critiques a "Taoist untruth" that tells how a certain Huang Ti, together with his entourage of over 70 people, mounted a dragon and flew away—except for those followers who grabbed the dragon's beard and pulled it out. In his critique of the story, Wang examines the etymology of Huang's name, concluding that Huang might have been someone who gained credit for pacifying a people, but that he was not an immortal who flew to heaven on a dragon's back. Besides, Wang notes, dragons do not go to heaven. They only leave their ponds when it storms, fly around for a bit, and then reenter their ponds when the rain stops. Therefore, had Huang ridden the beast, he would have drowned in its pond.

In the same section, Wang applies his naturalistic critique to other Taoist assertions that he finds to be patently incredible. Men, he concludes, do not rise to heaven. Men are creatures. If they were creatures capable of rising to heaven, they would have come equipped with feathers.

Wang conducts his critique in lively, colloquial language. He recommended that others do likewise. Vested interests, however, resist change. For a long time after Wang wrote, Chinese literature continued to be written in an artificially archaic literary language—as did Latin in the West. However, people are tenacious in their habits (literary style, religion, and so on) however absurd they may be. Thus, Wang fell into disrepute, and his works were not much read until the 19th century, when his advice about the use of the natural vernacular was once more taken seriously.

See also DAOISM.

Bibliography

Mair, Victor H., ed. *The Columbia Anthology of Traditional Chinese Literature*. New York: Columbia University Press, 1994.

Owen, Stephen. *Readings in Chinese Literary Thought*. Cambridge, Mass.: Harvard University Press, 1992.

Wang Chong. *Lun Heng*. Translated by Alfred Forke. New York: Paragon Book Gallery, 1962.

Watson, Burton. *Early Chinese Literature*. New York: Columbia University Press, 1962.

Lycophron (fl. early third century B.C.E.)
Greek dramatist

The name *Lycophron* is apparently associated with two different Greek writers of TRAGEDY. Both of them flourished in Egypt during the HELLENISTIC AGE. The earlier of the two, whose literary work is represented by extremely fragmentary remains, is usually included in lists of those outstanding Alexandrian tragic poets who were known as the PLEIAD OF ALEXANDRIA—the stars of the local poetic cosmos. This Lycophron was born in Chalchis and subsequently moved to Alexandria. In addition to 19 tragedies whose titles are known, he is thought to have written about 40 others and also a comedic SATYR PLAY on the subject of a banquet of the philosopher Menedemus. He worked, too, as a grammarian and was associated with the great Ptolemaic library at Alexandria. Among the fragments thought to be from his hand are glosses on some Greek comic poets.

Scholars disagree about whether or not more than one Lycophron wrote tragedy. Those who argue for two suggest that an apparently later person, who is often conflated with the first and who seems to have assumed the name of Lycophron as a pen name, is the author of a lengthy, extant tragic monologue, *Alexandra*.

The name *Alexandra* is an alternative for that of the priestess of Athena, Cassandra, who was the daughter of the rulers of Troy, Priam and Hecuba. In dactylic hexameter (see QUANTITATIVE VERSE) and in mind-numbing detail, the play's single speaker, a slave, reports to King Priam the dire prophecies of Alexandra concerning both the mythic and the historical doings of Greeks and Trojans and their progeny from the time of the Trojan War until the time of the play's writing.

Scholars who argue for a single Lycophron exercise considerable ingenuity in resolving perplexing issues of chronology and have to explain away allusions in *Alexandra* to events that seemingly occurred after the probable lifetime of the earlier Lycophron.

Bibliography

Lycophron. *Alexandra*. In *Callimachus and Lycophron*. Translated by A. W. Mair. New York: G. P. Putnam's Sons, 1921.

lyric poetry

In ancient Greece, early lyric poems such as those of SAPPHO were recited or sung to the accompaniment of a lyre by a single singer. Sappho's own instrument was constructed from tortoiseshell. These lyrics contrasted with choric songs—intended for singing by a choir or a chorus.

Lyrics continued to be instrumentally accompanied throughout most of the ancient period. Emperor Nero, for example, performed his own works in his quest for popular artistic fame. As publishing the texts of lyrics became a possibility, however, first in scrolls and later in boxed codices, the words of the poems and the tunes that accompanied them became separated so that eventually

the word *lyric* came to apply to any poem—usually on subjective or emotional topics—that is strongly rhythmic in its patterns of versification and personal and imaginative in its content.

Lysias (458–379 B.C.E.) *Greek prose writer*

Born in Athens to the family of a wealthy shield manufacturer, Lysias studied rhetoric at Thurii in Greek colonial Italy. As a result of political upheaval, his family had his property illegally seized by the state. In financial difficulty as a consequence, Lysias began supporting himself as an attorney, pleading cases eloquently before the tribunals of Athens. The first he argued was against Eratosthenes, one of the politicians that had dispossessed him and the man principally responsible for, as Lysias argued, the illegal execution of Lysias's brother Polemarchus.

Some 34 of the more than 200 speeches that Lysias gave have survived. An unusually successful advocate, Lysias owed his victories on behalf of his clients in part to his capacity to put himself in their emotional shoes and to speak as if he were they. Sometimes he wrote the speeches for his clients to deliver themselves.

Bibliography

Jebb, Richard Claverhouse, ed. *Selections from the Attic Orators*. Exeter, U.K.: Bristol Phoenix Press, 2005.

Lysias. *Lysias*. Translated by S. C. Todd. Austin: University of Texas Press, 2000.

———. *Selected Speechs of Lysisas*. Translated by Jeffrey A. Rydberg-Cox. Newburyport, Mass.: Focus Publishers, 2003.

Lysistrata Aristophanes (411 B.C.E.)

Produced in late winter 411 B.C.E., *Lysistrata* appeared at a moment when the Peloponnesian War was going particularly badly for Athens. As a member of the antiwar faction, ARISTOPHANES had used his comedies regularly to satirize the leaders of the war party and to proselytize for peace. In this brilliantly innovative play, Aristophanes tried a new tactic in his onstage campaign against the war. In doing so, he also invented the first comic heroine, the title character, Lysistrata.

Fed up with absent husbands and warfare, Lysistrata and her confederates have organized the women of all Greece in a rebellion against their husbands' penchant for fighting and their extended absences from home. She has called a meeting at her home of women from the various sectors of Greece, and as the play opens, she and her friend Calonice await the coming of their late-arriving guests. A good deal of bawdy humor characterizes the conversation of all the women as some wait and others arrive.

When the party has assembled, Lysistrata asks if the women pine for their absent husbands. All agree that they do and that if Lysistrata can come up with a plan to bring their men home from war, they all will cooperate. Their unanimity evaporates, however, when Lysistrata explains that the plan involves giving up sexual intercourse during their husbands' infrequent visits. Intrigued, the women ask for a fuller explanation. Lysistrata convinces them that they can frustrate their husbands into giving up warfare by denying them sexual gratification until they do.

The non-Athenian women doubt that the plan can succeed as long as the Athenians have a powerful fleet and as long as they own sufficient treasure to pursue the war. Lysistrata explains to her Spartan counterpart, Lampito, that the older women of Athens are about to occupy the Parthenon, where the city's treasure is kept, and deny men access to it.

There follows a merry scene in which Lysistrata has the women swear to deny sex to their husbands. If forced, they promise to remain unresponsive. The women all swear to cooperate with Lysistrata, and they drink a draught of wine to seal the bargain.

A hubbub outside indicates that the older women have occupied the Acropolis and the temple of Athena.

A CHORUS of elderly men enters. They bear logs for the purpose of building a giant bonfire and roasting the women who have rebelled. With much effort and complaining, they get the fire started. The women inside the temple, however, have friends outside, and a chorus of women comes bearing water jugs to quench the fire.

The old men and the women exchange insults. A magistrate and a crew of slaves enter with crowbars, and a series of jokes ensues based on the popular perception that both women and slaves drink too much. The slaves are about to use the crowbars when Lysistrata enters and stops them. As the men try to arrest Lysistrata, one woman after another comes to her aid. The men soon find that they are vastly outnumbered.

The men finally ask what the women hope to accomplish. They explain that they are keeping the money from the men so they cannot finance the war.

The women want to see some other changes too. They want the men to stop carrying arms to the marketplace. They explain that they will take over running the country and will do it better than the men have. Asked how, Lysistrata develops an extended comparison between running the state and the process of preparing yarn from wool and weaving it into cloth. She makes her point of view sound feasible.

In the next scene, just when the women seem to be getting the best of the men, Lysistrata enters with the news that the women are proving incapable of observing their vows of celibacy. She assures them, though, that their tactic is working and counsels them to stand firm a bit longer.

An extended encounter follows between the Athenian woman Myrrhine and her husband Cinesias. Visibly longing for his wife, Cinesias begs her to break her oath and lie with him. She agrees, but keeps putting him off with extended preparations and finally flees, leaving him unfulfilled. The costumes of the male actors now indicate that they are all in dire need of their wives' loving attention, and much ribald joking about this state of affairs takes place.

The general Panhellenic frustration finally forces the warring parties to parley. In their need, they submit all their disputes to Lysistrata for arbitration. Lysistrata calls in a naked young girl, the allegorical Reconciliation. As Lysistrata helps them resolve their disputes, the men remark on aspects of her attractiveness.

Finally, everyone is friendly again, and at a general party, Spartans and Athenians decide they really enjoy one another's company, and the prospect of warfare fades into memory. The play ends in a general dance and a hymn in praise of Athena, the goddess of wisdom.

Although the play is thoroughly bawdy, it is also thoroughly wise. It provides a telling if fictional instance of the power of determined women to defuse masculine disputes as men quibble over nonessentials to assert their predominance. One message of the play is the same as the one offered by the so-called flower children of the peace movement during the Vietnam War: "Make love, not war."

Bibliography

Henderson, Jeffrey, ed. and trans. *Aristophanes, Vol. 3: Birds; Lysistrata; Women at the Thesmophoria.* Cambridge, Mass.: Harvard University Press, 2000.

M

Macrobius (Macrobius Ambrosius Aurelius
 Theodosius) (fl. early fifth century C.E.)
 Roman prose writer

Of uncertain origin—perhaps Greek—Macrobius
seems to have risen to consular rank and to have
been widely known. He preserved important
mythological and philosophical information in a
Latin work that takes its cue from the dialogues
of Plato, particularly SYMPOSIUM. Entitled *The
Saturnalia* after the Roman holiday of that name,
the work imagines a group of banqueters gathered around tables in the homes of three hosts
and having a serious discussion about philosophy
and mythology.

The celebration takes place on December 17–
19, 384 C.E., during the feast of Saturnalia. The
hosts include historical persons: Praetextatus,
an authority on religious matters, politician, and
highly cultivated pagan; Flavianus, the praetorian prefect who was eventually made to commit
suicide for his support of Eugenius, a pagan
usurper of the Roman throne; and Symmachus,
a renowned orator and writer of both personal
and official letters. Symmachus opposed St.
AMBROSE by demanding religious freedom for
the pagans who were being oppressed by state-
sponsored Christianity.

The seven books of Macrobius's work are highly derivative, borrowing freely from such Roman
GRAMMARIANS as Gellius and such biographers
as PLUTARCH (see BIOGRAPHY GREEK AND
ROMAN). History and religion are among the topics that interest Macrobius's banqueters. So are
the works of ancient authors and Roman behavior
and customs. The banquet and the discussions
continue over a period of three days—a sort of
intellectual conference. Mornings are devoted to
serious discussion; the works of Virgil occupy
two mornings. More diverting topics occupy the
afternoons and evening. Then the discussion
turns to such matters as eating, drinking, and
joking. Though Macrobius has occasionally been
ranked among Christian adherents, both the
thrust of the conversations in *Saturnalia* and the
identity of the guests suggest that instead he was
an enlightened and intellectual Neoplatonist
pagan. Among the guests is one named Euange-
lus. Both ignorant and rude, he seems to be the
combative Christian foil for the learned and
peaceable pagans. Macrobius does not place himself among the company, though he makes clear
his authorial preferences.

A work influential in the Middle Ages and
early Renaissance was Macrobius's *Commentary
on the Dream of Scipio* as CICERO discusses it at

length in his *De Republica*. Macrobius considers the ways in which PLATO'S REPUBLIC and that of Cicero differ. Macrobius discusses the soul and concurs in Plato's view of it. Macrobius sees the *Dream* as having successfully combined the several subjects treated by philosophy. The principal philosophical thrust of Macrobius's work is Neoplatonist. In the *Dream*, Macrobius passes on to the Western tradition summaries of ancient scientific thinking concerning such matters as the nature of dreams, astronomy, and geography. He also discusses divination, music, morality, and mysticism.

Macrobius was also a grammarian and philologist. His third surviving work is a study of the differences and likenesses in Greek and Latin Verbs (*De verborum Graeci et Latini differentiis vel societatibus.*)

See also GRAMMARIANS OF ROME.

Bibliography

Conte, Gian Biagio. *Latin Literature: A History*. Translated by Joseph B. Solodow, Don Fowler, and Glen W. Most. Baltimore and London: Johns Hopkins University Press, 1994.

Macrobius, Ambrosius Aurelius Theodosius. *Commentary on the Dream of Scipio*. Translated by William Harris Stahl: New York: Columbia University Press, 1990.

———. *The Saturnalia*. Translated by Percival Vaughan Davies. New York: Columbia University Press, 1969.

Mad Hercules (*Hercules furens*) Seneca (before 54 C.E.)

Although SENECA borrows the plot of his version of Hercules' madness from the Greek original of EURIPIDES (see *HERACLES*), the Roman tragedian is at pains to unify the plot and to heighten the psychological realism of the story. Both playwrights deal with the same set of occurrences, though Seneca's erudition suggests a broad mastery of the genre of TRAGEDY and a loftier aim than simple adaptation. Most of the characters of the play have the same names in both the Greek and the Roman versions. There are, however, a few differences. The Greeks call the play's hero HERACLES instead of the Roman form, Hercules. The Romans call the queen of the gods Juno, while the Greeks addressed her Hera. Her husband, the king of the gods, is Zeus in Greek and Jupiter or Jove in Latin. Otherwise the characters' names are identical in both the Greek source and its Roman revision.

While Hercules is in Hell performing the last of his 12 great labors—capturing Cerberus the three-headed watchdog of Hades—a usurper named Lycus kills Thebes' rightful king, Creon, who is Hercules' father-in-law. Lycus also plans to kill Hercules' earthly father, Amphitryon, and his children by Hercules' wife, Megara.

In Euripides' version of the play, Heracles returns in time to save his relatives and kill Lycus. Once that has happened, however, Euripides changes the subject. Nursing her resentment against Heracles because Zeus had fathered Heracles with a human woman, Alcmene, the goddess Hera, Zeus's wife, decides to drive Heracles mad. She does so, and in his madness Heracles kills his own children. Thus, the Greek play divides into two essentially unrelated episodes, and the tragic part arises from the events of the second plot. The suddenness with which Euripides introduces this turn of events catches the audience by surprise and contributes to the effect of the play.

Seneca, however, prepares his audience for Juno's vengeance by having the goddess open the Roman version with a long soliloquy detailing her grievances against Hercules and her plan for revenge. Now the effect arises from the delayed fulfillment of the audience's expectation of the play's unhappy outcome throughout Hercules' successes against Lycus.

Seneca heightens Hercules' grievances against Lycus by introducing an element of jealousy. Lycus, who does not imagine that Hercules will ever return, is planning to marry Megara. She makes it clear that she would rather die.

Seneca also slows the pace of his play a bit with an apostrophe, or address, to fortune. At the end of the second scene of act 2, Amphitryon feels the earth quake and recognizes the approaching footfalls of Hercules as he returns from Hell. The entire third scene is devoted to a choral address to fortune and a synopsis of the story of Orpheus and Eurydice.

Another possible difference between the two plays is this. Euripides' version was unquestionably written for public performance. Seneca's may well have been intended as closet drama—a play to be read privately or by a group of readers who read the parts of the several characters to each other without an audience. Seneca's declamatory or oratorical mode favors long speeches and balanced exchanges.

Hercules has brought the Athenian king Theseus with him back from Hell, and Amphitryon quizzes Theseus about the underworld. His questions evoke long, melodramatic answers.

The long-anticipated madness of Hercules begins to affect him in the first scene of act 4—shortly after the hero has slain Lycus, but before he has performed the propitiary sacrifices his justifiable homicide requires. He mistakes his own wife and children for those of Lycus and slays them. Perhaps Seneca sought to heighten the credibility of this action by his earlier introduction of Lycus's attempt to seduce Megara. Hercules' homicidal spree ended, he falls asleep and his father, Amphitryon, has the servants disarm the hero lest he resume killing on awakening. The last scene of the act is given over to a choral dirge.

The final act begins with Hercules awakening in his right mind and recognizing his responsibility for the carnage in whose midst he finds himself. He is totally unaware that he has caused it until he recognizes his own arrows. Amphitryon confirms that Hercules is his family's murderer, but Amphitryon declares that the fault rests not with Hercules but with Juno. Aided by Theseus, Hercules seeks a place of exile where he can hide until the time for his final return to the underworld is at hand.

The tragedies of Seneca became the principal models for the so-called tragedy of the blood of the early modern period in Europe. In the man-

ner of Seneca, such practitioners as John Dryden strewed the stage with corpses.

Bibliography

Seneca. *Hercules; Trojan Women; Phoenician Women; Medea; Phaedra.* Edited and translated by John G. Fitch. Cambridge, Mass.: Harvard University Press, 2002.

Mahabharata Vyāsa (ca. 1500 B.C.E.; current form ca. 300–150 C.E.)

Attributed to the ancient priest, poet, and sage, Krishna Dwaipāyana VYĀSA, and perhaps in part actually composed by him, the *Mahabharata* is the great EPIC of India. It clearly, however, grew over time by accretion. In keeping with ancient custom, the poet authors who composed the later sections found greater merit in submerging their individual identities in the persona of their great originator than in crediting themselves with their own contributions. Though portions of the epic may very well survive from preliterate, early antiquity, much derives from later times.

In the form we now have it, the *Mahabharata* is written in the Sanskrit tongue. The longest national epic and longest poem extant, in its full form it contains some 200,000 lines deployed in *sloka*s, or couplets, through 18 cantos. In its shortest version, it runs to 88,000 lines. Hindus believe that merely reading the poem is an act of religious devotion that gains every good and perfect reward for the reader.

From a historical perspective, the poem finds its origins in the ancient conflicts that occurred as the Aryan peoples from regions to the north and west of India swept down in waves of conquest that overcame or displaced the original inhabitants of the subcontinent—people who were mostly speakers of Dravidian tongues. In the poem, these opposing forces are represented as being from different lineages of the family founded by Bharata—the founding father of India, or by its native name, Bharat. The opposing first cousins include, on the one hand, the sons of Raja Pandu, the five Pandava brothers. On the other, we find the 100 sons of a blind king, Raja Dhritarashtra. These brothers are collectively called the Kaurava. The epic's central event is the monumental battle of Kurukshetra between those opposing forces. Though the poem's 18 cantos evoke that conflict numerologically by suggesting the poem's 18 armies fighting a war that lasted 18 days, only about 4,000 lines of the epic concern themselves directly with this main plot.

From a generic perspective, the work is otherwise an episodic composite of history, legend, philosophy, saving theology, myth, love affairs, vengeance, ethics, politics, warfare, government, and physical and spiritual cosmology. In brief, it takes this life, future lives, and the release from the necessity for continual rebirth as its deepest subjects. Some of its sections are often published as freestanding works in their own right. An entry concerning the principal one of these, BHAGAVAD GITA, appears separately.

The opening section of the *Mahabharata* is called the *Ādi Parva*. As it begins, a king, Pariksit, has wounded a deer. Trying to follow it in the forest, he encounters a Brahman who had taken a vow of silence. The king asks about the deer. When the sage says nothing, the angry king hangs a dead snake around the holy man's neck and leaves. On the holy man's arrival home, the sight of the snake so angers the sage's son that he curses the king to die by the bite of the ruling serpent, Taksaka. That curse is fulfilled, and the king's son plots revenge against Taksaka by sacrificing a quantity of snakes. He does so but is stopped just before sacrificing Taksaka himself. Then the sage Vyāsa—the epic's legendary author—arrives, and the new king, Janamejaya, requests that Vyāsa tell the story of the Kaurava—also called Kurus—and the Pandava, for Vyāsa was the real father of the kings Pandu and Dhritarashtra, and he had seen their conflict with his own eyes.

Vyāsa complies with the king's request, appointing the first of the great epic's three narrators, Vaisampayana, to recount the story, and the *Mahabharata* gets underway in earnest. It first recounts the marriage of the wise king and bowman, Santanu, who marries in human form the goddess Ganga, tutelary deity of the River Ganges. Before leaving him to return to her divine state, the goddess bears the king eight godlike sons. She drowns the first seven so they can assume their heavenly identities. At the Santanu's request, she spares the last son, who is known by three names: Gangadatta, Gangeya, and Devavrata. The goddess takes that son and disappears. Later, the king encounters Devavrata as a young man with superhuman strength. He first disappears and then reappears to the king with his mother in all her divine beauty. Devavrata remains with his father. When the father wishes to remarry and his prospective father-in-law requires that the eldest son of the new marriage will succeed to the throne, Devavrata steps aside in his father's interest, and his half brother, Citrangada, succeeds Santanu on the throne.

Devavrata now acquires another name, Bhishma. This name reflects his vow never to marry or have children who will challenge the claim of his father's second family to the throne. Like many another vow in the course of the epic, this one has serious consequences, for when he rejects a woman, Amba, because of the vow, she in turn vows to kill him. None of the many vows in the epic proves inconsequential.

As matters evolve, Citragada's line dies out, and his widows want children. Since Bhishma sticks to his vow, he asks the poet-sage Vyāsa to substitute. Vyāsa agrees, but as a solitary holy man, he mortifies his flesh. As a result, he is filthy and he stinks. The princesses are displeased. One closes her eyes at the sight of him, and another grows pale at his touch. For these reasons, Vyāsa's son by the first princess is born blind and becomes King Dhritararastra. The son by the other is born light-skinned—King Pandu.

Pandu takes two wives, Kunti and Madri. Before either becomes pregnant, however, Pandu is cursed to die on the day he has sex. He therefore resigns his kingdom and takes his wives away. Kunti reveals that she has the power to call gods to her and bear their children. She does so and first bears the son of the god Dharma. This son's name, Yudhishthira, means "truthful" and "virtuous." She next bears the child of the wind god, Vayu. This son, Bhima, will be the strongest of men—possessed of the strength of 10 elephants. Finally she gives birth to Arjuna, the greatest of bowmen and a peerless warrior. He is the son of the god Indra. Kunti shares her power with her co-wife, Madri. Madri produces twin boys: Nakula and Sahadeva. All five Pandava brothers are now on the scene.

If all this strikes one as improbable, more follows. The blind king Dhritarashtra has married Gandhari in the meantime. To share his infirmity, she permanently blindfolds herself. She becomes pregnant and remains in that condition for two years, finally bearing a ball of flesh. On Vyāsa's advice, she divides the ball into a hundred sections and puts each in a jar of butter. When they have ripened there, they come forth, and the omens surrounding their appearance make clear that the 100 Kaurava brothers are the offspring of demonic forces.

If the poet in question were Edmund Spenser instead of Vyāsa and his surrogates, a reader might see in the foregoing passages preparation for the assault of the many subcategories of the deadly sins upon the five senses of the human creature. In the *Mahabharata*, however, the reader follows through many episodes the growing and increasingly violent rivalry between the demigods and the demidemons as they grow to manhood.

When the mighty bowman and warrior, Arjuna, has grown to manhood, he wins the hand of the lovely Draupadi in an archery contest. The catch is that, not knowing the nature of the prize, his mother, Kunti, had instructed him to share it with his brothers, and he has promised to do so. A vow is a vow, so all five Pandavas marry Draupadi, thereby answering five prayers for a husband that, in an earlier existence, she had addressed to the god Shiva.

The brothers agree to respect each other's privacy when they are with Draupadi, but Arjuna accidentally one day interrupts her with a brother. In penance, he exiles himself for a year. While he is gone, he cements alliances with other leaders by contracting three more marriages. One of these is with the sister of Krishna. Krishna is the incarnation of Vishnu—the preserver of the universe—come to earth to save it from the threat the Kauravas represent. Chaos threatens order, and evil threatens good. Divine intercession is called for. The literary critic, Larry Brown, suggests that the divinity of Krishna may be a late addition to the poem since he is also represented as a mortal, human prince with human failings.

Tensions continue to grow between the two sets of cousins, and the Kauravas eventually engineer a crooked game of dice in which they win control of all the Pandavas and Draupadi. As a result, the Pandavas spend 12 years in the wilderness and agree thereafter to live in disguise for a year. Books 3–5 of the epic follow them in their exile. In the 14th year, however, the Kauravas fail to honor their agreement to restore the Pandavas, and warfare becomes inevitable. Krishna makes an effort to dissuade the Kauravas, even revealing himself to them in his divine form, but all to no avail.

Before the battle is joined, however, the warrior Arjuna refuses to fight and slay so many of his kinsman. Overcoming his objections is the work of Krishna in the Bhagavad Gita, described in a separate entry. In the *Gita*, however, Krishna has revealed his divinity to Arjuna. At the same time, the blind king Dhritarashtra hears Krishna's words repeated by one of the *Mahabharata*'s narrators, Sanjaya. The enormous armies are drawn up in battle array, and Dhritarashtra fears that with Krishna on their side, the Pandavas will be invincible.

The 18-day-long battle begins with the unconquerable Arjuna leading the Pandava forces. In the Kauravas' ranks, some, including Bhishma and Drona, though they fight hard out of loyalty, really want the Pandavas to win and pray for their victory. Ironically, such persons all fall in battle, including Bhishma, who falls as a result of a subterfuge of the woman he had earlier rejected, Amba. Another vow is fulfilled.

Krishna has lost a son in the battle, and he vows to kill the unit commander of the troops who killed his son before sundown the following day. To thwart the defenses of a formation Krishna knows to be otherwise impregnable, he causes an eclipse of the sun. The Kauravan defenders think night has fallen, rendering Krishna's vow null and void. They lay down their defensive weapons, and Krishna fulfills his vow.

Many scenes of individual combat and heroism and many reports of victory through successful deceptions punctuate the story of the epic battle. The overall commander of the Kauravas' forces has been the field marshal, Duryodhana. The Pandavan hero Bhima challenges him to single combat. Like Achilles in HOMER's *The ILIAD*, Duryodhana has been rendered invincible by his mother's magic. Also like Achilles, Duryodhana has a vulnerable spot—in this case, his thighs since he has worn a loincloth because his modesty prohibits his fighting naked before his mother. Bhima breaks the rules and strikes his legs; Duryodhana's fall ends the war. The parallels with Homer are frequent and sometimes suggest common sources from the ORAL FORMULAIC TRADITION of a preliterate age.

As Duryodhana dies, his fellow soldier, Ashvatthama, reports that he had massacred all the Pandavan supporters, including the children of the family, while they slept the night before. Everyone on both sides—except for Ashvatthama and the five Pandava brothers—has died in the war or will soon die of their wounds. Some 6 million have fallen.

Recriminations, prophetic visions, and religious instruction follow the war and occupy books 11–18 of the epic. Among them is the assurance that in the fourth age of the world—of which our current times are a part—the world will be turned upside down, the forces of good become evil, and vice versa.

Gandhari, the mother of the 100 deceased Kauravas, curses Krishna and predicts his death at the hands of a stranger. She also prophesies the fall of the Pandavas after a period of 36 years. At the end of that period, the then-current king, Yudhishthira, dies and arrives at the gate of the Hindu heaven, *svarga*, carrying a dog. On being told that no dogs are allowed, Yudhishthira decides he will not enter. The dog, however, is really the god Dharma conducting a little test that Yudhishthira has passed. He faces one more test, in which all the other Pandavas and their common wife, Draupadi, seem to be suffering in one of the seven Hindu hells. Yudhishthira says he prefers being with them to being in heaven. This is the right answer, and all are reunited in Paradise. Residence there, however, is not a permanent condition. Until one escapes the cycle of death and rebirth through extraordinary merit, all sojourns in heaven or in one of the hells are temporary.

New York University Press is in process of issuing a new multivolume English translation of the great Indian epic. The best currently available, full-English verse translation remains that of P. Lal, listed in the bibliography below. Lal is currently revising that edition to include material that has traditionally been expurgated or neglected in popular editions.

Bibliography

Badrinath, Chaturvedi. *The Mahabharata: An Inquiry into the Human Condition.* New Delhi: Orient Longman, 2006.

Brown, Larry A. Mahabharata: *The Great Epic of India.* Available online. URL: http://larryavisbrown.homestead.com/files/xeno.mahabsynop.htm. Downloaded January 12, 2007.

Narasimhan, Chakravarthi V. *The Mahabharata: An English Version Based on Selected Verses.* New York: Columbia, University Press, 1965.

Vyāsa. *The Mahabharata.* 143 vols. Transcreated by P. Lal. Calcutta: Writers Workshop, 1968–80.

———. *The Mahabharata.* Rev. ed. 18 vols. Transcreated by P. Lal. Kolkatta, India: Writers Workshop, 2005–ca. 2008.

Mani (216–ca. 276 C.E.) *Babylonian-Syriac prose writer*

The founder of a Gnostic sect, Manichaeanism, that shared some features with early Christianity, Mani was probably born in Mardinu in northern Babylonia. His father and mother were both of noble Armenian descent, but Mani's birthplace made him a Babylonian. The young Mani grew up in a religious household whose pious observances were those of a non-Christian, vegetarian, abstemious sect that practiced baptism and encouraged celibacy. Babylon was a religious melting pot where ancient mystery religions of every description were practiced side by side with emergent Christianity, Zoroastrianism, the several varieties of idolatry, and the multitudinous cults of local deities.

Twice in his youth, in 228–29 and in 240–41, when he was 12 and 24, respectively, Mani received personal visits from an angel named at-Taum. The king of the Paradise of Lights had sent the angel to reveal to Mani his vocation as the preacher of a gnosis. *The New Catholic Encyclopedia* defines *gnosis* as: "a definitive and ultimate divine revelation."

Mani assumed the role of a missionary, traveling first to India, where Hindu thought deeply influenced his interpretation of his calling. On his return trip, he toured the Middle East, always preaching his new creed and building a reputation as a missionary. Recognizing in Mani a useful instrument for his political ambitions, the Persian emperor, Shapur I, summoned Mani to join his retinue as Sharpur pursued his anti-Roman program. As a member of the emperor's party, Mani first came into contact with Christianity, many of whose doctrines and principles he found congenial to his own way of thinking. He readily incorporated such views into his own composite religious ideas.

Mani won many converts, a number of whom also became missionaries, spreading his gospel into the Roman world, chiefly Egypt. Among those who subscribed, at least for a time, to the Manichaean faith was no less a subsequently Christian luminary than St. AUGUSTINE. Augustine, who had been reared as a Christian, converted temporarily to Manichaeanism before his final return to the Christian fold after hearing the sermons of St. AMBROSE.

For more than 30 years, Mani enjoyed the protection of the emperor and his immediate successor. When, however, a Persian devotee of the old Zoroastrian faith assumed the throne, his counselors judged Mani a heretic. He was jailed for 26 days and, at age 60, died in prison. His head was exposed on the gate of the city until his disciples collected his remains and buried them.

Like Judaism, Christianity, and Hinduism, Manichaeanism was and is a religion of the book. To help promote and spread the word of the religious system he had developed to preserve and share his revelation, Mani composed a series of works in the Syriac language as it was spoken at the city of Edessa (thus called Edessan Syriac). He also developed a distinctive script developed from Aramaic called Manichaean Sogdian. He used it for all but one of his works, some of which are considered canonical and some not.

The canonical works included *The Living* [or *Great*] *Gospel*, *The Treasure of Life*, *Pragmateia*, *The Book of Mysteries*, *The Book of the Giants*, and Mani's *Letters*. Also canonical was the single work tactfully, as its title reveals, written in Middle Persian, *Šāhburaghān* [Writings dedicated to his royal patron, Shapur I].

See also MANICHAEAN WRITINGS.

Bibliography

Daniels, Peter T., and William Bright. *The World's Writing Systems.* New York: Oxford University Press, 1966.

New Catholic Encyclopedia. Vol. 9. S.V. "Manichaeanism." New York: McGraw-Hill Book Company, 1967, pp. 153–160.

Wellborn, Andrew, ed. *Mani, the Angel, and the Column of Glory: An Anthology of Manichaean Texts.* Edinburgh: Floris, 1998.

Widengren, Geo. *Mani and Manichaeanism.* Translated by Charles Kessler. New York: Holt, Rinehart, and Winston, 1965.

Manichaean writings (third century C.E.)

Seven works of MANI, the founder of the Manichaean religion, were considered canonical: *The Living* [or *Great*] *Gospel*, *The Treasure of Life*, *Pragmateia*, *The Book of Mysteries*, *The Book of the Giants*, Mani's *Letters*; and his *Šāhburaghān*

[Writings dedicated to his royal patron, Shapur I]. Most of these works have largely perished; scholars know them through surviving fragments or because of allusions in the works of other writers.

From the few surviving fragments of the *Living Gospel*, we learn that it had 22 chapters—one for each of the 22 letters that composed the Syriac alphabet. We also know that, in its pages, Mani promoted himself as the Paraclete—the Holy Spirit—whose coming Christ had foretold. Beyond that, little is known except that Mani probably had access only to a single Syriac Christian gospel that circulated during his lifetime.

The Treasure of Life contained at least seven books detailing Mani's thinking about anthropology and psychology. The work also set forth Mani's theories about human beings as the constituents of a microcosm and considered the circumstances of those whom he called "dwellers in the realm of light." An Arab writer, Abu Rayhan Al-Biruni, has preserved a portion of that consideration in his book about India. Other substantial extracts appear both in the work of St. AUGUSTINE, *De Natura boni* (*On the Nature of the Good*), and in the work of the Christian controversialist Euodius, *On Faith: Against the Manichees*.

Nothing but the title remains of the *Pragmateia*, but judging from the title it is likely to have been a work on practical ethics. A similar informational void faces students of Manichaeanism interested in *The Book of Mysteries*. They know something of its form; it had 18 chapters. They also know the headings of three chapters. These suggest that those sections dealt with a Gnostic Christian splinter group in Edessa whose leader was named Bardesanes.

Matters take a turn for the better with respect to *The Book of the Giants*. Enough fragments have surfaced to make possible reconstructing most of the work. In this work, Mani combined an ancient Middle Eastern tale about the fall of the angels, retold in the HEBREW BIBLE's Book of Enoch, with an Iranian account of a giant named Ogia who lived after the great flood and who had killed a dragon. This, then, seems to be a work of mythohistory comparable to that of the Greek HESIOD.

The student of ancient religions, Geo Widengren, suggests that Mani's letters—again mostly lost—were a conscious imitation of the letters of St. Paul in which Mani, as the leader and pastor of his flock, gave advice to his fledgling congregations.

All of the above canonical writings were in the Edessan Syriac language. The one canonical exception to Mani's use of that tongue occurs in the writings that Mani addressed to Sharpur I. These were written in Middle Persian—presumably the king's native tongue. Recently discovered fragments suggest that this work contained Mani's views on the creation of the universe, the end of the world, and what would happen after that. The work also contained biographical information about Mani's birth and identified him as one in a succession of incarnations of a heavenly messenger. These included BUDDHA, ZOROASTER, Jesus, and Mani.

A number of noncanonical Manichaean writings exist that were penned by Mani's successors. Among them is a life of Mani that bears the earmarks of the lives of other religious leaders and of saints. It combines actual biography with accounts of miraculous works and his martyrdom. These works, which were not directly written by Mani, need not concern us here.

Bibliography

Wellborn, Andrew, ed. *Mani, the Angel, and the Column of Glory: An Anthology of Manichaean Texts.* Edinburgh: Floris, 1998.

Widengren, Geo. *Mani and Manichaeism.* Translated by Charles Kessler. New York: Holt, Rinehart, and Winston, 1965.

Man'yōshū (*Collection for a Myriad Ages*) (ca. 795 C.E.)

The earliest surviving and generally regarded as the best collection of Japanese poetry extant, the *Man'yōshū*'s 4,516 poems in 20 books represent a fairly narrow spectrum of forms with widely varying subjects. The work's title has also been translated as *Collection of Ten Thousand Leaves*. Among earlier examples of poetry, we find those of male and female poets who represent several social and economic classes from the most humble to the highest. The later examples tend to come from court poets—again of both sexes. Particularly, the collection is prized for the intensity of the emotion that it expresses. Some 450 of the poets represented are either named in the collection's pages or are otherwise identifiable, but many of the verses included spring from anonymous origins.

The composition of some of the poems collected in the *Man'yōshū* predates Japan's earliest book, the *Kojiki*, by almost a century. Many of the poems in the collection were probably sung—a fact to which some of them doubtless owe their preservation. They also show the influence of Chinese poetic practice and thus testify to the cultural contacts that regularly increased between China and Japan in the seventh century C.E. Nonetheless, it is clear that Japanese pronunciations are intended throughout the book except in the Buddhist poems of Book 16, and in two other minor instances.

Though more than one name has been offered as the compiler of the collection, the most authoritative view holds that a poet named ŌTOMO NO YAKAMOCHI performed the editorial work between 744–45 and 759 C.E. The ending date is also that of the last dated poem in the book. At least six known prior but now lost collections served as one of Yakamochi's sources: YAMANOUE NO OKURA's *Karin* (Forest of verses); the anonymously compiled *Kokashū* (Collection of ancient poems); and four collections bearing the names of poets who either compiled them or whose works were included in them. These are the KAKINOMOTO NO HITOMARO, Kanamura, Mushimaro, and Sakimaro collections.

From the perspective of form, most of the *Man'yōshū*'s poems are tanka (in ancient times called *waka*)—five-line poems with, first, a five-syllable line, then a seven-syllable line, then another line with five syllables, and finally two lines with seven syllables each. The best poems in the collection, however, are considered to be its 265 *chōka*—longer poems of 30–40 lines that

alternately have five or seven syllables. These sometimes tell stories, sometimes express sorrow at parting or grief over death, or sometimes congratulate prominent persons on notable achievements. The *chōka* apparently reached its apogee during the ancient period, and the examples contained in the *Man'yōshū* have not since been equaled. The literary historian Donald Keene attributes the excellence of these poems to the direct fashion in which the poets who composed the *chōka* of the *Man'yōshū* communicated their emotions to their readers.

Later Japanese poets strove for subtle implication of emotional quality with, as Keene thinks, a concomitant loss of directness. The ancient *chōka* succeed both in direct narration and in evoking strong feeling.

The poems of the first book appear in the order of their composition, beginning with a poem by Emperor Yūraku; its composition dates to 645. The poem describes a chance encounter between the emperor and a pretty maiden. He asks her for her name and address and identifies himself as her lord. The second poem is also from an imperial author, this time Emperor Jomei, who succeeded the last ruler named in the *Kojiki*. This was the Empress Suiko. Thus, the first two poems of the collection provide a transition from the *Kojiki* into the subsequent artistic endeavors of the Japanese. Many of the poems of the first book appear to have been written by female court poets who were responsible for composing the poetry that was performed on state occasions.

Many other poems are love poems, often verse exchanges between sometimes-illicit lovers. The Japanese tactfully allude to this poetic category as *mutual inquiries*. Exemplifying this sort of exchange, we find a poem addressed to the crown prince from his former wife, Princess Nukata (see FEMALE POETS OF ANCIENT JAPAN)—a woman now married to another man. She reproves him for waving at her during a royal hunt and fears his continued affection for her will be noticed. He replies with a courtly compliment in which he confesses his love despite her allegiance to a new husband.

As the chronologically arranged poems of the book move into verses composed during the second of the *Man'yōshū*'s four periods, the work appears of the most gifted poet included in the collection, Kakinomoto no Hitomaro, who seems to have served as the principal court poet to the widowed empress Jitō. The collection's longest poem is Hitomaro's ELEGY on the death of Jitō's husband, Prince Takechi. The poem both mourns the prince and celebrates his courage on the field of valor. Other works mourn other deceased members of the royal family, and others still sing the praises of the empress and the divinity of the royal family whom Hitomaro served.

Hitomaro's most celebrated elegies, however, do not concern the imperial family. One of them, instead, eulogizes a dead stranger whose corpse he observed on the island of Samine. The others are two elegies of parting that the poet wrote when he went on a journey, leaving his wife at home, and two eulogies that the poet offered on learning that she had died in his absence.

A powerful court figure and the father-in-law of two emperors, Fujiwara no Fuhito, strongly preferred Chinese to Japanese poetry. That preference may explain the temporary neglect of native poems during the dozen years of Fuhito's influence at court. An exception to that generalization was a poet who specialized in travel poetry and scenic descriptions, Takechi no Kurohito. Another poet who achieved considerable renown between 724 and 737 was Yamabe no Akahito, who combined nature poetry with courtly compliment.

The reputations of some of the poets featured in the *Man'yōshū* have waxed and waned at different periods over the centuries. One whose stock rose sharply in the 20th century was Yamanoue no Okura (ca. 660–733 C.E.). This revision of critical thinking arose from the 20th century's preference for the *chōka* form. Some of his poems deal with the conflicts that arise between one's official duty in serving the emperor and being a devotee of DAOISM who has renounced the world. Others deal with Okura's devotion to his children, with the brevity of human life and briefer love, and with the ills accompanying old age. He treats these universal themes with powerful expression. Okura wrote both in Chinese and in Japanese. His best-known poem is his "Dialogue on Poverty," in which a poor man complains of the cold and the miserable fare on which he subsists. But his thoughts turn to those even poorer than he, and he wonders how they live. A second verse answers this question with a poignant description of utter destitution made concrete by picturing a spider spinning its web in a cold and empty cooking pot and a growling tax collector insisting on payment. The poem itself speaks in its last three lines, passing judgment on the pain and shame in the world of men and lamenting the poem's inability to fly away as it lacks the wings of a bird.

The fourth and final period of the *Man'yōshū* (poems composed between 730 and 759 C.E.) centrally features the work of its compiler, Ōtomo no Yakamochi. At about the age of 14, Ōtomo began addressing ardent love poems to his 11- or 12-year-old cousin—the girl he married when she was 19 or 20. Ōtomo belonged to that class of poets who always seem to be in love with love. Beyond poems addressed to his wife and his aunt, the collection includes poems addressed to 14 named women and others unnamed. In at least one instance, Ōtomo includes the feminine responses in poems of mutual inquiry. A reader finds 29 poems by Ōtomo's literary paramour, Lady Kasa (see FEMALE POETS OF ANCIENT JAPAN), together with the poems he wrote that provoked her responses. At this remove, there is no way to know if their exchange was the product of an actual love affair or was a literary game. It may well have been both—an actual love for the lady and a literary game (perhaps with fringe benefits) for Ōtomo.

She complains that he does not return her affection, comparing her ardor to "bowing . . . behind the back of the famished devil." Ōtomo Yakamochi can't imagine what he was thinking about when the pair originally got involved since there was no chance that the relationship could go anywhere.

Beyond the verse of notable poets whose names and reputations are well known, numerous anonymous poems also appear in the *Man'yōshū*. Some were written in dialect and composed by frontier guards. Others were written by shepherds and, in the fashion of the European PASTORAL, by nobles pretending to be shepherds. A pair of "beggar poems" seems to have been composed by professional improvisers who performed in town markets. Their ostensible authors are a deer and a crab that are about to be turned, respectively, into useful artifacts and dinner.

Additionally, one finds poems expressing the feelings of the farm-girl mistress of a young nobleman, a poem to comfort a child when it thunders, and anonymous poems of longing for distant loves.

Within a century after its compilation, the *Man'yōshū* fell out of favor because of the soaring popularity of Chinese poetry. As a result, copies perished or were scattered, and whole sections disappeared from view. When the rising spirit of Japanese nationalism eventually overcame popular admiration for all things Chinese, efforts began to recover the full text. This was an enterprise that took centuries, and it was not until the 20th century that the full text was recovered and published in scholarly editions with full academic appraisal. The work of understanding and interpreting the poems is ongoing.

Bibliography

Keene, Donald. *Seeds in the Heart: Japanese Literature from Earliest Times to the Late Sixteenth Century.* New York: Henry Holt and Company, 1993.

1000 Poems from the Man'yōshū: *The Complete Nippon Gakujutsu Shinkokai Translation.* Translated by the Japanese Classics Translation Committee. Mineola, N.Y.: Dover Publications, 2005.

Marcus Aurelius (Marcus Aurelius Antoninus, Marcus Annius Verus) (121–180 C.E.) *Roman prose writer*

Born in Rome to Annius Verus and Domita Calvilla, Marcus Aurelius was chosen by the reigning emperor, Antonius Pius, to become both his son-in-law and heir to the Roman throne. Marcus was then 17 years old. He married the emperor's daughter, Faustina, and began his service as a Roman consul at age 18 in the year 140 C.E., serving in that capacity until he succeeded as emperor in 161. During his consulship, while he performed his duties with careful attention to justice, he also continued his studies. These principally included the Stoic philosophers (see STOICISM) and law.

On succeeding to the throne, Marcus Aurelius invited his adoptive brother, Lucius Aurelius Verus, to share the responsibilities of empire with him. Regrettably, he did not possess his brother's virtues, but he nonetheless became a successful military commander in the East. The times, however, remained difficult. Such natural disasters as plagues, earthquakes, and floods beleaguered Italy. Many of the subject peoples of the empire were in arms from Asia to Britain. Thus, the principal irony of Marcus Aurelius's life arose from the circumstance that a person of his peaceful disposition continually had to lead military campaigns.

Marcus Aurelius faced and decimated the Marcomanni in two engagements (168 and 173 C.E.) along the Danube River. Verus had shared command in the first engagement, but he died in 169. Marcus Aurelius was called to put down a rebellion in the Eastern Empire—a task eased by the death of the chief rebel. He made a grand tour of the trip home, stopping off in both Egypt and Greece. In Athens, he endowed professorships in each of the principal schools of Greek philosophy—the Epicurean, the PERIPATETIC (Neoplatonic), and the Stoic.

Late in 176, Marcus Aurelius was called again to Germany. There his always-fragile health broke down, and he died in the field. Fortunately, someone in his party had the foresight to preserve the emperor's *MEDITATIONS*, or *Communings with Himself*—a work whose 12 books he had chosen to compose in Greek.

Bibliography

Haines, C. R., trans. *The Communings with Himself of Marcus Aurelius Antoninus, Emperor of Rome. Together with his Speeches and his Sayings.* New York: G. P. Putnam's Sons, 1930.

Marcus Aurelius. *Marcus Aurelius in Love: Marcus Aurelius and Marcus Cornelius Fronto.* Edited and translated by Amy Richlin. Chicago: University of Chicago Press, 2006.

Martial (Marcus Valerius Martialis)
(ca. 40–103/4 C.E.) *Roman poet*

Born in Spain in the town of Bibilis to a mother named Flacilla and a father named Fronto, Martial acquired a good education before migrating to Rome, where he spent most of the rest of his life. There he became associated with another family with Spanish connections—that of the poet LUCAN and his powerful uncle, SENECA, first the tutor and then the close advisor to the emperor Nero. When the male members of Lucan's family were forced by Nero to commit suicide after they conspired against the emperor, Martial continued to receive patronage from Polla Argenteria, Lucan's brilliant and accomplished widow. He also forged connections with many of the principal literati of his day—such authors as FRONTINUS, JUVENAL, QUINTILIAN, PLINY THE YOUNGER, and STATIUS.

As far as posterity knows, Martial composed only EPIGRAMS: pithy, often witty, brief poems on a wide variety of subjects (see his *EPIGRAMS*). A good many of his epigrams were certainly occasional poems that he penned for clients who employed his services to write verses to grace anniversary celebrations, for example, or to accompany gifts. In short, he worked to order as a versifier.

In 80 C.E., Martial published a work known to posterity as his *Book on Shows* or *On the Spectacles.* It commemorates a series of spectacular entertainments presented by the emperor Titus in the then recently built Colosseum. That Martial had been chosen to write this work suggests that his reputation as an epigrammatist was already firmly and profitably established. Only a part of this work survives.

The year 85 saw two collections issued, *Xenia* and *Apophoreta.* These contain two-line verses written to accompany, in the first case, gifts of wine and food, and in the second, miscellaneous presents. Both sorts were exchanged at the Roman festival of Saturnalia, the Roman antecedent of Christmas, which took place on December 17. These collections now appear in the corpus of Martial's work as books 13 and 14.

Martial's laudatory poems in celebration of the emperors Titus and Domitian earned him the financial advantages that equaled those of fathering three children for Rome. In later times, the annual premiums that rewarded siring and rearing a large brood of children—future soldiers in the case of the males—came to be disbursed as a mark of imperial favor for anything the ruler found pleasing. At any rate, the emperor Titus awarded the "right of three children" to Martial, and Domitian renewed the grant. Martial's assiduous cultivation of royal personages also earned him the office of tribune for six months and, with it, automatic elevation to equestrian rank. (The free people of Rome were divided into plebeians, equestrians, and patricians, each rank enjoying progressively higher social status.)

Martial's collections of epigrams appeared with regularity beginning in the year 86 C.E., when books 1 and 2 appeared. They were followed in 87 by book 3; by books 4–9 between 88 and 94; and by book 10, first in 96 and afterward in 98 in a revised edition. The assassination of Domitian in September 96 required the excision of passages in praise of the now universally despised and discredited emperor. The revision, however, did not work for Martial. Domitian's successors, Nerva and Trajan, viewed the poet with suspicion, and Martial found it expedient to return to Bibilis in 100.

There, far from the urban attractions that he had so come to relish, Martial languished, and there, three or four years later, he died. When news of his death reached Rome, some of his friends and admirers genuinely mourned. Among them was Pliny the Younger, who wrote on many topics and who collected and published his own letters. In one of them, a letter to a friend, Pliny wrote a touching tribute to Martial and the value of his work.

Bibliography

Martial. *Epigrams*. 3 vols. Edited and Translated by D. R. Shackleton Bailey. Cambridge, Mass.: Harvard University Press, 1993.

———. *Select Epigrams*. Edited by Lindsay and Patricia Watson. Cambridge and New York: Cambridge University Press, ca. 2003.

Sullivan, J. P. and A. J. Boyle, eds. *Martial in English*. [Selections.] New York: Penguin Books, 1996.

Martyrdom of Polycarp, The   Marcion of Smyrna   (ca. early second century C.E.)

Surely the best-documented Christian person of the second century, Polycarp was the author, the recipient, and the subject of three of the letters included in the collection of early Christian, noncanonical writings known as the APOSTOLIC FATHERS OF THE CHRISTIAN CHURCH.

Marcion's letter describing Polycarp's martyrdom was written on behalf of the church at Smyrna to the church of Philomelium in the Roman province of Phrygia. Giving an account of Polycarp's death at the hands of the Romans, however, was not the letter's sole purpose. Rather, the missive's primary object was to set the whole subject of Christian martyrdom in a proper doctrinal perspective.

If faced with martyrdom, a good Christian will die bravely, steadfast in one's loyalty to the faith. The Christian martyr will not renounce the faith nor save himself by offering sacrifices to the deities of the Roman pantheon. The devout Christian will not, however, voluntarily seek to become a martyr.

To illustrate that point, Marcion recounts the story of a certain Quintus, who volunteered to become a martyr and counseled others to do likewise. Faced by the beasts in the arena, however, Quintus lost his nerve and recanted.

In the case of Polycarp, Marcion emphasizes the similarities between the passion of Christ and Polycarp's demise, saying that it was the martyr's special destiny to be a partner with Christ. Like Jesus, Polycarp anticipated that he would be arrested and condemned and had warned his followers to expect it. The 86-year-old Polycarp did not, however, voluntarily submit. Like Christ, persons close to him betrayed him—in Polycarp's case, members of his own household who were compelled by torture to reveal the bishop's whereabouts. Polycarp waited until the authorities apprehended him.

In other parallels with details of Christ's own martyrdom, Marcion reports that the chief of police who arrested him was called Herod, and a donkey carried Polycarp into the city. Repeatedly refusing to recant and to acknowledge Caesar as his lord, Polycarp remained courageous in the face of threats about wild beasts and burning at the stake. His persecutors chose the latter option, and a great pyre was prepared. His executioners were about to nail him to the stake, but Polycarp assured them that he would be able to stand on his own among the flames.

When the fire was lit, a miracle occurred. Instead of consuming him, the flames took the shape of a "vaulted room" around the martyr's body, and he stood in the center, not burning. Instead, "like baking bread" or like gold refined, he did not exude the stench of burning flesh but the sweet aroma of incense or other "precious perfume."

Despairing of dispatching him with fire, the authorities ordered an executioner to stab him. When he obeyed, a dove flew forth from the wound. Moreover, Polycarp bled so profusely that the blood extinguished the fire.

Once Polycarp was dead, the Romans refused to hand his body over to the Christians, but rather burned it so that only bones remained. The Christians collected these relics and preserved them. Marcion reports that Polycarp was the 12th martyr from Smyrna to die during that particular persecution. Marcion (or a later reviser) gives the date and time of Polycarp's martyrdom as "a great Sabbath," February 23, at 2:00 P.M. The year is not known.

Bibliography

Marcion of Smyrna. "Martyrdom of Polycarp." In *The Apostolic Fathers*. Edited and translated by Bart D. Ehrman. Cambridge, Mass.: Harvard University Press, 2003.

Medea Euripides (431 B.C.E.)

EURIPIDES' tragic masterpiece draws its subject from the ancient story of Jason and the Argonauts. At the behest of his uncle, Pelias, Jason and a crew of Greek heroes and demigods set off in the Argo, the first Greek ship, to steal the Golden Fleece revered and safeguarded in the distant land of Colchis—a land ruled by a king named Aeëtes. Pelias expected Jason to be killed on the voyage.

In the event, however, Aeëtes' daughter, a sorceress named Medea, fell in love with Jason. He accomplished his mission with her assistance, but this involved betraying her father and murdering her brother. When Jason, who was the rightful ruler of Iolcos, surprised his uncle by returning, Medea helped him overthrow Pelias, who had usurped the throne in his nephew's absence. Pelias's supporters, however, prevailed against Jason, and together with Medea and their two little boys, he fled to Corinth. There Jason's wandering eye and his desire to secure both his own safety and that of Medea and their sons led him to contract a marriage with King Creon's daughter. Medea, however, failed to understand the benefit of this politically motivated union. She was exclusively motivated by her love for Jason, for whom she had become both a traitoress and a murderess. His infidelity transformed her feelings into hatred and a desire for revenge.

It is at this point in the story that Euripides' TRAGEDY begins. Medea's nurse appears on stage alone, bemoaning the situation in which Medea finds herself. An attendant leads Medea's boys onto the stage. The attendant shares gossip with the nurse: Creon means to drive Medea and her children from Corinth. The nurse advises the attendant to keep the children away from their mother in "her evil hour." She says she has seen Medea eyeing the children "savagely."

The audience then meets Medea, chanting and cursing all the family: Jason, the children, and herself. Medea prays that Zeus and the Titaness Themis, probably in her character as the mother of the Fates, will achieve the destruction of Jason and his bride.

Next Medea addresses the members of the CHORUS in their role as citizens and airs her grievances before them. They sympathize with her. Then Creon enters and banishes Medea, her children, and her "sullen looks and angry thoughts" from Corinth.

Medea pleads that Creon has misjudged her and that, though she indeed hates her husband, she bears Creon and his daughter no ill will. She begs to be allowed to remain. Unconvinced of her sincerity, Creon refuses to yield and bids her to be gone. She begs for a single day to prepare for her exile. Creon grants her request but threatens her death if the next sunrise finds her in the city. Dark foreshadowings of death and destruction lie buried in this exchange, for the reprieve has given Medea sufficient time to accomplish her ends, and she gloats about her triumph over Creon.

Jason enters and criticizes Medea for bringing about her own banishment through her threatening demeanor. He says he means to provide for her and her sons. She reminds him of everything she has sacrificed for him, and berates him for deserting her. He responds with a speech that condemns women for valuing their marriages above all else and regrets that women are necessary to childbearing.

The chorus judges that he has spoken unwisely and has betrayed his wife. Medea's argument that, had he really been concerned about her, he would have sought her approval for his new match before making it, undermines any lingering credibility his sophistry might enjoy. He next tries to buy her off, but she refuses to accept his support.

Aegeus, the king of Athens, next enters and greets Medea. She tells him her situation and begs to be allowed to come in exile to his city. He agrees to receive her there provided she can get there without his help. He does not wish to incur the enmity of the Thebans. She binds him with an oath by the earth, by Zeus, and by all the race of the gods that he will not give her up nor throw her out if she can reach Athens safely.

Having thus guaranteed her own preservation with Aegeus's binding oath, she lays her plans for vengeance: She will send Jason's new bride a poisoned robe and headdress that, when she dons them, will kill her and anyone who touches her. She will next murder her own children, and then escape. "Let no one," she says, "think me a poor, weak woman."

Medea sets her scheme in motion. First she summons Jason and apologizes for her earlier words, saying that she has seen the wisdom in his actions. She tells her children to bid their father farewell. As Jason tells his sons he hopes to see them grown up and happy, Medea breaks into tears. When Jason asks why, however, she dissembles. She asks him to plead with Creon that the children may remain though she must leave. Jason agrees to ask.

Medea then gives the children the poisoned gifts to present to the new bride, and waits while they enter the palace with their father. An attendant brings back the children with the news that their exile has been remitted.

Medea wavers in her resolve to murder her own children, but her anger overcomes her compassion, and she sends the children into the house before her. They return, and she embraces and kisses them. This scene is one of the great portrayals of inner conflict in all the history of theater. She enters the house with them again, and, after a brief choral interlude, she returns alone.

A messenger runs on stage instructing her to flee. She asks why. Both the bride and Creon her father have succumbed to the poisoned garments. The messenger graphically details the scene of their horrible deaths, observing the convention that deaths in Greek tragedy do not occur on stage.

Once more Medea enters the house. The voices of the children are heard from within as they try to escape their mother's murderous blows. Jason belatedly arrives, hoping to save the children from their distraught mother. As he enters the house, Medea with the corpses of the children appears above the house in a chariot drawn through the sky by dragons.

Jason and Medea end the play with a lengthy exchange of recriminations—each blaming the other for the appalling outcome. He tries to curse her, but she says that no god will listen to a breaker of oaths. Finally the dragon chariot flies away, leaving Jason wishing he had never sired the children. The chorus ends the tragedy with an observation on the god's power to dispense variety of unanticipated fates.

Anyone who ever saw the great 20th-century Australian tragic actress Dame Judith Anderson depict Medea will have a visceral understanding of Aristotle's concept of catharsis—an audience's emotional cleansing as the result of viewing tragedy that somehow leads to the viewers' moral edification.

Bibliography

Euripides. *Medea. Greek Tragedy: Sophocles, Antigone; Euripides Medea and Bacchae.* Translated by Marianne McDonald et al. London: Nick Hern Books, 2005.

——. *Medea. Three Tragedies of Euripides.* Translated by Paul Roche. New York: Mentor, 1973.

Medea Seneca (before 53 C.E.)

In his version of *Medea*, Seneca follows quite closely Euripides' earlier Greek form of the play. Differences, however, do emerge. For example, Euripides generally enlists the audience's sympathies on the side of Medea against an opportunistic and unfeeling Jason. Seneca instead makes modifications that shift those sympathies in the direction of Jason.

In both plays, Medea has betrayed her father and murdered her brother to help Jason obtain the Golden Fleece that was the object of his voyage with the Argonauts (see *The Argonautika*). In both plays, she has married Jason and is the mother of his children, and in both Jason casts her off to marry Creusa, the daughter of Creon, the ruler of Corinth. In both versions, too, Jason excuses his action by explaining to Medea that he takes it to insure her welfare and that of the children.

That argument is less credible in Euripides' version than in Seneca's because in Euripides, Medea and the children must suffer exile. Seneca keeps them in Corinth, where Jason can at least exercise some fatherly responsibilities.

Seneca lays heavier emphasis than Euripides on Medea's mastery of witchcraft—a shift that tends to dehumanize the play's title character. In handling the choral commentaries on the events taking place, Euripides has the citizens of Corinth sympathize with Medea. Seneca has them favor Jason. One of the English translators of the Senecan version, Frank Justus Miller, suggests that Seneca's interest focuses less on "human suffering" and more on the title character as representative of "criminal psychology."

In both plays, Medea's vengeance is terrible. Not only does she murder her own children, she also inflicts painful deaths by means of a poisoned garment upon her rival, Creusa, and on Creusa's father, Creon. Seneca also stresses that Medea does not believe the loss of her husband's new intended bride will be adequate punishment for the suffering Jason has caused Medea. Jason's love has been the center of her being. Given that his feelings for Medea have proved to be so slight, only the deaths of his children can compensate the pain that his infidelity has caused her.

As is the case with Seneca's other tragedies, we do not know whether or not they were ever publicly performed, or indeed if they were intended to be. They may instead have been meant only for private reading alone or in small groups.

Bibliography

Miller, Frank Justus, trans. *Medea*. In *The Complete Roman Drama*. Vol. 2. Edited by George E. Duckworth. New York: Random House, 1942.

Seneca. *Hercules; Trojan Women; Phoenician Women; Medea; Phaedra*. Edited and Translated by John G. Fitch. Cambridge, Mass.: Harvard University Press, 2002.

Meditations Marcus Aurelius (ca. 177–189 C.E.)

While the Roman emperor MARCUS AURELIUS was leading his forces against Germanic tribes in the vicinity of the Danube River during the last 12 years of his life, he seized the opportunities afforded by breaks in hostilities to compose a work he intended to be a private reflection on his life. He wrote it in the Greek language and entitled it merely "To himself." He died in camp on the return journey from those wars, and some member of his party had the good sense to preserve the emperor's manuscript. It was subsequently published, becoming an instant classic and remaining so through the ages.

The work reveals that, although Marcus Aurelius's private views, moderate behavior, and unwavering virtue were grounded in the Stoic tradition, he did not always hew to the rational empiricism that characterized the thinking of STOICISM's mainstream thinkers. At Athens, Marcus Aurelius had been admitted to the Eleusinian mysteries associated with the worship of the new god, Dionysus, and of the goddesses Demeter and Kore. Suggestions do appear in the *Meditations* that he believed in a personal god. Though the emperor was clearly not a Christian, Christians through the centuries have nevertheless found his work congenial and even inspirational.

Marcus Aurelius begins his *Meditations* with a catalogue of his relatives and teachers and what he learned from each of them. From his grandfather, Verus, he learned good morals and how to control his temper. From the reputation of his deceased father and memories of him, Marcus learned "modesty and manly character." From his great-grandfather, he learned to value private education at home. He also learned from his private teacher to avoid such enthusiasms of the crowd as being a fan of a particular team of chariot racers. He learned to do physical labor, to mind his own business, and not to listen to slander.

From his teacher Diognetus, Marcus learned to disbelieve reports of miracles, exorcisms, and the like, and to avoid passionate attachments to games, contests, and gambling. He also learned to prefer simple living to luxury.

Marcus Aurelius devotes his lengthiest description to the things he learned from his true uncle and adoptive father, the Roman emperor Titus. Titus was modest, considering himself simply another citizen; he repressed lascivious appetites, was affable and courteous, and understood his own limitations of intellect and learning. Despite the pressures of his position, he took the time to study issues before making decisions.

A section of similar length details Marcus Aurelius's indebtedness to the gods. He is grateful that circumstances never led him to offend them, that he deferred sexual activity until the time was proper, and that both his father and his uncle were models of modesty whom he could emulate. He is grateful that his mother, who died young, nevertheless spent her last years in his company. He is grateful for the character and behavior of his wife and happy that he has been fortunate in finding good schoolmasters for his children. Finally, he is glad that he avoided the pitfalls of the sorts of education most Romans had: studying at the hands of SOPHISTS, reading history, constructing syllogisms, and learning astrology.

In Book 2, Marcus Aurelius gives himself 17 good pieces of advice for the conduct of what is left of his life. He knows that every day he will face a series of people whom he would rather avoid: the busybodies, the arrogant, the ungrateful, the deceitful, and so forth. He advises himself to bear with them patiently since they can do him no harm and observes a point he frequently repeats: People are made for cooperation.

Marcus reminds himself that he is old and need not let his time be wasted. What the gods send him is providential, and what chance sends is part of nature. He reminds himself to be grateful to the gods for what they have afforded him. The gods have afforded him a single opportunity—his life—for cogent action. He must make the best use of it. Several of his personal maxims remind him of the brevity of life and, especially, the life remaining to him. He also considers the brevity, regarded from the point of view of eternity, of all things. He recalls that he is a part of nature and that, as such, he must consider the relation of the part to the whole.

Marcus concludes that offenses committed from desire are worse than those committed from anger. Each individual must seek the "daemon"—the divine spark or spirit within each person—and strive, as SOCRATES did, to live according to its promptings. He considers that allowing oneself to feel vexed at anything that happens is an aberration of nature. Every act of the soul, he says, must be directed to some worthy end. Otherwise a person wastes the power of reason. He also concludes that nothing natural is evil.

Marcus Aurelius's third book of meditations begins from that conclusion. He lists a number of such unpleasant things as overripe figs, animal saliva, and ill-favored old people. He concludes that all should be considered natural and therefore comely. A person's conversation should reveal a simple and benevolent character. Everyone should remember that every "rational animal"—every human being—is one's kinsman. All should therefore labor in the common interest.

Marcus is convinced that the deity infused into each person will reveal that "justice, truth, temperance, fortitude, [and] right reason" are life's highest values. Nothing, he insists, is profitable if it involves breaking a promise. Doing so will cost one one's self-respect. However long posterity recalls a person, on the scale of eternity, that time is brief. Self-respect is the only important aspect of one's reputation.

Happiness results from performing the task at hand conscientiously, following right reason "seriously, diligently, calmly," and without distraction, and keeping one's "divine part" pure. Live, he advises, according to a fixed set of principles, for they have their origin in intelligence, not in appetite.

Book 4 calls for purposeful action. It advises that one's own mind rather than, say, a seashore villa, should be one's retreat. In that retreat, one should regard oneself as an individual, a human being, a citizen, and a mortal. One should also recall that "the universe is transformation, [and] life is opinion." Over and over again, Marcus Aurelius reverts to the advice to follow reason and to live in tranquility whatever happens.

A particularly revealing bit of wisdom to those interested in Marcus Aurelius's cosmological views occurs here. He counsels regarding the universe as "one living being" with a single substance and a single soul. As for the self, the emperor recommends: "Observe how worthless human things are." Today's mummy or urn of ashes was yesterday's speck of semen. Regard life as valueless.

The fifth book offers comfort to people of ordinary capacities. All of us can display sincerity, gravity, and endurance. We can be content in our circumstances, lead simple lives, and be benevolent and frank.

Marcus Aurelius suggests that the only appropriate prayer is a prayer for rain. It should be addressed to Zeus, by whom the emperor means the universe itself. From remark after remark, it is clear that the emperor considers seeking one's own pleasure both a snare and a delusion. He also enunciates a principle that all politicians everywhere should take to heart: "To seek what is impossible is madness."

Reverence is the proper attitude both toward the universe and toward what is best in oneself. As a ruler, Marcus Aurelius's guiding precept is this: What does the state no harm does not harm the citizen. If the state is harmed, repress anger and show the perpetrator his error. This advice appears again in Book 6 in another form: "The best way of avenging yourself is not to become like the wrongdoer." This precept appears a very hard one for polities to learn.

In Book 6, too, appears Marcus Aurelius's affirmation of faith. He considers that the universe must be one of two things. Either it is a disparate and involuted confusion—in which case he would not choose to remain in it—or it is, as he believes, unified, orderly, and provident. That being the case, Marcus Aurelius committedly worships and trusts the universe with its processes of bringing into and ushering out of existence. The universe that both creates and destroys is God (and the gods). People should be content with its processes as they find them.

Book 7 list 75 principles for and examples of governing one's thoughts, defining certain precepts, and conducting one's life. For instance,

Marcus Aurelius defines the perfection of moral character as living as if every day were one's last, remaining calmly interested in things, and not being hypocritical. In an interesting development of the idea of Providence developed in Book 6, Marcus Aurelius points out that current affairs are the consequence of unbreakable chains of cause and effect as the means by which the universe carries out that which it originally provided for.

For 23 years during the reign of his uncle Titus, while Marcus Aurelius was essentially in training to be emperor, Marcus studied philosophy at the same time that he occupied a series of important civic and imperial offices. He opens Book 7 with the reflection that the chains of cause and effect that he mentioned in Book 6 as the means by which Providence operates should console him for his loss of the opportunity ever to become a philosopher. He advises himself to accept that consolation and get on with the rest of his life. At the same time, he suggests that for every action a person contemplates taking, that person should consider whether or not taking the action would produce regrets. It is a person's duty, he reminds us, to live life well in every single act.

About wealth and prosperity, the emperor says, receive it without arrogance, and do not be afraid to let it go. He repeats in Book 8 his often-repeated opinion that striving after posthumous fame is folly. Many a poet, both before him and since, has so striven. As Marcus Aurelius ends Book 8, he offers, not for the first time, a sage bit of advice: "Men exist for the sake of one another. Teach them . . . or bear with them."

Book 9 opens with a syllogistic argument proving that people are guilty of impiety if they lie knowingly or if they pursue pleasure as a good and avoid pain as an evil. At several points throughout the work and again here, Marcus Aurelius develops the theory of the ruling faculty. Each person has one and it behooves each person to identify and develop it in socially beneficial ways. Here too, the emperor emphasizes once more the human responsibility for trying to reform rather than punish the aberrant behavior of fellow human beings.

Marcus Aurelius addresses Book 10 to his soul. It reviews much that has gone before, advising people to persist in behavior that is at once rational, true, good, modest, equable, and magnanimous. Though he himself has always had to be a man both of action and contemplation, he finds the contemplative way the more morally profitable of the two. Yet the rational person will be contemplative and active simultaneously and also will be reconciled to the inevitable operations of the natural world. We are all impelled by certain necessities. It is best to rest easy with them.

Book 11 contrasts the rational person's readiness to die with the Christian's desire for martyrdom. That desire, thinks the emperor, is mere obstinacy exercised against civic authority. Here too, Marcus Aurelius traces in brief the history of Greek theater with a view to revealing that, although much good was said and although the theater did please and, less often, instruct, the theater does not keep in mind the purposes for which human beings exist as philosophy does. No art, he reminds the reader, is superior to nature. Every person will find in his or her own soul the resources necessary to live in the best way. He ends the book with another list of sayings useful to recall in the project of living a good life.

Book 12 presents a grand summary of all that has gone before, once more emphasizing the emperor's advice to himself on the conduct of a good, even exemplary, life. Marcus Aurelius also raises a question that has concerned innumerable persons in all times and places. He wonders how it can be that the gods have apparently arranged matters so benevolently for human beings and yet have made no provision for the best people to live again. He concludes that whichever way that may be, it is right that it is that way. The grammar of his sentences, however, couched in clauses describing conditions contrary to fact, suggests that reincarnation or the survival of any egocentric essence is not something that the emperor feels to be terribly likely. Following the emperor's advice and hav-

ing no fear of the cessation of life seems to him by far the best road to follow.

Many consider that Marcus Aurelius was the best emperor Rome ever had. His modest and principled exercise of executive power could well serve as the standard against which to measure the success of decision makers in politics and business.

Bibliography

Marcus Aurelius. *The Communings with Himself of Marcus Aurelius Antoninus, Emperor of Rome, Together with his Speeches and Sayings.* Translated by C. R. Haines. New York: G. P. Putnam's Sons, 1930.

———. *Meditations.* Mineola, N.Y.: Dover Publications, 1997.

Mei Sheng   See SEVEN INCITEMENTS.

Meleager of Gadara (Meleagros) (fl. 100 B.C.E.) *Greek-Syrian poet*

Syrian by birth, Meleager was born in the city of Gadara. Later he lived both in Tyre and in Cos. He was a philosopher, a satirist, a poet, and a master of Greek and Phoenician as well as of his native Syrian.

Literature principally remembers Meleager for a work that inspired many imitators well into the modern era. He collected EPIGRAMS written by predecessor poets of the previous two centuries. To each of the poets represented, Meleager gave the name of a different flower—hence the title of the collection: the *Garland,* or in Greek, *Anthologia* (*Anthology*). The subjects of the epigrams, and of Meleager's own poems as well, included love, wine, death, and, sometimes, satirical characterization. For an example of the latter, one of Meleager's poems features a love triangle. One of its members is a Jew. He becomes an object of satire because his love does not cool down so he can properly observe the Sabbath.

Meleager artfully arranges the poems in his anthology, linking them by theme into an attractive verse bouquet. His innovation in presenting a poetic collection in this fashion was widely imitated during the European Renaissance and continues in vogue today, not only for verse but for many sorts of collections.

Meleager's own poetic works were largely autobiographical and principally included both hetero- and homosexual love poems. These were marked by a gift for apt, colorful imagery, and innovative expression. He also penned now lost SATIRES in the manner of Cynic philosopher, Menippus.

Bibliography

Cameron, Alan. *The Greek Anthology from Meleager to Planudes.* New York: Oxford University Press, 1993.

Lightfoot, Jane L. "Sophisticates and Solecisms: Greek Literature after the Classical Period." In *Literature in the Greek and Roman Worlds: A New Perspective.* Edited by Oliver Taplin. New York: Oxford University Press, 2000.

Meleager. *The Poems.* Translated and edited by Jeremy Clack. Wauconda, Ill.: Bolchazy-Carducci Publications, 1992.

Menander (ca. 342–292 B.C.E.) *Greek dramatist*

Famed and emulated as a comic playwright following his death, Menander's reputation did not fare as well during his lifetime. The most celebrated writer of the Greek New Comedy (see COMEDY IN GREECE AND ROME), he is thought to have composed around 100 plays. Only one of Menander's verse dramas, *DYSKOLOS (The Bad Tempered Man)*, survives in its entirety, having been discovered in Geneva in 1957. Beyond this, substantial sections of four plays were discovered at OXYRHYNCHUS in a 1328-line, fragmentary Egyptian papyrus early in the 20th century. These fragments include portions of *THE WOMAN FROM SAMOS* and *THE ARBITRATION*—the most complete of the fragments; *The Girl with Her Hair Cut Short*; and *The Hero.*

A much greater selection of Menander's work survived, of course, in antiquity, and subsequent playwrights admired and imitated his plays. The Roman essayist and rhetorician QUINTILIAN considered Menander the most important playwright among the Greek new comedians and also admired his mastery of rhetoric. The Roman playwrights PLAUTUS and TERENCE paid him the highest of compliments by imitating and borrowing his work. Renaissance playwrights in turn borrowed the Romans' work, so that, at one remove, the work of Menander remained influential in the early modern world.

Owing to later commentary and to the recycling of Menander's material by later writers, we know quite a lot about the sorts of plays he wrote. The literary historian T. B. L. Webster, who has reconstructed several of the plays in outline, divides Menander's subjects into three sorts of plays: "plays of reconciliation," "plays of social criticism," and "plays of adventure and satire." Menander's most recent editor, W. Geoffrey Arnott, offers reconstructions of his plays, both complete and fragmentary, filling three volumes.

Some of the plots Menander popularized remain the standard fare of popular entertainment to this day. Readers will find them familiar: A young woman becomes pregnant by means of seduction or rape. She bears a child whom she abandons or who is taken from her, but she always leaves the child with a memento by which the child is later identified. Often, the child's parents are reunited and eventually marry.

Stock characters also populate Menander's plays: cross and interfering parents; tricky, grasping servants; go-betweens; and prostitutes with hearts of gold. Yet while they conform to such types, Menander's characters nonetheless seem more individualized than their descendants, the stock characters of the Roman and Renaissance stages. Webster, who has closely studied the remnants in Greek, posits that Menander's stock characters are more differentiated from play to play than are those of his successors.

A friend and military companion of the philosopher EPICURUS, Menander had studied as a youth with THEOPHRASTUS OF ERESUS, the philosopher, scientist, and stylist who succeeded

ARISTOTLE as the leader of the PERIPATETIC (ARISTOTELIAN) SCHOOL OF PHILOSOPHY.

Menander is said to have met his death by drowning in the harbor at Pireus near Athens.

Bibliography

Arnott, Geoffrey w., ed. and trans. *Menander.* 3 vols. Cambridge, Mass: Harvard University Press, 1996 and 2000.

Webster, T. B. L. *Studies in Menander.* Manchester, U.K.: Manchester University Press, 1960.

Mencius (Meng K'o, Meng-tzu) (ca. 371–ca. 289 B.C.E.)

Mencius was a native of the Chinese state of Tsau (now Shantung) and connected with a noble family of CONFUCIUS's neighboring home state, Lu. As it has done with the name of Confucius, the West has considered Mencius important enough to Latinize his Chinese name, which simply means "Master Meng."

Apparently Mencius's father died when his son was very young, and Mencius's mother was at pains to support him and secure him an education commensurate with his evident capacities. Two or three stories purport to recount incidents from Mencius's childhood, but all have the ring of apocrypha about them. The tradition that he studied with Confucian scholars at a remove of about 115–120 years after the master's death, on the other hand, seems altogether probable, and Mencius himself reports that he studied with scholars in the line of Confucius's disciples. It seems likely that Mencius became a professor of moral philosophy. At about the age of 45, Mencius became an official of the state of Qi. But when its sovereign, Prince Hsuan, refused to implement Mencius's policies, he resigned his post.

Then there followed a period of wandering from state to state in search of rulers willing to put his humanistic Confucian ideals into practice. The time, however, was not ripe for the exercise of the gentler virtues, for military strife was everywhere. Eventually, around 319, he returned to Qi and resumed his former post. In 311 B.C.E., he retired. Though Mencius then disappears from the biographical record, the literary historian Herbert A. Giles credibly speculates that the sage spent the rest of his life teaching and, with the assistance of his students, beginning the work that they completed—the one by which history remembers him, *The Mencius*—an elaboration of Confucian humanistic idealism.

Mencius did not acquire his stature as the last of the ancient sages until the rise of neo-Confucianism some centuries after his death. Mencius was distinguished among Confucian philosophers by his firm belief in the innate goodness of human beings and in a human instinct to do the right thing.

Bibliography

Ildema, Wilt, and Lloyd Haft. *A Guide to Chinese Literature.* Ann Arbor: Center for Chinese Studies, University of Michigan, 1997.

Legge, James, ed. and trans. *The Works of Mencius.* New York: Dover Publications, 1970.

Mair, Victor H., ed. *The Columbia History of Chinese Literature.* New York: Columbia University Press, 2001.

Menippus of Gadara, Menippean Satire   See CYNICISM; SATIRE IN GREECE AND ROME; VARRO, MARCUS TERENTIUS.

Merchant, The (The Entrepreneur, Mercator) Plautus (second–third century B.C.E.)

In the prologue to the play, a young Athenian named Charinus shares with the audience that PLAUTUS based his play on a Greek original, the now-lost *Emporous* by PHILEMON. That citation made, Charinus goes on to indicate that, to please his father, Charinus left his lecherous ways at Athens and went off on a successful trading voyage to Rhodes. There, with money in his pocket and time on his hands, he went to a party, met and slept with a girl, and brought her home with him to Athens, where he has just arrived. Not yet ready for his father to know the truth, he has left the girl aboard ship with his slave Acanthio. As the prologue ends, Charinus sees Acanthio running toward him from the harbor. After much slapstick joking, Charinus reports that his father, Demipho, has boarded the ship and seen the girl. Acanthio had reported that Charinus bought the girl to be his mother's maid, and, besotted with the girl's beauty, Demipho started making passes at her.

The second act begins with Demipho's soliloquy. He first reports a strange dream of goats and monkeys—symbols of lust—from the night before. Then he confesses that he has fallen head over heels in love with the girl his son has brought home.

In the next scene, Demipho reports his condition to his neighbor, Lysimachus. Then Demipho turns his attention to finding a way to convince his son to sell the girl to him. Demipho sees Charinus coming and hides. Charinus soliloquizes for the audience as he racks his brain for a way out of his dilemma.

As matters develop, father and son end up bidding against each other for the girl, whom they agree would not work out well as a maid for Charinus's mother. In the event, the father exercises parental authority to trump both Charinus's bids and his arguments, and plans to have his friend Lysimachus, buy the girl on his behalf.

Now Charinus's friend, Eutychus the son of Lysimachus, shows up. He reminds Charinus that he already knows about the girl, and offers to go bid against Demipho for her. He promises to offer a hundred pounds more than Demipho's top figure.

As act 3 opens, however, we discover that Lysimachus has already purchased the girl, Pasicompsa, for Demipho and is leading her home. He explains that he has bought her for her own master, and she assumes he means Charinus. She confesses that they have already been together for two years. Lysimachus thinks she is speaking of Demipho. Leaving the girl at his house, Lysimachus encounters Demipho and convinces him he had better spruce up before going to see the

girl. Lysimachus also tells Demipho that he must get the girl out of his house before Lysimachus's wife comes home from the country.

In the fourth scene, Eutychus confesses to Charinus that the girl was auctioned off before he even got to the harbor. In desperation, Charinus decides to run away. Eutychus undertakes to find the girl.

Predictably, in act 4, Lysimachus's wife Dorippa and her slave Syra return from the country a day early and discover the girl in the house. Dorippa jumps to the obvious conclusion. Lysimachus cannot tell her the truth, and the spouses end the third scene in total misunderstanding. To add to the confusion, a cook whom Charinus and Lysimachus have hired to prepare a banquet now arrives with his entourage. Lysimachus tries to get rid of him, but the cook thinks that Dorippa is the new mistress. He quotes Lysimachus as having said that his wife is as "mean as a snake." Dorippa sends Syra to tell her father what a lecher Lysimachus has become. The father is not at home, and Syra encounters Eutychus instead. She explains that his father has brought home a girlfriend.

As act 5 opens, Charinus is bidding a melodramatic farewell to Athens when Eutychus finds him and explains that all will be well. Much addled misunderstanding by an apparently frenzied Charinus follows, but finally he settles down and accompanies Eutychus. In a brief third scene between the fathers, Demipho promises to make peace between Lysimachus and Dorippa, who has already understood the imbroglio. In the fourth, Lysimachus discovers that his wife is pacified, and Eutychus lectures Demipho for pursuing his son's girlfriend. That relationship is news to Demipho. Lysimachus further instructs Demipho about the inappropriateness of youthful passion in "autumnal men." Demipho gives Pasicompsa to his son and swears off lechery. Eutychus speaks an epilogue in which he proposes that men past 60 be exposed to public ridicule if they resume wenching, and the play ends.

Plautus's amusing comedy provides an example of the playwright's fascination with doubling:

two young men, two old men, two wives, and two slaves, all nincompoops and all caught in a maelstrom of laughable improbabilities whirling around one young woman.

Bibliography

Plautus. *The Entrepreneur* [*Mercator*]. Translated by George Garrett. In *Plautus: The Comedies.* Vol. 2. Edited by David R. Slavitt and Palmer Bovie. Baltimore and London: Johns Hopkins University Press, 1995.

Mesoamerican writing, ancient

Just how long true writing existed among the ancient cultures of Mesoamerica is unclear. Nonetheless, what researchers have been able to decipher about the Mesoamericans' astronomical observations suggest that some form of records keeping was practiced for millennia.

The oldest examples of true writing have been discovered on stones, pottery, and bark manuscripts in Oaxaca, on the Mexican gulf coast, and the Pacific Piedmont and highlands of Guatemala. These examples have been reliably dated to between 500 B.C.E. and 150 C.E. Though none of these ancient Mesoamerican scripts has been completely deciphered, the portions that have been suggest that the written symbols sometimes stood for entire words (logographs) and sometimes for syllables (syllabic script).

Insofar as the scripts have been read, it appears that, at a historic period contemporaneous with the flourishing of ancient Greek, Roman, and Chinese literary culture, the peoples of Mesoamerica had parallel manuscript cultures of their own. The linguistic historian Martha J. Macri suggests that every written language, such as Mayan or Zapotec, had signs representing the words for *paper*, *book*, *scribe*, and *writing*.

Bibliography

Macri, Martha J. "Logographic/syllabic Scripts: Maya Writing," and "Codified pictorial Systems." In *The World's Writing Systems.* New York: Oxford University Press: 1996.

Metamorphoses Apuleius   See GOLDEN ASS, THE.

Metamorphoses Ovid (ca. 8 C.E.)

Finished after the emperor AUGUSTUS CAESAR had exiled OVID from Rome to the city of Tomi on the Black Sea, the poet's *Metamorphoses* compose a work universally acknowledged to be his masterpiece. Both the poem's meter, dactylic hexameter (see QUANTITATIVE VERSE), and its length, 15 books, suggest that he cast the work in the EPIC mode—albeit the epic redefined, for *Metamorphoses* gave birth to an epic poem of a new sort. It takes a cue from Ovid's Greek predecessors of the HELLENISTIC AGE by bringing together a collection of supernatural transformations of shape. Looking even further back to such models as HESIOD'S THEOGONY, Ovid takes universal history and the changes that the gods have both wrought and undergone as his announced subject, and he establishes in his readers the expectation that the poem will proceed chronologically from the Creation until the poet's own time. That expectation, however, the poet soon and delightfully disappoints by, without altogether deserting chronology, changing the organizational principle into one arising from thematic correspondence and emotional effect. The poem achieves this by taking its readers through a compendium of the central myths of Greece and Rome.

Prologue

Moved to sing of bodies transformed into new and wondrous forms, instead of the traditional invocation of the Muses, Ovid instead invokes the immortal gods and shifts into a vision of primordial chaos—a sunless, formless, seething mass. Then, says Ovid, in the primal metamorphosis, either God or nature imposed order on the world, making it into a habitable and pleasant environment for creatures. That done, the stars spangled the heavens, and sentient life of all sorts was created. Then, wondering whether human beings were created by the Unknown God from divine seed or whether, as Greek myth had it, Prometheus shaped them from the soil of the newly created world, Ovid reports: "Shapeless clay put on the form of man."

Next Ovid describes the four ages of human habitation of the earth. First came the Golden Age, when justice ruled and weaponry and war were unknown, and when the earth produced sustenance for all without the intercession of human labor—when spring bloomed eternally, when rivers flowed with nectar, and oak trees brought forth honey. Saturn, the eldest of the gods, ruled that age.

But his successor, Jove, banished him and brought into being the Silver Age—one not quite so benign as the Golden Age. Spring became a brief season, and farming and husbandry with their accompanying need for human labor were introduced.

The Bronze Age followed. It saw the introduction of weaponry and warfare, but not of impious crimes. That development, says Ovid, was reserved for the Age of Iron, which also saw the development of private property, the mining of metals, impious war, rapacity, disrespect of the expectation of hospitality for strangers, and brother quarreling with brother. Filial piety, too, fell victim to the greed of children, and the goddess Astrea—the goddess of justice—"vanished from the blood-stained earth." The Age of Iron as the ancients envisioned it continues into our times.

Giants inhabited the earth in the early days of the Age of Iron, and in their pride and ferocity, they made war on the Olympian gods, piling up mountains to gain access to the gods' dwelling place. Jove, however, overcame the giants with thunderbolts, destroying them. From their reeking blood the earth brought forth human beings.

One of these, Lycaeus, to test the divinity of Jove, offers him human flesh to eat—a myth that Ovid first expects his reader to know but that he nonetheless repeats a little later. Incensed, Jove convenes a council of the gods, who unanimously call for revenge.

Now suddenly, Ovid's comparisons become anachronological. He compares the gods' call for vengeance against Lycaeus to the penalties that Ovid's contemporary, the Roman emperor Augustus, exacted for the assassination of his uncle, Julius Caesar. Jove reports that he has anticipated the gods' sentence, destroyed the dwelling of Lycaeus, and turned the man himself into a wolf.

Ovid next reports how Jove, incensed with the impiety of human beings, determined to destroy the world by flood. Amid the consequent universal carnage, however, Jove spots in the nick of time a single man and a single woman, praying and worshipping the gods. He causes the waters to recede and gives humankind another chance.

The remaining pair, Deucalion and Pyrrha, a brother and sister as well as husband and wife, despair of repopulating the earth in the ordinary course of nature. They therefore undertake a pilgrimage to consult the female TITAN and goddess Themis. Themis tells them to throw "the bones of their great mother" behind them as they walk along. The pair correctly interprets this to mean that they should throw rocks behind them as they walk. They do so, and the rocks Deucalion throws metamorphose into men; those thrown by Pyrrha transform into women, and so the breeding stock for the human repopulation of the world comes into being. The earth spontaneously repopulates itself with animals and insects and with a serpent so fearsome—a python—that the sun god, Phoebus Apollo, destroys it. In commemoration of that act, the Pythian games—athletic contests and horse races—were established.

Book 1

The mention of Apollo leads Ovid to an associative transition into the next instance of metamorphosis. Shot by a vengeful Cupid's golden arrow, the sun god, who, citing the python as an example, had boasted of the superior power of his arrows over Cupid's, falls in love with a nymph, Daphne—the daughter of a river god. To assure that Apollo suffers, Cupid then shoots Daphne with a leaden arrow—one that prevents her also falling in love.

When Apollo encounters Daphne, he pursues her, but she flees. Just as the god is about to catch her, Daphne prays to her father for protection, and on the spot he turns her into a laurel tree. For love of her, Apollo ordains that her immortal leaves become the victor's crown for athletes, military conquerors, Roman emperors, and artists in competition. So honored, the laurel tree, says Ovid, seems to nod to Apollo with answering love.

Ovid next recounts the story of Jove's love for another river god's daughter, the Naiad Io. When Io flees Jove's impassioned importunities, the god covers the earth with a cloud and ravishes Io. However, Juno (queen of the gods and Jove's sister and wife) surmises that such a cloud on an otherwise sunny day means that her husband is philandering—as he often does—and tries to catch him in the act. But Jove is equipped with almost perfect foreknowledge, and he changes Io into a snowy-white heifer. Juno expresses suspicions and asks about the heifer. Jove claims it was spontaneously generated from the earth, and Juno asks to have it as a gift. Jove agrees. Juno gives the heifer to the god Argos, who has a hundred eyes, to guard.

Io makes her identity known to her father, the river Inachus, by tracing her name on his banks with a hoof. Inachus understands and grieves at the disappointment of his hopes for Io's marriage and her children. Sympathetic to Io's plight, Jove sends Mercury to slay or deceive Argos.

Mercury enchants Argos by playing on reed pipes—a new art. Embedding a metamorphosis in the midst of another, Ovid has Mercury begin to recount the story of another Naiad, Syrinx, whom Pan had attempted to ravish. Made drowsy by the music and Mercury's verse, all of Argos's 100 eyes fall asleep at once, and Mercury seizes the opportunity to slay him by lopping off his head. For the benefit of his reader, Ovid finishes the story that Mercury interrupted, explaining how Syrinx was saved from Pan's embraces by being changed into the very reeds from which panpipes are fashioned.

Juno transplants the murdered Argos's eyes into the tails of the peacocks that draw her chariot as jeweled decorations. Then, venting her rage on the victim, she afflicts Io with a fury that goads her to wander the shores of the Mediterranean Sea and to cross the Bosporus Straits, which are named for her: "cow narrows." Eventually Io arrives in Egypt on the banks of the Nile, where, as well as she is able, she pleads for release from her transformation. A sympathetic Jove reconciles with Juno, who restores Io to her human shape. Because unions between gods and human beings are always fruitful, however, Io bears a son, the demigod Epaphus, and the Egyptians regard both as deities and build temples to them.

Book 2

Another coeval demigod, Phaeton, the son of Apollo the sun god, also inhabits Egypt at this time. In boasting of his parentage, Phaeton attracts the scorn of Epaphus, who needles Phaeton by requiring him to prove his paternity. Phaeton demands that his mother offer proofs of his lineage. She swears that Phaeton is Apollo's son and instructs him in the way to find his father. He immediately travels from his home in Ethiopia and through the Indies until he reaches the Land of Dawn.

There, in dazzling light, Phaeton stands in the presence of Apollo, who is attended by Day, Month, Year, Time, the Hours and the Seasons. Seeing his son, Phoebus Apollo addresses him as his "child beloved." When Phaeton pleads for a token of Apollo's parentage, with a mighty oath, Phoebus gives his son free choice. The foolish youth asked to be the sun's charioteer for a day.

Phoebus Apollo immediately regrets his rashness and tries to dissuade the mortal Phaeton from undertaking a task suited only for immortals, explaining that Apollo alone of gods or men has the capacity to do what Phaeton aspires to try. Apollo also explains the dangers that he daily faces. The god tries to convince his son that what he has wished for, if granted, will place him in mortal danger of an unimaginable sort.

Like many foolish youths, however, Phaeton will not be dissuaded, and he insists on driving the chariot of the sun. The horses that draw it, moreover, instantly know their master is not on board. They therefore take their own course, not the one over which Apollo regularly guides them.

As a result, disaster visits the earth. Cities, forests, and mountains are incinerated. The skins of Ethiopians darken with the heat. Rivers boil and run dry. The ground bursts open, letting light into Tartarus, the underworld of Greek mythology. Even the oceans dry up. Earth herself prays for relief from the devastation.

In response to the planet's prayer, Jove hurls one thunderbolt that incinerates Phaeton, who falls burning to earth like a comet. Jove hurls another bolt that extinguishes the fires destroying the earth.

Phaeton's charred and smoking remains fall into the Eridanus (Po) River of northern Italy. River nymphs collect them and bury them, marking his grave with a tombstone explaining who he was and what he tried to do. His mother Clymene and his sisters make a pilgrimage to the site of the tomb, and there as they mourn, Phaeton's sisters are metamorphosed into poplar trees.

Phaeton's father, too, is consumed by grief and almost decides to permanently deprive the world of light. The other gods, however, dissuade him with pleas, and in the case of Jove, with threats, from that course of action. The sun god vents his rage by beating his steeds into submission.

Jove, in the meantime, undertakes to assess and repair the damage that the sun's excessive heat caused in the heavens and on the earth. In the course of that journey, the ruler of the gods encounters the lovely nymph, Callisto, a devotee of the chaste goddess of the hunt, Diana. Finding Callisto asleep, Jove is once again moved to passion, and, careless of Juno's jealousy, he assumes the form of Diana and begins kissing Callisto. Once she realizes that her admirer is not Diana but a male, Callisto unavailingly struggles to free herself.

Having accomplished his desire, Jove flies off, and the real Diana comes. Callisto follows in Diana's train for nine months before her pregnancy is discovered. Then an angry Diana, who only allows herself the company of virgins, sends Callisto away. She has her baby, a boy she names Arcas.

Juno, in the meantime, has become aware of the situation and, true to form, vents her rage on Jove's victim, changing Callisto into a bear. At this point, Ovid lets his readers know that Callisto is a child of Lycaon, the wolf-man.

After 15 years have passed, Arcas, now a hunter, encounters his mother as a bear in the forest. Callisto recognizes her son and stands quietly while he Arcas prepares to spear her. In Ovid's version of the myth, however, Jove will not permit this matricide, and the god transforms both Callisto and Arcas into stars. She becomes the constellation Ursa Major, and he becomes Böotes. Stellification was the most glorious of all possible metamorphoses, for the stars and constellations were themselves thought to be deities.

Juno, of course, grows utterly enraged. She asks the TITANS, Oceanus and his consort Tethys, who rule the sea, to deny the stellified Callisto the privilege of bathing in the sea. They grant Juno's request, with the result that Callisto and Arcas never dip below the horizon in the northern hemisphere.

With another associational transition, Ovid considers a comparison between the tails of Juno's peacocks, now decorated with the eyes of Argos, and another metamorphosis that had turned the color of the originally white raven to black. This transformation occurred as the result of a raven, which had been Apollo's favored bird, becoming a tattletale.

In that story, the nymph Coronis of Larissa is the lover of Apollo and pregnant with his child. Hearing that she has been unfaithful to the god, the raven flies off to tattle and on the way tells a crow its news. The crow tries to warn the raven of the consequences of tattling, telling the story of her own transformation from a princess, also named Coronis, into a crow, and how she temporarily enjoyed the special protection of the goddess of Wisdom, Minerva, until that goddess replaced the crow with the owl—the metamorphosed former woman, Nictimene.

Not heeding the warning, the raven tells Apollo of Coronis's infidelity. Enraged, Apollo shoots Coronis with his bow and arrow. She confesses her fault, but asks why he could not wait until their child was born before killing her. Repenting too late of his rashness, Apollo tries to save Coronis. Failing, he saves the unborn child as Coronis lies upon her funeral pyre and gives the child, Aesclepius, to the centaur Chiron to be brought up. Apollo then punished the tattling raven by turning its plumes to black.

Chiron rears Aesclepius together with his own daughter, Ocyroë, a lovely prophetess. She predicts that Aesclepius, the archetypal physician, will bestow health upon the world and even have the power to raise the dead until he offends the gods with that power. Then he will be smitten into dust by a thunderbolt but will himself be raised from the dead to become a god. Continuing her prophecy, she predicts that the immortal Chiron, in agony from an envenomed arrow, will plead for death and that the gods will grant his prayer. Her prophecies, however, deprive her of human shape, and she becomes a mare.

In an associated instance of divine retribution, Ovid tells how Mercury, the messenger of the gods, spies Herse, a lovely, virginal devotee of the goddess of wisdom, Minerva. He approaches her co-worshipper, Aglauros, to help him win Herse's love. Aglauros agrees to help him for a substantial fee.

Minerva, however, is displeased at Aglauros's bargain and commands the allegorical figure Envy to instill her poison into Aglauros. Envy obeys, and Aglauros begins to suffer horribly at the thought of a happy liaison between her sister Herse and Mercury. When Mercury next comes to visit Herse, Aglauros attempts to renege on her bargain and bar his way. The angry god turns her into a statue—one black with envy's poison.

Book 3

Next follows the first in a series of tales organized around the house of the Phoenician Cadmus and the founding of the city of Thebes. Having changed himself into a bull for the purpose, Jupiter (Jove) kidnaps the lovely princess of Phoenicia, Europa, and bears her on his back across the sea. Distraught, her father, King Agenor, charges his son Cadmus, on pain of death, to recover his lost sister. With a body of armed men, Cadmus sets forth, but he never intends to return. Phoebus Apollo gives Cadmus a different set of orders. He must found a city in Boetia at the spot a heifer leads him to. At that place, however, the troops encounter a dreadful dragon that slays them all. Arriving last, Cadmus engages the dragon in battle. Under Minerva's protection, Cadmus prevails, and the goddess orders him to take the dead dragon's teeth and seed the ground wtih them. He does so, and armed warriors grow from the teeth.

As they spring forth, the warriors turn on one another and fight until only five remain alive. These become the companions of Cadmus in founding the city of Thebes. Cadmus rules happily until, in old age, he retires and then tragedy befalls his grandson, Acteon.

Acteon is a hunter, and one day in the forest he surprises the virginal goddess of the hunt, Diana, bathing naked with her attendant maidens. The goddess avenges her affronted modesty by changing Acteon into a stag. In that shape, he encounters his own pack of hunting dogs. Not recognizing their master, the dogs tear the metamorphosed Acteon to shreds in sight of his hunting companions, thus introducing a theme of dismemberment.

Juno, of course, ever angry with the victims of Jupiter's philandering and with their relatives, rejoices in the death of Europa's grandnephew. But Jupiter now turns his amorous attentions to Semele, a woman whom Ovid seems to have associated with the house of Cadmus, though why he did is uncertain.

Changing herself into the shape of Semele's nurse, Beroe, Juno counsels Semele to ask Jove (interchangeably called Jupiter in Roman mythology) to assume his own shape and to caress her in his godly form. Jupiter had promised Semele that he would grant her any request, and she fatally follows Juno's advice.

Jupiter sadly complies, revealing his true nature to her in the very mildest form of his essential thunder and lightning. Semele is instantly incinerated. Jupiter nonetheless manages to rescue his baby that was forming in Semele's womb. The god implants the embryo in his own thigh, from which, in due course, the god Bacchus—child of Jupiter and Semele—is born. The baby is hidden and nurtured by sea nymphs, including his aunt Ino, who had once been human but is now an immortal.

An interlude follows that introduces the blind prophet Teiresias. Unique among human beings, Teiresias had first been a man, then metamorphosed into a woman, then became a man once more. Jupiter and Juno appeal to Teiresias to settle their argument about whether men or women experience greater pleasure in lovemaking. When Teiresias agrees with Jupiter that women do, an incensed Juno blinds him. Jupiter, however, compensates Teiresias for his loss of physical vision by letting him know the future.

Following that transitional interlude, Ovid returns to tracing the metamorphic fortunes of the house of Cadmus, recounting the famous story of Narcissus and the nymph Echo.

Juno punishes Echo when the goddess discovers that the nymph had often detained Juno in idle conversation to allow Jupiter to make his getaway from philandering among the nymphs. Juno deprives Echo of the power of speech—except to repeat what another has said.

Later, Echo falls in love with the beautiful teenaged lad, Narcissus. Invisible to him, she has to wait until he speaks words that she can repeat that will express her feelings and inform him of her passion. Thinking he returns her feelings, she embraces him. Narcissus rejects her, and in her sorrow she dies. Her body wastes away to nothing, and her bones become stone, but her voice lives on among the hills, still echoing the words of others.

Narcissus continues to spurn both enamored maidens and love-struck youths until one of the latter prays that, if Narcissus ever loves, his love will be denied. The goddess Nemesis hears and grants the prayer.

In one of the most famous passages in Ovid's *Metamorphoses,* Narcissus gazes into a forest pool and falls in love with his own reflected image, which seems to return his his affection until he attempts to kiss and embrace it. Unable to embrace his beloved, Narcissus pines away, and Echo, present at the scene, repeats all his laments. At last, destroyed by unrequited love, Narcissus dies and his body is transmuted in the flower that bears his name.

Still tracing the mythical history of the descendants of Cadmus, Ovid next recounts the tale, also told by EURIPIDES in *The BACCHAE,* of the way that Pentheus—a descendant of Cadmus and of one of the five survivors of the dragon's teeth warriors—defied both the gods and Teiresias's gift of prophecy.

Teiresias predicts the arrival of a new god—Bacchus. The prophet warns Pentheus that, if he fails to erect a temple honoring the new deity, Pentheus's mother and her sisters will tear him to pieces.

When Bacchus appears and his devotees undertake the rites sacred to his worship, Pentheus tells his fellow Thebans that they are mad to believe such nonsense, and he orders his followers to arrest Bacchus as a prelude to debunking his divinity.

Unable to find the god, Pentheus's officers instead deliver a youth, Acoetes, who is a fisherman and a mariner and was among the first to recognize Bacchus as a deity. Acoetes tells how he took the youthful, half-intoxicated god aboard his ship. He also reports the way in which his doubting crew attempted to deceive Bacchus by rowing away from his announced destination of the Island of Naxos where he had been born. The mariners were amazed when their ship made no headway. Then Bacchus appeared to them in the glory of his deity, garlanded, armed, and surrounded by tigers, lynxes, and panthers. The deity changed the apostate sailors into sea creatures, and only Acoetes remained to take Bacchus ashore.

Unconvinced, Pentheus—after ordering Acoetes' imprisonment and execution—goes forth to quell the excesses of the worshippers of Bacchus who are practicing their rites in the woods and countryside. As Pentheus approaches the frenzied and intoxicated worshippers, his mother and his aunts (the first sisterly trio in a set) see him coming. To their sight, however, he appears to be a giant and dangerous boar, and, following the theme of dismemberment, they tear him to shreds and behead him.

Book 4

Ovid then continues his examples of the consequences of apostasy with the tale of how another trio of unbelievers—the daughters of King Mineus, women who worked while others worshipped—were changed into bats. But the poet now achieves variety by nesting the stories that the three daughters tell each other within that overarching account of the consequences of disbelief. The first daughter, unnamed in Ovid, recounts the famous story of Pyramus and Thisbe—forbidden lovers who live in adjacent houses and foil their unsympathetic parents by communicating through a chink in a wall.

Planning to elope, Pyramus and Thisbe agree to meet by night at the tomb of Ninus. Arriving first, Thisbe narrowly escapes a lioness whose jaws are still bloody after a kill. In fleeing, however, Thisbe loses her veil, and the lioness bloodies it with her jaws. Coming on the scene soon after, Pyramus finds the veil, assumes the worst, and stabs himself. Finding him dying, Thisbe prays that their parents will entomb the pair in a single sepulcher, and, falling on Pyramus's sword, follows him in death.

The second daughter, Leuconoe, tells the story, also recounted by HOMER in *The ODYSSEY*, of the way that Mars and Venus cheat Venus's husband, the lame blacksmith of the gods, Vulcan, and how, with a clever net, Vulcan catches the adulterous pair in bed.

Leuconoe then favors her sisters with a second tale that concerns Leucothea and Clytie—both beloved of Apollo, though Leucothea's beauty quenches Apollo's ardor for Clytie. So enamored of Leucothea does Apollo become that he drives the sun's chariot too early into the sky and lingers there too long, upsetting the natural order. At last, achieving his desire, Apollo consummates his passion for Leucothea, provoking Clytie's jealousy. She causes a scandal that reaches the ears of Leucothea's father, who punishes his daughter by burying her alive. Apollo tries but fails to resurrect her, and so instead he transmutes her corpse so that it becomes the frankincense plant. Apollo now disdains Clytie, who, always turning to view her beloved as he crosses the sky, metamorphoses into the heliotrope—the sunflower.

Feeling challenged to offer a tale that will produce pleasant thoughts, the third sister, Alcithoe, recounts the story of Hermaphroditus, son of the god Hermes. This youth chances upon a lazy, self-worshipping nymph named Salmacis. Seeing the youth, the nymph falls passionately in love with him and, after taking pains to look her best, proposes marriage to him. He rejects her. Salmacis hides and watches the boy bathe nude in the pool that she frequents. As he swims, she plunges in and embraces him. He resists, and she prays that he will never be allowed to escape her. Her prayer is granted, and the two are transformed into a single, bisexual creature. Hermaphroditus prays that the same fate will befall any man who enters the fountain of Salmacis, and the gods also grant his prayer.

Ovid now returns to the overarching plot into which he has embedded the sisters' tales. As they continue working at their weaving and ignore the feast of Bacchus, they hear the music of the celebrants approaching. As it does so, the girls' looms change into flourishing grapevines, and, as evening approaches, they themselves are transformed into bats.

Juno, however, is still nursing a grudge against Bacchus and his worshippers—especially against Ino, who nurtured Bacchus as a child, and against Ino's husband, Athamas. Juno therefore descends into the underworld to enlist the Furies as her agents of vengeance. The Fury of madness, Tisiphone, agrees to afflict Ino and

Athamas. Crazed, Athamas seizes his baby Learchus from Ino's arms and dismembers him by throwing him against rocks. Maddened herself, Ino takes her infant daughter, Melicerta, and leaps from a cliff into the sea. Pitying them however, Ino's grandmother, the goddess Venus, pleads with Neptune to immortalize them, and Neptune changes both into sea nymphs. Ino becomes the nymph Leucothea, who rescued Odysseus from the waves, and Melicerta becomes the nymph Palaemon.

Still venting her anger against the Bacchantes, Juno changes some of Ino's followers—all of them the offspring of Cadmus—into stone and others into seabirds.

Overwhelmed with the misfortunes his dynasty has endured, Cadmus goes into voluntary exile. As he grieves, he wonders if the dragon he slew long ago was sacred and the cause of all his troubles. If, he says, he is enduring the anger of the gods, then he prays he will himself be transformed into a serpent—a prayer the gods instantly grant. His wife prays for a similar transformation, and her prayer too is granted. They become a pair of serpents friendly to mankind, for they recall their human past.

Ovid next recounts the story of Perseus and Atlas. Seeking hospitality, the demigod Perseus, son of Jupiter, arrives at the dwelling of the giant Atlas after Perseus has slain the Gorgon, Medusa, and lopped off her snaky head. Atlas, fearful of a prophecy, disdains to welcome Perseus and tries to drive him off. Perseus unwraps the head of Medusa, which has the power to turn whoever gazes upon it into stone, and Atlas promptly metamorphoses into the mountain that still bears his name.

The poet follows that story with an account of the demigod Perseus's rescue of the maiden Andromeda, who has been chained to a rock as a sacrifice to a sea monster while her helpless parents cling to her and despair. Perseus asks to marry Andromeda, and when the parents assent, he slays the sea monster. Then, Ovid explains, Perseus turns seaweed into stone with Medusa's head. That original transformation explains why

coral—beginning as, Ovid thought, a sea plant—becomes stone when exposed to air.

At the nuptial celebrations between Perseus and Andromeda, Perseus tells the story of how he came to slay Medusa. He further explains how Minerva punished Medusa for being too proud of her hair by turning her beautiful locks to snakes.

Book 5

As Book 5 of the *Metamorphoses* begins, Andromeda's former fiancé, Phineas, interrupts the wedding feast, meaning to recover his intended bride by force of arms. A battle royal ensues that Ovid describes in the bloody manner of his predecessor epic poets. Eventually, Phineas and his allies corner Perseus. Until that moment, he has disdained to use his weapon of mass destruction, the Gorgon's head. To save himself, however, he does so now. All his enemies turn to stone except Phineas, who, true to form, looks away and begs for his life. Perseus, however, forces him to look upon Medusa's head, turning Phineas into a statue—a lasting monument to his cowardice. Ovid closes his account of Perseus's adventures with the metamorphosis into stone of King Polydectes—the person who, anticipating Perseus's death, had sent Perseus on his dangerous mission in the first place.

Minerva, goddess of wisdom, had been looking after her half-brother Perseus, but she now turns her attention to the nine MUSES, for the goddess wishes them to show her a new magic fountain that had been created by the stamping hoof of the winged horse, Pegasus.

As they entertain the goddess, the Muses tell how they escaped the forced attentions of the tyrant Pyraneus by flying away. When he attempted to follow them by leaping from a tower, he was killed. Next the Muses entertain their Olympian guest by explaining that the chattering magpies she hears were recently human women—the Emathian sisters—who had pridefully presumed to challenge the Muses to a contest. After the women had all competed, the muses nominated

Calliope, the Muse of epic poetry, to compete on their behalf.

Again nesting stories within stories, this time as part of a contest, Ovid has Calliope sing about the goddess of the harvest, Ceres, and her daughter, Proserpina, and the way that Pluto, the lord of the underworld, is struck by Cupid's arrow at Venus's behest, falls in love with Proserpina, and carries her off to the underworld. Venus wants to be sure that a third of the universe does not remain immune to the power of love.

The river nymph Cyane tries to persuade Pluto to ask Ceres for her Proserpina rather than ravish her, but Pluto turns Cyane into water for her pains. Ceres searches the world over for her daughter, at last finding her belt near the pool where Cyane had been transformed. Realizing that her daughter has been kidnapped, Ceres decides to withhold grain from the world and especially from the island of Sicily, where her daughter had been seized. However, another water nymph, Arethusa, a native of Pisa, gliding watery beneath the earth, has spotted Proserpina in the underworld, where she reigns as Pluto's queen consort. Arethusa reports her discovery to Ceres. She, in turn, complains to Jupiter. He objects that no injury has occurred since this was a deed of love. Nonetheless, he will release Proserpina from Hell if she has had nothing there to eat.

Proserpina, however, has eaten seven pomegranate seeds, observed by Ascalaphus, who tattles. She turns him into an owl. Zeus, trying to satisfy all parties, strikes a compromise. Proserpina will have to remain in Hades for six months of the year. The other six she can spend above ground with her mother.

Continuing her part in the contest, Calliope picks up on the story of Arethusa that she had introduced near the end of Proserpina's tale. She relates the story of Arethusa and Alpheus and the way that Arethusa became a sacred stream.

As the nymph Arethusa is swimming in the river Alpheus, its tutelary deity of the same name conceives a passion for her. She flees his forced embraces until, exhausted, she calls on Diana for help. Diana changes her into a stream, but Alpheus recognizes the waters as Arethusa and still seeks to encompass her waters with his own. The goddess has Arethusa sink into the ground and resurface as a stream on the island of Ortygia.

The focus shifts back now to Ceres. Mollified by the bargain, she begins to share her gifts with other parts of the world. She sends as her messenger Triptolemus, who, by traveling through the air, brings Ceres' gifts to Europe and Asia. When he arrives at Scythia in the northeastern region of Asia, his host, Lyncus, tries to murder Triptolemus in bed. Ceres saves her messenger by transmuting Lyncus into a lynx.

The nymphs who are acting as judges of the storytelling contest acclaim the Muses victors, and, as the challenging Emathian sisters complain, they are transformed into magpies.

Book 6

Continuing the theme of gods displeased by mortal presumption, Ovid opens Book 6 of the *Metamorphoses* with the story of the goddess Minerva's retribution against the pride of Arachne, who challenged the goddess to a weaving contest.

Minerva weaves, among others, scenes of the transformation of human beings into nonhuman forms—mountains or birds or even a temple. Arachne instead weaves scenes of sexual congress between gods and human beings. When both contestants have finished their labors, Minerva can find no fault in Arachne's weaving. Nonetheless, even though Arachne has at least equaled Minerva in weaving, for the woman's presumption in challenging an immortal, the goddess turns Arachne into a spider destined to dangle forever from a cord.

Though the story of Arachne's fate spreads to Phrygia, there another prideful but accomplished mortal, Niobe, a representative of the lineage of Cadmus, fails to heed the lesson and opposes the gods. Particularly, Niobe takes overweening pride in her children and in her own nobility and extraordinary beauty. She insists that people worhip her instead of the goddess Latona, mother of Apollo.

Latona complains of Niobe's impiety, and immediately Niobe's sons begin to fall dead, stricken by supernatural arrows shot principally by Apollo. Horrified, Niobe's husband Amphion commits suicide. Niobe curses Latona for venting her spleen on Latona's sons, and immediately Niobe's daughters also begin falling, until only one is left. Despite the now-chastened Niobe's pleas that her last child be spared, the little girl is also taken. The presumptuous queen finds herself transmuted into a marble fountain, weeping forever upon a mountaintop.

Hearing of these events, people begin to recall other and more ancient instances of Latona's vindictiveness. On one occasion, after the goddess had given birth to children and a group of rustic laborers denied her permission to drink at a pool, she changed them into frogs. Another time, the people remember, the satyr Marsyas wagered his life in a lyre-playing contest against the god Apollo and lost. As a result, Marsyas was transformed into a river.

Now Ovid focuses briefly on Niobe's brother, Pelops, whom the gods reassembled after his father had dismembered him. Finding a shoulder missing, the gods had supplied a substitute made of ivory.

There follows the tale of Tereus, king of Thrace, to whom an Athenian princess, Procne, is married. That marriage, however, proves to be cursed. After bearing her first child, Procne requests that her sister, Philomela, be permitted to visit her. Tereus accordingly sails to fetch his sister-in-law, but on first seeing her, he falls desperately in love.

Tereus's pleas on Procne's behalf finally overcome the resistance of the women's father, Pandion, and the king at last grants permission for the visit. Tereus sails with Philomela for Thrace and, on arriving there, imprisons her in an isolated dwelling and forces himself upon her. When she threatens to reveal her shame and tell everyone what has happened, Tereus cruelly cuts out her tongue. He then returns to Procne with a false tale of Philomela's death.

Philomela, however, cleverly weaves a tapestry that conveys the real story of Tereus's crimes and secretly sends it to her sister, who understands its message and resolves to avenge her husband's crimes. When the time comes to celebrate the rites of Bacchus, Procne, dressed as a bacchante, makes her way to Philomela's prison, disguises her sister as a celebrant, and sets her free. Then, acting together, the sisters exact a terrible vengeance. They murder and dismembered Tereus's child by Procne and feed his flesh to Tereus. When the king has dined, the women fling the child's head at him.

As Tereus pursues them with murderous intent, all three metamorphose into birds. Philomela becomes a nightingale, Procne a swallow, and Tereus a hoopoe. Learning of their fate, Pandion dies of grief at Athens. There, Erecthus succeeds him.

Considering that lineage, Ovid recounts the way that the North Wind, Boreas, fell in love with one of Erecthus's daughters, Orithyia. Despairing of winning her hand by diplomacy and entreaty, Boreas decides to gratify his desire by force since force is consonant with his nature. He therefore whisks Orithyia away to the far and frigid north, where she becomes the North Wind's bride and bears him two winged sons, Zetes and Calais, who, feathered like eagles, will later accompany Jason and his Argonauts on their quest for the Golden Fleece (see ARGONAUTIKA).

Book 7

The Argonaut association leads Ovid to think about Jason and Medea, and the poet opens book 7 with their story (see MEDEA). Ovid tells how Medea first resolves not to help Jason but, overcome with love, finally betrays her father and murders her brother to save Jason and run away with him to Greece as his wife. Protected by Medea's magic, Jason overcomes bulls made of brass and warriors from scattered dragons' teeth, sprinkles the guardian dragon with sleeping potion, and sails away both with the Golden Fleece and with Medea as his prizes.

Arriving home, the pair finds Jason's father, Aeson, depressed by the weight of his advancing years and the knowledge that he must soon die. Jason asks Medea to give his father some of Jason's own years through her magic arts. This she refuses to do, but she does agree to restore some of Aeson's lost years to him. Invoking the goddess of the moon in a marvelous incantation, she asks for transport to take her to the places where she can gather the herbs necessary to her magic. A dragon-drawn chariot takes her flying about the Mediterranean world as she collects what she needs. Then, in a complex ritual involving both black and white magic, she prepares the old man for the rejuvenating climax of her labors. Cutting his throat, she lets all his old blood run out and then refills his veins with the magical mixture she has prepared. When he awakes from his drugged slumbers, he is 40 years younger. Impressed with her witchcraft, the god Bacchus asks Medea to restore his nurses to their earlier vigor, and she does so.

The fame of this rejuvenation convinces the daughters of Jason's enemy, the aged king Pelias, to allow her to treat their father in a similar fashion. Medea enlists the daughters to spill their father's blood, and when he rises in perplexity and tries to defend himself, Medea administers the coup de grâce, cutting Pelias's throat. He dies, and Medea's dragon chariot spirits her away to safety through the air.

As she flies, Ovid gives his readers an aerial tour of the Mediterranean world, telling of mythical events that had earlier occurred in the locales below. Eventually she arrives at Corinth, where the more familiar events of Jason's desertion for another wife and Medea's murder of her children occur. Escaping her husband's wrath by dragon chariot, she finds protection at Athens and marries King Aegeus there.

As the poet prepares the reader for the story of Medea's efforts to overcome Aegeus's son, Theseus, a digression recounts the story of Hercules' victory over the three-headed guard dog of Hell, Cerberus.

Then, returning to his central theme, Ovid tells how Aegeus recognizes his son by the ivory hilt on his sword just in time to prevent his being poisoned. As usual, Medea decamps by air just in time to escape retribution.

The poet then rehearses Theseus's major triumphs in a series of couplets, ending the sequence with a transition to the preparations for war against Athens that King Minos of Crete is undertaking and his failure to secure King Aeacus of Agina as an ally. Though Aeacus disappoints Minos, he welcomes the Athenians and tells them a heartrending story of a plague that had depopulated his kingdom. In answer to his prayers, however, he dreamed that the birds shook ants from the trees, and, as they touched the earth, the ants changed form and became human beings. Upon awakening, Aeacus discovered that his dream was coming true, and the ants became his followers, the Myrmidons.

Ovid ends the seventh book by recounting the story of Cephalus and Procris—a story the poet also tells in *The Art of Love*. Procris, the sister of that Orithyia beloved by Boreas, is married to Cephalus but jealous because he often calls upon the soothing breeze, Aura, and confides his secrets to the wind. In her suspicion, thinking Aura to be a rival, Procris follows her husband one day on the hunt. Hearing her crashing through the bush and thinking her to be a game animal, Cephalus throws his spear and kills his beloved wife. As told in *Metamorphoses,* the story gains poignancy, for Ovid puts the account in the mouth of Cephalus himself, and the husband describes his feelings.

Book 8

As Book 8 opens, Ovid returns to a consideration of the fortunes of King Minos of Greece, who is waging war against King Nisus of Megara. Nisus's daughter, Scylla, conceives a violent passion for Minos and sets her mind to consider the circumstances in which she might become the wife of her enemy. Finally determining that she will betray her city to the enemy, she clips a lock of Nisus's hair, steals forth from the city, and presents herself and the lock of hair to Minos, explaining that her father's life is magically dependent on his hair.

Shocked at her treachery, Minos rejects the maiden, though he accepts the opportunity to overcome Megara. After imposing his rule upon the land, Minos leaves, abandoning Scylla to her fate. That fate Scylla bemoans in a lengthy soliloquy that ends with her casting herself into the sea, intent on following Minos's ships through the waves. Endowed with supernatural strength, she catches and clings to Minos's vessel. In the meantime, her father has been transformed into a hawk. Spying his daughter clinging to the ship, he swoops to tear her. Frightened, she lets go, and as she does so, she changes into a bird—a Ciris, whose name means "cut the lock."

Following Minos to Crete, Ovid now presents the episode of Minos and the Minotaur. The Minotaur, a creature with a human torso and a bull's head and lower body, is the offspring of Minos's wife, Pasiphae, and of a bull for which she had conceived an unnatural passion. She had consummated her desire by concealing herself in a wooden cow.

To hide his shame, Minos has the architect and inventor, Daedalus, build a complex labyrinth. There Minos imprisons the Minotaur, which feeds on human flesh. Each year thereafter, Minos requires that Athens send him young men as tribute, and he feeds them to the monster until, with the aid of Minos's love-stricken daughter, Ariadne, Theseus comes and kills the Minotaur. On the return trip to Athens, Theseus abandons Ariadne on the island of Naxos. There Bacchus finds her and immortalizes her name by setting her corona in the heavens as the constellation Ariadne's Crown.

Still concerning himself with Cretan legend, Ovid tells the story of Daedalus's and his son Icarus's escape from Crete, which Minos had forbidden Daedalus to leave, via the air, flying on wings of Daedalus's invention. But Icarus, in one of the most celebrated stories of antiquity, flies too near the sun. Its heat melts the wax that attaches his wings, and the boy plummets into the sea that now commemorates him—the Icarian sea. His grieving father finds his son's body, and as he buries it, a partridge lands nearby and whistles merrily. That partridge proves to be a metamorphosed student of Daedalus, Perdix. Daedalus had tried to kill Perdix for rivaling his master's art, and Perdix had been saved from death by his transmutation into the bird.

After burying Icarus, Daedalus continues to Sicily, where he seeks and gains the protection of King Cocalus of Sicily, who raises an army to protect Daedalus against the wrath of Minos at losing Daedalus's inventive skill. Daedalus always thought that Minos misused the artisan's skill for evil purposes.

Ovid now returns to the theme of divine retribution against human neglect, telling the story of Diana's punishing the land of Calydon by sending a giant boar to ravage the countryside. The hero Meleager raises a troop of sturdy youths: Castor and Pollux, Jason, Theseus of Athens and his friend Perithous, and many others. The troop includes a then-young Nestor, who will become the oldest of the Grecian generals at Troy during the Trojan War. Meleager includes in his company a sole woman, Atalanta, a huntress famed for fleet-footedness. When Meleager met her, he promptly fell in love with her, but the quest to kill the giant boar takes precedence.

When the hunters flush the boar from its hiding place, Diana protects it from their spears, and the boar's tusks take a deadly toll as it destroys several of its hunters. Finally, however, Atalanta's arrow draws first blood. Nonetheless, the boar continues to wreak havoc among its pursuers. At length, Meleager's spear proves mortal to the boar, and after he skins it, he presents its head and pelt to Atalanta. Displeased, the rest of the company force Atalanta to give up the prize. Infuriated, Meleager kills his maternal uncles, the brothers Plexippus and Toxeus.

Learning of her brothers' deaths at the hand of her son, Meleager's mother, Althea, takes from its hiding place a magic stick of firewood. At Meleager's birth, the Fates had predicted that he would die when the stick was burned, so Althea has kept it safe through the years. Now she determines to burn the stick in retribution for the deaths of her brothers by her son's hand. In a moving soliloquy,

Ovid catches the emotional conflict that the mother suffers as her desire for revenge and her love of her offspring collide. Several times she tries to throw the stick on the fire, and several times she cannot bring herself to do it. Finally, however, she does. As the stick burns, Meleager's life expires in fiery torment, and his last word is his mother's name. Similarly suffering from the maelstrom of her emotions, Althea commits suicide. Meleager's sisters, wild with grief, embrace his ashes and collapse upon his tomb. Finally relinquishing her vendetta against the people of Calydon, Diana transforms two of the four sisters into birds that fly off into the distance.

The poet next turns his attention to Theseus on his return to Athens. Delayed by the flooded river Achelous, Theseus and his companions accept the hospitality of the river's tutelary deity until the flood has receded. The river god has his nymphs prepare a banquet for his guests, and Theseus inquires about an island he can see. The god responds that because of the distance, Theseus is deceived. Not one but five islands, the Echinades, are there, and they are in fact metamorphosed river spirits or naiads. Achelous explains that he transformed them into islands for neglecting him at their altars. Another island beyond them, however, is the transformed nymph, Perimela. Her father Hippodamas discovered her pregnant with Achelous's child and threw her into the sea. Achelous saved her and called on Neptune to provide her with a place of safety. In response, the sea god changed her into a surpassingly lovely island.

Another guest doubts the tale of transformation and casts doubt not only on such metamorphoses but also on the existence of gods. Rising in the gods' defense, an old hero, Lelex, tells the story of Baucis and Philemon. This devoted couple had spent their lives together in perfect happiness. Unlike their wicked countrymen and despite their poverty, Baucis and Philemon had always managed to be charitable both to their neighbors and to strangers. In disguise, Jove and Mercury called at their humble dwelling, and the old couple entertained the gods to the best of their abilities. The elderly pair became frightened

and amazed, however, to see the wine bowl spontaneously replenish itself. As a result, they concluded that their guests must be deities.

They tried to kill the only goose they owned to prepare for the gods, but the gods would not accept that sacrifice. Instead, they led the old folks to a high place from which Baucis and Philemon witnessed the destruction of all the countryside except for their humble holdings. Their hut was transformed into a magnificent temple for the gods, and the gods ask them to name their fondest desire.

The pair discussed it and requested that, as they had "passed so many years in harmony," they be allowed to depart this life together and neither have to suffer the loss of the other. The gods granted their wish, and after many years spent together as keepers of the temple, the two transmuted together into intertwined oak trees, which the people of Tyana worshipped as gods. The story is one of the most touching of all the *Metamorphoses*.

The river god affirms that such metamorphoses do occur, and reminds the company of beings who take on many forms, such as the god Proteus. Among these was Mestra, the daughter of the unbeliever, Erysichthon. In his apostasy, Erysichthon cut down an oak sacred to the nature goddess Ceres—a tree that was in fact a nymph in a tree's shape. As the nymph died, she prophesied the miserable death of Erysichthon. Ceres sent another nymph to summon Famine from the northern wastes of frigid Scythia. Famine came and breathed her poison into the sleeping Erysichthon. After that, no matter how much he ate, Erysichthon wasted away, ever starving until he had consumed the value of everything he owned, always wanting more and more and never satisfied. Finally, he even sold his daughter, Mestra, beloved of the sea god Neptune, to have money to buy more food.

Calling on Neptune for protection from forced slavery, Mestra received the power of transmutation and transformed herself into a fisherman. Her owner asked the fisherman where she had gone, but Mestra assured him that, herself excepted, no woman had stood there. When her father discovered her newly gained power, he sold her frequently, and just as frequently she changed into various shapes. When he had consumed everything he could get by selling his daughter, Erysichthon began to eat his own flesh, but still derived no benefit and continued to starve.

As the book ends, the river-god host confesses to his guests that even he possesses the power of transformation. He regrets, however, that one of his horns is missing.

Book 9

In an unprecedented transition, Ovid moves to book 9 in mid-conversation. Theseus asks the god how he came to break his horn.

Sighing, the god confesses that he was among those once enamoured of the lovely Deiaenira. When, however, he asked her father for her hand, Achelous discovered that Hercules (see HERACLES) was a rival suitor. The two quarreled and fought. Bested by Hercules, Achelous sought refuge in a transformation and changed into a serpent. Hercules, who as a baby had strangled more dangerous snakes, remained unimpressed. Again shifting his shape, the river god became a savage bull. Hercules bested him and, adding insult to injury, broke off one of his horns.

A nymph enters bearing the horn, filled with apples to tempt Theseus's appetite. Ovid now recounts the story of Hercules and the centaur Nessus. Returning home with his new bride Deianeira, Hercules finds their route blocked by a swollen river. Nessus advises Hercules to swim, promising that he, Nessus, will bear Deianeira safely across. Trusting Nessus's word, Hercules does as he is advised. Nessus in the meantime attempts to kidnap and rape Deianeira, who calls for her husband's aid. Hercules brings down the centaur with an arrow. Nessus's blood soaks his tunic, and the centaur gives it to Deianeira as a charm against the day that her husband's love for her diminishes. The blood contains an admixture of the poisoned blood of the Lernaean hydra.

Years later, Hercules brings home a concubine, Iole. Hoping to preserve his affection, Deianeira sends a servant, Lichas, to give the tunic to her husband. When Hercules dons it, the poison from the robe melts into his flesh, and his body begins burning away. As it does so, he reviews his many triumphs and rushes about maddened. In this state, Hercules encounters Lichas and flings him into the sea, where Lichas changes into a flint rock that seaman still encounter.

Finally, unable to bear his suffering, Hercules builds a funeral pyre and asks his friend Philoctetes (see PHILOCTETES) to set it alight. Although his mortal flesh is consumed, because Hercules is the son of Jupiter and the greatest of human heroes, he joins the gods and is stellified.

Now Ovid imagines that Alcmena, Hercules' mother, and Iole—who, as Hercules' second wife, provoked Deianeira's jealousy—become close and that Alcmena recounts for Iole the tale of Hercules' birth and the role of her maid, Galanthis, in that event. Galanthis had guessed that Juno was interfering with Alcmena's delivery of Jupiter's son, Hercules. Arriving at the altar of Lucina, the goddess who presided at childbirth, Galanthis found Lucina tightly holding herself in, and guessed that by that means, Juno was interfering with Alcmena's delivery. The quick-witted Galanthis announced that Hercules had already been born, and as a surprised Lucina relaxed, Alcmena delivered the child without further difficulty. Lucina was not amused and transmuted Galanthis into a weasel.

Iole responds with the tale of her half sister, Dryope. Gone to enjoy an outing with her year-old son, Dryope was transformed into a lotus tree. Her voice was the last human quality that she lost, and she gave instructions that her infant was to play and nurse in the shade of the tree she had become. To her father and other relatives present, she bade farewell and completed her metamorphosis into a tree.

There now appeared at Alcmena's door an old man, Iolaus, whose youth had been restored to him. Learning of this gift, other gods began to pester Jupiter to grant similar gifts to their favorites. Jupiter, however, put them off by saying that Fate, not he, was responsible for Iolaus's rejuvenation. Moreover, Jupiter himself was subject to Fate's operation.

Ovid now turns to the story of the twin children of the nymph Cyane: Byblis and Caunus. Byblis conceives an incestuous passion for Caunus and dreams that her desire is fulfilled. Deeply torn between her ardor and her repulsion at the thought of incest, Byblis finally yields to her desire and writes a letter in which she confesses her feelings and rationalizes them.

When a servant delivers the letter, Caunus is so horrified that he almost kills the messenger, who reports the brother's rejection to Cyane. Byblis, however, again minimizes that response and seeks other means of fulfilling her forbidden desires. So obsessed does she become that she convinces herself that repeated overtures will overcome her brother's horror. Finally Caunus flees and founds a new city elsewhere.

At his departure, Byblis loses her reason altogether. Shrieking and howling, she pursues Caunus through forests, over mountains, and across rivers until she collapses, exhausted. Her sad plight evokes the pity of neighboring nymphs as Biblis lays weeping. She weeps until she dissolves in her own tears and changes into a fountain.

Ovid next turns to the story of a poor man of Crete, Ligdus, who instructs his wife that if their soon-to-be born child is a daughter, she must be put to death. But the Egyptian goddess appears to the wife, Telethusa, and instructs her to ignore her husband and to rear the daughter who will be born.

When a daughter is born in Ligdus's absence, Telethusa keeps the child's sex a secret from its father. Named Iphis, the child is reared as a boy for 13 years. Then Ligdus arranges a marriage for his supposed son to a lovely girl, Ianthe. Both youths burn to wed, but Ianthe expects a male and Iphis desires a female—though she is ashamed of a passion she thinks to be unnatural.

After several delays add to the suspense of the situation, at the very altar on the wedding day, Iphis is transformed into a man, with happy results for all concerned.

Book 10

Book 10 opens with an account of Orpheus and Eurydice—one of the most celebrated stories of ancient Greek mythology. Shortly after the wedding of the archetypal poet-singer ORPHEUS to his bride Eurydice, she is bitten by a deadly serpent and dies. The grief-stricken Orpheus descends into the underworld to share his grief with the dead and the gods below.

Making his way to the throne of Persephone and Pluto, Orpheus sings sweetly and eloquently of his love and his grief, pleading that Eurydice be allowed to return to earth. His song moves the ghosts to weep and causes a suspension of the punishments being administered to the wicked. Pluto grants Orpheus's request and tells him he may take Eurydice back to the world of the living. If, however, Orpheus should turn to look at his wife on the way, the favor will be revoked and the underworld will reclaim her.

Almost back in the world of the living, Orpheus yields to the temptation to glance at his beloved, and she immediately slips back into Hades. Though he tries to follow, Orpheus is denied a second chance, and he spends three years shunning all women and mourning his twice-dead love.

In the context of Orpheus's lyre playing and singing, Ovid sketches the metamorphoses of Attis into a bare-trunked pine and Cyparissus into a cypress tree. In the grove where both trees stand, the god Apollo had sung his grief for the loss of Cyparissus, and there Orpheus sings to an assembly of wild beasts. As he sings, Orpheus's song and that of Ovid meld into one, and the subjects of *Metamorphoses* now become boys who were favored by the gods and maids who were punished for wrongdoing.

Ovid/Orpheus sings of Ganymede, beloved of Jove, who became the cupbearer of the gods. He writes of Hyacinthus—accidentally killed by the rebound of a discus thrown by Apollo. Unable to restore the boy to life, Apollo changes Hyacinthus into the flower that bears his name, and as that flower he is annually reborn.

Ovid also sings of the way that Venus changes the guest-murdering Cerastes, who were horned men like the biblical Moses, into bulls. She also transforms the irreligious Propoetides, the first women to prostitute their bodies, into pale stones since they have lost their power to blush for shame.

The poet next tells the story of Pygmalion, who falls in love with the statue of a woman that he has carved from ivory. Praying to Venus that he might have a wife "like his ivory," Pygmalion receives the favor of the goddess. He returns home to find the ivory transformed to flesh, marries the girl, and fathers a daughter, Paphos, who is born nine months later.

Recurring now to his second announced theme—maids punished for wrongdoing—Ovid sings of an Arabian maiden, Myrrha. Myrrha is a woman who defies the customs against incest by falling in love with her father and, aided by the scheming and trickery of a rash and sympathetic nurse, becomes his mistress. When her father discovered Myrrha's identity, he tries to kill his pregnant daughter. She, however, escapes and flees. After nine months of wandering and on the point of giving birth, Myrrha prays for transmutation, saying she is fit neither to remain among the living nor to pass among the dead. She changes into the tree that is the source of the precious ointment myrrh, and as she undergoes the transformation, a sympathetic goddess of childbirth, Lucina, delivers the baby from her womb. That child is Adonis, later the beloved of Venus, and his story follows that of his mother.

Venus warns her beloved Adonis against the dangers of hunting and her fear of wild animals. When he asks why, she tells a tale within a tale, regaling him with the story of the runner, Atalanta. Warned to avoid marrying, Atalanta made every potential suitor race against her. Should she lose, she would marry the victor. But if the suitor lost, his penalty was death.

A young man, Hippomenes, heard of the harsh terms for wooing Atalanta and decided in advance that the risk was too great. When, however, he observed the maiden stripped for racing,

he changed his mind, even though he observed Atalanta best a bevy of suitors, all of whom paid the stipulated penalty.

Declaring his genealogy, which originated with the sea god Neptune, Hippomenes challenged Atalanta to race. For the first time, Atalanta felt moved by the importunities of a young man, and she fell in love without realizing it.

Hippomenes prayed to Venus for aid, and she received his prayer favorably. Invisible, the goddess provided the youth with three golden apples and whispered to him how to use them to win. The race began, and Atalanta often intentionally lagged, but still she led Hippomenes. Then he threw one of the apples. Seeing it, Atalanta fancied it and paused to pick it up while Hippomenes passed her. She caught him, and he repeated the ruse, but again she caught up.

With only one apple left, Hippomenes prayed to Venus for help. This time he threw it far out of the course. Atalanta hesitated whether or not to chase it, but Venus made her do so. Now, slowed by her detours and by the weight of the gold, Atalanta could not overtake Hippomenes, and he won.

Venus tells Adonis, however, that Hippomenes was ungrateful and did not reward her with the thanks of burning incense at her altar. Angered, she arranged to have both young people changed into lions, but she is afraid lest some vengeful lion or other wild beast might slay Adonis.

As soon as Venus has left him, Adonis goes boar hunting, and the boar he wounds fatally gores the hunter. Hearing her beloved's dying moans, Venus changes his blood into a perennial flower, the anemone.

Book 11

About such matters Ovid reminds the reader as book 11 opens and the Thracian Orpheus sings to the assembled animals, with the very stones responding to his music. However, a band of bacchantes Ciconean women—think that the singer with his lyre is mocking them, and they hurl weapons at him. Orpheus's sweet music protects him from them until the horns, drums, howling, and pounding of the Bacchantes drown out his lyre. Then the stones that formerly had dropped at his feet begin to strike him. His avian and animal audience also fall victim to the bacchantes' fury.

Peasants working nearby flee in terror, and the crazed women snatch up their hoes and mattocks and use them to dismember their farm animals. The bacchantes then turn on Orpheus and dismember him, flinging his head and lyre into the Hebrus River. There the lyre plays, and Orpheus's "lifeless tongue" murmurs while the riverbanks reply in kind. At long last, Orpheus and Eurydice are reunited in the underworld.

Bacchus, however, punishes the women for murdering his favored poet, turning them all into oak trees, before turning his back on Phrygia and going to Lydia, where he rewards King Midas with the golden touch.

This gift, of course, could prove fatal, as Midas can neither eat nor drink. He prays, therefore, to be restored to his former condition, confessing his greedy fault, and Bacchus grants his prayer. Midas bathes in the source of the Pactolus River near the Lydian city of Sardis, and the golden touch is transferred to the river.

The proximity of the mountain Timolus (sometimes Tmolus) reminds Ovid of a music contest between Pan playing his pipes and Apollo his lyre. Timolus acts as judge and finds in favor of Apollo. Midas disagrees with the judgment, and Apollo rewards Midas with the ears of an ass. These Midas disguises, but a slave tells his secret to a hole in the earth. Reeds growing nearby, however, whisper the secret abroad.

All the subject matter of Ovid's song is, in the annals of mythic history, roughly chronological, and with book 11 the reader arrives at what later became known as "the matter of Troy." Ovid sings of the way in which Apollo and Neptune assume human form and, for a stipulated fee, help the founder of Troy, Laomedon, build the walls of his newly founded city. The king reneges on payment, however, and in punishment, Neptune floods the countryside and demands the sacrifice of the king's daughter to a sea monster. Though she is

saved, the king reneges again, refusing to pay her rescuer, Alcides, who avenges himself by becoming the first conqueror of the city of Troy.

Now associatively, Ovid reverts to an earlier story of how Peleus, a mortal, wooed the sea nymph, Thetis. To avoid Juno's jealousy, Thetis had rebuffed Jupiter's advances. In retaliation, Jupiter condemns her to wed a mortal. Peleus tries to force himself on her, but she shifts her shape until, when she becomes a tiger, he let her go. Another shape-shifter, the god Proteus, counsels Peleus to hang on regardless of what shape she takes until she has exhausted her repertoire and resumed her own form. That done, Peleus has his way with Thetis, and their union conceives Achilles.

Ovid thinks that Peleus enjoyed a happy life except for having accidentally killed his brother Phocus in youth. To escape his father's wrath, Peleus fled with a few flocks and followers.

Arriving in the land of Trachin and concealing his crime, Peleus seeks and obtains the welcome of its king, Ceyx. Ceyx is feeling a bit disheartened and explains his mood by recounting the story of the genesis of the cruel bird the hawk, metamorphosed from his brother Daedalion. In that story he embeds another, telling of the serial rape of his niece, Chione, by two gods: Apollo and Mercury. Ceyx also reports the way in which Diana punished Chione with death for daring to criticize the goddess's beauty.

A herdsman interrupts this conversation to tell of a giant wolf that is ravaging the city's herds and also killing the cowherds. He summons the king and his warriors to destroy the wolf while there are still animals and men left to save. Ceyx immediately organizes a hunting party, joining it himself over the protestations of his wife, Alcyone. Instead of hunting, however, Peleus prays. Answering his prayer, Thetis transmutes the wolf into marble. After this, Peleus moves on to Magnesia, where at last he obtains absolution for his accidental fratricide.

Moved by a number of strange occurrences, Ceyx now resolves to undertake a trip to seek advice from the Delphic oracle. Alcyone argues against it and insists that, if he does go, he must take her with him. Eventually, promising a quick return, Ceyx persuades her to let him sail, but she has a premonition of disaster. As night falls on the journey's first day, a storm blows up. Ovid's description of the storm is magnificent.

At length a mighty wave plunges the doomed vessel to the bottom. Most of the sailors perish, but a few, including Ceyx, survive. He clings to a bit of flotsam as long as he could. Then he drowns with Alcyone's name on his lips and a prayer that she might find his corpse.

Alcyone in the meantime wearies Juno with her incessant prayers for her dead husband. Juno therefore sends her messenger, the rainbow Iris, to take Alcyone a vision in Ceyx's shape to inform her of her husband's fate. Iris delivers the vision to the god Sleep. Sleep has his son Morpheus assume Ceyx's form and deliver news of his death to Alcyone.

Alcyone awakens convinced of her husband's death. She grieves and goes down to the shore, where she discovers her husband's body. Mad with misery, Alcyone flings herself from a nearby seawall, but in midair is transmuted into a sea bird. The gods sympathetically resurrect Ceyx as a male of the same species, and Ovid says that they continue to mate and rear their young, brooding them in floating nests.

An old man identifies another sea bird—a Mergus—as another transmutation and also of royal birth. The Trojan prince Aesacus had pursued a maid who, while fleeing from him, was bitten by a serpent and died. Blaming himself, Aesacus attempted suicide by leaping into the sea, but he too was turned into a bird—one that dives for fish.

Book 12

As book 12 opens, we find Troy's king, Priam, grieving for the death of his son Aesacus. At the same time, the principal cause of the Trojan War, Paris's kidnapping Helen of Sparta, gets underway (see HELEN). Ovid reports the Greek fleet becalmed at Aulis. In his version of the sac-

rifice of Agamemnon's daughter Iphigenia (see IPHIGENIA IN AULIS), Ovid suggests that Diana substituted a doe for the girl, obscuring the eyes of the onlookers with a mist. After the sacrifice, of course, favoring winds took the Greek ships to Troy.

Following a description of the house of rumor—the clearing house for all news and situated just where earth and air and water meet at the center of the universe—Ovid begins his foreshortened account of the Trojan war itself. In the midst of that retelling, the poet has the ancient king of Gerania, Nestor (who claims to be in his third century of life), interpolate a lengthy campfire account, also told by VIRGIL, of the transformation of the female Caenis into the invulnerable warrior Caeneus. The god Neptune made this change of sex at her request after he had ravished her.

Still speaking, Nestor next recounts what happened at the wedding of Pirithous to Hippodame. Among the guests were several centaurs. Provoked both by the bride's beauty and by too much wine, the wildest of them, Eurytus, attempted to kidnap the bride from the wedding. A general melee ensued during which the human beings, led by Theseus of Athens, defeated the centaurs with great difficulty. As is usually the case in epic battle scenes, the carnage is graphically and minutely depicted. Clearly, Ovid could have chosen to become a major poet of warfare.

The poet lingers over a description of the most comely of the centaurs, Cyllarus, and his deep love for his devoted mate, Hylonome. When Cyllarus was killed in the wedding melee, Hylonome threw herself upon the same spear that had felled him.

At last the centaurs all focused their attention on Caeneus, but he was proof against all their weapons. They hit upon the expedient of burying him under a forest of trees, and though Caeneus could not be wounded, he could be overborne with a whole forest on top of him. He was finally pressed so deep that he had difficulty breathing. Ovid, however, admits uncertainty regarding Caeneus's end. Some say he was pressed all the way to Hades, and others say he was transmuted into a bird and escaped. The remaining human warriors so manfully resisted the Centaurs that the surviving half-humans eventually fled.

One of Nestor's auditors, however, is put out that the old king made no mention of Hercules' contributions to the fight. This prompts Nestor to admit that Hercules was his enemy and to rehearse the reasons. He ends his discourse, however, with a gesture of amity toward the Herculean relative who had asked the question.

Ovid ends book 12 by describing, first, the agreement between Neptune and Apollo that led to the death of Achilles when an apparently random arrow fired from Troy's battlements by Paris struck the otherwise invulnerable hero in his one vital spot, his heel, and killed him. Next he quickly glosses over the funeral, and finally he very briefly alludes to the dispute over the fallen hero's arms and armor.

Book 13

This disagreement carries over and begins the 13th book. As the principal Greek generals sit in judgment, the contenders for the arms state their cases. First comes Ajax, who pleads his mighty deeds, the duplicity of his rival Ulysses, and his superior genealogy as the great-grandson of Jupiter himself and his consanguinity as Achilles' cousin. Moreover, he accuses Ulysses of desertion and cowardice and of lacking the strength and will to stand in the face of the Trojan enemy without the protection of Ajax. Ajax is a man of action; Ulysses is clever and stealthy. Moreover, Achilles' armament is so heavy that Ulysses cannot sustain its weight. He ends by challenging Ulysses to vie with him in rescuing the arms from the midst of the enemy.

A cleverer orator, Ulysses first mourns Achilles and then reminds the Greeks that had it not been for Ulysses, the Greeks would never have enjoyed Achilles' services in the first place. Ulysses twits Ajax for being "slow of wit," softening the barb by granting that each person must make the most of his own powers. As for geneal-

ogy, Ulysses points out that he is no further removed from Jove than Ajax. Moreover, through his mother's line, Ulysses is descended from Mercury.

Ulysses reminds his listeners that it was he who saw through Achilles' disguise as a girl and recruited him against the Trojans. Then Ulysses enumerates his conquests. He persuaded Agamemnon to sacrifice Iphigenia to Diana. He had to fool the girl's mother into sending the girl to Aulis. It was Ulysses who served as the Grecian ambassador who denounced Paris and demanded Helen's return. It was he who, when all seemed lost, rallied the Greeks with his eloquence. It was he who acted as a spy, he who entered the enemy camp. He slew many an enemy, and unlike Ajax, Ulysses bears the marks of several wounds.

Ulysses suggests that Ajax in his boasting is claiming credit that belongs to all the Greeks. He refutes the claim that he is not strong enough to bear the weight of Achilles' arms and rejoins that Ajax does not understand their artistic value, not recognizing either the subject matter of the relief work or its fine quality.

After enumerating other distinguished accomplishments, Ulysses points out that all Ajax's accomplishments are those of the body, Ulysses' are those of the mind and, accordingly, are of greater value. His trump card, of course, is that he has taken the statue of Minerva from the city. As long as the image protected Troy, it could not fall.

Ulysses' eloquence carries the day, and the generals award him the arms. Ajax, in a fit of pique, commits suicide, and the hyacinth springs from his blood as it had from that of Hyacinthus.

Then Troy falls, and after achieving a measure of vengeance, Hecuba, its queen, is changed into a dog and begins to bark. Then Ovid lists the consequences of Troy's fall for those, such as the women of Troy (see *The Trojan Women*), whose fates have been recorded in poems and plays. He lingers over especially poignant stories like that of the Trojan princess Polyxena, sacrificed at the tomb of Achilles to appease the fallen hero's ghost. He also traces the grief of her mother, Hecuba, and her vengeance for her children's deaths (see *HECUBA*).

After recording the transformation of the rainbow goddess Aurora's son, Memnon, into birds called Memnonides, Ovid reminds his readers that the fates did not allow Troy's hopes to die with the city, and he summarizes the story of Aeneas, his accompanying survivors, their difficulties, and their eventual arrival in Italy, where they became the ancestors of the Romans (see *AENEID*).

In this section, Ovid also embeds the ostensibly self-told story of the nymph Galatea. She tells of the Cyclops Polyphemus's passion for her, of the manner of his wooing, and his vengeance when he discovers his love in the arms of Acis (see *DIALOGUES OF THE SEA GODS*). Polyphemus destroys Acis, but Galatea's lover is transmuted into a river bearing his name.

When Galatea has finished her discourse, her listeners disperse. Among them is the nymph Scylla. As she leaves the gathering, she is observed by Glaucus, once a man but recently transformed into a sea god. Glaucus conceives a passion for Scylla and pursues her. On reaching a place of refuge, Scylla examines her pursuer, and he explains that he is a merman and a sea god. He tells her the story of his recent transformation from human being to that state. Unimpressed, Scylla flees, and as book 13 ends, Glaucus rages off to sulk at the court of Circe, the witch who once converted Ulysses' crewmen into swine.

Book 14

Book 14 opens with a continuation of the story of Glaucus's passion for Scylla. He asks Circe for a charm to make Scylla love him. Circe counsels him to scorn the one who scorns him and to accept Circe as his love instead. His refusal, of course, enrages Circe, who mixes up a magic potion and skims over the sea in search of Scylla. Finding the pool in which the nymph habitually bathes, Circe poisons it. When Scylla next wades in waist deep, her torso changes into dogs' heads, and from the waist down she finds herself encircled with the forms of beasts. It was this transfor-

mation that, in an effort to avenge herself on Circe, caused Scylla to snatch the companions of Ulysses as he sailed between Scylla and Charybdis (see *ODYSSEY*). Ovid explains that Aeneas and his companions escaped a similar fate only because Scylla in the meantime had been further transmuted into a rock.

That transition leads Ovid back into summarizing the material of Virgil's *Aeneid*. Ovid follows Aeneus to Carthage and alludes to his marriage to Dido. Then the poet tracks the hero to the cave of the Avernan sibyl at Cumae and from there down into the underworld.

The sibyl tells Aeneas the story of her own situation. Wooed by Apollo, who offered any gift of her choosing, the sibyl asked for as many years of life as there were grains of sand in a nearby sand heap, but she forgot to specify that she remain young. As a result she has aged for 700 years and knows that she still has 300 more to go. She knows that her body will waste away to virtually nothing, but that the fates will leave her voice intact.

Arriving at Caieta, a landfall that ever since has borne the name of his nurse, Aeneas finds a Greek survivor of Ulysses' voyage whom Aeneas had earlier taken aboard and had left in Sicily. That sailor, Achaemenides, tells the story of the blinded Cyclops's attempts at vengeance against the Greeks who blinded him. The seafarer quotes Polyphemus at length as the Cyclops vents his despair at the loss of his single eye and his hatred of those who blinded him.

Then another member of the company, Macareus, tells how Ulysses' folly in trying to stay awake for nine days and nights cost his seafarers their homecoming. When their chief fell asleep, the sailors opened a bag they thought contained gold only to discover that instead it had imprisoned all the winds contrary to their voyage. In the ensuing discussion, Ovid has his characters summarize another famous episode of Homer's *Odyssey* that involves a metamorphosis—that of Circe's turning men into swine.

He also recounts a story told him by a woodpecker while he was in his swinish condition of the way in which the appetitive Circe fell in love with Picus, a youth who loved the nymph Canens. When Circe attempted to seduce him, Picus rejected her, with the result that she turned him into the very woodpecker that told the tale. The angry Circe also changed Picus's hunting companions into beasts. As for the nymph Canens, when Picus failed to return, she wore away to nothing and vanished into thin air.

Now the poet turns to tracing the arrival of Aeneus and his Trojan band in the region of the Tiber and of their encounters with the native peoples, both friendly and unfriendly (see *Aeneid*). He dutifully records such transformations as occur along the way, such as the metamorphosis of Acmon and others into swan-like birds when they offended the goddess Venus, or that of a shepherd transmuted to an olive tree for mocking dancing nymphs, and the way that the Trojan ships changed into sea nymphs.

Ovid then summarizes the victory of Aeneas over Turnus and Venus's successful plea for the success of her son Aeneas and his comrades in Italy so that they might become the forefathers of the Roman state and empire. He also records the deification of Aeneas as the god Indiges. He then traces the genealogy of the Roman state, pausing to detail the story of the love of the Etruscan god, Vertumnus, for the wood nymph Pomona. Vertumnus takes excessive pains to disguise himself in various ways so that he can approach Pomona. At last he disguises himself as an old woman and comes to admire the fastidious manner in which Pomona tends the trees and vines she cares for. Using the codependency of the trees and the vines as a parable for the mutual support of spouses, Vertumnus describes his own passion for Pomona and the benefits that will accrue for both if the nymph will only accept him. She will be his first and his last love.

To underscore the evils that arise from rejection, Vertumnus as the old woman tells the sorrowful tale of Iphis, who hanged himself when his love, Anaxarete, rejected him, and how she, when she tried to look away from his dead body, was turned into a marble statue in keeping with her stony refusal. Having finished his tutorial, Vertumnus reveals himself in his own form, and Pomona returns his love.

Returning to Rome and its history, Ovid outlines the Romans' war with the Sabines in the time of Romulus, and he ends the book with the deification of the Sabine, Quirinus, and his wife, Hersilla, who became the goddess Hora.

Book 15

Book 15 opens with the story of how Rome's second king, the perhaps legendary Pompilius Numa, hears the tale of Myscelus. In a dream, Hercules tells Myscelus to leave his homeland of Argos and move near the river Aesar. Leaving Argos is a capital offense, and learning of his intention, his neighbors bring Myscelus to trial. When a vote is taken on his guilt, all his jurors put black stones in a jar to condemn him. Hercules, however, miraculously changes all the stones to white. (Myscelus was credited with having founded Croton [Crotona] in Italy's toe in 710 B.C.E.)

Now Ovid introduces a novel form. The influential Greek thinker Pythagoras migrated from Samos to Croton in 530 B.C.E. There he established an influential school of thought that persisted for several hundred years. Into the text of the *Metamorphoses* Ovid inserts a lengthy lecture by Pythagoras, whom the poet credits with almost universal knowledge. The opening subject of Ovid's Pythagorean discourse is vegetarianism. Eating meat is hateful because it criminally requires the death of live creatures and because doing so makes the carnivore more savage. In the Golden Age, argues Pythagoras, people were vegetarians, consuming only the fruits of the field and not animal flesh. See *Lives of Eminent Philosophers*.

Pythagoras turns next to a critique of mythic punishment after death. Bodies are burnt to ash, and souls, says Pythagoras, are immortal. He argues for the transmigration of souls and their rebirths in various forms—another reason for not slaughtering animals.

Time is a continual round of seasons, following one another predictably. Our bodies undergo ceaseless metamorphoses as they age. Even earth, air, fire, and water—the elements of Greek physics—are subject to change. Nature continually creates new forms from old. Once-fresh rivers become brackish. The sea advances and retreats. Old land sinks; new land is formed. Streams like the river Ammon, cold at midday, is warm at morning and evening.

Pythagoras argues for the spontaneous generation of insects from putrefying flesh, and he cites the Phoenix as the only example of self-renewing creature. Cities and civilizations, too, rise and fall. Troy, Mycenae, Thebes, have all perished, except that while Rome lives, something of Troy will remain.

The speaker then returns to his theme of vegetarianism, citing many reasons why people should not consume the flesh of other creatures for nourishment.

Returning to his own poetic voice, Ovid then tells how a certain Virbius asserted that he was none other than the divinely resurrected Hippolytus, whose story the poet summarizes (see HIPPOLYTUS).

He then touches briefly on a number of transmutations associated with Roman history that have occurred since the founding of the city. Particularly, the poet calls upon the Muses to recall the story of the Aesculapius, Apollo's son, who, at the senate's invitation was miraculously wafted by ship from the city of Epidaurus to Rome. There, having arrived transmuted into the form of a serpent, he founded on the island in the Tiber river a notable cult of healing that has persisted in a series of forms from its founding in 291 B.C.E. until the present moment. Rather than a cult, now, however the therapeutic tradition of the island has transferred to the hospital of St. Bartholomew that occupies the site.

Aesculapius, however, on his first arrival in Rome quelled a pestilence that plagued the city. Ovid lovingly traces the god's progress by sea through the several stops along his route to the temple prepared to receive him. Having told the story, Ovid makes a sudden associative transition to the subject of JULIUS CAESAR—a god in his own city. Moreover, his principal achievement was to have been the (adoptive) father of the emperor, AUGUSTUS CAESAR. At this point, the exiled Ovid shamelessly flatters the emperor who had banished him in the fond hope of having his exile repealed. He has Venus appeal to the gods to stay the assassination of Julius Caesar. Even the gods, however, are subject to the fates, and they cannot comply. Before the murder, portents of disaster and unnatural occurrences took place. But such forewarnings could not forestall Caesar's death. "Naked swords," says Ovid, "were brought into the sacred curia."

Though the gods themselves could not preserve Caesar's life, they could receive him as one of themselves, and this they promised Venus. They also promised her that Caesar's heir Augustus would become the ruler of the known world and also be deified upon his death. Mollified, Venus took the soul of Julius Caesar as he died and bore it up to heaven. From the earth, it appeared as the comet that was observed on the night of Caesar's death. Now, just as Jupiter reigns in heaven, so Augustus reigns on earth. Ovid ends the body of his masterwork with a prayer for his emperor's long life before he too is deified and stellified.

There follows an envoi—the poet's address to his poem. It also serves as a none-too-tactful reminder to the emperor that the poet's fame is also inextinguishable. When his life has ended, Ovid's better part, his poetry, will be read as long as there are readers. Ovid's name will live in fame forever—"immortal," as he says, "beyond the lofty stars."

Bibliography

Ovid. *Metamorphoses.* Translated by Charles Martin. New York: W. W. Norton, 2004.

———. *Metamorphoses.* Translated by A. D. Melville. New York: Oxford University Press, 1990.

———. *Ovid in Six Volumes. Metamorphoses.* Vols. 3 and 4. Translated by Frank Justus Miller and G. P. Gould. Cambridge, Mass.: Harvard University Press, 1984.

Metaphysics   See ARISTOTLE.

Milesian Tales Aristides of Miletus
(ca. 100 B.C.E.)

Represented by only the most fragmentary of remains, *Milesian Tales* are supposed to have been a series of brief narratives penned by Aristides of Miletus around 100 B.C.E. They are reputed to have been lewdly erotic and to have exercised influence on both PETRONIUS ARBITER and APULEIUS.

Bibliography
Harrison, S. J., ed. *Oxford Readings in the Roman Novel.* New York: Oxford University Press, 1999.

Trenker, Sophie. *The Greek Novella in the Classical Period.* New York: Garland Publications, 1987.

Mimnermus of Colophon (fl. ca. 590 B.C.E.)
Greek poet

A transitional figure in the development of Greek elegiac poetry, Mimnermus was the first poet to move elegy away from its roots as a verse form used in songs of war. In the earliest Greek elegiac poetry, like that of CALLINUS OF EPHESUS or of TYRTAEUS, the term *elegy* described a meter in QUANTITATIVE VERSE that both poets used to inspire troops who sang the verses as they marched to battle.

Mimnermus employed the form for another purpose. The slender fragments of his verse that still exist lament the swift passage of youth, the afflictions of human life, and its brevity. After Mimnermus, the *elegy* came to be felt as a sad poem, often of considerable length, and regularly composed in hexameter and pentameter rather than in the original form.

See also ELEGY AND ELEGAIC POETRY.

Bibliography
Mimnermus of Colophon. *The Fragments of Mimnermus: Text* [in Greek] *and Commentary* [in English]. Edited by Archibald Allen. Stuttgart: F. Steiner, 1993.

———. *Poesia, Mimnermo.* Selections, translated into Spanish by Emilio Fernández-Galliano. Madrid: El Crotalón, 1983.

monastic farce   See COMEDY IN GREECE AND ROME.

Moralia (Ethical Essays) Plutarch
(ca. 100 C.E.)

Though PLUTARCH's plan for the essays that constitute his *Moralia* was evidently to present them as a series of letters, dialogues, and lectures, as his interest in his subject of the moment intensified, he tended to neglect the form chosen and simply develop an essay.

In its surviving form, this work is composed of 78 complete or almost complete essays and a few fragments of others. The collection holds special interest for anyone who is or who aspires to become an essayist, for it is the foundational document of this genre in the Western tradition. In their works, Renaissance writers such as the French and English essayists Michel Equem de Montaigne and Francis Bacon looked to Plutarch's example for models, often treating the same or similar topics to those of their Greek exemplar. Plutarch also provided useful examples for those who in the Renaissance specialized in writing essays describing the character traits of certain sorts of people.

The topics that Plutarch addresses range broadly in the course of his work. He writes several essays on subjects concerned with learning. "On the Education of Children," "How the Young Man should Study Poetry," and "On Listening to Lectures" exemplify essays addressing this topic.

Plutarch also offers advice for picking one's way through the pitfalls and vicissitudes of life. "HOW TO PROFIT BY ONE'S ENEMIES," "Advice about Keeping Well," "How to Tell a Flatterer from a Friend, and "HOW A MAN MAY BECOME AWARE OF HIS PROGRESS IN VIRTUE" typify Plutarch's friendly suggestions to his readers.

Still another set of essays examines the national characters of Greeks, Romans, and occasionally Persians. Sometimes Plutarch examines the question at a general level, as he does in "The Roman Questions" and "The Greek Questions." Sometimes he narrows the topic, as he does in "Were the Athenians More Famous in War or in Wisdom?" At other times, he approaches the issue through an examination of the sayings of an individual Greek, such as Alexander, or a Persian, such as Cyrus.

Plutarch discusses religious, moral, and psychological questions. He speaks of gods and prophecy, moral virtue, anger, and tranquility of mind. Beyond, that he concerns himself with such aspects of human personality as talking too much, being overly curious, or being consumed with jealousy. He also conducts discussions of aspects of Plato's work and of the philosophy of the Stoic philosophers (see STOICISM), and he propounds his disagreement with the manner of living proposed by EPICURUS. Music, too, becomes a subject for his consideration. Anticipating columnists who advise the lovelorn, he even offers suggestions for conjugal happiness to husbands and wives, and more than one of his essays discusses the bravery of women.

Bibliography

Plutarch. *Plutarch's Moralia* [Greek and English]. 15 vols. Translated by Frank Cole Babbitt. Cambridge, Mass.: Harvard University Press, 1960–64.

Moschus of Syracuse (fl. second century B.C.E.)

Moschus was a poet thought to be roughly contemporary with THEOCRITUS and sometimes classed with him as a pastoral poet. Only four complete idylls and a few fragments remain to illustrate Moschus's works. Of the works that survive in full, his mythological idyll entitled *The Seizure of Europa* is considered his best work. It tells of the god Zeus's kidnapping of Europa by turning himself into a bull and carrying her away across the sea on his back. Generally considered inferior to Theocritus, Moschus is nonetheless notable for his fine descriptive passages.

Bibiliography

Chamberlain, Henry Howard, trans. *Last Flowers. A Translation of Moschus and Bion.* Cambridge, Mass.: Harvard University Press, 1937.

Gow, Andrew Sydenham Farrar, trans. *The Greek Bucolic Poets.* Cambridge, U.K.: Cambridge University Press, 1953.

Holden, Anthony, trans. *Greek Pastoral Poetry: Theocritus, Bion, Moschus, The Pattern Poems.* Harmondworth, U. K.: Penguin, 1974.

Mozi (Modi, Moti, Mo Tzu, Master Mo) (ca. 480–390 B.C.E.)

Sometimes called literary history's "first true philosopher of China," Mozi (Master Mo) may have sprung from the ancient class of artisans or of craftsmen. Though he may have been a student of Confucianism at some point in his personal history, he broke with that tradition and founded a countermovement of his own, becoming the leader of an activist organization that was both antiaristocratic and opposed to wars whose purpose was the conquest of new territory.

Severely critical of the tenets of Confucianism, Mozi applied his own views to establishing a highly disciplined community of which he became the autocratic leader. In his view, a polity needed to share a common set of ideals, have a power structure that devolved from its leader, and be conducted in an orderly manner. In place of favoring family relationships as CONFUCIUS had, Mozi pursued universal brotherhood. He also took issue with Confucius's views concerning the central place of music in human life. Beyond that, he criticized as excessive the Confucian emphasis on funerals and mourning.

Whereas Confucianism centered both ethics and politics in the family, seeing the relationship of the citizen to the state as analogous to that of parent to child, Mozi saw a chain of command that began with God, descended to the sovereign, and so on down to the lowest echelons of society. Whereas Confucianism sought to promote good will among men, Mozi promulgated instead what the historian of philosophy, Philip J. Ivanhoe, calls "state consequentialism." That system's objectives included maximizing the wealth of a community or state, maintaining strict civic order, and increasing the state's population.

Mozi anticipated by more than two millennia the psychological theories of behaviorism. He believed that human behavior could be shaped quite easily by a system of rewards and punishments, and he put his theories to the test in the way he ran his community. Even the death penalty was not beyond his authority to impose.

Generally, Mozi believed that people would treat others in the way that others treated them and that they would, on the whole, try to please their rulers. For those exceptional persons outside these norms, his system of rewards and punishments came into play. Again for most persons, this system worked best when supplemented with carefully formed, rational arguments.

For a leader with such pragmatic views, Mozi held some surprising convictions. He believed, for instance, in ghosts and other sorts of spirits as well as in a literal heaven. Supernature, he was convinced, would enlist itself on the side of a polity's authority.

The antiaristocratic bias of Mozi's convictions led him to enlist his organization as a paramilitary group who would fight on the side of states that were victimized by wars seeking to add territory to aggressor states. This penchant for paramilitary activity, Ivanhoe believes, may have led to the demise of Mozi's community during the warring states period. (See ANCIENT CHINESE DYNASTIES AND PERIODS.)

The book that records Mozi's teachings bears his name (Mo) and his honorific (zi) as its title, The MOZI.

Bibliography

Idema, Wilt, and Lloyd Haft. *A Guide to Chinese Literature*. Ann Arbor: Center for Chinese Studies, University of Michigan, 1997.

Ivanhoe, Philip J., and Bryan W. Van Norden, eds. *Readings in Classical Chinese Philosophy*. New York and London: Seven Bridges Press, 2001.

Lowe, Scott. *Mo Tzu's Religious Blueprint for a Chinese Utopia: Mo Di the Will and the Way*. Lewiston, Me.: E. Mellen Press, 1992.

Mozi. *Mo Tzu: Basic Writings*. Translated by Burton Watson. New York: Columbia University Press, 1963.

Mozi, The *(The Mo Tzu)* Mozi (ca. fifth century B.C.E.)

Originally a work in 15 books organized into 71 chapters, *The Mozi* has come down to us in an incomplete state. Some 18 of the chapters are missing altogether. Given the repetitive nature of the work—at least insofar as its central tenets are concerned—this loss probably does not much affect our knowledge of the text. Some of its chapters, however, are considered to be the work of others.

Cast in the form of a series of questions and answers or as a series of pronouncements by the philosopher and utopian sect leader MOZI, the work pursues issues dear to his heart. The opening discussion addresses an issue of concern to Mozi. The state must be at pains to take care of its learned persons and foster education. Such persons are less likely to try to manipulate the state's leader with flattery and to give him farsighted and stern advice.

The second chapter suggests that superior people will be "incorruptible in poverty" and "righteous when wealthy." The third chapter, "On Dyeing," is demonstrably a late addition, though Mozi might have been struck with the potency of dyes during his lifetime. The chapter's advice is moral: one must be careful what one becomes involved in.

The fourth chapter proposes that state governments put in place the same sort of standards or benchmarks that guide artisans in making the goods they sell. The standard states must aim at, however, is one established by Heaven. Whatever universally benefits mankind is an action that

Heaven will approve. Mozi was convinced that Heaven redressed wrongs and singled out malefactors for punishment. States that exercise care for the populace will be singled out for blessings. Several of the subsequent chapters embroider that theme. The virtuous will be exalted.

In Book 3, chapters 11 and 12, Mozi argues that most people recognize that the war of all against all that prevails in a state of nature is a disorderly and unsustainable condition. Early on in human history, then, hierarchical forms of governance came into being, and in a well-ordered state, most people will identify with their leaders. The sage-kings of old earned the approval of heaven with their concern for all the people whom they led. The identification of the wills of the ruled with that of the ruler is the foundation of well-ordered government.

The exercise of the hierarchical system that he recommends will result, Mozi assures his readers in Book 4, in the eventuation of the universal love of humankind, giving "peace to the rulers and sustenance to the people." The effects of such universal love will be supranational. Therefore, offensive warfare will also cease. Just people will enlist in the defense of nations attacked by self-aggrandizing enemies. Book 5 contains the Mohist condemnation of offensive warfare. At the same time, Mozi was utterly realistic about the need of states for defense against expansionist neighbors, and to that end the members of his community became experts in the strategies and tactics of defensive warfare.

Like PLATO, Mozi espoused a version of the philosopher-king—the ruler-sage, a leader who would implement Mozi's program. Such a leader would also economize on state expenditures—the subjects of chapters 20 and 21 of Book 6. Similar motives of economy and good sense lead Mozi to criticize the elaborate funeral ceremonies and prolonged periods of mourning that characterized Confucian doctrine.

In the pages that follow, having dealt with that matter toward the end of Book 6, Mozi explores the subject of the will of Heaven. He firmly holds that rewards will come to those who succeed in acting in accord with Heaven's will, and punishments will follow for those who do not. The sage is convinced that Heaven dearly loves human beings. However, human beings do not always succeed in performing or even in discerning Heaven's will because, as he says in chapter 28, people understand trifles but not important matters.

In Book 8, chapter 21, Mozi takes up the subject of ghosts. To them and to spirits Mozi attributes the cause of confusion in the world. Seeking proof of their existence, Mozi prefers the authority of antiquity to the testimony of the living multitude. In support of his argument, he cites a number of old ghost stories. Though these are interesting, they would only convince those who already believed.

Mozi categorizes ghosts and other spirits as follows: heavenly spirits, spirits of hills and rivers, and ghosts of deceased persons. It behooves "the gentlemen of the world" to believe in them.

Chapter 32 of Book 8 contains a famous condemnation of music—one again grounded in what Mozi thought to be ancient practice and one diametrically opposed to Confucian teaching. He says flatly that "music is wrong." Among other things, it leads to dancing and lust.

In chapter 35, Mozi conducts a critique of the doctrines of fatalism. He does not believe that certain events have been fated to happen since the dawn of being. He thinks that careful planning and purposeful action can result in predictable outcomes that follow from the course of action taken and not from an inescapable destiny.

Chapter 39 once again mounts a direct attack on the tenets of Confucianism. This time Mozi complains that family-oriented Confucianism establishes a hierarchy of affection that undermines the principle of universal love.

The rest of *The Mozi* divides into two parts. The first essentially elaborates on many of the basic premises outlined above. It does so by presenting illustrative questions and answers in dialogue form. The second discusses defensive military tactics that can be used to dissuade self-aggrandizing states from attacking their neighbors. The defenses recommended either make victory impossible or so expensive that no advantage would accrue to an aggressor from winning.

Bibliography

Lowe, Scott. *Mo Tzu's Religious Blueprint for a Chinese Utopia.* Lewiston, Me.: E. Mellen Press, 1992.

Mo Tzu [Mozi]. *Basic Writings.* Translated by Burton Watson. New York: Columbia University Press, 1963.

———. *The Will and the Way.* Lewiston, Mass.: E. Mellen Press, ca. 1992.

Yi-Pao Mei, ed. and trans. *The Ethical and Political Works of Motse.* Westport, Conn.: Hyperion Press, 1973.

Musæus (1) (fl. sixth century B.C.E.)

Whether or not the early Musæus was a real person is unclear. His name, which means "He of the MUSES," is closely associated with that of ORPHEUS, and both were considered archetypal poets. Musaeus is pictured on an ancient piece of pottery as copying down the songs sung by the head of Orpheus after it had been severed by the bacchantes when Orpheus was observed spying on their secret rites.

Reputedly born in Thrace, Musæus was a pupil of Orpheus in some versions of his story. A collection of oracles was attributed to Musæus in ancient times, and a sixth-century Athenian scholar, Onomacritus, was employed by the Athenian leader Pisistratus to edit Musæus's works. The editor was caught adding at least one false oracle to the collection; his doing so has cast doubt on the reliability of the body of work attributed to Musæus. PLATO, however, speaks admiringly of Musæus's verse predictions concerning the world's final days.

Musæus (2) (fl. ca. 450–550 C.E.)

Possibly a Christian Greek poet, Musæus authored *Hero and Leander,* a tragic tale of Leander's wooing Hero by nightly swimming the Hellespont to see her in the lonely tower where she lived. Hero set out a light to guide her lover, but one stormy night Leander drowned. *Hero and Leander* is the source poem for the Renaissance British poet Christopher Marlowe's poem by the same name. The 19th-century British poet, George Gordon, Lord Byron, swam the Hellespont to prove it was possible.

Bibliography

Musaeus. *Hero and Leander.* Edited by Thomas Gelzer. Translated by Cedric Whitman. Cambridge, Mass.: Harvard University Press, 1975.

Muses

The Greek poet HESIOD (eight century B.C.E.). fixed the number and function of the Muses—the Greek divinities who presided over the arts and inspired their practitioners. Hesiod's list included Calliope, the patron goddess of EPIC poetry and the principal Muse; Clio, the Muse of history; Erato, the Muse of love poetry and lyrics in general; Euterpe, the Muse of music; Melpomene, the Muse of TRAGEDY; Polymnia, the Muse of sacred poetry and mimicry; Terpsichore, the Muse of dancing and choral singing (which on the Greek stage was accompanied by dance movement); Thalia, the Muse of COMEDY, and Urania, the Muse of astronomy.

From the perspective of literature, in keeping with the view of the poet as *vates,* or as priest, the artist was thought to act as a medium through which the deities spoke. Just as poets might accompany themselves on musical instruments, so the Muses used the artists as *their* instruments. HOMER and, following Homer, most epic poets ever after start their works by invoking the Muse. Homer begins his *ODYSSEY* by praying, "Sing in me, Muse [presumably Calliope], and in me tell the story . . . ," and the adventures of the wandering king of Ithaca unfold.

In iconography or mythography the Muses take traditional forms. Calliope is pictured with a writing tablet, Clio strumming on a lyre, Euterpe with a flute, Melpomene with the mask of tragedy, and Thalia with that of comedy. The thoughtful expression on Polymnia's face identifies her, while

Terpsichore is represented dancing and accompanying herself on a lyre. Urania is usually pictured holding either a terrestrial or a celestial globe. (See MYTHOGRAPHY IN THE ANCIENT WORLD.)

myth

Though the popular definition of *myth* identifies the term as one alluding to a fictitious story, perhaps a broader cultural definition would better serve to clarify the word's meaning: Myths contain the foundational stories of cultures. They are often collected together with history, poetry, moral wisdom, genealogy, and the like in the early literature of cultures or nations. Often, too, myths address such subjects as the origins of the universe, the creation of the earth and its creatures, the number and nature of the gods, the means through which human beings can communicate with or propitiate their deity or deities, and the moral and legal underpinnings of human society. They also tend to encompass the prehistoric and sometimes the historic figures of a cultural tradition, assigning them the status of gods or demigods. Such deification, for example, was frequently the case with the kings of ancient Sumer, with the emperors of Rome, and with the founders of major religions.

Collections of myths have often been elevated to the status of an official state religion. This was, for example, the situation in ancient Rome, Greece, Persia, Babylon, China, Egypt, Israel, India, and elsewhere. Even persons who do not literally credit the mythic stories of a culture often respect the restraints on antisocial human behavior imposed by believing in myths and behaving according to the moral codes they involve. CICERO provides an instance of one such person in ancient Rome.

Myths regularly have also had the opposite effect of encouraging antisocial behavior in persons or societies that become convinced of the exclusive truth of their particular set of myths. Beyond that, persons and groups principally interested in the exercise of power or in the accumulation of wealth have regularly and cynically appealed to the widespread belief in various systems of mythology in order to dominate or to gain the support of those systems' adherents.

A brief bibliography follows of representative ancient texts whose contents are in part mythical.

Bibliography

Budge, E. A. W., ed. and trans. The *Book of the Dead: An English Translation of the Chapters, Hymns, Etc. of the Theban Recension*. London: Routledge & Kegan Paul, Ltd., 1899. Reprint, New York: Barnes and Noble, 1969.

Henricks, Robert G. *Lao-Tzu: Te-Tao Ching: A New Translation Based on the Recently Discovered Ma-wang-tui Texts*. New York: Ballantine, 1989.

Hines, Derek, trans. *Gilgamesh*. New York: Anchor Books, 2004.

Homer. *The Odyssey*. Translated by Robert Fitzgerald. New York: Farrar, Straus & Giroux, 2004.

The New English Bible: The Old Testament. Oxford and Cambridge: Oxford University Press and Cambridge University Press, 1970.

The New English Bible: The New Testament. Oxford and Cambridge: Oxford University Press and Cambridge University Press, 1970.

Virgil. *Aeneid*. Translated by Stanley Lombardo. Indianapolis: Hackett Publishing, 2005.

Vyasa. *The Mahabharata: An Inquiry into the Human Condition*. New Delhi: Orient Longman, 2006.

mythography in the ancient world

Collecting and commenting on myths and tracing their origins back until they are lost in the mists of prehistory is an occupation that has fascinated many a mythographer through the ages. Preserving, explaining, and retelling the myths that formed part of the cultural heritage of every literate ancient people became a major literary enterprise very early after writing came into being.

We see examples of such collections in, for instance, the EGYPTIAN BOOK OF THE DEAD. It brought together all the stories necessary to assure the continued survival of human beings in the afterlife. Elsewhere in ancient Sumer, Assyria, and Babylonia, the invention of CUNEIFORM script, probably for the keeping of business records initially, soon gave rise to such collections of stories as those included in *The GILGAMESH EPIC* that tell of god-kings and heroes and recount a version of the flood story. Myths of origin also appear in the HEBREW BIBLE, including, among others, the two accounts of creation that appear in the first chapter of Genesis.

In India, the great national EPICS, *RAMAYANA* and *MAHABHARATA* coalesced over time, aggregating the stories surrounding the Hindu pantheon into powerful theological and ethical systems.

In Greece and later in Rome, mythical elements concerning gods and demigods and the interactions of mortals and immortals are everywhere apparent in the epics of HOMER and of those whom Homer inspired, including the Roman Augustan poet VIRGIL. The similarities among the myths of geographically distant peoples from Greece to India suggest regular contacts among their ancestors in the mists of preliterate history.

One such contact—that between early Hebrew and Canaanite farmers—has been brought into a sharper focus than the Judeo-Christian HEBREW BIBLE provides by the discovery of the RAS SHAMRA TEXTS. These fired clay tablets, incised with cuneiform writing in the Semitic language, shed light on the religious interactions and influences that occurred as the worshippers of Jehovah and of Baal became neighbors.

In China, we see the interaction of Buddhist myth (see BUDDHIST TEXTS) with native Chinese ancestor worship and efforts at cosmology and foretelling the future in the ongoing development of the *Daode jing* (see LAO TZU).

Such works as those mentioned above contain the myths themselves. Scholarly mythography, however, involves an effort to collect and explain myths and to set them in a frame of reference that will preserve their meanings for later generations. Mythography of this sort began in earnest in the Greco-Roman world with the writings of HESIOD. Another very early Greek mythographer was Palæaphatus of Athens. He probably flourished in the fourth century B.C.E. and is remembered for a book, *Peri apiston* (On incredible matters), in which he argued than mythological beings had originally been mortals whose achievements had resulted in their deification. To present that argument, of course, he had to recount the myths.

Later during the HELLENISTIC AGE, scholars—often employed by the great library at Alexandria, took pains to collect and explain all the mythical material they could find. One great collection of this sort has only recently emerged from the ongoing study of papyrus fragments discovered in Egypt. Called the *mythographus Homericus*, it later became part of the librarians' efforts to recover and interpret all the stories they could, and as a result, ancient commentary on hundreds of myths have survived from the epoch of Alexandrian scholarship. Persons associated with such efforts included ERATOSTHENES and CALLIMACHUS, both of whom had worked at the Alexandrian library.

The Romans, of course, largely borrowed their principal mythology from the Greeks, though vestiges of a native Italic mythology sometimes appear. Although the Romans renamed many of the gods and demigods, the deities fulfill the same functions and occupy the same status as they did in Greek religion. Though his works on the subject are now largely lost, the principal name associated with Roman mythography is that of MARCUS TERENTIUS VARRO. Fabius Planciades Fulgentius also wrote a three-book work dealing with the subject of myth. Later Roman mythographers borrowed from his work.

Bibliography

Bremmer Ian, ed. *Interpretations of Greek Mythology*. London: Croom Helm, 1987.

Botéro, Jean, et al. *Ancestor of the West: Writing, Reasoning, and Religion in Mesopotamia, Elam, and Greece*. Chicago: University of Chicago Press, 2000.

Roberts, Jeremy. *Chinese Mythology A-Z*. New York: Facts On File, 2004.

Vernant, Jean Pierre. *Myth and Thought among the Greeks*. New York: Zone Books, 2006.

Wiseman, T. P. *The Myths of Rome*. Exeter, U.K.: University of Exeter Press, 2004.

N

Nag Hammadi manuscripts   See GNOS-TIC APOCRYPHA AND PSEUDEPIGRAPHA.

Nart Sagas

A large body of myth and folklore that has survived from very ancient, preliterate times in the mouths of speakers of such languages as Abkhaz, Circassian, Abaza, Ossetic, and Kartvelian, the Nart Sagas have recently been the object of intense collection and study. Until the end of the 18th century, the speakers of these and of the other languages in which Nart Sagas principally occur occupied the Caucasus mountain region in a broad band between the Black Sea on the east and the Caspian Sea on the west.

Until the 20th century, the peoples who spoke the languages of the Nart Sagas included warlike pastoralists and traders who lived in clans and tribes with clearly defined class structures. These included, as the folklorist and linguist John Colarusso tells us, "princes, nobles, freemen, and serfs." Though the various clans remained largely independent in peacetime, when war threatened, they banded together into a formidable force. Just how formidable the former Soviet Union was to discover when it forcibly enveloped the Caucasus region in the years between the two world wars. Each Caucasian family's stone house had a tower and was a small fortress. Their resistance lasted for years.

The intensity of scholarly effort that has lately been expended in collecting the stories that comprise the Nart Sagas gains its principal impetus from the rapid disappearance of the native dialects in which the stories have been preserved—some apparently for millennia. All over the world, tongues with relatively few speakers are rapidly becoming extinct in the face of the electronic onslaught of such predominant world languages as Arabic, English, Spanish, Russian, and Chinese.

The stories that comprise the Nart Sagas resemble the myths of the Norse Germanic peoples and of the ancient Greeks as well. Some think them to be relics of cultures who spoke the OLD PERSIAN languages—cultures like the Scythians, described in XENOPHON OF ATHEN'S CYROPÆDIA. One of the principal editors of the sagas, John Colarusso, also sees analogues between stories in the Nart Sagas and myths found in several other cultures. With Greek myth, Colarusso sees a specific link with the story of the goddess of love, Aphrodite, and her shepherd lover, Anchises. Colarusso also notes parallels with Greek stories about Prometheus (see PROMETHEUS BOUND), Cyclops (see CYCLOPS) and the Amazons.

Beyond that, however, Colarusso finds links with the Rig-Veda of ancient India, particularly with its hero, Indra. Other links seem to exist with Norse myths involving Odin and those telling of the World Tree Yggrasil, which has a parallel in the Lady Tree saga of the Narts.

Less certain, but nonetheless attractive given Colarusso's convincing but highly technical linguistic arguments in their favor, are links between the Nart sagas, Hittite myth, and the unknown but assumed mythology of the ancient Indo-European linguistic ancestors of all the peoples mentioned above. If this is the case, then at least some elements of the Nart Sagas have persisted for more than 5,000 years. Links with Turkic and Mongol mythic traditions also seem possible.

To illustrate the character of the Nart Sagas, I have chosen to summarize two stories that suggest links to the myths of other cultures: "Tlepsh and Lady Tree" and the first fragment of "The Ballad of Sawseruquo." The first contains one of the links Colarusso identifies with Norse legend; the second seems associated with the Greek Titan Prometheus's theft of fire from the gods and also is reminiscent of the Sumerian Gilgamesh Epic, when Gilgamesh and his companion Enkidu destroy the giant Humbaba.

As for the Narts themselves, they appear to be the sorts of protohuman that occupy the mythical "dream time"—as the Australian aborigines put it—that featured in the origin myths of many ancient peoples.

Bibliography

Colarusso, John. *Nart Sagas from the Caucasus: Myths and Legends from the Circassians, Abazas, Abkhaz, and Ubykhs.* Princeton, N.J.: Princeton University Press, 2002.

Natural History   See Pliny the Elder.

Nemesianus (Marcus Aurelius Olympius Nemesianus) (fl. late third century C.E.)

An African by origin, likely from Carthage, Nemesianus moved to Italy and authored Latin works on fishing (now lost), hunting, and navigation (now lost). Despite his disclaimer in the introductory section of his longest-surviving work, the *Cynegetica* (on hunting), that this was the only sort of poetry he could write or, indeed, wanted to, we also have four eclogues (poems with shepherds' conversations) that he penned.

While the *Cynegetica* has instruction in the art of hunting as its object, it also presents opportunities for lovely descriptions of the countryside and lauds the sport as an opportunity for increasingly urbanized Romans to benefit from contact with wild nature.

The eclogues, which have Virgil's Eclogues as their example, used to be attributed to Titus Siculus Calpurnius, but it has become clear that significant novelty of theme and treatment differentiate Nemesianus's poems from those of Calpurnius.

Bibliography

Conte, Gian Biagio. *Latin Literature: A History.* Translated by Joseph B. Solodow et al. Baltimore, Md.: Johns Hopkins University Press, 1994.

Nemesianus, Marcus Aurelius Olympius. *The Eclogues of Nemesian and the Einsiedeln Manuscript.* Translated by James B. Pearce. San Antonio, Tex.: Scylax Press, 1992.

Williams, Heather J., ed. *The Eclogues and Cynegetica of Nemesianus.* Leiden: E. J. Brill, 1986.

New Testament

Considered as literature, the 27 books of the New Testament represent a narrower range of literary types than the more expansive Hebrew Bible. The Hebrew Bible traces the history and development of a people; of their trials, tribulations, and triumphs; of their leaders, heroes, and heroines; and of their ethical and religious development and understanding. Major portions of the document are verse compositions, and one can often trace whole stories or elements of those stories to analogous tales in earlier cultures.

The Hebrew Bible arrived at its final form by a slow process of accretion over almost two millennia. The composition of the New Testament's content, by contrast, was the work of less than two centuries. It had a much more specific goal in view than did the Hebrew Bible. First its authors and editors wished to preserve information concerning the life and teachings of Jesus Christ and his apostles. Biography, therefore, is a primary literary genre in the New Testament. Second, the compilers of the New Testament wished to underscore the global importance of the new religion that had coalesced around the figure of Jesus. Therefore instructional and persuasive material is incorporated into its pages.

Whether or not the official position of the young church would admit the account of Jesus' resurrection from the dead as doctrinal remained a matter of individual conviction until the Council of Nicaea (modern Iznik, Turkey). There, in 325 C.E., the literal resurrection became a matter of official doctrine whose essential features are preserved in the Nicene Creed.

The third objective of the works that came to be included in the New Testament was to trace the work of Jesus' followers and their successors in spreading the nascent faith from its place of origin in Palestine throughout Asia Minor, the Grecian archipelago, and the Western Roman Empire. At first, as new churches were established at various locations, letters written from figures of authority in the young church were sent to congregations in other places, read out in public, and often preserved as part of a library of papyrus scrolls treated as devotional literature. (See, for example, the LETTER OF POLYCARP TO THE PHILIPPIANS [ca. early second century C.E.] or the LETTERS OF IGNATIUS [ca. late first or early second century C.E.].) The inclusion of a body of important letters in the New Testament's official text thus makes epistolary prose an important scriptural genre.

The never-ending tendency of religious communities to splinter, however, soon made it alarmingly clear that Christian communicants needed an official body of scripture. Progress toward this goal gained impetus when, under the emperor Constantine, Christianity became the official religion of the Roman state. Whereas it was all very well for the members of peripheral religions to bicker among themselves about such matters as whether or not their founder had literally been resurrected, the official state religion of Rome could tolerate no such divisions. The Council of Nicaea had already pronounced on this crucial matter, and in his Easter letter of 367 C.E., the bishop of Alexandria, ATHANASIUS, listed the books now incorporated in the New Testament as official scripture. The Council of Trent confirmed Athanasius's catalog in 1546 C.E.

In addition to the literary genres mentioned above, the New Testament also contains history, legend, parable, oratory, sermons, short stories, and, particularly in the Book of Revelation, prophecy. From the perspective of those who follow the Christian ethos but who have reservations about such matters as the Virgin Birth or the Resurrection, the New Testament also contains the literary genre of mythology.

Gospel of Mark

The order of composition of the four gospels (from *godspel*: the Anglo Saxon word for "good news") is a matter of general agreement. The Gospel of Mark was the first to be written. Its author may have been the John Mark who personally knew the apostles Peter and Paul. Mark, like all the rest of the New Testament, was written in the Greek language. Unlike the other New Testament books, however, Mark may have had sources in the Aramaic language—the native tongue of Jesus. Mark's date of composition seems to have been a bit later than 70 C.E.

Mark's gospel may have been written at Rome, where early Christian sources (EUSEBIUS OF CAESAREA, Papias, and Aristion) report Mark to have been Peter's interpreter, clerk, and secretary. These early sources make clear that Mark did not personally know Jesus but wrote down everything that he learned from Peter. Modern textual critics suggest that as many as four distinct sources may underlie Mark's received text.

Mark has nothing to say concerning Jesus' birth and childhood, but rather begins his account with Jesus' baptism at the hands of John the Baptist. Mark proceeds to trace Jesus' ministry through Galilee and elsewhere until his final journey to Jericho and to Jerusalem. Mark reports miracles of healing that Jesus performed, including driving out devils and the miracle of feeding a multitude with seven loaves of bread and a few small fish. He also reports a divine voice from a cloud identifying Jesus as the son of God.

Embedded in Mark's text we find the short story of the beheading of John the Baptist. Mark also recounts several parables that Jesus used to teach those who had not been admitted into the ranks of his close disciples. Among others, these include the parable in which he proposes that any bodily suffering while one is alive is better than the risk of going to Hell. Another familiar parable from Mark is one suggesting that a camel can pass through the eye of a needle more easily than a rich man can enter God's kingdom.

Mark recounts Jesus' teaching at Jerusalem. There he gives his vision of the final days when the sun and moon grow dark, the stars fall, and the second coming eventuates. Thus, Mark also contains the literary genre of apocalyptic vision.

Dark forebodings of the coming death of Jesus grow more frequent as we reach Mark's 14th chapter. From that point, there follows the arrest and trial of Jesus and, in chapter 15, his crucifixion and entombment. In chapter 16, Mark recounts the story of Jesus' resurrection, his appearances, and his ascension into heaven. The book ends with the dispersion of the apostles to spread the good news.

Gospel of Matthew

Scholars have assigned the composition of the Gospel of Matthew to a period between that of Mark and ca. 130 C.E. Antioch has been proposed as its place of composition, but no one is sure. The Book of Mark, however, is certainly one of the major sources of the Gospel of Matthew, as about 500 of Matthew's verses rest on just over 600 of Mark's. Textual critics have proposed two other sources for another 550 of Matthew's verses.

Students of religion ascribe the utmost importance to the Gospel of Matthew, considering it to be the fundamental work of the Christian religion. The work begins with a genealogy of Jesus, tracing his descent through the paternal line—from Joseph through 14 generations to King David, and through 14 more to Abraham.

Despite that paternal genealogy, Matthew recounts the stories of Mary's miraculous conception of a divine offspring, of the astrologers from the east who came to Herod's court in search of a newborn king, of the child's birth at Bethlehem, of the family's flight to Egypt when Herod sought to assassinate the child and had all recently firstborn male children slaughtered, and of the angel recalling the family to Judea, where they settled in Nazareth.

There follows Jesus' baptism by John and then the new story of Satan's 40-day temptation of Jesus in the wilderness. Then, after the arrest of John the Baptist, Jesus begins his ministry, calling for repentance before the imminent arrival of the kingdom of Heaven. Matthew traces Jesus' career through the Sermon on the Mount (a model for the literary category of homily) and his ministry at Capernaum and elsewhere—a ministry in which he heals the sick, raises the dead, heals lepers, casts out demons, and encourages his disciples to do likewise. In Matthew, too, Christ teaches in parables. The parables, and indeed the style of the entire book, benefit from Matthew's preference for direct quotation. Matthew also recounts Christ's failed attempt to escape from the crowd that thwarts his solitude follows him after the death and burial of John the Baptist, and the reader once more learns of the miracle of the loaves and fishes. Thereafter, with minor variations, Matthew repeats in his own words Mark's account of Christ's passion, crucifixion, and resurrection. Matthew ends his book with Christ's appearances to the two Marys and to his disciples. On the last occasion, he charges the disciples with the mission of spreading his gospel.

Gospel of Luke

The Gospel of Luke, whose authorship is attributed with somewhat less conviction to Luke the physician at a place unknown, probably dates from between 100 and 110 C.E. Luke, too, used Mark for a source, following some 320 of his verses. Another primitive source—one not extant, but posited to have existed and called Q among biblical scholars—is thought to have provided material for 250 verses. The other half of the verses in Luke are thought to be uniquely his own.

Luke is the most self-consciously literary of the gospels. A full-blown biography with interspersed verse passages and an emphasis on its female characters, it begins with an address to a certain Theophilus—addressed as "your Excellency." That form of address suggests that Luke is attempting to instruct either a noble student or a patron. After that, Luke picks up the Christian narrative at a point earlier than either of his predecessors had done. He begins by talking about the parents of John the Baptist, a priest, Zachariah, and his wife Elizabeth, a couple who are childless and advanced in years. While Zachariah is attending to priestly duties one day, he is surprised by the appearance of the angel Gabriel. Gabriel explains that Elizabeth is going to conceive and bear a son who will be a predecessor of an even greater person.

Gabriel next appears to Mary, tells her Elizabeth's news, and informs Mary of her own role in the operation of eternal Providence. Mary, who is Elizabeth's cousin, goes to visit Elizabeth, and the fetus in Elizabeth's womb leaps for joy. At this point Mary speaks poetry, a paean of rejoicing at her selection as God's instrument. Luke puts a similar passage in the mouth of Zachariah on the occasion of the birth of his son, John.

The most familiar version of the Christmas story follows in chapter 2. So does a brief account of Jesus' childhood—though no mention of an Egyptian sojourn—ending with an account of Jesus debating with the learned at the temple in Jerusalem and his parents' amazement.

Now the narrative leaps ahead to a moment immediately before Jesus' baptism at the hands of John the Baptist and the descent, at that moment, of the Holy Spirit upon Christ. Next follow accounts of Jesus' teaching, healing, and preaching, and Jesus' selection of his apostles. Included as well is the account of Jesus' initial encounter with Mary Magdelene, who anoints and kisses his feet and washes them with her hair.

Luke recounts Jesus' acquiring 72 adherents who joyously go about exorcizing evil spirits in his name. He tells the parable of the man who fell among thieves with its consequent definition of "neighbor" as one who assists another. After numerous other parables and a prediction of the world's imminent end, Luke turns his attention to Jesus' betrayal by Judas Iscariot, Jesus' arrest, his denial by the apostle Peter, and his trial and initial exoneration by Pontius Pilate. King Herod then mocks Christ, and Pilate yields to the crowd's demands for Christ's crucifixion.

Luke's account of Christ's passion is the most graphic in the gospels, emphasizing at it does Christ's forgiving nature in the story of the thieves who were both crucified with him and brought into his fold. The Roman soldiers cast lots for Christ's garment. Joseph of Arimathea provides a tomb, and Christ is buried.

Luke goes on to explain how the stone was rolled away from the tomb and how an angel reported the resurrection to Mary Magdalene, Mary the mother of Jesus, and Joanna. Luke details Jesus' other appearances. In Luke's version, Jesus simply bids his apostles farewell without the fanfare of rising into the sky.

Gospel of John

The three preceding gospels, taken together, are called the synoptic Gospels. If one looks (optic) at the three side by side (syn = together), they are very much alike. The Gospel of John is different: It is a religious treatise of a high order of sophistication. It begins at the beginning of time and alludes to Christ as the Logos—that is, as the Word of God, the active creative principle in the universe without which nothing would have happened. In John are articulated the doctrines of necessary and salvific rebirth and of the love of God for the human race and his willingness to adopt humankind into godhead through the death of his son and human participation in the possibility of Christ's resurrection.

The gospel also contains the wonderful anecdote of the woman at the well whose personal history of five husbands Jesus recounts to her, and how his knowledge of that history so convinced many that he was the promised Messiah. John emphasizes Jesus' controversy with the Pharisees and how the Pharisees plotted among themselves to destroy him. As in the other gospels, he heals the sick and raises Lazarus from the dead. Here, in metaphoric anticipation of his death and burial, Mary anoints Jesus' feet with a costly ointment, nard, and wipes them with her hair.

Jesus' entry into Jerusalem on a donkey that symbolizes his humility is reported. So is the Last Supper and the duplicity of Judas Iscariot in betraying him. The atmosphere in the gospel grows tenser as the moment of Jesus' arrest approaches. That arrest occurs in John's 18th chapter, in which Peter fulfills Christ's prophecy that he will thrice deny Jesus before cockcrow.

In chapters 19 and 20, the stories of the crucifixion and resurrection are repeated in versions that are more circumstantial than those of the other gospels. In the final chapter, Jesus makes three appearances after the tomb has been found empty. For Christian believers, these are the greatest stories ever told.

Mythology and the Acts of the Apostles

For the majority of the ancient and the modern world's populations who did and do not regard the stories as factual, the accounts reported in Scripture are replete with representatives of another literary type—the myth. Some Christian apologists have been disingenuous enough to suggest in print that the events reported in the gospels would not, in the early first century, have made any sense if they were not literally true.

In assessing that claim, it is well to remember that for some 200 years prior to the beginning of the Common Era, Palestine had been occupied, first by the military heirs of Alexander the Great and then, succeeding them, by the armies of the Roman Empire. Both the Greeks and the Romans were polytheists who considered the Jews' monotheism to be stiff-necked. Moreover, under the Greeks and their surrogates an active policy of hellenization had long been implemented in Palestine. While such efforts may well have produced little effect on the priestly classes of the Jews, among the common folk who were the early adherents of Christianity, it seems hard to imagine that polytheism or superstitions rooted in polytheism did not make at least some inroads.

Ancient Greek religion is full of divine paternities, unusual births like that of Dionysus, and resurrections. Apollonius of Tyana, an historical figure, was credited with restoring life to the dead and was himself reported to have been resurrected. (See LIFE OF APOLLONIUS OF TYANA) Ancient Christian legend also shares numerous commonalities with the religion of ancient Egypt, and Egypt was the crucible of early Christianity. Osiris, for example, had been raised from the dead, and both the goddess Isis and the Greek Diana of Ephesus displayed attributes that paralleled qualities later attributed to the Virgin Mary. Nonbelievers, in any case, are likely to treat at least some of the stories in the four gospels as mythical.

With The Acts of the Apostles, we move into new territory. Its material is both narrative and anecdotal. Some commentators have even found EPIC qualities in its pages. The Acts are thought to have been written by the same Luke who wrote the gospel and to have been written around 90 C.E.

Chapter 1 through the first several verses of chapter 6 reports the doings of the Christian faithful in the first year or two following Jesus' crucifixion. The next two-plus chapters trace the nascent religion's growth in Palestine.

Christianity's spread through Asia Minor occupies the end of chapter 12 through the beginning of chapter 16. A reader then follows the career of Paul from the time of his conversion from Christian persecutor to Christian adherent through his missionary career in Macedonia and Greece. At chapter 20, Paul journeys to Jerusalem. There he is arrested, imprisoned, and, because he successfully pled his Roman citizenship, shipped off to Rome for judgment. He and his shipmates encounter a terrible storm and drift for two weeks before fetching up on an Adriatic strand. There, seemingly miraculously, he survives a viper bite.

Arriving in Rome at last, Paul pleads his case before the Jewish community there. Though some Jews are convinced by his arguments, many are not, and Paul finally announces: "The Salvation of God has been sent to the Gentiles." The last verse reports that he remained in Rome preaching Christianity unhindered for two years.

Letters and Revelation

The literary mode of the New Testament shifts at this point to the epistolary. Some 21 books compose the New Testament's corpus of letters. Of these, 10 can confidently be attributed to Paul, and consensus has emerged about the probable dates of many. These include his two letters to the Thessalonians (53 C.E.), two to the Corinthians and one each to the Galatians and the Romans (57–58 C.E.), and his letters to the Colossians the Ephesians (this last attribution is the subject of controversy) (62–63 C.E.). They also include a letter to Philemon and two written from prison to the Philippians (62–63 C.E.). The Pauline letters, which make up the earliest extant documents of the Christian religion, antedate the gospels. Among them, 1 Corinthians is the first authoritative statement of Christian doctrine on matters including immortality, charity or Christian love, and the earliest extant accounts of the Last Supper and the Resurrection.

Though some passages in the two letters to Timothy and one to Titus (all 65 C.E.) may have been written by Paul, no agreement has emerged concerning the identity of their primary author. A similar situation exists with respect to James (uncertain), Jude (ca. 100 C.E.), 1 and 2 Peter (66 and 150 C.E., respectively), and the three letters bearing the name John (ca. 100 C.E.). Hebrews—a sermon in letter form—probably was written ca. 75 C.E.. Hebrews is especially interesting as it blends together aspects of Judaism and late Alexandrian Platonism.

These letters fall into several subcategories. Letters such as those of Philemon and the third letter of John are simply personal. Others are formal treatises in letter form. These include all the letters to the Thessalonians and the Corinthians, 1 John, James, and Hebrews. One may be sure that, aside from such letters as were exclusively personal, these communications became parts of the devotional libraries of the congregations to which they are addressed.

The final book of the New Testament, Revelation, is a work sui generis. Unique in the Bible, it contains prophetic, foreboding dream visions of the end of the world and the final triumph of Christ over evil with the establishment of the New Jerusalem, the earthly dwelling of those who will occupy heaven—those who through their faith in the incredible qualified as brothers and sisters in Christ with the reward of direct participation in godhead.

Bibliography

Amit, Yairah. *Reading Biblical Narratives: Literary Criticism and the Hebrew Bible*. Minneapolis: Fortress Press, 2001.

Bloom, Harold, ed. *The Bible*. New York: Chelsea Publications, 2006.

The New English Bible: The New Testament. Oxford and Cambridge: Oxford University Press and Cambridge University Press, 1970.

Norton, David. *A History of the Bible as Literature*. New York: Cambridge University Press, 2005.

Sypherd, Wilbur Owen. *The Literature of the English Bible*. New York: Oxford University Press, 1938.

Nicander of Colophon (fl. ca. 146
B.C.E.) *Greek poet*

A Greek physician, grammarian, and poet of the HELLENISTIC AGE, Nicander's work survives in a pair of didactic, hexameter EPICS, the *Theriaka* (on poisonous serpents and beasts and remedies for wounds received from them) and *Alexipharmaka* (on antidotes). Nonetheless, the surviving titles of his otherwise lost works suggest that his poems may have been important sources for such later Latin poets as OVID, VIRGIL, and others. Nicander is known to have penned a mythological epic that Ovid used in his *METAMORPHOSES*, a poem on farming later reflected in Virgil's *GEORGICS*, a poem concerning Aetolia (*Aetolika*), and a poem on beekeeping.

Bibliography

Nicander of Colophon. *The Poems and Poetical Fragments.* Edited by A. S. F. Gow and A. F. Scholfield. New York: Arno Press, 1979.

Nicomachean Ethics, The Aristotle (ca.
323 B.C.E.)

ARISTOTLE's son Nichomachus probably compiled *The Nicomachean Ethics*—one of three ethical treatises deriving from the thought of Aristotle—shortly after the philosopher's death. Though a specific date cannot be ascertained, Nicomachus himself is known to have died young in battle, and he must have done the work fairly soon after his father died in 322. It seems that Nicomachus drew on lecture notes and on a treatise, the *Eudemian Ethics*—compiled by Aristotle's pupil Eudemus—which represented an earlier stage in his father's thought. Aristotle's third discussion of ethics, entitled *Magna Moralia* (Great Ethics) is probably a compilation drawn from the other two works by a successor member of Aristotle's peripatetic school of philosophy.

Aristotle defines human beings as political animals. For him, then, the science of ethical human behavior belongs to the realm of politics, and polities like the city-states of Greece are organized to promote human happiness. To accomplish that, however, one first needs to know what makes people happy. Next, one needs to know what sorts of social arrangements and institutions maximize the probability of happiness.

In the first book of *The Nicomachean Ethics*, Aristotle proposes that happiness results from the exercise of the virtues in human nature. These are of two sorts, intellectual and moral virtues, both of which derive from the human soul. In addition to animating the processes that sustain human life, the soul contains the rational intellect, from which flow the intellectual virtues. The soul also contains the human appetites and passions; these determine the second part of the soul, human character. When free human will subordinates appetites and passions to the power of reason, moral virtues result.

The second book examines moral virtue more closely; this Aristotle defines as habitually behaving with moderation—observing the golden mean. Those who legislate for the state assist individuals in achieving happiness by making laws that encourage moderate and rational behavior. Parents assist children in achieving happiness by training them to have good habits that are associated with positive moral qualities. "We become temperate," says Aristotle, "by abstaining from pleasures." We can, likewise, "best abstain from pleasures when we become temperate." Moral virtue results from habitually making temperate choices. The virtue of courage is, for example, the mean between fear that leads to cowardice and rash overconfidence. Liberality or generosity, a virtue, falls halfway on a scale between prodigality and meanness, both vices. The virtue of magnificence falls between the vice of excess and tastelessness and that of paltriness; the virtue gentleness between irascibility and lack of concern; truthfulness between boastfulness and self-depreciation; wittiness between buffoonery and boorishness; friendliness between flattery and surliness.

The third book opens with a consideration of free will and then, as the fourth book also does, examines in greater detail each of the virtues listed in the second book. In the fifth book, however, a separate examination of the virtue of justice occurs. This opens a three-book section of the *Nichomachean Ethics* that has been taken from the earlier *Eudemian Ethics*. Perhaps because actions can be just or unjust, but not often half-just, Aristotle elected to except justice from his general principle of defining virtue as conforming to a mean between polar opposites. In any case, Aristotle considers dealing justly with others and with oneself as the chief virtue. One can also, Aristotle continues, be unjust in one of two ways: one can either behave unlawfully or unfairly. The best judges are those who, in thorny cases, can properly determine what is fair and equitable and sometimes arrive at solutions to disagreements that both parties consider just. In such cases, the virtue of justice can conform to a mean.

Aristotle's discussion of justice concludes his consideration of the moral virtues or "the virtues of the character," and in the sixth book he focuses his attention on the intellectual virtues. These virtues he attributes to two subsections of the soul's rational capacity. He labels these divisions the "scientific faculty" (that is, the faculty of knowing) and the "calculative" or the "deliberative faculty." The function of both is to ascertain the truth. Associated with these faculties are five qualities that help determine what is true: art or technical skill, scientific knowledge, prudence, wisdom, and intelligence. The balance of the sixth book looks closely at the role each of these qualities plays in making the good choices that in turn lead to human happiness. Most important among these qualities is prudence, since it proves most helpful in ascertaining the mean between the excessive and the insufficient.

The seventh book goes off on a bit of a tangent. It explores the weakness of human will as it relates to the question of moral virtue. When willpower fails, Aristotle thinks, it generally does so owing to a person's being tempted by pleasure. Yet pleasure is not, in and of itself, intrinsically bad—a view that Aristotle develops at some length.

Friendship is the topic treated at length in the eighth and ninth books. The gist of Aristotle's argument involves the contribution that friendship makes to one's behaving in a virtuous fashion. Friends model virtuous behavior, and friendship encourages the mutual emulation of virtues observed in the friend. This chapter seems to be one of the most congenial and attractive portions of the document.

The tenth and final book begins with another and closer consideration of pleasure as it relates to ethics. Then Aristotle turns his attention to speculative wisdom, in his view the highest virtue of all. Exercising this virtue leads to a direct contemplation of truth. Contemplating truth is the activity that produces the highest human happiness. People cannot always achieve this virtue. Those who do cannot exercise it at all times and in all places. When, however, those with the capacity do sometimes achieve the contemplation of truth, they achieve a condition almost godlike.

Horace Rackham, a notable translator of *The Nichomachean Ethics*, observes that, though it does not do so, at this point the document should return to the issue of politics and point out that the business of politics should be organizing the state in such a way that the greatest possible number of its citizens will attain the virtue of speculative wisdom and the capacity to use it.

Bibliography
Aristotle. *The Nichomachean Ethics* [Greek and English]. Translated by Horace Rackham. Cambridge, Mass.: Harvard University Press, 1999.

Nihon Shoki (Chronicles of Japan)
(720 C.E.)

The second oldest work in surviving ancient Japanese literature, *Nihon Shoki* takes a more scholarly approach to the presentation of Japanese history that does its predecessor text, *Kojiki*. Unlike *Kojiki*, which was the work of a single hand, *Nihon Shoki* was a compilation undertaken by a dozen noblemen, each of whom recorded episodes in the national history from sources mostly not now extant, though *Kojiki* was among them.

Though the first version appeared in 720 C.E., the completed, official version did not reach its final form until 40 years after the project's inception. Moreover, the compilers of *Nihon Shoki* both wrote in Chinese and used Chinese source material. Only *Nihon Shoki*'s songs have recourse to the modified application of Chinese characters to represent Japanese speech as described in the *Kojiki* entry. Prince Toneri, third son of the emperor Temmu, seems to have headed up the editorial project.

When presenting legendary material, *Kojiki* presents a single version of events. The literary historian Donald Keene reports that, by contrast, *Nihon Shoki* may give as many as 11 variant accounts of a myth. The *Nihon Shoki* also includes material from foreign sources—particularly from Paekche, one of three kingdoms then on the Korean Peninsula.

From the perspective of historiography, *Nihon Shoki* is very precise. Whereas *Kojiki* approximated annual dates by normalizing them to correspond with the 60-year cycles of Chinese history, *Nihon Shoki* often gives day, month, and year, beginning with the coronation of the emperor Jimmu in 660 B.C.E. The accuracy of these dates is often dubious, however.

After dealing with much of the same legendary material that appears in the first book of *Kojiki* during the age of the gods, *Nihon Shoki* considers historical personages. Among these we find Prince Shōtoku (574–622), whose mother, according to the account, bore him painlessly in a stable. He is revered as the founder of Japanese culture and was worshipped after his death as one responsible for miracles. He was also the first Japanese person about whom a biography was written. He is credited with having established a polity along the Confucian lines of the Chinese, with having devised a constitution with 17 articles to guide the state, and with having fostered the spread of Buddhism (see BUDDHA AND BUDDHISM) in Japan. The constitution itself draws its articles both from the Buddhist system and from the *ANALECTS* of CONFUCIUS.

Nihon Shoki relies heavily on Chinese historical documents to fill in early epochs when facts about Japanese history were scant. From the perspective of actual Japanese history, *Nihon Shoki*, despite its scholarly provenance, cannot be relied upon except for the hundred years leading up to its completion.

Bibliography

Keene, Donald. *Seeds in the Heart: Japanese Literature from Earliest Times to the Late Sixteenth Century*. New York: Henry Holt and Company, 1993.

Wheeler, Post, ed. and trans. *The Sacred Scriptures of the Japanese: With All Authoritative Variants*. [*Kojiki* and *Nihon Shoki*.] Westport, Conn.: Greenwood Press, 1976.

Nukata, Princess

Japanese poet   See FEMALE POETS OF ANCIENT JAPAN.

O

Octavia Seneca (ca. 65 C.E.)

Though posterity has preserved fragmentary evidence for a dozen Roman plays on native Roman subjects, only one such play survives in its entirety. That play, *Octavia*, has customarily been listed among the works of SENECA, though a scene that accurately describes the death of the Roman emperor Nero, whom Seneca predeceased, makes Seneca's authorship unlikely.

The history of the Roman imperial family has regularly provided grist for the mills of writers, and that of Rome's fourth and fifth emperors, Claudius and his stepson Nero, is fraught with melodramatic material. Claudius reluctantly had his third wife, Messalina, put to death for treason when she took another husband during Claudius's absence from Rome. The following year, Claudius married the widow of Cneius Domitius Ahenobarbus. Her name was Agrippina, and as empress, she at once undertook a campaign to have her son by her first marriage succeed Claudius as emperor. Her efforts succeeded, and Claudius adopted Lucius Domitius, renaming him Nero. Agrippina bound Nero more tightly to the imperial family by arranging a marriage between him and Claudius's daughter, Octavia.

With the stage of history thus carefully set, Agrippina poisoned her husband on October 12, 54 C.E. On October 13, the 17-year-old Nero succeeded to the world's most powerful throne, and Agrippina, with the help of Nero's tutor, Seneca, and that of the captain of the Praetorian Guard, Sextus Afranius Burrus, became for a time the de facto regent of the Roman Empire. When Nero fell in love with Poppaea—a lovely woman of bad reputation—and wished to divorce Octavia, the imperious Agrippina objected. Annoyed with his mother's domineering ways, Nero arranged her murder. Then Octavia was falsely accused and convicted of adultery. Nero divorced and banished her and subsequently arranged for her murder as well.

The tragedy of *Octavia* picks up the story at the point when Poppaea has already been installed as Nero's concubine. Octavia enters, lamenting her father Claudius's death by the hand of Agrippina, and she bewails Octavia's own treatment at the hands of her husband's mistress Poppaea. In long set speeches that sometimes have more in common with declamation than with dramatic performance, Octavia and her nurse commiserate about their woes. Beyond those already listed, Octavia also mourns the murder of her brother Britannicus, who had been heir apparent before Nero's nomination. She lists Nero's crimes, including the murder of his own mother. The nurse does her best to comfort Octavia, citing historic and mythical examples of women who suffered and triumphed.

Then the chorus enters and reviews the sorry history of the women of the families of Claudius and Nero, particularly that of Agrippina. Then, abruptly, Seneca takes the stage. He thinks about his current unhappy state of affairs as a former power too near an unappreciative monarch, and regrets the loss of his former happiness while he was an exile on Corsica. He moves on to consider the history of the world and the way it moved from peace and justice in the golden age of Astrea—a maiden represented by the constellation Virgo and identified with justice.

Nero enters, and Seneca attempts to school the profligate ruler in a leader's responsibilities. The old scholar's words fall on empty ears, however, as the proud and impious ruler asserts executive authority in all matters. Their conversation then turns to love and wives, and while Seneca tries to convince Nero to found his hopes for a successor on Octavia, Nero praises the pregnant Poppaea. Wearied with Seneca's dull counsel, Nero suggests that the very next day would be a good one for his nuptials with Poppaea.

Now the ghost of Agrippina enters, bearing a flaming torch. She has come from the underworld to curse the union of Nero and Poppaea. She prophesies that the day will come when Nero will "give his throat to his enemies, abandoned and undone and stripped of all." On this quotation rest principally the arguments against Seneca's authorship of the play. It strikes me that the comment is entirely appropriate as it reflects the end of many deposed monarchs of ancient times. It may be that the naysayers protest too much in their objections to Seneca's authorship.

In any case, Agrippina's ghost regrets that she ever bore Nero. She wishes that instead she had been torn to pieces by wild beasts and he in the womb with her. Too ashamed to remain longer above ground, she returns to her place in Tartarus—the lowest depth of Hell.

Octavia reenters and tells the CHORUS that she is relieved by the turn of events that will free her from her monstrous husband.

Poppea and her nurse enter. The nurse congratulates Poppea on her coming triumph, but Poppea has been troubled by a nightmare in which her marriage chamber has been populated with mourners. She also dreamed that she followed Agrippina's ghost down to hell, and that Nero murdered Poppaea's former husband, Rufrius Crispinus. The nurse interprets Poppaea's nightmare, trying to put a rosy interpretation on everything. Unconvinced, Poppaea prepares to do sacrifice and to pray. A chorus of Roman women flutters about saying nice things about Poppaea's coming nuptials.

We then learn from a messenger that the majority of the citizens of Rome, utterly offended by Nero's behavior, are preparing to restore Octavia to her rightful place and role. Those citizens, however, are put down by military might.

The prefect of Rome enters to report on the unrest in the city. Nero blames Octavia and, to his prefect's horror, demands her execution. The emperor orders that she be exiled and, once arrived, be slain.

Octavia is dragged off prophesying her own end. The chorus comments on her fate and on the way the women of her house seem to lie under a curse that passes from generation to generation. Octavia tells her guard that she does not fear the end they are preparing for her and urges them to do their duty.

The chorus ends the play by observing how Iphigenia, in one version of her story, is borne away from the sacrificial altar wrapped in cloud. The chorus hopes that Octavia will elude her fate similarly. The chorus decides that places like Aulis in central Greece and Taurica (today's Crimea), where the gods are appeased by the blood of strangers, are less cruel than the gods of Rome, who seem to demand the blood of the city's own children.

Bibliography

Seneca. *Octavia* in *Seneca's Tragedies*. Vol. 2. Translated by Frank Justus Miller. New York: G. P. Putnam's Sons, 1917.

ode

Meaning simply a *song*, in ancient times the ode developed into a form of high poetic art, often ornamental and complex. In ancient verse, this form took on regularity as it was composed of a strophe (a unified group of lines on a given subject), an antistrophe (a group of lines identical in form to the strophe but with a different message), and an EPODE (a verse with a different structure whose content mediates between strophe and antistrophe).

The Greek poet PINDAR is at once regarded as the originator of the ode form in the Western world and as its most talented Greek practitioner. Pindar employed the form as described above to sing the praises and to celebrate the exploits of the winners of horse races and athletic contests (see VICTORY ODES). Pindar wrote his most famous ode. "OLYMPIAN I," for the Sicilian ruler of the city of Syracuse, Hieron, on the occasion of Hieron's horse winning the race at the Olympian games in 476 B.C.E. Both SAPPHO and ALCAEUS also employed the form, as did many others of lesser note. In all the foregoing cases, the poets intended their odes to be sung and accompanied by stringed instruments.

The most gifted poet of ancient Rome, HORACE, composed four books of 103 odes under the Latin title *Carmina* (Songs). Although Horace did not intend his works to be instrumentally accompanied or sung, he nevertheless achieves in them a notable musicality. That melodic quality results from variation of meter—he uses 19 different ones, all borrowed from the Greeks—and his happy choice of language. He suits both his vocabulary and his meters to the mood of each poem. Generally, too, his poems are addressed to a reader, a listener, a god, or even inanimate objects. His various subjects include moral advice, love, good food and fellowship, politics, regret at the brevity of human life, and many others. (See Horace's ODES.)

In ancient China, one of the foundational documents of Chinese Confucianism, the BOOK OF ODES (*Shi jing* or *Shih ching*) is a collection of 305 songs in four books dating to 700–600 B.C.E. At least five of the songs included reputedly were composed during the Shang Dynasty (ca. 1600–ca. 1028 B.C.E.). Chinese odes, too, were originally composed for musical accompaniment. Reputedly selected by CONFUCIUS himself from among 3,000 candidates, these precious relics of an age long gone served four main functions. Those in the first book made verse reports to the emperor about the lives and customs of common people from around the feudal states and provided an index of how well the local nobility was ruling. The second and third book respectively contained odes used to entertain at ordinary occasions and at conventions of feudal nobility. The fourth contained odes to be sung at religious sacrifices. Other topics of Chinese odes included love in all its manifestations and consequences, warfare, nature, antifeminist diatribes, politics, law, and the early Chinese view of the nature of deity.

Among the remnants of ancient libraries unearthed in the Middle East, similar poems address such members of the pantheon of Sumerian and Babylonian deities as the love goddess Innin or Innanna.

Throughout the world, intentional imitations of ancient odes or poems and songs resembling them have periodically enjoyed great popularity, as they did during the European Renaissance. Even in periods when popular taste turns in other directions, odes continue to be composed—sometimes by authors who are unaware that a long tradition precedes them.

Bibliography

Afanasieva, V. K. "Sumerian Culture." In *Early Antiquity*. Edited by I. M. Diakonoff and Philip L. Kohl. Translated by Alexander Kirjanov. Chicago: University of Chicago Press, 1991.

Birch, Cyril, ed. *Anthology of Chinese Literature*. New York: Grove Press, 1965.

Connery, Christopher Leigh. *The Empire of the Text: Writing and Authority in Early Imperial China*. New York: Rowman and Littlefield Publishers, 1998.

Horace. *Odes and Epodes*. Translated by Niall Rudd. Cambridge, Mass: Harvard University Press, 2004.

Race, William H. *Pindar: Olympian Odes, Pythian Odes.* [Greek and English.] Cambridge, Mass.: Harvard University Press, 1997.

Odes Horace (Books 1–3, 23 B.C.E.; book 4, ca. 13 B.C.E.)

As HORACE's recent translator, Niall Rudd, explains, Horace took pride in being the first Roman to write a significant body of lyric poetry, self-consciously modeling his *Odes* on Greek literary forebears. His exemplars included such early Greek lyricists as ALCAEUS, ANACREON, SAPPHO, and PINDAR, and the meters Horace employed echoed those his models had used.

Most of the poems in Horace's four books are deeply personal. He offers advice to friends, including in his counsel morsels of philosophy from such Greek thinkers as EPICURUS or PLATO. Some of them appear traditionally religious—as was Horace's own public religious stance, even though privately he seems to been a follower of Epicurus. An eighth of the poems in the first three of Horace's books of odes stem from the poet's nationalism, and in those 11 patriotic poems one particularly feels Pindar's influence. Other poems concern love—an emotion toward which Horace displays a wistful and ironic humor. As in Anacreon, one can find relief from lovesickness in drinking and in the musical qualities of poetry itself.

Book 1

The first book of odes is dedicated to Horace's patron, Maecenas, whose generosity and gift of a famous Sabine farm had freed Horace to follow his poetic program without fear of want and without unwelcome distractions. The first ode (1.1) gracefully and gratefully acknowledges that gift and promises that if his poems win his patron's approval, and if Maecenas ranks them with those of Horace's Grecian forebears, Horace will soar aloft and bump against the stars.

The second ode (1.2) is addressed to AUGUSTUS CAESAR, who had offered Horace the post of private secretary to the emperor—a post that Horace had declined. After a list of the natural and civic disasters that have afflicted Rome, the poet addresses the leader who at last has put everything right—the emperor, father, and first citizen, Augustus.

Ode 1.3 is addressed to the premier poet of the Roman state, VIRGIL, who is off on a journey to Greece. The poem opens with a prayer for Virgil's safety, and then recounts a list of natural and mythical disasters, most of them traceable to human folly and to HUBRIS—overweening human pride—that will not let Jove set aside his punishing thunderbolts.

The three dedicatory poems finished, Horace turns to his collection proper. The fourth ode contrasts the welcome arrival of spring with the inevitability of death and the absence of springtime joys thereafter. The fifth addresses a false girlfriend, Pyrhha, in the arms of a new lover. Its closing line suggests that the jilted lover has resolved to drown himself. In the sixth ode, Horace declines to sing the praises of the warlike Roman general Marcus Vipsoricus Agrippa (63–12 B.C.E.). The poet's talent, he insists, is too weak for that weighty subject. More suited to his pen are "drinking bouts" and "fierce girls" clawing young men with their fingernails.

Ode 1.7 ostensibly will leave it to other poets to sing of far-off places famous in history and legend. Horace is the poet of Rome, wine will drown sorrow, and the Tibur is the river Horace loves. Teucer, the Trojan, now confounds the poet's opening remarks by appearing in the poem. He is also drinking as he prepares to lead his followers to a new land on Cyprus.

In the eighth ode, Horace reproves a girl named Lydia because his friend Sybaris's adulation of her has destroyed his courage for martial exercise and risk. The ninth ode suggests that winter makes people merry because it reminds them to enjoy life while they can. The tenth is a hymn to Mercury. Horace is the source of the phrase *carpe diem*, and just as his fourth ode implied that subject, Ode 1.11 makes it explicit: Seize the day; tomorrow may not come.

Though Horace's principle of thematic organization (if there is one) is not always clear in his odes, his hymn to Mercury in the 10th ode seems to anticipate the 12th, in which he sings the praises of gods and heroes. He begins with an invocation of the Muse of history, Clio, which becomes the first of a series of rhetorical questions in which the poet seeks a subject. He decides that praising the gods is his first responsibility, and he does so. That done, the poet once more hesitates.

Horace's subject has shifted from mythic to Roman history, and he wonders where to begin. The alternatives he considers span Roman history from its beginnings to the elevation of Augustus Caesar. The poem ends as a prayer to Jupiter to endorse Augustus as his viceroy throughout the world.

Ode 1.13 concerns jealousy, and 1.14 addresses a ship. Scholars and readers have variously interpreted what Horace meant by the ship. Though that issue remains unresolved, the poem is clearly based on one by Alcaeus. The 15th ode glances back at the Trojan War and at the sea god Nereus's prophecy concerning Troy's fall.

Ode 1.16 addresses a goddess lovelier than her lovely mother—perhaps one of the MUSES. He asks that she condemn his angry satires and help him achieve a sweeter poetic voice as he forswears his earlier invectives. The following poem—which is among Horace's most beautiful—is an invitation to join the poet at his country estate and enjoy its pleasures. By seeming association, the next poem initially celebrates the pleasures of wine, but it ends by warning against wine's dangers. The 19th ode records the poet's infatuation with a girl named Glycera. The 20th invites Maecenas to join Horace at the Sabine farm, and the 21st encourages young people to sing the praises of the deities Diana, Cynthius (Apollo), and Latona, and to pray to Apollo that he will protect Augustus and the Roman people from famine, warfare, and plague.

In the 22nd ode, Horace celebrates the salutary effect of his love for a woman named Lalage in helping him lead a pure life and in protecting him from many dangers. In the 23rd, however, his amorous attention has shifted to Chloe.

The mood of Ode 1.24 darkens radically as Horace mourns the death of his good friend and Virgil's, the critic Quintilius Varus. The poet advises that patience will alleviate the loss that no one can restore. Grief is replaced in the next ode by wistful melancholy as the poet reflects on the circumstances of an aging courtesan, Lydia. Less and less often do impatient lovers accost her, and the day is not far off when her own lust will rage unsatisfied.

In 1.26, the speaker of the poem impatiently awaits the preparation of a garland for his beloved Lamia. Ode 1.27 recounts a drinking party at which the speaker entices a companion to name his beloved. When the friend does so, the speaker commiserates, telling the lover that he is caught in a whirlpool. The girl is a witch. The lover will not easily escape her toils.

Another funeral poem, Ode 1.28 is addressed to the drowned Archytas. After the usual observations on the inescapability of death, the drowned person speaks, asking passersby to bury his washed-up bones. His spirit can then rest, and the benefactor will enjoy blessing. If the passerby neglects this kindness, ill luck will follow him. The deceased begs for "three handfuls of dust"—a symbolic burial that will release his spirit.

The next ode reproves a philosopher who wants to trade his library for a Spanish breastplate, and the one that follows, Ode 1.30, calls upon the goddess Venus to come and pay tribute at the shrine of the poet's beloved Glycera. Horace asks Venus to bring with her Cupid, the Graces, and Mercury.

Ode 1.31 calls upon Apollo to grant the poet not lands and riches but, instead, the blessing of enjoying what he has in good health and a dignified old age still filled with music, by which Horace also means poetry. In the following poem, Horace invokes his "Greek lyre"—his talent—calling for a Latin song. He alludes to his predecessor poet and model, the Greek poet Alcaeus, and praises the lyre that symbolizes his own poetic talent and achievement.

Horace steps down from the lofty sentiment of the foregoing poem as he traces the complexities that embroil those lovers whose beloveds love others. He ends Ode 1.33 with the confession that he, too, had been smitten with the charms of a freedwoman when a "superior mistress" had shown an amorous interest in him.

Ode 1.34, reflects on Horace's transitions from religion to philosophy and back again to religion. He also considers the power of the gods to reverse or exchange the fortunes of the most and the least fortunate. This reflection leads the poet to invoke the goddess Fortuna herself in Ode 1.35. He observes that everyone prays to her—the lowly as well as those who wield power. "Ruthless Necessity," says Horace, always precedes Fortune. Hope and Loyalty accompany her and remain with her regardless of Fortune's granting or denying blessings. Her human worshippers, however, are unreliable. Following those reflections, Horace addresses a prayer to the goddess. He prays that she will protect Augustus Caesar as he leads a military expedition to Britain, and that she will grant her similar blessing to the young soldiers of the empire who are elsewhere engaged. Then the poet reflects on the shame that Rome accumulated in her recent civil wars. He hopes that the unworthy swords with which brother killed brother will be melted down, forged anew, and used against more appropriate enemies.

The 36th ode of the first collection celebrates the happy return of a traveler—probably a soldier—from Spain. The poem introduces the next one, which begins by celebrating the victory of the Romans over Marc Antony and Cleopatra at the Battle of Actium (29 B.C.E.). Horace then recounts Cleopatra's flight and her subsequent suicide. The poet admires the queen's courage in handling the venomous snakes that killed her and her pride in resolving to die rather than "be stripped of her royalty."

The final ode of the first collection addresses a servant and asserts the poet's preference for plain living. It also implies his happiness as he sits drinking in an arbor on his estate.

Book 2

The introductory ode of the second of Horace's collection is a reflection upon a work by Horace's fellow poet, the critic, tragedian, staunch repub-

lican, former soldier, and historian Gaius Asinius Pollio. Horace has been reading Pollio's history of the Roman Civil Wars, and the opening lines of the ode sound a warning. Pollio is treading on hot ashes. His pointed commentary and republican viewpoint are dangerous. Noting Pollio's triumphs as a defense attorney, an orator, and a victorious leader, Horace suggests that the historian return to writing theatrical tragedies.

A few lines convey the realistic images that Pollio's *History* calls up in Horace's mind. They in turn lead him first to consider the attitudes of the gods toward recent Roman history and then to mourn the carnage. Having grown too serious, Horace reproves his muse for making him sound more like SIMONIDES OF CEOS than like the love poet that Horace would prefer to be.

Ode 2.2 addresses the wealthy Sallustius Crispus, praising him for understanding the true value of money. Horace urges the reader to avoid greed. Virtue—by which Horace means manly and appropriate thought and behavior—appears only in the person who can look at "heaps of treasure" and pass on without a qualm.

Seizing the day and making the most of joyful life is the theme of the following poem. After that, Ode 2.4 encourages "Phocian Xanthia" not to feel ashamed for loving a slave girl. She might be the daughter of illustrious parents, but in any case her comportment testifies that she is of respectable birth.

Ode 2.5 begins with a reflection on the behavior of a young heifer not yet ready for breeding. It becomes clear that the poet really has in mind a woman he has mentioned before, Lalage. It seems she will soon marry. As the poem ends, however, Horace shifts to considering the effeminate appearance of a young man, "Cnidian Gyges."

The poet confides his preference for a burial place to a friend, Septimius, in Ode 2.6. Horace hopes to be buried in lovely Tivoli (ancient Tibur). Another epistolary Ode 2.7, invites an old comrade in arms, one Pompeius, to visit Horace on his estate. We learn that the friends had fought together in Greece during the civil wars. The god Mercury, however, had conducted

Horace through the enemy ranks and out of the battle. The god concealed the poet in a dense cloud, and Pompeius remained in the battle. Horace is jubilant at the prospect of a reunion with his friend.

A heartbreaker, Barine, is the addressee of Ode 2.8. All the oaths that she makes to her admirers, she breaks. But the gods do not punish her. Rather, she grows more attractive and prospers. Generations of young men worship at Barine's feet. Mothers, young brides, and the old men worried about what their sons are doing with their money—all have reason to fear Barine's appeal.

The ninth ode of the second collection reproves a fellow poet, Valgius, for too long lamenting his lost love, Mystes. Nothing else in nature mourns forever. Horace advises him to drop his sorrow and sing of the victories of Roman arms.

Ode 2.10 advises Horace's friend Licinius to steer a middle course and make his life an example of the golden mean. Ill fortune does not last forever; neither does the good. Apollo sometimes grants his inspiration, sometimes withholds. Wisdom dictates that canny seamen shorten sail before too favorable a breeze.

"Seize the day" is once again the subject of Ode 2.11, one that Horace addresses to "Hirpinian Quinctus." There is no point in making plans for infinity. Join me, Horace invites, in performing the rites of Bacchus, drinking a little wine mixed with water, and enjoying music played by Lyde, a local prostitute.

"Make love, not war" is the advice Horace offers in the 12th ode of his second collection. The poem is addressed to Horace's patron, Maecenas. It begins by suggesting that particular poetic forms best treat different subjects. One does not choose lyrics to describe battles. Therefore, if Maecenas wants to write about Rome's civil wars, Horace suggests that he do so in prose. Horace's own muse calls him to celebrate the "flashing eyes" and the singing of his sweet mistress, Licymnia. He wonders what Maecenas would exchange for a lock of Licymnia's hair, stolen when she bends her neck to receive a proffered kiss.

Ode 2.13 is an address to a tree that struck Horace's head when it fell. It gives Horace an occasion to comment on the frequency of accidental death. He reflects on some of the mythical consequences had the tree struck him: He would have met his predecessors, Alcaeus and Sappho, in the underworld and seen the ghosts and Hell's monsters entranced by the poets' songs.

The next ode reflects once more on death's inevitability despite whatever precautions one may attempt against it. Earth, home, beloved wife, and a cellar full of expensive wine—all must be left behind.

Conspicuous consumption, particularly that of agricultural acreage by luxurious dwellings, receives the brunt of the poet's criticism in Ode 2.15. Moreover, the privatization of hitherto public streams and ponds and open, public fields will diminish everyone's life. In the good old days, public temples were grand and private dwellings modest.

Ode 2.16 continues the theme. It praises the quiet and contented life that does not worry about the future beyond sensible provision for it. One cannot provide against any eventuality; one can be frugal.

Ode 2.17 assures Horace's patron, Maecenas, that he is not likely to die before Horace. Should Maecenas do so, Horace is resolved to end his own life as well. Maecenas, however, has already proved that he is fortune's darling, and the tree that struck Horace could easily have killed him. If Horace dies first, he hopes that Maecenas will offer a funeral sacrifice and dedicate a votive memorial. Should Maecenas die first, Horace promises to kill a humble lamb. He anticipates his own death.

Ode 2.18 once again stresses Horace's simple and contented mode of life. Then he rails against the foolishness of an old person who is still building mansions, still expanding the boundaries of his property in every direction, and still driving off his neighbors and trampling on their rights in his irrational pursuit of belongings and real estate. No amount of wealth will ward off Mercury, the escort of the souls of the dead to the underworld.

Ode 2.19 is a hymn in honor of the new god, Bacchus, and features the shout of praise—*Euhoe*—traditionally used by the god's adherents. He sings of the miracles performed by the god (see *The BACCHAE*), praises the god's unexpected prowess in battle, and recalls the way the guard dog of Hades, Cerberus, fawned on Bacchus and licked his feet when he descended into Hell.

The 20th and final ode of the second collection addresses Maecenas. The poem asserts Horace's expectation that he—or at least his poetic reputation—will live forever. Even as he writes, he is metamorphosing into a white swan whose song will sound throughout the world. Given the immortality of his verse, there is no point in a funeral, grieving, or even a tomb.

Horace originally intended his third collection of odes to be the last. In response to an imperial request, he later rethought that decision and added a fourth set. At the time he wrote the third collection, though, he intended it to close an epoch in his mastery of differing kinds of verse.

Book 3

The first ode of the third collection (3.1) asserts Horace's distaste for the mob, whose members are uninitiated to the joys of poetry. He understands differences in the tastes and capacities of different people, and he respects those, but he is free to choose his own manner of life and to avoid the annoyances that accompany others' choices. He thinks about the shrinking domain of fishes as contractors dump rubble into the sea to serve as foundations for the seaside villas of the rich. He reasserts his contentment in living a retiring life on his Sabine farm.

The second ode of the third collection contains one of Horace's most famous lines: "Dulce et decorum est pro patria mori" (It is sweet and fitting to die for one's country). The 20th-century poet Wilfred Owen called that line an "age-old lie." Horace, however, did not share Owen's view. He thought that military training and service toughened young men, and that death sought out cowardly youths who were likely to be hamstrung running from the battle.

A person's true worth, however, says Horace, changing the subject, is not measured by success in elections. It does not respect the whim of the governed. It takes its own way and soars above the vulgar crowd. Horace implies that he enjoys the confidence of the emperor and that he can be trusted with state secrets. He believes that retribution is likely to overtake a criminal.

Ode 3.3 looks to Pindar for its formal inspiration and dares to tread the edges of political matters. Horace approves of an imperial policy that remains steadfast in the face of the crowd, a popular tyrant, a dangerous south wind, or the disapproval of Jove himself. Augustus has the determination that Horace admires, and the poet is convinced that determination is the quality that will qualify the emperor to take his place among the immortal gods.

Horace now quotes a speech made by the goddess Juno after the fall of Troy. In it, she promises that she will withdraw her enmity from the descendants of Trojans, particularly Romulus, son of the war god Mars and a Trojan priestess. As long as the former site of Troy remains a wilderness, Rome will prosper—although greed can undermine that prosperity. If, however, the Romans should attempt to rebuild Troy as a new imperial capital—a plan that had been proposed—Juno herself will lead the host that will destroy the city as often as it is rebuilt. Reproving himself and his muse for straying into "momentous matters," Horace reminds himself to return to "trivial ditties."

The time for that return has not yet come. Ode 3.4, invokes the Muse of epic poetry, Calliope. She comes, and the poet recalls how as a child he could wander and sleep in the woodlands untroubled by snakes and bears. The poet rededicates himself to the Muses, crediting his love for them with his preservation at the battle of Philippi and with his escape from drowning at Palinurus—likely, as Niall Rudd tells us, in a battle against Pompey's son Sextus in 36 B.C.E. Horace also salutes the Muses as his protectresses against the falling tree. Given his history, he considers himself immune to violence and is willing to face any danger.

The poet credits the Muses with refreshing Augustus in the midst of his military exploits. In a lengthy epic simile, Horace compares Augustus's victories to that of the gods over the rebellious TITANS. With that simile, the ode concludes.

"Momentous matters" continue to occupy the poet through the next two odes. Ode 3.5, Horace disparages Crassus's captured Roman soldiers for marrying Barbarian wives and remaining in Parthia while serving in the army there. He contrasts that recent Roman behavior with the former fortitude of Marcus Attilius Regulus, a soldier in the first Punic War. Captured in Carthage in 255 B. C.E., Regulus was released to return to Italy and arrange an exchange of prisoners. Regulus appeared before the senate and advised them against bringing the army home. Having put the senatorial speech in Regulus's mouth, Horace then reports how Regulus, feeling unworthy in defeat, had refused to greet his wife and children. He concludes by reporting how Regulus unhesitatingly followed through on his determination to share his comrades' fates. The senate took his advice. Regulus returned to Carthage, where he was executed along with his fellows.

In Ode 3.6, Horace continues in the role of social critic. Until the profaned temples of the Roman gods are restored and until adultery no longer undermines the sanctity of Roman marriage, Rome will decline. His contemporaries compare unfavorably with their forefathers. Horace calls them "an inferior breed," one that will produce "degenerate offspring."

Lightening the mood a little, Horace moves from public to private matters. Ode 3.7 finds Gyges' wife Asterie, weeping for him while he is off on an extended business trip. Horace imagines the young man resisting the importunities of those who attempt to seduce him, and then advises Asterie not to look with too favorable an eye upon the accomplishments and virility of her neighbor, Enipeus. She is to lock up her house and resist his blandishments.

Ode 3.8 celebrates the poet's bachelorhood. It is March 1—"Matron's day." Responding to Maecena's question, the poet explains why he is surrounded with the paraphernalia of sacrifice. He says that he celebrates this day with a sacrifice to the "God of Freedom," Bacchus. He gives the god a delicious meal, including a white goat, and opens a jar of rare old wine. He asks Maecenas to join him in drinking a hundred ladles in honor of his "escape." The poet cites several examples of how well matters are going on the Romans' military fronts, and he advises his friend to put aside his civic responsibilities, join the celebration, and neglect the serious matters that occupy his time.

Ode 3.9 reports a conversation between former lovers who rehearse the grievances they have with one another, for they have both strayed. The male speaker, perhaps the poet, then proposes reconciliation. Lydia, the female, accepts him despite his flightiness and his bad temper. She would rather be with him than anyone else and would gladly die with him.

In Ode 3.10, a lover begs at his beloved Lyce's doorway to be admitted. Lyce's husband has a Muse for a mistress, but the lover is freezing on the rain-soaked doorstep with his hand on the latch, begging to be admitted.

Ode 3.11 invokes the god Mercury and sings for the benefit of Lyde, a girl who, "like a three-year-old filly," shies away from being touched. Mercury, a god of great power, should tell Lyde the story of Hypermestra (see The SUPPLIANTS). One of the 50 daughters of Danaus, Hypermestra was the only sister to spare her husband when all were supposed to kill the 50 sons of Aegyptus, their husbands, on their wedding night. Horace tells the rest of Hypermestra's story. Its moral is that virgin daughters deceive the fathers who want to prevent their daughter's marrying.

Ode 3.12 pities Neobule, a girl whom Cupid has struck with love for the youth Hebrus of Lipara. His accomplishments at sport are many. He can, ride, box, sprint, and hunt. The last line, however, hints darkly at his having been injured or killed by a charging boar.

The next poem, the 13th of the third collection, addresses the fountain of Bandusia. The poet promises that, on the day following, a young goat whose horns are just budding will be sacrificed to the nymphs of the spring in gratitude for the cooling waters that spring from it.

Ode 3.14 celebrates the return of Emperor Augustus from Spain in 24 B.C.E. Horace anticipates the welcome that Empress Livia will offer her triumphant husband. He also knows that the emperor's arrival will calm Horace's own fears about insurrection and violent death. In celebration, the poet sends his servant to find a jar of well-aged wine and to hurry along the singer Neaera.

In the next poem, the poet reproves an elderly woman who seeks many lovers. Following that, he turns once more to a weightier moral subject in Ode 3.16. It is a reflection on the power of money. He begins by recalling the story of Danae, whom Jupiter visited in the form of a shower of gold in her tightly locked room. Horace interprets the myth as the story of a bribe. Gold has a way of finding its way anywhere and ruining what it touches. Moreover, its acquisition is habit-forming. Horace thinks the gods will favor those who remain destitute, desire nothing, and do not seek out the company of the rich. He once again congratulates himself on his congenial way of life.

Ode 3.17 addresses the scion of a distinguished family, Aelius, and compresses his genealogy into a parenthetical interrupter. Continuing after this rather grandiose interpolation, Horace predicts a storm the following day. The harbinger of that storm is an aged crow that Horace keeps an eye on. In the poem that follows, Horace addresses a prayer to the rural deity Faunus, who both pursues nymphs and protects young goats from hungry wolves. His annual festival is celebrated on the fifth of December, when the wolf observes peace with the lambs, the forest sheds its leaves, and the country folk dance.

In Ode 3.19, an impatient Horace, bored by a pedantic conversation, is waiting for the drinking and the entertainment to begin at a celebration honoring a new month, a new day, and the installation of "Murena the augur" in a new political office. Scholars debate which of two possible Murenas Horace intended. Horace wants the party to grow noisy and wild so that the next-door neighbor, the grouchy Lycus, will be disturbed. In the last line, the poet's thoughts turn to his smoldering passion for his unnamed sweetheart. The organization of the ode follows the poet's stream of consciousness.

Ode 3.20 alludes to a rivalry between a man, Pyrrhus, and an unnamed woman for the affection of a handsome young man. The poet predicts victory for the woman, whom he compares to a lioness protecting her cubs.

The following poem, Ode 3.21, praises the qualities of wine in repressing the inhibitions of reserved persons, bringing hope to the worried and courage to the faint of heart. The poet intends to enjoy wine's advantages until sunrise.

In Ode 3.22, the poet presents the pine tree that shades his house to the goddess of the hunt, Diana, who is also Luna in heaven and Hecate in Hades. He makes the tree her altar so that he may annually sacrifice a young boar to her.

The 23rd poem of the third collection addresses a peasant girl, Phidyle. In his ode, the poet assures her that the simple offerings she can afford will please her household gods as much as the more expensive gifts she can not afford. The gods will favor her crops and her animals.

Ode 3.24 is a diatribe against the accumulation of wealth as the root cause of public immorality and lawlessness in Rome. Horace points to the nomadic Scythians and the Getae of Thrace as people who hold the basic necessities of life in common and live rigorously virtuous lives. Horace recommends that precious stones and the corrupting element, gold, either be locked up in temples or thrown into the sea. He also thinks that citizens should be invigorated with military training and give up soft living. Wealth without virtue leaves a fortune incomplete.

Horace next invokes the god Bacchus in Ode 3.25, asking for the inspiration of divine madness so that the poet can adequately sing the glories of Augustus Caesar.

The following poem, Ode 3.26, complains that, while the poet had formerly triumphed often in the ongoing battle of the sexes, overcoming girls' resistance with the tools of his poetic trade—here compared to crowbars, axes, and firebrands—his unaided successes are over. Haughty Chloe will require a flick of the whip of the goddess of love.

Ode 3.27 is a more complex and ambitious poem in which Horace adopts the persona of a seer, or one who interprets prophetic signs. He begins by invoking omens of bad fortune for evil people who travel, but for Galatea, who is leaving and who, Horace hopes, will remember him, he has only good wishes. The rest of the poem makes one wonder if Galatea is on her wedding journey.

Galatea is named for a sea nymph, and that association prompts what follows. The signs of the coming weather over the Adriatic Sea are unsettled, and Horace knows from experience what unpleasant consequences can follow in its waters both from an east wind and a south wind. Making a forced transition, he notes that the princess Europa had similar apprehensions when she rode across the sea on the back of the king of the gods, Jupiter, who had assumed the shape of a snow-white bull and made love to her. Horace imagines the qualms that Europa experienced as the bull carried her across the raging waters. He describes her second thoughts, her regrets, her father's imagined reproof, and her angry desire to punish or kill the bull. In her shame at her own folly, Europa prays to become "food for tigers."

The goddess of love, Venus, who with her son Cupid had led the princess astray, reproves Europa, however, The goddess explains that she has become the bride of the king of the gods. Europa must give up hysteria and tantrums and resign herself to her fated greatness; a continent will be named for her. Also, though Horace does not state it, Europa will bear Jupiter three boys—demigods who will become kings and leaders. One will be Minos of Crete. Another will be the judge of the dead, Rhadamanthys, who rules Elysium—first called the islands of the blest and later thought of

as the abode of the blessed in the underworld. In some versions of Europa's story, her third son is Sarpedon, one of the generals of the Lycians in the Trojan War.

Ode 3.28 sings Horace's celebration of the god Neptune's feast day with a jar of good old wine. The 29th poem of the collection addresses Maecenas, reminding him that he owes Horace a visit. The poet tells his wealthy patron to leave his luxury behind for a simple meal in a modest house. Horace describes the position of the stars. It is midsummer and hot, and the shepherds seek shade for their flocks. Horace also imagines Maecenas's weighty cares of state in his role as Augustus's chief minister. He advises him to let the gods worry about the plots being hatched in far-off places, since only their foreknowledge is accurate. Settle pressing problems calmly, is the poet's advice to the statesman. Horace iterates his conviction that when, at the end of a day, a person knows he has fully lived, that day has been well spent. As for Horace himself, he returns the gifts of fortune, wraps himself in virtue, and seeks out honest poverty. He ends the ode by recounting his stoic acceptance of adversity and his rejection of bargaining with the gods for favor.

Ode 3.30 is the final ode of the third collection. It is the piece with which Horace intended to close out his ode-writing career. Subsequent events would lead him to modify that intention. Nonetheless, the 30th poem contains Horace's evaluation of his own poetic worth. His judgment of his own merit has proved accurate. His poetry will outlast the pyramids. As long as he has readers, he cannot wholly die. His reputation will be worldwide. He has honored his muse, Melpomene (the Muse of tragedy), who deserves the credit for having inspired him. He hopes that she will crown him with bay leaves as Apollo's poet laureate.

Book 4

Though Horace intended to turn his attention to other sorts of poetic projects, his patron Maecenas and others hoped he would continue to write lyrics. He resisted their suggestions, but when Augustus himself officially requested a choral hymn for performance in 17 B.C.E. to celebrate the emperor's past accomplishments and the dawning of a new age in Rome, Horace was obliged to comply. That effort, his "Hymn for a New Age," invokes the gods and goddesses of the Roman pantheon—particularly Phoebus and Diana. It praises Rome's successes under Augustus's rule, and it calls for the gods' continued favor through a 110-year cycle of prosperity. Composing that hymn apparently stimulated the poet's lyric inspiration, and he produced a fourth book of 15 more odes.

The first ode of book 4 chides the goddess Venus for inflaming a no-longer-young poet's heart with passion for a youthful Ligurinus. Ode 4.2 addresses the son of Mark Antony, Iulus, who wrote poems in the fashion of Pindar. Horace's poem is itself a Pindaric ode, and it ironically explains that, as a Pindaric poet, Iulus must write the ode that celebrates Augustus Caesar's anticipated return from his wars in Gaul and Spain. Horace will contribute his praise as he can. Iulus, however, will give a larger sacrifice, though Horace's smaller one, the poet implies, will be at least as fitting.

Ode 4.3 addresses the poet's muse, Melpomene, crediting her with making Horace the poet of the Roman lyre. Horace follows that invocation with another Pindaric ode, this one celebrating the successes of Augustus Caesar's stepson, Drusus, as he led the Roman legions to victory against the warlike mountain people, the Vindelici, in the Rhaetian Alps. Horace attributes Drusus's bravery and his accomplishments both to nature and to nurture.

In an associative transition, the poet thinks back to a time when Roman arms proved less fortunate and the armies of the Carthaginians enjoyed temporary success in Italy. Horace puts a speech into the mouth of the Carthaginian general, Hannibal. In it, Hannibal acknowledges the invincibility of Roman arms as proved by the defeat of the army of Hannibal's brother, Hasdrubal, in 207 B.C.E. Hannibal utters his conviction that Jupiter protects Drusus and his brother Tiberius and that the god will keep them safe in war.

Still celebrating the benefits brought by Augustus's rule, Ode 4.5 addresses the emperor as a descendant of the gods. Venus was the mother of Augustus's supposed ancestor, the Trojan prince Aeneas. Horace wants the emperor to return quickly from the campaigns he is personally leading. Rome misses him just as a mother misses a son whom unfavorable winds have kept from sailing home. The emperor's return will assure the peace and safety of the motherland and the enforcement of her laws.

Augustus's presence also protects against the presumption of foreign enemies. His subjects offer prayers in the emperor's behalf. Horace ends the ode by quoting the customary prayer for the ruler, saying that the people repeat it both early and late.

Ode 4.6 addresses the god Apollo, the tutelary god of artists, thanking him for the destruction of the hero Achilles at Troy. Had Achilles not fallen, Horace imagines, the warrior's cruel vengeance among the defeated Trojans would have averted the successful voyage of the Trojan founder of Rome, Aeneas. The final verses of the song address the noble young men and maidens who will perform his "Hymn for a New Age" at Augustus's 10th-anniversary festival. He predicts that in years to come, they will recall that they performed his hymn for the gods' pleasure and that the priestly poet Horace taught them to sing it.

Ode 4.7 considers the cycle of nature and the lesson that it teaches. Like the year, like each day, life ends, and people should not hope to be immortal. Noble birth, eloquence, and piety, Horace tells his friend, the consul Torquatus, are all equally incapable of restoring life.

Addressing another consul, Censorinus, Horace sends him a gift of a poem, Ode 4.8. Such immortality as one can achieve results from being celebrated in long-lasting verse. The Muses immortalize a person worthy of verse. The same theme continues in Ode 4.9, where Horace points out how many worthy persons lie forgotten for lack of a poet to celebrate their deeds. Such will not be the fate of Augustus's general, Lollius, whom the poem praises for good judgment, for honesty, for preferring death to disgrace, and for having the courage die in defense of friends and country.

The 10th ode of the fourth collection addresses the same person as does the first—the youth Ligurinus. It warns the young man of coming old age and a time when he will regret not having seized the day. Horace regrets Ligurinus's continued absence.

Ode 4.11 invites a woman, Phyllis, to share a jar of nine-year-old wine with Horace and help him celebrate the birthday of Maecenas. The poet reflects that the man Phyllis loves, Telephus, is enamored of a wealthier and nobler mistress. If Phyllis aims so high, she is doomed to disappointment. Therefore, since Phyllis is the last of Horace's loves, she should keep him company and, from him, learn some songs that she can sing to drive black thoughts away from both of them.

The next ode celebrates the regreening of the world in springtime. As the world comes alive once more, the poet invites the poet Virgil—already dead if the poem was not written at a date earlier than the rest—or perhaps another person of that name to desert his serious concerns for a time, share a jar of wine and just be silly for a while.

Ode 4.13 gloats rather unattractively about Horace's being proved right. A woman he had pursued earlier, Lyce (see Ode 3.10) has grown old, white-haired, and wrinkled. She tries and fails to compete for the attention of men with the younger and more beautiful Chia. He asks rhetorically where Venus has fled—whither Lyce's formerly blooming complexion, her graceful carriage? Now Lyce has become a laughing stock.

The collection's penultimate poem, Ode 4.14, celebrates once again the military exploits of the emperor's stepsons, Drusus and Tiberius, in Rome's wars against several enemies. The 15th and last poem of Horace's final collection of odes is a graceful compliment to the emperor Augustus for pacifying both Italy and the Mediterra-

nean world and bringing the benefits of peace to all under his sway.

Bibliography
Horace. *The Complete Works: Translated in the Meters of the Originals.* Translated by Charles E. Passage. New York: F. Ungar Publishing Company, 1983.

———. *Odes and Epodes.* Translated and edited by Niall Rudd. Cambridge, Mass.: Harvard University Press, 2004.

Odyssey, The Homer (ca. eighth century B.C.E.)

Written some 400 years after the events it purports to chronicle, HOMER's *The Odyssey* and his other EPIC, *The ILIAD*, are the earliest surviving epic poems in any western European language. Together, these works establish the expectations to which subsequent epics in the Western tradition usually aspire. Typically, the poet calls on the Muses for inspiration. The hero, Odysseus, endures a journey into the underworld. The action begins in the middle of the story and includes numerous flashbacks. The principal human characters are drawn from the ruling and military classes, while gods and demigods interest themselves in the activities of the human beings and smooth or impede their progress. The events portrayed are usually of national, international, or even universal importance. The language of Homer's presentation is lofty, and the verse form of the poem is dignified.

The events in *The Iliad* concern themselves with the anger of the Greek hero-warrior Achilles and its consequences, as well as with the situation of Troy and the Trojans as they endure the 10-year-long siege that resulted in the destruction of their city and its civilization (The Trojan War). The events in *The Odyssey*, on the other hand, first concern the adventures of one of the Greek generals, Odysseus (Ulysses in Latin versions), as he endures adventures and hardships, partly brought on by his own folly, while sailing the Mediterranean Sea in an extended voyage home. Second, Homer recounts the passage from boyhood to manhood of Odysseus's son, Telemachus, and his search for his missing father. Third, *The Odyssey* relates the strategies and tactics of Odysseus's wife, Penelope, as she deflects and evades the uninvited attentions of a crowd of suitors—once by saying she must first weave a shroud for her father-in-law, Laertes. She weaves by day but unravels by night and makes no progress. Her admirers, uninvited guests in her palace at Ithaca, consume all her food and drink, try to convince her that her missing husband must be dead, and attempt to persuade her to return to her father so that he may bestow her on one of the suitors.

Book 1

As the epic opens, the poet, in his own voice, addresses the Muse (see MUSES), presumably Calliope, the Muse of epic poetry, praying that she will tell Odysseus's story through him. That story next receives a brief overview in the context of the continuing invocation. If, as some have thought, Homer was himself a performer who entertained by reciting his verse to the accompaniment of his lyre, the summary would have served to arouse listener interest. When Homer composed, there was as yet no reading public. We learn that the enmity of the god of the sea and earthquake, Poseidon, has been keeping Odysseus away from home. But in Poseidon's absence among his human devotees, Zeus and the other gods reflect on Odysseus.

Zeus, the father and ruler of the gods, has been thinking about Clytemnestra and Aigisthus's murder of Agamemnon (see *AGAMEMNON*), and the god concludes that human beings bring destruction on themselves despite warnings that the gods issue. Athena, the goddess of wisdom, takes the opportunity to remind Zeus of Odysseus. The hero is languishing on the island of the demigoddess Calypso, held there by her love for him and by the enmity of Poseidon. At Athena's suggestion, Zeus sends Hermes, the messenger of the gods, to tell Calypso to release Odysseus.

Athena herself goes to Ithaca to instruct Telemachus to mount an expedition to search for news of his father. With her, readers fly to Ithaca, where she assumes the aspect of Mentes, a Taphian sea captain, and calls at Odysseus's palace. Telemachus spots Mentes/Athena at the gate and welcomes the goddess, telling her to eat now and share news later. Servants and suitors also arrive to lay and consume a splendid banquet involuntarily provided by Odysseus's estate. After everyone is sated with food and drink, a minstrel, Phemios, begins the evening's entertainment, and Telemachus quizzes his guest about the purpose of the visit and what information he/she might share.

Athena speaks of Telemachus's grandfather, Laertes, and of Odysseus. She assures the boy that Odysseus cannot possibly be dead. Telemachus complains of the suitors' presumption and discourtesy in helping themselves to his inheritance. Athena advises Telemachus to call a communal assembly and demand the suitors' departure. She also suggests that he get a boat, assemble a crew, and sail to Pylos, where Nestor rules—Nestor being the eldest of the Greek generals who fought at Troy. Spend a year, she counsels, looking for news of Odysseus. If he lives, destroy the suitors. If he dies, conduct a funeral and give Penelope to another husband. Then, like a bird, Athena departs, and Telemachus realizes that a deity has visited him.

The minstrel Phemios has been singing about Troy and has saddened Penelope, who complains. Telemachus reproves his mother. She, impressed by his suddenly adult demeanor, withdraws, and he turns his attention to the suitors. He announces his intention to hold an assembly in the morning, when he will tell them to leave his house or face the fatal consequences of abusing his hospitality. The suitors variously threaten Telemachus or agree with his analysis. Presently they depart for the night, and Telemachus, assisted by his nurse, Eurykleia, prepares for bed.

Book 2

The assembly is held on the following morning, and before the citizenry of Ithaca, Telemachus states his case against the suitors. His charges are greeted with general approval until the most despicable of the suitors, Antinoos, responds. Penelope, he insists, is at fault for not choosing a husband. If Telemachus wants to protect his patrimony, he must send his mother back to her father so that another marriage can be arranged for her. Telemachus refuses, announces his intention to voyage in search of news of his father, and asserts that Zeus will punish the suitors for abusing the necessary institution of hospitality.

In affirmation of that threat, Zeus sends a pair of eagles who claw and peck at members of the assembly. An old man correctly interprets the omen as foretelling the suitors' doom and Odysseus's return. The suitors, however, dismiss both the prophecy and Telemachus; they will continue their predatory ways until Penelope chooses one of them. Telemachus's elderly guardian, Mentor, reproves the suitors. In their presumption, however, they ignore all portents and warnings.

Athena, assuming the aspect of Mentor, advises Telemachus about preparing for a sea voyage to Pylos. The suitors reconvene at his house and advise him to forget his plan. When they are unsuccessful, they begin muttering that he may be lost at sea, as his father presumably has been. Secretly assisted by his nurse and Mentor, Telemachus borrows a ship, assembles a crew, and sets sail for Pylos. The difference between men and boys, some say, is that men act while boys dream. When we first met Telemachus, he was dreaming; now he is taking action. The visits of the goddess can be interpreted as Telemachus's awakening maturity.

Telemachus successfully sails to Pylos, where, finding Nestor at a ceremony, he quickly develops a diplomat's sense of decorum. He does the right things, says the right words, tells Nestor his mission, and secures the king's friendship and assistance. At Telemachus's request Nestor recounts the story of his own return from Troy. He also mentions Athena's special regard for Odysseus.

After further discussion that includes accounts of voyages home from Troy and continual references to the fate of Agamemnon and to Orestes' vengeance on his father's killers (see Orestes)—references that ring like a funeral knell throughout this part of the poem—Nestor advises Telemachus to seek news of his father from Menelaus, king of Sparta. Nestor invites Telemachus to be his guest and offers him a chariot and his son as a guide. Pleased with this outcome, Athena-Mentor turns into a sea hawk and flies off. All recognize that they have been in the presence of divinity and that Telemachus is especially favored. After sacrifice and feasting, Telemachus and his guide, Peisistratus, travel by chariot to Pherai, where they spend the night. The next morning, they once more take to the road, and after dark they arrive at Sparta and the palace of Menelaus.

Book 3

At Sparta, a wedding feast is in progress, and in keeping with Greek traditions of hospitality, King Menelaus welcomes the strangers, who admire his sumptuous court. The king reminisces with the strangers and, in doing so, shrewdly admits how much he misses Odysseus. Telemachus weeps at the mention of his father's name, and Menelaos knows he has guessed right. As he speaks, Helen enters. We are introduced to the cause of the Trojan War—the woman whose face, Tennyson wrote, "launched a thousand ships / and burnt the topless towers of Ilion" (Troy). She too recognizes Telemachus as Odysseus's son.

After a good deal of reminiscing, Helen serves a mild sedative with the wine and begins to tell a story about Odysseus during the Trojan War. The careful reader at this point will bear in mind the difficult situation in which Helen finds herself. A wife who has run away with another man and who has been dragged home by force, she has few options other than to put the best face she can on her behavior.

Helen recounts an occasion on which Odysseus had entered the citadel of Troy disguised as a beggar. She nonetheless recognized him and confronted him. Eventually, she said, she convinced him to be her guest, bathed and anointed him, gave him fresh clothes, and swore an oath not to reveal him as Odysseus to the Trojans until he was safely back in the Greek camp. After that, she says, Odysseus told her the Greek plans and killed many Trojans as he fought his way out of the city. Helen says she repented "the mad day" that Aphrodite had made her forsake all she held dear, including a husband without physical or mental defect.

Menelaus compliments Helen on her tale and tells another. He recalls the way that, as the Greek detachment sat waiting in the Trojan horse for an opportunity to leap out and open the gates of the city to the attacking host, Helen walked around the horse three times, patting it and calling out the names of the best Greek fighters while imitating the voices of their wives. He remembers how Odysseus had clamped his hands over the mouth of Diomedes to keep him from calling out in answer and how Odysseus saved the Greek cause by keeping everyone quiet until Athena finally led Helen away.

In view of the subtext regarding Helen's true wishes that these stories imply, a reader can surmise that a considerable degree of tension had arisen between the spouses. Telemachus gives evidence of his mature tact by suggesting that everyone retire, thereby diffusing a brewing argument.

Book 4

The next day, Telemachus asks Menelaus for news of Odysseus. Menelaus recounts the details of his passage home via Egypt. He reports an encounter with the shape-shifting sea god Proteus, whom Menelaus held down until the deity had exhausted his repertoire of shapes: seal, other beasts, water, and fire. Then Menelaus could question Proteus, and the god had to answer truthfully. Menelaus asked about Odysseus, and Proteus reported that Calypso was keeping him on an island.

Having learned that Odysseus lives, Telemachus heads home to Ithaca. There the suitors have found out about his voyage and plot to ambush and kill him on the return trip. Penelope also finds out about her son's journey and, learning of the suitors' intention, grieves for him. Pallas Athena, however, comforts Penelope in a dream, assuring her that Telemachus is under the goddess's protection.

Book 5

The fifth book of *The Odyssey* opens with a reference to Aurora, the goddess Dawn, who is married to a former mortal, Tithonus. When she fell in love with him, she asked Zeus to make Tithonus immortal so he could forever remain her husband. She neglected, however, to ask for eternal youth for him as well. As a result, Tithonus grew ever older. The implication, of course, is that marriages between mortals and immortals violate the nature of things.

Athena then reminds Zeus that Calypso is still holding Odysseus prisoner. Zeus sends Hermes, the messenger of the gods, to tell Calypso to let Odysseus go. He does so, and despite her reluctance, she obeys, going to inform Odysseus of his liberation.

At last the reader directly encounters the hero, and our first view of him finds him sitting idly on the beach, weeping. Calypso tells him the time for his departure has come and that he must fashion a raft to cross the open sea. Odysseus is suspicious, but Calypso assures him that her intentions are good and her heart is kind. She does make a final effort to have him remain with her voluntarily, asking what is so attractive about Penelope. Odysseus assures the immortal that her beauty and agelessness leave no room for comparisons, but he nonetheless longs for his home. The pair enjoys a last night together.

The next day, Odysseus sets about building his raft—one that will be driven by both sail and oar. Its construction requires four days. Calypso provides food, drink, and a sea cloak that will protect him; she also instructs him in stellar navigation. He then sets forth and sails for 17 days and nights until the shoreline of the island of Skheria comes into view.

Just at that moment, returning home to Olympus, Odysseus's nemesis, the god Poseidon, spots him and realizes that the gods have released him from his bondage. Displeased, the god chooses to make things as unpleasant for Odysseus as possible and sends a fearful hurricane that destroys his rigging and plunges both raft and seaman under the waves. At that moment, however, the sea nymph Ino—previously a mortal girl named Leukothea—comes to his rescue. She advises him to abandon ship, cast off Calypso's sea cloak, and substitute for it her own immortal veil, which will protect him from drowning. Reluctant to abandon ship, Odysseus hangs on until his raft splinters; then he takes Ino/Leukothea's advice and trusts himself to the sea.

After swimming for two days and nights, on the third day Odysseus comes in sight of Skheria, and after narrowly avoiding being shredded by the sharp coastal rocks, he at last finds a river mouth into which he can swim. Exhausted, swollen, and covered with brine, he finally reaches land, where he makes a nest of fallen leaves and instantly falls asleep. This section of the epic has sometimes been read as an allegory of rebirth in which Odysseus is likened to a newborn child who has just passed through the birth trauma.

Book 6

As Odysseus sleeps, exhausted, on the riverbank, Athena brings a dream to Nausikaa, daughter of Alkinoos, the king of the Phaiakians who inhabit Skheria. The dream reminds Nausikaa to wash her clothes at the river so she will have fresh linen in the event of her betrothal and marriage. Going with her girl friends and maids to the river to do laundry, the princess stumbles upon the naked and terrifying Odysseus. She nonetheless retains her composure, speaks with him, and eventually advises him to seek her father at his palace, where, she says, the wanderer may be sure of a friendly welcome and assistance in reaching his homeland. He must, however, address his plea to the queen, Arete.

Book 7

Assuming the form of a child, Athena encounters Odysseus as he follows Nausikaa's counsel. The goddess shows him the way to the palace. Arriving at the court, Odysseus follows Nausikaa's advice. He kneels before the queen, embraces her knees in the manner of a suppliant, and begs passage to his homeland. He further abases himself by sitting among the ashes of the fireplace. Greek hospitality rituals immediately take over, and his hosts treat him as an honored guest, making sure that he is fed and comfortable before asking him any questions.

When the questions do come, however, Odysseus does not yet reveal his identity. Rather, he says he is a man of sorrows and begins the story of his adventures with a brief summary of his trials since leaving Calypso. His host suggests that Odysseus might perhaps be a suitable husband for Princess Nausikaa. If not, however, he promises his as-yet-unidentified guest passage home.

Book 8

The next day, a reception is arranged in honor of the stranger, and a blind bard, Demodocus, entertains after a sumptuous banquet. First he sings of the way the lame god Hephaistos caught his wife Aphrodite with her lover Ares in a clever net. Next he begins to sing about events in the Trojan War. Deeply moved, Odysseus weeps twice more, though he covers his head to disguise that fact. But the king, observing that Odysseus is saddened, suggests that Demodocus end his performance. The alert reader will notice that the outcomes of infidelity among the gods are inconsequential; among people, the outcome can be as awful as the Trojan War. It is the fact of mortality, Homer seems to imply, that makes human action meaningful.

Following the entertainment, the entire party moves outdoors to watch or to participate in athletic competitions. Odysseus watches until Prince Leodamas issues a ritual challenge to the unnamed guest. His subordinate, Seareach, then insults Odysseus—again ritually—to assure his participation in the contest. Affronted, Odysseus seizes a discus and flings it a country mile—far beyond the best of any other athlete at the gathering. He then boasts a bit, but he does not yet reveal his identity. So, having offered unstinting hospitality, the king directly questions Odysseus about his name and lineage, about his wanderings, and about the reason that tales of Troy move him so deeply.

Book 9

Odysseus first compliments the minstrel's performance and then considers his own. He reveals himself as Odysseus, son of Laertes. It is as if the sequence of events that he has endured since leaving Calypso has at last brought him into full possession of his human identity. Passing quickly over his interlude with the nymph, Odysseus flashes back to the beginning of his voyage home as he sailed from Troy.

He recalls how he played pirate among the Kikones and how greed held him and his mariners there too long, so that he lost six benches of oarsmen in every ship of his fleet to the Kikones' revenge. He recounts the way a nine-day storm drove his fleet ashore at the land of the Lotus Eaters, where his crew became addicted to the local narcotic and mired in inaction until he forced them back to the ships.

Next he reports on the episode that earned him the enmity of the god of sea and earthquake, Poseidon. The mariners beached on the land of the Cyclops, or Kyklopes—Poseidon's one-eyed volcanic offspring. There the men hunted goats and ate their fill. Odysseus then took a small body of men to reconnoiter. That group discovered the cave of a Cyclops who had driven his mature sheep and goats to pasture. However, the giant had left behind both lambs and kids and a number of curing cheeses. The men advised Odysseus to steal them and run to the ships. Odysseus, however, wanted a close look at the giant.

When the Cyclops, Polyphemus, returned, he blocked his cave's entrance with an enormous boulder and then noticed the sailors in his cave. Odysseus asked that Polyphemus share some of the cheese, as the laws of hospitality require. Zeus, Odysseus reminded the giant, will punish those who mistreat guests that give no offence. The Cyclops responded that he and his kind have no use for Zeus's laws, and he began to kill and eat Odysseus's men. Odysseus was just about to kill Polyphemus when he remembered that if he did so, he and his remaining men would be unable to move the rock and escape the cave.

After Polyphemus enjoyed another meal of crewmembers, Odysseus offered him a large bowl of wine to wash them down. After three bowls, Polyphemus grew quite drunk. Answering the giant's earlier question, Odysseus asserted that he was called Nohbody. Promising to eat Nohbody next, the giant collapsed in a drunken slumber.

Odysseus and his remaining men seized a green wooden spike they had earlier sharpened and laid in the fire to harden; then they ground it deep into Polyphemus's single eye. The Cyclops howled for help, but when his neighbors asked what happened, he replied that Nohbody had tricked or ruined him. Assuming that he was ill and having no skill in medicine, the neighbors ignored his shouts.

Knowing that the blinded giant would have to move the stone to let his animals pasture, the wily Odysseus slung his men and himself under their bellies, and rode to freedom the next morning, despite Polyphemus's efforts to discover them. Once back at their boats, Odysseus shouted taunts at the giant, who responded by heaving great boulders at the sound and nearly swamping the ships. Rowing out of range, Odysseus made the mistake of boasting and using his own name. Names were magic: If someone knew your name, they could use it to curse you. Polyphemus prayed to his father, Poseidon, to punish Odysseus, and the subsequent difficulties that have beset Odysseus all stem from that curse.

Book 10

In Odysseus's story, the adventures continue thick and fast. After the crew leaves the land of the Cyclops, the next landfall comes at the Island of Aiolia, the dominion of Aiolus Hippotades, the king of the winds. He gives Odysseus a bag containing all the adverse winds, and a following wind to take him home to Ithaca. Foolishly, Odysseus will allow no one else to steer and stays awake for nine days and nights. Inevitably he sleeps, and his crew, thinking he is keeping treasure from them in the bag, opens it. The resulting hurricane blows them all the way back to Aiolus, who concludes they must be cursed by the gods and refuses further help.

They next moor their ships near the cliffs of the island of giant cannibals, the Lystraigones. One mariner gets eaten, and many of the others are destroyed by boulders the islanders rain down on the anchored ships. Only Odysseus's own vessel escapes the carnage.

Next they reach the Island of Aiaia, where the demigoddess Circe, or Kirke, turns all the men but the cautious Eurylokhus and Odysseus into swine. Odysseus is proof against this magic by dint of having eaten an herb called moly at the behest of the god Hermes. Odysseus makes love to Kirke and masters her, and she restores the men to their former shapes, with one exception, Grillus. He has discovered that he prefers being a swine.

Kirke's attractions, nonetheless, deter Odysseus from his quest, and he lingers with her for over a year. Stirred by his mariners' complaints, however, he finally resumes his journey. Before he leaves, Kirke reveals to the seafarer's horror that before going home, he must first descend into the land of the dead and interview the shade of the prophet Teiresias (see OEDIPUS TYRANNUS). Teiresias is the only shade among the dead to be allowed to have his intelligence intact.

Book 11

Leaving the Mediterranean and sailing north in the Atlantic, the mariners come at last to the land of the dead. There they first encounter a seaman, Elpenor, who had died of a broken neck on Aiaia. Other shades crowd around. The shades that Odysseus allows to drink from a blood-filled pit temporarily regain the power of speech. Next, Odysseus sees the shade of his mother, Antikleia, who wishes to speak with him, but he holds her off until he talks to Teiresias. When Teiresias has drunk of the blood, he promises a rough voyage home. How rough will be determined by whether or not Odysseus is able to restrain his men from killing and eating the cattle of the sun god Helios when the ship lands on the island of Threnakia. If he can, most will get home; if he cannot, he alone will.

Once home, Teiresias continues, Odysseus will slay the suitors. Then he must resume his travels, take an oar, and walk inland till he comes to a country whose inhabitants do not know about the sea and think the oar is a winnowing fan. There he must plant the fan and make a sacrifice to Poseidon to defuse the god's enmity once and for all. Then, Teiresias assures him, he will enjoy a ripe old age until a "gentle, seaborne death" will claim him at last.

That talk at an end, Odysseus allows his mother's shade to drink. From her he learns the situation at home and how, longing for him, she herself had pined away and died. He tries to embrace her, but she is only shadow. There follows a long catalogue of women's ghosts from the annals of Greek history and myth.

Odysseus's recitation of the names of the shades he encountered is interrupted by conversation with his hosts at the palace of Alkinoos. They ask if he met the shades of any of his former comrades at Troy. He reports his encounter with Agamemnon, who reported the circumstances of his death. Odysseus's discussion, however, with the shade of Achilles is among the most informative of the epic. As a hero, Achilles enjoyed royal status among the dead, and Odysseus congratulated him because death need not pain him as much. But Achilles set him straight: "Better," he says, "to break sod as a poor farm hand" and to live on "iron rations" than "to lord it over all the exhausted dead."

Odysseus then reports his other experiences in the underworld, until, finally overcome by horror, he flees to the ship and entrusts himself to the sea once more.

Book 12

Returning by the route they had traveled, Odysseus and his crew land once more on Circe's island. After seeing the mariners well fed, she warns them of trials still to come. They must avoid the fatal attraction of the Sirens' song and steer clear of the drifting rocks. They must steer a course between Scylla and Charybdis—a monster and a whirlpool. Scylla will surely take six men from the ship, and if Odysseus tries to prevent it, he will lose more. Steer clear of the island of Thrinakia, Circe counsels, where the cattle of the sun god Helios are pastured, but if they must stop there, leave the cattle alone or destruction will follow, and Odysseus will arrive home old and alone.

Odysseus has his men tie him to the mast and stuff their ears with wax so that he can hear the Sirens' song with impunity. They barely negotiate the wandering rocks, and Odysseus drives on past Scylla, who, as Circe had predicted, snatches and eats six men as they pass. But when the now-hungry mariners hear the lowing of Helios's cattle, they threaten mutiny if their captain refuses to drop anchor. Having yielded to greed, curiosity, sexual appetite, and HUBRIS earlier in the epic, Odysseus now experiences a failure of leadership and capitulates. They land; the mariners go ashore, and they are stranded without food as the offshore winds die and for weeks refuse to blow. Eventually, the starving mariners can no longer resist the temptation to eat the cattle, and they convince themselves that sacrificing to Helios the sun god will render the curse ineffectual. They butcher and eat the cattle, and a breeze springs up. They set sail for the open sea, but Helios calls on Zeus for redress, and Zeus destroys the ship and all its crew except Odysseus. He clings to the mast and is blown back to the strait between Scylla and Charybdis, where this time he and his mast are caught in the whirlpool. He narrowly escapes by leaping for an overhanging branch and holding on till the whirlpool coughs up his mast. He clings to the mast for nine days, finally beaching on Ogygia, where we readers first met him.

Books 13–14

After the account of Odysseus's voyage, the Phaekians keep their promise. They shower him with precious gifts and take him home to Ithaca, where they deposit him and his treasure on the beach while he sleeps. On awakening, Odysseus is disoriented, but, in Book 14, he eventually reconnoiters, and gains an ally in his faithful swineherd, Eumaeus.

Books 15–16

In Book 15, Telemachus has returned to Ithaca, successfully avoiding a death trap that the suitors had set for him on the high seas. At about the same time, the swinherd Eumaeus tells Odysseus that the hero's aged father, Laertes, still lives. Book 16 sees the reunion of Odysseus and Telemachus. The hero reveals his identity, to his son.

Books 17–18

Discovering that Telemachus has avoided their trap, the suitors plot against him. In Book 17, Telemachus asserts his newfound authority and takes over the household—much to his mother's surprise. He also recounts his meeting with Helen and Menelaus.

Disguised as a beggar, Odysseus shows up at his own palace gates in Book 18. There, in a scene filled with pathos, Odysseus encounters his old dog, Argos, which had been left on the trash heap to die. Though the dog had only been a pup when Odysseus left, Argos recognizes his master and expires in a paroxysm of canine ecstasy. Book 18 also recounts Odysseus's powerful muscles as he strips for a fistfight with the formerly boastful but increasingly frightened Irus—a hanger-on of the suitors. One mighty punch leaves the braggart stunned, broken, and bleeding.

Books 19–20

Book 19 focuses on a scar that Odysseus carries from a childhood hunting accident when he had been almost fatally wounded by a boar's tusk. In addition to being an emblem of Odysseus's mortality, the scar becomes the token by which both his old nurse, Eurykleia, and his wife, Penelope, recognize him.

Storm clouds gather over the suitors' cause in Book 20. Odysseus recruits as allies his swineherd, his son, his father, and his nurse Euykleia. The Ithacan seer Theoclymenus predicts the suitors' destruction.

Books 21–22

In Book 21, Odysseus strings a bow that he alone can both string and draw and reveals his identity to all by making a trick shot that is his trademark. His arrow passes through the holes in 12 axe handles without touching any. This is the signal for general carnage to begin. Eurykleia locks the women of the household in their quarters; Odysseus's confederates seize weapons from the armory; the goddess Athena joins the fray in support of her favorite Odysseus; and the suitors are wiped out in Book 22.

Books 23–24

Vengeance is complete in Book 23 as Odysseus hangs the maids who had been the suitors' mistresses. In that book, too, Penelope has one further test for the man who claims to be her returned husband. She orders their bed made up in an impossible location. Odysseus complains, saying that his bed was fashioned from the trunk of a living tree and cannot be moved. He passes the test and Penelope accepts the returned Odysseus as her husband.

As *The Odyssey* ends in the 24th and final book, Odysseus settles the blood feuds that the deaths of the suitors have provoked with their families.

Taught for 3,000 years as an allegory of human life, and sometimes now approached as an existentialist novel, *The Odyssey* remains one of the principal literary glories of the Western tradition.

Bibliography

Homer. *The Odyssey.* Translated by Robert Fitzgerald. New York: Farrar, Straus & Giroux, 2004.

———. *The Odyssey.* Translated by Edward McCrorie. Baltimore: The Johns Hopkins University Press, 2004.

Oedipus Seneca (first century C.E.)

Based on SOPHOCLES' OEDIPUS TYRANNUS, and closely following the plot of his predecessor playwright, SENECA has different interests in telling the familiar story: As a child, Oedipus is exposed to die because of a prediction that he would kill his father and become his mother's husband. Rescued, he grows up as the adoptive son of the king of Corinth. While on a journey, Oedipus becomes involved in a disagreement over right of way with a party of travelers, and in a fit of road rage he kills all of them but one. Among the slain but unknown to Oedipus is his real father, King Laius of Thebes. Oedipus journeys to Thebes, where he unravels the Sphinx's riddle, becomes king, and marries the widowed queen Jocasta—his mother. In due course, she bears him children. Thereafter, a horrible plague afflicts Thebes. Oedipus insists on finding the reason, despite advice to the contrary from the blind prophet, Teiresias, who knows that Oedipus is a patricide, living in incest, and himself the reason that the gods have sent the plague. Sophocles dwells on the slow dawning of that truth on Oedipus and focuses on the horrible consequences of his discovery: the suicide of Jocasta and Oedipus blinding himself before going into exile.

Seneca, too, follows this sequence of events, but he was much more interested in magic, sorcery, and foretelling the future than was Sophocles. To accommodate that interest, Seneca dwells on such material at much greater length than Sophocles does, putting on stage not only the prophecy of Teiresias but also adding a long speech by the prophet's daughter Manto, who details the sacrifice. That speech reveals another Senecan interest that did not much concern Sophocles—oratory itself. Seneca rarely misses an opportunity to give a character a good and often lengthy speech.

To accommodate his interests in magic and oratory, and to appeal to the Roman taste for musical interludes, love scenes, and shorter drama, Seneca had to compress Sophocles' material substantially. Seneca therefore loses much of the effect produced in Sophocles' Greek original by Oedipus's slow recognition of his guilt, and his characterization suffers.

On the positive side, however, Seneca's version is more thrillingly horrible. His heightened use of foreshadowing produces credibility, and he achieves a degree of psychological analysis that is a hallmark of his drama.

See also TRAGEDY IN GREECE AND ROME.

Bibliography

Miller, Frank Justus, trans. *Oedipus*. In *The Complete Roman Drama*. Vol. 2. Edited by George E. Duckworth. New York: Random House, 1942.

Seneca. *Oedipus; Agamemnon; Thyestes; Hercules on Oeta; Octavia*. Edited and translated by John G. Fitch. Cambridge, Mass.: Harvard University Press, 2004.

Oedipus at Colonus Sophocles (ca. 406 B.C.E.)

SOPHOCLES' last treatment of the material in the Oedipus cycle and likely his final play as well, *Oedipus at Colonus* was staged by the playwright's son, Sophocles the younger, after his father's death.

Following the events chronicled in *OEDIPUS TYRANNUS*, the blinded and ill-starred Oedipus continued to live in Thebes as the subject of his brother-in-law, King Creon. With time, however, Creon and other influential citizens decided that Oedipus, whose unwitting patricide and incest had brought catastrophe upon his native city, still constituted a danger to the state and should be exiled. Eteocles and Polynices, his two sons by his incestuous marriage to his mother Jocasta, though destined to rule in Mycenae someday, made no effort to prevent their father's exile.

Therefore, accompanied only by his daughter, Antigone (see *ANTIGONE*), the sightless old man set out for the suburb of Colonus, just outside Athens in Attica and about a mile from the Acropolis—the place, as it happens, of Sophocles' birth. At that place is a grove sacred to the Furies, or Erinyes, who have become the Eumenides—the bearers of blessing, as recounted in AESCHYLUS's play of the same name (see *THE EUMENIDES*). It is at this grove that Antigone and Oedipus have arrived as the play opens.

Antigone seats the weary Oedipus on a stone and is about to go find someone to tell her where they are, when a peasant enters. He interrupts Oedipus's initial question by warning him to move, that his presence is polluting ground sacred to the Eumenides, to Poseidon (the god of sea and earthquake), and to the TITAN Prometheus (see *PROMETHEUS UNBOUND*). Oedipus takes this as an omen and declares himself a suppliant. He discovers that he is at Colonus and that Theseus, the ruler of Athens, rules at Colonus as well. The peasant tells him to remain there while he asks the inhabitants if Oedipus can stay or if he must resume his wanderings.

Oedipus prays to the Eumenides, and the audience learns that an oracle predicted that he should find his final shelter in the land sacred to the "dread goddesses."

In the guise of citizens of Colonus, the CHORUS comes seeking Oedipus, who first hides and then reveals himself. The chorus and Antigone cooperate in leading Oedipus away from the forbidden ground to a seat nearby, promising that he will find shelter among them as long as he wishes to remain.

At first Oedipus tries to conceal his identity, but when pressed, he admits it. The chorus is overcome by fear and tells him to leave. He reminds them of their promises, and a discussion follows in which the old man points out the distinction between someone who sins with foreknowledge and one whose fate has overcome him through no fault of his own. The citizens leave it up to Theseus to decide and inform Oedipus that a messenger has already gone to bring the king.

As they await his arrival, Antigone sees a woman approaching and recognizes her as her sister Ismene. In their ensuing exchange about the reason for Ismene's coming, Oedipus makes the play's first reference to his disapproval of the behavior of his sons who have no feeling for their father and display no filial piety. One is tempted to perceive an autobiographical subtext in this emphasis within the play, as Sophocles' sons had attempted to have him declared incompetent. The old playwright, then around 90, convinced the jury of his competence by reading aloud for them a draft of this play.

Asked for the reason she has sought her father out, Ismene first reports the events that comprise the substance of Aeschylus's play SEVEN AGAINST THEBES. Her brothers have quarreled; Eteocles has taken over the rule of Thebes and exiled Polynices, who in turn has gone to Argos and raised an army to assault his native city. Next, however, Ismene brings her father word of favorable Apollonian oracles concerning Oedipus himself. When he dies, the place where he is buried will be especially blessed. In order to gain control of Oedipus, Ismene warns, Eteocles has sent Creon to take Oedipus back closer to Thebes so that on his death his native city, not Athens, will profit from his passing. Oedipus vows not to return and inquires from the chorus what rites he needs to perform to apologize to the Eumenides for violating their grove and to put himself under their protection.

The citizens of Colonus recount in detail the steps he must take to achieve ritual purification and become an initiate of the Eumenides' cult. Ismene undertakes to perform the ritual on her father's behalf. While she is so engaged, the chorus prevails upon a reluctant Oedipus to recount for them the events that have led him to his current state. As that dialogue ends, Theseus arrives from Athens, anticipates Oedipus's need, and promises him shelter and protection in the Attic countryside. The chorus sings, praising the pleasures and the beauties of the region surrounding Athens and especially its olives.

Creon now arrives with an armed escort and attempts to persuade Oedipus to go home with him. Oedipus refuses and criticizes Creon's motives. Giving up on Oedipus, Creon orders his escort to seize Antigone and Ismene. The citizens of Colonus resist, and Creon attempts to seize Oedipus by force as well, but Theseus and his ret-inue arrive at this juncture. After much posturing and threatening by all concerned, it appears that the kidnappers are making off with Oedipus's daughters while Theseus and the citizens debate with Creon. Theseus places him under arrest.

The chorus reports a chase scene as Theseus's troops overtake Creon's escort, liberate the girls, and bring them back. They enter with Theseus. After a joyful reunion with his daughters, Oedipus learns from Theseus that another man is requesting an audience with him. Oedipus concludes that it must be his "hateful son." He is right.

Polynices enters and complains that the younger Eteocles has usurped the power due Polynices and exiled him from the city. Eteocles attributes this misfortune to the operation of the Furies, whose enmity was provoked by Oedipus's curse on his son. Polynices essentially asks his father to revoke his curse and give him a blessing so that the gods will favor his cause against his brother. Oedipus reminds Polynices that he exercised the city's power when Oedipus was exiled. He spits on his son and sends him off with his curses. Polynices take his leave of his sisters, and Antigone begs him to save himself and his city by abandoning his plans to invade Thebes. He refuses and departs.

Oedipus now hears thunder and recognizes it as a sign from Zeus that death is drawing near. He sends for Theseus so that he can tell the king about the benefit that Athens will gain by allowing Oedipus's body to be buried there. He tells Theseus that Athens will enjoy eternal protection if Theseus keeps secret the spot where Oedipus dies and is buried. Oedipus, Theseus, and the women depart, and the chorus prays for the spirit of Oedipus in the underworld.

A messenger enters to announce Oedipus's death and detail the manner of his passing. He tells how he shed his filthy travel garments, how his daughters ritually bathed him, and how the three embraced each other, the girls weeping and the father comforting them. Then a god's voice called out that it was time to go and that Oedipus was waiting too long. With that, Oedipus bade Theseus farewell and entrusted his children to the king. He urged his daughters to bear up courageously, and those who were in attendance escorted his daughters away. Then, observed only by Theseus, Oedipus disappeared, and no one else ever knew the manner of his death. Theseus saluted the earth and the sky. The messenger reports that Oedipus was taken by a miracle.

Antigone expresses a desire to go home. Ismene is doubtful as their dialogue dimly foreshadows the fate that awaits them in Thebes. They beg Theseus to take them to their father's tomb so they may perform due rites, but Theseus refuses, explaining that he promised Oedipus never to reveal his resting place.

The chorus ends the play, advising that there is no changing the past.

Bibliography

Bloom, Harold, ed. *Sophocles' Oedipus Plays: Oedipus the King, Oedipus at Colonus, and Antigone.* New York: Chelsea House, 1996.

Lloyd-Jones, Hugh, ed. and trans. *Oedipus at Colonus.* In *Sophocles.* Vol. 2. Loeb Classical Library. Vol. 21. Cambridge, Mass.: Harvard University Press, 1994.

Oedipus Tyrannus (*Oedipus Rex, Oedipus the King*) Sophocles (fifth century B.C.E.)

Generally considered to be SOPHOCLES' best play, *Oedipus Tyrannus* opens in the midst of a series of terrible misfortunes for the citizens of the city of Thebes. The crops are dying in the fields, the herds are expiring in the pastures, the children of the women of Thebes are stillborn, and plague is decimating the population. A priest—a member of the CHORUS—and the city's king, Oedipus, are discussing this situation, and the priest implores Oedipus to do something about it.

Oedipus reports that he has sent his brother-in-law, Creon, to the temple of Phoebus Apollo in Athens to learn the cause and the remedy for the city's suffering. Creon returns with the god's answer. To relieve the city's misery, it will be necessary to banish a man who is under the gods' curse and is defiling the city.

Under Oedipus's close questioning, Creon reports that the city's former king, Laius, and all his retinue, except for one man, were murdered on a visit to Delphi. That man could only report that a band of robbers had done the deed. A subsequent investigation led nowhere, and Thebes lies under the curse, in part, because King Laius's death is still unavenged. The Sphinx has darkly suggested that the fault lies closer home.

Oedipus vows to begin again at the beginning of the matter to solve the mystery and free his people from the curse. The chorus, representing the people of Thebes, sings the woes of the city and prays to the gods for relief.

Oedipus makes a public declaration in which he promises amnesty to anyone who has information about the murder of Laius and will report it. At the same time, he orders the populace to shun the murderer, neither to speak to nor shelter him, nor to admit him to the religious rites of the city. He prays that anyone disobeying will be destroyed by the afflictions that the city suffers. The leader of the chorus speaks for all, denying knowledge of the truth, but they advise Oedipus to speak with the blind prophet Teiresias—the wisest of living mortals.

A boy leads Teiresias onto the stage. Teiresias begs to be allowed to leave. The ensuing exchange between the prophet and Oedipus makes clear that Teiresias knows something but wishes to be excused from sharing what he knows. Oedipus grows angry and threatens Teiresias, suggesting that if he were not blind, Oedipus would suspect him of being the culprit. That accusation so offends the prophet that he declares what he knows: Oedipus himself is "the accursed defiler" of Thebes. Incredulous, Oedipus pushes for further information. Teiresias declares that Oedipus is the killer of Laius, that he lives in "unguessed shame" with his nearest kin, and that greater woe awaits him.

Oedipus thinks that his brother-in-law, Creon, has put Teiresias up to repeating these lies in an effort to usurp the throne. Teiresias denies the accusation and predicts that Oedipus will discover he is the foe of his own kin and will suffer under both his mother's and his father's curse. He foretells that the murderer will be found in Thebes: seemingly a stranger, but in fact a native who will become an exile; sighted now but soon to become blind; both brother and father of his children; son and husband of his mother; and the murderer of his father.

Following the chorus's reflection on this turn of events, an angry Creon appears to answer Oedipus's charges against him. Oedipus is irrationally upset, but Creon rationally defends himself against the charges, and Oedipus shifts to investigating the murder of Laius. Oedipus concludes that Teiresias would not have named him as the murderer of Laius had the seer not first conferred with Creon. Oedipus and Creon continue squabbling until Jocasta, Oedipus's wife and mother, enters and reproves them for folly. The chorus joins her until Oedipus withdraws his accusations.

In an effort to put Oedipus's mind at rest, Jocasta tells how Laius met his death at a place where three roads meet. She also recounts how, in an effort to avert his predicted fate of being slain by his own child, Laius took their firstborn, had his feet pinned together, and had him exposed upon a mountainside for the wild beasts to eat. On hearing this story, Oedipus is appalled. He asks Jocasta for further details and begins to be convinced that he is indeed the murderer whose presence in Thebes has provoked the wrath of the gods.

The genius of Sophocles' presentation of this material, familiar in all its details to his audience, lies first in the interaction between Oedipus's state of mind and the emergent details of the story. The psychological realism that Sophocles achieves is a remarkable accomplishment. At least as striking is the moral credibility that Sophocles achieves as he presents a public-spirited leader, attempting to resolve a realm-wide crisis, who finds himself ironically condemned by his own proclamations.

At this point, however, Oedipus still hopes that what he fears may not be true. He wishes to cross-examine the single witness to Laius's murder. Jocasta reports that when the man returned to Thebes and found Oedipus ruling, he asked for assignment as a shepherd outside the city—a request she willingly granted.

Oedipus now reveals that the oracle of Phoebus Apollo at Delphi had predicted that he would slay his father, marry his mother, and produce a brood of offspring in incest. Oedipus thought, however, that his father was Polybus of Corinth and his mother was Merope of Doria. To avoid the curse, he had left Corinth, and on the road he met and killed another wayfarer and his entourage in a dispute over right of way.

Oedipus and Jocasta begin looking for flaws in the evidence that will prove once and for all that he did not kill Laius. Moreover, she remarks that since her child perished as an infant, there is no way that she could become incestuously linked with him.

A messenger now arrives from Corinth, where King Polybus has died. The Corinthians want Oedipus to come and rule them. Both he and Jocasta take this as evidence that the predictions of the oracle are false. Yet Oedipus is still nervous about the prediction of incest. The messenger, trying to set his mind at ease, explains that he himself, once a shepherd on Mt. Cithaeron, received Oedipus as an infant from the hands of another shepherd who had been charged with exposing him as prey for the wild beasts. The messenger, in turn, presented the infant to King Polybus. The chorus identifies the other shepherd as the very man for whom Oedipus has already sent.

Jocasta turns pale and tries to dissuade Oedipus from further investigations. She declares herself miserable, tells Oedipus it is her last word, and rushes from the stage. Oedipus thinks that his humble birth has upset her.

Now the aged shepherd arrives, and he and the Corinthian messenger recognize one another as fellow shepherds in the time of their youth. Under duress, the Theban shepherd admits that he had given Oedipus to the Corinthian messenger and that the child he gave away was Laius's own. The

Theban shepherd confesses that he had pitied the child and spared its life.

Now Oedipus realizes that the prophecy has been fulfilled—that he is indeed the incestuous patricide it had foretold and the reason that Thebes lies under the curse. He cries out that he has looked his last on light and rushes into the palace.

A messenger enters and reports that Jocasta has taken her own life. She had locked herself in her chamber. Oedipus, frantic, had forced the doors and found her hanging, cut her body down, and then, with the pins of her golden broaches, blinded himself.

A second messenger obeys the blind Oedipus's command to show the people the cause of their affliction. The palace gate swings open, and a bloody, blinded Oedipus comes forth, attesting to the ironic operation of unavoidable fate.

Creon now assumes the leadership of Thebes. Oedipus begs to be sent from the city into exile. He asks Creon to rear Oedipus's two sons by Jocasta as his own. Then he sends for his daughters, Antigone and Ismene, and parts with them reluctantly when Creon reminds him that Oedipus no longer rules in Thebes.

The chorus ends the play with a bit of wisdom, already ancient when Sophocles borrowed it as his curtain line: Count no persons happy until they leave this life, free from pain.

Bibliography

Bloom, Harold, ed. *Sophocles' Oedipus Plays: Oedipus the King, Oedipus at Colonus, and Antigone.* New York: Chelsea House, 1996.

Sophocles. *The Complete Plays.* Translated by Paul Roche. New York: Signet Classics, 2001.

Old Persian (Avestan)

A tongue belonging to the southeastern satem branch of the Indo-European family of languages, Old Persian, or Avestan, was both spoken and written as early as the mid-sixth century B.C.E. Written first in alphabetical CUNEIFORM inscriptions on stone, it is also the liturgical language of

the Zoroastrian Scriptures, the *GĀTHĀS*. As a written language, Old Persian was displaced in ancient times by a form of the Semitic language that scholars call Imperial Aramaic. The Persian Empire required the official use of this tongue for all administrative purposes throughout the Middle East.

Bibliography

Daniels, Peter T., and William Bright. *The World's Writing Systems.* New York: Oxford University Press, 1996.

Old Testament   See HEBREW BIBLE; SEPTUAGINT OLD TESTAMENT.

"Olympian 1" Pindar (476 B.C.E.)

Among the ancients and probably still today, the best remembered among PINDAR's VICTORY ODES is one entitled "Olympian I." Pindar wrote it for the Sicilian ruler of the city of Syracuse, Hieron, on the occasion of Hieron's horse winning the single-horse race at the Olympian games in 476 B.C.E.

Water, gold, and fire, in that order, sings Pindar, are the best things in the world, but in athletics the Olympian games are preeminent, and the victor's song among those who honor Zeus at those games must be sung to celebrate Hieron and his horse, Pherenikos (the bearer of victory). By association, the poet then shifts the scene to an earlier time when the mythical hero Pelops, son of Tantalus, won a chariot race competing for the hand of Hippodamia. Pindar leaves untold the unpleasant outcome of the story, which involves a curse on the succeeding generations of Pelops's descendants, but the superiority of Hieron is nonetheless implicit.

Rather than tell that tale, Pindar's strategy moves the poem backward in time to a moment when Poseidon, the sea god, first kidnapped Pelops to be his lover and then whisked him to the abode of the gods on "golden steeds." Then the poet explicitly denies the part of Pelops's myth that says he was dismembered, cooked, eaten, and miraculously restored to life. Again by a process of association, Pindar shifts back in time to speak of Pelops's father, Tantalus, who was punished for greed in Hades by never being able to quench his thirst or satisfy his hunger.

Next Pindar moves forward again to Pelops and to his invoking Poseidon's gratitude for former favors in Pelops's attempt to win Hippodamia. Poseidon grants the prayer with the gift of a golden chariot and tireless, winged horses. Once the bride is won, Pindar speeds forward in time to Pelops's fathering six children, then to Pelops's tomb beside the altar of Olympian Zeus, and on to the games and his patron Hieron's victory. The poet hopes for a future victory in the chariot race. (In the year of "Olympian 1," Pindar's other patron, Theron, won the chariot race—a victory Pindar celebrates in "Olympian 2" and "Olympian 3.")

Pindar's poem at once celebrates his patron and reverences his gods. By implication, it acknowledges the dark side in human affairs—particularly mortality—but it principally celebrates the accomplishment that is possible even within the short span of one human life.

Bibliography

Bowra, C. M. *Pindar.* Oxford: Clarendon Press, 1964.

Race, William H. *Pindar.* Boston. Twayne Publishers, 1986.

———. *Pindar: Nemean Odes, Isthmian Odes, Fragments.* Cambridge, Mass.: Harvard University Press, 1997.

———. *Pindar: Olympian Odes, Pythian Odes.* [Greek and English.] Cambridge, Mass.: Harvard University Press, 1997.

On Literary Composition　Dionysius of Halicarnassus　(after 30 B.C.E.)

Written as a gift for the son of DIONYSIUS OF HALICARNASSUS's Roman friend, Rufus Metilius, *On Literary Composition* seems to address this subject for the very first time in the annals of Greek discourse. After promising to deal in a separate treatise with the question of the selection of vocabulary, Dionysius outlines the subjects that his composition will address. What is the nature of composition in its principal varieties? What is the distinguishing characteristic of each kind? Which sorts are most effective? What are the qualities of effective prose and poetry?

Dionysius then undertakes to illustrate the principles of effective composition using passages taken from fine authors. His first example is drawn from HOMER's *The ODYSSEY* and quotes the passage in which Odysseus arrives at the rustic hut of his swineherd, Eumaeus. Its genius, asserts Dionysius, lies in the passage's careful metrical arrangement of commonplace language that catalogues everyday events, and its beauty is the style with which Homer deploys his language. The critic turns next to a passage from HERODOTUS to illustrate the same principle with a passage of prose.

Dionysius next illustrates the importance of selecting a verse form appropriate to the effect a poet wishes to achieve. To illustrate this point, he quotes a passage from Homer in dactylic hexameter (see QUANTITATIVE VERSE). Then Dionysius revises the passage several times in alternative meters, leaving it to the reader's judgment to see that none of the alternatives work as well as Homer's original.

Turning his attention to grammar and the order of joining together clauses to construct sentences—or, as he labels them "periods"—Dionysius follows a similar method to illustrate the beauties that can arise from sentence construction. He also concerns himself with the melody of language, with rhythm and the cadences of emphasis, and with the variety arising from the combination of varying levels of pitch and length of pauses that characterize language but that become the raw materials of style in the hands of a skillful author. Lest his reader be confused, however, Dionysius carefully discriminates between the melodic qualities of speech and those of music.

Also careful to allow for the preferences of individual tastes, Dionysius instructs the would-be writer to vary his style to relieve monotony. Good style, Dionysius insists, "resembles a finely-woven net"; it "avoids everything rash and hazardous," as Stephen Usher translates the Greek.

SAPPHO, Dionysius finds, best illustrates the lyric style of poetic composition, which he proves by quoting in full her lovely *HYMN TO APHRODITE*. As it is the only complete example of an ODE of Sappho's left to us, history is indebted to Dionysius for rescuing it through his work.

Among historians, Dionysius admires the "rugged and austere" prose of THUCYDIDES as the best work of a group who stand in the second rank of writers, though he also has kind words for Ephorus and Theopompus, of whose work only fragments remain. Among EPIC poets, Dionysius admires the style of HESIOD; among tragedians, only that of EURIPIDES; and among orators, only the prose of ISOCRATES.

Persons aspiring to become good or better writers, even today, can profit from a careful reading of Dionysius's treatise.

Bibliography

Usher, Stephen, ed. and trans. *Dionysius of Halicarnassus: The Critical Essays.* Vol. 2. Loeb Classical Library. Vol. 466. Cambridge, Mass.: Harvard University Press; London: William Heinemann, 1985.

On the Crown *(De corona; In Defense of Ctesiphon)* Demosthenes (330 B.C.E.)

In 336 B.C.E., DEMOSTHENES' admirer and partisan, Ctesiphon, proposed awarding a golden crown to Demosthenes in consideration of the famous orator-statesman's singular services to Athenian interests. Demosthenes had previously enjoyed similar recognition. On this occasion, however, his political opponent and personal enemy, ÆSCHINES, immediately filed suit against Ctesiphon, charging that his proposal was unconstitutional. For reasons that are not altogether clear, this case was not heard for six years. When at length it did come to trial, it was argued before a jury of 500 Athenian citizens.

Æschines alleged unconstitutionality on the grounds that Demosthenes' accounts had not yet been properly audited, that the proclamation of the award at the great festival of the god Dionysus (see GREAT DIONYSIA) would amount to sacrilege, and that the grounds proposed for the reward contained errors of fact about Demosthenes' merits. In support of his charges, Æschines presented arguments based on Demosthenes' actions during four periods of his political life. The suit against Ctesiphon thus became a thinly disguised personal attack on Demosthenes—one calculated to assassinate the statesman's character.

Demosthenes' brilliant oration *On the Crown* destroyed Æschines' arguments, as much by emotional appeal as by factual argument, and resulted in the accuser's opting for voluntary exile.

In his speech, Demosthenes demonstrates that he had always supported Athenian interests against those of Philip and Alexander of Macedon. This, he convincingly demonstrates, was not the case with his opponent, who always supported Macedonian interests. Demosthenes traces the clever ways in which the Macedonians had manipulated Athenian embassies, deceiving them with friendly words while actively working against Athenian interests through military action and diplomacy.

Demosthenes also accuses Æschines of being an agent of the Macedonians. Responding to each charge made by Æschines, a city functionary reads aloud public documents several times at Demosthenes' behest. These documents, which include diplomatic letters from Philip of Macedon, substantiate the claims of the defense.

To the detriment of Æschines' accusations, Demosthenes recalls the comparative effectiveness of his and Æschines' public service—a strategy that puts the accuser at a distinct disadvantage. Essentially, Demosthenes shows that Æschines is probably guilty of both deception and treachery. By having the law read, Demosthenes also demonstrates that no sacrilege is involved in presenting a crown at the Great Dionysia.

To further undermine Æschines' credibility, Demosthenes mounts a vitriolic personal attack against him and his parents—even accusing his mother, who was a priestess, of performing weddings in a public latrine. He also accuses Æschines of being personally responsible for the chain of events that had led to the Macedonians taking up arms against the Athenians and, by implication, for the Athenians' defeat. The content of this considerable portion of the speech traces a detailed history of the demise of Athenian democracy.

The result of the oration was an overwhelming vote in favor of Demosthenes. Æschines got so few votes that his failure triggered an automatic penalty against those guilty of bringing frivolous lawsuits. Nonetheless, the outcome was ironic in a sense. The policy of appeasing Macedonia that Æschines espoused might have benefited Athens more in the long run than the policy of opposition to Macedonia that Demosthenes favored.

Bibliography

Demosthenes. *De Corona and De Falsa Legatione* [On the Crown and Concerning the Misconduct of an Embassy]. Translated by C. A. Vince and J. H. Vince. New York: G. P. Putnam's Sons, 1926.

On the Nature of the Gods Cicero
(ca. 45 B.C.E.)

Written during CICERO's most productive literary period, 44–45 B.C.E., *On the Nature of the Gods* (*De natura deorum*) takes the form of a conversation among three companions whose points of view represent those of the prevailing belief systems in vogue among the practitioners of ancient Greco-Roman philosophy. These systems included that of the followers of EPICURUS—the Epicureans. The first speaker, Gaius Velleius, presents their views. The host of the company, Gaius Aurelius Cotta, acts as the champion of the Academics—those who followed the religious precepts that had developed from the philosophy of Plato (see ACADEMIC [PLATONIC] SECT OF PHILOSOPHY). The third position argued is that of the Stoics (see STOICISM). Representing their point of view is Lucilius

Balbus. Cicero himself is also effectively present, and his personal views on theological matters—not entirely represented in his pages—is peculiarly complex and pragmatic.

Philosophically and intellectually, Cicero felt most comfortable and most closely aligned with the religious skepticism of the Academics. As a young man visiting Greece, however, he had been initiated into the Elusinian mysteries, and he considered that initiation one of the most enlightening and deeply moving events of his life. He subsequently enjoyed a lifetime appointment as the chief augur (a priest in charge of prophecy) of Rome. In that office, it was his responsibility to interpret the entrails of sacrificial animals and announce what the condition and appearance of the intestines indicated about the future and about the relative auspiciousness of various courses of action under consideration. He was utterly skeptical about the effectiveness of such procedures, but as a political pragmatist, he thought that the preservation and observation of a state religion was an absolute necessity in keeping the masses under control and encouraging the private observation of morality. Moreover, following the untimely death of his beloved daughter, Tullia, Cicero began to believe that, upon their deaths, persons like Tullia, whose souls were unspotted, went directly to join the gods. Thus, he announced his intention to build a shrine to a deified Tullia on one of his estates—a place where he could go to communicate with his goddess-daughter. He was writing about the gods, therefore, from a complex and personal point of view.

In prefatory remarks before the dialogue proper, Cicero observes that no subject provokes so many differences of opinion as theology. He also remarks that, while all those opinions could be wrong, only one of them can possibly be right. He announces that, as an Academic philosopher, he believes that while certainty seems unachievable regarding such questions, probability of truth is enough to lead a wise person to treat a precept as true.

Within the dialogue, Cicero characterizes the first speaker, Gaius Velleius, as a know-it-all Epicurean for whom certainty does exist. Velleius takes the company on a brief tour of the history of Greek philosophy, pausing along the way to scoff at each of the various conceptions of godhead—at least as he understands them—proposed by the various philosophers. All their opinions, Velleius thinks, are almost as absurd as those proposed by the "envenomed honey" of Egyptians, magicians, and poets' mythmaking.

Having scorned all views but his own, Velleius follows Epicurus in suggesting that the best proof of the existence of a god arises from the innate idea of blessed immortals that all human beings seem to have. He then quotes Epicurus on the nature of such a deity: "Whatever is blessed and eternal must . . . be free from trouble . . . cause others no trouble . . ." and remain "untouched by anger or affection."

Cicero himself considered such a view to amount simply to crypto-atheism. Besides, such a disengaged deity as Epicurus posited—one who not only did not punish human lapses but who also took no interest in them—would be of no practical use to the political managers of a state.

Velleius continues at some length to explain the corollaries that arise from Epicurus's view of the gods. There must be as many of them as there are mortal human beings; gods live the happiest of all imaginable lives, rejoicing in their wisdom and holiness and the certainty of eternal happiness. Moreover, the gods must have human form.

Throughout Velleius's diatribe, Cotta has waited patiently, and he speaks next. After praising Velleius as an incomparable exponent of the Epicurean point of view, he regrets that such an admirable person should hold opinions both irresponsible and ridiculous. After Cotta admits that he himself holds a religious office and has lingering doubts about the existence of gods, he undertakes a critique of Velleius's arguments. How can he claim that all people have an innate idea of god when he doesn't even know who all people are? How about people who deny the existence of gods? To agree with Epicurus, one must assent to his theories concerning all things arising from primordial atoms—theories that Cotta denies. He

accuses Velleius of presenting as self-evident matters that in fact are totally improbable. Particularly and vehemently, Cotta objects to the notion that gods must have human form; with apparent pleasure, he tears that notion to bits. He is equally hard on the ideas that the gods must be happy and that they live existences of continual enjoyment. Finally, Cotta declares that he has no use for gods to whom the doings of human beings are of no consequence, and he promulgates Cicero's point of view that Epicurus has paid lip service to the notion of the existence of gods while his characterization of them has, in fact, destroyed them.

As the second book begins, Velleius passes a favorable judgment on the form of Cotta's argument but an unfavorable one on its content, and he calls on Balbus to offer his viewpoint. Balbus first wants Cotta, who has attacked the false representation of the gods, to favor the company with a true depiction. Cotta reminds the company that he finds it much easier to say what he does not believe than what he does.

Balbus therefore proceeds. He says that the Stoic philosophers divide theology into four parts: They teach the existence of the gods, they explain the nature of the gods, they describe the way gods govern the world, and they show how the gods care for human beings. Owing, however, to the limitations of time, Balbus intends to speak only to the first two points. Cotta objects, saying that the discussants have plenty of time for the entire explanation.

Balbus's evidence for the existence of gods rests on reports of some of them having been seen in battle, fighting on the Roman side or bearing messages. He cites the fulfillment of priestly prophecies and predictions as evidence of the gods' existence. He is guilty of a *post hoc ergo propter hoc* (after this, therefore because of this) error of logic in attributing the loss of a sea battle to a commander's disregard for prophecies when he drowned the sacred chickens.

Balbus next turns to the blessings that human beings derive from the fecundity of the earth as evidence of the gods' existence and concern for humanity. He also cites the orderly processes of the sidereal universe and argues that only human egocentrism would imagine nothing greater, more rational, or more intelligent than human beings—that human intellective powers must be derivative from divine intelligence. This line of argument leads him to assert that "the universe and the divine are one." All the parts of the world have sense and reason, he argues, and he adduces many authorities in support of that view.

As Balbus discusses each part of the world, the earth, the stars, and the planets, he includes them among the gods. As he discusses the Roman pantheon, he explains how the names of the gods contribute to the revelation of their divinity. For the rest of Book 2, Balbus multiplies examples from the natural world demonstrating to his satisfaction that all parts of the universe are divine and that they reveal a concern with the well-being—principally, but not only—of human beings.

The third and final book of *On the Nature of the Gods* reveals signs, especially near its end, that the work probably had not reached the degree of editorial polish that Cicero had intended for it before he found it necessary to abandon his project. As this book opens, Cotta expresses the view that, as a Roman priest, the traditional religion of his forefathers, right or wrong, satisfies him, and the sophisticated arguments of the philosophers do not sway his belief in the benefits of the system that he practices. Nonetheless, Cotta challenges Balbus to produce reasons for believing in the gods.

When Balbus is unsure what Cotta is after, Cotta cites all Balbus's credulous examples about the appearance of deities in battle and so on. Item by item, Cotta none-too-gently undermines the arguments that Balbus has offered, scoffing at one point that if one follows his arguments about the universe to its logical conclusion, one will have a universe proficient at reading books. He also objects to the predictability of the behavior of natural phenomena being cited as grounds for positing their divinity. If the universe is a living creature, Cotta objects, then it cannot be immortal; like other living creatures, it will die, and thus

it cannot be an immortal god. Generally speaking, alluding to such natural phenomena as wine or grain as if they were gods is merely a figure of speech, not a serious attribution of divinity.

With mordant irony, Cicero has Cotta continue with a devastating critique of the entire Roman pantheon. In doing so, he reveals vast erudition concerning their folkloristic and mythic origins. This critique continues until the end of the book. There, Cicero brings his work to a hasty close, reporting that, while Velleius thought that Cotta had won the argument, Cicero himself thought Balbus came closer to seeing the truth of the matter.

Bibliography
Cicero, Marcus Tullius. *The Nature of the Gods, and On Divination.* Translated by C. D. Yonge. Amhurst, N.Y.: Prometheus Books, 1997.

On the Nature of Things   See DE RERUM NATURA.

On the Sublime   See °LONGINUS, ON THE SUBLIME.

Oppian of Corycus (Oppian of Corycus, Oppian of Apamea, Syria) (fl. ca. 170 C.E., fl. after 211 C.E.)

Oppian presents a perhaps insoluble problem. There are two poems, one on hunting and one on fishing, attributed to Oppian, but no one is sure if the poems are the work of one Oppian or of two. I shall mention both poems here, but I can offer no clarification on the subject of whether or not they were composed by the same hand. A comparative vocabulary index has already been done. A computerized textual analysis of grammatical structures might help.

In any case, both works are extant. The poem on fishing—a Greek didactic poem in five books of hexameters—is entitled *Halieutica.* The one on hunting, also a Greek didactic poem in the same meter and in four books of hexameters, is entitled *Cynegetica*. While the poems both offer instruction in the sports they celebrate, they also praise the benefits for people of being in a natural environment.

Bibliography

James, A. W. *Index in Halieutica Oppiani Cilicis et in Cynegtica poetaie Apameenis.* [Index of the "Fishing" of Oppian of Sicily and in the "Hunting" of the poet of Apamea.] New York: G. Olms, 1970.

Oppian of Corycus. *Oppian's Halieuticks of the Nature of Fishes and Fishing of the Ancients.* Oxford: Printed at the Theater, 1722.

oral formulaic tradition

Self-evidently, human language is far older than writing, and storytelling and singing must be almost as old as language itself. Language, in turn, is the principal identifying mark of the human species, so telling stories must be a very old practice indeed. Preliterate societies survived—and still survive—in odd corners of the world as late as the 20th and 21st centuries. This has given anthropologists, students of folklore, and others with a professional interest in such matters the opportunity to study at first hand what oral literary traditions were like before they became written.

One example of such an oral poetic culture survived among Yugoslavian shepherds into the mid-20th century, and the students of the poems those shepherds passed down through the generations discovered that their traditional works had much in common with the Homeric EPIC of ancient Greece. Their oral poems displayed a high degree of metrical regularity, and they used set phrases formulas to fill out lines where the singer's or the reciter's invention might momentarily fail. Phrases such as "rosy-fingered dawn" or "Atreus, king of men" both provided memnonic filler and met the metrical expectations of a line of verse. Verse, of course, is easier to memorize

than prose, and nonliterate cultures often develop specialists whose job it is to remember word for word the old stories that contain the cultural heritage of their people.

The same and other common literary characteristics typify such early Indian heroic epics as the MAHABHARATA and the RAMAYANA and the Sumerian GILGAMESH EPIC. Similar locutions and parallel stories characterize other national epics of ancient Eurasia, many of which seem to spring from a common ocean of story shared by the Indo-Aryan peoples long before their migrations took them as far east as Chinese Turkestan and as far west as the British Isles and, eventually, Iceland. There is evidence that their oral storytelling culture spread even further into the eastern part of Asia and at least to the Mediterranean coast of Africa. The cosmography of the two creation stories in Genesis in the Judeo-Christian HEBREW BIBLE and the story of Noah and the flood, among others, all have analogues in epics in other tongues spoken in regions far removed from the lands in which the stories were first recorded in writing.

The students of such matters have concluded that, with respect to the Homeric poems and the national epics of Middle Eastern and Indian origin, such poems preserve evidence of a transitional period in the development of literature as it moved from the mouths of storytellers and singers (including poets) onto the pages of manuscripts made of papyrus or palm leaves. Those early epics bear many of the characteristics of preliterate poetic practice over into the written literature of the cultures they represent.

Similar traditions emerged elsewhere in the world (or are descended at a great distance from very early common cultures). The peoples of Polynesian Oceania, for instance, developed a rich and complex oral literature that was preserved from generation to generation by remarkable feats of rapid memorization. In Polynesia in historical times, proof of identity and origin could be established by reciting one's genealogy through hundreds of generations and through numerous degrees of relationship. If the reason for the recitation was to prove land ownership, a mistake could be punishable by death.

Examples of African oral epic, though clearly infiltrated with elements of foreign culture, still survive, as do examples of folktales in India and among the indigenous peoples of North America.

Bibliography

Chadwick, H. Munro, and N. Kershaw Chadwick. *The Growth of Literature, Volume 3.* 1940. Cambridge: Cambridge University Press, 1986.

Cook, James Wyatt. "*The Odyssey between the Lines.*" In *Recognition, There You Are: Studies in Honor of John E. Hart.* Edited by Ingeborg Baumgartner and Myron Brick. Albion, Mich.: Albion Press, 1982.

———. "Oral Tradition." In *The Facts on File Encyclopedia of Renaissance Literature.* New York: Facts on File, 2006.

Diakonoff, I. M., ed. *Early Antiquity.* Chicago: University of Chicago Press, 1991.

Marko, Mathias "Composition and Theme in Homer and South Slavic Epic Poetry." *Proceedings of the American Philosophical Association* 82 (1951): 71.

Oratorical Institute (*On the Education of the Orator, The Orator's Education, Institutio oratoria*) Quintilian (ca. 94 C.E.)

Following his retirement as the first and most prestigious teacher and oratorical theorist ever to occupy the imperial chair of rhetoric in the city of Rome, around 92 C.E. QUINTILIAN began writing his most famous work, *Oratorical Institute*, also known as *On the Education of the Orator*.

Based on the program of education that Quintilian had pioneered in his own school, *Oratorical Institute* focused on turning male children into morally admirable adults who, because they were excellent orators, could fulfill their civic responsibilities. Quintilian proposed homeschooling at the elementary level and counseled methods of instruction that capitalized on the natural interests of children, recognized their individual differences both in ability and in predisposition for certain subjects, and also considered their psychological makeup. He also proposed what contemporary educational theorists, who regularly update him by renaming his concepts, would call "successive approximations to mastery"—a step-by-step approach. Quintilian posited rewarding children as they succeeded in mastering new material—positive reinforcement. In contrast to the practices of priests' and monks' medieval cathedral schools, Quintilian also proposed a wider-ranging curriculum. In further contrast, he argued against corporal and psychological punishment.

Other sections of the work are devoted to crafting speeches and to the necessary degree of emotional involvement that an orator must invest in his cause if he is to succeed. Quintilian makes clear that an orator's reading should be broad and should provide him with models that he can incorporate into his own oratorical style. He also believed that a good orator would of necessity be a good man.

Mutilated for centuries, but rediscovered whole in a surviving manuscript by the Italian humanist Gian Francesco Bracciolini Poggio in 1416, Quintilian's book became the foundational document for the educational innovations of the European Renaissance. It remains relevant in the 21st century.

Bibliography

Quintilian. *The Orator's Education.* [English and Latin.] 5 vols. Edited and translated by Donald Russell. Cambridge, Mass.: Harvard University Press, 2001.

Telligen-Couperus, Olga. *Quintilian and the Law: The Art of Persuasion in Law and Politics.* Leuven, Belgium: Leuven University Press, 2003.

orators and oratory

In the ancient world, literature comprised a much more inclusive category than it does in modern times. Whereas we now categorize works like novels, plays, and poems as literature, the ancients were inclined to consider any extended piece of writing as oratory, regardless of whether it was intended for private reading, for public performance, or for purposes of instruction.

Oratory, therefore, is included here as a branch of literature, and discussion of examples of the category appears under the names of the figures or works that significantly represent that branch. See ÆLIUS ARISTIDES; ÆSCHINES; ANDOCIDES; ANTIPHON OF RHAMNUS; APULEIUS; CAESAR, GAIUS JULIUS; CICERO, MARUCS TULLIUS; BIOGRAPHY, GREEK AND ROMAN; *CIVIL WAR (PHARSALIA)*; DEMOSTHENES; DINARCHUS; DIONYSIUS OF HALICARNASSUS; GORGIAS OF LEONTIUM; ISÆUS; ISOCRATES; *JEWISH WARS*; JUVENAL; *MAD HERCULES*; *ORATORICAL INSTITUTE*; PLINY THE ELDER; QUINTILIAN; *SATYRICON*; SENECA; SOCRATES; SOPHIST; TACITUS, PUBLIUS CORNELIUS; THEMISTIUS EUPHRADES. See also RHETORIC.

Oresteia Aeschylus (458 B.C.E.)

The group title of the only complete trilogy of tragic plays to have survived from ancient Greek theater, AESCHYLUS's *Oresteia* won the first prize for TRAGEDY at the Athenian city festival of the god Dionysus—the GREAT DIONYSIA—in the year of its composition. The trilogy includes *AGAMEMNON*, *The CHOEPHORI*, and *The EUMENIDES*.

Often considered as three acts of a single long tragedy, the *Oresteia* takes as its theme the operation of a curse on the house of Atreus (see *Agamemnon*) across several generations. The plays treat the role that the curse played in the Trojan War and its aftermath; in the death of King Agamemnon of Mycenae; in the vengeance that his son, Orestes, takes by killing his mother, Clytemnestra, and her paramour Aegisthus; and Orestes' own involvement in the curse as a matricide. In the context of the chilling consequences of the curse on the innocent and the guilty alike, Aeschylus examines the relationship between human beings and divine power and between people and fate and the avenging Greek Furies.

Universally regarded as the crowning achievement of Aeschylus's surviving drama, the trilogy evidences the command that a playwright at the height of his powers could exercise over the CONVENTIONS OF GREEK DRAMA, over the poetic resources of the language in which he wrote, and over the theological and philosophical issues implicit in the situations his plays examine.

Bibliography

Aeschylus. *Oresteia. English and Greek.* Translated by George Thompson. New York: Everyman's Library, 2004.

Orestes Euripides (408 B.C.E)

EURIPIDES' version of the final chapters on the effects of the curse on the house of Atreus, father of both Agamemnon and Menelaus, includes plays about both Electra and her brother Orestes. These two cooperated in killing their mother, Clytemnestra, who with her paramour Aegisthus had in turn murdered the siblings' father, Agamemnon.

The action of *Orestes* picks up six days after the burial of Clytemnestra. Orestes lies sleeping on a mat near the palace gate. His sister Electra speaks a soliloquy, commenting on the capacity of human beings to suffer. She reviews the salient features of the curse on the house of Atreus, bringing it down through the matricide of Clytemnestra to the suffering of Orestes in the toils of the Furies—goddesses whom Electra is afraid to name. The siblings have been adjudged outcasts, and this is the day on which the manner of their deaths is to be decided. Their only remaining hope lies in the fact that their father's brother, Menelaus, and the Spartan fleet have arrived at the nearby anchorage of Nauplia, bringing Helen of Troy. They intend to pick up their daughter, Hermione, left with Clytemnestra for safekeeping.

Helen enters and speaks. She accepts no responsibility for her infidelity but blames the god Apollo. After she establishes that, she also mentions that she is bereaved by the loss of her sister

Clytemnestra. Disregarding Electra's troubles and ambiguous feelings for her mother, Helen asks her niece to take the sacrifices she has brought to Clytemnestra's tomb. Asked why she does not do it herself, Helen confesses that she is an object of scorn among the Greeks. Electra suggests that Hermione run the errand, and Helen agrees. After mother and daughter exit, Electra lets the audience know that Helen's "sacrifices" to her sister were halfhearted.

The CHORUS enters, making noise. Electra tries to shush them so they will not disturb the still-sleeping Orestes, but they loudly deny they are making any racket—a comic moment in a mournful play. Electra and the chorus review the situation, and Orestes awakens. After a few cogent moments, his guilt surfaces and he is plagued by the Furies. After a few moments of raving, he recovers his senses. Electra departs, and he continues to waver between sanity and madness.

Menelaus enters in search of Orestes. The young man embraces his uncle's knees in the manner of a suppliant. Menelaus thinks his nephew looks like a corpse. After further discussion of his tortured state of mind, Orestes reveals that Phoebus Apollo ordered him to kill his mother. Under Menelaus's questioning, Orestes explains the hopelessness of his situation, the realities of the city's politics, and his enemies' control of the unfolding events that will culminate in his being stoned to death. Menelaus is the young man's only hope.

Now the elderly Tyndareus enters. The father of both Helen and Clytemnestra, Tyndareus expresses his displeasure at finding Menelaus talking with Orestes. He counsels his son-in-law to withhold help.

Orestes responds to Tydareus's arguments, suggesting that he is the one at fault for conceiving a wicked daughter. That attitude fuels the flames of the old man's wrath, and he upbraids Orestes as before. Orestes hurls an insult at the old man's retreating back and then finds Menelaus is faced with a dilemma. Orestes pleads for his intercession, but Menelaus explains that he has long wandered over the sea and that he does not have the men necessary to rescue Orestes by armed intervention. Resolved, apparently, only to do nothing, Menelaus walks out on his nephew. Orestes judges his uncle a coward.

Orestes' friend Pylades now arrives. Pylades was Orestes' confederate in making preparations for the murders of Clytemnestra and her paramour, Aegisthus. The two young men discuss the situation. They agree that matters look grim, but Pylades nonetheless promises to take care of Orestes. The contrast between the courageous Pylades and the cowardly Menelaus is abundantly evident. The youths agree that comrades are more desirable than blood kin, and they set off for the citizens' assembly.

The chorus reviews the events that have led to Orestes' confused state of mind, and Electra returns. A messenger brings the news that the assembly has sentenced Orestes and Electra to death. The messenger then details the speeches against and for the siblings. The former carried the day, and the death sentence passed. The messenger concludes that Apollo has destroyed the pair in ordering their mother's execution.

First Electra and then the chorus laments. Orestes enters and tells her to behave bravely. Electra resolves to die by her own hand. Brother and sister embrace in farewell, and Orestes also decides on suicide. Pylades joins the pair and resolves to die with them. He suggests, however, that they first punish the pusillanimous Menelaus by killing Helen, who is hiding in the palace. Since all the Greeks hate her as the cause of the Trojan War, Pylades thinks, killing her may prove to be the salvation of Orestes and Electra. Orestes is not so sure about that, but he thinks killing Helen will be a service to the world. Electra suggests that the three of them take Hermione, who is off making Helen's sacrifices at Clytemnestra's tomb, as a hostage to be bartered for their survival. All agree. They offer prayers to the dead Agamemnon, and the men leave the stage to Electra, who waits for Hermione with the women of the chorus.

Helen is heard screaming within the house, and Electra sends Hermione in to her captors. A Phrygian slave comes from the palace and reports the events that have transpired within. In brief, Pylades dealt with the palace guards, and Orestes was on the point of killing Helen when the killers were distracted for a moment and she disappeared.

Menelaus now appears and is about to storm the palace when Orestes, Pylades, Electra, and Hermione appear on the palace roof. Orestes has a blade at Hermione's throat, and he orders Menelaus to desist. Orestes confirms the disappearance of Helen. Orestes threatens to kill Hermione and burn the palace. Menelaus calls the citizens out to lay siege to Orestes and his confederates and then carry out the citizens' sentence. Matters have reached a seemingly irresolvable crisis.

At that moment, from a machine above, Helen and the god Apollo appear. Apollo orders everyone to do nothing and listen. On the orders of her father Zeus, Helen, like her brothers Castor and Pollux, will be deified as a protectress of seafarers. This is a reward for her being instrumental in the deaths of so many troublesome mortals. Orestes is ordered to go to Athens to be judged. There he will be found innocent and will eventually marry Hermione. Her current fiancé, Neoptolemus, will not live to marry her. Electra is destined to wed Pylades, and their union will be blessed.

The god instructs Menelaus to support Orestes as Agamemnon's successor. Menelaus is also to return to rule Sparta, regarding it henceforth as a dowry from Helen. Finally, Apollo confesses that he told Orestes to slay his mother. All the former enemies appear reconciled on stage, and the play ends.

Bibliography

Kovacs, David, ed. and trans. *Helen; Phoenician Women; Bacchae.* In *Euripides.* Vol. 5. Cambridge, Mass.: Harvard University Press, 2002.

Origen (ca. 184–255 C.E.)

Destined to become an influential Christian scholar and teacher, Origen was born the eldest of seven children to a Christian family in Alexandria, Egypt. His father, Leonidas, supervised his earliest studies, and Origen later attended the Catechetical School in his native city; he eventually became the school's devout headmaster. For reasons unknown, he reportedly took the advice of Matthew 19:12 literally and castrated himself. Later, he turned his attention to the study of philosophy, the better to defend Christianity against the arguments of the learned pagans. He fled Alexandria, however, during the persecution of Alexandrian Christians on the orders of the Roman emperor Caracalla (215 C.E.) Often an object of controversy, Origen was ordained a priest by Bishop Theoctistus while on a journey through Palestine, though Bishop Demetrius of Alexandria contested that ordination.

Origen's remarkable intellect and his capacity for hard work led him to aspire to furnish the Christians of his time with a reliable version of Scripture. He developed and applied new techniques for textual criticism. In his *Hexapla*, for example, he arranged in two columns the Hebrew and Greek texts of the HEBREW BIBLE. To these he added four more columns containing versions of the same Scripture by Aquila, Symmachus, and Theodotion. He also added the SEPTUAGINT OLD TESTAMENT version. Origen then identified variations in the texts with diacritical notations so that readers could readily compare versions. Only fragments of this prodigious labor survive. Examples do exist, however, of his textual commentaries and homilies on the Gospels of Matthew and John, the Song of Songs, Paul's Epistle to the Romans, and others.

Origen was the originator of a kind of Christian mysticism that involved the use of the interpretative techniques of PATRISTIC EXEGESIS to understand Scripture. His allegorical method of reading Scripture for its spiritual essence led him to part company with such believers as those who would subsequently subscribe to the Nicene Creed. Origen did not believe in the physical resurrection of Christ. Rather, he believed that at a Christian's baptism, Christ was born again in the recipient's spirit and would flourish there as the newly baptized person grew in faith and in the development of the spiritual senses, of which the five physical senses are the counterparts.

Modern Roman Catholic theologians handle Origen's speculative theology gingerly. They acknowledge that he was the most effective Christian apologist of his era, defending the faith in his *Contra Celsum*—an enormous, step-by-step rebuttal of *The True Doctrine*. The latter work, written by the Platonist philosopher Celsus late in the second century, criticizes Christianity—although it includes among the targets of that criticism much non-Christian, Gnostic thinking.

At the same time, the subsequent adoption of the Nicene Creed has banished much of Origen's mystical thinking and its methods to the realm of heresy. He would not have accepted the Nicene Creed's stipulation of belief in Christ's descent into Hell, his physical resurrection, and his ascension into Heaven. Other later developments in doctrinal thinking have contributed to the same effect. Nonetheless, the Roman Catholic Church treasures such works by Origen as *Commentary on John*, *On the Resurrection*, and *Treatise on First Principles*.

Despite the ex post facto judgments concerning Origen's orthodoxy, he died, as he had lived, as a defender of the Christian faith. When the Roman emperor Decius (ruled 249–51 C.E.) concluded that preserving the ancient cults of Rome was essential to the preservation of the empire against the onslaught of new creeds, Decius initiated a short-lived but brutal repression of the Christians. Origen was arrested at Tyre. Repeated sessions of torture undermined his health, and he died in his 69th year. The Catholic Church numbers him among its pre-Nicene Fathers.

Bibliography

Balthasar, Hans Urs von, ed. *Origen: Spirit and Fire: A Thematic Anthology of his Writings.* Edinburgh: T. & T. Clark, 2001.

Origen. *Commentary on the Epistle to the Romans, Books 6–10.* Translated by Thomas P. Scheck. Washington, D.C.: Catholic University of America Press, 2002.

———. *Contra Celsum.* Translated by Henry Chadwick. New York: Cambridge University Press, 1980.

———. *Homilies on Genesis & Exodus.* Translated by Ronald E. Heine. Washington, D.C.: Catholic University of America Press, 2002.

———. *Homilies on Joshua.* Translated by Cynthia White. Edited by Barbara J. Bruce. Washington, D.C.: Catholic University of America Press, 2002.

Trigg, Joseph Wilson. *Origen.* New York: Routledge, 1998.

Origines Cato the Elder (ca. 149 B.C.E.)

Dissatisfied with earlier historians' practice of writing Roman history in the Greek language, Marcus Porcius Cato (Cato the Censor, Cato the Elder; 234–149 B.C.E.) became the first Roman to undertake writing the history of his native land in his native tongue. He wrote the work, *Origines*, in his waning years.

Despite the title of his book, Cato devotes less attention in it to early Roman matters than he does to chronicling events nearer to and contemporary with his lifetime. The first book, for instance, discusses the founding of Rome. The next two record the establishment of the cities of Italy. In the fourth and fifth books, Cato respectively traces the history of the First and Second Punic Wars—the wars against the African city of Carthage. The final two books, 6 and 7, detail the fortunes of Rome until the year 152 B.C.E. As the author discusses more recent history, each chapter grows longer and longer. Cato was still occupied with the composition of his history at the time of his death.

Cato was himself what the Romans called a "new man." He had not grown up among the hereditary aristocrats of the Republic and therefore took the historical view that the creation of the Roman state and its republican institutions had been the work of the entire Roman people, not merely of the Roman upper classes. To emphasize the broadly democratic nature of the founding and growth of the institutions that had contributed to the greatness of the Roman republic, Cato rarely names great leaders and aristocratic persons. Rather, he identifies them by naming the office they occupy. The people he does name usually come from modest circumstances and are named because for Cato they symbolize the gallantry of the broader Roman population. He also concerns himself with the customs of peoples from Africa and Spain, and he suggests that his own ethnic forebears, the Sabines, had contributed both high standards of moral conduct and frugality to the essential Roman character. Cato's history survives in a highly fragmentary state.

Bibliography

Cato, Marcus Porcius, the Elder. *Opere* [Works]. Edited by Paolo Cugusi and Maria Teresa Sblendorio Cugusi. Turin, Italy: UTET, 2001.

Orpheus (fl. ca. 1250 B.C.E.) *Greek poet*

Although so many mythical elements have attached themselves to the story of Orpheus that sifting the facts, if any, from the fiction is virtually impossible, the ancient Greeks remembered Orpheus as a pre-Homeric poet and musician. He is thought to have been a native of the region of Thrace in the Eastern Balkan Peninsula and a devotee of the god Dionysus.

If Orpheus did compose poems and songs, nothing attributable to him survives. His legend, however, has inspired later poets and musicians down through the ages. So sweetly did he sing that animals were enamored of his song, and the very plants fanned their leaves in time with his music.

Orpheus is also remembered for his passion for his wife, the dryad or tree nymph Eurydice, and their story has inspired not only literary retellings but also ballets and operas. Fleeing Aristaeus, a potential ravisher, Eurydice stepped on a venomous serpent and died of its bite. Inconsolable at the loss of his wife, Orpheus descended into the underworld. There his music so charmed the king of the underworld, Hades, that the god shed an iron tear and released Eurydice from death—with one proviso. Eurydice would follow Orpheus back up from the underworld, but Orpheus must not look back at her. Nearing the world of the living, however, Orpheus could not

resist glancing back at his wife, and she slid back into the land of the dead.

Orpheus is said to have met his own death as a result of observing the secret, frenzied rituals that the god's Thracian female devotees—the Maenads—employed in their worship of Dionysus. When the worshippers caught Orpheus, they tore him to pieces and decapitated him, throwing his head into the river Hebrus, where, according to some versions, it continued singing.

Orpheus is also credited with founding a mystery cult that anticipated certain characteristics of early Christianity: The blessed enjoyed eternal life, the underworld became a place of punishment for the undeserving, the cult's adherents mortified the flesh as did early saints in the Egyptian desert, initiates ingested the god present in edible substances, and the god himself annually died and was resurrected.

Works of art inspired by the story of Orpheus and Eurydice include an early Italian opera by Ottavio Rinuccini, a later one by the German Christof Willibald Gluck, and poems by such poets as Isabella Andreini and John Milton. The literary historian Timothy Gantz has usefully traced the elements of the Orpheus myth to their earliest extant Greek sources.

Bibliography

Gantz, Timothy. *Early Greek Myth: A Guide to Literary and Artistic Sources*. 2 vols. Baltimore: Johns Hopkins University Press, 1993.

Ōtomo no Yakamochi (ca. 718–785 C.E.) *Japanese poet*

A poet, Ōtomo no Yakamochi was the first and possibly the only editor of the MAN'YŌSHŪ, Japan's earliest and best collection of poetry. That work's last four books principally feature Yakamochi's poetry.

Yakamochi was the only son of another poet, Ōtomo no Tabito. As Tabito's wife had borne no sons, Yakamochi's mother was a concubine, but his stepmother, the legal wife, reared the youngster until her death in 728. The Ōtomo clan served as the hereditary bodyguards—called *quiver bearers*—of the imperial family.

In 745, Yakamochi assumed the governorship of the province of Etchū on the seacoast of Japan. About the same year, he began his editorial work on the *Man'yōshū*—a work that occupied his attention until 759. His five years as governor of Etchū would also prove to be his own best and most productive poetic period.

Yakamochi was proud of his family's close connection with the imperial family, and he warned his kinsmen against the slanders of courtiers who had aroused the emperor's suspicions against a relative, the governor of another province. Yakamochi's warnings were well-founded. An influential enemy, Fujiwara no Nakamaro, took draconian measures against the clan, having its leaders rounded up, arrested, and executed.

Yakamochi managed to avoid this fate, but he did not escape suspicion. In 758, he was assigned to serve as the governor of a distant and unruly province, Inaba. He completed his editorial work there, but his poetic voice fell silent. Perhaps he was overburdened by the responsibilities of his office, or perhaps he deemed it wiser to keep silent. His composed his last dated poem on New Year's Day, 759.

In 785, Yakamochi died. Death did not, however, protect him from the implacable hatred the Ōtomo clan's enemies felt for all its members, and he was posthumously stripped of his offices and honors. Eventually, however, his name was cleared, and the honors and offices were later restored.

Bibliography

Keene, Donald. *Seeds of the Heart: Japanese Literature from Earliest Times to the Late Sixteenth Century.* New York: Henry Holt and Company, 1993.

Ovid (Publius Ovidius Naso) (43 B.C.E.– 17/18 C.E.) *Roman poet*

The son of a family of the Roman knightly or equestrian class, Ovid was born at Sulmo in Abbruzzi. His father hoped that Ovid and his brother would become influential public figures and sent the boys first to Rome and then to Athens for an education centered on the study of rhetoric. Ovid, however, was so passionately drawn to the study of literature and so intensely driven by poetic impulse that, as the poet himself admits, anything he wrote automatically took the form of verse. Perhaps in deference to his father's wishes, Ovid briefly occupied minor public office, but his passion for literary endeavor soon led him to abandon public affairs and pursue the usually hand-to-mouth existence of a poet. With the support, however, of a powerful literary patron, Marcus Valerius Messalla Corvinus, Ovid soon distinguished himself and eventually emerged as the leading poet of Rome.

Ovid married three times. The first two of his unions were brief and ended in divorce; the third lasted until his death and is thought to have produced a daughter, Perilla. Ovid's extramarital life was apparently sometimes colorful, and in the year 8 C.E., a supposed liaison with the granddaughter of the first Roman emperor, AUGUSTUS CAESAR, may have led to Ovid's banishment from Rome to the town of Tomi, far away on the shores of the Black Sea. There Ovid remained, poetically productive but cut off from the society and the pleasures of his beloved Rome, until his death.

From about the age of 20 until his death, Ovid's literary career falls roughly into three periods. During the first period, he produced most of his amorous verse, all of it written in elegiac couplets. One representative of this body of material, his *Amores* (Loves), includes a series of purportedly autobiographical, not terribly serious, sometimes racy encounters with a possibly fictive mistress, Corinna. The degree to which these early poems rely on the conventions of earlier Greek amatory verse suggests only a tenuous connection between the poems and the details of the poet's actual life.

Also belonging to this first period of Ovid's production is his *HEROIDES*. Still in elegiac couplets, the *Heroides* purport to be a collection of 21 letters written from mythical heroines such as Medea and Helen of Troy to their loves. In the cases of numbers 16–21, the heroines' letters answer epistles from their lovers, so that Helen's letter, for instance, responds to one from her lover, Paris.

Still representing Ovid's first or amatory period, we find the surviving 100 lines of an originally longer poem, *On Painting* (or, *Cosmetics for) the Female Face* (*Medicamina faciei femineae*). This piece celebrates contemporary fashion as compared with older styles and cleverly versifies the formulae for the preparation of cosmetics.

Two further excursions into the subject of love conclude the body of Ovid's work dating from his initial period. He wrote the first, The ART OF LOVE (*Ars Amatoria*), around the beginning of the Common Era. This work is a manual of instruction for would-be lovers. The first book gives lovers instructions about where to seek mistresses and how to win them, the second makes suggestions about keeping a mistress's love, while the third gives the same sorts of advice to women that men receive in the first two. *The Art of Love* reveals Ovid's growing interest in mythology and also, to a degree, parodies the DIDACTIC POETRY of such predecessor poet as VIRGIL in his GEORGICS. A companion piece, *Remedies for Love* (*Remedia Amoris*), turns the tables on Ovid's readers by offering advice about ways to withdraw from a no-longer-congenial love affair.

After his exile to Tomi, Ovid turned his attention to a new sort of work, producing what many would agree to be his masterpiece, his METAMORPHOSES. In this work, Ovid undertakes to reconstitute the EPIC mode. His choice of dactylic hexameter (see QUANTITATIVE VERSE) as the verse medium of this work immediately establishes its connection with epic poetry. Instead of a sustained narrative however, on a heroic subject such as the wrath of Achilles, Ovid follows the lead of some of his Alexandrian Greek predecessors of the HELLENISTIC AGE. The poet chooses to bring together a series of myths, all of which involve supernatural shape-shifting.

The form and content of this brilliant work reflect one another closely. After suggesting, for example, that the work will chronologically trace instances of metamorphoses—such as girls changing into trees or fountains—from the beginning of time to his own epoch, Ovid causes the poem's plan itself to undergo a metamorphosis. Chronology and linearity are displaced by pairings of metamorphoses, by thematic relevance, and by the complex ways in which his text and that of his predecessors speak to and interact with one another across time. As the classicist Stephen E. Hinds suggests, Ovid's poem both captures and redefines the traditions within which it purports to work.

Ovid's next work, albeit an unfinished one, is FASTI (Calendar). Ovid's plan had been to devote one book of his work to each month of the Roman year. Only six of the books remain—if more were ever finished. These are enough, however, to reveal the work's conceptual roots in the astronomy of ARATUS OF SOLI and in VARRO's now-lost discussion of the antiquities of Rome, and to suggest to 21st-century readers parallels between certain of their own political figures and the emperor Augustus, who appropriated, as Hinds puts it "Roman religious discourse." Ovid himself is a significant character in the poem. His exile to Tomi apparently interrupted the composition of this poem.

To that period of exile belong the poet's *Tristia* (Sorrows), a series of books to various persons in Rome in which the poet bewails his isolation in the intellectually, culturally, and climatically inhospitable vicinity of the Black Sea, and his hopes for repeal of the sentence that has isolated him there. Similar to *Tristia* in tone and intent, but differing from it in that the addressees are named, we find Ovid's *Epistulae ex Ponto* (Letters from Pontus, or Letters from the Black Sea).

Also surviving is Ovid's *Ibis*, an intricately crafted poem that catalogs and curses the poet's sufferings in exile.

Bibliography

Miller, Frank Justus, ed. and trans. *Ovid in Six Volumes.* 2nd ed. Cambridge, Mass.: Harvard University Press, 1984.

Ovid. *The Art of Love.* Translated by James Michie. New York: Modern Library, 2002.

————. *Epistulae ex Ponto*. Edited and translated by Jan Felix Gardner. Oxford and New York: Oxford University Press, 2005.

————. *Metamorphoses*. Translated by Arthur Golding. Manchester, U.K.: Carcanet, 2005.

————. *Metamorphoses*. Translated by Peter Green. Berkeley: University of California Press, 2005.

————. *Ovid: The Erotic Poems*. Translated by Peter Green. Harmondsworth, U.K.: Penguin Books, 1982.

————. *The Poems of Exile: Tristia and the Black Sea Letters*. Translated by Peter Green. Berkeley: University of California Press, 2005.

Oxyrhynchus

The name of the ancient Egyptian city Oxyrhynchus is now Behnasa. In the late 19th century, archeological excavations in an ancient trash heap in Oxyrhynchus unearthed an enormous treasure trove of papyrus fragments—many of them apparently torn into strips for mummy wrappings—dating from the second to the fifth centuries C.E. The site continued to yield truckloads of fragmentary papyri in the 19th and early 20th centuries, and even now it remains productive of ancient materials long thought utterly lost.

During the early years following the discovery, tons of documents were transported to England, and much of the material—including documents like receipts and deeds—is of greater interest to social than to literary historians. Students of ancient astronomy have been delighted by the discovery of papyri treating that subject. At the same time, remarkable literary finds have often turned up. A hitherto lost poem of SAPPHO, for example, has come to light. Lines by Sappho's contemporary and fellow citizen of Mytilene, ALCAEUS, have also been found, as have poems by PINDAR and documents concerning the scheduling of the Olympic, Pythian, Isthmian, and Nemean athletic contests held in Greece during the fifth century B.C.E. Knowing the dates of the games has made possible fixing the dates of some of Pindar's odes addressed to winners and sponsors of winners of events in those games (see VICTORY ODES). They have also confirmed that the longest of the guesses—80 years—for Pindar's lifetime is closest to being right. As a final example, a lost work of the poet CALLIMACHUS, his *Book of Iambi*, has also come to light.

More than 60 volumes publishing the discoveries at Oxyrhynchus have now appeared. No end is in sight as yet, and we may confidently look forward to further additions to our knowledge of ancient texts.

Bibliography

Bagnall, Roger S., Bruce W. Fries, and Ian Rutherford. *The Census Register: P. Oxy. 984: The Reverse of Pindar's Paeans*. Brussels: Fondation Égyptologique Reine Elizabeth, 1997.

Johnson, William A. *Bookrolls and Scribes in Oxyrhynchus*. Toronto: University of Toronto Press, 2004.

Jones, Alexander. *Astronomical Papyri from Oxyrhynchus (P. Oxy. 4133–4308)*. Philadelphia: American Philosophical Society, 1999.

Kerkhecher, Arnd. *Callimachus' Book of Iambi*. New York: Oxford University Press, 1999.

P

Pacuvius, Marcus (ca. 130–220 C.E.)
Roman dramatist

Born at Brundisium (modern Brindisi), Pacuvius was the nephew of the celebrated archaic Roman poet and playwright, QUINTUS ENNIUS. He was also a tragic playwright and the first really renowned Roman painter. Some 19 tragedies are attributed to him. Most of these were borrowed from Greek originals, but some were Roman in subject—the first such tragedies of the Roman world. Principal among them was Pacuvius's *Paulus*. Only five lines from it are known to survive, but it seems to have concerned an episode or episodes in the career of the Roman general Paulus Aemilianus Macedonicus, who brought Greece under Roman control by defeating the Epirotes after that Grecian tribe had succeeded Alexander as the rulers of the Greeks. Paulus had destroyed 70 of the Epirotes' cities.

Celebrated among Pacuvius's tragedies using Greek material was *Antiope*. He was also renowned for a scene in his *Iliona* in which the ghost of Polydorus appears to his sister Iliona, a princess of Troy. Pacuvius composed eight of the tragedies whose names survive on subjects connected with the Trojan War. The names of four other tragedies on Greek themes survive. These seem to have been translations of the tragedies written in Greece during the period following EURIPIDES.

Pacuvius seems also to have tried his hand at comedy, though the literary historian, Gian Biaggio Conte, regards the references to his satire as "vague." The late fifth-century Christian writer Fulgentius alludes to a Pacuvian comedy entitled *Pseudo*. In the late 1960s, the Italian playwright Pietro Magno made an effort to reconstruct one of the Trojan plays—*Teucer*—from its extant ancient fragments.

Bibliography

Conte, Gian Biagio. *Latin Literature: A History*. Translated by Joseph B. Solodow, et al. Baltimore, Md.: Johns Hopkins University Press, 1994.

d'Anna, Giovanni, ed. and trans. *M. Pacuvii fragmenta*. [Latin and Italian.] Rome: in aedibus Athenaei, 1964.

Magno, Pietro. *Tuicro: Tragedia tratta dai frammenti di Marco Pacuvio*. [Teucer: a tragedy drawn from fragments of Marcus Pacuvius.] Milan, Italy: Pegaso, 1967.

Palæphatus (fl. fourth century C.E.) *Greek prose writer* See MYTHOGRAPHY IN THE ANCIENT WORLD.

palimpsest

When any writing surface such as a tablet or a manuscript page has been scraped smooth so that it can be reused, sometimes the erasures are imperfect. Often, therefore, the text that lies under the new writing is recoverable. Such previously used writing surfaces are called *palimpsests*, which have been an important source for the recovery of ancient and medieval documents that were presumed lost.

Pāṇini (fl ca. fourth century B.C.E.) *Indian prose writer*

The definitive grammarian of classical Sanskrit, Pāṇini composed what is conceivably the most complete grammatical analysis that has ever been made of any language. Before Pāṇini's description of Sanskrit, that language had existed principally in the mouths of its speakers and, like every language, had been in a continual state of flux.

The earliest document to survive in Sanskrit's predecessor language and near relative, the Vedic tongue, is the Rig-Veda. As the Vedic language developed into Sanskrit, and as the hymns comprising the Rig-Veda were compiled and arranged into a liturgy, pressures increased among the Brahmins—the priestly class—to stablilize Sanskrit in a fixed liturgical form. Pāṇini's grammar made such a usually desperate hope a reality.

This is not to say that popularly spoken Sanscrit did not continue to change. It did, and it evolved into the various Indo-Aryan languages of modern northern India. Pāṇini's grammar, however, established a standard of liturgical speech and writing that the Brahmins could and did enforce for many centuries.

Bibliography

Burrow, T. *The Sanskrit Language.* London: Faber and Faber, 1965.

Cardona, George. *Pāṇini, His Work and its Traditions.* Delhi: Motilal Banarsidass, 1988.

Pāṇini. *The Astadhyayi of Panini.* Translated and edited by S. D. Joshi and J. A. F. Roodbergen. New Delhi: Sahitya Akademi, 1991–2006.

Parallel Lives (*The Lives of the Noble Grecians and Romans, Plutarch's Lives*) Plutarch (ca. 100 C.E.) *Greek biographer and essayist*

Owing to losses, additions, and possible authorial incompletion, *Plutarch's Lives*—more properly known as *Parallel Lives*—survives in a form substantially different from its original plan. Nonetheless, the biographies presented in it capture the spirit of the most genial of ancient biographers.

Plutarch's plan had been to present a series of two comparable biographies—one of a celebrated Greek and the other of a celebrated Roman. Following the pair, he would present a comparison of the two that focused principally on their moral characters rather than on the subjects' deeds. The document that survives is composed of 23 paired lives, each pair followed by a comparison. Four single lives follow—possibly not from Plutarch's pen but added later simply because they were biographies. For illustrative purposes in this volume, I have chosen Plutarch's first pair of lives, "Theseus" and "Romulus"; and his 10th pair, "Pericles" and "Fabius."

The first pairing in the collection presents the lives of the founders of two cities: Theseus, founder of Athens, and Romulus, founder of Rome. Plutarch's working method starts with a survey of the variant versions of his stories available to him. Though he sometimes weighs the credibility of the version he presents on the grounds of historical probability, he feels obliged to be broadly inclusive. He rarely distinguishes between the credible and the farfetched unless the story he is reporting offends the bounds of nature. Then, as with stories about heroes and heroines (including Romulus) whose dead bodies disappear and whose friends subsequently see them alive, he objects that such accounts are the work of fabulists who wish to claim divinity for their subjects. According to Plutarch, others whose surviving associates elevated them to the status of gods after their decease included Aristeas the Proconnesian and Cleomed the Astypalaean. Countering such claims, Plutarch suggests: "To mix heaven with earth is ridiculous." He quotes the poet PINDAR on the subject: "All human bodies yield to Death's decree, / the soul survives to all eternity"—a view that Plutarch endorses.

The other extant parallel lives that Plutarch treats include those of the Athenian general and politician Alcibiades (450–404 B.C.E.) paired with the legendary Roman hero Coriolanus whom Shakespeare treats in his tragedy of the same name. We also find the fifth century B.C.E. Greek statesman Aristides paired with the Roman patriot Cato the Elder (234–149 B.C.E.), the Athenian general Nicias (d. 423 B.C.E.) and the Roman triumvir and general Crassus (115–53 B.C.E.). Paired as well are the Greek statesman Demetrius and the Roman general and triumvir Marcus Antonius (83–30 B.C.E.); the Greek orator and statesman Demosthenes (384–322 B.C.E.) and his Roman counterpart CICERO (106–43 B.C.E.); the Greek patriot Dion and the Roman republican Marcus Junius Brutus (85–42 B.C.E.). Beyond these, other extant paired biographies include those of the wealthy Roman consul Lucullus (ca. 110–ca. 57 B.C.E.) with a Greek counterpart, the Athenian general and statesman Cimon (502–449 B.C.E.); the second king of Rome, Numa Pompilius (715–872 B.C.E.), with the Spartan lawgiver Lycurgus (ca. 820 B.C.E.).

Plutarch compares the Spartan conqueror of Athens in 404 B.C.E., Lysander, with the Roman general and dictator Sulla (138–78 B.C.E.). The author considers together the careers of the Theban general Pelopidas (d. 364 B.C.E.), who defeated the Spartans, together with that of the Roman hero Marcellus (266–208 B.C.E.) who was five times consul and the conqueror of Syracuse. Plutarch continues with a comparison of the Greek patriot and chief of the Achaean League, Philopoeman (ca. 252–183 B.C.E.), comparing him with the Roman general and censor Caius Flamininus (d. 217 B.C.E.). Also extant we find Plutarch's treatments of the Roman general and statesman Cneius Pompeius (Pompey the Great, 106–48 B.C.E.) paired with the Spartan king and conqueror, Agesilaus (ca. 444–360 B.C.E.); the Greek statesman Solon (638–558 B.C.E.) and the Roman Popli-

cola (d. 503 B.C.E.); the discussion of the Roman proconsul and general Sertorius (ca. 121–72 B.C.E. compared with his Greek counterpart, king Eumenes I of Cardia (ca. 362–316 B.C.E.); and the Greek liberator of Sicily, Timoleon (400–337 B.C.E.), paired with the Roman leader Aemilius Paulus.

Plutarch also varies his pattern of comparison by considering together two representatives of the powerful Roman Gracchus family Tiberius and Gaius Gracchus in tandem with the Spartan king Cleomenes (died 220 B.C.E.) and the Spartan king Agis IV (fl. ca. 262–291 B.C.E.). The biographer also includes four unpaired lives, those of the Greek governor Aratus of Sicyon, the Persian king Artaxerxes, the Roman emperor Galba (3 B.C.E.–69 C.E.), and the Roman emperor Otho (32–69 C.E.).

Known to have also existed but now lost are Plutarch's paired lives of Julius Caesar and Alexander the Great; of the Greek general Phocion (ca. 402–317 B.C.E.) and the Roman patriot and philosopher Cato the Younger (95–46 B.C.E.); of the Athenian statesman and architect of the city's naval policy, Themistocles (ca. 514–449 B.C.E.); and of the king of Epirus, Pyrrhus (d. 272 B.C.E.); and those of the Roman general and five-time consul, Gaius Marius (157–86 B.C.E.).

Bibliography

Plutarch. *The Lives of the Noble Grecians and Romans.* Translated by John Dryden with revisions by Arthur Hugh Clough. New York: Modern Library, 1932. Reprinted as *Greek and Roman Lives.* Mineola, N.Y: Dover Publications, 2005.

———. *Plutarch's Lives. [Greek and English.]* 11 vols. Translated by Bernadotte Perrin. Cambridge, Mass.: Harvard University Press, 1959.

Parthenius of Nicaea (fl. first century C.E.)
Greco-Roman poet

Brought to Rome as a prisoner of war in 73–74 C.E., Parthenius achieved his freedom and entered Roman literary circles. He tutored VIRGIL in Greek and recommended the use of Greek models to

Roman poets. Of the many elegiac verses he is thought to have written, only fragments of some survive. The most complete survival among his elegies is a work in praise of his wife, Arete.

Parthenius summarized Greek love stories in prose for the benefit of Roman poets, particularly GAIUS CORNELIUS GALLUS, to whom Parthenius dedicated his work. These summaries, *De amatoris affectibus*—or, in Greek, *Erotika pathemata* (Feelings of love)—were designed to provide grist for the mills of the Roman poets. In fact, the presence in Rome of a Greek poet like Parthenius lent impetus to Roman poetic experimentation already underway in the Roman poetic movement called the neoteric school—poets who adapted the conventions of poets of the Greek HELLENISTIC AGE to Roman verse.

See also ELEGY AND ELEGAIC POETRY.

Bibliography

Conte, Gian Biagio. *Latin Literature: A History.* Translated by Joseph B. Solodow, et al. Baltimore: Johns Hopkins University Press, 1994.

Parthenius of Nicaea. *Erotika pathemata: The Love Stories of Parthenius.* Translated by Jacob Stern. New York: Garland Publishing, 1992.

———. *Parthenius of Nicaea: The Poetical Fragments and the Erotika pathemata.* Edited and translated by J. L. Lightfoot. New York: Oxford University Press, 1999.

pastoral poetry (bucolic poetry)

About 280 B.C.E., the Sicilian-Greek poet THEOCRITUS took the simple songs of shepherds and developed from them three sorts of poems that were to prove influential throughout the ages. Some 22 poems are now confidently included in Theocritus's *IDYLLS*.

The first and most influential sort of pastoral poem later became the ELEGY of lament. Originally a sort of meter employed for military songs, the pastoral elegy became a poem of grief and reconciliation, under Theocritus's influence, so that the word *elegy* shifted in meaning to describe a mood instead of a meter. One finds an example of such a poem in BION OF SMYRNA's lament for the death of the handsome youth Adonis, Bion's only complete surviving poem.

Another often-emulated mode of Theocritan pastoral involved a singing contest between two shepherds. They sang original verses on a set subject before a third person who would judge their performances and declare one the winner of whatever goods had been staked as the prize. One also finds an example of this sort of pastoral in Bion of Smyrna's poems.

The third kind of Theocritan pastoral involved a poem, ostensibly written by a shepherd or other rural dweller, that celebrated country pleasures or a boy's or a mistresses's charms, or that bemoaned their unjustifiable neglect. Such a poem by Theocritus is his first *Idyll*, "The Passion of Daphnis." In the country-pleasures subcategory of this sort of pastoral, Theocritus may have to share honors as an originator with a third-century B.C.E. female lyricist, Anyte of Tegea, whose work is attested by only 18 surviving lines (see FEMALE GREEK LYRICISTS).

Another poet roughly contemporary with Theocritus is MOSCHUS OF SYRACUSE. Though his one fully surviving work is not pastoral in theme, his fine descriptive passages sometimes have led critics to include him among the pastoral poets.

The pastoral manner expanded from such verses into the GREEK PROSE ROMANCE or novel. Only one entire example of the mode survives in Greek: Longus's *PASTORALS OF DAPHNIS AND CHLOE*.

In Rome, VIRGIL's *ECLOGUES* belong to the pastoral mode, as do his *GEORGICS* and many of the *ODES* of HORACE. A poet contemporary with the emperor Nero, TITUS SICULUS CALPURNIUS, penned eclogues in imitation of both Theocritus and Virgil. Calpurnius also modified the genre in some of his poems to give it a more rhetorical cast. He may have thinly disguised actual persons under the characters in his poems. Some have suggested that his shepherd, Meliboeus, substitutes for the Roman tragedian SENECA.

The third century C.E. Afro-Roman NEMESIANUS authored works on hunting, fishing (now lost), and four surviving eclogues that illustrate the pastoral mode. The Renaissance republication of many of the ancient pastoral poems in their original languages prompted a vogue for the genre that saw a resurgence of pastoral verse published for private reading and of pastoral plays, monologues, and early opera.

Bibliography

Dunlop, J. E., ed. *Latin Pastorals by Vergil, Calpurnius Siculus, Nemesianus.* London: Bell, 1969.

Holden, Anthony, trans. *Greek Pastoral Poetry: Theocritus, Bion, Moschus, the Pattern Poems.* Harmondsworth, U.K.: Penguin, 1974.

Horace. *The Complete Works: Translated in the Meters of the Originals.* Translated by Charles E. Passage. New York: F. Ungar Publishing Company, 1983.

Hunter, Richard. *Theocritus and the Archaeology of Greek Poetry.* New York: Cambridge University Press, 1996.

Longus. *Daphnis and Chloe.* Translated by J. R. Morgan. Oxford: Aris and Phillips, 2004.

Theocritus. *Idylls.* Translated by Anthony Verity. New York: Oxford University Press, 2002.

Pastorals of Daphnis and Chloe   Longus

The only surviving GREEK PROSE ROMANCE whose subject matter is exclusively pastoral (see PASTORAL POETRY, this novel by Longus (fl. ca. second–third century C.E.) recounts in four episodes the story of the many difficulties besetting a pair of would-be lovers. In the first book, Lamo, a goatherd living near Mytilene on the island of Lesbos, finds an infant boy abandoned in the countryside together with valuable objects. Lamo takes the baby home and names him Daphnis. Two years later a shepherd, Dryas, finds a baby girl in similar circumstances, takes her home to rear, and names her Chloe.

Dreams forewarn the herdsmen about letting the growing children be seen much in public, so the adoptive fathers send the children to herd their flocks. Delighting in each other's company, the children play happily together as they tend the animals.

One day, Daphnis falls into a muddy pit that had been dug to trap a wolf. He is rescued unhurt but filthy, and as he strips and washes himself, Chloe sees him and admires his good looks. Chloe is growing into a beautiful young woman herself, and an admiring shepherd, Daphnis's rescuer Dorco, gives her gifts and becomes Daphnis's rival for her affections. She, however, is entirely in love's clutches, though as yet she does not understand her feelings for Daphnis

Daphnis returns her love, and the two kiss innocently as, despite their duties with the animals, they remain unaware of other methods for expressing their mutual ardor. When Dorco asks Dryas to give him Chloe in marriage, Dryas refuses. Disappointed and angry, Dorco formulates a plan to disguise himself in a wolf skin and kidnap Chloe, but the guard dogs attack him. Daphnis and Chloe, thinking Dorco was merely playing a prank, rescue him.

In the meantime, the foundlings' mutual, innocent affection and admiration of each other's bodies continue to increase.

One day, Tyrian pirates enter the fields; help themselves to a number of animals belonging to Daphnis, Chloe, and Dorco; and kidnap Daphnis. The pirates wound Dorco mortally. Before he dies, however, he gives Chloe his panpipes, tells her to play them so his animals will all run toward the sound, and begs for a kiss. This she grants him, and Dorco dies happy. As she plays the pipes, the animals all run to the shore side of the pirate ship and upset it. The ship sinks and the heavily armed pirates drown, but the lightly clad and shoeless Daphnis and the animals swim easily ashore. The first book ends with Daphnis suffering mightily from his as-yet-unfulfilled passion for Chloe.

The second book is set in late autumn when the grapes are harvested and taken to the wine presses and when the feast of Bacchus is celebrated along with the birth of the new vintage. An old man, Philetas, comes and reports an encounter with Eros, the god of love. Philetas informs the young people that the god predicts that they will love one another. He also instructs them briefly in the skill of innocent lovemaking: kissing, hugging, and lying side by side. A great deal of the suspense in the novel depends upon putting off the consummation of the couple's ardor until the last possible moment.

A group of seagoing partiers now arrives—young men from Methymna who want to join in the fun of the grape harvest and do some bird hunting. They secure their ship to the shore with a line made from green twigs. During the night, the goats gnaw through the line, and the ship, which is filled with treasures, is cast adrift. The young voyagers blame the goatherd, Daphnis, beat him soundly, and then go off on their hunting expedition. The wind shifts, the ship is blown back, and on their return, the youths beat Daphnis again, but this time his friends turn up to help him.

Cooler heads restore order, and a trial commences to determine Daphnis's degree of responsibility in the matter of the loose ship. When Daphnis is acquitted, the Mythynians depart angrily and return with a military squadron of 10 ships under the command of Bryaxis. They attack without warning and carry off everything in sight, including Chloe.

Now, however, the god Pan intervenes on behalf of Daphnis and Chloe. Pan sends a series of spectacles throughout the night to frighten the Mythynians at their nearby anchorage. The god also warns Bryaxis in a vision that he must return Chloe. He does so amidst other Pan-spawned wonders. Then, after an evening spent in storytelling and in other country pleasures, Daphnis and Chloe at last formally promise their love to each other in a ceremony where they swear their mutual affection before Pan. That, however, is not good enough for Chloe, who considers Pan a fickle god. She requires Daphnis to swear by his flock of goats that he will never desert his Chloe.

The third book is filled with more military adventures and with the advent of winter. The coming of winter means that Daphnis and Chloe must take their flocks to their separate folds. The lovers are disconsolate at their parting. While they are separated, many wealthy suitors seek to contract a marriage with Chloe. Her foster father,

Dryas, nearly consents. Daphnis, bemoaning his poverty, gets help from the nymphs of the field, who lead him to a treasure of silver, which Daphnis gives to Dryas. Dryas in turn approves the match. Daphnis's foster father, Lamo, however, decides to wait for the approval of his master, Dionysophanes, before consenting to the engagement.

The third book ends with Daphnis's reminding Chloe of Paris's awarding a golden apple to Aphrodite as the prize for her beauty in a contest against Hera and Athena. He then presents his beloved with an extraordinary apple he has picked for her.

The fourth book, after introducing further impediments to the union of the young people, including another kidnapping and rescue of Chloe, reveals the aristocratic identities of both the foundling children. Their true parents claim them and approve of their wedding plans, and their nuptials at last take place in their beloved countryside.

Bibliography

Longus. *Daphnis and Chloe*. Translated by J. R. Morgan. Oxford: Aris and Phillips, 2004.

Longus. *Daphnis and Chloe*. Translated by George Thornley and J. M. Edmunds. London and New York: William Heinemann and G. P. Putnam's Sons, 1924.

patristic exegesis

The fourfold system of explanation by which the early fathers of the church interpreted Scripture is called *patristic exegesis*. According to this system, the Bible can be read, understood, and interpreted on four different levels. The first is the literal level, which simply requires an understanding of what happens. The second, the moral level, seeks to understand the implications that biblical events hold for human behavior. Third is the allegorical level, which seeks to discover the multiple applications that Scripture may have for the conduct of human affairs and what the passages under consideration may reveal about divine expectations for people. The fourth level, the anagogical level, seeks to explain the mystical implications of Scripture for the state of the human soul in a condition of future glory.

St. AUGUSTINE learned to read and understand the Bible in this fashion from St. AMBROSE, the Bishop of Milan, opening him to scriptural riches that, as a younger man, he had failed to perceive.

Bibliography

Heine, Ronald E. *Reading the Old Testament with the Ancient Church: Exploring the Foundation of Early Christian Thought.* Grand Rapids, Mich.: Baker Academic, 2007.

Williams, D. H., ed. *Tradition, Scripture, and Interpretation: A Sourcebook of the Ancient Church.* Grand Rapids, Mich.: Baker Academic, ca. 2006.

Pausanias (fl. second C. C.E.)

A Greek born in Asia Minor, Pausanius traveled widely in Palestine, Egypt, Greece, and Italy. From a literary perspective, he is famous for his guidebook for tourists, ITINERARY OF GREECE (*Guide to Greece, Helladios Periegesis*). Each of its 10 sections deals with a region or with two adjacent regions of Greece. Pausanias describes temples, tombs, notable pictures, statuary, and the legends concerning them. He also assists the traveler by describing roads, rivers, and communities that the tourist will encounter on a journey to the various locations discussed. Sometimes Pausanias describes local delicacies, fauna, flora, and scenery. His reports largely draw on his own travels, and his accounts therefore are those of an eyewitness. He is often skeptical about tales of local marvels, even though he tells many of them for interest.

Bibliography

Pausanias. *Guide to Greece: Pausanias.* Translated by Peter Levi. Illustrated by John Newberry and Jeffrey Lacey. New York: Penguin, 1979.

———. *Pausanias' Description of Greece.* Translated by W. H. S. Jones. 5 vols. New York: G. P. Putnam's Sons, 1918–35.

Peloponnesian War, The (The History of the Peloponnesian War) Thucydides (ca. 430–411 B.C.E.)

The most significant work of history composed in an ancient European language, Thucydides' eight-book chronicle of the long (431–404 B.C.E.) and terrible war between Sparta and Athens and their respective allies focuses principally on military campaigns conducted in several theaters of operation during the second Peloponnesian War's first 21 years. The Peloponnesus—a region that lies at the southernmost extremity of the Grecian archipelago—is connected to the rest of Greece by a narrow isthmus. This isthmus, in turn, is commanded on the west by the city of Corinth and bounded on the east by the regions of Boeotia and Attica. Early on, the Spartans had established their de facto sovereignty over the Peloponnesus with their military culture and professional army.

Before turning his attention to his chronicle proper, however, Thucydides introduces himself (in the third person) and sets forth his reasons for undertaking the task to which he has set his hand. From the war's outset, he says, he recognized that it would be a great war—greater, perhaps, than any that the world had earlier seen in terms of both its scale and its consequences. He did not write his history, he says, "to win the applause of the moment." Rather, he intended it to be what it has become: "a possession for all time." Its lessons are so applicable to every powerful nation in any age that any leader of any nation would benefit from a thorough knowledge of the book's content.

To orient his readers to his subject, Thucydides considers the prehistory of Attica—the region around Athens—and the way that its unsuitability for agriculture and the growth of its population led to emigration, to the development of associated colonies, and to a federation of their inhabitants under the influence of the mother civilization. Then he turns his attention to greater Hellas (Greece and its colonies and possessions) and its history. He speaks of the development of differing modes of government in Athens and Sparta, and of the tendency to build cities far from the sea and the depredations of pirates. He considers the influence on the Peloponnesus of the arrival from Asia of the wealthy Pelops and his followers among the impoverished indigenous population and notes the authority the Asian king acquired among his newly subordinate and needy subjects. The historian also traces the sources of the power of King Agamemnon.

Thucydides considers in his preamble the preparations for the centuries-past Trojan War (ca. 1194–1184 B.C.E.) from a purely logistical perspective. He concludes that minimal financial resources were available to the Greeks and that their military expedition was limited to the minimum number of men needed to transport their munitions and to no more than could be expected to live off the land.

In any case, following the Greek victory in the Trojan War came a period of adjustment for all concerned. Whole populations migrated, and local conflicts multiplied. When matters stabilized, the Greeks colonized Italy, Sicily, other Mediterranean islands, and, after confronting the Persians, the Asiatic shore of the Aegean Sea.

Thucydides then traces the accumulation of wealth and the small but nonetheless growing sea power of certain of the Greek cities, such as Corinth, which, Thucydides claims, fought the earliest sea battle in history against their colonists in Corcyrea, an island off the northwestern shore of the Grecian Archipelago. The historian details further internecine struggles among the inhabitants of Greece, and then the lengthy and dangerous mobilization of Greek might against the threat posed by the expansionary ambitions of the Persians.

With some cooperation from other Greek cities, the Athenians defeated the Persians (whom the Greeks generally called the Medes) in a series of decisive battles at Marathon, Thermopylae, Salamis, and Platea. Abandoning many of their conquests along the eastern Aegean, the Persians retreated toward home. Many of the liberated cities willingly accepted Athenian hegemony and protection, with the result that Athens became the head of a considerable sea empire—a thalassocracy. Thucydides also observes that the rulers (tyrants) of cities on the Grecian mainland did not attempt to extend their powers with the same vigor as did those in colonial Sicily.

Having reviewed the general anthropological situation leading up to the initiation of hostilities, Thucydides pauses to acknowledge his debt to legend and EPIC story telling for his mastery of early history and to assure his readers that he has taken pains to include only that which strikes him as most probable. Thucydides believed that human history was cyclical. Situations like those that led up to the Peloponnesian War had earlier existed and would exist again in the future. What was new in the world, he emphasized, was the duration of the war and the scale on which it was conducted. What was most regrettable was that the good advice of the cautious and the experienced was often neglected in favor of the enthusiasms of the moment.

Nonetheless, Thucydides considered the war inevitable. The established dominion of the city of Sparta over the Peloponnesians was threatened by the rise of Athenian sea power. Similarly, the expansionary ambitions of Sparta were thwarted by Athenian might. A crisis was building.

The flashpoint of that crisis occurred when a Corinthian colony, Corcyra, failed to respond to a plea for military assistance from a besieged subcolony, the city of Epidamnus. Desperate for help, the Epidamnians appealed to Corinth. Corinth was already annoyed with Corcyra for asserting its independence, so it agreed to assist by sending fresh supplies of colonists to Epidamnus. This angered the Corcyrans, who prepared their fleet to stop the immigration. Corinth responded by mobilizing its fleet with assistance from its allies in the region. Outnumbered, the Corcyrans appealed to the Athenians for naval support. Both sides, Corinthians and Corcyrans, sent envoys to Athens. The Athenians heard both presentations and decided in favor of the Corcyrans.

An attractive feature of Thucydides' history is his handling of the speeches made by envoys on various occasions. Some of these, he reports, he heard himself. Others were reported to him. In all instances, given the difficulties involved in word-for-word recollection, he puts in the mouths of the speakers the words that, in the historian's best judgment, the occasions demanded of them.

After listening to the envoys representing both sides, the Athenians voted in favor of supporting the Corcyrans and sent ships in support of their blockade of the harbor at Epidamnus. The Corinthians and their allies set sail with every intention of landing the new settlers. When the two fleets met in battle, they more or less lay side by side, and the fighting was done by the hoplites—heavily armed infantrymen—who occupied the decks. The Athenians, Thucydides reports, tried to avoid direct confrontation with the Corinthians, for a peace treaty between the two powers was in effect. Eventually, however, the heat of battle overcame prudence, and the two sides engaged each other in combat.

In the initial engagement, the Corinthians routed the Athenians and butchered their defeated troops. On seeing 20 reinforcing Athenian vessels approaching, however, and in view of imminent nightfall, the Corinthians withdrew. The next day, the fleets stood off from one another and did not resume fighting. The Athenians maintained that despite the bloodshed, their treaty with Corinth was still in force as long the Corinthians left the Corcyrans unmolested.

Political intrigues involving the Macedonians, the Spartans, the Chalcidians, the Boetians, and the Potideans continued to swirl, however, and open hostilities once more broke out despite a truce agreement. That fiction evaporated entirely when Athens mounted a siege against the city of Potidea on the northern Aegean Sea.

At this critical moment, Thucydides reports the speech given by Corinthian ambassadors at Sparta blaming the Spartans for their inaction. Doing nothing encouraged Athenian aggression and expansionist ambitions. In Sparta on other business, Athenian ambassadors responded to the Corinthian complaints, noting the role of Athens in defeating the Persians just a few years earlier and suggesting that, given the provocations in the current circumstances, Athens had in fact been operating with restraint. The emissaries warned Sparta to act cautiously.

In response, the Spartan assembly declared that the Athenians were aggressors, and the assembly's members resisted the advice of the Spartan king, Archidamus, to act cautiously in the face of Athenian power. Despite the king's good counsel, the assembly voted for war, and over Sparta's objections, the Athenians strengthened their defense by building a new city wall while her ambassadors delayed the Spartans.

Thucydides now digresses from his announced subject to trace the history of Athens' rise to power as well as her occasional military embarrassments during the 50 years following their defeat of the Persians. Near the end of this period, in 446 B.C.E., Athens and Sparta concluded a 30-year peace treaty. The author explains this digression as arising from his conviction that other historians have not treated it adequately and accurately.

Returning to his principal subject, Thucydides continues his history by recounting further discussions and saber rattling between the Athenians and the Spartans and their contribution to the fall from power of the Athenian leader, Themistocles. In a famous passage, set in the context of a comparative discussion of the Spartan leader, Pausanias, and Themistocles, the historian analyzes the character and capacities of that extraordinary statesman who, after his exile from Athens, managed, to become the governor of a Persian province under the emperor Xerxes by dint of his uncommon gift for statesmanship.

As Thucydides ends his first book, the ties between Athens and Sparta have worn increasingly thin, and the Spartans at last send an ultimatum. The Athenian statesman and strategist, Pericles, gives a speech detailing his program for an Athenian victory over Spartan ambitions and advises Athens to go to war. Thucydides catalogues the attempts by the propaganda machines of all parties to claim divine authority for their own views and to discredit the leaders of their enemies. The Spartans, for instance, knew of Pericles' maternal connection with a family cursed for having committed sacrilege, and they tried unsuccessfully to have him banished.

The Spartans experienced greater success in implicating the Athenian Themistocles in plotting with the Spartan statesman Pausanias to subject all of Greece to Persian rule. The Spartans punished Pausanias by starving him to death at the temple of the goddess of the Bronze House, where he had sought sanctuary from retaliation.

Having established his reasons for writing his history and having laid down his essential method, Thucydides follows it through the next 20 years of the war. Year by year, he examines military events and relevant political action and public policy decisions in several grouped theaters of operation. Typically, these include: (1) Attica, Euboea, and Boeotia; (2) the Peloponnesus and its subregions; (3) western Hellas and its subregions; (4) Thrace and its subregions; and (5) other regions as relevant. Thucydides varies this plan, however, as events dictate. In the eighth book, for instance, he treats the first three regions together.

In book 2, hostilities begin in earnest. The Peloponnesians marched against Athens. Athens responded with a series of sea raids that forced the withdrawal of the Spartans and their ships, and Thucydides reports Pericles' stirring funeral oration for the Athenian war dead. Then, in the summer of 430 B.C.E., a plague struck Athens. Thucydides was himself among its victims, and he describes in detail both its symptoms and its moral consequences. People despaired and sought pleasure with no thought of law, honor, or religion.

After the plague and a series of military reverses, the Athenians rejected Pericles' leadership and sent peace envoys to Sparta. With difficulty, Pericles persuaded his fellow citizens to stay the course. Thucydides digresses to analyze Pericles' character, leadership, and accomplishments. The historian concludes that the Athenians ultimately lost the war by ignoring his good advice to wait, concentrate on naval preparations, attempt no new conquests, and secure their city. Unfortunately, Pericles died after two-and-a-half years of warfare, but Thucydides reports the Athenian leader's requirements for a statesman: "To know what must be done and to be able to explain it; to love one's country, and to be incorruptible."

In 428 B.C.E., the Peloponnesians encouraged the Athenian subject city of Mytilene on the island of Lesbos to rebel. The city did so, and its allies deserted it, leaving the citizens to suffer Athenian sacks and reprisals. A rising Athenian hard-liner, Cleon, proposed killing all adult Mytilenian males and enslaving all the city's women and children. This proposal earned Cleon the undying scorn of the playwright ARISTOPHANES, who never missed an opportunity to ridicule the demagogue as an inept swine feeding at the public trough. A more moderate politician, Diodatus, argued that Cleon's hard line would make enemies less disposed toward moderation if roles were reversed. Diodatus won the day, but high drama followed. A ship had already sailed for Mitilene with Cleon's solution and orders to put it into action. A following ship arrived just in time to save most of the population. Nonetheless, 1,000 men—perhaps a 10 of the male city's population—were executed without benefit of trial or appeal.

More moderate in his judgment than Aristophanes, Thucydides pictures Cleon as the most violent and at the same time the most influential of the Athenian politicians at this stage of the war. The historian wisely observes that men of lower intelligence, like Cleon, won out over the more intelligent by rushing into action. Their political opponents found the waste of lives and resources both unnecessary and contemptible, for they felt sure the same ends could be accomplished by brainpower and wise diplomacy. Though Aristophanes considered Cleon inept, Thucydides thought that, despite Cleon's bloody-mindedness, he was a shrewd politician with genuine military skills. These skills he demonstrated by joining DEMOSTHENES in resolving a stalemate by leading an Athenian force to the stunning defeat of a contingent of 420 heavily armed Spartan hoplites who were occupying a narrow spit of land at Sphacteria on the Bay of Navarino. The battle was particularly important since the 420 captured hoplites represented about a tenth of Sparta's most redoubtable fighters. Cleon accomplished that feat in 20 days, as he had promised the Athenian citizenry.

As the fortunes of war favored first one side and then the other, politics became increasingly contentious and the combatants increasingly inhumane. "Many and terrible things occurred," says Thucydides, "because of faction." He predicts that such things will continue to happen as long as human nature remains the same.

Commenting on the state of wartime politics throughout the Greek world, the historian Donald Kagan remarks: "Party membership and loyalty came to be regarded as the highest virtues . . . justifying the abandonment of all traditional morality." Kagan continues by saying that plotting "the destruction of an enemy behind his back" seemed "admirable."

The year 427 B.C.E. also saw the first of two major Athenian expeditions to Sicily, where the Athenians intervened in an effort to interrupt grain exports to the Peloponnesians. Until about 424 B.C.E., despite some important reversals in Sicily and despite plague and rising taxes at home, Athens fared remarkably well. In that year, however, fortune's wheel turned against the Athenian military. Fortune's agent was the Spartan general Brasidas, whose first coup was his capture of an Athenian dependency, the Thracian city of Amphipolis.

Thucydides himself was in charge of an Athenian naval squadron charged with supporting Amphipolis, but when the Spartan's surprise attack came, Thucydides and his ships were inexplicably 50 miles distant. Likely responding to signal fires, the squadron returned to base within 12 hours, but by then it was too late. This failure led to Thucydides' trial and 20-year-long exile. It also led to the leisure necessary for the composition of his history.

Partly as a result of the fall of Amphipolis, the Athenians at last became ready to consider cessation of hostilities and a formal peace treaty. The warring parties agreed to a yearlong truce to explore terms on which a lasting peace might be achieved. Despite the cities' agreement, the Spartan Brasidas ignored the truce, pursuing his own political and military agendas in Thrace. His violations impeded any progress toward peace.

Eventually Athenian patience wore thin, and Cleon himself led an Athenian contingent against Brasidas. In the ensuing engagement at Amphipolis, Brasidas outthought and outmaneuvered Cleon, who, with 600 other Athenians, died in the battle. Only seven Spartans fell at the second battle of Amphipolis, but one of them was their general, Brasidas.

With the war's two strongest proponents gone, peace suddenly became possible, and the Athenians and Spartans signed an agreement to keep the peace for 50 years. Officially, this agreement held for eight years. Unofficially, it was abrogated on many occasions before that. Not only were the interests of the two city-states too conflicted to allow the peace to stand, internal divisions inside Sparta also threatened the agreement.

Moreover, the double-dealing of the duplicitous Athenian statesman Alcibiades on at least one occasion prevented a final settlement of Athenian-Spartan differences. Yet afterward, Alcibiades came very close to achieving a lasting peace on Athenian terms. His failure to do so contributed to Athens' eventual rejection of his military leadership.

The fortunes of the combatants continued to ebb and flow. The Spartans, despite the inept field leadership of their king, Aegis, won the Battle of Mantinea (418 B.C.E.), costing the Athenians valuable allies.

Despite divided leadership in Athens, where Nicias's and Alcibiades' disagreements threatened to hamstring the war effort entirely, the Athenians conquered the island of Melos in the Cyclades. In the meantime, the two Athenian political rivals invented—or rediscovered—political spin, with Nicias playing up his religious piety and Alcibiades following suit with greater flair and public expenditure.

Disaster lurked in the wings, however, for in 415 B.C.E., Nicias misled the Athenians into mounting a major and probably foredoomed attack against

Sicily. Meanwhile, Alcibiades defected to Sparta. In Sicily, the Athenians suffered defeat at sea and on the land. In the final battle, led by Demosthenes and Nicias, the Syracusans routed the Athenians. The Athenian generals had ill-advisedly attacked the city without the necessary support of cavalry. Though the Syracusans' ally, the Spartan general Gylippus, wished to bring the losing commanders home in triumph, the Syracusans opted for a more direct approach and put both Nicias and Demosthenes to death.

Though Thucydides praises Nicias, his fellow citizens omitted his name from the Athenian role of military honor because he had voluntarily surrendered. Demosthenes, however, was included on the role since he was captured while attempting suicide after arranging a truce for his subordinates. Two other experienced Athenian generals, Lamachus and Eurymedon, had also fallen in the second Sicilian campaign.

To resolve the resultant crisis of leadership, the Athenians elected 10 citizens to serve as advisers on state matters and to propose necessary legislation. Only two names survive of that group's membership—a former general named Hagnon, and another man, then in his 80s, whose name is more familiar for poetry and drama than for his early military career: the tragedian SOPHOCLES.

Despite the near exhaustion of Athens's treasury, the loss of the bulk of her ground forces and a considerable portion of her navy, and notwithstanding further recurrences of the plague that had decimated the civilian citizenry, the Athenians remained in a tenable position owing to Sparta's weakness at sea. Into the near stalemate created by Sparta's land and Athens's sea superiority stepped Persia. The Persian ruler, Darius II, hoping to recover those portions of Persia's empire lost to the Athenians over 50 years before, sent emissaries to Sparta proposing an alliance. The traitorous Alcibiades also advised Sparta to offer support to such disaffected Athenian subject cities as Miletus in Ionia.

The Spartans' success at Miletus redoubled the Persians' efforts to strike a bargain. Alcibiades advised the Spartans to cooperate with the Persians, and the two powers negotiated the Treaty of Chalideus in 412 B.C.E. Athens responded by sending a naval squadron into the Aegean. The force reestablished Athenian control over cities whose disaffection had been encouraged by the revolt at Miletus. That city became the squadron's next target, but a spirited defense with Spartan and Persian support turned back the attempt.

A series of feints and counterfeints, attacks and counterattacks, and treaty renegotiations between Persia and Sparta followed, but the situation changed most materially in 411 B.C.E. when a Peloponnesian fleet in the Aegean at last demonstrated that they could hold their own against an Athenian armada. As a result, Athens lost its precarious advantage, and public dissatisfaction at home intensified. The aristocratic classes of Athens, increasingly fed up with the rule of the untutored majority, sought a return to oligarchy with themselves in charge. Into that situation stepped the ever-imaginative Alcibiades, who saw an opportunity to engineer his own return to Athens. He would come home, he said, bringing with him the support of the Persian governor Tissaphernes, who would abandon his support of Sparta—if the Athenians would agree to scrap democracy in favor of oligarchy. The success of Alcibiades' suggestion, Thucydides points out, principally resulted from the fact that powerful and influential Athenians had already concluded that ending democratic rule was the most intelligent course.

In his bid to return to Athens, Alcibiades found an unlikely ally in an antioligarchic moderate named Thrasybulus. This influential Athenian democrat prevailed on Alcibiades to moderate his position and not move all the way toward upper-class rule. A counterplot led by the Athenian statesman Phrynicus undermined Alcibiades' standing with the Persian nobleman Tissaphernes. (In addition to this, Tissaphernes' strategy all along had been to play both sides against the middle and eventually wear out both Athens and Sparta.) With the collapse of Alcibiades' apparent ability to bring Persia over to the Athenians, his hopes for a restoration evaporated.

So, for the moment, did the ambitions of the oligarchic party.

They soon resumed, however, and from fraud and political maneuvering, young members of the aristocratic class began a campaign of assassination against the leaders of the democratic coterie. What they had failed to accomplish by guile, they soon achieved through fear. A council of 400 who gained office in a complex and mysterious manner had succeeded in achieving dictatorial power in Athens, literally driving the elected officials from their council house and assuming plenary powers on June 9, 411 B.C.E.

Elsewhere in the Athenian sphere of influence, parallel attempts did not meet with such success. Democracy was preserved on the island of Samos in the threat of a similar oligarchic coup. Back on the mainland, oligarchs and democrats raised armies and faced off at Piraeus. The soldiers on both sides, however, favored the democrats, and after a mock battle, they joined forces to destroy the fortifications at Piraeus. In doing so, they unwittingly thwarted a coup by an attacking Spartan fleet in league with the 400. Despite the 400's usurpation of power in the city proper, the vigilance of ordinary democrats and a few moderate leaders saved Athens from falling to the Spartans. All this, of course, amounted to a failure of the policy of the 400, and the Athenians responded by formally deposing them and restoring the moderate council of the 5,000. In Thucydides' view, under the rule of this council, Athens enjoyed its best government during the historian's lifetime. About 10 months later, full democracy was restored in Athens, and a punitive reaction against aristocrats set in. A few were condemned and punished; others found it prudent to flee.

In the meantime, the focus of military operations had shifted to the Hellespont. There the Peloponnesian fleet fomented revolution in Byzantium and other neighboring locations, endangering Athens's food supply lines. Another Persian governor, Pharnabazus, lent encouragement to the Spartans but failed to send ships in their support.

A clever Spartan admiral, Mindarus, however, managed to elude his Athenian opposite number, Thrasyllus, and arrive safely in the Hellespont. In doing so, he shifted the principal location of hostilities. Despite Athenian naval successes (including that of Alcibiades, now reinstated as an Athenian general) at Cynossema, Abydos, and Cyzicus, the war in the region of the Hellespont put the Athenians on the pathway to ultimate disaster.

It is shortly after the battle of Cynossema in 411 B.C.E. that Thucydides' history ends, leading some to conclude that he died around this time. However, there is conflicting evidence that he lived to around 400–401 B.C.E. and perhaps even later. The contemporary historian Donald Kagan carried *The Peloponnesian War* to its ultimate conclusion, and here I follow his account.

The war's pathway still had many twists to take, and the first was that the Athenian naval successes noted above caused the Spartans to violate their treaty with the Persians and unilaterally sue for peace with Athens. The Athenians, though, rejected the Spartan overtures for good reason. The Spartans were not to be trusted; they wanted to keep conquered territory in the colonies, and if Athens relaxed its vigilance, the Spartans might very well take the opportunity to resume the war when the moment seemed favorable.

Now the tide of warfare turned in favor of the Spartans. A civil war on the island of Corcyra resulted in the defeat of the Athenian party. The Spartans overwhelmed the small Athenian stronghold on the Bay of Navarino. Attempting to take Ephesus, the Athenian general Thrasyllus was defeated. Teamed with Alcibiades, however, he enjoyed better success in 409 B.C.E. at Lampsacus and Abydos, where they defeated the Persians. Alcibiades and his confederates also managed to recapture the city of Byzantium by deception. When, however, the Athenians attempted to upstage the Spartans by means of a treaty with Persia, their slow-moving ambassadors, then on their way to the imperial capital at Susa, met a Spartan diplomatic mission returning thence. In the Spartans' hands was a treaty signed by Darius II himself, and in their company his son, Cyrus.

Alcibiades finally decided to return to Athens and did so at an unpropitious moment on the one day of the year when the holiest image of the city—the Athena Polias—was absent from public view and adoration owing to an annual cleaning. Many thought his arrival an ill omen. He recovered, however, by providing a military escort to a group of pilgrims walking on their way to Eleusis and making possible their participation in the ceremonies there for the first time in years. This success produced an outpouring of public affection so that the leaders confirmed the reformed Alcibiades in his role as a principal general.

While Alcibiades was thus engaged in polishing his public image, the Spartans in the Ionian and Aegean regions were reinforcing their military and coming to new agreements with the Persian prince Cyrus, who, though only 17 years old, was the new governor in the region formerly under the control of Tissaphernes, western Anatolia. Cyrus was the younger son, but he had his eye on the crown of the Persian Empire. Shrewd as well as ambitious, he searched for an eminent ally among the Spartans and found him in the person of the new Spartan admiral, Lysander, the subject of one of PLUTARCH's PARALLEL LIVES.

Common sailors who had deserted the Athenians for the better pay that Cyrus made possible reinforced Lysander's Spartan fleet, moored at Ephesus. Citing Plutarch, Donald Kagan tells us that Lysander's command had grown to 90 ships. Perhaps in an effort to get Lysander to engage in a sea battle, Alcibiades, now the commander of an 80-ship Greek fleet, withdrew his troop ships to Phocaea. He left his triremes (fighting ships) under the command of a petty officer who had served him a long time, probably because he thought he could be trusted to follow orders. He gave his deputy commander, Antiochus, a very important order not to attack Lysander's ships.

The opportunity, however, to strike a blow for Athens in Alcibiades' absence overcame Antiochus's obedience. He attacked with 10 ships, his own in the lead. Lysander's intelligence system was reliable. He knew the situation in the Athenian fleet and that he faced an inexperienced commander, not the formidable Alcibiades. Lysander rammed and sank Antiochus's ship, killing its commander; the other nine ships fled. Other Athenians attempted to come to the rescue, but their uncoordinated attack merely made them equally vulnerable. At the ensuing battle of Notium, the Spartans sank 22 Athenian ships and sailed back to the safety of the harbor at Ephesus before Alcibiades returned.

The Athenians properly blamed Alcibiades for the defeat that finally turned the tide of the Peloponnesian War in favor of the Spartans and their allies. He next incurred further blame by losing a land battle at Cyme. Anticipating the fate that would await him at Athens, Alcibiades retired in self-imposed exile to a fortified villa he had prepared at Gallipoli against just such an eventuality. He would not return to Athens again.

The Athenians appointed a new admiral, Conon, to take Alcibiades' command. In keeping with Spartan law, a new admiral, Callicratidas, also replaced Lysander. Callicratidas did not inspire the same regard in the Persian Cyrus, and Cyrus refused to pay the Spartan sailors. Callicratidas then moved his headquarters from Ephesus to Miletus and embarked on a policy and a publicity campaign that promised freedom to overseas Greeks.

Callicratidas proved himself superior as a naval tactician to the Athenian Conon. The Spartan admiral captured 30 ships of one of Conon's squadrons and blockaded another 40 in the harbor at Mytilene. In view of that success, Cyrus restored Persia's financial support. Athenian reinforcements, procured by an unprecedented flurry of shipbuilding and recruitment that finally utterly exhausted the Athenian treasury, arrived. But now it was the Spartans who had the experienced sailors and the tactical advantage. They felt assured of victory. Nevertheless, at the next engagement, the Battle of Arginusae (406 B.C.E.), brilliant Athenian planning produced a victory in which the Spartans lost 77 (well over half) of their ships to the Athenian's 25—about a sixth of their fleet. Athenian superiority at sea was reestablished, and the young Spartan admiral perished in the fight. Because of stormy weather and the distance from land where the battle was fought, both the living and the dead who were in the sea had to be abandoned. The Athenian public was so horrified by this decision that, their victory notwithstanding, the generals who returned to Athens were tried and executed.

As a result of their naval disaster, Sparta once again sued for peace, but the Athenian demagogue Cleophon, thinking that total victory was in sight, persuaded the Athenians to continue the war. The Spartans evaded their own laws by appointing a figurehead admiral but making Lysander his secretary. It was he who would give the orders.

The decisive battle of the Peloponnesian War was at last at hand—though no one knew it in advance. At the battle of Agospotami—not far from the residence in exile of Alcibiades—Lysander and his subordinates routed the Athenians both on land and at sea, and those who were captured were put to death. On receiving that news, the citizenry of Athens—even though their resources were utterly exhausted and the war definitively lost—decided to try to hold out at all costs lest they suffer a fate similar to their captured countrymen.

On his return to Greece in autumn 405 B.C.E., Lysander found the two kings of Sparta in the field with the entire army of the Peloponnesians encamped outside the walls of Athens. When the threat of that force failed to produce Athenian surrender, Lysander left some of his fleet to blockade Athens and starve the populace into submission while he sailed off to besiege a thus-far staunch Athenian colony, the island of Samos.

Eventually starvation overcame Athenian resistance. That, coupled with the initiative of an Athenian moderate, Theramenes, who was able to persuade Lysander not to destroy Athens utterly, led to the city's eventual surrender. The situation was touch and go, however. The Theban Erianthus, as Plutarch reports, wanted Athens razed and turned into a sheep pasture. But Theban

ambition may well have been the reason that Lysander decided to preserve Athens as a buffer against expansionary ambitions from the north. In any event, Lysander offered the Athenians severe but honorable peace terms. As Donald Kagan tells us in his completion of Thucydides' unfinished history of the war, the war officially ended March 404 B.C.E.

Bibliography

Kagan, Donald. *The Peloponnesian War*. New York: Viking, 2003.

Thucydides. *History of the Peloponnesian War*. Translated by David Crawley. Mineola, N.Y.: Dover Publications, 2004.

———. *The Landmark Thucydides: A Comprehensive Guide to the Peloponnesian War*. Translated by Richard Crawley. Edited by Robert B. Strassler. New York: Touchstone, Simon and Schuster, 1998.

"Pericles" and "Fabius" (from *Parallel Lives*) Plutarch (ca. 100 C.E.)

PLUTARCH's 10th set of biographies from his PARALLEL LIVES, together with the first, "THESEUS" AND "ROMULUS," provide samples in this volume of the 23 surviving pairs of biographies and the comparison of the subjects' moral qualities that, together with four individual lives, constitute Plutarch's biographical masterpiece.

The 10th set compares the Greek orator and statesman Pericles (ca. 500–429 B.C.E.) with Fabius Maximus (ca. 275–203 B.C.E.), nicknamed *Cunctator* (the delayer), the Roman general, consul, and dictator who from 217 to 209 B.C.E. opposed the Carthaginian invasion led by Hannibal. Fabius eventually defeated Hannibal through a long series of strategic delays and tactical retreats; ultimately, Hannibal's supply lines became so long that he could not sustain the invasion.

Plutarch begins his life of Pericles with an introduction that details the benefits of reading about acts of virtue, an activity that stimulates the reader to imitate virtuous behavior. Next he praises undertaking works of virtue and engaging in occupations of benefit to others, including writing the lives of famous people.

After reviewing Pericles' birth and education, Plutarch addresses the public image that the statesman cultivated. While Pericles felt his wealth, lineage, and capacities might attract the unfavorable notice of persons in power and could lead to his exile as a potentially dangerous person, he kept a low profile and confined his public service to distinguishing himself in the military. Later, when he considered the time ripe, he entered politics but kept very much to himself and appeared only when important matters justified his direct, public participation. On those occasions, he took care to speak eloquently and to say nothing inappropriate. He cultivated the favor of the Athenian citizenry by finding public employment for many of them and by carefully gauging and responding to public opinion.

Clearly an admirer of Pericles, Plutarch defends the statesman against the libels of other historians who, like Idomeneus, accused him of cruelty and dishonor. Plutarch, rather, finds in Pericles opposing tendencies toward populism on the one hand and aristocracy on the other. But as the parties of Athens displayed the same split, Pericles opted to side with the populists. He oversaw the redistribution of Athenian wealth through public work projects that benefited the citizenry by putting money in their pockets and improved the city by making it both more beautiful and more livable. To Pericles' initiative, for example, belonged the building of the Parthenon and improvements to the entrances to the Acropolis.

By such openhandedness, Pericles was eventually able to triumph over his principal rival for power, Thucydides (not the famous historian). After his rival's ostracism and exile, says Plutarch, Pericles felt himself to be in unopposed control of Athens and thus free to indulge his aristocratic tendencies. He became a regal and austere ruler, utterly free from any ignoble motive.

Plutarch also admires Pericles' military strategy, which held in check those who were enthusiastic for war while at the same time displaying Athenian power and seeking alliances with those whose ambitions might make them potential enemies. He told the Athenian citizens who were sometimes eager for military adventures that he wanted them to live forever and not die needlessly in some foolish foreign or domestic campaign. Nonetheless, when he thought the occasion warranted war, Pericles did not shrink from it, and Plutarch describes his campaigns against the Samians and the Athenians' eventual success (440–438 B.C.E.). Pericles was also drawn into the immediately subsequent Peloponnesian Wars. Again, however, he pursued his own strategies, sending a fleet to harass his enemies' coastal towns while keeping the Athenian foot soldiery within the city and leaving the countryside to invaders for a time.

Plutarch goes on to admire Pericles' demeanor in moments of adversity and at the time of his death from a sickness that afflicted many in Athens. The biographer recalls how, as Pericles neared his end, his friends and supporters gathered around his deathbed with many tokens of honor for his service to the city and stood recalling his triumphs as if he were already dead and could not hear him. Pericles, however, was conscious and finally reproved them, saying, "No Athenian, through my means, ever wore mourning." Pericles' life, his exercise of authority and his utter incorruptibility earns Plutarch's unwavering admiration.

Turning to the Roman, Fabius, Plutarch first traces his genealogy and then recalls his physical and behavioral characteristics in childhood. Thought to be backward and lacking energy as a child, Fabius instead proved himself to be a brilliant but stable, deliberate, constant, and prudent adult. With a severe regimen of exercise, he prepared his body for military service and his mind and tongue for leadership and public oratory.

Five times elected consul, and before the Carthaginian invasion, he had already proved his capacity for military leadership by defeating the

Ligurians of northwestern Italy. When Hannibal's Carthaginian army marched across the Alps and invaded the Italian peninsula from the north, won a battle near the river Trebia, and desolated the Tuscan countryside, Fabius wisely avoided the military confrontation that Hannibal wanted, choosing instead to harass the Carthaginian's over-extended supply lines and starve his army into submission. Fabius's fellow consul, Flamineus, on the other hand, resorted to an early trial by arms in a battle fought during an earthquake. The victorious Carthaginians killed Flamineus and 15,000 Romans; another 15,000 were taken prisoner.

The urgency of this situation resulted in Fabius's being named dictator. In that capacity, he attended to public relations, making the people regard themselves as favored by the gods in the engagement with the Carthaginians. Then, with the remaining Roman forces at his disposal, he flanked the enemy, repeatedly raiding Hannibal's supply lines, and scrupulously avoiding pitched battle—especially with Hannibal's cavalry, which included elephants.

Even after Flamineus's instructive defeat, not everyone approved of Fabius's strategy, and the consul Minucius succeeded in having the people proclaim him codictator with Fabius. With great wisdom and forbearance, Fabius allowed Minucius to assume command of half of the army and to fall into a trap that Hannibal had set for the unwary. Because of Fabius's foresight, however, he was able to trap the trapper and relieve Minucius. Minucius learned his lesson, resigned his codictatorship, and thereafter regarded Fabius as his father and the savior of Rome.

Lessons concerning the futility of confronting Hannibal, however, did not last long. Fabius now felt that he could resign the office of dictator. No sooner had he done so, however, than another consul, Terentius Varro, enlisted an army of 88,000 soldiers to confront Hannibal. In the ensuing melee near Cannae on the river Aufidus, as Fabius had feared and predicted, Hannibal decimated the flower of Roman youth. Varro and a "thin company" of his once-mighty army escaped.

The panicked citizens of Rome turned once more to Fabius, who calmly comforted them, assuaging their fears. Hannibal helped, too, by not following up on his victory and marching straight against Rome. Heartened, the Romans appointed another general, Claudius Marcellus, more skilled and judicious than any of his predecessors except for Fabius. While Fabius harassed the Carthaginians' rear and flanks, Claudius boldly engaged them in a series of successful battles, until he too at last fell victim to Hannibal's superior military tactics.

In Plutarch's view, Fabius, after retaking the occupied town of Tarentum with a combination of force and guile, momentarily yielded to ambition. As for Hannibal, after Tarentum fell, for the first time the Carthaginian general was overheard delivering the opinion that it was now impossible for him to master Italy with the forces at his command.

Rome now produced a new general, Scipio, afterward surnamed Africanus, who against Fabius's advice crossed the Mediterranean with a Roman force and took the war to Carthage. Scipio eventually forced Hannibal to leave Italy for the defense of his own homeland. Fabius predicted disaster but died before receiving news that he had at last been wrong. Scipio utterly decimated the Carthaginian forces under Hannibal.

Every Roman citizen contributed the smallest coin in his possession to defray Fabius's funeral expenses. Fabius did not need the money. The point was that by contributing to his funeral expenses, each Roman citizen acknowledged him as his father.

In his comparison of the two leaders, Plutarch judges that Fabius had the harder job since he came to power at a particularly difficult moment when the Roman commonwealth was in a "sinking and ruinous" condition. Pericles, on the other hand, took command when Athens was at the height of its power and prestige. The historian then compares Fabius's victory over Tarentum with that of Pericles over Samos and other campaigns waged by the two statesmen or their subordinates. In this instance, the historian's opinion is mixed. Fabius's rescue of Minucius trumps any exploit of Pericles. Pericles, on the other hand, was never outsmarted by his enemies, as Fabius was on an occasion when Hannibal convinced him that a herd of oxen with fire between the horns of each animal was an army marching by night.

The palm for prophecy goes to Pericles, whom Plutarch calls "a good prophet of bad success." Fabius, on the other hand, was a bad prophet of Scipio's success. The historian also suggests that, because of his greater authority, Pericles had an easier time of governing than did Fabius, whose power, especially when not in the role of dictator, was limited. In terms of public projects and adornment of his city, Pericles wins easily.

Plutarch's discussion of this pair of famous men is much more focused and better crafted than his treatment of his first duo, Theseus and Romulus. So striking is the contrast that some readers have called into question Plutarch's authorship of the first pair of parallel lives. While that issue is probably not resolvable, it may well be the case that, if "Theseus" and "Romulus" constituted Plutarch's first attempt at biographical comparison, the author grew into his art and learned to craft a more efficient and esthetically satisfying product.

Bibliography

Plutarch. *The Lives of the Noble Grecians and Romans.* Translated by John Dryden with revisions by Arthur Hugh Clough. New York: Modern Library, 1932. Reprinted as *Greek and Roman Lives.* Mineola, N.Y: Dover Publications, 2005.

——. *Plutarch's Lives.* [Greek and English.] 11 vols. Translated by Bernadotte Perrin. Cambridge, Mass.: Harvard University Press, 1959.

——. *Plutarch's Moralia.* 15 Volumes. Translated by Frank Cole Babbitt. Cambridge, Mass.: Harvard University Press, 1960.

Peripatetic school of philosophy
(Aristotelian philosophy)

When, in 335 B.C.E., the Greek philosopher ARISTOTLE finished his responsibilities as the tutor of Alexander the Great, he returned to Athens. He had been absent from the city since the death of his teacher, PLATO (347 B.C.E.). In Athens, Aristotle founded a school in a precinct sacred to Apollo, the Lyceum. This spot was available for public recreation and contained several walkways. Because of that and because of Aristotle's habit of strolling about as he discoursed with his students, the school took its name from the Greek word for walking and became known as the Peripatetic school. On Aristotle's death, the leadership of the school passed to THEOPHRASTUS OF ERESUS and then to a line of successors that included the eloquent but not very scholarly Lyco and the Stoic Ariston of Ceos.

The school took all knowledge as its province, and its first two heads initiated a program of research into every intellectual field then recognized. When the Romans conquered Athens in 87 B.C.E., their general, Lucius Cornelius Sulla, had the school's library taken to Rome. After a brief interval, the philosopher Andronicus of Rhodes reopened the school, and under him its focus became less specifically Aristotelian, becoming infused with elements of the ACADEMIC SECT OF PHILOSOPHY and that of the Stoic philosophers (see STOICISM).

In the second century C.E., the scholarly Roman emperor MARCUS AURELIUS became a benefactor not only of the Peripatetic school but also of the schools teaching the other branches of philosophy as well: the Platonists (Academic school), the Stoics, and the Epicureans. Thereafter, however, the Peripatetic institution faded away as the intellectual heritage of Aristotle passed into other hands.

Bibliography

Curren, Randall J. *Aristotle on the Necessity of Public Education.* Lanham, Md.: Rowan and Littlefield Publications, 2000.

Lynch, John Patrick. *Aristotle's School: A Study of a Greek Educational Institution.* Berkeley: University of California Press, 1972.

Too, Yun Lee. *Education in Greek and Roman Antiquity.* Boston: Brill, 2001.

Persians, The Aeschylus (472 B.C.E.)

The only extant Greek TRAGEDY to deal directly with contemporary historical events, *The Persians* commemorates the Athenian victory over the forces of Persia at the Battle of Salamis in 480 B.C.E. There the powers of a far-flung Persian empire mounted an attack by land and sea against Athens in particular and the Greeks in general. The king of Persia (modern Iran), Xerxes, had spanned the Hellespont—the narrowest strait separating Asia from Europe—with a bridge of ships and advanced into Greece. The Spartans' subsequent heroic stand at Thermopylae gave the other Greek states time to assemble their ships, and they destroyed the Persian naval force at Salamis, just south of Athens.

AESCHYLUS himself had served with the Greek forces at Salamis and had witnessed the events. It is a tribute to the playwright's innate humanity and his sense of moving dramaturgy, therefore, that he chose to set his play not in victorious Athens, nor at the scene of the battle itself, but rather in the royal Persian city of Susa. There the play opens at a moment when the citizens of Susa are awaiting word of the outcome of the Persian campaign. The CHORUS enumerates the embattled powers of Asia who pass in poetic review in such a pictorial fashion that the audience gains a sense of a bird's eye view of a seemingly endless parade of kings, soldiers, animals, and weaponry marching off to overwhelm Athens.

Mixed in among the Persians' paeans of martial pride, however, the audience detects an undercurrent of concern. No word has come from the front. The Persian cities have been emptied of their defenders and would be at the mercy of an attack should one come.

Atossa, the Persian queen, mother of Xerxes and wife of his deceased father, Darius, enters, and her monologue reinforces the repressed sense of foreboding that the chorus has initiated. In her second speech, Atossa recounts her dream of the preceding night—a dream that seems to auger ill success for the Persian venture. She asks her advisers for their interpretation of her vision, and they try to comfort her.

Feeling somewhat reassured, she asks questions about Athens: Where is it? How rich is it? What is its form of government? What is the nature of its military strategy? The answers she receives to her questions heighten her concern, and she exits to prepare to pray.

At that moment, a messenger arrives from the front and proclaims the annihilation of the Persian forces and their allies. Xerxes has himself survived, but an entire generation of the young men of Asia has been wiped out. The chorus laments Xerxes' loss of prestige and power throughout Asia.

Atossa reenters and goes to pray at the tomb of her husband, Darius. The chorus makes unflattering comparisons between the wise and peaceful ways of the father, Darius, and the warring folly of Xerxes, the son. Darius "wasted not his subjects' blood," they sing, in "realm un-peopling war."

The chorus calls up the ghost of Darius from the underworld. When the ghost appears, the chorus fears to recount to it the loss of the flower of Persia's youth, and this task falls to Atossa. Darius's ghost attributes Xerxes' utter failure to youthful HUBRIS and to the bad counsel of his youthful advisors. The ghost also faults the folly of the Hellespont strategy and the Persian attempt to tame the sea.

The ghost of Darius then foretells the future and predicts still worse to come. The ghost foresees the Persians' further defeat at Grecian hands and the mounds of Persian dead at the battle of Plataea (479 B.C.E.). Despite its harsh judgments of Xerxes' folly, the ghost counsels Atossa to array herself in her finest garb and greet her son with words of comfort rather than of blame. The chorus then catalogues Xerxes' successes, all fruitless in the light of his forces' total destruction at Salamis.

Xerxes himself now enters, and a dialogue ensues between him and the chorus in which the Persian losses are once more recounted (and the Athenian successes tacitly implied). Xerxes wends his woeful way home to lament his losses and utter humiliation.

In the final song, the chorus lauds the Grecian victory and bewails the Persian loss. The even-handed humanity with which Aeschylus treats the entire situation bears witness to the good judgment and essential kindness of a playwright who had viewed at first hand the horror of Salamis.

Bibliography

Aeschylus. *The Complete Plays*. Translated by Carl R. Mueller. Hanover, N.H.: Smith & Kraus, 2002.

———. *The Persians*. Translated by E. D. A. Morshead. In *The Complete Greek Drama. . . .* Edited by Whitney J. Oates and Eugene O'Neill, Jr. New York, Random House, 1938.

Persius (Aulus Persius Flaccus) (34–62 C.E.)
Roman poet

Like the poet LUCAN, the Roman satirist Persius studied under the Stoic philosopher Cornutus. According to a biography that Valerius Probus probably wrote and that SUETONIUS passed down for posterity, Persius was a member of the equestrian, or knightly, class of Roman citizenry, and he traced his ancestry to the ancient Etruscans. He had moved to Rome from his native town of Volaterrae in the district of Etruria.

The basis of the ideas and some of the vocabulary of Persius's SATIRES can be traced to HORACE. Nonetheless, though a thorough mastery of every aspect of Horace's work appears in Persius's satire, and though Persius himself acknowledges a debt to the Roman satirist LUCILIUS, Persius's work remains unmistakably distinctive.

That distinction appears first in the scornful stance Persius adopts with respect to his audience, to his contemporary society and its hypocrisy, to his contemporary poetic taste, and to his fellow writers. It also appears in the paucity of his output. His six satires were published posthumously, and their total length does not amount to 700 lines. His history as a student and ardent devotee of STOICISM informs his text at every turn.

Following Persius's early death, his satires were edited and published by the friend and fellow poet to whom the sixth satire is addressed, Caesius Bassus. Persius's works have long been translated into the modern languages of Europe and the New World. Notable among his English translators was an 18th-century fellow satirist and poet, John Dryden. A new and attractive prose translation of Persius's work is that of Susanna Morton Braund.

Bibliography

Braund, Susanna Morton, ed. and tran. *Juvenal and Persius*. Cambridge, Mass.: Harvard University Press, 2004.

Petronius Arbiter (Gaius Petronius[?], Titus Petronius[?]) (ca. 27–66 C.E.) Roman
prose writer and poet

A degree of irresolvable uncertainty surrounds the question of whether or not the author of what is now generally called the SATYRICON is the same courtier who was compelled to commit suicide at the imperial Roman court under the emperor Nero. If so, the Roman historian TACITUS gives an account of him that describes him as a person who "idled into fame," asleep during the day and wakeful through the night as he arranged and directed the extravagant and sensuous entertainments that occupied the emperor's nights. Petronius's popularity with Nero seemingly aroused the jealousy of the prefect of the Praetorian Guard, Ofonius Tigellinus. The upstaged Tigellinus vented his fury by contriving Petronius's downfall. Influenced by Tigellinus, Nero condemned Petronius to suicide. He sneeringly anticipated the emperor's order, but took his time and lengthened the process of dying by having his veins opened, then bound, then reopened. As he died, he engaged in the sorts of pleasures that he most enjoyed, and in his will he wrote a scathing exposé of the emperor's debauchery—debauchery that he had a hand in arranging but in which he probably did not participate himself.

If, as seems reasonably likely, the three men known to us as Petronius are one and the same, before coming to Nero's court, Petronius enjoyed a more active and distinguished career as an official of the Roman Empire. He served as the governor of the territory of Bithynia in Asia Minor in 60 C.E., and in the same year he became the interim commander of the Roman legions in Britain, holding that position through February 61 C.E. Immediately thereafter, he became the master of the emperor's revels. In that capacity, Petronius is said to have earned the title "arbiter of elegance"— whence the addition of Arbiter to his name. With Tigellinus's elevation in 62, however, the emperor withdrew his favor by degrees, with the eventual outcome described above.

Literary history remembers Petronius principally for the fragmentary remains of a work that originally ran to as many as 400,000 words. Its usual title is an invention of literary history. No one is sure what Petronius called his work, but the Latin word from which *Satyricon* derives is *satura* (a medley). An earlier title assigned to the work was *Satyrica* (the adventures of satyrs). The word *satire* as currently understood, of course, was also implicit in the title.

As a medley, the work is composed both in prose and in verse, and one subject freely follows another without a break for transition. What now survives of the work are sections taken principally from its 15th and 16th books. Some fragments of poems also survive.

Bibliography

Corbett, Philip B. *Petronius.* New York: Twayne Publishers, 1970.

Heseltine, Michael, trans. *Petronius.* New York: G. P. Putnam's Sons, 1925.

Petronius. *The Poems of Petronius.* [Selections.] Translated by Edward Courtney. Atlanta, Ga.: Scholars Press, 1991.

———. *Satyrica: Petronius.* Translated and edited by R. Bracht Branham and Daniel Kenney. Berkeley: University of California Press, 1996.

———. *The Satyricon.* Translated by P. G. Walsh. New York: Oxford University Press, 1997.

Phaedrus the fabulist (Gaius Iulius Phaeder) (ca. 15 B.C.E.–ca. 50 C.E.)
Roman poet

Brought from his native Thrace as a slave to Rome, Phaedrus fortunately became the servant of the emperor AUGUSTUS CAESAR, who set him free. He authored at least five books of FABLES that survive under his name; an additional 32 fables survive that are also likely attributable to him. Phaedrus relied for his stories principally upon the fables told by his predecessor, AESOP, and on stories from other sources that people attributed to Aesop. To both sorts of fables, however, he added brief tales about such figures as MENANDER, SOCRATES, or Aesop himself.

Phaedrus also made none-too-veiled references to current Roman politics. This practice brought Phaedrus to the unfavorable attention of the emperor Tiberius's prefect of the Praetorian Guard, Lucius Aelius Sejanus—a man not to be trifled with. Phaedrus may well have been imprisoned for a time over his real or fancied criticisms of imperial policy. It is likely they were real; though many of the fables are merely jocular, others seem to be straightforward social and political criticism. A principal Phaedrus lesson was this: When the immoral or the ignorant are in power, ordinary persons need to learn the virtue of resignation and wait out the storm. Resistance is futile.

If Phaedrus's versions of such stories as "The Fox and the Sour Grapes" or "The Wolf and the Lamb" do not reach the level of the Renaissance fabulist La Fontaine, his work is nonetheless a major vehicle for the transmission of the age-old plots. Phaedrus wrote in the verse style of archaic Latin. He used iambic, accentual verse rather than the Greek system of arbitrary syllabic length that the Golden Age writers of Rome had made common.

Bibliography

Perry, Ben Edwin, ed. and trans. *Babrius and Phaedrus: Newly Edited and Translated into English, Together with an Historical Introduction and a Comprehensive Survey of Greek and Latin Fables in the Aesopic Tradition.* Cambridge, Mass.: Harvard University Press, 1984.

Phaedrus. *Aesop's Human Zoo: Roman Stories about our Bodies.* Translated by John Henderson. Chicago: University of Chicago Press, 2004.

———. *The Fables of Phaedrus.* Translated by P. F. Widdows. Austin: University of Texas, 1992.

Pharsalia   See CIVIL WAR.

Philemon   (fl. ca. 368–ca. 265 B.C.E.)   *Greek dramatist*

A playwright of the Greek New Comedy (see COMEDY IN GREECE AND ROME Philemon's plays are principally known to posterity through almost 200 fragments of his work; through surviving lists of winning comedies in the Athenian January festival, the LENAEA; and through the comedies that the Roman playwright PLAUTUS based on Philemon's then-extant works.

Active throughout most of a life that may have spanned a century, Philemon is known to have written 97 comedies, although only around two-thirds of their titles survive. From the lists of winners, we know that Philemon's plays took first prize at the Lenaea on three occasions.

While the extant fragments tell us that Philemon's work sometimes tended toward wordiness and heavy-handed moralizing, Plautus's tighter, funnier, and better-crafted revisions of such plays as Philemon's *Emporos* (Plautus's *The MERCHANT*), *Thesauros* (Plautus's *Treasure*), and perhaps his *Phasma* (Plautus's *Haunted House*) give us a sense of the plots and outlines of Philemon's comedies. According to the classicist William Geoffrey Arnott, Philemon's plays enjoyed a brief Athenian revival after his death, and the citizens erected a statue of him. The absence of complete texts, however, suggests that his popularity soon dimmed.

Based on surviving lists of Greek New Comedy props, we can say something more about Philemon's characters, who represented types. The actors wore masks appropriate to the type that they portrayed. Thus, there were masks for old men and masks for slaves, for courtesans, for cooks, and so forth. The plays, too, were typical in being designed to meet audience expectations for light entertainment with an edifying moral resulting from predictable and often vicious difficulties that regularly involved older persons interfering in the love interests of younger ones. Coincidence and fate generally played major roles.

Though Philemon's plays sometimes defeated those of an apparently better dramatist, MENANDER, the latter playwright seems to have been in no doubt about whose plays were really superior. The essayist Gellius (fl. second century C.E.) quotes Menander as having asked Philemon if the latter were not ashamed that his play had been preferred to Menander's—suggesting that Philemon's play may have won owing to the support of a paid claque.

Bibliography
Aylen, Leo. *The Greek Theater.* London and Toronto: Associated University Presses, 1985.

Lefèvre, Eckhard. *Plautus und Philemon.* Tübingen, Germany: G. Narr, 1995.

Pickard-Cambridge, Arthur. *The Dramatic Festivals of Athens.* Oxford: Clarendon Press, 1953.

Philetas of Cos   (Philitas of Cos)   (ca. 330–270 B.C.E.)   *Greek poet*

A native of the island of Cos and the son of an islander named Telephus, Philetas became a learned poet and teacher. He tutored the second Greek pharaoh of Egypt, Ptolemy II (Ptolemy Philadelphus) and is also said to have taught other famous persons. Although only a few fragments of his works survive, his achievements are well attested to in the work of his successors. He provided a model for CALLIMACHUS and for other scholar-poets who rejected the EPIC as their preferred medium and chose instead to write shorter and more allusive poems that implied rather than stated much of their emotional meaning and achieved a high degree of verbal musicality.

Among the poetic works mentioned by successors and commentators, we find *Demeter*. This elegiac work told of the grief of the goddess of fertility when Pluto kidnapped Demeter's daughter Persephone (also called Kore) and made her queen of the underworld. Philetas's *Hermes* recounts an episode connected with HOMER's *The ODYSSEY*. In it, Odysseus has a love affair with Polymele, the daughter of Aeolus, the king of the winds. Another work, *Telephus*, may have been named for the poet's father. Most of its content is unknown, though it may have alluded to the marriage of the Argonaut Jason and Medea (see *MEDEA*). Philetas also brought together a collection of EPIGRAMS, and somewhere is said to have addressed a series of love poems to a woman named Bittis.

Among Philetas's lost prose works, we find references to a collection of glosses that clarify archaic forms used by Homer, explain dialectical variants, and define technical terms. This work was apparently treated as a benchmark reference by Philetas's successors.

Bibliography

Sbardella, Livio. *Filita: testimonianze e frammenti poetici.* [Philetas: witnesses and poetic fragments.] Rome: Quasar, 2000.

Philoctetes Sophocles (409 B.C.E.)

Philoctetes appears briefly in *The ILIAD* of HOMER as an archer and the leader of a squadron of seven of the Greek ships bound for Troy. Philoctetes' story as SOPHOCLES tells it, however, draws on legendary material about the Trojan War that had been recounted in a post-Homeric EPIC known as the *Little Iliad*.

Background: When the hero Heracles (Hercules) lay in agony about to be burned at his own request upon his funeral pyre (see *The TRACHINIAE*), the hero asked that the pyre be set ablaze by a youth named Philoctetes. As a reward for that service, Philoctetes received Heracles' bow and his arrows that had been poisoned with Hydra blood and were invariably fatal.

After some years passed, Philoctetes joined the Greek fleet bound for Troy. On the way, however, a prophetic forewarning required the Greeks to sacrifice to a local goddess, Chrysa, whose veneration was limited to a single small island in the Aegean sea, and only Philoctetes knew its whereabouts. He led the Greeks there. Incautiously, however, as the party prepared the sacrifice, Philoctetes trod profanely on hallowed ground. In retribution, a serpent bit his foot. Philoctetes' cries of pain interrupted the ritual and made it impossible to go on. Worse, his wound became gangrenous, and the smell overcame his comrades' concern for his welfare. The problem affected morale so severely that the matter came to the attention of the Greek generals Agamemnon and Menelaus. They ordered Odysseus to strand Philoctetes on Lemnos, an uninhabited island. There he remained, sustained by water from a spring, the flesh of game he shot with Heracles' bow and arrows, and such food as passing sailors would spare him throughout most of the 10 years of the Trojan War.

The Greeks, however, were not faring very well at Troy, and it looked as if the entire enterprise might fail. A prophecy, though, foretold that if two conditions were met, the Greeks' fortunes would improve, and Troy would fall. First, Achilles' son Neoptolemus must come to Troy and be armed with his father's weapons and armor. Second, Philoctetes must be rescued and bring Heracles' weapons to Troy. The Greek generals therefore sent Odysseus to round up the two young men.

As Sophocles' play opens, Odysseus has already collected Neoptolemus, and the two of them, together with an attendant and members of the CHORUS, appear before the entrance to Philoctetes' cave in a cliff on Lemnos. Odysseus tells Neoptolemus enough of the story to remind the audience where they are and why. Odysseus thinks that if Philoctetes sees him—the man who stranded the archer on the island—he will certainly shoot Odysseus with his invariably fatal arrows. The wily leader therefore instructs Neoptolemus on the strategy for recruiting Philoctetes to rejoin the Grecian adventure against Troy. The lad must trick the archer.

An idealistic youth, Neoptolemus says he would prefer to use force or persuasion, but Odysseus finally convinces the youth that only trickery can prevail. Neoptolemus has discovered signs of Philoctetes' encampment, and Odysseus withdraws to await the outcome of the encounter. After discussion with the chorus that further clarifies the play's background for the audience, Neoptolemus hears Philoctetes coming.

Seeing the strangers, Philoctetes greets them in a friendly fashion and inquires about them. They identify themselves as Greeks. Pleased, Philoctetes asks about their motives in coming. Neoptolemus identifies himself and denies any knowledge of Philoctetes. Philoctetes tells his story, the circumstances of his life on the island, and he reveals his natural antipathy for the Greek captains who abandoned him. Neoptolemus is sympathetic and says that he too bears a grudge against the Greek captains—particularly the sons of Atreus, Agamemnon and Menelaus, who denied him his father's arms. After further discussion in which they speak of those who have died at Troy and those who still survive, they conclude that the gods take the good men and let the evil flourish. Odysseus is Philoctetes' principal example of the latter.

Neoptolemus says he must be going, and Philoctetes begs him to take him along. He knows that the stench of his wound is a problem, but he is willing to ride anywhere, including in the bilge, and he is only a day's sail from home. Neoptolemus agrees to take him. The two are about to enter Philoctetes' dwelling to collect his belongings when they are interrupted by the arrival of a sailor and a merchant who supplies the Greek troops at Troy. The merchant has heard the prophecy concerning Philoctetes, and he further reports that Odysseus means to bring him to Troy. Philoctetes says he would rather go to Hell.

As Philoctetes gathers his belongings and some medicine that eases his foot, the chorus sings sympathetically of his plight. He allows Neoptolemus to examine his bow and arrows. Then Philoctetes suddenly suffers unbearable pain from his afflicted foot and begs Neoptolemus to cut off the offending heel. After describing his suffering, Philoctetes falls into a deep sleep.

When Philoctetes wakens, Neoptolemus is conscience-stricken about his role in deceiving his newfound friend. The youth confesses that Philoctetes must sail with him to Troy. Philoctetes begs the youth to give him back his weapons and leave him after all. Odysseus, however, enters, and reveals himself to be the master plotter, but he defends himself by saying that he is merely the instrument of the will of Zeus.

Philoctetes threatens suicide and moves toward the edge of a precipice. Odysseus orders two sailors to restrain the man. Philoctetes calls Odysseus evil and curses him. Odysseus threatens to take the weapons and leave Philoctetes on Lemnos after all. Neoptolemus sets about preparing his ship for the journey and encourages Philoctetes to change his mind and come willingly. The archer, however, has become totally distracted by finding himself in an impossible situation, and he speaks irrationally and at cross-purposes.

Neoptolemus now suffers another attack of conscience and announces to Odysseus that he intends to return Philoctetes' bow and arrows. Odysseus threatens the youth with his own reprisal and that of the entire Greek army. Neoptolemus again appeals to Philoctetes to change his mind, but when he remains firm in his decision to remain on Lemnos, Neoptolemus offers him his weapons. Before Philoctetes can believe it, Odysseus enters and forbids it. Philoctetes seizes the weapons and aims an arrow at Odysseus, but Neoptolemus prevents his shooting it, and in a lengthy speech again attempts to persuade the archer to come voluntarily to Troy. After exhausting every argument, Neoptolemus decides that, since he cannot persuade Philoctetes to go to Troy, the youth is honor bound to take him home as he had initially promised and to defend him against the anger of the Greek captains.

Having arrived at this impasse on stage, Sophocles has recourse to one of the CONVENTIONS OF GREEK DRAMA. The playwright has the hero Heracles appear as a demigod ex machina. Following his death, Heracles was taken to Mt. Olympus to dwell with the gods. Heracles informs Philoctetes that it is his destiny to go to Troy and to be cured of his disease by the divine physician, Aesclepius. Then Philoctetes will slay the Trojan prince Paris, be awarded the greatest prize in the army, and return in glory to his homeland. Heracles gives Neoptolemus similar advice. Both men accept Heracles' counsel, and all venture forth toward Troy.

Bibliography

Lloyd-Jones, Hugh, trans. and ed. *Philoctetes*. In *Sophocles*. Vol. 2. Loeb Classical Library. Cambridge, Mass.: Harvard University Press, 1994.

Philostratus, L. Flavius (Philostratus the Athenian) (fl. ca. 210 C.E.) *Greek prose writer and poet*

The second member of a literary family—all named Philostratus—whose production spanned four generations, the Athenian Philostratus is best remembered as a biographer. He composed a series of *Lives of the Sophists* that included portraits of rhetoricians and orators from the time of Protagoras in the fifth century B.C.E. until the early third century C.E.

Also attributed to Philostratus are: (1) two prose descriptions of pictures, entitled "Icons," an attribution that is sometimes disputed; (2) conversations among the ghosts of warriors killed during the Trojan War, his *Heroicus*; (3) a collection of philosophical studies (some of doubtful attribution) that includes a Greek poem upon which the Renaissance English poet Ben Jonson based his lovely poem "To Celia" ("Drink to me only with thine eyes . . .").

Beyond these, however, Philostratus deserves to be better remembered as the author of a fictionalized biography of a Pythagorean philosopher and mystic. Entitled *The Life of Apollonius of Tyana*, the work contains stories about Apollonius that find analogues in the career of Jesus Christ in the Christian New Testament. The

parallels made an early Platonist critic of Christianity, Celsus, suspicious enough that in his work *The True Doctrine,* he accused the Christians of borrowing accounts of Apollonius's raising the dead, of his having himself been resurrected, and of his having ascended bodily into heaven for the emergent Christian Scriptures. Not surprisingly, Celsus's work occasioned considerable consternation among the Christian community, and the Christian apologist ORIGEN responded in an effort to refute Celsus's accusations.

Others, however, took up the cudgels. A critic of the claims of Christianity, Hierocles, drew a point-by-point comparison between the miracles attributed to Christ and those attributed to Apollonius. Origen's pupil and friend, EUSEBIUS OF CAESAREA, also a Christian apologist, defended the Christian faith in his *Against Hierocles*, denying the comparisons that Hierocles had drawn between Christ and Apollonius of Tyana. Eusebius's refutation convinced the Christian community, which has since regarded Celsus and Hierocles as proved wrong.

Bibliography

Philostratus. *The Life of Apollonius of Tyana: The Epistles of Apollonius and the Treatise of Eusebius.* 2 vols. New York: G. P. Putnam's Sons, 1917.

Reimer, Andy M. *Miracle and Magic: A Study in the Acts of the Apostles and the Life of Apollonius of Tyana.* New York: Sheffield Academic Press, 2002.

Photius, St. (ca. 810–ca. 893 C.E.) *Greek Byzantine prose writer*

Photius was the son of a Christian family. His parents were exiled for a time from their native Constantinople owing to their devotion to the cult of images that temporarily was out of favor. Despite that transitory dislocation, Photius received a fine education, and his erudition brought him to the favorable attention of the authorities.

On her prime minister's recommendation, the Byzantine empress Theodora approved appointing Photius to be professor of philosophy at the

University of Constantinople—an institution that he then reorganized. In the usual atmosphere of disagreement that prevailed among ancient Christians, the church could reach not agreement about who should become the patriarch of Constantinople after the resignation of Ignatius. Finally, the bishops compromised on a layman as their patriarch and chose Photius. Photius hurriedly acquired the degrees necessary for him to take holy orders and was twice elevated to the office of patriarch.

Classicists remember Photius as the scholar who compiled a commentary on 280 chapters of secular and sacred books that he had read. Though many of the books containing those chapters did not survive, the commentary did. Posterity owes to Photius what little it knows about 60 or so lost secular books by ancient authors. Among these are the *Narratives of Konon*, cited in the bibliography below. A glossary by Photius, his *Lexicon*, also survives, as do some 200 of his letters and a number of his homilies.

Bibliography

Photius I, Saint. *The Bibliotheca: A Selection*. Translated by N. G. Wilson. London: Duckworth, 1994.

———. *The Narratives of Konon*. Edited and translated by Malcolm Kenneth Brown. Munich, Germany: Saur, 2002.

Phrynicos of Athens (fl. 512–476 B.C.E.)
Greek dramatist

Reputedly a disciple of the archetypal Greek playwright, THESPIS OF IKARIA, Phrynicos was the earliest Athenian author mentioned (in an inscription) as a tragic playwright. He is credited with having introduced the female mask to the Greek stage.

Phrynicos is known to have produced at least two plays—one a TRAGEDY and one a victory celebration. The latter, his *Phoenissae*, portrayed the Greeks' triumph over the Persians and Phoenicians in 480–79 B.C.E. This play is also remembered for the women who performed in the

CHORUS: They were the captured wives of the defeated Phoenician seafarers.

With respect to tragedy, the play or plays of Phrynicos made use of a single actor—who might portray more than one part by changing his costume and mask—and a chorus. Phrynicos's known tragedy, *The Destruction of Miletus*, was based on the Persian conquest of the Ionian Greek city of Miletus and the enslavement of its entire population in 494. Magnificently produced at the expense of the Athenian statesman Themistocles, *The Destruction of Miletus* won the prize for the best play presented that year, but reportedly it so moved the Athenian audience that Phrynicos was fined for saddening his fellow citizens and cutting too close to the bone with his portrayal of recent disheartening events.

Phrynicos is also remembered for preparing a word list that prescribed terms that playwrights should employ or avoid to be considered in step with the times by Athenian audiences.

Bibliography

Lightfoot, Jane L. "Romanized Greeks and Hellenized Romans: Later Greek Literature." In *Literature in the Greek and Roman Worlds: A New Perspective*. Edited by Oliver Taplin. New York: Oxford University Press, 2000.

Wilson, Peter. "Powers of Horror and Laughter: The Great Age of Drama." In *Literature in the Greek and Roman Worlds: A New Perspective*. Edited by Oliver Taplin. New York: Oxford University Press, 2000.

Physics See ARISTOTLE.

Pictor, Quintus Fabius (fl. 225–200 B.C.E.)
Roman historian

An early Roman annalist, Pictor is so classified because he recorded historical events in prose on a year-by-year basis. His language of composition was Greek, though almost all of his writings in that language are lost. The few Latin fragments that remain are later translations of his work.

Like other Roman historians, Pictor apparently began with the foundation myths of the city as they are recorded in VIRGIL and elsewhere. Having done so, he moved to the annual examination of more contemporary history. His work included discussion of the First and Second Punic Wars—Rome's first two wars with the North African city of Carthage. His annals were among the sources used by such later Roman historians as LIVY and POLYBIUS.

See also ANNALISTS AND ANNALS OF ROME.

Bibliography

Martini, Maria Cristina. *Due studi sulla riscrittura annalistica dell'età monarchica a Roma.* [Two studies on the annalistic rewriting of the monarchical age in Rome.] Brussels: Latomus, 1998.

Momigliano, Arnaldo. *The Classical Foundations of Modern Historiography.* Berkeley: University of California Press, 1990.

Pindar (ca. 518–ca. 438 B.C.E.) *Greek poet*

How little we know about Pindar's life may seem surprising since posterity generally regards him as the greatest lyric poet of ancient Greece. It is certain that Pindar was a citizen of the city of Thebes. Less certain is an assertion that he was born near Thebes in a village named Kynoskephalai (dogs' heads). There is, however, no doubt concerning the dates of the ODEs that he composed in honor of the victors in the Olympic games in the years ranging from 476 to 452 B.C.E. Anecdotes from various ancient biographies report the names of his teachers in flute playing, lyric composition, and music—respectively, Skopelinos, Lasos of Hermione, and either Agathokles or Apollodoros.

Because of the subjects of his ODEs and the fame of the figures they celebrate, Pindar's friendly relations with important and powerful contemporaries throughout the far-flung Grecian world are also a certainty. Less certain is whether or not he was personally present at all the events within the Greek sphere that his poems chronicle, but it seems safe to assume that he traveled far and wide. It is also likely the case that his cosmopolitanism and admiration of Athenian institutions did not always sit well with his fellow Thebans, who had long been in rivalry with Athens.

As with the writings of so many ancient Greek writers, the transmission of Pindar's texts relied in the first place on the skill of editors working at the library of Ptolemy II at Alexandria in Egypt. Between 194 and 180 B.C.E., an editor named Aristophanes of Byzantium prepared 17 papyrus scrolls containing the known writings of Pindar. One of these contained hymns to various gods. Another contained paeans—hymns addressed exclusively to Apollo. Dionysian hymns occupied another two scrolls. Three more recorded *parthenaia*—hymns sung by young boys and virgins. The next two preserved Pindar's *hyporchemes* (songs associated with ritual dance and addressed to gods). Two more collected Pindar's more secular poems—songs designed for singing at banquets in praise of important men. A single volume included his threnodies—songs of grief for deceased men—and four others brought together the work for which he is most celebrated, his *epinikia*—songs or VICTORY ODES in praise of the winners at athletic events and sometimes of their cities. As may seem self-evident from this list, Pindar's works were designed for public performance rather than for private reading.

Of this substantial body of material, only the last-named seemed to have survived into the 20th century in its entirety. A rubbish heap at OXYRHYNCHUS in Egypt, however, was found to contain substantial formerly lost portions of the paeans to Apollo.

Quite apart from the content of his work, Pindar's reputation as a poet rests first upon his mastery of the sonority of his language and of the metrical complexities of its prosody (see QUANTITATIVE VERSE). Second, it rests upon his capacity to combine the elements of its vocabulary into novel, allusive, and striking arrangements. Finally, it rests upon his command of the flexibility of Greek word order. Whereas English word order often determines the grammatical relationships among the words of a sentence, Greek grammatical relationships are signaled by endings on the words. This gives a skillful poet much greater latitude for manipulating rhythm and sonority. Pindar was among the most skillful of such manipulators. At the same time, his dazzling virtuosity makes extraordinary demands on a reader and must have made even more extraordinary demands on his initial audiences, composed not of readers but of hearers. Rendering Pindar into other tongues makes similar demands on his translators.

If Pindar's recent biographer, William H. Race, is right, Pindar lived about 80 years. His odes, particularly, became models for later writers in other languages, during classical times and also during the early modern and modern periods of our own epoch. Both HORACE and QUINTILIAN admired and emulated him. Ronsard in France and Cowley, Dryden, and Gray in England benefited from his example.

See also "OLYMPIAN 1"; "PYTHIAN 3."

Bibliography

Bowra, C. M. *Pindar*. Oxford: Clarendon Press, 1964.

Race, William H. *Pindar*. Boston: Twayne Publishers, 1986.

———. *Pindar*. [Greek and English.] 2 vols. Cambridge, Mass.: Harvard University Press, 1997.

Plato (ca. 428–ca. 348 B.C.E.) *Greek prose writer*

Arguably the preeminently influential philosopher of the Western world, Plato was born to a prominent but politically divided Athenian family. Various members of that family had urged opposing political points of view during the years of the Peloponnesian War, which had proved so disastrous for Athens. Some think that as a youth, Plato considered becoming a poet. Certainly the literary quality of his works suggests that he could have stood in the first rank. If his early ambitions were in fact poetic, however, he soon abandoned them when he met the Athenian thinker and teacher SOCRATES, who became Plato's mentor and model.

When, in a fit of foolish blood lust, the restored Athenian democracy condemned Socrates to death on a trumped-up charge of corrupting Athenian youth (399 B.C.E.), Plato and several other disciples of Socrates fled Athens for a time, at first finding shelter in the city of Megara with the philosopher Euclides. Then Plato undertook a grand tour of the western Mediterranean, traveling in Egypt, Italy, and Sicily. In the city of Syracuse, he found a good friend in Dion, the brother-in-law of the city's ruler, Dionysius I. Plato's later effort to turn the king's son, Dionysius II, into a philosopher failed utterly, however, and involved Plato in some personal danger.

On returning to Athens, Plato founded the academy that bore his name for more than 1,000 years—first in Athens, where the Roman emperor Justinian closed the school in 529 C.E., and then in Alexandria, where the institution survived for nearly a century more. Plato never married, investing his life in his students and in his thinking and writing rather than in a family. In his written works, he resurrects his teacher, Socrates, as a character who becomes Plato's voice and argues his viewpoints. He also pays Socrates tribute in three dialogues: *APOLOGY OF SOCRATES*, *CRITO*, and *Phaedo*. These contain accounts of Socrates' trial, last days, and death.

Plato never speaks in his own voice in his dialogues, his preferred literary form; rather, he usually—though not always—leaves the arguing to his imagined Socrates. Sometimes the dialogues follow the plan of narrative fiction, as does *The REPUBLIC* and all the dialogues from Plato's final period. Sometimes, instead, Plato writes his dialogues as if they were intended for stage performance, as is the case with *Timaeus*. Another mode that Plato employs is having someone read a dialogue to listeners, as is the case in the *Theatetus*. Sometimes Plato chooses, as in *SYMPOSIUM*, to have someone report a narrative the speaker has overheard.

Early Platonic dialogues on moral virtues, such as *Charmides* (a work about the virtue of temperance), *Euthyphro* (a dialogue between Socrates and Euthyphro, a soothsayer who claims to be the world's greatest expert on religion and piety), *Ion* (a gentle satire of an entertainer who recites epic poems), *Lachis* (a work about the virtue of courage), and *Lysis* (a work about the virtue of friendship) establish the pattern of an almost omniscient Socrates (who often claims to know nothing) tearing to pieces the ideas of his questioners. The ancients considered that these works contain accurate portraits of Socrates and the way he worked.

A more attractive Socrates and perhaps one more closely assimilated to Plato's thinking—a Socrates who puts forth his own viewpoints—appears in Plato's middle works. Among these works, we find *Alcibiades* (a discourse on the necessity for a statesman to possess real and accurate knowledge), *Cratylus* (an etymological treatise that suggests words have a natural affinity with the things or ideas they stand for), *Euthydemus* (a romping satire that pokes fun at the inability of two minor sophists to identify fallacies), *Gorgias*, *Menexenus* (a mock funeral oration), and *Meno* (which addresses the question of whether or not virtue is teachable). *Parmenides* is a rather odd work in which a youthful Socrates loses a debate and is advised to study dialectic harder. He meets that advice with a pyrotechnic display of his dialectical ability. The literary historian Herbert Jennings Rose has controversially suggested that in this essay Plato abandons one of his central teachings—the idea of forms.

Other works from Plato's middle period include: *Phaedrus* (a pleasant dialogue illustrating the difference between rhetoric that is used to confuse and mislead and that which instead clarifies by arising from dialectic and truth); *Protagoras* (in which the SOPHIST philosopher of that name is defeated in debate by an argument he cannot understand); and *The Republic, Symposium,* and *Theatetus* (an incomplete exposition of Plato's theory of knowledge—his epistemology—a subject that his *Sophist* further considers).

To Plato's third and final period belong such relatively straightforward dialogues as *Sophist* and *Politicus*—titles that suggest the subjects of the works. In a cosmological setting and for the

final time, *Timaeus* expounds Plato's theory of ideal forms as the ultimate reality and the intellectual substrate of the physical universe. *Timaeus* also begins the story of the lost continent of Atlantis. That story is continued in the unfinished *Critias*. From the last of all the dialogues, Plato's *Laws,* Socrates is entirely absent.

Socrates, in fact, appears less often as the interlocutor all through the last set of dialogues. We meet him for the final time leading a consideration of pleasure in *Philebus*, which examines the relations among pleasure, wisdom, and the good.

The ancients attributed a series of 13 surviving letters to Plato. Contemporary scholarship views these epistles with varying degrees of confidence. Three are regarded as definitely not his. Three others seem to have certainly come from Plato's hand, and the rest are regarded as likely to be his. Those with the clearest claim to authenticity concern Plato's connections with the ruling family of Syracuse in Sicily. One of the genuine letters, usually dated to around 353 B.C.E., contains otherwise unknown biographical details about Plato and expresses his sorrow at the murder of his Sicilian friend, Dion. It also defends his political ideas.

Plato's influence continues to reverberate through the corridors of history. His ideas contributed significantly to the theories adopted by early Christians, with respect not only to their political organization and ideas about Christian communism but also to their notions of good and evil, and even to their formulations concerning the nature of the afterlife and the system of rewards and punishments to be encountered there. Such an early Christian theorist as Saint AUGUSTINE, bishop of Hippo, found himself heavily indebted to Platonistic thinking.

Both in the ancient and in the modern worlds, Platonistic theology has exercised important influence. In the ancient, beyond their influence on Christian thinking, Plato's theories informed such thinkers as PLOTINUS, Iamblichus, PORPHYRY, Hypatia, and PROCLUS OF BYZANTIUM, who formed the backbone of the Neoplatonist theological school of thought in Alexandria and Byzantium in the third through the sixth centuries C.E. A serious school of Platonic Christianity also appeared in 17th-century England at Cambridge University.

In the European Renaissance, Platonistic religious ideas were central to thinkers such as Jehudah ben Isaac Abravanel (Leone Hebreo, ca. 1460–ca. 1521), whose *Dialoghi di amore* (Dialogues or conversations about love, 1535) develops the Platonic view that the true, the good, and the beautiful are the ground of being and that love, governed by reason, is the principle that makes these attributes perceptible to the human mind. But love is higher than reason, and, in the hierarchy of the real, beauty is the highest characteristic because it is the central quality of God from which all other qualities take their being. This elevated view eventually became secularized and developed into a platonic love cult whose objects involved more corporeal and less spiritual aims and led to popular games of stylized lovemaking throughout the courts of Europe. The ideas also informed European lyric poetry from the time of the Italian poet Petrarch in the 14th century until that of the English poet John Donne in the 17th. As the early cinema of the 20th century unwittingly adapted a good deal of platonic love theory to the silver screen, and as the 21st continues to follow that theory's conventions with a greater degree of explicit imagery, one could argue that Renaissance platonic love theory, developed from passages in the philosopher's *Symposium* and elsewhere, continues to underlie notions about the importance of romantic love in Western society.

On a more intellectual note, Plato's thought also continues to underlie philosophical thinking grounded in idealism. Idealistic philosophies argue the position that perceived phenomena are rooted, not in the external world, but in the thinking mind. Such philosophies also hold that one cannot finally demonstrate the existence of anything outside the perceptive intellect.

See also ACADEMIC SECT OF PHILOSOPHY.

Bibliography

Plato. *Dialogues of Plato*. 2 vols. Translated by Benjamin Jowett. New York: Washington Square Press, 2001.

Rose, Herbert Jennings. *A Handbook to Greek Literature From Homer to the Age of Lucian*. New York: E. P. Dutton and Company, 1934.

Plautus, Titus Maccius (254–184 B.C.E.)
Roman dramatist

The earliest Roman literary figure of whose work any complete example remains, the comic playwright Plautus was probably born in the town of Sarsina in the region of Umbria. From there, if the hints he gives us in his comedies are accurate, he migrated to Rome, where he found work as a carpenter building theatrical scenery. He saved some money, left Rome, and invested his slender capital in his own business. When that enterprise failed, he returned to Rome, where this time he found work as a miller, grinding grain into flour for a baker. While engaged in that work, he began writing plays. Where (or whether) he acquired a formal education, we do not know. It is, however, certain that he was a master of poetic form—all his plays are in verse—and he proved wonderfully skillful in deploying the linguistic resources at his command to amuse his audiences.

Although more than 125 plays have been attributed to Plautus at one time or another, most specialists think that a more accurate list is one prepared by the Roman philosopher and literary critic MARCUS TERENTIUS VARRO. That list includes the playwright's 20 complete surviving plays plus others, now largely lost, that Varro considered authentic. One considerable piece and other exceedingly fragmentary remains of perhaps 30 of Plautus's other productions also survive.

Plautus seems principally to have borrowed the plots of plays from the Greek New Comedy, though also perhaps from Greek Middle Comedy (See COMEDY IN GREECE AND ROME). The manner of his plays, however—especially his risqué humor and his tendency to satirize recognizable fellow Romans—smacks more of the Old Comedy of Greece. But Plautus did not merely slavishly recreate his models; rather, he reworked and revised them quite freely, sometimes omitting or adding material, changing characters' names, and achieving a poetic and verbal brilliance that was distinctively his own.

Not all passages in Plautine comedy were exclusively spoken. Many were sung as well, and the lyrics of the songs sometimes account for some of the poet's most distinguished verse. In many ways, Plautus set the stage for the later development of the Renaissance Italian commedia dell'arte with its stock characters and situations. He also anticipated contemporary musical comedy. Production notices called *didascaliae* (instructions) exist for two of Plautus's plays: *Stichus* and *Pseudolus*. (Plautus drew both titles from the names of characters in the plays.) The notice for *Stichus* suggests that the Greek comic playwright MENANDER's now-lost play *The Brothers* provided the framework of Plautus's piece. But Plautus has significantly heightened the musical elements of the production, moving it far along in the direction of comic opera or, indeed, of musical comedy. Regrettably, we have no way of knowing the tunes; only the poetry survives.

Plautus's works range across a wide spectrum of subject matter. Mythology provides the subject for his highly individualistic tragicomedy, AMPHITRYON. In this play, Plautus treats the legend of the king of the gods, Jupiter, and his love for the admirable human woman Alcmena, whom he visits in the form of her husband, Amphitryon. Called upon again on the same night by the real Amphitryon, Alcmena bears two sons. Jupiter has fathered one child, Herwles (see HERACLES), and Amphitryon the other twin, Iphicles. Plautus, who had an especial fondness for situations that developed from misidentifying twins, introduces further fun into his play by having the god Mercury also have a human double in the slave Sosia. The play's near-tragic element arises, on the one hand, from Alcmena's innocence in not knowing that she has entertained Jupiter in the form of her husband. On the other, domestic amity founders on the rock of Amphitryon's suspicions about Alcmena's fidelity. Jupiter, however, restores marital concord between the spouses and averts a tragic outcome.

Many of Plautus's surviving plays have inspired later imitators, and that is the case of his *Aulularia* (*The Pot of Gold*), whose major character, Euclio, provided the basis for the central character Harpagon when the 17th-century French playwright, Molière, penned his comedy *The Miser*. Of equal or greater interest to later playwrights were such Plautine comedies as *Miles Gloriosus* (The BRAGGART SOLDIER). The character type that Plautus developed in that play, the braggart military man, became the stock character Scaramuccia in the commedia dell'arte. The type also underlay such English theatrical characters as Nicholas Udall's Ralph Roister Doister and Shakespeare's Falstaff, and it continues to amuse modern audiences in such a character as television's cartoon antihero, Homer Simpson, and his more recent antecedent, Ralph, played by the late Jackie Gleason in television's early series *The Honeymooners*.

Menaechmi (*The Twin Brothers*) provides another example of Plautus's fondness for plots arising from the confusion of twins, in addition to being a Plautine drama that has influenced later playwrights—in this case William Shakespeare in *The Comedy of Errors* and, later, the American masters of musical comedy, Rodgers and Hart, in *The Boys from Syracuse*.

A different sort of confusion arises in *Mostellaria* (*The Haunted House*). In that play, a son tries to conceal from his father the fact that in the father's absence, the son has purchased the woman he loves and installed her in the family home. The 17th-century English playwright, Thomas Heywood borrowed elements of this play as a subplot for his work *The English Traveler*.

Both *PSEUDOLUS* (a character's name that roughly means "tricky") and *Rudens* (*The Rope*) belong to the boy-gets-girl subgenre of romantic comedy. In *Pseudolus*, a slave of that name succeeds in saving his young master's beloved from a forced career of prostitution. In *Rudens*, Plautus rings changes on a similar basic plot but and pulls out all the stops. The star Arcturus is an important character in the play, presents the prologue, and causes a storm at sea. There are shipwrecks and lost and recovered identities and treasures. The title's rope is responsible for hauling up from the seafloor both a lost treasure and tokens that establish the identity of the play's romantic heroine, Palaestra.

Not all of Plautus's plays provide audiences with such light fare, however. One of the surviving dramas among those usually considered his best, *Captivi* (*The Captives*), starkly illustrates, in the words of Richard Moore, the play's most recent translator, "man's inhumanity to man." Moreover, the bawdy sort of humor that Plautus is fond of using elsewhere is absent from this play. Slavery in its various manifestations is the subject of this dark study, which can be classified as comedy only in terms of a more or less happy ending.

TRINUMMUS (*The Three-Penny Day*—recently inflated with the title *The Thirty-Dollar Day*) employs a theme that appears in older literature in cultures as distant as China. Owing to a misplaced trust, a house containing a concealed treasure gets sold. To protect the treasure for the rightful owner, a friend buys the home, and further complications follow. Eventually, however, all turns out well.

Formerly considered to be of lesser interest was Plautus's play BACCHIDES—a romantic comedy about two sisters with the same name, Bacchis. One, a courtesan, lives at Samos and the other at Athens. The play features a clever slave, Chrysalus, and a fusty pedagogue, Lydus. Chrysalus is central to helping young love along. After a certain amount of predictable confusion arising from the identity of the sisters' names and one lover's concern that his friend is trying to steal his girl, all ends very well for the two central young couples.

Heightened interest in *Bacchides* has, as the play's recent translator James Tatum tells us, resulted from the 1968 discovery of a substantial fragment of the play's lost Greek source, MENANDER's *Dis exapaton* (*The Double Deceiver*). Having a 70-line sample of this play has made possible the sustained study of the way Plautus used his sources. Not altogether surpris-

ingly, Plautus translated closely or freely as it suited his dramatic purposes. The comparison confirms that achieving effective theater, not slavish imitation of his sources, was Plautus's goal. *Bacchides* is also of interest as the ultimate source of the inscription over Hell's gate in Dante's *Inferno*: "Abandon every hope, all you who enter here." In Plautus, however, the source reference to hope abandoned appears on the door of a brothel—a door characterized as a portal to Hades.

Sometimes also classed among the less important of Plautus's extant plays, we find *Asinaria* (*Asses Galore*) and *Casina* (the name of a slave girl who never appears on stage but who is loved by both an elderly man and his son—recently translated as "A Funny Thing Happened on the Way to the Wedding"). In a similar category, we find *Cistellaria* (*The Little Box*), another recognition play in which the contents of the box are crucial in the identification of a foundling as the daughter of a worthy citizen. Her improved status means she can marry her beloved. *Curculio* (*The Weevil*)—named for the central character, a stock parasite who is the literary ancestor of the British playwright Ben Jonson's smarmy Mosca in *Volpone*—tells another story of the triumph of true love over adversity and also revolves around hidden identities.

Also named for a major character, a slave, *Epidicus* once again exploits the stock situations of tricking an old man out of money to buy a young man's beloved—or in this case, two beloveds—out of slavery and captivity, respectively. However, the old man, Periphanes, forgives Epidicus when the second young woman proves to be his long-lost daughter, Telestis. *Mercator* (*The MERCHANT*, or *The Entrepreneur*) mines again the comic potential of the situation that arises when both a father and a son fall in love with the same young woman. In *Persa* (*The Persian*), a stock parasite named Saturio, posing as a Persian trader, deceives a procurer of women, Dordalus, by pretending that Saturio's daughter, Virgo, is an Arabian captive. Virgo goes along with the swindle out of filial piety, though she is miffed that her father seems willing to sell her for the price of decent meal.

Regularly translated into English under the title *The Little Carthaginian*, Plautus's *Poenulus* heaps on complications by reduplicating the stock situations of which the playwright was so fond. It features two stolen daughters, Adelphasium and Anterastilis, in the clutches of a particularly loathsome pimp named Lycus. We also find their stolen but well-adopted male cousin, Agorastocles, who loves one of the girls, and we meet the girls' father, Hanno, who has been roaming the Mediterranean world in search of his daughters, whom he eventually recovers. Agorastocles discovers his true identity and marries his cousin, Adelphasium. The pimp, of course, gets a satisfactory comeuppance. Some of Hanno's speeches are ostensibly in the Punic language of his home city, Carthage. The play's recent translator, Janet Burroway, has had wonderful fun rendering Plautus's probably phony Punic into delightful, quasi-English nonsense.

Plautus's remaining two complete plays, *Stichus* and *Truculentus,* both take their names from characters who are slaves. The word *stichus*, in fact, was a generic legal term often inserted in Roman contracts dealing with slaves in place of a person's actual name. The bad-tempered and quarrelsome character of the slave Truculentus is, of course, implicit in his name.

Stichus tells the story of two sisters, young wives whose husbands have been absent overlong on a trading expedition. Their father, Antipho, tries to convince the girls that, since their husbands must be dead, they should remarry. The husbands, now wealthy, reappear, and general rejoicing takes place.

The literary historian and translator James Tatum considers *Truculentus* to be "the sharpest delineation in Roman comedy of specifically male folly." The play explores the way that Phronesium, the madam of a house of prostitution, seduces man after man, including the originally wary Truculentus, in order to illustrate the moral of the play, which holds that lovers can spend their lives learning—but never learn—"how many ways there are to die for love."

Plautus's stock seems certain to rise again in the English-speaking world as the result of the excellent translations now available from the Johns Hopkins University Press. These include the texts, not only of the plays for which full or almost full versions survive but also of Plautus's exceedingly fragmentary *The Traveling Bag (Vidularia).*

Given the nonexistence of complete examples of Roman literary works earlier than the plays of Plautus, all of his dramas—even the most formulaic of them—are exceedingly important to our understanding of the development of Western letters.

Bibliography

Slavitt, David R., and Palmer Bowie, ed. *Plautus: The Comedies.* 4 vols. Translated by Constance Carrier *et al.* Complete Roman Drama in Translation. Baltimore: Johns Hopkins University Press, 1995.

Pleiad of Alexandria

This literary pleiad—a group of Greek poets of the HELLENISTIC AGE at Alexandria in Egypt—took its name from the seven stars in the old Greek constellation the Pleiades, now incorporated into the constellation Taurus. Different sources mention different poets as belonging to the group, and there may well have been more poets who required recognition than there were stars in the constellation to accommodate them.

All the poets so recognized wrote TRAGEDY. The list endorsed by the literary critic and editor of the *Oxford Classical Dictionary*, Simon Hornblower, includes the following Alexandrian tragedians: Alexander of Aetolia (fl. ca. 280 B.C.E); Homerus of Byzantion; Sositheus of Alexandria Troas; LYCOPHRON (fl. ca. 280 B.C.E); Philicus; Dionysiades of Tarsus; and Aeantiodes (fl. third century B.C.E). Most of their works have utterly perished. Fifteen hundred lines, however, of Lycophron's *Alexandra* have survived. The literary historian Jane Lightfoot finds it "quite the most repellent poem to survive from antiquity." The passage contains a prophecy of the doom of the Greeks homebound from Troy.

Knowledge of the Pleiad's existence as a stellar literary group persisted through the ages long after the honor of being so designated had disappeared. As a result, when the European Renaissance got under way in France, a similar group of outstanding literary figures was so named. Also, a small liberal arts institution, Albion College in Michigan, has adopted the name *Pleiad* for its weekly newspaper.

Bibliography

Hornblower, Simon. "Pleiad." In *The Oxford Classical Dictionary*. 3rd ed. New York: Oxford University Press, 1999.

Lightfoot, Jane L. "Sophisticates and Solecisms: Greek Literature after the Classical Period." In *Literature in the Greek and Roman Worlds: A New Perspective*. Edited by Oliver Taplin. New York: Oxford University Press, 2000.

Pliny the Elder (Gaius Plinius Secundus)
(23–79 C.E.) *Roman historian*

Born at Como to an equestrian (knightly) family, Pliny became a soldier, beginning a long and distinguished career of public service. Between the years 46 and 58 C.E., he fought in two long campaigns in Germany. It was there that his literary interests first found expression, for he composed a brief treatise, no longer extant, entitled "The Art of Using a Javelin on Horseback." He also wrote a now-lost biography of his friend and general, Pomponius Secondus, in two books His nephew and adoptive son, PLINY THE YOUNGER, reported that the elder pliny had also formed a plan to write and publish a history of the German wars in which he served. He was encouraged in his determination to do so by the appearance of the phantom of his commander, Drusus Nero, who wanted the memory of his conquests preserved. Pliny the Elder thus began his *History of the German Wars* (*Bella Germaniae*), and in due course, this work, also now lost, appeared in 20 volumes.

After the death of the emperor Claudius (54 C.E.), Pliny withdrew from public affairs owing to the hostility he harbored toward Claudius's successor, Nero. He probably occupied his time with the practice of law and with composing and delivering the associated orations. It may also be that during this time he wrote a handbook on oratory and rhetoric of which now only snippets remain, his *Studiosus* (The students), in three lengthy books. He also produced a grammatical or linguistic work, *Dubius sermo* (Linguistic theories). Because of numerous subsequent citations, several fragmentary passages from this work still exist. Another lost work was a one-book continuation of a 30-book history by Aufidius Bassus. The younger Pliny remarked that his uncle's industry was enhanced by his ability to get along on little sleep—principally catnaps.

When the emperor Vespasian succeeded to the throne (70 C.E.), Pliny reentered public life and occupied a series of imperial posts. He also pursued a busy legal career, never wasting a moment. He had books read to him at mealtimes and read to himself omnivorously whenever the occasion presented itself in his busy schedule. If he was not reading, he was dictating his own works to a writer of shorthand whom he kept constantly at his side.

The elder Pliny's greatest literary work, one still extant, was his 37-book encyclopedic work, *Natural History*. Of it Pliny the Younger said: "This is a work of great compass and learning, and as full of variety as nature herself." The work was Pliny's attempt to bring all knowledge into a systematic framework by mining the best-known works and giving the reader a guide to the information in them.

The first book gives a table of contents and a bibliography for each subsequent book. That bibliography alludes to 34,000 brief notices, to 2,000 books that Pliny had read, and to the 100 different authors who had composed them. It also includes references to 170 folders filled with Pliny's own notes and outlines. Book 2 covers cosmology and the physical geography of the known world. Books 3–6 deal with political geography, 7 with anthropology, and 8–11 with zoology. Books 12–19 concern themselves with botany, 20–32 with medicine, and 33–37 with mineralogy, metallurgy, and, perhaps idiosyncratically, with art history. The work was published in 77 or 78 C.E.

In one of his celebrated *Letters*, book 6, letter 16, addressed to the historian Tacitus, the younger Pliny describes the manner of his uncle's death at age 76 during the eruption of Mount Vesuvius in 79 C.E.

Bibliography

Pliny the Elder. *Natural History with an English Translation*. 10 vols. Translated by Horace H. Rackham and W. H. S. Jones. Cambridge, Mass.: Harvard University Press, 1949–61.

———. *Pliny on Art and Society: The Elder Pliny . . . on the History of Art*. Translated by Henrik Rosenmeir. Odense, Denmark: Odense University Press, 1991.

———. *The Elder Pliny on the Human Animal. Natural History, book 7*. Translated by Mary Begon. New York: Oxford University Press, 2005.

Pliny the Younger. *Letters and Panygyricus*. 2 vols. Translated by Betty Radice. Cambridge, Mass.: Harvard University Press, 1969.

Pliny the Younger (Gaius Plinius Caecilius Secundus) (ca. 61–ca. 112 C.E.)

The nephew and adoptive son of the Pliny the Elder (Gaius Plinius Secundus), Pliny the younger was born at Comum on the shores of Lake Como at the foot of the Italian Alps. A child of privilege, he was schooled in Rome both by Quintilian and by the Stoic philosopher Musonius.

Following Pliny's move to Rome, he remained deeply interested in and attached to his property on Lake Como as well as to the institutions and citizenry of the region. One of his best translators, the late Betty Radice, tells us of his benefactions to the town of Comum. These included building and stocking a library, supporting a portion of a resident teacher's salary, the support of needy children in the district, and a bequest of more than 2 million sesterces to the town.

A rising political star, the younger Pliny held a series of administrative offices under the emperors Domitian and Trajan. He began his career with military service in Syria when he was about 20 years old. On his return to Rome, he undertook the practice of law and, with the help of influential friends, was admitted to the Roman senate. There he conducted notable prosecutions of provincial governors accused of lining their own pockets by extortionate means. From that base, he rose to occupy important civic offices, serving first as praetor and later as consul.

Under the effective but arrogant emperor Domitian (ruled 81–96 C.E.), who had little use for Stoics (see Stoicism) and considered the senate an annoyance, Pliny was at some risk but managed to avoid imperial persecution. Domitian was murdered in 98, and after a two-year reign by the elderly emperor Nerva, the emperor Trajan succeeded to the throne.

Under Trajan's rule, Pliny's administrative career advanced. He became a prefect of the treasury, an associate consul, and then an important administrator responsible for the works controlling the flow of the Tiber River to avert flooding. Next he became an augur—one of Rome's official diviners who had charge of foretelling the likely success of proposed courses of action. In 111 C.E., Trajan appointed Pliny to be the governor of the province of Bithynia on the Bosporus Strait in contemporary Turkey. Pliny served in that office honestly and competently, if not always confidently, until his death. Though he was married three times, Pliny died without heirs.

The only example of Pliny's oratory that has survived is a speech in praise of Trajan on his succession to the throne—his *Panegyricus* (Panegyric). It expresses the senate's relief at being free of Domitian's oppression—an imposition so severe that the senate passed a bill condemning his memory.

Pliny's principal and priceless literary legacy, rather, are the 10 books of his *Letters*—especially the first nine, in which he constructs in part an epistolary history of his times. He also uses the letters to tell interesting stories—even ghost stories—and to give his opinions on a wide variety of subjects ranging from the parsimony of wealthy persons, through debates in the Roman Senate, to the moral attributes of his contemporaries. Especially notable is his description of the eruption of Mt. Vesuvius that buried Herculaneum and Pompey in 79 C.E. and also killed his uncle, Pliny the Elder. The 10th book contains Pliny the younger's official correspondence with Trajan. Among the letters of particular interest there, the 96th contains the earliest surviving non-Christian description of Christian worship. It also details the reasons why Pliny thought Christians should be put to death.

Bibliography

Hoffer, Stanley E. *The Anxieties of Pliny the Younger.* Atlanta, Ga.: Scholars Press, 1999.

Pliny. *Letters and Panygyricus.* 2 vols. Translated by Betty Radice. Cambridge, Mass.: Harvard University Press, 1969.

———. *Letters.* 2 vols. Translated by William Melmouth and W. M. L. Hutchinson. Cambridge, Mass.: Harvard University Press, 1952.

Plotinus (ca. 205–270 C.E.) *Greek-Egyptian prose writer*

Probably born in Upper Egypt, Plotinus migrated to Alexandria in 232 to study philosophy. After rejecting a series of teachers, Plotinus settled on the then-pagan but formerly Christian SOPHIST, Ammonius Saccas, and studied with him for the next 11 years.

Plotinus was not the only one of Ammonius's students destined for fame. Also under the Sophist's instruction at the time were the future Christian theologian, ORIGEN (ca 182–251 C.E.), and another notable Origen of Alexandria (a contemporary) who, like Plotinus, became a pagan Neoplatonist.

Hoping to broaden his philosophical horizons by making contact with the thinkers of India and Persia, Plotinus attached himself to an eastward-bound military expedition led by the Roman emperor Gordian III. In the vicinity of Ctesiphon on the River Tigris, Gordian died of wounds received in a disastrous military engagement, and Plotinus escaped, making his way to Antioch. His hope of adding the mastery of Eastern thought to his accomplishments remained unfulfilled. Instead, in 244 C.E. he went to Rome, where he established himself as a teacher of philosophy, writing a series of nine exploratory discussions that illustrated the central issues of his thinking. After his death, his student PORPHYRY organized these writings into six groups, each of which contained nine discussions. Porphyry entitled his professor's work Plotinus's *Enneads.*

Some central points of Plotinus's doctrine included his definition (which he borrowed from PLATO's *The REPUBLIC*) of the ground of being, or the first principle—at once both the One and the Good and also God. This principle is beyond being. From it springs intellect (*nous*), which contains all ideas and forms—the immaterial originals for everything in the material world. Intellect produces Soul, a part of which, in turn, becomes the World Soul. That agency rules the material universe and is organized hierarchically so that its lower echelons become Nature, to which belongs matter. When matter is formed, it is good. When it lacks form, it is deficient, and this deficiency is termed evil. Evil, however, is not an active principle in Plotinus's view of the universe. Moral evil arises when a soul, instead of seeking to rise and become one with the One and the Good, identifies instead with the material world.

Plotinus's view of the soul is quite complex. Each soul has three levels: the transcendent intellect, which is capable in the purified state of the true philosopher of contemplating the One and the Good; the intermediate soul; and the lower soul—that aspect of soul that gives life to the human body. The highest degree of unity involving the human soul and the One and the Good, though the philosopher occasionally can experience that unity in life, is not expressible in human language and is a state that can endure only after death.

The importance of Plotinus's thought for the ancient world from his time forward can hardly be exaggerated. In addition to refining the ideas of pagan Neoplatonism, Plotinus's language provided early Christians with the concepts that eventuated in the Christian idea of the Trinity. Whereas Plotinus saw the human, the spirit, and the One and the Good as three hierarchical conditions—a progression from flesh to spirit to God—the Christian concept of Trinity, instead, applied his language to three equal aspects of godhead. Christian mysticism also traces its roots to the thinking of Plotinus.

Bibliography

Abhayananda, S. *The Origins of Western Mysticism: Selected Writings of Plotinus.* Olympia, Wash.: ATMA Books, 2000.

Corrigan, Kevin. *Reading Plotinus: A Practical Introduction to Neoplatonism.* West Lafayette, Ind.: Purdue University Press, 2005.

McGroarty, Kieran, ed. and trans. *Plotinus on Eudaimonia: A Commentary on Ennead I.4.* New York: Oxford University Press, 2006.

Plotinus. *Collected Writings of Plotinus.* Translated by Thomas Taylor. Frome, Somerset, U.K.: Prometheus Trust, 1994.

———. *The Enneads: A New, Definitive Translation. . . .* Translated by Stephen Mackenna. Burdett, N.Y.: Published for the Paul Brunton Philosophic Foundation by Larson Publications, 1992.

———. *The Enneads: Plotinus.* [Abridged.] Translated by Stephen Mackenna. Edited by John Debbs. New York: Penguin, 1991.

Plutarch (ca. 46 C.E.–ca. 120 C.E.) *Greek prose writer*

A native of the small community of Chaeronea in the Greek region of Boetia, Plutarch spent most of his life in his native village, occupying local municipal offices and sometimes serving as a priest of Apollo at Delphi. Interested in Roman matters as well as Grecian ones, he more than once journeyed to Italy, where he was received with honor and respect, and where he gave lectures in Rome.

As an author, Plutarch is today remembered principally for the work often called *Plutarch's Lives* or *Lives of the Noble Grecians and Romans.* More properly, its title is PARALLEL LIVES. In its original form, it contained 23 pairs of extended biographical sketches—one portraying a Greek's life and one a Roman's. Their subjects, in Plutarch's judgment, merited pairing because of similarities in their moral characters, and each pair was followed by a brief summary that drew the comparisons Plutarch had observed. Beyond those pairings, we also find four unpaired lives.

Plutarch also authored another collection of essays, his MORALIA. The subjects of these essays range widely over Plutarch's various interests. They address issues of proper conduct, such as the way in which married couples should behave, and also include character writing, illustrating both major and minor vices such as anger and talkativeness and the predispositions of members of occupational groups. Additionally, the collection contains discussions of religion and superstition as well as speculation on such scientific questions as accounting for the face of the moon. One also finds treatments of Greek (but not of Roman) literary figures. The *Moralia* served as an important model for Renaissance essayists, especially Michel de Montaigne in France, and Francis Bacon in England.

Plutarch lived a long and useful life. Though he once remarked that being born in a famous city was a prerequisite for happiness, he himself was content to spend most of his days in the village of his birth, not willing to diminish it by the permanent removal of even one of its inhabitants.

Early Christians admired Plutarch and found in his eclectic brand of Platonism a pagan precursor of their faith. Some of them included Plutarch in their prayers, hoping that he might be included among the saved.

Bibliography

Plutarch. *The Lives of the Noble Grecians and Romans.* Translated by John Dryden with revisions by Arthur Hugh Clough. New York: Modern

Library, 1932. Reprinted as *Greek and Roman Lives*. Mineola, N.Y: Dover Publications, 2005.

———. *Plutarch's Lives*. [*Greek and English.*] 11 vols. Translated by Bernadotte Perrin. Cambridge, Mass.: Harvard University Press, 1959.

———. *Plutarch's Moralia*. 15 vols. Translated by Frank Cole Babbitt. Cambridge, Mass.: Harvard University Press, 1960.

Plutarch's Lives   See PARALLEL LIVES.

Poetics   Aristotle (ca. 355 B.C.E.)

ARISTOTLE's teacher, PLATO, famously considered poets untruthful and dangerous influences in a polity, and he banned them and their activities from his work *The* REPUBLIC. Aware, however, of the importance of Athenian theater to the city-state's religious, civic, and artistic life, and perhaps led by his disagreement with the elder philosopher's views in other intellectual arenas, Aristotle turned the full force of his analytical intellect onto a consideration of the history and characteristics of the verse theater of his time and of the private and public benefits that accrued from public theatrical performance.

Though not all of the resultant document survives, that which does is the oldest and the foundational literary-critical document in the Western European tradition. The considerable portion of the *Poetics* that we have begins with a statement of purpose. Aristotle means to examine the various genres of poetry, the requirements for constructing plot that lead to excellence, and the components of poetry. All the varieties of poetry and most music with which Aristotle is familiar, he says, share in common the quality of mimesis—that is, they are arts that somehow imitate life in their rhythms, language, and melody. The characters that poets draw also imitate life. Like people, they are elevated and admirable, low and blameworthy, or just ordinary. These generalizations apply equally to all the performing arts of Aristotle's time. TRAGEDY tends to imitate superior characters and COMEDY inferior ones. Charac-

ters, moreover, can act out their roles, be described as acting them out, or can merely have their actions narrated.

Aristotle considers nature to be the source of the human dramatic impulse and says that little children imitate the actions of others by their very nature. Melody and the rhythms of song and poetic meter, too, are natural. Having established these principles, Aristotle goes on to a discussion of several representative meters of Greek QUANTITATIVE VERSE and very briefly traces the beginnings of the comic and tragic modes among the Greeks. He then makes comparisons between tragedy and EPIC. All the resources of epic are to be found in tragedy, but not vice versa.

Aristotle then gives his famous definition of tragedy: "Tragedy . . . is the imitation of an action that is elevated, complete, and of a certain magnitude." Distinct poetic forms embellish the language of a tragedy in its various sections. A tragedy employs action and spectacle, not narration. It evokes in the audience members pity for the tragic hero or heroine, and fear lest similar horrible circumstances should overtake the viewers. The resolution of the drama purges the audience of these emotions, leaving them emotionally cleansed and somehow morally improved. For Aristotle, who arrived at his views as the result of seeing many tragedies and analyzing their common characteristics, any tragedy worthy of the name would be characterized by "plot, character, diction, thought, spectacle, and lyric poetry." A tragedy's plot and its objective are the most important considerations. The characters come next. They are important because they reveal the moral choices that lead to the events in the action. The thought implicit or explicit in making the choices is next most important, followed by the diction expressing the thought. Lyric poetry embellishes the whole. Spectacle, though effective, is not a necessary component of tragedy.

A tragedy is also not required to be a mere report of something that has happened. That is the historian's job. Responding to Plato's objections to poets as misrepresenters of the truth, Aristotle points out that a poet's job is to represent the *kinds* of things that might occur, in keeping with probability and necessity. Poetry represents universals, while history represents particulars.

Plots can be simple or complex. Complex plots are the better sort as they reverse the expectations of a principle character. To illustrate this point, Aristotle alludes to Sophocles' *Oedipus Tyrannus*, in which the title character expects to discover the identity of a villain whose crime has brought a plague to Thebes. Instead, Oedipus discovers that he himself is the culprit. Thus, two characteristics of a good plot emerge: reversal and recognition; a third necessary ingredient is suffering. Good tragic plots should be complex and involve a reasonably admirable character's falling from prosperity to adversity, not through depravity but through a flaw in his or her character—a flaw often arising from an excess of some virtue.

Aristotle counsels judicious and sparing use of a god from a machine (deus ex machina)—a device sometimes used to sort out complex plots by divine intervention. The philosopher wants nothing irrational to intrude into the structure of a tragedy. He also rejects improbable recognitions and coincidences.

Aristotle continues by offering advice on planning and writing tragedies, each point illustrated by examples. He makes further relatively minor distinctions among the varieties of possible tragedies, as usual providing his readers with copious examples. He interrupts his discussion of literary types with an extended disquisition concerning grammar and linguistics that attests to his analytical powers. He offers definitions of such terms as *metaphor* and *neologism* and draws distinctions among more and less effective word choices.

Following that digression, he returns to his central theme with a thoroughgoing discussion of epic that parallels his earlier analysis of tragedy. That analysis concluded, Aristotle discusses the relative merits of epic and tragedy. He decides that, in terms of the principle of mimesis and the impact that each sort of art has on its audiences, the tragedy is superior to the epic.

In Renaissance Italy, Ludovico Castelvetro published an influential treatise based on Aristotle's poetics. Castelvetro, however, embroidered Aristotle's treatise with the Italian's own views on what came to be called the unities of time, place, and action. Renaissance playwrights and others confused Aristotle's work with Castelvetro's pronouncements, and the latter became virtual rules that governed the work of many notable continental tragedians, especially in France.

Bibliography

Aristotle. *Poetics*. Edited and translated by Stephen Halliwell. Cambridge, Mass.: Harvard University Press, 1995.

Pollux, Julius   See GRAMMAR AND GRAMMARIANS IN GREECE.

Polyænus (ca. second century C.E.) *Greek historian*

Born in Macedonia, Polyænus was a rhetorician and lawyer who made and published a collection of historical military stratagems and deceptions drawn from the practice of such Romans as JULIUS CAESAR and AUGUSTUS CAESAR, and from the Carthaginian general Hannibal. In addition to historical military encounters, Polyænus also drew on mythology, recounting the tricks of gods and famous women as well as of soldiers. The work contains eight books and is entertainingly written in simple, straightforward Greek. Polyænus dedicated his volume to the Roman emperors MARCUS AURELIUS and Lucius Verrus. Verrus suffered from a reputation of being stupid and needed all the help he could get. A part of Polyænus's objective was to supply that help.

Bibliography

Polyænus. *Polyænus's Stratagems of War*. Translated by R. Shepherd. Chicago: Ares Publications, 1974.

Schettino, Maria Teresa. *Introduzione a Polieno*. Pisa: E. T. S., 1998.

Polybius (ca. 200–ca. 118 B.C.E.) *Greek-Roman historian*

Born in Megalopolis in Grecian Arcadia, Polybius distinguished himself both as a soldier and as a politician. For a long time, he lived at Rome, where, although he had arrived as a captive, he subsequently gained his freedom and moved in notable circles. He was, for instance a friend and adviser of the Roman soldier, diplomat, explorer, and administrator, Publius Cornelius Scipio Aemilianus. Polybius supervised Scipio's education and training as a public administrator and always remained a member of the distinguished group around Scipio that became known as the Scipionic circle.

In that connection, Polybius traveled with Scipio to Spain and Africa, and he was present at the Roman destruction of Carthage. Polybius also accompanied Scipio on an early voyage of exploration in the Atlantic Ocean and, with Scipio, crossed the Alps, tracing the route that the Carthaginian general Hannibal had followed to attack Rome in 218 B.C.E. Late in life, Polybius returned to Greece, spending his last six years in his homeland, helping to establish the Roman administration of Greece after its fall as an independent entity.

In the literary world, Polybius distinguished himself as a historian—a writer of a then-new sort of historiography that he called *pragmatic history*. Rather than simply chronicling events, he attempted to explain the causes and origins of those events and to follow them through to their consequences. His objective in following this method was to prepare his readers' minds to apply similar analyses to the situations in which they found themselves. Such a process, Polybius thought, would prepare people for citizenship and for political office. Perceiving and predicting chains of cause and effect would help officials avoid flailing blindly at the problems they confronted. His method of research involved the close examination of primary documents—state papers, diplomatic correspondence, and the like.

Polybius also paid close attention to characterization in his history, and he is anything but a disinterested historian. He passes judgment on the people and events that populate his pages. His history originally occupied 40 books. Of these, the first five survive as he issued them. We also have synopses of the first 18 books plus a few fragments or quotations from others. Several chapters are missing altogether.

Polybius attempted a compendious history that looked closely at the Mediterranean world for a period of 53 years, starting with the beginning of the second Punic War (218–201 B.C.E.) that Rome fought against Carthage and continuing until both Carthage in Africa and Corinth in Greece suffered destruction (146 B.C.E.). In order to clarify the underlying unity of Roman activity in the Mediterranean world, Polybius devised a novel mode of organization. He developed a system of treating a four-year slice of time (olympiads, as he called them). Within each time frame, he first followed events in the western Mediterranean, including northwestern Africa, Spain, Sicily, and Italy. He then focused on Greece, Macedonia, Asia, and finally, Egypt.

Before undertaking his history, Polybius had busied himself with other sorts of writing. All those works are lost, but they included a celebratory biography of the Greek general and statesman Philopoemen, a fellow native of Megalopolis and a symbol of Grecian resistance against the Romans. Polybius had carried Philopoemen's ashes in their funeral urn to their resting place. He also penned a history of the Numantine War, a work on military tactics, and a consideration of whether or not human beings could live at equatorial latitudes.

Polybius is said to have died from injuries sustained when he fell from a horse in his 82nd year.

Bibliography

Polybius. *Polybius on Roman Imperialism: the Histories of Polybius.* Translated by Evelyn S. Shuckburgh. Edited by Alvius H. Bernstein. South Bend, Ind.: Regnery/Gateway, 1980.

———. *The Histories* [abridged]. Translated by Mortimer Chambers. New York: Twayne, 1967.

———. *The Histories*. 6 vols. Translated by R. W. Paton. New York: G. P. Putnam's sons, 1922–27.

Wallbank, Frank W. *Polybius, Rome, and the Hellenistic World: Essays and Reflections.* New York: Cambridge University Press, 2002.

———. *Selected Papers: Studies in Greek and Roman History and Historiography.* New York: Cambridge University Press, 1985.

Polycarp   See LETTER OF POLYCARP TO THE PHILIPPIANS; MARTYRDOM OF POLYCARP, THE.

Porphyry (ca. 233–ca. 305 C.E.) *Syrian, Greek prose writer*

Born and brought up in Syria and possibly a native of Tyre, the immensely learned Porphyry migrated to Athens to continue his studies. From there, he moved on to Rome, where he studied with the anti-Christian, Neoplatonist philosopher PLOTINUS, whose biographer and disciple Porphyry would become. Porphyry expanded his work as a biographer to include a life of Pythagoras of Samos (see ITALIC SCHOOL OF PHILOSOPHY).

In addition to the work he did in spreading Plotinus's doctrines, Porphyry was the author of an anti-Christian diatribe, parts of which have survived in fragmentary condition. A gifted philosopher in his own right, Porphyry also wrote commentaries on treatises of PLATO and ARISTOTLE, as well as a *History of [or Introduction to] Philosophy.* The Roman polymath BOETHIUS was so impressed with Porphyry's Greek-language *Introduction* to the *Categories* (*Organon*) of Aristotle that Boethius translated Porphyry's work into Latin. Some modern historians of philosophy consider Porphyry's introduction to be among the best examples of its genre ever written anywhere, and it has remained influential among Western idealist philosophers into the modern era.

In his personal life, Porphyry was both an upstanding moralist and a vegetarian. These character traits appear in an explanation of the benefits of the philosophical enterprise that he prepared for his wife, Marcella. In it, he explained how the philosopher refines his soul until, having transcended his physical limitations, the philosopher ascends to the divine realm where his mind directly perceivers the ground of being. As a vegetarian, Porphyry also prepared a tract on the subject of refraining from killing animals and eating only a vegetarian diet, *De abstinentia.*

An allegorical, cosmological interpretation of a passage from HOMER's *The ODYSSEY*—*On the Cave of the Nymphs*—also survives, supplying Porphyry with additional credentials as a philosophical literary critic.

Bibliography

Porphyry. *Introduction [to Philosophy].* Translated by Jonathan Barnes. New York: Oxford University Press, 2003.

———. *On Abstinence from Killing Animals.* Translated by Gillian Clark. Ithaca, N.Y.: Cornell University Press, 2000.

———. *On Aristotle's Categories.* Translated by Stephen K. Strange. Ithaca, N.Y.: Cornell University Press, 1992.

———. *On the Cave of the Nymphs.* Translated by Robert Lamberton. Barrytown, N.Y.: Stone Hill Press, 2006.

———. *Porphyry's Against the Christians: The Literary Remains.* Edited and translated by R. Joseph Hoffman. Amherst, N.Y.: Prometheus Books, 1994.

———. *Porphyry's Letter to His Wife Marcella Concerning the Life of Philosophy and the Ascent to the Gods.* Translated by Alice Zeimern. Grand Rapids, Mich.: Phaner Press, 1986.

——— and Plotinus. *The Ethical Treatises of Plotinus with Porphyry's Life of Plotinus.* Translated by Stephen Mackenna. Boston: The Medici Society, 1926.

———. *The Homeric Questions.* Translated by Robin Schlank. New York: Peter Lang, ca. 1996.

Princess Nukata   See FEMALE POETS OF ANCIENT JAPAN.

printing, Chinese invention of

Primitive forms of block printing had likely been known as early as the seventh century C.E. and were probably first used to make available multiple copies of Buddhist devotional literature (see BUDDHIST TEXTS). By late in the T'ang dynasty, the technology had been employed in such applications as the production of almanacs, calendars, and dictionaries. The invention of the application of that technology to the production of a wide assortment of books, however, is attributable to Feng Dao (881–954 C.E.), a tutor in the imperial household. Thus, the Chinese achieved the capacity to mass-produce books about half a millennium before a comparable technology became available in Europe.

Bibliography

Giles, Herbert A. *A History of Chinese Literature.* New York: Grove Press, 1958.

Proba, Faltonia Betitia (fl. ca. 350 C.E.)
Roman poet

One of only two female Roman poets with substantial literary remains, Proba was an aristocrat and a Christian. She established an enviable literary reputation as a composer of CENTOS. The English word *cento*, in Proba's context, alludes to poems that she constructed on subjects taken from the HEBREW BIBLE and the NEW TESTAMENT by taking lines that VIRGIL originally wrote and cleverly rearranging them so that they addressed her subject.

The success among Christian readers of Proba's Virgilian centos was so great that Pope Gelasius named it on a list of works without authority as Christian text. For devout Christian Romans, however, the twin appeal of the authoritative poet of Rome's literary golden age and stories from Scripture seems to have been overwhelming.

See also SULPICIA.

Bibliography

Conte, Gian Biaggio. *Latin Literature: A History.* Translated by Joseph B. Solodow et al. Baltimore, Md.: Johns Hopkins University Press, 1994.

Proba, Faltonia Betitia. *The Golden Bough; the Oaken Cross; The Virgilian Cento of Faltonia Betitia Proba.* Chico, Calif.: Scholars Press, 1981.

Proclus of Byzantium (412–485 C.E.)
Greek prose writer

Born in Constantinople, Proclus was a devotee of the old gods who became a Neoplatonist philosopher. He studied at Xanthus in Lycia and at Alexandria, then moved to Athens, where he first studied and later taught, following his teacher, Syrianus, as principal of the Platonic academy in Athens, where he remained until his death.

Among Proclus's several surviving philosophical works, the one considered most important is his *Commentary on the Timaeus of Plato*. He commented as well on other dialogues of PLATO; these include *On the Alcibiades*, *On the Cratylus*, *On the Parmenides*, and *On The REPUBLIC*. Other philosophical writings of Proclus include: *Elements of Physics*, *Elements of Theology*, *On the Existence of Evils*, *On Fate*, *On Providence*, and *Platonic Theology*.

A synthesizing thinker, Proclus defended the old Greco-Roman religion against the onslaught of Christianity with an extensive and internally coherent body of thought, elements of which he largely inherited from his teacher Syrianus and from Iambichlus of Syria. He wrote some Platonic hymns, which survive, and also, perhaps, a little handbook about literature, now lost, of which we have summaries. In addition, he penned scientific treatises that include a work commenting on the mathematician EUCLID's *Elements*, another on PTOLEMY's *Tetrabiblos*, another about eclipses, and an *Outline of Astronomical Theories*. Proclus was the last great systematizer of classical, polytheistic thinking. Venerated as a Neoplatonic saint, he was the subject of a biography by his students.

Bibliography

Edwards, Mark, trans. *Neoplatonic Saints: The Lives of Plotinus and Proclus by their Students.* Liverpool, U.K.: Liverpool University Press, 2000.

Proclus. *Elements of Theology.* Translated by Thomas Taylor. Frome, Somerset, U.K.: Prometheus Trust, 1994.

——. *Elements of Theology.* Translated by E. R. Dodds. New York: Oxford University Press, 1992.

——. *The Fragments that Remain of the Lost Writings of Proclus.* Translated by Francis Taylor. San Diego: Wizard's Bookshelf, 1988.

——. *On the Eternity of the World.* Translated by Helen S. Lang, A. D. Macro, and Jon Mc Ginnis. Berkeley: University of California Press, 2001.

——. *On the Existence of Evils.* Translated by Ian Opsomer and Carlos Steel. Ithaca, N.Y.: Cornell University Press, 2003.

——. *The Platonic Theology.* 2 vols. Translated by Thomas Taylor. Kew Gardens, N.Y.: Selene Books, 1985–86.

——. *Proclus' Commentary on Plato's* Parmenides. Translated by Glenn R. Morrow and John M. Dillon. Princeton, N.J.: Princeton University Press, 1987.

Rosan, L. J. *The Philosophy of Proclus: The Final Phase of Ancient Thought.* New York: Cosmos, 1949.

Siegler, Julius A., ed. *The Nature of the Universe.* 2nd ed. Lanham, Md.: University Press of America, 1997.

Procopius (fl. sixth century C.E.) *Greek historian*

Born in the city of Caesarea in Palestine, Procopius migrated to Constantinople. There he became a lawyer and an important SOPHIST toward the end of the period known as the Second Sophistic. Associated with the Byzantine general Belisarius as his private secretary and legal advisor from as early as 527, Procopius accompanied Belisarius on his Persian campaign in 530 C.E. and was present when the Byzantines defeated an enormous Persian army at Dara.

Literature best remembers Procopius as an historian who wrote admirably clear and accurate prose. His best-known work is the eight-book *History of the Wars.* Written in Greek, this work's first four books, together called the Persic half of the work, recount the wars of the Romans against the Persians in the east and against the Moors and the Vandals in Africa. The second half includes the Gothic part, which details the Romans' campaigns against the Goths in three books. The final book is an overview of events throughout the empire. It takes the history up to about 554.

In his history, Procopius does not provide the sort of annualized account that ancient historians such as THUCYDIDES gave of events. Rather, he follows one set of events through from beginning to end before discussing another. While this approach generates greater reader interest, it also necessitates bearing in mind that the military actions described often overlap in time, for Rome fought simultaneously on more than one front. This work was the authorized, official history of the military accomplishments during Justinian's reign (527–565 C.E.). It documents Justinian's energetic but foredoomed effort to reestablish Rome's military control of the territory it had ruled at the height of Roman power. Importantly, Procopius's history of these wars is often an eyewitness account by a talented writer close to the commanding general. As Procopius himself observes, no one was better qualified than he to pen these histories. As the official chronicler of great events, Procopius perceived himself to be the scholarly heir of Thucydides and HERODOTUS. Evidence of this fact is to be found in his frequent borrowings of his predecessors' turns of phrase.

Procopius penned two other surviving works. The first of these is a *"secret history"* called *Anecdota* (Notes) that unofficially chronicles with bitter disapproval and perhaps exaggeration the scandalous events at the imperial court at Constantinople during the reign of Emperor Justininan.

Procopius privately considered the emperor to be two-faced and always willing to play both ends against the middle. Empress Theodora is the particular butt of Procopius's venom, for he disapprovingly recounts in lurid detail the history of her youth as a courtesan before Justinian ennobled her as his empress. Even Belisarius does not escape unscathed. In the view of Procopius's translator, H. B. Dewing, some of the history that Procopius retails in the *Anecdota* may not be true. Procopius wisely did not allow the work to be published during Justinian's lifetime. The book has provided such modern authors of historical fiction as Robert Graves with much grist for their mills.

Procopius's other work, entitled *Buildings*, describes the various construction and restoration projects undertaken by the emperor Justinian. The work is essentially an attempt to secure the emperor's favor by flattery. Despite that fact, and despite the florid style—atypical for Procopius—that the effort to flatter occasions, the book is an important document for students of the period because of the details it contains about imperial administration in the sixth century.

Bibliography

Cameron, Averil. *Procopius and the Sixth Century.* London: Duckworth, 1985.

Procopius. *History of the Wars, Secret History, and Buildings.* New York: Washington Square Press, 1967.

———. *Procopius with an English Translation.* 7 vols. Translated by H. B. Dewing. New York: Macmillan Co., 1914.

Prometheus Bound Aeschylus (after 478 B.C.E.)

Perhaps the first play in a trilogy that may have included *Prometheus Unbound* and *Prometheus the Fire-Bearer*, *Prometheus Bound* probably initiated AESCHYLUS's treatment of the second-generation Titan Prometheus who, after creating humankind from clay, stole fire from heaven against Zeus's express command and gave it to human beings to alleviate their suffering.

Prometheus belonged to a category of mythic beings called the TITANS. They were the children of the pre-Olympian, primeval gods Uranus and Ge, who represented heaven and earth. The union of Uranus and Ge produced 12 offspring, immortal giants. One of these, Iapetus, fathered Prometheus, whose name means "forethought." As we learn in Aeschylus's play, Prometheus was the ally of Zeus in establishing the reign of the Olympian gods. Once in power, however, Zeus decided to destroy the noxious race of humankind and forbade its access to fire. Prometheus resisted the destruction of his creatures.

Enraged by Prometheus's disobedience, a now almost omnipotent (though not omniscient) Zeus sentenced the Titan to be chained immobile to a mountainous promontory. Unrepentant and still rebellious, Prometheus was doomed to languish there, though his disdain for Zeus continually added new torments to his sentence. A vulture, for example, eventually began daily visits to the captive and tormented him by eating his liver. The destroyed organ regenerated each night, and Zeus intended the painful punishment to endure forever.

As Aeschylus's version of the story opens in the wastelands of Scythia, Prometheus enters as the prisoner of the allegorical figures Power and Force. With them also comes Hephaestus, the blacksmith of the gods, who will forge Prometheus's chains and immobilize him on the promontory.

Addressing Hephaestus, Power explains the object of their journey. Hephaestus expresses reluctance to carry out Zeus's harsh commands upon a fellow immortal, but the smithy has no choice in the matter. Prometheus must wear out the heat and frost of ceaseless eons alone, chained to the rock. As Hephaestus accomplishes his uncongenial task, Power, who feels no such compassion for Prometheus, spurs the smithy to tighten the bonds to make them more painful.

The task done and his captors departed, Prometheus bewails his fate but comforts himself with his ability to foresee the future. Prometheus is possessed of the omniscience that Zeus lacks.

The chained Titan articulates a central issue of the play: Why does the universe or the deity permit a good person who performs a kind act from a noble motive to suffer evil?

As Prometheus ends this speech, his cousins, the daughters of the Titan Oceanus, who are the first of a succession of visitors, arrive upon the scene in a winged chariot. The CHORUS recites their part. In the interchange that follows, the audience learns that Prometheus has knowledge of future events, and the prisoner explains that it is he who taught human beings all they know. That knowledge includes the interpretation of dreams, rituals of sacrifice and propitiation of the gods, metallurgy, medicine, husbandry, and so forth. The audience also learns that Prometheus knows things that Zeus does not. One day, the Titan promises, Zeus will have to ask Prometheus about the end of the Olympian deity's reign. We learn as well that Zeus's power is limited by Necessity. The Fates and the Furies in turn control Necessity. Prometheus assures the chorus that his bondage eventually will end.

Now the TITAN Oceanus comes calling, mounted on a four-legged bird that some believe to be the winged horse Pegasus. Oceanus bears warnings from Zeus and encourages Prometheus to apologize.

Prometheus, however, knows what Zeus does not—how Zeus will eventually fall from power. Prometheus, therefore, rejects Oceanus's advice, warning that he and Zeus should take care.

Prometheus's next visitor is Io, formerly a princess of Argos and a priestess of Hera. Zeus's love for Io, however, provoked his wife Hera's jealousy. Punishing Io, Hera turned her into a binatured half woman, half heifer. The goddess condemned the hapless girl to wander the world, continually driven on by the sting of a gadfly.

Io rehearses her story, and Prometheus predicts the path of her wandering, including the naming in her honor of the Bosporus—the crossing of the heifer. From Io's ongoing conversation with Prometheus, we learn that Zeus's eventual downfall will result from his own folly in seeking an ill-fated union with another mortal female.

The only way for Zeus to avoid his fate is to free Prometheus from his bonds. Io also learns that a member of the 14th generation of her descendants will be the person to deliver Prometheus.

The Titan then gives Io a choice: She may know either the troubles in store for her or the identity of the person who will deliver Prometheus. The chorus interrupts, asking Prometheus to tell it one of the two predictions and Io the other. Prometheus agrees. In high-flown language, he describes Io's future weary wanderings and their eventual end in Egypt. There in Canobus at the mouth of the Nile, Io is fated to return to her human shape and to bear Zeus a child named Epaphus. The member of the 14th generation of her descendants who will free Prometheus will be a child of the 13th generation's Hypermnestra (see *The SUPPLIANTS*). With that, Io's gadfly stings her, and she sets off on her wanderings.

The chorus reflects on the dangers inherent in matings between people and gods, and it describes the additional tortures that Prometheus must endure for refusing to cooperate with Zeus. Zeus, in the meantime, has overheard the foregoing discourse. He sends the messenger of the gods, Hermes, to demand the details of Zeus's eventual fall. Prometheus haughtily refuses.

Hermes predicts that Prometheus's only hope of deliverance rests on the unlikely circumstance that a god will appear who is willing to take Prometheus's place and voluntarily descend to Hades. As further punishment for his prideful resistance to Zeus's will, Prometheus sinks beneath the earth, and the play ends.

Early Christian commentators on the TRAGEDY almost a millennium later perceived in Hermes' prediction a foreshadowing of Christ's coming. Nineteenth and early 20th-century literary critics, instead, see in the character of Prometheus a blueprint for the character of the romantic hero—a person who opposes his freedom of will to the demands of authority, the operation of fate, and even the will of Divinity. Others perceive an argument for human nobility and purposefulness in the face of the insurmountable odds posed by weakness and mortality.

Bibliography

Aeschylus. *Prometheus Bound*. Translated by A. J. Podlecki. Warminster, U.K.: Aris and Phillips, 2002.

Propertius, Sextus Aurelius (ca. 53–15 B.C.E.) *Roman poet*

Born in the Italian region of Umbria, Sextus Aurelius Propertius appears to have been one of the unfortunate Romans whose land was confiscated in 48 B.C.E. for distribution to returning Roman legionaries in lieu of retirement pensions. Landless, Propertius migrated to the city of Rome and, having a natural affinity for poetry, joined a coterie of poets whose membership included such famous Romans as OVID; ALBIUS TIBULLUS; GAIUS CORNELIUS GALLUS; VIRGIL; and Ovid's patron, Gaius Maecenas, who became Propertius's patron as well.

From Propertius's pen, four books of elegiac couplets survive. He used as his Greek models the poems of CALLIMACHUS and the now-lost works of PHILETAS of COS. But Propertius also had a Roman model in Cornelius Gallus, who pictured himself as the love slave of a mistress named Lycoris.

Four books (originally five) of almost 100 poems by Propertius have survived. Many of them are love poems dedicated to a mistress of low status whom he calls Cynthia—one of the names of the moon goddess and the female form of one the names of Apollo, patron of the arts (Cynthius). Cynthia dominates Propertius's life—a total role reversal for the expectations of male-female love relationships in the Roman milieu. Yet despite Cynthia's ill treatment, Propertius stands firm in his dogged devotion to her.

The literary historian Llewelyn Morgan suggests that Propertius's role reversals in these poems, in which a dominant, low-status female mistreats and masters a servile, high-status male—are *intended* to be shocking. Morgan thinks, moreover, that Propertius was writing for a highly literate audience whose members would recognize the exag-gerated situations that Propertius describes as the poet's bid for an innovative place in the poetic canon of his day.

Among the poet's strategies for achieving that aim is creating a kind of verse that will both shock and titillate—one that makes the poet an immoral voice in his own verse and one that gives a predominantly male audience a voyeuristic experience. Propertius is witty, ironic, and both amoral and immoral—elements that have been and sometimes have not been perceived by different audiences reading his works in more prim or not-so-prim social environments over the millennia since he wrote.

See also ELEGY AND ELEGAIC POETRY.

Bibliography

Morgan, Llewelyn. "Creativity out of Chaos: Poetry between the Death of Caesar and the Death of Virgil." In *Literature in the Greek and Roman Worlds: A New Perspective*. Edited by Oliver Taplin. New York: Oxford University Press, 2000.

Propertius, Sextus. *Complete Elegies of Sextus Propertius*. Translated by Vincent Katz. Princeton, N.J.: Princeton University Press, 2004.

———. *Elegies: Book IV*. Edited by Gregory Hutchinson. New York: Cambridge University Press, 2006.

———. *Propertius in Love: The Elegies*. Translated by David Slavitt. Berkeley: University of California Press, 2002.

Protagoras Plato (ca. 400 B.C.E.)

The dramatic situation in this early Platonic dialogue features the arrival in Athens of the famous SOPHIST Protagoras of Abdera and the excitement that his presence generates among SOCRATES' friends. One of these, Hippocrates, identifies himself as a Sophist, but when Socrates questions him closely, he admits that he does not know just what a Sophist is supposed to know.

Socrates explains that a Sophist is a person who sells knowledge—the food of the soul. The buyer must beware lest the knowledge he buys be poison. This said, Socrates and his companions go to visit Protagoras. They find him discoursing to a band of listeners in the cloister of his residence. They introduce themselves, and Protagoras explains his role as a teacher of humankind.

Socrates flatters Protagoras by suggesting that others join them to benefit from his discourse, and when all the participants are assembled, Socrates asks Protagoras what Hippocrates can expect if he enrolls as the Sophist's student. Protagoras explains that Hippocrates will learn prudence in public and private matters.

Socrates asks if this means that Protagoras teaches politics and good citizenship. When Protagoras answers that it does, Socrates expresses his doubts that such matters can be taught. In response, Protagoras embarks on a mytho-historical discourse that begins with the creation of men and animals, proceeds through the introduction of fire by the TITAN Prometheus, to the assembly of human beings in cities. At that point, Zeus endowed people with the qualities of reverence and justice. These are universal gifts, and people who fail to practice them are punished. Since some people do not display these qualities, Protagoras thinks, they can be taught in the same fashion that good people teach virtue to their children. In adulthood, the laws themselves continue that education.

Now Socrates wants to know why the children of good men sometimes turn out to be bad. Protagoras suggests that parents teach virtue within their capacities, so that different persons learn different degrees of virtue.

Socrates inquires if the various virtues are really simply different aspects of the same overarching quality. Protagoras thinks that they are, just as different features compose a face. Socrates continues to pursue this line of questioning until it becomes clear that he is backing Protagoras into a logical corner—a method that Socrates regularly follows. In exploring the nature of the good, he has first led Protagoras to concur in identifying the expedient with the good, but then he traps Protagoras by also leading the Sophist to admit that some inexpedient things are also good.

Seeing that he has been trapped, Protagoras attempts to confuse the issue by giving a long-winded answer that directs the discussion down irrelevant paths. Socrates complains that he has a bad memory and cannot keep track of long answers. Protagoras refuses to accede to Socrates' request for short answers, and Socrates tries to leave. His friends restrain him and attempt to restore friendly relations between Protagoras and Socrates. One of the friends, Hippias, proposes to appoint a referee, but Socrates says that no better judge than Protagoras himself can be found. So, instead of remaining in his usual role of questioner, Socrates will let Protagoras ask the questions, and he will attempt to give short answers. Protagoras reluctantly agrees, and the discussion resumes.

Protagoras, in what is evidently one of his set pieces, cites an apparent ethical contradiction in the poetry of SIMONIDES OF CEOS. Socrates, however, by demonstrating the difference in the meanings of *be* and *become*, disproves Protagoras's analysis. A lengthy section follows in which the discussants offer analyses of the entire poem under discussion. When the analysis is complete, one of those present, Hippias, proposes to analyze another poem, but Alcibiades wants to go back to the main issue, and he shames Protagoras into resuming the discussion.

Protagoras now returns to a consideration of virtue. He argues that wisdom, temperance, justice, and holiness can be considered alternate names for the same quality, but that courage is different. An intemperate, unwise, unjust, and unholy person can nonetheless display courage in battle. Socrates proves him wrong by demonstrating that such courage is overconfidence and therefore madness. Protagoras complains that Socrates misrepresents his views.

Changing the subject, Socrates suggests the identity of good with pleasure and evil with pain. Protagoras objects to that identification but is unready to argue the matter. Socrates therefore shifts the focus of the discussion to knowledge, and Protagoras agrees with him that wisdom and knowledge are the highest of human qualities. Socrates then leads Protagoras to admit that both pleasure and pain can interfere with wise and knowledgeable behavior.

The argument goes on, and Socrates gradually gains the upper hand. As he does so, however, he leads Protagoras to assent to Socrates' original position, while Socrates undertakes to demonstrate that of Protagoras. By the end of the discussion, the opponents have switched sides on the basic issues of the discourse. The upshot of the entire argument is to undermine the sophistical enterprise.

The historical Protagoras was obliged to leave Athens for teaching atheism.

Bibliography

Plato. *Protagoras and Meno.* Translated by Robert C. Bartlett. Ithaca, N.Y.: Cornell University Press, 2004.

Prudentius, Aurelius (Clemens) (348–ca. 405 C.E.) *Roman poet and prose writer*

A poet, hymnodist, and Christian apologist and controversialist, Aurelius Prudentius was born in Spain. Some authorities argue for the Roman town of Calagurris (modern Calahorra) as his birthplace, and some for Caesarea Augusta (modern Saragossa). Trained in rhetoric, Prudentius first practiced law and became a functionary in civil government. He then became a soldier—an appointment that brought him to the attention of the Western Roman emperor.

After his 50th birthday, Prudentius retired from active participation in worldly affairs and devoted the rest of his life to pious occupations that included the composition of religious poems meant for singing as hymns. These survive in two small collections. One of them contains 12 hymns, some of which are designed for celebrating particular feast days and some for hours of prayer during the day. This collection bears the mixed Greek and Latin title *Cathemerinon liber* (Book for everyday, or *The Daily Round.)* A second collection contains 14 hymns, each honoring a Christian martyr. This work bears both Greek

and Latin titles *Peri Stephanon* (About the crowns . . .) and *De coronis* (About the [martyrs'] crowns).

As a Christian apologist, Prudentius penned a poem, "The Origin of Sin" ("*Hamartigenea*"). He also wrote "*Psychomachia,*" a poem describing the struggle between good and evil for a human soul.

As a Christian controversialist, Prudentius contributed to a renowned dispute between Roman Christians, led by the Roman Catholic bishop of Milan, St. AMBROSE, and Roman pagans, led by Symmachus, the pagan prefect of the city of Rome. The issue at stake involved an altar dedicated to the Roman goddess Victory. Ambrose, as the representative of what was now Rome's official state religion, wanted the altar destroyed. Symmachus, a learned and gentlemanly worshipper of the old religion, wished the altar to be preserved in a spirit of religious toleration. Prudentius took the side of St. Ambrose, arguing on the side of the Christians in two books entitled *Contra Symmachum* (Against Symmachus). Prudentius also penned another argument, this time against various heresies, entitled *Apotheosis.*

A metrical condensation of the life of Christ as depicted in the NEW TESTAMENT is sometimes also controversially ascribed to Prudentius.

Bibliography

Glover, T. R. *Life and Letters in the 4th Century.* Cambridge: Cambridge University Press, 1901.

Peebles, Bernard M. *The Poet Prudentius.* New York: McMullen Books, 1951.

Prudentius, Aurelius. *Hymns of Prudentius: The Cathemerinon or The Daily Round. . . .* Translated by David R. Slavitt. Baltimore, Md.: Johns Hopkins University Press, 1996.

———. *Poems.* 2 vols. Translated by Sister M. Clement Eagan. Washington, D.C.: Catholic University of American Press, 1962–65.

Thompson, H. J., trans. *Prudentius with an English Translation.* 2 vols. Cambridge, Mass.: Harvard University Press, 1949–53.

Pseudolus Plautus (191 B.C.E.)

Considered by the author to be PLAUTUS's masterpiece, *Pseudolus* displays all the characteristics for which the Plautine COMEDY has been celebrated through the ages. It is farcical, racy in language and action, and employs Plautus's innovations of using song and lyric rhythms to embellish the action, the gist of which he borrows from Greek originals.

As in his Greek models and as in Roman comedy generally, Plautus's characters tend to be types rather than individuals. They include clueless young lovers, heartless procurers, cross parents, and such crafty slaves as the title character, Pseudolus, who provides the brain power lacking in the others, moves the plot along, and provides its resolution. Pseudolus is legally the slave of Simo, but he effectively serves Simo's son Callidorus.

Set in Athens, the play opens with Pseudolus doing his best to get his clearly depressed master, Callidorus, to stop sighing and weeping long enough to explain his predicament. After much cajoling, Callidorus shows Pseudolus a letter from his beloved Phoenicium, a courtesan, begging for Callidorus's financial help. But Callidorus explains that he does not have the means to help her.

Phoenicium's letter explains that a pimp has sold her to a Macedonian soldier, and she will be taken away as soon as the soldier's representative pays the balance of the purchase price. She explains that the representative will identify himself with a wax tablet bearing the likeness of the soldier and that the deadline is the following day. Pseudolus agrees to find Callidorus the money he needs and get the girl for him. If finding the money proves difficult Pseudolus intends to weasel it from the young man's father, Simo.

Now the pimp, Ballio, enters, beating his slaves. The audience learns that this day is his birthday. He sings a song and remembers that he also requires his courtesans and calls for them, in Richard Beacham's wonderful translation, with the command, "Whores, out of doors!" The last to appear is Phoenicium. A lengthy interchange follows among Ballio, Pseudolus, and Callidorus, in which the latter two try to persuade Ballio to give them more time to raise money and buy Phoenicium's freedom. Ballio tells them she has been sold. Callidorus and Pseudolus compete in hurling insults at Ballio, but he parries them with good-humored, amoral wit. He finally promises that if the Macedonian soldier fails in his bargain, Callidorus will have another opportunity to buy Phoenicium's freedom. Pseudolus boasts that he will outwit Ballio, but after both Ballio and Callidorus exit, he admits that he has no plan to accomplish his boast.

Now Callidorus's father, Simo, enters with his neighbor, Callipho. Simo is complaining about Callidorus's spendthrift ways, but Callipho argues that someone must be slandering the lad. Besides, in his youth, Simo was a notorious womanizer.

Simo has already heard about the plot to have him finance his son's love life. To his surprise, Pseudolus confirms the rumor and assures Simo that before the day is over, the old man will give Pseudolus the necessary cash. Simo assures him he will not and makes a bet with Pseudolus. The two wager concerning that outcome. If Pseudolus wins and gets money from Simo, he will never be threatened with another beating; if he fails, he will be set to work at backbreaking labor in a mill. As the first act ends, Pseudolus addresses a song to the audience, and a musical interlude follows.

As the second act begins, Pseudolus observes the arrival of Harpax, the military aide of Phoenicium's buyer. Pseudolus pretends to be the pimp Ballio's slave, Surrus, and tries to get the money Harpax carries to pay the final installment for Phoenicium. Harpax mistrusts him Pseudolus with the money but is fooled into thinking that he can leave the letter and the identifying token for the pseudo-Surrus to pass along to his matter, the pimp Ballio. Pseudolus promises to find Harpax at his inn later on and to inform him when Ballio returns.

The lovelorn Callidorus now enters with his friend Charinus. Pseudolus explains that he has the token that identifies the messenger, and Charinus promises to supply the needed money to redeem Phoenicium. They agree to employ Charinus's slave, Simia, to impersonate Harpax and, equipped with both the necessary token and the money to get Phoenicium.

Now Ballio enters with a cook that he has hired to prepare his birthday feast. Like slaves, cooks are regularly among the stock characters of Greek and Roman comedy, and they are always rough and crooked pilferers. A good deal of slapstick interchange accompanies arrangements for the party. Then Simia enters, disguised as Harpax. He and Pseudolus exchange considerable banter on the subject of which of them is the greater scoundrel, and Simia, impersonating Harpax makes his attempt to deceive Ballio. The fact that Simia does not know the name of the master he is representing almost undoes the scheme, but he cleverly gets Ballio to name Polymachaeroplagides—a name suitable for a stock, braggart soldier. In the event, Simia gives Ballio the token and the money owed and makes off with the girl.

Certain that he has given Phoenicium to the right person and that Pseudolus has no hope of outwitting him, Ballio bags to Simo—who happens by—that he is safe from Pseudolus's tricks. So certain is he that he bets Simo 20 *minae* that Ballio has outwitted Pseudolus.

Harpax—Polymachaeroplagides's real emissary—now reappears to carry out his commission, and Ballio thinks he is a customer in search of a prostitute. When it becomes clear that Harpax is after Phoenicium, Ballio thinks that Harpax is an imposter sent by Pseudolus. The stage business surrounding this misapprehension occupies several lines, but when the truth finally dawns on Ballio, he realizes that he has not only been swindled out of Phoenicium but that—since the girl is gone—he owes Harpax the 20 silver *minae* already paid by Polymachaeroplagides as a down payment. Moreover, Ballio now owes Simo to whom he has lost his wages.

As Ballio goes off to get the money to pay Harpax, Simo goes home to get the cash to pay off his wager with Pseudolus. Simo now believes his slave to be the most clever fellow living, though he means to prepare a surprise for him.

Pseudolus arrives at the door drunk and crowned with a garland. He reports that the young lovers are entwined in one another's arms. Simo reluctantly pays him his money. Then Simo sets Pseudolus free, and Pseudolus restores Simo's cash. Pseudolus invites his former master to join him for a carouse, and the two exit arm in arm.

Bibliography

Plautus. *Pseudolus.* Translated by Richard Beachum. In *Plautus: The Comedies.* Vol. 4. Edited by David R. Slavitt and Palmer Bovie. Baltimore: Johns Hopkins University Press, 1995.

Ptolemy (Claudius Ptolemaeus) (ca. 90–168 C.E.) *Greek-Egyptian prose writer*

An Egyptian cartographer, geographer, musical theorist, astrologer, and astronomer, Ptolemy worked in Alexandria during the HELLENISTIC AGE. He is principally remembered for his astronomical work, *System of Mathematics,* better known by its Arabic title, *Almagest.* As an astronomer, Ptolemy derived his studies from the lost observations of predecessors, but as his was the earliest work to survive, his name has attached to the system that he promulgated: the Ptolemaic system of the universe.

Ptolemy subscribed to a geocentric theory of the solar system. Earth was the fixed center of a series of eight rotating spheres. Around it circled the moon, the sun, and the planets known to antiquity: Mercury, Venus, Mars, Jupiter, and Saturn. Beyond that was the sphere of the fixed stars, and beyond them the prime mover—the *primum mobile* that had started everything rotating. The mechanism for transferring the rotational power was a series of crystalline spheres that rubbed together, transferring their motion like a system of gears. The sound of their friction created the music of the spheres that could be heard, according to Neoplatonist philosophers, by the spiritual beings that were intermediate between the gods and men. The desire for consonance between the workings of the sidereal universe and the affairs of human beings may have been the factor that made Ptolemy a musical theorist as well as an astronomer. He wrote about musical matters as well in his *Harmonics*, and optics and the theory of vision also interested him.

Having the earth at the center of things created certain difficulties. It produced an apparently retrograde motion of certain stars, and Ptolemy and his predecessors exercised remarkable ingenuity to account for a problem that disappears when the sun is recognized as the center of the solar system.

His accomplishments, however, went further. Although his astronomy was largely derivative, his geography was original. His book on that subject, the *Geographike Huphegesis* (Geographical outline), lists many places, giving their correct longitudes and latitudes, and providing general descriptions of their features. He correctly calculates the size of a spheroid earth and provides a creditable world map.

Two works are ascribed to Ptolemy as an astrologer, his *Tetrabiblos syntaxis* (System of four books) and a work called *Karpos*, or *Centiloquium* (Hundred words).

See also GEOGRAPHY AND GEOGRAPHERS, GREEK AND ROMAN.

Bibliography

Ptolemy. *The Geography*. Translated and edited by Edward Luther Stevenson. Mineola, N.Y.: Dover Press, 1991.

———. *Harmonics*. Translated by Jon Solomon. Boston: Brill, 2000.

———. *Ptolemy's Almagest*. Translated by G. J. Toomer. Princeton, N.J.: Princeton University Press, 1998.

———. *Ptolemy's Geography: An Annotated Translation of the Theoretical Chapters*. Translated by J. Leeart Berggen and Alexander Jones. Princeton, N.J.: Princeton University Press, 2000.

———. *Ptolemy's Theory of Visual Perception with an English Translation of the Optics*. Philadelphia: American Philosophical Society, 1996.

Punica   See SILIUS ITALICUS.

Pythagoras of Samos   See ITALIC SCHOOL OF PHILOSOPHY; *LIVES OF EMINENT PHILOSOPHERS*.

"Pythian 3"   Pindar   (ca. 478 B.C.E)

One of the characteristics that contributed to PINDAR's reputation as the most notable lyric poet of ancient Greece appears in the remarkable variety that distinguishes his work. This quality appears in his prosody; in his choice of subjects; and in his deployment of word order, the lexicon, and the grammatical capacities of the Greek language. It also appears in his choice of subject and in the tonal shifts that he achieves.

Pindar's ODE entitled "Pythian 3" belongs to a category of Pindaric composition called VICTORY ODES. Pindar wrote them to celebrate the victories of his patrons or their horses in the major athletic contests of his time. Pindar composed "Pythian 3" for his longtime patron, Hieron, ruler of the city of Syracuse on the then-Grecian island of Sicily. The victory of Hieron's entry in the single-horse race held at the games in honor of Apollo at Pythia provides the nominal occasion for the poem's composition. The ODE's content, however, instead of directly celebrating that event, offers comfort and consolation to an ill and aging Hieron who has met the challenges of his life successfully and well. The literary historian and translator William H. Race calls Pindar's poem "one of the greatest consolatory poems in all of literature."

As is often Pindar's practice, he begins his poem by remembering a series of events from the mythic past. In the context of the race, he thinks about the centaur—half horse and half man—Chiron, offspring of Chronos and Philyra, the daughter of the TITAN Oceanus. Friendly to human beings, Chiron had nurtured Aesclepius and taught him medicine. Pindar wishes Chiron were again alive;

he implies but leaves unstated his patron's need for the centaur's medical expertise.

The poet's associative processes then regress further in time to consider the parents of Aesclepius: Apollo and Coronis. Pregnant with Aesclepius, Coronis had betrayed Apollo with another lover. Angered, Apollo killed her but pitied his child and rescued the baby from Coronis's burning funeral pyre. The cautionary tale of Coronis establishes a theme of the consequences of foolish excess and dissatisfaction with what one has. It also illustrates divine compassion as well as anger.

Aesclepius learned to treat the illnesses of all who sought his help, but he had also inherited his mother's folly. He overstepped his human limitations by yielding to the importunities of the goddess Artemis, who begged Aesclepius to bring back to life her human favorite, Hippolytus (see HIPPOLYTUS). Infuriated at this breech of human limitation, Zeus destroyed Aesclepius with a thunderbolt. From this tale, Pindar draws a moral. Human beings must "seek what is proper from the gods." Then, tactfully addressing himself instead of his royal patron, Pindar continues: "Do not, my soul, strive for the life of the immortals, / but exhaust the practical means at your disposal."

Returning to his original wish that Chiron were still living, the poet says he would use his song to persuade the centaur to "provide a healer" for the maladies of "good men"—presumably like Hieron. Were that the case, the poet would bring his patron two prizes for his horse's first-place finish, a "victory revel" and golden health.

Having proceeded until this point by indirection, Pindar now directly addresses his patron. The poet reminds the king that the gods apportion to human beings a pair of evils for every good. Fools, he continues, cannot handle this truth, but good men—as Hieron has implicitly done—take the gods' gifts and share them with others.

Pindar draws from mythology further examples of the intermixture of good fortune and misfortune that the gods dispense. He concludes the poem's fifth antistrophe with the observation that people's happiness, like "gusts of high-flying winds," does not last long.

With great tact, Pindar offers Hieron disguised advice in the concluding stanza of the poem. The disguise amounts to a statement of Pindar's personal intention to "be small in small times" and "great in great ones" and to "honor with [his] mind" the fortune that is allotted to him. Pindar concludes by hoping for fame that "endures in glorious songs," and he notes that few can easily become the subjects of poems. He seems to imply, however, that Hieron is among those whose fame has already been preserved in long-enduring song. It is the best that mortals can hope for.

Bibliography

Race, William H., ed. and trans. *Pindar: Olympian Odes, Pythian Odes.* Cambridge, Mass.: Loeb Classical Library, 1997.

———. *Pindar.* Boston: Twayne Publishers, 1986.

Q

quantitative verse

To analyze the metrical patterns of English and most other modern European verse, poets and their readers use a pattern of relative stress to determine a system of heavy and light emphasis on syllables: "The BOY/ stood ON/ the BURN/ing DECK" or "The AsSYR/ian came DOWN/ like a WOLF/ from the FOLD." In the first instance, the four groups of alternating lighter and heavier stresses creates a pattern called *iambic tetrameter*, and the second set of four three-syllable groupings of two light and one heavy stress is called *anapestic tetrameter*.

Though very ancient Latin verse employed such stress patterns (see SATURNIAN VERSE), in Greek and in the later Latin of CATULLUS, VIRGIL, and OVID, stress played no role in determining the chaining together of metrical measures. Theoretically, the relative length of a syllable was determined by the time a person took to utter it. In practice, a set of relatively complex rules determined a system according to which syllables were considered to be long or short. It helps to think of quantitative verse as measures of music. For example, a single dactylic measure, called a *foot* can be illustrated as a whole note followed by two quarter notes.

Six feet together comprise hexameter. For such serious poetry as the EPIC and TRAGEDY, Greek and later Roman authors favored a hexameter line composed principally of dactyls. To avoid tedium in the listener or reader, skillful artists varied their epic and tragic meters. Thus, the typical dactylic hexameter line ended with a spondee—two long syllables or two half notes in our musical analogy. Poets and playwrights often substituted any other metrical foot for a dactyl elsewhere in a line. Making use of the natural pauses that occur in language, they also typically inserted a break called a *caesura* in each line to give readers and actors a chance to inhale.

As Greek drama developed, plays began to rely less on set speeches and more on dialogue. This development resulted in a shift away from the statelier dactylic hexameter measure in dialogue and toward a more rapid iambic trimeter measure that was perfected by the poet ARCHILOCUS in the seventh century B.C.E. In quantitative verse, an iamb can be thought of as a quarter note followed by a half note. The Greek system of scansion considered two feet of iambic trimeter to be the durational equivalent of one foot of dactylic hexameter. As a result, the iambic trimeter pattern doubled in each line of the discourse in which it appeared. This development enriched the variety of verbal pace in the performance of tragedies.

Though not all the possible combinations of quantitative verse need be considered here, other frequently used patterns include the elegiac couplet (see ELEGY AND ELEGAIC POETRY), the sapphic stanza, the alcaic stanza, and scazon.

The elegiac couplet, also first observed in the seventh century and employed by such poets as CALLIMACHUS, was commonly used to lament or eulogize the dead. The first half line of this unrhymed couplet begins with two and a half dactylic feet whose last beat is silence—a caesura. The second half of the line is composed of dactylic hexameters whose third and sixth feet also contain silence instead of syllables. Two of these lines together give an impression of sobbing or catching the breath as one might do in the throes of grief.

The invention of the sapphic stanza is, of course, attributed to SAPPHO. Four lines of verse characterize it. The first three lines are each composed of two beginning and two ending trochees (long, short), with a dactyl (long, short, short) between the two trochees—a five-foot line. The fourth line, called an *adonic*, is formed from two feet, the first a dactyl and the second a trochee.

Taking its name from Sappho's fellow poet and contemporary, ALCAEUS, the alcaic stanza begins with two lines identical to the first three of the sapphic stanza, with these exceptions. The alcaic lines begin with an anacrusis—an extra syllable outside the metrical pattern—and end with a single long syllable. The third line also contains an anacrusis that is followed by four trochaic feet. The final line contains two dactyls followed by two trochees.

The scazon originated in Greek and then moved to Latin, where MARTIAL and Catullus employed it profitably. It is a six-foot line, the first five feet of which are iambic and the last of which is a trochee. The scazon is also called a *limping iambic* since the last foot drags.

See also HEPHŒSTION of ALEXANDRIA.

Bibliography

Harvey, Paul, ed. *The Oxford Companion to Classical Literature.* Oxford: Clarendon Press, 1937.

Thrall, William Flint, and Addison Hibbard. *A Handbook to Literature, with an Outline of Literary History, English and American.* New York: Odyssey Press, 1936.

Quintilian (Marcus Fabius Quintilianus)
(ca. 40–ca. 96 C.E.) *Roman prose writer*

The most famous Roman writer on the subjects of education, oratory, and rhetoric, Quintilian was born in Spain in the city of Calagurris. There were two towns with this name, but the larger and more likely of the two as Quintilian's birthplace was a Roman city on the Ebro River. The date of Quintilian's birth is uncertain, and, though it is often listed as 35 C.E., he was probably born a bit later. By 57 C.E., Quintilian was in Rome as a student of rhetoric, which suggests that he was then between ages 14 and 20. In 59, Quintilian returned to Spain and remained there until 68, when he returned to Rome.

The emperor Vespasian assumed the royal purple in 69, and in 71 he appointed Quintilian to a state professorship—a post he held until his retirement around 90 C.E. In that capacity, Quintilian opened a school and became the first rhetorician to receive a salary from the imperial treasury. He numbered among his pupils the children of the most prestigious families of Rome.

The most important occupations a man could perform in ancient Rome were fighting in the legions and speaking in the law courts and the senate. The preparation for speaking involved instruction in rhetoric and oratory, and it was in these subjects that Quintilian specialized. While still serving in his capacity of state professor, he published a now-lost treatise, *On the Causes of Corrupted Eloquence.*

Quintilian was not only a teacher, however. He was also a practitioner of the art he professed and maintained an active legal practice. In his known publications, although he made general mention of many cases, he specified only four. In one, he successfully defended Naevius of Arpinum against the charge of having thrown his wife to her death. Quintilian allowed his speech in defense of Naevius to be published. Other more or less corrupt versions of his legal speeches were published, but he did not authorize their circulation. A second case in which he is known to have served involved his successfully defending a woman against a charge of having forged her husband's will. A third case—one that underscores his fame—involved his defending the princess Berenice of Judea, sister to King Agrippa II. In the fourth and least-known case, Quintilian dealt with an allegation that a certain young woman was the sister of his client. Presumably he won.

Two collections of declamations controversially purporting to have been Quintillian's survive. Conceivably, some of them might have been schoolroom examples or exercises. There are 145 surviving *Minor Declamations*—about half the number known in antiquity—and 19 full-scale or *Major Declamations* on such issues as soothsayers and pirates. These do not seem in keeping with Quintilian's interests.

After his retirement, Quintilian published his masterwork: ORATORICAL INSTITUTE (*On the Education of the Orator, Institutio oratoria*) in about 94 or 95. Dealing not only with the intricacies of oratory but also, and most importantly, with the system of education necessary to the preparation of a good orator, the work proved enormously influential in the ancient world. In the aftermath of the dislocations that accompanied the fall of the Western Roman Empire, the work was known for centuries only in fragmentary condition. Petrarch read a portion of the partial manuscript and as a result began to understand Quintilian's deserved fame among the ancients. Then, in 1416, the Italian humanist Gian Francesco Bracciolini Poggio found a complete manuscript in the library of San Gallo. As a result, Quintilian resumed his importance for generations of educators, students, and orators.

Shortly after the publication of *Oratorical Institute*, the presiding consul of Rome for the first half of 95 C.E., Flavius Clemens, procured for Quintilian a signal honor: He was granted the right to dress in the clothing reserved for and exercise the privileges of persons who had once served as consuls of Rome. This honor, called the *ornamenta consularia* (consular insignia), also freed the recipient from the usual duties attendant upon former consuls—serving in the Roman senate. This acknowledgement of Quintilian's accomplishment came in the nick of time, for it is likely that he died in the following year.

Bibliography

Kennedy, George. *Quintilian.* New York: Twayne Publishers, 1969.

Quintilian. *The Lesser Declamations.* Edited and translated by D. R. Shackleton Bailey. Cambridge, Mass.: Harvard University Press, 1987.

———. *The Major Declamations Ascribed to Quintillian.* Translated by Lewis A. Sussman. New York: Verlag P. Lang, 1987.

———. *The Orator's Education.* [English and Latin.] 5 vols. Edited and translated by Donald Russell. Cambridge, Mass.: Harvard University Press, 2001.

Telligen-Couperus, Olga. *Quintilian and the Law: The Art of Persuasion in Law and Politics.* Leuven, Belgium: Leuven University Press, 2003.

Quintus Smyrnaeus (Quintus Calaber)
(fl. ca. third century C.E.) *Greek poet*

The author of a late post-Homeric Greek EPIC poem, Quintus lived in Smyrna in Ionia, a spot not far from HOMER's reputed birthplace. He undertook to fill in the gap in the events of the Trojan War that occurs between the material Homer covered in *The* ILIAD and that detailed in *The* ODYSSEY. Entitled *Posthomerica,* or *Paraleipomena Homero* (Matters omitted by Homer), the work relies on the verse of the Greek cyclic poets (see HOMERIDAE) as its source material and follows the siege of Troy from Hector's death at the hands of Achilles to the Greeks' departure from Troy. Not all the episodes included, however, were in fact omitted from Homer. There is some overlap with *The Odyssey,* as in the episode of the wooden horse and Troy's capture.

In composing his poem, Quintus took pains to emulate the manner of Homer while at the same time introducing a phraseology distinctively his own in an effort to avoid a style either too high flown or too pedestrian.

Bibliography

Quintus Smyrnaeus. *The Fall of Troy: Quintus of Smyrna.* Translated by Arthur S. Way. New York: Barnes and Noble, 2005.

———. *The Trojan Epic: Posthomerica: Quintus of Smyrna.* Translated and edited by Alan James. Baltimore, Md.: Johns Hopkins University Press, 2004.

———. *The War at Troy: What Homer Didn't Tell by Quintus of Smyrna.* Norman: University of Oklahoma Press, 1968.

White, Heather. *Studies in Late Greek Poetry.* Amsterdam: J. C. Gieben, 1987.

quipu (khipu)

At the time of European contact, the Incas of Peru had a sophisticated system of keeping records of such information as taxes collected by using a system of knots in colored strings, with subsidiary cords attached to a main cord. These might number from just a few cords to several thousand. While it seems clear that quipu, as these knotted cords are known, used a base-ten system to communicate numerical information, little evidence has yet emerged that quipu's system of knot-tying might also have been used to communicate linguistic information. Nonetheless, that intriguing possibility has often been suggested.

A recent discovery of a trove of quipu that antedates the Inca by 1,500 years suggests that the Inca borrowed the system from their ancestors. The archeologists who reported the find, Gary Urton and Carrie J. Brezine, believe they have identified a figure-eight knot that stands for the location to which the numerical information applies. If this is true and the knot in question is a place name and not merely something corresponding to a zip code, it represents the first such evidence of such a close correspondence between a quipu knot and a linguistic datum.

Bibliography

Daniels, Peter T., and William Bright, eds. *The World's Writing Systems.* New York: Oxford University Press, 1996.

Urton, Gary, and Carrie J. Brezine. "Khipu Accounting in Ancient Peru." *Science* Vol. 309 (August 12, 2005), pp. 1,008–09.

Qu Yuan (Ch'ü Yüan) (ca. 340–ca. 278 B.C.E.) *Chinese poet*

The earliest Chinese poet whose name we know, Qu Yuan was a member of the royal house of Qu (Chu) and was a courtier in the retinue of King Huai (329–299 B.C.E.). While later hands may have written some of the poems ascribed to him in the surviving collection, *Verses of Qu*, others seem genuine and even autobiographical.

As Tony Barnstone and Chou Ping tell Qu's story, a jealous colleague slandered Qu, and the king dismissed him from service. Nonetheless, Qu continued to warn the king against the State of Qin and its belligerent intentions. Failing to heed Qu's warnings, King Huai was taken captive and executed by the military forces of Qin. Huai's son succeeded to power, but he too rejected Qu's services, exiling the poet far to the south. Despondent there, Qu Yuan drowned himself in the River Miluo.

Qu Yuan wrote long, dramatic narratives as exemplified by his poem ENCOUNTERING SORROW (*Li sao*)—the most celebrated of Chinese poetic works and one thought to have been written in response to having fallen from the king's favor. Other sorts of works also appear in Qu's verses. One finds ritual songs and a series of verse riddles on the subjects of Chinese history, cosmology, and myth. There is a poetic dialogue between Qu and a fisherman in which the latter encourages Qu to remain among the living and continue to do his job. Several of the poems deal with the ritual activities of a priest or shaman. Qu Yuan became a Confucian model for the self-sacrificial honest courtier who is willing to risk criticizing his superiors. The annual Chinese

Dragon Boat Festival commemorates his death by drowning.

Bibliography

Barnstone, Tony, and Chou Ping, eds. "The Verses of Chou." In *The Anchor Book of Chinese Poetry.* New York: Anchor Books, 2005.

Mair, Victor H., ed. *The Columbia Anthology of Traditional Chinese Literature.* New York: Columbia University Press, 1994.

Watson, Burton. *Early Chinese Literature.* New York: Columbia University Press, 1962.

R

Ramayana Vālmīki (ca. fifth–third century B.C.E.)

The EPIC story of Rama has deeply and continually influenced Indian thought and letters throughout the ages. In its current form, the *Ramayana* is the earliest surviving poem in a language of India—Sanskrit. Commonly attributed to the poet Vālmīki (though also sometimes to VYĀSA), and sometimes called the Indian *ILIAD*, the poem seems to have a factual basis in the ancient wars of conquest that Aryan invaders fought in southern India and Sri Lanka. The *Ramayana* is a long, verse epic containing some 50,000 lines in 25,000 *slokas*, or couplets, organized into four principal sections.

Section 1

The first section recounts Rama's childhood and youth up to his wedding with his lovely bride Sita. Rama is the miraculous incarnation of the Hindu god Vishnu, the preserver of the universe. As the story begins, the elderly king of Kosala, Dasharata, has no children. While praying that he might still father some, a supernatural being appears to him in an annunciation scene, explaining that the king has pleased God and promising that the king's three wives will all conceive and bear children. Dasharata must first distribute among the women a bowl of supernatural rice pudding that the glorious being has provided. All three wives bear children; Rama is the eldest of them. His mother is Kausalya, and his half siblings include three brothers—one by Dasharata's second wife, Kaikeyi, and twins by the third, Sumitra.

As Rama reaches his mid-teens, his remarkable capacities began to reveal themselves. A holy man, Viswamitra, arrives and begs King Kosala to send the 15-year-old Rama to destroy a group called the Rakshasas, a company of demons who are interfering with the holy man's fire sacrifices. Taking with him his half brother Laksmana, Rama serially engages the giantess Tadaka, her son Maricha, and then all the other demons. He hurls Maricha miles away into the sea and kills the rest.

Then Rama and his brothers visit the city of Mithila, ruled by King Janaka, to perform the delayed fire sacrifice ceremony. Viswamitra has an ulterior motive: He wants Rama to marry Janaka's daughter, the lovely Sita. Before the king will assent, however, Rama must pass a test. Just as Odysseus in HOMER's *The ODYSSEY* must do to prove himself, Rama must string a bow. This one—the weapon of the god Siva—is so heavy

568

that no mere mortal can even budge it, much less string it. Rama can do it so easily that he snaps the weapon in two as he bends the bow. Sita is pleased, and the king assents to the wedding. The brothers also acquire brides, and a magnificent wedding ensues.

Section 2

The second section, entitled "Ayodhyā"—the name of both Rama's capital city and its district—picks up the story after Rama and Sita's honeymoon. Rama, not yet king, becomes regent of Ayodhyā, but jealous gods conspire to thwart his purposes. Queen Kaikeyi, deceived by a chambermaid who is the gods' emissary, prevails on the king to suspend Rama's regency, appoint her son Bharat in Rama's place, and exile Rama as a religious hermit to the forest for 14 years. The king resists this advice, but on hearing the plan, Rama thinks it a good idea. After much discussion and the king's fainting several times when he considers life at court without Rama nearby, Rama takes Sita with him, and the two depart for the forest. His brother Lakshmana also goes along, and Bharat follows them, becoming Rama's disciple for a while until he thinks the time has come to take up his regency. In the forest, they take up residence in an Edenic grove where they live in utter contentment.

The group has not dwelt there long before they are called back to Ayodhyā. Overcome by grief, the king has died, repeatedly uttering Rama's name with his last breaths. The time has now come for Bharat to assume the throne. He tries to defer to Rama, but Rama intends to fulfill his vow and spend 14 years in exile. In that case, Bharat says, he will only rule as Rama's regent until the latter's forest exile ends. He puts Rama's sandals on the throne to signify that Bharat rules in his name. The group's adventures on the journey to the forest, Rama's sympathy with the plight of the common people, and their recognition of Rama as the incarnation of the Lord occupy the rest of the second section. So does the theme of Rama's ascendancy over the entire pantheon of lesser Hindu deities who fear his power and try to resist with magic and guile what is fated to occur.

Section 3

In the third section, "The Forest," after locating another lovely spot to live, Rama must overcome a formidable army of 14,000 demons. They cannot match his strength, and his arrows cut the demons' entire host to pieces. Eventually Rama makes each demon see the other as Rama's image. The demons fight among themselves and finally kill each other.

What the demons cannot accomplish by combat, they attempt to achieve by guile. The 10-headed demon king, Ravan, kidnaps Sita—like Helen of Troy, the world's most beautiful woman—and, overcoming a rescue attempt by the Vulture King, carries her off to Sri Lanka in the south. In Ravan's clutches, Sita is ravished in every imaginable way.

Section 4

The epic's next part "Kiskindhā," is followed by a final part often split into "The Beautiful," and "Lankā." Together they recount the famous story of the recovery of Sita by the joint efforts of Rama, his brother Laksmana, and their wonderful ally Hannuman, the magical field marshal of all monkeys. Hannuman's magical talents and millions of monkey subjects locate Sita on the island of Sri Lanka, and they rescue Rama's wife from the demons, overcoming them both in battle and by trickery. Rama's forces, for example, cross the expanse of ocean separating India from Sri Lanka on a bridge supported by nothing but water. Eventually, after many changes in the fortunes of the warring parties, the battle's issue is decided in single combat between Rama and Ravan. The multiheaded demon keeps growing new heads each time Rama severs some. Finally, Rama remembers a magic arrow that Bhrama has given him, and with it he destroys the demon.

In Vālmīki's version of the often retold and sometimes bowdlerized epic, the prudish Rama then rejects the rescued Sita for suspected infidelity during her long captivity with the demon king. She objects that, despite her having been ravished, Rama never left her mind or her heart. Disconsolate, she has her funeral pyre built, meaning to burn to death rather than live rejected by Rama. When she mounts the burning pyre, however, the flames do not faze her, and her essential innocence is apparent to all. Yet when adversity strikes the kingdom in the form of famine, tongues wag once more, attributing this disaster to Sita's infidelity.

Rama's memory seems peculiarly short for a deity's, and he sends her unaccompanied into exile. Physically and spiritually exhausted, Sita half crawls to the hermitage of the poet sage, Vālmīki. There she bears twin sons, Lava and Kuça, and there she rears them for the next 20 years.

An elderly and irritable Rama, in the meantime, has begun to imagine that the gods are peeved with him for having killed Ravan because the demon was the son of a priest. To expiate his imagined guilt, Rama sends a valuable horse into the forest, where his twin sons capture it. In Rama's effort to recover the horse, his unknown sons' resistance first enrages their father. Finally, however, he is delighted to discover who they are.

This discovery prompts Rama to feel remorseful about his treatment of Sita. He finds out where she is and summons her. Sita, however, really wants no more to do with him, and at first she refuses to go. Eventually, however, Vālmīki and his wife convince her. She puts on her richest finery and stands before her erstwhile husband in all her beauty. To justify herself, she calls on the earth to witness the fidelity of her mind and heart. In answer, the earth opens and the earth goddess appears enthroned. She seats Sita beside her, and the two are transported to everlasting happiness. Rama gets his just desserts and lives with his guilt and regrets until the death of his human form.

The *Ramayana* enjoys the status of sacred scripture in the Hindu religion, and, as is the case with the *MAHABHARATA*, merely reading or reciting the work or portions of it confers spiritual benefits. New York University Press has prepared a bilingual, Sanskrit-English version in five volumes that splits the epic's fourth section in two.

Bibliography

Vālmīki. *The Ramayana.* 5 vols. *Book 1: Boyhood.* Translated by Robert P. Goldman. *Book 2: Ayodhya.* Translated by Sheldon Pollock. *Book 3: The Forest.* Translated by Sheldon Pollock. *Book 4: Kiskidhā.* Translated by Rosalind Lefebre. *Book 5: Sundara.* Translated by Robert P. Goldman and Sally J. Sutherland Goldman. New York: New York University Press, 2005–06.

———. *The Ramayana: A Modern Translation.* Translated by Ramesh Menon. New York: HarperCollins Publications; 2003.

Ras Shamra texts (ca. 1500–1100 B.C.E.)

A collection of fired clay tablets covered with CUNEIFORM, the works that comprise the Ras Shamra texts, were recovered from the topmost layer of five ancient cities, one built atop another since sometime in the New Stone Age, when the oldest of the cities was built. Once excavations of the site were begun, it quickly became clear that archaeologists had stumbled on the site of the city of Ugarit, whose name was well known from other sources.

Linguists recognized that the cuneiform inscriptions represented a language unknown before their discovery. Informed guesswork, however, led to the thesis that the unknown language might be Semitic—the immediate ancestor of Hebrew and Arabic. That theory proved valid, and it soon became possible to decipher the texts owing to the regularity of their divergences from Hebrew.

While some of the texts dealt with such business matters as the lading of ships and the like, by far the majority of them proved to be religious texts that bore directly on the ancient beliefs of Phoenicia and Canaan. Specifically, they are concerned with the annual death and resurrection of the fertility god Baal, as these events were celebrated in an autumn festival that featured weeping over his death and laughter over his resurrection and marriage.

Moreover, because of the close proximity of Israelite and Canaanite farmers after the former's invasion of Canaan, and, in some instances the interactions of and similarities in their modes of worship, the Ras Shamra texts have important implications for Hebrew Bible scholarship as well as for the study of the history of religious practice. Principal among these are: (1) the question of the degree of influence that native fertility religions had on the conquering Hebrews' understanding of the nature of Yahweh; (2) the form that such influence took; and (3) the long-term impact, if any, of such mutual development of religious ideas as may have taken place among Hebrew and Canaanite farmers.

Whatever else they do, the Ras Shamra texts make clear that the HEBREW BIBLE did not develop in a textual vacuum. The religion of the ancient Hebrews interacted with those of others in the course of their travels and those of their neighboring peoples.

Bibliography

Gibson, J. C. L., trans. *Ras Shamra: Canaanite Myths and Legends*. New York, T. & T. Clark International, 2004.

Habel, Norman C. *Yahweh vs. Baal: A Conflict of Religious Cultures*. New York: Bookman Associates, 1964.

Kapelrud, Arvid S. *The Ras Shamra Discoveries and the Old Testament*. Semitic texts translated by G. W. Anderson. Norman: University of Oklahoma Press, 1963.

Record of Ancient Matters   See *KOJIKI*.

"Record of the Peach Blossom Spring" (Taohuayuan, T'ao-hua yüan) Tao Qian (ca. 400 C.E.)

Contained in TAO QIAN's (T'ao Ch'ien's) 10-volume collection of 116 fairy tales and legends entitled *Sequel to "Search for the Supernatural,"*

"Record of the Peach Blossom Spring" is a utopian tale. It tells of an isolated people dwelling in peace in a location that, though a traveler has once discovered it, can never again be found. It finds its analogues in stories about the magical kingdom of Shangri-la in the Himalayan Mountains, or about the village of Brigadoon that only appears once each century in Scotland.

In "Record of the Peach Blossom Spring," a fisherman follows a narrow channel in his boat. The channel leads through a maze of high rocks to a pleasant land where people enjoy peace and plenty without the supervision of overlords or the expectation of military service. The people are happy to explain their circumstances to the visiting fisherman, asking only that he not reveal their existence to anyone in the outside world. He promises not to speak about them, but when he leaves, he carefully marks his route and immediately reports his experience to the authorities. When he tries to lead them to the happy land of the peach blossom spring, however, he can find no evidence of his markers, and he never succeeds in retracing his journey.

Bibliography

Tao Qian. *The Complete Poetical Works of Tao Yuanming* [Tao Quian]. Translated by Wang Rongpei. Beijing: Wai yu jiao xue yu yan jiu chu ban she, 2000.

Davis, A. R. *Tao Yüan Ming: His Works and Their Meaning*. New York: Cambridge University Press, 1983.

Records of the Grand Historian   See *SHIHJI*.

Republic, The Plato (ca. 411 or 410 B.C.E.)

Described by the 20th-century British writer Aldous Huxley as "a noble philosophical romance," the 10 books of PLATO's *The Republic* cover education, ethics, politics, religion, and sociology, among other subjects. Plato himself thought of his book as a serious but nonetheless playful fable about justice. In that context, the work provides a model for thinking about political systems rather than, as has sometimes been proposed, a blueprint for an ideal state. While Plato seriously examines the subjects that *The Republic* covers, and while careful readers can derive much intellectual profit as well as pleasure from its pages, those readers must always bear in mind that they have before them a work of sometimes playful and satirical fiction. The date ascribed above gives that which is sometimes proposed for the fictive conversations that occur in *The Republic*. The actual date of composition is uncertain.

Book 1

The story opens as SOCRATES and his companion, Glaucon, are about to leave a religious festival in the port city of Piraeus and return home to Athens. The servant of their friend Polemarchus asks them to wait for his master, who is coming along behind them. Catching up, Polemarchus persuades his friends to join him for dinner and to see the evening festivities. They accept, and at Polemarchus's home they encounter the virtuous, aged, and wise Cephalus, with whom Socrates discusses a variety of topics. Among these, we learn of Cephalus's relief at no longer feeling driven by sexual appetite. Cephalus says that old age is not as great a burden for persons of a temperate and cheerful disposition. He also praises living justly and piously with one's spouse and suggests that the chief benefit of comfortable wealth is being able to deal fairly with the gods and with other people.

Cephalus departs, and Socrates engages Polemarchus in a discussion of the concept of justice. Plato offers as a starting point the traditional Greek view of justice: It is that which benefits friends and harms enemies. Socrates, following his usual (and often tedious) method of leading his companion to change his mind or broaden his viewpoint, makes a series of assertions with which his friend agrees, finally leading him into a logical trap. In this case, Socrates suggests that if one

sticks to the above definition of justice, one must admit that justice so conceived amounts to a kind of stealing. Step by step, Socrates leads Polemarchus to admit: "In no case is it just to harm anyone." As a negative characteristic, however, that assertion will not serve as a definition of justice.

Blaming Socrates for his tactics, another character, Thrasymachus, defines justice as "the advantage of the stronger." He is extremely belligerent and rude to Socrates, who nonetheless leads him to admit that holding public office is an onerous task since the leaders are working for the advantage of the led and are paid for their labor. Socrates finally drags the cantankerous and reluctant Thrasymachus to the conclusion that "justice is wisdom and virtue." Having soothed the savage Thrasymachus, Socrates closes the first book of *The Republic* by observing that, since the subject changed in mid-discussion, he remains unsure about what "the just" is. Moreover, he finds it unclear whether or not "the just" is a virtue or its possessor happy.

Book 2

In Book 2, Thrasymachus has retired from the argument, but Glaucon, who is also present, seeks further discussion. He wants to hear Socrates praise justice unequivocally. To provoke the philosopher to do so, Glaucon is willing to try doing the same thing for injustice. After a lengthy discourse of the advantages of injustice to the unjust, Glaucon wonders what possible use anyone with "resources of mind, money, body, or family" would have for justice. Socrates guides the discussion from the consideration of justice as an attribute of an individual to a quality associated with city-states so that the quality of justice may appear in a broader context.

The origin of cities arises from the insufficiency of the individual to provide for all needs, as the discussants all agree. A certain number of persons with different but complementary skills are minimally required to constitute a city. Having achieved the requisite minimum, where in our hypothetical city, asks Socrates, are justice and injustice to be found? Deferring an answer to this question, the debaters consider that the city grows wealthier and enlarges, eventually needing a bigger agricultural base to feed its citizens and bringing it into competition for farmland with one or more neighboring cities. The resultant disagreements lead to the need for an army and, in turn, to the need for armament and training. For the entire city and army, a leader whom Plato calls a guardian is also needed—someone at once spirited, brave, forceful, kind, friendly, considerate, and a lover of wisdom. This leads into a discussion of the sort of education that might produce such a leader. Socrates thinks that a good education will be largely devoid of the sort of myths that poets tell about punitive deities and that attribute such human qualities as anger and lust to the gods. Socrates would banish from the city poets who tell such tales; children should instead hear stories of virtue.

As for the qualities of God, they are all good, and God is the cause of good only. Socrates advises that we must look elsewhere for the wellsprings of evil, and he dismisses the old story that Zeus has two jars—one of good fortune and one of ill—beside his throne. On the human beings Zeus dislikes, he pours ill fortune; on those he favors, he pours half and half. Not so, argues Socrates. No poet must be allowed to impute to a god the origins of evil, nor any falsehood. As Book 2 ends, the grounds for a definition of justice dimly begin to take shape in Socrates' discussion of the nature of deity.

Book 3

As we learn early in Book 3, poets' passages that characterize the afterlife of souls in the underworld will also be deleted from the education of children in Socrates' hypothetical city. Free people must be more afraid of slavery than of death. Indeed, the genuinely good person will not consider death a terrible thing.

There follows a consideration of poets' methods of composition and Socrates' general disapproval of mimetic art—where the poets speak their own words in the character of a person speaking—as opposed to descriptive art, where a poet reports what someone else has in fact said. If children imitate only proper and noble examples from an early age, the behaviors they practice will become habitual for them in later life.

A discussion of mimetic art ensues. While it is not limited to theatrical art, both theater and recited poetry of all sorts are implicit in the discourse. Only those poets who imitate exclusively good models will be admitted to the ideal city under discussion. The same restriction applies to musicians and musical instruments, though following the arguments in detail requires a close acquaintance with the metrics of Greek poetry and song. Suffice it to say that the speakers distinguish between better and worse rhythms and harmonies. This consideration strikes Socrates and his friends as particularly important owing to the way in which rhythm and harmony seize upon the listener's inmost soul.

The subject of the discussion has shifted to questions of the education of boys. After music, the most important subject is gymnastics, for practicing exercises in flexibility will better suit the youth for military training. Diet should also be moderate so that health can be maintained without recourse to physicians and the laws observed so that there will be less necessity for judges and sleepy jury men. The discourse naturally progresses to a discussion of physicians and their training and then to judges and their qualifications. A good judge should be an old man who has learned to understand the nature of injustice late in life. While those who are essentially bad can never acquire a knowledge of virtue, the virtuous can come to understand badness as a quality foreign to themselves.

The conversation drifts back to music and gymnastics, and all agree that training in both is necessary. Music without gymnastics makes one softer than he should be, and gymnastics unleavened by music tends to make one brutal and coarse.

Having satisfied themselves on the score of education and upbringing, Socrates and his companions turn their attention to the qualities of the rulers of the ideal city-state. They should be drawn from among the city's elders and have a long history of serving the public interest. Likely candidates should be selected in childhood and prepared for civic responsibility. The leader should be selected from among those who meet the criteria outlined. They also should own no private property and, like the young men of Sparta, must eat at a common mess.

Book 4

As Book 4 begins, one of the group, Adeimantus, objects that the ruling class being described does not seem very happy as the laws suggested cut them off from the common pleasures of people, such as owning lands, houses, and furnishings; giving to the gods and civic causes; entertaining guests; and so forth. Socrates replies that the objective is to provide for the maximum happiness of the city as a whole rather than for a single class of citizen. He then gives a long series of examples of the benefits of the well-governed city for all its citizens. Interestingly, progress is not an ideal that he aspires to. (Socrates probably would have objected to labeling as *progress* the technological changes that our century so admires.) Rather, he is interested in conserving the laws of and prescriptions for his ideal state. To this end, he resists innovations in the arrangements for the city's governance. He once again voices his particular concern about the insidious effects on character formation produced by innovations in music and poetry.

Once the city has been established in theory, Socrates is almost ready to return to the subject of justice. First, however, he proposes listing the qualities of the city that he and his companions have described. As the city's first quality, he suggests "well-advised." As its second, he proposes "brave." By bravery, Socrates means sticking to the founding principles and conserving in the citizens the sense of the dangers that originally led to banning poetry, music, and certain ideas. The third quality Socrates enumerates is sobriety, and the fourth is the quality toward which the entire development of *The Republic* has been moving: justice. Sobriety consists in self-mastery, and all concur that the city as described displays that quality.

Now, just as it seems the reader is at last on the point of arriving at Socrates' definition of the just, the philosopher interposes another anterior question. Does the soul contain in itself the forms of well-advisedness, bravery, and sobriety? (Socrates successfully introduces here the notion of ideal forms with no objection from his companions.) He leads his friends to admit three qualities that compose the structure of the soul: the rational quality, the appetitive quality, and something he calls *high spirit*. This last attribute is subject to the rational quality and allied with it. Finally, then, we find that the just and honorable action—justice— is the one that "preserves and helps to produce" a condition of the soul in which a person has achieved a "self-mastery" that leaves a person an integrated whole and that harmonizes the rational, the appetitive, and the high-spirited faculties within the soul. That harmony leads the just individual to seek virtue rather than vice. Excellence is the quality of the truly integrated soul. The forms of evil, says Socrates, are infinite.

Book 5

As Book 5 begins, Socrates, thinking the subject of the city closed, is about to enumerate four general categories of badness when Polemarchus interrupts him and asks instead that Socrates speak concerning the procreation and rearing of children and the community of women in a society.

Socrates holds that precisely the same education should be given to women and to men. He points out that in terms of qualities of mind and moral capacities, women and men are equal. The central difference is that women bear while men beget. Beyond that, on average, men have greater and women lesser physical strength. Yet both are equally capable of being, say, physicians or musicians. Just so, there are members of both sexes equally well suited to govern and fight for the city. Socrates also recommends eugenics—the arranged mating of the best-suited partners, and the continuing attempt to improve the breed by also allowing some of the best to cohabit with some of the worst. The numbers of children allowed will also be managed to keep the population of the city at approximately its original numbers. Parents will call all children born in the cohort of their own child either "son" or "daughter." The children, likewise, will consider one another brothers and sisters. The city is "best ordered" in which the greatest number of citizens call the same things "mine" and "not mine." A signal advantage of this system arises from the reduction in the number of lawsuits.

The discussion next turns to the conduct of war. Both men and women will fight, and the sturdiest children will be brought to observe the fighting from horseback so that they know what will be expected of them when the time comes. The book concludes by describing opinion as a kind of mean between ignorance and knowledge and preferring knowledge to opinion.

Book 6

Book 6 effectively begins with a definition of the term *philosophers* as "those who are capable of apprehending those things that are eternal and unchanging." After detailing the constituent attributes of such apprehension, Socrates asks if his friends would not want persons with the qualities of philosophers to be the rulers of their hypothetical city. All agree that they would, except that Adeimantus notes that most persons who linger too long in the study of philosophy become, in the translation of Paul Shorey, "cranks [and] rascals." Socrates replies with a parable whose essential point is that the labels Adeimantus has applied to philosophers come from persons who are ignorant of their pursuits, not to say their worth. The philosopher takes the opportunity to argue the degeneracy of the majority from whom

such low opinions of philosophers take their origin. Philosophy—the love of knowledge or wisdom—is an impossibility for most people. Moreover, the bad opinion that many hold of philosophy arises from the pronouncements and behavior of those—probably the majority—who practice the art of philosophy unworthily. Socrates insists that few if any have ever seen a virtuous city ruled by a person "equilibrated" and "assimilated" perfectly to virtue. Granting that very few will meet his criteria, Socrates lists the qualifications for a philosopher who would govern a city: "facility in learning, memory, sagacity, quickness of apprehension, youthful spirit, magnificence of soul . . . and a disposition to live [an] orderly, quiet, . . . stable [life]."

Socrates now turns to a consideration of the good—the concept underlying the positive attributes upon which he has constructed his model city-state. The good is perceptible by reason as the visible is perceptible to vision. From this observation, Socrates moves on to describe a section of the visible world, its images. By *images*, Socrates means phenomena like shadows and reflections. Next he discusses the objects that produce such images: animals, plants, and manufactured things. Socrates suggests that those image-producing-objects, including animals, plants, and manufactured things as people perceive them are not themselves realities. They are merely the shadows and reflections of the deeper reality that is imperceptible to human senses. The nature of that underlying reality is ideal. Social reality is perceptible to mathematical reasoning or dialectical analysis, but not its human senses. Socrates ends Book 6 by instructing his listeners to assume four capacities or "affections" in the soul: intellection, or reasoning; understanding; belief; and "picture thinking or conjecture."

Book 7

Book 7 of *The Republic* contains its most celebrated passage—the famous allegory of Plato's cave. "Picture men," Socrates begins, living in a subterranean cave. It has a long entrance that admits light. The men, however, wear leg and neck chains and can look only in one direction, away from the entrance of the cave. Behind them and between the people and the cave's entrance a fire burns. Between the fire and the prisoners is a circular road around which people carry images of all sorts of things: people, animals, and objects. The prisoners have never seen anything but the shadows of those objects, and when the carriers utter sounds, the prisoners think the shadows they see make the noises.

Socrates then imagines that one of the prisoners escapes and looks toward the painful light behind him. Though he can dimly perceive the objects carried, he prefers the shadows of them that he has known all his life. Finally dragged outside into the sunlight, he sees for the first time examples of the original people, animals, and objects. At first he has trouble believing what he sees, but by stages he comes to realize that his former companions had been looking upon nothing more than shadows of images of reality. The escapee might be anxious to share what he has learned about the nature of reality with his former comrades, but Socrates predicts that they would not believe him and, indeed, would try to kill him for denying the evidence of their senses.

Socrates interprets his own allegory. What human beings perceive in the physical universe is mediated by the operation of their sensory apparatus; thus, they are seeing images rather than absolute reality. To clarify with a current example, when one, for instance, touches a tabletop, the senses convey color, immobility, and solidity. At the atomic level, however, science tells us that the seeming solid is more emptiness than matter and its apparent immobility a swirl of atoms. So Socrates' prisoners see images of images of the real. Representatives of that reality, Socrates insists, exist beyond the range of human sensory perception as ideas. So reality in the allegory of the cave is trichotomous: the shadows on the wall are reflections of images analogous to the data that our sight, hearing, touch, taste, smell, and temperature perception convey to our brains. The images being carried about are like the objects that give rise to our perceptions of them. Those objects, in turn, take their being from ideal forms of them that exist—and, for Socrates and Plato, *really do exist*—as ideas on a plane accessible only to intellection.

True philosophers, Socrates goes on to argue, have minds able to contemplate the realm of ideas—a realm much more gripping and exciting that the realm of ordinary affairs. This capacity, however, also qualifies philosophers better than ordinary men to rule the hypothetical city-state, for they understand the essential nature of truth. Thus, they owe it to their fellows to use their special capacities to improve everyone's lot.

There now follows a lengthy debate about the utility of such studies as geometry, astronomy, harmony in music, and, principally, dialectics. The ultimate benefit of such studies, says Socrates, is that they prepare their students for eventually understanding the true and the good, which, as we shall learn, are both also one with the beautiful. The balance of Book 7 turns once again to the education of children and the preparation necessary to equip them as philosopher kings.

Book 8

Book 8 begins with a welcome recapitulation of the attributes of the ideal city-state thus far agreed upon. There must be a community of wives and children in the fashion described above, all education and all employments will be the same for both sexes, and the government will establish the living arrangements. Socrates now turns his attention to investigating the various sorts of social organization that typify states. His friends agree with him that there must be as many forms of government as there are patterns of individual souls. All agree that there are five such patterns. The first is government by aristocracy—by people who are both just and good. The next is government by those who are contentious and desire honor. The government of Sparta is an example of this sort, and Socrates dubs such a polity a *timocracy*. As the third form of government, Socrates names oligarchy, where a few wealthy persons govern the state. Then there is the democratic form of government where the majority of citizens, whatever their qualifications, rule. Finally, there is tyranny, where a single ruler—often of dubious character and ability—directs the government.

There follows a detailed discussion of eugenics and the consequences for the rule of the state of certain combinations of ability and personality types that Socrates characterizes as golden, silver, bronze, and iron. He predicts that the more the citizens pursue wealth and the more the wealthy are honored, the less citizens will prize virtue, and oligarchy will surely arise. Tyranny will take no heed of the rational principle and will not prize high-spiritedness. Democracy and the democratic personality indulge in the pleasures and the interests of the moment, says Socrates, and meander on an essentially directionless course thinking that it constitutes an existence of "pleasure, freedom, and happiness." He considers that democracy is the root from which tyranny springs, and that most democracies become de facto oligarchies, since it is the moneyed class from which the rulers spring, and their followers tolerate no dissent. Socrates calls the capitalistic class "the pasture of the drones." In general, the accuracy with which Socrates predicts the development of oligarchy and tyranny from democracies would seem uncanny if he had not had a detailed and instructive model of such developments in the history of his own city of Athens. Moreover, he thinks, tragic poets are complicit in such developments since they put the spin on tyrants' activities that win public approval for tyrannical leaders. He compares tyrants to parricides who destroy the father that bred them.

Book 9

In Book 9, Socrates examines the character and development of the tyrannical man. He concludes that the tyrant has "the soul of madness for his bodyguard" and considers himself the ruler of both men and gods. The truth of the matter, however, is that tyrants are always either masters or slaves and never experience either freedom or friendship. There is no city "more wretched" than one governed by a tyrant, and none happier than one governed by a "true king."

Socrates divides successful people into three categories: lovers of gain, lovers of wisdom, and lovers of honor. All three sorts enjoy honor because of their reputation, but only the lover of wisdom can taste the happiness that follows from the contemplation of "true being" and of "reality." Moreover, true philosophers let all the faculties of their souls be guided by the wisdom-loving part of it. In doing so, the philosopher experiences a greater measure of pleasure and of true happiness. The city ruled by such persons exists nowhere but is nonetheless an ideal worth striving toward.

Book 10

In Book 10, Socrates returns once more to a biting criticism of the mimetic arts, particularly dramatic poetry and the dangers that poets present to the ideal state. He suggests that God made only a single original for everything that is in nature or of everything that people fabricate. The mimetic arts, however, like painting and poetry, have the capacity to fashion ideas that do not correspond to the god-given originals but which boast powerful and attractive rhythms and music and thus have the capacity to mislead people. Socrates considers HOMER a "creator of phantoms." Nothing Homer ever did contributed anything to the well-being of any city-state. The arts, in so far as they represent truth at all, do so at third and fourth hand. So poetry must be banished—with the caveat that if anyone can, by clear argument, prove that poetry provides not only pleasure but benefit, the door is open for poetry's return to the city.

There follows a discourse on the immortality of the soul and its susceptibility to mutilation by evil. On the other hand, justice itself is the best remedy for keeping the soul in good condition. The gods, says Socrates, will never neglect the man who is both just and righteous. To illustrate this point, the sage tells the story of Er, a Pamphilian who was killed in battle, discovered undecayed after 10 days, and laid upon a funeral pyre on the 12th day after his death. There, however, he recovered his life, and he reported to his fellow countrymen what had happened to him while he was dead. He was taken to a place of judgment where righteous ones were told to turn right and journey upward, while the unrighteous were made to turn left and descend. Both wore tokens of their earthly existences. When Er, however, came to the place of judgment, he was appointed the messenger to mankind of what would happen after death.

Er saw squalid, dusty souls coming up from below and clean, pure souls descending from above. They met their arriving friends, the ones from below, with wailing and lamentation, saying they had just spent 1,000 years of torment. (The sentence is 1,000 years per offense.) The ones from above greeted their arriving friends with tales of the pleasures and wonders above. (It seems that Plato is not utterly opposed to playing the role of the poet.) Socrates details the punishments and sentences endured by the sinful souls. Tyrants, especially, suffer horrible torments being flayed and having their skinned bodies "carded" on thorns.

The blessed, on the other hand, experience delights for a time and then must choose a new life—often one involving suffering—into which to be reborn. Er reports seeing the soul of ORPHEUS choosing to be reborn as a swan because women had killed him, and he did not wish to be born from a woman. Beyond that, beasts become humans and humans beasts. Then all those to be reborn appear before the Fates, and when everyone's next life has been woven into the tapestry of inescapable destiny, the souls pass the Plain of Oblivion and, thirsty from its searing heat, drink from the River of Forgetfulness. Er was not allowed to drink and so carried his message to mankind.

From that tale, Socrates draws the final moral of *The Republic*. The soul is immortal and capable of undergoing every extreme of good and of evil.

It is therefore to people's benefit to preserve the soul unsullied by the world so that both here and in the hereafter, all will be well.

Plato. *The Republic*. 2 vols. Translated by Paul Shorey. Cambridge, Mass.: Harvard University Press, 1946.
———. *The Republic*. Translated by R. E. Allen. New Haven, Conn.: Yale University Press, ca. 2006.

Rerum Gestarum (History of deeds done) See AMMIANUS, MARCELLINOUS.

rhapsodes (rhapsodists)

In ancient Greece, a professional entertainer who recited EPIC poems or portions of epics came to be known as a rhapsode, or song weaver. At first the word *rhapsode* applied to bards who recited works of their own composition. The term later also applied to those who stitched together shorter lyrics into a relatively lengthy performance.

rhetoric

PLATO and SOCRATES shared the view that rhetoric made possible practicing the wisdom gained through philosophical activity. Rhetoric for them was a means to that end. For the Greek Sophists the purpose of rhetoric was political control of the state though the persuasion of the masses or was convincing jurors of the correctness of a speaker's point of view.

The Roman educator QUINTILIAN put rhetoric at the center of his instructional program as he examined the nexus between truth itself and its expression in words. He interested himself in rhetoric as the means for preserving truth when speaking to audiences with differing intellectual capacities and educational backgrounds.

As rhetoric developed in the Greco-Roman world during the period known as the Second Sophistic, about the beginning of the Common Era, rhetoric's role became that of an adjunct to artistic creation, and its practitioners often achieved the celebrity of our contemporary popular actors and musicians. The appeal of rhetoric might be based on *ethos*—that is, on the character of the speaker—on *logos*—logic or reason or on *pathos*—on emotion.

Rig-Veda (Rig Veda) (ca. 1000 B.C.E.)

A collection of 1028 Vedic hymns in the Sanskrit language, the Rig-Veda—or at least some of it—probably dates to very ancient, preliterate times in India. It is acknowledged as the most ancient authority on Hindu social and religious matters. The subjects and themes of the hymns cover a wide spectrum of subjects and purposes. Some of them are addressed to such gods and goddesses of the Hindu pantheon as Agni, Indra, and Vishnu, or to sun gods and weather gods. Others deal with cosmology; they sing of the creation. Some of them address the mysterious unknown god who preceded all the named gods of the pantheon—the uncreated progenitor of being, or the golden embryo that, from nothing, came into being. Others address the mysterious creation of lesser deities and provide sometimes-conflicting explanatory myths for their genesis.

The hymns also sing of the origins of sacred or liturgical language and of its connection with worship, almsgiving, the consecration of rulers, and sacrifice. One such set of hymns concerns the preparation for and then the sacrifice of a horse. This set also contains a requiem hymn for the horse as sacrificial victim.

Within the vast collection, one also finds hymns that function as magic charms and spells. One finds hymns designed to protect the singer (in this case female) against rival wives. Hymns appear that are sung to assure a safe pregnancy, the well-being of an embryo, and successful birth. Other hymns invoke or protect against demons, assure restful sleep, and ward off bad dreams.

Some of the Rig-Veda's hymns retell portions of familiar myths that also appear not only in such Hindu EPICS as the *MAHABHARATA* but also, in cognate form, in parallel myths in ancient Greece and elsewhere. One such set of hymns involves the sky god Varuna, a god parallel with Uranus in the Greco-Roman pantheon. In the Rig-Veda, hymns to Varuna picture him as concerned with the architecture of the universe and in his role as the monitor of human behavior. Some of the hymns are designed to propitiate Varuna's wrath when human beings fail to meet divine expectations.

Several hymns specifically address—from a masculine viewpoint—the activities of women and matters of concern to them. Such hymns fall into two categories: *conversation hymns* and *narrative hymns*. In the former category, one member of a pair of lovers attempts to persuade the other to join him or her in some sort of sexual behavior. The lovers are represented as both mortal and immortal. Sometimes the attempts at persuasion succeed, and sometimes they fail, but there is a pattern to the successes and failures. Mortal men and women and immortal men and human women always couple; mortal men and immortal females, however, never do. In the latter category, the narrative hymns, the subjects of marriage and rejection predominate.

The processing and effects of a certain hallucinogenic plant called Soma—treated in the Rig-Veda as a male deity—is also the subject of a category of the collection's hymns. The hymns describe how stones are used as pestles to press the plant in wooden bowls and the resultant fiber filtered through wool to produce an ingestible substance. Other hymns detail the heightened awareness, trances, assurances of immortality, and hallucinations that taking Soma produces. One hymn details the god Soma's arrival on earth from heaven.

A number of the hymns in the Rig-Veda concern themselves with death. As a principal translator of the Rig-Veda's hymns, Wendy Doniger O'Flaherty, points out in her discussion of representative selections, such hymns about death provide glimpses into ancient Vedic customs and beliefs. Both cremation and burial, for instance, were practiced. After death, expectations for what would happen next included reincarnation, going to heaven, a spirit's moving into a new body, resuscitation of the current body, and a return of the body to its constituent elements.

As for the company that the disembodied spirit of a dead person might keep, it encompassed various gods, including Yama, god of the underworld; ancestors and relations; mother earth; those who mourn; and death personified. Generally speaking, as depicted in the hymns of the Rig-Veda, though death provokes grief, it is not fearsome and promises reunion with friends and family who have gone before.

Bibliography
Frawley, David [Vamandevi Shastri]. *The Rig Veda and the History of India.* New Delhi: Actya Prakashan, 2001.
O'Flaherty, Wendy Doniger. *The Rig Veda: An Anthology: One Hundred and Eight Hymns.* New York: Penguin Books, 1981.
Wilson, H. H., trans. Rig-Veda *Sanhita: A Collection of Ancient Hindu Hymns of the* Rig-Veda: *The Oldest Authority on the Religious and Social Institutions of the Hindus.* 7 vols. 1850–88. New Delhi: Cosmo Publications, 1977.

romance fiction
See FICTION AS EPISTLE, ROMANCE, AND EROTIC PROSE; GREEK PROSE ROMANCE.

Rosetta Stone

Until the very end of the 18th century, Egyptian HIEROGLYPHS presented scholars with an undecipherable mystery. The most recent datable hieroglyphs had been carved in 394 C.E. A series of historical events that included conquest and foreign domination (Cleopatra was a Greek—not of African lineage); linguistic change; the development of increasingly stylized shorthand for noting the ever-changing Egyptian tongue; the loss of the ability, even among scribes, to understand the hieroglyphs; and the notion that hieroglyphs were mystic signs rather than written language had at last rendered hieroglyphs utterly incomprehensible.

Then, toward the end of Napoleon's Egyptian campaign in 1799, at the Egyptian town of Rosetta (Rashid) on one of the mouths of the Nile River, French soldiers discovered a black, basalt tablet into which were inscribed three texts. The topmost text—severely damaged—contained Egyptian hieroglyphs. The intact central text was inscribed in Egyptian demotic cursive. This was, as has been subsequently proved, a kind of shorthand for the hieroglyphs. The lower text gave a Greek translation of the Egyptian demotic inscriptions.

The texts slowly began to reveal their secrets to a pair of talented linguists, Thomas Young of England (1773–1829), and Jean François Champollion of France (1790–1832). Significant among them was the fact, formerly unrecognized, that some of the hieroglyphs had phonetic value. Such names as Cleopatra, Ptolemy, and Ramesses [sic] were among the first hieroglyphic words that the researchers read.

Young died in 1829, and Champollion died three years later without having unlocked all the secrets of the stone. Their successors, however, Richard Lepsius (1810–1884) and Edward Hincks, (1792–1866) respectively discovered that the hieroglyphs could represent more than one consonant, and that the hieroglyphs, like early Hebrew writing, contained no vowels. The main secrets of Egyptian hieroglyphs were finally deciphered.

The text of the stone contains a decree of the pharaoh Ptolemy V. The three scripts describe the repeal of certain taxes and give instructions for the installation of statues in various temples.

Bibliography
Daniels, Peter T., and Bright, William. *The World's Writing Systems.* New York: Oxford University Press, 1996.
Wilson, Hillary. *Understanding Hieroglyphs: A Complete Introductory Guide.* New York: Barnes and Noble, 1993.

Rutilius, Claudius Numantianus (fl. fifth century C.E.) *Roman-Gallic poet*

Born in Gaul, probably at Toulouse, Claudius Numantianus Rutilius enjoyed Roman citizenship and served in Rome as master of the offices and prefect of the city under the emperor Honorius. Rutilius's native estates in Gaul seem to have been damaged by tribal uprisings, and matters there required his attention. He retired from public life, and as he voyaged home along the Mediterranean coast, Rutilius composed two books of elegiac verse. Later editors have entitled Rutilius's work *Itinerary (Itinerarium)* or *About His Homecoming (De reditu suo).*

Much of Rutilius's poem is lost, but the parts that remain suggest that he was very accomplished as a poet. A master of the technicalities of his art, he also displayed verve and originality. The 18th-century British historian Edward Gibbon approved of Rutilius's unflattering depiction of a colony of Christian monks at Capraria and of the poet's evident attachment for the old paganism. If Rutilius was not himself a pagan, at least he admired the old Roman gods as an intrinsic feature of a Rome whose institutions and history he loved. In the surviving portions of the poem, there are invectives against Stilicho—the Western Roman emperor who had destroyed the books that preserved the prophetic utterances of the Sibylline oracle—and against the Jews. The Romans sometimes did not discriminate between Jews and Christians, even as late as the fifth century.

Bibliography

Rutilius, Claudius Namantius. *De reditu di Claudio Rutilio Namaziano.* Edited and translated [into Italian] by Emmanuele Castoria. Florence, Italy: Sansoni, 1967.

S

Sallust (Caius Sallustius Crispus) (86–35 B.C.E.) *Roman historian*

Sallust was born about 55 miles northeast of Rome at Amiternum, probably to a plebian family, and acquired a good Roman education.

He entered Roman politics at an early age. Indications are that became a *quaestor,* one of 20 minor civil magistrates who automatically became members of the Roman senate by virtue of their office. In 52 B.C.E. he certainly became tribune of the commons. In that office, he joined his two tribunal colleagues in their opposition to CICERO and other adherents of the preservation of the Roman republic. Two years later, however, Sallust was expelled from the senate on partisan, trumped-up charges. In the days preceding the Roman civil wars, he aligned himself with the party of JULIUS CAESAR against that of Pompey.

In 49 B.C.E., Caesar restored Sallust as a quaestor and senator and subsequently made him the commander of a legion. In his first two military assignments, Sallust met with ill success. Octavius and Libo defeated him in Illyricum, and when he was sent to quell a mutiny in Campania, he narrowly escaped the mutineers with his life. In 48, nonetheless, having now risen to the office of praetor—a military office in Caesar's time—

Sallust successfully commandeered the supplies that Caesar's opponent, Pompey, had stored on the island of Circina. This action played a significant role in Caesar's ultimate success.

In recognition of his services, Sallust was appointed the military governor of the Roman province of Numidia and Africa. It seems likely that he took that opportunity to enrich himself—a not unusual objective for Roman provincial governors. On his return to Rome, he was tried for extortion, but as an adherent of Caesar, he was duly acquitted. He built a magnificent pleasure garden in Rome, the *Horti Sallustiani.* After his death, the land passed into imperial ownership.

Following Caesar's assassination, Sallust retired from public life. He is said to have married Terentia, Cicero's divorced wife. Apparently childless himself, he adopted his sister's grandson.

From the time of his retirement, Sallust devoted himself to writing historical monographs. He took as models for his historiography the examples of THUCYDIDES and the *ORIGINES* of Cato the Elder. He made a happy departure from their annalistic mode of organization, however. Instead of plodding along year by year, he introduced sustained narrative, following a course of events from beginning to end without interruption.

Sallust's first subject was the war against Catiline, *Bellum Catilinae*. Catiline was a senator and frustrated patrician who aspired to usurp the republic. This monograph is apparently as much of a Caesarian propaganda piece as a history. Sallust prolongs the action by more than a year, and a concern for vividness and reader interest replace historical objectivity. As a literary production, however, Sallust's first effort was a great success. His depiction of character and the speeches that he puts in the mouths of his actors on the stage of history are especially compelling.

Sallust's second work, *The Jugurthine War*, traces Rome's war against the Numidian ruler, Jugurtha. Sallust says that he selected it for its populist implications. The work is carefully researched, making use of both Latin and Punic language sources. Sallust's translator, J. C. Rolfe suggests that the book works better as a historical novel than as "sober history." For instance, Sallust is willing to shift the actual sequence of events to tell a better tale.

Mostly lost now is Sallust's masterwork, his *Historiae (The Histories)*. Written in five books, it focuses on the events that occurred in Rome between 78 and 67 B.C.E. Ever loyal to his plebeian origins, Sallust's principal propagandistic objectives in this work were, first, to show the ineptitude of the noble classes for ruling the Roman republic, and, second, to show Pompey's unfitness to serve as chief of state. Only disconnected fragments of this work remain.

As a stylist, Sallust imitates Thycydides' brevity of expression. In his manner of expression, he prefers archaic language—a preference that endeared him to linguistic antiquarians in his own time.

Beyond the works listed above, others of doubtful attribution have sometimes been assigned to Sallust. Unlikely to be his, for example, is the *Invective against Cicero*.

Bibliography

Rolfe, J. C., trans. *Sallust*. New York: G. P. Putnam's Sons, 1931.

Sallust. *Bellum Catilinae*. Edited by J. T. Ramsay. New York: Oxford University Press, 2006.

———. *The Histories*. 2 vols. Translated by Patrick Mc Gushin. New York: Oxford University Press, 1992–94.

———. *The Jugurthine War*. Edited by M. R. Comber. Warminster, U.K.: Aris and Phillips, 1997.

Sanskrit grammar   See PĀNINI.

sapphic stanza   See QUANTITATIVE VERSE.

Sappho (Psappho) (b. ca 650 B.C.E.) *Greek lyric poet*

Probably the daughter of a woman named Cleis, Sappho was born on the Mediterranean island of Lesbos, perhaps in the town of Eresus. She almost certainly spent time in the island's principal town of Mytilene. She had brothers, one of whom, named Charaxus, she chided for becoming involved with an Egyptian courtesan. As an adult, she married and bore a daughter named Cleis. According to some, Sappho's husband and the father of Cleis was a man named Cercylas from Andros. As the scholar Margaret Reynolds tells us, however, this name means "Prick from the Island of Man," and so Cercylas may be the invention of later ribald tellers and dramatizers of the Sappho story.

It also seems that Sappho spent some time as an exile on the island of Sicily. This suggests that she played an actively subversive role in the politics of her homeland. It is likely, too, that she was a teacher and numbered among her students young women with literary aspirations. Several of their names and those of other female associates and of a rival are preserved in her verse: Andromeda (the rival), Atthis, Erinna, Climene, Dica, Gorgo, Mika (girls she admired or celebrated), and others. The names of contemporary male figures also appear.

Because a considerable number of Sappho's surviving love lyrics address women, literary tradition has appropriately conscripted her into the role of an archetypal lesbian—a name, of course, derived from that of the island of her birth. Stories about her death, though perhaps true, seem more consistent with the ongoing fictive embroidery that has for centuries been stitched onto the much simpler fabric of what can confidently be said about the historic Sappho. She committed suicide, so the story goes, when she cast herself from the white cliffs of an island in the Ionian Sea. Then called Leucadia or Leucas, the island is today labeled as St. Maura. Sappho's self-destruction is said to have resulted from her despair at her unrequited passion for Phaon—a name also applied to the demigod Adonis and to an aged ferryman whose youth Aphrodite restored. All this suggests at least a conflation of real and mythical stories.

As if this high degree of uncertainty were insufficient, more follows. It is unclear that Sappho herself *could* have written down any of her own works. Her composition stands on the very cusp of her native island's development of a script for representing her Aeolic dialect of the Greek language. Fragmentary remains of some of her verse, however, seem to suggest at least a nascent tradition of writing. Almost surely, like the preliterate poets and bards who preceded her, she sang her compositions while accompanying herself on a stringed instrument such as a lyre or harp. Probably her disciples then memorized her work, performed it, and taught it to others. The same method of dissemination had characterized the EPICS of HOMER composed 200 years before Sappho's time.

Nothing that Sappho wrote has come down to us directly. Nonetheless, by 150 years after her death, an active trade had developed in manuscripts, and much from Sappho was successfully transferred from the ORAL FORMULAIC TRADITION to the written one. In ancient times, members of the ACADEMIC SECT OF PHILOSOPHY are thought to have edited her then-surviving poems into nine volumes. Owing partly to a change in literary taste, partly to the marginalization of the Aeolic in which she composed, and partly to Christian disapproval of Sappho's pagan, lesbian, and bisexual material, many of these works were

lost. As tastes shifted and her language became obsolete, fewer copies of her poems were made. Some old copies were torn into strips and recycled for the funeral trade as mummy wrappings. Others were destroyed—the victims of Christian zeal. Zealots were probably responsible for burning Pharaoh Ptolemy I's 600-year-old library of classical manuscripts at Alexandria in 391 C.E., as Willis Barnstone tells us. Pope Gregory VII ordered Sappho's works burned both in Rome and in Constantinople in 1073, with the result that many irreplaceable manuscripts were committed to the flames. What, if anything, was left in Constantinople probably fell victim to crusader pillaging in 1204 and Ottoman destruction in 1453.

Nonetheless, some fragments of Sappho's verse were preserved in quotations made from her works by other writers. That some of these fragments have survived to be transmitted to us at all we owe to the most improbable and fortuitous circumstances. In the late 19th century, archeological excavations in an ancient trash heap near the Egyptian town anciently known as OXYRHYNCHUS and today called Behnasa unearthed an enormous treasure trove of papyrus fragments—many of them apparently torn into strips for mummy wrappings—dating from the second to the fifth centuries C.E. Amid the tens of thousands of bits of rubbish, a previously unknown poem by Sappho appeared and was painstakingly pieced together. Some 60-plus volumes of edited material later, the work of organizing and deciphering the still-daunting collection of remnants goes forward. Thus, the possibility of finding more Sapphic documents exists. At present, 213 fragments of her work are known.

Thanks to DIONYSIUS OF HALICARNASSUS, in what scholars categorize as Fragment 1 of Sappho's work, we do seem to have a single ODE to the goddess Aphrodite preserved in its entirety (see *HYMN TO APHRODITE*). Thanks to Longinus, who quoted Sappho in his famous essay, °*LONGINUS, ON THE SUBLIME*, a substantial remnant survives in Fragment 31 (see "I MORE THAN ENVY HIM").

Beyond that, we know Sappho's work as directly as we can principally from snippets of verse.

We also know her work, however, from the reputation that it enjoyed among the ancients who celebrated it, imitated it, and did homage to Sappho's memory. They regarded her, in PLATO's phrase, as a 10th Muse, and statues were erected to her memory. Across 2,600 years, her voice calls out to us, and, often unknowingly, we hear its echoes in the popular songs of love longing that continually sound in our ears. Sappho also feelingly explores such issues as the emotional consequences for the odd woman out in a love triangle involving two women and a man. Her great and continuing contribution to the vocabulary of lyric poetry is a language of desire.

That, however, is not her only contribution. In Greek, her poems are breathtakingly mellifluous. Her craftsmanship in melding sense and sound knows few equals in the Western tradition. The best translations of her work succeed in echoing something of her mastery. She also was an innovator of poetic form, developing, for instance, the sapphic stanza (see QUANTITATIVE VERSE). SOCRATES and PLATO admired her, and OVID, CATULLUS, and HORACE imitated her in Latin.

Some of Sappho's poems are epistolary—actual verse letters. Most of her love lyrics are addressed to women, though perhaps a few also address men. Other fragmentary poems invoke the gods and the Muses or contain prayers to Hera or Aphrodite. Others vent Sappho's spleen at the success of a rival, Andromeda. Still others are epithalamia—wedding hymns—celebrating either the unions of her contemporaries, some of them girls she admired, or imagined historical weddings such as that of Fragment 68, which describes the wedding of the long-dead Trojan prince Hector with Andromache.

In another verse (Fragment 102), a speaker complains to her mother that she cannot work her loom because the goddess of love has so smitten her with desire for "a slender boy." Still another rehearses a conversation begun by an apparently smitten young man, a poet named Alkaios, who tries to disguise his desire for "violet-haired" Sappho, who smells to him like honey. Her straightforward response makes clear that she knows what he wants and that he would do better to speak directly.

The poet and translator Paul Roche is among the best at conveying the music and delicacy of Sappho's verse in English. In his slender volume entitled *The Love Songs of Sappho,* he includes verses, numbered 55 and 152, snatched from almost certain oblivion.

Fragment 55 is an epistolary poem addressed "To a Soldier's Wife in Sardis: Anactoria." At one level, it praises the effects of military spectacles such as cavalry columns and flotillas of vessels. It contrasts that martial display, however, with a sight that Sappho prefers—the person one loves. Her perspective is that of a woman in love, as Helen was when she deserted her husband and children and home for love of the Trojan prince, Paris.

The poem's addressee, Anactoria, is presumably the soldier's wife who would much rather see her love than all the parades imaginable. But Anactoria is also beloved by Sappho, and in a graceful turn, the poem moves from implying Anactoria's feelings for her husband to asserting Sappho's feeling for Anactoria. The poet imagines her friend's walk, her style, the vivacity of her facial expression, all of which Sappho had rather see than "Lydian horse / and glitter of mail."

In fragment 152, "Ah, if my breasts could still give suck," by contrast, the reader or listener perceives the voice of a woman past childbearing. She declares that, were she still capable of bearing a child, she would unhesitatingly take another husband. In a touching acceptance of the facts of her situation, however, she comments upon her wrinkled appearance and on the way the god of love avoids her, no longer bringing her "His beautiful pain."

Today, Sappho studies are a thriving industry. The slender remains of the body of her work invite ever-new readings and interpretations. New images of her, moreover, continually emerge as each succeeding epoch reinterprets her significance in a new context. She and her work remain objects of ardent critical attention. Consulting the works in the bibliography below will afford readers a suggestion of the range and degree of interest that Sappho in her various scholarly and popular reincarnations has generated.

See also "I MORE THAN ENVY HIM."

Bibliography

Barnstone, Willis, trans. *Sweetbitter Love: Poems of Sappho.* [Bilingual edition.] Boston: Shambala, 2005.

Greene, Ellen. *Re-Reading Sappho: Reception and Transmission.* Berkeley: University of California Press, 1996.

———— et al. *Reading Sappho: Contemporary Approaches.* Berkeley: University of California Press, 1996.

Reynolds, Margaret. *The Sappho Companion.* New York: Palgrave, 2001.

Roche, Paul, trans. *The Love Songs of Sappho.* Amherst, N.Y.: Prometheus Books, 1998.

satire in Greece and Rome

The Roman orator and rhetorician QUINTILIAN claimed Roman origin for the literary genre of satire. The truth in this statement arises principally from the distinctive form that satire took in Rome. Though such a very early Roman poet as QUINTUS ENNIUS wrote verse that commentators categorized as *saturae*, satire in the later Roman world and in our contemporary sense of that term played a minor role. Ennius's work reflected the original meaning of the word *satura*—a medley or mixture that might include both verse and prose and address a variety of subjects.

The great Roman satirists HORACE, PERSIUS, and JUVENAL, however, consciously looked back to GAIUS LUCILIUS as their original model. Lucilius had written a collection of 30 books of works, now almost totally lost, that he termed *Sermones.* Composed in dactylic hexameter verse (see QUANTITATIVE VERSE), these reflections on his own life and the lives of his acquaintances also included passages of invective against the works of certain authors, against the machi-

nations of politicians, and against conspicuous consumption and gluttony.

Horace's *SATIRES* appeared early in his writing career—book 1 in the 35 B.C.E. and book 2 in 31 B.C.E. Among his models we find a Greek prototype, the somewhat elastic literary mode known as the diatribe. Diatribes were associated with Bion of Scythia (d. 241 B.C.E.) and included written lectures and philosophical discourse, particularly that of the Cynic philosophers (see Cynicism). One can also discern in Horace's satire echoes of passages from Greek comedy that poke sometimes-salacious fun at the objects of their humor.

Horace's satires, however, grow in their sense of humanity and in their urbane sense of purpose. If his early satires ridicule vice, his later ones ridicule vice with the object of helping the vicious reform their morals in the light of generally accepted social values. His satire becomes conversational, ironic, high-minded, and written in splendid verse. His attitude and his handling in verse of the issues that satire addresses become models for later satirists from his time to ours, whether those later satirists composed in verse or in prose.

Persius wrote a bit later than Horace and emulated him while claiming Lucilius as his model. The angriest of the Roman satirists, Persius did not, as Horace did, make peace with the social norms of his times. He abhorred current taste and remained utterly convinced that his contemporary Rome was not just on its way to hell but had already arrived there. The reform of public morals, though it may have been Persius's hope, was not his expectation. The best the moralist could do, he thought, was withdraw from the urban scene. Persius was also the most succinct of the Roman satirists and the least concerned with an audience. His total output was less than 700 lines, and he did not at all care whether or not anyone read them.

A contemporary urban European or American reading Juvenal might well imagine that she was reading the op-ed pieces in her daily newspaper. Juvenal's early voice in his *SATIRES* approaches the vehemence of Persius but also moderates as time passes. Licentiousness, gluttony, the dicey relationships between patrons and clients, the monstrosity of unchaste women, the immoral and relentless pursuit of money, and the decline into vicious notoriety of formerly venerated old families—all these are among the subjects upon which Juvenal casts his satirical gaze. In the process of doing so, an urbane and nihilistic sense of irony replaces the moral outrage with which the satirist began. Like Horace, however, Juvenal was a first-rate poet, and the manner of his verse is as attractive as its matter is interesting.

Conforming more closely to the original notion of the medley, the SATYRICON of PETRONIUS ARBITER is sometimes recounted in prose and sometimes in verse. Usually, as the text romps through a long menu of sexual misbehavior, gluttony, bad taste, and the implicit excoriation of virtually all the characters of the piece and their vices, its authorial voice does not moralize but leaves the readers to draw their own conclusions. From time to time, however, a judgment about degeneracy does emerge. When a principal character, Encolpius, asks the poet Eumolpus about the decadence of the present age, the poet attributes its depravity to drink, debauchery, the neglect of learning, and universal greed.

MARTIAL chose still another set of forms for presenting his satires. Although he did not name people, he drew character portraits of persons who also illustrated types. Among the vicious persons and the pretenders pictured in his EPIGRAMS, we find such sorts as would-be poets, a variety of hypocrites, drunkards, those guilty of many species of sexual misbehavior, and gluttons. He balances such figures—the majority—against a minority of virtuous touchstone characters: good judges of poetic worth, truly talented poets, faithful spouses, and reliable friends. Most of Martial's satiric EPIGRAMS are very short, and many of them were apparently first written at the request of clients. Martial made a living by writing verses to order.

In Greece, the satiric spirit certainly infused the older comedies of such playwrights as ARIS-TOPHANES. Aristophanes would sometimes mount direct satirical attacks on contemporary persons, as he did in his comedy The KNIGHTS. There Aristophanes skewered the Athenian politician and demagogue Cleon, picturing him as an embezzler of public funds. The playwright also makes SOCRATES a figure of ridicule in The CLOUDS, picturing the revered thinker and debater as a corrupt and ineffectual misleader of his students. Ridiculing a whole category of people, in The WASPS, Aristophanes pokes fun at elderly men who will go to almost any extreme to serve on juries. LYSISTRATA seriously satirizes the propensity of men to make war and lightheartedly pokes fun at the sexual appetites of both men and women. One can provide numerous examples from the Greek Old Comedy where satiric mockery was a standard part of the repertoire both of folk festival and dramatic competition (see COMEDY IN GREECE AND ROME).

Though little in the way of evidence survives concerning the Greek Middle Comedy, such vestiges as do remain suggest that the sort of personal invective that Aristophanes practiced in satirizing Socrates and Cleon disappeared from the public stage. Its place was taken by a generic sort of satire that depended on skewering identifiable types of characters. These, in turn, became the stock figures of the New Comedy with which we are principally familiar through Roman playwrights' practice of borrowing its plots. (Greek versions are almost all lost.) Such figures as the braggart soldier, the drunken but resourceful slave, the callow youth, the legacy hunter, and the credulous father became the butts of satirical but usually predictable stage business.

Menippean satire was a kind of verse satire written by the early Cynic philosopher Menippus of Gadara (fl. third century B.C.E.). Though only the titles of a few examples survive, the ancients generally thought that Menippus's work exercised influence on that of the Romans Horace, SENECA, and VARRO.

While the Romans, then, may have perfected the models that posterity has drawn on to inspire the later development of satire, we can see that the roots of the genre are to be found at least as far back as the Greeks and, given the predisposition of human beings both to folly and to passing judgment, likely further back still.

Bibliography

Braund, Susanna Morton, ed. and trans. *Juvenal and Persius*. Cambridge, Mass.: Harvard University Press, 2004.

Ennius, Quintus. *The Annals of Ennius Quintus*. Edited with commentary by Otto Skutsch. Oxford: Clarendon Press; New York: Oxford University Press, 1985.

Henderson, Jeffrey, ed. and trans. *Aristophanes*. 4 vols. Cambridge, Mass.: Harvard University Press, 1998–2002.

Horace. *The Complete Works: Translated in the Meters of the Originals*. Translated by Charles E. Passage. New York: F. Ungar Publishing Company, 1983.

Martial. *Epigrams*. 3 vols. Edited and translated by D. R. Shackleton Bailey. Cambridge, Mass.: Harvard University Press, 1993.

Petronius. *The Satyricon*. Translated by P. G. Walsh. New York: Oxford University Press, 1997.

Seneca, Lucius Annaeus. *Dialogues and Letters*. Translated by C. D. N. Costa. London and New York: Penguin Books, 1997.

Taplin, Oliver. *Literature in the Greek and Roman Worlds: A New Perspective*. Oxford: Oxford University Press, 2000.

Varro, Marcus Terentius. *Opere di Marco Terenzio Varro*. [The works of Marcus Terentius Varro.] Edited by Antonio Traglia. Turin, Italy: Unione Tipografico-editrice Torinese, 1974.

Satires Horace (Book 1, 35 B.C.E.; Book 2, 31 B.C.E.)

Addressed as a friendly letter to HORACE's wealthy patron Gaius Maecenas, *Satires* opens with the famous question *qui fit* (how does it happen that?). First, why are people not satisfied with their situations in life? Why can they not make do with what they have? Horace praises those who work hard in youth and middle life to accumulate enough to see them through old age, but he points up in his first SATIRE the folly of those who never cease trying to accumulate.

Adulterers and the consequences of their behavior become the focus of the second satire of Horace's first book. If one must dally with women, he thinks, prostitutes are a better choice than the seduction of others' wives. In the third satire, Horace appeals for as tolerant an attitude toward the failings of one's friends as one takes toward one's own.

The fourth satire takes satire as its subject, asserting that the archetype of Roman satirists, LUCILIUS, borrowed from the OLD COMEDY of the Greeks everything but the meter. Horace defends his own poetic practice and his conversational style. He notes that he does not recite his verses publicly but only among his friends, and then only when asked. Moreover, he insists, his satire is good-natured and free from malice; it does not lurk as judgment in the guise of compliment. The poet confesses that he has faults, but they are minor, and he judges himself free from major vices. Nonetheless, his minor lapses sometimes become the butt of his humor.

In the succeeding piece, Horace reports on a journey that included a mule-drawn boat trip down a canal to visit friends and on the discomfiting and the amusing incidents that occurred along the way. He then announces that he is proud of his heritage as both the son of a manumitted slave (a freedman) and as a former Roman army officer. He is also grateful that VIRGIL and VARRO had both commended him to Maecenas as a worthy object of literary patronage. He outlines the happy, productive, and uneventful life that Maecenas's patronage has made possible.

Sometimes Horace reports quite trivial incidents, such as a quarrel between two foul-tempered fellows in a courtroom. Sometimes he adopts the voice of an inanimate object, as when he speaks in the first person of the adventures of a carved idol. He reports a chance encounter with a bore who refuses to be put off.

In the final satire of his first book, Horace addresses his critics who apparently have blamed him for writing satire that is not in the manner of Lucilius, the archetypal Roman satirist. Horace responds that Lucilius invented the satiric mode in Latin, having borrowed something from the Greeks but also having invented a new Roman genre. If Lucilius were writing now, Horace insists, he would revise what he had written and prune away its imperfections. Good editing is the essence of good writing, and a good writer is satisfied if his work gives pleasure to his readers.

The first satire of Book 2 is cast as a dialogue between Horace and his companion, the lawyer Trebatius. This satire considers the difficulties that a satirist must face. Horace begins by summarizing the opinions that people hold about his verses: His satire is too harsh, and his poetry lacks liveliness. He asks Trebatius what he should do, and Trebatius tells him to do nothing, that he should just stop writing. This, however, Horace cannot bring himself to do. It is his nature to write. In that case, Trebatius fears, Horace will not live long. Trebatius advises Horace to be careful not to wander into difficulties with the law because the courts punish those who slander others. Horace asks if the courts will punish well-written, true statements. Trebatius replies that in such a circumstances, a court will dismiss the suit.

In the second satire of the second book, Horace gives a predinner lecture to a company of gentlemen on the virtues of the simple life. He begins by pointing out that simple fare is as healthful as delicacies and that chicken tastes the same as peacock. Overindulgence and gourmandizing depress the mind and enervate the body.

A plain meal followed by a nap, on the other hand, leaves a person refreshed and ready for work. An occasional holiday indulgence will not be harmful, but moderation protects health and vigor into old age. On ordinary days, Horace tells us, vegetables and "a hock of smoked pork" was his standard diet. On rainy days, when a friend came by, the holiday meal might include a kid or a hen (but not fish from a city market) and a dessert of fruit and nuts. Horace praises the fruitful sustenance provided by his farm and anticipates the future when the farm will provide for others.

He advises his readers to live courageously and not be daunted by ill fortune.

Book 2, satire 3 begins as a jocular exchange between Damasippus—a bankrupt trader in properties turned Stoic philosopher—and Horace. Damasippus chides Horace for seldom writing anything despite his good intentions. Horace thanks him for his worthless advice but, admitting that Damasippus is right, wonders how his friend knows him so well. Damasippus explains that ever since he lost everything, he has made it his practice to mind other people's business. He describes how, when he lost his business, he was about to commit suicide. His friend Stertinius talked him out of it, however, and encouraged him to become a Stoic philosopher instead.

Damasippus recounts the content of the lecture that saved his life. It was a lecture whose thesis held that all the world is mad—at least that portion of it governed by folly and ignorance. Some are afraid when there is nothing to fear. Others rush headlong into horrible danger or bankrupt themselves pursuing a passion for collecting certain objects. Still others pursue unworthy ambitions, are superstitious, or wear themselves out chasing money. These last are the maddest of all, and Damasippus gives many examples of that particular folly. Among them is the sort of person who, nearing the end of his life and richly provided for, lives like a pauper in anticipation of a need that will never arise. Drawing examples from the pages of history and literature, Damasippus illustrates the madness of those who kill their parents and of those who sacrifice their children on the altars of the gods.

Horace finally wants to know who is not mad. "The man who is not a fool," Damasippus replies. Greedy men are fools and therefore mad. So is anyone who believes in things untrue and whose beliefs are distorted by passion. The impious fall into this category, as do the extravagant. Being in love is madness. Those who seek to avoid death through prayer are mad, as are those who imagine that prayer and sacrifice will cure illness.

When Horace admits that to himself he appears quite sane, Damasippus assures him that many mad persons feel the same way. Horace asks Damasippus to point out symptoms of Horace's madness. Damasippus obliges by suggesting that Horace envies and imitates tall people, though he short. He also faults big people for being too large. As for Horace's poetry, it is fuel to the fire of Horace's madness and leads to "terrible ravings."

Horace interrupts at this point, but Damasippus continues, accusing Horace of living beyond his means and having insatiable sexual appetites. Horace cries for mercy, and the satire ends.

In the fourth satire of Book 2, Horace's friend Catius repeats for him a long series of precepts about food and a few about cleaning the house that he has learned from a lecture and that he finds more useful than the teachings of such famous philosophers as Pythagoras and SOCRATES. When Catius's summary seems interminable, Horace interrupts to inquire the name of the lecturer so that he too may benefit from a direct encounter with the sage.

Satire 5 in book 2 presents a dialogue between the homeward-bound Ulysses in the underworld and the shade of the blind prophet of Thebes, Tiresias, whose spirit Ulysses consulted in Hades. Horace has Ulysses ask the seer one non-Homeric question: How can Ulysses repair his ruined fortune? Tiresias advises Ulysses to become a legacy hunter and to cultivate and flatter wealthy old men. Beyond that, he must defend scoundrels in court. He must manage to be named as second in line for fortunes that have been bestowed on a nonrelative—and then see to it that he outlives the first in line.

To improve one's fortunes, Tiresias suggests allying oneself with the caretakers of wealthy old persons without heirs. He also instructs Ulysses to share the virtuous Penelope with a failing dotard. The hopeful person should not talk too much or too little and should flatter the potential source of a fortune. After further such useful advice, Ulysses' ghostly adviser explains that his time is up. He bids Ulysses farewell with the words: "Live long and prosper."

Horace's patron, Maecenas, the close adviser and friend of AUGUSTUS CAESAR and the wealthiest subject of the empire, had given the poet a farm, which became famous in the annals of literature as the Sabine Farm. The sixth satire of the second book details Horace's happiness there and his gratitude to the gods for his splendid possession. He contrasts the peaceful existence he leads on the farm with the bustle of Rome and the unremitting attempts of self-seekers to use Horace to curry favor with Maecenas.

Horace summarizes his contentment in the country by recounting the universally familiar story of the country mouse and the city mouse, and how the latter convinced the former that he would be happier amid the luxuries available in the city. Convinced, the country mouse tried his friend's mode of life in the city, but as the two were sampling the remains of a sumptuous banquet, the barking of watchdogs frightened the country mouse out of his wits, so that he rushed home and thereafter remained content with his rural manner of life.

In the seventh satire of book 2, Horace's slave, Davus, asks to say something, and Horace grants him "December privilege" to say what he likes. During the December festival of Saturnalia, masters and slaves customarily exchanged roles temporarily. Davus approaches his true subject obliquely, but when Horace chides him, Davus says that he really wants to talk about Horace, who often says one thing but means another and who cannot wait to get to the country when he is in the city and vice versa.

When Horace seems offended, Davus reminds him of his license to speak and proposes a conundrum. If Horace lusts after another man's wife, and if Davus seeks a prostitute, whose lust most deserves punishment? Though Horace is free and Davus is a slave, what person is truly free from obligation to some person or passion that controls him? It is only the wise person who fears neither poverty nor death, who resists the temptations of his passions, who "scorns unworthy ambition," who is not divided within himself, and who is not Fortune's servant. Davus asks Horace to examine his conscience to see if, on any single count, he is worthy to be counted among the wise. Tiring of Davus's sermonizing, Horace sends him away.

The final satire describes a sumptuous banquet hosted by the wealthy Nasidienus. A guest, Fundanius, tells Horace all about the occasion. Fundanius lists the expensive delicacies that were served, tells about a pair of rude guests who insisted upon larger drinking cups so they could get drunk faster, and describes the interruption of the banquet when a ceiling canopy fell, bringing with it a great cloud of dust.

The embarrassed host was comforted by trite remarks about the operation of fortune, and the banquet resumed with course after course of delicacies. A jest, however, lies at the end of the description. Fundanius and his friends, who apparently found the host's discussion of the food's preparation unappetizing, offended their host by running off without eating anything.

Bibliography

Horace. *The Complete Works: Translated in the Meters of the Originals.* Translated by Charles E. Passage. New York: F. Ungar Publishing Company, 1983.

———. *The Complete Works of Horace.* Edited by Casper J. Kramer, Jr. New York: Modern Library, 1936.

Satires Juvenal (ca. early second century C.E.)

In his series of 16 verse SATIRES, JUVENAL alludes to events datable to as early as 96 C.E. and as late, perhaps, as 127. At sometime within that window, or perhaps a little later, the satires were published.

Book 1

As the first of the satires opens, a reader encounters the voice of the satirist, who seems to be an audience member at a poetry reading. The satirist rhetorically asks himself why he must always be in the audience instead of being the poet. He certainly has the education to be a poet, for he has studied the classics of Greece and Rome. There are, however, so many poets that he is reluctant to add yet another voice to the yammer of versifiers—but he must. He is thoroughly enraged by the sorry state of an enfeebled and effeminate Rome. Eunuchs take wives, barbers make fortunes, wealthy old women hire lovers, conspicuous consumption thrives, and crooked politicians and civil servants on the take proliferate. The Roman world, in brief, is turned upside down, and the poet's persona, who is a conventional moralist if also a bit of a prig, quivers with rage at the state of Roman morality. His satiric voice must be heard. Yet he must be careful. Attacking powerful figures by name can be fatal to the attacker. He will be most secure if he vents his fury on famous (or infamous) figures already dead. If readers see parallels between them and the living, that is not the poet's fault.

As Satire 2 opens, the poet takes aim at those men who play the female role in homosexual relationships *and* who denounce others for doing the same thing. He waxes especially vehement when he reports that a male member of the famous Roman political family, the Gracchi, had been given in marriage as the bride. Cowardice and sexual bondage are rife. Religion is dead, and Rome exports its contemporary vices to the ends of the earth—at least as far as Armenia.

In the third satire, Juvenal turns his invective against the city of Rome itself. Her holy places have been let as tenements and her greensward paved over. The authorial voice of Juvenal in the person of one Umbricius asserts that Rome has become an uncongenial place for honest men. One can find a job as a hired assassin or a lookout for thieves. One can live by taking bribes or by becoming a yes-man.

Moreover, Rome has become overly fond of all things Greek. Umbricius complains about the great influx of Greek and other immigrants. Also, the courts have become the pawns of the rich, and a poor man's oath counts for nothing. Prostitution is rampant among all classes. Only wealth counts, class status is determined by property, and the cost of living is soaring so that everyone lives in "pretentious poverty." Everyone ignores the necessities of the impoverished. The noise of traffic is incessant, venturing forth at night is tantamount to taking one's life in one's hands, and one is lucky to make it home having suffered only a beating. Having ended his complaints, Umbricius bids Juvenal farewell.

Satire 4 opens with an invective against an Egyptian upstart, Crispinus, who was among the emperor Domitian's close advisors. Among his other vices, Crispinus is a spendthrift who will pay a fortune for a red mullet.

Having vented a part of his spleen against Crispinus, Juvenal opens a mock EPIC with an invocation of the MUSE of epic poetry, Calliope. He then recites the history of an enormous Adriatic turbot. Once they had netted the fish, the fisherman, rather than have the emperor Domitian's spies claim it had escaped from the imperial ponds, brought the fish as a gift to the emperor. He called a council meeting to determine what should be done with it. Seeing the fish, an imperial adviser, Fabricius Veiento, claimed that it was a harbinger of victory. He prophesied that Domitian would take a royal prisoner.

The council determines that the fish should be prepared whole, and that a special platter should be made to hold it. The meeting adjourns, and Juvenal ends the satire with a reference to the emperor's murderous blood lust.

An age-old feature of Roman social organization was the relationship between a person of high status as a patron and a circle of clients who supported his interests and who, in turn, received the patron's support and protection. In earlier times, both patron and clients understood their common humanity and their essential equality as Roman citizens. Juvenal's fifth satire bemoans the undermining of this ancient and formerly honorable institution by continuing his food metaphor.

In earlier days, both friends and clients used to enjoy the same menu at a patron's table. In Juvenal's satire, however, the patron Virro serves high-quality food and wine to friends and inferior-quality fare to clients. This inequity points up the gulf that Rome's new order has opened between the fabulously wealthy patrons and the clients to whose support the patron is indebted. Juvenal assures the client, Trebius, that his patron has intentionally arranged the feast to humiliate the client and rub his nose in his utter dependence upon the patron. Clients who endure such treatment, Juvenal thinks, are not much better than their patrons.

Book 2

The first five satires comprise book 1 of Juvenal's collection. The poet devotes book 2, however, to a single satire. In length, Satire 6 equals the entire poetic output of Juvenal's predecessor satirist, PERSIUS. This satire is a long diatribe against women and the disappearance of chastity from the earth. Juvenal scornfully reproves a notorious womanizer, Posthumous, for his decision to take a wife. Not only will she be unfaithful, she is also likely to poison her husband. Juvenal then begins to recount the sins of a series of women whom he names as he describes their sexual aberrations. Among the most notorious was Valeria Messalina, the third wife of the emperor Claudius, who worked in a brothel to satisfy her appetites.

Juvenal's picture of women is utterly misogynistic and his anger against them pathologically intense. The satire's women practice every vice, remain constant irritants to their husbands' peace of mind, and make use of potions that will induce abortion. Juvenal then allows himself to rant against the heroines of Greek epic and mythology. Despite all that, the possibility remains that the narrative voice of the satire is distinct from the voice of the poet. It may be that the satiric ranter who so excoriates all women based on the example of a few becomes himself the object of Juvenal's satire and that the poet trusts the reader to recognize the double objects of his invective.

Book 3

Satire 7 begins book 3 with a consideration of the poor financial prospects of poets, historians, advocates, and other intellectuals. Only the emperor himself is likely to become a literary patron, and in a time before royalty arrangements, independent means, or generous patronage provided poets and scholars their principal hope of income. Fine poets require peace of mind and freedom from want to create their best work. Yet Rome wallows in wealth while the talented starve. As for teachers of rhetoric and philosophy, they had better take up teaching music to the wealthy if they expect to earn a decent living. Then as now, though parents expected their children's teachers to assume the role of parental surrogates, they were unwilling to pay them as much in a year as they would give a talented athlete for a single match.

As many commentators have observed, the angry Juvenal of the opening satires has gradually been replaced with a voice that Susanna Morton Braund says belongs to "a nihilist with an acute sense of humour." In the eighth satire, the speaker assures his aristocratic auditor, Ponticus, that taking pride in one's ancestry is pointless. Juvenal lists the attributes that would lead him to respect a Roman diplomat abroad—someone who performs his mission with no thought of enriching himself.

The poet directs the force of his satire against persons of noble ancestry who betrayed their heritage: the emperor Nero, who longed to be a popular entertainer and often cast himself in that role, or the orator and Roman governor of Africa, Catiline, who led a conspiracy against his native land and was finally killed in rebellion against it. Finally, Juvenal argues that anyone who traces his ancestry back far enough will eventually arrive at humble, even disreputable origins.

In the ninth satire, Juvenal revisits the issue of relations between a patron and a client. The poet's persona engages in a dialogue (unique among these satires) with a certain Naevolus. Naevolus explains that his patron, though a married man, wishes to play the female role in sexual encounters, and that Naevolus himself has cooperated in his patron's accomplishing that aim. Moreover, Naevolus has performed the husband's office with his patron's wife and is the real father of the patron's two children. The name *Naevolus* suggests that the character may suffer from a syphilitic condition whose symptoms are evident in the eruptions on his skin. When Naevolus complains about his patron's treatment, Juvenal advises him to find another patron with similar tastes. As in the fourth satire, both patron and client become the objects of Juvenal's invective.

Book 4

Satire 10 begins book 4. In it, Juvenal raises a series of questions about and objections to the practice of prayer and its accompanying sacrifices, and he derides the irrational things that people pray for. Although he clearly finds the entire notion of prayer laughable, he nonetheless offers sound and often-quoted advice about the sorts of things that, if one must pray, one ought to pray for. Pray, he says in an endlessly quoted line, "for a sound mind in a sound body." Other appropriate gifts one might solicit through prayer include a courageous heart, fearlessness in the face of death, and a stout heart capable of "bearing any anguish"—one that does not know anger, that desires nothing beyond what it has, and that prefers toilsome virtue over easeful vice. These gifts, however, are already within the grasp of persons who live good and virtuous lives. Such gifts need not be begged from the gods that men create.

In the 11th satire, Juvenal returns to the image of gourmandizing as a metaphor for the decadence of his contemporary Rome. To show that he himself is immune from the excess that he abhors, he invites a friend to dinner at his country home—his "Triburtine farm." There the friend will find excellent, homegrown fare: a suckling kid, chicken, eggs, wild asparagus, fresh grapes, apples, and two varieties of pears. Such country fare, Juvenal continues, would have been considered sumptuous in the bygone days of Rome's virtue. But now the whole world can hardly supply the exotic dishes considered requisite to a luxurious feast. Moreover, at Juvenal's farm, the guest will be able to speak Latin to Juvenal's virtuous servants rather than Greek or Syrian to a foreign servant spoiled by vice. A guest at Juvenal's party should not expect lavish or licentious entertainment either. Instead, his guests may expect to hear readings from HOMER or VIRGIL. Returning to a consideration of the pleasures available only in the city—chariot racing and attendance at the public baths—Juvenal opines that a steady diet of such things soon proves tedious and concludes: "Pleasures are enhanced by rare indulgence."

Satire 12 ends the fourth book with a consideration of true versus false friendship. Juvenal opens by telling an auditor, Corvinus (whose name means *crow*), about an offering he is making to express his gratitude for the survival of Juvenal's friend, CATULLUS, when the ship in which he was traveling nearly foundered. Juvenal tells the story of Catullus's peril in a long, mock-epic passage. Then Juvenal explains to Corvinus that his attachment to Catullus stems from true friendship and not from the hope of becoming his friend's heir. The friend's name now becomes intertextually significant. For thousands of years, authors have chosen variants or translations of Corvinus as the name for villains who have been legacy seekers. Such false friends whose motive is eventual profit become the targets of the remainder of the 12th satire.

Book 5

The 13th satire parodies a standard rhetorical form: a consolation for persons who have been bereaved. The satire arises from the source of the consolee's bereavement—the loss by Juvenal's friend Calvinus of a paltry sum as the result of false testimony in a lawsuit. Juvenal tries to restore Calvinus's good humor by letting him see the perjurers' viewpoint and the silliness of their victims in hoping that some kind god will intervene on behalf of honesty.

This Juvenal follows with descriptions of similar lawsuits in which the perjuries were worse and the unjust verdicts costlier to the victims. Calvinus, however, is not mollified by these comparisons. He thinks that the gods *ought* to punish perjurers. Juvenal responds by suggesting that guilt punishes itself and that an obsession with revenge is a far worse and more ignoble than perjury. Nonetheless, he assures Calvinus that the perjurer will eventually suffer punishment.

Satire 14 addresses the way that the examples of parents lead their children into the paths of viciousness. Gamblers train gamblers, gluttons tutor gluttons, and philanderers coach philanderers. Bad examples at home corrupt with powerful authority. Masters who mistreat their servants will beget children who do the same. In passing, he also blames the Jewish faith for undermining Roman religion.

Parents pass miserliness along to children. How foolish, thinks Juvenal, to live like a pauper and die rich. Equally foolish is incessant acquisition of property, and most foolish of all is the risk of life and limb in pursuing wealth, particularly by seafaring.

Addressing the question of what constitutes adequacy, Juvenal responds that what thirst and hunger and cold require is enough. He cites the notably frugal examples of SOCRATES and EPICURUS as models for those who wonder how much is sufficient.

The satirist's listener, however, seems unwilling to assent to such modest goals, and when Juvenal suggests greater and greater amounts to answer the question, "How much is enough?"—he finally has to give up trying to reach agreement.

As the 15th satire opens, Juvenal asks Volusius of Bithynia if anyone exists who does not know how the "crazy" Egyptians worship monsters. Moreover, though they worship cats and fish and dogs, and though eating leeks and onions is sinful, cannibalism is condoned among them. While exceptions concerning cannibalism are permissible in times of famine, generally it is a reprehensible practice. There follows an extended example of such reprehensibility that followed when a group of frenzied and drunken Egyptian worshipers got to brawling. One group, the Ombri, routed the others, their neighbors the Tentyra. As the latter fled, one of them fell into the hands of the pursuing Ombri, who instantly tore him to pieces and ate him raw. The horror of the details reveals the depths of Juvenal's cynicism.

The apparent hard-heartedness of this discussion, however, evaporates when Juvenal insists that no true worshipper of the goddess Ceres/ Demeter (or for that matter of any other compassionate deity) "considers the distress of others irrelevant to themselves." This and only this separates rational human beings from the rest of animal creation. The gods expect human beings to cooperate, not always make war. It is a mark of the degree to which human beings fall short of fulfilling their destinies that "there is more harmony among snakes" than people, and that other species are kinder to their members than people are. Weapons are the products of anger. Rakes and hoes would be the better products of human ingenuity.

The last satire, the 16th, is only partly extant. Its manner is once again conversational or epistolary. Juvenal asks his friend Gallus to consider with him the advantages of a military career. The first of these derives from the fear and respect of civilians who know that if they beat you up, swift and overwhelming retribution will follow at the hands of your comrades. The same deterrent reduces the number of lawsuits filed against soldiers—and the number that soldiers find necessary to file since they have the means of taking the law into their own hands.

Other advantages of the military life include soldiers' ability to make wills while their fathers still live, an advantage denied to others under Roman law. After mentioning that some fathers try to get their soldier sons to make them their heirs, the poem breaks off unfinished. Neither ancient nor modern commentators had more of it. The reason that the poem stops is a matter of much critical debate.

Bibliography

Braund, S. H. *Beyond Anger: A Study of Juvenal's Third Book of Satires.* Cambridge and New York: Cambridge University Press, 1988.

Braund, Susanna Morton, ed. and trans. *Juvenal and Persius.* Cambridge, Mass.: Harvard University Press, 2004.

Juvenal. *The Satires of Juvenal.* Translated by Rolfe Humphries. Bloomington: Indiana University Press, 1958.

———. *The Sixteen Satires.* Translated by Peter Green. London and New York: Penguin, 1998.

Satires Persius (ca. 63 c.e.)

Written with utter contempt for the literary tastes of his contemporaries, PERSIUS's satires nonetheless claim a place in the mainstream of the Roman satiric tradition, first by everywhere echoing HORACE both in matter and manner. Second, Persius himself claimed literary kinship with the much earlier Roman satirist LUCILIUS (fl. second century B.C.E.), yet despite that kinship, Persius's satires are utterly distinctive both in their unflagging invective against readers with bad taste and the poets who pander to it and in their promotion of the ideals of STOICISM in an especially undiluted form. Persius's satires are short and pithy. They were edited and published after the poet's death by Caesius Bassus, the friend and poetic colleague to whom the sixth and last of the satires is addressed.

Persius precedes his satires proper with a brief prologue that presages a contrarian poetic performance. Instead of invoking the MUSES and drinking deep from the inspirational waters of the fountain of Hippocrene, Persius denies having wet his lips at "the nag's spring"—the fountain sprung from the hoof print of the winged horse Pegasus. Persius implies that the Muses and their worshippers, the poets, only serve their bellies and are interested only in cash. Persius's poetic form in his prologue supports his contrarian position as he chooses to begin his satires, not with the usual dactylic hexameters but with the scazon or limping iambic meter associated with invective. After the prologue, he reverts to the more usual meter. (See QUANTITATIVE VERSE)

In Satire 1, Persius draws an extended and sometimes subtle comparison between the practice of sodomy and the relationship between poets and their readers in the Rome of his day. Gone, he implies, is the manly virtue of the early Romans. Instead, his male audience is composed of overfed sensualists. Poets are worse. They have added "elegance and smoothness" to the "raw rhythms" of the old poetry that Persius clearly prefers. Contemporary taste runs to entertainments and games in public places and novels with incredible plots that rely on a standard palette of incident and coincidence to resolve their facile and predictable plots—novels like those of the Greek writer Chariton of Aphrodisias (see GREEK PROSE ROMANCE).

Persius's second satire berates the self-interested prayers of persons who feign honoring the gods and instead pray continually for the increase of their fortunes and flocks. Its last three lines suggest the sort of prayer and offering the gods would find acceptable in place of gold and sacrificial animals: justice and righteousness properly blended in the human mind and spirit, purity of thought, and a noble heart. Given these, the gods will find "a handful of grits" an acceptable sacrifice.

Satire 3 sustains a dialogue between a hungover student and an unidentified speaker—perhaps his conscience—who reproves the student's excesses and tries to guide him to a productive path. The unidentified speaker excoriates the student (and all like him) who repent such excesses as their habitual drunkenness when the excesses make them fall ill, but who, as soon as they feel recovered, resume their bad habits until, finally, they die from them.

In the fourth satire, Persius still employs the verse dialogue but sets it this time in the mouth of SOCRATES. The Greek philosopher reproves his student Alcibiades, ward of Pericles, for egocentrism and lack of self-knowledge. Persius's Socrates is an ill-tempered, foul-mouthed reviler of self-deception. Instead of kindly advice to "know thyself," the Socrates of the dialogue instructs his student to "spit out what isn't you!"—a revision in the spirit of the extreme Stoic minimalism that Persius practiced.

Persius's fifth satire begins in the poet's own voice as he tells his old teacher, the Stoic philosopher Cornutus, first of the excesses of poets and then of the debt of gratitude and affection that Persius owes Cornutus for teaching him that one's own rhetorical voice could be as effective as or more effective than a 100-tongued poet in finding and uttering the truth. The poet also acknowledges Cornutus's contribution to Persius's clear thinking. He offers a catechism for those who seek the truth: Do you have moderate desires? Is your household frugal? Are you kind to your friends? Can you pass up a profit? When one can answer yes to those questions, one is on the road to living freely. Persius then sneers at those who believe that achieving freedom from greed relies on imagining there is a life beyond the grave, on gratifying the senses, on flattery and ambition, and on the signs and portents that priests interpret.

The poet casts Satire 6 as a letter to his friend, the lyric poet Caesius Bassus. Written from Persius's retreat on the Ligurian coast of Italy, where he has withdrawn from Rome, this satire celebrates the freedom from apprehension that his isolation brings him. At the same time, he recognizes a responsibility to help a friend in need of money. Apparently, doing so brought Persius (or the persona that the poem creates) a reproof from an heir who thought the poet should be hoarding his cash to pass on at the time of his death.

Annoyed, the Persius persona ironically informs the heir that Persius is financing 100 pairs of gladiators in an entertainment to celebrate the emperor Caligula's military successes in Gaul—a clearly ironic suggestion since Caligula's principal success during the campaign of 39–40 was avoiding death at the hands of assassins. The point, however, is that Persius can do whatever he wishes with his own funds, and he need not concern himself with preserving his estate for the benefit of an heir. After growing quite hot-tempered about this topic, Persius breaks off the last of his satires.

Bibliography

Braund, Susanna Morton, ed. and trans. *Juvenal and Persius*. Cambridge, Mass.: Harvard University Press, 2004.

Ramsay, G. G., ed. and trans. *Juvenal and Persius*. New York: G. P. Putnam's Sons, 1940.

Saturnalia, The See MACROBIUS.

Saturnian verse

The prosodic system of classical Latin imitated Greek in using an arbitrary system of QUANTITATIVE VERSE meter. The native, primitive Latin system relied instead on patterns of stressed and unstressed syllables to give its poetry cadence, very much as modern English does. Primitive Latin verse also relied on the repetition of consonant sounds—alliteration—for its effect.

Saturnian verse was so called because it was thought to have survived from the first age of humankind—the age of Saturn, or the Golden Age. Very few representatives of Saturnian verse proper survive. One of the survivors is the text of a hymn sung by the Arval brotherhood. This was a college of 12 priests whose function was to invite the favor of the gods of the harvest—gods that included the guardian spirits of Rome and Mars, the god of war in later times but an agricultural spirit early in Roman history. Remnants also survive of hymns sung in Saturnian verse by the Salian college of priests whose particular function is not altogether clear. It too was probably agrarian in character. PLAUTUS and TERENCE used both accentual verse of the older Saturnian sort and quantitative meter of the Greek sort in their plays, many of which imitated Greek originals.

satyr plays

A satyr play was annually presented at the GREAT DIONYSIA in Athens in conjunction with three tragedies in a contest among playwrights. The satyr play was the last to be performed, featuring characters acted by performers wearing the same costumes they had worn in the TRAGEDY. A satyr play was similar in form to the tragedies that preceded it except that it dealt with bizarre incidents and the members of its CHORUS dressed in goatskin breeches to affect the appearance of satyrs—the half-human, half-goat spirits or creatures who were thought, like the god Pan, to inhabit the lonely reaches of the countryside. Satyr plays were associated with Greek tragedy from a very early epoch, and some argue that the tragic form arose from earlier satyr plays that may have been performed in connection with the ritual sacrifice of a goat.

Only one satyr play survives in its entirety, EURIPIDES' *CYCLOPS*. The classicist Richard A. S. Seaford tells us that satyr plays became separated from their accompanying tragedies in Greece and continued being performed independently after the mid-fourth century B.C.E. Seaford also suggests that the type appeared on the Roman stage as late as the second century C.E.

Bibliography

Seaford, Richard. *Cyclops, Euripides*. Oxford: Clarendon Press; New York: Oxford University Press, 1988.

Wilson, Peter. "Powers of Horror and Laughter: The Great Age of Drama." In *Literature in the Greek and Roman World: A New Perspective*. Edited by Oliver Taplin. Oxford: Oxford University Press, 2000.

Satyricon Petronius Arbiter (ca. 61 C.E.)

Nowhere else in the annals of literature does anything quite like PETRONIUS ARBITER's *Satyricon* exist. With exquisite literary taste and good humor, its fragmentary remnants mock the pretensions of rhetorical flourish that characterized Roman and Greek oratory under the continuing influence of the Greco-Sicilian rhetorician GORGIAS OF LEONTIUM. *Satyricon* also mocks most other pretensions, behavioral as well as literary, while it treats scandalously salacious material with unpretentious aplomb.

Often moving without transition from episode to episode, composed sometimes in prose and sometimes in verse, *Satyricon* frequently parodies and sometimes directly criticizes the literary claptrap of its time. What remains to us of a very much longer work begins, in fact, with the young protagonist Encolpius's critique of rhetoric as it is taught in schools, holding up the examples of PINDAR, HOMER, PLATO, DEMOSTHENES, THUCYDIDES, and Hyperides as correctives to the sterile and artificial conventions of schoolroom rhetoric and style as taught in Petronius's time.

A teacher of rhetoric named Agamemnon, however, interrupts Encolpius's diatribe. He points out that, though he knows what he teaches is twaddle, what he offers is what his paying students expect. He blames the parents for establishing such expectations and offers a piece of advice in verse to would-be poets: study Homer, then logic, and then the Socratic philosophers. Next, adopt as a rhetorical model the speeches of Demosthenes tempered by the Roman practice of CICERO. Such a regimen will invite the EPIC MUSE to claim the would-be poet as her own.

While the narrator is still listening to Agamemnon, Ascyltus, Encolpius's roommate, slips away unobserved. The narrator goes in search of him, and by chance the roommates encounter one another in a brothel to which both have been led—Encolpius by a female procurer and Ascyltus by an enamored pederast. Later, however, Encolpius finds that Ascyltus has been assaulting the lad, Giton, who cooks for the pair, and after an argument and reconciliation, Encolpius and Ascyltus decide to part company. Encolpius admits that the separation is motivated by his own desire for Giton. The episode ends with a returned Ascyltus catching the pair in bed and beating his former roommate with a leather strap.

The next fragment deals with the now-reunited roommates' recovery of a stolen garment with gold sewn into its seams. A missing portion of text seems to have described the pair's interruption of a fashionable woman named Quartilla as she and her maid Psyche participated in the rites of the god of masculine sexuality, Priapus. The text resumes with the appearance of the two women and a little girl at the inn of the young men, seeking a cure for Quartilla's malaria and assurance that the rites the lads observed will remain secret. The cure involves an extended though highly fragmentary orgy in which Encolpius, Ascyltus, and Giton become the principle

means for satisfying Quartilla and company's insatiable appetites, both participatory and voyeuristic.

The next section of *Satyricon* ranks among the most famous banqueting scenes in all of literature, the celebrated "Dinner with Trimalchio." The dinner itself parodies other famous literary banquets and discussions from the annals of classical literature, such as Plato's *SYMPOSIUM* or his *Timaeus*. The host of Petronius's banquet, Trimalchio, is a nouveau riche, egocentric millionaire who throws away silver serving dishes that happen to fall on the floor, serves wine rather than water for washing in fingerbowls, and offers his guest 100-year-old vintages as table wine. Trimalchio also enjoys a little joke at his guests' expense, serving them not-very-appetizing fare as the top layer of a two-tiered serving trolley whose second layer contained a sumptuous feast of the most expensive and appetizing foods imaginable.

The reader also meets Trimalchio's wife, Fortunata, risen from near untouchability to become a shrew whose likes and dislikes can make and break important persons. When a call of nature takes the host away from the table, the guests seize the opportunity to speak of the matters on their minds. They bewail the loss of the good old days. They speak of people disinherited of fortunes and fortunes left to strangers. The conversation parodies that of people looking for their main chance and hoping to make some money.

On Trimalchio's return, he reveals his utter lack of taste by sharing with the guests the details of the state of his innards and encouraging his guests to deal with any similar necessities that may develop. Encolpius imagines that entertainment of some sort will follow the enormous quantity of food that has already been served. Instead, three live hogs of varying sizes are led in, and the guests are asked to select the one they want prepared for dinner. They do so, and in a remarkably short time a roasted pig—seemingly larger than the largest of the three live ones—arrives from the kitchen. Someone announces, however, that the cook forgot to gut the animal before cooking it.

The cook is stripped, preparatory to being punished. The guests intercede, and the cook is ordered to gut the pig in everyone's presence. He hacks away at the carcass, and instead of intestines, fine sausages and blood puddings tumble forth.

A game follows in which guests receive humorous presents depending on what message appears on papers they draw from a jar. When Encolpius and his friends become amused by something and break into laughter, a former slave takes drunken offense and begins to threaten them. He perversely illustrates a kind of reverse snobbism as he takes pride in his former condition of servitude and imagines slights where none are intended.

After professional entertainment and gift giving, Trimalchio introduces his household gods: Fat Profit, Good Luck, and Large Income. Then the host invites a guest to tell a story. The guest obliges with the tale of a werewolf. Trimalchio himself responds with a story about witchcraft and a strong man killed by it.

Various displays of bad taste ensue. Among them, Trimalchio invites some of his slaves to join the guests at the table, where he announces to the assembled company his intention to free them all when he dies and to leave his money to Fortunata. He wants all his household to know his plans so that they will love him as much while he lives as they will after his death. He then describes in detail the sumptuous tomb that he plans for himself. Among other things, he specifies a statue of himself, another of his dog, a third of Fortunata, garlands of flowers, jars of perfume, and depictions of every fight that his favorite boxer has ever won. He also specifies his epitaph, shaped like a funeral urn and listing as chief among his accomplishments the fact that he never listened to philosophers. He then bursts into tears and mourns his own inevitable passing.

Recovering from his paroxysm of grief, Trimalchio invites everyone to his baths, where the water has been heated. Encolpius and Ascyltus agree to sneak away from the party, but they fail and so must join the others. Following the bath, the guests are led to a second dining room where drinking until dawn is the order of the night. Discovering that his slaves have not eaten anything as yet, Trimalchio sends them off to dine as a relief crew arrives. One of these is a very attractive boy. The attentions that Trimalchio lavishes on him incite Fortunata to rail at her husband, who strikes her in the face with a heavy wine cup. She weeps while Trimalchio recalls his wife's previous life as a prostitute. In his anger, he cancels his order for a statue of her in his tomb.

Utterly drunk, Trimalchio preaches his own eulogy, bragging of his mercantile accomplishments. Then he reverts to mourning his own death, orders his grave clothes brought in, anoints himself with spikenard—a perfume used to mask the odor of death—and orders the band to play a dirge. They do, but the neighborhood firemen think that the noise is a fire alarm and rush in with buckets and axes. In the ensuing confusion, Encolpius and company make their getaway.

Because of Giton's foresight in using chalk to blaze their path from the inn in which they were lodged to the party, the trio eventually makes its way home. There, however, they find themselves locked out until one of Trimalchio's agents happens by and forces an entry.

Once in their quarters, Ascyltus again snares Giton for his own bed and pleasure. This time, Encolpius insists that the roommates definitively part company. Ascyltus agrees, and the two share out the belongings they have held in common. Then, drawing his sword, Ascyltus insists on having his half of Giton. The rivals are about to fight when Giton intervenes and calms them. They agree to let Giton choose between them, and to Encolpius's chagrin, Giton chooses to leave with Ascyltus.

After three days of melodramatic self-pity, Encolpius grows angry once again, vows to kill them both, girds on his sword, and rushes off in search of the pair. A soldier, however, steals his sword, and when Encolpius's anger passes, he is glad that he has not murdered anyone.

In the 83rd chapter of *Satyricon*, Encolpius, while admiring the pictures in an art gallery, meets the poet Eumolpus, who tells him a story of pederasty. Billeted in a house in Asia where there was a handsome youth, Eumolpus pretended to be so offended at the very mention of pederasty that no one suspected his predilection for that activity. As a result, he was often entrusted with squiring the boy to school and supervising his activities. Eumolpus then details the way that he succeeded in seducing the lad, and the vengeance in kind that the boy visited on him when Eumolpus failed to produce a promised stallion.

When Encolpius asks the poet about the decadence of the present age, Eumolpus attributes its depravity to drink, debauchery, the neglect of learning, and universal greed. Then, observing Encolpius's interest in a painting of the fall of Troy, Eumolpus launches into his own poem commenting on the events depicted in the painting. Other gallery patrons respond to Eumolpus's impromptu recitation with a volley of stones. He flees, Encolpius follows, and the poet confesses that his audiences generally respond the same way when he recites in the theater.

The two visit the public baths, where Encolpius encounters a repentant Giton. Giton begs to be restored to his former favor. He claims that when two armed men were about to commit mayhem over him, he did the reasonable thing and went with the stronger, but his affections really lie with Encolpius. Pleased, Encolpius accepts the boy back. Eumolpus, however, arrives and, to Encolpius's annoyance, finds Giton attractive.

A growing rivalry for the lad's affection estranges Encolpius from Eumolpus, who finally suffers a beating at the hands of a drunken innkeeper and his equally drunken guests, while a jealous Encolpius refuses Giton's entreaties to unlock their door and save Eumolpus. He is saved nonetheless by one of the few admirers of his poetry, Bargates the caretaker.

In the meantime, Ascyltus has offered a reward for information leading to his recovery of Giton. While Ascyltus and a policeman begin a room-by-room search of the inn, Giton conceals himself in a mattress. The searchers fail to discover him. Eumolpus now enters and threatens to reveal all as his revenge for Encolpius's having allowed him to be beaten. Encolpius begs him not to accuse him and swears that Giton has run off. The lad's sneezes, however, expose that lie. Released from his hiding place, Giton manages to smooth things over between the two men, and as the 99th chapter ends, the three embark together upon a voyage.

Once the ship weighs anchor, Encolpius and Giton discover that the goddess Fate has delivered them into the hands of the very people they most wish to avoid—Lichas of Tarentum, the captain of the ship, and a woman, Tryphaena, who spends her life roaming about in search of pleasure. Both these persons have some unspecified score to settle with the two younger voyagers. After rejecting a series of suggestions for concealment and altering their appearances, Encolpius and Giton agree to be shorn and emblazoned with the marks of runaway slaves. A seasick passenger observes their shearing and curses them for inviting ill luck by emulating the last offering of shipwrecked sailors—shaving their heads.

Both Lichas and Tryphaena have dreams that reveal the presence of those they seek, and the seasick passenger identifies those who were shorn. Encolpius and Giton are sentenced immediately to suffer 40 lashes each. Encolpius bears his stoically, but Giton cries out and Tryphaena recognizes his voice. One incredible situation follows another as pleas for punishment and for forgiveness are bandied about. The ship's crew and passengers take sides until everyone except the ship's pilot is fighting. Finally, Tryphaena plays the role of peacemaker, and all resolve to become friends and observe certain conditions.

Wigs and false eyebrows restore their good looks to Encolpius and Giton, and Eumolpus volunteers to tell a tale that will prove all women can be seduced. He tells of an inconsolable widow who accompanied her husband's body to the tomb in the shadow of crosses upon which several thieves had been crucified. Assisted by the widow's maid, the soldier guarding the thieves' bodies laid siege to the widow's affections, which on that very night and for two more nights thereafter he enjoyed in the privacy of her former husband's tomb. The parents of one of the crucified thieves, however, noticed that the watchman was missing, and they stole their son's body. The watchman, fearing the horror of the punishment that would befall him for deserting his post and losing a body, prepared to commit suicide, but his beloved offered her dead husband's body as a substitute and resolved the problem. The next morning, the entire city was astounded that a dead man had managed to mount a cross.

While this tale is told, Tryphaena toys amorously with Giton, and Encolpius suffers from the flames of jealousy.

After a brief lacuna in the text, the story resumes with the description of a sea storm and shipwreck. As nearby fishermen struggle to save the passengers, Eumolpus makes his own rescue difficult by trying to immortalize the incident in verse.

The next day, the survivors discover the body of Lichas, which leads Encolpius to pronounce an *ubi sunt* (where are they?) epitaph. "Where are Lichas's anger and greatness now?" Encolpius wants to know.

The survivors make their way in the direction of an Italian city called Croton (Crotona), a place, as a wayfarer tells them, populated only by those who make wills and those who pursue will makers—that is, by the rich and by those who would inherit wealth through trickery. This intelligence gives Eumolpus an idea about how he and his companions might turn this new situation to their advantage.

By pretending to be a rich Roman of Africa attended by his servants, Eumolpus hopes to become a parasite sucking at the fortunes of those who would become a rich man's heirs. He becomes, in other words, one of the originals of the Renaissance English playwright Ben Jonson's *Volpone*.

As the company makes its way toward Croton, Eumolpus discourses about his views concerning the composition of poetry, illustrating them with his own verses on the subject of the Roman civil wars. At this point, it is hard to reject the notion that Eumolpus's poetic assertions have become a thin veil for Petronius's own voice. Among many of Eumolpus's conclusions, he suggests that "degenerates inherit Rome." He accuses them of sumptuary greed and makes reference to the building of lavish edifices whose foundations displace the bones of the honored dead. One thinks immediately of Nero's own proclivities for an immodest style of life. Into the text of a salacious romp, Petronius has suddenly inserted a serious poem on the decline and fall not only of the Roman republic but also of the ancient and virtuous Roman moral order.

The plan to bilk the inheritance seekers of their wealth, however, works admirably as those who aspire to inherit Eumolpus's supposed wealth shower him with gifts, and all his associates gain weight. The fragment breaks off as Encolpius describes the fears he is beginning to experience, fears that the scam will fail.

The story resumes with Encolpius's having unintentionally attracted the love of a lady named Circe. Her maid brings the two together, but at the crucial moment, Encolpius's manhood fails him as his thoughts turn to Giton. Circe forgives him, and he tries again. But once more he fails, and in her frustration and rage, Circe has him flogged and her entire household beaten as well. Utterly put out with himself, Encolpius makes several not very effective attempts at self-emasculation, but a little comic poem inserted in the text details his failure to achieve that aim. Then, in a mercurial change of mood, Encolpius speaks in what sounds suspiciously like Petronius's own voice, asserting Epicurean philosophy and the realism of the matters he chooses to write about and the purity of the style in which he writes of them.

Still afflicted by impotence, Encolpius prays to his patron deity, Priapus, and seeks the services of a witch, Onothea, to restore him to his former virility. This does not go well, though, and Encolpius has the misfortune to kill the god Priapus's pet goose. Bits and pieces of the attempted cure survive beyond that point, but the whole episode ends with the witch and her confederate chasing Encolpius down the street and crying "thief!"

In the succeeding and final fragments, first, Chrysis, Circe's servant, conceives a violent passion for Encolpius. Second, a fortune hunter named Philomela entrusts her teenaged children to Eumolpus for instruction in some rather acrobatic amatory engagements, and finally Encolpius recovers from his affliction. Beyond that, signs appear that Eumolpus's con game has about run its course. Eumolpus therefore makes his will, requiring that anyone wishing to share in his inheritance must be willing to eat his deceased flesh, and the final fragment ends with a recitation of several instances of similar cannibalism.

Among the many good translations of *Satyricon*, that of William Arrowsmith is particularly enjoyable.

Bibliography

Corbett, Philip B. *Petronius.* New York: Twayne Publishers, Inc., 1970.

Heseltine, Michael, trans. *Petronius.* New York: G. P. Putnam's Sons, 1925.

Petronius. *The Poems of Petronius.* [Selections.] Translated by Edward Courtney. Atlanta, Ga.: Scholars Press, 1991.

———. *Satyrica: Petronius.* Translated and edited by R. Bracht Branham and Daniel Kenney. Berkeley: University of California Press, 1996.

———. *The Satyricon.* Translated by P. G. Walsh. New York: Oxford University Press, 1997.

———. *The Satyricon.* Translated by William Arrowsmith. New York: New American Library of World Literature, 1964.

scazon   See QUANTITATIVE VERSE.

scholion, scolion

A scholion (plural scholia) is a note about or a commentary on a passage of literature. Where ancient literature is concerned, sometimes all we know about an ancient writer or about an ancient work is the commentary that remains in passages penned by later scholars. At other times, scholia give us glimpses into the reception encountered by ancient works among their readership.

Similar in spelling but with an entirely different meaning is a similar word, *scolion* (plural *scolia*), describes a particular sort of Greek lyric poetry. Examples of scolia included songs written for particular social events such as banquets and festivals. Guests or participants at such occasions sang scolia to harp accompaniment. The literary type flourished in Greece from about the seventh through the fourth centuries B.C.E.

Bibliography

Dickey, Eleanor. *Ancient Greek Scholarship: A Guide to Finding, Reading, and Understanding* Scolia, *Commentaries,* Lexica, *and Grammatical Treatises from Their Beginning to the Byzantine Period.* New York and Oxford: Oxford University Press, 2006.

Eschenburg, J. J. *Manual of Classical Literature.* Translated by N. W. Fiske. Philadelphia: E. C. & J. Biddle, 1850.

Scylax of Caryanda   See GEOGRAPHY AND GEOGRAPHERS, GREEK AND ROMAN.

Second Letter of Clement to the Corinthians, The (ca. second century C.E.)

Included as the second entry in the collection *The APOSTOLIC FATHERS OF THE CHRISTIAN CHURCH*, this document is not a letter, nor was it written by the Clement who was supposed to have written its predecessor document. Rather, as its most recent and authoritative translator, Bart D. Ehrman, tells us, it seems to be a somewhat later, but still very early, Christian homily delivered at a regular service of worship. It instructs the members of the congregation to regard with "awe, wonder, and gratitude" God's concern that has brought them, former pagans, into the fold of Christian believers.

The homily undertakes an interpretation of the Hebrew Bible text Isaiah 54:1, which exhorts the infertile and childless to rejoice aloud as they have more offspring than fertile parents. The preacher's interpretation is anagogical—that is, it strives to make an application of the text to the situation in which the early Christian congregation finds itself as it relates to future glory—to life in the world to come. The adherents of Christianity, says the preacher, must acknowledge their obligation to God, for they are the beneficiaries of Christ's sacrifice on their behalf. Christians must therefore renounce sinful ways and repent, focusing on their anagogical offspring, that is on their new lives in the next world, which will last forever, rather than on their existence in this fallen, temporal one.

Notable among the preacher's exhortations and scriptural citations are some drawn from such sources as the GOSPEL OF THOMAS—sources eventually excluded from received Scripture, but sources nonetheless thought of and preserved as Scripture among such ancient collections as the Nag Hammadi manuscripts (see GNOSTIC APOCRYPHA AND PSEUDEPIGRAPHA). Also compelling for those interested in the development of early Christian thought and ecclesiastical practice is the fact that, in addition to appealing to what is evidently an ORAL FORMULAIC TRADITION about the life of Jesus, the preacher of the homily also appeals to scriptural authority, not only to that of the HEBREW BIBLE but also to the writings of Paul and to an emergent tradition of compositions presumed to be those of the apostles—the nucleus of material from which the approved NEW TESTAMENT would eventually emerge.

All speculations about the author of the homily are so tenuous that nothing would be gained from reconsidering them here. Internal evidence leads Ehrman to guess that the homily has a mid-second-century provenance. This in itself lends the work the distinction of being the earliest non-canonical homily. It also illustrates the nature of early homiletic form and suggests that the interests of both preacher and congregation focused on ethical action and charity rather than on abstruse questions of theology. The homily also espouses a canon of Christian behavior that sets the members of the congregation apart from their pagan neighbors, among whom the congregation's members still lived.

Bibliography

Ehrman, Bart D, ed. and trans. "Second Letter of Clement to the Corinthians." In *The Apostolic Fathers.* Vol. 1. Cambridge, Mass.: Harvard University Press, 2002.

Sedulius, Caelius (fl. fifth century C.E.)

A Christian, devotional poet, Sedulius seems to have been a presbyter or an elder in the church. Possibly an Irishman, he is best remembered for *Carmen paschale,* an Easter song on the subject of divine miracles. He sent this work together with an explanatory letter addressed to a priest named Macedonius. He also wrote a poem about the Old and NEW TESTAMENTS in a complex and repetitive meter. The poem showed the way that the prophecies of the HEBREW BIBLE were revealed in the New Testament, and the form of the poem was chosen to reinforce its content.

His alphabetical poem "A solis ortus cardine," in which each of 23 lines begins with a different letter, is a hymn addressed to Christ. Another fragmentary remnant of Sedulius's work exists, but it is of more interest to cartographers than to students of literature. Though editions of Sedulius's work appeared in Polish, Dutch, and German in the 1990s, no English edition has emerged since 1922.

Bibliography

Sedulius. *The Easter Song.* Dublin: The Talbot Press, 1922.

Self-Tormentor, The (*Heauton Timorumenos*) Terence (163 B.C.E.)

In composing his Latin version of *The Self-Tormentor,* TERENCE took MENANDER's Greek

COMEDY of the same name and complicated it. In the first place, Terence doubled the plot, as he had also done in his *ANDRIA*. In the second place, he moved the recognition scene that closes the action in Menander's play; Terence put his recognition in the middle of the play so that it became a springboard for his plot's further complication. *The Self-Tormentor* was the third of his comedies to be performed on the Roman stage.

The play opens with a prologue that defends Terence against the criticisms of his enemies—especially that of a competing poet, Luscius Lanuvinus. The speaker of the prologue also hopes the audience will approve his performance so that he, an old actor, may aspire to better parts.

Act 1 begins with the arrival onstage of Chremes. Finding Menedemus already there and hard at work, Chremes reproves him for working too hard at his advanced age. Menedemus suggests that Chremes does not seem to have enough of his own business to mind, and says that he *must* work as he is a self-tormentor.

When Chremes snatches Menedemus's rake away, Menedemus tells his story. He has driven away his son, Clinia, by being overly harsh in blaming the youth for his love affair with a young woman. Clinia has run off to work for the king of Persia. To punish himself, Menedemus has sold off all his slaves and bought a farm where, as a form of penance, he will do everything himself until his son returns.

Chremes returns to his own door, for he has guests awaiting him. Just as he arrives, the door creaks open. Chremes conceals himself and over-hears his son, Clitipho, talking with the very Clinia who was supposedly in Asia but has just returned. We learn that Clinia is afraid of his father's reaction. He also fears that in his absence, his mistress may have ceased loving him.

Act 2 opens with a brief soliloquy in which Clitipho rehearses his own troubles. He, too, has a mistress, but she is overbearing and disreputable, and Clitipho is ashamed to admit that he has nothing to give her. In the second scene, Clinia is awaiting the arrival of his mistress with presentiments of ill success.

In the third scene of act 2, two slaves, Syrus and Dromo, enter. They have been escorting the women's sizable entourage, but as the slaves fell to gossiping, they outdistanced their charges, who are nowhere to be seen now. In addition to being burdened down with jewels and clothing and having a retinue of maidservants, Clinia's mistress does not know her way to the house, and Dromo goes to find the group.

Syrus puts Clinia's mind at ease by assuring him that his beloved Antiphila is still chaste, poor, and devoted to Clinia. The other lady is Clitipho's beloved Bacchis. Syrus assures Clitipho that he may enjoy Bacchis's company in his father's house. Moreover, as Clitipho has promised Bacchis money, Syrus promises to get it. For his plan to succeed, however, everyone will have to pretend that Bacchis is Clinia's mistress while Antiphila will be taken to stay with Clitipho's mother. Clitipho grudgingly assents to this plan.

In the fourth scene, Bacchis and Antiphila arrive. Bacchis praises Antiphila for leading a chaste and solitary life and says that it is in Antiphila's interest to be good, just as it is in Bacchis's interest to be otherwise. The devoted married life is a surer path for a woman than is the life of a courtesan who bids farewell to her livelihood when she loses her looks. Despite Syrus's plan, Clinia and Antiphila see one another and rush into each other's arms. Syrus hurries them into the house lest Menedemus see his son with the girl.

As act 3 opens, the next morning has dawned, and it occurs to Chremes to tell Menedemus that his son Clinia has returned. Chremes encounters Menedemus, who is soliloquizing about how much he misses Clinia. Chremes tells Menedemus that Clinia is in the former's house, but he advises his friend to wait and not appear to have given over his stern and critical ways.

That advice rests on Chremes' misapprehension that Bacchis is Antiphila. He believes that the formerly chaste young woman was driven by want to take up the life of a courtesan. Whereas in her former impoverished condition, Menedemus might have acquired her as a daughter-in-law with little expense, her price has now risen. In order to keep her price as low as possible, Menedemus must still seem to disapprove. At the very least, he must not be thought to be willingly generous with his money. Rather, he must appear to be deceived by the plots that the slaves are concocting—plots that Chremes has observed hatching. To do otherwise means that Menedemus will thereafter be subject to any whim of his son—whims that Menedemus must satisfy or risk his son's running off again.

In the next scene, Chremes encourages his slave Syrus to arrange a scheme to bilk Menedemus of some money. At the same time, the master challenges the slave not to imagine he can also pull the wool over Chremes' eyes.

In the third scene, Terence's plot grows even more complex. Syrus tells Chremes that Bacchis has brought with her a young girl, now with Chremes' wife. The girl was pledged as security for a debt. Bacchis wants Clinia to pay Bacchis the money, and she will hand the girl over. Answering for Menedemus, Chremes says that Menedemus will not pay. To Chremes' confusion, Syrus approves of that answer.

Just then, as act 4 begins, Chremes' wife Sostrata enters with a nurse. They are examining a ring that Sostrata believes was left with her infant daughter when, owing to his poverty, Chremes made her expose their infant daughter. (Leaving infants to die or be preserved by strangers was a not-uncommon practice in real life and a frequent one in fiction.) Sostrata tells Chremes that she did not herself expose the child; rather, she gave her to an elderly Corinthian woman. Chremes reproves his wife for not following through but, as usual, forgives her. Then he wants to know why she has brought up this issue.

Sostrata explains that Antiphila was wearing the ring, and Syrus is surprised to think that Antiphila may be Chremes' daughter. Syrus, who had a role in all this, begins to grow fearful, but Chremes, whom necessity forced to reluctantly expose his child, begins to grow hopeful.

In the next scene, Syrus racks his brain for a plan that will replace the one that the revelation about the ring destroyed. An idea comes to him.

In the third scene, Clinia enters. He is ecstatic over his coming marriage to Antiphila. Syrus says that if Clinia leaves with her, Chremes will know that Bacchis is Clitipho's mistress. The slave requires some delay in clarifying the situation if his plan to enrich himself at his master's expense is to succeed.

The courtesan Bacchis opens the next scene by saying that Syrus owes her 10 *minae*—a considerable sum—for her role in the slave's current plot. Syrus tells a fellow slave, Dromo, to move Bacchis and all her entourage and luggage into the house of Menedemus. This will lead to a ruse by which Syrus will convince Chremes to part with 10 *minae*.

In the fifth scene of act 4, Syrus explains to Chremes that Clinia has revealed to Menedemus that Bacchis is really the mistress of Clitipho. Syrus says that Bacchis and her companions moved to keep that knowledge from Chremes. Syrus cleverly manages to convince Chremes that, to set his daughter free, he must pay the money Bacchis demands. Chremes says that he will give her the money, but Syrus suggests that Clitipho deliver it instead, and they arrange the matter in this way. In the next scene, Syrus explains to Clitipho that the money is coming. In scene 7 of act 4, Syrus and Clitipho take the money into Menedemus's house, and Chremes contents himself by thinking that the 10 minae he has just spent have paid for his daughter's past board and lodging. He ponders the other expenses associated with a daughter's wedding and dowry and makes it clear that he will spare no expense.

It is easy to imagine that the confusion attending the complexities of this plot, beyond befuddling the play's characters, also mystified a considerable portion of the audience.

Scene 8 of act 4 portrays a happy Menedemus announcing to Chremes that Clinia wishes to marry Chremes' newly rediscovered daughter. Chremes is convinced that this is the trick that will bilk Menedemus of his money—money that Clinia will then give to Bacchis. The two fathers agree to appear to be deceived and to apparently assent to a wedding.

After further parental misunderstandings, Clinia is finally betrothed to Antiphila, and the matter of her dowry is settled. As Antiphila has proved to be Clitipho's long-lost sister, and as Clitipho's affair with the courtesan Bacchis has earned him his father's disapproval, Chremes decides that he will give all his money to Antiphila and make Clitipho her dependent. Clitipho avoids that indignity only by agreeing to take a wife—one his father chooses. Chremes selects the red-haired daughter of his friend Phanocrates. Clitipho objects and names the daughter of another family friend. This time all agree. Clitipho is restored to favor and successfully intercedes on behalf of the slave Syrus as the play ends.

The reappearance of characters from Terence's *Andria* and the similarities between the plots of the playwright's first and third efforts all suggest that Terence was riding a wave of audience approval for the stock characters and situations that characterized his plays.

Bibliography

Terence. *Works*. English and Latin. Edited and translated by John Barsley. Cambridge, Mass.: Harvard University Press, 2001.

Seneca, Lucius Annaeus (ca. 4 B.C.E.–65 C.E.) *Roman dramatist and prose writer*

Born to a notable father of the same name in Cordoba, Spain, Lucius Annaeus Seneca was the second of three brothers. His father was a historian and a writer on the art of public speaking. As a child, Seneca was sent in the company of an aunt to be educated in Rome. There he studied rhetoric and philosophy—a subject he particularly pursued so that, to distinguish him from his father, he earned the soubriquet *Seneca the Philosopher*. As a contributor to that subject, he was a member of the Stoic school (see STOICISM).

Engaging in Roman politics, Seneca was elected to the office of quaestor. Originally an investigative officer who tracked criminals on the orders of the Roman consuls, by Seneca's time a quaestor had become an officer of the Roman treasury. The office was elective and carried with it membership in the Roman senate. Seneca's abilities as a public speaker and legal advocate, however, provoked the jealousy of the demonic Roman emperor, Caligula, and he was obliged to go into exile, some say to save his life.

Recalled to court under the rule of Claudius, Seneca was accused, probably falsely, of having an affair with Claudius's niece, Julia Livilla. Both were sent into exile, she to her death at the hands of a judicial murderer and he to the island of Corsica. There he stayed, becoming famous as a writer. Then, in a reversal of fortune eight years later, Claudius's wife Agrippina called the now-celebrated Seneca back to court to tutor Nero, her son by an earlier marriage and the boy whom Claudius had adopted to succeed him as emperor.

Being tutor to Nero was no easy task. Perhaps the self-indulgent, amoral emperor displayed his proclivities for wanton mayhem and irresponsibility from early youth. If so, Seneca, with the help of the prefect of the imperial (praetorian) guard, Sextus Afranius Burrus, seems to have been able to check Nero's worst tendencies early in his reign, and a period of good government ensued. On the other hand, some believe that the taste that upper-class Romans developed for consuming lead acetate as a sweetener later drove Nero insane. In any case, as the emperor became increasingly self-indulgent and criminal in his behavior, Seneca and Burrus's influence with their ruler correspondingly waned.

When Nero wished to divorce his wife Octavia and marry instead Poppaea Sabina, his mother Agrippina objected. Nero vented his displeasure at Agrippina's interference by having his mother murdered in 59 C.E. Burrus did his best to stem the public furor the murder provoked, but as Nero spun further and further out of rational control, his advisers' counsel had little impact. When Burrus died, Seneca tried to resign and give all his enormous wealth to the emperor. The emperor refused the resignation and deferred accepting the wealth.

Finally and inevitably, however, responsible Romans began to plot against their mad ruler, and Seneca seemed to Nero to be implicated in one of the conspiracies. Nero therefore ordered his teacher and mentor to commit judicial suicide. An account of that occasion—one that Seneca was at some pains to model on the death of SOCRATES—survives in the pages of TACITUS.

From a literary perspective, Seneca was a major figure. While some of his works are only represented by fragments, we know that he wrote lost treatises on ethics, geography, and natural history. Twelve dialogues survive essentially intact; they treat subjects that include providence, the constancy of wisdom, the blessed life, leisure, the tranquillity of the mind, and the brevity of life. Beyond those, three more are prose consolations. One is addressed to a mother grieving a son's death, another to a mother bewailing her son's exile, and a third tried to flatter Nero in an effort to get back in his good graces.

As a philosopher, Seneca wrote about ethical subjects. Although he was not a Christian, he stood in the same tradition of Greek ethics that influenced early Christian thinking. As a result, his treatment of such subjects as death, wealth, the highest good, and happiness led Christians of the middle ages to consider Seneca a fellow communicant and even a correspondent of St. Paul's. Seneca also wrote about subjects of interest to the natural sciences. He did so, however, from a Stoic philosophical rather than from a scientific point of view. In addition, he was the author of several short poems, some of them autobiographical.

From the time of the European Renaissance until our own, Seneca's literary reputation has rested principally upon his tragedies. We have nine complete ones that have been confidently ascribed to Seneca. These include four probably based on plays by EURIPIDES: *Hercules furens* (MAD HERCULES); *Medea*; *Phaedra*; and *Troades* (*The Trojan Women*). One, *Agamemnon*, borrows its plot from AESCHYLUS. Two more, *Oedipus* and *Hercules Oetaeus* (*Hercules on Oeta*) rest substantially on the work of SOPHOCLES. Another, *Hippolytus*, rests on Sophocles and a second unknown source. Where the inspiration came from for the ninth tragedy, *THYESTES*, no one is certain. A fragment of Seneca's version of *The Phoenician Women* also survives. A 10th complete tragedy is sometimes doubtfully ascribed to Seneca. Because, however, it is the only Roman tragedy about native Roman history to survive in its entirety, the play, *OCTAVIA*, remains important whatever its authorship. As Seneca's editor and translator, Frank Justus Miller, tells us, the main objection to Seneca's having written *Octavia* arises from the play's circumstantial account of the death of Nero, which of course occurred after Seneca's suicide.

Although Seneca's plays do not always compare favorably with their Greek counterparts, that defect may arise more from performance expectations than from any lack of capacity on Seneca's part. Seneca apparently intended his tragedies for closet performance and for recitation among groups of friends or associates rather than for performance by trained actors on the public stage. In early modern England, at least, Seneca's tragedies provided models for such playwrights as George Gascoigne, Ben Jonson, and John Dryden.

See also TRAGEDY IN GREECE AND ROME.

Bibliography

Berry, Paul. *The Encounter between Seneca and Christianity*. Lewiston, N. Y.: Edwin Mellen Press, ca. 2002.

Seneca, Lucius Annaeus. *Dialogues and Letters*. Translated by C. D. N. Costa. London and New York: Penguin Books, 1997.

———. *Hercules; Trojan Women; Phoenician Women; Medea; Phaedra*. Edited and Translated by John G. Fitch. Cambridge, Mass.: Harvard University Press, 2002.

———. *Oedipus; Agamemnon; Thyestes; Hercules on Oeta; Octavia*. Edited and translated by John G. Fitch. Cambridge, Mass.: Harvard University Press, 2004.

———. *On the Shortness of Life*. Translated by G. D. N. Costa. London and New York: Penguin Books, 2005.

─────. *Seneca, The Tragedies.* Edited and translated by David R. Slavitt. Baltimore: Johns Hopkins University Press, 1992–1995.

Septuagint Old Testament

Many Jews migrated from Palestine into the Hellenic world during the three centuries before the Common Era. Over the generations, their descendants became absorbed into a Greek-speaking culture, and the emigrants' mastery of Hebrew deteriorated to the point that they required authoritative translations of the HEBREW BIBLE, or Old Testament. To meet this need, it is likely that a series of translations of portions of the Old Testament occurred about a hundred years into that period and that these translations were subsequently brought together.

An Alexandrian Greek scholar named Aristeas, however, reported that at the request of Egypt's bibliophilic Greek pharoah, Ptolemy II, for a Greek translation of the Torah, either 70 or 72 learned rabbis came from Jerusalem to Alexandria to accomplish the task. Over time, the story of their work expanded to include the entire Hebrew Bible.

Whether finished in that fashion or completed by a slower process of accretion, the task got done. A trustworthy Greek version of the Hebrew Bible in the dialect of the people (Greek *koine*) was in existence by the beginning of the Christian era. The story of the 70 or 72 translators stuck, and so the work became known as the version of the 70—the Septuagint. This was the version used both by Jews in the Greek-speaking diaspora and by early Christians.

Bibliography

Hengel, Martin, et al., eds. *The Septuagint as Christian Scripture: Its Prehistory and the Problems of its Canon.* Translated by Mark E. Biddle. Grand Rapids, Mich.: Baker Academic, 2004.

Knibb, M. A. *The Septuagint and Messianism.* Dudley, Mass.: Peeters, 2006.

Kraus, Wolfgang, and R. Glenn Wodden, eds. *Septuagint Research: Issues and Challenges in the Study of the Greek Jewish Scriptures.* Boston: Brill, 2006.

Seven against Thebes, The   Aeschylus
(467 B.C.E.)

The third and only surviving TRAGEDY of a first-prize winning trilogy, *The Seven against Thebes* recounts the fulfillment of Oedipus's curse upon his neglectful and abusive sons that each would die at the other's hands. The play was preceded by two other tragedies gleaned from the story of Oedipus. The first, entitled *Laius,* recounted the story of his father, and the second, *Oedipus,* gave AESCHYLUS's version of the central episode of the legend. A SATYR PLAY entitled *The Sphinx* followed the three tragedies. (See CONVENTIONS OF GREEK DRAMA and GREAT DIONYSIA) *The Seven against Thebes* provides a particularly clear example of the manner in which a play that features the siege of a city in a dramatic tradition that precluded onstage death could substitute declamatory verse description for action.

When the two sons of Oedipus, Eteocles and Polynices, succeeded to the throne of Thebes, they were supposed to share power by turns. Eteocles, however, refused to vacate the throne and exiled Polynices. He in turn raised an army in Argos and with it attacked his native city. As the play begins, a frightened Theban citizenry is awaiting the attack. A CHORUS of Theban women expresses the general fear as they pray at the city's altars. King Eteocles reproves them for spreading panic and suggests that doing so could undermine the resolve of the men defending the city. He also reassures the women by informing them how his spies have learned the enemy's strategy, and how he has already begun taking measures to counter it by defending the seven gates of the city against seven squadrons of troops to be led by seven heroes.

A spy enters and reports that the seven heroes have sworn a blood oath by the god of war, Ares, to overthrow Thebes. He reports the name of each hero and that of the gate his squadron will attack. As the spy does so, he also recounts the emblem that six of the heroes bear on their shields. One of the attackers, a soothsayer, has no device on his shield. As the spy names each attacking hero, Eteocles responds by naming the leader of the defenders who will guard each gate and resist the invading force. The seventh gate will be under attack from a force led by Polynices, and Eteocles himself will lead the force against his brother.

(For our contemporary audiences, accustomed to graphic battle scenes, the list and counter-list, with their accompanying verse descriptions of the arms of the leaders and their prowess, can grow a bit tedious. Athenian audiences, however, were accustomed to the way their theater handled such matters. Both HOMER and HESIOD had earlier featured such detailed descriptions of heraldic devices as part of the color of battle scenes. If the Athenian audience experienced any tedium, it did not affect the distribution of prizes.)

Shocked to learn that their king will hazard his own person in battle against his brother, the chorus attempts to dissuade Eteocles since his doing so will provide an opportunity for the operation of Oedipus's curse. Eteocles, however, scorns their advice, reminding them that if his death by his brother's hand is fated, it will occur one way or another.

Some critics have suggested that Eteocles is the archetype of ARISTOTLE's flawed tragic hero. A competent leader, public-spirited, concerned about the welfare of his people, he nevertheless allows himself to be blinded by his hatred of his brother, and this sets in motion the train of events that leads to the hero's fall.

As the battle rages offstage, the chorus onstage revisits the stories of Laius and Oedipus, telling how the father had been warned to die childless to avoid cursing his land, and how Oedipus, Laius's son, had fulfilled the curse and intensified its effect by adding unwitting parricide and incest to the list of crimes against the gods that his family had committed. The chorus darkly perceives the continuing operation of the curse against the generations of Laius's progeny.

The spy reenters and reports both the successful defense of the city and the death at each other's hand of Eteocles and Polynices. The chorus responds to the news with appropriate prayers—gratitude for their city's salvation and horror and grief at the death of the brothers and its manner.

Antigone and Ismene, the sisters of the fallen brothers, and a train of mourners now enter bearing the bodies, and all sing responsively concerning the tragedy. Then, in a scene that some have suggested may be a later addition to the play, as the mourners move off to bury the bodies of the brothers, a herald arrives from the city fathers to forbid the burial of Polynices' body. The politicians reason that since Polynices attacked his native city, he does not deserve decent burial and should simply be left for the vultures. Antigone, however, will have none of it. Even though she may be punished, she will not leave her brother's corpse unburied. Should she do so, according to Greek belief, his soul would not be able to cross into the underworld and would be condemned to wander forever. The chorus decides she has chosen rightly and joins the sisters in their funeral rites for their brothers. The play ends with the citizens praising Zeus for their salvation from the attackers.

Bibliography

Aeschylus. *The Complete Plays*. Translated by Carl R. Mueller. Hanover, N.H.: Smith & Kraus, 2002.
———. *The Seven Against Thebes*. Translated by E. D. A. Morshead. In *The Complete Greek Drama. . . .* Edited by Whitney J. Oates and Eugene O'Neill, Jr. New York: Random House, 1938.

Seven Incitements (Wenzhuan) Mei Sheng (ca. early second century B.C.E.)

In this FU POEM, Mei Sheng (d. 149 B.C.E.) imagines that a person from Wu visits a fictive prince of the state of Chu. The prince is ill, and the visitor offers to cure him.

The cure begins with the loving description of seven sensory pleasures in which the prince has a tendency to overindulge: (1) listening to lute music; (2) eating fine foods and drinking fine wines; (3) riding about in a luxury carriage; (4) spending too much time with courtiers, ladies-in-waiting, musicians and poets; (5) excessive hunting; (6) fighting in battles and over-celebrating victories; and (7) spending too much time at the seashore. Only the discussion of hunting seems to bring the prince much relief. Otherwise, at the end of the recitation, the prince feels as miserable as ever.

The visitor from Wu, however, restores the prince to instant perfect health by offering to arrange for some wise men to take over and manage his affairs. This very conventional ending was probably no more convincing then than it is now. What interests the poet are the descriptions of the excesses—not really their cure.

Bibliography
Watson, Burton. *Early Chinese Literature.* New York: Columbia University Press, 1962.

Seven Sages of the Bamboo Grove

This epithet applies to a coterie of antiestablishment poets and drinking companions whose most notable member was JI KANG (223–262 C.E.). Ji was put to death for "unfilial" behavior when he failed to show due deference to a powerful official. According to unverified folklore, they met for drinking as a means of experiencing the Tao and for jocular conversation in a bamboo grove. Another version of their story suggests they met also for Taoist conversation.

A second member, Shan Tao, is now remembered principally as the addressee of a letter from Ji Kang. Ji broke off his friendship with Shan when the latter sold out and joined the government.

Liu Ling (221–300 C.E.) was another affiliate of the group. His admiration for a mistress of the powerful warlord and superior poet, Cao Cao (Ts'ao Ts'ao), cost Liu his life.

Aside from Ji, Shan, and Liu, the group included Kong Rong (K'ung Jurg, 153–208 C.E.)—a 20th-generation descendant of CONFUCIUS who became the governor of Bohal (Po-hai) in Shandong (Shantung) province. His poems ran to laments such as one in which a traveler arrives home to find his family bemoaning his death. Perhaps there was prescience in this theme, for the same Ts'ao Ts'ao had Kong put to death with all the members of his family.

Also counted among the sages was Wang Can (Ts'an) (177–217 C.E.). A refugee, a poet, and a poetic theorist, Wang wrote his technical treatises in prose. His poems reflect the hardships and horrors of life as a fleeing refugee.

Other affiliates of the group included the otherwise unidentified Ying Yang, a poet whose subject was his dashed political ambition. Chen (Ch'en) Lin, completes the list. He contributed to a then-popular mode of writing called group composition, in which several poets would agree to write verses on a preassigned theme. Chen's FU POEM, "Rhapsody on the subject of agate," survives, as do two others on the same subject by his associates, Wang Can and Cao Bi.

Bibliography
Connery, Christopher Leigh. "*Sao, Fu,* Parallel Prose, and Related Genres." In Mair, Victor H. *The Columbia History of Chinese Literature.* New York: Columbia University Press, 2001.

Giles, Herbert A. *A History of Chinese Literature.* New York: Grove Press, 1958.

Severinus, Saint   See BOETHIUS, ANICIUS MANLIUS SEVERINUS.

Shepherd, The   Hermas (ca. 110–140 C.E.)

One of the most widely disseminated Christian documents of the second and third centuries, Hermas's Greek-language *The Shepherd* was regarded as a part of the NEW TESTAMENT by such early Christian writers as Clement of Alexandria, but as noncanonical by such others as ATHANASIUS. Regardless of their points of view concerning *The Shepherd*'s scriptural status, however, numerous early Christian commentators cited the work. Beyond those already mentioned, these included such figures as St. AUGUSTINE, St. JEROME, ORIGEN, Tertullian, and others. As it has been transmitted to us and as it is included in the modern collection, *The APOSTOLIC FATHERS OF THE CHRISTIAN CHURCH*, *The Shepherd* consists of five "visions," 12 "commandments," and 10 "parables."

The Visions

From a literary point of view, the work begins as a sort of Christian romance. Ostensibly the author, Hermas, a former slave in Rome but now a freed man, having always loved his former owner, Rhoda, as a sister, observes her bathing in the River Tiber some years after his manumission. He helps her ashore, admires her beauty, and reflects that he would be fortunate to marry such a wife.

Some time later, during a moment of religious reverie, Hermas falls asleep, and his report of what next occurs takes on the character of a series of dream visions. In the first, a spirit takes Hermas across a river to a deserted place where he begins to pray. As he does so, the soul of the now-deceased Rhoda addresses Hermas from Heaven. She says that she has "been taken up to accuse [Hermas] before the Lord." Hermas denies any fault, but Rhoda insists that he has entertained sinful thoughts about her. She counsels him to repent and pray.

As Hermas reflects on the state of his soul and wonders how he can be saved, an elderly woman in radiant garments appears with a book in her hand, takes a seat in a chair made of snow-white wool, and questions him about his uncharacteristic sadness. The woman tells Hermas that even if he unconsciously entertained an evil thought about Rhoda, what God is really angry about stems from Hermas's too-tolerant indulgence of his children's folly. She then offers to read from her book. Subsequently, Hermas, though he has forgotten most of what the woman read, nonetheless remembers how he felt amazed. He does remember the woman's last words to him. They celebrate the wonder of God's foreknowledge, his creation, and the blessings in store for God's elect.

A year later, Hermas experiences a second such vision in the same location as earlier. This time, the same woman gives Hermas a document to copy. The document reproves Hermas's wife and children for their sinful behavior and calls on Hermas to lead them to repentance. Though Hermas is at fault for failing to chastise them, he receives indications that all will yet be well.

Now a young man enters Hermas's ongoing vision and identifies the elderly woman as the church for whose sake the world was created. She then reappears with instructions for Hermas about what he must do with the information he has copied from her books. Hermas must write two little books and send them to "Clement and to Grapte." Clement will disseminate his among the foreign cities, Grapte will use his to admonish widows and orphans, and Hermas must read his copy to the presbyters who lead the church of his own city (perhaps Alexandria?).

Hermas's third vision comes in answer to his prayer that the elderly woman provide him with a revelation. She agrees to meet him in a field that Hermas farms, and when he arrives there, he finds an ivory bench set up. The lady arrives with six young men whom she directs to go and build. Then she directs Hermas to sit on the bench. He tries to defer to her, but she insists that he obey her instructions, and when he tries to sit on the right side of the bench, she makes him move to the left. Hermas takes offense, but the lady explains that the right-hand side is reserved for those who have already pleased God and who for God's sake have suffered "floggings, imprisonments, great afflictions, crucifixions, and wild beasts."

Now, in answer to Hermas's plea for a revelation, the lady shows him a vision of a tower rising from the surface of the water and being built of stone by the six young men. Stones are brought from land and sea. They are of several sizes and shapes. Some are used in the building, which is seamlessly crafted, and others are rejected. Hermas asks, essentially, for an explanation of the allegory, and the lady accedes to his request. The tower, she explains is herself—the church. The six young men who are building are God's first-created holy angels. Those bringing the stones are lesser angels.

The squared stones that fit seamlessly into the tower are the "apostles, bishops, teachers, and deacons who perform their functions harmoniously as God would have them do." Those drawn from the depths of the sea represent those who have suffered on God's account. Those who have sinned but who will repent are cast away, but not too far as repentance will turn them once again into worthy building materials. If they do not repent, however they will remain outside the church's edifice. Those cast far away from the tower are the lawless and the hypocritical, neither of whom will enjoy salvation. The lady also explains the significance of each of the other sorts of stones. One sort, with rounded edges, represents the wealthy who put their business affairs ahead of their religious devotion. Their only hope lies in having their wealth cut off and squaring up their edges. A sort of hope exists for those who do not measure up, but it is feeble when compared with the rewards to be expected for those who do.

The lady now points to seven women standing around the top of the tower. She tells Hermas that they are Faith, Self-restraint, Simplicity, Knowledge, Innocence, Reverence, and Love. Not altogether satisfied that he has fully understood the visions, Hermas prays for further elucidation, and the Lord, somewhat testily, answers his prayer, giving tropological interpretations to every detail of the visions that Hermas has been privileged to see.

In subsequent visions, Hermas escapes destruction by a sea monster—tropologically standing for Satan—owing to the protection of an angel on account of Hermas's faith. All aspects of the beast, including the meaning of its colors, are explained to Hermas.

In the fifth of Hermas's visions, a shepherd appears. The shepherd is identified as the "angel of repentance," the one to whom Hermas has been entrusted as a guide to salvation. A reader might have expected that the shepherd would have been identified as Jesus Christ, but rather mysteriously that name never occurs in the entire work. The shepherd nonetheless instructs Hermas to write down his commandments and parables, and those sections then follow.

The Commandments

The shepherd first commands Hermas to believe "that God is one, [that he] created and completed all things," making everything out of nothing, and that, though God contains all things, he alone is uncontained.

The second commandment enjoins Hermas to "hold on to simplicity and be innocent" and neither to slander not to listen to slander. He must be reverent, good, and generous.

The third commandment is: "Love the truth." If, in the conduct of business affairs, Hermas knows that he has lied, the shepherd encourages him to behave so as to make that lie into a truth.

Fourth, the shepherd instructs Hermas to "guard [his] holiness" by excluding from his thoughts any reflection on a woman other than his wife. Also, a husband should divorce a wife who has an affair and does not repent. Thereafter, however, the husband should live a celibate life, unless his wife repents, in which case he can take her back. Healing and reform make the sin of adultery forgivable.

Hermas wants to know, after one has been baptized and redeemed from one's former sins, whether or not other opportunities for forgiveness are possible should someone backslide. The shepherd replies that one can be forgiven one more time. If, however, one sins and repents repeatedly, one has exhausted one's reservoir of grace.

Hermas then asks if remarriage after the death of a spouse is a sin. The shepherd replies that it is not, but that "superior honor" attaches to life as a widow or widower. This, of course, is the Catholic Church's historically orthodox view of that matter.

The shepherd's fifth commandment requires patience and prohibits irascibility, whose ill effects he describes at length. In the sixth, the shepherd recurs to the first. He wants to discuss in more detail the benefits of faith, fear, and self-restraint. Staying on the right path will avoid temptation. Each person, the shepherd avers, has two angels: one righteous and one wicked. The wicked one can be recognized if a person feels angry or bitter, or feels extravagantly desirous of too much food or drink, lusts after sex, or easily grows haughty, proud, or angry.

The seventh commandment requires that a person "fear the Lord . . . and guard his commandments." It also suggests fearing the works of the devil.

The eighth commandment requires refraining from evil, but not from good. If Hermas had been in any doubt about what was evil, the Shepherd gives him a list of prohibitions. He must avoid: "adultery and sexual immorality . . . lawless drunkenness . . . evil luxury . . . overabundant food . . . extravagant wealth . . . boasting . . . pride . . . haughtiness . . . lying, slander . . . hypocrisy . . . bearing grudges, and speaking . . . blasphemy." Other lesser wickedness is also to be avoided: "robbery, fraud, false witnessing, greed, evil desire, deception, vanity, arrogance," and other similar vices.

The shepherd encourages works and words that reveal "faith, fear of the Lord, love, harmony, . . . righteousness, truth, and endurance." Performing such works and saying such words carries the promise of happiness in this life and the next.

The ninth commandment precludes doubtfulness and encourages bringing one's burdens to the Lord despite whatever sins one may have committed in the assurance that the Lord is always open to the sincere sorrow of the faithful and to their desire for forgiveness.

The 10th commandment requires giving up grief and sorrow, as they are both related to irascibility, and always being of good cheer.

The 11th commandment requires discriminating between true and false prophets and joining one's petitions to those of the former. The shep-herd gives a number of tests by which one can decide if a prophet is reliable or not. Above all, one should trust in the Holy Spirit to render false prophets powerless.

The 12th commandment requires the extermination of every evil desire and steadfastness in desiring the good. Having given that general instruction, the shepherd repeats many of the examples of each that he had previously given. At Hermas's request, he also gives a general review of what has gone before, thereby observing the threefold form of the Trinity that has come to characterize everything from sermons to three-point student research paper.

Hermas objects that keeping the commandments is hard because of the devil's power. The shepherd, in his role as the angel of repentance, assures Hermas that the devil is weak when faced with godly fortitude.

The Parables

Now the shepherd turns to the parables that he wishes Hermas to share. All the "slaves of God" must live as if they are residents in a foreign land, expect to be excluded from the accumulation of worldly riches, and persecuted because they do not revere the laws of their places of dwelling above those of God.

In the next parable, the shepherd compares rich and poor believers to an elm tree and a grape vine. The elm tree bears no fruit, but if it supports a vine, the vine will flourish and bear much fruit. Similarly, the rich are distracted by their wealth and so not very fruitful from a spiritual point of view. If, however, they will support the poor who are rich in their petitions and confessions, the rich will thereby play the role of the elm tree in making it possible for the vine to bear a fruitful harvest and not simply bear a little fruit that rots on the ground as it would were it not for the elm's support. Like the elm and the vine, therefore, both rich and poor will benefit from mutual dependency.

The shepherd next shows Hermas how trees that have no leaves are like the people of the second century: One cannot tell by looking at them whether they are alive or dead—that is, whether they are upright or sinners. The parable that follows this one contrasts that situation with the age that is coming, when one can discern the living trees by their buds and the dead by their lack thereof. The upright, in other words, will be identifiable by their acts, and all others fit only to fuel fires.

In the fifth parable, the shepherd reproves Hermas for fasting physically and instructs him to fast spiritually by avoiding evil desires. To further illustrate this parable, the shepherd incorporates another, telling the story of how a slave, by exceeding his master's expectations in caring for the vines in his field, became the joint heir of his master's estate together with his son.

Hermas insists on an explanation, and the shepherd explains that the master is the creator of the world, the son is the Holy Spirit, and the slave is the Son of God. The vines represent the human race. The shepherd explains other details in the same way: Fence posts, for instance, are guardian angels. But Hermas has still not understood why God's Son was represented as a slave. The explanation is a bit convoluted, but essentially the shepherd explains that the Holy Spirit has donned human *flesh* as God's Son on earth. That flesh is the Spirit's "blameless slave" that will be sacrificed for human beings, but not the Spirit. The Son's flesh will be sacrificed for people so that they too can participate in godhead by accepting the sacrifice and becoming coheirs of the kingdom of God. The shepherd counsels Hermas to emulate the slave and keep both his flesh and his spirit pure.

As the sixth parable opens, Hermas is reflecting on all the good advice he has received and speculating that if he takes it, he will be fortunate. The Lord, however, objects to that "if" and reproaches Hermas for doublemindedness. The Lord shows Hermas a vision of a flock of frisky, well-fed sheep being tended by a yellow-clad shepherd. But the Lord explains that the shepherd is really an evil angel intent on ruining people (the sheep) with "vain deceits and luxuries." Eventually, the misled sheep find themselves amid

thorns and brambles being beaten by a shepherd who is in reality the good angel of punishment. After appropriate chastisement—a year for each day they lived in luxury and deceit—if they repent, the Lord receives them as his own, and their suffering ends.

Hermas next complains that the punishing angel is afflicting him and asks that the angel leave his house. The Lord tells Hermas that he deserves punishing, not only because of his own many sins, but also because his household is sinful and lawless. So Hermas resolves to "endure every affliction" until his time of punishment ends.

The eighth parable recounts a tale of persons to whom an angel has given the green branches of a willow tree. Despite having so many of its branches pruned, the tree remains healthy and vigorous. Then the people begin returning the sticks of willow they had taken away. They vary in condition from withered and moth-eaten to green, budding, and bearing fruit. The shepherd and the angel are very pleased with the latter, and they confer crowns on those whose sticks are green and fruitful and send them to the tower. Those whose sticks are budding without fruit are also rewarded, as are those whose sticks have merely remained green.

The shepherd directs that the sticks returned in withered condition be planted in the ground and watered in the hope that many of them will live. He then explains that the willow tree stands for the law of the Son of God, and all whose sticks were either merely green or green and flourishing represent those who have observed the law with varying degrees of fortitude. The withered sticks, of course, represent those who have not observed the law. Yet many of those, once planted and watered, revive, and the persons they represent have repented and been saved. The unrepentant, however, who both dissent and break the Son of God's law are condemned to spiritual death. The trope of this parable becomes tedious as it continues long after its point has been clearly made.

The ninth parable finds Hermas amid 12 mountains of varying degrees of pleasantness and unpleasantness observing the construction of yet another stone tower. This one, unfinished but left in the care of a company of virgins, awaits the coming of the master of the tower to examine each of its stones. Some are found to be rotten and removed. The scenario described in the building of the tower is very similar to that summarized in Hermas's third vision above.

The shepherd leaves Hermas overnight in the care of the virgins and returns the next day to explain the allegory of all Hermas has seen. An ancient rock stands for the Son of God who is older than all creation. A new gate in the rock is the passageway that the Son has provided into his kingdom for all those who enter in his name.

As he regularly does, Hermas asks for detailed explanations of the tropological meanings of all he has seen. He learns that the names of the virgins are Simplicity, Faith, Self-Restraint, Power, Patience, Innocence, Holiness, Cheerfulness, Truth, Understanding, Harmony, and Love. Having those qualities and taking the name of the Son of God qualifies a person for entrance into the kingdom. Contrasted with them, however, is a group of women clad in black in whose names are Disbelief, Lack of Self-Control, Disobedience, Deceit, Sorrow, Wickedness, Licentiousness, Short Temper, Lying, Foolishness, Slander, and Hatred. Every detail receives careful explanation—the meaning of the dwellers on the 12 mountains who represent believers and disbelievers of various temperaments and spiritual accomplishments or failings.

In the final parable, Hermas learns that he has qualified for the confidence of the shepherd and of the angel who sent him, and that the virgins will come to dwell in his house. The shepherd advises Hermas to carry out his ministry in a manful way, telling everyone to continually do good works and participate in building the church and the kingdom. Many candidates for authorship of *the shepherd* have been suggested. Least likely is a Hermas mentioned by St. Paul. Most likely is the brother of Pope Pius I, which would put the composition of the work after 140–155 C.E.

Bibliography

Osiek, Carolyn. *Shepherd of Hermas. Humeia.* Minneapolis: Fortress Press, 1991.

"*Shepherd of Hermas.*" In *Apostolic Fathers.* Vol. 2. Edited and translated by Bart D. Ehrman. Cambridge, Mass.: Harvard University Press, 2003.

Wilson, J. C. *Five Problems in the Interpretation of the Shepherd of Hermas: Authorship, Genre, Canonicity, Apocalyptic, and the Absence of the Name Jesus Christ.* Lewiston, Maine: Mellen Biblical Press, 1995.

Shihji (*Shih-chi, Historical Record, Records of the Grand Historian of China*) Sima Qian (ca. 86 B.C.E.)

A monumental work of history and one of the few surviving chronicles of early China, the *Shiji* (*Historical Record* or *Records of the Grand Historian of China*) contains 130 chapters and some 526,500 words. It is organized into five major divisions. The first of these, "Basic Annals," contains 12 chapters. For dynasties preceding the Han, the ruling house that employed Sima Qian, the historian presents overview histories of the ruling families. For the Han dynasty, Sima draws individual portraits of the emperors.

Next come 10 chronological tables containing lists of important events and their dates. Following those graphs, Sima turns his attention to such issues as astronomy, economics, music, rites, and religious matters. He next deals in 30 chapters with "Hereditary Houses," in which he examines the autonomous regional rulers who governed before the unification of China under the first Qin (Ch'in) emperor (see ANCIENT CHINESE DYNASTIES AND PERIODS).

In the last major section of his work, Sima devotes 70 chapters, first, to the lives of the notable men of Chinese history. Second, he discusses all the foreign peoples and countries that China had relations with or knowledge of. When Sima discusses very early Chinese history, the paucity of reliable source material forces him to fill out his treatment with legendary material and with folk stories. As he turns his attention to Qin and Han times, however, the historian finds himself on much surer ground. His characters cease to be simply types and become individualized portraits.

Like historians in all times and places, Sima is interested in drawing from history the lessons that it can teach the present. He concerns himself with the affairs of human beings and cares little for accounts of supernatural beings or occurrences—topics that he approaches with skepticism.

Like the European historians of antiquity, Sima is not above supplying his characters with the speeches they might have given if the ones they did give are absent from the record. In fact, his historical approach often tries to recreate the past in dramatic fashion rather than to give merely a running retrospective account. The result is a highly readable, often novelistic account of Chinese antiquity.

Bibliography

Giles, Herbert A. *A History of Chinese Literature.* New York: Grove Press, Inc., 1958.

Mair, Victor H., ed. *The Columbia History of Chinese Literature.* New York: Columbia University Press, 2001.

Sima Qian. *Records of the Grand Historian: Han Dynasty.* 2 vols. Translated by Burton Watson. New York: Columbia University Press, 1993.

———. *The Grand Scribe's Records.* 7 vols. Edited by William Nienhauser, Jr. Translated by Tsai-fa Cheng et al. Bloomington: Indiana University Press, 1994–2006.

shi poems

Written Chinese is a monosyllabic language. This does not mean that *all* words in Chinese have one syllable and one only. Indeed, in the spoken language, words may very well be polysyllabic. The monosyllabic classification does mean, however, that the great preponderance of Chinese written words have just one syllable. Chinese, however, is also a·tonal language, so that the same syllable—

wu, for example—might mean one thing when spoken with a level pitch, another when spoken with a rising pitch, and yet another when spoken with a falling pitch. Thus, three separate characters, or *sinographs,* would be required to render the three possible combinations in this hypothetical example.

Sinographs in ancient times were scratched or painted onto surfaces such as bamboo or silk before the invention of paper in about 100 C.E. made brush and ink the preferred mode for rendering them. The pictorial qualities of the graphs themselves can make the writing of Chinese poems equally an art to delight the ear and the eye.

Shi poems were written in what were considered to be the lyrical or song meters. Typically their lines were five or seven syllables in length, and sometimes the composition of each verse would contain as many vertical lines as horizontal characters, giving the resultant verse a square appearance. I do not read, write, or speak Chinese. I have therefore simply chosen a set of symbols at random to approximate the appearance of a square, five-syllable, *shi* lyric:

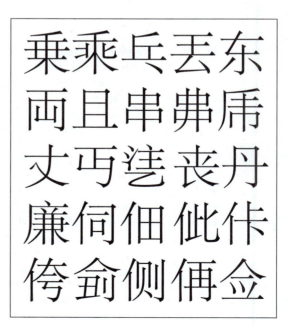

More usually, however, both verse and prose were simply strung across the surface without indication of line endings or punctuation. As the literary historian Lois Fusek suggests, the regularities of the *shi* metric encouraged artists to select literary devices associated with balance, such as parallelism and antithesis.

Bibliography

Daniels, Peter T., and William Bright, eds. *The World's Writing Systems*. New York: Oxford University Press, 1996.

Mair, Victor H., ed. *The Columbia Anthology of Traditional Chinese Literature*. New York: Columbia University Press, 1994.

sibyls and sacred verse

Sibyls were women thought to have the power of prophecy. Possibly the word *sibyl* originally designated a woman of that name. If so, however, the word soon came to apply to any of several priestesses who were inspired by gods—often the god Apollo—to utter or to write down predictions and hard-to-interpret solutions to thorny problems.

The Grecian sibyl (also called the *pythia*) who served as the Delphic oracle of Apollo answered questions put to her by those in need of predictions and advice. As she sat above a fissure in the earth from which, as modern investigations have proved, there issued toxic gases, her answers were generally incomprehensible. Priests of Apollo, however, were present and wrote down in verse their interpretations of her answers on oak leaves. These they presented to the questioners. As the interpretations also regularly required interpretation, hindsight was often required to determine whether or not the prediction had been accurate.

Another particularly famous sibyl was the prophetess who occupied a cavern at Cumae near Lake Averna, not far from contemporary Naples. Again, the escape of volcanic gases probably had much to do with the prophetic and ecstatic utterances of the Cumaean sibyl. It was she who showed Aeneas the path leading to the underworld in Virgil's *Aeneid*.

Sibyls served as the mouthpieces of the gods they represented—most often but not exclusively Apollo. The Roman author Marcus Terentius Varro compiled a list of catalogues of sibylline utterances from Italy, several places in Greece, Asia Minor, Persia, and elsewhere. Sibyls also prophesied in Egypt and in Palestine, where 200 years of Greek rule and an active program of hellenization had conflated Judaic monotheism and the trappings of Hellenic polytheism in the popular mind to a degree. Early Christians seem also to have been fascinated with sibyls and sought predictions of Christ's coming among their utterances. Later, however, such a Christian Renaissance poet as Petrarch adopted the sibylline prophecies written on leaves that fly away on the winds as a metaphor for untrue scatterings. Those scattered false prophecies contrast, the Christian poet thought, with the gathered truths bound together in a codex whose prime example was the Bible.

In Rome from a very early date—at least the fifth century B.C.E.—texts containing sibylline prophecies were entrusted to the hands of priests who would consult and interpret them on orders from the senate. Such collections were also to be found in private hands, and these continued to be consulted well into the Christian era in Europe.

Bibliography

Collins, John J. *Seers, Sibyls, and Sages in Hellenistic-Roman Judaism*. Boston: Brill Academic, 2001.

Potter, David S. *Prophets and Emperors: Human and Divine Authority from Augustus to Theodosius*. Cambridge, Mass.: Harvard University Press, 1994.

Terry, Milton S. trans. *Sibylline Oracles: Translated from the Greek into English Blank Verse*. El Paso, Tex.: Selene Books, 1991.

Silius Italicus (Tiberius Catius Silius Asconius) (26–102 C.E.) *Roman poet*

The author of the longest (12,000-line) EPIC poem in Latin, *Punica*, Silius Italicus does not command much literary attention among modern readers.

He is nonetheless of considerable interest to Roman history quite apart from his literary work.

Before he retired to the poetic life, Silius enjoyed a distinguished career as a public official and a jurist. He served as a consul of the Roman state under the emperor Nero. On Nero's death, Silius tried to negotiate between conflicting claims to the imperial throne made by Nero's general in northern Europe, Vitellius, and by Nero's commander in Asia, Vespasian. Though the negotiations succeeded and Vitellius agreed to abdicate in favor of Vespasian, the mass desertion of Vitellius by his troops left him at the mercy of a hostile crowd of Romans who demeaned, mutilated, and murdered him.

The victorious Vespasian advanced Silius's career. Already a member of the Roman senate, Silius rose to become the proconsul of Asia. Thereafter, he retired to his extensive estates and began his massive literary undertaking. For his poetic model, he chose VIRGIL's AENEID, although his debts to LUCAN also abound. For historical detail, he consulted LIVY.

Silius begins *Punica* from the premise that Dido's dying curse against a faithless Aeneas in the *Aeneid* was fulfilled by the second Punic War fought between Rome and Carthage. He restores to his epic the gods that Lucan had excised from his CIVIL WAR, and like many ancient and modern politicians and poets who claim divine authority for their actions or godly provenance for their inspiration, Silius drafts the victorious gods into the service of the Roman cause, leaving the anti-Roman goddess Juno in a continuing state of frustration about the successes of the Roman descendants of Venus's son, the Trojan Aeneas. The great Roman victor over the Carthaginians, Scipio Africanus, is celebrated in Silius's lines.

Silius probably completed his work around 96 C.E. Not long thereafter, his health failed and he fell victim to a painful and incurable sickness. Rather than suffer needlessly, Silius took his own life by ceasing to eat.

Long thought to be lost, the *Punica* resurfaced in 1417. New studies, some of them underway at this writing, may lead to a resurgence of interest in Silius's epic.

Bibliography

Marks, Raymond. *From Republic to Empire: Scipio Africanus in the* Punica *of Silius Italicus.* New York: Peter Lang, 2005.

McGushin, Patrick. *The Transmission of the Punica of Silius Italicus.* Amsterdam: M. Hakkert, 1985.

Silius Italicus, Tiberius Catius. *Punica, with an English Translation.* 2 vols. Translated by J. D. Duff. New York: Putnam, 1934.

Silloi See DIDACTIC POETRY.

Sima Qian (Ssŭ-ma Ch'ien) (ca. 145–86 B.C.E.) *Chinese historian*

The first major Chinese historian, Sima Qian was a child prodigy. By the age of 10, he had already distinguished himself in scholarship, and by 20 he had undertaken a grand tour of the Chinese empire. Sima's father, Sima Tan, served as the empire's principal astrologer and "prefect grand historian," and when he died in 110 B.C.E., Sima inherited the post. In addition to completing a project started by his father to update the calendar, Sima also undertook the task of completing the history of China that the old scholar had begun. This became Sima's great life work.

So dedicated to his task was Sima that when he angered Emperor Wu and was punished with castration, he did not, as was usual in such circumstances, commit suicide. As the historian explained in a letter to a friend, Jen An, though he was shamed by his punishment, he would have been more greatly shamed to think that posterity would not know his writings. To preserve them, he declared, he would suffer a thousand mutilations.

Sima's magnum opus covers almost 3,000 years of Chinese history from the earliest known times down to his own day. The work, entitled SHIHJI (Shih-chi, *Historical Record, Records of the Grand Historian of China*) is massive: It contains 526,500 words—not quite twice as long as this present volume. It was an unprecedented undertaking that presented daunting physical and intellectual challenges. In the first place, paper had not yet been invented. Sima presumably had scribes to assist him, but nonetheless he or they would have been constrained to paint on expensive silk or, more likely, to scratch their words with ink and stylus onto narrow bamboo strips that served as the common writing materials of the day.

From an intellectual point of view, Sima had few models to follow. Though chronicles had been kept before his time, many of them had been destroyed in a notable book burning during the Qin (Ch'in) dynasty (see ANCIENT CHINESE DYNASTIES AND PERIODS). Even with respect to surviving models he may have had, he organized his materials innovatively. In 130 chapters, he arranged his discussion under several major (capitals) and minor (lower-case) categories that included: a) annals of the emperors; b) chronological tables; c) rites; d) music; e) pitch-pipes; f) the calendar; g) astrology; h) imperial sacrifices; i) watercourses; j) political economy; k) annals of the feudal nobles; and l) many biographies of outstanding men. This last feature was particularly innovative.

Not surprisingly, this monumental achievement became the model for all subsequent Chinese historians. As the literary historian Herbert Giles tells us, histories in its likeness were kept from Sima's time forward until, in 1747, all 24 dynastic histories of China were gathered into a uniform edition running to 219 large volumes.

Bibliography

Giles, Herbert A. *A History of Chinese Literature.* New York: Grove Press, 1958.

Mair, Victor H., ed. *The Columbia History of Chinese Literature.* New York: Columbia University Press, 2001.

Sima Qian. *Records of the Grand Historian: Han Dynasty.* 2 vols. Translated by Burton Watson. New York: Columbia University Press, 1993.

———. *The Grand Scribe's Records.* Edited by William Nienhauser, Jr. Translated by Tsai-fa Cheng et al. 7 vols. Bloomington: Indiana University Press, 1994–2006.

Sima Xiangru (Ssŭ-ma Hsiang-ju)
(177–119 B.C.E) *Chinese poet*

A poet at the court of the former Han dynasty emperor Wu (reigned 141–87 B.C.E.), Sima Xiangru wrote FU POEMS that established the norms for the genre that poets thereafter followed. His most celebrated work, entitled "Master Void Rhapsody," or "Mr. Fantasy" (Zixufu, or Tzu hsü fu), is reported to have been the work that made him a member of the emperor's personal entourage.

The literary historian Lai Ming speculates that several attributes of Sima's *fu* appealed to the emperor. The poet combined the literary form of the "question and answer mode" with moralistic overtones in the context of lengthy, highly decorative verse.

The emperor first became acquainted with Sima's verse by reading a copy that someone had given him. The ruler assumed that the writer was dead. On being told that he was a living poet, the emperor immediately sent for Sima, making the poet a court official so that the emperor could enjoy his companionship.

Sima assured himself of the emperor's continuing favor by writing a poem, *Shang Lin Fu* (The Imperial Hunting Preserve), that, in a triumph of the poet's art, celebrated the emperor's favorite pastime and the sumptuous venue in which the emperor followed this passion. The poem employs detailed, gorgeous descriptions of every plant and every animal, both real and mythic, associated with the art of hunting.

In his private life, before becoming a court official, Sima had the reputation of being a lady's man. Penniless himself, he pursued the widowed daughter of the wealthy Cho family and won her by playing and singing love songs. At first cut off from her family, the daughter, Wen Chun, and Sima contrived to support themselves by running a small inn and serving wine. This created a scandal from which Wen Chun's wealthy father finally extricated his family by presenting his daughter with 100 servants, an enormous sum of money, and many valuable presents for her dowry. She and Sima closed their inn and thereafter enjoyed the style of life appropriate to the idle rich until the imperial summons to court.

As time went on, the emperor discovered in Sima a trusted diplomat who was able to enlist the leaders of independent states under the imperial standards. Beyond that, the story is told of the way in which the empress Chen, who was estranged from the emperor because of her jealousy, hired Sima to write a poem of fewer than 1,000 words, the *Chang Meng Fu* (the Chang Meng palace poem). The work so moved the emperor that he repented his former displeasure with the empress, and the pair made up their differences. The empress paid Sima 130 pounds of gold for his poem.

Sima ended his successful life as the Master of the Imperial Literary Academy at the age of 61. Some six of the 29 *fu* poems that he reportedly wrote survive.

See also SIMA XIANGRU'S *FU* POEMS.

Bibliography

Hervouet, Yves. *Un poeté de cour sous les Han: Sseuma-Siang jou.* Paris: Presses universitaire de France, 1964.

Lai Ming. *A History of Chinese Literature.* New York: The John Day Company, 1964.

Ssu-ma Hsiang-ju. "Rhapsody on the Shang lin (Hunting park)"; "Sir Fantasy." Translated by Burton Watson. In *The Columbia Anthology of Chinese Literature.* Edited by Victor H. Mair. New York: Columbia University Press, 1994.

Watson, Burton. *Early Chinese Literature.* New York: Columbia University Press, New York, 1962.

Sima Xiangru's *fu* poems

Six FU POEMS of the 29 that SIMA XIANGRU wrote are known to survive. These include "Zixufu" ("Tse Hsu Fu"; Mr. Non-being, or Sir Fantasy) and "Shanglingfu" ("Shang Lin Fu"; The imperial hunting preserve), which I describe below. The other survivors include "Darenfu" "Ta Jen Fu" (The immortals), Ch "Chang Meng Fu" (The Chang Meng Palace poem), "Meirenfu" ("Mei Jen Fu"; The beauty), and "Ai Ershi" ("Ai Erh Shih"; Lamentations for Ershi).

The poet expanded the first poem named above to include the second when he was called to the imperial court. The two poems sometimes appear together and sometimes separately. Both of them concern the subject of hunting.

The first opens by explaining that Sir Fantasy, Master No-such, and Lord Not-real are discussing hunts in the states of Qi (Chi) and Chu. Sima tells how, in Qi, 1,000 carriages and 10,000 horsemen set off to catch every imaginable sort of game, and as they clear the land of its animals, the king of Qi asks Sir Fantasy if the state of Chu can offer such fine hunting.

Sir Fantasy obliges by describing a wondrous landscape filled with exotic flora and fauna whose names he lists and whose features he sometimes details. Then he describes the king of Chu and his companions. Next, Fantasy admires the beauties and the skill at archery of the maidens who also ride to the hunt. Then he explains how musical instruments give the signal to end the hunt, how everyone reassembles in proper order, and how the king of Chu ascends to his pavilion to dine in perfect comfort. He concludes his description with an invidious comparison between the gentility of the king of Chu when compared with the less-dignified hunting practices of Qi.

Offended, the king of Qi falls silent, and one of his retainers reproves Fantasy for his ill manners. The retainers then undertake to praise the superiority of Chu. Lord Not-real, however, rebukes both Sir Fantasy and the Qi retainer who should have used the occasion to try to clarify for the kings of Chu and Qi their responsibilities, and for their failure to reprove their sovereigns for their lapses—in other words, for not doing the things that good Confucian ministers are supposed to do for their kings.

Then Lord Not-real undertakes the description of the emperor's Shang-lin Park (the second poem). In his description, in detail, gorgeousness, and musicality of language, Lord Not-real out-does the wonders that the preceding speakers had detailed. When Lord Not-real describes the imperial banquet, however, he makes the emperor himself remark on the "wasteful extravagance" that has marked the occasion. The emperor worries that he has set a bad example for the rulers who will follow him, and he sends everyone away. He gives orders that the hunting preserve be turned into farmland and that the lakes be stocked with fish to help feed the common people. The poor need to be fed. The emperor, in short, proposes a new order with new laws and regulations that will benefit the masses of the populace and not merely the wealthy.

The emperor himself undertakes to master a series of skills, virtues, and texts that characterize the learning of a properly educated Confucian gentleman: "etiquette, music, archery, charioteering, writing . . . mathematics . . . ," and the contents of the BOOK OF ODES, Book of Documents, and BOOK OF CHANGES.

Having given an example of the way a judicious lord prepares his ruler's mind to take instruction from his officials, Lord Not-real explains to his predecessor speakers that it is their job to instruct their emperors and not waste their time in idle comparisons of grandeur. He also observes that the kings of Qi and Chu both "merit pity," since they devote nine-tenths of the arable land in their domains to private pleasure, and their people will certainly suffer.

Ashamed of their previous boastful performances, Sir Fantasy and Master No-such apologize for their uncouth ignorance and for talking too much. They thank Lord Not-real for his good instruction.

Bibliography

Hervouet, Yves. *Un Poète de cour sous les Han: Sseuma-Siang jou*. Paris: Presses Universitaire de France, 1964.

Lai Ming. *A History of Chinese Literature*. New York: The John Day Company, 1964.

Ssu-ma Hsiang-ju [Sima Xiangru]. "Rhapsody on the Shang Lin (Hunting Park)"; "Sir Fantasy."

Translated by Burton Watson. In *The Columbia Anthology of Chinese Literature*. Edited by Victor H. Mair. New York: Columbia University Press, 1994.

Watson, Burton. *Early Chinese Literature*. New York: Columbia University Press, New York, 1962.

Simonides of Ceos (ca. 556–468 B.C.E.)
Greek poet

Born on the island of Ceos to the family of a man named Leoprepes, Simonides became one of the most renowned poets of his epoch.

Poets in the Greek world fulfilled in part the function that press agents and spin doctors now perform. Sometimes poets celebrated the victories of athletes and warriors; sometimes they wrote occasional poetry for weddings or funerals. Good poets were generously rewarded for their work, and their reputations spread throughout the Greek Mediterranean world. Moreover, competitions frequently pitted poets against one another, and Simonides is said to have won 57 such contests.

Though only fragments of Simonides' works survive, his reputation has endured. He was a widely respected lyric poet who may have begun his career in the service of Hipparchus, the younger son of an early ruler of Athens, Pisistratus. Thereafter, Simonides' pen was for hire by anyone who needed it. He apparently worked for individual athletes, singing their triumphs and accomplishments. He also wrote to order for the princes of Thessaly. A famous though surely apocryphal story has survived concerning one such commission.

Contracted to write a poem in praise of the ruler, Scopas, Simonides did so. He also included in this work the customary praises of the gods, in this case of the Dioscuri, Castor and Pollux, the stellified sons of Zeus in the form of a swan and their human mother, Leda. Apparently offended at having to share the poem's spotlight with the twin immortals, Scopas only paid Simonides half of the sum agreed upon when the poet read his work at a banquet. Scopas told Simonides to collect the other half of his fee from the Dioscuri, who had received half the poem's praise.

Shortly thereafter, so the story goes, Simonides was summoned to the palace gate where two young men were asking for him. He left the dining hall, but found no one at the gate. In his absence, however, the roof of the hall fell in, killing Scopas and the other guests. Other such stories decorate the legend of Simonides.

More credible reports and a few fragments—some discovered at OXYRHYNCHUS—give firmer evidence of the poet's accomplishment. In addition to athletes and rulers, he wrote for cities and for private individuals. His range of poetic varieties was broad. It included two sorts of choral lyric, hymns of praise, laments, and poems celebrating his patrons' accomplishments. He also wrote ELEGY AND ELEGAIC POETRY as well as historical poetry. Celebrated examples of the latter include his now-lost poems about the battles of Platea (479 B.C.E.) and Artemesium (480 B.C.E.). He is also credited with many EPIGRAMS. He was capable of writing poems of the highest nobility as well as highly erotic verse in his elegies.

The Roman poet HORACE translated at least two lines from Simonides and incorporated them into the second ODE of Horace's third book of ODES. Simonides lived a long and famous life. He died on Sicily at the court of Hiero, the tyrant of Syracuse.

See also VICTORY ODES.

Bibliography

Doty, Ralph E., trans. *Hiero: A New Translation.* Lewiston, N.Y.: Edwin Mellen Press, 2003.

Gentili, Bruno, and Carolus Prato, eds. *Poetae elegiaci testimonia et fragmenta.* (Evidence about and fragments of the [work of the] elegiac poets.) Munich: K. G. Saur, 2002.

Molyneux, John H. *Simonides: A Historical Study.* Wauconda, Ill.: Bolchazy-Carduuci Publishers, 1992.

Oates, Whitney Jennings. *The Influence of Simonides of Ceos upon Horace.* Princeton, N.J.: Princeton University Press, 1932.

Socrates (469–399 B.C.E.) *Greek philosopher*

A native of Athens, Socrates spent his whole life there, supporting himself as a cobbler. Socrates did not write books. Although he taught in his own fashion, he established no educational institutions. Yet, along with PLATO and ARISTOTLE, Socrates acquired a reputation as one of the three preeminent philosophers of ancient Greece.

What we know about Socrates comes from three sources written by people who knew him. One of these is XENOPHON OF ATHENS, whose *Memorials of Socrates* (*Memorabilia*) sketches the character of Xenophon's revered teacher at the ethical and practical rather than at the philosophical level. In this work, Xenophon treats Socrates' religious views, his moderation in all things, and his willingness to discourse with anyone. Like Plato, Xenophon also wrote a *Socratic Apology*, in which he reported Socrates' defense when the Athenians put him on trial for impiety. As Xenophon was off on an expedition with the Persian prince Cyrus at the time, he had to rely on the descriptions reported by his friend Hermogenes. In Xenophon's version, though Socrates, as in Plato and elsewhere, is innocent of the charges against him, he is nonetheless willing to die to avoid the afflictions that accompany old age rather than, as Plato suggested, on principle.

Also notable among Xenophon's Socratic writings is his *Symposium* (Banquet). In this work, he reports the doings at a banquet held in 421 B.C.E. at the home of Callias. Xenophon describes the entertainment and activities at the banquet and pictures Socrates as a relaxed, jovial, and genial companion. Socrates' more serious reported conversation centers on the inferiority of carnal love to spiritual love.

Like Xenophon, Socrates had also been a soldier, fighting for Athens in three notable military engagements. He fought at Potidea (432–29 B.C.E.), at Delium (424 B.C.E.), and at Amphipolis (422 B.C.E.). Socrates distinguished himself by his remarkable endurance on these campaigns. He was able to walk barefoot on frozen ground and stand lost in thought all night long without fatigue. The consumption of alcohol did not seem to affect him. In a work on household management (*Oeconomicus*) Xenophon has Socrates discussing agriculture, leadership, daily life among the Athenian wealthy, and the roles of women as wives and household managers.

The second source of our knowledge about Socrates is Plato. In his Socratic dialogues, Plato made Socrates into a literary hero. Although it may be the case that in real life the views of Socrates and Plato were identical, it seems more likely that in Plato's works, Socrates becomes Plato's spokesman. It is also the case that, as far as we know, none of Plato's contemporaries accused him of misrepresenting Socrates' views.

In Plato's first set of Socratic dialogues, Socrates' views emerge by inference as he raises questions about others' convictions without presenting his own. This set of dialogues include: *Alcibiades*, APOLOGY OF SOCRATES, *Charmides*, *Cleitophon*, CRITO, *Euthyphro*, *Hippias Major*, *Hippias Minor*, *Laches*, *Lysis*, *Menexenus*, and PROTAGORAS. Two other Socratic dialogues exist whose attribution to Plato has been questioned: *Lovers* and *Hipparchus*. In these dialogues, Socrates emerges as a not altogether sympathetic know-it-all and gadfly.

A second set, the so-called middle dialogues, are preceded by two transitional ones: *Gorgias* and *Meno*. In the middle dialogues, Socrates retreats from continually challenging the views of others, offering his own views instead. This group of dialogues includes *Phaedo, Phaedrus, The* REPUBLIC, and SYMPOSIUM. In this group, Socrates emerges as an admirable and congenial figure with firm, consistent, and noble convictions. In Plato's later dialogues, Socrates takes a back seat and Plato speaks mainly for himself.

Although the views of Socrates presented by Plato and by Xenophon differ, they are not essentially incompatible. When we come to the third source of our information about Socrates, however, a very different perspective emerges.

The comic playwright ARISTOPHANES makes Socrates the object of vitriolic SATIRE in his play *The* CLOUDS. Here Aristophanes represents Socrates as a SOPHIST who runs a private school in his home—a tuition-accepting institution called "the Thoughtery." Pupils there learn to address such problems as "How many times the length of its legs can a flea jump?" or "Does a gnat buzz through its proboscis or anus?"

Although the play was not a great success, given the popularity of Athenian theater, Aristophanes' mockery may well have established the popular perception of Socrates—one that conceivably played a role in the decision of the Athenians to accuse Socrates of the crime of impiety and to sentence him to commit suicide by drinking hemlock in his 70th year.

History, in any case, rejects Aristophanes' portrait of Socrates as a conniving charlatan and instead remembers him as a cobbler, a soldier, the husband of a shrewish but nonetheless beloved wife named Xantippe, and the patriotic father of Athenian children. His appearance was odd. He seems to have been ugly and potbellied, but at the same time people found him utterly charming. He considered himself to have an interior "divine sign"—one that warned him from any action that would be wrong or unjust. He preferred the spoken to the written word lest reliance on the latter impair the memory.

Because Socrates comes to us through the eyes of three very different writers, trying to discover the unvarnished views of the historical Socrates in their pages may be an exercise in futility. With respect to his influence on philosophy, he founded a philosophical milieu in which thinkers concerned themselves principally with questions about the origins of the universe and the operations of natural phenomena. By the time he died, his conversational teachings had played a major role in shifting the focus of philosophical inquiry to questions of ethics and to the investigation and analysis of concepts.

Bibliography

Ahbel-Rappe, Sara, and Rachana Kamtekar. *A Companion to Socrates*. Malden, Mass.: Blackwell Publishing, 2006.

Aristophanes. *The Complete Plays*. Translated by Paul Roche. New York: New American Library, 2005.

Plato. *Plato Unmasked: Plato's Dialogues Made New*. Translated by Keith Quincy. Spokane: Eastern Washington University Press, 2003.

———. *The Trial and Death of Socrates: Four Dialogues*. Translated by Benjamin Jowett. New York: Barnes and Noble, 2004.

Xenophon. *The Shorter Socratic Writings*. Translated and edited by Robert C. Bartlett. Ithaca, N.Y.: Cornell University Press, 1996.

Solon (fl. ca. 594 B.C.E.) *Greek statesman, poet*

Said to be descended from Codrus, the last of Athens's legendary kings, Solon was born at Salamis on the island of Cyprus. Tradition has it that he spent time in his youth traveling to Egypt and other Mediterranean countries while engaging in trade. Perhaps his ventures succeeded, for he was able to retire to Athens while still relatively young and to spend his time there in literary and philosophical pursuits.

The state of Athenian politics, however, compelled Solon's attention. By means of a martial poem, he encouraged the Athenians to make war against the neighboring city-state of Megara. Taking a command himself, he overcame his native city of Salamis. His success as a general led to his appointment as archon of the city—that is, as head of the Athenian state. In that capacity, Solon promulgated laws whose effectiveness has made his name a byword for wisdom. He cancelled all debts, including the traditional responsibility of tenant farmers to give a sixth of their produce to landlords. He broke the power of the hereditary nobility by organizing the rest of the citizenry into property classes, each of which could elect members to certain civic offices. He gave all citizens the right to sue and initiated an appeals process against the arbitrary decisions of magistrates. Naturally, as with any political reform, some were satisfied, but most were not. Nonetheless, Solon's reformation of the Athenian legal code laid the foundation for Athens' subsequent ascendancy as a successful democracy.

When he had done what he could to remedy Athens's political and diplomatic difficulties, Solon retired once more to his literary and philosophical occupations. The remains of these are slender. A collection of moral proverbs in elegiac verse (see ELEGY AND ELEGAIC POETRY) bears his name. A few letters and a fragment concerning a well-spent life are also ascribed to him.

Bibliography

Blok, Josine H., and André P. M. H. Lardinois. *Solon of Athens: New Historical and Philological Approaches*. Boston: Brill, 2006.

Irwin, Elizabeth. *Solon and Early Greek Poetry: The Politics of Exhortation*. New York: Cambridge University Press, 2005.

Solon. *Frammenti dell' opera poetica: Solone*. Edited by Herwing Maehler. Translated by Marco Fantuzzi. Milan, Italy: Biblioteca Universale Rizzoli, 2007.

Wallace, Robert W. "Revolutions and a New Order in Solonian Athens and Archaic Greece." In *Origins of Democracy in Ancient Greece*. Edited by Kurt A. Raaflaub et al. Berkeley: University of California Press, 2007.

Song Yu (Sung Yü) (fl. ca. 290–223 B.C.E.) *Chinese official, poet*

The nephew of the poet QU YUAN, Song Yu was an official at the Zhou (Chou) dynasty's court and an influential poet. Little else is known concerning his life. Song Yu is historically credited with a number of compositions. Some of those credits, however, are certainly mistaken, others are in doubt, and still others are presumed to be accurate.

A major work in the second category is a work in several sections that runs to almost 300 lines—*The Nine Changes* (*Jiu Bian, Chiu Pien*). This work is in an elegiac mood that seems to characterize Song's composition and looks to China's most famous poem, *Li Sao* (ENCOUNTERING SORROW), as its model. According to SIMA QIAN, who included a biography of the poet Qu Yuan in his monumental history the SHIJI, Song Yu wrote a famous poem, *The Summons of the Soul (Zhao Hun, Chao Hun)* that had mistakenly been attributed to Song's uncle Qu Yuan. Sima also reprovingly includes Song Yu among a group of poets who lacked the courage to correct the Chou emperor's misjudgments. Partly as a result, says Sima, the Zhou (Chou) dynasty fell victim to the Qin (Ch'in) 30 years later.

Song Yu seems to have been a master of the genre of ancient Chinese verse known as FU POEMS. *Fu* is variously translated as *rhapsody*, *rhymeprose*, or *prose poem*. Among the poems attributed to Song Yu is a "Rhapsody on the Lechery of Master Tengtu." He is also credited with a pair of rhapsodies celebrating a love goddess who had earlier appeared in *Encountering Sorrow*. In the first, "Rhapsody on Mount Gaotang," the goddess appears in a king's erotic dream. In the other, "Rhapsody on the Goddess," the poet himself dreams of the goddess, but she eludes his embraces and, as the literary historian Anne Birrell points out, reverses the usual ancient Chinese literary presentation of male-female roles by becoming the rhapsody's dominant figure.

Song Yu's rhapsody "The Wind" is anthologized in English translation in *The Columbia Anthology of Traditional Chinese Literature*.

See also ANCIENT CHINESE DYNASTIES AND PERIODS.

Bibliography

Mair, Victor H., ed. *The Columbia Anthology of Traditional Chinese Literature*. New York: Columbia University Press, 1994.

———. *The Columbia History of Chinese Literature*. New York: Columbia University Press, 2001.

Ssu-ma Ch'ien [Sima Qian]. *Records of the Grand Historian*. Vol. 1. Translated by Burton Watson. New York: Columbia University Press, 1961.

Sophist

Though the term *Sophist* originally denoted a wise or learned person, it later came to be applied in the Greco-Roman sphere to teachers of mathematics, politics, and especially rhetoric. As those who taught rhetoric in ancient, democratic Athens came increasingly to focus on the form and manner of presenting a speech or an argument and to de-emphasize content to the point that arguments sometimes became nonsensical, the word *Sophist* acquired a negative sense. Sophists came to be perceived as nitpicky hairsplitters who would argue any position regardless of how trivial or absurd it might be. It was in that light that SOCRATES and PLATO viewed such Sophists of their time as GORGIAS OF LEONTIUM and Protagoras (see PROTAGORAS).

Later, by the time the Roman Empire had established its power through the Mediterranean world, the Sophists who taught rhetoric, mathematics, and politics had recovered their respectability and their reputation for wisdom. This period of the renewed importance of Sophists is called the Second Sophistic—a term coined in *Lives of the Sophists* by L. FLAVIUS PHILOSTRATUS, (fl. ca. 210 C.E.). He composed a series of biographical sketches that included portraits of rhetoricians and orators from the time of Protagoras in the fifth century B.C.E. until the early third century C.E.

During the Second Sophistic, Sophists acquired great intellectual authority. The fourth-century C.E. Sophist and Byzantine THEMISTIUS EUPHRADES, for example, established an important school at the capital of the Eastern Roman Empire, tutored the children of the imperial family, and served creditably in a number of important political and administrative offices. Other Sophists at Rome and at Athens offered rhetorical instruction to such men as CICERO—men who would be at the heart of the intellectual and political life of their times.

Many of those second-period Sophists who specialized in delivering orations acquired the same sort of fame and adulation accorded 21st-century celebrities. These Sophist orators would travel the Roman world with an entourage of disciples and followers, presenting oratorical set pieces before enormous and enthusiastic audiences.

Although the persons called Sophists recovered their reputation for wisdom and acquired fame through their public speaking abilities, the word *sophist* itself continued then and continues now to carry a pejorative overtone and is often applied, for example, to those who formulate empty arguments designed to attract adherents to particular points of view.

Bibliography

Dillon, John, and Tania Gergel, trans. *The Greek Sophists*. New York: Penguin, 2003.

Goldhill, Simon, ed. *Being Greek under Rome: Cultural Identity, the Second Sophistic, and the Development of Empire*. New York: Cambridge University Press, 2001.

Lendering, Jona. "Second Sophistic." *Articles on Ancient History*. Available online. URL: http//www.livius.org/so-st/sophistic/second_sophistic. Downloaded 3 January 2007.

Philostratus, L. Flavius. *Lives of the Sophists*. In *Philostratus and Eunapius*. Translated by Wilmer Cave Wright. Cambridge, Mass.: Harvard University Press, 1952.

Plato. *Plato's Sophist: A Translation with a Detailed Account of Its Theses and Arguments*. Translated by James Duerlinger. New York: P. Lang, 2005.

Whitmarsh, Tim. *The Second Sophistic*. New York: Oxford University Press, 2005.

Sophocles (496–406 B.C.E.) *Greek tragic playwright*

The son of a well-to-do manufacturer of armor, Sophocles was born just outside Athens at Colonus. He spent his long life in Athens at the height of the city's wealth and renown. Most of his professional effort went into playwriting.

His translator and editor, Hugh Lloyd-Jones, lists the titles of 124 of Sophocles' tragedies, of which seven survive in their entirety. A significant fragment of an eighth entitled *Ichneutae* (The hunters) was discovered in an ancient trash heap in an Egyptian city called OXYRHYNCHUS in ancient times and Behnasa today. That fragmentary play concerns the theft of the cattle of Apollo,

the sun god, by the messenger of the gods, Hermes. Less sizable fragmentary remains exist for more than 90 other plays. More have been uncovered that are unassignable. Beyond Sophocles' tragedies, Lloyd-Jones lists the titles of 24 lost SATYR PLAYS attributed to Sophocles with varying degrees of confidence. The works surviving in their entirety include *AJAX, ANTIGONE, ELECTRA, OEDIPUS AT COLONUS, OEDIPUS TYRANNUS, PHILOCTETES,* and *TRACHINIAE.*

In the GREAT DIONYSIA, the annual Athenian competition held in connection with the city's celebration of the great festival of the god Dionysius, Sophocles' entries won 18 times. His first victory came in 468 when his entry triumphed over that of AESCHYLUS. To be a contender, a playwright's submission had first to survive a preliminary competition. Only the top three aspirants had their entries selected. Each entry comprised a tetralogy—three examples of TRAGEDY and a satyr-play.

As a dramatist, Sophocles earned a reputation for innovation. Whereas the tetralogies of Aeschylus, for example, contained linked tragedies that functioned like the acts of a single long play (see *ORESTEIA*), Sophocles introduced the practice of letting each of the three tragedies stand on its own. Aeschylus seemed more interested in the religious implications of his drama than did Sophocles, who was principally interested in the operation of the human will. When Sophocles' characters suffer, they suffer the consequences of actions that arise from their own psychological and moral makeup rather than from a general curse inflicted on the generations of a family, as in Aeschylus's treatment of the curse on the house of Atreus (see *AGAMEMNON*.)

The tragic flaws of Sophocles' heroes and heroines arise, as ARISTOTLE said they did in good tragedy, from an excess of a character's virtue. His heroines and heroes are all rather idealized, noble persons. In *POETICS*, Aristotle quotes Sophocles as remarking that "he drew men as they ought to be; EURIPIDES as they are." No love was lost between the two dramatists, who apparently exchanged accusations of plagiarism.

As an Athenian citizen, Sophocles achieved both renown and extraordinary personal popularity. He was handsome and approachable, and the citizens reposed confidence in his capacities to deal competently with public affairs, including military ones. On two occasions, they elected him to the post of *strategus*. In this capacity, Sophocles served as one of 10 Athenian military commanders of a regiment of the heavily armed foot soldiers called hoplites, and he was a general in a naval expedition against Samos in 440 B.C.E.

Sophocles lived an unusually long life, and he remained productive till its end. His *Oedipus at Colonus* was produced posthumously by his son, Sophocles the younger. Late in life, Sophocles invited an Athenian courtesan to share his quarters. His children filed suit alleging his incompetence to manage his own affairs. To defend himself against the charge he read the jury a draft of his *Oedipus at Colonus*. The court found Sophocles competent, and, perhaps as the children had feared, he left his money to his companion.

See also TRAGEDY IN GREECE AND ROME.

Bibliography

Haddas, Moses. *Ancilla to Classical Reading*. Morningside Heights, N.Y.: Columbia University Press, 1954.

Harvey, Paul, ed. *The Oxford Companion to Classical Literature*. Oxford: Clarendon Press, 1937.

Lloyd-Jones, Hugh, trans. and ed. *Sophocles, Vol. 3: Fragments*. Loeb Classical Library. Vol. 483. Cambridge, Mass.: Harvard University Press, 1996.

Scodel, Ruth. *Sophocles*. Boston: Twayne Publishers, 1984.

Spring and Autumn of Mr. Lü, The
(Lü shih ch'un-ch'iu, The Spring and Autumn Annals, The Annals of Lü Buwei) Lü Buwei (ca. 220 B.C.E.)

Purported to have been anonymously compiled at the request of the merchant statesman Lü Buwei (Lü Pu-wei), the *Spring and Autumn of Mr. Lü* is an innovative document that bears the name of its sponsor rather than that of its compiler. Although its content comes largely from predecessors, its form is the first Chinese work designed to make the work's organization reflect the nature of the universe.

The book's three principal sections reflect the interdependence of heaven, earth, and humankind. The first section, entitled "Prescriptions"—the heavenly section—contains 12 chapters, one for each month of the year. Each chapter begins with a description of the month and of the initiatives of government that are appropriate to that month. For the earthly section, entitled "Considerations," the numerological key is eight. To the ancient Chinese, the number eight symbolized earth, and each chapter in the section is further divided into eight smaller sections. The third section is keyed to the number six, symbolizing humankind. Therefore the section, called "The Six Discussions," contains six chapters, each one of which is further divided into six subdivisions. The literary historian Burton Watson suggests that this careful formal structure is meant to imply that the work is a "compendium of knowledge" about the "celestial, natural, and human worlds."

Political issues occupy most of the work's attention. Topics treated in its pages include agriculture, judging the capacities of men, avoiding being fooled by flatterers, and appointing men to the offices for which they are best suited. Conversations between sages and questioners often serve to illustrate the points under discussion, so CONFUCIUS might speak to a politician or a disciple about the topic at hand.

Aside from its organization, not much new appears in *The Spring and Autumn of Mr. Lü*. It draws its content principally from such earlier annals as SIMA QIAN'S *SHIHJI*. Watson reports that Lü Buwei's work does preserve a few legends not found elsewhere.

Bibliography

Lü Buwei. *The Annals of Lü Buwei: A Complete Translation and Study*. Translated by John Knoblock and Jeffrey K. Riegel. Stanford, Calif.: Stanford University Press, 2000.

Watson, Burton. *Early Chinese Literature.* New York: Columbia University Press, 1962.

Statius (Publius Papinius Statius) (d. 96 C.E.) *Roman poet*

Born in Naples to a father who later became a teacher in the household of the Roman emperor Domitian, Statius displayed poetic talent at an early age. He was educated in Rome and thereafter became a professional poet—one favored by the Emperor Domitian, as it seems, since Statius three times took first place in dramatic competitions held at the games near the emperor's villa at modern Alba.

Imperial favor notwithstanding, Statius seems to have suffered from poverty. He managed to eke out a living by selling dramatic pieces to actors. In addition to whatever these pieces may have been, Statius also wrote two known EPICS. The most celebrated of the pair, *Thebais*, uses some of the same narrative material that informs AESCHYLUS's *The SEVEN AGAINST THEBES,* tracing the competition and warfare between the brothers Polynices and Eteocles for control of the city and its eventual capture by Theseus. Statius's other epic, *Achilleis*, follows the career of Achilles before the Trojan War. That poem survives in a very incomplete state.

Also extant from Statius's pen we have five books of miscellaneous lyrics grouped together under the title *Sylvae.* The quality of the pieces in this compilation is very uneven.

Perhaps the emperor made a grant of land to Statius to relieve his poverty, for while he was still a young man, he retired to his place in the country and died there at a comparatively early age.

Bibliography

Slavitt, David, trans. *Broken Columns: Two Roman Epic Fragments.* [The *Achilliad* of Statius; *The Rape of Proserpina* of Claudius Claudianus.] Philadelphia: University of Pennsylvania Press, 1997.

Statius. *Statius.* 3 vols. Edited and translated by D. R. Shackleton Bailey. Cambridge, Mass.: Harvard University Press, 2003.

———. *The Silvae of Statius.* Translated by Betty Rose Nagel. Bloomington: Indiana University Press, 2004.

———. *The Thebiad: Seven against Thebes.* Translated by Charles Stanley Ross. Baltimore: Johns Hopkins University Press, 2004.

Stoicism

The Stoic philosophy is named for the locale in Athens at which one of Stoicism's founders, Zeno of Citium (333–264 B.C.E.), a native of the island of Cyprus, propounded his views. This was a colonnade or, in Greek, a *stoa.* The Stoics pursued three avenues of study as they sought to advance their philosophical point of view: ethics, logic, and physics. The last of these was crucial to the Stoic position, for Stoic philosophy regarded the essential ground of being in the universe as material rather than spiritual. This materiality, however, in no way diminished being's capacity for creative activity. The Stoics perceived it as an eternal, living fire with the same creative impulses that PLATO attributed to God and to the realm of spirit. Their viewpoint on the universe had something in common with that of the ancient Hindu thinkers in that the Stoics believed the eternal fire periodically created, destroyed, and then recreated the universe in a thoroughly deterministic and endless cycle of identical events.

For the Stoics, a human being's unique reflection of the universal creative fire was reason. Reason compelled those who followed the Stoic path to concentrate on matters that lay within their ability to influence. These included their own actions and the operations of the social and political systems within which they functioned. At root, the Stoics were rational empiricists. They found it pointless to worry about what they could not do anything about: death, natural disaster, or the end of the world. They instead tried to live ethically and moderately and to avoid illicit sensual gratification, the exercise of unreasonable power, and the pursuit of fame. Civic virtue, they felt, had to be based on the virtuous qualities of individual citizens. Otherwise, civic virtue would be a sham.

In Greece, thinkers who advanced the Stoic position included such philosophers as Ariston of Chios (fl. 250 B.C.E.), Herillus (fl. ca. 3rd c., B.C.E.), Cleanthes (ca. 330–ca. 230 B.C.E.), and the especially important Chrysippus of Soli (ca. 280–ca. 206 B.C.E.). Chrysippus systematized the Stoic viewpoint and marshaled its most convincing arguments. Later Stoics in the Greek world softened the Stoic position somewhat, incorporating into it some of the more spiritual views of Plato and the thinking of Aristotle. A similar trajectory seems to have been followed by the ancient Indian atheistic philosophy represented in the LOKĀYATA, which may have given rise to the viewpoints both of BUDDHA and of early Jain philosophers.

In Rome, it is perhaps fair to say that Stoicism became more of a personal and sometimes state ethical program than a philosophical movement. One sees its operation in such political and literary figures as Cato the Censor (see ORIGINES); CICERO; SENECA; or St. AUGUSTINE's friend, Symmachus, the imperial prefect of Rome. Symmachus was a part of the rearguard action of Roman intellectuals who mounted a foredoomed effort to preserve the toleration of conflicting religious points of view in the face of the religious intolerance of state-sponsored Christianity.

For a time, Stoicism had a powerful spokesman in the person of the Roman emperor MARCUS AURELIUS ANTONINUS, whose MEDITATIONS, written in Greek, reveal the character of a man who resisted the tendency for absolute power to corrupt absolutely and who believed in the power of reason over credulity.

Bibliography

Inwood, Brad, ed. *The Cambridge Companion to the Stoics*. New York: Cambridge University Press, 2003.

Marcus Aurelius. *Meditations*. Mineola, N.Y.: Dover Publications, Inc., 1997.

Strabo   See *GEOGRAPHY;* GEOGRAPHY AND GEOGRAPHERS, GREEK AND ROMAN.

Suetonius Tranquillus, Caius (ca. 70–ca. 160 C.E.) *Roman historian*

A member of the equestrian (knightly) class of Roman citizens, Suetonius was the son of a a tribune, a senior officer of the 13th Roman Legion. As a young man in Rome, Suetonius practiced law. He was a friend of PLINY THE YOUNGER, and Pliny formally requested that the emperor Trajan grant Suetonius exemption from the payment of certain taxes.

Roman emperors continued to look upon Suetonius with favor, and he occupied a series of responsible offices within the imperial household. Under Trajan and his successor Hadrian, Suetonius performed the offices of research secretary, chief librarian, and private or corresponding secretary. In the latter post, he well may have been a member of Hadrian's retinue when the emperor visited Gaul, Germany, and Britain in 121–22 C.E.

For reasons unknown, Suetonius was summarily dismissed from the imperial service around the time of the emperor's return. By that time, though, he had already acquired a reputation as a writer on a wide range of topics from BIOGRAPHY to clothing to meteorology. Many of his works have been lost, but we know some of the matters they concerned. Composing in both Latin and in Greek, Suetonius wrote biographies of courtesans, discussions of Greek games and Roman customs, and character sketches. He also wrote a commentary on CICERO's *Republic* and interested himself in the meanings and origins of words.

Suetonius compiled a group of bibliographies of illustrious men. Arranged into occupational groupings, most of these have disappeared over the centuries, though a section on grammarians

(*De illustribus grammaticis*) and another on rhetoricians (*De claris rhetoribus*) have survived.

Suetonius is principally remembered, however, as the earliest biographer of the Roman emperors, with the exception of Cornelius Nepos. His book, *Lives of the 12 Emperors* (*Vitae XII. Imperatorum*) begins with JULIUS CAESAR, whom he counts as the first, and continues through AUGUSTUS CAESAR, Tiberius, Caligula, Claudius, Nero, Galba, Otho, Vitellius, Vespasian, Titus, and Domitian. Suetonius had completed this work before his dismissal from imperial service denied him access to the authoritative documents upon which his discussion rests.

Presumably, Suetonius continued to live in Rome and to write until the time of his death.

Bibliography

Suetonius. *De grammaticis et rhetoribus: C. Suetonius tranquillus.* Translated by Robert A. Kaster. New York: Oxford University Press, 1995.

———. *Lives of the Caesars.* Translated by J. C. Rolfe. New York: Barnes and Noble, 2004.

———. *Suetonius with an English Translation.* [Includes *Lives of Illustrious Men.*] 2 vols. Cambridge, Mass.: Harvard University Press, 1997–98.

———. *The Twelve Caesars.* Translated by Robert Graves. New York: Penguin, 2003.

Sulpicia (fl. first century B.C.E.) *Roman poet*

A member of the household and the niece of Marcus Valerius Messalla Corvinus—the patron of the poet ALBIUS TIBULLUS—Sulpicia is thought to have authored the only poems by a pre-Christian Roman woman that have survived in their entirety. There are only six of them, each one an ELEGY, and in their surviving form, they may be revisions that Tibullus made of Sulpicia's originals.

The occasion for the composition of the poems was the ardor that Sulpicia felt for a young man whom she addresses as Cerinthus but who, as the translator Hubert Creekmore speculates, may have been the man she eventually married, Cornutus. The chronological arrangement of the poems in Creekmore's English translation is the translator's. Creekmore also intersperses poems by Tibullus so that the grouping tells the story of Sulpicia and Cerinthus both from the lovers' points of view and from that of a well-wisher. Creekmore assigns this grouping the title *No Harm to Lovers*

The first poem—one by Tibullus—celebrates Sulpicia's careful dress and adornment to celebrate the *Matronalia*, a Roman holiday in honor of Mars that was celebrated on March 1. She is so lovely in her attire that, should Mars himself descend from heaven, the war god would fall in love with her and embarrass himself by letting his armor drop. Sulpicia is the most worthy of the celebrants.

The second elegy—just eight lines long and Sulpicia's—is an epistolary poem addressed to Cerinthus and complaining that her uncle is insisting that she spend her birthday in the country away from her beloved. Though she must go, her heart and soul, she says, will remain with her beloved. In the third poem, Sulpicia's, the birthday plans have changed, and she joyfully announces that she will spend it in Rome after all.

In the fourth poem, the birthday has arrived, and Tibullus's elegy, written as though Sulpicia were sometimes speaking, takes the form of a prayer to Juno. Although Sulpicia's mother is present and offers advice about the content of her prayer to her patron goddess, Sulpicia prays silently in her heart for the fulfillment of her love as she makes her offerings to Juno.

Sulpicia lies ill with fever in the fifth poem (Sulpicia's) and hopes that Cerinthus is thinking tender thoughts of her. If not, then she fears she will be unable to overcome her illness if her lover proves indifferent. The sixth poem, by Tibullus, continues this theme with an invocation of Phoebus as the god of physicians to come and heal Sulpicia. At the same time, the god will relieve Cerinthus from his worry over the girl's health.

The seventh poem (Sulpicia's) is an apology to Cerinthus because, feeling consumed by her love for him, she fled from his company.

Tibullus assumes the role of Sulpicia in the eighth poem—one celebrating Cerinthus's birthday. Her voice in the poem prays that she and Cerinthus will burn for each other with equal passion.

Sulpicia speaks herself in the ninth poem, thanking Cerinthus ironically for his care of her virtue. He has apparently exceeded the bounds of propriety. In the next poem, however, one by Tibullus in Sulpicia's voice, Cerinthus is forgiven for his lapse. The poem concerns a hunting party to which Cerinthus has been invited, and Sulpicia's voice urges him to return quickly to her arms.

The final poem in the little collection is Sulpicia's own. Her love for Cerinthus has been consummated with the urging of Venus, and Sulpica is glad but also guilty. In her excitement, she hates having to "calm her features" to ward off gossip. She suggests that instead she and Cerinthus simply tell what happened.

Creekmore's translations are charming and his arrangement perfectly plausible and sensible.

See also PROBA, FALTONIA BETITIA.

Bibliography

Creekmore, Hubert, trans. *The Erotic Elegies of Tibullus with the Poems of Sulpicia Arranged as a Sequence Called No Harm to Lovers.* New York: Washington Square Press, 1966.

Sumerian literature (ca. 3000–2500 B.C.E.)

The historian of early Sumerian culture, V. K. Afanasieva, has reported that in 1991 we knew of more than 150 Sumerian literary works, many of them in fragmentary form. These works include verse MYTHS and EPICS. Love songs for the celebration of marriages between living, deified kings and priestesses also appear. Sumerian hymns include both funeral songs of mourning and songs about grief occasioned by disasters. There are hymns in honor of rulers and literary embellishments of royal inscriptions. We also find anecdotes, collections of fables, and proverbs. Beyond these, various instructional texts also exist.

The genre most widely represented is that of the hymn. Most of those surviving originated in the city of Nippur, and like many of the hymns of contemporary Hinduism, they often invoked the names of the gods to whom they were addressed and recited their deeds. Other hymns were addressed to those rulers who had been deified during their reigns, but not all kings were so honored.

An ancient Sumerian analogue exists for a story shared in different forms by later fertility cults and mystery religions that include, among others, Christianity. This comparable story appears in a series of songs or poems that begin by recounting a myth about the goddess of sexual love and animal fertility, Innin. Innin falls in love with the shepherd god or hero, Dumuzi, and marries him. She then descends into the underworld to challenge the power of its queen. For her rashness, she is killed there.

As soon as Innin dies, however, the animals on earth cease to procreate. The gods therefore restore Innin's life rather than have the world die. There is, however, a condition for her return to earth. She needs a volunteer to replace her in the world below. As the goddess of love and fertility, Innin (or Innanna, as she was known in the AKKADIAN tongue) has married deified husbands or taken official lovers in all the cities of Sumer, but these god-men all beg off when asked to replace her in the land of the dead. Only the shepherd god, Dumuzi, is willing to volunteer, but his sister Geshtinana resists his effort to die and calls on Utu, god of the sun, to hide Dununzi. Utu cooperates, three times disguising Dumuzi by transforming him into an animal. Eventually, however, Dununzi carries out his promise. He is killed and taken to the underworld. Anticipating the Greco-Roman myth of Proserpina, Geshtinana makes a deal with the gods of the netherworld. By its terms, she and Dumuzi each take turns spending six months in the land of the dead, so that they annually die and are annually reborn.

Undoubtedly, this myth that explains in anthropomorphic terms the annual regreening of the springtime world has oral roots that anticipate its written form by centuries and perhaps by millennia. Its Sumerian form also displays complications of plot that set it apart from Greco-Roman-Judeo-Christian versions.

A number of Sumerian myths survive that explain certain creative activities of the gods. These are not stories about universal beginnings like those one finds in Hebrew or Greco-Roman myth; the cosmos is beyond their ken. Such myths do include, however, an explanation of the creation of the world. They also concern the ordering of things. They discuss the creation of those gods whose responsibilities included overseeing earthly order. Among such gods one finds a pair named in The GILGAMESH EPIC, Enlil and Enki. Within the province of such deities fell such matters as populating the earth with creatures of all sorts, the invention of farming implements, and seeing that matters on earth proceeded more or less according to plan. Many of these myths are preserved in dialogue form and are the product of schools established as early as the third millennium B.C.E.—schools called *e-dubba*. Most of the literary texts that now survive seem to have been prepared by teachers or by students at such schools. The point of such texts, however, was not to prepare clay tablets that would circulate among a reading public. Rather, the objective was to prepare didactic material that would serve as an aid in memorizing such texts in the same way that the later texts of HOMER were memorized in Greek and Roman schools. One may feel certain that the oral literature of ancient Sumer was richer than the portion of it that survives incised on clay tablets.

We find the accomplishments of hero-kings recounted in nine surviving verse legends traceable, according to the king lists (see CUNEIFORM), to the First Dynasty of the city of Uruk—legends that include *The Gilgamesh Epic* and also stories concerning the kings Enmerkar and Lugalbanda.

Unlike *The Gilgamesh Epic*, most surviving Sumerian stories appear to represent a stage in the development of stories about heroes—a stage that precedes the formation of an actual unified epic. Composed of rather heterogeneous groups of stories, they tend to concern human heroes. Occasionally, similar cycles do feature divine heroes or heroines. Included in this group one finds a story in which the goddess Innin fights against a diabolical mountain—"Mount Ebekh." In another such example a deified ancestor-hero, Ninurta, fights against the demon Asak or Anzu.

Bibliography

Afanasieva, V. K. "Sumerian Culture." In *Early Antiquity*. Edited by I. M. Diakonoff and Philip L. Kohl. Translated by Alexander Kirjanov. Chicago: University of Chicago Press, 1991.

Alster, Bendt. *Wisdom of Ancient Sumer*. Bethesda, Md.: C. D. L. Press, 2005.

Cooper, Jerrold I., trans. *The Return of Ninurta to Nippur. An-gim dimma*. Rome: Pontificium Institutum Biblicum, 1978.

Kramer, Samuel Noah. *Enmerkar and the Lord of Aratta; A Sumerian Epic Tale of Iraq and Iran*. Philadelphia: University Museum, University of Pennsylvania, 1952.

Sung Yu   See FU POEMS.

Suppliants, The Aeschylus (ca. 492 B.C.E.)

The sole representative of a trilogy of plays, *The Suppliants* is thought to be the earliest surviving drama in any Western European language. The text of *The Suppliants* is almost certainly very corrupted in the form we have it, but at least it exists. AESCHYLUS took its subject from the myth of Io, a priestess of Hera and princess of Argos, whom the jealous goddess Hera turned partly into a heifer when Zeus's eye wandered in Io's direction. Distraught and terrified, Io fled to Egypt, where Zeus, in the form of a bull, made love to her and then restored her to her proper shape.

All intercourse between gods and human beings proved fruitful, and in due course Io bore a son, the demigod Epaphus. Epaphus in turn fathered a daughter, Libya. She gave birth to a son, Belus, and he became the sire of Danaus and his brother, Aegyptus. The scions of the fifth generation of this family each proved exceedingly fruitful. In the sixth generation, Danaus fathered 50 daughters and Aegyptus 50 sons. Aegyptus, who was a king in Egypt, intended his sons to marry his brother's daughters, forcibly if necessary. The girls and their father took exception to this proposal and, pursued by Aegyptus, fled back across the sea to Argos, where they intended to seek the protection of its king, Pelasgus.

It is at the point of the arrival of Danaus and the 50 girls on Argos that Aeschylus takes up the story in *The Suppliants*. The 50 girls are represented by a 50-woman CHORUS who present most of the play's dialogue, always in verse and often in song. They offer varying viewpoints whose shifts are emphasized by the chorus's dancelike movements, called *strophes* and *antistrophes*, about the stage. Aside from the chorus, only two actors perform. ARISTOTLE says that using a second actor was Aeschylus's innovative contribution to Greek drama. Performing in masks, the two actors represent the three male characters of the play: Danaus, Pelasgus, and a herald of King Aegyptus.

Arriving on the island of Argos, Danaus and his daughter seek out the temple of the votive gods of the island and lay wands of supplication on their altars, begging that the gods will preserve them from forced marriage to their first cousins. Finding a group of women dressed in foreign costume so employed, King Pelasgus challenges them to reveal their identities. In a series of questions and answers between a skeptical Pelasgus and members of the chorus, Pelasgus has the women tell the myth by rehearsing their genealogy. By that means, they both inform the audience of the play's background and establish their bona fides and their hereditary right to claim his protection from forced, incestuous marriage.

Even after he becomes convinced of the strangers' identities, Pelasgus remains cautious about promising them sanctuary. Such a policy would be tantamount to a declaration of war against Egypt. The suppliants invoke justice, but the king pleads that he must consult the citizenry of Argos lest they complain that he has "slain the state" in support of strangers. Desperate, the girls threaten

to commit suicide by hanging themselves from the images of the gods.

King Pelasgus sends Danaus to the city's shrines to lay the maidens' offerings before the gods of Argos and to acquaint the citizens with the suppliants' plight. Pelasgus seems to be coming round to the suppliants' point of view. While Danaus is absent, the chorus revisits the myth of Io, focusing on her state of mind as a binatured creature—half human, half cow—harassed by Hera and desperate in a strange land as a reflection of the state of mind in which the daughters of Danaus find themselves.

Danaus returns with the news that the citizens of Argos have voted in favor of protecting the women. They all offer grateful prayers for the success of their cause. These prayers have hardly been uttered, however, before the first of a fleet of Egyptian pursuers sails into view. Danaus runs to rouse the Argives to the promised defense, while the chorus repeats the fears of the maidens and their resolve to die rather than become forced brides.

A frenzied dance on stage represents the efforts of the vanguard of the Egyptian forces to tear the maidens from the altars of the Argive gods, while the herald of Aegyptus speaks the parts of all the would-be ravishers who are trying to tear the girls from the altars. The Egyptians are on the point of success when Pelasgus reappears and announces the intention of the Argives to defend the women. Threats, counterthreats, and a declaration of war ensue, and the herald and his followers are forced to leave empty-handed.

Pelasgus invites the maidens to dwell in Argos as his guests in the manner of their own choosing, and Danaus exhorts his daughters to be grateful. Then the chorus divides into halves that sing responsively of their gratitude and their fears for the future, knowing that Fate will determine the outcome of their situation, and the surviving and presumably first play of Aeschylus's trilogy comes to a close.

The rest of the history of the descendants of Io is well known, making it possible to reconstruct the plots, as well as, perhaps, the titles of the other two plays in Aeschylus's trilogy. The literary historians Whitney J. Oates and Eugene O'Neill, Jr., suggest the titles *The Egyptians* and *The Daughters of Danaus* for the lost plays. If, like the first, the subsequent plays follow the outline of the myth, the maidens are eventually forced to return to Egypt and go through with the marriages. Although Danaus publicly finally assents to the unions, privately he commands his daughters to kill their husbands on their wedding nights. Though 49 of the 50 daughters obey, one, a girl named Hypermnestra, happens to love her husband, Lynceus, and lets him live. Tried for disobedience to her father, Hypermnestra is defended from that charge by the goddess of love, Aphrodite, who argues that love takes precedence over filial obedience.

Bibliography

Aeschylus. *The Complete Plays*. Translated by Carl R. Mueller. Hanover, N.H.: Smith & Kraus, 2002.

———. *The Suppliants*. Translated by E. D. A. Morshead. In *The Complete Greek Drama. . . .* Edited by Whitney J. Oates and Eugene O'Neill, Jr. New York: Random House, 1938.

Hadas, Moses. *Ancilla to Classical Reading*. Morningside Heights, N.Y.: Columbia University Press, 1954.

Symposium (The Banquet) Plato
(385 B.C.E.)

Among the most celebrated of PLATO's dialogues, his *Symposium* recounts in dramatic fashion the speeches delivered on the subject of love and the accompanying conversation at a banquet held some years earlier in Athens at the house of Agathon. Plato establishes a dramatic situation in which Apollodorus describes the banquet's events, which he had learned about from Aristodemus, for the benefit of Glaucon and his nameless companion, who had already heard enough about the occasion to be curious.

On his way to the banquet, SOCRATES encounters Aristodemus and invites him to come along as a surprise guest. Agathon welcomes Aristodemus, but Socrates—as he regularly does—has been distracted and has disappeared. He soon reappears, however, and takes his place at the table, reclining next to his host, Agathon.

After dinner, customarily followed by a drinking bout, the banqueters agree to drink moderately and to dismiss the usual entertainment of flute girls. They choose instead to devote the allotted time to conversation, consenting to hear a series of speeches on the subject of love and about the god whose name is Love (Eros).

The first speaker, Phaedrus, quotes HESIOD to suggest that Love is the oldest of the gods and also the source of the greatest benefits to people. These benefits accrue from the honorable love of one person for another. A lover always wishes to impress his beloved by following the most honorable course of action. Ideal states and ideal armies should be composed of persons who are lovers, for they would rather die than have their beloved observe them perform any but the most admirable and heroic deeds. Phaedrus offers the examples of Achilles and Patroclus from HOMER's *The ILIAD* as proof of his assertions.

The next speech that Apollodorus recalls is that of Pausanias. Pausanias objects that Phaedrus has been insufficiently discriminating in his praise of love because there are in fact not one but two deities of love: the heavenly and the earthly Aphrodite. That of the earthly Aphrodite, says Pausanias, is the lower sort felt by "the meaner sort of men for women and youths." The higher sort of love, he argues, is inspired by the heavenly Aphrodite and is the sometimes homoerotic love of man for man—a love that delights in a "valiant and intelligent nature." (When this sort of love included a physical dimension, it was variously regarded by different city-states throughout Greece.)

Often, Pausanias continues, earthly lovers indulge in foolish behavior that in others would be considered blameworthy but that is tolerated and even approved in lovers. Moreover, even the gods are not angry with lovers who break their oaths. Nevertheless, true love is the unshakable love of soul for soul, stable, and lifelong. Love that is rooted in material considerations is dishonorable. Only love that makes the lovers eager for their own improvement belongs to the heavenly sort.

As Pausanias ends his oration, the dramatist ARISTOPHANES is to speak next. Just at that moment, however, he is seized with an attack of the hiccoughs, so Aristophanes exchanges turns with the physician Erixymachus.

Erixymachus begins by prescribing a cure for Aristophanes' hiccoughs and then turns to the subject at hand. Not surprisingly, he takes a medical view of the matter. In an extended and recondite Platonic doctor joke, Erixymachus defines medicine as "the knowledge of the loves and desires of the body, and how to satisfy them or not." The best physician is the one capable of discriminating healthy from unhealthy love. The humor arises from the age-old view that, in general, doctors are hard-pressed to discuss anything other than medicine.

Erixymachus suggests that love is the compelling principle in all life forms, not merely in human beings but also in the orderly but perhaps nonsentient processes of the universe as well. Health-giving love results in universal harmony and in health in men, animals, and plants. The entire process of sacrifice and divination to which religion devotes itself, says Erixymachus, concerns itself with the preservation of the good love and curing the conditions produced by the evil love. The good love, both among men and gods, is the source of happiness.

Aristophanes, now recovered from his hiccoughs as a result of sneezing as recommended by Erixymachus, jokes at the doctor's expense. The doctor warns the playwright that two can play the joking game.

Aristophanes explains that at the beginning of humanity, things were different from their current status. There were three, not just two, sexes. There was a male, a female, and an androgynous sex. Moreover, the original human being was a round creature with four hands, four feet, a single head with two identical faces on opposite sides, and two sex organs. This creature's locomotion

included the choice of walking upright but also included doing a series of rolling somersaults when speed was essential instead of running. These protohumans were so fearsomely strong that they attacked the gods. In punishment, the gods decided to split the mortals so that they walked about on two legs only. Moreover, should people continue their obstreperous ways, Zeus threatened to split them again so that they would have to hop about on one leg only.

The newly divided creatures, however, instantly became so insecure that they sought out their former halves and embraced them. In their depression, they began dying off at a startling rate. Pitying that outcome, Zeus moved the organs of procreation around to the front so that those who had originally been male-female and their descendants could temporarily approximate the original condition of the species and procreate. Likewise, those who were born with a predisposition toward same-sex counterparts could find love and fulfillment in the new circumstances. This myth has the benefit of accounting—albeit at the level of FABLE—for the actuality of human circumstances without making sexual preference or predisposition blameworthy. Moreover, the myth accounts for humanity's yearnings for happiness through finding a life-completing partner to love.

At the same time, impiety may result in still further alienation from humanity's original nature, so Aristophanes exhorts everyone to praise the god Love, who promises through love to restore pious people to their original state and make them blessed and happy. He also counsels Eryximachus to forego ridicule.

Now Socrates, Agathon, and Phaedrus begin to chat. Socrates tries to lead Agathon into one of his famous dialogues, but Phaedrus interrupts, warning Agathon against falling for Socrates' game. Instead, Phaedrus encourages Agathon to make his speech.

Acceding to the request, Agathon begins his discourse. He objects that the previous speakers have discussed the benefits that the god of Love confers upon mankind. Instead, Agathon objects, the god should be praised for his own attributes: youthfulness, tenderness, softness, the fairness of the god's complexion, his beauty, his gracefulness, his justice, and his temperance.

Agathon praises Love as well for the god's accomplishments in poetry and the fine arts. The devotees of Love walk in the light and not in darkness. Love is responsible for the discovery of the healing arts, the musical arts, and even the industrial and the household arts. Love is, moreover, a peacemaker and the savior of mankind. The attributes of Love, as Agathon proclaims them, anticipate many of the attributes of Christ by several centuries.

At the conclusion of Agathon's remarks, a reader learns that Socrates has been trying to avoid participation in the debate, excusing himself on the grounds that he did not understand the rules. Finally, however, he agrees to tell the truth about Love.

With characteristic subtlety, Socrates leads Agathon to admit that Love is neither good nor great, but rather aspires to become good and great. Having essentially destroyed Agathon's argument, Socrates now proposes to repeat the wisdom concerning Love that he learned from the wise woman Diotima of Mantineia. She had convinced Socrates that, just as a right opinion that cannot be proved represents a mean between ignorance and provable wisdom, so Love is neither fair and good nor foul and evil, but rather a mean between the two poles. Diotima explained that Love is a great spirit that mediates between the divine and the mortal. Love bears the prayers and sacrifices of human beings to the gods, and their replies and commands to mortals.

Socrates reports the myth of the parentage of Love that Diotima shared. Love, she explained, is the child Poverty—Love's mother—and was fathered by Plenty. Diotima described Love as always poor but at the same time bold, strong, and always plotting. Love is a philosopher, but also a SOPHIST; he is alive sometimes, and sometimes dead. Though love is not himself wise, he loves wisdom. Love is not beautiful, but that

which is truly beautiful, instead, is the person or thing beloved.

In discussing the nature of the beloved, Diotima explained that the beloved is at once the beautiful, the good, and, in consequence, the happy. Love is a process of creation, of bringing into being. Its expression in human lovemaking reflects the generative processes of the universe in bringing existence into being and thus also illustrates the quest for immortality.

All creative human activity, according to Diotima, is in essence a quest after immortality. Because the true, the good, and the beautiful are unified as a single entity that is also the ultimate ground of reality, the essential task of the human being must be to pursue those beautiful and virtuous objects and acts that will serve as stepping-stones to the eventual capacity to contemplate beauty directly with the active intellect. Achieving that end, said Diotima, will engender and nourish "true virtue," make the person so engaged "a friend of God," and lead directly to whatever degree of immortality human beings can aspire to.

This, Socrates tells his auditors, is what he learned from Diotima and is what he believes about the nature of love.

Just then a hubbub at the door announces the arrival of the drunken Alcibiades, who takes a place near Socrates. Socrates asks for protection against Alcibiades' violent affection for him. Alcibiades decides to entertain the company by demonstrating Socrates' remarkable ability to drink vast quantities of wine without visible effect. Socrates obediently drains a two-quart wine cooler but remains perfectly sober.

Now Alcibiades claims the privilege of pronouncing an encomium in praise of Socrates. Alcibiades compares the Athenian sage to busts of the satyr Silenus that conceal within them the images of the gods. His words have the power of music to charm the soul and evoke mysteries, and among orators only Socrates is perfect. Even Alcibiades would be convinced by Socrates' oratory to improve his manner of life, if Alcibiades could always remain near Socrates. But whenever

Socrates is absent, Alcibiades is overcome again by his love of popularity.

Alcibiades goes on to praise Socrates' self-control and his firm and nonjudgmental resistance to the homoerotic advances of Alcibiades. He recalls Socrates' self-mastery in other situations, such as in the battle of Potidea during the Peloponnesian Wars. There, Socrates seemed indifferent to such hardships as hunger, fatigue, and cold. He could, for instance, march barefoot on ice without seeming to experience discomfort. His powers of concentration made it possible for him to stand lost in thought throughout the night. Alcibiades recalls an occasion when he himself lay wounded on the field and Socrates saved his life, rescuing both Alcibiades and his weapons.

Alcibiades concludes his oration in praise of Socrates by repeating his comparison between Socrates and the busts that conceal images of the gods. In reply, Socrates accuses Alcibiades of only feigning drunkenness to have the opportunity to try a new tactic in his ongoing attempt to seduce Socrates. He also thinks Alcibiades is attempting to stir up a quarrel between Socrates and his friend Agathon.

Just at that moment, a new band of revelers bursts in at the door, and the orderly speechifying at the banquet is irretrievably interrupted. Everyone falls asleep except Socrates, Aristophanes, and Agathon. When a cock's crowing awakens Aristodemus, he discovers Socrates discoursing to the other two about the essential identity of the geniuses of COMEDY and TRAGEDY. When his last two listeners also fall asleep toward daybreak, Socrates rises, goes to the public baths to bathe, passes the day as he usually does, and goes home to rest at the day's end.

In *Symposium*, Plato provides us with a dramatic performance that contains a philosophical clarification of his thinking about the subject of love in the dialogue reported between Socrates and Diotima. The drama also draws for us one of antiquity's most compelling portraits of Plato's teacher, Socrates, who is also the central character of many Platonic dialogues.

Bibliography

Plato. *Symposium*. Translated by Christopher Gill and Desmond Lee. New York: Penguin Books, 2000.

T

Tacitus (Publius (?) Cornelius Tacitus)
(ca. 55–ca. 117 C.E.) *Roman historian*
The birthplace of Cornelius Tacitus—universally respected as the premier historian of the Roman world—is uncertain, though somewhere in northern Italy seems likely. His marriage in 78 to the daughter of Agricola, a respected governor of Britain, suggests that Tacitus's family was well-to-do and well-connected. This is also indicated by the rhetorical education that he apparently received.

Tacitus seems to have pursued first a military and then a political career. In the latter capacity, he served both the emperors Vespasian and Titus and subsequently, perhaps, became the governor of one of the empire's lesser provinces from 89 to 93 C.E. Upon his return, he became praetor under the reign of the emperor Domitian. After the consuls, who were the heads of the Roman republic, the praetor was the next most responsible official of the city of Rome. In addition to performing the offices of the consuls in their absence, a praetor also could serve as the general of an army when the need arose.

In the office of praetor, Tacitus, whose attitude toward Domitian was influenced by the historian's affinity for the Roman Senate, had the opportunity to observe at first hand the excesses of Domitian's arrogance toward the senate and the emperor's propensity for executing former consuls. At least 12, and possibly more of them, died on Domitian's orders.

Tacitus also served as one of the 16 members of a college of Roman priests responsible for guarding and interpreting ancient Greek books of ritual texts that the priests consulted when the senate required a religious interpretation of unusual events. Tacitus himself tells us that each of the emperors Vespasian, Titus, and Domitian (whom he abhorred) all advanced his career.

Tacitus began his literary work with the publication of a biography of his father-in-law, Iulius Agricola, in 98. In addition to chronicling that life, Tacitus asserted his opposition to Domitian and offered a much-admired consolation on the demise of Agricola. Later in 98 appeared a work of GEOGRAPHY and ethnography, *Germania*, in which Tacitus describes the peoples of Germany, their manner of life, and their government. The 18th-century British historian Edward Gibbon praised the work for "accurate observation" and for the "diligent inquiries" Tacitus had made in preparing to write it. Following that work came a dialogue treating the subject of the contemporary decline of the art of public speaking, *Dialogus de oratoribus* (A dialogue about oratory).

Tacitus began working next on his *Histories* and on *Annals*. When the *Histories* were finished (date uncertain), they included as many as 12 or 14 books that dealt with events between the years 69 and 96 C.E. The *Annals* included as many as 14 or 16 books. In their original form, the *Histories* dealt with the period running from 69 to 96 C.E. Owing, however, to imponderable accidents of history, only four of the books and a bit of the fifth have survived. Even these are known only from single manuscripts.

The *Annals* began with the death of Rome's first emperor, AUGUSTUS CAESAR, in 14 C.E. and continued through the death of Nero in 68. The remaining portions of the *Annals* include all of books 1–4 and books 12–15. Most of book 6 and portions of books 5, 11, and 16 also exist.

Quite apart from being the source from which stories about Rome during the empire's early years have been regularly unearthed by more modern literary figures such as Robert Graves, Tacitus's pithy and original style is much admired by those who comment on his Latin. The renowned classicist Moses Hadas, in his introduction to the Modern Library edition of Tacitus's complete works, quotes Tacitus: "*solitudinem faciunt pacem appellant*"—the ancient historian's description of pointless wars waged to occupy the attention of the populace. Hadas translates the phrase: "They make a wilderness and call it peace." Tacitus is a historian for all ages.

Bibliography

Mellor, Ronald. *Tacitus*. New York: Routledge, 1994.

Tacitus, Cornelius. *The Annals*. Translated by Alfred John Church and William Jackson Brodribb. Mineola, N.Y.: Dover Publications, 2006.

———. *The Annals and The Histories*. Translated by A. J. Church and William Jackson Brodribb. New York: Barnes and Noble Books, 2005.

———. *The Complete Works of Tacitus*. Translated by Alfred John Church and William Jackson Brodribb. Edited by Moses Haddas. New York: Modern Library, 1942.

———. *Tacitus' Agricola, Germany and Dialogue on Orators*. Indianapolis: Hackett Publishers, 2006.

Tao Qian (T'ao Ch'ien, Tao Yüan Ming)
(365–427 C.E.) *Chinese poet*

Earlier known as Tao Yüan Ming, Tao Qian contrived to earn appointment as a magistrate, but the expectation that he must behave deferentially to superior officers of the civil service annoyed him. Therefore, after serving in office for only 83 days, Tao retired to private life. This decision earned him enduring admiration as a man of principle.

In his private capacity, Tao cultivated flowers, particularly chrysanthemums, and occupied his time with music and with writing FU POEMS. One of these reflects on his decision to avoid a public career and the pleasures that arise from his alternative pursuits. He delights in the company of his family, in reading, and in performing on his lute. The fact that Tao owned land made possible his retirement as a gentleman farmer, and he reflects on the way that his laborers will keep him informed when his attention is required during the passage of the seasons. Otherwise, the work celebrates his rural pleasures and reflects on the joy and freedom from care that will characterize the brief days of his earthly existence.

Chinese letters also remember Tao Qian as a composer of picture eulogies—verses written to accompany pictures on a painting or on a fan. He was the author of one of the earliest such works to survive. In five-syllable and sometimes four-syllable rhymed verse, he wrote poems celebrating the lives of early Confucian recluses. His "Eulogy on Shang Chang and Ch'in Ch'ing," as the scholar Charles Hartman tells us, is perhaps the earliest surviving example of this particular art form.

Late in his life, Tao Qian is thought to have compiled a 10-volume collection of 116 fairy tales and legends entitled *Sequel to "Search for the Supernatural."* Among those legends is an analogue to the modern Scottish story of Brigadoon—*T'ao-hua yüan chi* ("RECORD OF THE PEACH BLOSSOM SPRING").

Bibliography

Davis, A. R. *Tao Yüan Ming: His Works and Their Meaning.* New York: Cambridge University Press, 1983.

Hartman, Charles. "Poetry and Painting." In *The Columbia History of Chinese Literature.* Edited by Victor H. Mair. New York: Columbia University Press, 2001.

Hu Ying. "Records of Anomalies." In *The Columbia History of Chinese Literature.* Edited by Victor H. Mair. New York: Columbia University Press, 2001.

Tao te ching   See LAO TZU.

Terence (Publius Terentius Afer) (ca. 195– ca. 159 B.C.E.) *Roman dramatist*

The classicist Walter E. Forehand, a biographer of the Roman playwright Terence, cautions us that the ancient sources of biographical and critical information about Terence may not be altogether trustworthy. These sources include, first, a biography of the playwright by SUETONIUS in his collection *On Poets.*

According to Suetonius, Terence's life spanned the years 185–159 B.C.E. Suetonius also asserts that Terence was a Carthaginian—an African (hence the name Afer) brought to Rome as the slave of a senator, Terentius Lucanus. Later the senator adopted Terence as his own son. Then, before he turned 25, perhaps with the help of powerful Roman patrons and a master of COMEDY named Caecilius Statius, Terence brought to the Roman stage a series of six plays whose plots he had borrowed from his Grecian predecessors: ANDRIA (*The Woman of Andros*), *The SELF-TORMENTOR, The Eunuch, Phormio, The Mother-in-Law,* and ADELPHI (*The Brothers*). These proved highly successful, and, armed with that success, Terence set out for Greece, presumably in search of new material. There he wrote some new plays, but they were lost and the poet may also have drowned when he was shipwrecked on the return voyage. Forehand presents alternatives that call almost all of Suetonius's facts into question, without opting strongly for one view over another.

Forehand has also examined another set of ancient sources that purport to give us information about Terence's theatrical career. This set includes ancient production notices for all of the plays except *Andria,* and another ancient source gives the pertinent information for that play. The central bone of scholarly contention about the content of these notices arises from the uncertainty they introduce into establishing the order of some of Terence's work. Further evidence suggests that, on his return voyage from Greece, Terence may have been bringing with him not only whatever new plays he had written there, but also 108 texts of other Greek plays—enough to supply him with a lifetime of plots. Thus, if the poet did lose his life and his plays at once, an unhappy accident deprived the world of a good deal of amusement.

As is the case with the Greek originals on which Terence modeled his surviving plays, Roman comedy as he helped to shape it was highly conventional. The plays featured stock situations: Shipwrecks (ironically), mistaken identities, kidnapping by pirates, disguises, separations and reunions, and young lovers kept apart by venal elders all figured prominently. Characters were also predictable: Old misers, lickspittles, blusterers, foolish youngsters, and hypocrites peopled Terence's stage. A part of the playwright's charm, however, arises from his ability to make his characters fresh and engaging within the confines of their predictability.

Bibliography

Forehand, Walter E. *Terence.* Boston, Mass.: Twayne Publishers, 1985.

Terence. *Terence, the Comedies.* Translated by Palmer Bovie et al. Baltimore: Johns Hopkins University Press, 1992.

———. *Works: English and Latin.* Translated by John Barsby. Cambridge, Mass.: Harvard University Press, 2001.

Thales of Miletus   *Greek prose writer* See *LIVES OF EMINENT PHILOSOPHERS.*

Thaletas of Crete   (fl. seventh century B.C.E.) *Greek poet*

Virtually nothing of the poems attributed to Thaletas of Crete survives. What little does exist under his name is of dubious attribution. Legend has it, nonetheless, that, encouraged by the Spartan lawgiver Lycurgus, Thaletas moved from his birthplace, the town of Gortyn on the island of Crete, to Sparta on the Grecian mainland. There he founded a school for boys. As a poet and a musician, Thaletas composed verse or song of such power that his works are credited with either having averted civil war or having cured a plague. If the poems attributed to him are really his, stopping the war seems more likely as his verse encouraged observation of the law. Tradition also credits Thaletas with the introduction of novel rhythms to Greek verse and with having written songs designed to accompany choral dancing.

Bibliography

Cambell, David A. *The Golden Lyre: The Themes of the Greek Lyric Poets.* London: Duckworth, 1983.

Santos, Sherod. *Greek Lyric Poetry: A New Translation.* New York: W. W. Norton, 2005.

Themistius Euphrades   (fl. fourth century C.E.)

Born in Paphlagonia near the Euxine Sea, Themistius Euphrades moved to Constantinople, where he earned a notable reputation as an orator, as a SOPHIST, and, in his own school, as a teacher of philosophy and rhetoric. He also spent some time in Rome, where he instructed St. AUGUSTINE.

A pagan, Themistius enjoyed the confidence of the Roman emperor Julian the Apostate. A lost oration by Themistius seems to have encouraged the emperor in his suppression of the Christians, and it produced a surviving letter from Julian that outlined his plans for his anti-Christian campaign. As a mark of Themistius's capacities, however, he remained a trusted adviser to the Christian rulers who succeeded the pagan Julian—particularly the emperor Constantine. Themistius also served as a member of the senate in Constantinople. Theodosius the Great employed Themistius as a tutor in the imperial household and entrusted him with his heir's education. The same emperor also appointed Themistius as prefect of Constantinople. Themistius, who strongly believed in tolerating all religious viewpoints, also made friends with such Christian intellectuals as Gregory Nazianzen, who greatly respected Themistius's capacities.

Themistius's surviving work includes 34 discourses. Many of these are formal addresses to the emperors he served in which he sometimes offers useful observations on the conduct of monarchical government. Sometimes they contain standard praises of the emperor currently enthroned. Themistius delivered one of the surviving orations at his father's funeral. Others paraphrase works of ARISTOTLE, including that philosopher's discourses "On the Soul," "Physics," "Posterior Analytics," and others. These orations are distinguished by their clarity, organization, and vividness of idiom. The designation *euphrades* means "the eloquent one." (See JULIANUS.)

Bibliography

Themistius. *On Aristotle's "On the Soul": Themistius.* Translated by Robert B. Todd. Ithaca, N.Y.: Cornell University Press, 1996.

———. *On Aristotle's "Physics 4": Themistius.* Translated by Robert B. Todd. Ithaca, N.Y.: Cornell University Press, 2003.

———. *Politics, Philosophy, and Empire in the Fourth Century: Select Orations of Themistius.* Translated by Peter Heather and David Moncour. Liverpool, U.K.: Liverpool University Press, 2001.

———. *Private Orations of Themistius.* Translated by Robert J. Penella. Berkeley: University of California Press, 2000.

Theocritus (ca. 310–ca. 270 B.C.E.) *Greek poet*

The first and most important Greek bucolic or pastoral poet, Theocritus was born on Sicily, probably at Syracuse, and later migrated, first to the island of Cos near Asia Minor and then to Alexandria in Egypt. There he was certainly acquainted with the verse of CALLIMACHUS and probably knew the poet personally. Theocritus took Callimachus's side in a literary dispute with a critic who favored traditional EPIC poetry over short lyrics.

Some of Theocritus's extant verse is nonetheless semi-epic in its content. His most famous and characteristic poetic productions, however, the pastoral *IDYLLS*, focus on life in the countryside and were seminally influential in the later development of the mode of PASTORAL POETRY. His work provided a model for the Roman poet VIRGIL's *ECLOGUES*. Also much admired during the European Renaissance, Theocritus became the model for such poets as Edmund Spenser and John Milton in England, for such playwrights as Torquato Tasso in Italy or Luis de Góngora y Argote in Spain, and such novelists as Honoré d' Urfé in France.

Often in his *Idylls*, Theocritus adopts the fiction that shepherds, traditionally in the Sicilian countryside but also in that of Cos, are engaged in a poetic contest or are mourning a lost friend. The characterizations and the emotional tone that emerge are true to life, as are Theocritus's treatments of animals and his descriptions of the rural landscape. Above all, his style is straightforward, unaffected, and beautiful.

Not all of Theocritus's *Idylls* take place in a rural landscape. Some, like "The Ladies of Syracuse," are set in a metropolitan landscape; some, like "Polyphemus and Galatea," treat mythological subjects; and some, like his poem in praise of the Greek pharaoh of Egypt, Ptolemy II Philadelphus, contain addresses to rulers.

About the details of Theocritus's personal life, virtually nothing—other than his parents' names: Praxagoras and Philinna—is certain. Some 22 surviving idylls can confidently be associated with his name.

Bibliography

Theocritus. *Idylls.* Translated by Anthony Verity. New York: Oxford University Press, 2002.
———. *Encomium of Ptolemy Philadelphus.* Translated by Richard Hunter. Berkeley: University of California Press, 2003.
———. *A Selection: Theocritus.* Translated by Richard Hunter. Cambridge: Cambridge University Press, 1999.
Walker, Steven F. *Theocritus.* Boston: Twayne Publishers, 1980.

Theognis (ca. mid-sixth century B.C.E.) *Greek poet*

Probably born in the mainland city of Megara, Theognis composed elegiac verses that took among their principal subjects the benefits of hereditary oligarchy as opposed to the evils of democratic politics and majority rule. The works of Theognis survive in a unique manuscript of almost 1,400 lines, but it appears that the work of other poets also comprise a part of the collection. Some poems on the subject of love are attributed to Theognis, but that attribution is highly suspect.

In the political poems, Theognis chooses the elegiac form that alternates lines of dactylic hexameter—the meter of HOMER—with lines of dactylic pentameter (see QUANTITATIVE VERSE). An aristocrat by birth, Theognis believed that humankind was sharply divided into two sorts: those who were born of noble parentage and were therefore good, and those who were not so born and were therefore bad. Education brought no benefit in the reformation of the moral predispositions of the bad ones, so that when the rule of cities fell into their hands, political corruption and the ruin of aristocrats inevitably followed.

The virtues of the aristocratic class included judgment, moderation, justice, restraint, and reverence. The lower classes were distinguished by a total absence of those virtues. Theognis thought it easier to "beget and rear a man" than it was "to put good sense in him." Fools did not become wise; neither did bad people suddenly turn good. Teaching did not lead to improvement of virtue.

Theognis complains of the role that the wicked, risen to important positions, were playing in debasing the citizenry of Megara, in replacing noble motives with the quest for power and profit, in approving injustice to achieve those goals, and in turning "gentlemen into nobodies." Apparently this was the fate that the poet himself had suffered, for he laments his former wealth and status in lines 667–682 of the collection.

In another subcategory of poems most confidently attributable to Theognis, his "Maxims," he gives high-minded advice to a youth named Kyrnus. The poet advises his friend to exercise prudence and not to employ base or unjust means in seeking honors, prestige, and fortune. Theognis held unwavering friendship in the highest esteem and considered it a refuge from the vagaries of fortune.

See also ELEGY AND ELEGAIC POETRY.

Bibliography

Banks, J., ed. and trans. *The Works of Hesiod, Callimachus, and Theognis.* London: George Bell and Sons, 1876.

Kagan, Donald. *The Peloponnesian War.* New York: Viking, Penguin, 2003.

Lattimore, Richmond, trans. *Greek Lyrics.* Chicago: University of Chicago Press, 1955.

Romilly, Jacqueline de. *A Short History of Greek Literature.* Translated by Lillian Doherty. Chicago: University of Chicago Press, 1985.

Theognis. "The Elegiac Poems of Theognis." In *Elegy and Iambus.* Vol. 1. Edited and translated by J. M. Edwards. Cambridge, Mass.: Harvard University Press, 1965.

Theogony Hesiod ca. 8th c., B.C.E.

A dactylic hexameter poem of slightly over 1,000 lines (see QUANTITATIVE VERSE), *Theogony* traces the genealogy and history of the Greek gods. The poet HESIOD begins his song with a description of the activities of the nine Muses in their mountain home on Mt. Helicon. He tells how they sing and celebrate the gods of the Olympian pantheon; the TITANS who came before them; and the oldest of the gods—Chaos, Chronos (time), Gaia (the earth), Uranus (the heavens), Oceanus, Night, and others.

The Muses, Hesiod tells us, spoke to him as he tended his flocks on the slopes of Mt. Helicon near his home. Into the rustic shepherd they breathed a poetic voice with the power to sing about the future and the past. They instructed the poet that, when he sang, the Muses should begin and end his song. He therefore obeys, tracing their genealogy and recording their birth as the daughters of Zeus and Mnemosyne (memory). He speaks of their power to sing and to inspire poets and singers, and invokes their power to help him sing of the origins of the gods; of their power, riches, and privileges; and of the universe and its phenomena.

The Muses inspire Hesiod, and he begins his account of the gods' genealogy, in the order of their appearance: Chaos; Gaia; Tartaros (the worst pit of the underworld), and Eros, the god of love, who overpowers intelligence and strength in gods and in men. Hesiod continues his account of the gods and of mythic beings like the Cyclops and the hundred-armed Kottos, Briareos, and Gyes—giants who hated their father Uranus and conspired with their mother Gaia to emasculate him. Uranus's seed nonetheless impregnated Gaia with the Furies, giants, and wood nymphs. His genitalia ended up in the sea, and from the resultant insemination, Aphrodite, the goddess of love, was born.

Having dealt at some length with Uranus's progeny, Hesiod turns his attention to the children of Night. Night required no consort, but in a series of births by parthenogenesis, she produced numerous offspring. Among others, these included Fate or Fortune; End; Death; Sleep; Dreams; the three Fates named Klotho, Lachesis, and Atropos; Deception; the Furies (a second version of their origin); Discord; malignant Old Age; Hardship; Battles; Murders; Lawlessness; and, in short, most of the personifications of human-kind's afflictions.

Pontos, the great Sea, on the other hand, lay with Gaia, and their progeny displayed their father's characteristics of gentleness, thoughtfulness, and trustworthiness. Notable among the descendants of Pontos we find Oceanus, the great river that early Greek geographers thought encircled the earth, and Nereus, who always tells the truth. Nereus, in turn, produced 50 lovely daughters with his consort Doris.

After almost 500 lines detailing the genealogies of the pre-Olympian gods, nature spirits, and the personifications of aspects of creation, Hesiod turns his attention to the origin of the Olympians. He tells how Uranus's son Cronus parented the infant Zeus with his consort Rheia, who represents the principle of fertility. At Zeus's birth, Cronus asked that the baby be brought to him, but, fearing Cronus's motives, Rheia instead presented him with a stone wrapped in swaddling clothes. Thinking the object to be the child who a prophecy had foretold would displace him, Cronus instantly swallowed the stone, swaddling and all. The infant Zeus grew up and replaced his father as the chief of the gods, as the prophecy had foretold.

At line 509, Hesiod digresses to discuss the parentage of the Titan Prometheus, the benefactor of humankind. He details the strife between Zeus and the Titans as the two sets of immortals struggled for supremacy, until the hundred-armed giants overcame the Titans in warfare. The poet remarks on the unkind treatment that both Prometheus, who had helped Zeus prevail, and his brother Atlas endured at Zeus's hand, and how at long last Zeus imprisoned the rebellious Titans in an exhaustively described "moldy place" under the earth forever. We also learn of Zeus's ill treatment of people.

Following this section of *Theogony*, Hesiod treats his readers to a detailed lesson in the topography of the world of myth and then to Zeus's struggle against the giant Typhoeus. This monster had a hundred serpents' heads, eyes of fire, and an eardrum shattering voice. Zeus was narrowly able to overcome Typhoeus with thunderbolts, set him aflame, and confine him in Tartarus, the lowest pit of the underworld. Had Zeus lost, Typhoeus would have become master of the universe. Typhoeus is the sire of all winds that blow loudly and wetly, like hurricanes and tornadoes.

When the Olympian gods finished the battles against their predecessors, they forced the Titans to share their titles and privileges, and on the advice of Gaia, the Earth, Zeus was appointed the chief god. Hesiod next details Zeus's relationships with a series of wives. First came Metis, with whom he conceived Athene, goddess of wisdom. Metis enjoyed unparalleled intelligence, and a brother for Athene was prophesied—one who would eventually supplant Zeus. To avoid that outcome, Zeus hid the pregnant Metis away in his belly so that she could do his thinking.

Zeus's second wife, Themis, gave birth to the Seasons, Lawfulness, Justice, Peacetime and the Fates (for a second version of this origin, see above.). To these offspring fell the responsibility of supervising the actions of human beings. Others among Zeus's numerous liaisons mothered the three Graces, Persephone, the Muses, Apollo, and Artemis. Finally he married Hera, who gave birth to Hebe, Ares, and the goddess of childbirth, Eileithyia. With no help from Zeus, Hera also mothered the blacksmith of the gods, Hephaistos. At length, Zeus himself bore the child of the concealed thinker, Metis. That child, Athene, sprang fully armed from the right side of Zeus's head.

Through the 964th line of his poem, Hesiod continues to chronicle the genealogies of the Olympians and the offspring of their amours. He next turns his attention to goddesses who slept with mortal men and catalogues their offspring for the next 70 lines. He brings his account down to the time of the Trojan War, which historians believed to have ended around 1184 B.C.E. Some of the details he recounts there suggest his direct knowledge of HOMER's *The ODYSSEY*, a work he was most likely to have known as an oral recitation.

As *Theogony* ends, lines occur that suggest Hesiod next meant to turn his attention to mortal women and their progeny. These lines provide grounds for thinking Hesiod to be the author of a work called *Catalogue of Women* (*Eoeae*). This attribution, however, is far from certain, and that fragmentary catalogue could well spring from a later author writing, as many did, in the manner of Hesiod.

Hesiod's example remained influential throughout the ancient world and into the Renaissance, when Boccaccio's *Genealogy of the Gods* revived a genre that Hesiod, as far as we know, had fathered. In his admirable translation of major works authored by or associated with Hesiod, Richmond Lattimore includes a very useful genealogical chart that summarizes in graphic form the familial relationships among the gods that Hesiod details in song.

Bibliography

Hesiod. *Hesiod: The Works and Days; Theogony; The Shield of Herakles*. Translated by Richmond Lattimore. Ann Arbor: University of Michigan Press, 1962.

———. *Theogony, Works and Days, Shield*. Translated by Apostolos N. Athanassakis. Baltimore: Johns Hopkins University Press, 2004.

——— et al. *Works of Hesiod and the Homeric Hymns*. Translated by Daryl Hine. Chicago: University of Chicago Press, 2005.

Theophrastus of Eresus (ca. 371–ca. 287 B.C.E.) *Greek prose writer*

Born on the Island of Lesbos, Theophrastus succeeded his teacher and friend, ARISTOTLE, as the principal of the PERIPATETIC SCHOOL OF PHILOSOPHY at Athens. A prolific author, Theophrastus wrote scientific treatises about such subjects as botany, physiology, and meteorology. He also authored numerous philosophical works that included one on metaphysics. Beyond that, Theophrastus interested himself in stylistics, writing a work, *On Style*, that CICERO admired.

Literature best remembers him, however, for a kind of work that writers through the ages would emulate: character writing. To write a character, Theophrastus would choose a trait or failing that someone displayed and then would give amusing examples of that characteristic as his subject displayed it. The characters tend to be stylized and are recognizable as the same sort of types that stock characters represented on Theophrastus's contemporary comic Athenian stage. Like MENANDER's stage types, Theophrastus's characters convey amusing glimpses of ancient Athenian foibles.

As a literary type, the character has enjoyed periods of renewed popularity throughout the centuries. The 17th century in England, for example, was such a time. Earlier, in 14th-century England, Geoffrey Chaucer alluded to the *Book of Wicked Wives* as a work consulted by Jankyn, Alice of Bath's fifth husband in Geoffrey Chaucer's *The Wife of Bath's Tale*. Theophrastus's essay on marriage was among the sources for Jankyn's book.

From Theophrastus's own point of view, however, the characters he composed, while intended to amuse, were more importantly intended to instruct. He used them as examples in teaching rhetoric.

Bibliography

Hanna, Ralph, et al. *Jankyn's Book of Wicked Wives*. Athens: University of Georgia Press, 1997.

Sharples, R. W. *Theophrastus of Eresus. Commentary, Vol. 31: Sources on Physics; Sources for His Life Writings, Thought, and Influence*. Boston: Brill, 1998.

Theophrastus of Eresus. *Characters: Theophrastus*. Edited and translated by James Diggle. New York: Columbia University Press, 2004.

———. *On Sweat; On Dizzyness; and On Fatigue*. Edited by William W. Fortenbaugh, Robert W. Sharples, and Michael G. Sollenberger. Boston: Brill, 2003.

———. *On Weather Signs: Theophrastus of Eresus*. Edited by David Sider and Carl Wolfram Brunschön. Boston: Brill, 2007.

"Theseus" and "Romulus" (from *Parallel Lives*) Plutarch (ca. 100 C.E.)

PLUTARCH's first set of biographies from his *PAR-ALLEL LIVES*, "Theseus" and "Romulus," together with his 10th set, "PERICLES" AND "FABIUS," provide samples in this volume of the 23 surviving pairs of biographies and the comparison of the subjects' moral qualities that, together with four individual lives, constitute Plutarch's biographical masterpiece.

In the collection's first pair, Plutarch traces the childhood of his subjects, Theseus, the ruler of Athens and Romulus, Rome's founder. He recounts the dangers through which they pass and the unusual circumstances of their early survival—as when Romulus and his brother Remus were suckled by a she-wolf and fed by a woodpecker. He recounts his heroes' bravery and ferocity in battle, as when the Romans, under Romulus's leadership, go in search of wives, overcome the Sabines, and kidnap some of their virgin daughters, or when Theseus seeks out and destroys the Minotaur, a mythical half bull/half man who annually kills a group of Athenian youths sent to Crete as tribute. Revealing a naturalistic bent, Plutarch suggests that the Minotaur was in reality a fearsome gladiator who had regularly routed the Athenian young men in combat but whom Theseus successfully overcame.

In his method as a biographer, Plutarch sometimes tends toward wordiness. He cannot resist including a good and sometimes a not-so-good story, even if it leads away from the main thrust of his narrative. At the same time, the encompassing quality of his interest and his willingness to suspend judgment give us clear insight into the attractive qualities of mind of the author. Ironically, very little of the external circumstances of Plutarch's own life is known to us.

In the process of the first set of paired biographies, a reader learns much about the founding of Athens and Rome. Theseus, who was the hereditary king of Troezen, traveled to Attica, where he gathered people from small, autonomous city-states and brought them together as one polity under the umbrella of Athens. Moreover, in establishing the city, he gave up his role as king. He reserved to himself the military role of general, but representatives of the people would rule. Theseus fulfilled this promise. Arthur Hugh Clough, a modern editor of Plutarch, trusts this version of the story, pointing out that in HOMER's *The ILIAD*, the name of the ship the Athenians send to join the invasion of Troy is simply *People*. Plutarch admits that he cannot always discriminate between history and myth, and so this pair of biographies allows for both.

As in most of his other comparisons, when Plutarch comes to "The Comparison of Romulus with Theseus," the author mainly concerns himself with the moral character of his subjects. Essentially, he awards Theseus the palm on the front of public-spiritedness. Theseus voluntarily gave up rule and sought out public dangers, destroying them to improve conditions, as when he hunted down and killed the Crommyonian sow, Phaea. (Plutarch suggests she may have been a female bandit rather than a dangerous wild pig.)

Romulus, on the other hand, was moved to his accomplishments by fear and out of the necessity for self-preservation. On another front, the biographer equates his subjects: Both were meant to be governors, and neither lived up to the expectations of a king. Theseus avoided the job and sought popular approval. Romulus became self-important and tyrannical. Both were rapists, but no advantage to Theseus's citizens accrued from his private behavior and his winning his wives by force. Romulus, on the other hand, needed wives for himself and his men, and after carrying off some 800 of the Sabine women, he distributed them among his men, keeping only one for himself. Those women eventually came to love their husbands and the children that resulted from their unions. When the Sabines made a belated effort to rescue their daughters, the women ran between the combatants and begged their kinsmen to reconcile themselves to the women's condition as Roman wives and mothers.

Carefully hedging his final judgment, Plutarch assesses the relative degree of approval each member of his pair received from the gods. Here Romulus gets the palm since the gods took an active role in preserving his life. On the contrary, Theseus was conceived when his father Aegeus directly disobeyed the gods' order to abstain from intercourse.

Bibliography

Plutarch. *The Lives of the Noble Grecians and Romans.* Translated by John Dryden with revisions by Arthur Hugh Clough. New York: Modern Library, 1932. Reprinted as *Greek and Roman Lives.* Mineola, N.Y: Dover Publications, 2005.

———. *Plutarch's Lives.* [Greek and English.] 11 vols. Translated by Bernadotte Perrin. Cambridge, Mass.: Harvard University Press, 1959.

———. *Plutarch's Moralia.* 15 vols. Translated by Frank Cole Babbitt. Cambridge, Mass.: Harvard University Press, 1960.

Thespis of Ikaria   (fl. ca sixth century B.C.E.)
Greek dramatist

Often credited with having invented TRAGEDY, Thespis's story contains some elements that many think are legendary. He is thought to have *invented* tragedy in the sense that he introduced an actor, or *answerer* (Greek: *hypokritos*), into what had earlier been exclusively choral performance. This had several effects. First, it provided a break for the singers of the CHORUS. Second, the resultant interchange heightened the dramatic possibilities of the presentation. Thespis is also sometimes credited with having dignified dramatic presentation in Attica and toning down the licentious character of earlier performances.

According to some, Thespis—from whom the word *Thespian* comes—himself took the role of the actor in the plays he wrote (of which only dubious and fragmentary attributions survive). The likelihood of his existence at Athens, however, gains credence from a marble fragment that was brought to England in the 18th century by a representative of Thomas Howard, the earl of Arundel. This stone, now at Oxford University's Ashmolean Museum, bears a chronicle of events at Athens and elsewhere in the Greek world from the city's legendary first king, Cecrops, down to 354 B.C.E. Among the events receiving notice on the marble is a tragedy (from the Greek *tragos*, "goat," and *aeidein*, "to sing") produced by Thespis and likely performed between 542 and 519 B.C.E.

The literary historian Herbert Jennings Rose also considers it likely that, as his own actor, Thespis used makeup of white lead and a mask. Less verifiable are stories suggesting that he toured the area with a kind of pageant wagon that served both as stage and transportation.

Bibliography

Gastis, Theodor Herzl. *Thespis: Ritual, Myth, and Drama in the Ancient Near East.* New York: Norton, 1977.

Hartigan, Karelisa V. *Legacy of Thespis: Drama Past and Present.* Lanham, Md.: University Press of America, 1984.

Rose, Herbert Jennings. *A Handbook of Greek Literature from Homer to the Age of Lucian.* New York: E. P. Dutton and Company, 1934.

Thucydides   (ca. 460–ca. 401 B.C.E.)   *Greek historian*

As the historian Victor Davis Hansen points out, the few certainties that have come down to us concerning the life of the most famous historian of ancient Greece are all to be found in Thycydides' monumental history, *The PELOPONNESIAN WAR.* From that source, we know that he authored the work and that he was an Athenian. In the course of his book, we also learn that he was a military commander in Thrace and that his father was named Olorus—a name that further suggests a noble and wealthy Thracian heritage. Thucydides confirms that suggestion by explaining that he owned the right to work gold mines in Thrace and consequently enjoyed great influence among the local population there. In his narrative, Thucydides also incidentally recalls that he caught and survived the plague that ravaged Athens between 430 and 427 B.C.E.—a plague that killed the Athenian statesman Pericles.

During the Peloponnesian campaign, Thucydides was called to help the defenders of the Thracian city of Amphipolis near the mouth of the Strymon River on the Strymonian Gulf at the northern extremity of the Aegean Sea. The Spartan general Brasidas had shrewdly attacked Athens's distant possession instead of its homeland. The Spartans defeated the Athenians at Amphipolis, and the Athenian citizens blamed Thucydides for this. They expressed their displeasure by relieving him of command and exiling him. He remarked that spending the subsequent 20 years in exile among the Peloponnesians gave him "leisure to observe affairs more closely."

Other information concerning Thucydides, though some of it may be accurate, is not subject to confirmation in documents contemporary with him. One tradition holds that he was assassinated and buried outside the walls of Athens. The evidence concerning his death is conflicting, though, and some think he died later than 401 B.C.E.

Bibliography

Kegan, Donald. *The Peloponnesian War*. New York: Viking Penguin, 2003.

Strassler, Robert B., ed. *The Landmark Thucydides: A Comprehensive Guide to the Peloponnesian War*. Translated by Richard Crawley. New York: Simon and Schuster Touchstone, 1998.

Thyestes   Seneca (first century C.E.)

Earlier playwrights both in Greece and Rome had penned tragedies about Thyestes, the brother of Atreus, the king of ancient Argos. In Greece, both SOPHOCLES and EURIPIDES had done so; in Rome, ENNIUS, Varius, and Accius had each written a TRAGEDY on the subject. Regrettably, all these previous versions have perished.

Seneca's version is a bloody representation of one of the most horrifying of ancient stories. On the death of their father Pelops, former king of Argos, Thyestes and Atreus quarreled over the succession to the throne. As a part of his plan to prevail, Thyestes seduced his brother's wife and stole a wondrous ram whose fleece was made of gold. Local wisdom had it that the owner of the ram was heir to the throne.

Although Thyestes' ruse failed, and though Atreus exiled his brother for the attempt, Atreus's thirst for revenge remained unquenched. He therefore pretended to forgive his brother and called him home, seized Thyestes' sons, and killed them. Atreus then invited Thyestes to a banquet where the main dish was his children's flesh. That horrid deed so offended the gods that they cursed the house of Atreus forever. The operation of the curse through successive generations—including, for instance, that of Oedipus (see *OEDIPUS*)—became a principal subject of Greek myth and tragedy.

Seneca's usual dramatic practice provides clues about possible differences between his play and its lost sources. One of these appears in the dark foreshadowing that occurs in the first scene, in which appear the Fury Megaera, and the ghost of Thyestes' and Atreus's ancestor, Tantalus, who has been condemned to stand forever thirsty in a pool of water that recedes when he stoops to drink. Tantalus wonders why he has been called from Hell to the palace where he once ruled. The Fury orders him to drive all of his descendants mad and instructs him to urge on the deeds that took place before the play began and that will be enacted in the drama. The ghost objects that though it is right that he suffer, he ought not to be made an instrument for punishing his descendants. Megaera, however, insists that he perform her will.

The play, in five short acts, then recounts the events outlined above. Seneca emphasizes the sense of foreboding that seizes Thyestes. He also underscores the hypocrisy of Atreus, who misleads Thyestes with promises of friendship at the very moment he is having his children murdered and planning the horrifying banquet. The consummate evil of Atreus appears in his expectation that his people will not only put up with his criminality but praise him for it. Moreover, Atreus takes pride in his sadism. He boasts that death is a favor that people seek eagerly as an escape from his cruelty.

Seneca graphically illustrates that cruelty in the play's fifth act, when Thyestes, having wined and dined sumptuously, ironically wishes that his sons were there to share his enjoyment. Atreus assures Thyestes that the sons are indeed there, that they are in his embrace, and that no part of them will be lost to their father. Even after Atreus has revealed the deaths of the children, he tantalizes the father by withholding the truth about their bodies' whereabouts.

The maniacal cruelty of Atreus make one wonder whether or not Seneca is using this play to conduct a veiled critique of his former student, the emperor Nero, whose advisor Seneca had been. Nero eventually forced Seneca to commit suicide.

Bibliography

Seneca. *Oedipus; Agamemnon; Thyestes; Hercules on Oeta; Octavia.* Edited and translated by John G. Fitch. Cambridge, Mass.: Harvard University Press, 2004.

Tibullus, Albius (ca. 56–ca. 19 B.C.E.)
Roman Poet

A Roman elegiac poet of the Augustan Age (under the first Roman emperor, AUGUSTUS CAESAR), Tibullus, of equestrian (knightly) rank by birth, was a member of the circle of authors who enjoyed the patronage of Marcus Valerius Messalla Corvinus. Corvinus was the scion of an old Roman aristocratic family who had supported the Republican cause but who, under an imperial reign, undertook the support of poets instead. Tibullus had served with Messalla during several military campaigns and was his patron's lifelong companion.

Tibullus was counted among the two or three most distinguished Roman elegists of his epoch and was particularly valued for the tender and natural qualities of his verse, his elegance, his eroticism, and the linguistic propriety of his diction. Many of the poems are addressed to Tibullus's mistress, Delia, though some also address a lad, Marathus. APULEIUS claimed that Delia was a real woman named Plania. The tone of Tibullus's poems tends toward the melancholy. QUIN-TILIAN considered Tibullus to be the foremost Roman elegist.

Four surviving books containing 35 elegies and a poem praising Messalla constitute the works of Tibullus. While the first two of these books and the poem in praise of Mesalla near the beginning of the fourth are almost universally accounted to be Tibullus's work, the rest of books 3 and 4 are either certainly not his or are matters of dispute. Some critics properly ascribe several of them to the female Roman poet SULPICIA. Other poems, with less justification, are attributed to other writers, including one named Lygdamus about whose existence some doubt lingers. Some think "Lygdamus" to have been the nom de plume of the young OVID.

See also ELEGY AND ELEGAIC POETRY.

Bibliography

Catullus and Tibullus. *Catullus and Tibullus.* Translated by Francis Ware Cornish and by J. P. Postgate, respectively. Cambridge, Mass.: Harvard University Press, 1988.

Tibullus, Albius. *Elegies.* Translated by Guy Lee. Liverpool, U.K.: F. Cairns, 1982.

———. *The Poems of Tibullus.* Translated by Constance Carrier. Bloomington: Indiana University Press, 1968.

——— and Sulpicia. *The Erotic Elegies of Albius Tibullus with the Poems of Sulpicia Arranged in a Sequence Called No Harm to Lovers.* Translated by Hubert Creekmoner. New York: Washington Square Press, 1966.

Titans

According to HESIOD in *THEOGONY*, the Titans were a species of giant immortals that appeared and ruled before the establishment of the Olympian gods of the Greeks. The first Titans, six male and six female, were the sons and daughters of the archetypal deities Uranus (who stood for the heavens) and Gaia (who stood for the earth). The male Titans included: Oceanus, Hyperion, Iapetus, Coeus, Crius, and Cronus; the females were Mnemosyne, Phoebe, Rhea, Tethys, Theia, and

Themis. Not all the Titans are equally important from a literary perspective.

Among those who do figure prominently in literature, one finds Oceanus and his consort, Tethys. In some versions of myth, they were thought to have been the parents of the Olympian gods. Hyperion was the sun god and sometimes thought to be the sun itself; the Olympian deity Apollo displaced him. Iapetus and Themis parented the second generation Titan, Prometheus, whose story appears in AESCHYLUS's tragedy *PROMETHEUS BOUND*. Prometheus was thought to have fashioned human beings out of clay and to have taught them useful arts like husbandry and medicine. He was punished for bringing the gift of fire to humankind. His mother Themis served in HOMER's work as a functionary in the court of Zeus. She was responsible for maintaining order and decorum at the banquets of the gods.

Cronus, the son of Uranus, overthrew Uranus and fathered the principal Greek deity, Zeus, who in due course supplanted Cronus. Mnemosyne (memory) was the mother of the Muses—the tutelary deities of the fine arts. In later mythology, the Titaness Phoebe became associated with the moon. Rhea became similarly connected with the earth and the mythology of its fertility and the harvest. In the most common versions of the myth, she was the mother of the Olympian gods by Cronus.

From the perspective of the history of religion, it may be that the Titans personified gods who once had been worshipped in what eventually became Greek territory by the peoples whom the Greeks displaced, conquered, or absorbed early in their period of expansion in the Mediterranean area.

Bibliography

Gantz, Timothy. *Early Greek Myth: A Guide to Literary and Artistic Sources*. Baltimore and London: Johns Hopkins University Press, 1993.

"Tlepsh and Lady Tree"

A representative of the NART SAGAS, an ancient body of folklore, "Tlepsh and Lady Tree" tells in the Circassian language the story of an artisan, Tlepsh, who lacked the necessary knowledge to fabricate the things that his people, the Narts, needed for their lives. Narts were protohumans who lived in the distant, mythical past, making a living, as this story implies, by rustling cattle.

Recognizing his need of further skills, Tlepsh goes to Lady Setenaya, who seems to have been a matriarchal figure, and asks her to remember the mastery he needs. Instead, she sends him on a worldwide mission to acquire the knowledge he lacks.

Equipped with a pair of steel shoes of his own fabrication and with the confidence that strangers will not let him starve, Tlepsh sets out, traveling through forests, stepping over cliffs, and leaping across rivers until he reached the Taingyiz Sea (the Sea of Azov). *Taingyiz*, as the translator John Colarusso tells us, means *heaven* in the Turkic language. On the shore, Tlepsh builds a raft and sails it over the sea to a land populated with lovely women. Though he tries to catch them, they elude him. Finally he begs them to tell him about themselves. They explain that they are disciples of Lady Tree.

The women lead Tlepsh to their ruler. Partly human and partly deciduous, Lady Tree has roots reaching down into the depths of the earth. Her cloudlike hair reaches high into the sky, but she has two arms and a lovely human face. Lady Tree instantly falls in love with Tlepsh, feeds him, and invites him to rest. Late at night, however, Tlepsh remembers his quest and announces his departure. When Lady Tree objects, saying he is the first human to have found her, Tlepsh replies that he is one of the gods and makes love to her. Then he explains his mission: to travel to the edge of the earth to discover knowledge for the Narts.

Lady Tree begs him to stay. She can teach him all he needs to know, she says. The world has no edge. She can give him everything.

But Tlepsh will not be dissuaded. He pursues his quest, and it is an utter catastrophe. Dejected, he returns to Lady Tree and admits his failure. Lady Tree tells him that the Narts will perish from pride and stubbornness, but she also presents him with his child, whom she has borne in his absence. She has filled the baby boy with all the knowledge the Narts will need, and she tells Tlepsch to take the baby home and rear it.

One day the baby disappears. Thinking that he has returned to his mother, Tlepsh seeks him there. But Lady Tree does not know his whereabouts. She suggests that some day the child may return, and Tlepsch returns home dejectedly.

The story shares elements in common with that of HOMER's *ODYSSEY*—particularly the section in which Odysseus finds himself a love captive on the island of Ogygia, home of the witch Calypso. Additionally, Colarusso has pointed out the parallel between Lady Tree and the great ash tree from Norse mythology, Yggdrasil, whose roots and branches bind the universe together.

Bibliography
Colarusso, John, trans. and ed. *Nart Sagas from the Caucasus: Myths and Legends from the Circassians, Abazas, Abkhaz, and Ubykhs.* Princeton, N.J.: Princeton University Press, 2002.

Homer. *The Odyssey.* Translated by Robert Fitzgerald. New York: Farrar, Strauss, and Giroux, 2004.

Trachiniae, The (The Women of Trachis)
Sophocles (ca. 450 B.C.E.)

Because of apparent influences (such as a poisoned robe) from the younger playwright EURIPIDES, *The Trachiniae* is thought to be among SOPHOCLES' later compositions. It draws its subject from the legendary material surrounding the mythical hero Heracles (Hercules).

As Sophocles' audience would have known, in Heracles' youth and following the tragic death of his first wife, Megara, and their children at his hands during a fit of madness, he married Deianeira, whom he won in a wrestling match with the river god Achelous. As the newlywed couple journeyed toward home, they had to rely on a centaur, Nessus, to carry them across the flooded river Euenus. As Nessus carried Deianeira across, the centaur attempted to rape her. Observing the situation, Heracles shot Nessus

with a poisoned arrow. As he died, the centaur instructed Deianeira to preserve some of the blood that had clotted around the wound. Should Heracles ever prove unfaithful to Deianeira, the dying Nessus promised, she could apply it to a garment. When Heracles donned the garment, his love for her would be restored.

Eventually Heracles, who possessed the strength of many men, had to endure Zeus's punishment because he had deceitfully murdered a man. Zeus sentenced the hero to a period of slavery performing woman's work in the household of Omphale, the queen of Lydia. As Nessus had surmised, Heracles did indeed fall in love again, this time with Iole, a princess of Oechalia in Euboea, whom he eventually carried off by force.

When Deianeira learned that Heracles loved another, to regain his affection she sent him a robe smeared with Nessus's blood. The poisoned blood, however, burned into the hero's flesh and caused unendurable suffering. To end his agony, Heracles had himself carried to the summit of Mt. Oeta and immolated on a funeral pyre.

Sophocles' version of the later portion of these events begins 15 months after Heracles has left his home in Trachis to perform a year's service to Queen Omphale. Deianeira has had no word from her husband. In fact, she has no idea where he has gone. A nurse, Deianeira's companion, suggests that she send her son Hyllus in search of his father. Hyllus enters, and in the ensuing conversation we learn that he has more idea of his father's whereabouts than Deianeira does. Heracles, Hyllus thinks, is either waging or contemplating waging war on Euboea.

Learning this, Deianeira becomes agitated. Oracles have predicted that this is the turning point in Heracles' life. He will either die or ever afterward have rest from his labors. At his mother's urging, Hyllus goes off in search of his father. The CHORUS attempts to comfort Deianeira. Just then a messenger arrives with the news that Heracles lives and will soon be home, and this is confirmed by a herald, Lichas, who has come directly from Heracles. Lichas recounts the wanderings and accomplishments of Heracles since he left home. Lichas has also brought with him some captive exiles from Euboea. Among these is Iole. Deianeira tries to draw her out, but Iole refuses to speak, and Deianeira respects her silence.

As Deianeira is about to leave the stage, the earlier messenger detains her and informs her that Lichas was untruthful for her benefit. The messenger confirms that Heracles sacked the city of Oechalia in Euboea because of his passion for Iole. Under pressure, Lichas confirms the truth of this. Deianeira goes within to prepare her message and gifts for Heracles, and the chorus rehearses her history and the story of her marriage to Heracles. Deianeira recounts the story of Nessus's gift and produces the robe. The leader of the chorus encourages her to send it. She does, but she suffers a sense of foreboding. She reports to the chorus that a ray of sunlight fell on a bit of cloth that she had anointed, and she tells how the cloth crumbled away to dust. She fears she has done a horrible thing in sending Heracles the robe. She resolves that if it causes Heracles' death, she too will die.

Hyllus reenters with the news that the robe did indeed kill, or is in process of killing, Heracles. He gives a detailed, gruesome, eyewitness account of Heracles' sufferings, and he tells his mother that he has brought his father for her to see, either alive and suffering or by now perhaps dead. She exits, and the chorus sings of the events just past. The nurse enters to report Deianeira's death by her own hand in the bed that had belonged to her and Heracles. The nurse also reports Hyllus's discovery of his mother and his grief at her suicide.

Hyllus and an old man now enter along with Heracles, who is borne in on a litter. Heracles wants Hyllus to produce his mother so that Heracles can avenge himself upon her. He details the pangs of his agony and promises to kill Deianeira.

Hyllus tries to calm his vengeful father and reports Deianeira's death. He also informs Heracles that his wife's intention was only to regain his love, and the vengeance was that of the centaur Nessus, not Deianeira. Heracles realizes that the oracle of his death has been fulfilled; a living person could not kill him. He commands that Hyllus

prepare his funeral pyre on Mount Oeta and that he marry Iole. Hyllus agrees, Heracles is borne offstage on his litter, and the chorus reflects on the unreality of all existence except that of Zeus.

Though not one of Sophocles' best plays, *The Trachiniae* is particularly notable for its sympathetic portrayal of the character of Deianeira and for its concomitantly unsympathetic portrayal of the vengeful Heracles.

Bibliography
Gantz, Timothy. *Early Greek Myth: A Guide to Literary and Artistic Sources.* Baltimore and London: Johns Hopkins University Press, 1993.

Sophocles. *The Complete Plays.* Translated by Paul Roche. New York: Signet Classics, 2001.

Sophocles. *The Women of Trachis.* [Bilingual Greek and English edition.] Translated and edited by Hugh Lloyd-Jones. In *Sophocles.* Vol. 2. Cambridge Mass.: Harvard University Press, 1994.

tragedy in Greece and Rome

The word *tragedy* derives from the Greek *tragos* ("goat") and aeidein ("to sing"). In its earliest manifestations in Europe, Egypt, and the Middle East, tragedy seems to have been associated with religious ritual, with the cycle of death and rebirth in the vegetative world, and with such deities as the Egyptian Osiris or the Greek Dionysus who were connected with that cycle. Mythical figures such as the Greek god Adonis and, in Greece, the sacrifices of goats at Dionysian rites also seem related to tragedy.

Some argue that ancient Greek theatrical tragedy sprang partly from eulogies given at the funerals of influential people. One scenario suggests that the most interesting episodes of the lives of notable persons began to be acted out at graveside and attracted such large audiences that someone got the idea of staging the action in a larger venue.

THESPIS OF IKARIA (fl. ca sixth century B.C.E.) is usually credited with having invented Greek stage tragedy by adding an actor who responded to the CHORUS's song. The first Athenian author whose name is recorded as a tragic playwright was PHRYNICOS OF ATHENS. The only tragedy whose title survives is his *The Destruction of Miletus*, based on the Persian conquest of the Ionian Greek city of Miletus and the enslavement of its entire population in 494 B.C.E. Phrynicos's play or plays involved only a single actor—who might portray more than one part by changing his costume and mask—and a chorus.

Early on, the word *tragedy* applied to any serious play, even those with happy endings such as SOPHOCLES' *PHILOCTETES*. Together with Sophocles, AESCHYLUS and EURIPIDES were the principal Greek tragedians.

About 70 years after the death of Euripides (406 B.C.E.), ARISTOTLE developed a theory of tragedy in his *POETICS*. He thought of tragic figures as persons who, owing to a "tragic flaw," somehow contributed to their own downfall or destruction. The phrase *tragic flaw* translates Aristotle's Greek word *hamartia*, a term used in archery that means missing the target or what one aims at. It is the same word usually translated as "sin" when it occurs in English versions of the Greek NEW TESTAMENT. Thus, to Aristotle, a tragic hero was a person whose judgment or character was flawed but who was otherwise a person of some importance, with high morals and with intellect sufficient to her or his station and responsibilities.

Aristotle arrived at his definition of tragedy and his analysis of its elements empirically—that is, he attended the theater, watched many tragedies, and conducted an analysis of the way they seemed to operate. He noted that the action of tragic plays regularly took place in a 24-hour span, usually (but not always) occurred in a space limited by the distance one could travel in that time, and always swept inescapably from beginning to end without interruption or remission. (This observation later became the basis for the Italian Ludovico Castelvetro's concept of the unities of time, place, and action—a concept Aristotle himself never mentioned.) Aristotle's analysis proposed that the action be complete in itself and of a sufficient magnitude, and that its language (always verse) be lofty. Because the flaw led to the protagonist's downfall, the tragic hero's situation finally had to reach a turning point (a peripeteia). This resulted in the hero's suffering in a way audience members identified with. That identification evoked in them the emotions of pity and fear, and the end of the play served to purge the audience of those emotions. The resultant catharsis, or cleansing, left the audience morally improved.

In the classical Grecian world, the performance of tragedy was intimately bound up with religious observance. Tragic playwrights competed annually to have their work selected as winner at such religious festivals as the Athenian festival of LENAEA or the festival of the wine vats, which occurred annually after the winter solstice in honor of the god Dionysus. The more important such festival, the GREAT DIONYSIA, honored the same god in the spring.

During the HELLENISTIC AGE, Greek tragedy survived at Alexandria, Egypt, and elsewhere in the Greek world in the hands of such poets as the PLEIAD OF ALEXANDRIA. These writers included Alexander of Aetolia, Homerus of Byzantium, Sositheus of Alexandria Troas, LYCOPHRON, Philicus, Dionysiades of Tarsus, and Aeantiades. To represent this group, only 1,500 lines of Lycophron's tragedy *Alexandra* have survived. It concerns a prophecy of doom for the Greeks returning home from the Trojan War.

Roman tragedy relied heavily for its subjects on its Greek forebears. The first Roman to write tragedy was LIVIUS ANDRONICUS, whose work survives in about 40 fragments. On the basis of these fragments, we know the titles of five examples of his war tragedies: *Achilles, Aegisthus, Ajax Mastigophorus* (Ajax with the whip), *Equos Troianus* (The Trojan horse), and *Hermiona*. We also have the names of three tragedies drawn from myth: *Andromeda, Danaë*, and *Tereus*. It is clear from the fragments that Livius Andronicus introduced innovative elements into the plays and stories that he borrowed from his Greek predecessors.

The first Roman to write a tragedy based on Roman history rather than on Greek originals was MARCUS PACUVIUS (d. 220 C.E.) Entitled *Paulus*, his tragedy seems based on the career of the

Roman general Paulus Amelius, who had brought Greece under Roman control and had destroyed 70 cities in Greece. Pacuvius also translated into Latin now-lost Greek tragedies composed after the career of Euripides. Only the names of four such translations survive. Beyond this, Pacuvius composed at least eight tragedies on subjects connected with the Trojan War. The Italian playwright Pietro Magno has tried to reconstruct one such play—*Teucer*—from its fragmentary remains.

The tragedies of several Roman authors, including Varius and Accius, have utterly perished. Fragments of 20 tragedies by QUINTUS ENNIUS, however, survive. These remains suggest that Ennius freely translated from Greek originals and that he particularly revered Euripides.

Among Roman tragic playwrights, SENECA remains by far the most celebrated. We have nine complete tragedies that have been confidently ascribed to Seneca. These include four probably based on plays by Euripides: *Hercules furens* (MAD HERCULES); *MEDEA*; *Phaedra*; and *Troades* (*The TROJAN WOMEN*). One, *Agamemnon*, borrows its plot from AESCHYLUS. Two more, *OEDIPUS* and *Hercules Oetaeus* (*Hercules on Oeta*) rest substantially on the work of SOPHOCLES. Another, *HIPPOLYTUS*, rests on Sophocles and a second unknown source. Where the inspiration came from for the ninth tragedy, *THYESTES*, no one is certain, though precedent Greek and Roman versions existed and Seneca could have used any one of them or used them in combination. A fragment of Seneca's version of *The Phoenician Women* also survives.

A 10th complete tragedy is sometimes doubtfully ascribed to Seneca, but because it is the only Roman tragedy about native Roman history to survive in its entirety, the play, *OCTAVIA*, remains important whatever its authorship. As Seneca's editor and translator, Frank Justus Miller, tells us, the main objection to Seneca's having written *Octavia* arises from the play's circumstantial account of the death of Nero, which of course occurred after Seneca's judicial suicide.

Senecan tragedy is the source of a subcategory of tragedy that became widely popular on the European stage during the early modern period— the *tragedy of the blood*. Seneca's tragedies are the only complete Roman representatives of the form to survive. He may have intended them both for stage performance and for being read, either as closet drama or by a single performer in the manner of a declamation. His plays reflect a preference for brevity that the literary historian Gian Biaggio Conte attributes to the influence of Asiatic rhetoric.

We know the names of such subsequent tragedians as Mamercus Scaurus, whose veiled references to the emperor Tiberius in his play *Atreus* resulted in Mamercus's judicial suicide. The political and military dislocations that accompanied the fall of the Western Roman Empire along with a popular taste that valued spectacle more highly than traditional performance perhaps meant that fewer tragedies were written and enacted.

Late in the ancient period, the Christian church co-opted theater, moving performance into sacred spaces and focusing on such subjects as the lives of saints, so tragedy was little represented. Although plays based on the lives of Christian martyrs came to be performed in abundance, such plays were examples of pathos insofar as they concerned the physical deaths of martyrs and of high comedy insofar as they concerned the eternal lives of their souls. For the Christian faithful, ultimate tragedy afflicts only condemned souls.

Bibliography

Conte, Gian Biaggio. *Latin Literature: A History.* Translated by Joseph B. Solodow et al. Baltimore, Md.: Johns Hopkins University Press: 1994.

Gastis, Theodor Herzl. *Thespis: Ritual, Myth, and Drama in the Ancient Near East.* New York: Norton, 1977.

Green, Peter, ed. *Hellenistic History and Culture.* Berkeley: University of California Press, 1993.

Hartigan, Karelisa V. *Legacy of Thespis: Drama Past and Present.* Lanham, Md.: University Press of America, 1984.

Seneca, Lucius Annaeus. *Hercules; Trojan Women; Phoenician Women; Medea; Phaedra.* Edited and

Translated by John G. Fitch. Cambridge, Mass.: Harvard University Press, 2002.

———. *Oedipus; Agamemnon; Thyestes; Hercules on Oeta; Octavia.* Edited and translated by John G. Fitch. Cambridge, Mass.: Harvard University Press, 2004.

Warmington, E. H., ed. and trans. *Remains of Old Latin: Ennius and Caecilius.* Vol. 1. Cambridge, Mass.: Harvard University Press, 1935.

Wilson, Peter. "Powers of Horror and Laughter: The Great Age of Drama." In *Literature in the Greek and Roman Worlds: A New Perspective.* Edited by Oliver Taplin. New York: Oxford University Press, 2000.

Trinummus (The Three-Penny Day, The Three-Bob Day, The Three-Dollar Day, The Thirty-Dollar Day) Plautus (late second century B.C.E.)

Thought to be among PLAUTUS's later plays, *Trinummus* (a three-penny piece) shares some of the characteristics of later medieval morality plays and is distinguished from other Plautine comedy by having an all-male cast. A comedy of manners, the play affirms the benefits of conventional morality.

In brief, the plot is this: Journeying abroad, Charmides appoints his friend Callicles to manage Charmides' affairs. Charmides' wastrel son Lesbonicus, however, immediately spends all of his father's money that he can lay his hands on and then sells his ancestral home to Callicles. The wastrel's profligacy, we hear, has deprived his unnamed sister of the dowry she was to have brought with her into an arranged marriage. Another young man, Lysiteles the son of Philto, wishes to marry Lesbonicus's sister without a dowry. Lesbonicus, however, is mortified by that notion. (In the ancient world, a dowry was a woman's insurance policy. If a marriage broke up, the dowry had to be restored to her.) Moreover, Lesbonicus feels guilty about his prodigality and no longer considers his financially ruined family the social equals of Philto and Lysiteles.

Callicles is about to confer a dowry on Charmides' daughter when Charmides himself returns. At first, finding Callicles in possession of his home, he thinks that Callicles has betrayed him. All misunderstandings are eventually resolved to everyone's satisfaction, generous dowries are bestowed, and Lesbonicus reforms and settles down.

As the play opens, two allegorical figures, Luxury and her daughter Want, take the stage and speak the prologue. Luxury sends Want into Charmides' house and then addresses the audience, explaining that the son has run through the father's entire fortune and now must dwell with Want. Luxury also explains that Plautus has translated the Greek playwright Philemon's comedy, *Thensaurus*, into Latin and given it a new title. The play's most recent English translator, Daniel Mark Epstein, takes his cue from Plautus and, allowing for inflation, has reentitled the piece *The Thirty-Dollar Day.* It is that version which is used here.

As act 1 opens, an elderly gentleman, Megaronides, enters and bewails the state of contemporary morality: Vice is ruining the country. Callicles calls his wife to worship their household god and prays for his wife's death as soon as she is out of earshot. Megaronides greets him, reveals that he too dislikes his own wife, and the two argue about which wife is worst.

Now Megaronides gets to the point of his visit. He has come to reprove Callicles for his handling of Charmides' trust. He blames Callicles for having paid the son 100,000 dollars for Charmides' house and says that the boy will instantly squander the money.

Callicles feels forced to betray Charmides' trust and tells Megaronides that, before leaving, Charmides had walled up 30,000 gold coins in the house, and Callicles has bought the house to take it out of the son's hands and to properly exercise his guardianship of his friend's property. If Charmides returns safely, his money is secure; if not, it will pay his daughter's dowry. We learn that both Charmides' children are still living in the house as part of the sale bargain.

A much-chastened Megaronides leaves, blaming himself for having believed idle gossip against his friend.

Act 2 begins with the soliloquy of the young Athenian, Lysiteles. He is pondering the question of whether to concentrate on love affairs or on business and wonders which option would bring the greater happiness. Business with integrity wins his internal conflict. His father, Philto, now enters spouting a fountain of moral advice. After assuring his father that he always observes his counsel punctiliously, Lysiteles tries to borrow money to help a young friend out of financial difficulty. Philto's high principles, however, do not usually extend to rescuing the financially foolish, but as Lysiteles keeps insisting, Philto begins to weaken until he hears that the friend is Charmides' son, Lesbonicus. Then he once more grows reluctant to help a wastrel.

Lysiteles suggests that he be allowed to wed Lesbonicus's sister and to take her without a dowry. Shocked at such an unprecedented idea, the doting father nonetheless yields and agrees to arrange the marriage on terms he regards as unfavorable. As he does, he sees Lesbonicus coming with his slave Stasimus, and Philto hides to eavesdrop on their conversation. The two are trying to sort out where 100,000 dollars has disappeared to in the past two weeks. Philto interrupts them and tries to arrange the marriage, but Lesbonicus refuses the contract on the grounds that, because he has wasted his father's substance, the families are no longer social equals. He is also unwilling to put his sister into a situation in which she does not have the protection that a dowry affords. After some persuasion, Lesbonicus agrees to the match provided that Philto will accept a remaining family farm as his sister's dowry.

The slave Stasimus, trying to keep the farm in his master's family, interrupts and tells Philto awful stories about the farm's imperfections. In the end, Philto refuses the farm but still insists on the match, and Lesbonicus finally appears to agree. When Philto exits, however, Lesbonicus reveals that, if he can not provide his sister with a dowry, he has no intention of following through.

As act 3 opens, Stasimus explains the situation to Callicles, who goes in search of Megaronides to ask his advice. Then Lysiteles and Lesbonicus meet and discuss the ruinous fact that, unlike Lysiteles, Lesbonicus chose love affairs instead of business as the road to happiness. Lesbonicus continues to try to save some shred of his self-respect by refusing to allow his sister to marry without a dowry, and Lysiteles argues that, if he allows his friend to ruin himself financially by providing a dowry, Lysiteles' own reputation will be in tatters.

Stasimus interrupts them with a bit of slapstick humor, and the friends move off to avoid him and then take their leave of one another. Stasimus concludes that he may have to join the army.

Scene 3 of the third act opens with a dialogue between Megaronides and Callicles, who hatch a plot to make it appear that Charmides has sent money for his daughter's dowry. Callicles is going secretly to dig up the gold, and agrees to hire some local lowlife as the fake messenger who is bringing the money.

Charmides himself opens act 4 with a prayer of gratitude to the sea god Neptune for having brought the old man home safely, though unexpectedly. As he nears his house, he sees approaching the swindler whom Megaronides and Callicles have hired for the 30 dollars that give the play in this version its title. Charmides decides that the swindler bears watching. As the two encounter one another, the swindler plays the role he has been hired for, saying that he is Charmides' messenger—except that he does not know Charmides' name. Charmides prompts him to remember it and then questions him about the places that they supposedly have spent together. The swindler claims to have 200,000 in gold belonging to Charmides. Charmides identifies himself and demands that he hand it over.

After an exchange of insults, the swindler departs, and as Charmides sees Stasimus approaching at a drunken jog, he first hides and then confronts Stasimus, whom he does not at first recognize. Stasimus discourses like an orator about the sad state of public morality and manners, and Charmides eventually recognizes him. It takes a while, though, for the sodden Stasimus to recognize his master, and Plautus milks the situation for its comic potential. Then Stasimus reveals that Lesbonicus has sold the house, and Charmides thinks that Callicles has betrayed him, but soon all is explained. Charmides sends Stasimus to supervise unloading the ship he arrived on.

The two old friends unravel the mystery of the swindler for Charmides, who is pleased to find that his daughter is betrothed to a young man of good family. Lysiteles arrives and introduces himself as Charmides' new son-in-law. Charmides awards a dowry of 200,000 dollars. He recalls, however, that this is his son's friend and blames him for having led Lesbonicus astray. Lysiteles denies the accusation and reconciles the father to his son. Lesbonicus agrees to the marry Callicles' daughter, and Charmides utters one more misogynist and misogamist remark, saying: "One wife is punishment enough for any man." Callicles disagrees, saying that Lesbonicus's sins would require 100 wives as just retribution. Lesbonicus promises to reform. All agree that the wedding will occur the next day, and the play ends.

The Epstein translation of this play is often appropriately free. However, one device that Epstein introduces seems to ring false: He employs stereotypical, Hollywood-slave-era-plantation verbal humor in the speeches of the Greek slaves. While it is true that Greek and Roman stage slaves were often stereotypical figures and often associated with low humor, the analogy that Epstein tries to establish strikes me as outdated for contemporary readers. George E. Duckworth's older translation provides interested readers with a more literal alternative.

Bibliography

Plautus. *The Thirty-Dollar Day.* In *Plautus: The Comedies.* Vol. 3. Edited by David R. Slavitt and Palmer Bovie. Translated by Daniel Mark Epstein. Baltimore and London: Johns Hopkins University Press, 1995.

———. *The Three Penny Day.* In *The Complete Roman Drama.* Vol. 2. Edited and translated by George E. Duckworth. New York: Random House, 1942.

Tristia and *Epistulae ex Ponto* Ovid
(8–ca. 17 C.E.)

For more than 2,000 years, literary scholars and historians have advanced numerous theories concerning the reasons that Rome's first emperor, AUGUSTUS CAESAR, decided to expel OVID from Rome in the eighth year of the Common Era. None of the scenarios that the scholars suggest is impossible, but neither is any one of them certain. No uncertainty, however, surrounds Ovid's permanent banishment by imperial decree to a remote and uncongenial outpost of Roman control—Tomis on the shores of the Black Sea.

Technically, Ovid's banishment did not amount to exile, otherwise he could not have retained his property and his rights as a Roman citizen as he did. The literary historian Hermann Frankel sensibly suggests that, whatever the deciding occasion had been, the aging and increasingly conservative Augustus perceived in Ovid's amatory freethinking and risqué humor a threat to the family values that the emperor cherished for Rome. Though Augustus allowed the private circulation of Ovid's works to continue, he had them removed from public libraries. In any case, there was no legal appeal from the decree. Only if the emperor changed his mind could Ovid hope to escape the bitter cold and what he considered the provinciality of Tomis.

Despite the poet's depression at this unlooked-for turn of events, he discovered that his capacity for writing first-rate poetry had not diminished. While Ovid was still aboard ship on the outbound journey, he turned his attention to composing the first of many collections of elegies that would flow from his pen during the last nine years of his life. He titled this first collection of 5 books of elegies *Tristia* (Sadness, or *Elegies of Gloom*).

Tristia, Book 1

The first of Ovid's elegies is an extended address to the book he is writing. He imagines that it will visit the beloved places in Rome where he cannot go, and he charges the book to greet those places for him. He also warns the book that readers may take no pleasure from it. He begs the book to try to intercede with Augustus on the poet's behalf and to withdraw the edict that has left him isolated from his friends and his family. He imagines that his book at last comes to rest in the "round book-cases" of Ovid's home, where *Tristia* will find itself lodged among its brothers. Ovid warns *Tristia* to avoid those of his books that "teach how to love"—his ART OF LOVE. He tells his book to make haste while he himself continues "to dwell at the edge of the world."

In the second elegy, Ovid describes a storm at sea and his responses to the storm's fury. Among those responses is his vain prayer that he will be drowned. His thoughts turn to the wife he left in Rome and her grief for him. But the violence of the storm does not long allow him to think about her, and his thoughts turn again to dying. He decides that he prefers to bear "Caesar's wrath" with him to the appointed place of his banishment. He makes explicit his continued and former loyalty to Augustus and insists that no guilty deed incurred his punishment.

In the third elegy, Ovid revisits in his imagination his final night at home before his exile and leave-taking from his wife and friends. He regrets that his daughter was in Libya and had not heard about his circumstances. He recalls his fruitless prayers, his three attempts to leave his home for the final time. He remembers his wife's offer to accompany him and her frenzied grief as he left. Ovid entertains the hope that her staying in Rome will present opportunities for her to intercede on his behalf and bring him home at last.

The sea roars again in the fourth elegy as Ovid remarks on the boldness to which his fear of seafaring has forced him. He sees the mariners pale with fear and notes that even the helmsman has given over any attempt at steering. He prays that, like him, the adverse wind will yield to the desires of the divine Augustus. If Ovid were not already dead, he thinks, he would like not to die.

A lengthy epistolary elegy, the fifth, addresses an unnamed friend—the first among his comrades. Ovid credits the friend with having dissuaded him from suicide after the decree of banishment. The poet ruminates on the fickleness of fortune, considers examples of friendship from the annals of mythology and literature, and then remarks that he knows the quality of his own friendship with the ODE's addressee through experience of the anonymous friend's kindness. He makes one of many veiled references to the reason for his banishment, asserting yet again that his naiveté, not his malice or fault, was the cause of Augustus's displeasure.

Ovid then whines a bit about his own frailty, which does not suit him to withstand the hardships he anticipates. He contrasts himself with Ulysses, a hardened warrior used to adversity. An urban poet, Ovid can expect no homecoming of the sort that awaited HOMER's hero—unless Augustus relents.

The sixth elegy of the first book of *Tristia* is both a love letter and an encomium to his wife, who has stood by him through all of life's vicissitudes. Now all he can promise her is what hopeful poets always promise their ladies—immortality for as long as the poems are read. In Ovid's case, we are at 2,000 years and counting.

A certain degree of theatrical exaggeration attends the seventh elegy of the first book. In his grief over his banishment, Ovid had burned a copy of his greatest work, METAMORPHOSES. He treats this act as if he had destroyed the only extant copy. In fact, of course, many copies were in circulation as they have been ever since.

The eighth and ninth elegies make a pair. The first of them reproves a "traitorous friend" for having dropped him when Ovid lost imperial favor. The other appreciates a true friend who stuck by the poet despite his ill fortune and who seems to be laboring at having the emperor withdraw Ovid's decree of banishment. The 10th elegy traces Ovid's course, first from Italy across the

Adriatic Sea to Greece, then to the Dardanelles, and finally to the Black Sea (also called the Euxine Sea) and the city of Tomis. His ship bears a figurehead of the goddess Minerva on its stern, and to her he promises a sacrificial lamb if he makes it safely to his place of exile.

The 11th and final elegy of the collection addresses the reader. Ovid assures his audience that every preceding word was written at sea—often during perilous circumstances. Even as he writes the final words of the first book, a storm is raging.

Tristia, Books 2 and 3

The entire second book of *Tristia* represents a probably foredoomed effort on Ovid's part to change Augustus Caesar's mind about him. Ovid hopes, fondly as it proved, that he can lead Augustus to revoke Ovid's banishment by pleading his poetic talent. Ovid pulls out all the stops and observes that two faults—a poem and a blunder in seeing something that he should not have—have resulted in his ruin. He argues at length that poetry has no power to corrupt if the mind of the reader is pure. He clearly thinks he knows the cause of Caesar's decision respecting him. He ends the book by asking not for pardon but for a more salubrious place of exile.

Book 3 begins with Ovid imagining his book's arrival in Rome. Then, in the second elegy, Ovid shivers in the Scythian cold and longs for Rome. The third poem is a letter to Ovid's wife that he dictated to a scribe as he lay ill in Tomis. He sends her his love, praises her undoubted loyalty, and imagines that he may soon die. He asks that, should that happen, his bones be returned to Rome for interment or cremation. He also wrote his own epitaph. In the translation of Arthur Leslie Wheeler, it reads: "I, who lie here, with tender loves once played, / Naso, the bard, whose life his wit betrayed. / Grudge not, O Lover, as thou passest by, / A prayer: "Soft may the bones of Naso Lie!"

The fourth elegy has two parts. The first part warns a friend against being too familiar with the mighty of the earth. Danger lurks in their compa-

ny. The second part declares that though his body is in a godforsaken part of the world, Ovid's mind is with his wife and friends in Rome. He cautiously does not name his friends lest they be tarred with his brush.

A series of affectionate epistolary elegies follows. Two are to friends and another to Ovid's daughter, Perilla, to whom he gives fatherly advice. The eighth elegy is another prayer to Augustus for a more congenial place of exile.

Associatively, Ovid now turns his attention in the ninth elegy to Tomis itself. He traces its origin as a Grecian colony of settlers from Miletus who made their homes among the tribesmen of the Scythian Getae. He recalls the story of Jason and the Argonauts, who came to Scythia's shores in search of the Golden Fleece, and the way Medea became involved in his plot (see MEDEA). Tomis, he concludes, is the place where Medea tore her brother's body apart after she had murdered him.

The 10th elegy spins tales—accurate enough—of Tomis's icy climate and the way the inhabitants dress to deal with it. Ovid also details how, when the rivers freeze over, Tomis is exposed to the raids of mounted barbarians, with the consequent theft of both people and livestock. He finds the place to be without any redeeming qualities.

Ovid's next elegy addresses an unnamed enemy whom he holds responsible for inflaming Augustus against him. He hopes that man can experience Tomis in his own person. In elegy 3.12, as spring begins to melt the ice of Tomis but not that of Ovid's exile, he hopes that he may meet a sailor who speaks Latin or at least Greek and get some news of Italy. The 13th elegy is addressed to Ovid's birthday deity, who arrives to find himself surprised at Ovid's new location and circumstances. Instead of another year of life, Ovid longs for a funeral pyre. In an epilogue, the 14th elegy of book 3, Ovid complains that the Gothic language is beginning to adulterate his Latin.

Tristia, Book 4

The introductory elegy of book 4 addresses the MUSES who inspire Ovid's verse. When they seize control of his mind, he can forget his misery for a time and share with his Muses the creative joys of Mt. Helicon.

Among the troubles Ovid faced in Tomis, apparently, was a responsibility for serving in the civil guard. When pirates attacked from the sea, as they do in the 2nd elegy, and the signal was given, he had to don sword, armor, and helmet, and join the other citizens to repel the raid. He confesses that he had always done his best to avoid military service, and he has not learned to like it any better than before. In this military mood, Ovid next celebrates in his mind's eye the Roman triumphs over the Germanic tribes, and he congratulates Augustus in absentia.

Elegy 4.3 is a touching epistolary poem to Ovid's wife. He expresses his fear that she may have grown ashamed of being his wife. He comforts her, assuring her that his guilt has not touched her nor tinged her reputation. On the contrary, adversity provides opportunity for the display of genuine virtue. The following elegy, also epistolary, addresses a noble friend. Ovid assures this friend, perhaps Messalinus, that the friend's regard for him will do the friend no harm since Augustus realizes that Ovid's fault was unintentional. Ovid closes the poem by reciting some of the mythical history of his place of exile. He notes here, as elsewhere, that the Euxine Sea—the *hospitable* sea—is a misnomer. The sea on whose shores he now dwells should instead be named the Axine—*inhospitable*—Sea.

The fifth elegy of book 4 addresses another friend and expresses Ovid's frequent concern that his friendship may be dangerous to his associates. Ovid praises the friend and sends warm wishes for him and his family. The following poem laments the poet's failing health and the fact that time's passage has not eased his sense of loss. He lives in the hope that death will release him from his woes. The next verse letter chides a friend who has not written, and the next after that again rehearses the poet's woes and warns against arousing the wrath of the emperor, who is a living god.

The ninth elegy of book 4 atypically threatens revenge against the person whom Ovid blames

for his banishment. In the 10th and final elegy, he summarizes his autobiography and thanks his Muse for his talent and the relief that she offers from his psychological misery. He also gratefully thanks his readers for the fame and wealth that their eager acceptance of his poems has brought him. He feels certain that his fame will survive, though the earth will claim his body.

Tristia, Book 5

The fifth book of *Tristia* opens with a poem that is also an apology. Ovid expresses the fear that his epistolary poems from exile with all their complaining may burden the friends to whom he sends them. He explains that he sends them as a way of being with them if only by an exchange of thoughts. In the second poem, a letter to his wife, he imagines that she must pale with fear whenever a letter arrives. He rehearses his depression and lists some of the many sorrows that oppress him. He ends his address to his wife by saying that he will seek refuge at the holy altar—that is, appeal to Augustus—even though he knows himself to be hated there. The balance of the poem contains a direct address to the emperor, imploring once again a more pleasant and healthful place of exile. Such pleas continued to fall on deaf ears.

Since Ovid's pleas have failed to move Augustus, the poet appeals to higher authority in his next verse letter, one addressed to the god Bacchus. He begs the god to intercede with the emperor. He also hopes that poets, drinking the wine that marks the god's festivals, will recall the name of Naso (Ovid's family name) and drink to his health. Another letter of complaint to a friend follows, and after that comes a birthday greeting to his wife, expressing the hope that she may live happily even though her husband is banished from her side. It is the poet's fervent wish that his wife be spared grief that she has done nothing to deserve.

The sixth letter-poem of the fifth book seems to respond to his wife's apparent impatience with all of Ovid's self-pity. He begs her to overcome her anger and bear with him lest he utterly despair. The seventh epistolary poem describes Ovid's neighbors—the descendants of the Greeks who founded Tomis as well as the Gothic tribes people, the Getae and the Sarmatae. The latter two, hairy and violent, go armed with bows, poisoned arrows, and knives. The former speak a variety of Greek whose vocabulary and pronunciation has been invaded by the language of their barbarous neighbors. The poet comments on the news that his verses are being performed in Roman theaters to accompany dancing. He says that, though he has no interest in applause, anything that keeps his reputation alive is pleasing.

The eighth verse letter addresses someone whom Ovid hates. The poet says that, however low he himself has fallen, the addressee is lower still. Ovid warns his enemy that he may yet be restored to Rome. When that happens, he will endeavor to see the addressee sentenced to a worse form of exile.

The ninth verse letter is to an unnamed friend who has apparently provided Ovid with continual support during his period of exile. Ovid expresses his gratitude and credits the friend for preserving the poet's life. The 10th elegy again expresses Ovid's distaste for Tomis and for the barbarians who laugh at his Latin and threaten him when they believe that he makes fun of them. Moreover, the very sheep in the fields fear the frequent warfare and raiding parties more than they fear wolves. Ovid closes the poem by upbraiding himself for his madness in offending Augustus and bringing this exile on himself.

The 11th elegy of the fifth and final book of *Tristia* addresses Ovid's wife. Someone had offended her by calling her an "exile's wife." He advises her to endure such slights courageously. He reminds the unkind name-caller that, technically, Ovid is not an exile. Although he is like a disabled ship, he is nonetheless still afloat. He closes by cautioning the offending person against lying by calling Ovid an exile.

The following poem addresses a well-wisher who has offered Ovid the advice that he ought to spend his time writing. Ovid points out that writing verse is a joyful occupation best accomplished by a peaceful mind. Moreover, the poet's hardships have sapped his strength. After detailing all the reasons that he ought not to try to write, Ovid at last confesses that his "Muse cannot be restrained from composing verses." Most of these, however, he consigns to the flames. Such verses are emblems of the way in which Ovid's art has ruined him and left his life a heap of ashes.

The 13th elegy, composed while Ovid was ill, reproves a friend for neglecting to write. The 14th and last elegy of the collection addresses his wife. Again the poet reminds her that his readers will forever remember her. She is also the sole guardian of his fortune. He compares her to the faithful wives of mythology and epic—to Penelope, Alcestis, Andromache, and Evadne. He observes that by reminding her to do what she is already doing, he is expressing his praise and approval.

Epistulae ex Ponto

Ovid spent the rest of his life in Tomis; he died there in 17 C.E. Before his death, he wrote a similar, four-book collection of epistolary elegies, which were gathered in his *Epistulae ex Ponto*— Letters from Pontus, or Letters from the Black Sea. The tone and the subjects of the elegies in this collection often recapitulate those described above. The principal difference between the two collections is that, in the poems from Pontus, Ovid names most of the friends to whom he writes. Only one of the letters, book 3, elegy 1, is addressed to his wife, and the final letter, 4.16, is addressed to an unnamed enemy.

See also ELEGY AND ELEGAIC POETRY.

Bibliography

Ovid. *Ovid: Tristia; Ex Ponto.* Vol. 6. Translated by Arthur Leslie Wheeler and G. P. Goold. Cambridge, Mass.: Harvard University Press, 1988.
———. *The Poems of Exile: Tristia and the Black Sea Letters.* Translated by Peter Green. Berkeley: University of California Press, 2005.

Trojan Women, The Euripides (415 B.C.E.)

Produced shortly after the Athenian attack on and capture of the island of Melos, EURIPIDES' verse play explores the dehumanizing effect of war on the conquerors and elucidates the misery to which war's aftermath regularly subjects the conquered. In real life, the inhabitants of Melos had merely wished to maintain their neutrality in Athenian disagreements with other polities. In punishment, the Athenians slaughtered all the men of the island and sold the women and children into slavery. This outrage seemingly shattered Euripides' earlier faith in the justice and fairness of Athens and its democratic institutions, and the playwright's disillusionment reflects itself in the play.

It would have been too dangerous politically for Euripides to present the Melosian situation directly, as the policy makers who perpetrated the Melosian debacle remained in power. The playwright therefore displaces his grief at the suffering of the islanders and his disillusionment with the democratic institutions of his native land by setting his play four centuries earlier and at a geographical distance. The audience finds itself surveying the battlefield before the ruined walls of Troy. The flower of Trojan manhood already lies dead. The women of Troy who are destined to become the concubines of the Greek conquerors are housed in a series of shacks around the battlefield, and an older woman, the Trojan queen Hecuba, lies sleeping on stage.

One of Troy's tutelary deities, the god of the sea and earthquake, Poseidon, speaks first. He reviews the cause of the desolation and identifies Hecuba and others, including her daughter, the priestess Cassandra, among the women awaiting deportation to the beds of their conquerors. Poseidon also mourns some of the fallen Trojans and bids farewell to a city he has especially favored.

The goddess Pallas Athena enters and speaks next. Poseidon has credited her with the Trojan defeat, but she surprises him by announcing that she wishes "a bitter homecoming" for the Grecian fleet. Poseidon finds that, although Pallas Athena supported the Greeks, she has been offended by the outrages offered her priestess Cassandra by one of the Grecian warriors, and the divinities join forces to punish the Greeks. Poseidon then pronounces judgment on those who initiate warfare: "How are ye blind, / Ye treaders down of cities, ye that cast / Temples to desolation, and lay waste / Tombs, the untrodden sanctuaries where lie / The ancient dead; yourselves so soon to die!" [Translation by Gilbert Murray.]

Hecuba awakens and mourns the multiple losses she has sustained: children, city, husband, and king, and calls forth the other women to help her grieve. They appear from the doors of the huts, bewail their circumstances, and utter their deepest fears about their futures. The arrival of a Greek herald, Talthybius, interrupts their keening. He has come to announce which Greek has won each woman for his prize. Questioned, he reports that King Agamemnon himself has chosen the priestess Cassandra.

When Hecuba asks about another daughter, Polyxena, Talthybius temporizes, saying that she watches Achilles' tomb. He does not say that she has been murdered there. Hecuba continues asking about women of her family. Her daughter-in-law Andromache has fallen to the lot of Pyrrhus the son of Achilles. Hecuba herself is intended for Odysseus, the king of Ithaca.

Cassandra enters; out of her mind with grief, she takes joy in the prospect of becoming Agamemnon's thrall as it will give her the chance to kill him, which she swears to do. She continues darkly to predict the future until the herald leads her away to Agamemnon, and Hecuba collapses.

A CHORUS of watchers comments on the action, and some of the women go to Hecuba's assistance. She, however, refuses it and distractedly continues to examine her fate and remember her past. As she weeps for Troy's fate, a chariot comes. It is loaded with booty, and in it too are a weeping woman and a child. The woman is Prince Hector's widow, Andromache, and the child, Astyanax, is Hecuba's grandson by that union. Andromache and Hecuba share remembrances, their grief, and their fears of the future while the leader of the chorus interjects observations on the action of the play and on the history that led up to it.

The Greek herald, Talthybius, reenters and with great difficulty and sorrow informs Andromache that Odysseus has persuaded the Greek council that allowing Astyanax to live will be too dangerous because, when he grows up, he may seek vengeance against the Greeks. The child is to be flung from a tower and his broken body allowed no burial. This last detail is particularly heartless. The Greeks traditionally thought that the soul of an unburied person would wander forever, unable to cross over the river Styx into the underworld. Moreover, such a sentence amounted to sacrilege since the dead were no longer the enemies of any living person and belonged to the gods. A soldier seizes the child to perform his commission, and Andromache is borne away on the chariot. The chorus sings a lengthy lament on the action. They conclude that the events they have witnessed have destroyed their love of the gods.

Now King Menelaus enters and, after justifying the war on the grounds that Paris seduced and abducted Helen, commands that his faithless wife be dragged before him. Hecuba warns him that he must kill Helen at once lest her wiles once more ensnare him. Hecuba even promises to bless Troy's destroyer if he will do the deed.

Helen asks leave to speak, and, after declaring his intention to kill Helen, Menelaus yields to Hecuba's request that Helen be allowed to talk. Helen reviews the story of the way in which three goddesses, Pallas Athena, Hera, and Aphrodite, contended for first prize in the world's archetypal beauty contest. Each goddess sought to rig the contest, offering respectively (in this version) military success, royal power, and the love of the world's most beautiful woman—Helen herself—to Paris, who was foolish enough to agree to be judge. Compounding his folly, Paris chose beauty. Thus, Helen argues, she was not at fault when she deserted Menelaus for Paris. She was merely the pawn of Aphrodite.

The chorus is both unmoved and unconvinced by Helen's disclaimer of responsibility for deserting Menelaus. So is Hecuba, who criticizes Helen's performance and calls on Menelaus to pronounce judgment and kill her. Menelaus resolves to do so, but Helen embraces his knees and asks him to "remember all." Despite Hecuba's encouragement, Menelaus weakens and instructs the soldiers to take Helen to the ships.

The chorus now takes the part of citizens, and its verse songs convey the feelings of citizens about to be enslaved and transported across the sea to uncertain fates.

Talthybius and soldiers enter bearing the corpse of Astyanax, which the chorus recognizes and bemoans. Only one ship remains, Talthybius reports, to carry off his detachment, Hecuba, and the remaining women. He cannot, however, bring himself to observe the sacrilege of his instructions by leaving Astyanax unburied. Instead he announces the respectful funeral arrangements that he has decided on, and he blames Helen for all the Trojan women's troubles. Hecuba pantomimes the funeral rites over the child's dead body, and the chorus mourns the boy's death.

Hecuba behaves as if she is in a trance and announces her vision: She has, she says, seen God's open hand, and there is nothing in it. She pronounces a nihilistic view of the purposes of the universe—a view that has perhaps become Euripides' as well.

The Greek soldiers set fire to the ruins of Troy. Hecuba attempts to immolate herself, but the Greeks restrain her. Then she and the chorus in turn lament the passing of Troy, and after a final farewell to her past, her fallen kin, and her city, she sets her face toward the future and the fate that awaits her. A trumpet sounds, and she and the other Trojan women march to the waiting Greek ship—just as, presumably, the women of Melos had been constrained to do.

Bibliography

Bloom, Harold, ed. *Euripides: Comprehensive Research and Study Guide.* Philadelphia: Chelsea House Publishers, 2003.

Euripides. *The Trojan Women.* A 16mm. television kinescope. Surry Hills, NSW, Australia: Barrie Patterson, 2003.

———. *The Trojan Women and Hippolytus.* Translated by Edward P. Coleridge. Mineola, N.Y.: Dover Publications, 2002.

———. *Women of Troy.* Translated by Kenneth McLeish. London: Nick Hern, 2004.

Turnus (fl. first century B.C.E.) *Roman dramatist*

Only a single fragment of PASTORAL POETRY and one fragment of a drama survive as evidence of Turnus's talent. Allusions to him by such other ancient writers as MARTIAL and JUVENAL suggest, however, that Turnus's contemporaries principally valued him as a satirical playwright—one who perhaps dealt with themes of social justice and risked the wrath of the emperor Nero. Some evidence also survives to suggest that Turnus may have been a freed slave.

Bibliography

Eschenburg, Johann J. *Manual of Classical Literature.* Translated by N. W. Fiske. Philadelphia: E. C. & J. Biddle, 1850.

Martial. *Epigrams.* Vol. 2, 7.97, and Vol. 3, 9.10. Translated by Shackleton Bailey. Cambridge, Mass.: Harvard University Press, 1993.

Tusculan Disputations Marcus Tullius Cicero (45 B.C.E.)

Cast in the form of a dialogue between CICERO and an unnamed respondent, the *Tusculan Disputations* are dedicated to Brutus and represented as having taken place at Cicero's villa at Tusculum. The work is composed of five books, each of which considers happiness from the point of view of Stoic philosophy (see STOICISM) in the context of the following subjects: death, grief, sadness, spiritual disquiet, and whether or not virtue can assure happiness. Because these questions interest Cicero not only as academic considerations but also as deeply felt personal issues, a reader feels the emotional urgency of Cicero's personal involvement as he works his way through the principal ethical issues that had concerned the ancient world.

The method that Cicero develops for conducting his explorations is this: He defers forming his own opinion until he articulates all the points of view that he knows to have been offered. Having done so, he compares the several viewpoints in terms of their internal consistency and their probability. He strives to give each view a fair representation and to avoid argumentative discourse and direct contradiction. The result is almost always a courteous and reasonable exchange of viewpoints between Cicero and his companion.

Only when the discussion turns to the subject of EPICURUS and Epicureanism does Cicero's discourse become heated. As a statesman, Cicero abhorred the positions taken by Epicurean apologists. He felt that following their lead made people disdain participation in public affairs—a view that was anathema to the public-spirited Cicero. Second, Epicureanism, though it asserted the existence of deity, held that no immortal being living in a state of bliss would take any interest in the doings of its creatures. While Cicero himself may not have actually believed in the pantheon of Roman gods, he nonetheless thought that an approved state religion led to better behavior among the citizenry. Moreover, he did believe in Providence. Therefore, for him, a national religion was the foundation of ethics.

Cicero's prose style represented the ideal toward which writers strove as late as the 20th century of the Common Era. Nowhere, perhaps, in the pages of his extensive work does that style achieve more poignant effect than in his heartfelt discussions in the *Tusculan Disputations*.

Bibliography

Cicero, Marcus Tullius. *Tusculan Disputations: On the Nature of the Gods: and the Commonwealth.* Translated by C. D. Yonge. New York: Cosimo Classics, 2005.

Everitt, Anthony. *Cicero: The Life and Times of Rome's Greatest Politician.* New York: Random House Trade Paperbacks, 2001.

Two Sisters Named Bacchis Plautus   See BACCHIDES.

Tyrant, The Lucian   See FERRYBOAT, THE.

Tyrtaeus (fl. ca. 647 B.C.E.) *Greek poet*

Only the elegiac poet CALLINUS is known to have flourished before another ancient Greek practitioner of that poetic form: the Athenian Tyrtaeus. Reported to have been a lame schoolmaster at Athens, Tyrtaeus was held in low esteem by his fellow citizens, who thought him weak-minded and odd.

When an oracle revealed to the Spartans that, if they wished to succeed in their battles against the southwestern Peloponnesian city of Messene, they needed to find an Athenian general, they sent to Athens in search of one. Wishing the Spartans ill success, the Athenians sent them Tyrtaeus. Contrary to Athenian expectations, the young man proved to be an extraordinarily effective general. His war songs in the elegiac meter, moreover, heartened the Spartan troops and encouraged them to extraordinary acts of valor. After 20 years of previously fruitless warfare, the Spartans under Tyrtaeus's command took Messene, and they razed the city to the ground. Athenaeus the SOPHIST reported, moreover, that in view of the success at Messene, Spartan soldiers thereafter adopted the custom not only of reciting Tyrtaeus's verses in preparation for battle but also of marching in time to them as they repeated them from memory.

Tyrtaeus's poetic reputation rests on the fragmentary remains of his hortatory verse and on ancient opinion of him. PLUTARCH, as the literary historian J. M. Edmonds tells us, called Tyrtaeus "a good poet for sharpening the courage of the young." (See ELEGY AND ELEGIAC POETRY.)

Bibliography

Edwards, J. M., ed. and trans. *Elegy and Iambus . . . The Greek Elegiac and Iambic Poets from Callinus to Crates with the Anacreontea.* 2 vols. Cambridge, Mass.: Harvard University Press, 1954.

U

Upanishads

A collection of Hindu wisdom literature, the Upanishads are thought by the devout to contain (in the words of their translator, S. Radhakrishnan) "a complete chart of the unseen Reality . . . [an] immediate, intimate . . . convincing light on the secret of human existence."

A composite word that literally means "to sit down near," the term *Upanishad* suggests a long, oral history in which the works' inherent wisdom was passed from teacher to student over the generations. A more metaphorical interpretation of the word suggests that Upanishad conveys "bhrama-knowledge by which ignorance is loosened or destroyed." Both philosophy and spiritual enlightenment are implicit in the term.

While the numbers of texts that have come to be included under the Upanishads umbrella have grown over the centuries to more than 200, the ancient list of texts connected with the earliest Vedic schools seems to number between 10 and 14. Eight of these texts are in prose and are held to be the earliest extant philosophical documents. Dating from the eighth and seventh centuries B. C.E., they are considered to be "revealed literature," and they enjoy the same status among devout Hindus that the Bible does among Christians and that the Koran does among Muslims. The Upanishads contain the central doctrines as well as the goal of enlightenment that Hindus revere according to their individual and collective capacities.

Among the concerns that the Upanishads address are the origins, processes, and ends of the universe, the differences between the gods and goddesses that people create—deities that are genuine despite their origins and that populate polytheistic pantheons—and the "one light of universal creation." The Upanishads focus principally on subjective as opposed to objective reality. They are critical of ritualistic religion and eschew all sacrifices other than individual human will and selfhood. They find in Brahman both the creative principle and the first thing created. Brahman is the ultimate reality: It is intellective, and it recognizes itself in the thinking capacities of human beings.

Bibliography

Radhakrishnan, S., ed. and trans. *The Principal Upanishads.* New York: Harper and Brothers Publishers, 1953.

Valerius Flaccus, Gaius (d. ca. 90 C.E.)
Roman poet

A Roman poet about whom little is known, Gaius Valerius Flaccus left eight books of an unfinished EPIC, his *Argonautica*. Using as his principal source the ARGONAUTIKA of APOLLONIUS OF RHODES, Valerius Flaccus modified some incidents in the story, sometimes using HOMER or VIRGIL as models for some of his changes. Others seem to have been the work of his powers of invention.

Valerius displays a deeper concern and a greater psychological sympathy for the character of Medea than do his models (see MEDEA). The poet understands Medea as a woman torn between her loyalties to her parental family and to the lover for whom she feels a passion so intense that she is willing to murder a brother and betray her father.

Valerius also takes a less sympathetic view of Jason than does Apollonius. In Valerius's version, Jason emerges as immature, weak, and vacillating. Beyond that, Valerius feels the relevance of the voyage of the Argonauts—which was the archetypal Greek voyage of discovery—to a pattern of Greco-Roman ascendancy and to the eventual establishment of the Roman imperium. The sole representative of Valerius's talent suggests that he was a very able poet indeed and that his talent was more than adequate to renovate an old story by making it entirely relevant to his own times and their temper. QUINTILIAN considered Valerius's death to have been "a great loss."

The poem disappeared in ancient times and had been completely forgotten until, in the 15th century, a manuscript of the first four books was discovered.

Bibliography

Valerius Flaccus, Gaius. *Argonautika, Book One: A Commentary by A. J. Kleywegt.* Boston: Brill, 2005.

———. *Argonautika, Book VI: A Commentary by Henri J. W. Wijsman.* Boston: Brill, 2000.

———. *Voyage of the Argo. The Argonautica of Gaius Valerius Flaccus.* Translated by David R. Slavitt. Baltimore: Johns Hopkins University Press, 1999.

Valerius Maximus (fl. first century C.E.)
Roman prose writer

A Roman of the patrician class, Valerius Maximus collected a miscellany that he entitled *Factorum ac dictorumque memorabilium libri ix ad Tib. Caes. Augustum* (Memorable actions and

667

sayings in nine books dedicated to the Emperor Tiberius Caesar). Valerius organizes the nine books by the sort of material to be handled in each. The first book deals with religion, and each chapter handles a subtopic under that heading. Beyond that, Valerius deals with largely Greek foreign examples (which he calls *external)* and with Roman examples (which he calls *internal).* The topics so treated under religion include such matters as "religion feigned" and "augury."

The second book handles ancient institutions in a similar manner, examining such subjects as "Military Discipline." Book 3 considers the wellsprings of human valor. "Moderation" is the topic of the fourth book and "Humanity and Mercy" of the fifth. Book 6 treats the virtue of chastity, giving examples such as that of a Greek woman called Hippo who, when captured by enemy sailors, drowned herself rather than submit to their lust.

In Book 7, Valerius turns his attention to "Good Fortune." Among the attributes of the fortunate, he lists wisdom displayed in speech and in action. He then, however, wanders about among subtopics whose relation to the overarching consideration are not altogether clear, as when, for instance, he considers the operation of necessity in human affairs and the difficulties that coping with necessity sometimes imposes.

The eighth book considers the reasons that defendants with bad reputations were either acquitted or condemned for crimes of which they were accused. The final book examines viciousness of various kinds: "luxury and lust," "cruelty," "anger and hatred," and the like. The titles of chapters were probably the later innovations of copyists, so it may well be that when some subtopic strikes a reader as peculiar given the chapter title, the copyist guessed wrong about the organizing concept that Valerius had intended.

In bringing together such a volume as this, Valerius intended to collect in one place examples that people might find useful for purposes such as speaking and writing. His object was to save his readers—including, as he hoped, the emperor—time that would otherwise be devoted to individual research.

Though some have found his style artificial and overblown, his attributions faulty, and some of his personal asides silly, critics generally praise the content of Valerius's work. The ancients apparently did find his compendium helpful, as indicated both by its survival and by later summaries that scholars made of the work.

Bibliography
Valerius Maximus. *Memorable Doings and Sayings.* Edited and translated by D. R. Shackleton Bailey. Cambridge, Mass.: Harvard University Press, 2000.

———. *Memorable Deeds and Sayings: One Thousand Tales from Ancient Rome.* Translated by Henry John Walker. Indianapolis, Ind.: Hackett Publications, 2004.

Vālmīki   See RAMAYANA.

Varro, Marcus Terentius (116–27 B.C.E.)
Roman prose writer

Ancient Rome's most important and most productive scholar, Varro is credited with a life work of some 75 different compositions written in over 600 papyrus scrolls. Born in the town of Reate (now Rieti) to the north of Rome, as a child Varro moved to Rome, where he studied philosophy, letters, and antiquities. Like many of his gifted contemporaries, Varro undertook a career of public service, rising eventually to the post of praetor—the leading official of the city after the two heads of state during the republic, the consuls. In addition to serving as head of state in the absence of the consuls, the praetor chaired the senate and was empowered to lead an army if the occasion arose.

Varro's career coincided with the tumultuous period that preceded Rome's civil wars, the end of republican Rome, and the establishment of the Roman Empire. In the struggles that accompanied that changeover, Varro aligned himself with Pompey the Great—the odds-on-favorite to become the head of an imperial Roman state. In the event, however, JULIUS CAESAR overcame

Pompey, and after Caesar's assassination, Mark Antony banned Varro from holding public office and had Varro's library at his estate in Casinum plundered. This was not only Varro's loss but also that of the literary persons to whom Varro had granted free access to his collection.

Varro himself, however, escaped Antony's agents and devoted the rest of a long life to study and writing. The range of his interests was astounding. He wrote about language, producing a work, *De lingua Latina*, on Latin vocabulary and syntax in 25 books (papyrus scrolls). Of these, the fifth and sixth books survive in their entirety, as do portions of the seventh through the 10th. He also wrote an amusing little treatise about agriculture and animal husbandry, *De re rustica*, which survives in its entirety.

Everything else Varro wrote, except the titles and some representative surviving fragments, has apparently been irretrievably lost to us. From those remains, however, we can gain an idea of the subjects that Varro addressed. These include education, a topic addressed in his *Disciplinae*, where he outlined the subjects to be mastered by an educated individual. These were the subjects included in the traditional liberal arts education.

Varro also compiled a collection of some 700 biographical sketches of famous Greeks and Romans, appending a relevant EPIGRAM to each portrait. Beyond that, he composed a collection of dialogues that he titled by associating the name of a notable person with the subject under consideration. He prepared a series of 150 amusing verse and prose essays, entitled *Menippean Satires*, exploring human foolishness and vice. The work derived its title from the fact that in it Varro imitated the pithy style of a Greek model, Menippus of Gadara (fl. third century B.C.E.). (See SATIRE IN GREECE AND ROME.)

In 41 books, Varro also explored topics associated with ancient Rome. He discussed the peoples of early Italy as well as the places, the tenor of the times, and the things that were to be found there. Varro dedicated the 16 final books in that collection to Julius Caesar in his role as the *pontifex maximus*—the leading member of the college of priests responsible for controlling the Roman state cult. In these works that dealt with religious matters, Varro explored the way that human beings make divinities in their own images. He discussed priests and their organizations, sacred places, the natures of the gods, rituals, and sacred occasions.

Varro also wrote on mythology, the cults of the gods, the founding of the city of Rome, and the history of philosophy. At least some of his writings were well known to St. AUGUSTINE, who borrowed from Varro in *The City of God*.

Though both *On Agriculture* and the extant portions of *On the Latin Language* have been several times translated into English, the fragmentary remains of Varro's other works are as yet available only in the original Latin and in German and Italian translations.

See also GRAMMARIANS OF ROME.

Bibliography

Varro, Marcus Terrentius. *On Agriculture*. Translated by Harrison Boyd Ash. Cambridge, Mass.: Harvard University Press, 1934.

———. *On the Latin Language*. Translated by Roland G. Kent. 2 vols. Cambridge, Mass.: Harvard University Press, 1951.

victory odes (fifth and sixth centuries B.C.E.)

Television has schooled those of us who follow athletic events to expect them to be accompanied by the commentary and analysis of former athletes who endlessly repeat pretty much the same things. Similarly, for a span of time that was only slightly longer than the 80 years of the Greek poet PINDAR's probable lifetime, the victors in the athletic events of the ancient Greek world were celebrated by poems in their honor. Three ancient Greek poets are remembered for writing victory ODEs that, accompanied by musical instruments, were sung (and probably danced) in praise of winning athletes or of the owners of winning horses. Only the lyrics have survived the ages.

Two of these poets were SIMONIDES OF CEOS (ca. 556–468 B.C.E.) and Simonides' nephew, Bacchylides of Ceos (ca. 505–ca. 450 B.C.E.). Slightly senior to Bacchylides was Pindar, universally regarded as the greatest lyric poet of the ancient Greek world. After the work of the three poets named, the genre they all successfully practiced, as it related to athletics, disappeared from the literary scene.

To understand the emergence of the victory ode, one must have a sense of the importance of athletic events in the ancient Greek world, of the way such events were organized, and of the utility and function of the poems themselves.

The first Olympic games in ancient Greece occurred in 776 B.C.E. The Greeks so venerated that beginning that they dated the beginning of Greek history from those games. The games at Olympus honored Zeus and gave the competitors the opportunity to demonstrate for the immortal the excellence that mortals could aspire to and achieve through innate strength and courage, training, and hard work. As time went on, as the literary historian William H. Race explains, other communities organized games. The major ones were the Pythian games at Delphi in honor of the sun god Apollo; the Isthmian games at Corinth in honor of the god of sea and earthquake, Poseidon; and the Nemean games, held sometimes under the sponsorship of the city of Kleonai and sometimes of Argos, also in honor of Zeus. These were the major contests. Dozens of local ones also sprang up.

The games were organized so that they occurred serially and did not compete for audiences. This meant that athletes successful in one location could also compete in others, and some famous athletes swept their events in all of the games. In fact, some athletes extended their winning streaks to as many as 25 contests. The events included boxing and wrestling, both separately and in combination; a pentathlon that included throwing both the discus and the javelin, wrestling, the long jump, and a 200-meter dash; a 400-meter race with the participants wearing full armor; and a 4,800-meter run. These were called the gymnastic events.

Additionally, equestrian events were staged. These varied from time to time, but while Pindar was active, they included as the main event a four-horse chariot race, an ordinary horse race, and sometimes a mule-cart race. The chariot race was viewed as the most important of all the events. When the major games were in progress, if there happened to be a war going on among the Greek city-states, anyone en route to the games was granted safe passage.

Like our contemporary horse racing, chariot racing was an expensive enterprise. The owners of the horses and chariots made a significant investment in animals, their transportation to the sites of the races, chariots, training, and usually in hiring the charioteers. Rarely did the owner himself drive. Regardless of who did the driving, the owner was nonetheless regarded as having won.

When an athlete or a winning horse's owner achieved the distinction of a victory, the athlete's sponsors or the owner would hire a poet to compose a celebratory poem. Pindar was clearly the poet of choice, and as a result some 43 of his poems have survived.

Pindar enjoyed the patronage of several important persons. Particularly notable among them was Hieron, the ruler (tyrant) of the important city of Syracuse in Sicily—a Greek island at that time. Other powerful Sicilian patrons included the ruler of Agrakas (today's Agrigento); Theron, his brother, Xenocrates; and his nephew, Thrasyboulos. Arkesila of Cyrene in Libya also commissioned poems from Pindar, as did others. Although Pindar is known to have traveled widely, it is not clear that he was necessarily present at the events his poems commemorate. His verses did not involve descriptions of the events themselves. Rather, they tended to draw universal wisdom from situations somehow thematically connected with the contest or the patron.

See also "OLYMPIAN 1"; "PYTHIAN 3."

Bibliography

Bowra, C. M. *Pindar.* Oxford: Clarendon Press, 1964.

Race, William H. *Pindar: Olympian Odes, Pythian Odes.* [Greek and English]. Cambridge, Mass.: Harvard University Press, 1997.

———. *Pindar: Nemean Odes, Isthmian Odes, Fragments.* Cambridge, Mass.: Harvard University Press, 1997.

———. *Pindar.* Boston. Twayne Publishers, 1986.

Virgil (Vergil, Publius Vergilius Maro)
(70–19 B.C.E.) *Roman poet*

Born in the village of Andes near Mantua in what was then Cisalpine Gaul, Virgil is thought to have had a working-class father, perhaps a farmer or a potter, and a priestess or sorceress (*magia*) mother named Polla. He received an extensive formal education, first at Cremona, then at Milan (Roman Mediolanum), and finally in Rome itself, where among other subjects he studied philosophy and rhetoric. One of his teachers is known to have been the Epicurean philosopher, Siron. That Virgil was able to afford this extensive education suggests that his family had independent means.

Following his education, Virgil returned to Mantua in 43 B.C.E. to begin writing his ECLOGUES (published 37 B.C.E.). In the unsettled years following the slaying of JULIUS CAESAR, party faction, civil strife, and punitive actions became the Roman norm for a time. It appears that Virgil lost possession of his ancestral lands through confiscation in 41 B.C.E., had them restored, and then once again was forced to flee from them. His teacher Siron sheltered Virgil for a period, but Virgil's influential friend and patron, Gaius Maecenas, introduced him to the first Roman emperor, AUGUSTUS CAESAR. From that time forward, Virgil enjoyed imperial patronage. As a result, in addition to dwelling for a time in Rome, he acquired estates in Naples and at Nola in Campania, as well as a considerable independent fortune.

Virgil's second major publication, GEORGICS, appeared in 30 B.C.E., and thereafter he devoted his energies to the composition of his great national Roman EPIC, the AENEID. Around 20 B.C.E., Virgil traveled to Greece and elsewhere to view some of the scenes he was describing in the *Aeneid.* He fell ill on that journey, however, and passed away on the trip home before finishing the *Aeneid* to his own satisfaction. Though he had given instructions to have the manuscript destroyed, no one obeyed them. Other, shorter poems are also attributed to Virgil, though often controversially so.

Other hands may have lightly corrected the *Aeneid* before its publication, though it seems that no substantive alterations in its fabric have been made. Once it appeared, Virgil's masterpiece occupied an unchallenged place as *the* national epic of Rome, and its author became the poet-seer of the golden-age Roman Empire. The *Aeneid* conducts an intertextual conversation with the epics of HOMER from which it drew its founding mythos, some of its material, and its clear inspiration. After its appearance, it joined and often superseded Homer's epics as the repository of incident and meaning upon which subsequent works in the Western literary tradition would draw to achieve both depth and allusiveness. Dante's *Commedia* provides the most notable example.

Bibliography

Levi, Peter. *Virgil: His Life and Times.* New York: St. Martin's Press, 1999.

Taplin, Oliver. *Literature in the Greek and Roman Worlds: A New Perspective.* New York: Oxford University Press, 2000.

Vyāsa (Krishna Dvaipāyana, Vedavyā)
(fl. ca. 1500 B.C.E.) *Indian poet*

In the folklore of India, Vyāsa receives credit for having written or at least assembled the great Indian EPIC, the MAHABHARATA. He is sometimes credited for the epic RAMAYANA, though that is more commonly attributed to the poet Vālmīki. Vyāsa is said to have been a holy man who dictated this longest of the epics of the ancient world to the elephant-headed deity of the Indian pantheon, Ganesha, the remover of obstacles.

W

Wang Chong (Ch'Ung) (27–97 C.E.)
Chinese prose writer

A scholar of the later Han dynasty (see ANCIENT CHINESE DYNASTIES AND PERIODS), Wang Chong set out to debunk the wildly superstitious nonsense that over time had spread from popular culture into the teachings of ill-educated Confucian preachers and teachers. He even leveled his critique at those portions of the standard Confucian canon that he found offensive to reason and common sense. He conducted his examination in a series of stylistically elegant, lively, conversational essays entitled *LUN HENG* (*Critical Essays,* or *Balanced Discussions*), deployed in 85 sections. In its pages, he scathingly exposes the silliness of many of the supernatural fictions that had crept into the Confucian fold.

Wang wrote other works of a similar nature, but all have been lost. Victor Mair, the historian of Chinese literature, tells us that another of Wang's titles was *Satires against Customs and Usages*. There, according to surviving commentary on the work, Wang proposed abandoning the artifices of the stylized Chinese literary language in favor of straightforward contemporary vernacular exposition in writing. Mair observes that such an outcome would have been "salutary [and] liberating" for Chinese thinking and letters. Vested interests, however, made such a revolution in literature impossible.

Wang's rationalist stance also did not sit well with his superstitious contemporaries. Until the 19th century, few read him. Then his advocacy of using vernacular language in writing earned him a wider readership. Not until the 20th century did the revolutionary government of China resuscitate Wang's reputation as a philosopher, celebrating him as an early rational materialist.

Bibliography

Mair, Victor H., ed. *The Columbia Anthology of Traditional Chinese Literature.* New York: Columbia University Press, 1994.

Owen, Stephen. *Readings in Chinese Literary Thought.* Cambridge, Mass.: Harvard University Press, 1992.

Wang Chong. *Lun Heng.* Translated by Alfred Forke. New York: Paragon Book Gallery, 1962.

Watson, Burton. *Early Chinese Literature.* New York: Colombia University Press, 1962.

Wasps, The Aristophanes (422 B.C.E.)

ARISTOPHANES produced his political COMEDY, *The Wasps,* at the Athenian festival of LENAEA, where it won the first prize. The play succeeds as an admirable piece of stagecraft even though Aristophanes had probably not yet attained to his fullest powers as a comic playwright.

The play's principal character, the elderly Philocleon, finds himself utterly addicted to serving in the capacity of juror at lawsuits. So problematic has this obsession become that the old man's son, Bdelycleon, has had the entire house surrounded with a gigantic net and posted two slaves, Xanthias and Sosias, as guards to keep his father away from the court. As the play opens, the drowsy guards are trying to keep one another awake by recounting their dreams and attempting to interpret them. Xanthias interrupts his conversation with Sosias to address the audience directly. He explains that, unlike Aristophanes' *The* ACHARNIANS *and The* KNIGHTS, this play will contain little by way of attack on the Athenian demagogue, Cleon. Instead he explains Philocleon's mania for jury duty and his invariable judgment of guilty. This assertion, however, merely alerts the audience to look for unflattering references to the hated Cleon. The play is full of them, in fact. The names of the principal characters, Philocleon and Bdelycleon, for example, can be respectively translated as "one who loves Cleon" and "one who loathes Cleon."

Bdelycleon awakens on the roof and calls to the men below that he hears his father in the stove chamber. A moment later, the old man pokes his head out of the chimney and says he is just the smoke. Thwarted, the old man explains that an oracle warned that if he ever voted for an acquittal, he would die of consumption. Finding no sympathy for that story, he says he will gnaw his way through the net. His guardians remind him that he has no teeth. He then says that he wishes to sell his jackass, but his son replies he will sell the beast on his father's behalf. Philocleon agrees, and when the animal is led out, the old man is found clinging to its belly like Odysseus escaping from the Cyclops's cave.

Discovered, the old man calls for assistance from his fellow jurors. No sooner has he been locked in than he reappears among the roof tiles, trying to escape that way. As soon as the slaves have secured him again, the members of the CHORUS appear costumed as wasps and representing the other oldsters who comprise the jury. They sing their concern that their fellow juror, Philocleon, has not appeared to join them.

Singing as well, the old man appears at a window behind the net and explains his problem. Encouraged by his fellow wasps, he decides that gnawing through the net is best, and he attacks it with his toothless gums. Succeeding in getting through, he slides down a rope to his waiting compatriots, but his noise awakens Bdelycleon. He calls the slaves to help restrain his father, but the old jurymen who await him shed their cloaks, and all discover them equipped with the stings of wasps. A rousing battle ensues in which the strength of the younger contestants eventually prevails, and the waspish old men are exhausted.

Now Bdelycleon undertakes to convince his father that, far from fulfilling an important office, he is actually the slave of ruthless masters. Philocleon and Bdelycleon agree to argue the case before his colleagues, the wasps, and abide by their judgment.

Philocleon argues that a juryman is more powerful than a king. He describes the ways that accused persons attempt to influence him before a trial. He speaks of the disregard of the jurors for the wills of deceased persons and the authority they exercise over the goods and children of deceased persons. He then speaks of the high regard in which the demagogue, Cleon, holds this particular group of jurors.

Bdelycleon encourages his father to keep talking, with an unsavory comparison between the power he thinks he is exercising and an anus. When Philocleon has exhausted his arguments—which have earned the admiring approval of the jury of wasps—Bdelycleon responds. First he makes the jurors understand what a small percentage of state revenue their payment represents. They are surprised and want to know where the rest goes. He tells them how their theoretical subordinates, who are really their masters, enrich themselves at state expense, while the jurors receive a pittance for their services. His examples convince his father of the venality of Athenian statesmen.

The other jurors also find themselves convinced, and they beg Philocleon to forego judging. For the old man, however, working at the court has become a drug. He is hooked and cannot face the consequences of withdrawal.

Sympathetic to his father's addiction, Bdelycleon proposes a solution. Philocleon can do his judging at home, ruling on all matters touching the household and fining offenders in keeping with the nature of their crimes and with their means to pay. Philocleon likes the idea, but he wonders who will pay him. Bdelycleon assures him that he will pay and goes to arrange the home court. He provides a chamber pot, a fire with a crock of lentils to snack from, a rooster whose crowing will keep the judge from dozing, and a picture of the hero Lycus, a former king of Thebes.

They are about to look for a case to judge when Philocleon realizes that there is no bar for an accused to plead before. He rushes off in search of something that will serve. In his absence, the slave Xanthias enters and explains that the dog, Labes, has snatched and eaten a Sicilian cheese in the kitchen. Bdelycleon decides that this will make an admirable first case for his father. After more sending after forgotten paraphernalia, the case begins with solemn libations and prayers. When all is in readiness, two actors costumed as dogs are led onstage. One, the accuser, wears a mask that looks like the SOPHIST Laches, and the other, the defendant, wears a likeness of the demagogue Cleon.

Having heard the case against Labes, Philocleon instantly wishes to rush to a harsh judgment. Bdelycleon, however, insists that his father hear the other side, and since the dog cannot speak, Bdelycleon speaks for him. He praises his qualities as a sheep dog and a guard dog, but says that he is ignorant. A group of children costumed as puppies now enter and paw at Philocleon for mercy. The judge weeps, but nonetheless determines to condemn the dog.

The tears in his eyes, however, blind Philocleon so that Bdelycleon must lead him to the jar into which the old man must drop the pebble of judgment. This, of course, is the jar of acquittal. The old man is certain that he will die of consumption; his last reason for insisting on being a judge dies within him, and the principal actors leave the stage.

The chorus now berates the audience for their prior mistreatment of the poet and explains to them the utility of poets in helping them think through political problems. They also praise the older generation of war heroes—a generation they themselves represent—the men who saved Greece from the threat posed by Persian invasion. They have, they say, come by their stings honestly while fighting in defense of their homelands. They admit, however, that some among them are drones, and that such citizens—doubtless including Cleon—are parasites on the body of the state.

In the ensuing scene, the principals return. Bdelycleon is trying to get his father to dress and talk like a member of the leisured upper classes of Athenian society. He reproves his bawdy humor and his juridical shoptalk in favor of urbane banter. Aristophanes, however, cannot long stray from his enmity for Cleon, which resurfaces here as Bdelycleon tries to prepare his father for life in society. They go to the party.

Xanthius the slave returns and reports what happened. Philocleon got roaring drunk, insulted everyone, and made off with a totally nude flute girl whom, when we next see him, he is escorting to his home for nefarious purposes. Bdelycleon rescues her, and a parade of persons with complaints against Philocleon begins to occupy the stage. In his drunken state, he has ruined merchandise and started fights. Those he injured are pursuing him with summonses. Ironically, Bdelycleon has achieved the objective he sought. His father is no longer obsessed with pleadings at law. Moreover, the old man has conceived a passion for dancing, after a manner that wildly parodies the dances often performed in EURIPIDES' tragedies. A trio of dancers attired as crabs joins the old man on stage, and the four dance frenziedly together as the chorus sings an accompaniment and ends the play.

Bibliography

Aristophanes. *The Complete Plays.* Translated by Paul Roche. New York: New American Library, 2005.

Woman from Samos, The *(The Marriage Contract)* Menander *(ca. 320 B.C.E.)*

Restored from a variety of fragmentary sources to a reasonably complete condition, this play, under the title *The Girl from Samos,* appears as the sole representative of MENANDER's work in the literary historian Harold Bloom's selection of works in the Western canon of literature. Since that choice, however, a complete drama of Menander's, DYSKOLOS *(The Bad Tempered Man)*, has been discovered and probably should be added to Bloom's list as a second representative of Menander's work.

Though Menander peopled his stage with stock characters, a number of his dramatis personae seem to have been drawn from life. This, as the literary historian W. Geoffrey Arnott tells us, is surely the case with some of the characters in *The Woman from Samos.* The title character, Chrysis, has come to Athens from Samos as a refugee, worked as a hetaera (a courtesan), and eventually cohabited with an elderly Athenian named Demeas—also one of the play's characters. Without belaboring the point, the likelihood exists that details of the plot of this play are drawn from events that actually occurred in the Athens of the fourth century B.C.E.

Set in an Athenian street near the houses of the wealthy Demeas and the impoverished Nikeratos, the play opens with Moschion, the adopted son of Demeas, addressing the audience and giving the play's background. He tells how Demeas adopted him and brought him up affectionately and carefully, providing him with many luxuries. Then Demeas fell in love with the Samian courtesan and took her to live with him. At this point, a number of lines are lost or imperfect.

When intelligible discourse resumes, Moschion confesses that he got drunk and raped Nikeratos's daughter, Plangon. Moreover, a baby had been born from the union, and Moschion has brought the child into Demeas's house for Chrysis to help nurse. Both Demeas and Nikeratos have been away on a journey together for some months and are unaware of the events that have transpired. Moschion hopes to conceal his paternity of the baby from both men, and Chrysis suggests that they pretend the child is hers. She thinks Demeas's love for her will disarm his anger. In their absence, however, Demeas and Nikeratos have decided that their children should be joined in marriage.

The second act probably began with Demeas expressing his displeasure over finding Chrysis nursing a baby. Moschion enters and finds his father angry and threatening to send Chrysis and the baby—which at this point he thinks is his— away. Moschion argues against this, and after more lost lines, he seems to have prevailed. When the action resumes, Demeas suggests that his son marry Plangon and is surprised when his adoptive son eagerly agrees.

Demeas then convinces Nikeratos, against the latter's better judgment, that the wedding should take place at once—that very day. Demeas sends his servant Parmenon to invite the wedding guests and go off to the market for the necessary goods.

Act 3 opens with Demeas's accidental discovery that the baby's father is Moschion, but of course Demeas thinks the mother to be Chrysis. Deciding that Parmenon will know the truth, Demeas crossexamines him. Parmenon lies. Demeas says he knows that the baby is Moschion's and threatens to beat Parmenon.

Now Demeas considers his situation. He decides that Moschion is not at fault since he has so willingly consented to marry Plangon. Demeas concludes that the fault lies with Chrysis, and he resolves to send her away. He immediately acts on his decision and locks her out. At this point Nikeratos arrives, and he and Chrysis conclude that Demeas's unpredictable behavior suggests that he has gone mad. Nikeratos takes Chrysis and the baby into his house, hoping that Demeas's illness will soon pass.

Act 4 opens with Nikeratos telling his wife that Demeas's callous behavior is an ill omen for a wedding day. Moschion arrives. Impatient for the wedding, he has been trying to while away the hours until the appointed time. Nikeratos reports the problem. Demeas enters, and Moschion tries to plead on Chrysis's behalf. Moschion's defense of Chrysis convinces Demeas that his son has taken his mistress's part against him.

Eventually Moschion confesses to his father what has really happened, and Demeas is pacified. Nikeratos, however, stumbles in on his daughter, Plangon, when she is nursing the baby; he realizes what has really happened and becomes furious. After further complications—including Moschion's temporary decision to run away and become a soldier—and after additional misunderstandings and more reconciliations, everything gets sorted out. The wedding takes place, everyone becomes friends again, and Demeas speaks the epilogue.

The play is lively and full of fun and good humor. It also illustrates a penchant of Athenian playwrights of the New Comedy for satirizing some of their fellow citizens on the stage.

See also COMEDY IN GREECE AND ROME.

Bibliography

Bloom, Harold. *The Western Canon: The Books and School of the Ages.* New York: Harcourt Brace and Company, 1994.

Menander. *Samia* [The Woman from Samos]. In *Menander.* Vol. 3. Edited and translated by W. Geoffrey Arnott. Cambridge, Mass.: Harvard University Press, 2000.

Women at the Thesmophoria (The Parliament of Women, The Assembly Women) Aristophanes (ca. 411 B.C.E.)

Probably performed at the GREAT DIONYSIA in the same year as LYSISTRATA's debut at the Athenian Festival of LENAEA, *Women at the Thesmophoria* subordinates to professional and sexual satire the politics that so often attracted ARISTOPHANES' dramatic attention. The treatment of wives and women in EURIPIDES' tragedies becomes the particular object of Aristophanes' scorn in this play.

The Thesmophoria was a festival that only women could attend. As the play opens, a character representing Euripides is leading a reluctant kinsman to the home of the tragic poet and effeminate homosexual Agathon. Euripides has learned that at their festival—one that Aristophanes has here turned into a mock governmental assembly—the women intend to sentence Euripides to death for his unflattering portrayal of women in his tragedies. Euripides hopes to enlist Agathon as his ally. He plans to persuade Agathon to dress as a woman and speak in Euripides' favor at the assembly.

The two kinsmen find Agathon in feminine attire. The poet explains that dressing the part assists him in his art. Euripides explains his errand, but Agathon refuses his request. The women, he suggests, will find him more attractive than they are and will turn on him.

Euripides is forced to turn to his kinsman for aid and, with Agathon's help, shaves him and dress him as a woman. So attired, The Kinsman makes his way to the festival where the chair, Critylla, calls the assembly to order and leads the prayers to the various patron deities. The last such prayer invokes punishments on Euripides and on others who expose women's misbehavior.

A speaker named Mica succeeds Critylla. It is she who brings charges against Euripides, accusing him of having acquainted husbands with the devices that wives formerly could use to deceive the men. She proposes that the women plot the playwright's destruction. Her views are seconded by a garland seller who complains that Euripides is sowing disbelief in religion with the result that her sales of votive flowers have fallen off.

Euripides' kinsman is the third to speak. He defends Euripides by suggesting that he has only revealed a few of the tricks women use to deceive their husbands, and that the women have thousands more. The examples that he gives so incense his listeners that the women threaten him, and Critylla restrains them with some difficulty.

Just then, an effeminate male, Cleisthenes, enters with the intelligence that Euripides' kinsman has infiltrated the meeting. The kinsman is shortly identified as the spy, and a brief physical confirms his masculinity. Concerned that there might be other infiltrators, the women begin a search. Seizing his moment, the kinsman grabs Mica's baby from her arms and races to seek sanctuary at an altar.

The women decide to gather firewood and burn the kinsman. He unwraps the child in his arms and discovers that he holds not a baby but a skin full of wine. As the kinsman seeks other strategies to extract himself from his difficulties, the CHORUS enumerates a series of complaints against husbands.

Euripides' kinsman has an idea and begins to parody his cousin's tragicomedy, *HELEN*. In that play, Menelaus, shipwrecked in Egypt, discovers that the real and virtuous Helen has been there all along, and that the woman over whom he fought the Trojan War was an evil phantom. Menelaus conspires to rescue his wife.

In *Women at the Thesmophoria*, as the kinsman plays virtuous Helen, Euripides enters in the guise of Menelaus. Still parodying the play, Euripides attempts to lead his kinsman/Helen away from the altar and out of harm's way. Critylla, however, stops them and points out that a marshal and an archer are on their way. Euripides decides to beat a hasty retreat, while promising not to desert the kinsman. The marshal announces that the kinsman has been condemned to die in the feminine apparel he wore to the festival. The archer drags the kinsman away to chain him to a plank.

Returned to the stage so chained, the kinsman spots Euripides in the distance, this time costumed as Perseus from Euripides' play *Andromeda*. Assuming that Euripides has a plan for his rescue, the kinsman takes the role of the chained Andromeda and begins reciting lines satirizing that play. Another character, Echo, comes and repeats the final words of each of Andromeda's speeches. The exchanges become increasingly insulting and funny, and Echo takes up the same routine with the archer, who grows more and more incensed.

Euripides arrives through the air via the stage crane, just as Perseus arrived in the borrowed winged sandals of Hermes in the source myth for *Andromeda*. When, however, Euripides attempts to unchain his kinsman, the archer threatens to behead the playwright. Euripides must invent another stratagem and exits to do so. After a choral interlude, he reenters dressed as a female procurer with a girl dancer, a boy piper, and a travel bag. In his own person, he offers to effect a peace treaty with the women of Athens. If they will release his kinsman, he promises never to insult them again. If they do not, however, he promises to tell their husbands, who are away fighting the Peloponnesian War, what the women have been up to in the men's absence.

The women agree. Euripides sees that the archer becomes occupied with the dancing girl and spirits his kinsman away. When the archer returns, he finds his prisoner gone and his bow stolen. The chorus misdirects his pursuit, and the play ends with a choral blessing.

Bibliography

Aristophanes. *The Complete Plays*. Translated by Paul Roche. New York: New American Library, ca. 2005.

Henderson, Jeffrey, ed. and trans. *Women at the Thesmophoria*. *Aristophanes III*. Cambridge, Mass.: Harvard University Press, 2000.

Works and Days Hesiod (ca. 710 B.C.E.)

A poem of 828 Greek dactylic hexameter verses (see QUANTITATIVE VERSE), HESIOD's *Works and Days*, though it contains a good deal of mythological material, differs from the EPIC poetic tradition in which HOMER composed. Hesiod's is the earliest Greek poetry to concern itself with agriculture and with the situation of the ordinary citizen to a degree victimized by the judges and leaders of his community. The poem opens a window through which one can view the life of a Greek farming village in the eighth century B.C.E.

Thus, Hesiod's work can be studied profitably by those principally interested in literature, sociology, or history. It can also shed light on ancient autobiography to a degree since Hesiod often alludes to his own circumstances.

After opening with a brief and conventional invocation to the MUSES, Hesiod declares that he wants to present the facts of a certain situation to his brother, Perses. Two sorts of strife exist, the poet says. One is the evil kind that leads to war and ill-natured disagreement. The other is a good kind: It is the sort of disagreement whose careful discussion by the disagreeing parties leads to a settlement that may not entirely please anyone, but with which everyone can live. It appears that Perses and Hesiod disagreed over the disposition of their father's holdings and that perhaps Perses bribed or otherwise influenced the civic fathers to find in his favor.

Hesiod next looks back on the way in which troubles came into the world. He recites the myth of Pandora, who, in the version told here, opened a jar and released upon the world the troubles the jar contained. Before that time, and before Zeus and Hesiod's contemporary Greek pantheon, the god Cronus created from gold people who populated a golden age. They lived in peace and plenty and died easy deaths. Next, however, the gods created human beings from silver, and they introduced violence into the world. Eventually they all passed on. A race made of bronze succeeded them. These people developed violence into warfare and wiped each other out.

Until this point, Hesiod borrows from standard mythology. Next, however, he invents a fourth group. Zeus brings forth the race of heroes who populate Greek myth and legend—heroes such as Heracles, Agamemnon, Achilles, and Odysseus. These too pass away.

Hesiod and his contemporaries, however, have the misfortune, as do we, to belong to the iron age. They are dishonest; they do not honor their aged parents; they lie, are foul-mouthed, and rejoice in evil. These people are doomed never to cease from labor, never to enjoy good unmixed with evil, and eventually to be destroyed when

they begin to be born already gray-headed. Hesiod regrets that he is one of them.

Again addressing his brother Perses, Hesiod advises him to seek good judgments instead of crooked ones, and he tells a fable illustrating the latter. He then advises those who sit in council and pass judgment in disagreements to find wise solutions and to avoid being influenced by bribery and the like. Turning once more to Perses, Hesiod loads him with much brotherly advice: Work hard. Organize carefully. Be trustworthy. Seek solutions to problems that all can assent to. Treat your guests well since Zeus protects the traveler. Be hospitable to friends and avoid enemies. Be constant in familial relationships. Do not associate with promiscuous women.

Hesiod next advises Perses to get himself a little homestead. He instructs him in fascinating detail about the things he will need to equip it properly and the people he will need to staff it. Modern sociology has learned much about ancient farming arrangements and economy from Hesiod's extended instructions to Perses. These include instructions for building a plow and other implements needed in farming and for selling produce profitably.

Dispersed throughout Hesiod's poem are instructions for the best times of year for performing certain sorts of farm work. Cut wood when the rains start and the constellation Sirius is mostly visible. When the Pleiades are setting and the cranes migrating, do your plowing. Prune vines when Arcturus rises at twilight and the swallows are in evidence. When the Pleiades rise and the fig leaves grow, it is a good time for sailing and time for the harvest. After the summer harvest is finished, the time is ripe for drinking, and the grapes one harvests in September will produce the wine for the following season. Hesiod continues with advice about sheep shearing and against sowing grain on the 13th day of any month.

The poem also provides a treasure trove of superstitions on a broad variety of subjects. These appear mostly in the context of advice on how to avoid unwanted consequences of various sorts. It ends by listing the days that are propitious for building narrow ships, for conceiving, and for being born. Hesiod finally advises that many days are of "mixed thunder" and imply neither good fortune nor bad. It behooves a person, nonetheless, the poet says, to take into consideration all of Hesiod's good advice.

Bibliography

Hesiod *Theogony, Works and Days, Shield*. Translated by Apostolos N. Athanassakis. Baltimore, Md.: Johns Hopkins University Press, 2004.

———— et al. *Works of Hesiod and the Homeric Hymns*. Translated by Daryl Hine. Chicago: University of Chicago Press, 2005.

Nelson, Stephanie A. *God and the Land: The Metaphysics of Farming in Hesiod and Vergil* [sic], *with a Translation of Hesiod's Works and Days*. Translated by David Greene. New York: Oxford University Press, 1998.

Tandy, David W., and Walter C. Neale, eds. and trans. *Hesiod's Works and Days: A Translation and Commentary for the Social Sciences*. Berkeley: University of California Press, 1996.

Xenophon of Athens (ca. 429–ca. 357 B.C.E.) Greek historian

The son of a prominent Athenian family, Xenophon was a memoirist, writer of fictionalized history, essayist, and student and protégé of SOCRATES. As an adventurer and observer, he attached himself to a Persian military campaign led by the young Persian prince Cyrus against his elder brother and king, Artaxerxes II. When that effort failed and Cyrus and the leaders of his Greek mercenaries died (401 B.C.E.), it fell to Xenophon to lead the 10,000 Spartan soldiers of fortune who had been serving with Cyrus from the frozen mountains of Armenia to Greek colonial territory on the Black Sea and finally to the Hellespont. Xenophon was then able to negotiate permanent appointments for himself and for the men who followed him in the Spartan army—an act for which Athens at first banished him, though its citizens ultimately relented.

Xenophon never returned to Athens, but spent the final decades of his life writing at places of retirement in the countryside, first at Scillus and then at Corinth. The model of government that he most admired, however, was always that of Sparta—a constitutional monarchy.

Literary history remembers Xenophon for four principal sorts of compositions. The first of these include his straightforward historical writings. His *Hellenics* details the history of Greece for a period of 50 years during the author's own lifetime. He begins with 411 B.C.E.—the point at which THUCYDIDES' discussion of *The PELOPONNESIAN WAR* breaks off—and carries the narrative down to 362 B.C.E. This was the period during which Sparta triumphed over Athens and temporarily emerged as the principal military power of Greece. Then Sparta, in turn, found itself eclipsed by the rise of Thebes. Thebes defeated Sparta at the battle of Leuctra (371 B.C.E.), and again at Mantinea (362 B.C.E.). On the second occasion however, the brilliant Theban general Epaminondas was killed in action, effectively thwarting further Theban ambitions.

As compared with Thucydides, says the literary historian Carleton L. Brownson, Xenophon's historiography is filled with disappointing omissions and with a failure to make connections between his own narrative and the one that he tries to continue. He also displays a pro-Spartan bias that sometimes clouds his reporting of events. In the final analysis, Brownson finds Xenophon less than trustworthy as a historian of this period.

Xenophon's *Anabasis,* however, is a different story. This is Xenophon's own memoir of the campaign of Cyrus against his brother, Artaxerxes II. It recounts the remarkable leadership role that the young scholar Xenophon, who in the beginning was a sort of military sightseer, came to play. The opening paragraph of this entry gives the framework of the story, but the importance of Xenophon's achievement in leading his 10,000 Spartans back across hundreds of miles of hostile Persian territory can hardly be exaggerated. Xenophon had to invent tactics to ensure the safety of his rear guard. His success in defeating Asiatic armies much larger than his own revealed to the entire world the soft military underbelly of the enormous Persian Empire. A 19th-century writer on military tactics, Theodore F. Dodge, remarked of the *Anabasis*: "After . . . 23 centuries, there is no better military textbook."

Perhaps the least highly regarded of Xenophon's historical works is his funeral appreciation of the Spartan king Agesilaus—the descendant at a remove of 25 generations of the hero Heracles (Hercules). Despite its author's preference for Spartan government and its military virtues, Xenophon treats his subject in an uncharacteristically perfunctory fashion. Probably the necessity for the hasty composition of a funeral oration is at the source of the compositional defects it displays, including wholesale borrowing from the author's previously written works.

In his CYROPÆDIA (The education of Cyrus—not the would-be usurper with whom Xenophon marched, but Cyrus the Great who founded the Persian empire), Xenophon creates a kind of historical fiction. The literary historian Walter Miller calls it the pioneering work of Western literature in the field of "historical romance." Though Xenophon had a firm firsthand acquaintance with Persia, the system of government and training that the author attributes to Persians comes straight out of Sparta. So do the practices of soldiers going into battle and the tactics they employ.

The work is much more historically reliable when it comes to reporting the customs of the Armenians and Chaldeans, peoples whom Xenophon knew from having fought against them. Yet the book's principal purpose is not histori-

cal; rather, it is educational. It strives to paint an ideal society as Xenophon conceived of one. His Cyrus is guided, as Xenophon tried to be, by the principles of Socrates. Cyrus's imagined subjects enjoy freedom of speech and legal equality—benefits unrelated to the Persian system of ruling. Roman writers and statesmen such as CICERO and Cato nonetheless found in the book a model for the Rome they hoped would evolve. When considered as didactic fiction rather than as history, *Cyropaedia* deserves its place as Xenophon's masterpiece.

Among Xenophon's lesser writings we find his *Hiero*, an imagined dialogue between the poet SIMONIDES OF CEOS and King Hiero of Syracuse in Sicily. Their conversation presents a dialogue in the manner of Socrates on two subjects: First, who is happier, an absolute ruler or a private citizen? Second, if the ruler is less happy, can that ruler become happier by gaining the subjects' affection? Critics generally judge this essay to be a lesser work than PLATO's on the same subject.

Beyond the works mentioned above, Xenophon also wrote essays on miscellaneous subjects, including one about the constitution of his beloved Spartans: "Constitution of the Lacedemians." He wrote another pair called "Ways and Means" and "Athenian Finance," on the way in which the city of Athens might replenish the treasury it had exhausted in warfare. A fourth essay treats the subject of horsemanship, a fifth—a military treatise—discusses "The Cavalry Commander," and a sixth considers the art of "Hunting."

Others among Xenophon's surviving works commemorate his beloved teacher and master, Socrates. His *Memorials of Socrates* (*Memorabilia*) sketches the character of Xenophon's revered teacher at the ethical and practical rather than at the philosophical level. Like Plato, Xenophon also wrote a *Socratic Apology*. In it, Xenophon reports Socrates' defense when the Athenians put him on trial for impiety. As Xenophon was off on his expedition with Cyrus at the time, he had to rely on the descriptions reported by his friend Hermogenes. In Xenophon's version, though Socrates, as in Plato and elsewhere, is innocent of the charges against him, he is nonetheless willing to die to avoid the afflictions that accompany old age rather than, as Plato has it, on principle.

Also notable among Xenophon's Socratic writings is his *Symposium* (Banquet), in which he reports the doings at a banquet held in 421 B.C.E. at the home of Callias. Xenophon describes the entertainment and activities at the banquet and pictures Socrates as a relaxed, jovial, and genial companion. Socrates' more serious reported conversation centers on the inferiority of carnal love to spiritual love.

Bibliography

Brownson, Carleton L., ed. and trans. *Xenophon: Hellenica; Anabasis.* 2 vols. Vol. 1: London: William Heinemann Ltd., 1950; Vol. 2: New York: G. P. Putnam and Sons, 1930.

Hendrick, Larry. *Xenophon's Cyrus the Great: The Art of Leadership and War.* New York: St. Martin's Press, 2006.

Marchant, E. C., ed. and trans. *Xenophon: Scripta Minora.* New York: G. P. Putnam's Sons, 1925.

Miller, Walter, ed. and trans. *Xenophon's Cyropaedia.* 2 vols. Cambridge, Mass.: Harvard University Press, 1952–53.

Xenophon. *The Shorter Socratic Writings.* Translated and edited by Robert C. Bartlett. Ithaca, N.Y.: Cornell University Press, 1996.

Xenophon of Ephesus (fl. second or third century B.C.E.) *Greek prose writer*

A member of a category of writers sometimes described as Greek erotic novelists, Xenophon of Ephesus composed a story that is sometimes called *An Ephesian Tale* (*Ephesiaca*) and is sometimes known by the names of its protagonists, Abrocomes and Antheia. Typical of the genre, Xenophon of Ephesus's tale recounts in six books the trials of a young couple separated soon after their wedding. As is often the case in such works, pirates kidnap the bride. After five books of stylized adventures common to the genre, the couple are reunited. Such novels became models for Renaissance imitators of their plot elements. Sir Philip Sidney's *Arcadia*, for instance, introduced elements of Greek romance to England.

See also GREEK PROSE ROMANCE.

Bibliography

Xenophon of Ephesus. *Ephesiaca* in *Three Greek Romances.* Translated and edited by Moses Haddas. Indianapolis, Ind.: Bobbs-Merrill, 1964.

Xunzi (Hsün Tzu) (ca. 312 B.C.E.) *Chinese prose writer*

What little we know of the Chinese philosopher Xunzi's life has been gathered from occasional snippets in his own work and from a short biography of him that the historian SIMA QIAN (SSU-MA CH'IEN) wrote about a century after Xunzi's death. The first biographical notice we have of Xunzi appears when, at about the age of 50, he traveled from his native Zhao (Chao) to the state of Qi (Chi) to teach and to study; he arrived there about 264 B.C.E. Sometime during the period 266–255, B.C.E., Xunzi himself wrote that he had debated military matters before King Xiaocheng (Hsiao-ch'eng) of Zhao.

For a time after his arrival in Qi, Xunzi was welcomed and honored, but jealousy produced slander, and he moved on to the state of Chu. There the prime minister appointed him to be the magistrate of Lanling in Shandong (Shantung) Province. He remained in this post until the assassination of his patron in 238. Though he lost his appointment on that occasion, he remained for the rest of his life in Lanling and was buried there. The date of his death is not known.

As a philosopher, Xunzi ardently rose to the defense of traditional Confucianism, writing mostly in prose but also in verse against the positions of such opponents to Confucian doctrine as MOZI. Mozi had disparaged two central doctrines of Confucianism—the value of ritual for instilling right thinking and the ethical benefit of music. Xunzi considered both necessary to a functioning and upright human society.

Xunzi also argued against revisionist thinkers who were responsible for the rise of neo-Confucianism. In that group Xunzi included his predecessor MENCIUS. Xunzi took issue with Mencius's argument that basic human nature is good. Such a view, Xunzi argued, contradicts the authority of ritual, which provides models for emulation in the human effort to become good. The assertion that essential human nature is good also marginalizes the necessity for education, and it contradicts universal human experience. People require external restraint to avert wrongdoing, and ritual provides it. In his own time, however, Xunzi lost the argument to Mencius's adherents.

Xunzi was a prolific writer, and his works have survived to be collected for us in three substantial volumes in John Knobloch's English translation.

Bibliography

Knobloch, John. *Xunzi: A Translation and Study of the Complete Works*. 3 Vols. Stanford, Calif.: Stanford University Press, 1988–94.

Xunzi. *Basic Writings*. Translated by Burton Watson. New York: Columbia University Press. 2003.

Wing-Tsit Chan, ed. and trans. *A Source Book in Chinese Philosophy*. Princeton, N.J.: Princeton University Press, 1963.

Y

Yamanoue no Okura (ca. 660–ca. 733 C.E.)
Japanese Poet

Born in Korea in the kingdom of Paekche, Okura was a child of three or four when he arrived in Japan as a refugee. The literary historian Donald Keene suggests that, given Okura's mastery of Chinese as well as Japanese and his acquaintance with the thought of CONFUCIUS, BUDDHA, and the LAO TZU (*Daode jing*), his father had probably educated him in Chinese philosophy. In any case, his Japanese poems on subjects connected with such matters often appear in the MAN'YŌSHŪ, Japan's earliest surviving anthology of poetry, with lengthy explanatory prefaces in the Chinese language.

In 701, Okura went to China as a junior diplomatic official, remaining there for perhaps two or perhaps five years. During that stay, he composed the only poem in the great collection that was penned outside Japan. Eventually he rose to become the governor of Hōki and, later, a tutor to the crown prince. His pupil eventually became the emperor Shōmu, who assigned Okura the important post of governor of Chikuzen, a major province where many people with literary interests dwelled.

In his verse, Okura objected to the Taoist (see DAOISM) rejection of worldly responsibilities and encouraged Buddhist asceticism and Confucian devotion to the family. His most eloquent poem, his "Dialogue on Poverty" is described in the entry on the *Man'yōshū*.

Okura himself compiled a lost anthology, *Karin* (Forest of verses) that became a source for the *Man'yōshū*. Okura's reputation as a poet has recently risen because of the 20th century's preference for the longer sort of poem that Okura wrote over the shorter poems that came to characterize Japanese letters after the ancient period.

Bibliography

Keene, Donald. *Seeds in the Heart: Japanese Literature from Earliest Times to the Late Sixteenth Century.* New York: Henry Holt and Company, 1993.

1000 Poems from the Man'yōshū: *The Complete Nippon Gakujutsu Shinkokai Translation.* Translated by the Japanese Classics Translation Committee. Mineola, N.Y.: Dover Publications, 2005.

Yang Xiong (Yang Hsiüng) (53 B.C.E.–18 C.E.)
Chinese poet and prose writer

A poet, literary critic, scholar, ethicist, and statesman, Yang Xiong had been a precocious child. He read widely, thought much, and, owing to a bad case of stuttering, spoke little.

Yang combined the roles of poet and ethicist in a collection of FU POEMS, six of which survive. Couched in the form of debates, these poems deal with such issues as moderation in the use of wine or as a consideration of the negative and positive attributes of hunting. His poem "Changyangfu" (Tall poplars) suggests that the aristocratic sport of hunting imposes on the common people by drawing them from their labors to trap game for the nobility to chase. On the positive side, hunting provides a useful adjunct to diplomacy, for it impresses foreign guests with the hosts' generosity and the warlike qualities that the huntsmen display in the chase. Yang's verse self-consciously imitated the work of older poets and therefore seemed archaic to his contemporaries.

As a scholar, Yang interested himself in the science of acupuncture, musical theory, and the origins and development of language. The old-fashioned style that manifested itself in his verse appeared elsewhere in his writing. He found the BOOK OF CHANGES to be a compelling document and wrote a companion volume pointing out its excellences—his *Taixuanjing* (*T'ai hsüan ching*).

As a literary critic, however, Yang later came to disavow his own verse. He felt that the rhymed prose (*fu*) in which he had composed led people into idle and lascivious thoughts. Moreover, he found his own verse false rather than genuine and *fu* verse in general no better than "worm carving."

Posterity principally remembers Yang for a work on ethics, *FAYAN*, in which he modifies some of the principles of CONFUCIUS. The *Fayun* argues that essential human nature is neither good nor evil but can be shaped to go either way.

Relatively late in life, Yang became an official in the government of the usurper Wang Mang, who had briefly overthrown the Han dynasty. Yang was not happy in his official role and once attempted suicide by jumping out a library window. Nonetheless, his affiliation with a disreputable sovereign adversely colored the Confucians' evaluation of Yang's work for 1,000 years.

Bibliography

Giles, Herbert A. *A History of Chinese Literature.* New York: Grove Press, 1958.

Idema, Wilt, and Lloyd Haft. *A Guide to Chinese Literature.* Ann Arbor: Center for Chinese Studies, University of Michigan, 1997.

Mair, Victor H. *The Columbia History of Chinese Literature.* New York: Columbia University Press, 2001.

Owen, Stephen. *Readings in Chinese Literary Thought.* Cambridge, Mass.: Harvard University Press, 1992.

Yang, Xiong. *The Elemental Changes: The Ancient Chinese Companion to the I Ching: the Tai Hsüan Ching of Master Yang Hsüng.* Translated by Michael Nylan. Albany: State University of New York Press, 1994.

Yantielun (*Yen t'ieh lun, Debates on Salt and Iron*) Huan Kuan (ca. 80 B.C.E.)

During the reign of the Han dynasty emperor Wu, a leader who saw warfare as a principal tool of diplomacy, the Chinese government created state monopolies that controlled the distribution of salt and iron. These assertive policies, though they were strongly endorsed by the imperial civil servants, the Legalists, both oppressed the common people and offended the adherents of the humanistic Confucian way.

If the accounts are true, representatives of the two sides engaged in an extended series of debates in which they argued their respective views of the state monopolies and economic policy. A scholar named Huan Kuan (fl. 1st c., C.E.) recorded and edited the debates, and he produced the lively, 60-section account of them that has come down to posterity.

Whereas the Legalists uphold the benefits of foreign wars, the Confucians are dead set against them. The Legalists insist that such wars are necessary to defend the empire against militaristic tribal people who must be destroyed. Besides, the wars bring glamorous goods into the marketplace as a side effect. The Confucians object, citing the universal brotherhood of man, and insist that diplomacy and friendship can win the barbarians to China's side.

The Legalists favor stern laws and harsh punishments as the proper means for keeping the common people in line. The Confucians describe the wretchedness and want of the common people and call for social programs to relieve their misery. The Legalists feel sure that such programs only encourage slothfulness. The Confucians insist that proper educational programming can lead the untutored commoners to virtue. Besides, the Confucians argue, the idle rich have no concept of the misery and drudgery that make up the ordinary lot of common folks.

Huan Kuan manages to catch the flavor of the debates. While the rhetoric is high-flown and the speeches are often set pieces, insults are sometimes exchanged, tempers flare, and they occasionally become so bitter that personal quarreling and name-calling ensue.

Bibliography

Huan Kuan. *Discourses on Salt and Iron: a debate.* Trans. by Esson M. Gale. Leiden: E.J. Brill, 1931.

Idema, Wilt, and Lloyd Haft. *A Guide to Chinese Literature.* Ann Arbor: Center for Chinese Studies, The University of Michigan, 1997.

Watson, Burton. *Early Chinese Literature.* New York: Columbia University Press, 1962.

Yanzi chunqiu (Yen Tzu Ch'un-ch'iu, Spring and Autumn of Master Yen) (ca. 500 B.C.E.)

The hero of this eight-chapter series of rigidly moralistic anecdotes, Yen Ying, was a younger contemporary of Confucius who shared some of Confucius's views but was not always the great sage's admirer. Specifically, Yen took issue with the Confucian penchant for long periods of mourning and elaborate funeral rituals. He also disapproved of the Confucian fondness for music. Instead, he seemed to favor the view of

Mozi, who considered music to be tainted with lascivious overtones.

The literary historian Burton Watson suggests that much of the material contained in this work has been borrowed from the *Zuozhuan*. That fact alone rules out this work's sometimes-proposed claim to be an early representative of Chinese biography.

Yen Ying is portrayed as an unwittingly sententious courtier—one in the mold of Shakespeare's Polonius in *Hamlet*. In the role of the good adviser to his ruler, Duke Jing (Ching), Yen must thwart the duke's evil advisers, Liang Chu Qu and I Quan. The duke is predisposed to a remarkable array of vices, and Yen reproves his sovereign for every one of them. The duke is a glutton, a drunkard, and a sensualist. He neglects affairs of state so he can go hunting. He is fond of expensive clothes, luxurious palaces, and lavish gardens and watercourses. He also likes musical performance. Yet the only harping that Yen Ying will allow his master to hear is Yen's own perpetual reproof. Not very credibly, the reprobate duke docilely follows his counselor's priggish advice.

Sometimes, however, the onus of providing the duke with a moral example shifts to another character, as it does when Duke Ching tries to arrange the marriage of his favorite daughter to the already married Yenzi (Yen Tzu). The duke opens the negotiations by commenting on the age and ugliness of Yenzi's wife. He then proposes to present Yenzi with the ducal daughter as a more attractive second spouse.

Groveling respectfully on the floor, Yenzi declines on the grounds that he married his wife when she was young and beautiful and in the expectation that time would work its ravages. The couple remains happy, and Yenzi feels certain that Duke Jing will not force him to turn against his lifetime partner. The authority of Yenzi's moral fortitude trumps the Duke's arbitrary exercise of power.

Bibliography

Watson, Burton. *Early Chinese Literature.* New York: Columbia University Press, 1962.

Yosami *Japanese poet* See FEMALE POETS OF ANCIENT JAPAN.

yuefu (*yüeh-fu*) (poems and ballads)
(ca. 120 B.C.E.)

According to Burton Watson, the historian of Chinese literature, in the late Han dynasty Emperor Wu established an official bureau of music to write ritual songs to be performed in connection with religious and civic sacrifices. This bureau survived from around 120 until 6 B.C.E. After that date, its 829 employees lost their jobs or were reassigned, and other civil departments assumed the functions of the bureau. The compositions they wrote amounted to old-fashioned liturgical works, patterned on those in the Confucian BOOK OF ODES. The bureau's *yue fu* songs served their public purposes, but they contributed little to the cause of good poetry.

In addition to cranking out hymns, however, the bureaucrats also collected anonymous folk ballads from around the empire. These songs—the second kind of *yuefu* verse—were intended to inspire the officials and to acquaint them with popular taste. In quality, the surviving examples of such works vary from being merely quaint relics of a long-dead past to moving poems that convey and recreate sincere feelings in the reader.

A third subcategory of poem falling under the *yuefu* rubric, and one that has occasioned considerable controversy among students of ancient Chinese letters, includes examples of poems that, using a five-word meter, emulate the early ballads. The controversy about these works centers on the degree to which they are or are not expressive of an individual, self-consciously poetic, authorial personality. Those who favor the 19th and early 20th century formulations that envision poets as lonely geniuses starving in garrets tend to follow the view that the idea of the expression of individual subjectivity emerged in such works in China in the late Han period. Those, instead, who find postmodern critical positions more convincing—critics like Christopher Leigh Connery—argue that such works were often the result of active collaboration among groups of poets. The works represent the spirit of the times and linguistic expressive capacities and limitations rather than the emergence of a cult of authorial personality.

From the point of view of their subjects, *yuefu* poems often concerned such topics as life on farms or in villages. Orphans, foot soldiers, the wives who would accompany them to battle, and singing girls populate their lines. Such subjects, however, do not preclude persons outside those classes from authorship. Those who argue for folk origins to a considerable degree must support oral composition, since most country commoners were illiterate. The scholarly debate concerning the class of authors who produced the best *yuefu* verse will not be resolved in these pages.

Bibliography

Barnstone, Tony, and Chou Ping, eds. *The Anchor Book of Chinese Poetry*. New York: Anchor Books, 2005.

Connery, Christopher Leigh. *The Empire of the Text: Writing and Authority in Early Imperial China*. Lanham, Md.: Rowman and Littlefield Publishers, 1998.

Watson, Burton. *Early Chinese Literature*. New York: Columbia University Press, 1962.

Z

Zeno of Cittium   See STOICISM.

Zhuangzi (Chuang Tzu, Chuangtse, Kuan
Tzu) (fl. ca. 350 B.C.E.) *Chinese prose writer*
A prose writer, philosopher, and humorist,
Zhuangzi generally receives credit for elevating
the beliefs of DAOISM into a unified philosophical
position. Though there is general agreement that
not all of the book that bears his name, the
Zhuangzi, is his, Zhuangzi advances a nontheistic
view of the operations of the universe in its pages.
The universe comes into being spontaneously,
unmediated by any divine intention. It changes
according to the internal principles associated
with its being and is not always susceptible to
human understanding.

Zhuangzi thinks that the moral systems about
which human beings argue—particularly those
of CONFUCIUS and MOZI—are the constructs of
the schools that argue them. Human beings are
neither essentially good nor essentially bad. They
simply are what the universe has made them.
Their goal, then, should be to operate as spontaneously as the universe does and to seek to behave
just as naturally. Any attempt to do otherwise
will result in failure.

Life and death are simply different modes of
existence, neither of which is better than the
other. Therefore, when a beloved person dies, the
survivors mourn for themselves and their sense
of loss. Immortality of individual consciousness
does not exist. Some interpreters, however, think
that a sort of unself-conscious life force persists as
a part of the universal processes.

Zhuangzi, insofar as he constructs arguments
at all, does so by telling stories. He relates, for
example, the tale of a keeper of monkeys who provided three nuts for the monkeys' breakfast and
four for their dinner. The monkeys were highly
displeased with this arrangement, so the keeper
changed it. He gave them four nuts for breakfast
and three for dinner, and the monkeys were
entirely satisfied with this arrangement. The point
is that likes and dislikes follow from subjective
evaluation. The wise person will bring together
such evaluations and decide on the most acceptable by trying out the alternatives.

The wise person will also always seek the natural path of least resistance, as did the cook whose
knife never needed sharpening since he always
carved up the animals he prepared in such a way
that the knife missed the bone and gristle and
only passed through flesh and internal interstices.

His prince congratulated the cook on this method, commenting that the cook had taught the prince how to conduct his life: Find the natural path.

Many of the stories Zhuangzi tells both teach and amuse. This one concerns himself. Two high officials of the Prince of Chu came from the ruler as emissaries. Their mission was to invite Zhuangzi to become Chu's chief minister. Zhuangzi replied that he had heard of a sacred tortoise that had died at the age of 3,000 years and that the prince kept its remains in his ancestral temple. Would the tortoise rather, Zhuangzi asked the messengers, have its remains venerated there or wag its tail in the mud? The messengers agreed that the tortoise would have preferred the latter. Zhuangzi sent them away with the message that he too preferred to wag his tail in the mud.

Bibliography

Roth, Harold D. A *Companion to Angus C. Graham's Chuang-tzu: The Inner Chapters*. Honolulu: University of Hawaii Press, 2003.

Zhuangzi. *Basic Writings*. Translated by Burton Watson. New York: Columbia University Press, 2003.

———. *Chuang-tzu: The Inner Chapters*. Translated by A. C. Graham. Indianapolis, Ind.: Hackett Publishing Company, 2001.

———. *Chuang-Tzu: A New Selected Translation with an Exposition of the Philosophy of Kuo Hsiang*. Translated by Yu-Lan Fung. New York: Paragon Book Reprint Corporation, 1964.

Zoroaster (Zarathustra Spitama)
(ca. 630–ca. 553 B.C.E.) *Persian poet*

An ancient Persian poet, prophet, and religious leader, Zoroaster may have been the founder or the head of a reform movement within the religion of ancient Persia. Reference to him as a historical figure appears at the beginning of Zoroastrianism's holy book, the Avesta.

The historian W. B. Henning finds Zoroastrianism to be an essentially dualistic kind of mixed religion whose beliefs varied with time. Whether Zororaster initiated or inherited the religious beliefs that came to be associated with his name, Henning enumerates the following central points. Zoroaster believed in one god called Ahura Mazda—the god of light. He also believed that god had an adversary, an evil spirit named Anra Mainyu—a force of darkness. Zororaster also thought that human activity played an important role in the eventual outcome of the struggle between light and darkness.

From Zoroaster's own hand we have about 900 lines of surviving verse. These are dispersed in 17 poems called *GĀTHĀS* and arranged into five groups according to their meter. From them we learn that, in addition to being a dualist who saw universal history as a struggle between the powers of light and darkness, Zoroaster was also an agrarian reformer who had at heart the interests of small farmers against those of the great landowners who exploited them. He also supported the establishment of permanent settlements of farmers and herders who took precautions against the raids of roving bands of nomads who would use force to carry off the farmer-herders' animals and provisions.

Zoroastrianism became a world religion and, before Christianity, had an impact on the thought and theology of the ancient Greeks and Romans that was almost unique among Asian religions. That the religion of Zoroaster shared some points of correspondence with early Christianity is perhaps attested to by the fact that the three wise men, the Magi of the Christmas story, were adherents of the Zoroastrian faith.

Bibliography

Henning, W. B. *Zoroaster: Politician or Witch-Doctor?* London: Oxford University Press and Geoffrey Cumberlege, 1951.

The Hymns of Zoroaster. Translated into French by Jacques Duchesne-Guillemin and from French to English by M. Henning. Boston: Beacon Press, 1963.

Zosimus (fl. ca. 500 C.E.) *Greek prose writer*
The treasurer of the Roman Empire at Constantinople, Zosimus undertook writing a history of the decline of the Roman Empire in Greek. This resulted in a well-written document in six books (papyrus scrolls). Zosimus's *New History (Nea Istoria)*, which emulates POLYBIUS's work on the rise of Rome, takes an unusually clear-eyed look at the role that the propagation and establishment of the Christian religion played in the dwindling of Roman power from the ascension in 30 B.C.E. of Rome's first emperor, AUGUSTUS CAESAR, until 476 C.E.

Bibliography

Zosimus. *New History.* Translated by Ronald T. Ridley. Canberra: Australian Association for Byzantine Studies, 1982.

Zuozhuan *(Tso Chuan, Commentary of Zuo)* (ca. 475 B.C.E.)

Written by a Confucian disciple named Zuo (Tso), this expansive commentary on CONFUCIUS's *ANNALS OF SPRING AND AUTUMN* has been incorporated with its source document into the essential canon of Confucian writing.

Confucius's own work provides brief notices of occurrences in his native state of Lu between the years 722 and 484 B.C.E. At the head of each entry, Confucius recorded the year, month, day, and season of the noted event's occurrence. Confucius included summer under spring and winter under autumn, thus giving rise to the common title of the work. In the *Annals* that Zuo used as an index to help locate Confucius's sources, the sage points out natural phenomena such as meteor showers and political events such as raids by warriors from other states, victories and defeats in feudal warfare, and treaties resolving disagreements with neighboring rulers. Confucius also takes note of such unfortunate occurrences as deaths from natural causes and from murders.

Onto this bare-bones list, Zuo grafted the flesh of incident and significance that revealed much of the meaning implicit in Confucius's original catalogue. An illustrative example recorded by the literary historian Herbert A. Giles was listed by Confucius in the Spring section of the 21st year of the government of Duke Xi (Hsi). "In summer there was a great drought" is all that Confucius says about the matter, but Zuo gives the following additional information: As a remedy for the drought, the duke proposed burning a witch. An adviser retorted that such a remedy would not help. The duke would do better to repair the city's walls, eat less, spend less, and encourage the people to assist each other. Witches were not involved. If God wanted this one slain, why did he bother to let her be born? Besides, if she did cause the drought, burning her would make matters worse.

Zuo's expansion clarified the reasons that Confucius had selected the incidents he listed. Beyond that, other commentaries augmented every sentence of Confucius's brief entries with interpretive significance. Zuo, however, was not only a good conceptual Confucian, he was also the first great master of Chinese prose writing, and many subsequent writers looked to his work for their inspiration.

Beyond such commentary, the *Zuozhuan* also contains its author's comments about music and about music's role in governing a polity. Superior men, thought Zuo, would not listen to "lascivious or seductive airs." Good people played their instruments to help regulate their conduct, not simply for aesthetic pleasure or to stir their emotions.

The *Zuozhuan* is also the source of such inspirational maxims as its definition of "the three things that do not decay—establishing oneself by virtue; establishing oneself by deeds; [and] establishing oneself by words."

Bibliography

Giles, Herbert A. *A History of Chinese Literature.* New York: Grove Press, 1958.

Legge, James, trans. *The Confucian Classics.* Vols. 5 and 6. Oxford: The Clarendon Press, 1893–95.

Owen, Stephen. *Readings in Chinese Literary Thought.* Cambridge, Mass.: Harvard University Press, 1992.

SELECTED BIBLIOGRAPHY

Armstrong, Rebecca. *Cretan Women: Pasiphae, Ariadne, and Phaedra in Latin Poetry.* Oxford and New York: Oxford University Press, 2006.

Barnstone, Willis, trans. *Sweetbitter Love: Poems of Sappho.* Boston: Shambala, 2006.

Barrett, W. S. *Greek Lyric, Tragedy, and Textual Criticism: Collected Papers.* Edited by M. L. West. Oxford and New York: Oxford University Press, 2007.

Beyes, Charles Rowan. *Ancient Epic Poetry: Homer, Apollonius, Virgil with a Chapter on the Gilgamish Poems.* Wauconda, Ill.: Bolchazy-Carducci, 2006.

Bingham, Jane. *Classical Myth: A Treasury of Greek and Roman Legends, Art, and History.* Armonk, N.Y.: M. E. Sharp, 2008.

Black, Brian. *The Character of the Self in Ancient India: Priests, Kings, and Women in the early Upanishads.* Albany, N.Y.: State University of New York Press, 2007.

Bloom, Harold, ed. *Homer.* New York: Chelsea House, 2007.

———. *Sophocles'* Oedipus Rex. New York: Chelsea House, 2007.

Briggs, Ward W. ed. *Ancient Roman Writers.* Detroit, Mich.: Gale Group, 1999.

Carawan, Edwin. *Oxford Readings in the Attic Orators.* Oxford and New York: Oxford and New York: Oxford University Press, 2007.

Casiday, Augustine, and Frederick W. Norris. *Constantine to c. 600.* [Essays on the development of ancient versions of Christianity.] Cambridge and New York: Cambridge University Press, 2007.

Claren, James L., ed. *Chinese Literature: Overview and Bibliography.* Hauppauge, N.Y.: Nova Science Publishers, 2002.

Conte, Gian Biagio. *Latin Literature: A History.* Translated by Joseph B. Solodow. Revised by Don Fowler and Glenn W. Most. Baltimore, Md.: Johns Hopkins University Press, 1994.

Crane, Gregory, ed. *Perseus 2.0* [computer file]: *Interactive Sources and Studies on Ancient Greece: The Perseus Project.* New Haven, Conn.: Yale University Press, 2000.

Daniels, Peter T., and William Bright. *The World's Writing Systems.* New York and Oxford: Oxford University Press, 1996.

De, Sushil Kumar. *Ancient Indian Erotics and Erotic Literature.* Calcutta: Firma K. L. Mukhopadhyay, 1969.

De Jong, Irene, Rene Nünlist, and Angus Bowie. *Narrators, Narrative, and Narrations in Ancient Greek Literature: Studies in Ancient Narratives.* Leiden and Boston: Brill, 2004.

Dell, Pamela. *Socrates: An Ancient Greek in Search of Truth.* Minneapolis: Compass Point Books, 2006.

Doak, Robin S. *Thucydides: Ancient Greek Historian.* Minneapolis: Compass Point Books, 2007.

Dominick, William, and Jon Hall. *A Companion to Roman Rhetoric.* Malden, Mass.: Blackwell, 2007.

Dover, K. J., ed. *Ancient Greek Literature.* Oxford and New York: Oxford University Press, 1994.

Drozdek, Adam. *Greek Philosophers as Theologians.* Aldershot, U.K., and Burlington Vt.: Ashgate, 2007.

Easterling, P. E., B. M. W. Knox, and E. J. Kenney. *The Cambridge History of Classical Literature.* 2 vols. Cambridge: Cambridge University Press, 1982–85.

Fotopoulos, John. *The New Testament and early Christian Literatures in Greco-Roman Context: Studies in Honor of David E. Aune.* Leiden and Boston: Brill, 2006.

Graziosi, Barbara, and Emily Greenwood, eds. *Homer in the Twentieth Century: Between World Literature and the Western Canon.* New York: Oxford University Press, 2007.

Grice, Ettalane Mears, et al. *Chronology of the Larsa Dynasty; Patesis of the Ur Dynasty. An Old Babylonian Version of the* Gilgamesh Epic. New York: AMS Press, 1980.

Gutzwiler, Kathryn J. *A Guide to Hellenistic Literature.* Malden, Mass.: Blackwell, 2007.

Haddas, Moses. *Ancilla to Classical Reading.* New York: Columbia University Press, 1957.

Hallo, William W. *The Exaltation of* [the Sumerian goddess] *Inanna.* New York: AMS Press, 1982.

Heine, Ronald E. *Reading the Old Testament with the Ancient Church: Exploring the Formation of Early Christian Thought.* Grand Rapids, Mich.: Baker Academic Press, 2007.

Hollihan-Elliot, Sheila. *The Ancient History of China.* Philadelphia: Mason Crest Publishers, 2006.

Hornblower, Simon. *Thucydides and Pindar: Historical Narrative and the World of Epinikian Poetry.* Oxford and New York: Oxford University Press, 2006.

———, and Antony Spawforth, eds. *The Oxford Classical Dictionary.* New York: Oxford University Press, 1999.

Horowitz, Wayne. *Mesopotamian Cosmic Geography.* [Illustrated from literary sources.] Winona Lake, Ind.: Eisenbrauns, 1998.

Husayn, Muhammad Ahmad. *Origins of the Book: Egypt's Contribution to the Development of the Book from Papyrus to Codex.* Translated by Dorothy Jaeschke and Douglas Sharp. Leipzig: Edition Leipzig, 1970.

Johnson, Scott Fitzgerald, ed. *Greek Literature in Late Antiquity.* Aldershot, U.K., and Burlington, Vt.: Ashgate Publishing, 2006.

Konishi, Jin'ichi. *A History of Japanese Literature.* Translated by Aileen Gatten and Nicholas Teele. Edited by Earl Miner. Princeton, N.J.: Princeton University Press, 1991.

Kramer, Samuel Noah, and John Maier, eds. *Myths of Enki, the Crafty God.* [Sumerian and Akkadian.] New York: Oxford University Press, 1989.

Kraus, Chris, ed. *Visualizing the Tragic: Drama, Myth and Ritual in Greek Art and Literature: Essays in Honor of Froma Zeitlein.* Oxford and New York: Oxford University Press, 2007.

Legg, James. *Chinese Classics: With a Translation, Critical and Exegetical Notes, Prologmena, and Copious Indexes.* 2nd ed. 7 vols. Oxford: Clarendon Press, 1893–95.

Lévy, André. *Chinese Literature: Ancient and Classical.* Translated by William J. Nienhauser, Jr. Bloomington: Indiana University Press, 2000.

Ley, Graham. *A Short Introduction to the Ancient Greek Theater.* Rev. ed. Chicago: University of Chicago Press, 2006.

Lichtheim, Miriam. *Ancient Egyptian Literature: A Book of Readings.* Berkeley: University of California Press, 2006.

Lind, Richard E. *The Seat of Consciousness in Ancient Literature.* Jefferson, N.C.: McFarland & Company, 2007.

Louden, Bruce. *The Iliad: Structure, Myth, and Meaning.* Baltimore, Md.: Johns Hopkins University Press, 2006.

MacDonald, Marianne, and J. J. Michael Walton. *The Cambridge Companion to Greek and Roman Theater.* Cambridge and New York: Cambridge University Press, 2005.

Marcus, Joyce. *Mesoamerican Writing Systems: Propaganda, Myth, and History in Four Ancient Civilizations.* Princeton, N.J.: Princeton University Press, 1992.

Mellor, Ronald J., and Marni McGee. *The Ancient Roman World*. Oxford and New York: Oxford University Press, 2004.

Minchin, Elizabeth. *Homeric Voices: Discourse, Memory, Gender*. New York: Oxford University Press, 2007.

Morello, Ruth, and A. D. Morrison, eds. *Ancient Letters: Classical and Late Antique Epistolography*. Oxford and New York: Oxford University Press, 2007.

Nagy, Gregory. *Greek Literature: Critical Studies* [by period]. 9 vols. New York: Routledge, 2001.

Ō no Yasumaro. *The Story of Ancient Japan: or, Tales from the* Kojiki. Edited by Yarchiro Isobe. Tokyo: Sankaku sha, 1929.

Osborne, Catherine. *Dumb Beasts and Dead Philosophers: Humanity and the Humane in Ancient Philosophy and Literature*. New York: Oxford University Press, 2007.

Pedersén, Olof. *Archives and Libraries in the City of Assur: A Survey of the Material from the German Excavations*. Uppsala, Sweden: Uppsala University Press, 1986.

Pedrick, Victoria. *Euripides, Freud, and the Romance of Belonging*. Baltimore, Md.: Johns Hopkins University Press, 2007.

Powell, Barry B. *Homer*. Malden, Mass.: John Wiley, 2007.

Putnam, George Hovens. *Authors and Their Public in Ancient Times: A Sketch of Literary Conditions and of the Relations with the Public of Literary Producers from the Earliest Times to the Fall of the Roman Empire*. New York: Cooper Square Publishers, 1967.

Raaflaub, Kurt A., et. al. *Origins of Democracy in Ancient Greece*. Berkeley: University of California Press, 2002.

Reed, J. D. *Virgil's Gaze: Nation and Poetry in the Aeneid*. Princeton, N.J.: Princeton University Press, 2007.

Rogers, Effie Baker. *An Outline of the History of Ancient Japanese Literature*. New York: Greenwood Book Publishers, 1965.

Rothwell, Kenneth S. *Nature, Culture, and the Origins of Greek Comedy: A Study of Animal Choruses*. Cambridge and New York: Cambridge University Press, 2007.

Schomp, Virginia. *The Ancient Greeks*. New York: Marshall Cavendish Benchmark, 2007.

Shapiro, Alan H. *Cambridge Companion to Archaic Greece*. Cambridge, U. K. and New York: Cambridge University Press, 2007.

Shaffer, Aaron. *Literary and Religious Texts: Third Part*. [Sumerian] London: British Museum Press, 2006.

Shuter, Jane. *The Ancient Chinese*. Chicago: Heinemann Library, 2007.

Spaulding, Oliver Lyman. *Pen and Sword in Greece and Rome*. Cranbury, N.J.: Scholar's Bookshelf, 2006.

Trenckner, Sophie. *The Greek Novella in the Classical Period*. New York: Garland Publishing, 1987.

Vinci, Felice. *The Baltic Origins of Homer's Epic Tales: The Iliad and The Odyssey and the Migration of Myth*. Translated by Felice Vinci and Amalia De Francesco. Rochester, Vt.: Inner Traditions, 2006.

West, M. L. *Indo-European Poetry and Myth*. New York: Oxford University Press, 2007.

White, Emmons E. *The Wisdom of the Tamil People, as Illustrated by Translated Selections from their Ancient Literature*. New Delhi: Munishiràm Manoharlal Publisher, 1975.

Whiting, Jim. *The Life and Times of Herodotus*. Hockessin, Del.: M. Laine Publishers, 2007.

William, Brian. *Ancient Roman Women*. Chicago: Heinemann Library, 2003.

Wills, Lawrence M. *The Jewish Novel in the Ancient World*. Ithaca, N.Y.: Cornell University Press, 1995.

Worthington, Ian, ed. *A Companion to Greek Rhetoric*. Malden, Mass.: Blackwell Publishing, 2007.

Wright, Anne. *Philosophy and Writing*. [Greek] Armonk, N.Y.: M. E. Sharp, 2008.

Yasuda, Kenneth, trans. and ed. *Land of the Reed Plains: Ancient Japanese Lyrics from the* Manyoshu. Rutland, Vt.: C. E. Tuttle Co., 1972.

Annual and Occasional Bibliographies of Ancient Literatures and Related Subjects

Bibliotheca philologica classica. 1874–1938. Leipzig: Reisland, 1875–1941. [No longer published, this bibliography remains useful as a guide to older scholarship and commentary concerning the Greek and Roman classical world.]

Datta, Amaresh, et al., eds. *Encyclopaedia of Indian Literature*. 6 vols. New Delhi: Sahitya Akademi, 1987–92.

Davidson, Martha. *A List of Published Translations from Chinese into English, French and German*. 2 vols. Ann Arbor, Mich.: J. W. Edwards for the American Council of Learned Societies, 1957.

De Bary, William Theodore, et al. *A Guide to Oriental Classics*. New York: Columbia University Press, 1989.

Emeneau, Murray Barnson. *A Union List of Printed Indic Texts and Translations in American Libraries*. New Haven, Conn.: American Oriental Society, 1935.

Fung, Sydney S. K., and S. T. Lai. *25 Tang Poets: Index to English Translations*. Hong Kong: Chinese University Press, 1984.

Gonda, Jan, ed. *A History of Indian Literature*. 10 vols. Wiesbaden: O. Harrassowitz, 1973– [work ongoing]. [Vols. 1–3 deal with the literature of ancient India.]

Hospers, J. H., ed. *A Basic Bibliography for the Study of Semitic Languages*. 2 vols. Leiden: Brill, 1973–74. [Contains sections of interest to literary scholars about such languages as Akkadian, Sumerian, Anatolian, Ancient Persian, dialects of Hebrew, Syriac, and Aramaic, among others, together with bibliographies of studies of literary works in the Semitic languages. The second volume focuses on Arabic in all its varieties in all times and places.]

Kai-chee Wong, Pung Ho, and Shu-leung Dang. *A Research Guide to English Translation of Chinese Verse (Han Dynasty to T'ang Dynasty)*. Hong Kong: Chinese University Press, 1977.

L'Année philologique: Bibliographie critique et analytique de l'antiquité gréco-latine. Edited by J. Marouzeau et al. Paris: Societe d'Éditions Les Belles Lettres, 1928–. [The most complete source for scholarly literature concerning the Greek and Latin classical world, this bibliography has been published annually since 1928. Starting with volume 36, an American branch commenced publication at Chapel Hill, North Carolina. Notes to the entries in the American version appear in English.]

Lynn, Richard John. *Guide to Chinese Poetry and Drama*. 2nd ed. Boston: G. K. Hall, 1984.

Mamola, Claire Zebroski. *Japanese Women Writers in English Translation: An Annotated Bibliography*. 2 vols. New York: Garland, 1989–92. [Volume 1 addresses belle lettres composed between 794 and 1987 C.E.]

Marks, Alfred H., and Barry D. Bort. *Guide to Japanese Prose*. 2nd ed. Boston: G. K. Hall, 1984.

Miner, Earl Roy, Hiroko Odagiri, and Robert E. Morrell. *The Princeton Companion to Classical Japanese Literature*. Princeton, N.J.: Princeton University Press, 1985. [An indispensable research tool for serious inquiry.]

Paper, Jordan D. *Guide to Chinese Prose*. 2nd ed. Boston: G. K. Hall, 1984.

Rimer, J. Thomas, and Robert E. Morrell. *Guide to Japanese Poetry*. 2nd ed. Boston: G. K. Hall, 1984.

———. *A Reader's Guide to Japanese Literature*. Tokyo and New York: Kodansha International and Harper and Row, 1988.

Sen'ichi Hisamatsu, ed. *Biographical Dictionary of Japanese Literature*. Tokyo: International Society of Educational Information, 1982. [Addresses all periods of Japanese literature.]

Waxman, Meyer. *A History of Jewish Literature*. 5 vols. New York: T. Yoseloff, 1960. [Vol. 1 is relevant to literature written from the close of the Hebrew canon, ca. 200 B.C.E., to the end of the ancient period.]

Winternitz, Moriz. *A History of Indian Literature*. 3 vols. Translated by V. Srinivasa Sarma. Delhi: Motilal Banarsidass, 1981–85.

Yang, Winston L. Y., et al. *Classical Chinese Fiction: A Guide to Its Study and Appreciation: Essays and Bibliographies*. Boston: G. K Hall, 1978.

Yohizaki, Yasuhiro. *Studies in Japanese Literature and Language: A Bibliography of English Materials*. Tokyo: Nichigai Associates, 1979. [The first of three parts specifically addresses Japanese literature.]

INDEX